Constructing Frames of Reference

The publisher gratefully acknowledges the generous contribution
to this book provided by the General Endowment Fund of the
Association of the University of California Press.

Constructing Frames of Reference

An Analytical Method for Archaeological Theory Building
Using Hunter-Gatherer and Environmental Data Sets

LEWIS R. BINFORD

UNIVERSITY OF CALIFORNIA PRESS
Berkeley   Los Angeles   London

University of California Press
Berkeley and Los Angeles, California

University of California Press Ltd.
London, England

Library of Congress Cataloging-in-Publication Data

Binford, Lewis Roberts, 1930–
    Constructing frames of reference: an analytical method for archaeological theory
building using hunter-gatherer and environmental data sets / Lewis R. Binford.
      p.   cm.
    Includes bibliographical references and index.
    ISBN 0-520-22393-4 (cloth : alk. paper).
    1. Hunting and gathering societies. 2. Human evolution. 3. Social evolution.
4. Social archaeology. 5. Environmental archaeology. I. Title.
GN388 .B56   2001
206.3′64—dc21
                                                    00-28714

Printed in Canada
08 07 06 05 04 03 02 01
10 9 8 7 6 5 4 3 2 1

This book is dedicated to the memory of
Julian H. Steward
John J. Honigmann
Joseph B. Birdsell
and
Wendell H. Oswalt
four inspiring investigators of hunter-gatherer life ways

Contents

    Spotlight on the Group Size Model   317
    Risk Pooling or Nested Hierarchies of Decision Makers?   351
    Too Many Models and Constants!   351
    More Interesting Problems Raised by the Frequency Distributions of "Basal Units"   352
    The "Population Pressure" Controversy and the General Issue of Density-Dependent Changes
    in Organization   354
    Reflections   357

PART IV   *Putting Ideas, Second-Order Derivative Patterning,*
           and Generalizations Together: Explorations in Theory Building

CHAPTER 10   *A Disembodied Observer Looks at Hunter-Gatherer Responses to Packing*   363

    Habitat Variability, Potential Niche Diversity, and the Spatial Structure of Resource
    Accessibility   364
    Two New Instruments for Measurement: Spatial Packing and Niche Effectiveness   372
    Pattern Recognition Using Instruments for Measurement   375
    Intensification and Technology: More Responses to Packing   387
    Conclusion   399

CHAPTER 11   *The Evolution of System States: Complexity, Stability, Symmetry, and*
              System Change   400

    The Once and Future Processual Archaeology   400
    Recent Archaeological Research on Complexity: Issues of Stability and Instability   401
    Applying New Knowledge about Stability and Instability to Questions of Specialization and
    Diversification   406
    One Route to Complexity: Emergence through Internal Differentiation   417
    Conclusion   432

CHAPTER 12   *The Last Act Crowns the Play*   434

    How Hunter-Gatherers Become Non-Hunter-Gatherers   434
    Conclusion   461

    Epilogue   465
    Glimpses of Processes beyond the Packing Threshold   468
    Have I Established a General Research Procedure?   471

    Notes   473
    References   493
    Author Index   535
    Index of Ethnographic Cases and Archaeological Sites   539
    Subject Index   541

Figures

Tables

Acknowledgments

Four people have each worked long and hard to help make this book a reality. Without their efforts, the form and content of the manuscript would have been much less interesting and the experience of writing it would have been much less enriching for me. Three of them have served as my research assistants at Southern Methodist University during the time that the manuscript was evolving. In order of participation, they are Russell Gould, SMU Ph.D. student and resident of Fairbanks, Alaska; Amber Johnson, Ph.D., research associate at the Institute for the Study of Earth and Man in Dallas, Texas; and Joseph Miller, graduate student in archaeology at SMU and my assistant for the past two years.

Russell worked with me daily in the early 1990s, and much of the material summarized in chapters 4 and 5 will certainly be familiar to him. He also assembled most of the hunter-gatherer case references cited in the text and, then as now, acted as my advisor in all matters related to the complex world of computer programming. Amber came on board when I was heavily involved in developing the equations for estimating net aboveground productivity and trying to obtain a reasonable estimate of animal biomass. Successful completion of this aspect of the research set me up to cope with the difficult task of developing the Terrestrial Model presented in chapter 6. Amber worked with me on most of the pattern recognition work leading up to and including the writing of chapter 9, and she also cheerfully entered more data than any person ever wants to do in life. I salute her patience and persistence and the lengths to which she will go for a friend.

Joe took over from Amber and faced the daunting task of learning the names of all of the computer files and mastering the protocols that manipulate the series of complicated programs used to translate selected variables into patterned relationships. Ultimately, Joe's attention has been focused on the production of all of the computer graphics used in the book. I think that even this brief statement of what these three

colleagues have contributed to this book indicates the depth of my indebtedness to them and my appreciation for their splendid companionship during my extended intellectual journey.

The fourth person I want to recognize has played a very different role in this process. My former wife, Nancy Medaris Stone, has been with me every step of the way since my decision in 1990 to concentrate on the research that represents the foundation of this book. Early on it became clear that, in addition to enlarging my hunter-gatherer data base, as much or even more time and effort was needed to develop the frames of reference in terms of which I would eventually examine relationships in the hunter-gatherer data. I had realized that—regardless of how well this body of information might have been collected by ethnographers—only the diversity and informational content of well-chosen frames of reference would provide the aperture I needed to make sense of the patterns in the data.

The day that I decided to move toward assembling a climatological frame of reference, Nancy and I made a commitment to devote endless hours to data entry and to making tedious measurements using maps that in some cases had been very hard to find. Although this effort enabled me to do some early and very provocative pattern recognition work, it also convinced me that I did not yet have a real frame of reference. This unwelcome realization sent us back to square one as we coped again with the rigors of developing a much more comprehensive environmental frame of reference.

In subsequent chapters, the reader will encounter discussions of hunter-gatherer labor organization and the different contributions that males and females make to the subsistence effort. Nancy and I have had our own division of labor with respect to this book, and our work has been complementary. Typically, I would produce the first rough draft of a chapter, which I would then hand to her. Often there would be silence for the longest time as she read and, sometimes, had to decipher what I was trying to say. Then I would hear the *click-click-click* of her computer keyboard as she rewrote the chapter. Finally she would come up with a title and hand the new draft back to me for review. Upon reading my ideas and arguments in her words, I would frequently smile and say, "That's great—why didn't I say that myself?"

In an endeavor like this, there are those wonderful moments when, in discussion with others, new points are offered and ideas emerge. I have had many such moments over the past nine years, and that has been the real joy of working with Nancy, Russell, Amber, and Joe. We have all shared an exciting learning experience, and I cannot thank them enough.

If this book can be said to have a godfather, then that benevolent éminence grise is William Woodcock, my longtime friend and publishing ally. He has been responsible for the transformation of the majority of my manuscripts into printed volumes, and when this book existed as only a rough outline in my head he provided the encouragement I needed to begin work. As evidence of his faith in the project, he wrote a publishing contract for me in 1991. Now, eight years after the due date has passed—and because of his continued support—this book is at last in print. It is with the greatest relief and gratitude that I express my thanks to Bill.

At a very different scale, a number of people have influenced my thinking in general and my ideas about hunter-gatherers in particular. Very early in my career as a graduate student in anthropology, John J. Honigmann strongly guided me in the direction of hunter-gatherer studies and, perhaps equally forcefully, toward an interest in cross-cultural comparison and analysis. His vast ethnographic experience was an inspiration to me, and emulating him intellectually became my goal.

My first experience as an instructor in a comparative course on hunter-gatherers occurred in 1966–67 at the University of California at Los Angeles, where I enjoyed the companionship of Joseph B. Birdsell, Wendell H. Oswalt, and—during a short visit—Norman B. Tindale. Birdsell attended my first class, and since my office was across the hall from Oswalt's I was the grateful recipient of knowledge and vast experience from these pioneers of research. Coming after the many intellectual feasts that I had shared with Joe and Wendell, Tindale's brief presence in our midst was like an elegant dessert. All in all, I had the wealth of experience and teaching skills of these three excellent role models to draw on when I began the first of my many years of teaching courses about hunter-gatherers

Beginning in 1966 and continuing to the present, the students in my classes at several universities have been a constant source of intellectual stimulation and have contributed significantly to the growth of my knowledge about hunter-gatherers. I am fortunate to have been able to maintain contact with many of them, and they continue to provide me with an opportunity to share their interests and the results of their hard work. In chapter 1, I discuss at some length many of the researchers whom I never met, or knew only slightly, who have played pivotal roles as "founders" of the hunter-gatherer research field. I have great respect and admiration for these early researchers, and I am thankful to be able to build upon their pioneering work.

Finally, I celebrate the contributions to life, to scientific learning, and to my efforts in particular that have been made by the many women, children, and men who, as hunter-gatherers, welcomed me into their lives and allowed me to interview and observe them and to get to know them as friends. In a very real sense, they educated me well to deal with the subject matter of this book, and they have been my most important teachers. To them and the traditional knowledge that they represent, I am immeasurably grateful.

The National Science Foundation, the Wenner-Gren Foundation, the Australian Institute of Aboriginal Studies, the L. B. Leakey Foundation, and the Department of Anthropology at the University of Capetown, South Africa, have all provided me with funding for field research on hunter-gatherers. Jean and Ray Auel generously provided me with the funds to obtain the Human Relations Area Files on hunter-gatherers. Additional support from the University of New Mexico through the Leslie Spier Professorship and Southern Methodist University through the University Distinguished Professorship has made the comparative and integrative work discussed in this book possible.

Prologue

We will draw the curtain and show you the picture.

—William Shakespeare, *Twelfth Night*

This book has had a very long gestation period. It began life in 1971 as a book-length manuscript that I used as the basic text for the hunter-gatherer course I taught for twenty years at the University of New Mexico. Some of my former students still recall the tattered, yellowed, foolscap pages, littered with typos, which they photocopied and exchanged with one another in their effort to learn more about the world of hunter-gatherers. By 1974, however, I had given up all thought of publishing "the H & G book" in its initial incarnation. My own field work had convinced me that organizing hunter-gatherer data in a case study or topical format would not be very useful to archaeologists—and besides, there were many other books that presented descriptions of ethnographic groups as examples of the life ways of small-scale societies.

My early manuscript had included tables of comparative data—some based on Murdock's early cross-cultural research and others assembled from data presented by students in earlier classes, who had reported on those aspects of hunter-gatherer organization that were relevant to their own research. Unfortunately, the ethnographic groups for which there were "good data" were few in number. Even though cross-tabulations of data and some statistical tests filled many pages of my manuscript, I could never figure out how to use the results to develop an understanding of what the hunter-gatherer world was like and, more importantly, how it was organized.

True, I had chapters on demography, the use of space, mean household size, and other topical features that documented domains of cultural variability. In some instances, the patterns in these data even gave me some insight into how segments of a cultural system might be organized. Overall,

however, it seemed as though the harder I worked and the more traits or attributes I tabulated, the more unattainable a systems view of my subject matter became. As the number of paired comparisons—and the combinations and permutations of pairwise comparisons—increased, the less hopeful I felt that my mountain of information would ever lead me to an understanding of how hunter-gatherer systems were organized.

My former graduate students can verify that, from the outset, my efforts to develop a hunter-gatherer data base were accompanied by an exploration of various properties of the environments in which these groups lived. Using weather data, I had calculated various measures of temperature, and I had experimented with indices for evaluating rainfall in a biologically meaningful way. I discovered that more interesting and provocative relationships emerged when continuous environmental variables could be used to organize the comparisons among nominal variables. It also became clear that comparisons between continuous environmental variables frequently resulted in the organization of ordinal cultural variables into interesting patterns, especially when both the environmental and cultural variables were continuous in character. Unfortunately, there were very few reliable values for continuous variables in the ethnographic literature of hunter-gatherers.

One other major frustration in the 1970s was that the computer hardware to which I had access was anything but "user friendly" and the mainframes that I had begun to use while I was still a graduate student were simply not interactive on anything other than a geologic time scale. Today's generation of graduate students must find it inconceivable that one would attempt to process data using the dinosaur computers of the 1960s, and there were times when I thought so too, particularly when I was trying to wrangle large boxes of punch cards, which were inevitably full of errors and minor formatting problems—not to mention the problem of lost or mutilated cards.

As a result of these technological difficulties, along with a large body of field-based observations that I had accumulated and was committed to writing up, I had less and less interest in coping with my hunter-gatherer manuscript, and it gradually moved lower and lower on my list of intellectual priorities. I remained convinced, however, that finding a way to maximize the information in the ethnographic literature about the variability among hunter-gatherer societies had to be a major research priority for archaeologists who were interested in the 30,000-year time period between the Upper Paleolithic and the transformation to ways of life not based on hunter-gatherer strategies. The problem was not simply how to maximize the information accessible to archeologists but, much more importantly, how to use that information as part of a methodology for learning about the past—particularly a past that was different in its range of organized system variants from what we know about the ethnographic present.

I was particularly disillusioned by the way most archaeologists used their knowledge about hunter-gatherers. The standard operating procedure was to extract isolated facts or behaviors from an ethnographic monograph and use them to "interpret" archaeological sites. Interpretations were then assumed to explain the features and properties of the archaeological record at specific sites, and this accommodative fit was then cited as the warranting argument for the accuracy of the interpretation. The dazzling circularity of this explanatory method guaranteed that making more ethnographic sources available to archaeologists would only make the situation worse!

I cannot emphasize strongly enough that the major problem this book addresses is *the development of a method for productively using ethnographic data in the service of archaeological goals.* This is not to say that the method I present in this book is the *only* procedure, but it is the only methodological tool that I have been able to develop which results in knowledge that is germane to archaeological problems. Former students will soon appreciate that this book bears very little resemblance to my 1970s manuscript. Its evolution was definitely gradual and occurred concurrently with the realization that my earlier attempts to record germane information about environments and habitats did not equip me to undertake a realistic study of human adaptations.

For example, I have learned that temperature is not just temperature. Some plants are more responsive to the prevailing temperature throughout the growing season, whereas others react to extreme temperatures during the nongrowing season. Similarly, rainfall occurring at the beginning of the growing season may be more important to horticulturists in some climatic settings than rainfall that comes at the end of the growing season. This understanding of some aspects of what the world was like forced me to take a very different approach to the documentation of environments. I needed to devise many different ways of measuring temperature and available water in order to understand the differences among habitats and the diverse challenges faced by hunter-gatherers seeking subsistence security in different settings. It was clear that I needed to return to methodological square one, and I began to research in a much more comprehensive way the environments in which ethnographically documented hunter-gathers have lived.

It took me two years to develop the data bases dealing with the world's environments and the geographical distribution of documented hunter-gatherers. Once this aspect of the work was completed, it became clear that the limited range of hunter-gatherer characteristics upon which traditional cross-cultural studies had focused was not really relevant to most of the issues that I hoped to address in my book. I spent a great deal of time researching traditional anthropological interests, such as kinship, as well as the phenomena representing variability among hunter-gatherer educational systems. I also targeted areas of special interest to archaeologists, such as mortuary practices and the character of public rituals, as well as housing, settlement size and distribution, mobility, subsistence practices, and demographic properties.

Quite early in my research, I realized that many of these areas of interest were very difficult to describe dimensionally.[1] In other words, I needed continuous ethnographic variables that I could relate to the many continuous environmental variables that documented the diversity in hunter-gatherer habitats. The lack of precise information in many of the ethnographies that I consulted was disappointing, but I concluded that continuous variables with substantial noise would probably work better in analysis than ordinal variables. This decision meant that I spent many hours developing quantitative estimates and guesses to augment the observational data sometimes provided by ethnographers and observers. As a result, I was able to obtain a number of mean or normative values for settlement size by types, house size by types, mean household size, age at marriage for males and females, percentage of polygamous marriages, mobility variables, demographic variables, and many other categories of information.

These data were very important since I assumed that habitats varied quantitatively within and between nominal or ordinal classifications of habitat. If it were possible to identify truly adaptive responses to continuously varying environmental variables, there should be significant variability within so-called culture or ethnic areas as well as between them, in which case "Galton's problem" (Naroll 1961) would lose its problematic status (Harner 1970:73). It is also possible that the geographic distributions of entities and formal properties that archaeologists refer to as *diffusion* may really represent fine-grained adaptive adjustments to environmental conditions. If this is so, I would expect changes in the synergistic social relationships among adjacent groups to result not from the spread of a good idea but, instead, from conditioning processes rooted in adaptive variability when studied analytically across geographic space. The idea that diffusion could be explained—that it might be possible to say when it would occur, when it would not, and how it would pattern—was an appealing possibility.

I also concentrated on other properties usually considered to be indicative of system state differences. I was well aware of the ecological principle that the same climatic changes acting upon a population of mice and elephants would have very different effects on each species. This is another way of saying that one would expect that the prior state of a system could potentially condition very different responses to similar or identical environmental variables. Throughout my intellectual journey, I realized that I would not be able to categorize a priori many important features of hunter-gatherer life as either continuous or even ordinal variables.

The preceding comments are part of the background or scenery revealed by opening the metaphorical *Twelfth Night* "curtain," but they do not present a comprehensive "picture" of what to expect in this book. Three of the points presented previously are, however, central:

1. The primary problem that this book addresses is the development of a method for productively using ethnographic data to serve archaeological goals.
2. The possibility that the patterning which has been termed "diffusion" can be explained and that one might be able to predict when it would and would not occur—and what shape it would assume—has great appeal.
3. It is reasonable to expect that the prior state of a system may condition very different responses to similar or identical values for environmental variables.

These three statements can be visualized as providing the defining coloration in the intellectual background of the analytical hunter-gatherer picture, but details about the actors and their visages remain unclear. In an effort to sharpen some of the picture's blurred outlines, I offer the following comments about material that is *not* included in this book. I do not analyze any archeological data directly, I do not discuss the ideas of many contemporary archaeologists, and I do not attempt to cope with paradigmatic diversity in the field of archaeology.

This book is unapologetically written from a scientific perspective. It is largely an exercise in inductive reasoning, in that it asks questions regarding the character of the world of

organized variability among ethnographically documented hunter-gatherer groups. As such, it addresses many alleged empirical generalizations that appear in the archaeological literature which turn out to be inaccurate or, at best, only marginally useful.

From a methodological perspective, the picture is built up gradually, chapter by chapter. Because some of the material is detailed and requires considerable concentration, I think it is important at the outset to give readers a brief guide to the book's contents. Unlike a novel, whose writer tries to keep the ending of the book a secret until the climactic chapter, this book will mean more to the reader who has been given some idea about where the argument is heading at any given moment.

The metaphorical picture that develops in this book is one in which particular devices for structuring data—called *frames of reference*—appear in the foreground as the way to organize prior knowledge and make it useful to archaeologists. Two major frames of reference are featured, one of which is designed to document the primary variables conditioning habitat variability. Use of this frame of reference in turn permits archaeologists to relate archaeological facts to a multitude of environmental variables so that the characteristics of adaptive responses to habitat variability can be documented and identified.

As I have already indicated, very different responses to environmental variables can be expected, depending on the prior conditions extant within the cultural systems that are experiencing environmental fluctuation, change, or variability. This problem brings us to the second frame of reference developed in this book. The variability documented among ethnographically known hunter-gatherers is organized into a basic frame of reference for comparison to archaeological remains. In principle, from the equations developed in this book, an archaeologist can anticipate many of the properties of hunter-gatherer groups that might be expected to occur at a given location, at an archeological site, or at a series of sites. These anticipated characteristics can then be used in a variety of ways to learn more not only about hunter-gatherers but also about the archaeological record. And, since one of the goals of this book is to explain variability among hunter-gatherers, the explanatory theory that I have developed is available for archaeologists to use deductively by reasoning to or simulating changing conditions and thereby providing patterns of change that can be expected to occur in the archaeological record at specific locations.

Most of this book is concerned with the development of procedures and methods that can be used directly by archaeologists or that can be used as models by other scientists. At the same time, I hope to illustrate the general principles of and the benefits to be derived from using environmental frames of reference to study patterning among hunter-gatherer cases. I hope that the archaeological reader realizes that the same procedures could be used with archaeological data. The organizational insights derived from using environmental frames of reference to study hunter-gatherers also make it possible to construct a *hunter-gatherer frame of reference* with which archaeologists can productively study the archaeological record. Last, I address the subject of cultural responses to changed climatic conditions by applying a hunter-gatherer frame of reference to changing climatic sequences at locations where there are provocative archaeological sequences.

Although there are many graphs in this book that display the relationships among the several data sets that I have assembled during my research, the "picture" that this material presents is essentially an intellectual one. It becomes "graphic" to the degree that the reader understands the organization of the data and my tactics and strategies for transforming patterning into new knowledge. The book is divided into four parts, each of which uses—in different ways—the prior knowledge available to me in the pursuit of different goals.

The three chapters in *Part I* survey some of the prior knowledge available to me about hunter-gatherers. Although I spent years assembling and ordering this ethnographic information, earlier researchers devoted whole lifetimes to observing and recording the life ways of the small-scale societies that are at the core of my information base. In chapter 1, I summarize the work of several important anthropological researchers whose ideas about hunter-gatherers have shaped the thinking of their intellectual descendants up to and including the contemporary era. Following this "founder's effect" chapter, I address contentious assumptions and ideas about the role of human actors in the explanatory process. I also use the stage in chapter 2 to clarify my position on many of the issues that are of great concern to humanists. Chapter 3 is devoted to a discussion of science as the learning strategy whose precepts will be implemented in subsequent chapters when I actually develop frames of reference and use prior knowledge within the broad framework of inductive research.

Part II of the book is fairly well described by its title: "Methods for Using Prior Knowledge: Building Frames of Reference and Models." Chapters 4 and 5 describe the mechanics of building an environmental frame of reference and developing the means for making projections from hunter-gatherer data. In chapter 6, I demonstrate how to use prior knowledge to build models with which to analyze one's subject matter. I conclude this section with an illustration of how to apply these models, using the constructed frames of reference for the analysis of European archaeological data dealing with the appearance of domesticated plants and animals. These three chapters outline the logic and actual construction of intellectual models and frames of reference and are central to the tactical exploration of the procedures developed in subsequent chapters.

In *Part III,* the dialogue becomes more complicated. Instead of presenting a linear sequence of information, strategies, reasoning, and warranting arguments, I begin to demonstrate some strategies that have strong philosophical implications for such controversial subjects as objectivity and the ability of science to go beyond the circularity of "theory-dependent" observations and reasoning. These issues reflect complicated interactions in what the reader will discover is the drama unfolding in the metaphorical "scientific theater," where researchers engage their colleagues in a debate of ideas.

One intellectual engagement in the scientific theater has arisen from several points that I first encountered in a fascinating paper delivered by Patty Jo Watson (1986) at the fiftieth anniversary meeting of the Society for American Archaeologists. Watson was responding to an argument that I had made (Binford 1981:29; Binford and Sabloff 1982:149) denying the empiricist assumption that the past was directly and self-evidently accessible. I had argued that the past was only knowable through disciplined inferential reasoning and that, up until then, I had encountered nothing in the archaeological literature that indicated archaeologists could cope with the magnitude of the methodological problem they faced. More specifically, I said that "the dependence of our knowledge of the past on inference rather than direct observation renders the relationship between paradigm (the conceptual tool of description) and theory (the conceptual tool of explanation) vague; it also renders the 'independence' of observations from explanations frequently suspect and commonly standing in a built-in relationship, thereby committing the fallacy of 'confirming the consequent'" (Binford 1981:29).

Watson's response to this argument surprised me, particularly what she perceived as my skeptical attitude. Although I had publicly confessed that I doubted that many of the forms of reasoning presented in the archaeological literature would get us to the past, I had never doubted that the problem could be solved. In fact, in the monograph in which the preceding quotation appeared, I was working to reduce some ambiguities associated with the problem of inference. This point was overlooked, as was my earlier argument (Binford 1982) that the intellectual independence of propositions formed the basis for a modern idea of objectivity. Not many years later, Alison Wylie (1989) seemed to appreciate this issue and, unlike many other critical voices, acknowledged my attempts to solve some of the problems associated with the secure growth of knowledge in archaeology, at least at the methodological level.

I have long admired the solution developed by the discipline of geology to deal with the fact that it is impossible to observe directly the dynamics that occurred in the past (Kitts 1977:56–68). By means of warranted, uniformitarian assumptions demonstrating the linkages between circumstantial evidence from the past and direct observations in the present, the dynamic geologic processes that operate in the world today are argued to have also been operative in the past. The use of uniformitarian assumptions, however, implies tactical reasoning and not a dogmatic assumption that the past was like the present, as many have imagined.

Throughout my research career I have been an advocate of the use of cross-cultural comparisons as a uniformitarian strategy for learning in anthropology. Despite the fact that this was the method of choice during one phase of anthropology's development, I always felt that the potential value of this technique had gone unrealized. This is partly because—in my opinion—researchers always asked the wrong questions of their comparative data and also because the standard comparative tactics ensured that the results would be ambiguous. In *Part III* of this book, I use cross-cultural comparisons differently and, I believe, more productively by looking at selected attributes and characteristics of a global sample of diverse hunter-gatherer groups in terms of multiple frames of reference. The patterns I isolate using this technique provide clues to dynamic processes that were operative in the world of nearly contemporary, ethnographically documented hunter-gatherers; they do not simply represent an "interpretation," with its attached logical fallacy of confirming the consequent.

The title of *Part III*—"Recognizing Patterns and Generalizing about What the World Is Like: The Transition from Pattern Recognition to Theory Building"—fairly accurately describes the challenges of the subject matter of chapters 7–9. In chapter 7, I use generalizations derived from pattern recognition studies to build a model of the factors that *might* contribute to the variability in hunter-gatherer group sizes,

and in chapter 8, I get feedback from the hunter-gatherer data set about how group size actually varies in a wide range of specific circumstances. In chapter 9, I shift focus and discuss the observations and reflections of the scientific observer who is engaged in an effort to understand what the world is like and why it is the way it appears to be.

Part IV of the book, which is called "Putting Ideas, Second-Order Derivative Patterning, and Generalizations Together: Explorations in Theory Building," places the reader more directly in the scientific theater in which the researcher is engaged in theory building. This section also demonstrates that the learning strategies and tactics that have been focused on ethnographic investigation can have productive results when they are applied to archaeological research. I urge the reader not to jump immediately to chapter 10 ("A Disembodied Observer Looks at Hunter-Gatherer Responses to Packing"), chapter 11 ("The Evolution of System States: Complexity, Stability, Symmetry, and System Change"), and chapter 12 ("The Last Act Crowns the Play"), because much of the value of these chapters will be lost unless the reader follows the development of the patterning and arguments that precede them.

I hope that once the reader has made the considerable effort required to digest the material presented in this book, he or she will be motivated to apply this approach to the many intriguing problems that archaeologists confront in all regions of the world. One could say that the end of this book is, in fact, a beginning, since what has been learned from the research upon which the book is based cries out in the Epilogue for elaboration, expansion, and application to other sources of data that may be organized fruitfully into frames of reference.

Exploring Prior Knowledge and Belief

One of the purposes of this book is to develop a method for productively using ethnographic data to serve archaeological learning goals. The next three chapters introduce some of the ideas guiding earlier researchers as they reported and commented on the variability they observed among hunter-gatherers. This background provides a set of fundamental ideas that guide the consideration of new observations and the creation of data. The principles that underlie the use of science as a learning strategy and their relevance to this endeavor are also discussed.

1

"Founder's Effect" and the Study of Hunter-Gatherers

Culture, or civilization, . . . is that complex whole which includes knowledge, belief, art, law, morals, custom, and any other capabilities and habits acquired by man as a member of society.

—E. B. Tylor (1871:1)

A comparison of the discipline of anthropology as it existed in the middle of the nineteenth century with what it has become at the beginning of the twenty-first century would reveal that the founding and contemporary states appear radically different. Early investigations into the scope and nature of human diversity were led by a handful of scholars; now tens of thousands of anthropologists contribute to almost every domain of human endeavor. Despite the expansion of the range of subjects addressed by anthropologists, however, the ensemble of concepts in terms of which questions are posed and answers are pursued has not expanded in the same way as the field's purview. Many of the ideas that were initially proposed in the first fifty years of research, in addition to having exerted a profound impact in their own time, remain with us in essentially unaltered form.

The Explanatory Challenge of Complex Wholes

From its inception, anthropology took as its goal the study and explanation of cultural variability. It is clear that for E. B. Tylor, one of the discipline's nineteenth-century founders, the capabilities and habits that he designated as cultural were extrasomatic, or learned, and were not referable to what today are thought of as genetic processes of differentiation. For Tylor and his contemporary colleagues, the pathway to an understanding of cultural diversity led through the doorway of the past. Tylor made this point most distinctly when he observed that "civilization [culture], being a process

of long and complex growth, can only be thoroughly understood when studied through its entire range; that the past is continually needed to explain the present, and the whole to explain the past" (Tylor 1878:2). There is no ambiguity about what Tylor meant when he affirmed that a knowledge of the past is a prerequisite to an understanding of the present, but when he referred to "the whole" as essential to an explanation of the past, his intent is considerably less clear.

An examination of the history of anthropology up until the 1930s reveals that research and debate were focused on the best use of the present to reconstruct the past. All of the early evolutionists and diffusionists addressed the issue of what the past had been like. Diffusionists used ethnohistoric sources to plot the geographic distribution of traits, customs, attitudes, house forms, and burial practices in an effort to reconstruct the histories of diverse peoples, particularly those who had been documented during the colonial era in North America. These unique, reconstructed histories were then cited as the causes of the cultural variability noted at the time of earliest description.

Evolutionists, on the other hand, considered these reconstructed histories inadequate and proposed instead that general processes of diversification and change continually modified the cultural behavior of humankind. By the 1930s, however, voices in anthropology were being raised in opposition to a focus on the past as an explanation for the present. One had to understand the present *in terms of the present*, it was argued. Tylor had been wrong when he targeted a knowledge of the past as a precondition to an understanding of the present. Although today we would agree that the ideas of process contemplated by the nineteenth-century evolutionists were inadequate and in many cases simply wrong, we should not reject Tylor's commitment to an explanatory perspective that attempted to encompass variability at the largest scale imaginable—that of "the whole."

Throughout the period in which the discipline of anthropology coalesced and defined its mission, increased exploration of the archaeological record produced a body of data and a host of explanatory concerns that were similar to the interests of social anthropology. As a result of this alignment, at least in the New World, both ethnology and archaeology became linked as subdisciplines under the same anthropological aegis. During this era of disciplinary definition and expansion, however, Tylor's prescription that the whole was needed to explain the past was ignored by archaeologists at the methodological level. Most early archaeologists attempted to reconstruct prehistory by partitioning their data into as many different categories as possible and then plotting the spatial distribution of separate material traits, much as their ethnographic colleagues had done with ethnohistoric and ethnographic data. The methods of inference were identical in each subdiscipline (i.e., the most widely distributed materials were the oldest), and archaeologists, too, attempted to reconstruct culture histories.

Clearly Tylor considered that "histories"—whether reconstructed or not—were necessary to an explanation of the present, but why did he discuss the explanation of the past in different terms? Any satisfactory effort to explain the past would require access to "the whole," which presumably meant total knowledge about both the past and the present! We may never know exactly what Tylor meant by this equivocal pronouncement, but it emphasizes that the explanatory challenge faced by those who try to understand the past can only be met by a higher-order understanding of the present and the past.

In the 1930s, reactions to the predominance of the cultural historical method prompted a reconsideration of the utility of an evolutionary perspective. It was argued that one could not explain the present by appealing to the particulars of unique cultural histories; rather, ongoing processes shaped the present as they had the past. In ensuing decades, research undertaken to develop this perspective has generated considerable controversy, and the anthropological arena of today echoes with faint as well as clearly audible challenges flung at one another by contemporary evolutionists and diffusionists, materialists and idealists, scientists and historians.

The idea that specific processes may operate in the present as well as in the past was the central formulation responsible for the growth of the sciences of geology and paleontology, two related disciplines that also deal with the dilemma of knowing the past and the present. Could Tylor

have been referring to the development of uniformitarian principles when he declared that in order to explain the past the researcher must address "the whole" of present and past?

This book accepts Tylor's challenge and regards those events reported or inferred to have occurred in the past, as well as those documented in the present, as the consequences of a fundamental set of processes that are common to the past and the present. It goes beyond this particular goal by seeking to develop what is known about the present into a baseline body of knowledge for evaluating some aspects of the character of past system states (*system states* are defined and discussed in chapters 6 and 7). This book explores how we, as archaeologists, can use our knowledge of and in the present to make defensible statements about what the past was like. An equally important concern is how we explain the past, once we are convinced that something reliable is known about it.

Was the past different from what we know of the present? Most researchers would agree that the view of the past that is available through analysis of the archaeological record indicates that human behavior was different in many respects from hunter-gatherer life ways recorded during the era of colonial expansion and more recently. The fundamental synthesis that emerges from archaeological research reveals patterned change through time and the existence of cultural systems with no apparent contemporary counterparts. I will attempt to demonstrate how archaeologists may profitably use the knowledge base developed about ethnographically documented hunting and gathering peoples as a tool in the search for an explanation of cultural variability, both past and present.

This book is Darwinian in the sense that it wrestles with the same problem that Darwin faced: that is, how to take an awareness of great variety in the present and develop explanatory arguments that encompass all similar variety, regardless of time and place. Understanding the complexities of evolutionary processes has preoccupied the biological sciences since Darwin's day. I do not argue that the processual solutions proposed by Darwin will resolve the anthropological challenge of explaining sociocultural diversity and change. I merely maintain that the specification of process, or how the world works, is the key to the growth of further knowledge about evolutionary processes and, ultimately, to understanding.

In the science of biology, the isolation and successive transmission of a subset of the total genetic composition of a population, with little additional admixture, are referred to as the "founder's effect." I propose that a roughly comparable intellectual process has occurred within anthropology generally and particularly with respect to the study of hunter-gatherers. This chapter explores that intellectual legacy—what has been learned about hunter-gatherers in the last 150 years—as well as what remains unknown. The discussion of a series of important efforts to understand and explain variability in hunter-gatherer life ways undertaken by some of anthropology's "founders" frames a sense of problem for us in the present and suggests the direction in which relevant contemporary studies of hunter-gatherers might proceed.

Several Perspectives on Hunter-Gatherer Variability

MARCEL MAUSS AND SEASONAL VARIATIONS

One of the earliest and most thought-provoking treatments of hunter-gatherer settlement patterns and what today would be called the autocorrelated dynamics of social organization was published in 1906 by Marcel Mauss in collaboration with Henri Beuchat (1979). Given the limited ethnographic materials available to the authors, their monograph—entitled *Seasonal Variations of the Eskimo: A Study in Social Morphology*—provided a provocative description of the organizational differences or, as I have previously referred to them, the "structural poses" (Binford and Binford 1966 after Gearing 1962) within a society that can be observed seasonally. From the standpoint of interaction and internal organization, Mauss and Beuchat pointed to significant differences between larger and smaller Eskimo camps and between the winter and summer phases of organized life.

> There is, as it were, a summer religion and a winter religion: or rather, there is no religion during the summer. The only rites that are practised are private, domestic rituals: everything is reduced to the rituals of birth and death and to the observation of certain prohibitions.... By contrast, the winter settlement lives in a state of continuous religious exaltation....
>
> It would appear that there are two kinds of family: one in which kinship is collective, conforming to the type that Morgan called classificatory, and the other in which kinship is individualized.... one is the summer family, the other [former] the winter family.... During the winter the rules of domestic life are entirely different. The nuclear family, so clearly individualized during the summer, tends to disappear to some extent within a much wider group, a kind of joint-family which resembles that of the Zadruga Slavs, and which constitutes domestic society *par excellence*: this is the group who together occupies the same igloo or long-house....
>
> Seasonal variations affect property rights even more significantly than they affect personal rights and duties. First, the objects used vary according to the seasons; food and implements are entirely different in winter and in summer. Second, the material relations that link individuals to one another vary both in number and in kind. Alongside a twofold morphology and technology there is a corresponding twofold system of property rights.... The hunter [in summer] must bring back his entire catch to his tent, no matter how far away he is or how hungry he may be. Europeans have marveled at how strictly this rule is observed. Game and the products that can be extracted from it do not belong to the hunter, but to the family, no matter who hunted it.... The rules for winter are completely different. In contrast to the egoism of the individual or the nuclear family, a generous collectivism prevails. First, there is communal regulation of fixed property. The long-house belongs to none of the families who live in it; it is the joint property of all the "housemates."... Collective rights over food, instead of being limited to the family as in the summer, extend to the entire house. Game is divided equally among all members. The exclusive economy of the nuclear family totally disappears.
>
> (Mauss and Beuchat 1979:57, 62–64, 70–72)

Religion, the family, and property rights are only three of the components of Eskimo life about which Mauss noted important organizational differences between summer and winter. Seasonal contrasts were also reported in the size of settlements and their occupational duration, in the degree to which labor was organized cooperatively or independently, and in the procurement and consumption of food. Differential aggregation and dispersion across the landscape of segments of the larger Eskimo social formation that today might be called regional "bands" compose another set of distinctions in terms of which Mauss compared winter versus summer and interior versus coastal settlement distributions. Settlement patterns at this larger scale of integration were characterized as internally variable and responsive to shifts in seasonal conditions in the environment.

Although more contemporary ethnographic studies of Eskimo peoples have provided many details that to some extent undercut the sweeping generalizations offered by Mauss and Beuchat, the authors' basic point remains valid. More recent studies have confirmed that the major seasonal contrasts typical of the ways in which Eskimo social units were constituted, organized, and positioned are also a feature of hunter-gatherer life in many nonarctic settings.

Unfortunately, Mauss and Beuchat were somewhat vague about the causal factors that might be responsible for the alternating occurrence of different societal states that were identified as coincident with seasonal environmental change. "We have proposed, as a methodological rule, that social life in all its forms—moral, religious, and legal—is dependent on its material substratum and that it varies with this substratum, namely with the mass, density, form and composition of human groups" (Mauss and Beuchat 1979:80). This statement would appear to be a fairly straightforward materialist proposition except for its failure to specify the factors that would operate determinatively on the "mass, density, form and composition of human groups." With regard to this critical omission, earlier in the monograph Mauss and Beuchat made two interesting statements:

> All this suggests that we have come upon a law that is probably of considerable generality. Social life does not continue at the same level throughout the year; it goes

through regular, successive phases of increased and decreased intensity. . . . We might almost say that social life does violence to the minds and bodies of individuals which they can sustain only for a time; and there comes a point when they must slow down and partially withdraw from it. . . .

Instead of being the necessary and determining cause of an entire system, truly seasonal factors may merely mark the most opportune occasions in the year for these two phases to occur.

(Mauss and Beuchat 1979:78–79)

The explanatory framework of Mauss and Beuchat has been interpreted by some researchers (e.g., Fox 1979:1–17) as consistent with the principles of historical materialism in the original sense of this term. I think, however, that the two preceding paragraphs appear to relate alternating Eskimo organizational strategies to a putative limited tolerance of intense sociality and a need for restorative periods of solitude. The monograph's translator, James J. Fox, refers in his foreword to the somewhat different view of Mary Douglas, for whom *Seasonal Variations* represented "an explicit attack on geographical or technological determinism in interpreting domestic organization. It demands an ecological approach in which the structure of ideas and of society, the mode of gaining a livelihood and the domestic architecture are interpreted as a single interacting whole in which no one element can be said to determine the others" (Douglas 1972:512–14).

Although I might agree with Douglas that *Seasonal Variations* presents a systems view of hunter-gatherer society in which distinguishable features are strongly integrated and therefore appear *autocorrelated* with one another—in other words, organized—I am not sure that a holistic view of society in which cause cannot be discussed is implied. Mauss and Beuchat seem to be saying that their "law" has reference to basic or essential human properties that govern the pursuit or avoidance of intense social life and that perhaps the oscillation between social poles determines the pattern of Eskimo aggregation and dispersal, with attendant shifts in structural poses that were noted by the authors.

In spite of the uncertainty about the authors' views on the causes of Eskimo organizational variability, *Seasonal Variations* is a provocative work that sets the stage for future archaeological considerations of settlement pattern. It challenges the normative assumption that societies are internally homogeneous, in both action and organizational poses, and leaves open for investigation the explanation of documented forms of internal variability.

There are, however, additional implications for the methods of study that might or might not be appropriate to the inductive study of social forms. If, as I have suggested, the work of Mauss and Beuchat represents an argument about the organizational integration of social systems, then I would expect many autocorrelations among the apparently different phenomena that are selected when a system is described. Autocorrelations may well be informative about how the system is organized, but they do not reliably signal the causes responsible for the phenomena so organized. In short, autocorrelations may suggest important vectors of organization but may not be indicative of the direction that an explanatory argument about the causes for the organization itself should take. This distinction must be kept in mind as I pursue possible explanations for the variability among hunters and gatherers.

JULIAN STEWARD AND THE BAND

The primary and fundamental cultural medium in terms of which small-scale societies are articulated is referred to by anthropologists as "kinship." Kinship conventions are the tools used to recognize and grade relatedness among persons and, by extension, among families, and they therefore provide the terms for the potential integration and organization of families into larger social formations. There is little doubt that the focus on kinship prevalent in American anthropology in the 1920s had a formative effect on the interests and arguments of Julian Steward. In Steward's student years, many of the arguments in the North American literature had to do with the "explanation" of clans, moieties, sibs, and other forms of kinship-based social categories that were (1) relatively large, (2) commonly multilocal in their spatial and social distributions, and (3) representative of institutions or networks that commonly crosscut observable groups of living people.

When Steward turned his attention to the ethnographic record of hunter-gatherers, he noted that spatially extensive, large-scale, kinship-based institutions were seldom characteristic of the life of the formerly mobile persons among whom he worked. His challenge was to develop a systematic assessment of the observable variability in hunter-gatherer social life, including many groups to whom the terms then being debated in the North American literature did not apply. The product of this research was one of the earliest arguments about variability among hunter-gatherer societies that was not based upon either diffusionist principles or the value-laden idea of progressive development.

Steward recognized three "types" of hunter-gatherer societies when viewed from the perspective of the principles of sociocultural integration: (1) the family level of integration, (2) the band level of integration, and (3) a level of integration characterized by clans and other forms of extended, lineage-like units that were multilocal in their spatial patterning. The empirical model for what was called a *band* appears to have been largely based on nineteenth-century ethnohistoric accounts of Plains Indian societies. Within the band category, Steward identified (a) the lineal band, (b) the composite band, and (c) the predatory band.

One of the points about kinship that loomed large in Steward's thought concerned the relationship between different forms of kin affiliation and observable patterns of group formation. Kinship as the organizing principle underlying many types of group formations is a subject that, over time, has absorbed the attention of numerous anthropologists, among them Meyer Fortes (1969:276–310).[1] Fortes argued that attempts to correlate systems for calculating descent with the social composition of specific human groups can produce confusing results. Although actual human aggregations may in some cases embody relationships defined by a set of kinship principles (as in the case of lineal descent conventions that operate according to rules of inclusion and exclusion), in other situations—such as those in which kin relations are tracked bilaterally—co-resident persons *may be* affiliated by kinship ties, but the group itself cannot be defined in terms of descent.

I think Fortes was correct when he argued for the use of the term *filiation* in reference to cultural conventions—variable from case to case—that direct the way individuals are scaled in terms of social distance and establish expectations for the behavior of persons so differentiated. In other words, filiation can be thought of as the culturally specific conventions for calculating social distance when viewed from the individual perspective. Filiation is fundamentally rooted in the relationship of parent to child, and it shares with genetic distance the fact that the point of reference for a filial structure is simply a knowledge of the parentage of a given individual. Derivative relationships, such as the identification of persons with whom marriage would be permissible or prohibited, are all dependent upon this primary relationship. As Fortes said, "I have considered filiation as the primary credential or set of credentials for activating the initial status relationship of what must necessarily expand into a hierarchy of status relationships for a person to be a complete right- and duty-bearing unit in his society" (1969:276).

Filial relationships are always egocentric since, in all situations, ego is socially defined by the parent-child relationship. Because the parent-child relationship includes both a male and a female parent, any given individual participates in equal, parallel, filial relationships with both parents. Any given individual is therefore doubly defined by his or her parents' relationships and is positioned, as in the case of genetic distance, with equal filial distance to the recognized kin of both male and female parents.

The attempts by anthropologists to uncover within extant or historically documented social groups a set of organizational principles that were fundamentally filial in form have, however, presented great difficulty. In contrast to matrilineal descent conventions, according to which it is not uncommon for sons to marry mother's brother's daughters, bilateral kinship reckoning often results in a situation in which the kinpersons of one's spouse are different from one's own kin. Therefore, co-resident sets of persons that calculate descent bilaterally are frequently characterized by no direct filial linkages, although persons within the group will be related to other persons through their bilateral kin networks. Julian Steward's identification of hunter-gatherer groups that were composed of families unrelated to one another in direct *lineal* terms led him to designate these groups as "composite" bands.

Steward (1936:344) suggested that two very different kinds of factors promoted the existence of or, perhaps more appropriately, transformed lineal bands into composite bands. One set involved demographic or environmental conditions thought to "influence" band endogamy:[2]

1. Unusual band size, produced by greater population density (Cupeno and many tribes who are on a higher subsistence level than those considered here); or unusual ecology such as reliance on migratory herds (Eastern Athabaskans).
2. Remoteness of bands into which to marry (Central African Negritos, Philippine Negritos).
3. Matrilocal residence as conditioned by
   a. Shortage of men in the wife's family or more favorable conditions (subsistence) in the territory of the wife's family (Algonkian).
   b. Lack of a woman to exchange with the wife's band in marriage (Congo Negritos).

Another set of circumstances that Steward (1936:344) cited as contributing to the formation of the composite band resulted from modifications of the customary rules for social inclusion or exclusion dictated by specific kinship conventions:

1. Adoption of children between bands (Andamanese).
2. Legitimacy of parallel as well as cross-cousin marriage (Cape, Namib, and !Okung Bushmen and Philippine Negritos).
3. Desire to secure the assistance of the wife's mother in child rearing (Naron Bushmen).
4. Sufficient strength of borrowed matrilineal institutions. The last may tend to produce matrilineal bands or even societies that are not classifiable as bands.

Steward's analysis of the factors promoting the development of composite bands has several interesting features. First, and perhaps most revealing, is the fact that demographic and environmental conditions, as well as cultural practices or choices, are cited as relevant causes for changes in group composition. Second, there is no attempt at theory building here. Steward simply listed the unique circumstances that he believed produced social arrangements that were exceptions to the "conventional" practice of lineally defined groups and then classified those groups as composite bands.

Steward's listing of correlates, particularly those in the social domain, reveals a somewhat different viewpoint from that of Mauss and Beuchat, provided that one concludes that the sub-liminal message in *Seasonal Variations* argues that within an organized system there would be many autocorrelations that might not betray cause. This point aside, if there *is* an implicit theory underlying the list of conditions that, for Steward, explained the transformation from lineal to composite bands, it is one based on demographic scale. Steward seems to be arguing that in some situations, factors impinge on large social units in such a way that exogamy becomes impossible, whereas, in other cases, the demographic structure interferes with the stability of some set of conditions that are essential to the maintenance of lineal band forms.

Some significant assumptions about human society are also implicit in Steward's discussion of group structure. Of primary interest is his statement that mutual aid, coopera-tion, and sharing are "natural" benefits of group living. Greater security is found in the superfamily group than is avail-able to either isolated families or individuals: "In practically all human groups several families cooperate in some economic activity and frequently share game and even vegetable foods communally. This provides a kind of subsistence insurance or greater security than individual families could achieve" (Steward 1936:332).[3]

Steward seems to regard this assertion as a statement of self-evident reality that requires no explanation. Furthermore, the multifamily, mutualistic or communalistic social unit is assumed a priori to be a *landowning* unit: "Greater human intelligence eliminates the strife of unrestricted competi-tion for food by developing property concepts. Because of these facts, human groups will reach an equilibrium in which land is parceled among definite social groups" (Steward 1936:332).

It is Steward's apparent acceptance of primordial group ownership of land that makes the existence of bilateral kin-ship and the composite band so troubling. Kin reckoning in terms of filiation ensures that the identity of (1) who is a group member and (2) who owns the land presumably controlled by the "group" remains totally ambiguous when viewed from the perspective of egocentric kinship. There seems to be little doubt that Steward considered the composite band as a special case derived from the "normal" patrilineal band (Steward 1955:150). He assumed that in order for there to be "kin-defined" concrete groups, the ambiguity of filiation must be eliminated by the stipulation—necessary for the defi-nition of group boundaries—of a relationship to only one parent. Otherwise, the concrete group would not be kin-defined and the identity of the actual persons entitled to "landowner" status in any particular "landowning" group would be ambiguous.

In his list of factors contributing to the transformation of lineal into composite bands, Steward attempted to summa-rize the conditions that would tend to introduce persons into the local group who were nonkin, in the *emic* sense of the word, and result in a group that was not kin-defined. It is therefore something of a paradox to consider that the unit which is most often cited by anthropologists as the funda-mental social component of larger-scale social systems is *the family.* This unit is always a "composite" unit from the filial perspective of the "egos" who establish such a unit, that is, the married couple. This condition creates the often-discussed reality of a male or female, living with their spouses, either of whom may not be a member of the kin group to which their marriage-based family belongs. Instead, they remain socially defined members of the lineal group of their family of origin and not of their primary life course unit, the fam-ily of procreation.

One can argue that kinship and the kin conventions that Steward focused on were taken for granted, were considered fundamental properties of humankind, and were therefore only subject to examination and generalization in terms of the factors that were presumed to interfere with the normal operation of the conventional patterns of social integration. These assumptions about social organization and the limit-ing factors operating upon its several forms also constitute the basis for Steward's later arguments regarding multilineal evolution (Steward 1953, 1955).

Equally important to an understanding of the develop-ment of Steward's ideas is the fact that in his 1936 paper on hunter-gatherers there is no reference to the "family level of sociocultural integration," a principle that he later devel-oped and discussed in *Theory of Culture Change* (1955). The genesis of this concept, however, lies without question in his work with Great Basin hunter-gatherer materials. In Stew-ard's most important publication on this subject, *Basin-Plateau Aboriginal Sociopolitical Groups* (1938), the term *family level* is not used, but the following statements of great interest appear: "Western Shoshoni, probably Southern Paiute, and perhaps some Northern Paiute fall outside the scope of the previous generalizations [the 1936 classification of bands], which were too inclusive. *They lacked bands and any forms of landownership.* The only stable social and politi-cal unit was the family. Larger groupings for social and eco-nomic purposes were temporary and shifting" (Steward 1938:260; emphasis added).

This statement reveals that Steward's two fundamental cri-teria for identifying a "band" are (1) a relatively permanent or stable census of persons associated as a group, and (2) landownership by such a group. Steward proceeds to offer an explanation for the absence of these properties among the Western Shoshoni and other Great Basin groups:

> The radical departure of these peoples from the band pat-terns, however, is explainable by ecological factors not previously encountered. It has been shown that the unusually great economic importance of seeds largely

restricted the economic unit to the family. Communal enterprises did not always align the same families, so that there were no large groups having political unity. It has also been shown that the peculiar occurrence of certain foods, especially seed species, entailed interlocking subsistence areas which militated against land ownership.

(Steward 1938:260)

The interesting point in the preceding statement relates to the factors that Steward considered responsible for the composite band. In the set of causal conditions outlined in his earlier paper (1936:344), Steward was thinking primarily about the circumstances that would result in a shift from band exogamy to endogamy. When considering the environmental conditions that would favor the formation of composite bands, he had proposed that large group sizes were made possible by highly productive environments or large aggregations of attractive resources, such as migratory herd mammals.[4] In contrast, his 1938 paper proposed that human occupation of *unattractive* environments was the fundamental "reason" accounting for the absence of bands and the presence of the "family level of sociocultural integration."

In Steward's discussion of the family level of sociocultural integration, he overlooked the ambiguities of filiation and focused instead on a pattern of economic independence atypical of the articulations that were assumed to exist among families organized into bands. He observed that "virtually all cultural activities were carried out by the family *in comparative isolation from other families*" (Steward 1955:102; emphasis added). This pattern of economic independence was underscored for Steward by a lack of continuity or perpetuity in the association of and related patterns of cooperation among family units: "I classify the Shoshoneans as an exemplification of a family level of sociocultural integration because in the few forms of collective activity the same group of families did not co-operate with one another or accept the same leader on successive occasions" (Steward 1955:109).

In other words, local groups varied in size, duration of co-residence, and degree of redundancy in household composition, and there was no apparent cooperation or filial regularity to the actual composition of multifamily camps. Steward's diagnosis of familial independence was also supported by related spatial patterning in settlements, notably by the reported lack of close spatial proximity among family residential locations. *There was, therefore, a site structural correlate of the "family level of sociocultural integration"*:[5]

These winter quarters have sometimes been called villages, but they were not tightly nucleated settlements which constituted organized communities. Instead, family houses were widely scattered within productive portions of the piñon zone. The location of each household was determined primarily by its pine nut caches and secondarily by accessibility to wood and water. The scattered families were able to visit one another to dance, gamble, and exchange gossip, and the men occasionally co-operated in a deer or mountain sheep hunt.

(Steward 1955:114–15)

An interesting aspect of Steward's argument is that if one adhered strictly to his criteria for discriminating between lineal and composite bands, the Shoshoni-speaking peoples of the Great Basin would be classified as composite bands since the membership in on-the-ground groups was shifting and unstructured by strict kinship conventions, and therefore the local groups could not be defined by kinship criteria. Why did Steward classify the Shoshoni, the Eskimo (he did not specify which groups), and the Nambicuara, Guato, and Mura groups of South America as different and claim that they represented a different level of sociocultural integration from that of composite bands? The answer to this question rests with the demographic scale or size of the groups with which Steward was working. Composite bands were described by Steward as large relative to the size of patrilineal bands, size was considered the factor responsible for the practice of endogamy, and endogamy enlarged still further the aggregations of families unrelated by kinship conventions. The Shoshoni, however, were organized in even smaller units than those considered characteristic of lineal bands and, therefore, required a separate category.

By focusing on group size, or what Mauss and Beuchat would have called social morphology, Steward was approaching the ethnographic record from a similar perspective: "We have proposed, as a methodological rule, that social life in all its forms—moral, religious, and legal—is dependent on its material substratum and that it varies with this substratum, namely with the mass, density, form and composition of human groups" (Mauss and Beuchat 1979:80). He differed, however, in his belief that the "mass, density, form and composition of human groups" were conditioned quite directly by characteristics of the environment; for Mauss and Beuchat, environmental conditions merely determined when and how the dual human needs of both solitude and social intensity would be indulged.

Another major difference concerned the essential properties of the band level of social organization. Steward's extended arguments with Omer Stewart[6] about whether Great Basin groups were landowning emphasized his criterion of landownership. A second criterion was based on two other attributes of social groups, demographic scale and degree of integration. The connection between these two attributes is demonstrated in the example of composite bands. These groups were large and tended to be endogamous; therefore in Steward's judgment they were integrated.

In the Great Basin, Steward had observed many very small units that related to one another in terms of interpersonal ties and created a network of articulations that apparently lacked integrating institutions, consistent leadership, and sustained economic ties. There was no ownership of land nor any periodic social aggregation except in extemporaneous, situational contexts. Northern Athapaskan peoples, on the other hand, were thought to aggregate in a regular and predictable manner. What Steward meant by a criterion based on the scale of integration is made clear in his later work:

> A striking illustration of the shift of interest from the maximum group, or what was formerly called "band," to the smaller divisions is the contrast between Helm's and Father Morice's reports. Morice's data on the Dogrib Athapaskans gave the band average as 287 persons (1906a). Helm has distinguished these large groups as "regional bands" and shown that they are no more than groups of identification, whereas the "local band" of some 10 to 20 persons constitutes the permanent subsistence unit (Helm 1968, 1969).   (Steward 1970:115)

The difference between what Steward meant by the term *band* and the meaning assigned to that term in the hunter-gatherer literature generated since the mid-1960s resulted from the availability of detailed studies of on-the-ground groups containing observations that contrasted considerably with the way groups had been imagined by earlier researchers. The latter had worked primarily with memory culture information and—in the Americas, at least—with an empirical model of band organization based on the Plains Indians. It is clear from Steward's 1970 statement that he recognized the importance of this difference in observational perspective.

If the seminal works of Julian Steward were the only intellectual resources available to a contemporary archaeologist wishing to explore hunter-gatherer variability, Steward's legacy would consist of the following fundamental assumptions:

1. The formation of social units larger than the biological family is a natural or essential feature of human social existence. Persons belonging to these larger units engage in sharing and communal or cooperative activities in order to insure against misfortune.
2. These suprafamilial communal units are landowning units.
3. Although Steward is not as explicit as a researcher might like, it appears that he considered the original form of the hunter-gatherer band to have been patrilineal, as he defined the term. He states: "Social factors which made for composite bands where patrilineal bands normally occurred include . . ." (Steward 1955:150), after which he lists the circumstances quoted previously (see page 13) as "causes" of composite bands.

In the course of Steward's lifetime, his research in the Great Basin appears to have led him to question the second assumption and to have doubts about at least some aspects of the first. He postulated a family level of sociocultural integration for some, if not most, of the Paiute and Shoshoni groups of the American Great Basin, and he repeatedly included unspecified Eskimo groups in this category. (At the Man the Hunter Conference in 1966 I was told by Fred Eggan that Steward was referring to the Copper Eskimo.) He also argued that in these groups there was little cooperative effort extending beyond the immediate family and that they were not landowning.

Steward lived long enough to be able to examine his assumptions in the light of knowledge gained from more recent field work, reports of which were presented at Canadian conferences in 1965 and 1966, as well as at the Man the Hunter Conference, also held in 1966. These ethnographic studies questioned whether mobile hunter-gatherers were characteristically landowning and whether Steward's earlier ideas about band size were accurate, at least as far as on-the-ground groups exploiting the landscape were concerned (Steward 1969:290–94). From an archaeological perspective, however, the allusions to spatial phenomena embedded in Steward's descriptions of Great Basin peoples were truly provocative. In light of the characteristics of hunter-gatherer society that were emerging from more contemporary research, his depiction of social units camping in small, widely dispersed aggregates and characterized by dispersed intrahousehold spacing illustrated the need for further investigation.

ARGUMENTS ABOUT ACCULTURATION BY STEWARD, SPECK, AND EISELEY

Contemporary with Steward's work, an ongoing set of arguments debated the precontact character of socioeconomic life among the northern Algonkian peoples. Frank Speck (1915) had argued that nuclear families of northern Algonkian hunter-gatherers in eastern Canada were landowning units. Speck was convinced that this characteristic was not restricted to northern Algonkian peoples but was, instead, prevalent in a wide variety of ethnic groups (the Veddah; Australian Aborigines; many groups in northeastern Asia; the Aleuts, Ona, and Yahgan; some Athapaskan cases; and Northwest Coast groups) (Speck 1926). Supporters of Speck's position (e.g., Cooper 1939) cited the Punan and other, mostly reindeer-herding, groups from Asia as additional examples of landowning at the family level of organization.

The context of these arguments was made explicit in a 1942 paper by Speck and Eiseley, which suggested that there were two types of hunter-gatherer societal form in the Labrador area of Canada:

> One is nomadic and communal in structure as regards the grouping of biological family units to form a collective band. . . . The second type is based upon the more sedentary limited nomadic family principle and seems to remain confined to the coniferous forest area. *The factor operating chiefly to determine the two is, we believe, traceable in large degree to the natural history of the game*

animals which alone furnish the natives of the Labradorean area with their subsistence.
        (Speck and Eiseley 1942:219; emphasis added)

In short, Speck and Eiseley argued that ecological factors were responsible for the presence of communal versus family-based forms of landownership and that these factors had operated in the past to produce the same effect. They concluded, therefore, that the family-based form of landownership was an aboriginal pattern with considerable time-depth in the human experience,[7] and they situated their arguments in the context of a wider debate within the anthropological community:

> Does band ownership, for example, precede the family system? Does the assignment of land to individual families by the head man … precede the direct handing down of territories within the family? … These and many other questions present themselves for an answer. Their shadow must inevitably be troubling to those who, like Morgan, and many present-day Russians, would see the culture of the lower hunters as representing a stage prior to the development of the institution of individualized property.   (Speck and Eiseley 1942:238)

This view challenged the more general consensus, subscribed to by Steward, that Morgan was essentially correct in his depiction of the character of early society as communalistic. It is interesting to recall that throughout Steward's active career, his view was consistent with the prevalent contemporary assessment, which interprets the landowning practices documented by Speck among the northern Algonkians as a response to changes brought about during the "culture contact" period initiated by the fur trade. This view argues that familial landownership was the consequence of acculturation and not an aboriginal state of affairs. The argument over landownership remains unresolved and is discussed in the work of Eleanor Leacock in the recent era (Leacock 1954; Leacock and Lee 1982).

STEWARD ON ACCULTURATION

In 1956, Robert F. Murphy collaborated with Steward on a paper entitled "Tappers and Trappers: Parallel Process in Acculturation." The authors presented a variant of Leacock's acculturation argument to explain the postcontact appearance of family hunting territories that Speck had documented so extensively among the northeastern Algonkians. Acculturative event sequences, as they were described by Leacock and others, were compared to analogous event sequences documented by Murphy among the Mundurucu of Brazil. In the northeastern Algonkian cases, an increasing number of articulations with traders had produced changes in basic subsistence strategies, and, as a result, communal activities were gradually replaced by individual family units trap-

ping for their own benefit. This change ultimately led to the distribution of small, relatively isolated social units in a diffuse settlement pattern and to a system of land tenure in which families attempted to maintain control of their trapping territories by claiming property rights to ranges that they had once exploited as part of a societally sanctioned, usufruct monopoly.

Although aboriginal Mundurucu social organization was thought to have been very different from what is known of northeastern Algonkian social structure, the cases are similar in one respect. Exploitation of the latex in a tract of rubber trees is a solitary activity that involves tapping the trees, processing the collected latex, and maintaining on a daily basis the path (called an "avenue") through the lowland undergrowth that defines the boundary surrounding the one hundred or more trees maintained by one individual. As Murphy and Steward noted, "the distribution of rubber trees is such that each avenue gives access to trees within an area of about three to five square miles" (1956:343), depending on the density of the rubber trees. As the Mundurucu involvement in latex extraction increased, rubber tree avenues became more extensive and tappers and their families became more dispersed. The parallel centrifugal trajectories of both the northeastern Athapaskans and the Mundurucu were said to have resulted in the geographic dispersal of family-level units and a dissolution of integrative institutions, leadership, and cooperative endeavors. It was in this context that access monopolies were maintained by individual families over trapping and tapping areas.

Based on the ethnographic case material discussed in their paper, Murphy and Steward presented two general propositions summarizing changes in subsistence strategy and social organization in acculturative contexts:

> *When goods manufactured by the industrialized nations with modern techniques become available through trade to aboriginal populations, the native people increasingly give up their home crafts in order to devote their efforts to producing specialized cash crops or other trade items in order to obtain more of the industrially made articles. …*
> *When the people of an unstratified native society barter wild products found in extensive distribution and obtained though individual effort, the structure of the native culture will be destroyed, and the final culmination will be a culture type characterized by individual families having delimited rights to marketable resources and linked to the larger nation through trading centers.* Tappers, trappers, and no doubt other collectors come under this general statement.
> (Murphy and Steward 1956:353; emphasis in original)

These two processes have been documented in many encounters between native peoples and the global expansion of western industrial-capitalist society. One interesting feature of this argument is the linkage Murphy and Steward made between ownership of land or property rights and a very specialized subsistence strategy. In the situations they describe, one set of related tasks is performed and the products therefrom are used to acquire most of a family's subsistence necessities (in most instances, some minor component is obtained while engaged in the very specialized task). It is important, however, to note in the second proposition the use of the phrase "*wild products found in extensive distribution and obtained through individual effort.*" This phrase should be compared with the previously quoted proposition by Speck and Eiseley: "The second type [the noncommunal familial form] is based upon the more sedentary limited nomadic family principle and seems to remain confined to the coniferous forest area. *The factor operating chiefly to determine the two is, we believe, traceable in large degree to the natural history of the game animals which alone furnish the natives of the Labradorean area with their subsistence*" (Speck and Eiseley 1942:219; emphasis added).

It is apparent that both Murphy and Steward, as well as Speck and Eiseley, believed that the distribution and character of exploited resources determined which alternative—cooperation or independence—was characteristic of residential labor units. The same environmental factors also conditioned the size of those social units that were economically independent. Steward and Speck differed only over the issue of landownership, which Steward specifically denied was characteristic of the Shoshoni, and not over the actual existence of widely dispersed family units lacking strong interfamilial economic ties. This similarity in views is not surprising since I have already discussed Steward's recognition, within the range of hunter-gatherer variability, of the family level of sociocultural integration exemplified for him by the Great Basin Shoshoni. Steward was certainly aware of the possibility that ecological factors could contribute to a family level of organization, and he had discussed them in detail only a year before the "Tappers and Trappers" paper was written. Clearly, Steward felt that a small social unit consisting of the family as the core economic entity was a predictable feature of particular aboriginal conditions in certain environmental settings.

THE ATOMISTIC SOCIETY

The Murphy and Steward paper was roughly contemporary with a general reconsideration by anthropologists of the types of hunter-gatherer social formations observed by ethnographers. One particular focus of this wider inquiry involved the Canadian communities that had experienced a long period of Euroamerican interaction prior to extensive ethnographic documentation. Although some researchers began to use the term *atomism* to refer to the kinds of social articulations documented in Canada and other regions, the

term itself had been introduced into the anthropological literature several decades earlier. For example, in the work of William G. Sumner, sometimes referred to as one of the major advocates of Social Darwinism, the term *atomism* appears in the following context:

> There are observed cases where the close-knit world-society of civilized mankind finds its prototype in the scarcely more than temporary and scattering kin-groups of the Australian natives or the African Bushmen and Pygmies. Not only are these societies small, unstable, and disconnected, but their members harbor sentiments toward outsiders and even toward each other that cannot, by any stretch of the imagination, be interpreted as brotherly. Where men are existing with slight resources on the edge of catastrophe—and, except in certain favored spots, we take this to have been the original state—they are full of hostility, suspicion, and other anti-social feelings and habits.
> (Sumner and Keller 1927, 1:16)

> The account of Homer concerning the Cyclopes, the representatives to him of utter savagery, is typical of *atomism:* "Each rules his consorts and children, and they pay no heed to one another."
> (Sumner et al. 1927, IV:1; emphasis added)

Although Sumner is not cited in the 1960s revival of the concept of "primitive atomism" and its introduction is usually attributed to Ruth Benedict, the concept is nevertheless similar to some of Sumner's ideas. The essential features of atomism were established in a series of articles characterizing this societal state: "The atomistic-type of society . . . is a society in which the nuclear family represents the major structural unit and, indeed, almost the only formalized social entity" (Rubel and Kupferer 1968:189).

John Honigmann, an ethnographer reporting on many different North American groups, including Eskimos, outlined the characteristics of societies to which the term *structural atomism* would be applied:

> Structural atomism, corresponding to the empirical level, includes such observable characteristics of behavior as the following:
> (1) Primary concern is put on a person's own individual interests and on great freedom from, or avoidance of, social constraint. As a result, interpersonal behavior strongly manifests the property of individualism. This has been the core meaning of atomism, and the word was so used by Ruth Benedict in her Bryn Mawr lectures to describe "the very simple societies as atomistic." "They recognize only individual allegiances and ties," she said. "They lack the social forms necessary for group action."
> (2) People reveal a tendency to retreat from too intense or unnecessary contact with neighbors, with the result that interpersonal relations are marked by empirically demonstrable reserve, restraint, or caution . . . interest is most often confined to short-term con-

sequences or expected reciprocities; such relationships do not give rise to long-term structural obligations. . . .

(3) A reluctance of people to commit themselves to large groups, even when ecological conditions allow such forms to appear. . . . The nuclear family represents the major structural unit and, in fact, almost the only formalized social entity. . . . Benedict in her Bryn Mawr lectures maintained that when mutual helpfulness does occur in an atomistic social setting, the individual helps others "on their enterprises as they help him on his, rather than carrying out enterprises which some permanently constituted group engages in together, where the results are common property." Subsequently, she observed that "anthropologists have not found any atomistic society with high synergy"—that is, with a social system geared to mutual advantage. . . .

(4) Weak and ineffectual leadership and reluctance to delegate or even to assume political authority are further features of social atomism, . . .

(5) Finally, social relations in an atomistic community are marked by strain, contention, or invidiousness.
(Honigmann 1968:220–21)

Honigmann regards atomism as a characteristic of "simple" societies and seems to expect that "simple" hunter-gatherers would exhibit the defining atomistic attributes whether or not they had also experienced a period of acculturation. The following summary of the attributes of atomistic society demonstrates that the anthropologists who were concentrating on this issue were attempting to define a social type or, as Steward would say, a level of sociocultural integration:

Structural atomism is characterized by a lack of cooperation beyond that of the immediate family. Interpersonal relations beyond the family are weak and short-lived, occurring primarily to achieve individualistic short-range goals rather than persisting group goals. Such societies are frequently encountered among the hunting peoples of the world—for example, Steward's family level of social integration, and many of the groups which Service classifies as on the band level but with primarily familistic bonds of interpersonal relationships. These are the societies that illustrate Benedict's notion of atomism due to the lack of those social forms which unite larger groups of people into concerted action. On the surface, the causal factor would seem to be the low level of technology which prohibits large population aggregates. (Lévy 1968:230–31)

Instead of involving any communal sharing of goals or ongoing commitment of persons to one another beyond the family unit, structural atomism was a social form in which individualism was dominant, communal obligations and actions were minimal, and cooperation took the form that Sahlins (1972) would later call balanced reciprocity. Those who explored the notion of atomism, particularly with reference to northern hunter-gatherers, argued that society was simply an integration of individuals rather than an integration of statuses:

Allegiances and ties of social obligation, in other words, are not lacking in social atomism. On the contrary, the individual member of an atomistic society "may attain his goals by helpfulness to other individuals, but he helps them on their enterprises and they help him on his, rather than carrying out enterprises that some permanently constituted group engage in together. . . . Individual acts [of helpfulness] are at the discretion of the individual.
Munch and Marske (1981:161) quoting Benedict in Maslow and Honigmann (1970:323)

Among those persons contributing to hunter-gatherer research and debate today, Peter Gardner was the first to argue that atomism was characteristic of recently documented hunter-gatherer systems (Gardner 1965, 1966, 1969, 1972, 1978, 1982, 1983, 1985, 1988). In his 1965 Ph.D. thesis, the social life of the Paliyans of South India was such that "individualism, familism, general social atomism, and covert revenge join forces with demography so that reliance can be placed only on primary kin bilaterally reckoned. . . . Weak leadership is one of the implications of atomism, symmetric respect, and avoidance of overt aggression. Supernatural sanctions are similarly consistent with lack of cooperation and lack of authority hierarchy" (Gardner 1965:103–4).

In attempting to explain the factors responsible for the atomistic character of Paliyan social life, Gardner identified three causal domains: (1) the cultural environment, (2) the natural environment, and (3) demographic patterns. The features that prompted Gardner to classify the Paliyans as an atomistic society were, however, attributed primarily to the cultural environment:

The Paliyans dwell in the hills, but, conspicuously, their habitat is further limited to just the lower slopes. Above live the shifting agriculturists and below, the Tamils. This particular zone lacks all of the requisite resources for profitable agriculture, and is, in fact, most forbidding to gatherers too. . . . The Paliyan is vocal on all these points; he is aware of his lack of fortune. It is not the area that persons with unlimited freedom would choose, whatever their subsistence pattern. In other words, the Paliyans have withdrawn, or been pushed, into their present natural environment. Further validity to this finding is given by our review of the history of culture contact. . . .

Pressure from outsiders leads to retreat. It is clear that in the event of unavoidable contact, the Paliyans have little alternative but to act submissively. It is the expected response and the one which most quickly brings cessation of hostility from the outsiders. This aspect of environment is a contributor to the whole complex of retreat, avoidance of overt aggression, and framing interpersonal relations in terms of symmetric respect.
(Gardner 1965:101–2)

The Paliyans clearly exhibited many of the social characteristics implied by the term *structural atomism,* and Gardner advanced an argument attributing at least some of the features of the complex—particularly their withdrawal response in a competitive situation as well as their refugee status—to cultural pressures from more powerful neighbors. He then examined a sample of twenty-seven social groups in terms of a list of characteristics that he considered integral to the cultural state of the Paliyans and identified six different types of hunter-gatherer sociocultural organizations in the data set. The type most relevant to the history of hunter-gatherer research is the suite of cases most like the Paliyans in their response to intercultural pressure from more socially dominant neighbors. This set consisted of (1) the Malapandaram (referred to as the Hill Pandaram in this study), who lived in the same region as the Paliyans and have been more recently studied by Brian Morris (1982a); (2) the Kadar, also located in South India and described by Ehrenfels (1952); (3) the Semang of the Malay Peninsula, who have been characterized by Fox (1969) as "professional primitives"; (4) the !Kung of Botswana and Namibia, who were presented in the anthropological literature (in the year after Gardner's thesis submission) as an archetypal form of hunter-gatherer society, previously isolated from outside contact (Lee 1968);[8] (5) the Mbuti, another group claimed to exemplify an original hunter-gatherer social form (Meillassoux 1972); and (6) the Paiute-Shoshoni, whom Steward (1936) identified as an example of the family level of sociocultural integration.

The 1960s discussion of social atomism emphasized societal forms and features that contrasted sharply with the views of researchers who assumed that "primal" hunter-gatherer societies were characterized by a kind of "primitive communism." Investigators of structural atomism also ignored earlier arguments about family ownership of territory that had represented a challenge to the assumption that "original" hunter-gatherer societies were communalistic. Gardner's analysis ignored the issue of landownership and attributed the similarities between the Paliyan and the Great Basin Shoshoni to the consequences of intersocial competition and acculturation rather than to the distribution and scarcity of resources (sensu Steward). He also argued that a similar set of dynamics had affected the !Kung in the Kalahari.

During the 1960s, Gardner was not the only anthropologist to claim that social atomism was attributable to processes of acculturation and its social consequences. The primary advocate of this viewpoint was Elman Service, although Gardner does not cite his research.

ELMAN SERVICE AND THE ACCULTURATION VIEW

The intellectual ancestry of Service's formulations can be traced to two arguments by Julian Steward, one of which concerned the circumstances promoting the formation of composite bands. Another logically parallel discussion claimed

that hunter-gatherers differed in the character of the basic economic units into which local groups were organized. Steward had recognized that nuclear and even minimally extended families were invariably organized within local groups as subunits. There did, however, appear to be differences among hunter-gatherer groups in the degree to which economic principles or forms of behavior assumed to be characteristic of families could be said to characterize the broader economic interaction among households living together in camps.

The emphasis by both Steward and Speck on the character and distribution of resources as causal factors in the development of social forms was replaced in Service's arguments by the elevation of acculturation to the position of an explanatory principle. For Service, the band was an integrated and familially linked social formation that constituted the primal, fundamental cooperative unit of hunter-gatherer society. Bands were communal and were characterized economically by what Sahlins (1972) later referred to as "the domestic mode of production." Since bands were by definition kin-based, the ambiguously defined, composite local groups noted by Steward were to be understood in the following terms: "The causes of the modern fluid, informal, composite band clearly lie in the initial shocks, depopulation, relocation, and other disturbances in the early contact period which produced refugee-like groups of unrelated families among the Indians even before the time of the American Revolutionary War. Depopulation owing to European diseases had the first and most devastating social effects" (Service 1962:88; see also page 108).

Steward's characterization of Shoshoni and Eskimo economic organization as operating at the family level was explainable, in Service's view, as the product of a sequence of historical events that disrupted the "natural state" of hunter-gatherer social organization and was therefore epiphenomenal:

> Most of the bands under survey here, including patrilocal bands like the central Australians, are composed of nuclear family units that themselves undertake most of the economic tasks. The families are rarely all together in a total meeting of the band or bands. The big difference in any of these bands is whether reciprocal exogamy between groups or sodalities and virilocal residence rules are operative; this is what determines whether several nuclear families, *scattered or not*, are a structured band of families or are at a "family level," with the larger society being merely informal, haphazard, and *ad hoc*.   (Service 1962:95; emphasis in original)

Service paid relatively little attention to economics. Instead, his concept of the band rested heavily on one set of implicit preconditions that included territoriality (or what Steward would have called landownership) as well as the formal rules for marriage and postmarital residence governing the behavior of territorial or geographically bounded corporate groups. In Service's typology of human social organization, hunter-gatherers constituted the band level, and it was argued that there were no ecological or environmental correlates of the archetypal or primal organizational form, the patrilocal band: "It is truly an important, even astonishing, fact that we find this social structure in all the major quarters of the earth and in such tremendously varying habitats as deserts, seacoasts, plains, and jungles, in tropical, polar, and temperate zones, with great variations in kinds and amounts of food, and with seasonal and yearly alterations in the supplies. This is an even better reason for thinking that the patrilocal band is early; it seems almost an inevitable kind of organization" (Service 1962:107–8).

Service makes two key points in this revealing statement. First, the distribution of the patrilocal band, which appears to vary randomly with environmental variables, justifies his rejection of the relevance of ecology to an understanding of social variability among hunter-gatherers (Service 1962:73). And second, by appealing to diffusionist principles from an earlier era of anthropology—in particular the "age area hypothesis," which argued that the traits with the most general distribution were the oldest—Service posits the patrilocal band as the original form of social structure among ancient hunter-gatherers.

Earlier in his monograph Service had discussed the conditions responsible for the formation of the primal, patrilocal band: "It has been argued so far that rules of reciprocal band exogamy are related to peacemaking alliance and offense-defense situations, that is, to the superorganic environment rather than to food-getting alone. The rule of virilocal residence is also related to male cooperation in offense-defense, and not always to hunting alone. . . . Band exogamy and virilocal residence make a patrilocal band" (Service 1962:75).

It is clear that if one accepts that the patrilocal band was the original, generic form of hunter-gatherer organization, one must also accept that the alleged causes (conflict and its social ramifications) were early and essentially perpetual and ubiquitous. Second, one would have to be comfortable with the essentialist notion that territoriality and its correlates—local band exogamy and virilocal residence—were the essential, defining features of hunter-gatherer social life.

Service's arguments were so well insulated by sweeping claims for the effects of culture contact that counterarguments based on empirical evidence could always be dismissed by asserting that the challenging cases were not representative of primal conditions. Despite the fact that Service's arguments were discussed and accepted by many anthropologists, they were never tested in any technical sense and were, instead, merely replaced later with an alternative argument purporting to identify a different primal form of hunter-gatherer society.

Implications for spatial phenomena that archaeologists could pursue were embedded in Julian Steward's arguments, but there were no similar implications for archaeologists in Service's arguments. The issue generated by Service's views was, instead, the relevance of ethnographic experience to an understanding of the past. His arguments indirectly challenged the generalizations from ethnographic experience previously discussed here, i.e., the work of Mauss, Speck, Steward, and the proponents of social atomism, which all addressed some aspect of social organization among ethnographically documented cases. Service's argument postulated an invariable primal form of social organization for past hunter-gatherers and related observed organizational variability to the more recent historical, colonial context. This static view of the past referred variability in the present to conditions of acculturation in the present—in other words, it was a historical explanation.

Service specifically denied the relevance of the ecological factors that were explored by Steward, Speck, and even Mauss and were implicit in Leacock's critique (1954) of Speck's position. There was little discussion of the issue of individualism versus communalism, but the form of past society imagined by Service was consistent with a communalist formulation.

THE CONFERENCE SYNTHESIS

The Conference on Band Societies held in Canada in 1965 (Damas 1969) and the 1966 Man the Hunter Conference in Chicago (Lee and DeVore 1968) had a tremendous impact on the anthropological view of hunter-gatherers and, for a large group of students, defined what was considered germane to know about them. Certainly, the summary characterization by Richard Lee and Irvin DeVore (1968) of the "nomadic style" has set the tone for discussion up through the present time. The following statement about hunter-gatherers is particularly important: "The economic system is based on several core features including a home base or camp, a division of labor—with males hunting and females gathering—and, most important, a pattern of sharing out the collected food resources" (Lee and DeVore 1968:11).

What Lee and DeVore are doing here—that is, characterizing hunting and gathering as a way of life or a mode of production by abstracting a set of essential characteristics of a normatively conceived life way—is still very much in the tradition of preceding authors, although the typifying terms are different. (A contrasting approach would involve a consideration of variables that might be expected to vary across cases and perhaps be seen as responsive to other variables in terms of causal processes.) If Lee and DeVore's static characterization of the "organizational base line of the small-scale society from which subsequent developments can be derived"

(1968:11) is accepted as the primal human condition (Isaac 1978a, 1978b; Leakey and Lewin 1977) or as an archetypal form, then the task of researchers is to uncover the factors that disrupted, modified, or distorted this original "persistent and well-adapted way of life" (Lee 1968:43).[9]

Lee and DeVore's formulation of the five essential characteristics contributing to the character of the "organizational base line" was rather clearly drawn from Lee's experiences with the !Kung Bushmen. Their normative or archetypal view of the original form of hunter-gatherer society has remained relatively unchanged in Lee's writing over the years. For instance: "Historical materialism argues that there exists a core of culture in primitive society that is intimately linked to mode of production. It is much longer lived, has a much deeper time-depth, than our own Western capitalist culture. Historical materialism further argues that this culture core is communal: the collective right to basic resources and the egalitarian political culture. By a dictionary definition of communism, our ancestors were communist" (Lee 1990:232).

This perspective shaped Lee's thinking prior to his initial field work among the !Kung and has been expressed more and more clearly in recent years, although, as Gellner has pointed out, it represents a reversion to nineteenth-century ideas: "Social anthropology was born of the hope of using the contemporary savage as a time machine, and modern Western anthropology emerged from the rejection of this aspiration" (Gellner 1973:537–38).

By "modern Western anthropology" Gellner is referring to the view that variability in cultural phenomena does not simply represent deviations from a primal form but is instead the consequence of contingent processes in which variables interact differentially and affect one another to produce variety. In light of the variability documented in contemporary ethnographic cases, the research challenge is to isolate, study, and understand the causal processes responsible for the observable range of differences. If one adopts a position claiming that there was an original, invariable form of social organization, then the intellectual goal is to identify it and to explain how subsequent diversity occurred. Either the primeval state was good (sensu Rousseau) and the problem is to identify the factors that led to the corruption of the ideal condition (which has been the quest of historical materialists and others who are less easy to label), or the primeval state was bad (sensu Hobbes) and the challenge is explain what factors caused conditions to improve and were responsible for human progress.

Except for the occasional intrusion of antiquated nineteenth-century notions of essential social forms, the terms in which hunter-gatherers were discussed in the conferences of 1965 and 1966 demonstrated that significant knowledge growth had occurred. For example, the recognition that a static model of social units was no longer a productive perspective was illustrated by Woodburn's (1968) descriptions of the

Hadza. Lee (1968) and Turnbull (1968) stressed the same observations that had impressed Julian Steward: that is, families were reported to change their associations regularly, and thus the composition of local groups could be highly variable from one time to another within a single camp and also varied as camps were established and abandoned. This observation was even extended to societies that appeared to exhibit strict lineal definition of corporate groups, such as the Australian Aborigines, although this view of Australian systems was also criticized (Hiatt 1962; Stanner 1965).

The issue of territoriality, which earlier anthropologists had assumed was an original feature of human life, was reassessed in light of reports that many mobile hunter-gatherer claims to exclusive use of territory were not in any way comparable to the ownership of private property. It was argued that their relationships to the habitat were organized in very different terms than previous notions of corporate control of territory had specified.

In another important development at the conferences, the assumption that hunter-gatherers were overworked and underdeveloped because of the difficulty of meeting basic subsistence needs was challenged. Implicit in the old idea that "starvation stalks the stalker" (Sahlins 1968:85) was the belief that hunter-gatherers did not have sufficient leisure time to invent more complex cultural forms. If anything, the pendulum swung to the opposite pole of opinion with regard to the amount of leisure time available to hunter-gatherers.

All of these topics, as well as the issue of sharing, continue to be investigated and discussed in the contemporary hunter-gatherer literature. At the Man the Hunter Conference, sharing was viewed by some participants as a behavioral manifestation of the primeval communal ethic, even though it was clear that there were many situations in which hunter-gatherer groups did not share. Some researchers felt a more productive approach was to attempt to explain the continuum of sharing behavior rather than label those cases that did not fit the archetypal model as deviant or progressive (depending upon whether one accepted Rousseau's or Hobbes's view of the original condition of man). The contrast in views is made vivid by comparing Lee's statement on hunter-gatherers and sharing (see page 21) with Fred Eggan's (1968) remarks at the conference:

> I want to follow up one of Washburn's points on adaptation versus flexibility. There is a series of norms or sanctions with regard to the sharing of food. It seems to me that they often differ with the kind of food—meat, fish, or vegetable—with the size of the animals involved, and with the latitude of the location. I remember looking at the Siberian-central Asian data, and in that area food-sharing increases to the north and decreases to the south. I wonder whether these patterns of sharing, if we worked them out, might not give us something relevant to the problem of adaptation, even an index to it.
>
> (Eggan 1968:85)

The focus in the anthropological literature on sharing behavior has increased since the Man the Hunter Conference, but unfortunately not enough attention has been devoted to reporting and attempting to explain the "patterns of sharing" to which Eggan referred. Instead, an increasingly integrated argument has been developed and systematically presented by Marshall Sahlins, defining the relationships between communalism, social solidarity, economics, sharing, and the spatial relationships among households, as well as scales of social integration.

SAHLINS AND THE DOMESTIC FOCUS

If I were to ask several anthropological theorists to enumerate the propositions that they accept as justified uniformitarian assumptions, their statements would provide a logical baseline in terms of which to compare their theories. If one of the theorists was Marshall Sahlins, he would probably offer two uniformitarian assumptions as the foundation of his arguments. The first would be that the fundamental building block of society is the family, which is also the fundamental reproductive unit, and that all societies in the precapitalist world were organized articulations of these fundamental units. The second assumption would be that human societies articulate such units into larger social formations using extrasomatic or cultural mechanisms. Sahlins might add that the cultural definitions of just what constitutes a family, the ways that families are socially articulated, and the conventions for recognizing and organizing more distant kin are emic phenomena and may therefore be expected to vary from setting to setting.

Probably the arguments most commonly invoked by archaeologists when they attempt to make inferences about social organization in the past have been derived from Sahlins's work. These arguments may be considered transformational in that various domains such as kinship, economics, family well-being, social distance, interactional intensities, and knowledge of others are viewed as integrated and therefore *autocorrelated phenomena*. That is, everything is embedded in the single social phenomenon of kinship, which is said to be the conventional locus for the organized features of small-scale societies, particularly those of hunter-gatherers.

Sahlins's argument, which has several components, was first introduced in his much-misunderstood article in the book *Man the Hunter* (1968), entitled "Notes on the Original Affluent Society." His point was elaborated more fully in his own book, *Stone Age Economics* (1972:1–39). It represents an argument that can be viewed in several ways. I prefer to see it as a particularly important challenge to the idea, prevalent in the anthropological literature in the mid-1960s, that life was so difficult and uncertain that hunter-gatherers had no

alternative than to spend all available time searching for food. The temporal demands of the hunter-gatherer food quest had been held responsible for the apparent stability, documented archaeologically, in hunter-gatherer life ways. There had been no time, it was argued, for the development of social complexity, philosophy, art, and other highly valued features of Western industrialized society.

Sahlins's "leisure time hypothesis" challenged the view that "man's wants are great, not to say infinite, whereas his means are limited" (Sahlins 1968:85). Sahlins argued (1) that hunter-gatherers *did* have leisure time and that temporal investment in subsistence could not be the factor inhibiting "progress"; and (2) that the essentialist assumption that all people had unlimited "wants" was questionable. Despite suggestions by subsequent authors (Bettinger 1991:100; Foley 1988:207; Hawkes and O'Connell 1981; Riches 1982:213) to the contrary, Sahlins was not suggesting that life was easy or secure. He was saying, rather, that there was no vitalistic force in the form of unlimited needs that drove hunter-gatherers to produce surplus and "build culture" (Sahlins 1968:85). It was in this context that he later proposed the "domestic mode of production" as characteristic of hunter-gatherer and other societies that he claimed were organized by a "production for use" strategy that resulted in chronic underproduction (Sahlins 1972:86). Sahlins argued that the family was the unit that produced for use and that when its needs were met production ceased:

> The DMP [domestic mode of production] harbors an antisurplus principle. Geared to the production of livelihood, it is endowed with the tendency to come to a halt at that point. Hence if "surplus" is defined as output above the producers' requirements, the household system is not organized for it. Nothing within the structure of production for use pushes it to transcend itself. The entire society is constructed on an obstinate economic base, therefore on a contradiction, because unless the domestic economy is forced beyond itself the entire society does not survive.   (Sahlins 1972:86)

Sahlins is making a classic Marxist argument here, the structure of which involves establishing a contradiction and then proceeding to define a dialectic through which the apparent contradiction is resolved. Sahlins himself commented on his use of this logical device: "The determination of the main organization of production at an infrastructural level of kinship is one way of facing the dilemma presented by primitive societies to Marxist analyses, namely, between the decisive role accorded by theory to the economic base and the fact that the dominant economic relations are in quality superstructural, e.g., kinship relations" (Sahlins 1972:102, note 1).

This statement introduces another important component of Sahlins's argument, the assertion that "primitive societies" are kin-based societies. For Sahlins, kinship is the ideological (superstructural) context in which the domestic mode of production is embedded and integrated, and the vitality of the larger multifamily society is derived from this context. Crucial to this argument is acceptance of the premise that within communities there is a quasi-normal distribution of household production such that some households produce below their needs and others produce beyond their needs. Sahlins also suggested that some *communities,* relative to their needs, overproduce while others underproduce. It is at this juncture that kinship plays a pivotal role in the argument: "The kinship relations prevailing between households must affect their economic behavior. Descent groups and marital alliances of different structure, even interpersonal kin networks of different pattern, should differentially encourage surplus domestic labor. And with varying success, too, kinship relations counter the centrifugal movement of the DMP, to determine a more or less intensive exploitation of local resources" (Sahlins 1972:123).

Clearly the superstructural principle of kinship is viewed as a scale of social distance that differentially incorporates persons into larger domestic and quasi-domestic units. Sahlins made this point in the following example: "Where Eskimo kinship categorically isolates the immediate family, placing others in a social space definitely outside, Hawaiian extends familial relationships indefinitely along collateral lines. The Hawaiian household economy risks an analogous integration in the community of households. Everything depends on the strength and spread of solidarity in the kinship system. Hawaiian kinship is in these respects superior to Eskimo . . . specifying in this way a wider cooperation" (Sahlins 1972:123).

As the solidarity of the domestic unit expands to include a broader social formation, the negative properties of the domestic mode of production—Sahlins used the terms *antisurplus, antisocial, centrifugal, a segmentary fragility,* and *a species of anarchy* to characterize the DMP—are offset. (The term *primitive atomism* might be added to Sahlins's list of negative properties.) "Maximum dispersion is the settlement pattern of the state of nature. . . . Left to its own devices, the DMP is inclined toward a maximum dispersion of homesteads, because maximum dispersion is the absence of interdependence and a common authority, and these are by and large the way production is organized" (Sahlins 1972:97).

Having advanced this perspective, Sahlins proceeded to discuss the relationship between kinship and economics in terms of a scale of economic transactions ranging from generalized reciprocity to negative reciprocity (Sahlins 1972: 193–96). Generalized reciprocity borders on altruism and is said to characterize economic transactions within the domestic unit. It embodies behaviors that in the archaeological literature are usually referred to as *sharing,* and it is frequently assumed to be a basic characteristic of hunter-gatherer sociality. Balanced reciprocity occurs at the midpoint of the scale and involves direct exchanges in which "reciprocation is the

customary equivalent of the thing received and is without delay" (Sahlins 1972:194). Negative reciprocity is the polar opposite of generalized reciprocity, involving the attempt to get something for nothing, as in an exploitative relationship.

After outlining the continuum of economic relationships, Sahlins linked reciprocity to its determining criteria: "The span of social distance between those who exchange conditions the mode of exchange. Kinship distance, as has already been suggested, is especially relevant to the form of reciprocity. Reciprocity is inclined toward the generalized pole by close kinship, toward the negative extreme in proportion to kinship distance" (Sahlins 1972:196).

This statement provides not only an intellectual framework within which we may accommodate our expectations for social forms at the dawn of human existence but also a scalar focus for accommodating the variability that is documented in small-scale societies. It reflects a Marxist perspective in which changes in the superstructure determine the character of the observed system states, and it is in opposition to "vulgar materialist" notions that the means of production and the fundamental character of work are the major determinants of social forms and their scales of organization.

Sahlins was aware of the variability in labor organization and forms of cooperation observable among hunter-gatherers:

> I do not suggest that the household everywhere is an exclusive work group, and production merely a domestic activity. Local techniques demand more or less cooperation, so production may be organized in diverse social forms, and sometimes at levels higher than the household. Members of one family may regularly collaborate on an individual basis with kith and kin from other houses: certain projects are collectively undertaken by constituted groups such as lineages or village communities. But the issue is not the social composition of work. *Larger working parties are in the main just so many ways the domestic mode of production realizes itself. Often the collective organization of work merely disguises by its massiveness its essential social simplicity. A series of persons or small groups act side by side on parallel and duplicate tasks, or they labor together for the benefit of each participant in turn. . . . Cooperation remains for the most part a technical fact, without independent social realization on the level of economic control.* It does not compromise the autonomy of the household or its economic purpose, the domestic management of labor-power or the prevalence of domestic objectives across the social activities of work.
>
> (Sahlins 1972:77–78; emphasis added)

This is just another way of expressing the recurrent view that neither ecology, nor the articulation of humans with their environments (both natural and social), nor subsistence strategies, nor the means of production are germane to the investigation and explanation of social change. Ingold has made this point quite forcefully: "It cannot be emphasised too strongly that the concept of adaptation loses all significance unless it is combined with a demonstrable principle of selection. . . . If this principle is contained within the social system, it is evident that the latter cannot be the object of a selective process" (Ingold 1981:126).

For the neo-Marxist, evolutionary ecology is irrelevant and general explanations are futile since it is the superstructure—the ideological domain—that directs change and manifests itself as historically particular variability.

Sahlins was attempting to transform emic phenomena into *etic* phenomena. Kinship distance becomes social distance and social distance becomes transactional distance once the spectrum of reciprocal relations has been introduced. The fundamental social unit—the family—becomes extended through emic kinship conventions, a process that widens the social domain of the domestic mode of production to include more and more persons. These extensions represent scales of solidarity that should be distributed isomorphically with economic connections in those situations in which generalized reciprocity is extended to larger and larger sets of persons, producing larger and larger communal units. Given Sahlins's linkage of these scales, there is a clear autocorrelational equation in which (1) kinship distance, (2) social distance, and (3) physical distance or spatial association constitute a measure of communal solidarity.

It should therefore be clear that for the archaeologist who seeks interpretive guidance by invoking Sahlins's principles, variability in both site structure and settlement pattern would be referred for explanation to the domains of kinship, social distance, and mutual aid and sharing. Variability in the size and dispersion of social units within a settlement system would be thought to reflect a single scale of degree of relationship, ranging from familial independence (atomism) to the integration of families into a broader-scale social formation in which the economic solidarity of the domestic mode of production is extended to others.

With regard to site structure, those camps in which residences were placed close to one another would be thought to exemplify solidarity, whereas camps with widely spaced residences would reflect household independence, a lack of interhousehold integration, and, by extension, a lack of solidarity. This same scale would be expected to reflect the emic scaling of kinship distance since, as Sahlins suggested, variability in familial inclusion and assimilation fosters integration and therefore solidarity. Another implication of this view is that as the kin-integrated unit becomes larger, productivity and "culture building" will increase.

Sahlins's scalar arguments about kinship and economic integration are consistent with the original proposals of Lewis H. Morgan regarding aboriginal house design. Ever since the publication of Morgan's seminal work, *Houses and House-Life of the American Aborigines* (1881), many anthropologists have regarded communal shelter as a direct clue to the char-

acter of the economic articulations between persons occupying the same residence. For his time, Morgan made a convincing case. He certainly influenced the thinking of Marx and Engels, and his assumptions are a fundamental component of the argument for "primitive communism" (Lee 1988). They also underlie the efforts by archaeologists (e.g., Movius 1965, 1966) to infer communal living based on archaeological house forms and camp plans:

> Communism in living had its origin in the necessities of the family. . . . Several families, related by kin, united as a rule in a common household and made a common stock of the provisions acquired by fishing and hunting, and by the cultivation of maize and plants. They erected joint tenement houses large enough to accommodate several families, so that, instead of a single family in the exclusive occupation of a single house, large households as a rule existed in all parts of America in the aboriginal period. . . . *To a very great extent communism in living . . . entered into their plan of life and determined the character of their houses.*
> (Morgan 1881:63; emphasis added)

To use Sahlins's terms, the construction and use of multifamily dwellings were the ultimate manifestations of the principles of kinship-based scaling according to which many families are integrated into a large domestic unit to which all of the characteristics of the domestic mode of production are said to apply.

It is not unreasonable to suggest that implicit in this argument is an additional normative expectation. Since the emic kin terms employed within societies and the social formations they imply are not, according to Sahlins, modified drastically in short-term situations, normative patterning in both site structure and settlement patterning should be expected. For Sahlins, kinship and scale of kin distance are the factors conditioning social integration, which, in turn, is directly reflected in spatial association and proximity among fundamental family units. (It is hard to accommodate these normative views to the within-systems variability emphasized by Mauss in describing Eskimo societies.)

Another set of expectations contained in Sahlins's arguments may be anticipated in experience. The differences between strong and weak social solidarity, selfishness instead of sharing, and minimally integrated as opposed to strongly integrated social forms are said to be caused by factors belonging to the superstructure (in Sahlins's argument the domain would be kinship conventions). Social organization would therefore be expected to remain unaffected by the character of task groups, the forms of cooperative labor, and the organization of work in general. One would expect the scale of social solidarity to vary independently of labor organization and its attendant, cooperative characteristics as conditioned by the nature of the tasks themselves. In short, there should be little variability in either settlement pattern or site structure in response to the many quite different demands that a range of subsistence strategies place on individuals in terms of the organization of labor and the amount of work required to operationalize those strategies.

The arguments proposed by Sahlins contrast in their entirety with earlier views expressed by Chang, who believed that settlement pattern was "directly related to ecology and subsistence of the inhabitants," whereas site structure—or community pattern as he preferred to call it—would be referable to "those aspects that can best be interpreted in terms of social organization and social psychology" (Chang 1962:36). Sahlins instead attributed spatial separation in either settlement pattern or site structure to a simple scale of variability in social integration—that is, to an expanded or contracted state of the domestic mode of production.

It is reasonable to say that, in spite of their deficiencies,[10] Sahlins's views are central to or at least underlie most of the arguments currently offered by archaeologists regarding the importance of sharing. Not only is sharing invoked to provide an understanding of hunter-gatherer socioeconomic organization, it also forms the basis for the interpretation of variability in site structure, particularly for such features as interhousehold spacing in the layout of hunter-gatherer camps (Gargett and Hayden 1991).

From one perspective, Sahlins's formulations are concerned with the structure and extension of relationships among persons for whom sharing is the characteristic transaction. Food sharing in particular has become the definitive and pivotal criterion of human relationships for many archaeologists. The following passage from Speth (1990:148–49) is a good example of this point of view:

> Food sharing, particularly sharing involving meat from larger mammals, is widely held to be one of the principal hallmarks of so-called "egalitarian" hunter-gatherer or "band" societies (e.g., Isaac 1978a; Lee and DeVore 1968; Service 1971). Almost every ethnographic study of foragers mentions the occurrence of some form of food sharing, and most comment on the importance of meat from larger mammals in these exchanges. The reciprocal give and take of hunted foods as well as other resources, assured among egalitarian foragers by powerful social sanctions, is thought to play a crucial role in maintaining amicable and cooperative relations among the society's members. . . . Sharing of food, especially meat, is believed by many anthropologists to be so basic a part of the forager way-of-life that archaeological evidence for its apparent emergence more than one-and-a-half or two million years ago in the Plio-Pleistocene has been taken as one of the first clear signs of true "humanness."   (Isaac 1978a)

Several recent publications on archaeological site structure contain propositions that reflect Sahlins's emphasis on communalism. Sharing is considered to be a clue to, if not the basis of, communalism, and the absence of sharing is thought to be indicative of individualism or the lack of communal ties: "In sharing, the rule is that a subunit engages in exchange only with a larger unit which includes it. That is, each unit is obliged to give only to the whole of which it is a part, and is entitled to receive only from that whole, or as an undifferentiated part of it. Recipients do not become indebted to the sponsor of the moment: their obligation is only to the group as a whole" (Gibson 1988:175). Of course, one way to ensure that sharing represents collectivism is to define it as such.

The tendency to equate sharing with communalism is well represented in an argument by Parkington and Mills (1991), who contend that close interhousehold spacing is one means of reinforcing and educating new recruits to the communal-egalitarian ethic. Tight interhousehold spacing also acts to "guarantee the evenness of resource acquisition and the relative egalitarianism of interpersonal relations" (Parkington and Mills 1991:357). This functional argument is consistent with Sahlins's expectations that the caring-sharing egalitarian ethic of the domestic unit is extended to those living in tightly clustered houses.

As interesting as all of the preceding arguments may be, they cannot contribute significantly to an understanding of the organization of human behavior until their accuracy is examined. For instance, it is essential to determine whether or not the "atomistic" Paliyan camps are widely spaced and whether the !Kung, Paliyan, and Great Basin Shoshoni camps are similar in site structural terms. It would be equally important to know what are the spatial relationships of structures in Montagnais and Naskapi camps that date to the fur trade era. The site structural implications of all of the competing arguments about "atomism" and "communalism" simply have not been evaluated, in spite of the ethnographic resources that could be brought to bear on this problem. It is especially dimwitted that archaeologists, rather than using their data to evaluate the accuracy of these arguments, instead appeal to them as justifications for the inferences that they make about the past!

HUMAN SOCIAL ORGANIZATION FROM THE PERSPECTIVE OF EVOLUTIONARY BIOLOGY

Subsequent to the work of Marshall Sahlins, the single most important discussion of sharing, cooperation, task group formation, and related behavior to appear in the anthropological literature is found in the work of evolutionary biologists (the initial label for this research focus was sociobiology). Crucial to many of the early debates out of which the sociobiological perspective coalesced was the controversy over what unit constituted the fundamental element of evolutionary process. Opposing sides argued about whether change occurred at the level of the individual organism or whether selection operated on social groups. According to the former perspective, social behavior was viewed as a consequence of evolutionary processes operating on the individual as the fundamental processual unit (e.g., Axelrod 1981; Axelrod and Hamilton 1981; Hamilton 1963). It was in the context of this initial argument over units of processual dynamics that research attention was directed toward altruism or behavior that appeared to serve the needs of others rather than those of the altruist (Trivers 1971).

Another important set of arguments, now referred to as "optimal foraging theory," emerged directly from the fields of ecology and microeconomics and was adopted and elaborated upon by researchers in the field of evolutionary ecology (see Stephens and Krebs 1986 for a review). Optimal foraging theory has implications not only for sharing behavior but also for the controversy over which units of analysis should be used in investigating the role of evolutionary processes in the diversification of human systems of adaptation.

Perhaps the greatest impact of efforts to develop an evolutionary theory explaining variability will be on those explanatory approaches that postulate the existence of "original human conditions" and "primal states" that are subsequently corrupted by the accidents of history.[11] These arguments become irrelevant when the original conditions are expected to have been variable and the history of change is in fact what one seeks to explain. One of the earliest attempts to challenge an explanatory argument based on alleged "primal conditions" was made by Elizabeth Cashdan and focused on the !Kung Bushmen. The citation of !Kung social organization as the quintessential example of primitive communism—a "group selectionist" proposition writ large—has been dealt with by Cashdan:

> The literature of anthropology is rich in theories and discussions on the causes of stratification, while egalitarianism has largely been considered to be simply the baseline upon which stratification develops. Material from !Kung ethnographers, however, indicates that the egalitarianism found among most Bushman groups is a phenomenon resulting from stringent constraints, not simply a natural condition that represents the absence of stratification. These constraints arise from high spatial and temporal variability in food supply, together with a paucity of means to buffer this variability.
>
> (Cashdan 1980:116)

Cashdan then discussed the social sanctions that were implemented among the !Kung to ensure that sharing occurred at the group level. (In this regard see the description by Richard Lee [1969b] of the !Kung response to his display of "wealth" on the occasion of Christmas dinner.) She contrasted her observations among the !Kung with her experiences among the //Gana, who live south and slightly to the east of the !Kung. The //Gana, Cashdan noted, were less

dependent upon "the insurance provided by the economic leveling mechanisms typical of other Bushman groups" (Cashdan 1980:118). Leveling mechanisms include both direct sharing between social units and household mobility as a means of reducing security differentials among geographic ranges. Implied in this argument, as well as in earlier discussions by Draper (1975) and Wiessner (1977, 1982), is the proposition that sharing was selected for and is advantageous only under certain ecological conditions. Precedence for this conclusion is found in Steward (1936, 1955) and in Eggan's (1968:85) comments at the Man the Hunter Conference.

During the time that Hillard Kaplan was working on his doctoral dissertation, he participated in a major study of sharing among the Ache of eastern Paraguay (Kaplan 1983). This research formed the basis of a series of important papers dealing specifically with sharing and the arguments that had previously been offered to account for this behavior (Jones 1983; Kaplan et al. 1984; Kaplan and Hill 1985; Kaplan et al. 1990). This body of literature is methodologically sophisticated, internally consistent, and comprehensive, and it is the most provocative examination of the subject of sharing currently available.

Throughout the remainder of this book I refer to pertinent observations and arguments presented in the research of evolutionary biologists. At this juncture, however, I prefer to deal with the issue of sharing as a risk-reducing mechanism—that is, one in which variance in productive success is leveled by sharing among cooperating producers. (The term *leveling* describes a situation in which the mean value of the food acquired by a set of producers is available to all within the set, as opposed to each producer having to rely on the product of his or her individual efforts during the term of the cooperation.)

In order to understand variability in this domain of hunter-gatherer social phenomena, a set of cooperating producers and a term or duration of the cooperation must be specified so that behavior can be monitored and risk reduction strategies can be evaluated. To obtain a measurement of mean and variance in the results of work effort within a socially defined labor unit, both categories of data are required, not only for field research but also for theory building. Thus far, data are available for only one group of hunter-gatherers, the Ache, although observations germane to the proposition of risk reduction are available for other groups.

The following summary of detailed research on sharing is abstracted from recent work by Kaplan et al. (1990):[12]

1. *Risk:* Risk is defined not as danger or insecurity[13] but rather as temporal variability in the amount of food available for consumption, resulting from the productive efforts of a finite set of producers over a given time period of observation. Risk may be thought of as a particular conse-

quence of exploiting certain types of foods, in the course of which the skill, knowledge, and ability of different producers is not considered to vary during the period of observation. Nevertheless (a) the number of occasions on which a single producer is successful in a series of efforts is variable and (b) the total productivity of the set of producers is itself variable when the time frame is held constant (e.g., a day or a week). This kind of variability is frequently referred to as "luck" by many researchers.

2. *Risk management decisions:* A number of decisions are made in the course of implementing any particular risk management strategy. Food producers must decide with whom to cooperate in a risk-pooling unit, how many persons to include in the group (see E. A. Smith 1991 for extensive field-based research focused on task group formation), and what productive output to aim for during the period of cooperation. Whether producers envision a long-term cooperative effort or a task-specific cooperation must be established before rational discussion may proceed. (Remember that in order to calculate mean productivity and variance, a set of outcomes must be distributed across individuals when time is held constant or among outcomes for a single individual across a suite of events, or both.)

In the Ache study, it was necessary to distinguish between male and female behavior in terms of the extent to which they pursued a risk-prone versus a risk-averse strategy. This distinction illuminates another set of decisions having to do with the production targets or biased prey choices observed in cooperative action. As Kaplan et al. ask: "do they consistently choose either the high variance (unstable food supply) or the low variance (stable food supply) option?" (Kaplan et al. 1990:110–11). When detailed Ache data were used to evaluate the proposition that food sharing represents a risk reduction strategy, it was found that "*without* food sharing, families are likely to experience 2 weeks in which they acquire less than 50% of their caloric needs about once every 2 years" (Kaplan et al. 1990:114; emphasis in original). The risk reduction argument was therefore empirically supported in the Ache case.

Perhaps of even greater importance were the results of research that focused on the relationship between prey choice and variance in returns. Here the authors noted that "*the amount of reduction in variance conferred by food sharing appears to depend on the acquisition pattern of food*" (Kaplan et al. 1990:118; emphasis added). In other words, sharing is conditioned both by the character of the environment and by the labor organization appropriate to the exploitation of given prey targets. The sharing argument is therefore directly linked to the optimal foraging argument regarding prey choice.

For purposes of this discussion, the observations of Ache foraging and sharing behavior, as well as the optimal forag-

ing theory to which they are linked, directly challenge arguments claiming that "superstructure" conditions the relations of production. These data have similar implications for the viewpoints of Service and others who consider social solidarity or integration an essential property of small-scale society and attribute the existence of societies in which sharing is minimal to processes of social disintegration.

Kaplan et al. have presented a set of propositions based on the definition of risk as "temporal variation in individual returns and . . . inter-individual variation in returns at single points in time. . . . When both kinds of variation are present (that is, when the returns of individuals vary over time and that variation is not synchronized across individuals), food sharing confers the greatest reduction in risk" (1990:118–19).

This proposition covers those situations in which hunters collectively experience stochastic variance in their combined productivity while at the same time the productivity of each individual hunter also varies stochastically relative to other hunters in the risk pool: "If individual returns vary over time but that variation is synchronized across members of a social group, as in the case of seasonal gluts and shortages, food sharing does little to reduce variance because when food supply is low for some it is also low for others. When the inter-individual variance is high but temporal variance for individuals is low, food sharing does not reduce risk" (Kaplan et al. 1990:119).

This second proposition is important since it acknowledges that a change in security simultaneously experienced by all of the participants in a risk-pooling labor group is not buffered by sharing associated with any one production event, such as one animal kill. The content of this proposition contrasts sharply with the meaning inherent in the expression "risk-minimizing strategies" used by some authors, who are simply referring to all of those strategies that tend to enhance subsistence security in an otherwise "poor" habitat (Gould 1980:87). (Later in this book I discuss the kinds of strategies adopted by hunter-gatherers when gluts and shortages characterize seasonal variability in the habitat.)

> When interindividual variance is high but temporal variance for individuals is low, food sharing does not reduce risk. It simply raises the mean of low producers and lowers the mean of high producers. While from a group perspective this reduction in interindividual variance may or may not be beneficial, it does not benefit high-producing individuals. Under these circumstances, high producers are not likely to elect to share food unless there are other compensatory benefits, or alternatively, unless there are costs associated with not sharing food.   (Kaplan et al. 1990:119)

This proposition will assume more importance when I discuss differential productivity as a function of individual age and, in particular, the role of young unmarried males as producers in the labor force. Situations in which food sharing may occur as a result of other compensatory benefits, or those in which the refusal to share results in social sanctions, are variable among hunter-gatherers and will be kept in mind as I discuss variability in organizational forms among hunter-gatherers.

Kaplan et al. (1990) have raised some additional issues regarding the preconditions for effective sharing as a risk-reducing strategy and make some assessments about the likelihood that these conditions occur in real-life social situations. They point out that sharing does not work as a risk-reducing strategy if some participants in the risk-reducing labor pool do not share or if they hoard food for their exclusive use. In short, in order to be successful, sharing must be a "response-contingent" strategy, which means that failure to share by participants in a risk-pooling group is dealt with by withholding shares to freeloaders or applying other negative sanctions. A successful response-contingent strategy implies that members of a risk-pooling unit must have extensive and dependable prior knowledge of the persons with whom they plan to share labor and output or the anticipated successful outcome will be jeopardized. For food sharing to either evolve or be maintained,

> group size, group stability, and the value of reciprocal food sharing will interact in determining whether it will evolve. . . . As group size increases or stability decreases (such that old partners leave and new partners enter the group), the value of food sharing must also increase. . . .
>
> If food sharing evolves in order to reduce variance, then, all other things being equal, it is most likely to occur when . . . [there is] high temporal variability in food acquisition which is not synchronized across the pool of potential sharers, repeated interactions, and small group size.　　　(Kaplan et al. 1990:120–21)

These statements constitute a bare bones outline of a theory of sharing, which is justification for some excitement since, in fact, theories are rare in the anthropological and archaeological literature.[14] Theories are the fundamental tools of the learning strategy that is generally referred to as science, and as such they outline dynamic relationships and permit the reasoned derivation of hypotheses that stipulate when a condition can be expected to occur and when it will not. The use of theory is well illustrated in the investigations conducted by Kaplan et al. among the Ache, and their work contrasts starkly with another kind of variability in the field of hunter-gatherer studies that is derived from the adoption by various authors of particular intellectual postures. It is not possible to review this voluminous literature here, but it may be summarized as advocating the utility of particular cognitive criteria for characterizing hunter-gatherer societies. A currently popular example distinguishes between social groups in terms of immediate- versus delayed-return reciprocity (Morris 1982b; Woodburn 1980, 1988) whereas another heated set of arguments disputes the essential characteristics of "real" hunter-gatherers (Bower 1989; Headland and Reid 1989; Kent 1992; Lee 1992; Lewin 1988; Schrire 1984a, 1984b; Wilmsen 1983, 1989).

I do not find either of these characterizing exercises useful. Arguments about "real" hunter-gatherers proceed from a failure to address the question of what is an explanatory theory, and they ignore the vital concern of how knowledge—which exists in the present—is most productively used to structure research to accomplish the goal of making knowledge grow. My approach to the strategic use of contemporary knowledge is described as part of a set of fundamental arguments that I make in subsequent chapters of this book.

Conclusion

This chapter has been concerned with what has been learned about hunter-gatherers from some of our intellectual predecessors in the discipline of anthropology and about how this knowledge contributes to a definition of the challenging research problems to be addressed by the contemporary generation of researchers.

The work of Mauss and Beuchat was introduced to demonstrate that some early scholars who investigated organizational variety in hunter-gatherer life ways had tried to establish that behavior in many small-scale societies was organized in ways that were neither normative nor static. Their research demonstrated that hunter-gatherer behavior appeared to exhibit regularities that were at least influenced, if not caused, by large-scale environmental cyclicities. For the greater part of the twentieth century, this approach to research was frequently cited, but the processual implications were ignored until quite recently. Work at the pattern recognition level has repeatedly informed us that hunter-gatherers are *variable* in the extent to which their social and labor organization is stable or cyclically changing, and yet little work has been directed to explaining why within-systems variability should or should not occur. One could say, then, that Mauss and Beuchat's intellectual bequest to future generations of hunter-gatherer researchers was inadvertently placed in trust and remained there for several generations. We believe that the time has come to gain access to that bequest and manipulate it productively.

The work of Julian Steward illustrates very graphically what happens when the units of observation in terms of which variability is monitored are ambiguous or indistinct. Steward's idea of the band was stated clearly enough. For him "the functional basis of band organization, then, was the habitual cooperation of its members in joint enterprises and its objective expression was the common name, chieftainship, and ownership of territory" (Steward 1938:51).

The problem was that no amount of definitional specificity could make reality correspond to Steward's terms. The Shoshoni did not appear to demonstrate much cooperation among spatially dispersed, small social units, nor did they maintain a chieftainship or appear to exercise property rights over the territory that they exploited. Steward's response to the lack of correspondence between his definitional units and reality was to conceive of a new unit, the family level of sociocultural integration, which fit the observations that he had made on Great Basin peoples. Steward later acknowledged that the size criterion embedded in his notion of a band was misguided, and he modified his view in light of more detailed field work.

Since Steward's time, the term *band* has been used to refer to a number of different kinds of observational units, some defined by proximity criteria, or by the social composition of residential camps, or by criteria that monitor levels of economic integration. One pattern emerges in this chapter from my overview of the stipulative approach: observational units require constant redefinition in order to accommodate the variability that is sequentially uncovered in the world of dynamics. The unproductiveness of a stipulative research strategy has prompted me to follow a more pragmatic approach to unit conceptualization in the research and analysis reported in this book.

By recognizing and concentrating on the *variability* in settlement pattern and site structural data, both within and among hunter-gatherer systems, it becomes possible to propose that patterns of organization relate to conditions external to the examined systems and to begin to do pattern recognition studies in these domains. Steward, of course, was a pioneer in the investigation of the ecological relationships that hunter-gatherers maintained with their environment, and it may be that of all his work, his research in this domain constitutes our most important inheritance.[15]

The research by Speck, Leacock, and Murphy and Steward pointed to interesting patterns of social organization in the present and took the view that traditional interpretations of the past could not explain them. These authors argued instead that processes operating in the present accounted for some features of a pattern of organization that was referred to as "atomism." It was theorized that a lack of economic integration among some groups of hunter-gatherers who had become productive specialists in the context of a market economy was accounted for by their exposure to forces of acculturation.

It was argued that these processes were unique to their historical context, but is it not reasonable to ask whether singular historical events are themselves the outcome of ongoing, more fundamental processes and, if so, might not some of the same conditioning variables have been at work in the past? A processual perspective is strongly opposed to the view that events cause events, and to the extent that historicism is a major explanatory theme in anthropology,[16] archaeologists would be well advised to reject this aspect of our intellectual patrimony.

Social types and primal forms were important conceptual tools for Steward, Service, the atomists, and researchers like Richard Lee. Lee has argued that the original condition of hunter-gatherers was one of primitive communism and that this original form is extant in the modern world (e.g., the Dobe peoples of the Kalahari area). I would suggest that the whole purpose of tools, intellectual or otherwise, is to facilitate doing work, and if our theoretical tools tell us that we *already know* what the past was like and why it was that way, then we have to conclude that there is no significant work left to be done. Obviously I believe that constructs such as *primal social forms* are useless when we explore the research challenges facing our discipline.

In Sahlins's work there is a strong emphasis on the systemic characteristics of domestic life. Sahlins makes many arguments about the bases of culturally organized life, but these all proceed from an assumption about what human life was like in a "state of nature." His bias regarding where or in what domain we are to look for the causes of variability places causation in the superstructural realm of ideation. Suggestions that causal relationships occur in the interrelations between humanity and the environment are generally denied.

Sahlins's work has provided archaeologists with a clear-cut set of expectations for site structure and settlement pattern and for what the variability might mean in terms of social integration. It is therefore unfortunate that these expectations are stipulative and derived from Sahlins's a priori assumptions about human nature. I suspect that those archaeologists who interpret their data in terms of Sahlins-like precepts will inevitably be surprised by the results of more rigorous theory building.

In this review of some of the more recent anthropological literature, it is clear that many elements of Sahlins's work remain relevant—particularly those having to do with sharing and the pooling of resources as fundamental forms of cooperation—but these elements are now embedded in some new and interesting perspectives. Recent studies suggest that sharing is not just an idiosyncratically expressed human characteristic but that, instead, it varies in practice with different environmental contexts according to whether there either is or is not a tangible payoff. If this pattern is sustained by continued research, such an understanding would be particularly germane to the problems posed by earlier writers who viewed cooperation, sharing, and communalism as essential to human life, particularly in prehistory, and it would lead us to expect much greater variety in the archaeologically documented settlement patterns and features of site structure remaining from the past.

Overall, this review of the utility of the intellectual tools bequeathed to subsequent generations by the "founders" of hunter-gatherer research has provided an opportunity to evaluate the state of our knowledge and, by reflection, our ignorance. It has also stimulated a process of conceptual selection, as a result of which some elements of our inheritance are discarded and replaced by new formulations. For instance, I argue in this book that in order to address productively problems related to organizational variability among hunter-gatherers, it is necessary to investigate patterns of variability in environmental properties, in group sizes (both within and among social organizations), and in mobility patterns and their consequences for group sizes, as well as spatial patterning in settlements. The sticky issue of integration must also be addressed if we are to succeed in discussing organization meaningfully. Sharing, cooper-ation, differential degrees of mutualism and independence among societal segments (particularly involving subsistence), and the social relations of the distribution of the products of labor are all relevant topics demanding rigorous investigation.

Finally, although the issue of within-systems variability is largely ignored in most contemporary discussions, the kind of dynamics noted by Mauss and Beuchat among the Eskimo must be addressed in the same explanatory terms as between-systems variability. After all, the extent to which the contemporary generation of hunter-gatherer researchers is able to meet the research challenge facing us determines whether or not we will be able to leave a worthwhile theoretical inheritance for *our* intellectual descendants.

CHAPTER

2

Human Actors and Their Role in the Evolutionary Play

Over thirty years ago, the eminent biologist G. E. Hutchinson published a book entitled *The Ecological Theater and the Evolutionary Play* (1965), in which he expanded on his insightful recognition of the resemblance between the structure of biological dynamics and certain aspects of the dramatic arts. Hutchinson visualized an ecological community as a locus of action similar to a theater in which an audience—in this case made up of scientific researchers—watches the ongoing interplay of evolutionary forces and events that constitute the drama. Respectfully borrowing Hutchinson's metaphor, in subsequent chapters I visit many different environmental theaters in an effort to understand the way the world works, in both ecological and evolutionary terms, for the human actors in these different settings.

Actors in Hyperspace

I am also indebted to Hutchinson for his role in the development of several important ecological concepts that will figure prominently in the arguments presented in this book. In a sequence of articles (Hutchinson 1953, 1958, 1959, 1965, 1967) and the discussion they generated, Hutchinson formulated a proposition stipulating that, at any given time, an individual species or population thereof—which can be thought of as a unit of *actors*—occupies an analytical domain referred to as *hyperspace*. Hyperspace can be visualized as an infinite array of gauges and dials, each corresponding to one of the known dimensions in terms of which individual states of being can be recorded at one particular time and place. The settings on the dials and gauges may change from moment to moment in response to changes in the forces that are being monitored, or the settings may remain constant, indicating no fluctuation in the dynamics of interest.

In the ecological literature, the analytical concept of hyperspace is partitioned into three different sets of variables

(or gauges)—those relating to *habitat, niche,* and *population* (Whittaker et al. 1975:327)—and there are important differences among the three sets that it is necessary to review. Variables associated with *habitat* can be measured independently of a consideration of the species or group of actors occupying any specific habitat. These are frequently referred to as environmental variables and can include such domains as temperature, rainfall, biomass, and species diversity, as well as numerous others.

Discussion of *niche,* on the other hand, requires a consideration of the characteristics of a given group of actors, since a niche is a complex, systemically conditioned, multidimensional state of a species or population (Whittaker et al. 1975:333) that results from the interactions between the specific attributes and capabilities of a set of actors and the organizational properties of their habitat. Within any specific habitat, the actors constituting a group will exhibit certain patterned properties and therefore occupy a specific niche. On the other hand, when this same species is studied in many different habitats, variability is observable in the other components of hyperspace, particularly in niche variables.

When the hyperspace associated with an individual theater is examined in greater detail, it may be obvious that the play is not being performed all in one place. For instance, within any given area exploited by a particular species, density gradients for groups of individuals may frequently appear as extended, three-dimensional, normal curves featuring an optimal zone where individuals are concentrated, surrounded on either side by zones of lesser density.

A closer inspection indicates, however, that a species is rarely dispersed in a single distribution. Instead it has many discrete population aggregations of variable density that can be thought of as a swarm of microdistributions. Each population concentration occupies a semi-independent hyperspace, yet interacts within the larger-scale hyperspace of the area as a whole. It is thought that this pattern occurs in response to the interaction of multiple, unevenly distributed variables within the living system of which the species is a part and that these microvariations in the properties of a habitat result in minor adjustments in niche. Niche, then, may be said to be conditioned in two ways from one habitat to another: localities may differ with respect to gross climatic variables, and they may also reflect different distributional patterns in the components of the larger ecological communities.

Niche has particular reference to the suite of articulations between a group of actors of one species and the nutritional resources that it regularly exploits within the habitat. Because niche properties are the result of a set of interactions going on within an ecological community, they constitute intra-community states that may be analyzed in terms of many dimensional axes, including the number of species within the community, the prey size normally exploited by the actors of interest, and their trophic bias in food procurement. None of these variables, however, can be measured, studied, or understood without attendant consideration of habitat variables and the relevant properties of a particular set of actors. Invoking Hutchinson's metaphor once again, it can be said that niche is the way that the evolutionary play is enacted, given differences in the character of the theater and the responses of the actors to this variability.

Relationships that result from the relative success or failure of the species within its niche fall into a different category, however. They can be imagined as part of the dramatic action and can only be monitored as the play unfolds. Such measurements as changes in population density and fitness are the populational consequences of the effect of niche dynamics on the species or unit of study. These characteristics, like those of habitat, may be measured independently of any consideration of niche. They are properties of specific guilds of actors performing in many different regional theaters.

All three suites of habitat, niche, and populational variables are required in order to conduct a comprehensive investigation of the behavior of actors in different theaters and at different times. Any two sets of variables taken together can provide some understanding of what the evolutionary play is about, but it will be a static, mechanistic script. When all three suites of variables are considered, however, the world of dynamic open systems becomes accessible and the investigation of organizational change and evolution becomes possible.

The actors of interest in this study are hunter-gatherers, and the interaction of habitat, niche, and population variables across a broad range of ecosystems will provide the organizing framework for the presentation and analysis of the data developed for use in this book. Based on my review of the explanatory arguments in chapter 1, I suspect that the adoption of an ecological perspective would have been viewed with tolerance by Julian Steward and Frank Speck—despite their vigorous disagreements over the primal form of hunter-gatherer society—but that Elman Service and Marshall Sahlins would find my intellectual framework somewhat disturbing.

Sahlins and Service dismissed the important effects of ecological factors on the forms assumed by hunter-gatherer societies, although for different reasons. Sahlins proposed that expansion of the kinship networks integrating the domestic mode of production both changed the characteristics of production and acted as the driving mechanism behind the appearance of more complex and productive forms of society. A unique and particular characteristic of human actors—their capacity for culture—removed them from a state of nature and set them on a course toward progressive cultural growth. Ingold (1981, 1986:173–221), too, is among the ranks of anthropologists who proclaim that the unique characteristics of human actors exempt them from the effects of interactive habitat, niche, and populational variables, and he would dispute the suggestion that ecological studies can contribute to an understanding of the different, changing behavior of human actors.

Some anthropologists take an additional step and claim that because of the uniquely human characteristics of our species, the methods of science are inappropriate when applied to the investigation of human behavior. (This point of view is so prevalent, in fact, that a list of relevant citations would be immensely long.) Inherent within this assertion of uniqueness is the claim that human beings are, in effect, actors in a play-within-a-play, which can have themes, events, and outcomes that are independent of the larger drama of which they are a part.

In evaluating such a postulation, the first issue to be dealt with is whether uniqueness is exclusively a human characteristic. It is, in fact, well known that all species are unique with regard to certain features, so uniqueness per se is not exclusively a property of human beings. The uniqueness claim as such is therefore insufficient justification for a rejection of the thermodynamic grounding of behavior emphasized in ecological studies or the claim that science is an appropriate learning strategy to apply to human behavior.

Exploring the Properties of the Actors: A Prerequisite for Understanding Niche

I have already said that although habitat variables can be measured independently of any consideration of the properties of particular species, except for their placement in environmental space, niche has reference to a special kind of observation that is relational in character. Consequently, germane characteristics of the actors under investigation become fundamental to a discussion of niche. In broadly focused ecological studies, these frequently take the form of behavioral capabilities, such as the ability to fly, the quality of night vision, climbing ability, passive as opposed to aggressive responses to predators, and flight versus fight responses to provocation. An identification of the relevant properties establishes the initial conditions that remain stable or constant during the investigation of the nature of the actors' interaction with or responses to habitat variables, and they form the boundary conditions for any argument mounted subsequently. For human beings, there are many relevant characteristics, of which the regular use of technological aids such as clothing and housing to cope with habitat variables and the use of technology to enhance the effectiveness of food-accessing strategies are only two examples.

An equally controversial problem has to do with a related question: in what *ways* are human beings unique? The set of properties at the center of debate in the social science arena may be broadly characterized as relating to the human capacity for culture itself. The ability to think abstractly, to invent symbols, to anticipate events not yet experienced, to engage in volitional action, to plan behavior and organize actions directed toward achieving desired future events—these are the attributes most frequently cited as quintessentially and uniquely human.

Considerations of singularly human capacities frequently lead to discussions about the appropriate human units for study. For instance, it is commonly argued that since individual human beings make decisions and choose to act in anticipation of future events, the individual is therefore the only ontologically justifiable unit for study. One of the most frequently repeated claims by archaeologists calling themselves "postprocessualists" is that the individual human actor is the "natural" unit in terms of which the investigation of cultural processes should proceed (Hodder 1986:6–15). Similarly, many anthropologists are comfortable with the generalization that variability in social organization can be scaled in terms of the differences between individual human beings in status, role, and other properties related to the organizational structures in which they participate.

Since the emergence of new societal segments and distinctions in social form result in a corresponding change in units and organizational segments, it is not unreasonable to ask whether there is only one "natural" unit appropriate to the study of human behavior, as suggested by postprocessual arguments. I would argue that the question of what units and scales are the appropriate focus for investigation is not an ontological problem but rather a pragmatic one and that a researcher's choice of units and scales should be determined by the potential for knowledge growth inherent in the alternatives.[1]

Since the term *knowledge growth* implies that a researcher hopes to structure the investigative process so that the outcome goes beyond the boundaries of what is currently known, knowledge growth is therefore incompatible with any explanatory schema that would constrain the possible outcomes of investigation by stipulating them in advance. Those researchers in anthropology who have mandated that the past must be written in exclusively human terms, and who have a very narrow definition of what an appropriate human past should be about, have cut themselves off from the explanatory goals of science—from the exploration of cause and consequence—in favor of the domain of "thick description," where dynamics are cast in terms of reasons and motivations rather than causes. The quotations from Edmund Leach that follow support such a modus operandi:[2]

> The intentionality of human action implies that, where human beings are concerned, we can never predict what will happen next. . . .
>
> The proper analogy for human behavior is not natural law of the physical kind—but a game of chess. . . . What is the relevance of that? . . . Please recognize your limitations. As soon as you go beyond asking "what" questions such as "What is the nature of my material?" and start asking "How" and "Why" questions, such as "How did this deposit come into existence?," 'Why does my series of deposits change over time?," or by analogy, "How was the prehistoric game of social chess played out?," now you are moving away from verifiable fact into the realm of pure speculation. This does not mean that you should not speculate, but you need to understand what you are doing and when you are doing it. In speculative areas of this sort, because you are dealing with *human* materials, there are no intrinsic probabilities and science and statistics can give no answers at all.
> (Leach 1973:764; emphasis added)

I would argue that reasons are mental constructs that defend the rationality of human behavior in a particular set of circumstances. They differ in focus from other constructs—such as plans, tactics, and strategies—that are concerned with the relationship between the informational content of a design for action and the character of subsequent outcomes. If, for example, in response to the question "why are you burning holes in that piece of canvas with your cigarette?" I said, "I want to insert grommets into this mainsail and the burned holes are just the right size," the answer is likely to be considered rational once the goal has become clear.

On the other hand, if I said, "I am burning holes because if I do not, my grandmother will die of yaws," this would only be considered an acceptable reason if the questioner shared with me a belief in the relationship between burning holes in canvas and grandmothers recovering from yaws. If the validity of such a relationship is rejected, doubts about my sanity might arise or I might be suspected of lying about my motives. In neither case, however, is acceptance of the offered reason related in any necessary way to conditions in the world of general experience.

A reason is only plausible if it is consistent with one's own beliefs or prior knowledge about a set of relationships, either real or imagined. Reasons are perhaps most easily understood in the context of excuses for behaving in unexpected ways. For instance, in an interesting essay in defense of historical explanation, Hexter (1971) presented the "muddy pants" example, in which a father questioned his young son about why the boy came home with mud on his pants when he knew his father expected him to keep his pants clean. The son replied that after school he was chased by bullies and that, in trying to escape, he slipped and fell, getting his pants muddy. The father accepted this explanation because it demonstrated that his son did not intentionally disregard his father's injunction to keep his pants clean, but got them dirty as the result of an acceptable human response to aggression—hasty flight.

It should be clear from this example that reasons are not linked in any predictable way with outcomes. They have reference only to a person's motivations in the pursuit of particular goals or, in the "muddy pants" example, the substitution of one goal for another. If the object of interest is an individual's motivation for his or her own behavior, then Leach's view that predictability is impossible is at least partially correct. Inspiring stories can be spun about human intentions, and when reasons are linked metaphorically with abstract symbols, values, or relativist social "principles" (Gibson 1988) such stories can appear convincing, since the reader validates them by referring to his or her own experiences.

A counterargument, however, asks the question: is a reason a cause? Riches (1982), Mithen (1990), and many others hold the view that—in order to make causal arguments—strategies, tactics, and decision making must be investigated. Riches restates a view previously articulated by Barth (1966, 1967) in proposing that "social activity (or behavior) should be understood in terms of the goals realized through it, and in terms of the knowledge through which people judge that it is appropriate to these goals' attainment" (1982:5). In spite of my sympathy with Riches's arguments, I believe that he ignores or makes only ambiguous reference to a number of important issues. There is, for instance, no discussion of the epistemological issue of functional explanations and the frequently invoked form of argument in which future goals are cited as causes for antecedent behavior (Hull 1974:101–24). Riches also neglects to specify the appropriate units among which dynamic interaction operates causally.

Assessing Risk and Uncertainty When Considering Volition and Planning

Determining the place that considerations of tactics and strategies should occupy in the explanatory lattice presents difficulties for archaeologists. For instance, in their introduction to an edited volume on archaeological site structure,

Kroll and Price take Susan Kent (1991; Kent and Vierich 1989) to task for her contention that at least some site structural characteristics are explained by the "anticipated mobility" or, more accurately, the duration of occupancy anticipated by the residents of a site. Kroll and Price reject this argument and ask "how does one measure the intangible concept of anticipated mobility in an ethnographic context let alone in an archaeological context?" (1991:9).

A more productive restatement of the problem archaeologists face might be to ask how do we reconcile what we know from experience—that persons make plans, devise tactics to fulfill them, and achieve desired goals—with the byproducts of the operation of past cultural systems that are observed in the archaeological record? One starting point might be an investigation into the factors that condition the outcomes of human planning and tactics, because the patterned relationships that archaeologists observe among the components of the archaeological record directly reflect those outcomes.

Let us think about planning for a moment and ask why the expression of human intentions frequently corresponds to patterned or regular outcomes. In the first place, intentions are manifested as effects and consequences in the broader world beyond the individual. They are therefore not part of a closed system but must relate in some regular way to the world beyond the intending individual. This is a world of variable risk and uncertainty in all forms of interaction, affecting even a creature capable of volitional acts: "Problems of risk concern the effects of stochastic variation in the outcome associated with some decision, while uncertainty refers to the stock of information processed by an actor as compared to some objective measure of the state of relevant variables" (Smith and Boyd 1990:168).

Rephrasing this statement in more human terms, I would say that uncertainty refers to the adequacy of the knowledge available to and used by persons as they develop their strategies and tactics. Risk, on the other hand, has reference to unpredictable variability with regard to specific outcomes in the performance domain—the world in which tactics and strategies are executed—that cannot be assessed by an individual's prior knowledge and experience. Human beings pursue a range of tactics and strategies that attempt to cope with risk itself, and these always entail some knowledge of the conditions under which stochastic variability can be anticipated. In fact, any tactical or strategic measures undertaken in order to achieve future goals must involve an understanding of the relationship between antecedent and future conditions in order to succeed.

In addressing the issue of intentionality it is necessary to introduce the distinction between the terms *projection* and *prediction*. When a public opinion poll is conducted prior to an election, many persons are asked to state how they intend to act at a future time—how they intend to vote on election day—and the poll reports the total of these declared intentions as the best estimate of collective future behavior on election day. The pollster does not need to know why the respondents intend to vote for Candidate A or B—only that they do. *In order to anticipate the results of the future election, the only assumption the pollster must make is that the world will stay the way it now appears to be.* No theory about the way the world works is involved in this example. The validity of the poll rests on an expectation that the germane conditions, whatever they may be, will remain stable. This kind of anticipation of outcomes is a projection—it is *not* a prediction—and depends for its utility on the accuracy of the initial assumption of stability in voting preferences.

It is possible to argue that one reason why intentional or planned behavior frequently corresponds to regular, reliably projected outcomes is that human actors experience conditions that are stable or relatively stable. In such instances, planning pays off in accurately anticipated outcomes when those stabilities guide the formulation of plans. This is only true as long as the stable conditions persist, however.

The human capacity for assessing stabilities and planning tactics is one of the most important characteristics of human actors, but is it the *cause* of the outcomes associated with planned or tactically organized acts? Just as in the example of the opinion pollster,

---

Generalization 2.01

The capacity to assess and plan is a necessary condition for behavior, but the causes of the outcomes rest with the accuracy of the assumptions about stability in the initial conditions with respect to which plans were made.

In a tactical situation, outcomes are always caused by external conditions and their states—stable or unstable—coupled with the accuracy of human projections of these prior conditions to some future time. Knowledge of the state of the external conditions makes successful volitional action possible, and therefore cause is to be sought in those external conditions, given the human actor's capacity for learning.

It was necessary to make the preceding distinctions in order to expand our discussion of the previously introduced concepts of risk and uncertainty. Considering first the issue of uncertainty, if I could imagine a situation of absolute uncertainty, I would also have to imagine that the human capacity for planned, volitional action would be of little utility. Projection would be pointless since any prior knowledge would be unreliable under conditions of total uncertainty. I might try to obtain new information upon which to plan my actions, but if I simply continued to act by trial and error no reliable estimate of outcomes would be developed, and the patterning of outcomes would appear chaotic.

Given the fact that, at least some of the time, the human capacity for informed, volitional action coincides with stabilities in external conditions and results in beneficial outcomes anticipated by the human actors, one wonders how Leach can so emphatically assert that "the intentionality of human action implies that, where human beings are concerned, we can never predict what will happen next" (Leach 1973:764). Although he uses the word *predict*—which in contemporary usage means to foretell the future—perhaps Leach really is referring to the ability to make projections about outcomes. If this reading is correct, though, Leach seems far too dogmatic in his generalization, since it is possible to demonstrate many instances that contradict his premise.

The word *predict*, however, has a more restricted meaning that is specific to science. It means to anticipate the character of future observations, based on deductions reasoned from a theory. If Leach is using *predict* in the scientific sense, he could be saying either (1) that no theory yet exists that makes this kind of expectation possible, or, more likely, (2) that because of the human ability to act volitionally, no theory is possible.

This is not the place for an extensive discussion of the role of theory in modern science, but it is necessary to point out that in the early days of science, a theory was considered to be a trial statement about the empirical regularities demonstrable in the world. It consisted of empirical generalizations—often referred to as "laws"—and, as such, was a projection in the sense that I have used the term. The success of any theoretical statement was dependent upon the relative stability, at or near equilibrium, of the systems described in the generalizations.

In modern science, however, a theory is an argument about the way the world works. As such, not only is a theory dependent upon the recognition of stabilities germane to a given argument, it may also acknowledge variability in relevant domains that is not easily generalized, except in gross statistical ways. A theory may posit dynamic linkages between variables in such a way that the outcomes of specific interactions may be different from anything currently observed. Such a theory would go beyond the stabilities of the world as known—which are reversible and therefore equilibrium-based forms of order—to imagine worldly conditions thus far unknown.

Assuming that such a theory existed about some aspect of human behavior, its success would depend upon the validity of its assumptions of stability in many different components of the integrated argument. If nothing is certain, then no argument can be reasonably mounted. One thing I can argue is that although many unexpected events occur in the "messy" world of human behavior, the goal is nevertheless the growth of knowledge and an increase in the intellectual utility of the ideas I use. Leach takes a different view, one which gives human actors a genuinely unique role—that of playwright—based on the putative ability to choose a future that cannot be projected from the present state. Alternatively, Leach would have human beings determine the future by means of an inner dynamic that is rooted exclusively in human unpredictability.

These and similar views have considerable cachet in contemporary anthropology. They are vigorously promoted as preferable alternatives to the conventions of Newtonian physics that defined a mechanistic world of strict determinism, or to the principles of classical dynamics in terms of which the properties of entities were seen as unchanging and their interactions predictable in terms of equilibrium states. Historians and students of human variability have seen a different world—one in which human properties are variable, appear emergent, and can therefore be judged from a particular historical point in time as progressive, conservative, desirable, or undesirable. This latter conception includes an expectation that events will not necessarily materialize in the future the way we might imagine or desire.[3]

Blaming Human Uniqueness for the Lack of Productive Theory

In the wake of the Darwinian conceptual revolution, which introduced a new understanding about how the world works in some of its fundamental dynamic properties, the inability of any extant theory of evolution to predict the forms that might be assumed by new genetic variety and novelty remained a bedeviling problem. Practical experience with the temporal directionality of biological phenomena appeared to some researchers to warrant a view of the world and a way of knowing that differed from the strategies and tactics used in other scientific disciplines (see Mayr 1982:36 versus Wicken 1990:150–56).[4] It was recognized that even complete knowledge of the world was inadequate when the organizational properties of that world underwent change, which—of course—is a limitation of all strategies that depend upon an assumption of stability when anticipating future conditions.

Within the discipline of archaeology, it was argued that the unique characteristics of human actors explained emergent changes in history (Dunnell 1971:130; Hodder 1982a:9). It has even been suggested that unique human features form a continuous dynamic of "becoming" and that the essence of uniqueness is its own dynamic character (Hodder 1986:6–17). Archaeological advocates of uniqueness-based theory building (Dunnell 1992:218; Flannery 1986a:513; Leonard and Jones 1987; O'Brien and Holland 1990) have based their arguments on the explanatory perspective of biologist Ernst Mayr. Mayr has advocated unique methods and epistemologies for biology to account for the fact that there still appeared to be no way to anticipate future events, given a com-

plete knowledge of all the initial conditions and the state of dynamics within any particular system prior to major changes (Mayr 1982:35). Although some archaeologists consider Mayr's work to be relevant to their concerns, it has been labeled "whiggish" (Wicken 1990:151) by another researcher who requires that explanatory schemata include a recognition of how dynamics relate to the appearance of organizational novelty and irreversible processes.

Even though unpredictability in experience may still appear to many anthropologists to be a unique characteristic of human behavior, in the new synthetic discipline coalescing to investigate the phenomena of emergence in many contexts (Prigogine and Stengers 1984) the explanatory targets have become the world of irreversible process, the mental construct of time that is produced by irreversibility, and the problem of the emergence of life itself. I would argue that much has already been learned as a result of the shift in observational scale—from a view in which one variable population gives rise to another variable population to a focus on the organization of systems and the production of new organizational phenomena[5]—and in this light, Ernst Mayr does appear "whiggish" and Edmund Leach seems to represent a bygone intellectual era (see popularly written summaries of emergence theory by Gleick 1987; Lewin 1992; Waldrop 1992).

Human Uniqueness Is a Constant, Not a Cause

It is lamentable that, with a few exceptions (Allen 1982; Rosen 1982; Zeeman 1982), most archaeologists, as well the argumentative literature of archaeology, have ignored the formulations of emergence theorists and have continued to engage in debates about uniqueness versus determinism. In my opinion, it would be wise to reject claims for a unique epistemology and a uniquely human view of the human experience. Just as for any other species defined in terms of unique properties, uniquely human properties must be recognized and evaluated to determine the extent to which they are germane to any given argument about niche dynamics. Even if germane, however, these properties function only as *constants* in any consideration of dynamics. The problem is always to determine how these capabilities—in dynamic articulation with other conditions of existence—result in variable, changing, or stable forms of relational phenomena. As with other animals, the ways in which these relational states condition the outcome of human actions are most productively explored as part of a consideration of niche dynamics.

To illustrate the role of human intentionality as a constant in discussions of niche variability, I return to the concept of risk. It will be recalled that for Smith and Boyd risk is concerned with "the effects of stochastic variation in the outcome associated with some decision" (1990:168), and in this context the word *stochastic* implies the inability to anticipate the outcome of a given action. If, however, we accept the statement that an outcome cannot be anticipated because it is subject to stochastic variability, how can we reasonably speak of planned or rational volitional action?

A useful example in this regard concerns the strategy of a man who leaves home to go hunting. He is always guided by the same knowledge about the natural world and uses the same tactics and strategies, yet on some days he is successful and on other days he fails. The different outcomes of these hunting experiences are frequently chalked up to luck, but hunter-gatherers are known to cope advantageously with unpredictability, or luck, by relying on the human capacity for planned volitional action. Resolution of the apparent contradiction between unpredictability and the successful anticipation of risk will emerge from a discussion of the niche relativity of units.

For the individual hunter whose luck varies in apparently unpredictable ways, risk is said to have reference to stochastic variability in outcomes relative to a prior decision. Tactics for dealing with this situation are termed *risk-buffering strategies* because they mitigate the effects of stochastic variability on individuals by distributing the risk among a set of individuals. This is accomplished by pooling the net hunting returns of a group of individual participants, even though each member of the pool may be operating individually. The effectiveness of buffering strategies such as risk pooling is documented both by empirical studies (Bailey 1985) and by mathematical demonstrations, which is undoubtedly why numerous examples of hunter-gatherer risk pooling are found in the ethnographic record.

There are, however, two basic conditions that must be met if a buffering strategy is to work consistently. First, there must be a reasonable expectation that all of the persons in the risk-pooling unit intend to participate equally in terms of time and energy invested, and, second, the distribution of the products of successful hunting must be equal (Smith and Boyd 1990:178). In other words, the success of risk pooling is, in the long run, a frequency-dependent phenomenon. It is based on the frequency of interaction and the accumulation of knowledge about the predisposition of potential group members either to share or not to share, to cooperate or not to cooperate (Smith and Boyd 1990:179). Certain stabilities in the behavior of others must be correctly *projected* if planned outcomes that depend on cooperative interaction are also to be projected successfully.

This conclusion directly implies what anthropologists refer to as "social organization" and in the process it targets ideology as a particularly important integrating capability. The linkage between kinship and risk pooling opens the door to opportunities for explanation and theory building when the issue of variability in niche is addressed. Many features of social organization reduce a hunter's uncertainty

about the expected behavior of potential collaborators and, in turn, make possible accurate projections of human behavior in future situations involving groups of individuals. From this perspective, many of the conventional terms used to describe hunter-gatherer life ways and cited as diagnostic of system state variability—such as kin-based, egalitarian, based on mutual sharing of the products of labor (Gould 1981:434) and the communal use of goods and resources (Lee 1990), typified by family-centered economics (Service 1966:8) or mode of production (Sahlins 1972:41–99)—can be seen for what they really are: different organizational features requiring an explanation rather than essential properties of hunter-gatherer system states.[6]

By identifying the necessity for accurate knowledge and information about patterned regularities and stabilities in both the habitat and social setting of decision makers as a precondition for successful outcomes of planned actions, it is possible to integrate some fundamental anthropological domains. Most importantly, analytical tools can be brought to bear on Tylor's pioneering definition of culture as "that complex whole which includes knowledge, belief, art, law, morals, custom, and any other capabilities and habits acquired by man as a member of society" (1871:1).

Received Knowledge, Volition, and the Outcomes of Future Events

A contemporary philosopher of science might say that Tylor's definition of culture simply refers to received knowledge or to knowledge and understanding obtained from previous generations or other persons. Viewed in the context of a discussion of planning and projection, one would expect there to be some relationship between (1) the stability of phenomena about which knowledge is transmitted, (2) the frequency with which planned actions based on received knowledge are undertaken, (3) the degree that received knowledge actually applies and is reliably projected to the venue of planned action, and (4) the extent to which projected stabilities are irrelevant to conditions in a particular planning context but are nevertheless autocorrelated with relevant real-world stabilities that are at least somewhat accurately projected and result in successful planned action. It is important to remember that because of the prevalence in nature of systemic integrations among many apparently different types of phenomena, many autocorrelations reflecting organizational stabilities can be expected, although these are not causes in any satisfactory sense.

It should be possible to point to properties of habitat and niche that would directly affect decisions to adopt risk pooling as a buffering strategy and, even more importantly, might predict when levels of risk that require risk-buffering strategies might occur. Since by definition risk is restricted to stochastic variability in the outcomes of planned strategies, *if there is no stochastic variability, then there is no risk to be buffered against.* Food procurement strategies that focus upon widely available resources—as well as resources that require little or no pursuit time because, once located, they are relatively stationary and exhibit few effective avoidance behaviors (plants, shellfish, small mammals)—present the forager with the probability of greatly reduced risk. Similarly, resources obtained and placed in storage for future use expose dependent consumers to relatively little risk, although there is always the possibility that some stored resources will be lost, depending on the environment, either to other animals (bears are a problem for the Nunamiut) or to spoilage (Panowski 1985:103–13). This type of risk is not, however, a procurement problem but instead relates to the maintenance of resources once they have been obtained.

The Nunamiut strategy for dealing with the risks associated with stored foods involves establishing storage caches at many different sites. This practice distributes the risk among a number of locations so that at least some (and in reality most) caches survive the effects of damaging agents. In addition, the margin of probable loss is anticipated by hunters as they procure game for storage, and, to provide a buffer against storage loss and the uncertainty of the timing of the next caribou migration, they usually take a few more animals than the minimum number required for a household (see Binford 1978:139–44 for a discussion of sharing).

Do procurement and distribution strategies designed to compensate for potential storage losses fall within the definitional boundaries of risk-pooling strategies? The location of storage facilities in many different places *can* be considered a risk-pooling strategy from the perspective of the cache units—the risk pool in this case being all of those caches included in a given pool—just as the example of hunters working as a task group on a given day constitutes a risk pool. If the goal is to develop useful theories about risk responses, the unit that from an organizational standpoint is said to be integrated into a risk pool becomes a subject of great interest.

Most anthropologists would be comfortable with the definition of risk as stochastic variability in the luck of individual hunters who are observed over a relatively short period of time—on any given day, for instance. A focus on individual decision making permits detailed discussion of the factors influencing an individual's decision to participate or reject participation in a risk pool, as well as the decision to initiate risk-buffering strategies (Smith 1991). Edmund Leach notwithstanding, studies show that human actors respond predictably to apparent unpredictability in hunting outcomes by changing the scale of the response unit from individual to group participation in a risk pool (Smith 1991). Another strategy is to organize behavior with respect to a suite of caches in such a way that the caches, in fact, become a risk pool. Research indicates that in this context, the size of the

human unit is a product of organization and not the other way around.

A well-researched example of risk pooling by human actors involves the Ache, a group studied intensively by Kaplan, Hill, Hurtado, Hawkes, and O'Connell (Kaplan and Hill 1985; Kaplan et al. 1984, 1990). These authors have documented the movement through the landscape of foragers who are grouped into multiple family units. Male members of the group hunt in advance of the females and children, who move more slowly as they gather fruits and vegetables. The prey killed by the males is commonly, though not exclusively, turned over to the females as the entire group traverses an area. At the end of the day, instead of the male hunters dividing the meat equally among themselves, the products of all activities are pooled for consumption by the group.

In such a situation, what are the units making up the risk pool? Kaplan believes that his team has observed "cooperative hunting" and that males are directly pooling risk at the level of the consumer unit or family that they each represent. Organization at this level is different from situations in which males simply make up a hunting party as, for instance, Lee reports is common among the !Kung (Lee 1979:200). I think a convincing argument can be made that risk pooling can be organized in terms of a number of different units, ranging from individual producers or families to nonhuman units such as meat caches. Risk can be pooled among any units judged to be subject to stochastic variability in the outcomes resulting from planned strategies.

Similarly, risk-pooling units may differ in terms of their duration. For instance, a risk pool may be formed on a daily basis by persons who decide to go hunting on a given day. The following day, the composition of the risk pool may change, and, in fact, each day it is possible to have a risk pool made up of different members. On the other hand, membership in a risk pool may remain stable over longer durations.

The analytical challenge is to determine not only what factors affect the decision to adopt risk-buffering strategies, but also what factors are responsible for different scales of inclusiveness in risk pools and for differences in their duration. It is not necessary, however, to be able to account for all variability in risk-pooling behavior in order to appreciate the inutility of pronouncements that postulate a priori, empirically verifiable, "real" units in nature. Research with the Ache and others demonstrates that the composition of human social units is the result of the interaction of organizational phenomena and is neither immutable nor given by nature.

Additional permutations of risk-pooling behavior are apparent in a Nunamiut example in which hunters killed more animals than were needed as insurance against the possibility that some of their caches might be destroyed or as a way of coping with uncertainty about when caribou herds might reappear in spring. This was a planned response, but was the pooling of risk among a number of at-risk units required? *This strategy insures against the effects of risk, should chance events occur,* but it does not buffer against the acknowledged effects of risk among participants in a risk pool. It is not a risk-buffering phenomenon but rather a precaution against the possibility of stochastic variability. Overproduction as a strategy to insure against risk—should it occur—is a security strategy and not a risk-buffering strategy, as exemplified by risk pooling among producers with associated sharing in the context of demonstrable risk.

In situations in which a similar security strategy of a given household fails, the distribution of risk among households to deal with the possibility of cache loss might be organizationally recognized. For instance, it has been noted that sharing occurs in these situations (Binford 1978:140) *but only after the fact.* It is difficult in this context for a short-term observer to determine whether a long-term risk pool exists that is made up of different households or whether situational, altruistic sharing is taking place in response to the infrequent and specifically unanticipated effects of risk.

Data on these infrequent events do not permit a conclusion about Nunamiut organization, although for the Chippewayan—described so thoroughly by Fidler (1934)—the presence of a long-term, multifamily risk pool was noted. In this case, information regarding the state of spatially separated social units was regularly gathered by messengers reporting to the headman or chief of a larger social unit.

Among the Nunamiut, there is little regularity in the kinds of kin ties linking the persons who are engaged in sharing to offset potential cache losses. Campmates simply share with the affected family once a loss has occurred (Binford 1978:140–41). This type of sharing resembles what Sahlins (1972:193–95) referred to as *delayed reciprocity,* and, in the example of cache failure, the reciprocity is among households, many of which are not directly linked by recognized kin ties. Nevertheless, the expectation would be that if the donors were to lose their stored food at some future time, their campmates could be counted upon to help out by sharing.

In order for such households to constitute a risk-pooling unit, the unit would have to have some perpetuity, as well as stable membership, and there would also have to be long-term stability in the behavioral responses of the units in the pool to the system state conditions affecting those units. In addition, an effective flow of information about the system states impinging upon the units in the pool would be a necessary condition for success. Is such a risk pool maintained by organizational structures and ideological conditioners? Many situations involving risk pooling over the long term are made up of socially constituted subunits that are not operative at the individual level of organization.

The Need for Organizational Approaches to Variability

The discussion so far suggests that *a behavioral definition of sharing is analytically inadequate.* If sharing is defined simply as the distribution of the products of labor between producers and nonproducers, it is unreasonable to expect that explanations for sharing behavior can be developed. The ethnographic record reveals differences in the temporal scale over which a risk-pooling unit may be organized, differences in the nature of the units so organized, and, importantly, differences in the organized relationships and stabilities in differently organized risk-pooling units within a single system. These may occur as a nested set of differently organized units, with the result that sharing may be observed among the participants of a short-term labor unit as one set of events. Subsequently, sharing may take place among a differently constituted risk-pooling unit made up of groups—rather than individuals—and conducted in a different manner.

Organizational variability of this kind greatly affects the human behavior recorded by short-term ethnographic observers and accounts for much of the controversy in the anthropological literature about the prevalence and extent of sharing. Short-term behavioral observations would appear to be inadequate when the goal is an understanding of the importance of risk-pooling units within a society.

Successful ecological research is critically dependent upon the recognition of the unique properties of the actors being studied, but these unique properties—insofar as they are common to a class of actors—function as constants in any discussion of variability in behavior and its organization. These properties are studied most productively from the perspective of *niche*—the intellectual tool by means of which the locus of dynamics is designated—and, in this interactive and relational domain, constants play out in relation to changing and variable conditions in the habitat and result in variable forms of behavior and its organizational context.

I have focused on the human capacity for planning and volitional action to illustrate how stabilities in habitat are the fundamental properties that render this capacity an effective coping mechanism in real-world settings. As part of this argument, I introduced the terms *projection* and *prediction* and the concepts of *risk* and *uncertainty* in order to distinguish between different kinds of stabilities and instabilities, as well as different ways of utilizing the human capacity for planning. These distinctions will facilitate my later discussion of niche dynamics.

In the context of discussing risk and uncertainty, I introduced but did not elaborate upon another constant or feature of human beings as a class—the assumption that human actors would universally regard the reduction of risk as desirable. When cast in these terms, this assumption brings us face-to-face with another controversial question: do human actors regularly maximize their efforts or behave in a consistently goal-directed way? Many current anthropological arguments take this assumption for granted. It is claimed that human actors are motivated to enhance their prestige, to acquire competitive advantage over other actors, to maximize their reproductive fitness, to achieve a better life through maximizing social solidarity, and to maximize their longevity.

Ethnic differences have even been attributed to maximizing or minimizing behaviors. For instance, proponents of atomism have claimed that in atomistic societies individuals attempt to maximize their individuality and to minimize social entanglements, whereas anthropologists who have characterized societies as communalistic suggest that participants maximize social solidarity at the expense of individuality. Characterizations of this kind are usually wrong, but, more importantly, they represent inadequate ways of dealing with variability. Conceptualizing variability in terms of niche differences, on the other hand, implies an awareness of different articulations with causal variables that are, of course, amenable to further investigation.

In the vocabulary of evolutionary biology, a *currency* is any property that is subject to maximization in any set of acts that are directed toward an optimizing outcome. Although the terminology may not be identical, in the anthropological debate over the role that different properties of human actors play in the outcome of events, the issue is really what currencies are relevant to an explanation of the observed human behavior. Humanists claim that reasons and motivations constitute the appropriate currency for the evaluation of specific human behaviors, and, not infrequently, reasons are reduced to particular character traits of individuals or societies (see the discussion of atomism in chapter 1). A similar reduction, but one involving a different currency, is a feature of the scientific subdiscipline of sociobiology, which views most human behavior as a simple byproduct of natural selection operating through genetic mechanisms, and most—if not all—behavioral variability as ultimately referable to the argument that all human actors seek to maximize their reproductive fitness.

In contrast to arguments that maintain the primacy of one currency in all explanatory contexts, my research has convinced me that the choice of currencies themselves will vary with niche dynamics and that the specification of goal-directed action in a given currency may be niche-dependent (for example, prestige maximizing). Alternatively, one may use a currency that is a habitat variable, and therefore common to all niches, but perhaps varies in value in different niches for actors of equal capacity. Energy would be an example of such a currency, although to be meaningful energy must be expressed as a relational phenomenon. (Properties of the interaction between a human actor and specific habitat variables are what one monitors by a ratio such as efficiency, or the energy expended per unit of energetic return.)

Many informative niche-state variables might be developed using surrogate measures of energetic investment, such as time spent working, which would be indicative of system states within niches. The value of these and similar measures as indicators of habitat or niche variables is dependent, however, upon the maximizing capacity of the actor.[7] In this study, I will assume that *actors maximize niche state conditions* and that many different currencies may be involved. This assumption makes it reasonable and possible to speak of trade-offs between currencies—that is, decisions must be made continuously about the types of energetic investments that individuals or groups may make, since investments in one currency may preclude adequate investment in others. Discussions about trade-offs are common (for example, trade-offs between investing labor in obtaining food at the expense of child care in the context of fitness arguments), demonstrating that the subject is really niche states and not currencies per se.

For heuristic purposes I will argue that

Generalization 2.02

A constant characteristic of human actors is that they attempt to maximize their vital security in any habitat, limited only by their capacities and means.

This is a restatement of two frequently invoked ecological principles: the *principle of the inoptimum* ("no community encounters in any given habitat the optimum conditions for all of its functions" [Dansereau 1957:257])[8] and *the law of tolerance* ("organisms are controlled in nature by . . . the quantity and variability of materials for which there is a minimum requirement and physical factors which are critical and . . . the limits of tolerance of the organisms themselves to these and other components of the environment" [Odum 1959:93–94]).

To my enumeration of the properties of human actors required for a discussion of the dynamics of human niches, only two need be added: the capacity for behavioral plasticity and the capacity for culture itself. The former was the first property discussed by E. O. Wilson in his introduction to human beings and their behavior within the much broader inquiry entitled *Sociobiology*:

> Monkeys and apes utilize behavioral scaling to adjust aggressive and sexual interactions; in man the scales have become multidimensional, culturally adjustable, and almost endlessly subtle. Bonding and the practices of reciprocal altruism are rudimentary in other primates; man has expanded them into great networks where individuals consciously alter roles from hour to hour as if changing masks. . . . The variation exceeds even that occurring between the remaining primate species. Some increase in plasticity is to be expected. . . . What is truly surprising, however, is the extreme to which it has been carried.   (Wilson 1975:548)

The extreme plasticity of human behavior is expressed by many quick, interactive responses to habitat conditions and by a complex procedure for distinguishing among individuals in human social contexts. In terms of the currently accepted view of biological evolution, this means that genetic mechanisms operate on phenotypes in response to long-term stabilities. Any conditions that increase phenotypic variety (resulting in a polytypic species such as *Homo sapiens sapiens*) and at the same time decrease response time in phenotypic change (behavioral plasticity) must create for the observer extreme ambiguity about the relationship between the phenotypic properties and long-term stabilities, acting through genetic mechanisms, that molded a given phenotype.

The relationship between cultural and genetically based evolution is certainly an important concern, but the stipulation that most human phenotypic variability, in both individual and group behavior, is accounted for by genetic factors (see Beatty 1987 for a discussion of this problem) overlooks the reality of extreme plasticity in human behavior. The consequences of this capacity for short-term, and in most cases demonstrably reversible, phenotypic expressions are a source of ambiguity or "white noise" in the overall pattern of much slower, genetically based evolutionary change. In subsequent chapters I focus on plasticity and ignore the issue of the longer-term relationships between plasticity and genetically based phenotypic change. The human capacity for culture itself is both an extension of the concept of plasticity and the source of human behavioral variability, and it makes possible an enormous range of different phenotypic behaviors as well as a dazzling array of organizational variety in that behavior.

The features of Tylor's "complex whole" that represented the products of the human capacity for culture—"knowledge, belief, art, law, morals, custom, and any other capabilities and habits acquired by man as a member of society" (1871:1)—appear diverse but are similar in one respect that is relevant to the concerns of this chapter. They all represent received knowledge that is transmitted from persons to other persons. In discussing risk and risk-coping strategies, it was noted that the success of planned behaviors is critically dependent upon an accurate projection of stabilities to future events, and that any planned and organized cooperative behavior depends on the knowledge available to potential participants about the behavior of other possible participants. Similarly, successful outcomes of planned behavior depend on the accuracy of the stabilities assumed to apply to both habitat conditions and the behavior of participants in planned events. This means that the contribution of culture to any adaptation (the niche state of the moment) lies in the quality of the transmitted information; that is, it adds to knowledge about habitat variables and about the ways in which human actors will behave.

As far as human actors are concerned, many cultural signals may be totally arbitrary but nonetheless quite effective in reducing uncertainty about the behavior of others. In the twentieth century, a traffic light is used to control urban vehicular flow, but any clearly visible on-off device will have the same effect under some habitat conditions as long as all participants are enculturated to respond in a predictable manner. This stabilization of behavior reduces chaos and lowers the risk that any given decision to drive through an intersection might otherwise entail.

Most moral or ethical belief systems operate in a similar way in human society. They stabilize the potential chaos of individualistic decision making and reduce the hazards to individuals wishing to act in social settings and to plan cooperative actions. Beliefs may focus on any phenomena—persons, the environment, the cosmos—or combinations of phenomena. They frequently center on how the world works when instability is perceived and provide answers to questions such as, Why do thunderstorms occur? or Why do very skilled men who habitually go out in kayaks and return safely through rough water sometimes unexpectedly capsize and drown?

Examples abound, but in this context it is more relevant to point out several characteristics of ideologies. First of all, *ideologies stabilize the behavior of persons vis-à-vis one another;* they provide a model of the way the world works that defines the role of humankind in both natural and social dynamics. One would expect these models to bear some relationship to the world of human experience and to vary with the intensity of instabilities, so that if the social experience is chaotic, there will be more ideological investment in that source of instability.

If, on the other hand, the dynamics of the environment are less predictable and impinge in undesirable ways on human existence, there will be a corresponding investment in coping strategies dressed up as ideology. Ideology—or "superstructure" in Marxist terminology—may change the meaning of life for the participants within a system, but it does not change the character of life itself. Explanations for material changes must be sought in the dynamics of niche states and in the conditions that systemically change such states.

I would conclude, therefore, that the human capacity for culture is a constant that must be considered in discussions of human systems, but that this capacity is a boundary condition for considerations of cause and effect and is not a cause in itself. Appealing to various cultural forms is never an explanation for either cultural variety or change itself. Rather, cultural variability in all its forms—including ideology—should be the object of anthropology's explanatory efforts.

Conclusion

In this chapter I have focused on several issues. One has to do with variables and how they are measured, both independently of any consideration of the properties of the actors being investigated and as a means of identifying niche. Niche has been defined as the dynamic juncture at which the properties of the experiential world interact with the properties of human actors and result in variable organizations and social forms among hunter-gatherers.

Before embarking on a discussion of specific habitat, niche, and populational variables, it was necessary to discuss the unique properties of human actors that operate as initial conditions for any subsequent exploration of niche dynamics. I have focused on planned or volitional action and on the associated idea that goal-directed behavior, extreme behavioral plasticity, and the capacity for culture itself are important human characteristics that must be considered as constants in any discussion of humans as actors in the eco-

logical theater and the evolutionary play. Although these constants serve as important boundary conditions for any arguments that might have explanatory potential, they can never be explanations for niche dynamics.

Finally, throughout this chapter I have argued *against* the position that these features of the human species warrant a different kind of learning strategy when the focus is human behavior, *against* the assertion that science is an inappropriate learning strategy, and *against* the view that the best explanation of cultural variability lies in the attitudes of persons incorporated into different cultural systems.[9] Having offered these caveats, I am ready to consider the roles that habitat, niche, and populational variables play in the development of theories about variability in hunter-gatherer life ways.

3

The Play of Ideas in the Scientific Theater

The archaeological and ethnohistoric records provide observers with incomplete, tantalizing glimpses of innumerable evolutive dramas that have unfolded since the appearance of the human species. The former record consists of a sequence of remnant props, stage settings, and, in some cases, skeletal remains of the human actors themselves. In the latter record, there are reports of the physical appearance and mise-en-scène of a cast of characters who are often brought to life through dialogue and a description of their actions. Neither the static nor the dynamic vignettes, however, provide sufficient information to allow the observer to grasp what the evolutionary play may have been about and whether or not the performance remained the same or changed over time.

The scientific investigation of the human past and the ethnographic present has many of the attributes of a theatrical presentation whose theme is the growth of knowledge. But unlike the conventional stage—where action is organized in terms of a plot with a beginning, a middle, and an end—the drama in this metaphorical example is more open-ended and improvisational. It depends for its direction and pace on the goals and strategies of a group of scientific researchers who—in this instance—have a common interest in hunter-gatherers. These dramatis personae work to reduce their ignorance, sometimes collectively but more often in isolation, with varying degrees of success. The results of their efforts are communicated in a public forum where the dialogue is frequently contentious and the argument is often ad hominem, but where there are also heroic achievements and insights to applaud and, after a suitable intermission, new goals to be defined and debated. In this chapter I am concerned with what happens on- and offstage as the play unfolds. I outline what I believe to be the salient characteristics of science that provide the context for learning and direct the outcomes of the actors' efforts. I explore the intellectual tools and the conventions for using them that, in my experience, most efficiently

contribute to the growth of knowledge, thereby setting the stage for my own contribution to the ongoing dialogue about how to make profitable use of ethnographic and environmental data as a baseline for the study of the past.

Prologue

Some plays begin with an introductory statement preceding the first act in which a character addresses the audience about the theme of the play or outlines the dramatic conventions or rules of the game that will be observed by the players. A similar prelude inaugurates the play of ideas in the scientific theater. In it the participants define as explicitly as possible the terms in which they have chosen to describe the material properties of the world of experience. An archaeologist working in the American Southwest, for instance, might specify in a site report all of the properties of ceramic artifacts that he or she has chosen to record. These could include temper, type and placement of decoration, rim diameter, and many others. Precise definition benefits not only the audience but also the players themselves, who will evaluate and respond to their colleagues' ideas or suggestions. Agreement on the terms of observation is critical at this juncture because it enables other players, should they so choose, to replicate these observational experiences at a future time, presumably with comparable results.

In the *prologue,* players also describe the steps that they have taken to define a class of observations. An archaeologist might say, for instance, "In order to measure rim diameter, I will place each rim sherd on a piece of cardboard containing the magic marker outline of rim sherds of nine different diameters ranging from 4 to 12 centimeters. The sherd will be assigned the value of the outline that it most closely resembles." *Operational definitions,* as these specications are called, are intended to prevent confusion and mis-understanding as the play of ideas develops.

Not all of the descriptive criteria that will later play a part in argument and analysis can be identified initially, however, since the direction that research sometimes takes is dependent upon what the players learn about the validity of their ideas as the action of the play unfolds. If some or all of a player's corpus of knowledge is discovered to be irrelevant to the investigation of a particular problem, he or she must develop another set of propositions that appear to be germane to the current research trajectory. Such midstream regrouping does not necessarily represent failure. The process of recognizing one's ignorance—or better, the limits of one's knowledge—is itself a form of knowledge expansion if it stimulates the player to search for new, more relevant information and then reformulate his or her argument.

Archaeologists are participants in a play of ideas that attempts to transform ignorance of the past into secure knowledge. The fact that the past itself is gone and is therefore unavailable for them to observe has a profound effect on the tactics available to players wanting to know about the past. One challenge is to learn how to use the archaeological record as a source of circumstantial evidence—to borrow legal terminology—regarding the character of the past. Success in this endeavor then helps to define the questions that can be dealt with through the strategic use of accumulated prior knowledge, whether it concerns ethnographically documented hunter-gatherer peoples or the chemical changes occurring in clay as it is heated at high temperatures in a kiln.

Earlier in the play of ideas represented by this book, I aligned myself with Tylor's dictum that a knowledge of both the present and the past (or *the whole* in Tylor's terms) was necessary to explain the past. I have refined my ideas about which domains in the vast continuum of available knowledge would be relevant to such a pursuit (elsewhere referred to as *middle-range research* [Binford 1981:21–34]), and I am now prepared to make an argument about the relevance of ecological and environmental factors to some of the events in the past that created the archaeological record.

The dramatic sequence of my play of ideas therefore reflects the logical sequence of my argument in this book. It progresses, in Part II, from a definition of environmental and ecological variables to their use, in Part III, as frames of reference and as components of models. I use both kinds of constructs as tools for recognizing patterns in the ethnographic data that may implicate causal and conditioning processes affecting various properties of human organizational systems. Finally, in Part IV, I tackle the difficult task of building theory to explain some of the provocative configurations that have been identified in the ethnographic data during the extensive pattern recognition work undertaken in previous chapters.

Act I, Scene 1: Data Production

In the opening scenes of most theatrical productions, the playwright introduces a set of characters and events in a way designed to tell the audience "this is what's going on, and we're going to take it from here." In the play of ideas in the scientific theater, exposition takes the form of data production. A researcher says, in effect, "I have looked at events in the material world and this is what I have seen." Just as a playwright does not attempt to focus on an infinite number of characters and events, it is understood in science that although any single event has an almost infinite number of properties, infinities are impossible to deal with productively. The experienced researcher therefore selects for observation a specific number of properties of the event of interest and ignores all the rest.

By convention, the properties or aspects of an event observed by a researcher are referred to as *facts*, a word derived from the Latin root *factum*, which means "something done" (*Webster's Encyclopedic Unabridged Dictionary*, 1st ed., s.v. *fact*). *Done*, in this case, refers to something that occurs and can be apprehended by the senses, as opposed to something thought or something imagined, both of which occur but have no physical manifestation. Facts, therefore, are aspects of reality that have an existence that is independent of the observer, and they remain in their "doing" mode regardless of whether or not any attention is paid to them.

When a researcher records his or her observation of a fact or a multitude of facts, the factual record is referred to as either *a datum* (from the Latin word meaning "a thing given") or, more often, *data*. Since data are systematically recorded observations, organized in terms of some criterion of similarity or difference, the act of transforming observed facts into data that will be useful in pattern recognition[1] studies and data analysis is referred to as *data production*.

The same event or object can prompt different researchers to make very different observations and to produce very different kinds of data. Take, for instance, the example of the diary of a very well-known person, which, after the person's death, is donated to an academic archive, along with numerous manuscripts, letters, and sketches. The diary contains a daily record of events over a twenty-year period, but the author has described some days in great detail, while entries such as "nothing much happened today" appear on other days. One researcher might be interested in the diary for what it will reveal about the author's daily comments on such subjects as the weather or events occurring in connection with his professional obligations, or perhaps his relationship with his wife and offspring, or the state of his health. All of the references to these topics could be recorded and tabulated by category, in which case data production might enable a researcher to generalize about the author's changing social, intellectual, or emotional states over a particular period of time. A different researcher, however, might not be very interested in the author himself and would choose to search the diary for references to *another* person, in which case a very different body of data would be produced from the very same entity, the diary.[2]

When some archaeologists are asked to describe what they do, they often say "I study the past." Actually this statement is incorrect: no one has or can obtain any facts (in the sense of *things being done*) about past events because the events that would have produced them are over and done with. All that remains of past events is circumstantial evidence. Archaeologists do, however, make observations on events in the *present*: we record the events connected with excavating the archaeological record; with examining the sediments, features, and items of which it is composed; and with classifying our observations in terms of innumerable criteria. We record the facts generated by our investigation of the archaeological record.

The challenge facing archaeological researchers is to decide which properties of our observational events can be linked most securely to events that occurred in the past. Since all arguments about what the past was like are based on circumstantial evidence, they must be judged by how well they link observations in the present to dynamic events inferred from such evidence. Only strong arguments of causal necessity are acceptable. There is, for instance, very little ambiguity about the physical consequences of the human use of a hammer stone on a nodule of flint to produce stone tools. The entire process has been replicated and documented thousands of times in controlled settings, allowing observers to relate energetic input and stone-working technique to their material consequences. The physical structure of numerous types of lithic material has been investigated with sufficient thoroughness to enable archaeologists to diagnose the sequence of blows and fractures occurring in the past that produced the lithic artifacts they examine in the present.

Archaeologists who want to learn about the establishment and operation of extinct state-level societies might try to generate data that would help them assess the level of political complexity achieved by the human systems once operating at their archaeological sites. What observations on which classes of archaeological remains would unambiguously produce such data? First of all, researchers would have to be able to discriminate between political and nonpolitical phenomena. This capability would permit the development of a scale of "politicalness," with values ranging from one (completely nonpolitical) to ten (totally political), so that items recovered from archaeological sites could be ranked according to their degree of politicalness. A comparable set of criteria would be necessary before a dimension of "complexness" could be defined and used to evaluate the properties of the same archaeological observations.

At present, however, no clear set of criteria exists for the assignment of archaeological facts to a dimension such as politicalness or complexness, although many researchers act as though these scales exist. Even in ethnographic research, which is based on the direct observation of human behaviors and events, there are few universally accepted dimensions in terms of which data are organized. Should a researcher stipulate that the size of the retinue serving a political leader is a circumstantial indicator of organizational complexity? Or should size of retinue be interpreted as an indicator of despotic rule in a relatively noncomplex system?[3] The answer is probably "it could be either," which suggests that it would be a good idea to establish one scale for tabulating facts relating to the size of a political leader's retinue and another scale for distinguishing between members of the retinue who served in staff positions and those who were kinpersons of the leader and dependent upon him for support.

The preceding example illustrates the important role that *dimensionalizing data* plays in organizing facts—both archaeological and ethnographic—into units in terms of some defining criteria that we, the researchers, decide are relevant to our knowledge goals. The operational definitions that we apply to our archaeological observations serve the same purpose as those a physician might make when measuring the weight and age of all of his patients. The data enable the physician to say, "Patient X belongs *here* on the age dimension [or scale] and *here* on the dimension of body weight, and when I look at my practice as a whole, it consists overwhelmingly of elderly, obese patients."

Having uncovered this pattern in his office records, the physician might then decide to compare his patients in terms of several other dimensions (perhaps the presence and severity of heart disease relative to caloric intake) to see if patient obesity might occur in conjunction with and be influenced by other health problems. This simple example illustrates the dictum that dimensionalizing data is one of the most useful tools available to all researchers who want to make their knowledge grow. A corollary would be that, as a profession, archaeologists tend to foreclose the possibilities inherent in their subject matter by ignoring the dimensionalizing imperative.

Equally pervasive is the habit of classifying data in terms of a particular dimension, then arguing that the dimension is germane by appealing to some other body of experience, and then elevating the body of experience itself to the level of an explanatory principle that is invoked to "explain" any similar observations in the future.[4] Such a procedure also provides a basis for the accusation—hostile to science in its intent and meant to demonstrate that the logic of science is tautological—that all researchers *create* their own data. I would argue that creating dimensionalized data from archaeological evidence is *essential* to all subsequent steps in the analytical process (in Binford 1989:34–39 I discuss further the difference between creating data and creating *evidence*), which is why it occurs primarily in Act I of the play of ideas.

Act I, Scene 2: Dimensionalizing Data

Once a researcher has recorded his or her observations on material phenomena and has selected the initial dimensions in terms of which these observations are to be organized, the scientific dialogue can begin. This is the juncture at which, if one resists the temptation to make accommodative arguments that stipulate what the data represent, the data have the opportunity to "talk back." The generic term for all subsequent investigation is *analysis,* which embraces all of the tactics and strategies a researcher might implement in the search for relationships in a data set. Analysis is the study of how vectors of dimensionalized data interact with other, independently dimensionalized data either in the same or another data set. Once relationships are identified, the "conversation" between the researcher and the data begins as he or she attempts to link the identified patterns to other sources of secure knowledge.

The example of the physician whose curiosity is stimulated by what he thinks might be some commonalities among his patients will help me illustrate. Of the many observations that the physician made on his patients over time, for analytical purposes he has initially chosen to examine two: age and weight. When he discovers that the interaction between these two categories of dimensionalized data reveals a startling correlation, he is observing a patterned relationship among two of the classes in his total data set.

For archaeologists, regularities in the way vectors of circumstantial evidence distribute with respect to each other signal organized phenomena that have been structured by past dynamic processes. Both the archaeologist and the physician have observed *first-order derivative patterning* in their data, and, although each has chosen what observations to make and how to dimensionalize them, the first-order patterns themselves *were not stipulated* by either researcher. First-order patterns cannot be used directly, however, as the basis for any nontautological or nonstipulative statements about either obesity in elderly patients or about the past. Interpretation of the data at this stage would be by stipulation or convention and would reflect the intellectual "culture" of the person doing the interpretation.[5]

The investigator has a tactical choice to make at this juncture. He or she may decide to look at the provocative first-order patterning in terms of another independent dimension in the original data set, or he or she could array the first-order patterning against another, independent data set. The physician could, for example, select the oldest and most obese patients (in whom some sort of relationship was shown to exist between age and weight) and plot their physical distri-

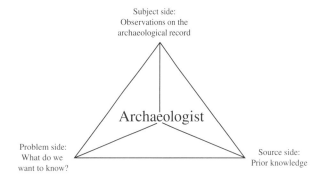

FIGURE 3.01

Model of an archaeologist's intellectual mix.

bution on a city map (the dimension of space) to see whether the patients were clustered or randomly distributed across the overlying north-south-east-west municipal grid.

For purposes of illustration, let us assume that a significant proportion of the elderly, obese patients were clustered in a section of the city where many retirement villages were located. This pattern, which I would call *second-order derivative patterning,* would probably prompt the physician to look at his patient records to see if there were another relevant category of data against which he could array his second-order patterns.

Another way of representing how analysis works is to imagine a researcher who is standing in the middle of an equilateral triangle (figure 3.01). One leg of the triangle is labeled "source side" because all of the received knowledge that can be appealed to in argument or cited as warranting certain beliefs about process, dynamics, and cause is located here. The label "subject side" is attached to the triangle's second leg because the phenomena selected for study have been arrayed here. This is the side with all of the question marks, because it represents the domain of ignorance that a researcher hopes to transmute into knowledge. For archaeologists, the subject side consists of the various properties of the archaeological record that will be organized for investigation (Watson 1979b).

On the triangle's third side are found all of the tactical options available to an investigator for articulating the source side with the subject side of the triangle—including a few that I wish could be eliminated from the roster. How many times do archaeologists skip the opportunity to dimensionalize and analyze their data and instead routinely accommodate their observations to some domain of knowledge on the source side of the triangle? This kind of linkage is usually justified by a claim that the connection either is self-evident or can be validated by an argument from analogy about resemblances between source-side and subject-side data.

One very productive tactical option is to intensify the effort to increase source- and subject-side knowledge bases.[6]

Ethnoarchaeological research, improvements in dating technology, phytolithic research, and cross-cultural ethnographic analysis are only a few domains that have contributed to recent increases in source-side knowledge. Similarly, improved methods of excavating, recording, and documenting the archaeological record have greatly increased knowledge on the subject side of the triangle. Without a doubt, however, the most useful tactic available to archaeologists for articulating source- and subject-side knowledge is the construction of frames of reference.

Act II, Scene 1: Building and Using Frames of Reference

A *frame of reference* allows the researcher to juxtapose one domain of knowledge about which there is a history of productive learning with another, less well-known domain. Frames of reference vary directly in their utility as a function of how organizationally germane they are to the domain of data being investigated. In the broadest sense of the word, everyone uses current knowledge as a frame of reference when examining archaeological remains and determining that they are, in fact, *archaeological* phenomena instead of phenomena unrelated to events in the human past. One of the greatest challenges in doing good science is to develop and use multiple, relevant frames of reference during data analysis.

One of the more exciting experiences in science is to project one's dimensionalized data against a frame of reference and observe a patterned distribution of the data relative to the phenomena constituting the frame of reference. When this step is repeated using a different frame of reference, the processual implications of the data may shift as the knowledge base incorporated into the frame of reference also shifts. The ability to tease out implications from repetitively patterned relationships among variables (classes of data) provides the clues to the way the world is organized and how it works in a dynamic sense.

The initial frame of reference in terms of which most archaeologists begin an examination of their data is the simple one of Cartesian space. The first step in field work is usually to lay out a grid on the site and relate all observations to their placement in three-dimensional space. As points accumulate on the site map corresponding to different observational units or properties of the site itself, first-order derivative patterning slowly emerges. The properties of the site that the archaeologist chooses to observe may have relatively unambiguous implications. This would be true for concentrations of ash and charcoal in circumscribed areas within a site. All of the stipulated criteria for recognizing charcoal and ash, however, and all of the prior knowledge that an excavator has about how ash and charcoal concentrations are produced, as well as what their presence could imply about past

dynamics, do *not* determine whether any concentrations will be observed. Neither does this knowledge affect the patterned distribution of concentrations in Cartesian space.

It is worth repeating that as long as the observational conventions remain the same, all of an excavator's definitions and stipulated conventions for making observations determine neither the properties of the spatial patterns produced by distributions of ash and charcoal nor the presence or absence of these materials at different archaeological sites. The patterning itself defines a new domain of data that may have more direct implications for ancient (or at least prior) dynamic processes.[7] To investigate these patterns, the excavator may wish to change the frame of reference from simple Cartesian space to some type of *property space*.[8]

For instance, I could structure a property space map by plotting two independent, continuous variables, such as the number of retouched tools and the amount of excavated anthropogenic deposit measured in terms of cubic meters. Then I could perform an intersite comparison by plotting points (each representing a different site) in terms of the number of cubic meters of ashy deposit, or the mean size of ashy concentrations at each site, or as a ratio with another of the site's characteristics, such as numbers of houses. If I were to note clusters in the resulting scatter of coded points, I might then have some clue (although it would probably be incomplete) about the factors conditioning differential consumption of fuels on archaeological sites relative to some indirect measures of site formational duration.

This is an example of *second-order derivative patterning*. It is second-order because the patterning is made visible by plotting first-order observations against another frame of reference—a Cartesian property space map—and shifting the scale to an intersite comparison that is displayed in a property space defined by the relationships between additional variables. Likewise, if the second-order patterns (which are also referred to as observations at this point) were then displayed against a new frame of reference, *third-order patterning* would be generated. I could continue to generate multiple orders of derivative patterning by exposing each new pattern to a different frame of reference.

Because investigators select their frames of reference to suit their knowledge goals,[9] they must decide at the outset what is the appropriate *scale* of the referential domain in terms of which they will look at their research subject. Since the subject I am investigating in this book is hunter-gatherers, I have had to decide whether to look at hunter-gatherers in only one climatic setting or in several different settings, on one continent or from a global perspective. Since I have chosen the most inclusive of referential domains—the entire earth—for purposes of comparison, I must adopt a global perspective.

Selection of such a large-scale perspective presents me with another critical decision. The referential domain of this study—the earth—is characterized by an infinite number of properties, many of which may be relevant to the search for patterning. Clarity demands, however, that initially I select only one set of properties to act as the *frame* in my frame of reference in terms of which the hunter-gatherer data will be arrayed.

I could, for example, choose to array the data in terms of a classification of all of the earth's plant formations like the one developed by Eyre (1968). At this juncture I would need to specify a currency in terms of which the measurements within the frame of reference will be expressed for purposes of comparison. In this case the currency will be spatial units of 100 square kilometers each, and I will measure how many 100-square-kilometer units of each type of plant community in Eyre's classification can be found within my referential domain, which is the earth. Next I will compare the number of such units to the frequency with which hunter-gatherer cases from the global sample are found in each type of plant community. I might also have chosen to observe the patterning produced by a more typical geographical frame of reference in which the earth is separated into continents and countries.

Much of the information and many of the variables that are presented in subsequent chapters are used to develop frames of reference that I believe are essential to making sense of archaeological phenomena. Throughout this study I use location in geographical space (as identified by longitude and latitude) as the basis for linking archaeological and ethnographic observations to one another and to environmental properties at these places. Using longitude and latitude as the linking properties for the development of frames of reference should make it clear that an almost infinite number of useful frames of reference could be developed for both ethnographic and archaeological observations at different places on the earth.

Sometimes I assume that ethnographic data are subject-side phenomena, and in these instances they are displayed against various frames of reference. At other times these phenomena function as source-side information against which archaeological data are arrayed. I also build frames of reference using field studies of animal biomass and data from other ecological investigations as a way of exploring the climatic variables that condition plant biomass.

Frames of reference are not, however, the only way that prior knowledge can be organized and used tactically by archaeologists. Another helpful tactic is to project secure knowledge onto locations or settings—and into eras and contexts—about which there is little direct knowledge.[10]

Act II, Scene 2: Projection

In chapter 2 I argued that projection is the primary strategy used by human beings when they anticipate the course of future events. The tactic of projection is based on the simple

assumption that the world is likely to remain the same as it was the last time one looked. If the assumption of stability is justified, then the outcome of planned or volitional action can be accurately anticipated. If, on the other hand, the world is not stable, then human actions may not have the desired results. (When I use the word *stable* I do not mean static or unchanging. I mean that the dynamic properties and organizational relationships stay the same even though some of the formal properties may have changed.)

The logic of projection is one of the fundamental tools of scientific research. In science, as in life, it is the fit between what is projected and what is experienced that informs us about the utility of our prior knowledge as well as its limitations. Most of us have no difficulty recognizing when the results of our carefully thought-out plans fall short of our expectations or when our strategies fail to yield the desired results. Investors receive prompt feedback when their stock-purchasing strategies fail to anticipate the market's behavior: they make or lose money, depending on whether the value of their stocks goes up or down.

Science as a learning strategy relies on the disciplined use of this projective capacity. As scientists, we put our knowledge and ideas about process on the line through projection and then see if our understanding of dynamics is correct. We often refer to the "future" in this context, but what we really have in mind are the subsequent observations that we make and not the future course of the events or conditions being projected.

The recurrent distinction between the *historical sciences*—about which it is claimed that experimental learning is not possible because the events studied are long over—and the *natural sciences*—which permit projections about the "real future" and thereby test projective arguments in the same way that an investor's financial success or failure tests his or her strategies—is methodologically false. For the scientist, the future refers to his subsequent observations and not to some "real," chronologically distant future of the phenomena being studied. Projection, in this case, refers to some situation in which germane observations are made on germane data. A scientist's future (or subsequent) observations inform him or her whether or not a projection, based on prior knowledge and argument, is supported by events in the world of controlled observations, regardless of whether the subject of observation consists of material remains from ancient events or aspects of events in the future world of general experience.

The role of statistics in science is based exclusively on projection. Eons ago it became apparent that, in general, there are two reasons why human plans or scenarios fail. One reflects the fact that although a knowledge of current conditions was accurate and adequate when the plans were made, the world did not stay the way it was, and this change in conditions made all plans obsolete. The other reason is that knowledge about some critical aspect of the world was inadequate to begin with, either because of problems connected with observation or because the terms chosen to describe the world were irrelevant.[11] If distorted views or irrelevant ways of conceptualizing are projected onto the world, the anticipated future will not be realized, not because the world has changed but because not enough was known about it in the first place.[12]

It is possible, for instance, to waste considerable time and energy trying to explain why the earth is flat or to explain the physics of flipping coins by reference to the graphic contrasts between heads and tails. The irony is that it is necessary to have germane knowledge of the world and its properties in order to decide what is a rational way to look at it further so that we might "know" it even more accurately!

What is the best way to proceed in a situation in which there is insufficient accurate knowledge about the world to make any projections—as in the world of the past, for instance? How does a researcher construct a projection that puts prior knowledge and argument on the line to be evaluated by that ultimate arbiter, future observations?

Proposition 3.01

Good science consists of strategically using prior knowledge to make projections from better-known domains to less well-known domains. When observations on the less well-known phenomena are inconsistent with our projections, this is an important clue to the way in which the world may have been different from our conception of it. When ideas that we have considered germane are shown to be irrelevant, or at least poorly conceived relative to the way the world is organized, an opportunity for learning has been identified.

This is the way in which we learn what questions are important to research and what domains will be the most productive to explore.

A reasonable response to the preceding statement would be to note that archaeologists have frequently used their prior knowledge to make projections to unknown contexts by means of arguments that can be lumped under the heading of *ethnographic analogy*. This approach has been used to interpret the archaeological record or to distinguish between archaeological and nonarchaeological phenomena at particular places.[13] Not surprisingly, these arguments are frequently debunked by empirical arguments to the contrary, or some form of cautionary tale that cites a situation in which very different dynamics have been responsible for the same distributional patterns (Bonnichsen 1973).[14]

Although these demonstrations illustrate ambiguity in the *meaning* of observations, they do not necessarily contribute to a growth of knowledge. Most of the time these responses have the unfortunate consequence of discouraging innovative thinking about archaeological observations.[15] No matter how interpretations of archaeological materials may be warranted, they are most often an accommodation of archaeological phenomena—and by implication the past—to what we think we know or believe to be "true."[16] When an unknown context is interpreted in familiar terms, what might be called a "meaning-added" enhancement of archaeological observations occurs. The real opportunity for learning comes when we use our prior knowledge to tactically enhance our ability to learn rather than simply put our subjective stamp on the remains from the past.

Act III, Scene 1: Developing a Dialogue between Researchers and Hunter-Gatherers

I now introduce some of the tactics available to archaeologists who want to use the ethnographic record of hunter-gatherer peoples as a frame of reference for the study of variability in the archaeological record. I begin by looking at variability among hunter-gatherer life ways when viewed through an environmental frame of reference (see chapter 5). Searching for patterns in hunter-gatherer data from this perspective can provide the basis for causal arguments about why hunter-gatherers differ. As Wylie points out, researchers must establish "the principles of connection—the considerations of relevance—that inform the selection and evaluation of analogies. . . . expanding the base of interpretations and elaborating the fit between source and subject. . . . the inquiry . . . must be specifically designed to determine what causal connections hold between the material and cultural or behavioral variables of interest" (1985:101). I would affirm that analogical reasoning is a tactical approach to theory building and not an interpretive end in itself.

Since pattern recognition techniques—such as projection and the patterning it produces—provide an insight into how the world appears to work in a dynamic sense, once I observe a set of patterns in ethnographic data I can begin building theories that account for the patterned variability. Dipping into my store of prior knowledge, I can create arguments that link pattern A to variables A, B, and C; then I can compare my theoretical template to the patterns in archaeological data generated by ancient hunger-gatherers. I hope, of course, that the outlines of my explanatory construction conform to those in the archaeological data for which I would like to account, but even if there is no correspondence I am still in a learning posture.[17] Similarly, if it is possible to relate variability in hunter-gatherer behavior and organization to variability in environmental variables, then through the use of summary equations I can directly project some expected properties onto any location for which there is basic environmental information.

Of course, one assumption is that the entire earth is populated by hunter-gatherers who were similar to those who have been documented ethnographically. I also assume that the patterned relationships in environmental variables have been stable for at least the recent past. This uniformitarian assumption must be warranted, however, by arguments positing a necessary ecological linkage between environmental variables and the organizational properties of hunter-gatherers. This is called a *relational projection* because it depends for its utility on a convincing argument for the necessity of the linkage.

When properties about which I have less secure knowledge are involved, an alternative tactic is to employ a simple *proportional projection*, using, for instance, the Eyre classification of the earth's plant communities as a frame of reference. To develop a proportional projection I would first obtain the means of various properties, such as the total area occupied by an ethnic group, from the hunter-gatherer cases occurring within the area covered by each plant community in the classification. This information could then be projected to the entire earth by dividing the total area occupied by each plant community by the mean area occupied by an ethnic group in each class of plant community.

The result of such an operation would be a statement of the projected number of ethnic groups per plant community; the sum of all types of plant communities would correspond to the number of ethnic groups projected for the entire earth. Even though there is clearly much less information and more faith in the adequacy and accuracy of the sample associated with a proportional as opposed to a relational projection, this will still be a useful tactic at certain junctures in the research on which I report in this book.

Act III, Scene 2: Learning about Variability through Pattern Recognition Techniques

Relational projections (illustrated in chapter 4 by the calculation of expected prey values) and proportional projections (which in chapter 5 link several properties of hunter-gatherer peoples) are not the only tools for expanding the relevance of an admittedly limited knowledge base. Second-order derivative patterning is potentially more informative about how variability in one or more variables in a data set may pattern when arrayed against other variables.

So far I have chosen to illustrate the use of frames of reference by examples based on the dimension of geographic space. Another major dimension along which variability in ethnographically and archaeologically documented systems can be expected to be arrayed has to do with organizational complexity. The frequently cited classification of human societies into units, ranging from bands to states, and the very term *hunter-gatherer* (which presupposes other subsistence strategies, such as horticulture, agriculture, pastoralism, and

industrialism) imply a developmental sequence or series of *system states* that constitutes a trajectory of directional changes at a given location.

The term *system state* is used frequently in this book to refer to the fact that any dynamic system may exhibit significantly different properties when observed at different times. Some of the variability noted in the hunter-gatherer cases in my ethnographic sample may reflect the fact that directional, nonreversible, organizational changes have occurred between two different points in time. On the other hand, some of the differences between cases reflect the fact that while some characteristics of human groups may change cyclically, the cycle of change is itself recurrent and therefore stable.

Many of the properties of the groups in the ethnographic sample were selected for study because I suspected that they were indicative of different system states or were conditioned by such changes. Through the study of the way system indicators relate to one another and to other potentially conditioning variables, I expect to learn more about dynamic system states themselves and how they are affected by processes contributing to directional change in hunter-gatherer organization.[18]

Although it is plausible to imagine that a significant amount of the variability among the hunter-gatherer groups in the sample may relate to variability in habitat, it is equally plausible that some, and perhaps much, of the variability reflects different trajectories of stability and change that have characterized the different evolutionary plays enacted in different ecological theaters. My sample of ethnographic cases is composed of societies that represent very different system states, reflecting different tempos and modes of evolutionary change prior to their ethnographic documentation.[19]

Basic to the diagnosis of system states is the ability to approximate the divergence in state from some basic organizational standard. For archaeologists, hunter-gatherers have represented the point of departure for evaluating the organizational level of more complex social formations. Since one of my goals is an examination of variability among the hunter-gatherer cases in the sample, an a priori assumption about which groups fall into the "least-developed" category leaves little to be learned about organizational complexity and diversity.

Instead of adopting a typological approach, I build a model and illustrate its potential for knowledge growth. I do not, however, use the model as a projection to which the data from the archaeological record are accommodated, thereby creating a meaning-added interpretation for archaeological observations. Since a model is a very explicit use of prior knowledge to simulate a specified state—or the determinants of that state—in nature, a totally stipulated set of conditions can be used as a baseline against which to compare real-world conditions. Because there is complete knowledge of all the simulated conditions and ensuing interactions, the observed deviations from anticipated values or properties are a direct clue to relationships and conditions not included in the model.

The alternative (and invalid) tactic of using some descriptive characterizations of a given hunter-gatherer case as the zero point on a scale of system state complexity is unproductive because it is not known what factors are conditioning the system state of the chosen case. With a constructed model, all of the conditioning components are specified when the model is built, an approach that permits both qualitative and quantitative comparisons with observed systems.

I hope that this brief introduction to some of the tactics for developing and using source-side knowledge to deal with variability on a broad scale of comparison will sufficiently orient observers of the play of ideas unfolding in subsequent chapters.

Methods for Using Prior Knowledge

Building Frames of Reference and Models

The three chapters that follow represent a fairly linear accumulation of prior knowledge that is organized systematically for future use with various frames of reference. The equations necessary for making projections—incorporating the relationships discovered or selected for use in frames of reference—are also developed.

Based on a reasoned use of prior knowledge, the Terrestrial Model is designed and constructed to play a methodological rather than an explanatory role in subsequent studies and comparisons. This model can be used as a standard for measurement as well as a baseline for comparing observed conditions. Differences between the observations and values projected by the Terrestrial Model also play an important role in exploring the world of hunter-gatherer dynamics.

Finally, a demonstration of the utility of the Terrestrial Model leads to a consideration of those sequences in the archaeological record in Western Europe that document the appearance of domesticated plants and animals. This examination prompts the question: do the archaeological statics indicate the appearance of a new niche in the region?

4

Setting the Stage for the Evolutionary Play

The Earth's Climates, Plants, and Animals

In this chapter, the variability in environments within which hunter-gatherers are known to have lived is documented and the habitat variables that I consider germane to an understanding of hunter-gatherer life ways are dimensionalized. I also illustrate how an ecologically informed description of the earth's environments permits the definition, with intellectually productive results, of the environmental property space of any given location. A relational projection for estimating moderate body size, ungulate biomass (which is important in subsequent models, frames of reference, and projections), is presented, and I illustrate how all of these data and variables can be used as frames of reference for both ethnographic and archaeological data.

Habitat variables were defined in chapter 2 as those properties of the environment that can be measured without reference to the attributes of any particular organism occupying a specific habitat. In this chapter, some of the habitat variables that are basic to the operation of ecosystems are considered, and specific values for some environmental properties characteristic of the locations where hunter-gatherers have lived are obtained. I have also developed a data base of 1,429 weather stations from around the world in which case frequencies are roughly proportional to the documented variability in the earth's climatic regimes. These data provide a frame of reference against which to view and assess any bias that might be demonstrable in the environments that hunter-gatherers are known to have exploited. Analysis of these data also identifies links between specific ecological patterns and some organizational properties of the hunter-gatherer cases included in this study.

The biosphere of the earth varies from place to place in the magnitude of its biological activity and in the number and forms of organisms that are present. One way of monitoring this array of variability is to compare the amount of energy that passes through an ecosystem with the amount that is stored biologically in different regions of the world. Two terms will be used repeatedly in discussions of these dynamics. *Production* refers to the synthesis of energy within an ecosystem, measured in terms of the number of grams of *new cells* generated per square meter per year. *Biomass,* on the other hand, represents the amount of synthesized energy that is *stored* by plants or animals in an ecosystem.

Like all other animal species, human beings ultimately depend upon the plant species that in any ecosystem act as the initial biological transformers of energy. The amount of energy stored within an ecosystem in the form of animals is therefore considered *secondary production* because it is derived from and supported by primary plant producers. It is reasonable to expect that certain dependent relationships exist between human populations and the primary producer component of their habitats, and that similar niche-conditioning relationships occur between human populations and other animals.

Ultimately I would like to be able to compare the behavior of hunter-gatherers in relation to quantitative variability in their environments in terms of the production and biomass of plant producers and plant consumers (animals). Before I can anticipate how human actors might fit into different habitats, however, it is necessary to understand the factors that affect both primary and secondary production.

The fundamental principle of ecological dynamics is that all stored energy in an ecosystem has been synthesized from the solar radiation that penetrates the earth's atmosphere. A strong relationship can therefore be expected between the amount of energy synthesized by plant communities and the duration and intensity of their exposure to solar radiation. Other things being equal, the gross primary production occurring in an ecosystem is linked to its location relative to the equator: the greater the distance from the equator, the lower the ecosystem's gross production.

Photosynthesis—the process by which plants convert or "fix" solar energy—requires the presence of at least three ingredients: solar radiation, water, and carbon dioxide. Carbon dioxide is present at a fairly uniform level (0.02%) over most of the earth, and because it is a constant, it may be eliminated as a source of meaningful variation in plant production. Water and solar radiation are, therefore, the two major variables whose interaction determines the irregular and complicated pattern of biotic production observable across the surface of the earth.

Climate: A Baseline for the Study of Ecology

Solar radiation is distributed globally in a pattern of graded reduction as the distance from the equator increases. The distribution of water, however, is not as easily summarized. Global differences in the amount of rainfall are the result of complex interactions between gases of varying temperatures, atmospheric circulation patterns, and interactions with topographical features that may modify these patterns, such as landmasses, bodies of water, and differences in surface elevation. Rainfall is somewhat irregularly distributed as a result of the temperature and related movement of circulating air masses in response to different pressure levels. For instance, when rising bodies of air expand as a result of decreasing pressure at high altitudes, this expansion is accompanied by heat loss, and, as a consequence, the air becomes cooler. Warm air is therefore characterized by high pressure and cool air by low pressure, and, as a general rule in the atmospheric matrix, air from high-pressure centers moves in the direction of low-pressure centers.

Due to the differential distribution of solar energy over the earth's surface, air is warmed maximally in equatorial zones and minimally in polar regions, which means that convection, or the presence of rapidly rising and expanding air, will be particularly characteristic of equatorial settings. In response to pressure differentials at the earth's surface, the movement of cooler air occurs from the polar regions toward the equator while, coincidentally, a similar band of warmer air moves at high altitudes toward the poles. This rather simple picture is further complicated by the effect of the earth's rotation, which I do not attempt to explain but merely describe in terms of patterned results.

The model of atmospheric circulation presented here—in which air masses rise along the equator, move at high altitudes toward the polar areas, are cooled, drop to the surface in response to cooling, and then move along the surface toward the equator, where warming occurs once again—results in three interacting circulation cells: (1) the equatorial or major convection cell, (2) the middle or "horse latitude" cell, and (3) the polar cell (see Trewartha and Horn 1980:100–91 for more information). The interaction of these three circulation cells is illustrated in figure 4.01.

The air moving at higher elevations in the equatorial zone is sufficiently cool at a latitude of about 30 degrees to drop again to the earth's surface. Some of this cooler air moves at low elevations back toward the equator and some moves in a polar direction, but in both cases the air from the upper atmosphere becomes warmer as it moves over the earth's surface. When warm air moving along the surface in a polar direction encounters cold air moving toward the equator from within the polar cell (figure 4.01), it is forced to rise over the cold air, which causes an initial expansion of the warm air followed by cooling and condensation. Rainfall is produced in the zone of overlap (usually located between 45 and 60 degrees latitude) between the polar and middle circulation cells.

Within the polar cell, a looplike circulation pattern prevails, with warm air moving toward the pole at higher elevations and then dropping to the surface near the poles. The now-cool, dry air then moves across the surface in an equatorial direction until it meets warm air moving in a polar direction in the middle or north temperate cell. These

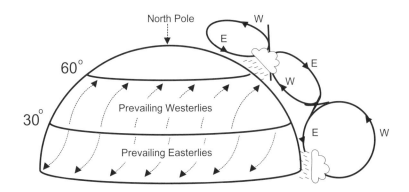

FIGURE 4.01

Model of the earth's circulation patterns. Adapted from Trewartha and Horn (1980:100–128).

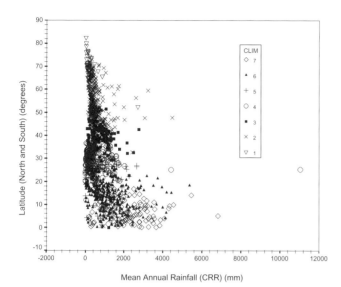

FIGURE 4.02

Scatter plot of data from the 1,429 weather stations included in the sample of the earth's environments showing the relationship between latitude and mean annual rainfall. Marker is an ordination of the earth's climates by temperature (CLIM): (1) polar, (2) boreal, (3) cool temperate, (4) warm temperate, (5) subtropical, (6) tropical, and (7) equatorial.

circulation patterns produce two broad bands of heavy rainfall over the earth's surface: the convection or thunderstorm zone along the equator (0 to 18 degrees latitude) and the polar front zone between 45 and 60 degrees. This generalization is strongly warranted by the patterns in figure 4.02, which are derived from the large data set of the world's weather stations referred to earlier.[1]

Figure 4.02 is a scatter plot of data from 1,429 weather stations with latitude plotted on the y axis and total annual rainfall summarized in millimeters and displayed on the x axis. High-rainfall zones are indicated by the points spread to the right of the graph. The equatorial convection zone is represented by the scatter between 0 and 18 degrees north and south latitude. Similarly, the zone of interaction between the air of the polar zone and the central cell is shown by the points to the right of the graph between 45 and 60 degrees latitude.

The north and south middle latitude zones—which lie on either side of 30 degrees latitude—are traversed by dry, upper-atmosphere air that converges on the earth's surface at a latitude of 30 degrees. This dry air, which may move either southward or northward, generates relatively low rainfall, whereas the equatorial and polar front zones have relatively high and sustained rainfall.

Figure 4.03 illustrates the latitudinal distribution of some of the earth's great desert areas. It is clear that the lowest-rainfall zones are concentrated in the latitudes between 15 and

30 degrees, with a more rapid increase in rainfall occurring as air moves toward the poles from the 30 degree zone. The midlatitude zone in which dry upper atmospheric air returns to the earth's surface is visible in figure 4.02 as the "hole" (between 40 and 18 degrees latitude) in the scatter of points resembling a wishbone that extends from 45 to 25 degrees latitude.

This is the zone in which either dry upper atmospheric air dominates the circulation pattern and results in very dry settings (the left margin of the distribution) or cyclonic and anticyclonic storm tracks interact to produce higher rainfall. Cyclonic tracks and prevailing westerlies may also interact along the polar side of 30 degrees latitude. This zone is characterized by *either-or* environments—either dry or fairly wet—and there are very few areas within these geographic boundaries that have climatic regimes intermediate between the two extremes. The few points occurring more or less in the center of the "hole" are primarily weather stations from northern Mexico and Texas in the Northern Hemisphere and from South Africa, Botswana, Mozambique, and Australia in the Southern Hemisphere.

All of these areas are within the 30 degree zone with relatively small landmass when compared with the adjacent ocean regions with their massive high-pressure cells. They represent convergence zones in which moisture-laden winds having their origin in two different high-pressure systems meet and overlap across a narrow landmass with lowered pressure. Vast areas of North Africa and Asia that fall within the 30 degrees latitude boundaries are not included in the *either-or* climatic dichotomy because they either are landlocked or share minimal coastal boundaries with adjacent oceans.

The wet areas forming the right side of the wishbone distribution in figure 4.02 support three basic types of vegetation: the southern pine forests of the southeastern United States; the midlatitude deciduous forests of the eastern United States, China, and adjacent areas in Asia; and the subtropical, broadleaf evergreen forests of both the southeastern United States and a vast area of China. Minor contributors to the distribution are regions with predominantly winter rainfall, including parts of California and the Mediterranean areas of Albania, Greece, and Italy, as well as the mountainous areas of Algeria and Tunisia.

Figure 4.02 is explored more fully in subsequent sections of this chapter. In the meantime, with regard to the model of the earth's climatic circulation pattern, it should be noted that the primary factors responsible for deviations from the model are the presence of physical features such as mountain ranges, as well as the different thermal properties of land and water surfaces and proportional differences in their distribution. Cyclical temperature differentials related to seasonal changes from winter to summer constitute another factor conditioning deviations from the circulation model. It will be necessary to monitor all of these factors

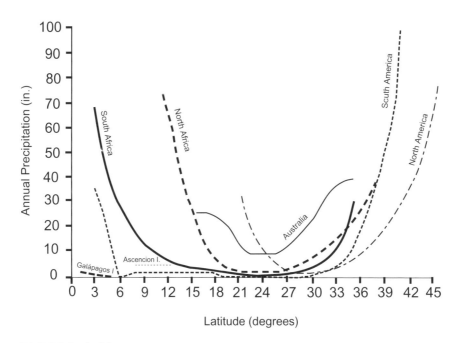

FIGURE 4.03

Distribution of deserts by continent and latitude. Redrawn and adapted from Trewartha and Horn (1980: figure 12.10).

in order to identify the variables that affect the lives of hunter-gatherers when they are viewed from an ecological perspective.

This brief introduction to air circulation patterns provides a background for several generalizations about the earth's biological activity. Since carbon dioxide levels are more or less uniform worldwide and therefore do not contribute to variability in biological productivity, solar radiation and rainfall are the two remaining variables affecting differential productivity among the earth's ecosystems. If the only available knowledge about the earth's ecosystems consisted of a simple sketch of the air circulation patterns, coupled with diminishing levels of solar radiation as distance from the equator increased, several expectations would still be justifiable. Simply by considering water as a limiting factor in plant production, maximum primary productivity would be expected in the equatorial zone and in the vicinity of 55 degrees latitude. The middle zone at around 30 degrees latitude should be characterized by greatly reduced primary productivity, given the probability of low rainfall in the areas where dry upper-altitude air descends to the surface.

If these expectations are coupled with a scalar reduction of solar energy as distance from the equator increases, polar areas would be expected to have low levels of production, temperate areas to have moderate levels, and equatorial areas to have high productivity. This expectation is tempered by the limitations of available moisture in the middle latitudes, which may reduce primary productivity still further.

BASIC CLIMATIC INGREDIENTS: SOLAR RADIATION AND TEMPERATURE

Basic temperature data in this study consist of mean annual temperature (CMAT) and the monthly values from which this annual value was obtained. This information can, of course, be organized in different ways to produce more technical measures serving different analytical functions. For instance, *effective temperature* (ET) is a measure that was specifically designed by Bailey (1960) to examine the biological implications of ambient warmth, which is another way of referring to the amount of solar energy available at any given location. ET is calculated in terms of three empirically determined constants:

1. The minimal mean temperature (18°C) of the coldest month of the year that will sustain tropical plant communities (those having 365-day growing seasons).
2. The minimal mean temperature (10°C) expected at the beginning and end of the growing season along the zonal boundary between polar and boreal environments.
3. The minimal mean temperature (8°C) at the beginning and end of the growing season, or—at the earth's poles—the warmest month.

The choice of these constants permits the calculation of effective temperature values that relate directly to the major biological boundaries recognized empirically as marking transitions in biological activity.

The relationship between ET and the earth's biotic communities can be visualized as a scale along which ET values range. An ET value of 18°C or higher corresponds to those places in the world where there is no killing frost during the year. Locations that have an ET value of 10°C or less are characterized by fewer than thirty days of the year without a killing frost. Effective temperature provides more biologically relevant information than simple mean annual temperature, and, in addition, the magnitude of the value is directly indicative of the duration of the growing season.

The following formula is used to calculate ET when temperature is measured in degrees centigrade:

(4.01)

$$ET = [(18 * MWM) - (10 * MCM)]/(MWM - MCM + 8)$$

where   MWM = mean temperature in degrees centigrade for
            the warmest month of the year and
        MCM = mean temperature in degrees centigrade for
            the coldest month of the year.

ET values have been calculated for all of the 339 documented groups of hunter-gatherers that make up the comparative data base of this study,[2] and in table 4.01 ET and some other basic climatic variables are listed for specific locations associated with each hunter-gatherer case. Because the human adaptation to environmental conditions differs so drastically from strictly biological responses, such as plant production, table 4.01 includes some additional measures of temperature. Mean temperature during the coldest month of the year (MCM) has a direct impact on the human investment in shelter and clothing, so this value, along with the range of mean temperatures between the coldest (MCM) and warmest (MWM) months (TRANGE), can be calculated.

Other conventional measures for summarizing basic climatic data—such as *biotemperature* (BT), first used by Holdridge (1947) in a well-known classification of the earth's vegetation based on climatic data—were calculated. Biotemperature is a measure of central tendency calculated by dividing by twelve the sum of all mean monthly temperatures greater than 0°C.[3] The relationship between BT and ET, both of which summarize climatic data relating to temperature and solar radiation, is illustrated in figure 4.04 relative to the more familiar measure of mean annual temperature, CMAT.

Although it might be assumed that these three measurements would be closely related since they represent different ways of measuring approximately the same thing—the solar energy available at any given location—this assumption is not

supported by the pattern in figure 4.04. In the comparison between mean annual temperature (CMAT) and biotemperature (BT) in graph A, these measurements are identical until BT reaches a value of 13.68, the point at which the first monthly mean value equal to or less then zero appears. Thereafter, a cascading scatter of points diverge from the straight line that otherwise dominates the graph. This difference holds only for cold environments, where the means of the warmer months deviate from the mean of all the months. In contrast, a predominantly curvilinear relationship occurs in the plot of CMAT and ET in graph B, which has a substantial scatter of points both higher and lower than an ET value of approximately 14.4.

Figure 4.04 clearly illustrates that summary measurements based on only the means of the warmest and coldest months (ET) or the means of all months (CMAT) or the means of only those months with values above zero (BT) produce very different results. Since temperature extremes play such a crucial role in the observable deviations between these summary measurements, some calculation of temperature variability throughout an annual cycle (or "evenness") has been considered a desirable goal.

Bailey (1960:10) has developed a variable that he refers to as *temperateness* (TEMP), which combines aspects of evenness with a "comfort" judgment based on human experience. This measure tracks differences in temperature range between adjacent months at specific locations, with a positive bias in favor of locations where mean winter temperatures are above 0°C. When large month-to-month differences are noted, the location is said to lack temperateness, whereas the location is referred to as "temperate" when temperatures are very similar. Temperateness values may be calculated from the basic meteorological data available for each hunter-gatherer group in the sample, using the same constants used to calculate values of ET. The formula for calculating temperateness is

(4.02)

$$TEMP = 161.7 - 41\log_{10}[(MWM - 10)^2 + (MCM - 18)^2]$$

The variables ET and TEMP measure different aspects of the same set of environmental characteristics. Effective temperature tracks the effect of intra-annual temperature differences on the length of the growing season, whereas temperateness measures the constancy of temperature throughout the year relative to the earth's mean effective temperature. Figure 4.05 displays the patterned relationship among mean annual temperature (CMAT), effective temperature (ET), and biotemperature (BT) when plotted against temperateness (TEMP), and it is clear that the overall pattern is very similar for both ET and BT. In each case there is great variability in the temperature measure for similar val-

TABLE 4.01

BASIC CLIMATIC VARIABLES FOR USE WITH HUNTER-GATHERER DATA SETS

NO.	STATE	NAME	LATITUDE	LONGITUDE	CMAT	CRR	MCM	MWM	RHIGH	RLOW	RRCORR2	ET
1	Indonesia	Punan	3.00 N	114.00 E	26.45	3,444.31	26.00	26.80	361.02	211.58	9.25	25.27
2	Philippines	Batek	10.00 N	119.11 E	27.65	2,546.75	26.89	28.78	445.26	26.04	7.50	25.19
3	Indonesia	Kubu	3.04 S	102.69 E	26.31	3,138.13	25.50	26.89	378.42	141.98	11.50	24.39
4	Nicobar Island	Shompen	7.00 N	93.77 E	27.84	3,189.80	26.70	29.70	485.80	49.10	9.50	24.33
5	Andaman Islands	Onge	10.70 N	92.47 E	26.79	3,081.84	26.04	28.29	521.72	28.70	6.50	24.27
6	Andaman Islands	Jarwa	12.19 N	92.37 E	26.59	2,301.48	25.36	27.71	388.75	12.95	6.50	23.69
7	Philippines	Ayta-Pinatubo	15.50 N	120.33 E	26.84	3,051.20	25.39	28.39	753.87	9.14	7.50	23.37
8	Andaman Islands	North Island	13.32 N	92.89 E	26.36	1,752.74	25.11	27.86	391.92	0.02	7.50	23.29
9	Malaysia	Semang	5.86 N	101.00 E	24.58	2,560.70	24.02	25.18	349.44	144.08	10.00	23.26
10	Sri Lanka	Veddah	8.58 N	81.25 E	27.97	1728.16	25.56	29.94	375.36	18.54	10.50	22.89
11	India	Hill-Pandaran	9.25 N	77.25 E	28.99	850.62	25.56	31.89	177.16	18.54	9.50	22.22
12	Philippines	Agta (Casiguran)	17.33 N	122.13 E	26.37	2,713.71	23.72	28.39	420.12	125.35	9.50	21.61
13	Philippines	Agta (Isabela)	17.48 N	122.05 E	26.77	1,806.97	23.72	29.17	257.39	39.62	9.50	21.40
14	Philippines	Agta (North Luzon)	17.82 N	121.80 E	26.52	1,941.83	23.47	28.83	275.17	54.61	9.17	21.28
15	India	Chenchu	16.25 N	78.97 E	25.34	1,410.24	22.47	29.08	404.11	3.05	7.50	20.45
16	Thailand	Mrabri	18.41 N	100.47 E	26.34	1,141.75	21.53	29.50	241.43	5.61	9.00	19.77
17	India	Paliyans	9.75 N	77.50 E	21.60	1,124.60	19.03	24.22	201.34	23.03	10.00	18.62
18	India	Birhor	23.41 N	84.38 E	23.79	1,367.21	16.19	31.72	391.67	4.42	7.50	17.38
19	India	Kadar	10.25 N	77.17 E	14.22	1,672.30	12.50	16.56	274.07	32.00	10.50	14.35
20	India	Cholanaickan	10.18 N	76.40 E	14.25	1,282.26	12.50	16.53	208.96	22.01	9.83	14.34
21	India	Nayaka	11.90 N	77.21 E	14.18	1,008.28	12.50	16.50	177.63	11.60	9.50	14.33
22	Japan	Ainu (Hokkaido)	44.01 N	144.17 E	6.26	807.06	-7.43	20.30	115.32	37.00	5.50	12.31
23	China	Orogens	51.91 N	122.50 E	-2.46	406.48	-26.46	19.22	105.73	2.54	4.75	11.37
24	Russia	Ket	62.00 N	90.00 E	-3.81	524.88	-24.17	17.39	72.90	17.02	5.50	11.19
25	Russia	Gilyak	51.54 N	140.00 E	-1.73	440.64	-21.56	16.50	90.55	5.46	4.60	11.13
26	Russia	Yukaghir	70.00 N	145.00 E	-13.19	158.66	-36.92	12.06	26.04	5.97	5.00	10.29
27	Russia	Nganasan	73.83 N	90.00 E	-11.62	288.87	-28.06	8.39	54.48	10.02	5.00	9.71
28	Russia	Siberian Eskimo	65.96 N	170.08 E	-6.91	330.79	-20.47	6.64	67.60	14.61	5.50	9.23
35	Venezuela	Paraujano	9.90 N	72.41 W	28.30	1,453.04	27.39	29.39	209.30	34.67	4.60	25.51
36	Venezuela	Shiriana	3.86 N	66.17 W	27.13	2,294.35	26.22	27.89	283.72	105.41	8.00	24.80
37	Suriname	Akuriyo	3.00 N	55.00 W	26.64	2,039.06	26.06	27.61	276.48	50.04	6.00	24.75
38	Venezuela	Yaruro-pume	6.85 N	68.77 W	27.38	1,839.05	26.54	29.00	552.80	0.10	9.50	24.53
39	Colombia	Guahibo	5.38 N	68.31 W	26.87	2,571.14	25.72	27.75	337.06	107.30	4.00	24.16
40	Colombia	Nukak	2.56 N	71.81 W	23.10	2,470.54	22.28	23.44	289.18	155.26	9.50	21.74
41	Brazil	Bororo	16.52 S	55.00 W	24.27	1,721.35	22.50	25.42	307.09	19.56	7.75	21.30
42	Brazil	Guato	18.00 S	57.50 W	25.35	1,218.72	22.08	27.00	192.91	16.00	7.50	20.53
43	Bolivia	Siriono	15.00 S	63.58 W	25.60	1,466.61	22.06	27.61	241.05	34.54	6.00	20.40
44	Bolivia	Yuqui	16.46 S	64.97 W	25.55	2,358.02	21.97	27.50	399.03	62.61	6.00	20.35
45	Brazil	Nambikwara	12.73 S	59.55 W	23.54	549.50	21.00	26.00	96.77	15.34	10.50	19.85
46	Florida	Calusa	26.50 S	82.00 W	23.11	1,351.30	17.61	27.94	226.95	31.50	4.00	17.83

47	Paraguay	Guayaki (Ache)	25.70 S	55.38 W	21.86	1,534.16	16.83	26.06	161.80	62.86	5.49	17.46
48	Brazil	Botocudo	18.71 S	41.86 W	20.62	1,297.60	16.81	23.17	270.43	16.38	3.00	17.34
49	Brazil	Heta	23.52 S	53.68 W	19.61	1,505.20	15.11	23.14	173.74	67.95	4.00	16.56
50	Brazil	Aweikomo	28.00 S	50.00 W	19.11	1,587.07	14.56	23.69	160.02	108.46	4.00	16.39
51	Argentina	Tehuelche	46.00 S	68.70 W	11.86	182.16	5.50	18.28	26.03	9.02	8.50	13.19
52	Chile	Chono	45.00 S	73.83 W	9.57	2,399.86	4.78	14.78	290.20	127.38	6.50	12.12
53	Chile	Alacaluf	49.55 S	74.52 W	8.83	3,649.84	5.14	12.11	363.09	255.65	8.50	11.13
54	Argentina	Ona	53.90 S	68.62 W	5.28	476.32	1.11	9.50	55.03	31.33	6.50	9.76
55	Argentina	Yahgan	60.00 S	68.66 W	5.57	524.80	1.78	9.22	56.52	33.27	6.50	9.60
60	Congo	Aka	2.00 N	17.00 E	25.55	1,758.11	24.72	26.50	247.90	22.10	11.50	23.50
61	Congo	Bayaka	3.58 N	17.76 E	25.56	1,751.09	24.72	26.50	214.19	46.10	12.25	23.50
62	Zaire	Bambote	6.64 S	28.26 E	24.11	1,241.07	23.28	24.78	216.54	4.57	8.00	22.45
63	Cameroon	Baka	2.39 N	15.31 E	24.05	1,648.50	23.28	24.89	228.47	57.91	9.50	22.40
64	Zaire	Efe	2.70 N	27.64 E	23.23	1,556.46	22.36	24.19	189.48	43.05	10.00	21.55
65	Zaire	Mbuti	1.54 N	28.61 E	22.01	1,576.71	21.11	23.11	192.41	55.50	10.50	20.49
66	Madagascar	Mikea	22.32 S	43.81 E	24.49	397.36	20.39	28.11	126.62	2.79	5.00	19.22
67	Zambia	Hukwe	16.93 S	24.32 E	22.32	763.60	16.97	26.81	172.97	0.02	7.50	17.54
68	Namibia	Hai//Om	18.65 S	16.12 E	22.25	517.16	16.33	25.61	120.14	0.01	6.50	17.23
69	Tanzania	Hadza	3.82 S	35.32 E	19.60	780.65	16.50	21.22	149.78	2.55	7.00	17.06
70	Kenya	Dorobo (Okiek)	0.00 S	36.00 E	17.45	1,246.33	16.28	18.76	169.23	36.51	7.50	16.69
71	Angola	Sekele	16.42 S	19.53 E	22.02	618.50	14.42	27.42	147.32	0.03	6.50	16.64
72	Botswana	!Kung	20.00 S	21.18 E	20.60	405.60	14.78	24.22	90.60	0.001	8.25	16.52
73	Botswana	Nharo	21.64 S	21.61 E	20.44	385.60	12.98	25.66	82.90	0.50	3.50	16.06
74	Botswana	G/Wi	22.46 S	23.39 E	19.35	333.84	12.93	23.52	137.73	0.001	7.50	15.82
75	Botswana	Kua	22.88 S	24.41 E	19.32	354.20	12.65	23.78	66.00	0.001	5.50	15.76
76	Botswana	!Ko	23.86 S	22.20 E	18.54	281.50	10.72	25.50	77.50	0.001	5.50	15.44
77	South Africa	/Auni-khomani	27.37 S	19.82 E	18.27	123.77	10.79	23.45	22.97	1.27	6.50	15.21
78	South Africa	//Xegwi	26.28 S	30.23 E	16.65	918.72	11.50	20.22	156.97	10.92	3.50	14.89
79	South Africa	/Xam	31.47 S	19.77 E	16.30	209.04	9.50	22.78	28.96	7.11	10.50	14.80
82	Australia—Queensland	Kaurareg	10.77 S	142.12 E	26.14	1,749.39	24.57	27.50	370.87	6.36	7.50	22.81
83	Australia—Northern Territory	Larikia	12.60 S	130.78 E	27.70	1,811.75	24.89	29.60	429.70	0.66	7.50	22.34
84	Australia—Northern Territory	Gunwinggu	12.43 S	134.12 E	28.09	1,391.51	25.15	30.44	332.37	0.89	6.50	22.30
85	Australia—Northern Territory	Mirrngadja	12.31 S	135.20 E	27.15	1,351.21	24.31	29.28	313.87	0.67	5.50	21.89
86	Australia—Northern Territory	Anbara	12.20 S	134.73 E	26.98	1,303.74	23.98	29.16	296.78	0.41	7.50	21.63
87	Australia—Northern Territory	Gidjingali	12.18 S	134.40 E	26.81	1,256.38	23.65	29.05	308.63	0.16	7.50	21.37
88	Australia—Northern Territory	Murngin (Yolngu)	12.93 S	135.84 E	27.08	1,245.70	23.60	29.66	305.39	0.93	5.50	21.19
89	Australia—Western Australia	Jeidji (Forest-river)	15.55 S	128.19 E	28.92	638.82	24.22	32.22	172.47	0.51	6.50	21.11
90	Australia—Queensland	Wikmunkan	13.47 S	142.00 E	25.89	1,750.10	23.02	28.22	489.78	0.00	7.50	21.04
91	Australia—Northern Territory	Kakadu	13.13 S	132.95 E	26.61	1,315.80	23.09	28.80	317.70	2.46	5.50	20.97
92	Australia—Northern Territory	Nunggubuyu	13.76 S	135.98 E	27.23	956.06	23.02	30.51	233.97	0.11	6.50	20.59
93	Australia—Queensland	Yintjingga	14.00 S	143.50 E	25.61	1,723.90	22.39	27.94	408.18	13.46	7.50	20.59
94	Australia—Queensland	Yir-yoront	15.00 S	142.17 E	26.83	1,145.51	22.76	29.69	299.55	1.15	6.50	20.55
95	Australia—Northern Territory	Tiwi	11.59 S	130.87 E	25.92	1,681.39	21.97	28.14	359.71	1.17	6.50	20.24
96	Australia—Queensland	Kuku-yalanji	15.92 S	145.32 E	25.29	1,906.86	21.89	27.81	449.36	19.50	7.50	20.23
97	Australia—Northern Territory	Groote-eylandt	14.00 S	136.62 E	25.98	1,122.62	21.89	28.99	267.57	0.98	7.50	20.06

(continued)

TABLE 4.01 (continued)

NO.	STATE	NAME	LATITUDE	LONGITUDE	CMAT	CRR	MCM	MWM	RHIGH	RLOW	RRCORR2	ET
98	Australia—Queensland	Walmbaria	14.34 S	144.22 E	25.49	1,128.28	21.61	28.56	306.32	1.91	6.50	19.93
99	Australia—Northern Territory	Mulluk	13.58 S	130.58 E	26.94	1,498.27	21.49	30.27	359.36	0.22	7.50	19.66
100	Australia—Western Australia	Worora	15.32 S	124.72 E	26.31	1,280.67	20.94	29.61	384.05	1.02	5.50	19.41
101	Australia—Western Australia	Lungga	16.91 S	127.83 E	27.36	587.13	20.94	31.47	159.68	0.93	6.00	19.30
102	Australia—Queensland	Lardil	16.30 S	139.30 E	26.10	1,207.20	20.55	29.74	318.84	0.73	5.50	19.19
103	Australia—Queensland	Kaiadilt	16.94 S	139.28 E	26.10	1,155.31	20.55	29.74	305.24	1.94	5.50	19.19
104	Australia—Western Australia	Karadjeri	18.92 S	121.21 E	26.31	445.97	20.25	30.11	119.21	0.93	5.33	19.01
105	Australia—Queensland	Mamu	17.64 S	145.84 E	23.27	3,534.41	19.17	26.72	686.82	80.52	6.50	18.60
106	Australia—Western Australia	Kariera	20.88 S	118.27 E	25.29	303.86	18.67	31.11	83.40	1.95	6.00	18.26
107	Australia—Queensland	Warunggu	18.41 S	145.61 E	23.13	2,122.25	18.50	26.83	485.72	24.59	5.50	18.24
108	Australia—Western Australia	Djaru	19.16 S	130.00 E	25.41	413.86	17.53	30.89	119.51	1.65	5.00	17.82
109	Australia—Northern Territory	Walbiri	20.00 S	130.57 E	25.23	334.50	17.39	30.94	76.10	6.22	5.50	17.77
110	Australia—Queensland	Ngatjan	17.36 S	145.56 E	21.66	1,901.20	17.50	25.14	359.51	39.68	6.00	17.74
111	Australia—Western Australia	Mardudjara	22.79 S	125.06 E	24.63	298.01	15.49	31.95	54.76	5.28	6.50	17.18
112	Australia—Western Australia	Ildawongga	22.93 S	127.18 E	24.04	317.08	15.46	30.29	67.65	4.99	4.50	17.11
113	Australia—Northern Territory	Pintubi	22.86 S	129.44 E	23.71	314.47	14.56	31.33	55.92	6.45	4.50	16.89
114	Australia—Queensland	Undanbi	27.28 S	153.24 E	20.54	1,017.79	15.00	25.17	145.29	27.18	4.50	16.68
115	Australia—Queensland	Jinibarra	27.25 S	152.87 E	20.55	1,018.20	15.00	25.17	145.29	27.18	4.50	16.68
116	Australia—Queensland	Karuwali	24.41 S	141.64 E	22.90	248.91	13.50	30.94	47.63	4.32	5.50	16.58
117	Australia—Northern Territory	Alyawara	22.27 S	135.17 E	22.10	300.31	13.54	28.96	69.54	5.65	5.00	16.48
118	Australia—Western Australia	Ngatatjara	25.32 S	127.27 E	22.46	244.47	12.89	30.83	45.08	6.89	5.50	16.42
119	Australia—New South Wales	Badjalang	29.59 S	152.78 E	20.36	881.22	14.06	25.67	115.82	23.62	4.50	16.39
120	Australia—Northern Territory	Pitjandjara	26.00 S	130.00 E	22.01	245.37	12.59	30.56	30.96	7.98	6.50	16.33
121	Australia—South Australia	Dieri	28.54 S	139.09 E	21.84	184.08	12.69	30.16	31.60	8.38	5.00	16.33
122	Australia—Northern Territory	Arenda (southern)	26.09 S	135.52 E	21.55	175.88	12.56	29.96	28.90	9.00	5.50	16.29
123	Australia—South Australia	Jankundjara	27.00 S	131.95 E	20.74	189.27	11.99	29.11	32.60	3.27	5.50	16.09
124	Australia—Northern Territory	Arenda (northern)	23.70 S	133.76 E	20.84	277.63	11.73	28.62	41.11	8.93	5.50	15.98
125	Australia—New South Wales	Ualaria	29.30 S	147.25 E	20.53	403.55	11.78	28.40	52.81	19.60	4.50	15.98
126	Australia—Western Australia	Nakako	27.31 S	128.19 E	20.25	213.80	11.47	28.17	26.88	5.35	6.50	15.88
127	Australia—Western Australia	Ooldea	30.38 S	131.81 E	18.20	200.20	11.48	24.11	21.37	11.31	3.50	15.47
128	Australia—New South Wales	Barkindji	32.40 S	142.25 E	18.37	215.31	10.38	26.03	22.92	14.67	5.50	15.42
129	Australia—South Australia	Karuna	34.56 S	138.40 E	17.18	535.60	11.44	23.17	74.42	19.20	8.50	15.34
130	Australia—New South Wales	Wongaibon	32.14 S	146.09 E	18.23	348.64	9.46	26.65	39.27	24.13	5.50	15.29
131	Australia—South Australia	Jaralde	35.06 S	139.29 E	16.21	346.81	10.74	21.79	37.06	16.54	10.50	14.95
132	Australia—Western Australia	Mineng	34.95 S	117.81 E	15.57	1,007.61	12.00	19.17	152.40	26.16	9.50	14.83
133	Australia—Victoria	Tjapwurong	35.86 S	141.38 E	15.28	356.46	8.61	21.83	40.51	16.76	10.50	14.46
134	Australia—Victoria	Bunurong	38.93 S	145.07 E	14.11	760.56	10.00	18.50	84.58	37.08	10.00	14.12
135	Australia—Victoria	Kurnai	37.59 S	147.42 E	12.83	633.84	7.03	18.56	64.52	42.93	1.50	13.51
136	Tasmania	Tasmanians (eastern)	42.62 S	147.49 E	11.35	610.61	6.72	15.89	62.73	41.02	1.50	12.74
137	Tasmania	Tasmanians (western)	41.38 S	145.21 E	10.88	1690.19	7.17	15.00	192.79	77.47	10.50	12.51

#	Region	Language	Lat	Lon								
143	Mexico	Seri	29.59 N	112.18 W	24.34	285.86	16.72	31.36	79.63	2.16	5.50	17.55
144	California	Cahuilla	33.59 N	116.24 W	22.95	79.81	12.11	33.83	16.76	0.25	10.50	16.41
145	California	Cupeno	33.26 N	116.59 W	21.12	209.43	11.50	31.39	34.16	0.76	3.00	16.14
146	Mexico	Kiliwa	31.44 N	115.25 W	19.47	203.88	12.25	26.83	42.04	2.41	10.00	15.96
147	California	Diegueno	32.44 N	116.49 W	17.24	275.41	11.36	23.52	50.32	1.65	10.50	15.37
148	California	Lake Yokuts	36.00 N	119.83 W	18.33	168.28	8.44	29.06	32.34	0.10	12.50	15.33
149	California	Serrano	34.52 N	117.00 W	17.48	235.34	9.06	27.00	43.05	2.29	12.50	15.24
150	California	Luiseno	33.42 N	117.30 W	16.89	314.33	11.07	23.15	65.19	0.68	13.00	15.24
151	California	Wukchumi	36.45 N	118.96 W	17.41	654.23	7.89	28.50	124.71	1.02	12.50	15.17
152	California	Tubatulabal	36.00 N	118.32 W	17.63	211.47	7.14	29.03	37.34	1.40	13.00	15.09
153	California	Nomlaki	40.00 N	122.56 W	16.41	510.73	6.93	27.04	99.82	1.40	10.50	14.85
154	California	Northern Foothill Yokuts	37.44 N	120.44 W	15.94	472.42	7.19	26.00	90.68	0.34	10.50	14.77
155	California	Patwin	39.08 N	122.05 W	16.33	445.67	7.46	25.59	88.90	0.16	13.34	14.77
156	California	Gabrielino	34.00 N	118.00 W	15.07	518.72	9.22	21.92	106.55	0.32	10.25	14.61
157	California	Monache	36.60 N	117.08 W	15.87	128.73	4.83	27.72	29.97	1.52	10.50	14.59
158	California	Eastern Pomo	39.03 N	122.94 W	15.44	819.96	7.56	23.58	170.81	1.40	10.50	14.52
159	California	Clear-Lake Pomo	39.12 N	122.94 W	15.12	913.62	7.72	23.17	191.26	1.27	10.50	14.49
160	California	Wintu	40.90 N	122.35 W	15.23	986.25	5.69	25.72	191.87	3.81	10.30	14.49
161	California	Chumash	34.63 N	119.60 W	14.87	390.03	11.22	18.26	86.36	0.43	9.17	14.39
162	California	Chimariko	40.85 N	123.30 W	14.94	1522.88	5.61	24.94	308.61	5.08	10.50	14.37
163	California	Nisenan	39.03 N	121.15 W	14.84	958.86	6.42	23.94	188.72	0.77	10.30	14.37
164	California	Salinan	35.47 N	120.84 W	14.89	422.89	9.30	20.07	93.27	0.25	10.00	14.29
165	California	Pomo (Southern)	38.54 N	122.88 W	14.78	889.61	8.02	21.09	186.86	0.76	10.50	14.21
166	California	Sinkyone	40.10 N	123.96 W	14.29	1,357.40	6.83	22.39	273.56	0.51	10.50	14.21
167	California	Lessik	40.18 N	123.16 W	13.82	1,126.43	5.72	22.86	231.33	2.48	10.50	14.09
168	California	Miwok (Coast)	38.24 N	122.88 W	14.08	807.34	8.28	18.89	169.80	0.51	10.50	13.82
169	California	Mattole	40.17 N	124.04 W	13.50	1,298.42	7.78	19.22	259.59	2.20	9.83	13.79
170	California	Miwok (Lake)	38.79 N	122.48 W	13.99	718.42	8.09	18.83	154.37	0.89	10.25	13.77
171	California	Yuki (Proper)	39.70 N	123.15 W	12.89	1,186.35	4.83	21.69	243.25	2.12	10.00	13.76
172	California	Wappo	38.59 N	122.54 W	13.88	861.16	8.03	18.72	188.38	0.59	10.50	13.73
173	California	Pomo (Northern)	39.34 N	123.29 W	13.37	1,264.85	8.25	18.42	264.48	1.46	9.50	13.71
174	California	Yana	40.38 N	122.89 W	12.14	941.20	3.01	22.24	166.62	2.86	10.00	13.60
175	California	Miwok	38.00 N	119.77 W	12.02	867.96	2.94	22.00	151.64	2.54	10.50	13.55
176	Oregon	Tekelma	42.44 N	123.48 W	12.09	767.59	3.94	21.22	142.24	4.83	10.50	13.55
177	California	Yuki (Coast)	39.64 N	123.74 W	12.96	1,546.68	7.81	18.03	318.64	1.59	10.00	13.53
178	California	Tolowa	41.87 N	123.92 W	12.35	1,513.70	5.97	18.67	290.83	8.76	10.00	13.35
179	California	Shasta	41.62 N	122.70 W	11.63	1,095.93	2.12	21.24	213.21	7.16	13.10	13.32
180	California	Hupa	40.93 N	123.61 W	11.42	1,374.97	4.81	18.36	251.33	6.98	10.00	13.10
181	Oregon	Tututni	42.61 N	124.04 W	11.70	1,573.62	6.67	17.00	269.58	10.75	8.83	13.06
182	California	Karok	41.58 N	123.47 W	10.85	1,161.77	4.25	17.64	220.34	10.92	10.00	12.86
183	California	Atsugewi	40.75 N	121.12 W	9.73	565.14	0.25	19.75	102.49	4.06	10.00	12.84
184	California	Wiyot	40.75 N	124.14 W	11.81	1,079.38	8.53	14.89	205.61	1.90	10.00	12.72
185	California	Maidu (Mountain)	40.28 N	120.56 W	8.57	454.32	-1.39	19.19	85.22	2.79	10.50	12.57
186	California	Yurok	41.40 N	123.89 W	11.08	1,812.74	6.94	15.17	316.23	8.64	9.50	12.55
187	California	Achumawi	41.32 N	121.19 W	8.46	477.88	-1.47	18.83	78.40	3.89	0.00	12.50

(continued)

NO.	STATE	NAME	LATITUDE	LONGITUDE	CMAT	CRR	MCM	MWM	RHIGH	RLOW	RRCORR2	ET
188	Oregon	Modoc	42.00 N	121.31 W	7.97	258.96	-1.39	18.22	33.66	4.83	9.50	12.38
189	Oregon	Klamath	42.62 N	121.50 W	6.34	808.33	-2.81	16.61	133.11	9.82	9.83	11.93
190	Mexico	Guaicura	25.00 N	111.54 W	22.19	137.32	14.00	30.50	46.23	0.03	6.50	16.69
191	Mexico	Chichimec	22.00 N	100.00 W	20.22	527.48	15.06	24.22	103.12	6.48	7.50	16.63
192	California	Death Valley	36.52 N	116.81 W	25.03	41.42	11.39	39.00	6.35	0.51	10.50	16.52
193	Texas	Karankawa	28.44 N	96.91 W	21.86	839.19	13.61	29.08	117.35	38.99	6.00	16.50
194	Mexico	Coahuilenos	26.00 N	102.07 W	21.81	253.89	13.31	28.15	64.94	3.73	5.50	16.36
195	California	Panamint Shoshoni	36.37 N	117.33 W	19.17	96.84	7.63	30.78	17.86	1.69	10.50	15.34
196	Arizona	Yavapai	33.37 N	110.50 W	18.14	327.42	7.39	29.69	53.09	6.10	5.50	15.20
197	California	Koso Mountain Shoshoni	36.12 N	117.70 W	17.35	122.64	5.89	29.61	23.75	1.65	13.00	14.95
198	Arizona	Walapai	35.95 N	114.50 W	16.37	276.98	6.33	27.89	38.86	3.81	5.50	14.84
199	California	Kawaiisu Shoshoni	35.37 N	118.00 W	16.00	195.95	4.97	27.83	36.70	4.25	13.00	14.62
200	California	Saline Valley Shoshoni	36.65 N	117.79 W	14.13	135.41	3.58	25.53	26.61	2.29	13.00	14.15
201	Colorado	Antarianunt Southern Paiute	37.86 N	110.72 W	13.73	163.54	0.74	26.07	22.27	9.82	5.83	13.86
202	California	Owens Valley Paiute	36.88 N	118.18 W	12.78	141.96	2.67	23.78	30.73	1.90	10.50	13.79
203	Nevada	Kawich Mountain Shoshoni	37.92 N	116.45 W	12.23	214.08	1.64	24.22	27.18	6.98	13.00	13.72
204	Arizona	Kaibab Southern Paiute	36.90 N	112.55 W	12.01	288.55	0.81	24.00	35.18	9.14	2.50	13.59
205	California	Mono Lake Paiute	38.11 N	118.85 W	11.74	205.86	1.50	22.97	37.42	5.33	13.00	13.52
206	California	Deep Spring Paiute	37.28 N	118.00 W	11.66	131.37	0.69	23.31	25.91	3.05	0.00	13.48
207	Idaho	Salmon-eater Shoshoni	42.94 N	115.30 W	10.98	219.05	-1.78	24.94	30.73	3.30	10.50	13.44
208	Nevada	Pyramid Lake Paiute	40.00 N	119.60 W	11.07	160.11	-1.03	24.00	23.72	2.92	10.00	13.39
209	Utah	Ute-timanogas	40.22 N	111.81 W	10.79	405.04	-1.72	24.14	44.20	18.88	12.50	13.34
210	Nevada	Cattail Paiute	40.12 N	118.37 W	10.86	120.19	-1.17	23.72	17.27	3.81	10.50	13.34
211	Nevada	Fish Lake Paiute	37.69 N	118.14 W	10.54	105.18	-1.28	22.83	16.51	3.30	1.50	13.20
212	California	Honey Lake Paiute	40.27 N	120.44 W	10.29	285.09	-0.97	22.33	49.28	3.39	9.83	13.15
213	Utah	Hukunduka Shoshoni	41.55 N	112.22 W	9.92	374.36	-4.06	24.00	41.40	11.85	1.83	13.11
214	Utah	Gosiute Shoshoni	39.88 N	114.00 W	9.66	183.26	-2.83	23.22	24.30	10.16	2.50	13.11
215	Nevada	Spring Valley Shoshoni	39.19 N	114.48 W	8.71	295.74	-2.14	21.89	35.31	15.32	1.83	12.97
216	Nevada	White Knife Shoshoni	41.00 N	117.31 W	8.95	265.03	-1.92	21.64	31.33	7.79	2.17	12.95
217	Nevada	Rainroad Valley Shoshoni	38.33 N	115.78 W	9.01	239.44	-2.76	21.72	27.43	11.18	1.50	12.89
218	Nevada	Reese River Shoshoni	39.25 N	117.32 W	8.49	301.86	-1.94	21.11	40.64	12.70	1.50	12.86
219	California	North Fork Paiute	37.00 N	119.07 W	9.50	813.04	1.61	19.11	158.23	1.40	12.50	12.86
221	Utah	Grouse Creek Shoshoni	41.59 N	113.94 W	8.24	204.16	-4.64	22.36	22.61	12.83	2.50	12.83
222	Utah	Utewimonantci	37.67 N	109.00 W	8.97	309.40	-3.61	21.76	36.77	14.16	6.00	12.82
223	Oregon	Bear Creek Paiute	43.94 N	120.49 W	9.16	294.76	0.06	19.69	39.50	7.87	2.00	12.81
224	Nevada	Antelope Valley Shoshoni	40.19 N	114.24 W	7.96	293.30	-3.28	21.28	33.95	13.04	12.50	12.77
225	Nevada	Washo	39.08 N	119.82 W	8.75	326.28	-1.18	19.71	60.13	4.19	10.50	12.69
226	Nevada	Surprise Valley Paiute	41.50 N	120.06 W	8.66	364.18	-1.53	19.86	54.10	6.22	10.00	12.68
227	Wyoming	Wind River Shoshoni	43.19 N	108.86 W	7.73	292.56	-7.39	22.64	62.48	8.16	2.17	12.66
228	Nevada	Ruby Valley Shoshoni	40.36 N	115.39 W	7.73	312.57	-3.61	20.28	38.86	10.92	0.50	12.58
229	Idaho	Bohogue–Northern Shoshoni	43.00 N	112.00 W	7.62	250.28	-5.98	21.28	29.04	11.60	2.83	12.56

230	Utah	Uintah-ute	40.47 N	110.22 W	7.21	222.26	−9.59	21.52	23.05	13.02	4.50	12.36
231	Oregon	Harney Valley Paiute	43.25 N	119.14 W	7.23	282.40	−3.61	18.89	36.75	8.64	0.84	12.33
232	Idaho	Sheep-eater Shoshoni	45.17 N	113.84 W	6.51	227.40	−8.00	20.00	34.29	11.94	3.50	12.22
233	Nevada	Little Smoky Shoshoni	39.33 M	115.84 W	6.20	221.38	−5.69	18.69	25.06	13.55	3.50	12.15
234	Utah	Uncompahgre Ute	38.14 N	107.80 W	4.51	520.84	−5.61	15.35	64.26	28.89	5.50	11.48
240	Texas	Lipan Apache	28.96 N	98.48 W	20.18	778.73	10.97	28.83	92.33	44.07	4.50	15.83
241	Texas	Comanche	36.83 N	100.50 W	17.81	432.47	6.78	28.17	72.47	12.62	2.17	14.95
242	Texas	Chiricahua Apache	32.52 N	101.76 W	16.33	303.62	6.44	27.46	68.20	5.33	5.50	14.81
243	Kansas	Kiowa	36.90 N	99.10 W	15.71	677.41	3.28	28.06	110.87	24.64	2.50	14.41
244	Texas	Kiowa Apache	35.83 N	98.90 W	14.03	488.00	0.83	27.39	72.90	12.70	2.50	14.02
245	Colorado	Cheyenne	38.83 N	102.35 W	10.52	387.47	−1.83	23.83	63.16	8.30	3.83	13.29
246	Colorado	Arapahoe	40.13 N	102.72 W	10.09	411.69	−2.85	23.87	69.26	8.38	2.83	13.20
248	Wyoming	Crow	45.83 N	108.48 W	7.82	289.94	−7.46	22.78	62.40	8.55	3.17	12.67
249	South Dakota	Teton Lakota	44.50 N	102.27 W	7.53	391.88	−6.98	22.52	76.71	9.74	3.50	12.67
250	Montana	Kutenai	47.48 N	114.08 W	7.01	434.58	−4.75	20.11	78.99	19.05	3.00	12.46
252	Idaho	Bannock	43.66 N	112.32 W	6.64	225.62	−7.36	20.58	32.26	11.18	3.00	12.35
253	Montana	Gros-Ventre	48.12 N	105.60 W	5.51	309.99	−10.06	20.69	78.32	6.77	3.50	12.21
254	North Dakota	Plains Ojibwa	47.60 N	97.25 W	3.99	456.87	−15.03	20.75	90.04	11.81	3.50	11.96
255	Alberta	Peigan	49.34 N	111.21 W	4.66	239.10	−10.56	19.17	64.69	0.25	3.50	11.94
256	Alberta	Blackfoot	51.01 N	110.76 W	2.64	227.74	−14.94	18.50	54.99	0.03	3.50	11.64
257	Saskatchewan	Assiniboine	49.49 N	102.43 N	2.42	308.80	−16.15	18.54	86.19	0.10	3.50	11.60
258	Saskatchewan	Plains Cree	51.86 N	102.67 W	1.44	272.84	−18.00	18.54	70.78	0.03	3.50	11.53
259	Alberta	Blood	52.79 N	113.86 W	2.53	317.28	−13.17	17.06	75.69	0.03	3.50	11.48
260	Alberta	Sarsi	53.15 N	111.04 W	1.87	300.08	−15.44	16.85	77.13	0.19	4.50	11.36
268	British Columbia	Squamish	49.77 N	123.19 W	10.68	904.88	4.06	17.52	141.82	18.03	9.50	12.80
269	Oregon	Alsea	44.42 N	123.84 W	10.83	1,319.45	4.52	17.15	219.96	11.43	5.50	12.77
270	Washington	Puyallup	47.11 N	122.04 W	10.42	1,102.00	3.58	17.58	167.13	23.11	9.50	12.76
271	Washington	Twana	47.55 N	123.16 W	10.46	1,778.39	3.02	17.85	288.21	23.88	9.50	12.75
272	Washington	Chehalis	46.87 N	123.67 W	10.30	1,515.39	3.52	17.13	246.72	24.47	8.83	12.64
273	British Columbia	Nootka	49.34 N	125.74 W	9.68	1,397.41	2.00	17.83	236.22	31.16	9.17	12.63
274	Oregon	Chinook	46.06 N	123.75 W	10.53	1,725.85	4.07	16.69	281.77	25.99	8.83	12.60
275	Oregon	Coos	43.43 N	124.11 W	11.16	1,629.09	7.26	15.11	273.98	12.53	9.17	12.58
276	British Columbia	Lillooet	50.46 N	123.00 W	8.75	413.86	−3.89	20.28	69.43	14.90	6.50	12.56
277	Washington	Lummi	48.84 N	122.34 W	9.83	659.84	3.35	16.24	95.67	19.14	9.50	12.39
278	Washington	Quinault	47.38 N	123.82 W	9.87	2,597.94	3.98	15.80	415.04	47.07	8.83	12.34
279	British Columbia	Stalo	49.23 N	122.70 W	9.55	785.99	2.74	16.24	114.13	20.66	9.50	12.32
280	British Columbia	Cowichan	48.41 N	123.64 W	9.74	861.04	3.28	15.86	146.22	20.15	8.83	12.28
281	Oregon	Tillamook	45.40 N	123.82 W	10.32	2,354.42	5.56	14.89	372.81	32.26	8.50	12.26
282	British Columbia	Comox	50.00 N	125.50 W	8.76	1,249.18	2.86	15.56	198.37	36.49	7.83	12.15
283	British Columbia	Bella-bella	52.87 N	127.87 W	8.64	3,152.68	2.25	15.53	431.63	135.64	6.83	12.08
284	Washington	Quileute	47.77 N	124.14 W	9.50	2,692.45	4.11	14.72	422.40	51.65	8.50	12.03
285	Washington	Clallam	47.95 N	123.55 W	9.00	1,061.77	3.30	14.69	183.56	20.91	8.50	11.94
286	Washington	Makah	48.22 N	124.58 W	9.21	2,372.87	4.07	14.15	387.10	45.64	8.50	11.84
287	British Columbia	Haisla	53.50 N	128.42 W	6.86	3,472.40	−3.56	16.11	556.60	135.89	7.17	11.77
288	British Columbia	Kwakiutl	50.42 N	126.67 W	8.59	1,462.14	3.44	14.06	224.11	49.02	7.83	11.74

(continued)

TABLE 4.01 (*continued*)

NO.	STATE	NAME	LATITUDE	LONGITUDE	CMAT	CRR	MCM	MWM	RHIGH	RLOW	RRCORR2	ET
289	British Columbia	Tsimshim	54.00 N	129.58 W	7.05	1,839.64	-1.83	15.48	304.63	73.57	6.83	11.73
290	British Columbia	Haida	53.54 N	132.29 W	7.88	1,778.16	2.11	14.33	261.70	68.07	7.17	11.71
291	British Columbia	Bella-coola	52.32 N	126.58 W	6.15	1,986.22	-3.94	15.26	290.24	81.45	6.50	11.55
292	Alaska	Tlingit	57.00 N	133.59 W	6.24	1,958.37	-0.96	13.50	294.39	86.53	7.50	11.25
293	British Columbia	Gitksan	55.65 N	128.06 W	4.32	664.74	-7.65	14.15	127.68	17.19	7.17	11.11
294	Alaska	Konaig	57.93 N	153.16 W	4.80	1,479.00	-1.22	12.89	169.42	95.25	6.50	11.05
295	Alaska	Eyak	60.48 N	144.00 W	0.91	1,291.42	-12.58	12.92	201.04	49.66	6.50	10.70
296	Alaska	Kuskowagmut	61.01 N	161.55 W	-2.01	509.00	-16.72	12.92	125.35	13.21	5.50	10.62
297	Alaska	Chugash	61.21 N	147.61 W	1.13	1,373.58	-9.09	11.69	215.56	54.61	5.83	10.47
298	Alaska	Aleut	55.00 N	162.85 W	3.16	897.86	-2.11	10.72	124.21	40.89	4.50	10.28
299	Alaska	Nunavak	60.03 N	166.30 W	-1.49	385.67	-12.00	9.94	59.94	14.73	4.50	9.98
315	Washington	Tenino	45.59 N	120.45 W	11.97	218.64	0.00	23.94	32.85	4.32	10.50	13.49
316	Washington	Umatiela	45.49 N	119.94 W	11.48	259.72	0.30	22.87	34.80	5.50	10.50	13.37
317	Washington	Wenatchi	47.41 N	120.31 W	10.18	398.57	-3.50	22.94	72.64	5.97	9.50	13.01
318	Washington	Yakima	46.33 N	120.27 W	10.04	238.47	-2.09	21.83	39.96	3.81	10.17	12.96
319	Washington	Wishram	45.72 N	121.13 W	10.38	535.06	-0.22	20.67	99.23	4.57	10.17	12.95
320	Idaho	Coeur d'Alene	47.42 N	116.34 W	8.45	697.00	-2.61	19.83	93.64	19.30	9.50	12.58
321	Washington	Sinkaietk	48.78 N	119.56 W	8.18	317.89	-5.61	20.92	37.34	12.06	9.50	12.53
322	British Columbia	Okanogan	49.46 N	119.63 W	7.80	341.04	-5.74	20.41	46.74	15.92	5.50	12.44
323	Washington	Sanpoil	47.94 N	118.44 W	7.97	374.66	-4.97	19.92	49.19	11.26	9.83	12.41
324	Idaho	Nez-perce	46.25 N	116.46 W	7.34	547.04	-3.11	18.83	69.09	24.64	2.50	12.36
325	British Columbia	Thompson	51.26 N	121.75 W	7.83	200.28	-5.39	19.80	32.34	5.08	3.50	12.36
326	Idaho	Kalispel	47.94 N	115.67 W	6.97	721.07	-4.33	18.72	98.04	22.27	9.50	12.25
327	Michigan	Ojibwa (Kitchibuan)	45.21 N	85.10 W	6.17	754.08	-7.63	19.35	86.87	37.08	3.83	12.14
328	Wisconsin	Kitikitegon	45.00 N	91.00 W	4.55	811.90	-11.97	19.69	122.43	24.51	3.50	11.95
329	New Brunswick	Micmac	46.99 N	65.00 W	4.75	735.41	-8.85	18.63	92.88	22.52	4.83	11.95
330	Montana	Flathead	46.28 N	113.26 W	5.57	405.43	-6.17	17.26	58.76	20.07	3.50	11.85
331	Ontario	Rainy River Ojibwa	45.21 N	85.10 W	3.09	594.10	-15.65	19.35	94.74	15.83	4.50	11.74
332	Ontario	Northern Saulteaux	52.28 N	96.78 W	2.05	375.60	-18.24	20.00	83.65	0.18	3.50	11.73
333	Alberta	Shuswap	53.41 N	119.53 W	4.92	427.11	-8.43	16.80	62.91	5.33	5.50	11.64
334	Ontario	Pekangekum Ojibwa	51.84 N	93.85 W	1.11	389.45	-18.69	18.67	81.66	0.03	5.00	11.53
335	Ontario	Round Lake Ojibwa	52.71 N	90.62 W	-0.92	452.67	-21.22	17.64	98.04	0.14	4.50	11.30
336	British Columbia	Alcatcho	51.32 N	124.02 W	4.62	617.50	-6.76	14.61	89.24	30.40	8.50	11.26
337	Ontario	Nipigon Ojibwa	49.34 N	88.31 W	-0.51	456.19	-18.85	16.83	81.70	0.42	4.50	11.25
338	Quebec	Mistassini Cree	51.75 N	72.66 W	0.53	602.35	-17.96	16.46	102.87	2.29	4.50	11.22
339	Ontario	Ojibwa (Northern Albany)	51.22 N	83.10 W	-0.76	465.93	-20.28	16.56	86.28	0.68	3.50	11.17
340	Quebec	Waswanip Cree	49.78 N	76.64 W	-0.24	677.23	-18.89	16.11	98.55	4.07	3.50	11.14
341	Ontario	Weagamon Ojibwa	52.79 N	90.64 W	-2.17	404.92	-23.03	16.50	94.36	0.14	4.50	11.09
342	Quebec	Montagnais	52.42 N	63.33 W	0.72	509.48	-14.50	15.11	85.26	3.47	6.17	11.09
343	Alberta	Sekani	56.14 N	120.00 W	2.15	269.60	-13.26	14.83	53.34	0.69	3.83	11.07
344	Alberta	Beaver	58.51 N	115.76 W	-1.21	243.63	-21.75	16.11	59.31	0.03	4.50	11.07

345	Northwest Territories	Slave	61.15 N	119.50 W	-3.74	222.61	-25.70	16.31	56.30	0.02	4.83	11.01
346	British Columbia	Kaska	59.73 N	125.00 W	-1.84	242.49	-23.31	15.92	58.42	0.03	4.00	11.00
347	British Columbia	Tahltan	57.66 N	127.85 W	1.85	266.38	-14.52	14.44	45.13	3.56	4.50	10.96
348	British Columbia	Chilcotin	51.68 N	124.00 W	2.78	225.18	-10.00	13.63	42.93	2.89	3.50	10.91
349	British Columbia	Carrier	53.33 N	123.15 W	2.39	196.37	-10.44	13.56	49.53	0.02	3.50	10.89
350	Northwest Territories	Mountain	63.68 N	125.37 W	-6.21	195.31	-28.14	15.72	58.04	0.03	5.50	10.88
351	Yukon	Han	64.79 N	141.20 W	-4.78	246.44	-26.44	15.50	50.37	5.17	4.83	10.88
352	Northwest Territories	Hare	67.47 N	125.00 W	-6.85	180.11	-29.00	15.56	53.93	0.03	5.50	10.85
353	Ontario	Attawapiskat Cree	53.62 N	83.88 W	-2.64	454.55	-22.69	14.80	84.20	0.89	4.00	10.84
354	Alaska	Koyukon	66.52 N	153.78 W	-4.95	350.50	-23.72	14.89	77.64	6.18	5.50	10.84
355	Saskatchewan	Chippewyan	59.47 N	106.19 W	-4.45	221.56	-26.39	15.17	56.98	0.10	4.50	10.83
356	Yukon	Kutchin	65.94 N	135.23 W	-5.94	156.16	-27.00	14.67	47.37	0.02	5.50	10.75
357	Alaska	Ingalik	61.82 N	157.75 W	-2.63	488.29	-19.35	13.87	107.44	13.21	5.50	10.75
358	Northwest Territories	Satudene	65.75 N	122.89 W	-6.08	173.35	-27.74	14.59	47.07	0.03	5.17	10.73
359	Alaska	Nabesna	63.44 N	143.12 W	-4.30	271.76	-24.78	14.28	58.59	5.59	4.50	10.73
360	Quebec	Rupert House Cree	51.08 N	77.81 W	-2.64	464.33	-21.67	13.94	96.60	0.76	4.50	10.72
361	Northwest Territories	Dogrib	63.85 N	115.61 W	-6.25	150.48	-27.76	14.54	45.13	0.02	5.50	10.72
362	Alaska	Tanaina	61.74 N	150.45 W	1.10	500.25	-10.70	12.83	91.78	18.54	5.83	10.71
363	Alaska	Tutchone	61.24 N	138.21 W	-2.47	158.14	-21.39	13.65	37.08	0.03	5.07	10.68
364	Alaska	Holikachuk	63.33 N	157.54 W	-2.18	521.55	-16.25	12.92	131.57	11.56	4.81	10.63
365	Quebec	Naskapi	56.19 N	68.92 W	-4.08	327.01	-22.02	11.69	77.22	1.02	4.83	10.32
369	Alaska	Norton Sound Inuit	63.98 N	160.75 W	-3.86	472.81	-20.17	13.50	98.04	18.41	5.50	10.67
370	Alaska	Kobuk Inuit	66.95 N	156.94 W	-6.09	287.45	-22.58	13.08	67.44	8.00	5.50	10.56
371	Alaska	Kotzebue Sound Inuit	66.77 N	161.53 W	-6.26	239.69	-20.89	11.78	68.07	7.11	5.50	10.35
372	Newfoundland	Labrador Inuit	57.97 N	62.02 W	-3.58	325.90	-20.47	11.39	76.45	1.52	5.00	10.28
373	Quebec	Great Whale Inuit	55.32 N	77.69 W	-5.05	304.10	-23.72	10.61	69.85	0.14	4.50	10.11
374	Northwest Territories	Caribou Inuit	64.33 N	96.20 W	-11.88	150.52	-33.00	10.72	44.96	0.02	5.50	10.11
375	Alaska	Noatak Inuit	68.09 N	160.00 W	-8.77	231.68	-25.47	10.28	51.18	7.11	5.50	10.05
377	Alaska	Nunamiut Inuit	68.18 N	151.71 W	-9.36	225.47	-25.30	9.31	44.83	5.97	5.50	9.87
378	Northwest Territories	Mackenzie Inuit	69.96 N	132.09 W	-10.62	142.97	-28.42	9.08	32.26	2.68	5.50	9.84
379	Alaska	Sivokamiut Inuit	63.49 N	170.31 W	-4.99	304.53	-17.74	9.17	61.47	10.50	5.17	9.81
380	Alaska	Point Hope Inuit	68.29 N	166.62 W	-8.95	181.76	-24.08	8.97	51.82	5.08	5.50	9.80
381	Northwest Territories	Copper Inuit	68.58 N	106.61 W	-13.60	85.40	-32.98	8.61	30.90	0.03	4.83	9.78
382	Northwest Territories	Utkuhikhalingmiut	66.99 N	95.18 W	-14.06	106.86	-33.56	7.67	36.32	0.02	5.50	9.62
383	Northwest Territories	Aivilingmiut Inuit	65.16 N	88.12 W	-12.18	114.51	-31.22	7.52	34.71	0.03	5.17	9.58
384	Northwest Territories	Ingulik Inuit	69.44 N	81.51 W	-12.48	91.58	-30.83	7.22	30.86	0.02	5.50	9.52
385	Greenland	West Greenland	69.31 N	50.21 W	-3.31	331.93	-12.14	7.61	53.47	12.45	6.50	9.31
386	Northwest Territories	Baffin Island Inuit	65.00 N	65.00 W	-10.46	117.73	-27.08	6.33	40.77	0.03	5.21	9.29
387	Northwest Territories	Netsilik Inuit	71.46 N	94.93 W	-16.24	63.19	-34.33	4.61	27.69	0.02	5.50	9.08
388	East Greenland	Angmaksaslik	65.63 N	37.64 W	-0.32	869.50	-6.89	7.28	93.98	44.96	8.50	9.02
389	Alaska	Tareumiut Inuit	71.32 N	156.78 W	-12.35	113.56	-28.00	4.22	22.86	3.05	5.50	8.85
390	Greenland	Polar Inuit	77.49 N	69.50 W	-10.60	120.05	-23.33	4.00	20.45	4.06	4.50	8.64

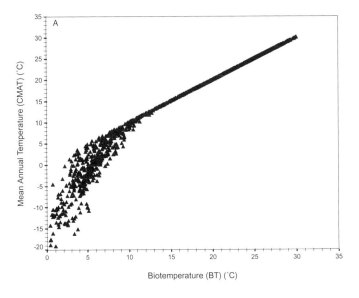

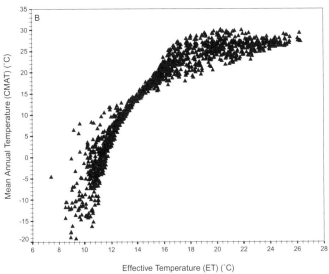

FIGURE 4.04

Comparative distribution of two measures of temperature—bio-temperature (A) and effective temperature (B)—from the world weather station sample. Each is shown relative to mean annual temperature.

ues of temperateness above 43.45, and the spread of values diminishes as temperateness values increase. This correspondence is to some extent a function of the patterned variability in temperature itself, since temperateness is standardized relative to a comfort value for temperature. (Note that the highest values for temperateness lie between ET values of 13.00 and 16.00 and include the earth's mean biotemperature, which occurs at an ET value of 14.84.)

In order to examine temperature constancy in greater detail, an additional measure, MTEMP, was calculated by means of the following formula:

(4.03)

$$MTEMP = [(MCM + 45)/(MWM + 45)] \times 100$$

where MCM = mean of the coldest month and
MWM = mean of the warmest month.[4]

The results of this equation can be arranged on a scale between 0.0 and 100.0, where a value of 0 would indicate the least evenness or the most extreme contrast between warm and cold months of the year and a value of 100.0 would indi-

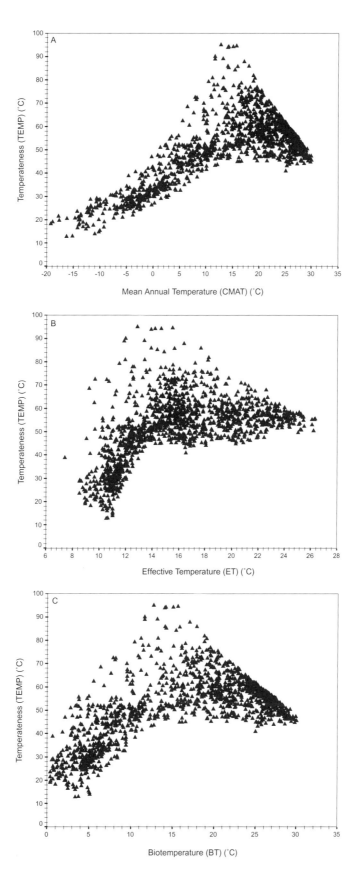

FIGURE 4.05

Comparative distribution of three measures of temperature—mean annual temperature (A), effective temperature (B), and biotemperature (C), expressed relative to a modeled measure of temperateness—from the world weather station sample.

TABLE 4.02

TEMPERATURE ORDINATION OF CLIMATES (CLIM)

CLASS NUMBER	CLASS
1	Polar climate, defined as all locations where the value of effective temperature (ET) is less than 10.00
2	Boreal climate, defined as all locations where the value of ET is greater than 9.99 and less than 12.50
3	Cool temperate climate, defined as all locations where the value of ET is greater than 12.49 and less than 14.56
4	Warm temperate climate, defined as all locations where the value of ET is greater than 14.55 and less than 16.62
5	Subtropical climate, defined as all locations where the value of ET is greater than 16.61 and less than 18.16
6	Tropical climate, defined as all locations where the value of ET is greater than 18.15 and less than 22.58
7	Equatorial climate, defined as all locations where the value of ET is greater than 22.57

cate no difference between the warmest and coldest months. In human terms, values of MTEMP provide a measure of the scale of temperature extremes with which an inhabitant of a specific locality would have to cope. Two additional indices of variability have also been calculated for use in subsequent comparisons: the standard deviation of an array of mean temperature values across the twelve months of the year (SDTEMP) and the coefficient of variance (CVTEMP) for such an array.

Over the years, a number of different systems of classifying temperature-based data have been developed by ecological researchers, each reflecting a judgment by its author about which data are germane to a particular research goal. As my research progressed, it became necessary to develop my own classification of gross temperature-related climatic variability, in which temperature and its correlative measurement, latitude, serve as the primary basis for a general classification of climates. The following system, defined in table 4.02, is based on an ordination of seven temperature classes. These range from coldest to warmest, in which a value of one is assigned to the coldest climates and a value of seven to the warmest. The ordinal variable is referred to as CLIM.

Now that the procedures for measuring temperature and its correlate, available solar energy, have been introduced and a temperature-based classification of climates that is relevant to the needs of this study has been presented, it is time to discuss measurement of the second major conditioner of biological activity on the earth—the water available to the plant community.

RAINFALL AND WHERE THE WATER GOES

Basic information about monthly rainfall levels was obtained for each of the ethnographic cases in this study and *mean annual rainfall* (CRR) was then calculated for each case. From these data, a suite of related indices and measures has been derived. One of these, REVEN, will be used to moni-tor the evenness of rainfall distribution throughout the year. It is calculated using two observations included in table 4.01: RHIGH, which is the mean monthly rainfall occurring during the wettest month of the year, and CRR. (A related value—RLOW, which is the mean monthly rainfall occurring during the driest month of the year—will figure in subsequent calculations.)

REVEN is a straightforward measure resulting from a two-step calculation: first, total annual rainfall is divided by 12.0 to obtain the value expected for any one month, assuming that all months had identical rainfall. Then the value of the month observed to have the highest rainfall (RHIGH) is divided by the expected monthly value. REVEN is distributed so that a value of 1.0 would occur if all months received the same amount of rainfall, and it increases as the magnitude of the wettest month rises relative to the mean annual value. The highest possible value would be 12.0, which indicates that all rain occurred in one month and no rain occurred in any other months. The relationship between these measures is represented in the following formula:

$$(4.04)$$

$$REVEN = RHIGH/(CRR/12)$$

REVEN is very similar to Mohr's Index (Whitmore 1975:44–66) and, like the latter scale, it is not corrected for the effect of frozen water stored during the winter months. Rainfall variance (CVRAIN) has also been calculated, as has the standard deviation for the array of mean monthly rainfall values, which is referred to as SDRAIN.

In order to develop variables that effectively measure seasonal differences in rainfall, the season in which rainfall occurs must be specified, as well as the length of the growing season, which represents the access window available to the plant community for the effective use of water. Seasonality in rainfall is easily measured in this study since, at the time of data collection, both the warmest and the wettest months were recorded. Using the warmest month as a ref-

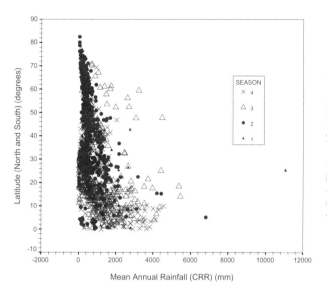

FIGURE 4.06

Scatter plot of the data from 1,429 weather stations included in the sample of the earth's environments showing the relationship between latitude and mean annual rainfall. Marker is for season of greatest rainfall (SEASON): (1) spring, (2) summer, (3) fall, and (4) winter.

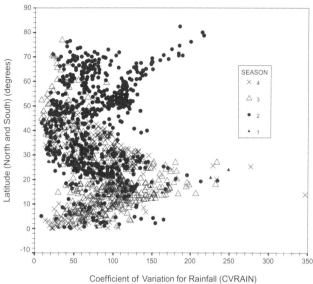

FIGURE 4.07

Dramatic latitudinal pattern in the coefficient of variation for rainfall, coded for season of greatest rainfall. Marker is for season of greatest rainfall (SEASON): (1) spring, (2) summer, (3) fall, and (4) winter.

erence point, the number of months or parts thereof, positive or negative, that separate the wettest month from the warmest month was calculated and assigned the term RRCORR. All positive values of RRCORR refer to the number of months *after* the warmest month.

Although these conventions were used in the initial tabulations of monthly weather data, in subsequent analysis the positive and negative scale became confusing, so a value of 4.5 was added to the recorded scale and any negative values remaining after this addition were subtracted from a value of 12.0. The result is a positive scale running from 0.0 to 12.0 and referred to as RRCORR2. This scale proved to be less confusing and could be separated into a seasonal ordination of three-month segments, termed SEASON, in which spring (season 1) values range from 0 to 2.99, summer (season 2) values range from 3.0 to 5.99, fall (season 3) values range from 6.0 to 8.99, and winter (season 4) values range from 9.0 to 11.99.

In addition, the variable RRCORR3 was defined to accommodate the fact that in environments with a twelve-month growing season, identification of those months with high rainfall is less important than in other habitats. In this study, therefore, for those cases with a twelve-month growing season the value of RRCORR3 is set at 4.5, which is the mean value of summer or growing season rainfall in seasonal settings. On the other hand, in all those cases in which the growing season is not year-round, the values of RRCORR3 and RRCORR2 are the same.

The scatter plot in figure 4.02 illustrating the relationship between latitude and mean annual rainfall (CRR) has been redesigned in figure 4.06 so that all data points are coded for season of rainfall (SEASON). The value measuring variance in the mean values for monthly rainfall (CVRAIN) replaces mean annual rainfall (CRR) on the *x* axis in figure 4.07, and these points are also then coded for SEASON.

These two scatter plots each contain several striking features, one of which is that locations with very high values for annual rainfall are dominated by autumn or winter rainfall patterns, particularly in the 40 to 60 degree latitude zone of high rainfall. Greater variability in the season of rainfall is found in tropical zones, but there the highest rainfall also tends to occur during the coolest months. Another interesting pattern is the high density of cases with winter-dominated rainfall that runs diagonally across the graph. It begins at about 24 degrees latitude with very-low-rainfall cases and runs diagonally up into the high-rainfall zone, where it peaks at about 48 degrees and then falls steeply to 55 degrees.

This pattern illustrates the dynamics of two significantly different climatic regimes. The first is the maritime climate of coastal western Europe and northwestern North America, and it includes the Southern Hemisphere equivalent along the Chilean Pacific coast, where autumn and winter rainfall is heavy but rain also occurs during other seasons. The other variant is the classic "Mediterranean" climate in which the summer months are dry and rainfall is concentrated during the winter months.

Although these two rainfall patterns are quite distinct, they tend to grade into one another in both the Mediterranean region and California. Figure 4.08 illustrates the gradual transition from a classic Mediterranean rainfall pattern to the weak winter-autumn–dominated pattern along the narrow coastal areas of western Europe. A "Mediterranean" climate prevails along the North African coast of the Mediterranean Sea, as well as along the eastern end of the Mediterranean coast and over most of California. In the Southern Hemisphere, the Mediterranean rainfall pattern occurs in a small part of Chile, at the western tip of southern Africa, and along the south coastal areas of western Australia and in parts of the states of South Australia and Victoria.

A Mediterranean climate indicator (MEDSTAB) was calculated to reflect the seasonality of rainfall and de-emphasize the measured dryness that occurs during the growing season. MEDSTAB is determined by the following equation:

$$(4.05)$$

$$MEDSTAB = 10 ** \{[\log_{10}ET^2 - \log_{10}(7.5 * \text{sqrt } CRR)] * RRCORR^2 * \log_{10}REVEN\}/10$$

By squaring RRCORR, the sign is eliminated and the resulting value simply measures the temporal distance between the months with the warmest temperature and the highest rainfall. Rainfall occurring during the growing season results in a low value whereas a high value indicates winter rainfall, when coupled with lower values of CRR and REVEN.

Referring back to Figure 4.07 we note a striking reversal of rainfall patterning as latitude changes. The coefficient of variation in rainfall (CVRAIN) is generally highest in those areas with low annual rainfall and dramatic contrasts between wet and dry seasons of the year. Above 50 degrees, a latitude that corresponds to the northern boreal and polar environments, rainfall is strongly summer dominated and CVRAIN is distributed over a very wide range of values. The lowest variance is localized discretely at 45 degrees and at 0 degrees latitude whereas the greatest variability occurs in the latitudinal zone characterized by dry environments, which are roughly clustered at 20 degrees latitude.

Subsequent chapters will explore the relationship between hunter-gatherer system structure and the fundamental climatic patterns that have been presented in this chapter thus far, but some additional habitat variables must first be introduced and discussed. One of these variables is MRAIN, a measure of rainfall evenness that is calculated by dividing the mean monthly rainfall occurring during the driest month of the year (RLOW) by the value for the mean monthly rainfall occurring during the wettest month (RHIGH) and multiplying the result by 100:

$$(4.06)$$

$$MRAIN = (RLOW/RHIGH) * 100$$

This calculation results in a scale of values from 0 to 100 in which 0 indicates the least evenness or the greatest extremes of variation between high- and low-rainfall months. MRAIN is thus the rainfall equivalent of the MTEMP measure of temperature.

In addition to the preceding indicators of seasonality, two measurements of the effect of rainfall on vegetation provide at least a partial basis for classifying plant communities in terms of production. Thornthwaite and Mather's (1955) *moisture index*[5] (MI) and Holdridge's (1959) *rainfall*

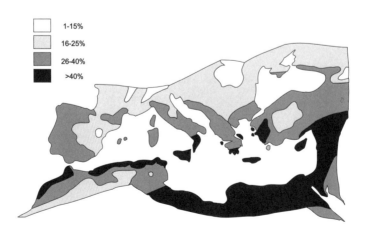

FIGURE 4.08

Percentage of annual precipitation falling in the three winter months over the Mediterranean region of southern Europe and North Africa. Redrawn and adapted from Trewartha (1961:figure 5.26).

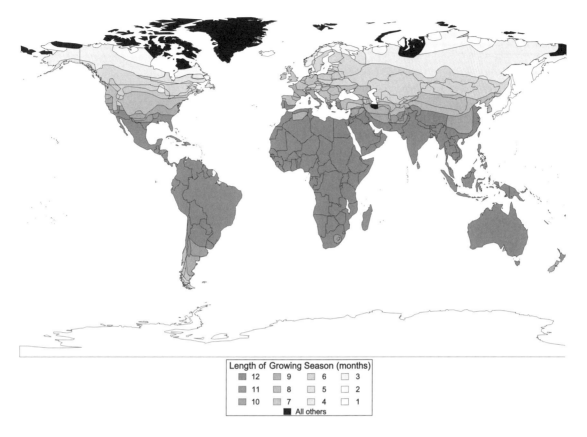

Length of Growing Season (months)
12	9	6	3
11	8	5	2
10	7	4	1

All others

FIGURE 4.09

World map with ordinal zones for the length of the growing season.

index[6] (HIRX) are introduced in this section but will be explored more fully following a discussion of techniques for measuring production in the plant community.

Two important properties of environments that have implications for productivity are the length and quality of the growing season. *Growing season* is itself a term that has been defined in different ways. For instance, it can refer to the length of time—measured in consecutive days—without "killing frost," which is usually defined as a temperature of 0°C. But because the data used in this study are monthly *means* of temperatures, a related but slightly different measure (GROWC) has been developed by counting the number of consecutive months in which the mean exceeds 8°C. This measure takes into account the fact that although many plants are not killed at temperatures approaching freezing, few will germinate under near-freezing temperatures. For example, some common agricultural crops of the temperate zone will not germinate if temperatures go below 4°C, whereas others require temperatures higher than 10°C for germination. A constant of 8°C is used because Bailey (1960) found that this value best summarized the temperature at the beginning and end of the growing season in the coldest places on earth.

In the global distribution of growing season indicators depicted in figure 4.09, truly remarkable differences between North America and western Europe are observable in the relationship between growing season and latitude. For example, agriculture can be practiced at much higher latitudes in western Europe than in North America. With this illustration, the introduction of basic measures of temperature and moisture is now complete, and it is time to consider how to measure the earth's biological activity as it is affected by these variables.

Biomes and Habitats: Structures of Accessible Resources

NET PRIMARY PRODUCTIVITY: DETERMINANTS AND MEASUREMENT

The amount of energy that human actors are able to access from the biological components of a habitat is strongly influenced by both the sources of potential energy available for exploitation within the ecosystem and the tactics and strategies available to humans for extracting that energy. Since all stored energy in a terrestrial ecosystem is derived from the conversion of solar energy penetrating the earth's atmosphere, it is reasonable to expect that there will be some relationship between productive intensity and the duration of exposure to solar radiation. Other things being equal, the distribution of net production occurring in an ecosystem is related to its position relative to the equator—the greater the distance from the equator, the lower the net production.

This simple generalization has led to attempts—the most successful by Rosenzweig (1968)—to relate net production to those climatic variables that seem to be at least partial determinants of biological activity. One basic climatic process is summarized by the term *actual evapotranspiration* (AE), which, according to Rosenzweig,

> may be defined as precipitation minus runoff, minus percolation . . . it may be thought of as the reverse of rain. It is the amount of water actually entering the atmosphere from the soil and the vegetation during any period of time. . . . Obviously, this atmospheric entry simultaneously requires water and sufficient energy to make the phase transfer of the water possible. Thus AE is a measure of the simultaneous availability of water and solar energy in an environment during any given period of time.   (1968:67)

Rosenzweig demonstrated a $\log_{10}$ relationship between annual evapotranspiration (in millimeters) and net annual aboveground productivity (measured in grams per square meter per year), and he explained why AE is a good predictor of biological activity and productivity:

> The fact that AE is a measure of the simultaneous availability of water and energy in an environment suggests to me an explanation as to why it should be a successful predictor of production. Gross productivity may be defined as the integral rate of photosynthesis throughout the year. The rate of photosynthesis depends on the concentrations of its raw materials, and water and solar radiational energy are two of these. In terrestrial environments, the third, CO_2, is a more or less constant 0.029 percent. Thus the AE is a measure of the two most variable photosynthetic resources.   (1968:71)

Although Rosenzweig's arguments and the demonstrations upon which they were based are impressive, there nevertheless remains a real-world problem of obtaining a reliable estimate of annual actual evapotranspiration. A number of years ago, after spending considerable time describing the detailed and expensive methods then available for measuring primary productivity, Odum (1971:56–62) sounded an optimistic note in a discussion of the ability of researchers to obtain reliable estimates of net aboveground productivity using basic meteorological data:

> Despite the many biological and physical complications, total evapotranspiration is broadly correlated with the rate of productivity. For example, Rosenzweig (1968) found that evapotranspiration was a highly sig-

nificant predictor of the annual aboveground net primary production in mature or climax terrestrial communities of all kinds (deserts, tundras, grasslands, and forests): however, the relationship was not reliable in unstable or developmental vegetation. . . . Knowing the latitude and mean monthly temperatures and precipitation (basic weather record), one can estimate [AE] from meteorological tables (see Thornthwaite and Mather, 1957), and then with the above equation [Rosenzweig 1968:71] predict what a well-adjusted, mature, natural community should be able to produce.
(Odum 1971:376–77)

Odum's optimism—prompted by Thornthwaite and Mather's "Instructions and Tables for Computing Potential Evapotranspiration and Water Balance"—was not wholly justified because the procedure developed by Thornthwaite and his associates, although methodologically elegant, was very awkward at the operational level. It is, for example, very difficult to follow all of the steps involved in the procedure and, even if somehow this obstacle were to be surmounted, several of the steps are primarily germane to estimating conditions affecting agricultural plant species rather than naturally occurring plant communities.[7]

In an attempt to eliminate some of these impediments, Thornthwaite's associate, John Mather, published a six-part series of articles entitled "Average Climatic Water Balance Data of the Continents" (Mather 1962, 1962a, 1963, 1963a, 1963b, 1964, 1965, 1965a), in which each article dealt with a different geographic region of the earth. By *water balance,* Mather meant temporal variability in the relationship between the moisture available to the plant community from rainfall and other sources and the maximum availability of solar radiation in an annual cycle. It should be clear that if most precipitation occurs in the winter, when solar radiation is least abundant, the effect on plant production will be very different than if rainfall occurs during the growing season, during which the highest rates of biological activity in the plant community occur.

Mather's series of articles contained a large sample of the earth's weather stations and provided data on the longitude, latitude, topographic elevation, and number of years that meteorological data had been recorded at each station. Although Mather's series of articles contained a wealth of important data in an accessible tabular format, the equations by means of which the data were produced were, unfortunately, never published. This meant that if the locations of interest to a researcher were not listed in the Mather series, it was unlikely that water balance values could be used in that particular analysis.

Mather's series was sufficiently comprehensive, however, for the purposes of several researchers. For instance, in *Vegetation of the Earth* (1973), Heinrich Walter used water balance as the organizing principle for a discussion of the earth's vegetation and the basis for excellent graphic summaries of environmental conditions affecting seasonality and vegetation. Water balance plays an equally important role in a number of textbooks on physical geography (e.g., Strahler and Strahler 1984).

Thornthwaite and Mather's logic and reasoning are so sound and elegant that I was prompted to invest the time and effort necessary to generate the equations upon which the water balance data were based.[8] The logic was to work backwards from the tables of meteorological data presented by those authors (1957) and, once the water balance equations were derived, to develop a computer program to calculate the data dimensions required for a description of weather station locations in the terms developed by Thornthwaite and Mather.[9]

In table 4.03, water balance data gathered from the region occupied by the Ngatatjara peoples of Australia are presented in the terms devised by Thornthwaite and Mather (1957) and Mather (1962, 1963a, 1963b, 1964).[10] Comparable data are presented in table 4.04 for the area of the Kalahari desert of Botswana occupied by the !Kung. These tabulations illustrate how a simple format can be used to provide a quick and informative way of comparing basic habitat parameters.

Thornthwaite and Mather also used innovative graphing techniques to illustrate the relationships among water balance variables (Mather 1962:fig.1). Some of their conventions are included in the climatic diagrams in figure 4.10, in which the horizontal axis is scaled from left to right in terms of the months of the year, from January to December for the Northern Hemisphere and from July to June for the Southern Hemisphere. The vertical axis is scaled in increments of 50 millimeters of water. Since all of the values in figure 4.10 are in millimeters of water, all of the curves can be overplotted, which permits easy visualization of the dynamic state of the plant community over a yearly cycle at a chosen location.

The advantage of graphic overplotting is demonstrated by a comparison of graph A in figure 4.10, which presents water balance data for the region of Australia inhabited by Ngatatjara peoples, and graph B, in which similar data are plotted for the Botswana home range of !Kung Bushmen. It has been alleged (Gould and Yellen 1987:86) that these two groups occupy "similar environments" and that environment can therefore be regarded as a constant when other properties of the two ethnographic cases are compared. Examination of the critical habitat variable of water balance as illustrated in figure 4.10 indicates, however, that Gould and Yellen's assumption is unjustified. The question of what the obvious difference in water balance between the Ngatatjara and !Kung habitats might mean in terms of divergent niche boundaries between the two groups must, unfortunately, remain unanswered, since there has been no systematic investigation of the relationships between habitat variables and system state properties.

Before Thornthwaite and Mather could plot the seasonal differences in photosynthetic processes that result from variations in water balance at any given location, they first had to obtain estimates of the potential amount of water lost to the soil and the plant community in the form of water vapor dissipated into the atmosphere. Whereas AE is the amount of water, measured in millimeters, that is *actually* transpired and evaporated from the soil and the plant community during a given period of time, *potential evapotranspiration* (or PET) is the amount of *potential* water loss to the soil and the plant community, measured in millimeters, assuming that the only limiting factor is the availability of solar energy.

Any difference between AE and PET values at a given location is therefore a direct measure of the degree to which water limitation affects the production of new cells in a specific plant community. If, for example, AE is less than PET, the difference is attributable to the fact that actual rainfall was less than the amount that *could* have been metabolized by the plant community given the level of available solar energy. The deficit in available water relative to the amount that could have been metabolized is referred to as *water deficit* (WATD) and is also measured in millimeters.

Thornthwaite and Mather were aware that moisture already retained in the soil could fuel both evaporation and transpiration and directly affect the productive capacity of a plant community. They also realized that the value of AE could not be based exclusively on the amount of rain falling during a given time period (CRR) but must also take into account the quantity of moisture already stored in the soil (WATRET). Further, if rainfall levels tabulated as CRR exceed the amount of moisture that can be evaporated or transpired (PET), then the excess water either increases the level of water already present in the soil (WATRET) or is lost to the location through runoff. The term *runoff* (RUNOFF) includes water that is rendered inaccessible to the plant community—either through surface flow away from the area or through storage below the level of plant root penetration—and ultimately constitutes a region's water table and contributes to bodies of water such as lakes and ponds. In some climates, snow accumulation, or SNOWAC, also contributes to a region's water surplus or deficit and therefore to the amount of water either stored in the soil (WATRET)[11] or released seasonally through runoff.

The information summarized in Thornthwaite and Mather's approach to water balance is useful in several ways:

1. It introduces variables based on the dynamic interaction between moisture and solar energy, particularly within the terrestrial plant biome, that cannot be calculated as long as attention is focused strictly on climatic conditions per se. For instance, instead of relating exclusively to hydrological dynamics, runoff is now more meaningfully represented as that water which falls in excess of the amount

TABLE 4.03
WATER BALANCE DATA FOR THE NGATATJARA OF AUSTRALIA

	JANUARY	FEBRUARY	MARCH	APRIL	MAY	JUNE	JULY	AUGUST	SEPTEMBER	OCTOBER	NOVEMBER	DECEMBER	TOTAL
PET	195.38	162.87	152.26	87.62	41.46	20.68	18.07	29.35	59.89	110.46	155.60	186.29	1,219.92
AE	28.08	45.08	33.98	17.20	21.20	18.43	10.50	10.13	6.89	8.35	19.07	25.56	244.47
MRR	28.00	45.00	34.00	17.00	21.00	18.00	11.00	10.00	7.00	8.00	19.00	25.00	244.00
WATRET	0.00	0.00	0.00	0.00	0.00	0.00	0.00	0.00	0.00	0.00	0.00	0.00	0.00
WATD	167.30	117.79	118.28	70.42	20.26	2.25	7.57	19.22	53.00	102.11	136.53	160.73	975.45
SNOWAC	0.00	0.00	0.00	0.00	0.00	0.00	0.00	0.00	0.00	0.00	0.00	0.00	0.00
RUNOFF	0.00	0.00	0.00	0.00	0.00	0.00	0.00	0.00	0.00	0.00	0.00	0.00	0.00

Note: PET = potential evapotranspiration; AE = actual evapotranspiration; MRR = mean monthly precipitation in millimeters; WATRET = water retention in millimeters; WATD = water deficit in millimeters; SNOWAC = snow accumulation in millimeters; RUNOFF = water surplus in millimeters.

TABLE 4.04

WATER BALANCE DATA FOR THE !KUNG OF BOTSWANA

	JANUARY	FEBRUARY	MARCH	APRIL	MAY	JUNE	JULY	AUGUST	SEPTEMBER	OCTOBER	NOVEMBER	DECEMBER	TOTAL
PET	114.88	95.73	97.51	80.38	54.01	34.29	34.56	50.09	85.70	123.65	115.05	116.30	1,002.15
AE	99.07	95.73	97.51	26.00	1.30	0.80	0.00	0.00	5.40	19.50	38.50	73.50	457.32
MRR	79.00	91.00	82.00	16.00	1.00	1.00	0.00	0.00	5.00	20.00	38.00	74.00	406.00
WRET	20.57	27.15	10.10	0.00	0.00	0.00	0.00	0.00	0.00	0.00	0.00	0.00	57.82
WATD	15.81	0.00	0.00	54.38	52.71	33.49	34.56	50.09	80.30	104.15	76.55	42.80	544.83
SNOWAC	0.00	0.00	0.00	0.00	0.00	0.00	0.00	0.00	0.00	0.00	0.00	0.00	0.00
RUNOFF	0.00	1.45	1.14	0.00	0.00	0.00	0.00	0.00	0.00	0.00	0.00	0.00	2.58

Notes: PET = potential evapotranspiration; AE = actual evapotranspiration; MRR = mean monthly precipitation in millimeters; WATRET = water retention in millimeters; WATD = water deficit in millimeters; SNOWAC = snow accumulation in millimeters; RUNOFF = water surplus in millimeters.

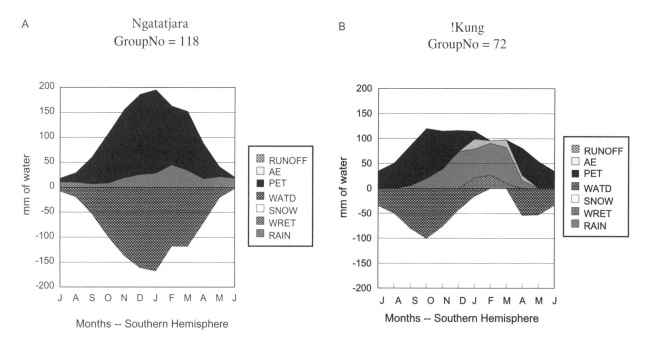

FIGURE 4.10

Water balance graphs featuring examples from the Ngatatjara of Australia (A) and the !Kung of Botswana (B).

that can be evaporated or transpired, given the available solar energy at a given location. Similarly, seasonality of runoff can be evaluated relative to the growing season, so that moisture that was "in storage" as snow or ice can be seen to be a source of water during the early part of the growing season, released by the same increasing temperatures that also make plant growth possible.

2. It provides values for variables that are required to calculate estimates of net above-ground productivity as envisioned by Odum.

3. It facilitates the creation of informative graphs that plot the basic variables conditioning plant production in terrestrial biomes.

At this juncture, another set of variables used in analysis must be defined. These measure ecologically important properties that can now be standardized relative to potential evapotranspiration (PET), thereby making it possible to compare properties as though potential evapotranspiration were being held constant. These variables include the following:

1. PTOAE: This term refers to the value that is obtained by dividing potential evapotranspiration (PET) by the sum of actual evapotranspiration (AE) and 1.0. It should be clear that low values of AE will result in high values of PTOAE while low values of PTOAE signify AE values very close to or identical to PET. The numeral one is added to AE

so that the lowest values of AE will yield a value equal to PET. The importance of the PTOAE variable is underscored by the fact that many researchers concerned with plant communities have found that forest maintenance depends on more rain than is indicated by PET values; in other words, more water is required than can be potentially transpired or evaporated. Researchers have also found that a transitional zone between forests and grasslands—composed of botanical communities termed "forest steppe" in cooler settings and "savanna" in warmer environments—occurs regularly in places where values of PET divided by CRR (mean annual rainfall) are just slightly greater than 1.0.

In this study, the PET/CRR index is referred to as HIRX and is similar to one reported by Holdridge (1947) (see note 6 to this chapter). All locations with values of less than 1.0 support forests, while values greater than 1.0 apply to arid plant communities—semidesert, desert, and various transitional forms of vegetation such as steppe, savanna, thorn woodland, and most "Mediterranean" vegetation types. In the era since water-balance formulas were developed and more detailed information has become available on the water resources actually serving plant communities as measured by AE and other variables, there have been some attempts to develop more accurate indices for anticipating types of vegetation using climatic data (Strahler and Strahler 1984).[12]

2. PTOWATD: This term refers to the value of PET divided

by the sum of WATD plus 1.0, where WATD is the total amount of water that could have been utilized by the plant community annually had it been present in sufficient quantity or at the correct time of the year. As in the previous example, high values of WATD yield low values of PTOWATD. In contrast to the previous example, however, low PTOWATD values are not positive indicators. On the contrary, the lower the value, the greater the water deficit and therefore the less growth potential there is in the plant community.

3. PTORUN: This term refers to the value of PET divided by the sum of the value of RUNOFF plus 1.0 and measures the water that is lost to the plant community through runoff or absorption by the soil beyond the limits of root penetration. It is also a measure of the amount of excess water that may be present at a location, either seasonally or in general, measured by values of HIRX or (PET/CRR) that were less than 1.0. As such, PTORUN is considered a predictor of all true forest plant associations.

In addition to the three preceding coefficients, several others were calculated using the water balance approach to measure or count some feature or characteristic of the growing season:

1. WILTGRC is a term for the number of months during the growing season—as defined by GROWC—in which rainfall (CRR) is less than or equal to 38 percent of PET. On average, in each month of the growing season included in the WILTGRC variable, available water is below the level at which plants wilt because of water deprivation.
2. WATDGRC is a term for the number of months during the growing season, as defined by GROWC, in which the value for WATD is greater than zero.
3. RUNGRC refers to the number of months during the growing season, as defined by GROWC, in which RUNOFF is greater than zero.

These three variables will be of considerable help in dealing with the types of plant communities from which hunter-gatherers must obtain their food.

Using the preceding measures that summarize relevant properties of the growing season, it is possible to calculate an additional set of useful percentage values with which to document variability in the water balance properties of the growing season. In each of the next three itemized paragraphs, the number of months during the growing season characterized by particular water balance conditions is tabulated, and this count is then divided by the number of months in which the mean monthly temperature equals or exceeds 8°C (GROWC). The product of this calculation is the percentage of the growing season during which a given set of conditions occurs.

1. The term PERWRET refers to the percentage of the growing season, measured in months, during which water is stored in the soil (the scale is from .001 to 1.00):

(4.07)

PERWRET = WATRGRC/GROWC

2. The term DEFPER refers to the percentage of the growing season, measured in months, during which a water deficit occurs (less water delivered as rainfall than could be evaporated or transpired given the potential evapotranspiration values for the months of the growing season; the scale is from 1 to 100):

(4.08)

DEFPER = (WATDGRC/GROWC) * 100

3. The term PERWLTG refers to the percentage of the growing season in which the water available to the plant community is at or below the wilting point for plants, which occurs when the sum of rainfall and water stored in the soil is 40 percent or less than the PET value for the month:

(4.09)

PERWLTG = WILTGRC/GROWC

In preparation for the introduction of another classification of both climate and vegetation, table 4.05 presents an ordination of climates referred to as AVWAT. This classification of the earth's environments is based exclusively on a biologically important set of differences in the amount of water available to plant communities in different environmental settings. It consists of eight classes of vegetation that range from a low of 1.0, which refers to the driest locations, to a high of 8.0 for rain forests.

Describing the relationships among some of the important climatic indicators associated with water balance dynamics now makes it possible to fulfill Odum's dream of developing estimates of net aboveground productivity (NAGP) from climatic data. NAGP represents the new cell life added to a habitat as a result of photosynthesis and growth (measured in grams per square meter per year) and can be calculated by inserting the estimates of actual evapotranspiration or AE into the formula derived by Rosenzweig (1968:71):

(4.10)

$$\log_{10}NAGP = \{[1.0 + (1.66 \pm 0.27)] * [\log_{10}AE]\} - (1.66 \pm 0.07)$$

where   NAGP = net annual aboveground productivity in grams per square meter per year and
AE = annual actual evapotranspiration in millimeters.

Another useful value is POTNAGP, which represents potential net aboveground productivity as if the only limitations were from temperature as a surrogate measure of solar radiation. The formula for POTNAGP is

TABLE 4.05
MOISTURE ORDINATION OF CLIMATES (AVWAT)

TYPE	PTOAE RANGE AND CONDITIONS
1	If PTOAE is greater than 5.0, conditions are very dry.
2	If PTOAE is less than or equal to 5.0 and greater than 2.25, conditions are dry.
3	If PTOAE is less than or equal to 2.25 and greater than 1.61, conditions are moderately dry.
4	If PTOAE is less than or equal to 1.61 and greater than 1.41 and DEFPER is greater than 50, conditions are transitional dry.
5	If PTOAE is less than or equal to 1.61 and greater than 1.41 and DEFPER is less than 50, conditions are transitional damp.
6	If PTOAE is less than or equal to 1.41 and PTOWATD is greater than 3.40, and if PTOAE is less than or equal to 1.41 and greater than 1.23, conditions are damp.
7	If PTOAE is less than or equal to 1.41 and PTOWATD is greater than 3.40, and if PTOAE is less than or equal to 1.23 and greater than 1.01, conditions are moist.
8	If PTOAE is less than or equal to 1.41 and PTOWATD is greater than 3.40, and if PTOAE is less than or equal to 1.01, conditions are wet.

(4.11)

$$\log_{10}\text{POTNAGP} = \{[1.0 + (1.66 \pm 0.27)] * [\log_{10}\text{PET}]\} - (1.66 \pm 0.07)$$

where   POTNAGP equals potential net annual aboveground productivity in grams per square meter per year and PET = potential evapotranspiration in millimeters.

The variable POTNAGP is therefore an estimate of the projected level of net annual aboveground productivity, given the unlikely possibility that unlimited water is available at all locations. In reality, this measure is a little misleading since cloud cover is related to rainfall and tends to depress temperatures and the amount of available solar radiation. Similarly, dry environments tend to lack cloud cover and are therefore characterized by higher temperatures.

ECOLOGICAL PROPERTY SPACE

As the analysis of the large environmental and ethnographic data bases at the heart of this study proceeds, it should become clear that the descriptive generalizations and theoretical conclusions that are produced have resulted from the application of inductive principles of investigation. The inductive method consists of a search for relationships between classes of entities or properties, and a researcher's goal is usually to identify the character of a relationship (or to illustrate a nonrelationship) between two factors or properties assigned to the axes of a two-dimensional graph. The field of possible data points within the boundaries of such a Cartesian graph can be thought of as an analytical "space"— often referred to as *property space*—against which distributions of properties of interest to the researcher assume different forms that reflect the relationships between those properties.

It is possible to project onto property space some of the environmental dimensions previously defined in this chapter, such as AE, PET, and POTNAGP, whose differing values are likely to be strong conditioners of hunter-gatherer niche differentiation. The graphic pattern that is created in such a display is called a *property space map*, and the different spatial forms that the environmental data of my study assume can be thought of as "habitat continents." As the two scatter plots in figure 4.11 illustrate, these analytical continents are in some ways comparable to the physical earth with its warm equatorial zones and cold polar regions. They demonstrate the relationships between latitude, plotted on the *y* axis, and the two measures of solar energy, ET and PET, plotted on the *x* axis.

Both graphs feature a familiar pattern: a slightly curvilinear distribution with high energy (warm) values in the low latitudes and lower energy values in the high latitudes. A more surprising observation, however, is an increasing spread in the energy values as one approaches the lower latitudes (less than 20 degrees on the ET chart and less than 30 degrees on the PET chart). This pattern records the increasing effects of altitude and other conditions, such as ocean temperatures, on the energy variance as a function of increased potential values for warmth in the tropics. As displayed in property space, the pattern or "habitat continent" resembles a beanie or skullcap with a feather emerging from the upper left side.

Figure 4.12 illustrates the relationship between the geographic distribution of weather stations in the global sample and the temperature-based classification of climates (CLIM) that will be used in some subsequent comparisons. Without any other relevant information, however, the CLIM categories would constitute a very limited frame of reference for looking at habitat variability. Similarly, solar energy equivalents scaled relative to latitude in figure 4.11 (which also appear in figure 4.02), although useful, are nevertheless only single climatic approximations of fundamental energy states.

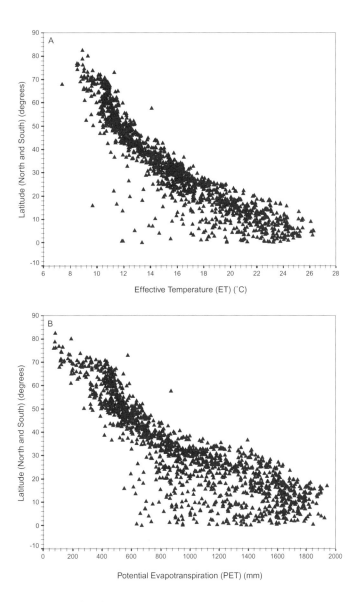

FIGURE 4.11

Property space graphs, compiled from the world weather station sample, defined by latitude, effective temperature, and potential evapotranspiration.

In an effort to endow the "habitat continent" depicted in figure 4.12 with greater information and therefore more realism, the relationship between latitude (y axis) and the $\log_{10}$ value of net aboveground productivity (NAGP) in the plant community (x axis) is shown in figure 4.13. This distribution should be compared with a plot of latitude (y axis) against the $\log_{10}$ value of the net annual productivity expected if water were not a limiting factor (figure 4.14). (It should be recalled that primary productivity as estimated by either NAGP or POTNAGP is a direct estimate of the amount of new plant cells added to the plant community per unit area per year.)

The addition of NAGP and POTNAGP has a dramatic effect on the shape of the habitat continent. Instead of the beanie-with-feather pattern produced when solar energy was the only defining parameter, now the continent is very much wider. A pronounced peninsula of low net aboveground productivity forms a high-latitude arc pointing to 90 degrees and another broad, triangular peninsula converges to the left at 20 degrees latitude. The former peninsula represents the limitations on plant productivity that are almost exclusively conditioned by diminished solar energy, whereas the latter peninsula corresponds to situations in which there is insufficient rainfall to ensure maximum productivity from the amount of available solar energy. The peninsula that converges on 20 degrees represents the concentration of very dry environments—identified earlier in a discussion of

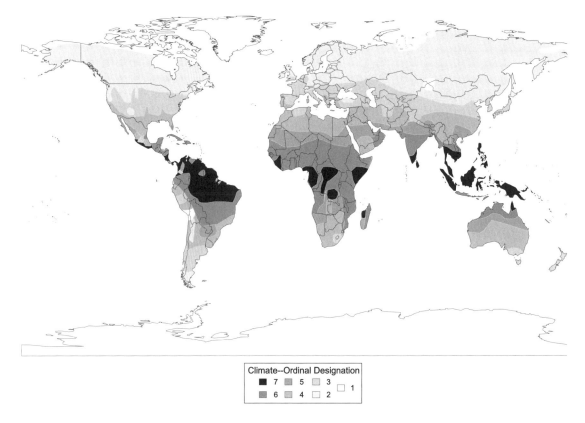

Climate--Ordinal Designation

■ 7 ■ 5 □ 3 □ 1
■ 6 ■ 4 □ 2

FIGURE 4.12

World map with ordinal zones by effective temperature, compiled from the world weather station sample. Marker is for temperature (CLIM): (1) polar, (2) boreal, (3) cool temperate, (4) warm temperate, (5) subtropical, (6) tropical, and (7) equatorial.

weather circulation patterns—that includes the deserts of the world and occurs just below 30 degrees latitude on a model of the earth.

In fact, all of the points in figure 4.13 that fall either below or to the left of the right edge of the distribution represent situations in which insufficient water, relative to PET, results in less productivity than would otherwise be possible, given the amount of available solar energy. This pattern is indicated by the distribution of points that is coded in terms of the eight-point AVWAT scale in table 4.05, which measures the annual water deficit in each case. In this graph, the larger, open, circular markers correspond to locations with the least water deficit. The projection of a smooth, curved line along the upper right margin of the distribution represents the upper limit of productivity, conditioned by solar energy, on the earth as it is geographically constituted.

Similarly, the graph in figure 4.14 demonstrates that any deviation between the amount of solar radiation, measured by PET, and net productivity (NAGP) results from either of two conditions: (1) the amount of annual rainfall (CRR) is less than the amount that could be evaporated or transpired at a given location, or (2) variations in geography, such as land-

mass size and elevation, affect the temperature regime at a location in response to the interaction of such meteorological factors as ocean currents and air circulation patterns.

The plots in figures 4.11–4.14 illustrate what is meant by the concept of property space and demonstrate the potential utility of graphic tools such as property space maps in a complex, comparative study of hunter-gatherer ecology. After I have introduced some additional variables that appear to condition sociocultural variability, more property space maps will be generated as part of my examination of the interaction of pertinent variables and their effect on hunter-gatherer life ways. The huge spread at the top of the graph in figure 4.14 illustrates the relationship between the amount of water in a region and net aboveground productivity. It should also be clear from this example that the closer an area is to either polar region, where PET approaches zero, the less effect water has on NAGP values.

Primary Biomass

Any consideration of habitat variability in terms of net aboveground productivity leads directly to the subject of biomass—that is, the amount of synthesized material pres-

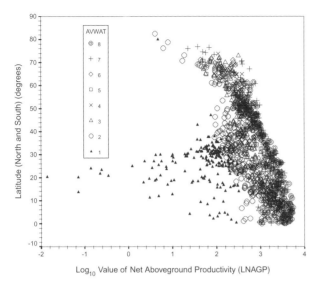

FIGURE 4.13

Property space map defined by latitude and the $\log_{10}$ value of net aboveground productivity in the plant biome, from the world weather station sample. Marker is for available water (AVWAT): (1) very dry, (2) dry, (3) moderately dry, (4) transitional dry, (5) transitional damp, (6) damp, (7) moist, and (8) wet.

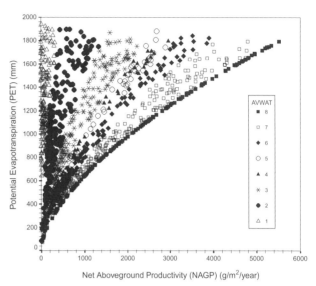

FIGURE 4.14

Demonstration of the relationship between potential evapotranspiration and rainfall as joint conditioners of net aboveground productivity in the plant biome, from the world weather station sample. Marker is for available water (AVWAT): (1) very dry, (2) dry, (3) moderately dry, (4) transitional dry, (5) transitional damp, (6) damp, (7) moist, and (8) wet.

ent or maintained in the producer component of an ecosystem. Although levels of biomass and production are the direct result of gross climatic conditions, they respond independently to the impact of specific climatic variables. Think for a moment of a dense forest in which much of the biomass is concentrated in tree trunks, limbs, and roots. In this setting, production may be low relative to the amount of biomass that is present. On the other hand, in a grassland, where most of the biomass is represented by reproductive tissue (e.g., blades of grass), production is relatively high and biomass is low.

Table 4.06 documents some of the variability in biomass and production that has defined the opportunities and limitations on subsistence that hunter-gatherers in different habitats have had to cope with. The various levels of primary biomass that are listed in column 3 for a range of habitat types have considerable impact on the subsistence efforts of human foragers. Primary biomass is greatest in high-rainfall zones such as boreal-temperate forests and tropical and subtropical forests. Any location where water is restricted will place limits on both net primary productivity and primary biomass, although primary biomass does not respond to energetic limitations such as temperature in the same way as net primary productivity. In the face of variations in available solar radiation, the amount of primary biomass is tempered by the variable metabolic rates that characterize the different quaternary forest types and results in a partial independence between the distributions of biomass and net primary productivity.

These patterns have significant implications for all animal species, including human beings. For instance, the higher the *biomass accumulation ratio* (table 4.06, column 6), the lower the proportion of primary production available for browsing and grazing animals to eat. *Secondary biomass*—the amount of animal tissue supported by the habitat—is even more directly signaled by the percentage of biomass represented by leafy plant material (column 4). Those habitats with the highest values for percent of biomass represented by leaves—temperate steppe, arctic tundra, dry steppe, immature temperate broadleaf forest, and dwarf scrub tundra—are also habitats with the highest secondary biomass.

The arctic tundra biome is characterized by vast caribou herds, the steppe by bison and horse herds, and the subtropical savannas by mixed herds of wildebeest, zebra, and other ungulates. In fact, other things being equal, it is reasonable to expect that the lower the leaf percentage of a habitat is, the less secondary or animal biomass is likely to be present in that habitat. The lowest values in column 4 occur in temperate mature forests, followed by deserts and subtropical forests, strongly indicating that a subsistence strategy based primarily on animal resources will be difficult in these settings.

This brief comparison of some of the data in table 4.06 is sufficient to indicate that the distribution of biomass is crucial to the niche definition of both human and nonhuman foragers. The next step is to develop a measure of primary

TABLE 4.06

BIOMASS, PRODUCTION, AND BIOMASS ACCUMULATION
IN DIFFERENT HABITATS

HABITAT		BIOMASS (B)		NET PRODUCTION (P)	BIOMASS ACCUMULATION (B/P)
Type	Subtype	Total	Percent leaves		
ARCTIC TUNDRA	True	0.50	15.00	0.10	5.00
	Dwarf-scrub	2.80	11.00	0.25	11.20
BOREAL FOREST	Northern taiga	10.00	8.00	0.45	22.20
	Middle taiga	26.00	6.00	0.70	37.10
	Southern taiga	33.00	6.00	0.85	38.70
MATURE TEMPERATE	Northern coniferous	26.00	1.00	2.00	13.10
AND BOREAL FOREST	Beech	37.00	1.00	1.30	28.40
	Oak	40.00	1.00	0.90	44.40
	Temperate broadleaf	43.20	2.80	2.16	20.00
IMMATURE OR MANAGED	Secondary birch	8.77	3.60	1.08	8.10
FOREST	Northern coniferous	8.05	4.20	1.11	7.20
	Acacia plantation	9.33	7.60	2.94	3.20
	Beech-poplar	2.20	7.70	0.86	2.40
	Temperate broadleaf	6.20	11.60	2.80	2.20
	Bamboo	1.30	3.50	1.60	0.70
STEPPE	Temperate	2.50	18.00	1.12	2.20
	Dry	1.00	15.00	0.42	2.40
DESERT	Subtropical	0.60	3.00	0.25	2.40
	Dwarf/semishrub	0.43	3.00	0.12	3.50
SAVANNA	Dry	0.27	11.00	0.73	3.70
	Moderate	6.66	12.00	1.20	5.60
SUBTROPICAL FOREST	True	41.00	3.00	2.45	16.70
TROPICAL RAIN FOREST	True	50.00	8.00	3.25	15.40

Note: Total biomass and net production values are calculated as kg/m^2 per year. Data are taken from Krebs (1972:449) and Odum (1971:376).

biomass so that this variable can be reliably incorporated into the frame of reference used in this study as a tool to investigate the organization of hunter-gatherer groups. A search of the ecological literature has revealed that independent estimates of biomass are not available for many specific areas where measures of other habitat variables could be obtained. This discovery has necessitated the use of the data in tables 4.01 and 4.07 to ground empirically the procedures for estimating biomass.

To do this, the locations at which biomass values were summarized in table 4.06 were identified and additional meteorological data relevant to these locations were obtained, thereby linking biomass values to other variables used in this study. Those cases were plotted for which maximum biomass was expected—that is, where actual evapotranspiration (AE) equaled potential evapotranspiration (PET) and rainfall exceeded potential evapotranspiration by at least 1.75 times PET.

The preceding criterion is derived from a number of studies of the relationship between rainfall relative to potential evapotranspiration and biomass. For example, true rain

forests generally occur only in regions in which annual rainfall is greater than potential evapotranspiration. Similarly, empirical information has been summarized by Holdridge (1959) and Thornthwaite and Mather (1957) which demonstrates that biomass increases as a function of increases in rainfall of between 1.75 and 2.0 times PET—the interval within which maximum plant biomass occurs.[13] Plant biomass therefore appears to be a function of the availability of water beyond that which is evaporated or transpired by the plant community, which makes good sense given the fact that maximum biomass is achieved when water is not a limiting factor for the plant community. The more continuously that excess water is available—while not resulting in long periods of standing water—the higher the biomass in a plant community will be.

For the documented cases in this study that spanned the total range of the earth's environments, a curve was fit defining the relationship between primary biomass and the maximum net aboveground productivity that could be supported at a given location,[14] using the following equation:

$$\text{(4.12)}$$

$$
\begin{aligned}
\text{MAXBIO} = [&{-}1514.10169014 + \\
&(23.7869109052 * \text{POTNAGP}) + \\
&(-0.0609287524512 * \text{POTNAGP}^2) + \\
&(6.46993574054\text{E}{-}05 * \text{POTNAGP}^3)]/ \\
[1 + &(-0.00230688794979 * \text{POTNAGP}) + \\
&(1.30111054427\text{E}{-}06 * \text{POTNAGP}^2) + \\
&(7.5212956032\text{E}{-}10 * \text{POTNAGP}^3)]
\end{aligned}
$$

Once an estimate of MAXBIO or the maximum biomass that can occur at a given location has been determined, it is possible to calculate the maximum biomass accumulation ratio, or MAXBAR, that would correspond to this value:

$$\text{(4.13)}$$

$$\text{MAXBAR} = \text{MAXBIO}/\text{POTNAGP}$$

With two maximum estimates for biomass at any climatically documented location—and assuming maximum water availability—it becomes possible to scale observed conditions against this maximum estimate to obtain an estimate of actual primary biomass. Before outlining the steps involved in the development of this important environmental parameter, a brief recap of the research standing behind MAXBIO might be helpful. Numbers of empirical studies have demonstrated that in order for maximum primary biomass to occur, water in considerable excess of PET is required. In fact, total rainfall levels nearly equal to or double PET are common in areas in which maximum biomass values have been observed. Regular shifts in the character of a forest, as well as shifts to nonforest habitats, have been noted to scale with the proportions of rainfall to PET. Although it is easy to think of the real world in these terms, the actual relationship between rainfall levels and PET is curvilinear, which made it necessary to use $\log_{10}$ conversions in estimating primary biomass (BIO5).

Equation development step one:

If   AE/PET is less than 1.0
then   BIO5 = 10 ** [$\log_{10}$CRR – ($\log_{10}$1.75 + $\log_{10}$PET)] *
        a modified value for MAXBIO to be
        described in step two,
otherwise BIO5 = MAXBIO.

This equation outlines only part of the dynamics, since water is only one of several limitations on primary biomass that include reduced solar radiation and differences in the metabolic rates of plant communities at different latitudes. It is necessary to build into the equation such factors as the effects of temperature limitations, as well as constraints that involve the interaction between temperature (growing season conditions) and water availability. These conditioners of primary biomass are summarized in the next analytical step.

Equation development step two:

MAXBIO * [(2.5 * PGROW/36) + PPPER]/3.5

where   PGROW is a weighted measure of the simultaneous
        presence of both water and solar radiation
        available to the plant community and PPPER is the
        percentage of potential evapotranspiration realized
        as actual evapotranspiration.

This weighting is obtained through the following series of steps:

If   CRR is ≤ .40 * PET

then   PGROW = 0.0 for the month in question.
Else if CRR is ≤ 1.2 * PET
then   PGROW = 1.0 for the month in question.
Else if CRR > 1.2 * PET
then   PGROW = 3.0 for the month in question.

The sum of monthly PGROW indices for all months is then divided by thirty-six, or the maximum value that could occur if all twelve months had a value of 3.0. This percentage value is then multiplied by 2.5 and added to the percentage value obtained when CRR/(1.75 * PET). Annual rainfall is divided by 1.75 times annual potential evapotranspiration (PET), and the entire value is then divided by 3.5 to obtain an average percentage for the weighted sum value. This value is then multiplied by MAXBIO, and the resulting value is then multiplied by the values obtained from the first step in the equation. This result has the effect of a squared percentage value, but the two values are different ways of obtaining estimates of similar conditioners of primary biomass. The final equation used for estimating primary biomass is

If   AE/PET is less than 1.0
then   BIO5 = 10 ** [$\log_{10}$CRR – ($\log_{10}$1.75 + $\log_{10}$PET)]
        * MAXBIO * [(2.5 * PGROW/36) +
        PPPER]/3.5
otherwise BIO5 = MAXBIO.

The preceding equations now make it possible to obtain primary biomass (BIO5) estimates from climatic data. Values for biomass accumulation ratio,

$$\text{(4.15)}$$

BAR5 = BIO5/NAGP

and turnover rate (TURNOV),

$$\text{(4.16)}$$

TURNOV = NAGP/BIO5

can now be calculated using values presented for each group in the hunter-gatherer data set in table 4.07.

Figure 4.15 illustrates the distribution of latitude and primary biomass (BIO5) for the global sample of weather

TABLE 4.07

DERIVATIVE ENVIRONMENTAL INDICATORS FOR USE WITH HUNTER-GATHERER DATA SETS

NO.	STATE	NAME	PET	AE	BIO5	BAR5	NAGP	WATD	SNOWAC	GROWC	WLTGRC	WATRET	DEFPER
1	Indonesia	Punan	1,637.66	1,637.66	56,660.51	11.96	4,738.19	0.00	0.00	12	0	174.52	0.00
2	Philippines	Batek	1,778.69	1,445.65	30,378.80	7.89	3,852.15	333.05	0.00	12	3	84.98	25.00
3	Indonesia	Kubu	1,609.52	1,609.52	56,157.12	12.120	4,603.80	0.00	0.00	12	0	174.52	0.00
4	Nicobar Islands	Shompen	1,794.49	1,794.47	59,274.80	10.75	5,514.85	0.00	0.00	12	0	306.71	0.00
5	Andaman Islands	Onge	1,679.34	1,566.25	57,386.48	13.05	4,400.17	113.09	0.00	12	0	259.95	25.00
6	Andaman Islands	Jarwa	1,650.56	1,414.14	29,082.34	7.83	3,713.79	236.42	0.00	12	2	196.74	41.67
7	Philippines	Ayta-Pinatubo	1,678.16	1,224.17	57,366.23	19.63	2,922.91	453.99	0.00	12	4	65.8	41.67
8	Andaman Islands	North Island	1,605.91	1,235.08	2,0875.11	7.04	2,966.27	370.84	0.00	12	3	178.00	41.67
9	Malaysia	Semang	1,320.69	1,320.69	50,350.34	15.19	3,315.37	0.00	0.00	12	0	174.52	0.00
10	Sri Lanka	Veddah	1,779.68	1,305.34	17,266.13	5.31	3,251.70	474.32	0.00	12	2	129.28	41.67
11	India	Hill-Pandaran	1,867.69	850.62	3,916.20	2.45	1,597.21	1,017.07	0.00	12	5	9.00	83.33
12	Philippines	Agta (Casiguran)	1,590.15	1,590.15	47,941.20	10.62	4,512.19	0.00	0.00	12	0	113.49	0.00
13	Philippines	Agta (Isabela)	1,633.04	1,400.41	23,670.98	6.48	3,654.14	232.63	0.00	12	1	51.75	41.67
14	Philippines	Agta (North Luzon)	1,601.79	1,446.63	26,951.88	6.99	3,856.52	155.15	0.00	12	0	63.27	33.33
15	India	Chenchu	1,428.30	946.74	15,645.89	8.20	1,907.85	481.56	0.00	12	3	78.07	50.00
16	Thailand	Mrabri	1,573.28	1,088.39	9,571.19	3.98	2,404.72	484.89	0.00	12	3	28.99	66.67
17	India	Paliyans	1,033.43	1,015.75	17,804.35	8.30	2,144.19	17.68	0.00	12	0	76.56	16.67
18	India	Birhor	1,306.81	936.14	13,839.86	7.39	1,872.51	370.67	0.00	12	3	77.54	41.67
19	India	Kadar	698.73	698.73	36,049.30	31.29	1,152.28	0.00	0.00	12	0	363.18	0.00
20	India	Cholanaickan	699.02	699.02	36,054.52	31.27	1,153.06	0.00	0.00	12	0	166.28	0.00
21	India	Nayaka	697.84	695.51	22,638.52	19.80	1,143.48	2.32	0.00	12	0	292.12	8.33
22	Japan	Ainu (Hokkaido)	565.29	550.42	21,509.67	27.74	775.45	14.88	106.14	6	0	88.69	16.67
23	China	Orogens	491.47	422.87	8,175.25	16.34	500.62	68.60	44.72	5	0	24.18	80.00
24	Russia	Ket	465.09	358.30	8,724.06	22.95	380.24	106.79	190.84	3	0	44.10	66.67
25	Russia	Gilyak	452.85	378.82	6,895.30	16.53	417.06	74.03	124.63	5	0	62.17	60.00
26	Russia	Yukaghir	331.97	153.59	875.62	9.40	93.19	178.38	68.87	3	2	35.41	100.00
27	Russia	Nganasan	250.51	171.06	1,219.11	10.94	111.44	79.44	109.28	1	0	52.19	100.00
28	Russia	Siberian Eskimo	223.66	189.93	1,235.29	9.32	132.57	33.73	124.51	0	0	51.77	0.00
35	Venezuela	Paraujano	1,842.08	1,370.66	13,800.41	3.91	3,526.19	471.42	0.00	12	3	14.25	58.33
36	Venezuela	Shiriana	1,717.92	1,644.54	36,721.40	7.70	4,771.26	73.38	0.00	12	0	87.32	25.00
37	Suriname	Akuriyo	1,654.70	1,611.05	30,257.05	6.56	4,611.08	43.65	0.00	12	0	190.66	16.67
38	Venezuela	Yaruro-pume	1,742.83	1,217.25	18,920.42	6.53	2,895.55	525.58	0.00	12	4	145.32	50.00
39	Colombia	Guahibo	1,676.08	1,667.86	42,207.45	8.64	4,884.11	8.22	0.00	12	0	299.64	16.67
40	Colombia	Nukak	1,144.33	1,144.33	46,251.29	17.70	2,613.32	0.00	0.00	12	0	373.93	0.00
41	Brazil	Bororo	1,291.23	1,152.33	26,175.82	9.90	2,643.73	138.90	0.00	12	1	96.32	16.67
42	Brazil	Guato	1,462.16	1,341.13	13,715.39	4.03	3,400.97	121.03	0.00	12	0	98.28	50.00
43	Bolivia	Siriono	1,487.55	1,385.18	18,304.27	5.10	3,588.40	102.37	0.00	12	0	84.50	25.00
44	Bolivia	Yuqui	1,482.57	1,482.57	43,035.30	10.71	4,016.87	0.00	0.00	12	0	127.85	0.00
45	Brazil	Nambikwara	1,211.40	801.58	4,806.06	3.32	1,447.29	409.82	0.00	12	4	61.87	50.00
46	Florida	Calusa	1,234.85	1,233.17	19,445.02	6.57	2,958.67	1.68	0.00	12	0	110.62	8.33

	Country	Group										
47	Paraguay	Guayaki (Ache)	1,108.86	1,108.86	31,611.53	12.75	2,480.26	0.00	0.00	12	0	154.16	0.00
48	Brazil	Botocudo	978.44	935.41	22,041.49	11.79	1,870.10	43.02	0.00	12	0	101.29	25.00
49	Brazil	Heta	930.89	930.89	37,881.40	20.42	1,855.11	0.00	0.00	12	0	174.52	0.00
50	Brazil	Aweikomo	914.24	914.24	37,074.12	20.59	1,800.37	0.00	0.00	12	0	152.68	0.00
51	Argentina	Tehuelche	690.24	206.91	1,322.77	8.65	152.83	483.33	0.00	9	7	5.49	88.89
52	Chile	Chono	613.71	613.71	34,097.80	36.70	929.01	0.00	0.00	7	0	174.52	0.00
53	Chile	Alacaluf	599.25	599.25	33,546.36	37.57	892.96	0.00	0.00	6	0	143.03	0.00
54	Argentina	Ona	485.00	392.84	8,600.41	19.41	443.00	92.16	0.00	3	0	43.35	100.00
55	Argentina	Yahgan	508.63	414.50	10,603.66	21.90	484.28	94.13	0.00	3	0	45.54	100.00
60	Congo	Aka	1,472.02	1,443.27	25,461.31	6.63	3,841.66	28.75	0.00	12	0	177.95	16.67
61	Congo	Bayaka	1,472.30	1,472.30	28,448.64	7.16	3,970.77	0.00	0.00	12	0	226.79	0.00
62	Zaire	Bambote	1,258.56	927.34	16,752.04	9.09	1,843.38	331.22	0.00	12	3	81.58	41.67
63	Cameroon	Baka	1,249.95	1,246.66	30,880.84	10.25	3,012.60	3.29	0.00	12	0	300.96	8.33
64	Zaire	Efe	1,157.54	1,154.09	30,072.33	11.35	2,650.44	3.46	0.00	12	0	289.85	8.33
65	Zaire	Mbuti	1,048.96	1,043.32	33,168.24	14.80	2,241.67	5.64	0.00	12	0	324.97	8.33
66	Madagascar	Mikea	1,345.27	397.36	1,065.74	2.36	451.48	947.91	0.00	12	10	0.00	100.00
67	Zambia	Hukwe	1,122.66	688.80	6,994.88	6.22	1,125.21	433.86	0.00	12	4	48.91	58.33
68	Namibia	Hai//Om	1,130.89	616.70	3,060.41	3.27	936.53	514.19	0.00	12	4	14.04	83.33
69	Tanzania	Hadza	899.93	732.73	11,372.16	9.12	1,246.84	167.20	0.00	12	2	61.91	41.67
70	Kenya	Dorobo (Okiek)	798.18	795.41	25,774.44	18.04	1,428.85	2.77	0.00	12	0	133.95	8.33
71	Angola	Sekele	1,147.65	700.45	4,469.83	3.86	1,156.98	447.20	0.00	12	3	26.12	66.67
72	Botswana	!Kung	998.50	457.32	2,081.68	3.65	570.12	541.18	0.00	12	8	4.82	83.33
73	Botswana	Nharo	1,024.23	385.60	2,110.81	4.91	429.52	638.63	0.00	12	6	0.00	100.00
74	Botswana	G/Wi	934.94	333.84	1,521.00	4.50	338.12	601.09	0.00	12	9	3.42	91.67
75	Botswana	Kua	942.07	354.20	2,008.09	5.38	373.04	587.87	0.00	12	6	0.00	100.00
76	Botswana	!Ko	916.00	281.50	909.82	3.57	254.76	634.49	0.00	12	9	0.00	100.00
77	South Africa	/Auni Khomani	900.39	123.77	124.22	1.91	65.12	776.62	0.00	12	12	0.00	100.00
78	South Africa	//Xegwi	799.29	742.61	17,513.66	13.74	1,274.87	56.68	0.00	12	0	48.43	33.33
79	South Africa	/Xam	810.07	236.12	1,028.31	5.40	190.29	573.95	0.00	12	7	3.40	66.67
82	Australia—Queensland	Kaurareg	1,569.36	997.90	17,620.21	8.46	2,082.03	571.46	0.00	12	4	55.14	50.00
83	Australia—Northern Territory	Larikia	1,754.19	1041.45	16,168.63	7.23	2,235.02	712.74	0.00	12	5	59.32	58.33
84	Australia—Northern Territory	Gunwinggu	1,791.86	969.83	11,366.31	5.72	1,985.71	822.02	0.00	12	6	53.31	58.33
85	Australia—Northern Territory	Mirrngadja	1,678.19	976.04	10,146.53	5.06	2,006.86	702.15	0.00	12	6	55.90	58.33
86	Australia—Northern Territory	Anbara	1,652.76	960.48	9,860.92	5.05	1,954.04	692.28	0.00	12	6	53.47	58.33
87	Australia—Northern Territory	Gidjingali	1,627.61	945.63	9,573.19	5.03	1,904.13	681.99	0.00	12	6	45.45	58.33
88	Australia—Northern Territory	Murngin (Yolngu)	1,656.69	965.00	9,420.35	4.79	1,969.32	691.69	0.00	12	6	49.34	66.67
89	Australia—Western Australia	Jeidji (Forest River)	1,834.81	638.82	2,131.21	2.15	992.95	1,195.99	0.00	12	8	0.00	100.00
90	Australia—Queensland	Wikmunkan	1,513.15	983.44	16,648.36	8.19	2,032.18	529.71	0.00	12	5	54.38	50.00
91	Australia—Northern Territory	Kakadu	1,603.68	1,042.59	11,138.53	4.97	2,239.09	561.08	0.00	12	6	47.83	66.67
92	Australia—Northern Territory	Nunggubuyu	1,652.81	896.22	6,275.31	3.60	1,741.85	756.59	0.00	12	6	27.41	66.67
93	Australia—Queensland	Yintjingga	1,476.92	1,062.81	18,003.14	7.79	2,311.62	414.11	0.00	12	4	53.16	58.33
94	Australia—Queensland	Yir-yoront	1,620.94	899.50	8,576.32	4.89	1,752.44	721.44	0.00	12	6	40.24	58.33
95	Australia—Northern Territory	Tiwi	1,517.62	1,052.17	16,400.11	7.21	2,273.33	465.45	0.00	12	5	55.83	58.33
96	Australia—Queensland	Kuku-yalanji	1,435.67	1,097.66	21,477.13	8.81	2,438.82	338.01	0.00	12	3	59.68	50.00
97	Australia—Northern Territory	Groote-eylandt	1,509.97	957.95	10,129.69	5.21	1,945.50	552.02	0.00	12	5	41.95	58.33

(continued)

TABLE 4.07 (continued)

NO.	STATE	NAME	PET	AE	BIO5	BAR5	NAGP	WATD	SNOWAC	GROWC	WLTGRC	WATRET	DEFPER
98	Australia—Queensland	Walmbaria	1,456.20	858.81	9,113.49	5.62	1,622.82	597.39	0.00	12	7	42.42	58.33
99	Australia—Northern Territory	Mulluk	1,625.29	1,017.53	13,576.86	6.31	2,150.46	607.75	0.00	12	5	58.22	58.33
100	Australia—Western Australia	Worora	1,544.83	909.11	9,543.11	5.35	1,783.62	635.72	0.00	12	7	34.73	58.33
101	Australia—Western Australia	Lungga	1,631.88	587.13	2,118.17	2.45	863.18	1,044.75	0.00	12	8	0.00	100.00
102	Australia—Queensland	Lardil	1,520.08	878.98	9,481.53	5.62	1,686.58	641.10	0.00	12	7	45.53	66.66
103	Australia—Queensland	Kaiadilt	1,521.27	895.09	8,669.90	4.99	1,738.21	626.18	0.00	12	7	43.77	66.67
104	Australia—Western Australia	Karadjeri	1,528.09	445.97	1,302.20	2.38	546.82	1,082.13	0.00	12	9	0.00	100.00
105	Australia—Queensland	Mamu	1,211.90	1,211.90	47,864.82	16.65	2,874.45	0.00	0.00	12	0	154.21	0.00
106	Australia—Western Australia	Kariera	1,398.59	303.86	657.34	2.27	289.23	1,094.73	0.00	12	10	0.00	100.00
107	Australia—Queensland	Warunggu	1,206.87	1,144.95	47,746.43	18.25	2,615.68	61.92	0.00	12	0	103.45	25.00
108	Australia—Western Australia	Djaru	1,432.30	413.87	1,063.79	2.20	483.04	1,019.12	0.00	12	9	0.00	100.00
109	Australia—Northern Territory	Walbiri	1,419.12	334.50	756.27	2.23	339.23	1,084.62	0.00	12	10	0.00	100.00
110	Australia—Queensland	Ngatjan	1,061.83	1,061.83	44,229.26	19.16	2,308.07	0.00	0.00	12	0	112.08	0.00
111	Australia—Western Australia	Mardudjara	1,369.51	298.01	524.32	1.87	280.04	1,071.50	0.00	12	11	0.00	100.00
112	Australia—Western Australia	Ildawongga	1,331.81	317.08	468.23	1.51	310.41	1,014.73	0.00	12	11	0.00	100.00
113	Australia—Northern Territory	Pintubi	1,300.40	314.47	886.85	2.90	306.18	985.93	0.00	12	9	0.00	100.00
114	Australia—Queensland	Undanbi	1,012.21	982.93	14,698.17	7.24	2,030.41	29.28	0.00	12	0	43.65	16.67
115	Australia—Queensland	Jinibarra	1,013.01	983.17	14,695.53	7.23	2,031.27	29.84	0.00	12	0	43.73	16.67
116	Australia—Queensland	Karuwali	1,243.02	248.91	538.75	2.59	207.70	994.11	0.00	12	10	0.00	100.00
117	Australia—Northern Territory	Alyawara	1,261.29	300.30	850.55	23.00	283.64	960.98	0.00	12	9	0.00	100.00
118	Australia—Western Australia	Ngatatjara	1,215.88	244.47	644.52	3.20	201.58	971.41	0.00	12	9	0.00	100.00
119	Australia—New South Wales	Badjalang	1,017.25	877.98	12,888.24	7.66	1,683.40	139.27	0.00	12	0	25.70	41.67
120	Australia—Northern Territory	Pitjandjara	1,192.01	284.49	711.99	2.75	259.28	907.52	0.00	12	7	4.85	75.00
121	Australia—South Australia	Dieri	1,173.73	184.08	355.58	2.82	125.87	989.65	0.00	12	10	0.00	100.00
122	Australia—Northern Territory	Arenda (southern)	1,149.40	175.88	338.19	2.90	116.70	973.53	0.00	12	9	0.00	100.00
123	Australia—South Australia	Jankundjara	1,093.38	189.27	485.19	3.68	131.81	904.11	0.00	12	8	0.00	100.00
124	Australia—Northern Territory	Arenda (northern)	1,094.03	277.63	862.00	3.46	248.97	816.40	0.00	12	9	0.00	100.00
125	Australia—New South Wales	Ualaria	1,078.66	478.89	2915.04	4.74	615.44	599.77	0.00	12	5	15.64	66.67
126	Australia—Western Australia	Nakako	1,054.35	247.10	848.04	4.13	205.19	807.25	0.00	12	7	5.11	75.00
127	Australia—Western Australia	Ooldea	891.90	200.20	737.40	5.10	144.69	691.70	0.00	12	8	0.00	100.00
128	Australia—New South Wales	Barkindji	937.42	215.31	783.20	4.80	163.26	722.11	0.00	12	8	0.00	100.00
129	Australia—South Australia	Karuna	845.84	428.41	6,801.93	13.30	511.56	417.42	0.00	12	4	33.41	50.00
130	Australia—New South Wales	Wongaibon	941.58	406.42	2,808.65	5.99	468.70	535.16	0.00	12	4	17.25	58.33
131	Australia—South Australia	Jaralde	801.73	374.60	3,307.30	8.08	409.38	427.13	0.00	12	4	9.84	58.33
132	Australia—Western Australia	Mineng	759.21	550.68	17,590.48	22.67	776.07	208.52	0.00	12	2	53.40	33.33
133	Australia—Victoria	Tjapwurong	780.19	356.49	3,812.81	10.11	377.01	423.73	0.00	12	4	14.77	58.33
134	Australia—Victoria	Bunurong	721.54	596.51	14,340.08	16.18	886.20	125.03	0.00	12	0	50.57	25.00
135	Australia—Victoria	Kurnai	696.90	568.81	12,535.66	15.31	818.92	128.09	0.00	12	0	38.41	50.00
136	Tasmania	Tasmanians (eastern)	658.31	575.94	12,091.62	14.46	836.05	82.36	0.00	10	0	45.98	33.33
137	Tasmania	Tasmanians (western)	640.60	640.60	34,871.13	34.96	997.54	0.00	0.00	9	0	143.00	0.00
143	Mexico	Seri	1,350.78	306.23	644.35	2.20	292.99	1,044.54	0.00	12	8	0.85	100.00

144	California	Cahuilla	1,269.97	117.47	3.72	222.03	59.71	1,152.50	0.00	12	8	2.82	83.33
145	California	Cupeno	1,143.68	204.68	7.40	1,111.30	150.10	939.01	0.00	12	6	9.25	66.67
146	Mexico	Kiliwa	988.19	196.68	8.378	1,177.00	140.49	791.50	0.00	12	8	6.81	66.67
147	California	Diegueno	846.94	244.57	11.53	2,324.81	201.72	602.37	0.00	12	6	12.83	66.67
148	California	Lake Yokuts	983.44	174.83	9.63	1,112.48	115.54	808.61	0.00	12	6	12.51	58.33
149	California	Serrano	910.07	210.37	10.83	1,701.29	157.09	699.71	0.00	12	6	16.20	58.33
150	California	Luiseno	834.18	238.83	13.76	2,668.39	193.92	595.35	0.00	12	6	13.62	58.33
151	California	Wukchumi	9,30.61	321.43	23.64	7,506.25	317.52	609.17	0.00	11	5	74.36	45.45
152	California	Tubatulabal	955.62	255.22	7.64	1,653.91	216.51	700.40	0.00	11	5	30.09	63.64
153	California	Nomlaki	886.75	287.96	21.37	5,653.81	264.54	598.79	0.00	10	4	48.35	60.00
154	California	Northern Foothill Yokuts	845.91	284.43	19.86	5,146.86	259.19	561.48	0.00	10	5	53.23	50.00
155	California	Patwin	864.97	265.15	20.39	4,702.85	230.68	599.81	0.00	11	5	45.03	54.55
156	California	Gabrielino	765.42	295.72	20.28	5,606.47	276.48	469.70	0.00	12	5	36.96	50.00
157	California	Monache	876.96	201.91	6.45	946.14	146.74	675.05	0.00	9	5	22.08	77.78
158	California	Eastern Pomo	809.49	325.92	30.78	10,002.09	324.91	483.57	0.00	11	4	43.76	54.54
159	California	Clear-lake Pomo	792.10	335.97	33.46	11,433.60	341.71	456.13	0.00	11	4	48.68	45.45
160	California	Wintu	831.02	367.28	34.62	13,717.91	396.18	463.74	0.00	10	4	66.41	40.00
161	California	Chumash	736.85	332.06	13.48	4,518.86	335.14	404.79	0.00	12	5	40.37	50.00
162	California	Chimariko	810.88	452.79	68.18	38,231.51	560.78	358.09	0.00	9	3	97.51	44.44
163	California	Nisenan	793.75	320.47	42.38	13,389.29	315.94	473.28	0.00	10	4	49.49	50.00
164	California	Salinan	755.30	315.22	15.33	4,712.60	307.39	440.08	0.00	12	5	44.82	50.00
165	California	Pomo (southern)	767.47	346.78	32.02	11,534.93	360.15	420.69	0.00	12	4	47.95	41.67
166	California	Sinkyone	763.50	431.10	72.09	37,259.99	516.89	332.40	0.00	10	3	96.84	40.00
167	California	Lessik	754.31	371.67	45.21	18,266.87	404.08	382.64	0.00	9	3	72.02	44.44
168	California	Miwok (Coast)	731.93	377.74	26.98	11,200.64	415.09	354.19	0.00	12	3	62.73	41.67
169	California	Mattole	720.59	425.54	72.05	36,448.62	505.88	295.05	0.00	11	3	66.75	36.36
170	California	Miwok (Lake)	731.30	365.07	25.17	9,873.17	392.24	366.22	0.00	12	4	53.91	41.67
171	California	Yuki (Proper)	722.32	372.37	49.31	19,987.89	405.34	349.95	0.00	9	3	78.93	44.44
172	California	Wappo	727.19	349.13	32.23	11,741.79	364.21	378.06	0.00	12	4	47.85	41.67
173	California	Pomo (northern)	711.77	451.60	64.99	36,287.22	558.32	260.17	0.00	12	3	91.57	25.00
174	California	Yana	706.80	385.53	35.45	15,222.43	429.40	321.27	0.00	7	3	86.44	42.86
175	California	Miwok	696.01	364.98	35.77	14,023.43	392.08	331.02	0.00	8	3	75.91	50.00
176	California	Tekelma	706.56	345.62	33.66	12,055.83	358.16	360.93	0.00	8	3	62.86	50.00
177	California	Yuki (Coast)	700.29	464.55	61.66	36,077.82	585.15	235.75	0.00	11	3	90.75	27.27
178	California	Tolowa	695.74	482.68	57.72	35,994.43	623.55	213.06	0.00	9	2	100.93	33.33
179	California	Shasta	693.13	388.39	44.57	19,376.48	434.69	304.74	0.00	8	3	80.64	50.00
180	California	Hupa	670.54	447.34	64.63	35,519.58	549.61	223.20	0.00	8	3	94.91	37.50
181	Oregon	Tututni	671.63	521.60	50.11	35,541.01	709.22	150.03	0.00	9	1	110.75	33.33
182	California	Karok	654.65	453.80	62.53	35,193.32	562.86	200.85	0.00	7	2	101.30	42.86
183	California	Atsugewi	630.07	304.59	30.25	8,782.52	290.38	325.48	83.24	7	3	64.26	71.43
184	California	Wiyot	660.47	464.69	33.68	19,717.44	585.46	195.78	0.00	12	3	90.51	33.33
185	California	Maidu (Mountain)	591.07	257.65	30.60	6,729.62	219.94	333.42	166.67	6	3	73.34	83.33
186	California	Yurok	648.99	510.86	51.18	35,068.30	685.14	138.13	0.00	9	1	114.83	33.33
187	California	Achumawi	589.94	281.85	29.64	7,567.83	255.29	308.09	167.75	6	3	66.16	83.33
188	Oregon	Modoc	573.00	239.71	20.29	3,958.39	195.11	333.30	84.14	6	3	43.11	83.33

(continued)

T A B L E 4 . 0 7 (*continued*)

NO.	STATE	NAME	PET	AE	BIO5	BAR5	NAGP	WATD	SNOWAC	GROWC	WLTGRC	WATRET	DEFPER
189	Oregon	Klamath	518.50	302.28	15,322.20	53.44	286.73	216.22	285.29	5	2	83.25	60.00
190	Mexico	Guaicura	1,170.04	173.80	195.77	1.71	114.41	996.24	0.00	12	9	1.85	91.67
191	Mexico	Chichimec	973.32	653.53	3,788.91	3.67	1,031.20	319.79	0.00	12	3	17.89	66.67
192	California	Death Valley	1,395.53	87.06	68.18	1.88	36.32	1,308.47	0.00	12	8	3.14	83.33
193	Texas	Karankawa	1,173.22	821.01	10,689.81	7.09	1,505.97	352.21	0.00	12	1	32.93	50.00
194	Mexico	Coahuilenos	1,167.46	287.09	754.92	2.87	263.21	880.38	0.00	12	8	1.73	91.67
195	California	Panamintshoshoni	1,066.02	96.84	379.35	8.75	43.34	969.18	0.00	11	8	3.85	81.82
196	Arizona	Yavapai	993.38	297.83	2,434.57	8.70	279.76	695.55	0.00	10	6	15.23	80.00
197	California	Koso Mountain Shoshoni	961.24	122.05	774.54	12.17	63.63	839.20	0.00	10	6	8.25	80.00
198	Arizona	Walapai	889.57	268.85	2,168.30	9.19	236.04	620.72	0.00	10	6	18.24	70.00
199	California	Kawaiisushoshoni	879.37	160.17	1,368.73	13.70	99.91	719.20	0.00	9	6	14.36	88.89
200	California	Saline Valley Shoshoni	788.72	131.06	984.53	13.75	71.62	657.66	0.00	9	6	9.93	88.89
201	Colorado	Antarianunts Southern Paiute	811.54	248.81	1,434.38	6.91	207.56	562.72	11.46	8.	4	20.51	75.00
202	California	Owens Valley Paiute	731.87	128.91	1,091.25	15.66	69.67	602.96	0.00	7	6	11.76	100.00
203	Nevada	Kawich Mountain Shoshoni	722.02	183.84	1,921.01	15.29	125.60	538.17	0.00	7	6	15.09	85.71
204	Arizona	Kaibab Southern Paiute	714.31	225.47	3,252.46	18.45	176.24	488.85	32.17	7	5	19.30	85.71
205	California	Mono Lake Paiute	698.40	185.97	1,786.88	13.96	128.02	512.43	0.00	7	5	21.44	85.71
206	California	Deep Spring Paiute	698.61	131.37	1,053.53	14.65	71.90	567.24	24.28	7	6	11.66	100.00
207	Idaho	Salmon-eater Shoshoni	710.18	156.92	2,051.78	21.25	96.57	553.26	29.80	7	6	20.59	85.71
208	Nevada	Pyramid Lake Paiute	693.57	220.22	1,465.46	8.65	169.48	473.35	44.85	7	5	38.40	71.43
209	Utah	Ute-timanogas	692.44	336.91	5,959.34	17.36	343.30	355.53	118.99	7	3	60.19	71.43
210	Nevada	Cattail Paiute	687.49	176.58	1,044.20	8.89	117.46	510.92	28.23	7	5	20.57	85.71
211	Nevada	Fish Lake Paiute	665.98	126.55	681.13	10.08	67.57	539.42	16.63	7	6	7.33	85.71
212	California	Honey Lake Paiute	658.98	231.56	3,645.01	19.79	184.22	427.42	96.31	7	4	55.05	71.43
213	Utah	Hukunduka Shoshoni	677.65	257.16	5,240.48	23.90	219.25	420.49	89.13	7	4	28.34	85.71
214	Utah	Gosiute Shoshoni	652.89	171.08	1,988.45	17.84	111.46	481.81	36.87	7	5	15.37	85.71
215	Nevada	Spring Valley Shoshoni	602.03	225.11	4,384.23	24.94	175.78	376.92	60.51	6	4	23.80	100.00
216	Nevada	White Knife Shoshoni	613.01	194.71	3,770.34	27.29	138.16	418.30	80.93	6	4	24.51	100.00
217	Nevada	Rainroad Valley Shoshoni	615.38	181.73	3,202.16	25.99	123.21	433.65	54.09	6	4	21.50	100.00
218	Nevada	Reese River Shoshoni	589.79	199.29	4,777.80	33.27	143.60	390.50	83.14	6	4	26.14	83.33
219	California	North Fork Paiute	606.03	313.75	1,4123.51	46.30	305.02	292.28	0.00	6	3	75.96	66.67
221	Utah	Grouse Creek Shoshoni	614.08	170.68	2,700.44	24.32	111.03	443.40	54.55	6	4	20.76	100.00
222	Utah	Ute Wimonantci	622.97	246.55	4,396.30	21.50	204.44	376.42	66.28	7	3	23.24	85.71
223	Oregon	Bear Creek Paiute	617.45	315.44	4,696.67	15.26	307.75	302.01	27.73	7	3	44.24	57.14
224	Nevada	Antelope Valley Shoshoni	583.61	205.67	4,311.22	28.49	151.31	377.93	53.82	6	4	25.70	100.00
225	Nevada	Washo	595.14	190.71	4,482.79	33.58	133.48	404.43	81.83	6	4	37.84	100.00
226	Nevada	Suprise Valley Paiute	598.69	292.79	5,789.72	21.29	271.94	305.90	144.31	6	3	70.16	66.67
227	Wyoming	Wind River Shoshoni	619.76	268.13	4,814.55	20.49	235.00	351.63	65.70	6	3	29.16	83.33
228	Nevada	Ruby Valley Shoshoni	576.01	192.72	4,541.17	33.43	135.83	383.29	95.03	6	4	28.64	100.00
229	Idaho	Bohogue–Northern Shoshoni	601.46	217.20	3,523.25	21.27	165.65	384.26	67.40	6	4	30.98	83.33
230	Utah	Uintah-ute	609.95	217.80	3,107.02	18.67	166.40	392.16	57.62	7	4	28.42	85.71

No.	Name	State/Province											
231	Harney Valley Paiute	Oregon	558.33	273.32	4,464.95	18.40	242.59	285.01	88.43	6	3	58.51	66.67
232	Sheep-eater Shoshoni	Idaho	581.37	227.39	3,278.51	18.34	178.75	353.97	61.53	5	4	27.68	100.00
233	Little Smoky Shoshoni	Nevada	528.83	169.04	2,880.07	26.36	109.27	359.78	86.72	5	4	26.96	100.00
234	Uncompahgre Ute	Utah	468.34	384.62	8,781.20	20.53	427.72	83.71	175.84	4	0	75.87	75.00
240	Lipan Apache	Texas	1074.62	681.45	9,929.81	8.98	1,105.34	393.17	0.00	12	1	25.09	50.00
241	Comanche	Texas	989.59	515.77	4,101.51	5.89	696.11	473.83	0.00	10	4	21.47	60.00
242	Chiricahua Apache	Texas	867.93	415.08	2,645.77	5.45	485.39	452.86	0.00	10	4	22.21	70.00
243	Kiowa	Kansas	890.07	635.05	11,490.80	11.69	983.25	255.01	0.00	9	1	43.31	33.33
244	Kiowa Apache	Texas	827.15	542.61	7,083.70	9.35	757.26	284.54	11.79	7	2	31.43	57.14
245	Cheyenne	Colorado	681.55	395.81	6,532.32	14.56	448.56	285.74	30.35	7	1	19.18	71.43
246	Arapahoe	Colorado	678.91	455.76	7,277.78	12.84	566.90	223.15	30.18	7	1	26.78	57.14
248	Crow	Wyoming	634.00	273.34	4,536.61	18.70	242.63	360.55	56.58	6	3	21.44	83.33
249	Teton Lakota	South Dakota	619.71	384.96	6,870.95	16.04	428.34	234.75	61.80	6	1	31.66	83.33
250	Kutenai	Montana	575.21	408.15	8,364.15	17.68	473.18	166.46	99.58	5	1	64.64	60.00
252	Bannock	Idaho	578.20	202.85	3,168.93	21.43	147.88	375.35	82.21	5	4	34.55	80.00
253	Gros-Ventre	Montana	581.12	364.62	5,536.30	14.14	391.44	216.49	43.80	5	2	34.94	60.00
254	Plains Ojibwa	North Dakota	585.12	468.07	10,336.32	17.44	592.53	117.05	74.85	5	0	44.87	80.00
255	Peigan	Alberta	558.92	340.07	4,191.69	12.02	348.66	218.85	4.41	5	2	19.36	60.00
256	Blackfoot	Alberta	540.22	333.93	3,918.71	11.58	338.28	206.28	4.22	5	1	19.24	60.00
257	Assiniboine	Saskatchewan	533.90	407.71	6,207.44	13.17	471.17	126.19	6.54	5	0	27.59	60.00
258	Plains Cree	Saskatchewan	535.17	351.02	5,240.62	14.26	367.50	184.14	3.94	5	0	14.01	80.00
259	Blood	Alberta	527.64	419.27	6,371.04	12.91	493.56	108.37	4.02	5	0	23.27	60.00
260	Sarsi	Alberta	519.48	395.29	5,628.49	12.57	447.60	124.19	4.59	5	0	20.04	60.00
268	Squamish	British Columbia	667.78	466.94	18,563.15	31.45	590.17	200.84	0.00	7	2	93.80	42.86
269	Alsea	Oregon	657.66	487.32	35,257.78	55.65	633.54	170.34	0.00	7	1	97.19	42.86
270	Puyallup	Washington	656.29	527.50	23,858.77	33.02	722.59	128.79	0.00	7	1	112.08	42.86
271	Twana	Washington	659.23	518.36	35,290.62	50.28	701.91	140.87	0.00	7	1	108.33	42.86
272	Chehalis	Washington	650.61	527.84	35,104.62	48.53	723.36	122.76	0.00	7	1	106.92	42.86
273	Nootka	British Columbia	643.54	491.74	34,942.13	54.33	643.11	151.80	0.00	7	1	103.47	42.86
274	Chinook	Oregon	652.37	580.46	35,143.66	41.49	846.96	71.91	0.00	7	1	116.32	28.57
275	Coos	Oregon	652.04	547.70	35,136.31	45.69	769.09	104.34	0.00	10	1	114.20	30.00
276	Lillooet	British Columbia	651.04	314.07	6,819.72	22.32	305.53	336.98	88.90	7	3	71.81	57.14
277	Lummi	Washington	639.70	444.66	13,045.84	23.97	544.17	195.03	0.00	7	2	81.85	42.86
278	Quinault	Washington	634.97	610.67	34,729.48	37.69	921.38	24.30	0.00	7	0	123.61	14.29
279	Stalo	British Columbia	634.97	461.82	15,827.69	27.31	579.45	173.15	0.00	7	2	92.46	42.86
280	Cowichan	British Columbia	636.85	452.22	16,646.70	29.75	559.60	184.63	0.00	7	2	89.38	42.86
281	Tillamook	Oregon	637.58	546.50	34,796.22	45.41	766.29	91.09	0.00	8	0	16.67	25.00
282	Comox	British Columbia	609.40	451.51	33,945.90	60.82	558.14	157.90	0.00	6	0	12.65	66.67
283	Bella-bella	British Columbia	612.18	612.18	34,044.99	36.80	925.17	0.00	0.00	6	0	174.52	0.00
284	Quileute	Washington	622.60	618.41	34,383.32	36.55	940.84	4.19	0.00	6	0	141.92	14.29
285	Clallam	Washington	612.19	461.38	23,332.60	40.33	578.55	150.81	0.00	7	1	90.23	42.86
286	Makah	Washington	615.11	611.09	34,145.23	37.03	922.43	4.03	0.00	7	0	123.13	14.26
287	Haisla	British Columbia	574.00	574.00	32,220.84	38.76	831.37	0.00	825.90	5	0	174.52	0.00
288	Kwakiutl	British Columbia	602.51	576.30	33,681.48	40.24	836.90	26.21	0.00	6	0	117.15	16.67
289	Tsimshim	British Columbia	571.85	571.85	32,080.96	38.83	826.21	0.00	476.66	5	0	138.61	0.00

(continued)

NO.	STATE	NAME	PET	AE	BIO5	BAR5	NAGP	WATD	SNOWAC	GROWC	WLTGRC	WATRET	DEFPER
290	British Columbia	Haida	585.75	582.12	32,905.27	38.67	850.97	3.63	0.00	6	0	140.91	16.67
291	British Columbia	Bella-coola	547.97	547.97	30,164.86	39.19	769.72	0.00	390.74	5	0	148.89	0.00
292	Alaska	Tlingit	542.21	542.21	29,593.31	39.13	756.34	0.00	504.05	5	0	156.87	0.00
293	British Columbia	Gitksan	517.88	436.59	14,806.47	28.05	527.86	81.29	96.82	5	0	109.14	40.00
294	Alaska	Konaig	472.27	469.11	19,558.85	32.89	594.72	3.17	428.43	4	0	157.96	25.00
295	Alaska	Eyak	459.14	459.14	17,420.94	30.36	573.90	0.00	481.01	4	0	136.00	0.00
296	Alaska	Kuskowagmut	421.63	360.35	6,814.29	17.75	383.86	61.27	165.61	3	0	114.41	33.33
297	Alaska	Chugash	424.87	424.87	12,456.48	24.69	504.55	0.00	512.96	3	0	160.68	0.00
298	Alaska	Aleut	388.73	388.73	8,646.98	19.86	435.32	0.00	224.91	3	0	146.06	0.00
299	Alaska	Nunavak	333.35	299.74	2,503.76	8.86	282.74	33.61	127.25	2	0	91.24	50.00
315	Washington	Tenino	742.01	252.49	2,326.58	10.94	212.68	489.52	32.85	7	4	41.95	71.43
316	Washington	Umatilla	714.7	278.67	2,936.51	11.72	250.52	436.12	34.13	7	4	46.12	71.43
317	Washington	Wenatchi	700.55	263.52	4,984.83	21.83	228.33	437.02	182.56	7	4	76.91	71.43
318	Washington	Yakima	672.50	240.69	2,738.23	13.94	196.44	431.81	70.40	7	4	53.14	71.43
319	Washington	Wishram	670.14	311.77	7,618.60	25.24	301.82	358.37	64.18	7	3	81.63	71.43
320	Idaho	Coeur d'Alene	616.32	378.10	13,515.44	32.51	415.74	238.22	177.48	7	2	85.89	42.86
321	Washington	Sinkaietk	639.04	273.84	4,552.07	18.71	243.35	365.20	98.82	7	3	55.59	71.43
322	British Columbia	Okanogan	628.10	282.04	4,990.19	19.52	255.58	346.06	113.80	7	3	59.69	71.43
323	Washington	Sanpoil	618.76	266.11	5,690.89	24.52	232.06	352.65	120.09	7	4	53.92	71.43
324	Idaho	Nez-perce	571.40	424.26	11,373.33	22.60	503.35	147.14	133.270	6	1	92.90	50.00
325	British Columbia	Thompson	630.69	274.24	2,525.15	10.35	243.94	356.45	22.65	6	4	28.64	66.67
326	Idaho	Kalispel	573.12	371.57	15,294.97	37.89	403.90	201.54	196.73	5	2	90.71	60.00
327	Michigan	Ojibwa (Kitchibuan)	571.29	465.09	18,090.10	30.86	586.28	106.20	169.98	6	0	40.40	33.33
328	Wisconsin	Kitikitegon	562.02	556.64	21,718.49	27.49	790.04	5.39	141.45	5	0	46.55	20.00
329	New Brunswick	Micmac	533.22	451.45	17,980.64	32.22	558.01	81.78	123.63	5	0	42.83	40.00
330	Montana	Flathead	526.05	347.88	7,157.57	19.77	362.06	178.17	158.27	6	1	70.46	66.67
331	Ontario	Rainy River Ojibwa	546.08	475.93	14,256.87	23.40	609.14	70.15	89.18	5	0	31.96	60.00
332	Ontario	Northern Saulteaux	562.48	375.60	7,518.73	18.29	411.20	186.88	11.79	5	0	5.16	100.00
333	Alberta	Shuswap	545.89	416.93	9,302.59	19.02	488.99	128.96	73.54	5	0	55.97	60.00
334	Ontario	Pekangekum Ojibwa	525.27	385.78	8,500.37	19.78	429.85	139.49	8.58	5	0	12.72	60.00
335	Ontario	Round Lake Ojibwa	476.10	411.92	8,370.43	17.46	479.28	64.18	12.32	4	0	30.70	75.00
336	British Columbia	Alcatcho	506.92	374.75	11,669.18	28.48	409.66	132.17	224.70	5	1	99.57	60.00
337	Ontario	Nipigon Ojibwa	437.71	402.16	7,242.04	15.72	460.58	35.54	35.46	3	0	39.15	66.67
338	Quebec	Mistassini Cree	475.15	444.71	11,943.50	21.94	544.26	30.45	73.04	4	0	45.13	50.00
339	Ontario	Ojibwa (Northern Albany)	460.68	395.51	81,77.04	18.25	448.00	65.17	39.32	4	0	39.84	50.00
340	Quebec	Waswanip Cree	458.57	452.28	12,826.40	22.92	559.73	6.30	98.05	4	0	49.75	25.00
341	Ontario	Weagamon Ojibwa	444.97	388.95	6,377.49	14.64	435.73	56.03	16.04	4	0	24.21	50.00
342	Quebec	Montagnais	439.97	383.87	7,721.32	18.11	426.34	56.09	72.32	4	0	44.87	50.00
343	Alberta	Sekani	505.08	269.60	4,462.15	18.82	237.14	235.47	21.19	5	0	11.60	100.00
344	Alberta	Beaver	497.80	285.12	3,980.58	15.30	260.22	212.69	3.34	5	0	5.17	80.00
345	Northwest Territories	Slave	479.24	222.61	3,456.11	20.03	172.55	256.64	12.13	3	0	5.74	100.00

346	British Columbia	Kaska	489.39	333.50	12.22	4,124.34	337.55	155.89	10.37	5	0	10.93	100.00
347	British Columbia	Tahltan	501.12	320.20	13.98	4,410.89	315.50	180.92	32.53	5	0	36.48	80.00
348	British Columbia	Chilcotin	472.19	295.59	10.33	2,854.82	276.28	176.60	40.61	4	1	30.73	100.00
349	British Columbia	Carrier	471.88	256.12	11.33	2,466.40	217.78	215.76	6.13	5	1	6.91	80.00
350	Northwest Territories	Mountain	454.73	310.95	8.90	2,674.83	300.51	143.78	5.32	3	1	9.23	66.67
351	Yukon	Han	474.66	238.26	18.38	3,550.31	193.15	236.40	58.65	3	2	27.59	100.00
352	Northwest Territories	Hare	462.43	180.11	18.68	2,267.59	121.40	282.32	4.85	3	2	2.24	100.00
353	Ontario	Attawapiskat Cree	425.43	369.06	16.15	6,448.43	399.37	56.37	39.23	4	0	40.22	50.00
354	Alaska	Koyukon	464.50	269.04	20.75	4,902.67	236.32	195.46	111.01	3	1	42.84	100.00
355	Saskatchewan	Chippewyan	423.51	221.56	13.85	2,370.59	171.20	201.95	17.59	3	0	10.18	100.00
356	Yukon	Kutchin	439.68	183.05	13.54	1,688.05	124.70	256.63	6.94	3	1	5.59	100.00
357	Alaska	Ingalik	442.01	378.59	17.05	7,103.03	416.64	63.42	168.47	3	0	104.81	33.33
358	Northwest Territories	Satudene	445.62	173.35	16.97	1,933.35	113.92	272.27	8.16	3	2	4.35	100.00
359	Alaska	Nabesna	452.22	245.90	17.40	3,541.57	203.55	206.31	69.80	3	1	35.10	100.00
360	Quebec	Rupert House Cree	398.92	374.32	13.44	5,496.17	408.87	24.60	28.22	4	0	43.95	50.00
361	Northwest Territories	Dogrib	423.14	150.48	15.41	1,387.74	90.08	272.66	11.20	3	2	7.54	100.00
362	Alaska	Tanaina	454.50	389.03	18.31	7,980.49	435.88	65.47	143.55	4	0	103.35	75.00
363	Alaska	Tutchone	440.60	158.14	16.49	1,612.90	97.81	282.46	18.35	3	2	10.46	100.00
364	Alaska	Holikachuk	423.84	346.40	18.07	6,495.36	359.50	77.43	111.05	3	1	52.37	33.33
365	Quebec	Naskapi	340.29	291.85	8.91	2,415.18	270.50	48.44	56.13	2	0	34.48	100.00
369	Alaska	Norton Sound Inuit	426.32	275.06	22.88	5,609.51	245.16	151.25	183.77	3	1	50.18	66.67
370	Alaska	Kobuk Inuit	393.30	217.53	15.33	2,546.58	166.07	175.77	88.59	3	1	41.97	100.00
371	Alaska	Kotzebue Sound Inuit	331.57	221.60	8.67	1,484.89	171.26	109.97	78.91	2	1	39.02	100.00
372	Newfoundland	Labrador Inuit	342.46	287.11	9.66	2,542.70	263.25	55.35	53.86	2	0	35.05	100.00
373	Quebec	Great Whale Inuit	317.45	259.92	9.14	2,039.60	223.17	57.53	23.95	2	0	37.21	100.00
374	Northwest Territories	Caribou Inuit	281.18	150.52	8.04	724.73	90.12	130.66	13.36	2	1	12.21	100.00
375	Alaska	Noatak Inuit	305.56	189.26	9.75	1,285.11	131.80	116.30	88.56	2	1	49.07	100.00
377	Alaska	Nunamiut Inuit	284.45	178.63	9.32	1,115.98	119.74	105.82	92.13	1	0	60.71	100.00
378	Northwest Territories	Mackenzie Inuit	272.69	142.97	7.24	598.97	82.73	129.73	46.32	1	0	26.53	100.00
379	Alaska	Sivokamiut Inuit	290.37	201.77	10.33	1514.5825	146.58	88.59	132.81	2	0	49.30	100.00
380	Alaska	Point Hope Inuit	266.35	163.54	7.36	761.4264	103.42	102.81	60.98	1	0	34.34	100.00
381	Northwest Territories	Copper Inuit	223.71	95.44	5.92	250.4341	42.30	128.27	7.78	1	0	6.79	100.00
382	Northwest Territories	Utkuhikhalingmiut	198.52	106.86	5.20	265.2573	51.02	91.66	25.09	0	0	20.60	0.00
383	Northwest Territories	Aivilingmiut Inuit	207.22	114.51	5.55	317.7130	57.24	92.71	21.85	0	0	17.58	0.00
384	Northwest Territories	Ingulik Inuit	197.93	91.58	5.39	212.7756	39.50	106.35	20.46	0	0	16.53	0.00
385	Greenland	West Greenland	263.98	169.87	14.02	1544.5499	110.16	94.10	123.36	0	0	51.75	0.00
386	Northwest Territories	Baffin Island Inuit	188.58	117.73	4.48	268.4011	59.93	70.85	6.60	0	0	10.64	0.00
387	Northwest Territories	Netsilik Inuit	118.49	104.89	0.56	27.4751	49.48	13.61	4.77	0	0	7.69	0.00
388	Greenland	Angmakaslik	293.69	233.07	19.57	3644.7700	186.23	60.61	485.70	0	0	53.84	0.00
389	Alaska	Tareumiut Inuit	123.18	98.06	0.93	41.1707	44.25	25.12	59.20	0	0	40.33	0.00
390	Greenland	Polar Inuit	133.09	88.18	0.84	31.33	37.10	44.91	71.91	0	0	41.12	0.00

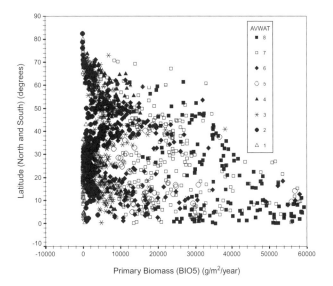

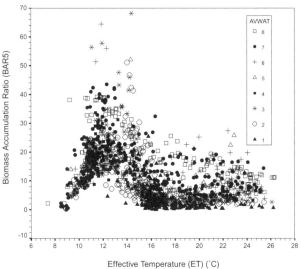

FIGURE 4.15

Demonstration of the property space defined by latitude and primary biomass as coded for available water (AVWAT), from the world weather station sample: (1) very dry, (2) dry, (3) moderately dry, (4) transitional dry, (5) transitional damp, (6) damp, (7) moist, and (8) wet.

FIGURE 4.16

Demonstration of the property space defined by the biomass accumulation ratio and effective temperature as coded for available water (AVWAT), from the world weather station sample: (1) very dry, (2) dry, (3) moderately dry, (4) transitional dry, (5) transitional damp, (6) damp, (7) moist, and (8) wet.

stations included in this study. It should be clear that at any latitude there is a range in BIO5 values, but the greatest variability occurs at the equator. Even though the range in variability decreases as latitude increases, it nevertheless remains wide until a latitude of approximately 60 degrees. The relationship between BIO5 and net aboveground productivity is conventionally summarized by the biomass accumulation ratio (BAR5), which is simply primary biomass (BIO) divided by net aboveground primary productivity (NAGP).

Figure 4.16 illustrates the distribution of the biomass accumulation ratio (BAR5), expressed with respect to effective temperature (ET). It should be clear that BAR5 is at its absolute maximum in boreal forests and in rare, slow-metabolism, temperate oak forests, while in tropical forests BAR5 is significantly below boreal and temperate oak forest levels. This range refers primarily to variation in metabolic rates in different plant communities.

Habitat Variability Described in Formal Terms

Thus far I have introduced a number of environmental variables that I suspect are particularly germane to understanding and modeling variability among plant communities in such basic conditions as biomass and productivity. I have discussed the earth's climatic variability and the impact of climatic dynamics on the biological domain considered exclusively in terms of plant abundance, but many important, qualitative differences between plant and animal communities have been temporarily ignored. Even though humans live in

a world of habitat variability that is structured in quantitative terms, more often than not we cognize the world around us in very different terms.

We perceive that boreal forests are different from deserts and that tropical rain forests have very little in common with southern pine forests. Our responses to these environmental differences are usually in terms of the impact they have on our sensory apparatus—on the signals we can receive with our eyes and ears and skin. In short, we tend to think of habitat variability in *formal* terms and to classify the differences we perceive in terms of a set of observed properties and characteristics. Very often, in daily living, our folk classifications of habitats begin with vegetation; the word "desert" evokes an image of a cactus and "forest" might bring to mind a giant redwood tree.

As an introduction to qualitative differences in habitat variability, I begin with the classification of the earth's plant formations initially summarized by Eyre (1968) and projected in his text onto world maps.[15] A few of the vegetational distinctions made by Eyre were merged into a classification by Strahler and Strahler (1984:420–40), and in most instances I have followed this simplified classification, augmented at the descriptive level by reference to Walter (1973).

According to Eyre, his classification represents "climatic climax," which means that empirical reports of vegetation have been smoothed and the earth is described as if there has been no destruction of vegetation by human beings and other agents. A further assumption is that climax vegetation is uniformly present, in contrast to the real-world situation, in which formations consist of a mix of different, successional stages as a result of intermittent, destructive events such as fires, volcanic eruptions, and the death of individual plants from natural causes. This is an appropriate assumption in light of the fact that hunter-gatherers are widely assumed to have rarely affected climax vegetation to the point that a habitat would consist solely of lower successional stages.[16]

Eyre's global classification identified thirty-one different types of vegetative communities. Strahler and Strahler reduced this number to twenty-eight types by eliminating separate categories for several formations, such as Scottish bog communities and Russian forest steppe zones. Using these two sources, I have identified the types of vegetation at each location in the hunter-gatherer data base and in the world sample of weather stations. This was difficult because the maps used by Eyre and Strahler and Strahler differed in scale—although all were relatively large-scale—and overlapped in complicated ways. Another problem was that while a longitude-latitude grid was superimposed on those portions of the maps representing bodies of water, it was omitted on all land surfaces, an omission that made the identification of specific locations very difficult.[17] The fact that the published maps appeared to be tracings from other, presumably more accurate, base maps was another complication in identifying vegetative formations for specific locations of relevance to this study.

Nevertheless, using both sets of maps (Eyre 1968: appendix I; Strahler and Strahler 1984:420–40), I was able to assign plant communities to specific formations using one or, in some cases, two different designations. The term VEGTAT applies to those locations that were clearly positioned well within the boundaries of a given vegetative formation, so any marginal inaccuracy in my estimate of longitude and latitude would not affect their assignment to a particular type of formation. In other cases in which the location of interest was very close to a boundary between vegetative types, a second identification, referred to as VEG, was also recorded. For example, it is not uncommon for montane forest zones to be surrounded by tropical rain forest formations.

If a particular weather station for which I knew the longitude and latitude *appeared* to be located on the montane forest side of a boundary between montane forest and tropical rain forest zones, I would give it a VEGTAT designation of *tropical montane forest* (FMT-6). To cope with the fact that I could not determine with complete confidence whether the weather station was actually on the tropical rain forest side of the boundary, I would also assign it the VEG designation of *tropical rain forest* (FE-1).

The type of vegetative formation (VEGTAT) was stipulated for each case in the ethnographic file of 339 hunter-gatherer groups, for all 103 cases in the animal field studies file, and for the world sample of 1,429 weather stations. All

of these, taken together, total 1,871 cases. It should be noted that although Eyre's classification of vegetative communities functioned as a Rosetta Stone by permitting me to link measured areas of the earth to properties of the earth's vegetation coded for each case in this study, its use represents a compromise. For instance, classificatory inconsistencies in Eyre's maps reflect his inclination to be a "lumper" in one instance and a "splitter" in another. Most of the classification is based on soil type rather than on specific climatic variables, and some groupings are not easily defended when compared with, for example, state-of-the-art empirical forest ordination studies such as those undertaken for the state of Wisconsin (Curtis 1959). For future researchers, a further problem with Eyre's classification is inaccessibility, although this is offset by the fact that the maps offer the correct cartographic projections and permit the accurate measurement of pertinent vegetative formations.

In this study, which uses climate as a frame of reference, one useful category refers to the Mediterranean environment, a set of meteorological dynamics characterized by long, hot, and very dry summers followed by warm, moist winters. Five geographically separate regions are included in this category: (1) large areas of California, (2) a section of the Chilean coast of South America, (3) southern portions of both Spain and Portugal as well as other coastal regions surrounding the Mediterranean Sea, (4) the southernmost tip of Africa, and (5) areas of southern Australia. Although these regions have very different species inventories, they share many features that are attributable to particular characteristics of the rainfall-to-temperature cycling. Eyre's classification accommodates this type of environmental setting very well and does not tie itself to particular plant species.

On the other hand, when distinguishing between plant formations that occur in very dry regions, in some instances Eyre appears to lump species in terms of rainfall and to ignore differences in potential evapotranspiration, but in other cases—such as the taxon *desert alternating with porcupine grass* (DSP-25)[18]—he defines the dry plant community in terms of particular sets of species. For example, the formation termed *boreal forest* (FBO-19) includes xerophytic, mesophytic, and hydrophytic species, whereas *taiga* formations are ordinated in terms of temperature differences, although this criterion is not specified in the classification. Eyre's propensity for lumping seems to account for the mixture of species included in the boreal forest class, the tropical rain forest category (FE-1), and all settings drier than the Mediterranean formation, with the exception of Australian formations.

My work with climatic variables suggested that I could produce a classification similar to Walter's taxonomy (1973) that would enhance the analysis and pattern recognition studies that I planned to undertake and could be assigned to cases through the use of climatic data. In a sense, I used Eyre's classification as a "seed" by converting it to an ordinal scale of increasing values of net aboveground productivity (NAGP) ranging from one to twenty-eight. The conversion made it possible to use the scale as the dependent variable in a discriminant function analysis, which confirmed that 56.32 percent of all the cases were correctly assigned to the same Eyre classes. Classes with the highest number of reassignments included most of the very dry settings and some of the highest-biomass regimes, such as tropical rain forests, tropical-subtropical monsoon forests, boreal forests, and the categories of tallgrass prairie and temperate deciduous forest.

The next step was to rerun the discriminant function analysis using the results of the initial analysis, which produced an 89.99 percent fit between the first derivative classification and the results of the second run. This same procedure was repeated for twenty iterations, at which point there was a 100 percent fit between the last classification and the results of the previously iterated classification. This result seemed to be the best operational classification to use once I had discussed the problem of sampling weather stations and hunter-gatherer cases in numbers proportional to the areas covered by the vegetative classes of the Eyre classification (see table 4.06).

As a result of the discriminant functions analysis, I made one change in the Eyre classification. It was clear that the class called *alpine tundra* (TA-26) was a nonclass, vegetationally speaking, because a number of cases originally assigned to the *boreal forest* (FBO-19) class had been lumped into it, at the same time that most of the taxon's original cases were assigned elsewhere. It appeared that the classificational criteria of temperature and moisture were responsible for the reassignments and that the new locations in the restructured class—termed *dry boreal parkland* (BPK-23)—were colder than the classic boreal forest but not as cold as those of the boreal larch forests of Siberian Russia.

Some of the reclassified locations are characterized by microhabitat clusters of dwarf and scrub boreal species and by stands of willows in stream beds, with tundra interspersed between the patches of taller vegetation. These were the driest cases in the boreal forest category and comprised the xerophytic segment of the lumped boreal forest class, which also had the lowest primary biomass and production.

It is likely that the original Eyre category would have remained intact if weather station data from Tibet and the nearby Asian highlands had been available and there had been a larger sample of Andean stations. At the time that I and my graduate assistants were working with Eyre's maps,[19] we also used a polar planimeter to measure the area covered by different types of plant formations on Eyre's equal area projection (homolographic) biogeographic maps. These measurements provided the data on the total area covered by various plant communities that are presented in table 4.08 and that were used to calculate the percentage of the earth's total land area covered by different types of vegetative com-

munities summarized in that table. Table 4.08 also summarizes the mean values for those climatic variables that vary in informative ways among the vegetative types.

VIEWING VARIABLES AND FORMAL CLASSES IN PROPERTY AND GEOGRAPHIC SPACE

The linkage between climatic variables, vegetative types, and the areal distributions of plant communities, summarized in table 4.08, provides a currency for discussing differences in the geographic distribution of living systems, regardless of whether they are composed of nonhuman animal species or hunter-gatherers. With the definition of that currency, all of the germane environmental variables that can be isolated without reference to properties specific to human foragers and their niches have now been briefly presented in this chapter. The analytical utility of property space plots has also been suggested, but geographic space itself has been referred to only in terms of longitude and latitude.

This narrow focus on spatial coordinates is replaced in figure 4.17 by a global perspective in a map of the world on which the distribution of the 1,429 weather stations included in this study is represented. In this sample, the number of weather stations in each vegetational formation is proportional to the percentage of the world's area that is characterized by each formation. Several features of the sample become apparent when their distribution is examined.

First, the map's mercator projection produces a reduction in the density of sites in the polar areas of the world. Second, there are obvious blank spaces or holes in the distribution, such as in western China and Tibet, for which no weather station data were available. There are also very few stations in truly desertic regions, and those that are present frequently do not report time-transgressive data on temperature. Similarly, holes in the distribution of stations occur in tropical rain forests as well as tropical savanna woodlands, not necessarily because of a lack of coverage but, more frequently, because stations in equatorial regions often fail to report temperature data.

Because a goal of the study was to make the number of stations in a particular environmental zone correspond to the percentage that each zone represents of the world's total area, one strategy for coping with a lack of representation was to exclude regions such as western China and Tibet from the world's total area. Approximately one-third of the world's desertic areas were also excluded because weather station data were not available for those locations.

The symbol code in figure 4.17 represents generic groupings of the twenty-eight different types of vegetative communities that are identified and described in table 4.08. These and other plant associations form a consistent geographic pattern and provide clues to the types of climate and

I. Water-stressed communities: 36.12 percent of the earth's area

D-28   *Desert.* Usually located between 18 and 28 degrees latitude with a mean of 26.44 degrees, which places them at the upper extreme of the tropical vegetation zone. The wettest month is in autumn (RRCORR2 = 8.04 ± 2.86 months). The growing season is 11.54 months ± 1.34 months.

DSS-22   *Subtropical semidesert scrub.* This formation represents 13.48 percent of the earth's vegetative surface (164,204.86 units of 100 square kilometers). It occurs in North Africa, Australia, the southwestern United States, northern Mexico, and Afghanistan. This is the most common plant formation on earth in terms of areal extent. Succulent plants are prevalent, spacing between plants is considerable, and plant height is limited. Plants have very superficial roots. Grasses are generally rare or absent. In the New World, cactus may be an important subsistence resource. In terms of rainfall, this is a transitional formation that is somewhat wetter than a true desert. Mean annual rainfall is 242.22 mm ± 252.07 mm. Transitional zones of this type usually occur at a mean latitude of 27.12 degrees ± 6.97 degrees. As in true deserts, rainfall occurs primarily in autumn (RRCORR2 = 7.05 ± 2.52 months). This formation supports more potential prey animals in the ungulate class than does a true desert. Formations have essentially a twelve-month growing season (GROWC = 11.61 months).

DSP-25   *Desert alternating with porcupine grass semidesert.* This formation represents 0.82 percent of the earth's vegetative surface (9,994.90 units of 100 square kilometers). It occurs primarily in Australia. Australia's faunal and floral species differ considerably from species at many other places on earth. Spinifex (neither a shrub nor a succulent) is dominant in this formation in the niche that shrubs and succulents might be expected to occupy. Mean annual rainfall averages just under nine inches (227 mm ± 61.65 mm). This formation is centered on 26.09 degrees latitude ± 2.78 degrees, which places it largely in the tropical-subtropical climatic zones. The wettest month is usually during the summer (RRCORR2 = 5.3 ± 0.895 months). Expected prey values for this formation are much lower than in the DSS-27 formation. There is essentially a twelve-month growing season (mean = 11.93 months).

DSD-24   *Midlatitude semidesert scrub and woodland.* This formation represents 2.40 percent of the earth's vegetative surface (29,216.23 units of 100 square kilometers). It occurs primarily in North America, Asia, and Patagonia. Rainfall averages just slightly more than in the porcupine grass semidesert zone. Mean latitude for the occurrence of this formation is approximately 39.7 degrees ± 7.32 degrees. The wettest month occurs at the end of summer and the beginning of autumn, although there is a wide range of variability (mean RRCORR2 = 6.75 ± 3.76 months). Of the world's classic dry environments, this zone has the shortest average growing season (7.53 months).

DTG-19   *Lower tropical thorntree-desert grass savanna.* This formation represents 3.86 percent of the earth's vegetative surface (47,024.16 units of 100 square kilometers). It occurs primarily in Australia, Africa, and Patagonia. Annual rainfall averages almost fourteen inches (342.0 mm ± 207 mm). This is the driest formation to occur in true tropical areas. Formations occur at 18.27 degrees latitude ± 8.97 degrees. This formation is never transitional to desert or semidesert; it is simply the driest tropical zone, which, with increased rainfall, grades into more woody savanna and forest. Maximum rainfall follows the warmest month by about 1.77 months (RRCORR2 = 6.50 ± 2.21 months). Potential prey animals may be abundant in this formation, with an average expected value of 1,518 kilograms per square kilometer. Most documented locations have a twelve-month growing season (average = 11.87 months).

DTW-11   *Upper tropical thorn forest and thorn woodland.* This formation represents 3.74 percent of the earth's vegetative surface (45,564.13 units of 100 square kilometers). It may be transitional to forest formation. It occurs primarily in Brazil, Bolivia, Australia, and the west coast of Mesoamerica. Rainfall averages 22.72 inches (577.16 mm ± 332.9 mm). Formations are found on average at 24.19 degrees latitude ± 7.36 degrees. Maximum rainfall occurs in late summer, following the warmest month by about 1.5 months (RRCORR2 = 6.14 ± 1.82 months). Expected prey is 662.33 kilograms per square kilometer. The growing season is just slightly short of twelve months (GROWC = 11.94 months).

GS-18   *Midlatitude short grass prairie.* This formation represents 6.12 percent of the earth's vegetative surface (74,498.34 units of 100 square kilometers. This formation centers on 43.32 degrees latitude ± 6.45 degrees. Mean value for rainfall is 16.98 inches (431.49 mm ± 177.9 mm). This formation may grade between semidesertic formations (DSD) and tall grass prairie (GP), which in turn grades into midlatitude steppe-forest savannalike formations. In these latitudes transitional savanna zones are generally less extensive than in tropical and equatorial zones. Maximum rainfall follows the warmest month (RRCORR2 = 5.73 ± 3.29 months). Expected prey equals 6,686.73 kilograms per square kilometer. The growing season is the shortest of all dry environments thus far discussed (GROWC = 6.94 months).

II. Water-graded biomes transitional to forests: 12.92 percent of the earth's area
A. Savanna biome: 9.05 percent of the earth's area

SSA-15   *Upper subtropical Australian sclerophyllous tree savanna.* This formation represents 0.40 percent of the earth's vegetative surface (4,866.84 units of 100 square kilometers). Mean annual rainfall is 433.79 mm ± 111.05 mm. Formations occur on average at 33.00 degrees latitude, ± 2.46 degrees. Maximum rainfall occurs in early autumn (RRCORR2 = 7.78 ± 3.09 months). The growing season is twelve months long. Expected prey equals 831.72 kilograms per square kilometers.

(continued)

TABLE 4.08 (*continued*)

STG-7   *Tropical thorntree-tallgrass savanna.* This formation represents 5.93 percent of the earth's vegetative surface (72,231.63 units of 100 square kilometers). It occurs primarily in Africa and Asia. A savanna is a grassland with more-or-less evenly spaced woody plants or trees. This formation may grade into grassland or into the savanna-woodland zone in which trees are more prevalent than grassland. Annual rainfall is on average 795.52 mm ± 335.15 mm. Locations are centered on 16.16 degrees latitude but range between 23.22 and 9.1 degrees. This formation tends to grade into more open grasslands or, more commonly, tropical monsoon forests. Maximum rainfall follows the warmest month by 2.39 months and occurs in autumn. In this classic African savanna the mean value for expected prey is 4,212.78 kilograms per square kilometer, making it the highest mean value of any plant community. There is a twelve-month growing season with a standard deviation of 0.00.

SW-2   *Upper equatorial savanna-woodland/broadleaf tree savanna.* This formation represents 2.72 percent of the earth's vegetative surface (33,181.75 units of 100 square kilometers). It occurs primarily in Africa, Asia, and South America. The mean annual rainfall is 61.5 inches (1,563.74 mm ± 559.77 mm). Formations are centered on 9.71 degrees latitude ± 6.23 degrees. This formation grades to damp forest and can include some dry equatorial forests with a closed canopy and patches of grassy understory. Maximum rainfall follows the warmest month by 2.84 months, making this technically winter rainfall. There is, however, a twelve-month growing season. Expected prey is 1,813.9 kilograms ± 2,044 kilograms per square kilometer.

B. Sclerophyllous (thick- or hard-leafed plants) biome: 2.52 percent of the earth's area

FSS-23   *Upper subtropical sclerophyllous scrub-dwarf forest.* This formation represents 1.40 percent of the earth's vegetative surface (17,106.47 units of 100 square kilometers). It is a chaparral formation that may be transitional to desert formations. Mean annual rainfall is 543.10 mm ± 241.76 mm. This value overlaps that for the subtropical savanna, but this formation is also heavily conditioned by predominantly late fall–early winter rainfall (RRCORR2 = 9.08 ± 2.04 months). Formations are centered on 33.21 degrees latitude ± 7.99 degrees. Expected prey values are 176.45 kilograms ± 187.81 kilograms per square kilometer. On average the growing season is 11.38 months ± 1.55 months.

FSA-10   *Lower midlatitude Australian sclerophyll scrub forest.* This formation represents 0.28 percent of the earth's vegetative surface (3,389.40 units of 100 square kilometers). Mean annual rainfall averages 726.03 ± 92.95 mm. Formations are found primarily between 31.6 and 40.81 degrees latitude. This formation is conditioned by predominantly early winter rainfall (RRCORR2 = 7.32 ± 3.61 months). The average growing season is 11.40 months ± 1.34 months. Expected prey is 1,499.83 kilograms ± 1,597.21 kilograms per square kilometer. This formation is one of the most variable with regard to ungulate abundance.

FSM-16   *Midlatitude Mediterranean evergreen mixed forest.* This formation represents over 0.84 percent of the earth's vegetative surface (10,250.62 units of 100 square kilometers). It includes the cedar forests of North Africa and Lebanon. Mean annual rainfall averages 724.78 mm ± 264.43 mm. Formations are centered on 39.35 degrees latitude ± 3.06 degrees. This formation is heavily conditioned by predominantly winter rainfall (RRCORR2 = 7.80 ± 2.59 months). The average growing season is 10.28 months ± 2.19 months. Expected prey is 327.86 kilograms ± 200.08 kilograms per square kilometer.

C. Grass-parkland transitional biome: 1.35 percent of the earth's area

GP-8   *Tall grass prairie-forest steppe.* This formation represents 1.35 percent of the earth's vegetative surface (16,494.76 units of 100 square kilometers). It includes the pampa of Argentina, the eastern prairie of the United States, and the moist prairie of Poland. It also includes so-called forest-steppe or the transition from deciduous forest to more water-stressed formations. Mean annual rainfall is 717.07 mm ± 257.12 mm. Formations are centered on 40.29 degrees latitude ± 6.35 degrees. Rainfall occurs predominantly in midsummer (RRCORR2 = 4.39 ± 2.55 months). The growing season averages 7.95 ± 2.21 months. Expected prey is 1,098.82 kilograms ± 630.73 kilograms per square kilometer.

III. *Water-abundant biomes: 45.82 percent of the earth's area*

A. Forests of the equatorial, tropical, and subtropical zones: 20.09 percent of the earth's area

FE-1   *Equatorial and tropical rain forests (broadleaf evergreen forests).* This formation represents 7.72 percent of the earth's vegetative surface (93,998.97 units of 100 square kilometers). It occurs in Asia, South America, and Africa. Mean annual rainfall averages 2,499.53 mm (98.4 inches) ± 1,281.88 mm. Formations are centered on 9.30 degrees latitude ± 6.95 degrees. Most rainfall occurs in autumn (RRCORR2 = 7.64 ± 2.91 months). There is nearly a full twelve-month growing season. Expected prey is 352.18 kilograms ± 565.42 kilograms per square kilometer.

FMT-6   *Tropical montane forest (may also include some conifers).* This formation represents 2.22 percent of the earth's vegetative surface (27,056.56 units of 100 square kilometers). It occurs in Asia, South America, and Africa. Mean annual rainfall is 1,314.58 mm ± 801.86 mm. Formations are centered on 12.04 degrees latitude ± 9.23 degrees. Rainfall is predominantly in early autumn (RRCORR2 = 6.53 ± 2.46 months). Expected prey equals 2,386.10 kilograms ± 2,179.92 kilograms per square kilometer. The growing season is twelve months ± 0.00 months. This formation tends to grade into classic thorntree savanna (STG).

FMO-3   *Monsoon (raingreen) forest (tropical deciduous forest).* This formation represents 7.27 percent of the earth's vegetative surface (88,514.40 units of 100 square kilometers). It occurs primarily in Africa, Asia, and Australia. Mean annual rainfall is 1,509.27 mm (59.42 inches) ± 694.40 mm. Rainfall occurs predominantly in autumn (RRCORR2 = 7.11 ± 2.00 months). There is a full twelve-month growing season. Expected prey equals 1,358.44 kilograms ± 2,054.15 kilograms per square kilometer.

FBE-4   *Subtropical broadleaf evergreen forest (laurel forest that may include needle-leaf trees).* This formation represents 2.88 percent of the earth's vegetative surface (35,127.82 units of 100 square kilometers). Mean annual rainfall averages 1,428 mm (56.22 inches) ± 597 mm. Formations occur at 30.12 degrees latitude ± 6.4 degrees. Rainfall occurs predominantly in late summer (RRCORR2 = 5.03 ± 2.13 months). The growing season is 10.68 months ± 1.73 months. Expected prey equals 648.52 kilograms ± 698.75 kilograms per square kilometer.

     B. Forests of the midlatitude and subarctic zones: 25.73 percent of the earth's area

FD-10   *Midlatitude deciduous (summergreen) forest.* This formation represents 3.30 percent of the earth's vegetative surface (40,204 18 units of 100 square kilometers). It occurs primarily in eastern Europe, the eastern United States, western Europe, China, and Korea. Mean annual rainfall averages 959.53 mm (37.77 inches) ± 481 mm. Formations cluster around 44.04 degrees latitude ± 7.96 degrees. Rainfall occurs primarily in late summer (RRCORR2 = 5.61 ± 2.66 months). The growing season averages 6.87 months ± 1.72 months. Expected prey averages 543.17 kilograms ± 520.18 kilograms per square kilometer.

FC-11   *Coastal forests (largely needle-leaf evergreen forests).* This formation represents 0.36 percent of the earth's vegetative surface (4,441.07 units of 100 square kilometers). It is common on the northwest coast of North America but also occurs on the west coast of Chile. Mean annual rainfall averages 2,022.43 mm (79.62 inches) ± 898.03 mm. Formations are localized around 47.9 degrees latitude ± 7.31 degrees. Winter rainfall predominates (RRCORR2 = 9.43 ± 2.14 months). The growing season is on average 6.16 months ± 2.14 months. Expected prey is 265.45 kilograms ± 457.56 kilograms per square kilometer.

FL-14   *Lake forest.* This formation represents 0.26 percent of the earth's vegetative surface (3,110.67 units of 100 square kilometers). It is most common in the Great Lakes area of North America. It is largely a needle-leaf forest. Average mean annual rainfall is 660.59 mm (26.0 inches) ± 130.9 mm. Formations are localized around 47.50 degrees latitude ± 2.08 degrees. It is characterized by predominantly summer rainfall (RRCORR2 = 4.21 ± 0.58 months). The growing season averages 5.25 months ± .50 months. Expected prey equals 197.01 kilograms ± 191.31 kilograms per square kilometer.

FSP-5   *Southern pine forest* (and other small analogous communities). This formation represents 0.42 percent of the earth's vegetative surface (5,092.83 units of 100 square kilometers). It occurs as a major formation exclusively in the southeastern United States. Mean annual rainfall is 1,172.36 mm (46.16 inches) ± 478.9 mm. Formations are localized around 31.45 degrees latitude ± 2.83 degrees. Rainfall occurs predominantly in late summer-autumn (RRCORR2 = 8.37 ± 4.17 months). The growing season averages 11.71 months ± 0.75 months. Expected prey equals 495.66 kilograms ± 343.60 kilograms per square kilometer.

FBD-12   *Mixed boreal and deciduous forest.* This formation represents 2.51 percent of the earth's vegetative surface (30,588.25 units of 100 square kilometers). It occurs primarily in northern Europe and Asia as well as northern North America. Mean annual rainfall averages 1,013.92 mm (39.91 inches) ± 659.8 mm. Formations are localized around 45.86 degrees latitude ± 4.84 degrees. Rainfall is predominantly in late summer-early autumn (RRCORR2 = 5.46 ± 2.08 months). The growing season averages 6.00 months ± 1.48 months. Expected prey equals 644.54 kilograms ± 760.51 kilograms per square kilometer.

FBO-19   *Boreal forest.* This formation represents 10.26 percent of the earth's vegetative surface (124,959.23 units of 100 square kilometers). It is largely a needle-leaf evergreen forest occurring across North America northern Europe, and Asia. North American and Asian boreal forests tend to have somewhat greater species diversity than European forests. Mean annual rainfall is 517.93 mm (20.39 inches) ± 306 mm. Formations are localized around 55.01 degrees latitude ± 8.21 degrees. Rainfall occurs predominantly in late summer (RRCORR2 = 5.37 ± 1.62 months). The growing season averages 4.22 months ± 1.52 months. Expected prey equals 265.55 kilograms ± 397.98 kilograms per square kilometer.

FBL-21   *Boreal forest dominated by deciduous larch-aspen.* This formation represents 4.44 percent of the earth's vegetative surface (54,058.95 units of 100 square kilometers). It is most common in northern Asia and occurs in regions with little soil development above permafrost layers. Because trees tend to have shallow roots, tall conifers are generally absent. These conditions are reflected in low values for primary biomass (BIO5 = 3,894.57 grams ± 2,285.56 grams per square meter). Mean annual rainfall averages 345.73 mm (13.61 inches) ± 192.8 mm. Formations are located at 58.40 degrees latitude ± 7.16 degrees. Predominantly summer rainfall occurs (RRCORR2 = 4.88 ± 0.47 months). The growing season averages 3.0 months ± .56 months. Expected prey equals 384.26 kilograms ± 790.69 kilograms per square kilometer.

BPK-22   *Moderately dry boreal parkland.* This formation was not developed by Eyre or discussed by Strahler and Strahler (1984). It occurs in well-drained locations or locations with some water deficit during the growing season, in regions otherwise having boreal forest characteristics. Many cases classified by Eyre as "TA" belong in this category because they are well drained. Many other cases are ecologically similar in terms of rainfall deficit but these occur at lower elevations. This is essentially a dry transition to tundra. This formation is concentrated around 61.13 degrees latitude ± 4.88 degrees. It has roughly half the mean annual rainfall of the classic boreal forest (229.71 mm ± 73.39 mm). Rainfall tends to occur in midsummer (RRCORR2 = 4.74 ± 0.63 months) and the growing season averages 3.60 months ± 0.96 months. Expected prey averages 65.40 kilograms ± 72.91 kilograms per square kilometer.

     IV. Tundra biome: 8.30 percent of the earth's area

T-26   *Polar tundra.* This formation represents 4.12 percent of the earth's vegetative surface (50,242.10 units of 100 square kilometers). Mean annual rainfall averages 233.21 mm (9.17 inches) ± 185 mm. Formations occur near the Arctic Ocean at 69.05 degrees latitude ± 4.81 degrees. Rainfall occurs primarily in late summer (RRCORR2 = 5.41 ± 0.90 months). The growing season averages less than one month (0.98 ± 1.16 months). Expected prey equals 24.76 kilograms ± 36.72 kilograms per square kilometer.

(continued)

TABLE 4.08 *(continued)*

TA-21   *Alpine tundra and boreal forest.* This formation represents 5.18 percent of the earth's vegetative surface (63,050.04 units of 100 square kilometers). The largest areas are in Tibet and parts of central Asia, as well as in the Andes and the northern Rocky Mountains of Alaska and western Canada. Mean annual rainfall averages 210.57 mm (8.29 inches) ± 135 mm. Formations are localized around 42 degrees latitude, but variability measures ± 11.95 degrees. Rainfall occurs primarily in late summer (RRCORR2 = 5.96 ± 2.17 months). Expected prey is 1.62 kilograms per square kilometer. This taxon was originally called "Alpine tundra (includes boreal forest)" but did not hold up as a type of vegetation when climatic variables were used in analysis. For instance, the largest area assigned to this classification is in the Himalayas, centered in Tibet. No weather station data were available for this region, but examination of many photographs indicates that the vegetation grades to what is called "DSD" in this classification and bears little resemblance to arctic tundra. Another area demonstrated no internal consistency in terms of climatic parameters, and for these reasons this remains a nonuseful category.

the ranges of values that are likely to occur at different places in geographic space. Graph A in figure 4.18, on the other hand, illustrates differences in property space between two of the basic vegetative groupings—moderate- to high-biomass forest (TF) and savanna communities. Differences in the annual variability in rainfall are dramatically illustrated by a comparison of the water-starved savanna (graph A) and grassland plant communities plotted in figure 4.18 (graph B) with two different kinds of forest communities—high-

biomass tropical and midlatitude—in the same property space in graphs A and B.

PLANTS TO ANIMALS: ESTIMATING SECONDARY BIOMASS

Having developed techniques for monitoring and ways of understanding global variability in both climate and vege-

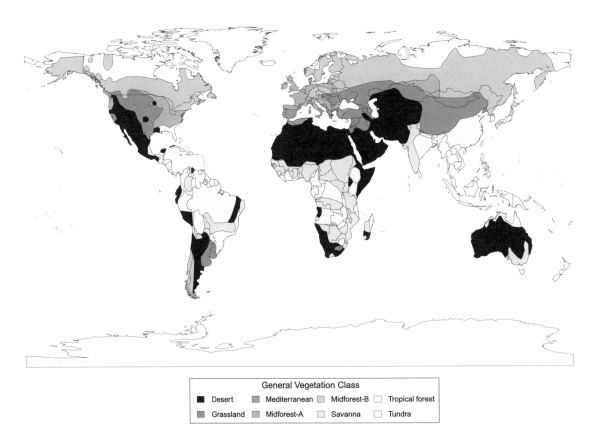

General Vegetation Class

■ Desert   ▨ Mediterranean   ▨ Midforest-B   □ Tropical forest
▨ Grassland   ▨ Midforest-A   ▨ Savanna   □ Tundra

FIGURE 4.17

World map with zones defined by large-scale plant formations according to the world weather station sample.

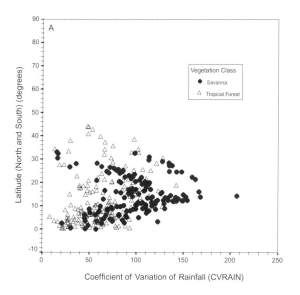
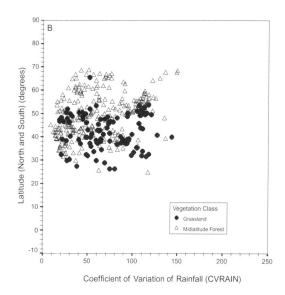

FIGURE 4.18

Comparative distributions of two major plant associations from the world weather station sample—savanna and tropical forest (A) and grassland and midlatitude forest (B)—illustrating their different locations in the property space of latitude and the coefficient of variation for rainfall.

tation, I now turn to a consideration of the nonhuman animal species with whom humans share a dependence, either direct or indirect, on the earth's plant producers. The term *hunter-gatherer* acknowledges that—although it is variable from place to place—a substantial proportion of the human diet come from the animal kingdom. This generalization imposes on us the necessity of investigating the ways in which animal species vary in both abundance and distribution among the world's many different types of plant communities. Any rigorous investigation of human dependence on animal food resources must begin, therefore, with the accumulation of data documenting the distribution of animal species, which in this analysis are referred to collectively as *secondary biomass.*

I had expected that the literature focusing on community ecology would include detailed faunal analyses of various ecological settings, but I discovered, unfortunately, that complete tabulations of all of the animal species at a given location were extremely rare. Studies of secondary biomass are available, but, more often than not, they have recorded the number of individuals in only a single species such as mule deer or moose. My survey of the literature on animal biomass has also revealed that although many studies are available from all parts of the world, they are not all equally reliable. Another unwelcome discovery was that most long-term studies have focused on the animal species found in tropical savanna settings. It seemed that if I wanted cases from the full range of the earth's climatic and biotic zones, I would have to accept studies that focused on only a few species.

After a very informative conference with John Eisenberg,[20] I settled on an approach that used data from two different kinds of biomass studies. In environments in which ungulates of moderate body size are represented by one or at most two species, I have used combinations of single-species studies. On the other hand, in environments characterized by the presence of many different species, I have relied on community studies. Since settings with multiple species are more frequently located in the tropics and subtropics, it is not surprising that most community studies have, in fact, been carried out in these settings.

The term *ungulates of moderate body size* refers to animals that are equal to or larger in size than an impala or pronghorn antelope and that range up to and include a giraffe. Large herbivores such as elephants were excluded from consideration because their numbers are so variable from study area to study area. This variation is primarily due to the effects of poaching, at one extreme, as well as to the negative effects of habitat destruction on confined populations at reserves, such as Amboseli in Kenya, and to species proliferation at other localities. When the data on elephant and hippopotamus were removed from community ecology biomass estimates, secondary biomass values varied convincingly with climatic variables.

Table 4.09 lists the 107 localities—spanning the earth's major biotic communities—for which studies documenting variability in ungulates of moderate body size were available. In addition to providing bibliographic citations for the species data for each locality, it lists values for two variables for each case: BIOMASS, which is the total value of all

TABLE 4.09
A GLOBAL SAMPLE OF ANIMAL BIOMASS VARIABILITY
FOR UNGULATES OF MODERATE BODY SIZE

GROUP NO.	STATE	NAME	BIOMASS	BIOSMALL	EXPREY	REFERENCE(S)
1	Sri Lanka	Wilpattu	766	330	398.32	Eisenberg and Seidensticker 1976; McKay and Eisenberg 1974
2	Sri Lanka	Gal Oya	886	458	662.80	Eisenberg and Seidensticker 1976; McKay and Eisenberg 1974
3	Java	Udjung Kulon	492	492	406.36	Hougerwerf 1970; McKay and Eisenberg 1974
4	India	Gir	6,800	6,800	410.01	Eisenberg and Seidensticker 1976; Schaller 1967
5	India	Kanha	2,437	2,437	748.12	Eisenberg and Seidensticker 1976; Schaller 1967
6	India	Jaldapura	984	600	339.35	Eisenberg and Seidensticker 1976; Schaller 1967
7	India	Bharatpur	4,160	1,617	474.61	Eisenberg and Seidensticker 1976; Schaller 1967
8	India	Kazaranga	2,058	900	386.69	Eisenberg and Seidensticker 1976; Schaller 1967; Spillett 1967
9	Nepal	Royal Chitawan	5,370	1,790	1,245.98	Eisenberg and Seidensticker 1976; Schaller 1967
10	Panama	Barro Colorado	542	169	222.14	Eisenberg 1980; Eisenberg and Thorington 1973
11	Venezuela	Calabozo	8,684	3,654	2,303.81	Eisenberg et al. 1979
12	Venezuela	Hato	7,460	3,730	3,694.37	Eisenberg 1980; Eisenberg et al. 1979
13	Chile	Chono Island	175	175	375.75	E. Piana (pers. comm.)
14	Argentina	Tierra Del Fuego	125	125	93.00	E. Piana (pers. comm.)
15	Kenya	Lake Rudolf	405	205	53.96	Coe et al. 1976
16	Ghana	Tano Nimri	94	150	191.37	Collins 1958
17	Kenya	Tsavo Park	4,210	1,690	1,933.40	Coe et al. 1976
18	Uganda	Kabalega Falls	10,164	2,258	1,370.15	Lock 1977
19	Tanzania	Mkomasi	1,731	1,731	1,357.66	Coe et al. 1976
20	Uganda	Queen Elizabeth	18,352	8,282	9,768.28	Field and Laws 1970; Spinage 1982
21	Rwanda	Akagera Park	3,650	2,259	2,421.58	Coe et al. 1976
22	Tanzania	Ngorongoro	7,561	7,339	4,197.01	Coe et al. 1976
23	Cameroon	Boubaldijidah	2,164	1,788	1,870.49	VanLavieren and Bosch 1977
24	Kenya	Samburu	2,018	1,300	1,012.11	Coe et al. 1976
25	Tanzania	Serengeti	8,352	8,142	8,929.25	Coe et al. 1976; Lamprey 1964; Sinclair and Norton-Griffiths (eds.) 1979
26	South Africa	Kruger Park north	984	659	446.64	Coe et al. 1976
27	Zimbabwe	Sengwa	2,824	1,581	2,796.35	Coe et al. 1976
28	Zimbabwe	Victoria Falls	2,715	3,117	2,983.57	Dasmann and Mossman 1962
29	South Africa	Kruger Park south	3,783	2,554	922.56	Coe et al. 1976
30	Tanzania	Ruaha	3,909	664	9,104.00	Barnes and Douglas-Hamilton 1982; Coe et al. 1976
31	Kenya	Lake Nakura	6,688	5,799	7,863.57	Coe et al. 1976
32	Kenya	Nairobi Park	4,824	4,438	7,169.79	Coe et al. 1976; Lamprey 1964
33	Namibia	Etosha Park	1,050	526	622.82	East 1984; Hofmeyer 1980; Joubert and Mostert 1975
34	Tanzania	Doma Mikumi	2,722	1,048	2,984.52	Lamprey 1964
35	Zambia	Luangwa	11,576	4,141	2,546.25	Caughley and Goddard 1975; Naylor 1973

TABLE 4.09 *(continued)*

GROUP NO.	STATE	NAME	BIOMASS	BIOSMALL	EXPREY	REFERENCE(S)
36	South Africa	Umfolozi	4,385	2,197	3802.57	Mentis 1970
37	South Africa	Hlu-Hluhluwe	8,094	6,588	1,097.29	Bourquin et al. 1971; Mentis 1970, 1980
38	South Africa	William Pretorius	3,344	2,493	300.42	Coe et al. 1976
39	Tanzania	Lioliondo	5,423	5,000	4,696.91	Coe et al. 1976
40	Australia	Bond Springs	19	19	79.24	Newsome 1965, 1965a
41	Australia	Charlie Creek	78	78	127.41	Newsome 1965, 1965a
42	Australia	Derwent	4	4	119.92	Newsome 1965, 1965a
43	Australia	Hamilton Down	23	23	93.01	Newsome 1965, 1965a
44	Tasmania	Mount William	2,339	1,200	785.74	J. F. Eisenberg (pers. comm.)
45	Florida	Everglade	88	88	334.54	Loveless 1959
46	California	Imperial Valley	15	15	24.76	Longhurst et al. 1952
47	California	Kern River	137	137	162.89	Longhurst et al. 1952
48	Texas	Llano Basin	2,063	2,063	1,915.73	Teer et al. 1965
49	Mississippi	Greenville	695	695	530.62	Sigler-Eisenberg ca. 1993
50	Arizona	3-Bar Ranch	146	511	373.85	Swank 1958
51	South Carolina	Greenwood	303	303	617.69	Sigler-Eisenberg ca. 1993
52	Oklahoma	Wichita Mountain	815	815	1,235.53	McHugh 1958
53	Tennessee	Bolivar	465	465	322.85	Sigler-Eisenberg ca. 1993
54	Arizona	Mingus	199	298	231.30	Swank 1958
55	California	Lake County	792	367	188.14	Taber and Dasmann 1957
56	California	Jawbone deer	510	246	287.13	Leopond et al. 1952
57	California	Hayfork	411	411	317.24	Longhurst et al. 1952
58	California	Sacramento	745	745	144.79	Longhurst et al. 1952
59	Nevada	Belted Mountains	58	58	66.14	Rue 1978
60	Japan	Sendai deer	1,162	650	539.91	Ito 1967
61	Nevada	Trinity Mountains	19	19	72.64	Rue 1978
62	Arizona	Prescott	183	325	375.84	Swank 1958
63	California	White Mountains	17	17	38.72	Longhurst et al. 1952
64	Utah	Oak Creek deer	761	414	291.60	Robinette et al. 1977
65	California	Yosemite deer	228	228	231.81	Longhurst et al. 1952
66	California	Mono Lake deer	165	165	51.82	Longhurst et al. 1952
67	Washington	Hoh elk	1,143	179	262.68	Schwartz and Mitchell 1945
68	Nevada	Battle Mountain	26	26	34.77	Gruell and Parez 1963
69	Washington	Humtulips	90	135	307.99	Schwartz and Mitchell 1945
70	Michigan	Reserve	678	550	330.83	McCullough 1979
71	Nevada	Schell Creek deer	314	314	108.04	Reference misplaced
72	Utah	Uncompahgre deer	547	246	375.83	Kuffeld et al. 1980
73	Arizona	Kaibab deer	235	235	127.01	Russo 1964; Swank 1958
74	Montana	Crow Reservation	1,655	1,055	882.18	McHugh 1958
75	Colorado	Ouray deer	612	489	622.50	Kuffeld et al. 1980
76	South Dakota	Wind Cave	1,437	862	961.21	McHugh 1958
77	California	Orick Prairie	132	132	272.16	Harper et al. 1967
78	California	Hat Creek	128	128	185.23	Longhurst et al. 1952
79	Montana	Missouri Breaks	1,312	650	861.82	Mackie 1970
80	Washington	Queets	599	199	252.18	Schwartz and Mitchell 1945
81	Montana	Sun River elk	595	659	1,366.79	Knight 1970
82	Washington	Elwha elk	670	340	293.37	Schwartz and Mitchell 1945
83	Idaho	Big Wood	296	296	168.59	Tanner 1965
84	Newfoundland	Zero	690	328	168.24	Bergerud 1974; Bergerud and Manuel 1969
85	Minnesota	Deer herd	97	97	199.59	Floyd et al. 1979
86	Scotland	Rhum Island deer	1,388	1,041	422.13	Clutton-Brock et al. 1982
87	Michigan	Isle Royal	674	303	198.28	Mech 1966
88	Canada	Alberta moose	179	179	227.20	Rolley and Keith 1980
89	Canada	Fort McKay, Alberta	274	274	195.33	Hauge and Keith 1981
90	Wyoming	Yellowstone	1,538	769	466.28	McHugh 1958

(continued)

TABLE 4.09 *(continued)*

GROUP NO.	STATE	NAME	BIOMASS	BIOSMALL	EXPREY	REFERENCE(S)
91	Alaska	Fortymile herd	181	181	72.53	Hemming 1971
92	Alaska	Yukon moose	129	129	85.22	Evans et al. 1966
93	Alaska	Beaver herd	12	12	92.37	Hemming 1971
94	Alaska	Porcupine herd	95	95	59.54	Hemming 1971
95	Alaska	Kenai moose	246	196	152.20	Evans et al. 1966
96	Alaska	Valdez	66	66	167.73	Hemming 1971
97	Alaska	Peninsula caribou	425	255	127.92	Hemming 1971
98	Canada	Kaminuriak herd	95	952	41.57	Parker 1972
99	Alaska	Arctic herd	55	55	37.71	Hemming 1971
100	Greenland	W. Greenland caribou	32	32	19.58	Thing 1981
101	Russia	Coastal Siberia	10	10	17.35	Poulov et al. 1971
102	Canada	Boothia Peninsula	10	10	10.88	Parker 1972
103	Kenya	Amboseli Park	4,848	3,539	58.85	Coe et al. 1978; Western 1975
104	Zimbabwe	Henderson's Ranch	2,869	2,582	842.61	Dasmann and Mossman 1962
105	Upper Volta	Arli	1,831	1,831	1,516.40	Green 1979
106	Nigeria	Kainji Lake	1,200	1,200	1,324.85	Milligan et al. 1982
107	Ivory Coast	Comoe	212	212	528.55	Geering and Bokdam 1973

herbivores reported in the cited studies, including animals of large body size such as elephants, and BIOSMALL, which is the adjusted value of only ungulates of moderate body size.

In the fifty-three cases in which the value of BIOSMALL is lower than that entered for BIOMASS, the difference is due to one or more of the following conditions at the study location: (1) values for elephant, hippopotamus, and rhino were subtracted from the community totals; (2) secondary vegetation reported at the study location (i.e., the mature plant community) had been harvested by humans prior to the study (managed elk populations in North America were particularly affected, as was the Tasmanian marsupial population); or (3) game managers maintain the animal population at the study site by supplemental feeding (this applies to most bison populations within the United States). Some areas for which animal biomass data are available were characterized by more than one of these conditions. In 8 of the 107 cases in table 4.09, the BIOSMALL estimate is higher than the BIOMASS value. In these cases, a single-species study was augmented by information about other species in the same area, including domesticated animals.

Although it might appear that I have jumped ahead of myself by describing the data collection strategies involved in this aspect of my research and that a more appropriate discussion would focus on the reasons that I was collecting data in the first place, the sequence in which I have introduced my research on animal biomass may seem more logical when viewed in the context of ecological research as a whole. Ecologists have worried for some time over two major questions: (1) What factors limit the biomass of animals? (2) How do the dynamics of animal biomass fluctuations dif-

ferentially condition the abundance of animals at different times and places within a habitat?

In a seminal work on this issue entitled *The Distribution and Abundance of Animals* (1954), two Australian zoologists, H. G. Andrewartha and L. C. Birch, addressed the question of how animal abundance is differentially conditioned in space and time. The authors distinguished between four major components of the problem: (1) a factor they referred to as "a place to live," (2) the subsistence strategies of different animals, (3) the social geography of different species, and (4) the climatological context of the species and its habitat. Because Andrewartha and Birch addressed their concerns using data drawn primarily from insect species, many of their colleagues were critical of the results, arguing that the unique features of insect organisms made it unlikely that knowledge gained from the study would be relevant to mammalian and, particularly, human behavior.

Before accepting the majority verdict and dismissing Andrewartha and Birch's research entirely, I present one of the major conclusions of this study:

The numbers of animals in a natural population may be limited in three ways: (a) by shortage of material resources, such as food, places in which to make nests, etc.; (b) by inaccessibility of these material resources relative to the animals' capacities for dispersal and searching; and (c) by shortage of time when the rate of increase r is positive. Of these three ways, the first is probably the least, and the last is probably the most, important in nature. Concerning c, the fluctuations in the value of r may be caused by weather, predators, or any other component of environment that influences the rate of increase. For example, the fluctuations in the value of *r* which are determined by weather may be rhythmical in response to the progressions of the seasons, or more erratic in response to "runs" of years with "good" or "bad" weather. . . . The fluctuations in *r* which are determined by the activities of predators must be considered in relation to the populations in local situations. . . . How long each newly founded colony may be allowed to multiply free from predators may depend on the dispersive powers of the predators relative to those of the prey.   (Andrewartha and Birch 1954:661)

These conclusions challenge the views on animal distribution and abundance advanced by Australian animal ecologist A. J. Nicholson (1933, 1954a, 1954b, 1957, 1958), who developed the *density-dependent* approach to species numbers and differential dispersal. A basic tenet of this argument states that as the number (density) of individuals of a species increases at a particular location, processes are activated that dampen or reduce the rates at which the population grows. One of these inhibiting factors is intraspecific competition, which was referred to by Nicholson as the "governing reaction." According to Begon et al., "density-dependent processes play a crucial role in determining the abundance of species by operating as stabilizing or regulating mechanisms" (1990:516).

Despite the fact that this view of population dynamics, with its cycles of growth and decline, has been widely accepted, Andrewartha and Birch (1954) nonetheless minimize its role. In their study, which was remarkable for the quality of its data and the duration of research, multiple regression analysis of population counts were run against environmental variables. The results indicated that 78 percent of the variation in population levels could be accounted for by weather variables (Andrewartha and Birch 1954:660–61), a conclusion that led the authors to conclude that density-dependent responses played little or no role in determining animal population levels.

Andrewartha and Birch's challenge to Nicholson's assertions set in motion a debate (McLaren 1971) that has ramified into many different fields, including anthropology (see the criticism of *equilibrium* topics by postprocessual archaeologists [Hodder 1982:2] and Hassan's review [1981:144–75] of discussions in the 1960s and 1970s). The contemporary view is well stated by Begon et al.: "it is important to note that because all environments are variable, the position of any 'balance-point' is continually changing. Thus, in spite of the ubiquity of density-dependent, regularizing processes, there seems little value in a view based on universal balance, with rare nonequilibrium interludes. On the contrary, it is likely that no natural population is ever truly at equilibrium" (1990:520–21).

This view focuses on dynamics and variability in dynamic patterning rather than ideas of stable versus unstable system states. It may well be that a growing system is organizationally more or less stable than an oscillating one, but confirmation of either alternative must await further research.

Although a major concern of this chapter is the distribution and abundance of animals, particularly human animals, my interest at this juncture is the biomass of animals, which represents the standing crop of potentially accessible food for a human actor in a particular habitat. I especially want to be able to estimate the ungulate biomass at any location for which climatological data are available, and several studies offer encouragement that such a goal is attainable. The comparative study by M. J. Coe, D. H. Cumming, and J. Phillipson (1976) demonstrated a relationship between the standing crop biomass of herbivores from the game-rich east African grasslands and mean annual rainfall (CRR), which is certainly one of the major conditioners of plant productivity upon which ungulate populations depend. Coe et al. (1976:349) obtained a correlation coefficient of 0.96 for the relationships summarized by the following equation:

$$\text{(4.17)}$$

$$\text{Large herbivore biomass} = 10 ** [1.685(0.238) * (CRR) - 1.095(0.661)]$$

where   large herbivore biomass is measured in kilograms per square kilometer and CRR equals mean annual rainfall.

These researchers stressed that this equation accurately projected conditions in African settings in which mean annual rainfall ranged between approximately 250 and 1,100 millimeters. They noted that the relationship was curvilinear with an inflection point at around 850 millimeters (Coe et al. 1976:347).

An earlier, more global examination of ungulate biomass by Eisenberg and McKay (1974) had a more general ecological focus and dealt more specifically with tropical forests. One of the authors' observations will play an important role in ideas developed in later chapters of this book:

the carrying capacity of a mature forest region is reduced for the terrestrial herbivores. In order to effectively graze and browse in a forest, a terrestrial herbivore is obliged to live at thin densities and, if the species is nonmigratory, then intraspecific spacing mechanisms become important. An open forest condition or an interface between forest and grassland allows for the maximum in diversity and density of herbivores for the tropical regions, but the true forest itself supports a less diverse ungulate fauna at thinner densities.
                    (Eisenberg and McKay 1974:586)

Specific climatological data from the study sites in their biomass comparisons were not available to Eisenberg and McKay, so they used an approximate classification of vegetation types based on an ordination of rainfall levels to demonstrate some interesting patterning in herbivore biomass. The following equation best fits the distribution that is presented in Eisenberg and McKay's graph (1974:587) of their data:

(4.18)

$$y = [(a + cx + ex^2)/(1.0 + bx + dx^2)]^2$$

where y = ungulate biomass in kilograms per square
          kilometer,
          x = mean annual rainfall in millimeters (CRR),
          a = −2.4449724,
          b = −0.0023505657,
          c = 0.034561408,
          d = 1.759661E–06, and
          e = −3.6542129E–06.

Both the Coe study and that of Eisenberg and McKay illustrate the strong relationship between herbivore biomass and climatic variables, particularly rainfall, but subsequent studies have recognized that a single variable is not likely to account for fine-grained variability across a global range of different habitats. McNaughton, Oesterheld, Frank, and Williams (1989; Oesterheld et al. 1992) have shifted from simple rainfall measures to estimates of net aboveground productivity, which is strongly conditioned by both rainfall and temperature, and their findings offer considerable support for the claim that herbivores are strongly food limited. Eisenberg and McKay's reports of the reduced role of ungulates and other herbivores in high-biomass forests have also been validated and further documented by McNaughton et al. (1989:143). In fact, in the latter study, when the proportion of net aboveground productivity that is converted to standing biomass in the form of tree trunks and limbs was excluded from calculations and only foliage production was included, an even closer relationship was demonstrated.

Another contentious issue troubling researchers who do comparative studies of animal biomass is whether contemporary, domestic range animals can be regarded as representative of a locality's past populations of undomesticated animals. Oesterheld et al. (1992:235) found that higher animal biomass was correlated with net aboveground productivity in *both* wild and domesticated animal populations. The slope of the line in each case was similar, although the intercepts were different, and domesticated animals as a group behaved at a higher biomass level than wild animals (17% more biomass per unit of net aboveground productivity). The introduction into the equation of a new variable, soil quality, reduced the difference between domesticated and wild animal biomass and made contrasts between African and South American grassland-savanna regions appear less pronounced.

Previous interregional comparisons had shown that secondary biomass was strongly related to net aboveground productivity, and, when cases from roughly the same regions and ecotypes were compared, rainfall was also a good predictor, at least up to the 1,000-millimeter level. Evidence also suggested that, relative to net aboveground productivity, terrestrial herbivore biomass was considerably reduced

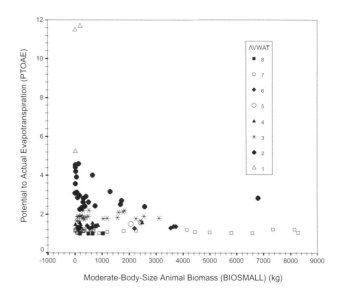

FIGURE 4.19

Scatter plot of observed biomass of animals of moderate body size and the ratio of potential to actual evapotranspiration. Cases are coded for available water (AVWAT): (1) very dry, (2) dry, (3) moderately dry, (4) transitional dry, (5) transitional damp, (6) damp, (7) moist, and (8) wet.

in high-biomass forests. Since my goal has been to project herbivore and, more particularly, ungulate biomass to the entire earth as a way tracking hunter-gatherer habitat differences, I have approached the problem somewhat differently than is customary in ecological studies.

I had assembled a wide range of climatic information on the locations for which biomass estimates of herbivores, especially ungulates, were available, so I decided to perform a series of multiple regression analyses[21] on the data file of 103 cases in which BIOSMALL was the dependent variable and all of the environmental variables presented earlier in this chapter constituted the suite of independent variables. The major variables were converted to $\log_{10}$ values so that the multiple regression (which is a linear model) could retain or eliminate either the $\log_{10}$ or the normal scale value of a variable, depending upon the measures used for retaining variables in the equation.

Independent analytical runs were made on a series of different ways to segment the data file into various subsets. Previous ecological studies had focused on rainfall as an important variable, and, not surprisingly, I discovered that grouping subsets of the cases in terms of rainfall-related criteria produced the highest correlations with the fewest variables contributing to the solution.[22] The partition was made in terms of the variable AVWAT, which represents a dimensional ordination of variability of rainfall-related criteria. Since PTOAE was the primary variable used to define the eight-step ordination of environments by AVWAT value, the reason that this segregation produced the best results is illustrated in figure 4.19, which presents a graph with PTOAE plotted on the *y* axis and BIOSMALL on the *x* axis.

By taking this approach, I learned that when a small sample is partitioned into still smaller samples and multiple regressions are performed, two complications are common: (1) As a result of distributional bias in the subset sample, a smooth transition from one subset to another frequently does not occur. (2) With small samples that do not represent the full range of variability in the population targeted for projection, the equations will frequently yield impossible values when run on cases with values outside the range represented in the sample. Attempting to project expected ungulate biomass accurately to all of the earth's environments on the basis of a data set composed of 103 cases invariably means that the sample does not adequately represent all environmental settings. For instance, in this sample of animal biomass locations there are only four cases from true rain forest zones, so it is not likely that my projections will be within acceptable limits of precision in true rain forests.

Another problem is that I lacked a critical environmental control variable to measure the quantity and seasonal distribution of unearned water in dry environments. (It should be recalled that unearned water falls as rain somewhere else and is transported to plant communities in very different types of settings.) Rivers may bring unearned water to otherwise very dry places and various processes may distribute and make ground water abundantly available to plants at locations where there is very little rainfall. Such a situation occurs at

Amboseli Game Park in Kenya (Coe et al. 1976:350), and figure 4.20 illustrates the large number of animals that are found adjacent to the park's spring-fed marshes and streams. The vegetation in these areas is not maintained by earned rainfall, which means that there will be bias in my results depending upon the number of dry setting cases that are supplemented by unearned water as opposed to those that are not. The probability is strongly in favor of supplemented cases since, in truly dry settings, one would expect no ungulates of moderate body size. If they are reported from otherwise dry locations, it is nearly certain that unearned water resources are involved.

I concluded that no matter how I solved the problem of selecting the most useful summary of the relationships between animal biomass and basic environmental variables, I could still expect inflated values in very dry environments since my sample is almost certainly biased in favor of higher biomass values at study locations with substantial unearned water. In fact, many of the study locations feature constructed dams, ponds, and tanks designed to exploit both earned and unearned water, providing animals with more and longer-duration "drinking spots" than they would find in the natural landscape. Contrast the setting in figure 4.21, in which elephants are provided water in the southern part of the Kruger National Park in South Africa, with the water resources along the Olifants River in the park's northern area (figure 4.22). In both settings animals depend on unearned water resources, but the dammed-up pond in figure 4.21 would never be anticipated by my rainfall-only data.

FIGURE 4.20
Large herds of ungulates in Amboseli Game Park, Kenya.

FIGURE 4.21

Artificial pan in Kruger National Park, South Africa.

It is also likely that my projections will overestimate the amount of animal biomass for very wet environments because my sample included only four cases representing the full range of the earth's variability in these settings. Uncontrolled variability among the cases in the sample is not, however, the cause of the overestimate. It derives instead from the very abrupt transitions between low-biomass forests and high-biomass savanna depicted in figure 4.19. Since the cases are not evenly distributed across the full range of variability but are concentrated at the drier end of this variability, a line fitted to these cases projects more biomass for animals in extremely wet locations. My only recourse is to note this condition

FIGURE 4.22

Elephants on the Olifants River in the northern area of Kruger National Park, South Africa.

and expect that biases of this kind will occur for locations onto which the best-fit equations developed here may project expected values.

As I tried alternate ways to make the best use of the information contained in the animal biomass file, I would sometimes get a set of equations that would anticipate the sample very well. But when the equations were used to calculate expected values for the large file of 1,429 global weather stations, I would sometimes have negative values for very dry locations and unreasonably high values (e.g., 3,456,238 kilograms of animal biomass per square kilometer) for some locations that were not represented in the range of environments for which I had animal data. As a result, I took two different approaches to developing the best equations for projecting values of expected ungulate prey biomass for the whole earth.

First, I would use only a single equation, which would eliminate the problem of disjunctures between merged equations calculated on subsets of the total number of cases. Then I developed a "reality check" for the results so that I could identify wild values for those cases in which my equations were not well constrained by the range of variability in the sample when compared with the global range of variability in certain important environmental variables.[23] I also discovered that by forcing the equations through the origin, I partially solved the problem of negative values for low-rainfall cases. Another finding was that better correlation coefficients and lower standard error values resulted when I ran the environmental variables against the $\log_{10}$ value of BIOSMALL.

The best-fit multiple linear regression[24] that I obtained using a stepwise method for anticipating the $\log_{10}$ value of BIOSMALL had a squared multiple R value of 0.99206 with an r^2 value of 0.98418, an adjusted r^2 value of 0.98258, and a standard error of the $\log_{10}$ value of 0.34978 when the equation was forced through the origin. The equation takes the following form:

$$(4.19)$$

EXPREY = 10 ** [(ELEV * 5.30810E–05) +
        (LLAT *–0.300235) + (LNAGP * 1.200771) +
        (LWATD * –0.116610) +
        (LWATRGRC * 0.216493) +
        (NAGP * –4.26495E–04) +
        (RRCORR2 * –0.028577) +
        (WRET * –0.008066) +
        (WSTORAGE * 0.005171)]

This equation is provocative when viewed from the perspective of previous work on the conditioners of net aboveground productivity and the quantity of secondary biomass. First, the three variables most frequently cited as conditioners of secondary biomass are represented. Obviously, net aboveground productivity (NAGP) plays an important role since it is represented by both its natural value and the $\log_{10}$ expression of that value. This is not surprising since each form is represented with opposite signs and therefore interacts to define the threshold of the relationship between secondary biomass and primary production. In addition, four variables measuring different aspects of the water balance characteristics of habitats are included:

1. Negative LWATD, which is the $\log_{10}$ value of the total annual water deficit or the amount of additional water that could have been evaporated or transpired had it been present. LWATD is inversely correlated with secondary biomass and strongly supports other water-related variables, but it provides more information relative to NAGP because its values imply what is frequently called the wilting point.

2. LWATRGRC, which is the $\log_{10}$ value of the number of months during the growing season in which water was retained in the soil at the end of the month. This is another way of saying that rainfall levels were high enough, in spite of evaporation or transpiration, to result in water stored in the soil. This variable makes a positive contribution to the equation.

3. WATRET, which is the yearly total of water stored in the soil. WATRET is an indicator of the difference between wet, high-biomass forests and dry-to-savannalike settings. As the value of WATRET increases, the biomass of ungulates decreases, negatively conditioning the equation.

4. RRCORR2, which is the measure of the seasonality of rainfall relative to the warmest and potentially most productive months of the year. Animal biomass is expected to be higher when RRCORR2 values are low and lower when they are high. This means that spring and summer rainfall contributes to high animal biomass whereas autumn and winter rainfall is correlated with lower levels of ungulate biomass. In the animal kingdom, dynamics related to RRCORR2 affect seasonal birthing patterns and increases in primary plant productivity in response to rainfall.

Another provocative variable included in the equation, WSTORAGE, is an ordinal scaling of soil type in terms of water storage potential. Poor, sandy soils have low storage capacity whereas rich mollisols, at the other end of the scale, have high storage capacity. This scaling of soil quality supports other research demonstrating that soil quality is a major conditioner of animal biomass levels above and beyond relationships attributable to net aboveground plant productivity (Fritz and Duncan 1993).[25]

In my equation solving for EXPREY, topographic elevation is included as a positive contributor and the $\log_{10}$ value of latitude represents a negative contributor. This means that increases in elevation are correlated with increases in ungulate biomass, whereas increases in latitude correspond to decreases in net aboveground productivity and ungulate biomass. In a real-world context, these statements about the relationships between variables translate into the challenges to survival, in addition to food limitation, that ungulates face in settings of increasing coldness, where the primary problem is maintenance of body temperature.

Different species have different coping mechanisms, ranging from growing thicker pelts to hibernation, so latitude is used in this equation as a surrogate for many of the problems that ungulates must solve in cold settings. On the other hand, elevation is a surrogate for habitat diversity and the fact that the security of ungulates increases through their access to different food resources. There are, of course, other ways of evaluating the significance of these variables, but my goal was to develop—using habitat variables—an accurate projection of what is already known about ungulate biomass that could be applied to locations for which there is little if any knowledge.

Let us examine the results of applying this equation to the cases from which it was generated. Figure 4.23 displays observed values of BIOSMALL and expected values of EXPREY, both of which are expressed as kilograms per square kilometer. In three rather extreme cases, observed and expected values are quite different: (1) Ruaha Park in Tanzania (664 observed; 9,097 expected); (2) Hlu-Hluhluwe Park in South Africa (6,588 observed; 1,105.8 expected); and (3) Gir National Park in Gujarat, India (6,800 observed; 409.7 expected). These differences are so large that some attention must be paid to these cases.

1. Ruaha Park values for BIOSMALL came from Coe et al. (1976),[26] who estimated the total elephant and non-elephant biomass to be 3,909 kilograms per square kilometer. Six years later, Barnes and Douglas-Hamilton (1982)

reported a total animal biomass value of 5,422 kilograms per square kilometer, of which elephant biomass amounted to 4,157 kilograms, or 76.67 percent of the total. This percentage was used as a guide to eliminate elephants from the biomass value reported by Coe et al., with the understanding that it might not correspond to current biomass values at the park. The next question was whether an expected prey value of 9,097 kilograms per square kilometer is totally off the mark, and here I have to admit that I simply do not know. One thing is certain, however: Ruaha does not represent a climax or stable animal population relative to the productivity and character of the plant community.

2. Hlu-Hluhluwe Park in South Africa is very close to Umfolozi Game Reserve and, like the latter, contains a protected and managed population of black and white rhino, as well as other ungulate species, including nyala, impala, waterbuck, greater kudu, blue wildebeest, buffalo, giraffe, and Burchell's zebra. The proportion of rhino to other species is unreported, and—since hippo, rhino, and elephant were subtracted from the biomass value to obtain BIOSMALL— it was impossible to perform such a correction in this case. This undoubtedly accounts for most of the discrepancy between the observed and expected values of BIOSMALL.

3. Gir National Park in India was recently carved out of an area previously occupied by seminomadic cattle herders to provide a habitat for the rare Asiatic lion of India. The forests are reported to have been "depleted by decades of grazing cattle" (Krishnan 1984:54). The biomass values used here were taken from Eisenberg and Seidensticker (1976:300), who reported that 6,171 kilograms of the total represent domestic stock that feed in the park. Only

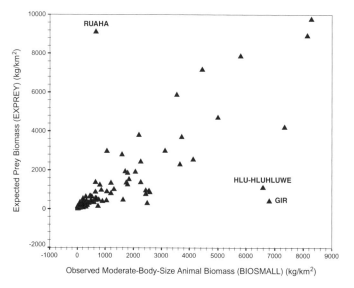

FIGURE 4.23

Scatter plot of observed and expected biomass of animals of moderate body size.

383 kilograms were reported to be wild ungulates, a value that is very close to the 409 kilograms projected by the expected prey equation.

Other cases with lower expected than observed values of BIOSMALL include the Scottish island of Rhum, Bharatpur and Kanha Parks in India, Ngorongoro Crater in Tanzania, and William Pretorius Game Reserve and the southern sector of the Kruger National Park in South Africa. Unearned water is suspected as a major contributor to the discrepancies in each of these cases:

1. The red deer populations on the Scottish island of Rhum constitute the only case in which expected animal biomass values are lower than the observed values for reasons that are unrelated to unearned water. The higher than expected biomass value is likely to be related to the destruction of the island's forests during the seventeenth and eighteenth centuries, which resulted in the complete extirpation of all woodlands by the dawn of the nineteenth century. Since 1957, the island has been a nature reserve supporting wildlife, with a vegetation cover of heath, blanket bog, and grassland heath. Prior to a study initiated by zoologists, there was also some feeding of animal populations by humans on the island (Clutton-Brock et al. 1982:27). Another relevant point is that although eagles have sometimes been observed killing calves, there are no larger predators affecting animal populations on the sland (Clutton-Brock et al. 1982:85). The climatic data, of course, anticipate a forested area that would support considerably fewer animals on a sustainable basis.

2. Bharatpur, or the Keoladeo Ghana Animal Park, consists of 32 square kilometers surrounding a 29-square-kilometer lake that is the breeding area for so many species of water birds that the park is thought of primarily as a bird sanctuary. The size of the lake expands considerably during the rainy season. Schaller reports even higher biomass levels than were reported by Eisenberg and Seidensticker (1976), noting that the buffalo population primarily feeds in the swamp and the area around the lake is "deteriorating rapidly to desert conditions" (Schaller 1967:202–3). It is clear that the lake is a major source of water and that animals seasonally aggregate there; this is having a very negative effect on the plant community. Inflated biomass values are expected under such conditions.

3. Ngorongoro Crater Conservation Area is another location at which unearned water resources support more animals than could be supported by locally earned rainfall in a more conventional topography.

4. William Pretorius Game Reserve in South Africa is a 34.7-square-mile park with an artificial lake that provides water for park animals (Guggisberg 1970:175). Inflated biomass values are expected under such conditions.

5. The southern part of the huge Kruger National Park in South Africa is dotted with artificially dammed ponds and tanks. These facilities not only conserve local rainfall that would otherwise be lost as runoff but also allow game animals to be dispersed over a much larger area than would be possible with only a few sources of naturally occurring water during the dry season. Once again, observed biomass is higher than the expected value, which was based exclusively on rainfall levels.

There are only four cases in which the observed BIOSMALL value is less than the expected value. These include Lake Nakura Park in Kenya, which is a small reserve of 24 square miles that is best known as a bird sanctuary owing to its location adjacent to a lake that is considerably larger than the park itself. Large game is strictly managed in the park in order to reduce predation on the bird populations and to mitigate the destruction of bird habitats. Two other parks where animal populations are strictly regulated are the Umfolozi Park in South Africa and Nairobi Park, which is only four miles from the center of the capital of Kenya. Last, there is the Mikumi Park in Tanzania, but I know very little about this location.

Except for the preceding locations, the data are quite remarkable, and, as I have noted, the outliers are almost exclusively understandable in terms of conditions that my equation does not accommodate. The results are better at anticipating conditions in a "natural" state than is any simple summary of the data itself, and—simply by projecting the knowledge summarized in the EXPREY equation—it is now possible to provide an ungulate biomass estimate for any location on earth for which there is adequate weather data.

The equation was run on the world sample of weather station cases and yielded an expected prey (EXPREY) value in units of biomass measured as kilograms per square kilometer for all of the 1,429 locations in the world sample. Figure 4.24 illustrates how ungulate biomass would be globally distributed *if the rest of the world were like what is known about the set of cases documenting animal biomass.*

Many features of this distribution make good sense in light of what was learned about the natural world at the time it was first documented in the historical and anthropological literature. The high-animal-biomass areas of Africa are well defined in figure 4.24 as a semicircular scatter of dark shading around a core of moderately dark units extending along the West African coast and around the Congo drainage. Both north and south of this region of graded secondary productivity there is the wide zone of low to absent productivity represented by the Saharan zone that is defined by adjacent regions of Mauritania, Mali, Algeria, Niger, Chad, Libya, Sudan, Egypt, and Saudi Arabia on the north and Namibia, Botswana, and most of central and western South Africa on the south.

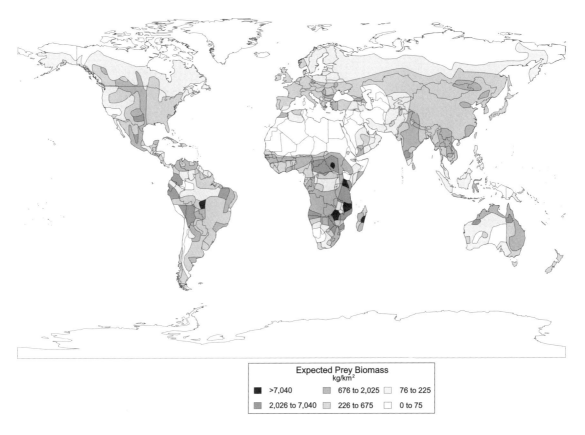

FIGURE 4.24

World map with zones defined by an ordination of projected biomass for ungulates of moderate body size according to the world weather station sample.

Regions analogous to the Namibia–Botswana–South Africa area, where hunter-gatherers and pastoralists were reported at the time of initial European exploration, include Patagonia in southeastern Argentina and the entire continent of Australia, both of which were occupied exclusively by hunter-gatherers at the time of initial European exploration. (It is tempting to ask at this juncture why so many hunter-gatherers were found in these regions, or, reversing the perspective, why agriculturists were absent. Hunter-gatherers operated next to state-level societies in South America and adjacent to both agriculturists and pastoralists in southern Africa. It is only in Australia that a case can be made for isolation, and that argument can be effectively challenged. I am, of course, jumping ahead of myself here—but only because the environmental information developed for comparative work is so provocative.)

Another region with a history of high ungulate productivity is the Great Plains of North America, which is defined in figure 4.24 by an inverted, backwards, L-shaped distribution There is an east-west distribution along the border between Canada and the United States that includes the southern parts of Alberta and Saskatchewan and a small

western corner of Manitoba, and a similar distribution across Montana and North Dakota that turns south through western South Dakota, Nebraska, and Kansas, into Texas and along the gulf coast of Mexico.

The only other location on earth with such an extensive distribution of moderately high animal productivity is in Asia, where it runs along the Russian-Mongolian border into Manchuria and turns southwest to Beijing and Tientsin in China. An analogous but much smaller area is found in central Europe, beginning on the Turkish Plateau; jumping over to Bulgaria, Romania, eastern parts of the former Yugoslavia, Hungary, and Czechoslovakia and into southern Poland; and covering much of the Ukraine as well. Other fascinating features of this map include the distributions in India and the contrasts in the distribution of ungulates between the Old and New Worlds.

I will have to defer another demonstration of the rewards of large-scale, multivariate comparison (in this case, an examination of the geographic patterning in the projected abundance of animals of moderate body size) while I introduce two other frames of reference for examining distributional variability in the abundance of ungulates. In figure 4.25,

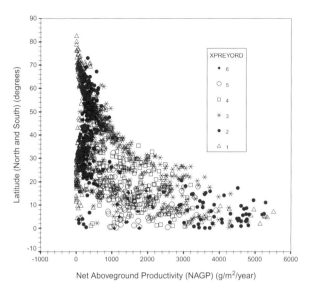

FIGURE 4.25

Property space map for primary net aboveground productivity and latitude, with zones defined by an ordination of projected biomass for ungulates of moderate body size, from the world weather station sample (XPREYORD): (1) very low, (2) low, (3) scant, (4) moderate, (5) high, and (6) very high.

for instance, the ordination of ungulate abundance is plotted on a property space map with the $\log_{10}$ value of net aboveground productivity (NAGP) on the *x* axis and latitude on the *y* axis. This projection makes it clear that regions with the highest and lowest primary biomass support the lowest biomass for ungulates of moderate body size. On the other hand, the highest biomass for the animals in this study occurs at latitudes below 15 degrees and in settings with primary net aboveground productivity of between 1,000 and 2,220 grams per square meter. The second highest biomass occurs below 35 degrees in regions with NAGP values of between 500 and 3,900 grams per square meter.

The other feature of the distribution in figure 4.25 is that the property space defined by maximum values for animal biomass is by no means homogeneous. Values as low as 226 grams per square meter may occur in the same property space as much higher levels of NAGP. This is a clear indication that variables other than NAGP are strongly conditioning animal biomass. This set of relationships was demonstrated in equation (4.19), which included important conditioning variables representing the season of rainfall, soil storage capacity, and the amount of water retained in the soil during the growing season, in addition to the more basic variables conditioning generic plant productivity.

Using the results of the EXPREY equation, I can examine the relationship between my classification of vegetation

and the abundance of ungulates of moderate body size. An ordination of the mean values for expected prey at locations identified by the twenty-eight vegetative communities used in this study and described in table 4.08 was obtained. The resultant pattern corresponds roughly to what is already known about this issue: the highest values of ungulate biomass per unit area are found in tropical montane forests (FMT-6), tropical thorntree tallgrass savannas (STG-7), tropical savanna woodlands (SW-2), and tropical-subtropical monsoon raingreen forests (FMO-3). Conversely, the lowest level for biomass of ungulates of moderate body size is found in tundra settings (T-26), followed by porcupine grass semi-desert (DSP-25), true deserts (D-28), and coastal forests of the temperate zone (FC-11).

The first three cases are perhaps no surprise, but the last case includes the classic Douglas fir and redwood forests that are found along the west coast of North America from northern California to Valdez, Alaska. These forests were home to many well-documented hunter-gatherer groups—often referred to collectively as the Northwest Coast Native Americans—whose bold graphic styles and social complexity have preoccupied the public imagination for many years. A pertinent question to ask at this juncture might be: is this pattern related in any way to the natural absence of prey? This is, of course, a question that I will investigate later in this study, but the fact that it comes to mind demonstrates the utility of the referential tools I have been building.

Conclusion

In this chapter, I have introduced a robust body of information and some of the analytical tools that will be used to build various frames of reference for the comparative study of hunter-gatherer peoples. I have even demonstrated that when these tools are used to analyze my data sets, some interesting patterns become visible. The experience of reading this chapter, however, may provoke some readers to compare it to swallowing a maximum-strength vitamin pill. That is, almost everything that is needed to provide a realistic ecological basis for tackling the explanation of ethnographic variability has been concentrated into one unit, and it may produce the slightly queasy feeling that sometimes accompanies the consumption of the day's concentrated dose of nutrients.

I certainly hope, however, that as I proceed in subsequent chapters to project ethnographic and even archaeological data onto various environmental frames of reference, the effort of digesting this large intellectual capsule will fade from memory, to be replaced by an appreciation for the growth of knowledge that an environmental baseline makes possible.

5

Designing Frames of Reference and Exploring Projections

The Plot Thickens

In chapter 3, I discussed two different kinds of analytical tools—frames of reference and projections. In chapter 4, I introduced and defined numerous ecological variables that can be used to record specific, relevant properties of the world's environments. In this chapter, I integrate these two domains and look at some aspects of hunter-gatherer behavior through several different sets of lenses. And because this book is concerned as much with how to do analysis as it is with the results of my endeavors, at every juncture I examine the utility of the tools I use and the logic directing their use, reporting where appropriate either the patterns and insights they produce or their failure to contribute to my knowledge goals.

I begin by constructing an environmental frame of reference that will be used to study a sample of ethnographically observed hunting and gathering peoples of the relatively recent past. Of course, such a tool could be used just as effectively to study archaeological data derived from an unknown past. Most of the environmental variables are taken from weather station data, which means that they are based on observations that are global in distribution and standardized in terms of collection procedures. This consistency, and the fact that well-understood environmental dynamics inform us about critical factors producing habitat variability, will permit the construction of very robust frames of reference.

I also intend to use information tabulated in a sample of 339 hunter-gatherer cases as the basis of another frame of reference that can be used in a search for patterns in archaeological data. The immediate methodological challenge is, of course, to develop a globally comprehensive hunter-gatherer frame of reference from an ethnographic data base that is admittedly biased in many ways, including spatial distribution.

The brief survey of hunter-gatherer research presented in chapter 1 illustrated an additional research problem: the discipline of anthropology has yet to develop a coherent statement of the factors conditioning hunter-gatherer variability, although there are some germane descriptive resources. Since archaeologists cannot simply suspend their efforts to account for archaeological patterning until ethnological researchers develop a comprehensively descriptive, explanatory body of knowledge about hunter-gatherers, they must themselves do the middle-range research necessary to create and experiment with the intellectual tools that will make patterning in the archaeological record meaningful.[1]

Because it is impossible for contemporary researchers to observe the behavior of ancient peoples and then record its archaeological consequences, many archaeologists have been less than discriminating in using ethnographic data to inform themselves about the patterns documented in archaeological sites. Indeed, they have been encouraged in this practice by the prevalent belief that living hunter-gatherers constitute a surviving remnant of past human populations.[2] The argument for historical continuity made by Elman Service in the 1960s had particularly powerful repercussions:

> The paleolithic era . . .—from the beginning of culture until the beginning of the domestication of plants and animals—was a time when there were no forms of economy higher than hunting-gathering bands. Once the Neolithic era began and the tribes gradually expanded, some bands were transformed, others possibly obliterated and the remainder pushed into, or confined to, ecological areas where domestication of plants and animals was not feasible. Still higher stages of cultural development, culminating in industrial civilizations, came to dominate these earlier levels of culture until remnants of the original kind of hunting-gathering bands which once covered the face of the earth are found in modern times only in marginal out-of-the-way places.
>
> (Service 1962:59)

It is true that in the decades since Service discussed supposedly remnant hunter-gatherer populations anthropologists of all persuasions have become much more aware of the folly of using extant peoples as discrete exemplars of pre-historic life ways. Among southern African researchers the pendulum has even swung to the opposite extreme. Wilmsen (1983, 1989) and others challenge the characterization of mobile San peoples as the latest practitioners of an unbroken foraging tradition in the Kalahari, extending without interruption from the distant past (see also Bower 1989; Headland and Bailey 1991).

Implicit in Wilmsen's argument is the assumption that a break in occupational and organizational continuity—which probably did, in fact, occur in the Kalahari area—renders a group of hunter-gatherers irrelevant to an investigation of what life is like for food producers exploiting domesticated plants and animals. I hope to make a strong case to the contrary and to demonstrate how knowledge of nearly contemporary hunter-gatherers may profitably serve the goal of learning about a past that may have been altogether different from the present and, in many places, created by persons with no extant descendants in the present era.

Two middle-range research alternatives are available to me. I can attempt to develop a theoretical understanding of the variability among ethnographically documented hunter-gatherers and thereby answer such questions as "why are some groups mobile and others sedentary?" Or I can devise ways to use the descriptive wealth of hunter-gatherer ethnography as a frame of reference for studying archaeological materials. In this case, the documented variability among hunter-gatherers becomes a baseline for studying variability in the archaeological record.

It is undeniable that the more success I have with the former approach, the greater the likelihood that the latter approach will be successful. I have chosen, however, to begin with the problems associated with the latter approach, because understanding the nature of the bias in any data set is central to the success of *both* approaches. I hope to demonstrate some useful research tactics for converting a biased data set into a useful frame of reference instead of dismissing such data as irrelevant to generalizing research goals.

Hunter-Gatherer Niche Diversity

Although all human actors share a number of important characteristics—they are omnivorous, behaviorally flexible, and capable of planning and acting intentionally, and, in a variety of different circumstances, they organize their efforts cooperatively—they differ profoundly from one another in terms of niche state. If one were to ask what role human actors occupy in ecosystems, the answer would have to reflect the fact that sometimes human beings act as predators at the top of the food chain (figure 5.01), where predation on other animals is the predominant strategy, and in other settings they may behave primarily as herbivores, like the Pume, as illustrated in figure 5.02. Some human groups are organized to cope with their status as a food-limited species, whereas others modify the ecosystem and change the character of nutrient production in their favor:

FIGURE 5.01

Nunamiut butchering caribou. Photo by Robert L. Rausch.

FIGURE 5.02

Pume women engaged in cooperative household plant food processing. Photo by Rusty Greaves.

The evolutionary play was going on in the ecological the-ater when as part of the plot man entered, romping and stamping on the stage and bringing it almost to the point of collapse. The feedback between ecosystems and evolving species is obvious in the relations between man and nature. The second part of the circuit involves the impact of man on nature.... The evolution of man has not been in the direction of passive adjustment to more mature ecosystems but is actively sustained through a regression of the rest of the biosphere.

(Margalef 1968:96–97)

The factors that are responsible for the many different niches occupied by so many different groups of individuals of a single human species are of some interest, but how does one determine what they are? The first step is to address the issue of *niche diversity* itself; then it will be possible to focus on the dynamic properties of a particular niche. By niche diversity I am referring to the characteristics of humanity that anthropologists have undertaken to explain: the astonishing variety in life styles, levels of organizational complexity, beliefs, customs, social rituals such as marital and burial practices—in short, all of the organizationally different ways in which human beings engage each other and the world.

The ethnographic record of hunter-gatherers is not orga-nized in terms of niche diversity per se. It is composed of observations and descriptions of life ways that are docu-mented with different degrees of accuracy and comprehen-siveness. Since, however, it is impossible to anticipate accurately the different properties of niches by considering the universally shared physical and cognitive characteristics of human actors,

researchers have no choice but to examine human behavior and organized life ways relative to some other standard, which in this study will be a suite of observed and derivative habitat variables.

Just as in chapter 4 it was necessary to specify the terms in which I intended to describe some properties of the earth's environments, I must also specify the terms I will use to describe hunter-gatherer peoples and conduct an analysis of niche diversity. I will not, however, introduce all of the descriptive criteria at one time. I prefer instead to trace the development of my argument about what is germane knowl-edge at each juncture and to introduce the criteria for obser-vation in that context.

Hunter-Gatherer Variability

Although hunter-gatherer societies differ from each other in many significant ways, in one respect they are all members of a single class: they do not organize themselves to control food production through strategic modifications in the organization of the ecosystems that they exploit. This distinction does limit to some extent the range of variability with which I will be work-ing, but it does not isolate a unit, such as a species or subspecies, that has clear niche implications. As a class, in fact, hunter-gatherers encompass an enormous variety of niches compared with the range observable in nonhuman animals.

Between 1971 and 1978, I was engaged in a systematic study of the ethnographies dealing with all 196 hunter-gatherer cases included in the *Ethnographic Atlas* (Murdock 1967), focusing exclusively on groups with subsistence strategies designated by Murdock's codes as "fishing," "hunting," and "gathering." During the same interval I accumulated information about a number of hunter-gatherer cases that were not included in Murdock's tabulation and began to explore various ways of classifying and documenting environments. Work on this project was intermittent in the decade between the mid-1970s and mid-1980s, but in the late 1980s I began to concentrate on expanding the sample of ethnographic cases and acquiring the monographs, reports, and other records that documented them. A suite of 163 variables was initially identified as important for comparative analysis, and a data base was established as a repository for the rapidly increasing volume of coded data. As it became clear that fewer and fewer ethnographic resources remained to be explored, I began to concentrate on documenting various characteristics of the environments in which the cases in the ethnographic sample were located.

In table 5.01, the 339 hunter-gatherer groups that now make up the comprehensive, comparative data base used in this study are presented, along with seventeen categories of ethnographic and environmental data. The first data category, SUBPOP, is a nominal variable that reflects my judgment about the character of a group's system state at the time of documentation. Groups are designated as either *normal* (*n*) or *suspect* (*x*).

A classification of *n* means that at the time of initial contact, subsistence was based exclusively on hunting, gathering, or some combination of both strategies. No domesticated resources were exploited except perhaps the dog or plant substances such as tobacco. A classification of *x* means that although the group may be organized similarly to hunter-gatherers, subsistence is based primarily on mutualistic articulations with non–hunting and gathering peoples. Classic examples of groups in the *x* category include the Nayaka of India, the Mbuti of the Ituri forest of Zambia, and the Mikea of Madagascar. Groups also receive a classification of *x* if there are claims that, prior to European contact, subsistence was based on hunting and gathering even though all records describe them as exploiting domesticated plants. The Cahuilla of California, the Ayta of the Philippines, and the Hai//om of Namibia all have an *x* in the SUBPOP category.

The next variables to be tabulated are TLPOP, which refers to the total number of persons to whom the ethnographic description applies, and AREA, which represents ethnographers' estimates of the total land area occupied by the group, calculated in units of 100 square kilometers. Dividing TLPOP by AREA produces the variable DENSITY, which is the number of persons per 100-square-kilometer unit.

The next three variables in table 5.01 deal with subsistence[3] and are estimates (calculated as percentages) of a group's dependence upon terrestrial plants (GATHERING),[4] ter-

restrial animals (HUNTING), and aquatic organisms (FISHING) as reflected in the diet of "average" members of the group. The summary variable SUBSP indicates what food type supplies the majority of a group's nutritional intake. A SUBSP value of 1 corresponds to terrestrial animal resources; when SUBSP equals 2, it refers to terrestrial plant resources; when SUBSP equals 3, aquatic resources are indicated.

The next six variables refer to group size and degree of mobility. GRPPAT is a nominal variable that distinguishes between those cases that are mobile and move the entire group from camp to camp as they go about the subsistence round (coded as 1) and other cases that either move into and out of a central location that is maintained for more than one year or are completely sedentary (coded as 2). GRPPAT is followed by three measures of group size, each with a different meaning, depending upon the coding for GRPPAT. For instance, in those cases for which GRPPAT equals 1, GROUP1 records the mean size of the mobile consumer unit that camps together during the most dispersed phase of the yearly settlement cycle. If, however, GRPPAT equals 2, the entry indicates the size of the mobile task group operating out of a relatively permanent settlement, as in the case of family units moving together in a "walkabout" strategy during some season of the year.

For cases in which GRPPAT equals 1, the variable GROUP2 represents the mean size of the consumer group that regularly camps together during the most aggregated phase of the yearly economic cycle. When GRPPAT equals 2, the GROUP2 entry refers to the mean size of the villages that are maintained by the group for two or more years. In cases with a GRPPAT value of either 1 or 2, the value for GROUP3 records the mean size of the multigroup encampments that may aggregate periodically, but not necessarily annually or for immediate subsistence-related activities.

In order to provide an additional perspective on the mobility strategies of the ethnic units in the sample, the variable NOMOV records the average number of residential moves made by household units within the group on an annual basis. A related variable, DISMOV, records the estimated total distance that these residential moves represent each year. Both of these values are documented in table 8.04. The last two variables in table 5.01 summarize properties of the environment within which the hunter-gatherer cases are found. VEGNU refers to the classification by vegetative type, such as "boreal forest" or "tropical savanna woodland," that was discussed in detail in chapter 4. SOIL indicates the primary soil type that is characteristic of a group's range.

Although many other tabulated properties of environments and social systems will be introduced subsequently, at this juncture my immediate concern is tactical. Operating on the assumption that until one has demonstrated the nature of the problem there is no way of evaluating whether the

TABLE 5.01

ENVIRONMENTAL AND SOCIOCULTURAL VARIABLES DEFINED
FOR THE HUNTER-GATHERER DATA SET

GROUP NO.	NAME	SUBPOP	TLPOP	AREA	DENSITY	GATHERING	HUNTING
1	Punan	x	349	29.6	11.8	65	30
2	Batek	x	424	9.8	43	65	30
3	Kubu	x	11,800	1,282.6	9.2	70	25
4	Shompen	n	342	8.6	39.54	50	15
5	Onge	n	393	9.8	40.1	35	20
6	Jarwa	n	255	5.7	44.65	50	20
7	Ayta—Pinatubo	x	1,645	17.9	91.89	87	8
8	North Island	n	464	13.9	33.38	60	35
9	Semang	x	366	20.8	17.57	50	40
10	Veddah	x	72	3.9	18.5	65	30
11	Hill Pandaran	x	556	7.9	70.37	82	16
12	Agta—Casiguran	x	609	7	87	45	15
13	Agta—Isabela	x	1,644	39.1	42	35	20
14	Agta—North Luzon	x	46	1.2	37.94	50	35
15	Chenchu	x	426	3.4	123.3	85	10
16	Mrabri	x	139	6	23.16	75	20
17	Paliyans	x	3,000	311.6	9.63	85	14
18	Birhor	x	629	28.6	22	65	35
19	Kadar	x	565	11.3	50	90	5
20	Cholanaickan	x	254	3.6	70.5	75	15
21	Nayaka	x	70	1	70	90	10
22	Ainu—Hokkaido	n	122	3.5	34.8	10	15
23	Orogens	n	3,200	744	4.3	10	65
24	Ket	n	1,000	625	1.64	5	45
25	Gilyak	n	1,481	76.7	19.31	3	12
26	Yukaghir	n	2,360	3,868.8	0.61	5	55
27	Nganasan	n	876	1,904.3	0.46	1	55
28	Siberian Eskimo	n	1,292	274.9	4.7	1	30
35	Paraujano	n	5,000	142.8	35	30	10
36	Shiriana	x	1,200	76.9	15.6	60	35
37	Akuriyo	n	66	16.4	7.04	55	40
38	Yaruro—Pume	x	164	8.2	19.95	41	6
39	Guahibo	x	1,540	87.4	17.63	60	20
40	Nukak	n	282	30.1	9.34	76	11
41	Bororo	x	850	16.5	51.36	70	20
42	Guato	x	450	66.8	6.74	20	10
43	Siriono	x	94	15.6	6	45	50
44	Yuqui	x	43	25.8	1.66	35	60
45	Nambikwara	x	235	30.2	7.78	75	20
46	Calusa	n	5,500	142	38.73	25	10
47	Guayaki—Ache	x	100	28.7	3.48	30	62
48	Botocudo	x	2,346	239.4	9.8	60	30
49	Heta	n	30	3.1	9.6	55	35
50	Aweikomo	x	106	26	4.1	35	60
51	Tehuelche	n	9,000	4,753	1.89	30	65
52	Chono	n	2,100	153.9	13.64	5	20
53	Alacaluf	n	3,400	226.9	14.98	5	20
54	Ona	n	3,497	481	7.27	5	75
55	Yahgan	n	2,500	88	28.42	5	25
60	Aka	x	1,088	120	9.06	79.5	20
61	Bayaka	x	1,223	70	17.47	90.3	9
62	Bambote	x	937	37.5	25	85	14
63	Baka	x	3,000	220	13.63	85	14
64	Efe	x	750	47	15.96	88.2	11
65	Mbuti	x	1,496	34	44	90	9
66	Mikea	x	300	68.8	4.36	85	15
67	Hukwe	n	124	43	2.9	60	35
68	Hai//Om	x	2,000	520	3.84	55	45

FISHING	SUBSP	GRPPAT	GROUP1	GROUP2	GROUP3	NOMOV	DISMOV	VEGNU	SOIL
5	2	1	22	30	62	45	240	1	U
5	2	2	19	58	0	6	50	1	H
5	2	1	12	0	0	7	140	1	U
35	2	1	19.3	31	0	0	0	1	O
45	3	1	10	23	70	8	40	1	O
30	2	1	8.6	25.8	65	9	59	1	O
5	2	2	11	35	200	0.1	0	1	H
5	2	1	11	43	80	12	76	1	O
10	2	1	17	34	71	36	147	1	U
5	2	1	14	29	72	3	36	2	O
2	2	1	10	34.1	141	45	150	6	A3
40	2	1	17	30	82	27	135	1	H
45	3	1	12	21	70	10	170	1	H
15	2	1	18.9	43.3	0	29	120	1	H
5	2	2	19.3	48	0	4	14	6	A3
5	2	1	19.5	40	0	12	95	2	A3
1	2	1	14	25	107	5	55	3	A3
0	2	1	26.8	46	160	8	90	2	A3
5	2	2	17.5	31.7	187	1.5	19	7	O
10	2	1	10.2	20.5	0	4	75	7	A3
0	2	2	13.8	69	0	0.1	0	7	O
75	3	2	6	30.3	122.6	1.5	8	17	H
25	1	1	20	60	265	15	350	17	H
50	3	1	19	33	182	13	420	17	A1
85	3	2	23	90	0	0.1	0	17	H
40	1	1	12.3	55	180	17	410	20	T
44	1	1	14	29	116	12	375	26	T
69	3	1	15	35	90	3	90	26	T
60	3	2	0	0	0	0	0	2	D
5	2	1	0	50	0	33	171	1	H
5	2	1	18.5	28	66	49	285	1	O
53	3	1	15.1	57	70	7	33	2	O
20	2	2	20	60	179	40	175	1	O
13	2	1	18.8	47	94	55	225	3	O
10	2	2	0	118	0	0.1	0	3	A3
70	3	1	16.6	37	0	0	0	2	O
5	1	1	16	70	0	17	210	2	A3
5	1	1	18	43	0	53	312	1	U
5	2	1	17.5	47	75	13	70	6	O
65	3	2	35	62	700	0.1	0	4	U
8	1	1	26.7	60	130	58	290	4	U
10	2	1	0	50	84	7	135	7	U
10	2	1	6	30	0	0	0	4	U
5	1	1	27	0	110	30	170	7	U
5	1	1	25	75	225	17	360	25	D
75	3	1	0	0	0	0	0	12	U
75	3	1	13.4	0	0	0	0	12	H
20	1	1	20	45	290	24	320	10	A2
70	3	1	13	24	250	7	90	10	A2
0.04	2	1	18	36	111	6	75	1	O
0.7	2	1	19.7	30	73	10	37	1	O
1	2	1	19.7	60	95	7	60	6	U
1	2	1	16	31.7	90	16	85	1	O
0.8	2	1	17.8	33	100	12	65	3	O
1	2	2	30.2	104	252	13	64	3	O
0	2	1	0	40	0	0	0	19	A3
5	2	1	0	23	70	8	125	6	A3
0	2	1	0	60	166	0	0	19	A3

(continued)

GROUP NO.	NAME	SUBPOP	TLPOP	AREA	DENSITY	GATHERING	HUNTING
69	Hadza	*n*	600	25	24	60	40
70	Dorobo—Okiek	*x*	151	3.7	40.81	45	55
71	Sekele	*x*	3,500	2,300	1.52	65	35
72	!Kung	*n*	726	110	6.6	67	33
73	Nharo	*x*	7,500	600	.5	67	32.5
74	G/Wi	*n*	528	180	2.93	55	45
75	Kua	*x*	954	150	6.36	55	45
76	!Ko	*n*	122	118	1.03	55	45
77	/Auni-khomani	*n*	364	570	0.64	52	48
78	//Xegwi	*x*	280	78.4	3.57	40	50
79	/Xam	*n*	300	123.5	2.43	70	30
82	Kaurareg	*x*	140	4	35	35	0
83	Larikia	*n*	1,560	39	40	20	15
84	Gunwinggu	*x*	1,302	73	17.84	40	35
85	Mirrngadja	*x*	77	2	38.5	40	10
86	Anbara	*n*	35	0.8	43.7	35	10
87	Gidjingali	*x*	400	5.5	72.7	35	10
88	Murngin—Yolngu	*n*	588	50	11.76	55	35
89	Jeidji—Forestriver	*n*	442	26	17	60	15
90	Wikmunkan	*n*	1,602	83	19.31	50	30
91	Kakadu	*n*	528	60	8.8	55	20
92	Nunggubuyu	*n*	1,610	70	23	30	10
93	Yintjingga	*n*	217	7	31	20	5
94	Yir-yoront	*n*	104	13	8	65	25
95	Tiwi	*n*	2,662	71	37.5	40	25
96	Kuku—Yalanji	*n*	650	13	50	35	10
97	Groote Eylandt	*n*	595	26	22.9	30	10
98	Walmbaria	*n*	75	1.3	58	25	5
99	Mulluk	*n*	445	10	45	30	10
100	Worora	*n*	1,114	104	11	60	30
101	Lungga	*n*	562	125	4.5	60	35
102	Lardil	*n*	120	4	30	35	5
103	Kaiadilt	*n*	165	2.5	66	13	7
104	Karadjeri	*n*	536	143	3.75	55	40
105	Mamu	*x*	585	13	45	68	7
106	Kariera	*n*	1,111	117	9.5	55	10
107	Warunggu	*n*	1,562	96	16.28	24	42
108	Djaru	*n*	1,345	338	3.98	65	30
109	Walbiri	*n*	1,598	1,378	1.16	70	30
110	Ngatjan	*x*	299	5	59.8	65	15
111	Mardudjara	*n*	169	226	0.75	70	30
112	Ildawongga	*n*	354	787	0.45	80	20
113	Pintubi	*n*	343	229	1.5	65	35
114	Undanbi	*n*	500	23	21.74	20	5
115	Jinibarra	*n*	219	13.7	16	55	30
116	Karuwali	*n*	660	330	2	65	35
117	Alyawara	*n*	560	463	1.21	65	35
118	Ngatatjara	*n*	312	780	0.4	75	25
119	Badjalang	*n*	804	60	13.4	35	25
120	Pitjandjara	*n*	358	598	0.6	65	35
121	Dieri	*n*	420	218	1.93	55	25
122	Arenda—southern	*n*	500	455	1.1	65	30
123	Jankundjara	*n*	572	572	1	65	35
124	Arenda—northern	*n*	2,045	767	2.66	55	45
125	Ualaria	*n*	1,080	120	9	45	35

FISHING	SUBSP	GRPPAT	GROUP1	GROUP2	GROUP3	NOMOV	DISMOV	VEGNU	SOIL
0	2	1	16.5	42	0	7	80	6	A3
0	1	2	17	46	75	0.1	0	7	U
0	2	1	12	31	65	0	0	2	A3
0	2	1	10.4	24.3	87	5.5	75	6	A3
0	2	1	6	20.2	70	2	31	6	D
0	2	1	5.6	36	85	11.5	270	6	D
0	2	1	8	20.8	42	9	215	6	D
0	2	1	13	54	111	12	310	19	D
0	2	1	9	21	77	13	352	19	D
10	2	1	0	0	100	0	0	7	A2
0	2	1	8	24	0	0	0	23	D
65	3	1	17.5	50	116	4	32	2	U
65	3	1	0	0	0	7	60	2	A3
25	2	1	18.5	44	128	14	140	2	A3
50	3	1	16	34	77	6	14	2	A3
55	3	1	10	35	250	3	17	2	A3
55	3	2	16	34	80	0.1	0	2	A3
10	2	1	18	36	290	15	160	2	A3
25	2	1	17	32	125	14	218	19	A3
20	2	1	8	45	150	14	238	2	U
25	2	1	9	32	200	12	150	2	A3
60	3	1	17	30	225	10	85	2	A3
75	3	1	15	0	0	6	25	2	U
10	2	1	14.3	30	0	13	145	2	U
35	2	1	18	32	0	10	75	2	A3
55	3	1	14.3	0	250	6	18	4	U
60	3	1	10	32	0	8	60	2	A3
70	3	2	0	35	60	4	30	2	U
60	3	1	18	30	150	7	40	2	A3
10	2	1	18	35	150	13	150	2	A3
5	2	1	0	0	0	0	0	19	A3
60	3	1	0	45	0	4	35	2	A3
80	3	1	15.4	29	85	7	35	2	A3
5	2	1	0	0	0	0	0	19	D
25	2	1	20	45	285	12	70	1	U
35	2	1	11	31	0	8	130	19	H
34	1	1	9	25	250	0	0	2	U
5	2	1	16	50	0	13	350	19	D
0	2	1	9	42	200	14	380	19	D
20	2	1	8	25	130	0	0	4	U
0	2	1	8	25	180	15	416	24	D
0	2	1	11.5	0	0	15	380	24	D
0	2	1	8.5	21	300	15	325	24	H
85	3	1	0	0	150	0	0	4	H
15	2	1	20	60	400	8	32	4	H
0	2	1	0	0	0	13	275	24	D
0	2	1	10	30	230	14	325	19	D
0	2	1	11	25	150	14	373	24	D
40	3	1	14	40	250	8	90	9	H
0	2	1	10	23	256	15	289	27	D
20	2	1	6.7	22	350	0	0	24	D
5	2	1	0	0	0	0	0	24	D
0	2	1	9.5	28	225	12	298	24	D
0	2	1	9.6	30	310	14	285	24	D
20	2	1	0	0	0	0	0	16	H

(continued)

TABLE 5.01 *(continued)*

GROUP NO.	NAME	SUBPOP	TLPOP	AREA	DENSITY	GATHERING	HUNTING
126	Nakako	*n*	429	494	0.87	50	45
127	Ooldea	*x*	300	637	0.47	55	45
128	Barkindji	*n*	3,008	195	15.43	40	25
129	Karuna	*n*	1,296	72	18	45	20
130	Wongaibon	*n*	3,589	701.1	5.12	40	35
131	Jaralde	*n*	200	5	40	45	15
132	Mineng	*n*	889	127	7	40	30
133	Tjapwurong	*n*	2,450	70	35	35	20
134	Bunurong	*n*	1,953	78	25.04	35	25
135	Kurnai	*n*	336	19	17.7	45	30
136	Tasmanians—eastern	*n*	700	85.7	8.17	25	35
137	Tasmanians—western	*n*	450	33.7	13.35	15	25
143	Seri	*n*	550	21.6	25.48	30	10
144	Cahuilla	*x*	3,675	84	43.75	75	25
145	Cupeno	*x*	195	4	48.8	75	25
146	Kiliwa	*n*	445	36.4	12.25	55	15
147	Diegueno	*n*	3,000	166	18.1	55	25
148	Lake Yokuts	*n*	6,500	170.7	38.1	50	20
149	Serrano	*n*	3,500	199	17.58	60	40
150	Luiseno	*n*	5,500	81.2	67.9	60	15
151	Wukchumi	*n*	92	3.8	24.21	45	40
152	Tubatulabal	*n*	1,000	58	17.2	50	35
153	Nomlaki	*n*	1,575	45	35.0	60	30
154	North Foothill Yokuts	*n*	360	9.4	38.29	50	25
155	Patwin	*n*	1,517	18.5	82	50	30
156	Gabrielino	*n*	5,000	77	64.9	40	10
157	Monache	*n*	387	13.5	28.7	50	30
158	Eastern Pomo	*n*	940	7.4	127	60	15
159	Clear Lake Pomo	*n*	2,099	5.4	308.7	65	10
160	Wintu	*n*	4,000	68	58.82	35	25
161	Chumash	*n*	2,124	18	118.2	25	5
162	Chimariko	*n*	450	9.9	50	30	30
163	Nisenan	*n*	4,770	120	39.75	50	30
164	Salinan	*n*	3,500	94	37.4	50	20
165	Pomo—southern	*n*	2,250	20.3	110.8	45	15
166	Sinkyone	*n*	1,300	9.54	136.44	40	15
167	Lessik	*n*	1,770	18.2	97.2	45	20
168	Miwok—Coast	*n*	1,500	28	53.57	40	10
169	Mattole	*n*	652	5.6	116.4	40	10
170	Miwok—Lake	*n*	227	3.5	65	60	10
171	Yuki—Proper	*n*	4,000	30.4	131.6	50	15
172	Wappo	*n*	1,170	9.7	120.6	55	15
173	Pomo—northern	*n*	3,360	31	108.4	50	20
174	Yana	*n*	1,820	58.1	31.3	45	25
175	Miwok	*n*	1,212	49.5	24.54	55	35
176	Tekelma	*n*	900	70	12.85	35	20
177	Yuki—Coast	*n*	750	11.2	66.96	25	15
178	Tolowa	*n*	2,562	21	122.0	25	10
179	Shasta	*n*	2,925	117	25	45	25
180	Hupa	*n*	1,000	12.5	80	35	10
181	Tututni	*n*	2,200	32.8	67.07	10	30
182	Karok	*n*	1,500	32	46.9	35	10
183	Atsugewi	*n*	1,300	72.5	17.93	35	40
184	Wiyot	*n*	1,390	13.2	107.93	30	5
185	Maidu—Mountain	*n*	1,900	81	23.5	50	30

FISHING	SUBSP	GRPPAT	GROUP1	GROUP2	GROUP3	NOMOV	DISMOV	VEGNU	SOIL
5	2	1	10.6	0	0	17	360	27	D
0	2	1	0	0	0	0	0	24	D
35	2	1	0	0	0	0	0	13	D
35	2	1	0	0	0	8	100	23	A4
25	2	1	0	0	0	0	0	13	V
40	2	2	0	0	0	0	0	16	A4
30	2	1	9	50	300	0	0	9	A4
45	3	2	25	175	350	0	0	16	A2
40	3	1	7.3	44	275	10	90	9	A2
25	2	1	10	50	270	0	0	9	A2
40	3	1	7.5	35	52	12	165	9	H
60	3	1	7.5	33	75	7	65	11	H
60	3	1	17	45	188	7	95	27	D
0	2	2	20	75	180	4	40	27	D
0	2	2	0	97	195	0.1	0	27	D
30	2	1	0	62	130	7	90	23	D
20	2	1	0	39	120	7	80	23	D
30	2	2	0	91.6	150	1	4	23	A4
0	2	2	0	68	0	7	90	23	D
25	2	2	14	110	300	2	18	23	D
15	2	1	0	40	350	5	50	23	U
15	2	1	10	21	110	9	110	23	U
10	2	2	13	65	130	3	33	18	A4
25	2	1	16	40	130	6	70	18	A5
20	2	2	0	53	189	2	14	18	A4
50	3	2	0	0	0	0.1	0	23	D
20	2	1	13	32	70	9	85	25	U
25	2	2	0	0	235	3	36	18	A4
25	2	2	0	150	450	0	0	18	A4
40	3	2	20	50	150	6	139	18	A
70	3	2	0	557	0	0.1	0	23	A5
40	3	2	0	42	0	2	34	17	U
20	2	2	11	45	165	1	5	18	A4
30	2	2	0	0	0	0	0	23	A5
40	2	2	0	150	0	0.1	0	11	A4
45	3	2	0	23	0	4	60	11	U
35	2	2	0	0	0	0	0	11	U2
50	3	2	0	26	0	0	0	11	M5
50	3	2	0	45	0	0	0	11	U2
30	2	2	0	90	192	0	0	18	M5
35	2	2	0	25	150	0	0	11	M5
30	2	2	0	95	154	2	8	23	A4
30	2	2	0	127	0	0.1	0	11	U
30	2	1	0	0	0	4	85	17	U
10	2	1	19	45	250	4	32	17	U
45	3	1	18	50	0	6	70	17	U4
60	3	1	0	0	0	8	100	11	U
65	3	2	18	96	0	5	60	11	U
30	2	1	0	48	0	3	55	11	M5
55	3	2	0	113	0	0.1	0	11	U
60	3	2	0	60	0	5	75	11	U
55	3	2	0	30	0	0.1	0	11	U
25	1	1	0	0	0	0	0	11	M5
65	3	2	0	33	0	1	12	11	U
20	2	1	0	40	0	4	28	25	U

(continued)

TABLE 5.01 *(continued)*

GROUP NO.	NAME	SUBPOP	TLPOP	AREA	DENSITY	GATHERING	HUNTING
186	Yurok	*n*	2,500	19	131	20	10
187	Achumawi	*n*	1,700	98.5	17.25	30	40
188	Modoc	*n*	2,000	90.0	22.89	45	30
189	Klamath	*n*	1,200	89.8	13.36	30	20
190	Guaicura	*n*	977	162.9	6	70	15
191	Chichimec	*n*	3,000	333	9	65	20
192	Death Valley	*n*	42	32.7	1.29	75	25
193	Karankawa	*n*	2,800	133	21	30	15
194	Coahuilenos	*n*	600	373	1.68	65	30
195	Panamint Shoshoni	*n*	500	236	2.12	65	35
196	Yavapai	*x*	600	405	1.48	60	35
197	Koso Mountain Shoshoni	*n*	222	25.9	8.57	60	40
198	Walapai	*x*	1,000	259	3.86	65	35
199	Kawaiisu Shoshoni	*n*	500	42	11.9	60	40
200	Saline Valley Shoshoni	*n*	65	28	2.32	60	40
201	Antarianunts—Southern Paiute	*n*	234	68	3.45	50	35
202	Owens Valley Paiute	*n*	2,100	55.2	38.04	65	30
203	Kawich Mountain Shoshoni	*n*	105	52.6	1.99	55	45
204	Kaibab Southern Paiute	*n*	425	114.6	3.71	60	40
205	Mono Lake Paiute	*n*	170	28.8	5.9	48	45
206	Deep Spring Paiute	*n*	23	6.5	3.54	55	45
207	Salmon-eater Shoshoni	*n*	400	57.9	6.9	30	50
208	Pyramid Lake Paiute	*n*	485	26.2	18.53	50	20
209	Ute—Timanogas	*n*	480	138.8	3.47	40	30
210	Cattail Paiute	*n*	481	21.8	22	50	30
211	Fish Lake Paiute	*n*	100	25.7	3.89	50	30
212	Honey Lake Paiute	*n*	385	36.3	10.6	40	50
213	Hukunduka Shoshoni	*n*	1,000	337.6	2.96	45	35
214	Gosiute Shoshoni	*n*	435	259.7	1.67	50	40
215	Spring Valley Shoshoni	*n*	378	62.6	6.09	45	55
216	White Knife Shoshoni	*n*	500	42.7	11.71	40	45
217	Rainroad Valley Shoshoni	*n*	250	58.4	4.28	55	45
218	Reese River Shoshoni	*n*	390	23.4	16.7	45	40
219	North Fork Paiute	*n*	385	24	16.04	40	45
221	Grouse Creek Shoshoni	*n*	200	122	1.64	40	45
222	Ute—Wimonantci	*n*	405	156	2.6	35	55
223	Bear Creek Paiute	*n*	60	54	1.1	45	50
224	Antelope Valley Shoshoni	*n*	78	58.4	1.13	50	40
225	Washo	*n*	1,877	126	14.9	48	37
226	Suprise Valley Paiute	*n*	367	27	13.59	50	30
227	Wind River Shoshoni	*n*	1,500	960	1.87	20	65
228	Ruby Valley Shoshoni	*n*	450	32.6	13.79	55	37
229	Bohogue North Shoshoni	*n*	380	365.4	1.04	30	55
230	Uintah Ute	*n*	1,750	233.7	7.48	40	35
231	Harney Valley Paiute	*n*	200	160.8	1.24	45	35
232	Sheep-eater Shoshoni	*n*	550	88.1	6.24	20	55
233	Little Smoky Shoshoni	*n*	96	52.6	1.82	45	55
234	Uncompahgre Ute	*n*	1,100	256.4	4.29	35	50
240	Lipan Apache	*x*	500	980	0.51	60	35
241	Comanche	*n*	3,500	1,500	2.33	20	80
242	Chiricahua Apache	*x*	1,425	1,228.5	1.16	60	40
243	Kiowa	*n*	392	280	1.4	20	80
244	Kiowa Apache	*n*	1,908	460	4.14	10	90
245	Cheyenne	*n*	2,750	570	4.82	15	80
246	Arapahoe	*n*	3,000	400	7.5	20	80
248	Crow	*n*	4,650	800	5.81	20	80

FISHING	SUBSP	GRPPAT	GROUP1	GROUP2	GROUP3	NOMOV	DISMOV	VEGNU	SOIL
70	3	2	0	45	0	2	24	11	U
30	1	1	0	23	275	3	64	25	M5
25	2	2	15	92	157	9	45	25	M5
50	3	1	18	31	97	6	84	17	M5
15	2	1	11.7	45	128.3	8	135	27	D
15	2	1	0	0	0	0	0	13	M
0	2	1	7.5	22.5	45	13	225	17	D
55	3	1	0	0	225	0	0	8	V
5	2	1	9	31	153	0	0	27	D
0	2	1	7.5	22.5	0	11	220	27	D
5	2	2	0	107	0	9	18	23	D
0	2	1	13.5	55	0	14	220	27	D
0	2	2	7	27.8	60	4	105	23	D
0	2	1	15	31	45	9	150	25	D
0	2	1	9	30	65	14	180	25	D
15	2	1	0	0	0	10	200	25	M
5	2	2	13	64	300	2	17	25	D
0	2	1	9.5	19.5	42	12	270	25	D
0	2	1	10.1	21.2	70	8	200	25	D
7	2	1	9.6	25	0	11	215	25	D
0	2	1	0	23	0	8	195	25	D
20	1	1	11.2	34	119	12	210	25	D
30	2	1	0	50	320	3	33	25	M
30	2	1	17.5	50	160	0	0	25	U
20	2	1	18	46	130	5	90	25	U
20	2	1	10.5	27	101	9	150	25	D
10	1	1	0	0	0	9	165	25	U
20	2	1	0	24	138	12	250	25	D
10	2	1	10	33	150	13	228	25	D
0	1	1	11	24	180	0	0	25	D
15	1	1	11.4	23	180	0	0	25	D
0	2	1	11	32	70	5	90	25	D
15	2	1	10	30	132	8	130	25	D
15	1	1	0	29	0	0	0	11	U
15	1	1	16	38	78	14	315	25	D
10	1	1	0	37	102	0	0	25	D
5	1	1	16	40	0	0	0	25	M
10	2	1	12.5	20	110	0	0	25	D
15	2	1	9	29	0	7	198	25	D
20	2	1	12.9	28.4	100	9	210	25	M
15	1	1	16	50	200	0	0	18	D
8	2	1	21	48	65	7	120	25	D
15	1	1	12	60	0	0	0	25	D
25	2	1	16	43	169	0	0	25	U
20	2	1	11	0	0	11	250	25	M
25	1	1	18.3	0	300	13	270	25	D
0	1	1	16	0	96	11	260	25	D
15	1	1	17	45	150	0	0	25	U
5	2	1	25	75	166	18	480	18	D
0	1	1	60	269	650	0	0	13	M
0	2	1	34	95	200	0	0	25	A3
0	1	1	35	313	620	0	0	8	D
0	1	1	0	291	0	0	0	8	M
5	1	1	45	275	687	18	390	18	D
0	1	1	36	325	750	0	0	18	M
0	1	1	66	330	1,500	31	570	18	D

(continued)

T A B L E 5 . 0 1 *(continued)*

GROUP NO.	NAME	SUBPOP	TLPOP	AREA	DENSITY	GATHERING	HUNTING
249	Teton Lakota	*n*	12,725	1,450	8.77	10	90
250	Kutenai	*n*	1,200	595	2.01	15	45
252	Bannock	*n*	1,500	649	2.31	30	50
253	Gros-Ventre	*n*	2,260	670	3.37	20	80
254	Plains Ojibwa	*n*	2,000	716.8	2.79	10	75
255	Piegan	*n*	1,525	600	2.54	20	80
256	Blackfoot	*n*	2,425	700	3.46	20	75
257	Assiniboine	*n*	4,500	1,400	3.21	20	70
258	Plains Cree	*n*	4,650	1,700	2.73	10	75
259	Blood	*n*	3,110	700	4.44	10	85
260	Sarsi	*n*	700	400	1.75	10	82
268	Squamish	*n*	1,700	30	56.5	15	25
269	Alsea	*n*	1,500	15.5	96.8	10	15
270	Puyallup	*n*	441	12	36.75	15	15
271	Twana	*n*	965.5	29.8	32.4	10	20
272	Chehalis	*n*	4,000	182	21.97	15	20
273	Nootka	*n*	14,000	91	153.9	5	5
274	Chinook	*n*	5,000	148	33.8	15	10
275	Coos	*n*	2,000	19.2	104.2	10	10
276	Lillooet	*n*	4,000	170	23.5	10	40
277	Lummi	*n*	459	4.1	104.63	10	15
278	Quinault	*n*	1,661	28.3	58.7	10	15
279	Stalo	*n*	1,650	25	66	10	15
280	Cowichan	*n*	347	10	34.75	10	30
281	Tillamook	*n*	1,500	36.3	41.32	30	25
282	Comox	*n*	2,475	45	55	10	15
283	Bella-bella	*n*	2,000	97.5	20.51	10	20
284	Quileute	*n*	1,324	12.7	104.3	10	15
285	Clallam	*n*	2,400	33.9	70	10	20
286	Makah	*n*	332	2.7	123	10	10
287	Haisla	*n*	1,300	68.2	19.1	10	35
288	Kwakiutl	*n*	14,500	211	68.7	5	10
289	Tsimshim	*n*	10,100	241	41.9	5	20
290	Haida	*n*	10,000	103	97.09	1	10
291	Bella-coola	*n*	1,950	150	13	5	25
292	Tlingit	*n*	12,000	1,050	11.42	1	15
293	Gitksan	*n*	3,000	127.2	23.58	1	30
294	Konaig	*n*	8,800	287	30.6	1	5
295	Eyak	*n*	156	26.6	5.86	0.01	10
296	Kuskowagmut	*n*	7,200	416	17.3	5	20
297	Chugash	*n*	3,170	262	12.1	0.01	10
298	Aleut	*n*	13,500	247	54.65	1	5
299	Nunavak	*n*	864	45	19.22	1	15
315	Tenino	*n*	1,510	79.5	19	30	20
316	Umatiela	*n*	1,155	110	10.5	30	30
317	Wenatchi	*n*	5,000	84.5	50.17	20	25
318	Yakima	*n*	3,780	140.8	27	30	25
319	Wishram	*n*	2,132	9.2	231.7	25	15
320	Coeur d'Alene	*n*	1,000	666	1.5	20	55
321	Sinkaietk	*n*	875	60.3	14.51	15	25
322	Okanogan	*n*	1,500	113.1	13.27	25	30
323	Sanpoil	*n*	687	61.4	11.2	25	35
324	Nez-perce	*n*	4,000	450	8.88	33	15
325	Thompson	*n*	5,150	155	33.2	20	25
326	Kalispel	*n*	1,000	666	1.5	20	35
327	Ojibwa—Kitchibuan	*n*	3,000	600	5	15	40
328	Kitikitegon	*n*	76	24.6	3.09	15	45

FISHING	SUBSP	GRPPAT	GROUP1	GROUP2	GROUP3	NOMOV	DISMOV	VEGNU	SOIL
0	1	1	38	283	500	0	0	18	M
40	1	1	0	122	0	13	285	18	M
20	1	1	43	170	650	0	0	18	U
0	1	1	34	188	445	24	420	18	M
15	1	1	40	250	500	0	0	18	M
0	1	1	45	254	762	21	560	18	M
5	1	1	70	346	1,100	30	540	18	M
10	1	1	55	159	850	0	0	18	M
15	1	1	40	75	285	0	0	10	M
5	1	1	42	250	800	0	0	18	M
8	1	1	43	140	300	18	440	22	M
60	3	2	0	106	0	2	34	11	U
75	3	2	0	0	0	3	22	11	U
70	3	2	28	145	0	2	50	11	M
70	3	2	0	80	0	4	65	11	U
65	3	2	0	110	0	0	0	11	U
95	3	2	0	195	0	3	25	11	U
75	3	2	0	52	0	2	28	11	U
80	3	2	0	58	0	0.1	0	11	U
50	3	2	0	85	0	8	90	18	U
75	3	2	0	140	0	2	20	11	U
75	3	2	0	36	0	2	12	11	U
75	3	2	0	37	0	4	40	11	U
60	3	2	0	48	0	6	60	11	U
45	3	2	0	65	0	2	16	11	I4
75	3	2	0	240	0	0	0	11	I4
70	3	2	0	181	0	0	0	11	U
75	3	2	29	112	225	0.1	0	11	U
70	3	2	0	166	0	4	45	11	U
80	3	2	0	164	0	2	15	11	U
55	3	2	0	650	0	0.1	0	11	U
85	3	2	0	420	0	3	31	11	U
75	3	2	0	389	0	3.5	40	11	U
89	3	2	0	577	0	0	0	11	U
70	3	2	0	58	0	0	0	17	U
84	3	2	0	197	0	3	30	11	U
69	3	2	0	179	0	4	45	17	U
94	3	2	0	162	0	0.1	0	17	U
89.99	3	2	0	57	130	2	25	11	U
75	3	2	19	108	0	0.1	0	17	U
89.99	3	2	0	53.5	0	2	40	17	U
94	3	2	0	55	0	0.1	0	17	U
84	3	2	0	54.6	133	0.1	0	17	U
50	3	1	0	0	212	6	70	25	M
40	3	1	0	0	0	0	0	25	M
55	3	2	0	275	500	2	19	25	M
45	3	1	0	0	0	0	0	25	M
60	3	2	25	205	700	0.1	0	25	M
25	1	1	21	60	350	11	300	18	U
60	3	2	20	83	230	7	90	25	U
45	3	2	23	50	245	3	40	25	U
40	3	1	0	50	0	5	75	25	U
52	3	1	0	134	438	0	0	18	M
55	3	2	18	113	265	0	0	18	U
45	3	1	22	75	350	0	0	17	U
45	3	1	15	65	200	14	225	14	S
40	1	2	0	76	0	14	280	14	A1

(continued)

TABLE 5.01 *(continued)*

GROUP NO.	NAME	SUBPOP	TLPOP	AREA	DENSITY	GATHERING	HUNTING
329	Micmac	n	4,393	1,017	4.32	10	55
330	Flathead	n	800	533	1.5	20	60
331	Rainy River Ojibwa	n	230	190.1	1.21	10	60
332	North Saulteaux	n	185	154.2	1.2	5	65
333	Shuswap	n	14,582	1,176	12.4	15	30
334	Pekangekum Ojibwa	n	382	124	3.08	10	60
335	Round Lake Ojibwa	n	250	142.9	1.75	15	65
336	Alcatcho	n	405	54	7.5	10	55
337	Nipigon Ojibwa	n	221	255	0.87	10	55
338	Mistassini Cree	n	450	779	0.58	0.9	74
339	Ojibwa—Northern Albany	n	225	157.4	1.43	5	60
340	Waswanip Cree	n	150	358	0.41	5	55
341	Weagamon Ojibwa	n	250	490	0.51	10	55
342	Montagnais	n	2,700	6,600	0.41	10	50
343	Sekani	n	656	800	0.82	10	60
344	Beaver	n	1,000	1,947	0.51	10	55
345	Slave	n	2,454	2,453.7	1.0	10	60
346	Kaska	n	540	600	0.90	10	65
347	Tahltan	n	810	700	1.16	10	60
348	Chilcotin	n	2,500	217	11.52	10	40
349	Carrier	n	525	70	7.59	10	47
350	Mountain	n	780	1,000	0.78	10	75
351	Han	n	1,000	550.8	1.8	10	70
352	Hare	n	572	1,734	0.33	10	65
353	Attawapiskat Cree	n	4,460	3,120	1.43	5	40
354	Koyukon	n	2,000	1,825	1.09	5	60
355	Chippewyan	n	2,850	6,194	0.46	5	70
356	Kutchin	n	4,863	2,861	1.70	2	65
357	Ingalik	n	1,500	690	2.71	2	43
358	Satudene	n	825	1,500	0.55	3	75
359	Nabesna	n	162	210	0.77	3	40
360	Rupert House Cree	n	450	500	0.9	3	56
361	Dogrib	n	1,590	1,809	0.88	3	66
362	Tanaina	n	4,500	925	4.86	3	51
363	Tutchone	n	1,500	1,620	0.92	2	62
364	Holikachuk	n	330	216.4	1.52	2	36
365	Naskapi	n	400	960	0.42	1	73
369	Norton Sound Inuit	n	1,600	210	7.61	1	15
370	Kobuk Inuit	n	500	187	2.67	1	63
371	Kotzebue Sound Inuit	n	975	147	6.63	1	21
372	Labrador Inuit	n	1,460	525	2.78	0.01	29
373	Great Whale Inuit	n	450	242	1.86	0.1	18
374	Caribou Inuit	n	700	2,365	0.3	0.1	55
375	Noatak Inuit	n	550	250	2.2	0.1	75
377	Nunamiut Inuit	n	240	249	0.96	0.1	89
378	Mackenzie Inuit	n	2,500	650	3.84	0.1	38
379	Sivokamiut Inuit	n	600	40	15	0.1	10
380	Point Hope Inuit	n	450	107.1	4.2	0.01	35
381	Copper Inuit	n	2,000	4,620	0.43	0.01	25
382	Utkuhikhaling-miut	n	164	431	0.38	0.01	30
383	Aivilingmiut Inuit	n	130	400	0.32	0.01	35
384	Ingulik Inuit	n	1,193	2,210	0.54	0.01	15
385	West Greenland	n	5,112	1,080	4.73	0.01	15
386	Baffin Island Inuit	n	6,000	3,706	1.26	0.01	5
387	Netsilik Inuit	n	500	1,970	0.25	0.01	25
388	Angmakaslik	n	567	73.5	7.72	0.01	10
389	Tareumiut Inuit	n	550	142.5	3.86	0.01	25
390	Polar Inuit	n	300	731	0.41	0.01	30

FISHING	SUBSP	GRPPAT	GROUP1	GROUP2	GROUP3	NOMOV	DISMOV	VEGNU	SOIL
35	1	1	15	25	150	12	252	14	S
20	1	1	24	73	300	0	0	18	U
30	1	1	21	57	190	13	350	14	S
30	1	1	15	45	185	15	375	22	S
55	3	2	0	108	266	4	60	18	U
30	1	2	22	55	160	0	0	17	S
20	1	1	7	50	150	0	0	17	S
35	1	1	20	85	235	5.5	90	17	U
35	1	1	18	36	126	14	350	17	S
25.1	1	1	6	37	215	16	450	17	S
35	1	1	0	50	225	14	2.75	12	A1
40	1	1	12	58	235	0	0	17	S
35	1	1	10	50	140	0	0	17	S
40	1	1	22	95	245	19	318	17	S
30	1	1	18	40	164	15	400	17	A1
35	1	1	20	58	110	20	400	17	T
30	1	1	13	39	220	13	445	22	T
25	1	1	16	58	139	9	280	22	U
30	1	1	0	71	165	0	0	17	U
50	3	2	0	0	0	0	0	18	U
43	1	2	18	54	170	12	275	17	A1
15	1	1	15	60	0	0	0	17	U
20	1	1	0	0	214	0	0	22	T
25	1	1	13	26	120	16	450	17	T
55	3	1	17	55	172	8	215	17	A1
35	1	1	14	38	105	14	350	17	T
25	1	1	23	75	295	18	496	26	S
33		1	32	78	210	16	450	22	T
55	3	2	0	77	0	4	64	17	U
20	1	1	12.5	29	0	14	375	22	T
57	3	2	17	39	0	14	320	22	T
41	1	1	12	55	225	16	340	17	S
31	1	1	22	60	162	13	450	22	T
46	1	2	0	68	0	2	36	17	U
36	1	1	17	60	0	19	450	22	T
62	3	2	0	66	300	0.1	0	17	T
26	1	1	23	39	117	16	420	17	T
84	3	2	27.5	48	0	0.1	0	17	T
36	1	1	18	30	0	9	225	17	T
78	3	2	24.5	49	350	0.1	0	26	T
70.99	3	1	11	35	158	4	135	17	T
81.9	3	1	20	40	65	3	85	17	T
44.9	1	1	19.5	40	75	16	440	26	T
24.9	1	1	17.5	30	105	12	360	26	T
10.9	1	1	18.5	25.1	75	11	501	26	T
61.9	3	2	12	45	135	6	145	26	T
89.9	3	2	19	121	0	2	16	26	T
64.9	3	2	13	79	0	2	75	26	T
74.99	3	1	18	105	264	14	444	26	T
69.9	3	1	18	35	0	15	380	26	T
64.9	3	1	13	26	64	14	400	26	T
84.99	3	1	20	60	120	12	385	26	T
84.99	3	1	16.5	31.5	0	3	70	26	T
94.99	3	1	12	70	143.9	4	175	26	T
74.99	3	1	22	85	150	11	307	26	T
89.99	3	2	14	30.9	137	2	13	26	T
74.99	3	2	14	309	0	3	60	26	T
69.99	3	1	11.5	35	150	11	350	26	T

proposed solutions are rational, I begin by examining a sub-set of the total data set in order to expose the types of problems that may be recognized through analysis.[5]

Productive Results from Biased Data

My demonstration will begin with a map of the world and with the data set of 339 ethnic groups that constitute the universe in this study. The first question to be asked is: what can be learned by situating each group in a two-dimensional map of geographic space? An initial inspection of figure 5.03, which illustrates the spatial distribution of the comprehensive sample of hunter-gatherer groups, reveals that the black dots representing individual cases are not evenly distributed across the surface of the map. Of the 51,349,234 square miles of the earth's terrestrial surface, the 339 groups occupy only 4,965,340.76 square miles, or 9.66 percent of the total land area.

As I have noted, this sample does not include all of the hunter-gatherer groups that were known to exist during the colonial and more recent eras, but it does include all of the cases that were described with sufficient detail to be included in a comparative analysis. Omissions bias figure 5.03 in the following ways. At the time of initial European contact, for instance, all of the continent of Australia, which has a total land mass of 1,967,741 square miles, was occupied by 592 distinct ethnic groups of foragers, only 56 of which were doc-umented at the level of detail required by this study. The neighboring island of Tasmania, consisting of 26,000 square miles, was occupied at close to maximum capacity by nine groups of hunter-gatherers, of which only two are included in our study. The only other geographic unit inhabited exclusively by hunter-gatherers at the onset of the European colonial expansion was the Andaman Island group in the Bay of Bengal, where twelve ethnic groups were observed in a 2,508-square-mile area.

Although sixteenth-century Spanish, English, French, Dutch, and Portuguese explorers of the New World encountered both large, centralized, state-level polities and looser networks of small-scale, agrarian communities, nearly one-third of the total land mass of both North and South America was nevertheless occupied by hunter-gatherers at colonial contact. An estimated ninety-four ethnically distinct groups of hunter-gatherers, twenty of which are included in our sample, inhabited southeastern South America (figure 5.04) and occupied approximately 21 percent, or 1,511,716.21 square miles, of the continent's total area. At the time of initial observation by literate Europeans, approximately 250 ethnically distinct groups of hunter-gatherers were distributed across 46 percent of the total land area of North America (4,235,317.16 square miles). Of these groups, 215 (86 percent of the contact-era population) are included in this study.

Twenty of the cases in the global sample (including one case from Madagascar) were located in southern and central Africa, occupying 1.75 percent of the continental land mass.

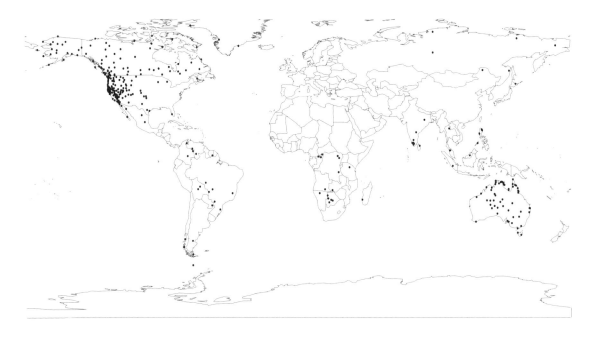

FIGURE 5.03

World map showing the location of the 339 ethnographically documented cases of hunter-gatherers used comparatively in this study.

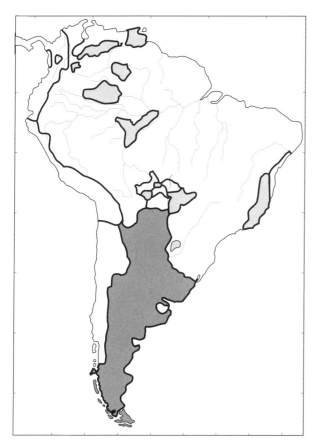

FIGURE 5.04

Map of South America showing the areas occupied by hunter-gatherer groups documented during the colonial period. Adapted and redrawn from Wilson (1999:figure 5.1).

In contrast, thirty foraging groups are thought to have been extant during the fifteenth and sixteenth centuries, inhabiting approximately 313,016 square miles or roughly 2.67 percent of the continental land surface. Similarly, compared with the size of the Asian land mass, a disproportionately small number of Asian hunter-gatherer groups are observable in figure 5.03. Of the thirty-nine ethnically distinct groups referred to in sixteenth-century documents, twenty-eight cases are included in the global sample. The colonial era populations had access to 2.55 percent of the Asian land area (434,949.42 square miles), but this is reduced for groups in my sample to 358,932.55 square miles or 2.1 percent.

In some areas of the world—primarily western and central Europe, the Near East, North Africa, and the central Eurasian steppe—a subsistence strategy based on the exploitation of hunted and gathered resources by highly mobile peoples has not been an option for thousands of years. Not only are these regions blank on the map in figure 5.03, they would also have been featureless on a map of the global distribution of hunter-gatherers produced in the fifteenth or sixteenth century.

Similarly, in the colonial era—as now—the area of eastern North America from the Great Lakes south to the Gulf of Mexico would have had no hunter-gatherer populations. This is also true for most of Mesoamerica and major regions of South America. On the latter continent, the only exception is a huge contiguous area composed of most of the modern states of Argentina and Uruguay, parts of Paraguay, the eastern region of Bolivia, and southwestern Brazil. Despite the likelihood that this large region was well populated by hunter-gatherers at the time of European intrusion, the thin scatter of points across this area in figure 5.03 reflects the fact that little information about the region's indigenous peoples remains in the ethnographic record.

In table 5.02, I look at the problem of lack of representation from a global perspective and present estimates of the

TABLE 5.02

COMPARISON BY GEOGRAPHIC REGION OF THE GLOBAL SAMPLE OF HUNTER-GATHERERS WITH ESTIMATES OF HUNTER-GATHERER DISTRIBUTION IN THE COLONIAL ERA

	AFRICA	ASIA	SOUTH AMERICA	AUSTRALIA	NORTH AMERICA	TOTAL
AREA:[1]						
a. Colonial era	8,128	11,294	39,255	77,739	109,980	246,396
b. Global sample	5,419	9,320	6,331	11,039	96,826	128,936
PERCENT OF (A) REPRESENTED BY (B)	66.7	82.5	16.3	14.2	88.0	52.3
NUMBER OF ETHNIC GROUPS:						
a. Colonial era	30	49	94	601	250	1,024
b. Global sample	20	28	20	56	215	339
PERCENT OF (A) REPRESENTED BY (B)	66.6	58.1	21.3	9.3	86.0	33.1

Note: 1. Areas are expressed in 100-square-kilometer units.

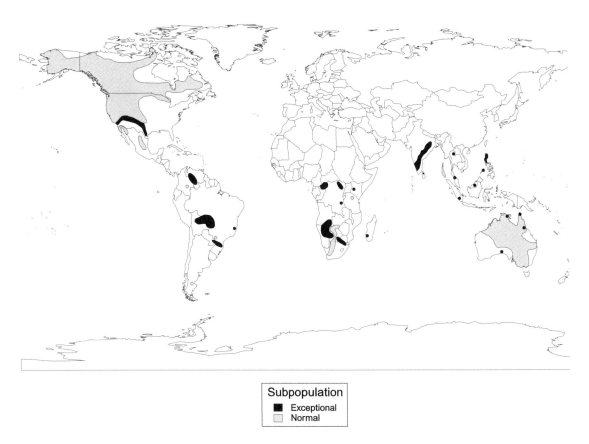

Subpopulation
■ Exceptional
▢ Normal

FIGURE 5.05

World map showing the location of ethnographically documented hunter-gatherer cases, differentiated into those in settings with other hunter-gatherers and those that were integrated into non-hunter-gatherer systems at the time of description.

number of hunter-gatherer groups encountered by early European explorers as well as the size and continental placement of their territories. I contrast this distribution with the geographic location and area occupied by the 339 ethnographically documented groups forming the informational baseline of this book. The differences between the two samples are to some extent the result of decisions by observers about the feasibility of undertaking field work and the likelihood that research would be productive. Much more responsibility for the loss of ethnic identity, amalgamation, or outright extinction standing behind the two-thirds reduction in hunter-gatherer cases in my sample lies, however, with the appropriation and destruction of foragers' territories and resources by indigenous and colonial agents of change.

Of the five continental areas included in table 5.02, North America is represented by the largest number of cases, and it also has the highest percentage of cases remaining from the colonial era. In contrast, the greatest attrition recorded in table 5.02 between the colonial era and my comprehensive sample—and the greatest loss of information—has occurred in Australia and South America. A corresponding reduction in the

size of hunter-gatherer territories is noticeable in all five regions between the time of initial contact and the period of ethnographic documentation. Hunter-gatherer groups living in large, contiguous regions of North and South America—and throughout the continent of Australia—differed from similar groups in Asia and Africa in that their territories were part of larger geographic units composed of a number of other ethnically distinct hunter-gatherer groups.

The organizational differences between hunter-gatherer groups that operated in a competitive matrix of similar but economically independent units—as in Australia, for example—and those that occupied a specialist role in a complex, mutualistically organized system such as the Efe in Zaire will be discussed in greater detail in chapters 7 and 8. An initial picture of the geographic distribution of the hunter-gatherer groups belonging to each of these two different organizational types is provided in figure 5.05.

I distinguish between those groups that were independently organized, active foragers at the time of ethnographic description and those that are suspected to have participated in complex arrangements integrating various occupational

TABLE 5.03

TABULATION OF THE SUBPOP VARIABLE BY GEOGRAPHIC REGION

	AFRICA	ASIA	SOUTH AMERICA	AUSTRALIA	NORTH AMERICA	TOTAL
NUMBER OF NORMAL HUNTER-GATHERER CASES (CODED *n* = "NORMAL" IN DATA FILE)	7	11	9	49	209	285
NUMBER OF SUSPECT HUNTER-GATHERER CASES (CODED *x* = "SUSPECT" IN DATA FILE)	13	17	11	7	6	54
PERCENTAGE OF TOTAL "SUSPECT" CASES IN REGION	65.0	60.7	55.0	12.5	2.8	15.9

Note: Cases from Australia and North America are primarily classified as "suspect" because nineteenth-century ethnographic descriptions were incomplete or inaccurate and not because the original status of the groups is uncertain.

specialists into an economic mosaic. Groups in the latter category—as well as groups whose recent status as hunter-gatherers is not disputed but who were practicing agriculture or working as wage laborers at the time of ethnographic description (usually as the result of intense regional competition)—have been identified by the variable SUBPOP. A tabulation of cases by geographic region and organizational status is provided in table 5.03.

A SUBPOP designation of "suspect" applies to more than 3 percent of the hunter-gatherer cases from Asia and Africa, a high percentage due largely to the mutualistic articulation of many hunter-gatherer groups with societies of non-hunter-gatherers. Many of the cases in the "suspect" category are assumed to be survivors of historically known hunter-gatherer groups, which may be correct, but I also think that at the time of ethnographic description, many were specialists who contributed nonagricultural products to a regional system dominated by non-hunter-gatherers. Some of the cases that have been assigned to the "normal" category might also be challenged because their classification was not based on their history but, instead, on whether their internal organization proceeded primarily from the integration of hunting and gathering activities.

By taking another look at figure 5.03 and—instead of focusing on the areas of the world where ethnographically documented groups of hunter-gatherers have been found—by concentrating on where they have *not,* a geographic bias becomes clearly evident. All hunter-gatherer groups for which eyewitness reports exist have consistently been distributed in areas of the world that are peripheral to those places in Europe, Africa, and Asia where agriculturists, pastoralists, and ancient complex societies once developed. Since the archaeological record reveals that there was a time when all human groups depended upon wild resources for their subsistence, this is an appropriate point at which to ask an epistemological question. Is the accumulated knowledge of hunting and gathering peoples that is depicted schematically in figure 5.03 so historically and geographically circum-

scribed that I cannot justify any attempt I might make to learn about past hunter-gatherers who lived in geographic areas where hunter-gatherers are unknown in the modern era?

I believe that the answer to this question is *no, I am not constrained by my ignorance of the past as long as I can find other relevant knowledge to bring to bear on the problem.* Even though the distribution of my sample of documented hunter-gatherers is in no way representative with regard to the earth's geography and is relatively marginal to the regions where so-called "great civilizations" arose (particularly western civilization, with its post-fourteenth-century colonial expansion), the relevant question is: *is this bias particularly germane to my efforts to understand the conditioners of variability among hunter-gatherers?* Since no one has yet systematically investigated the factors that contribute to societal variability, it is not known what the geographic bias of the data set implies in processual terms. As a first step in exploring this question, therefore, I will substitute an information-laden environmental frame of reference in place of a deficiency-ridden geopolitical and historical frame of reference and take a look at the data against this new background.

As the first step in my attempt to evaluate the utility of the ethnographic data base and generate useful information, I develop a proportional projection based on the use of the environmental variable VEGNU as a frame of reference. Initially I want to answer the following question: is the sample of hunter-gatherers as strongly biased relative to the VEGNU classification of the earth's vegetation as it is when I look at the same ethnographic data in terms of simple historical geography? If it is not, then it may be possible to use the observable relationships between organizational properties of hunter-gatherers and some specific properties of their ecological theaters as the basis for subsequent relational projections of "what we know" to geographic areas where no hunter-gatherer groups have ever been documented. As I have argued previously, decisions about what is germane analytical practice are not an ontological issue but rather a tactical one, and my choices at any given juncture are based primarily on my learning goals.

TABLE 5.04

DISTRIBUTION OF ETHNOGRAPHIC SAMPLE OF HUNTER-GATHERER
CASES ACCORDING TO PLANT COMMUNITY TYPE

PLANT COMMUNITY TYPES			HUNTER-GATHERER CASES		
Vegetation code (1)	Area[1] covered (2)	Percentage of earth (3)	Area occupied (4)	Percentage of column 2 (5)	Percentage of cases (6)
FE-1	93,998.97	7.72	2,075.50	2.21	5.9 0
SW-2	33,181.75	2.72	439.20	1.32	1.47
FMO-3	88,514.40	7.27	3,294.00	3.72	8.26[2]
FSP-4	5,092.83	0.42	0.00	0.00	0.00
FBE-5	35,127.82	2.88	215.50	0.61	1.76
FMT-6	27,056.56	2.22	634.00	2.34	2.06
STG-7	72,231.63	5.93	1,187.00	1.64	2.94
GP-8	16,494.76	1.35	873.00	**5.29**	0.88
FD-9	40,204.18	3.30	1,813.00	**4.51**	0.88
FSA-10	3,389.90	0.28	489.70	**14.44**	1.17
DTW-11	45,564.13	3.74	2,729.10	**5.99**	1.17
FBD-12	30,588.25	2.51	551.20	1.80	1.17
FC-13	4,441.07	0.36	3,054.00	**68.76**	**12.29**
FL-14	3,110.67	0.26	1,813.70	**58.30**	1.17
SSA-15	4,866.84	0.40	75.00	1.54	0.59
FSM-16	10,250.62	0.84	0.00	0.00	0.00
DTG-17	47,024.16	3.86	3,866.80	**8.22**	3.24
GS-18	74,498.34	6.12	14,835.00	**19.91**	**8.55**
FBO-19	123,375.93	10.13	40,539.70	**32.44**	**12.29**
FSS-20	17,106.47	1.40	1,773.20	**10.37**	**4.42**
FBL-21	53,815.44	4.42	3,868.00	**7.15**	0.29
DSS-22	164,204.86	13.48	2,032.10	1.23	1.94
BPK-23	21,926.45	1.80	14,622.70	66.68	2.94
DSD-24	29,216.23	2.40	10,212.30	**34.95**	**13.86**
DSP-25	9,994.90	0.82	5,001.00	**50.03**	2.94
TA-26	45,844.81	3.52	0.00	0.00	0.00
T-27	50,242.10	4.12	27,545.30	**54.82**	**5.90**
D-28	69,702.93	5.72	20.06	2.88	0.00

Notes: 1. Area is expressed in 100-square-kilometer units.
2. **Bold** type in columns 5 and 6 indicates that the values exceed the percentage-of-earth-area values in column 3. The differences in value indicate the positive bias in the habitats occupied by hunter-gatherers.

The attributes of each vegetative type included in the classification of the earth's plant formations have been presented in detail in table 4.08, but in order to use these twenty-eight types I must specify a *currency* in terms of which measurements within my frame of reference will be expressed for purposes of comparison. I have chosen a standardized currency of 100-square-kilometer units, and I will measure how many such units of each type of plant community in the classification are found in my referential domain, which is the earth. I will then compare this number of units to the number of units of each vegetative type that each hunter-gatherer group in the global sample occupies.

The results of this comparison are summarized in table 5.04, using the following conventions. The table is ordinated from beginning to end in terms of the net aboveground productivity (NAGP) value of each plant community, proceeding from the highest value, which is the equatorial and

tropical rain forest community (FE), to the lowest, which is the desert formation (D). Column 2 of the table summarizes the total area covered by each plant formation, and in column 3 the percentage of the earth's land area represented by the formation is listed. The total number of 100-square-kilometer units that hunter-gatherers occupy in each plant community is listed in column 4, and the figures in column 5 correspond to the percentage of a plant community's total area that is occupied by hunter-gatherers (column 4 divided by column 2 and multiplied by 100). Column 6 lists the percentage of cases in the global sample that is found in each plant community.

In order to provide a different perspective on the issue of the "representativeness" of my sample of surviving hunter-gatherers (Lee and DeVore 1968:5), I rework some of the data in table 5.04 so that I may ask in what environments there is a rough proportionality between the amount of the earth's

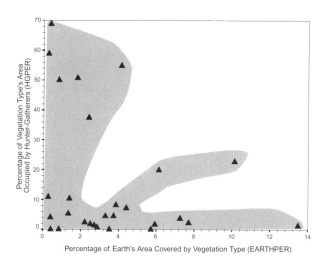

FIGURE 5.06

Percentage of the earth's area covered by identified plant communities graphed relative to the percentage of each community occupied by documented hunter-gatherers.

surface covered by a particular vegetation type (column 2) and the percentage of the global sample of hunter-gatherer cases found within a given plant community (column 6). A plot of this information on the graph illustrated in figure 5.06 reveals four vegetative subgroups distinguished in terms of the percentage of the area occupied by hunter-gatherers within a particular vegetative formation (HGPER) when arrayed against the percentage of the earth covered by that formation (EARTHPER). A fifth, less visible, distribution consists of the vegetative communities for which there are no documented cases of hunter-gatherers.

The first subset consists of examples of rather small vegetative communities for which the percentage of resident hunter-gatherer cases is substantial. These include the coastal forests of northern California and the Pacific northwest (FC-13), the so-called lake forests of northern North America (FL-14), the boreal parkland located primarily in North America (BPK-23), the Australian deserts that alternate with porcupine grass (DAP-9), and the Australian sclerophyllous forests (FSA-10). It is likely that if I had adequate ethnographic information, the congruence between EARTHPER and HGPER would be 100 percent because these plant formations occur only in regions that were also exclusively occupied by hunter-gatherers. In any case, from a sampling perspective there is more than adequate coverage of these environments. All possible cases are represented except for Australian sclerophyllous forests, which are distributed widely over the area of the earliest European settlement in Australia, where, unfortunately, there was minimal ethnographic documentation.

In the second subset in figure 5.06, the percentage of the earth covered by a vegetative type (EARTHPER) and the

percentage of the area of each vegetative community occupied by hunter-gatherer cases (HGPER) are linearly related, but the number of cases rises steeply relative to EARTHPER. Plant formations in this category include tundra (T-27), temperate zone semidesert scrub and woodland (DSD-24), sclerophyllous scrub–dwarf forest and chaparral (FSS-20), tallgrass prairie (GP-8), and Australian sclerophyllous tree savanna (SSA-15). Here also the list of vegetative communities can be understood in terms of the geographic bias in the distribution of hunter-gatherers. The tundra, the semidesert scrub of the Great Basin of North America, the tallgrass prairie, and the dwarf forest–chaparral of California are major plant communities characteristic of the regions of North America where hunter-gatherers were continuously distributed. The Australian sclerophyllous tree savanna is also found only in a region exclusively occupied by hunter-gatherers. With the exception of the latter vegetative type, all of the preceding plant communities cover considerably larger areas of the earth than do the hunter-gatherer cases in the global sample.

In other words, there are areas of the earth with identical or similar vegetative types but no ethnographically documented history of hunter-gatherer occupation. These include the tundra of Eurasia, a large semidesert scrub region in central Asia and another in Argentina, a zone of sclerophyllous scrub–dwarf forest and chaparral around the Mediterranean basin, and a large area of tallgrass prairie in Uruguay and northern Argentina, as well as smaller areas in Poland, Czechoslovakia, parts of eastern Hungary, western Ukraine, and northern Romania. The absence in these regions of ethnographically documented hunter-gatherer groups makes them prime candidates for proportional projection, followed by archaeological verification.

A relatively large number of hunter-gatherer cases have been documented in the vegetative communities making up the second subset. There is, however, a distinct geographic bias associated with their location relative to the actual geographic distribution of the vegetative communities to which hunter-gatherer habitats have been assigned. Nevertheless, as representatives of vegetative communities rather than geographic areas, these cases can be expected to be informative about the role of conditioning variables in these plant communities and their effect on hunter-gatherer variability in analogous settings, if not in general. At the very least, these cases inform us about probable dynamics in geographic regions where there are no known hunter-gatherers.

The third subset of vegetative types in figure 5.06 is the largest and, as in the second, there is a linear correlation between HGPER and EARTHPER. The only difference between the two is that in the third the slope of the line is much less steep, which means that the proportion between the values of HGPER and EARTHPER in each vegetative type is much closer. This pattern indicates that of all the vegetative types the ones in the third subset most closely resemble a numerically unbiased sample. The plant communities included in this subset are boreal forest (FBO-19), shortgrass prairie (GS-18), boreal forest dominated by deciduous larch-aspen (FBL-21), thorntree–desert grass savanna (DTG-17), deciduous forest (FD-9), equatorial mountain forest (FMT-6), mixed boreal and deciduous forest (FBD-12), tropical and subtropical savanna woodland (broadleaf tree savanna) (SW-3), and subtropical broadleaf evergreen forest (FBE-5).

Initial observation of this cluster of plant communities reveals that it includes most of the vegetative types that are found in Europe west of 60 degrees east latitude and north of the Mediterranean basin or Saudi Arabia. The exceptions are polar tundra (T-27), which leads the list of overrepresented groups of hunter-gatherers in the second subset, and Mediterranean evergreen mixed forest (FSM-16)—including cedars of Lebanon in better-watered areas and mixed pistachio and juniper in less well-watered regions where no hunter-gatherers are found. This pattern confirms that my sample of hunter-gatherer cases is numerically adequate and can be projected to the areas of the earth where no groups were recorded historically. There is also a huge geographic bias in the particular locations where hunter-gatherers have been documented.

The question remains, however, whether it is reasonable to project what has been learned from this geographically biased sample to climatically and vegetatively analogous regions of the earth where hunter-gatherers have not been observed. I think that the geographic bias is relatively unimportant in light of the fact that the number of documented hunter-gatherer cases is almost perfectly correlated with the actual area of the earth covered by the twenty-eight plant communities in my classification. In other words, there is little relational bias among these plant communities relative to the environmental variables that condition the similarities in vegetation.

The fourth subset of figure 5.06 is composed of four vegetative communities: tropical rain forest (FE-1), tropical-subtropical monsoon (raingreen) forest (FMO-3), thorntree-tallgrass savanna (STG-7), and subtropical semidesert scrub (DSS-22). Each of these plant types covers a considerable area of the earth, but the total area exploited by hunter-gatherers is relatively small, although other subsistence strategies have permitted human presence. These plant communities are characterized by formations with very low primary productivity (DSS, for example) as well as two of the *most* productive communities: tropical rain forests, which have very high plant productivity, and thorntree-tallgrass savanna, where the second highest standing crop of ungulates is usually found. Tropical-subtropical monsoon forests, which have the third highest levels of ungulate biomass, are also in this subset.

The final subset in figure 5.06, which represents only 10.74 percent of the land surface of the earth, includes four plant communities in which there are no hunter-gatherer presence. On balance, this is a relatively small proportion of the earth for which there are no exemplars to act as guides in imagining a world populated exclusively by hunter-gatherers. The plant communities in the fifth subset include true deserts (D-28), which are the most marginal of habitats in terms of plant productivity, and alpine tundra or Puna (TA-26), comprising the high, mountainous areas of Tibet and analogous regions in the South American Andes. Also in this subset are Mediterranean forests (FSM-16), such as the cedars of Lebanon and the forested areas of western North Africa, and southern pine forests (FSP-4) in the southeastern United States (and analogous zones in south China). Both of the forest communities are relatively small areas and are components of regional plant communities in which agriculture was a relatively early feature.

Although desert and alpine tundra–Puna plant communities are two of the least productive vegetative settings on earth, if conventional anthropological wisdom were correct one would expect that hunter-gatherers would have been quite common in these settings. According to a popular anthropological origin myth, hunter-gatherers once occupied most of the earth's "best" environments. With the onset of human food production, it is argued, hunter-gatherers were rapidly replaced by agriculturists in the "best" environments and were forced to become food producers or to retreat into what Service (1962:59) referred to as "areas where domestication of plants and animals was not feasible."

This view has been restated so many times that hunter-gatherer survival into the modern era is expected to have occurred only in the most "marginal" of the earth's habitats (see also Ammerman and Cavalli-Sforza 1984:24). According to Steward and Faron, "at the time of their discovery, the nomads lived in regions that were economically marginal, inferior, or relatively unproductive, such as swamps, deserts, and other hinterlands" (1959:374–75). Lee and DeVore expressed the similar view that "neolithic peoples have been steadily expanding at the expense of the hunters. Today the latter are often found in unattractive environments, in lands which are of no use to their neighbors and which pose difficult and dramatic problems of survival. The more favorable habitats have long ago been appropriated by peoples with stronger, more aggressive social systems" (1968:5).

The evidence arrayed in figure 5.06 and table 5.04, however, contradicts these assertions and prompts me to make the following empirical generalization:

Generalization 5.01

Hunter-gatherers are not found in true desert settings, which are the most marginal habitats in terms of plant productivity. They are rarely found in zones of semidesert scrub (DSS), which is the world's most prevalent plant formation and the second driest environment when measured in terms of total annual rainfall. Hunter-gatherers are not found in the high mountain areas of Tibet and analogous regions of South America (vegetative type TA).

In other words, in heavily water-stressed areas, pastoralists or agriculturists who use some form of irrigation or other unearned water source predominate.

The absence of hunter-gatherer survivors in the world's most water-deficient habitats suggests that knowledge about the range of hunter-gatherer niches in the past is seriously incomplete. The preceding generalization also prompts me to question the conventional view that the use of domesticated sources of food was primarily responsible for population growth. The data in table 5.05 suggest that, as a consequence of domestication, it became possible to support human beings in some settings that were "marginal" to or previously unoccupied by hunter-gatherers. It also suggests that the evolutionary importance of the domestication of plants and animals stems from the fact that their existence opened up new niches while increasing the productivity of old ones.

Another way to use the data from table 5.05 to address the issue of marginality is to ask if there is any statistical relationship—measured in terms of primary productivity—between the locations where hunter-gatherers are found and specific plant communities (see notes to table 5.05). When I do a chi-square analysis, I find that there is no significant relationship, which supports my assertions about marginality and supports the conclusion that there is no bias to the distribution of ethnographically documented hunter-gatherers if "marginality" is judged relative to plant productivity. I should, therefore, be able to use the global sample of ethnographically documented hunter-gatherer peoples to study the relationships between the organizational properties of social groups and basic environmental conditioners of plant productivity. Any observed regularities could then be projected to the total earth as relational analogies that are relatively unbiased with respect to the conditioners of primary plant productivity.

On the other hand, with regard to the distribution of hunter-gatherers vis-à-vis the estimates of secondary biomass in table 5.05, a low probability value was obtained for the biomass of ungulates of moderate body size (EXPREY), which suggests that there is some bias in the spatial distribution of hunter-gatherers relative to rank order variability in the estimated standing crop of ungulates (see ranks for animals data in table 5.05). I conclude, therefore, that

---

Generalization 5.02

When hunter-gatherers occupy a high percentage of the area covered by a given plant community, there is a bias in favor of settings in which ungulates are not present in large numbers. In settings that feature a strong proportional relationship between the area covered by a plant community and the percentage of the area occupied by hunter-gatherers, there is a bias in favor of plant communities in which ungulates do moderately well. On the other hand, in settings in which hunter-gatherers are absent or only minimally represented, there is a bias in favor of plant communities in which ungulates should be common or present in moderately high numbers.

These provocative patterns reveal that the areas in which hunter-gatherers are absent are the regions in which agriculturists, pastoralists, and industrial states predominate in the contemporary world. The latter regions are also places in which ungulate biomass would be expected to be high to moderate, provided that the impact of human exploitation was minimal. This pattern may be surprising to researchers who have argued that domestication, particularly of plants, might have been expected to occur in settings in which hunter-gatherers were primarily dependent upon plants. In such scenarios, domestication is viewed as the "logical" outcome of the intensified use of a plant species already basic to hunter-gatherer diet (Rindos 1984). This could be true, but the major impact of domestication may be to open up new niches in very different areas from the ones in which domesticates were originally produced.

Research thus far has shown, however, that there is no bias with respect to plant productivity in the distribution of ethnographically documented hunter-gatherers. This fact alone casts doubt on the credibility of the assertion that hunter-gatherers of the contemporary era were found in marginal and out-of-the-way places or "impoverished ecological settings" (Martin 1969:244). It might be argued that there are exceptions to this assertion, but whereas it is true that the arctic tundra region can be accurately described as a marginal environment from a subsistence perspective, and it is certainly "out-of-the-way" relative to the areas where much of recent human history has been centered, this region was also marginal to the areas occupied by hunter-gatherer peoples until rather recently.

It is apparent in figure 5.07, which illustrates a commonly accepted distribution of hunter-gatherers at 10,000 B.C., that the vast zone of northern tundra was uninhabited across Eurasia and most of North America. Hunter-gatherers expanded into the New World—and particularly into polar regions—in response to a suite of dynamic processes that opened up a new niche in their habitats. They were not marginalized by agriculturists and pastoralists who, in fact, arrived on the scene much later in time.[6]

Hunter-gatherer niche diversity during the colonial period can be deduced from a reconsideration of the distribution of the global sample depicted in figure 5.03. There is a northern-temperate-to-arctic distribution, which is almost exclusively a North American phenomenon, and a spotty, scattered

TABLE 5.05

SUBSETS OF VEGETATIVE COMMUNITIES ORDINATED FROM HIGH TO LOW BY PERCENTAGE OF AREA OCCUPIED BY HUNTER-GATHERERS AND AREA COVERED BY A SPECIFIC PLANT COMMUNITY

OVERINFORMED SETTINGS

Subset 1			Subset 2		
A. 58.28%			A. 34.32%		
B. 3.52%			B. 9.67%		
C. Ranks[1]			Ranks		
Vegetation type	Plant	Animal	Vegetation type	Plant	Animal
FC	13	23	T	28	28
FL	14	22	DSD	24	23
BPK	23	24	FSS	17	21
DSP	25	27	GP	08	05
FSA	11	07	SSA	15	08

PROPORTIONALLY INFORMED SETTINGS

Subset 3		
8.25%		
36.03%		
Ranks		
Vegetation type	Plant	Animal
FBO	20	19
GS	19	09
DTG	18	16
FBL	21	18
FD	10	13
DTW	09	06
FMT	06	01
FBD	12	14

UNDERINFORMED SETTINGS

Subset 4			Subset 5		
1.90%			0.00%		
40.0%			10.74%		
Ranks			Ranks		
Vegetation type	Plant	Animal	Vegetation type	Plant	Animal
DSS	22	20	D	27	26
FE	01	12	TA	26	15
FMO	03	04	FSM	16	17
STG	07	02	FSP	05	11
SW	02	03			
FBE	04	10			

Notes: A = percentage of the total area for the set that is occupied by hunter-gatherers. B = percentage of the earth's total area represented by the set of plant communities.
1. The two columns of ranks for each subset represent the rank ordering of the mean values for the plant community measured in terms of net aboveground productivity (NAGP) and the biomass of ungulates present (EXPREY). Low numbers correspond to the greatest amount of production and biomass. The chi-square value corresponding to high equals 1–9, to medium 10–18, and to low 19–28. Tabulation of plant rankings by subset yields a chi-square of 8.72 (df = 8, $P = 0.39$). The tabulation of EXPREY ranks yielded a chi-square value of 18.10 (df = 8, $P = 0.22$).

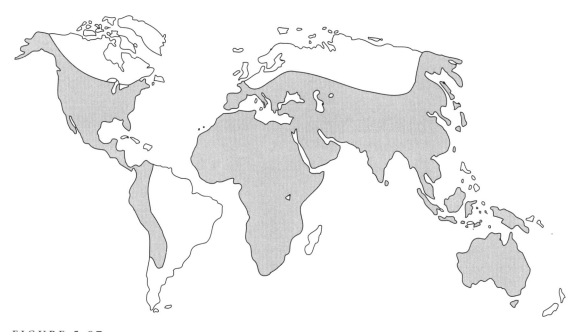

FIGURE 5.07

Estimated distribution of hunter-gatherers just prior to 10,000 B.C. Adapted and redrawn from Lee and DeVore (1968: figure facing title page).

distribution of groups in the subtropics and tropics who live among non-hunter-gatherer peoples. A third, southern temperate distribution is situated on large, contiguous areas of South America, Africa, and Australia that share many climatic and ecological properties.

Around the western and northern perimeters of the South American temperate zone distribution, hunter-gatherer groups have interacted with complex states as well as with less complex agriculturists and pastoralists. In the southern part of Africa occupied by hunter-gatherer peoples, which includes parts of Angola, Zimbabwe, Namibia, Botswana, and South Africa, interaction with agriculturists and pastoralists was common. In contrast, the entire continent of Australia was occupied exclusively by hunter-gatherers who lived in a slightly greater range of habitats than analogous groups in Africa and South America.

Although unique mixes of plant communities were characteristic of each of these three continents, various dispersions of three different plant formations were found in the areas inhabited by hunter-gatherers. The driest of the formations, all of which may be transitional to woodland, is thorntree–desert grass savanna (DTG-17), which is followed in terms of increasing moisture by desert thorn woodland (DTW-11) and thorntree-tallgrass savanna (STG-7). The tropical thorntree-tallgrass savanna is the venue of some of the better-documented hunter-gatherers of the Kalahari region of southern Africa, particularly the !Kung (Lee 1979; Marshall 1976) and the /Gwi (Silberbauer 1981; Tanaka

1980). Desert thorn woodland is the setting of the Hadza in Tanzania, of the Chenchu and Paliyans in India, and of the Nambikwara in Brazil. All four of these groups either are partial agriculturists or maintain mutualistic relations with neighboring agriculturists.

Two other New World groups inhabiting different localities within this vegetative class are the Chichimec of Mexico and, in the southern plains of the United States, the Comanche. Both of these groups exploited naturally occurring food resources in areas in which agriculturists were also known to have flourished. The best-known of the Australian cases found in a similar desert thorn woodland community are the Northern Arenda peoples, whose range encircled Alice Springs in the center of the continent.

The driest of these plant formations, the thorntree–desert grass savanna, is found in the sections of the Kalahari inhabited by the !Ko and the Hai//om (who were pastoralists at the time of documentation), as well as in regions of Madagascar occupied by the Mikea, who appear to have been situated in a mutualist-specialist niche that is common in various parts of India. A number of well-known Australian cases—including the Alyawara, Walbiri, and Kariera—have also met their subsistence needs while situated in this formation.

A common feature of the preceding suite of cases from Africa and the Americas is that they have all occupied what might be called a tension zone shared by agriculturists, pastoralists, and hunter-gatherers. This observation prompts me to ask why the ethnographic record is characterized by the

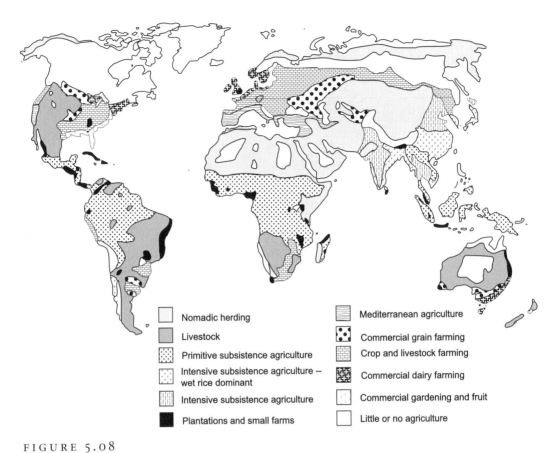

FIGURE 5.08

Nearly contemporary world distribution of the use of domesticated plants and animals.

huge underrepresentation of hunter-gatherer groups in deserts, semidesert scrub formations, and high-altitude deserts adjacent to tundra formations—where agriculturists and pastoralists have predominated—yet in regions that are more productive in terms of both plant and animal resources, hunter-gatherers competed successfully with agriculturists and pastoralists until the contemporary era.[7]

What properties of these environments appear to give hunter-gatherers an edge, while in less productive habitats foragers are either not present to begin with or are replaced by agriculturists or pastoralists? Is it simply that the latter found a niche in regions that were never previously occupied by, or were marginal to, hunter-gatherers? Why would a replacement by agriculturists and pastoralists occur consistently in the most marginal of nonpolar environments—deserts and near-deserts—while hunter-gatherers held on in more productive environments?

Another perspective on the three-continent distribution of hunter-gatherers in the Southern Hemisphere is provided by a comparison of this pattern with the global distribution in the contemporary era of domesticate-based food production, illustrated in figure 5.08. Contemporaneously, live-stock production predominates in those areas of the continents

of the Southern Hemisphere characterized by hunter-gatherer occupation. A similar land use pattern prevails in those regions of North America formerly occupied by hunter-gatherers, with the exception of California and the coastal regions of the states of Oregon and Washington. These similarities are consistent with earlier findings that ungulate prey can be expected in moderate numbers in those regions in which hunter-gatherers occupied plant communities proportionately to the size of a plant community itself (table 5.05).

The patterning that triggered the preceding discussion has implications for a process frequently referred to as the "spread" of agriculture and pastoralism. I would suggest that changes in basic subsistence strategies may not be related to the transmission of a way of making a living that is "superior" to that of one's neighbors, who struggle to maintain themselves by means of an "inferior" dependence on non-cultivated foods. The alternative supposition that hunter-gatherers were simply replaced by more advanced agriculturists and pastoralists appears equally dubious to me. I am skeptical that "by about 5,000 B.C., peasant farmers from western Asia had begun to penetrate Greece and push northward to the Danube in the vicinity of Belgrade. Moving along the river and its tributaries, agriculturists practicing shifting cultiva-

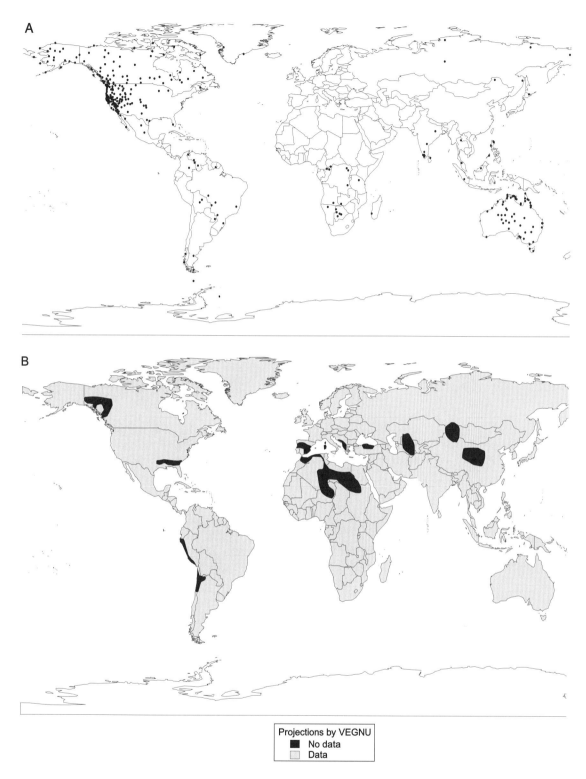

Projections by VEGNU
■ No data
▨ Data

FIGURE 5.09

Comparative world maps illustrating the geographic distribution of hunter-gatherer cases (A) with information from those cases projected through plant community associations to the world, based on the world weather station sample (B).

tion occupied central Europe and reached the Rhineland no later than 4,000 B.C." (Atkinson 1964:115). I also doubt that "to early agriculturists . . . crops and livestock came to represent much more than food and it was in part these subsidiary qualities that made agriculture such an attractive alternative to hunting and gathering. With agriculture, for the first time in history, humans could harness labour by using food as a currency and a medium of exchange. This idea, like that of domestication itself, spread very quickly" (Hole 1992:377–78).[8]

One further characteristic of the geographic distribution of hunter-gatherers may be related to the issue of explaining variability. Many of the cases in the global sample from tropical and subtropical regions of Africa, South America, and Asia have provoked arguments about the validity of their status as foragers. For example, according to Brosius (1988), the Punan represent remnant survivors of a way of life that is being replaced by more developed systems. An alternative view states that many of these tropical and subtropical groups have been encapsulated by more "complex" peoples, which explains some of their social features (Woodburn 1988). Still another view argues that these groups have "devolved" from peoples who were once more complex (e.g., Gardner 1965:141; Hoffman 1984; Martin 1969). It is also suggested that in some settings the presence and needs of agriculturists have created a hunter-gatherer niche that some persons have adopted as a "secondary" specialization (Bower 1989; Headland and Bailey 1991).[9]

Although these arguments have largely been proposed in discussions focusing on a search for "real" hunter-gatherers and are therefore concerned with accurately tracing historical trajectories, at least they recognize and document the range of variability in hunter-gatherer organization that must be explained before an understanding of what the past was like is possible. In one way or another, all of these views express concern that processual convergences are being treated as homologous forms,[10] a perspective that is based on a belief in the existence of a "real" or natural hunter-gatherer unit.[11] Presumably this unit would be characterized by a shared suite of features, and all groups in this class would share a common set of initial conditions that would account for their observable properties.

If this argument were true, it would validate claims that an ethnoarchaeologist's observations in the present would be representative of the archetypal past and therefore justify the projection of specific, contemporary observations to past hunter-gatherers in general (Lee 1968). Of course, if another researcher had different experiences, the claim could be made that *these* were more valid according to a set of more privileged criteria (Hill 1982), and the argument could go on indefinitely.

The research reported in this book does not proceed from a belief in organizational archetypes and the characteristics that define them. The global sample I have assembled has demonstrated that, as a class, hunter-gatherers are so organizationally variable that the investigative challenge is to explain that variability. I have shown that geographic bias in the sample of ethnographic cases looks different when the frame of reference shifts to a classification of the earth's plant communities, only four of which are not characterized by documented cases of hunter-gatherers in the nearly contemporary era. This diversity of settings represents 89.22 percent of the total area of the earth, and one would expect that some germane information about hunter-gatherers might be generalizable to almost 90 percent of the earth's land area.

Although bias still exists in the documented ethnographic variability of the global sample, bias must always be measured relative to some germane frame of reference. This point is demonstrated by the two maps in figure 5.09, which illustrate the geographic distribution of bias in case distribution (figure 5.09, map A) and compare it with the geographic distribution of *information* about the relationship between hunter-gatherers and their habitats (figure 5.09, map B). This comparison illustrates the wealth of germane information that is available about the earth's temperate, boreal, and polar regions and confirms the fact that, although hunter-gatherer groups in tropical and subtropical habitats are underrepresented in the sample, some productive information can nevertheless be used to tease out what is unknown about these zones. The appropriate analytical technique at this juncture would appear to be proportional projection, which I discussed in detail in chapter 3.

Projecting Hunter-Gatherer Populations to the Entire Earth

A knowledge of the diverse settings within which hunter-gatherers have been documented allows us to look at the earth in hunter-gatherer terms. Since groups have been documented in almost all of the earth's plant communities during the colonial era (table 5.04), it is possible to project the properties of this distribution to the earth as a whole, since the following variables have been coded for the 339 groups in the global sample: (1) the number of persons in each documented group (TLPOP), (2) the total area occupied by each group (AREA), and (3) the vegetative community within which each group lived (VEGNU). Once these variables were defined and quantified, a sequence of operations produced the results that are presented in table 5.06.

First, the area covered by a given plant formation (column 2) was divided by the mean area (AREA) used by the groups occupying that formation (column 4), producing an estimate of the number of groups that would exist worldwide in that plant community (column 5). In step two, the projected number of cases was then multiplied by the mean number

TABLE 5.06

PLANT COMMUNITY TYPES AS A FRAME OF REFERENCE
FOR THE GLOBAL DISTRIBUTION OF HUNTER-GATHERER CASES

PLANT COMMUNITY TYPE		HUNTER-GATHERER CASES				
Vegetation code[1] (1)	Area[2] covered (2)	Observed number of cases (3)	Case area (4)	Projected number of cases (5)	Persons[3] per case (6)	Projected number of persons (7)
FE	93,998.97	20	103.78	905.75	1,354.10	1,226,530.24
SW	33,181.75	5	87.84	377.75	1,275.60	481,857.90
FMO	88,514.40	28	117.64	752.42	858.75	646,140.67
FSP	5,092.83	0	380.34*	13.30	1,690.92	22,489.24
FBE	35,127.82	7	32.65	319.34	1,042.57	332,934.30
FMT	27,056.56	7	90.57	298.74	918.00	274,243.32
STG	72,231.63	10	118.70	608.52	1,258.60	765,886.52
GP	16,494.76	3	291.00	56.68	1,700.00	96,361.14
FD	40,204.18	3	604.33	66.53	2,296.67	152,797.45
FSA	3,389.90	5	73.94	45.85	936.40	42,933.94
DTW	45,564.13	3	676.00	67.40	3,169.33	213,620.95
FBD	30,588.25	3	179.40	170.50	1,908.33	325,376.11
FC	4,441.07	42	72.72	61.07	2,892.17	176,627.19
FL	3,110.67	4	457.92	6.79	1,416.25	9,620.64
SSA	4,866.84	3	65.00	74.87	1,243.33	93,093.66
FSM	10,250.62	0	380.34*	26.95	1,690.92	45,572.33
DTG	47,024.16	11	351.53	133.76	812.73	108,718.87
GS	74,498.34	29	511.55	145.63	3,197.07	465,597.51
FBO	124,959.23	42	675.74	184.92	1,888.55	349,228.82
FSS	17,106.47	15	118.22	144.70	2,335.13	337,894.02
FBL	54,058.95	1	2,623.03	20.61	844.80	17,411.32
DSS	164,204.86	9	222.91	736.64	814.00	599,626.56
BPK	37,363.68	10	1,215.87	30.73	1,254.90	38,563.08
DSD	29,216.23	49	223.25	130.86	1,064.79	139,338.42
DSP	9,994.90	10	500.10	19.99	567.50	11,344.32
TA	63,050.04	0	—	—	—	—
T	50,242.10	20	1,377.27	36.47	1,329.60	48,503.12
D	69,702.93	0	3,868.00*	18.02	560.00	10,091.20
TOTAL		339		5,454.79		7,032,402.79

Notes: 1. Vegetation types are arranged by NAGP value in descending order of magnitude.
2. Area is expressed in 100-square-kilometer units.
3. The total number of persons represented by the 339 cases is 573,224.

of persons per case documented in that plant community (column 6), and an estimate of the total number of persons living in the plant community worldwide was obtained (column 7). Using these two steps, an estimated global population of 7,032,402 persons was derived, which represents a mean population density of 5.27 persons per 100 square kilometers, or 0.136 persons per square mile. *In this projection, the information about hunter-gatherers as summarized by plant community is projected proportionally to the earth as a whole.*

It must be kept in mind that for past eras about which no estimates of population size exist, any estimates that I make are primarily projections from what is known about nearly contemporary hunter-gatherers, weighted by various biases derived from archaeological observations. Table 5.07 illustrates

that the population estimate of more than seven million persons falls halfway between Hassan's (1981) estimates of population levels (in column 6) during the Upper Paleolithic and Mesolithic eras. The projection from my data is also higher than both Birdsell's (1975:292) and Deevey's (1960) estimates for the Upper Paleolithic (columns 3 and 5).

In my judgment, the projection from ethnographic information is more likely than other estimates to represent population levels during the Mesolithic era, close to the initial appearance of domesticated plants and animals between approximately 9,000 and 11,000 B.P. Hassan's (1981:7–10) Mesolithic projection is considerably higher than mine but it is based on Baumhoff's (1963) population estimates of California hunter-gatherers and Yesner's (1977) estimates of Pacific northwest coast population levels. I believe that the

TABLE 5.07

ESTIMATES OF GLOBAL POPULATION LEVELS,
LOWER PALEOLITHIC ERA TO THE PRESENT

TIME PERIOD	DEEVEY (1960)		BIRDSELL (1972)		HASSAN (1981)		COMPTON'S ENCYCLOPEDIA	
	Density	No.	Density	No.	Density	No.	Density	No.
LOWER PALEOLLITHIC	0.425	0.125	1.5	0.400	2.25	0.600	—	—
MIDDLE PALEOLITHIC	1.2	1.0	3.2	1.0	3.0	1.2	—	—
UPPER PALEOLITHIC	4.0	3.34	3.9	2.2	10.0	6.0	—	—
MESOLITHIC	—	—	—	—	11.5	8.63	—	—
1960	—	—	—	—	—	—	2,249.9	3,000.0
1987	—	—	—	—	—	—	3,749.8	5,000.0
1997	—	—	—	—	—	—	4,499.8	6,000.0

Note: The cited authors disagree about the area of the earth occupied by humans at different time periods in the past. Comparisons are therefore difficult except for population density values. My estimates are projected to the entire earth and are perhaps most accurate during the European Mesolithic-epipaleolithic period. Although Hassan's estimates are inflated, they are nevertheless based upon Baumhoff's (1963) and Cook's (1955, 1956) population estimates for California and Yesner's (1980) estimates for the Pacific Northwest (Hassan 1981:7–10).

latter estimates are inflated and that, if they are used to project population levels in other parts of the world, generally inflated levels will result. If, however, the estimates had included a knowledge of variability among hunter-gatherers and had been measured against the geographic distribution of entities such as the plant communities included in my study, I believe the results would have had a higher probability of accuracy.

Even though I am fairly confident that my projections are defensible from the standpoint of the use of available knowledge, does this mean that the projected values are accurate? Unfortunately, no; it simply means that this is a good use of contemporary knowledge and that the value is probably somewhere in the ballpark. This is a claim, however, that at least Hassan and perhaps others could also make for their projections, which required much less work and many fewer steps to produce! On the other hand, if I were not content with such an uncertain approximation and wanted to pursue other analytical techniques, what are the choices available to me?

USING SAMPLES AS FRAMES OF REFERENCE

As a first step, I can examine my assumptions regarding stability. Hidden in my projection of population levels is an unstated assumption:

Proposition 5.01

The greater the amount of space occupied by a given plant community, the greater the likely diversity in the properties of hunter-gatherer peoples living there.

Suppose, for instance, I were to suggest that I needed a proportionally representative sample of hunter-gatherers and pro-

posed that the number of hunter-gatherer cases from each plant community should be proportional to the percentage of the earth covered by that plant community. Such a proposal would make sense only if I believed in some relationship between area and diversity in which a larger number of cases would be required to represent the diversity adequately.

Now it should be clear that I do *not* know what factors condition diversity in cultural systems—in fact, one of my research goals is to learn more about the conditioning factors—but, since I have to begin somewhere, it is at least plausible to assume there *is* a relationship between area and diversity and to select a sample of hunter-gatherer cases based on these terms. As it turns out, I discovered that a sample size of 142 cases was the most that I could derive from the data set of 339 hunter-gatherer groups if my goal was an areally proportioned representation of the earth's plant communities, excluding the true desert and alpine desert-tundra categories that were characterized by no hunter-gatherer cases.

Table 5.08 summarizes information on three different sets of data that will be used repeatedly as samples in this study. One set (HG339) consists of the global sample of documented hunter-gatherer cases, while another (HG142) consists of a subset of those cases designed to correspond as closely as possible to the proportions of the earth's surface covered by the twenty-eight different plant communities adapted in this study from Eyre's classification (1968). If, for instance, the tropical rain forest plant community constitutes 7.72 percent of the earth's surface, then 7.72 percent of the ethnographic cases in sample HG142 were drawn from regions characterized by tropical rain forest vegetation. The third data set (WLD1429) consists of a sample of the earth's weather stations that also were selected so that the percentage of weather stations from each plant community corresponds to the proportion of the earth's surface occupied by that plant community.

TABLE 5.08

DATA SETS AND THEIR RELATIONSHIPS TO A GEOGRAPHICALLY PROPORTIONAL REPRESENTATION OF THE EARTH'S PLANT COMMUNITIES

PLANT GROUP	HG142 Expected no. of cases[1]	HG142 Actual no. of cases	HG339 Actual no. of cases	WLD1429 Expected no. of cases[2]	WLD1429 Actual no. of cases
FE-1	11.50	15	20	123.52	128
SW-2	4.08	5	5	43.52	44
FMO-3	10.91	14	28	116.32	121
FBE-5	4.32	6	7	46.08	48
FSP-4	0.63	0	0	6.72	7
FMT-6	3.33	4	7	35.52	37
STG-7	8.90	10	10	94.88	98
GP-8	2.03	3	3	21.60	22
DTW-11	5.61	3	3	59.84	56
FD-9	4.95	3	3	52.80	56
FSA-10	0.42	1	5	4.48	5
FBD-12	3.77	3	3	40.16	43
FC-13	0.54	4	42	5.76	6
FL-14	0.39	1	4	4.16	4
SSA-15	0.60	1	3	6.4	7
FSM-16	1.26	0	0	13.44	14
FSS-20	2.10	4	15	22.40	**13**
DTG-17	5.79	7	11	61.76	64
GS-18	9.18	12	29	97.92	99
FBO-19	15.19	15	42	162.08	161
FBL-21	6.63	1	1	70.72	**48**
DSS-22	20.22	9	9	215.00	**174**
BPK-23	4.59	5	10	48.96	**10**
DSD-24	3.60	5	49	38.40	41
DSP-25	1.23	2	10	13.12	13
TA-26	5.28	0	0	56.32	**12**
D-28	8.58	0	0	91.52	**31**
T-27	6.18	9	20	65.92	67
TOTAL	163.27*	142	339	1,619.30*	1,429

Notes: 1. Values in column 2 are derived by multiplying the values in table 5.04, column 3, by 150 and dividing the result by 100.
2. Values in column 5 are derived by multiplying the values in table 5.04, column 3, by 1,475 and dividing the result by 100.
An asterisk (*) indicates that the differences between the total and initial target totals are due to the exclusion of D-28 (deserts) and TA-21 (alpine tundra) from the sums as the samples were originally conceived.
Bold type signifies situations in which sufficient cases could not be found to meet the numbers required for a truly representative sample and still maintain adequate geographic coverage.

Inspection of table 5.08 reveals that both HG142 and WLD1429 represent a compromise with regard to my selection criteria, because in order to maintain a credible sample size some of the proportionality had to be sacrificed for those plant communities in which there were either no hunter-gatherer cases or insufficient coverage of the plant communities by weather stations of record. To evaluate how representative the samples may be, I must use environmental properties to obtain some perspective, since the samples are designed to permit me to see biased distributions in

hunter-gatherer cases. I chose six environmental variables to guide my evaluation of between-sample comparisons: mean annual temperature (CMAT), total annual rainfall (CRR), net aboveground productivity (NAGP), primary biomass (BIO5), water retention or the total amount of water stored in the soil annually (WATRET), and the biomass of ungulates as calculated from equations developed in chapter 4 (EXPREY).

Using these variables, I calculated means and standard deviations for each vegetative community within each of the three data sets listed in table 5.08 (HG142, HG339, and

TABLE 5.09

TABLE 5.09

t TEST COMPARISONS OF SIX ENVIRONMENTAL VARIABLES
IN THREE DIFFERENT DATA SETS

PLANT GROUP	HG142 AND HG339		HG142 AND WLD1429		HG339 AND WLD1429		TOTAL
	Variance	*Mean*	*Variance*	*Mean*	*Variance*	*Mean*	
FE-1	100.0	100.0	100.0	83.3	83.3	66.6	77.0
SW-2	100.0	100.0	83.3	83.3	83.3	83.3	*88.8*
FMO-3	100.0	100.0	33.3	83.3	33.3	83.3	55.5
FBE-5	100.0	100.0	66.6	83.3	66.6	83.3	55.5
FSP-4	No hunter-gatherer cases						
FMT-6	100.0	100.0	100.0	100.0	100.0	100.0	**100.0**
STG-7	100.0	100.0	100.0	83.3	100.0	83.3	*88.8*
GP-8	100.0	100.0	100.0	83.3	100.0	83.3	*88.8*
DTW-11	100.0	100.0	83.3	100.0	83.3	100.0	*88.8*
FD-10	100.0	100.0	100.0	66.6	100.0	66.6	*88.8*
FSA-9	100.0	100.0	100.0	100.0	100.0	100.0	**100.0**
FBD-12	100.0	100.0	88.8	88.8	88.8	88.8	*88.8*
FC-13	88.8	100.0	50.0	100.0	100.0	66.6	77.7
FL-14	100.0	100.0	100.0	100.0	100.0	100.0	**100.0**
SSA-16	100.0	100.0	100.0	100.0	88.8	100.0	**94.4**
FSM-16	No hunter-gatherer cases						
FSS-20	100.0	100.0	100.0	100.0	66.6	66.6	*88.8*
DTG-17	100.0	100.0	88.8	100.0	88.8	100.0	*88.8*
GS-18	100.0	100.0	88.8	100.0	88.8	100.0	*88.8*
FBO-19	100.0	100.0	100.0	88.8	66.6	88.8	*88.8*
FBL-21	No hunter-gatherer cases						
DSS-22	100.0	100.0	88.8	100.0	88.8	100.0	*88.8*
BPK-23	88.8	100.0	100.0	100.0	100.0	100.0	**94.4**
DSD-24	100.0	100.0	100.0	88.8	88.8	66.6	**94.4**
DSP-25	100.0	100.0	100.0	100.0	100.0	100.0	**100.0**
TA-26	No hunter-gatherer cases						
D-28	No hunter-gatherer cases						
T-27	100.0	100.0	100.0	100.0	100.0	100.0	**100.0**
MEAN	**99.2**	**100.0**	82.2	92.7	87.6	88.1	88.1

Notes: **Bold** type signifies a majority of comparisons. *Italic* type signifies a high number of comparisons.

WLD1429). Double-tailed *t* tests were then performed for the comparisons of mean values among the different data subsets from identical plant communities for each of the six environmental variables. Levene's test for equality of variance was also calculated by vegetative community for all of the variables within each of the three data subsets. In all cases, probability values of less than .05 were considered indicative of bias and deviations from an unbiased, sampling-based variability. In table 5.09 the results of all of these tests are summarized in terms of the percentage of "hits and misses" for probability values in each test. For each among-subset comparison, 168 *t* tests and an additional 168 Levene's tests for equality of variances were calculated (twenty-eight vegetative communities multiplied by six variables).

Table 5.09 is arranged so that there are separate columns for the comparison of means and the comparison of variances

in each pair of data sets being compared for identity of means and variances. An entry of 100.00 in either column would indicate that no comparison varied by more than the range expected from sampling error alone. If, for instance, a value of 66.6 were entered, it would signify that of six comparisons for variance, four were not considered different but two deviated more than would be expected from sampling error alone.

Several features of the comparisons are worth noting. I would expect more deviations from simple sampling error in the variance comparisons than in the comparisons of means, and this expectation is supported by the percentage means in each column. I would also expect less deviation from sampling error for the HG142 sample when compared with the HG339 data set, since the former is, in fact, selectively drawn from the latter. This expectation is met by the results

TABLE 5.10

PROJECTED MEAN VALUES FOR ETHNOGRAPHICALLY DOCUMENTED HUNTER-GATHERERS, SUMMARIZED BY PLANT COMMUNITY (339 CASES)

VEGETATIVE CLASS	DENSITY	AREA	GATHERING	NOMOV	GROUP2	MHS
FE-1	31.26 (20)	103.78 (20)	59.74 (20)	21.48 (19)	36.73 (19)	9.01 (16)
FMO-2	27.08 (28)	117.64 (28)	40.82 (28)	8.50 (24)	38.44 (25)	5.35 (14)
SW-3	26.06 (05)	87.84 (05)	81.84 (05)	17.02 (05)	65.40 (05)	5.21 (05)
FBE-4	28.48 (07)	32.64 (07)	40.71 (07)	18.03 (04)	48.80 (05)	14.97 (03)
FSP-5	— (00)	— (00)	— (00)	— (00)	— (00)	— (00)
STG-7	28.17 (10)	118.70 (10)	68.90 (10)	11.20 (10)	35.54 (10)	4.03 (09)
FMT-6	34.29 (07)	90.57 (07)	62.14 (07)	7.12 (06)	43.44 (05)	9.10 (06)
GP-8	8.85 (03)	291.00 (03)	20.00 (03)	— (00)	302.00 (02)	7.66 (02)
FSA-9	14.26 (05)	73.90 (05)	32.00 (05)	10.00 (03)	44.80 (05)	6.17 (03)
FD-10	13.45 (03)	604.33 (03)	6.67 (03)	15.50 (02)	48.00 (03)	6.49 (03)
FC-13	67.03 (42)	73.75 (42)	20.52 (42)	2.60 (32)	131.56 (39)	14.15 (28)
FBD-12	10.02 (03)	179.40 (03)	5.00 (03)	14.00 (01)	50.00 (01)	7.25 (01)
DTW-11	8.92 (03)	682.27 (03)	41.67 (03)	— (00)	269.00 (01)	6.28 (01)
FL-14	2.91 (04)	457.92 (04)	12.50 (04)	13.25 (04)	45.75 (04)	6.96 (04)
FSM-15	— (00)	— (00)	— (00)	— (00)	— (00)	— (00)
SSA-16	28.00 (03)	65.00 (03)	41.67 (03)	— (00)	175.00 (01)	5.00 (01)
FBO-19	10.79 (42)	675.74 (42)	10.02 (42)	7.40 (34)	59.81 (41)	10.51 (30)
GS-17	31.96 (29)	495.51 (29)	29.24 (29)	12.44 (16)	153.44 (27)	8.45 (21)
DTG-17	4.63 (11)	351.53 (11)	61.55 (11)	12.57 (07)	37.56 (09)	4.29 (04)
FBL-21	0.61 (01)	3,868.80 (01)	5.00 (01)	17.00 (01)	55.00 (01)	7.85 (01)
TA-26	— (00)	— (00)	— (00)	— (00)	— (00)	— (00)
BPK-23	0.99 (10)	1,462.27 (10)	5.80 (10	14.56 (09)	60.89 (09)	6.96 (08)
FSS-22	37.48 (15)	118.22 (15)	49.67 (15)	4.71 (13)	101.18 (13)	6.28 (07)
DSP-25	1.23 (10)	500.10 (10)	65.00 (10)	14.00 (07)	25.17 (06)	4.31 (03)
DSD-24	14.67 (49)	217.28 (49)	42.76 (49)	8.36 (36)	50.10 (41)	6.17 (29)
T-27	2.81 (20)	1,377.26 (20)	0.43 (20)	8.46 (20)	72.07 (20)	8.46 (20)
DSS-22	14.51 (09)	203.21. (09)	63.33 (09)	9.38 (08)	46.37 (08)	5.53 (07)
D-28	— (00)	— (00)	— (00)	— (00)	— (00)	— (00)

in column 3, which illustrate that 100.0 percent of all tests of means yielded values that deviated within expected ranges of sampling error only; consistent with these observations, the variance comparisons were slightly reduced (99.2 percent is the mean value).

The comparisons between the 142-case set of hunter-gatherers and the 1,429-case set of weather stations produced interesting results. The mean percentage of cases within sampling error ranges drops slightly from the values observed when the HG142 data set was compared to the HG339 set. The mean value for *t* tests of means is 92.7 percent, and the mean for Levene's test of equality in variance yielded a percentage value of 82.2. The relative reliability of the means is fairly high, but, given the much smaller sample (142 versus 1,429 cases), the variance is less reliable in the small sample.

A similar comparison between HG339 and HG142 was made using six coded properties of the hunter-gatherer cases: (1) total area occupied by ethnic group in number of 100-square-kilometer units (AREA), (2) population density calculated in terms of persons per 100 square kilometers (DENSITY), (3) estimates (in percentages) of the dependence upon terrestrial plants (GATHERING), (4) mean size of the largest annual social aggregation as a regular feature of the settlement round (GROUP2), (5) mean number of residential moves made annually (NOMOV), and (6) mean household size or mean number of persons associated with each residential structure (MHS). When values were calculated using the same procedure as in table 5.09, only slightly lower percentage values were obtained for the suites of comparisons for mean values (98.6 as opposed to 100.0 percent for the environmental variables) and the comparisons of standard deviation (97.2 percent versus 98.5 percent for the environmental variables).

This exercise indicates that I am justified in projecting to the world the variability documented among hunter-gatherers, given that I expect to warrant the projections by reference to habitat variability. My assumption in proposition 5.01 that the size of a given habitat conditions diversity is supported by the Levene's tests for equality of variance. My goal is to be able to project information in such a way that archaeologists working in different places could use current knowledge about hunter-gatherers to structure direct comparisons between the archaeological record as it is reported in different locations. I also need to be able to project information from recent hunter-gatherers so that the archaeological record can be used to evaluate the accuracy of my projections, which would enable me to recognize variability and conditioning variables that are *not* well represented in the sample of recent hunter-gatherers. I will use the data in table 5.10 to illustrate what I mean.

In table 5.10, mean values for six different hunter-gatherer variables are summarized by vegetative community. These include population density (DENSITY), the percentage of the total diet obtained from terrestrial plants (GATHERING), the number of residential moves per year (NOMOV), the mean size of the residential group during the most aggregated phase of the annual cycle (GROUP2), and the mean household size of the average number of persons associated with one residential structure (MHS). Because each weather station in the WLD1429 data set was coded for type of vegetation using the Eyre (1968) world vegetation maps, I could project onto these discrete weather stations the mean values for all of the variables listed in table 5.10. This allowed me to produce a world map of summary information about the geographic distribution of the properties that I want to illustrate (figure 5.10). Since the pattern resulting from a projection of twenty-eight separate symbols for vegetative type onto a two-dimensional representation of the earth is very confusing to interpret, ordinal shading was used for population density so that the gross patterning would be clear.

Two assumptions stand behind the projections in figure 5.10. It is assumed that the whole earth is filled with hunter-gatherers who are exactly like those documented in the recent past and summarized in the sample file used in this example. I also assume that the documented relationships between the variability in the HG339 sample and the patterned distribution of the earth's vegetation is maintained over all areas of the earth. A look at the results of the projections involving the full suite of 339 hunter-gatherer cases (figure 5.10, map A) compared with the projection using the proportional sample of 142 cases (figure 5.10, map B) reveals that the difference in patterns is striking. Overall contrasts are greatest for symbols indicative of population densities greater than thirty-two persons per 100 square kilometers.

Figure 5.10, map A, illustrates a pronounced cluster of high population projections in the North American region characterized by shortgrass prairie. There is similar but less dense clustering in the prairie areas north of the Black Sea and across the Turkish plateau. In light of reliable historical knowledge about these areas, however, there is little reason to have much confidence in these projected values, and the archaeological record does not suggest that these areas were

characterized by high population density during the Mesolithic era, just prior to the appearance of agriculture.

The cause of this projected patterning, which is in conflict with two different sources of knowledge about the past, becomes clear from a comparison of map A with map B, in which projected population density is based on the proportionally drawn sample of hunter-gatherer cases (HG142). There is a greater correspondence between what I accept as true and the latter sample, and it should also be noted that the shortgrass prairie areas of the world are no longer characterized as some of the most densely occupied. This difference results from the inclusion of a number of California cases (Wintu, Patwin, Nomlaki, Nisenan, Eastern Pomo, Clear Lake Pomo, and Lake Miwok) with rather high population densities, which are classified as occupying regions of shortgrass prairie.[12] These cases dramatically inflate the mean values for the HG339 sample but are less important sources of bias in the proportional sample (HG142).

The problem appears to originate with Eyre's classification of grasslands, which equates the Mediterranean grasslands of California with both the short- and tallgrass prairies of North America (Eyre 1968:appendix I, map 5). The projection in map A of figure 5.10 is useful, however, because it allows me to reemphasize that a frame of reference must be realistic and accurate in order to produce useful proportional projections.

Further examination of the two distributions reveals that the only other major differences occur in the projected coding for Australia. There is very little contrast in the internal part of the continent, but the north and south coastal areas display different scales of projected values. This comparison simply confirms what was already known, which is that if one is projecting summary information in terms of a proportionally variable target population, the sample of cases must also be proportional in terms of a common set of criteria. It is clear that the projections from the proportional 142-case sample of hunter-gatherer cases are more reliable, although the problem with the classification of grasslands is reduced but not eliminated in this sample.

Another set of projections based on the HG142 sample is illustrated in the three maps that make up figure 5.11. These include (1) map A, an illustration of the percentage dependence upon terrestrial plants in the total diet (GATHERING); (2) map B, the size of the largest regular residential aggregation during the annual round (GROUP2); and (3) map C, mean household size (MHS). Before I discuss what the relationships demonstrated in these patterns may imply vis-à-vis well-known archaeological patterning in some regions of the world, I must acknowledge that, in addition to my skepticism about projecting to the entire earth the information drawn from ethnographically documented hunter-gatherers, I am also aware that there are inaccuracies in my frame of reference. This problem is due primarily to Eyre's classification of

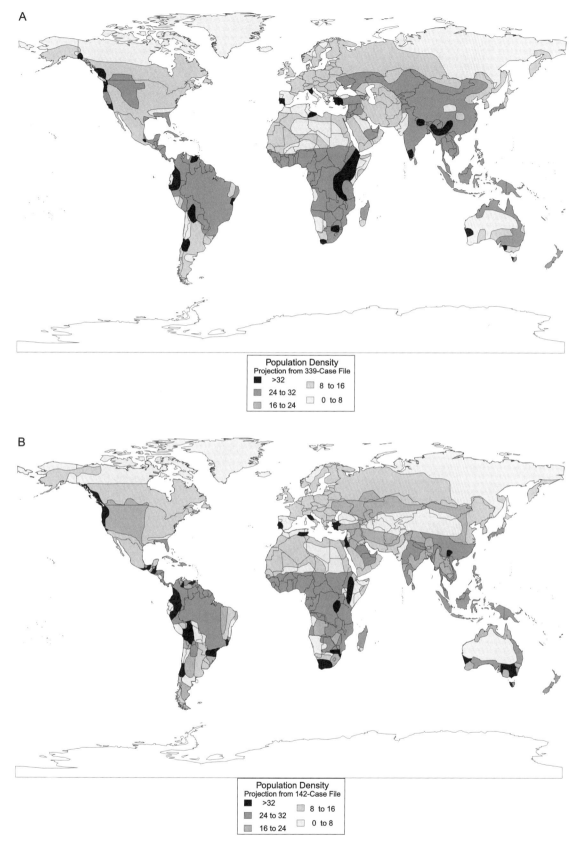

Population Density
Projection from 339-Case File
■ >32   ▨ 8 to 16
▨ 24 to 32 ☐ 0 to 8
▨ 16 to 24

Population Density
Projection from 142-Case File
■ >32   ▨ 8 to 16
▨ 24 to 32 ☐ 0 to 8
▨ 16 to 24

FIGURE 5.10

Comparative world maps for projected hunter-gatherer population density: map A uses the biased but complete suite of 339 cases from the world weather station sample while map B uses the proportional sample of 142 hunter-gatherer cases.

A

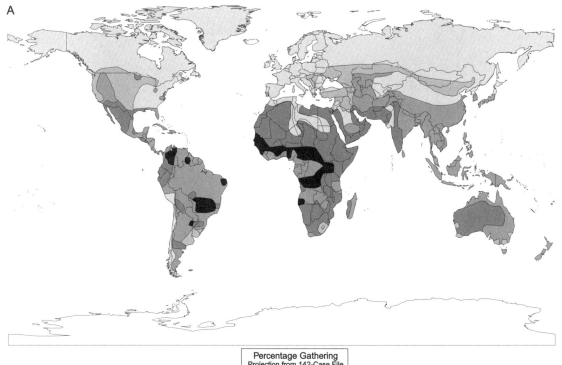

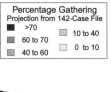

B

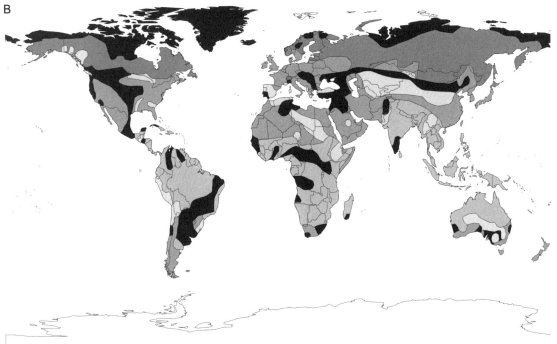

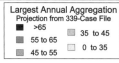

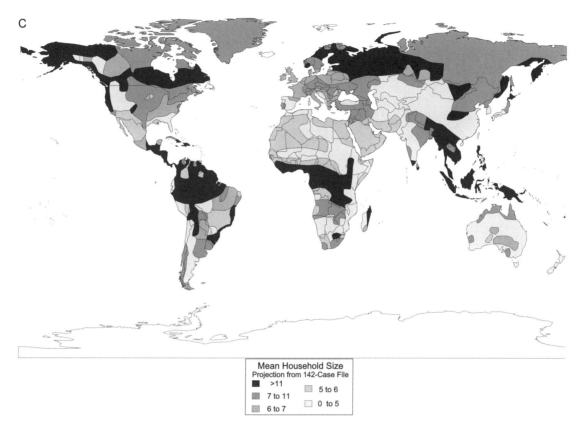

FIGURE 5.11

Three proportional projections from the sample of 142 hunter-gatherer cases from the world weather station sample: map A shows the percentage dependence upon terrestrial plants, map B features the size of the largest residential aggregation during the annual round, and map C illustrates mean household size.

grasslands, which does not discriminate between very different plant communities and therefore identifies as similar a number of hunter-gatherer cases that have very different relationships to different habitats.

Before I proceed any further, it is also necessary to deal explicitly with the issue of similarity in places, things, or systems and how unconformity affects the production of frames of reference and the pattern recognition work carried out on subject-side observations expressed relative to frames of reference. Whereas the earth may be regarded as variable in terms of the distribution of vegetation, hunter-gatherers differ from one another in numerous properties that are likely to be indicators of system state and therefore suggest the outlines of past evolutionary plays. The distributions observable in the maps in figures 5.10 and 5.11 demonstrate that

—————— *Proposition 5.02* ——————

Population density and other variables correspond in regular ways to geographic differences in vegetation and, therefore, implicate other environmental variables that could be expected to affect both population density and vegetative differences. It is reasonable to suspect that system state differences among hunter-gatherer groups may also relate in regular ways to population density, resulting in different patterning because of their interaction with otherwise similar environmental variables.

———————————————

The maps in figure 5.12 illustrate just this kind of difference. In map A, population densities are projected to the whole world using the proportional sample of 142 hunter-gatherer cases. Only those cases are included, however, that have a value of *n* or "normal" for the variable SUBPOP, which indicates that their subsistence is based on the acquisition and consumption of undomesticated foods. Groups that have hunted or gathered for the purpose of trade with more complex, non–hunting and gathering peoples are generally excluded from this category, as are cases that are reported to have

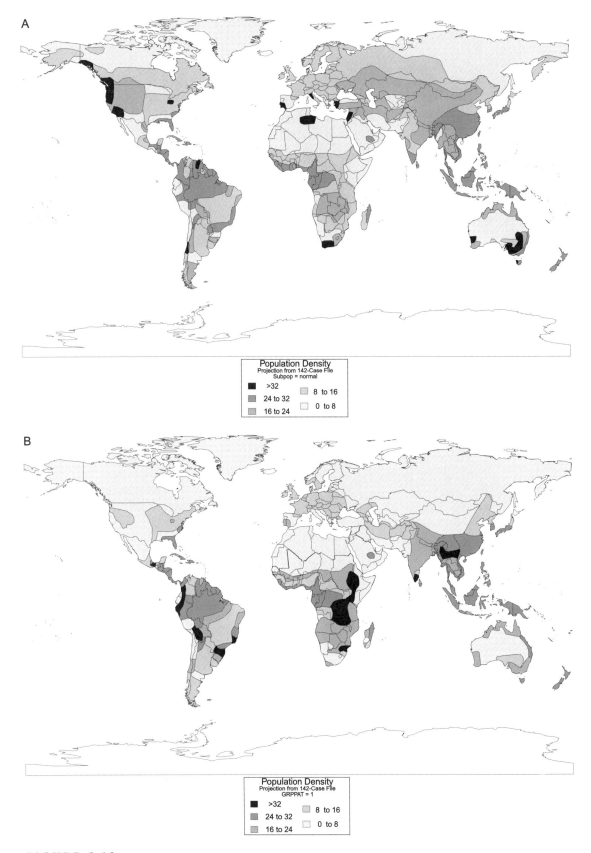

FIGURE 5.12

Two proportional projections from the sample of 142 cases from the world weather station sample: map A illustrates the population density of cases that are relatively unaffected by larger non-hunter-gatherer systems, while map B features the same projected variable, but the distribution now includes only groups from the 142-case sample judged to utilize mobility as a basic food procurement tactic.

been hunter-gatherers in the past but were practicing agriculture at the time of observation.

The projected pattern in figure 5.12, map A, is comparable to map B, in which the same sample is used but the projected values have been summarized using only nonsedentary, residentially mobile hunter-gatherer cases with a classification of 1 for the GRPPAT variable. By varying the features that serve as the basis for the projection, it is possible to see impressionistically how system state indicators may differentially condition the geographic patterning of different variables.[13]

A comparison of the patterns in the two maps in figure 5.12 produces the initial impression that population density varies strongly with mobility, since the number of locations with high-population-density cases is significantly reduced in map B, which included only residentially mobile hunter-gatherers in the projection. Although this kind of trial-and-error pursuit of system state indicators can be informative—as in the previous example, which demonstrates the geographic consequences of holding different features constant—fortunately it is possible to develop more direct ways of recognizing system state differences.

I noted earlier that, other things being equal, it might be expected that variability in the form of hunter-gatherer systems would be correlated with the size of the area covered by a given plant community. This view was supported by Levene's tests for equality of standard deviations, listed in table 5.09. I can reverse this expectation and explore the possibility that cases whose standard deviations vary *inversely* with the area covered by a plant community might, in fact, provide a clue to major system state differences. This approach is illustrated in the graph in figure 5.13, which summarizes and presents on the *y* axis the standard deviations of the size of the largest group (among cases found in the same plant community) to associate residentially on an annual basis (GROUP2). On the *x* axis, the percentage of the earth's total land area that is occupied by each plant community is displayed.

It is clear from an examination of figure 5.13 that the coastal forest (FC-13) and Mediterranean sclerophyllous scrub (FSS-20) plant communities have very high standard deviations for GROUP2 sizes, yet both types cover very small areas of the earth compared with other vegetative types. That this unexpected pattern is informing us about the system state differences that are concentrated in these two vegetative communities is verified by an examination of the cases contributing to this pattern. The coastal forest (FC-13) biome is the vegetative community in which almost all of the ranked societies of the Pacific northwest coast of North America are found. This is true also of the complex and largely sedentary coastal peoples of northern California, including the Yurok, Coast Yuki, Wiyot, and Tolowa. The

region is characterized by high variability and differentiation in system state, which ranges from the expansionist Kwakiutl to the small California Mattole. There is also a wide range of variability in GROUP2 size in the sclerophyllous scrub (FSS-20) formation, which includes the Chumash, Gabrielino, Lake Yokuts, Luiseno, Salinan, and Tubatulabal groups of California; the Karuna of South Australia; and the /Xam of South Africa.

The plant community with the third highest standard deviation in figure 5.13 is the shortgrass prairie, which was identified in the comparisons in figure 5.10 as a roughly analogous suite of grasslands differing in the seasonality of rainfall. Plains Indian cases are included in this category, as are hunter-gatherer groups from the interior valleys of California. The cases in this grouping represent different evolutionary trajectories whose different phases appear to have had a major effect on the high values of the standard deviation of mean values from different plant communities.

All three of the preceding plant communities are characterized by moderately high biomass and are found in areas in which winter rainfall changes gradually across space into zones of very low summer rainfall. These classic Mediterranean formations are typical of locations with either great variability in the availability and productivity of the adjacent aquatic biomes or dramatic contrasts between the productivity of the terrestrial and aquatic biomes. A great deal of the variability can be directly attributed to a corresponding variability in the productivity and seasonal scheduling of resources in the aquatic biome. Up to this point, I have not considered this fact in my discussion of environmental variables or when I developed habitat frames of reference. Additional sources of variability may reflect hunter-gatherer dependence on different combinations of terrestrial and aquatic resources.

It is also apparent in figure 5.13 that there is an obvious linear subset of cases associated with plant formations designated as VEGNU classes 3, 8, 18, 22, and 26. I have already discussed VEGNU class 18, which is the shortgrass prairie formation occupied by Plains Indians and hunter-gatherer groups occupying interior valleys of California, where salmon runs are among the mixed terrestrial-aquatic resources that are exploited. All the other groups in this projection rely on either exclusively terrestrial resources or a mixture of terrestrial and aquatic resources, except for VEGNU class 3, which includes the Bororo, who were agriculturists at the time of documentation; the Efe and Mbuti, who are mutualists exchanging forest products with non-hunter-gatherer peoples in return for horticultural products; and the Paliyans of India, who are an encapsulated group. In VEGNU class 3, only the Nukak of Colombia are mobile hunter-gatherers.

I would again point to high variability in the subsistence base, the overall system state relative to neighboring groups, and different mixes of major food resources as the sources

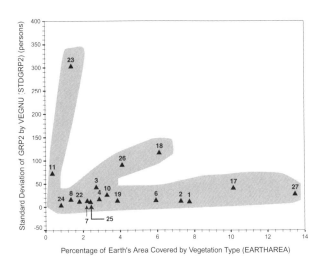

FIGURE 5.13

Scatter plot of the standard deviation of GROUP2 sizes among groups living in the same gross plant community displayed against the percentage of the earth's total land area occupied by each plant community. Cases are Eyre's vegetation types.

of the higher standard deviation values for GROUP2 sizes in figure 5.13. In procedural terms, this exercise has allowed me to isolate an additional source of bias in the data having reference to the treatment of systems that are fundamentally different in some important organizational dimensions and to treat them as if they were all examples of a single "natural kind" (Quine 1991). That hunter-gatherers do not constitute a "natural kind" in any organizational sense was demonstrated by the use of a vegetational frame of reference. Therefore, if I am correct in suggesting that systems in different formal states might well respond differently to similar environmental variables, then simple correlational approaches using the total sample of hunter-gatherers would appear to be inappropriate for the study of many system properties. This also means that more powerful *relational projections* must be designed for my analytical endeavors.

USING RELATIONAL PROJECTIONS AS FRAMES OF REFERENCE

If I can develop continuously scaled equations that summarize the relationships between the properties of hunter-gatherer systems and suites of environmental variables, it is likely that these equations could be used to project estimates for habitats from which there are few, if any, actual cases of hunter-gatherers documented in the recent past. But since such equations summarize interactive ecological relationships

that are not confined to particular time periods, they may furnish strong clues about hunter-gatherer organizational variability that will provide a strong platform for subsequent theory building.

As a first step in developing a relational projection using hunter-gatherer data, I created a computer file that included all of the environmental variables described so far in this study and some not yet introduced, as well as the values of all the variables recorded for each hunter-gatherer case in the HG339 suite of cases. Using SPSS software (version 6.1.2), I then ran stepwise multiple regressions on the entire file of environmental variables and several specific hunter-gatherer variables. This set constituted the independent variables in my equation; the single dependent hunter-gatherer variable was AREA, which represents the total area utilized relatively exclusively by an ethnic group, recorded in units of 100 square kilometers. Co-lineality indicators were calculated so that variables could be eliminated from the list as a function of their redundancy relative to the dependent variable. I then accepted the best multiple regression equation based on several measures of correlation: multiple r, r-square, adjusted r-square, and the standard error. The equation takes the following form:

$$(5.01)$$

$$\begin{aligned}
AREA = 10**[&3.421431 + (0.004732 * HUNTING) + \\
&(-0.387229 * LBIO5) + (0.186574 * LCOKLM) + \\
&(-0.110286 * LRUNOFF) + \\
&(0.175157 * WATRGRC) + \\
&(-0.164604 * MEDSTAB) + \\
&(-0.743144 * PERWLTG) + \\
&(0.004706 * RLOW) + \\
&(-0.080339 * RUNGRC) + \\
&(0.024755 * SDTEMP)]
\end{aligned}$$

where the following variables are positive contributors (that is, higher variable values increase the anticipated area of the ethnic unit's home range):

HUNTING = the percentage contribution to the diet of foods obtained from terrestrial animals;
LCOKLM = the log$_{10}$ value of the distance from the marine coast;
LWATRGRC = the number of months during the growing season when water remains stored in the soil;
RLOW = the number of millimeters of rainfall during the driest month of the year; and
SDTEMP = the standard deviation of mean monthly temperature readings.

The relationships between these variables make considerable sense. Both dependence upon hunting and inflated values for the distance to the coast condition higher AREA values. These variables are negative relative to a dependence upon marine resources and positive relative to the exploitation of terrestrial game. These basic conditions are modified by two rainfall-related variables, with the effect that, since both measure the absence of real annual drought conditions, larger ethnic areas would be expected when associated with either higher values for the percentage of the growing season in which water is stored in the soil or higher values for rainfall during the driest month of the year. It also makes sense that as the standard deviation for monthly temperatures increases home range size would increase correspondingly.

An additional suite of variables act as negative conditioners on the size of an ethnic group's home range; that is, as values of these variables increase, the projected size of the ethnic area decreases. These include (1) LBIO5, the $\log_{10}$ value of the standing biomass of the plant community measured in grams per square meter; (2) LRUNOFF, the $\log_{10}$ value of the number of millimeters of water that is neither evaporated nor stored in the soil and represents excess relative to the needs of the plant community; (3) MEDSTAB, an indicator of successional stability or a measure that highlights cases with winter rainfall and a high probability of fire during warm months; (4) PERWLTG, the percentage of months in the growing season when insufficient rainfall produces plant wilting; and (5) RUNGRC, the number of months with runoff during the growing season.

I noted in chapter 4 that primary biomass increases with rainfall, especially when rainfall increases beyond the level at which it can be evaporated or transpired. This relationship is implied by the presence of $\log_{10}$ values for BIO5 and RUNOFF, both of which condition smaller ethnic home ranges. Stability in the plant community seems to be related to smaller home range sizes, as indicated by the inclusion of MEDSTAB and PERWLTG as negative conditioners. The inclusion of RUNGRC, a rainfall indicator that has the opposite effect of MEDSTAB and PERWLTG, also suggests stability, but home range sizes are equally depressed by excessive rainfall during the growing season. The factors that appear correlated with small ethnic areas are the presence of marine coasts in the region, high plant biomass, and environmental stability in seasonality of temperature and rainfall variability. When these factors all have negative values indicating opposite conditions, large ethnic areas are unlikely.

The property space graphs in figure 5.14, which feature $\log_{10}$ values of net aboveground productivity on the x axis and latitude on the y axis, illustrate the relationships among the preceding suite of variables. In both graphs, hunter-gatherer cases occupying small ethnic areas are clustered in low latitudes that are characterized by high plant productivity. This placement corresponds to terrestrial settings that have very high productivity and low variance patterns of annual rainfall and temperature variation. Another loosely scat-tered set of cases appears on the display of the world sample in graph B, beginning around 30 degrees latitude, where cases are scattered between NAGP values of 0.5 and 2.5, and moving toward higher productivity zones at approximately 40 degrees latitude.

A partial expression of this pattern can be seen in graph A, where hunter-gatherer cases with small areas are found along the marine coasts of Mexico and Australia, as well as in California and the Pacific northwest. Hunter-gatherers in these regions were heavily dependent upon marine resources in the temperate zones. Drier and more interior locations at similar latitudes have larger areas for each ethnic group, while locations with latitudes above 50 degrees have high frequencies of ethnic units characterized by very large areas.

One way to think about these results is to consider the size of an ethnic group's area to be at least a partial indicator of the geographic scale of social networks. Small areas are indicative of small, inward-looking groups that are relatively self-sufficient and whose social customs do not foster the maintenance of social ties to distant neighbors. For the cluster of high-biomass tropical cases in figure 5.14, these properties may well be consistent with indicators of habitat stability, but they do not fit well with the temperate zone cases located between 20 and 45 degrees latitude. Cases in the latter distribution have the highest primary biomass in the temperate-boreal zone (the coastal forests of the Pacific northwest of North America) and in some very-low-primary-biomass locations, such as the western coast of Sonora in Mexico. Some Australian cases are also ethnic groups that control very small areas.

Another suite of cases is distributed across a wide range of productivity zones, including the very-high-primary-biomass forests ranging from the northern coast of California up to Vancouver, British Columbia. Almost without exception these cases are heavily dependent upon marine resources and only minimally dependent upon terrestrial food resources. (The scattering of cases farther north of this zone consists of *all* coastal peoples.) Since two very different habitat contexts appear to be favoring small ethnic areas, how is it possible to isolate the relevant variables and begin to envision the causal processes that stand behind such interesting patterning?

The habitat indicators included in the projectional equations seem to be providing some clues to human organizational dynamics, and they support my assertions about the research value of relational projections. In addition to isolating relevant variables, relational projections also allow me to make projections to the entire earth that are unaffected by the geographic bias in the original sample. They also provide a tip-off to system state differences associated with different ecological settings. Both the equations and the patterns produced when they are displayed against property

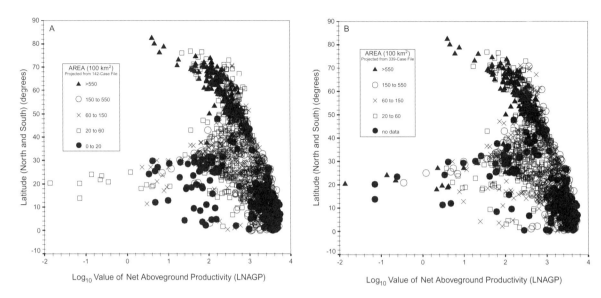

FIGURE 5.14

Comparative property space defined by latitude and the $\log_{10}$ value of net aboveground productivity among terrestrial plants coded for size of ethnic areas. Comparison is between projections from the total sample of 339 cases and the proportional sample of 142 cases from the world weather station sample.

space maps provide thought-provoking clues to process, which was one of my research goals.

RELATIONAL VERSUS PROPORTIONAL PROJECTION

The differential utility of relational and proportional projection is illustrated in the two property space maps in figure 5.15. The relational projection of the variable AREA is arrayed in map A, while map B presents a proportional projection for AREA using means from the VEGNU classes. I pointed out previously (see figure 5.14) that the world relational projection is very faithful to the actual data when both are displayed in common property space. The maps in figure 5.15 demonstrate that there is much greater resolution in the relational projection. The proportional projection suffers from taking the mean value of a major plant community, which is very misleading when applied to habitats in which there are diverse niches. This effect is visible in figure 5.15, map B, in which mean values between 60 and 150 square kilometers predominate in the zone of lowest latitude, while a range of smaller values is found in the low-latitude wet zones. This pattern is also apparent in the actual hunter-gatherer data presented in figure 5.14.

Another problem is that the use of VEGNU as a frame of reference is limited by the fact that it encompasses only terrestrial plant communities, whereas hunter-gatherers also exploit aquatic biomes, and VEGNU provides no clue about when this might occur. The relational frame of reference, on the other hand, includes variables such as distance from the marine coast (COKLM) and a number of surrogate indicators of aquatic variables, such as RUNOFF, as well as the subsistence variables that were included in the multiple regression analysis.

If one assumes that the entire earth is populated with hunter-gatherers as they are known from the recent ethnographic record, relational projections are the most useful tools, provided that the correlation with environmental variables is high. In those situations in which these correlations are low—perhaps as a result of very different system state conditions in the sample—proportional projections might be less misleading at the scale of specifics. I have illustrated how the use of property space projections provides clues to the types of habitat in which similar formal conditions prevail or where high variability is expected for proportional projections owing to high standard deviations within plant communities (figure 5.15, maps A and B).

Conclusion

I began this chapter with the suggestion that data from ethnographically documented hunter-gatherers could be developed to serve two interesting purposes. Not only would it provide a useful frame of reference for the study of the

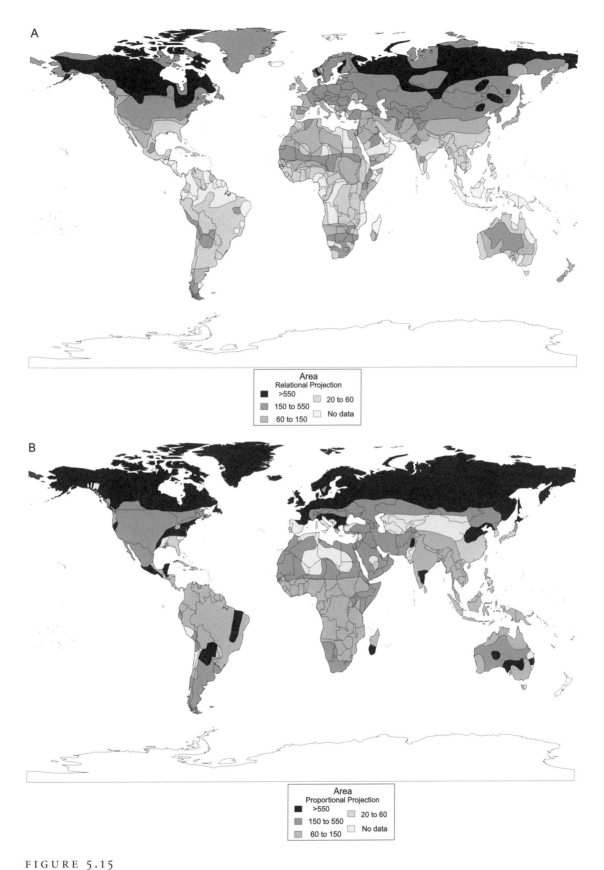

FIGURE 5.15

Contrast in the accuracy of relational (A) and proportional (B) projection from the world weather station sample for size of the area occupied by an ethnic group.

archaeological record, but it could also form the basis of models that would embody the initial conditions of human systems that subsequently evolved from a dependence on some combination of hunted and gathered resources into cultural systems with non-hunter-gatherer forms of subsistence. I also argued that the study of hunter-gatherers relative to an environmental frame of reference would provide information pertinent to the goal of developing theories explaining hunter-gatherer organizational variability. As an initial illustration of a useful frame of reference for assessing the bias in information collected about ethnographically documented hunter-gatherers, I chose Eyre's (1968) classification of the earth's plant communities. I discovered to my surprise that there were no documented hunter-gatherers in true deserts and alpine tundras, as well as very few cases recorded in the earth's second driest plant community, the semidesertic scrub plant formation. In spite of numerous generalizations in the anthropological literature asserting that hunter-gatherers could be found in the recent era only in the most marginal or nonproductive habitats, I discovered that *truly* nonproductive habitats were occupied exclusively by pastoralists and agriculturists.

Looking at the global sample of hunter-gatherers from a geographic and environmental perspective, I also noted that in those habitats in which no cases in my sample occurred ungulate biomass is projected to have been substantial. In contrast, those locations in which hunter-gatherers were found in the recent era constitute settings in which, using my projections, ungulates are not expected to proliferate, and indeed these areas are characterized by relatively low secondary biomass. These are provocative observations relative to the issue of which conditions in the past favored human intensification of subsistence and resulted in the use of domesticated plants and animals. I am not convinced by claims that the domestication of plants was a "natural" consequence of heavy plant dependence (Rindos 1984), and I will explore my observations further in subsequent chapters.

This chapter has demonstrated the utility of several techniques for looking at one set of data in terms of another. Proportional projection techniques allowed me to estimate the total hunter-gatherer population of the earth, assuming that the earth was peopled by groups similar to those documented in ethnographic sources. Then I designed an environmentally proportional sample of hunter-gatherer cases (HG142)—and a similar sample of the earth's weather stations (WLD1429)—and evaluated the relative reliability of these populations for use in projection and as target locations for projection. I discovered that estimates of reliability could be made for projections to different plant communities, and this ability allowed me to see the limitations of proportional projections.

Mean values of five different properties of hunter-gatherer systems were then summarized by vegetational community, and these demonstrated provocative differences in habitats. One variable, population density, was proportionally projected to the world sample of weather stations. This exercise allowed me to evaluate the utility of a sample that is proportional relative to an underlying environmental frame of reference. I noted that error in the underlying frame of reference can produce high-variance associations of hunter-gatherer cases in common vegetative communities. I also demonstrated that a relational projection represents a more powerful use of the information in the environmental frame of reference than a proportional projection.

In the course of my analytical trajectory I also learned more about hunter-gatherers. This result demonstrates the way in which the play of ideas in the scientific arena tends to unfold: subject-side growth of knowledge is to a great extent tied to the intellectual tools that one builds by using source-side knowledge. My analytical efforts helped me to realize that although identical suites of environmental variables underlie the abstract terms *variability* and *system state,* these variables may interact in different ways to produce human cultural systems that can be either organizationally similar[14] or different in their fundamental organizational properties, depending on system state conditions. Systems of the latter kind might be expected to relate in different ways to a common set of environmental variables as a function of their important organizational differences.

The concept of system state was introduced in the context of exploring inadequacies in my underlying frame of reference, the Eyre classification of vegetative communities. I discovered serendipitously, however, that by examining the standard deviations of ethnic area sizes within plant communities I had found a reliable clue to system state variability.

In chapter 2, one of the reasons I proposed that properties of human actors were important initial conditions for discussing different evolutionary plays was my recognition that different species with different organizational properties might well react to common environmental conditions in different ways. I noted that important generic properties of human beings structure organized life ways quite differently than it is structured in nonhuman animals.

One of the human properties that appears at least quantitatively unique is the ability of our species to occupy very different niches, in an ecological sense, and yet remain a cohesive single species. The evolutionary plays in which humans participate produce different organizations of life, but we, the participants, in spite of phenotypic behavioral variability, remain biologically unchanged, at least in the sense indicative of speciation.

These facts prompt me to ask the following question: if the species is the entity or "natural kind" that designates

organizationally different units upon which subsequent biological evolution must act, what are the units or "natural kinds"
of variability among cultural systems? It is also pertinent to
ask a related question: what produces variability when cultural systems respond in similar ways to similar stimuli, and
what produces variant systemic forms that respond differently
to similar stimuli? In the next chapter, I develop techniques
specifically designed to deal with some aspects of this problem.

Building a Baseline for Analyzing Niche Variability among Ethnographically Documented Peoples

A Minimalist Terrestrial Model of Hunting and Gathering

Ecosystems, Sociocultural Systems, and Evolution

In chapter 4, I introduced a basic set of environmental variables with which I summarized some fundamental properties contributing to variability in the earth's ecosystems. Similarly, in chapter 5, I discussed some aspects of hunter-gatherer organizational variability drawn from the ethnographic record, and I provided global projections of organizational properties such as the size of an ethnic area. I used the examples in chapter 5 to illustrate the logic and procedures giving structure to my research and to highlight some of the problems of using ethnographic data that had to be addressed before an elucidation of hunter-gatherer variability could be productively attempted.

Because the human species is polytypic and the behavioral plasticity of human actors allows them to organize their lives in a variety of ways, the concepts of *niche* and *system state* (discussed in chapters 2 and 3) are central to the understanding that I seek. The term *niche* implies ecological organization and suggests that differences in niche integration reflect the operation of many diverse conditioning factors. In order to explore the range of variability in human cultural systems, it is necessary to consider the spectrum of human niches in their ecological context. To do this, it must be recognized that the environmental variables introduced in chapter 4 not only serve as a frame of reference against which diversity in hunter-gatherer systems may be projected but will also provide a frame of reference for exploring organizational variability between habitats themselves, which is more commonly referred to as ecological variability.

In this chapter I identify the range of energetic domains— or habitats—within which hunter-gatherers are known to have participated. As a prerequisite, however, I need a basic knowledge of the energetic levels required to maintain human life, as well as the physical limits on the human capacity to expend energy. Once I have reliable knowledge about these

fundamental properties of human actors, I can begin to identify some particularly germane properties of the environment with which such a species of actors might interact in a biased way.

Different initial ecological conditions, in interaction with the fundamental energetic properties of a group of actors, are expected to produce different outcomes in the evolutionary plays in which human groups participate. The actors may be limited or constrained by some forms of ecological dynamics, or, alternatively, some interactions may present new career opportunities for the human species. Information about these dynamics is essential in order to study niche diversification and the tempo at which it occurs and to address the fact that these diverse niches are, nevertheless, all occupied by a single species.

In order to make headway with the somewhat daunting task I have just outlined, at this juncture I must discuss a pertinent element of current evolutionary arguments describing how evolutionary processes produce new forms and new kinds of organized life. Adjusting my perspective for a moment to encompass the history of intellectual problems that archaeologists have customarily addressed, I think it is clear that they seem to fall into two primary categories: (1) variety in the forms of artifacts, assemblages, and (by implication) ways of life in the past, and (2) variability in sociocultural complexity. Interest in the latter issue has always been accompanied by a concern with "transformations," events of emergence, and changes in sociocultural organization.

According to this view—which frequently proceeds from a "holistic" perspective that sees similarities between the structure of nature and nested Chinese boxes—systems that are smaller and made up of relatively small numbers of different components are expected to become the building blocks of systems at more complex levels of organizational integration. It is argued here, however, that even a complete knowledge of lower-level systems is insufficient to anticipate accurately the organizational properties of higher-level integrations—or systems of more complex form—even though some lower-level systems may be incorporated as sub-systems. A more colloquial way of summarizing this view is that an emergent system is more than the sum of its parts.

Approaching the world with this set of expectations results in a habitual concern with identifying organizationally defined units, because complexity implies organization. It is not surprising, then, that the issues most frequently discussed by archaeologists are "the origins of culture," "the origins of agriculture," and "the appearance of complex systems." Usually the defining properties of complex systems are said to include social stratification and coercive, power-based autocracy. If, however, an archaeologist were to ask what are the processes that foster changes in organizational complexity, as opposed to changes in morphology and form among organizationally similar systems, he or she would be brought face-to-face with one of archaeology's most important, unsolved problems.[1]

Organizational complexity in the natural world has itself been the subject of significant research in recent years, although thus far there has been little impact on archaeological thinking.[2] Some of this research has contributed to the development of a synthetic argument about the systemic world which posits that evolutionary processes operate over time to produce systems that differ in size, organizational scale, flexibility in energy transfers, and overall levels of system complexity. In an intellectual bailiwick that is sometimes referred to as "complexity studies," "emergence theory," or, more self-consciously, as the evolutionary "grand synthesis" (see Laszlo 1987), it is argued that the same processes are involved in such diverse domains as the appearance of complex forms of sociocultural systems in the recent past and the origins of life itself.

The seminal ideas underlying this new explanatory focus developed from early attempts by L. Bertalanffy (1950, 1968), Anatol Rapoport (1953, 1956, 1966), and Kenneth Boulding (1956) to establish a "general systems theory," as well as from research in cybernetics by Norbert Wiener (1954) and W. Ross Ashby (1964). Exposure to these ideas, coupled with Leslie White's energy-based arguments (1949, 1985),[3] stimulated me in the 1960s to begin thinking and writing about process and a systems approach. Somewhat later, the research of Robert MacArthur (1972) and his colleagues and students, which explored the dynamics of ecosystems, was equally influential. These researchers did some of the earliest work with supralevel organizations and rejected from the outset a taxonomic approach positing that higher-level systems require different forms of explanation than lower-level subsystems.

Like Leslie White, MacArthur used energy as a master currency, in conjunction with a series of simplifying models, to address the complex problems of ecosystem organization and

the issue of species versus niche.[4] The knotty problem of subsystem and suprasystem relationships was also dealt with without resort to an all-or-nothing position on the issue of reductionism versus holism. Equally productive research was going on simultaneously in the domain of nonequilibrium thermodynamics (see particularly Prigogine and Stengers 1984) and in an early attempt at complex, dynamic system theory known as catastrophe theory (Renfrew 1978; Renfrew and Cooke 1979; Thom 1975; Zeeman 1979, 1982). More recent research has been summarized by Laszlo (1987), and concurrent developments in complexity research have been reported by Lewin (1992) and Waldrop (1992).

Essential to the growth of knowledge in this domain has been the recognition that all physical systems may exhibit properties indicative of three basic states. When a system is at or near equilibrium, it is stable and relatively inert, it resists motion or action, and it is chemically inactive. A system in such a state is internally homogeneous, and the elements of the system are internally unordered. Systems that are *near* equilibrium are characterized by some internal differentiation in temperature and disposition of matter. Their internal structure is neither homogeneous nor random, and the system is responsive to changes in both sources and scales of perturbation that tend to be destabilizing. When the limiting factors abate, the system tends to move toward equilibrium. The system is entropic when in a state of nonequilibrium, but as it approaches equilibrium, entropy diminishes to nearly zero.

A third type of system includes living systems of many forms that are not characterized by thermal or chemical equilibrium. Changes in these systems tend to be nonlinear and, under some conditions, may appear to be indeterminate. Organizational properties may, nevertheless, dramatically amplify fluctuations and move the system's structure to new organizational levels.

The propensity of living systems to become more energetic over time, with corresponding increases in organizational complexity, appears to violate the second law of thermodynamics, which generalizes that systems gradually *lose* energy and experience an associated reduction in structure or organization. This apparent paradox is resolved by the knowledge that living systems are open or energy-capturing, whereas the second law applies only to closed systems. Exclusively internal processes obey the second law of thermodynamics, as do internally organized components of living systems, but energy may nevertheless be introduced or imported across the system boundaries of macroscale living systems. This possibility results in a spectrum of potential system state conditions that can include a condition of *dynamic equilibrium,* or *steady state,* in which free energy is imported in quantities roughly equal to the internal energetics of the system. The term *dynamic equilibrium* is more appropriate than *steady state,* however, since there are likely to be instabilities in the environments of open systems that result in the presence of varying levels of free energy in the environment available for capture or importation.

Additionally, changes in entropy levels within open systems are not determined exclusively by irreversible processes internal to such systems. Instead, the dynamics of living systems are a function of the "connectivity" among nets and nodes of energy-based interaction, both within and across the interior systems that are linked to energy sources outside the system. According to this organizationally oriented perspective on evolution, dynamic processes—particularly those leading to internal reorganizations and changes in organizational complexity—are driven by the dynamics of energy flows as well as the scales and forms of energetic networks. Arguments of this kind are concerned with and attempt to explain changes at the macro level of systemic organization.

The better-known—or at least more widely discussed—neo-Darwinian view of evolution is derived from the synthesis of Darwinian principles and modern genetics (Mayr 1982). Its view of dynamics is strongly tied to mechanistic views of process. In the terminology associated with a concern for energy-based, macrolevel processes, neo-Darwinian arguments *may* apply to living systems near a state of dynamic equilibrium, but they are unable to explain changes in either the level of energy flow through a system or the level of organizational complexity surrounding nonequilibrium states.

Competing evolutionary schemata can be easily distinguished from one another by comparing the answers they provide to the following three questions: (1) How does variety arise? (2) How is variety transmitted to future states of a system? (3) What process of selection biases the transmission of variety to subsequent generations? Proponents of creationist, Lamarckian, Darwinian, and neo-Darwinian theories of evolutionary change—including neo-Darwinian variants such as sociobiology (Wilson 1975), evolutionary ecology (Dupré 1987), and "selectionism" (Dunnell 1989, 1995)—would deal with the preceding questions very differently. And, if I were to ask what are the units or carriers of variety and upon what units does selection operate, still other views of evolution would present themselves.

Finally, a query about the implications that any given suite of answers to the preceding questions would have for the character of temporal patterning in the results of evolutionary process would return me full circle to at least some variant of the macrosystemic perspective with which I introduced this discussion. Contrasts between a macrosystemic view and the "replacement" view of some current fitness-driven arguments are illustrated in discussions of gradualism versus punctuated equilibrium (Eldredge and Gould 1972; Eldredge and Tattersall 1982), in discussions of micro- versus macroevolution (Stanley 1979), and in the contemporary interest in emergence and complexity studies (Lewin 1992; Waldrop 1992). There is indeed little doubt that evolutionary viewpoints abound. Regrettably, no single theory is sufficiently developed to permit fine-tuned testing and evaluation.

In spite of many claims for the existence of a "true" evolutionary theory (see Dunnell 1980; Rindos 1989; Teltser 1995;[5] and O'Connell 1995, for instance), many interesting issues remain unresolved and many stipulations about the way the world works have not been adequately researched[6] (e.g., Binford 1992[7]). One controversial issue that is central to many conflicting views of evolution revolves around the role of human "tendencies" to solve problems and to plan and execute goal-directed actions. I discussed some of these properties in chapter 2 in the context of clarifying what I mean by the term *projection*. I noted that projections are always based on expectations of stability and that successful, goal-directed actions based on projections are by nature conservative. Human actions that are based on a limited experience of all possible outcomes are therefore not likely to result in "directed change," despite the arguments mounted by critics of the so-called "adaptational" approach.

An awareness of these characteristics of human decision-making has led to the suggestion that cultural evolution, although not directed at the macro-evolutionary scale of process, may exhibit some bias in the production of variety that allows potentially new phenotypic variety to arise from the recognition of problems and attempts to solve them (Rosenberg 1990). According to this view, the bigger is the problem requiring human action, the greater will be the effort to solve it. Therefore, the production of variety would be stimulated by both the intensity of the stress experienced by human actors and the problem-solving effort that the stress stimulates. I would therefore expect that the production of variety in human cultural history would not be a random, continuous process, as has been maintained by Rindos (1984:59–61) among others, but that it may be "punctuated" relative to system state conditions.

Problem-solvers frequently select alternatives by trial and error. In such situations they must combine prior information in new ways that, in their judgment, are germane to the new problems they confront. Because problem-solvers produce new variety, the possibility exists that they will act as agents of evolutionary change, based on the consequences of their accumulative, decision-making experiences, as they transmit their experiences to subsequent generations. This process of transmission seats human actors securely in the evolutionary process and contrasts sharply with the selectionist construct of a passive human phenotype that is detached from the processes producing variety and governing trait replacement and selection.[8]

I think there is little doubt that some directed bias operates in the domain of problem-solving when persons filter experience and pass on information to the next generation. I cannot claim to be guided by a codified evolutionary theory, however, because such a comprehensive theory does not yet exist. I nonetheless have some expectations regarding evolutionary processes and how they operate in the causal domain of systems change, which make it imperative to know something about the properties of human actors relative to variations in the quantities and changing tempos of energy that flow through the living systems in which they participate.

This means that any conditions that cause an imbalance in the relationship between the amount of available free energy and the demand for that energy, and result in either the demands being less readily met or an increase in the energetic costs of meeting the demands, or in the failure to meet the demands, will condition some or all of the following responses:

1. Tactical shifts in the energy-capturing activities of the actors.
2. Increased competition among the actors both within and between socially integrated systems.
3. The appearance of new tactical variants that may include either technological aids or new organizational means of extracting energy or the matter necessary to such extraction, or energy conservation.
4. Exploration of and experimentation with the extraction of energy from new or previously untapped sources of energy or the matter required to extract free energy from new energy sources.

All situations in which energy is expended in the course of capturing free energy are intrinsically economic. In addition, all situations involving the extraction of energy or the transfer of energy across system boundaries exhibit the characteristics of an economically defined cost-benefit relationship. Among hunter-gatherers, the cost-benefit relationship is usually expressed as the relationship between the cost in energy expended to do work and the potential energetic returns acquired or captured by that work.

Recent research has demonstrated that human actors attempt to maximize their energetic returns in contexts of energy expenditure; in short, they commonly optimize (Smith 1991:32–52). Humans also seek to synchronize the flow of free energy into the human system relative to the human demand curve for food and other energy sources, such as firewood. Humans tend to organize their labor and their activities in a way that reduces the risk associated with accessing critical resources, and they tend to organize into cooperative social units in order to minimize any uncertainty associated with the dynamics of their social and ecological environments. Knowledge about the dynamics of patterned flow, state changes, and distribution of potential energy sources, as well as the matter required to access such sources, is a prerequisite to adaptive behaviors such as volitional or planned risk reduction strategies.[9]

I introduced the term *risk* in chapter 1 and pointed out that it refers to temporal variability in the amount of food that is available for consumption as a result of the productive efforts of a single producer over a given period of time. Other things being equal, risk pooling, or cooperation and subsequent pooling of products, is based on a sense of trust among those persons cooperating as food producers. Consequently I would expect social groups to use many different mechanisms to instill trust among those who cooperate in labor- and risk-pooling forms of organization. Indeed a variety of kinship conventions and other constructions and elaborations of social identity have been developed to reduce uncertainty about an individual's level of participation in cooperative efforts and the interaction among competitive groups.

Risk and cost-benefit constructs are essential to the arguments of many micro-evolutionary or neo-Darwinian schemata. They may be woven into a complex cognitive fabric of assumptions about proximate and ultimate causation or they may be linked to reductionist arguments about fitness that are unconvincing when based on phenotypic characteristics. On the other hand, when these propositions are considered in the context of energy-based arguments about macrosystemic change, they can be synthesized into a single, comprehensive theory that is not dependent upon holistic or reductionist preferences and biases. To evaluate my claim, however, it is necessary to explore further some of the observations and arguments that have emerged from general systems research.

> The processes of evolution unfold in all domains of the empirical world.... They produce systems in the third state—dynamic matter-energy systems far from equilibrium. These systems form a continuum that bridges the traditional boundaries of classical disciplines.... The relevant parameters include size, organizational level, bounding energy, and level of complexity.... As we move from microscopic systems on a basic level of organization to macroscopic systems on higher organizational levels, we move from systems that are strongly and rigidly bonded to those with weaker and more flexible binding energies. Relatively small units with strong binding forces act as building blocks in the formation of larger and less strongly bound systems on higher levels of organization. These in turn become building blocks in still larger, higher-level and less strongly bonded units.... On a given level of organization, systems on the lower level function as subsystems; on the next higher level of organization systems jointly form suprasystems.   (Laszlo 1987:21–25)

Laszlo's views are based on Prigogine's seminal work on entropy and energy flows, which demonstrates that emergent forms of organization are derived from nonequilibrium states. This research has resulted in the development of a more precise argument consistent with the earlier proposition that "cultural systems evolve as the energy harnessed per capita per year increases" (White 1949:368). In today's terminology, such a relationship is referred to as the "free-energy flux density" (Laszlo 1987:28) of a system and is expressed as energy per unit time per unit mass. The current focus on energetic systems and the investigation of *chaos* and other dynamic properties of systems have been responsible for still other changes in the way evolution may be conceptualized:

> The relationship between energy flow over time and change in entropy and free energy is essential for answering not only the question as to *how* systems in the third state evolve, but also whether they evolve *necessarily,* under certain conditions. Until the 1970s investigators leaned to the view—exposed most eloquently by Jacques Monod—that evolution is due mainly to accidental factors. But as of the 1980s many scientists are becoming convinced that evolution is not an accident, but occurs necessarily whenever certain parametric conditions are fulfilled.
> (Laszlo 1987:28–29; emphasis in original)

Although I do not pretend to contribute to the basic research effort to understand the structure and operation of energetic systems, I do agree with the content of general theories describing suprasystemic levels of organization such as ecosystems and sociocultural systems. A basic principle of the study of macrolevel forms of organized integration is that such systems cannot be understood simply in terms of their subsystemic components, whether considered individually or in the aggregate. This same principle also renders pointless any effort to understand sociocultural systems of organized variability, or the appearance of sociocultural complexity itself, exclusively by means of an examination of the individuals who participate in the system. Energetic processes are clearly the basis for systemic organization, structure, and dynamics, and they also underlie the restructuring of organizational properties in response to changing energy flows and networks.

Consistent with my affirmation of the utility of energy-based approaches to the study of systemic organization, I would also expect interesting organizational parallels, and even direct similarities, between aspects of ecosystems and sociocultural systems. For this reason, I think that hunter-gatherer groups can be viewed most productively as subsystems within organizationally more comprehensive ecosystems. Some types of changes that have occurred in the human evolutionary experience, however, have resulted in situations in which some components of ecosystems—if not ecosystems in their entirety—have become organized as subsystems of supralevel sociocultural systems. Ecosystems themselves, then, would appear to be a logical subject for study since the investigation of such a supralevel organization might well help us learn how to study macrolevel organizations in general and, ultimately, lead to a serious consideration of the interactive

dynamics between ecosystems and sociocultural systems in particular.

I begin my focus on ecosystems by identifying some properties of the environment that particularly contribute to the generation of diversity in human niches. In this effort I use whatever knowledge I have about human behavior and the dynamics of environments to outline a few basic conditions that may limit hunter-gatherer access to all of the food resources available in an environment. I use my knowledge of more generic aspects of human environments as a guide to the construction of a bare-bones, minimalist model of probable human responses to different environments.

The model is minimalist in the sense that it assumes human actors will behave exclusively as terrestrial hunter-gatherers, exploiting only terrestrial plants and animals as food resources. The model also assumes that hunter-gatherers are nearly perfect generalists, which means that they include food resources in their diet in almost direct proportion to the availability of resources in the habitat. The construction of this model provides some analytical advantages, since it is concretely defined and the assumptions standing behind it are explicit.

Initially I explore only some of the geographic and property space distributions of selected human behavior to see how the subject of the model responds to differences among the world's gross environments. I also explore the differences between a modeled and a projected frame of reference and the contributions that these analytical tools will make to research into variability and temporal trends in the archaeological record. In the final section of this chapter I apply the tools that have been developed—both the model and the projections from ethnographically documented hunter-gatherers—in an examination of some archaeological features related to the spread of domesticates throughout Europe in the sixth and seventh centuries B.C. I also examine how a concern for processes of emergence (the appearance of new forms that a full knowledge of preceding events would not permit one to anticipate)—which are energy based and not simply the result of gradual, accumulative, incremental change—will modify the ways in which the archaeological record is interpreted.[10]

Environmental Properties Germane to an Understanding of Variability among Hunter-Gatherers

At this juncture, I am interested in those properties of ecosystems that will help me to recognize specific environmental dynamics that condition organizational diversity in the niches occupied by human actors. The properties of interest derive from the nature of the interactions—the "fit"—between human performance capabilities and the differential distribution and character of the products of nature in varying habitats. These conditions can be described as variables that would not have seemed relevant had I not known something about both the range of human behavioral variability and the differential organization of productive variability in the world's environments. The recognition of new variables is stimulated by a growing understanding of human *effective environments* studied in conjunction with a recognition of the limiting factors that affect modern human participation in ecosystems. These constraints, of course, condition the character of the system states that could be achieved by participating sociocultural systems.

SYSTEM STATES AND HUMAN EFFECTIVE ENVIRONMENTS

Even though ecologists often invoke a state of optimal or perfect balance in the natural world to serve as an intellectual standard against which real-world dynamic states are measured, it is accepted that their use of such a conception is purely heuristic. In the 1950s, this understanding was embodied in the ecological principle of the inoptimum, which states that "no community encounters in any given habitat the optimum conditions for all of its functions" (Dansereau 1957:257). This is another way of saying that no adaptation[11] is ever optimal or balanced with reference to its habitat.

Subsistence security is defined by the environmental setting relative to the tactical capabilities and options of the organism that confronts it. For hunter-gatherers, solutions to the problem of subsistence insecurity are derived from the strategies or tactical arrays of behavior designed to cope with specifically inoptimum environmental conditions. Some environments may place strict limits on the ways in which security may be obtained, whereas others may tolerate the application of a strategy to a much broader range of situations. In this sense, one can speak of environments that differ in their levels of security potential, other things being equal. Other things, in this case, would be the range of knowledge and learned behaviors from which strategies could be built.

The term *effective environment* is a useful way to refer to the components of the gross environment with which a given group of human actors is most closely articulated, including the particular species within the habitat that are regularly exploited for food. Different groups of hunter-gatherers are known to vary in their relative dependence upon plant, animal, and aquatic foods. They are also known to vary in the amount of the earth's surface across which they range for food, in their pattern of movement within the habitat, in their techniques for organizing labor to procure resources, and in the ways they utilize foods.

From its inception, the discipline of anthropology has been preoccupied with the relationship between the character of all of the various attributes of an environment and the effec-

tive environments characteristic of different groups, although anthropologists have used different words to voice their concerns. There has been no consensus, however, about whether people simply choose their effective environments because they like to eat fish or honey or whether ecologically influenced, selective conditioning pushes and pulls human actors into different niches. I agree with the latter proposition, even though to suggest that some kind of environmental conditioning is a factor in the choices made by human actors prompts many archaeologists to dismiss supporting evidence as just another example of "environmental determinism."[12]

In order to explore the claim that niches are conditioned and not chosen, I build a minimalist terrestrial model of human behavior to which I will then compare documented human behavior in a variety of organized forms. The model will assume that, like other animals, human actors are constrained by properties of the gross environment to participate only in certain types of ecological plays that are characterized by a particular kind of plot. Possession of an explicit model rooted in ecological dynamics allows one to compare the differences between modeled variability and documented real-world cases.

The model is quite literally like the zero point on a scale of values in terms of which real-world cases can be arrayed to observe their deviation from the modeled values. If I were to express this relationship in terms of system state variability, I would say that the model represents the assumption of a particular response state relative to actual response states in given habitats. The model assumes that the response of the actors will be the same in all situations and that the environmental situation in which the actors find themselves is what is varying. Deviations from the modeled values are, therefore, some measure of the actors' organizational divergence from the modeled conditions and can be interpreted as potential indicators of system state differences.

Both modeled values and deviations from them can be projected onto either property space maps or the more familiar geographic representation of the earth's surface. The patterning visible in these projections can form the basis for arguments about the causes of emergent evolutionary episodes and their temporal and spatial discontinuities. Although building a minimalist model of human terrestrial subsistence is the goal of this chapter, my initial concern is to identify some of the generic properties of the effective environments of hunter-gatherers and to develop additional measures of those properties that are particularly germane to human actors.

BETWEEN-HABITAT DIVERSITY

Most of the variables introduced in chapter 4 are environmental attributes that make it possible to specify in some detail the differences between environmental conditions at a variety of locations. All of these variables, therefore, may be considered potential conditioners of the between-habitat diversity that characterizes the totality of different places where hunter-gatherers have lived. All of the variables that I have introduced thus far, however, defined climatic and associated energetic conditions. I did not explore how habitats themselves are "grounded" by topographic variability arising from the earth's internal energetics.

Topographic variability is not conditioned by the same kind of dynamic causation as variability in biomass in the plant community. Diversity in the topographic placement of a habitat nevertheless affects how many basic climatic variables are modified and redirected. Extant habitats are considerably more varied than if they were situated on a perfectly smooth sphere with no irregularity in the elevation of land surfaces and bodies of water.

Topography and Geography

Topography is the defining context in which the differential juxtaposition of biological species in space creates between-habitat diversity. Vertical and horizontal topographic differences produce microclimatic multiformity in habitats that has considerable impact on the composition of ecological communities. Although some differences among habitats may be referable to differences in *habitat states*—which, as we have seen, are affected by supraregional factors such as rainfall and solar radiation—these structural differences are not included in the category of between-habitat diversity but are instead various expressions of within-habitat states. The term *between-habitat diversity* refers exclusively to variability in the spatial juxtaposition of biotic communities that results from the character of the habitat base or land surface itself.

One of the most useful studies of between-habitat variability was undertaken by Simpson (1964), who examined the species density of mammals in North America from Panama to the arctic. In addition to describing the graded distributions of species and their correlations with latitude, Simpson also pointed out that "there is certainly a relationship between topography and species density, although the correlation is neither perfect nor simple" (1964:68).

One of Simpson's particularly provocative observations was that species density is greater in areas of broken topography. He also noted that peninsulas exhibit lower species densities than analogously placed, continuous land masses (1964:73), and he summarized his empirical observations with the overarching generalization that species density is negatively correlated with rainfall at equivalent latitudes (Simpson 1964:72). This means that species density is higher in the southwestern United States than it is in the forests of eastern North America, if latitude is held roughly constant. Several related differences come to mind as a result of Simpson's

correlations (e.g., the forests of eastern North America have higher biomass and there are lower elevational differences per unit area), but at the time that his research was published there were few explanatory arguments to account for the patterning.

More recent ecological research has produced additional patterns, most notably that species heterogeneity is conditioned by the nutrient level available to plant communities (Tilman 1982), and this factor may be implicated in some of the contrasts that Simpson observed relative to rainfall. Additional field studies of desertic species and their densities have greatly expanded what is known about diversity in dry environments (Hallett 1982; Pianka 1969, 1971; Rosenzweig and Winakur 1969), and attention has also focused on the structure of ecological communities on islands and peninsulas (Case et al. 1979). Explanations of this variability are, however, less important to this study than the facts of the patterning itself.

As a way of controlling for at least some of the factors contributing to between-habitat diversity—and the impact these factors have on human subsistence strategies—I have assembled topographic data for the regions inhabited by the hunter-gatherer groups in this study. The same procedure was applied to each case: a point in the center of each region was identified, and I then recorded the highest and lowest elevations in the area defined by a set of circles inscribed at ten, twenty-five, and fifty miles from the central point.

Six elevational values were determined for each region, and two different measures were calculated using these data. A modal elevation, ELEV, was calculated by adding the lowest and highest values noted within a ten-mile radius of the central point of the group's range and dividing this sum by two. In those cases in which the only available source of elevation data was a weather station, the station's elevation was recorded. The second value, MAXRANGE, is more germane to habitat variability. It was calculated by subtracting the lowest elevation value from the highest value recorded within a fifty-mile radius of the center of the territory. I also calculated the standard deviation (SDELEV) of a region's six elevation values and the coefficient of variation (CVELEV), which was calculated using the observations taken from a fifty-mile radius. When only weather station data were available, the preceding measures of within-area variability were not calculated.

Although the local elevational characteristics contribute significantly to habitat variability and diversity within the ranges of human sociocultural systems, they must be considered in conjunction with the fact that humans are omnivorous feeders whose habitat breadth has expanded in some settings to include the exploitation of aquatic resources.

Aquatic Biomes and Human Habitats

So far my discussion of habitats has focused on the properties of terrestrial biotypes because human beings are terrestrial animals who are biologically incapable of living in aquatic environments without technological assistance. Nevertheless, as I noted in chapter 5, many past and present hunter-gatherer groups have expanded their niches to include the aquatic biome as a component of their habitat. The degree to which this expansion has occurred is conditioned by slightly different variables than those that structure terrestrial habitats.

Although human actors are capable of direct participation, ecologically speaking, in a terrestrial setting, they may be thought of as outsiders in aquatic biomes; they intrude at times, but always at very restricted locations and under rather specific conditions. To exploit aquatic resources, humans must be positioned on aquatic-terrestrial ecotones. This positioning, together with the fact that successful human exploitation of an aquatic biome is severely limited, ensures that specific properties of the ecotone from which human intrusions are launched condition to a large extent how and when aquatic resources are tapped for human use. This ecotonal constraint often results in a linear distribution of the human groups who regularly incorporate aquatic resources into their niche space.

Most generalizations about the geographic patterning of variability in terrestrial habitats do not apply to marine habitats because the marine biome is energetically conditioned by the mobile properties of liquids. These properties tend to modify the temperature and salinity of the marine world quite independently of the actual distribution of solar radiation over the surface of the earth. Tides, ocean currents, and particularly the depth of the ocean affect not only the distribution of important biological parameters but also the local variability and stability of these parameters. As a result, from a global perspective the biogeography of marine production and biomass is very different from that of terrestrial biomes.

In contrast, the patterns of production and biomass distribution in riparian and lacustrian biomes are linked to the bioenergetics of the terrestrial habitats in which they are located, being strongly related to the same variables that regulate terrestrial production—rainfall and solar radiation. Runoff from rainfall provides the water for riparian and lacustrian biomes, and solar radiation provides the energy for most of the production in these terrestrially linked aquatic settings. Another link between riparian and lacustrian settings and the terrestrial habitat in which they are embedded results from the fact that much of the production in streams and rivers is the result of a truncated trophic structure. Many of the habitat's consumers are not dependent upon production in the aquatic domain because they feed on detritus derived ultimately from terrestrial production. Still other consumers feed on organisms whose reproductive success is directly conditioned by the bioenergetics of the terrestrial biome (e.g., insect larvae). As might be expected, production in streams and lakes is correlated with terrestrial production.

The exception to the preceding generalization occurs in those instances in which the flow of water to the sea is through areas of low or reduced rainfall. The term *unearned water*[13] is used to describe settings of this kind, in which the water occurring within a habitat is not produced by rainfall in the region. Many of the world's major river systems—including much of the Nile River valley, the Rio Grande valley, the Colorado River valley, and the better part of the Murray River drainage in Australia—are good examples of regions in which rivers supply unearned water. These systems support much higher productivity and biomass in riparian settings than would be possible from earned water alone.

The productivity of these streams and rivers is also much greater than would be anticipated from the level of adjacent terrestrial production. As a river nears the ocean, unearned water accumulates from very large drainage catchments and causes accelerating increases in productivity. In some settings, like the lower Columbia River drainage, productivity is enriched not only by unearned "extra" water but also by earned water that occurs in a zone of high earned rainfall near the river's mouth. These features are not directly related to terrestrial productivity per se but are produced by the coincidence of the topographic characteristics and bioenergetics of terrestrial habitats.

I had originally intended to include data in my study estimating the amount of aquatic resources available to hunter-gatherers in various locations by directly measuring production in the world's oceans, inland lakes, and rivers. I quickly discovered, however, that global data on productivity were scanty and that there was no consistent procedure for measuring productivity levels for those data that were available.

Many of the conventions that have been applied to the interpretation of archaeological data are based on ethnographic information about the location and size of a group's territory. In those situations in which relevant information is available, such as those reported by Baumhoff (1963), estimates of the number of miles of streams or coastlines within a group's territory have been used successfully to anticipate population density or fishing dependence. One of the goals of this research is to develop a frame of reference for archaeologists who do *not* know the ranges or territories of the prehistoric peoples responsible for the archaeological sites that they excavate. I asked myself what knowledge would allow me to anticipate intense use of aquatic resources at any given location when it was unknown how the landscape was partitioned into ranges. It seemed to me that a study of the topography and character of drainage systems was an obvious way to assess the likelihood that different localities would have usable aquatic resources.

This approach required that I make a number of distance measurements in the drainage systems in which hunter-gatherer groups in my study were documented. Their location in space was known, so I measured the distance in miles from a central point in their territory to the headwaters of the streams and rivers draining into the area within which they lived (HEADWAT). The distance from the central point to the mouth (at the sea) of the larger drainages was also measured in miles and added to HEADWAT, resulting in a measure in miles of the total length of the drainage system (DRAIN) passing through the area of interest. In order to develop a scale in terms of which drainages could be compared, the length of each drainage (DRAIN) was divided by 4,132 miles, which is a constant based on the length of the Nile (the world's longest river system), and each percentage value was then multiplied by ten. The resulting variable, DRANK, ranks drainages on a scale from zero to ten: the higher the value, the larger the drainage system.

Because there is a positive relationship between drainage size and the volume of water flowing at different points along the trunk drainage, I calculated an index value (DGROSS), which is simply DRANK multiplied by DPOSIT (a variable determined by dividing HEADWAT by DRAIN). The values are distributed from zero to ten: the higher the value, the greater the amount of unearned water expected at the location serving as the reference point for the measurements. The water resources of all hunter-gatherer cases in this study were then evaluated and a categorical classification, called SETTING, was defined. This classification is presented in table 6.01.

The final variable developed as part of my investigation of the exploitation of aquatic resources is the crow-flies distance from hunter-gatherer habitats to the nearest coast, measured in kilometers (COKLM). It should be pointed out that DRAIN, HEADWAT, DRANK, DPOSIT, and DGROSS do not apply to all coastal settings or to many settings with only intermittent streams or waterless deserts. In some cases, a group's position may be coastal but located at the mouth of a major river—for example, the Chinook of Oregon—and in such a situation the drainage can be measured and the values calculated.

Similarly, continuously flowing internal drainages such as the Humboldt River of Nevada may also be measured, but in many internal drainages these riparian measures do not apply. Several conventions have been used in this situation. For coasts, SETTING = (C), a DRAIN value of 1.0 and a HEADWAT value of 1.0 are entered, yielding a DPOSIT value of 1.0, which indicates maximum positioning relative to an exclusively marine biome. For internal drainages, SETTING = (P), but not lakes or regularly flowing internal drainages capable of supporting significant aquatic resources, a value of 1.0 is entered for DRAIN and a value of 0.01 for HEADWAT, indicating the absence of a significant aquatic biome.

TABLE 6.01
DRAINAGE CATEGORIES (SETTING)

TYPE	DEFINITION
1	Coastal locations (C): includes some groups located on islands and peninsulas as well as cases on the coasts of major continents, in major utilizing bays, and in tidal estuarine settings.
2	Rivers and streams (S): includes cases located in terrestrial settings with defined drainage systems and outlets to the sea.
3	Lakes and swamps (L): includes cases that are also terrestrial in that drainage systems are classified as rivers and streams, but there is a major lake or accumulation basin in the drainage, either within or immediately adjacent to the range.
4	Pans and all internal drainages (P): includes locations with spring water or access to underground water only. Good examples of this type are found in the Humboldt River drainage of Nevada and the Cooper's Creek drainage of southeastern Australia. Both systems are quite long but dissipate in sinks—Lake Eyre in the Australian case and Humboldt Lake and Carson Sink in Nevada. These locations may support either lakes with varying degrees of salinity, seasonally filled pans, or water holes. In very dry settings, vegetation may seasonally fill the role of water sources. Intermittent streams are, however, the most common form of drainage in these settings.

A More Dynamic View of Between-Habitat Variability

In chapter 4, I was concerned with the global climatic factors that condition at least some of the organizational characteristics of ecological communities. Thus far I have not explored any of the local dynamic responses to variability in global climatic variables, although dynamics have been implied. The dynamics of local communities may condition properties of the habitat, such as the number of species per unit area or species density. For instance, species density has been shown to vary regularly with succession, or the reversible cyclical dynamics within a particular habitat and biotic community at a given latitude. Monk (1967) has shown that, other things being equal, greater species diversity has been observed in climax plant communities than in the early stages of succession, and this finding has been confirmed by studies of forests in the eastern United States (Woodwell and Whittaker 1968:21–22).

On the other hand, Whittaker (1956) discovered that in the high-biomass forests of the Great Smoky Mountains diversity did not vary directly with either production or biomass (Woodwell and Whittaker 1968). Loucks's (1970) study of succession demonstrated that in Wisconsin forests the greatest diversity occurs in the understory layers and the least diversity is found among upperstory species, an observation also made by Monk (1967). As succession proceeds, however, diversity increases in the upperstory and decreases in the understory (Loucks 1970:20).

Using comparative data, Loucks was able to demonstrate that if no disturbance interrupts the continuation of a successional trend, diversity in the upperstory tends to decrease as more and more of the species are replaced by maturing individuals of shade-tolerant species, which in his study area were sugar maples. It was Loucks's (1970) contention that under normal conditions fires periodically interrupted this sequence and returned the forest to lower stages of succession. Over time, the maximum diversity in the upperstory tended to be the inflection point in an oscillating steady state in which maximum diversity was associated with the modal maturity level of forests in the region.

This research is important for several reasons. It confirms that, for animals, the greatest variety of potential foods is present during the early stages of succession and decreases in maturing forest associations.[14] Second, it illustrates the shift in diversity from understory to upperstory growth, which favors the increased presence of small-body-size, secondary consumers concentrated in the upperstory zones. Finally, it renders intelligible Whittaker's observation (1956) that diversity was generally lower in the isolated and exceedingly mature "cove forests" of the Great Smoky Mountains.

The mere mention of the term *succession* implies perturbations, the most common of which are violent storms and fires,[15] that reduce or change the biomass-production relationships in particular places. I have not accumulated global data on lightning strike frequencies and the seasonality of burns resulting from this phenomenon, but it should be kept in mind that on a global basis lightning strike frequencies vary in a patterned way from one location to another (Komarek 1964). Two major factors that condition the incidence of fire are, of course, lightning strike frequencies and the predominance of winter rainfall coupled with the severity of rainfall deficits during the summer months.

In tropical settings in which growing season temperatures are high, potential evapotranspiration is also very high, which means that very large quantities of rainfall are required to maintain water balance. The fact that forest vegetation will be maintained only in areas of exceedingly high rainfall, combined with the fact that thunderstorm frequencies generally increase as the distance from the equator decreases (Komarek 1964:142), ensures that a steady state with regard to immature successional stages is likely. The African savanna is at least partially a fire-maintained ecosystem, as are most temperate steppic areas. In the temperate zone, potential evapotranspiration is reduced because decreased solar radiation results in shorter growing seasons, which—other things being equal—increase the probability that water balance will be achieved.

On the other hand, rainfall is substantially reduced in the zones on both sides of 30 degrees latitude, although local conditions may modify global circulation patterns and result in local patches of higher rainfall. This means that the middle latitudes will, on the whole, have fewer areas with high-biomass plant communities and more areas where fire hazard is high, in spite of lower frequencies of thunderstorms. Still farther to the north and south, potential evapotranspiration is correspondingly reduced, and in the zones bordering 60 degrees latitude rainfall tends to increase. Thunderstorm frequencies in these regions are reduced still further, which means that destructive fires are less likely because of lower thunderstorm frequencies and increased rainfall. This generalization does not apply to areas with pronounced seasonality in rainfall, particularly areas with predominantly winter rainfall regimes, where the probability of significant, cyclically occurring fires is high. Much of California and the western region of the United States, parts of British Columbia, and even Alaska are characterized by significant forest destruction from fires caused by lightning strikes.

In a fifteen-year study of a major stand of ponderosa pine in northern Arizona, Wadsworth (1943) found that one-third of the individual tree deaths were caused by lightning strikes. In the forests of Yellowstone Park, Taylor (1969:279) reported that of the 1,228 fires documented between 1931 and 1967, 54 percent were caused by lightning strikes. Also in Yellowstone, 35 percent of the lodgepole pine trees larger than four inches in diameter were fire-scarred (Taylor 1969:289). In both of these study areas, significant fire scarring occurred. Applying these observations and their implications for successional dynamics to concrete case material, Hardy and Franks (1963) estimated that in Alaska during the month of June alone, 511,000 acres would be burned as a result of fires caused by lightning.

I have developed a numerical indicator for those regions in which successional dynamics are likely to exhibit greater amplitudes, based on the following patterns and assumptions. The first pertinent observation is that thunderstorm frequencies must correspond roughly to effective temperature levels. The only departure from this pattern is a slight increase in storms in zones bordering 60 degrees latitude north and south, where polar convection cells may be overridden by the northward-moving, warmer surface air of central circulatory cells. The frequency of fires, therefore, results from a combination of thunderstorm activity and dry conditions in the plant communities. These conditions usually occur in regions with dry summers or in areas dominated by either winter rainfall or very low levels of annual rainfall.

Based on the climatic conditions that interact to produce meteorologically induced fires, the following equation has been developed to provide an indicator, termed SUCSTAB, of the conditions likely to result in extensive, periodic burning

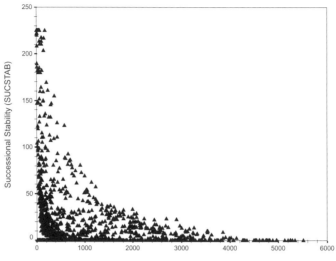

FIGURE 6.01

Demonstration of an inverse relationship between predominantly winter rainfall (SUCSTAB) and net aboveground productivity (NAGP) based on the world weather station sample.

and subsequent cyclical primary biomass reduction in regions inhabited by hunter-gatherers (table 4.01):

$$(6.01)$$

$$\text{SUCSTAB} = 10^{**}\{\log_{10}\text{ET}^2 - \log_{10}(7.5 * \text{sqrtCRR})]\} * \{10^{**}[\log_{10}(\text{PERWLTG}/100) * \text{LREVEN}]\}/10$$

This measure tends to inflate the differences between areas with very dry growing seasons and those with wet growing seasons. Values that are close to zero suggest low probabilities of fire-induced community destruction; the higher the value, the greater the probability of fires and community destruction. In the preceding equation, SUCSTAB includes variables that relate only to the rainfall and temperature conditions favoring fire and does not actually deal with the other necessary condition, which is adequate fuel. One can imagine, for instance, a setting near the equator with optimal conditions of low rainfall and high temperatures, yet fires would not occur if the rainfall level was zero and there was no unearned water because truly desertic conditions would exist and there would be no vegetation to burn. To make the SUCSTAB index more realistic, a corrective procedure was therefore added to the preceding equation to take into account the partially independent distributions of fuel and the optimal temperature and moisture conditions favoring fires.

The distribution in figure 6.01 illustrates a very distinct, inverse relationship between SUCSTAB and net aboveground productivity (NAGP). As the values for productivity decrease, the value of SUCSTAB increases, which would suggest that

with zero productivity the probability of fire is highest. I have already pointed out, however, that this is impossible since fuel is required in order for fires to start and burn. An examination of the cases represented in the distribution in figure 6.01 leads me to define a cutoff value for NAGP of 500 grams per square meter. For cases in which this value is exceeded, the value of SUCSTAB calculated in the preceding equation would be accepted, indicating that fuel is not considered a limiting factor. In cases characterized by an NAGP value of less than 500, a straight-line equation was fitted between the lower part of the distribution in figure 6.01, where NAGP approaches zero, and an upper value of 500. According to this equation,

$$(6.02)$$

$$Y = a + bX$$

where $a = 1.2699958$
$b = 0.27247497$
and Y = a new variable called MAXSUC and
X = an NAGP value of less than 500.

This equation sets an upper limit for the value of SUCSTAB simply as a function of increasing values of NAGP. In settings in which there is no fuel, there is a zero value for SUCSTAB, regardless of temperature and moisture conditions. By using this value, I reverse the distribution of SUCSTAB shown in figure 6.01 for cases with high SUCSTAB values but low to zero values of NAGP, my surrogate measure of the quantity of fuel present. To correct for fuel absence, the following procedure was implemented:

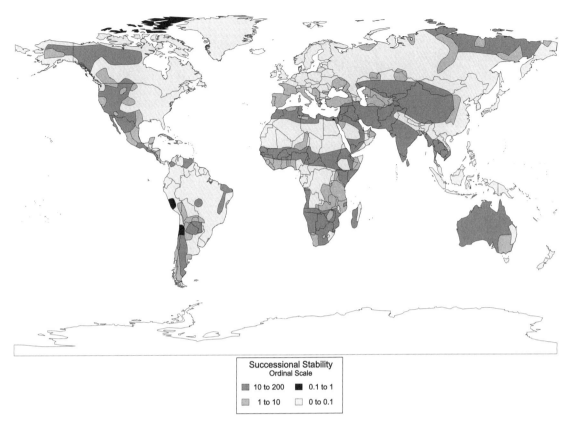

FIGURE 6.02

World distribution map for scaled values of successional stability (SSTAB2) based on the world weather station sample.

(6.03)

If NAGP is greater than 499.99, then SSTAB2 equals SUCSTAB.

If NAGP is less than 500.00 and SUCSTAB is less than MAXSUC, then SSTAB2 is also equal to SUCSTAB.

If, however, NAGP is less than 500.00 and SUCSTAB is greater than MAXSUC, then SSTAB2 is equal to {1.0 − [(SUCSTAB − MAXSUC)/(225 − MAXSUC)]} * MAXSUC.

When 225 is the maximum value allowed by the default setting used in calculating SUCSTAB, MAXSUC is the estimated value for SUCSTAB that could occur given the previous equation for correcting the limiting effects of low fuel availability.

When MAXSUC and SUCSTAB are used in the context of the preceding equation, the result is an inverted percentage value that produces low percentages in cases in which SUCSTAB values far exceed those of MAXSUC, thereby adjusting the cases to the realities of fuel deficits. The fuel-corrected value, SSTAB2, is illustrated in figure 6.02, which presents the distribution of this variable in a proportional

sample of the earth's weather stations. SUCSTAB is a very realistic indicator of the probability of successional turnover in the earth's environments.

The variable MEDSTAB, which was introduced initially in chapter 4, is similar to SUCSTAB but emphasizes the seasonality of rainfall and de-emphasizes relative dryness during the growing season. Like SUCSTAB and SSTAB2, it is an indicator of gross environmental conditions, but the latter variable is a much more sensitive indicator of between-habitat variability. Figure 6.03 illustrates the relationship between $\log_{10}$ values of SUCSTAB and MEDSTAB. The interaction of these indices delineates an eight-part classification of habitats based primarily on the quantity of rainfall and its effect on the role of fire and the seasonality of precipitation.

In chapter 4, I introduced equations that permit the projection of current knowledge about ungulates and their relative success when measured by their biomass. In light of my discussion in this chapter about fire and the fact that successional reduction enhances the habitat for animals, it is not surprising that positive values of SUCSTAB are an important conditioner of higher ungulate biomass values.

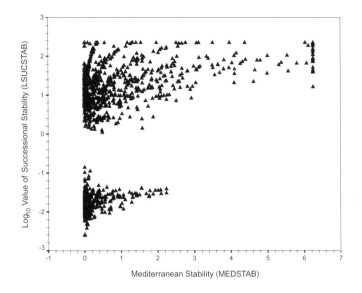

FIGURE 6.03

Relationship between two measures of winter-dominant rainfall, SUC-STAB and MEDSTAB, based on the world weather station sample.

ECOLOGICAL ORGANIZATION OF
WITHIN-HABITAT DIVERSITY

When MacArthur (1965) introduced the distinction between within- and between-habitat diversity, diversity was defined as the difference in the numbers of species present per unit area at different locations. MacArthur's construct emphasized the scalar differences between features of the ecosystem that were due to widespread climatic variability (between-habitat diversity) and those features resulting from organizational differences arising in the context of the internal dynamics of ecological communities themselves (within-habitat diversity). MacArthur's interest was initially focused on the assumption that two species utilizing the same resources could not occupy the same niche, which was a prelude to arguments about competition. He was also concerned with the observation that, for tropical species but not for species in higher-latitude settings, diversity also seemed to correlate with some features of niche breadth, which was evaluated in terms of diet breadth. In other words, more tropical species exhibited specialized feeding strategies and fewer were more generalized feeders who resorted to what MacArthur termed "jack-of-all-trades" strategies.

Arguments attempting to account for within-habitat diversity may be grouped into several sets that differ largely in terms of scale shifts in the way the problem is envisioned. The most widely cited arguments link a locality's system state properties, such as stability or predictability, and more formal characteristics, such as diversity, into a single argument. For many years it was thought that a system state property such as stability simply referred to stability in basic climatic variables. Researchers then began to explore the possibility that aspects of stability in the gross environment should be considered independently of measures of ecosystem stability. It was also thought that there were differences between community stability and instability among the particular breeding populations of species participating in the same ecosystem. Variability in particular breeding populations was thought to be responsive to within-ecosystem dynamics rather than simply to reflect the meta-stabilities of the gross environment providing the systemic envelope for the ecosystem.

Conventional wisdom had stipulated that complexity in ecosystems resulted from environmental stability, but this view has been challenged on many different fronts by recent research. It was argued convincingly that environmental "steadiness" or lack of high-amplitude variability in basic climatic variables fostered ecological stability. Pielou (1975:130) took the argument one step further by proposing that "high environmental stability leads to high community stability, which, in turn, permits (but is not caused by) high diversity." Pielou should have qualified his statement by including the phrase "other things being equal," since local conditions dampen climatic fluctuations in temperature and rainfall quite independently of tropical or high-latitude placement on the earth. This seems, nevertheless, to have been what Pielou had in mind, since he observed that "to survive in a seasonal or unpredictable environment, a species needs to be 'flexible in its responses' or, equivalently, to have a 'wide niche,' . . . as a result a given type of habitat can contain fewer niches and hence fewer species the more strongly seasonal, or unpredictable, the conditions" (Pielou 1975:131).

The preceding statement touches upon a subject that ecologists have debated at length—the distinction between a feeding generalist and a feeding specialist. Other things being equal, the members of a species are called specialists if they feed on very few other species, and they are said to be generalists if they feed on many species. The phrase "other things being equal" is very important in this context, and its omission has led to many strange arguments about the implications of feeding strategies.[16]

One critically important characteristic of habitats is simply the number of species present at different locations. For instance, a "generalist" in an environment containing only seven species might feed on four of the seven (57 percent of those present), whereas a species feeding on four species in a setting containing sixty species would be exploiting only 6.6 percent of the resident species and would be considered a specialist.[17]

The confusion in the archaeological literature between the terms *specialist* and *generalist* results from a failure to consider not only the number of species that a group exploits but also that number *relative to the total number of species present in the habitat.* Confusion also arises from a misunderstanding of the ecological implications of differences in strategic feeding behaviors. For those ecologists who study nonhuman systems, species diversity is essentially isomorphic with niche diversity. *Generalist* and *specialist* are terms that have reference to between-species niche comparisons of diet breadth, and these comparisons are always made relative to the gross environment within which niches are structured.

There are, in fact, other ways of looking at system stability besides Pielou's mechanistic generalizations. It is possible to compare systems in terms of their actual responses to perturbations in variables affecting the system's energetics. A system may be viewed as stable or unstable depending upon whether a perturbation tends to be amplified or rapidly dampened by internal system dynamics. Recent research has tended to confirm that if one measures the number of species and the "connectance" in the interaction matrix among species in an ecological community (Auerbach 1984:413–28), an estimate of stability is indicated.

Recent studies also suggest that various probability models, frequently referred to as neutral models (Sugihara 1980; Tilman 1982:190–204; Wiens 1984), may be as useful in anticipating stability as more conventional arguments based on mechanistic reasoning (Crowder 1980). Development of nonlinear and probability-based analysis has rendered problematic the old idea that increased species diversity itself results in increased complexity and, therefore, greater stability.

Contemporary research does not emphasize only species numbers and the limitations that low numbers place on the combinations and permutations that can be regarded as

some measure of complexity. Of equal concern is how species are organized and articulated. Current research supports the following generalization:

Generalization 6.01
As the number of energetic linkages between species increases, overall stability decreases.

Other things being equal, omnivores and trophic generalists tend to reduce systemwide stability, whereas an increase in the number of specialists seems to enhance it (May 1972:414). Additionally,

Generalization 6.02
The more organized or partitioned into feeding guilds the group of species in a habitat may be, the greater the stability relative to the total number of species represented. In contrast, the presence of intraspecific feeding guilds reduces the connectance links among all species in the community.

Much more work must be done before the diversity-stability connection can be fully understood, but the evidence appears to support a third generalization:

Generalization 6.03
Other things being equal, the fewer fluctuations in the basic variables conditioning production and biomass structure, the greater the potential stability and complexity of the system.

This generality is mediated, however, by a large number of fascinating organizational possibilities within ecosystems themselves, which prompt me to ask what rules govern this variability.

In the course of my research, I developed some tools for analyzing gross environments in terms of their stability differentials, some of which were introduced in chapter 3. I believe that a number of the variables directed toward measuring the magnitude of annual climatic fluctuations are important since the coincidence of high rainfall with high temperature affects subsistence, mobility, and sheltering requirements very differently than does a coincidence between high rainfall and low temperatures. I need, nevertheless, to increase my ability to monitor organizational variability, not only in the articulation of human units into the broader organization of the ecosystem in which they participate, but also in the articulation of different human groups to one another within an ecosystemic context. How does this "human ecoystem within an ecosystem" differ from the articulations of nonhuman systems that ecologists study?

I have already pointed out that for ecologists studying nonhuman systems, niche differentiation is basically signaled by species difference. Given that genetically based species differentiation in terms of behavior, morphology, and niche is a consequence of the same processes of natural selection that condition the differential reproductive success of breeding individuals, it is reasonable to think of niche and behavioral flexibility as aspects of the differences between species. In contrast, vastly different levels of organization are observed among human populations, the differences in niche are extreme, there is variability in the behavior-based tactics and strategies employed in analogous niches, and yet there is universal acknowledgment that human beings all belong to only one species. These correlates of phenotype that (for students of nonhuman ecosystems) would be clear and unequivocal indicators of species differences have been observed in contrasts between cultural systems past and present.

This fact alone indicates that there is something emergent about organized human participation in ecosystems. This is not a unique phenomenon; it happened earlier when life emerged from nonlife, when mammals emerged from nonmammalian species, and so on. It does mean, however, that a successful explanation of diversification among nonhuman species, although not irrelevant, is inadequate to explain the processes occurring in ecosystems after the new and different human participant arrived on the scene. Since phenotypic differentiations are not simultaneous steps in the speciation process, differentiations in the organization of cultural systems do not necessarily appear to be the phenotypic building blocks of species differentiation.

In chapter 2, I discussed some uniquely human properties and argued that those unique properties could never explain the diversity of outcomes from various planned events. I suggested that those unique properties must be considered constants; that is, they are the boundary conditions for arguments about organized human variability and therefore can never directly explain the variability. In this chapter I am suggesting that humans may perform unique roles in ecosystems and that researchers really do not know the degree to which the human species operates by the same rules as other species participating in ecosystems. Nor is it known how human behavioral flexibility (very nearly the definition of a generalist in ecological terms) may condition the appearance of within-species specializations and many other organizational building blocks of species differentiation. It is also unknown whether some of the generalizations about ecosystems may well be applicable to various forms of cultural systems and at the same time not apply to the roles those cultural systems actually play in the broader ecosystem.

Model Building: Further Considerations of Species-Specific Properties and Initial Conditions for Imagining Dynamics

One way of addressing the questions that have been posed is to construct a model of human behavioral responses to between-habitat variability. This model should specify in explicit terms the behavioral role of the human species in variable environments. It is also necessary to anticipate some of the characteristics of the human species that would limit the possible niches that it could occupy.

Body size is a feature of paramount importance because it places limits on the range of locations within an ecosystem in which the modeled species could perform. The body size of humans basically limits our species to a terrestrial role in the biosphere. Because we cannot fly, we are unable to play an effective role in exploiting foods from, for instance, the upper canopy of trees in a tropical rain forest. Humans are also unable to digest wood cellulose, so tree trunks and fallen branches lie outside the human dietary range. It should be clear that successfully casting species as actors in evolutionary plays depends initially on the behavioral capabilities of the actors. In turn, a knowledge of the behavioral range of a species conditions the features of the gross environment that, in interaction with the actor, may further limit the roles that a specific actor could perform.

CASTING HUMAN ACTORS IN EVOLUTIONARY PLAYS

A discussion of the role of human actors in evolutionary plays, performed in a variety of ecological theaters, can be approached most economically by limiting the roles and desires of actors. In this initial exploration of modeling, all of the plays are about subsistence and all the actors want to ensure their own security. By security—and in this example security refers to the food supply—I mean a system state or a set of relationships between human consumer demands and human producer capabilities to meet those demands. When demands can be met, one can say that an adaptation offers subsistence security. When demands are not met, a state of insecurity prevails. Given what is known about human actors and their subsistence needs, as well as the environments constituting the locus of potential foods, I will make an argument about how differences in the ecological theater may determine where in their gross environment human actors might be expected to achieve the greatest success.

It is suggested that, other things being equal,

Proposition 6.01

Optimum security would be possible in environmental settings with minimal temporal variability in the availability and abundance of potential foods.

I have already pointed out that variability in the periodicity of rainfall and the levels of temperature and solar energy throughout an annual cycle tends to result in cyclical shifts in the magnitude of primary biotic production. The intensity of this productive periodicity increases along temperature or latitudinal gradients. Similarly, it varies with global rainfall patterning in such a way that higher periodicity is expected in the middle latitudes, both north and south of 30 degrees latitude, in rain shadow areas of equatorial zones, and occasionally in areas approaching 60 degrees latitude. I also suggest that, other things being equal,

Proposition 6.02

Potential subsistence security will decrease as a direct result of seasonality in primary production stemming from either annual periodicity or long-term variability in rainfall or from concentrations of solar radiation at terrestrial locations.

If one reflects on this statement, it is reasonable to ask how this generalization has much to do with humans, since I have already demonstrated that (1) potential net aboveground productivity varies latitudinally in a rather regular fashion and (2) deficiencies in both solar radiation and rainfall result systematically in lowered net aboveground productivity (see figures 4.13 and 4.14) Why, therefore, is similarly patterned regularity in human behavior not simply an autocorrelation relating to the broader trends in habitat variability?

The answer to this question is very important: the periodicities of human energetic needs are very different from the metabolic trajectories of habitats. The human need for water is such that comparatively little time elapses between recurring states of critical need. Similarly, the human need for food, although scaled to a slightly longer duration, is nevertheless short relative to the cycles of productivity in plant communities. The human species does not have the widely varying fluctuations in metabolic rate that characterize some plant and animal species. There is a big difference between the resources produced in a habitat and the resources that are accessible, given the energetic needs of humans. In this case, the word *accessible* is used in the sense of resources being present when they are needed and being obtainable when they are both present and needed.

MODELING ACCESSIBLE PLANT FOODS

A knowledge of how much plant biomass is present in a given habitat in an average year is very different from a knowledge of the amount of potential plant foods that are accessible to human beings in any habitat at a given time during the year. Humans do not usually consume plant biomass per se but concentrate primarily on plant parts resulting from annual gross production, such as nuts, seeds, leaves, and honey.[18] There are exceptions to the productivity rule, particularly in dry environments in which the consumption of underground tubers and roots is common. Similarly, it is not uncommon in tropical settings for entire trees, such as the sago palm, to be exploited. Nevertheless, the majority of the food resources taken from the plant community are technically products of net annual production and not components of the plant community's standing biomass.

In order to estimate the potential food available for human consumption in a habitat, I have selected net aboveground productivity as the baseline parameter in terms of which to create an index of plant foods. The following equation, in which net aboveground productivity is expressed as the number of kilograms per 100 square kilometers, measures the potential maximum amount of consumables present in a habitat, expressed at a scale[19] consistent with population measures:

$$(6.04)$$
$$\text{NAGP per 100 square kilometers} = (NAGP/1000) * 100,000,000$$

Primary productivity is not the only factor conditioning the amount of food in a habitat that is available for human consumption. Access to food resources is also affected by the length of the growing season and by correlated environmental variables such as the measurements of temperature developed in chapter 4. Complex interactions among these factors influence how much primary productivity humans might reasonably exploit throughout a full and potentially variable annual cycle. My model assumes that

Proposition 6.03

Most human food is obtained from sources that are referred to as production and in settings in which production (and therefore food accessibility) slows or ceases for periods of variable length during the year. Humans, on the other hand, have a nearly continuous demand curve for food and a maturational period that exceeds the length of the annual cycle. Given these conditions, the amount of food that is available during the least productive period of the year will limit the level of sustainable population within an area.

This statement represents the application to the human species of one aspect of Shelford's *law of tolerance*, which states that the "presence and success of an organism depends upon the completeness of a complex of conditions. Absence or failure of an organism can be controlled by the qualitative or quantitative deficiency or excess with respect to any one of several factors which may approach the limits of tolerance for that organism" (Odum 1971:107).

Experimentation with environmental variables, together with the available information about hunter-gatherers, has demonstrated that the most reasonable weighting of a variable encompassing human access to shifting levels of plant productivity—resulting from the annual cycle of temperature fluctuations at a given location on earth—could be approximated by the following equation:

(6.05)

Accessibility-weighted production =
    Measured production * [1.0 − (GROWC/12)^2] *
    1.0 − [(ET − 7.0)/23] = [1.0 − (GROWC/12)^2] *
    1.0 − [(ET − 7.0)/23]

Human access to edible plant products is limited as a curvilinear function of both the length and the warmth of the growing season, other things being equal. The preceding equation approximates this limiting relationship with respect to plant foods by dividing the variable measuring the length of the growing season (GROWC) by twelve months of the year and squaring the result, which is then subtracted from 1.0. The value obtained is a percentage that, when multiplied by a measure of potential plant food productivity, is decreased in a way that parallels the effect of the availability of solar energy on the productive activity in the plant community. This limitation on production, taken together with variability derived from the amount of energy available to drive photosynthesis, is weighted by a percentage scale based on effective temperature (ET). When these segments of an equation are multiplied by the total plant productivity present in a habitat, they yield a value for the quantity of inaccessible plant productivity characteristic of the location.

The preceding propositions and mathematically structured statements attempt to approximate the access limitations affecting human feeders in a particular habitat, but they are admittedly inadequate because it is well known that other conditions place further limitations on human access to potential foods. I suggest that

Proposition 6.04

Other things being equal, optimal security would exist in environmental settings in which there is a maximum amount of food accessible per unit of energy expended in its procurement.

Obviously, many different factors—such as habitat structure, species diversity, and habitat stability—will affect the labor costs that humans, other things being equal, can expect to pay in the process of obtaining food.

Ecologists frequently speak of complexity as a variable property of ecosystems although complexity, as such, is a difficult property to measure. Estimates of species diversity are often used to approximate what is implied by the term *ecological complexity,* but at the simplest level species diversity simply refers to the number of species present in a specified area (the technical term is actually *species density*). Another more complicated meaning attached to species diversity refers to the relationship between the number of individuals of a particular species and the number of other species present in the same area (another term for this relationship is *species equability*).

If I were interested simply in species density and discovered, for instance, that two different regions of identical size each contained two species, this knowledge would reveal very little about the habitat to a potential consumer of those species. On the other hand, if in one region almost all of the individuals encountered were from one species and the second species was quite rare, while in a second region the two species were represented by roughly equal numbers of individuals, it is clear that these differences in equability might require that hunter-gatherers in the two regions develop different procurement strategies. Accurate analysis requires that measures of both species density and species equability be developed.

One of the most widely accepted generalizations about species density was stated with notable emphasis by Fischer, who observed that the "correlation of floral and faunal diversity with latitude is one of the most imposing biogeographic features on earth" (Fischer 1960:64). Attempts to explain the geographic patterning of diversity have occupied the attention of many ecologists, and recent research has begun to uncover some of the complications (Connell and Orias 1964; Pianka 1966; see MacArthur 1965 for a review of work through the mid-1960s; see Pielou 1975 and Bonner 1988 for more recent research). For my purposes, attempts to explain this phenomenon are provocative, but the phenomenon itself is interesting because of its potential conditioning effect on the labor costs incurred by human actors in obtaining food.

Species equability—or the relationship between the number of individuals and the number of species in a given habitat—is highly variable from habitat to habitat. MacArthur and Connell have provided a graphic example of differential equability:

> In these forests [tropical rain forests] the number of species is astonishing. Although the pattern of many species is found in most organisms, we illustrate it with trees. In an undisturbed rain forest at latitude 17 degrees south in North Queensland, Australia,[20] there were 141 species among 1261 trees over one inch diameter on an area of 1.25 acres (Connell et al. 1964). This diversity is difficult to comprehend for someone from a temperate

country, where such an area of woods may have ten or fifteen species of trees. Another feature of these forests is the lack of a "dominant" species that would account for most of the trees. By summing up the "basal area" (i.e., the cross-sectional area of tree trunks, measured at breast height) of all trees of each species, it is possible to obtain a rough estimate of the relative amount of organic matter contained in each species. In North Queensland the commonest tree accounted for about 9 percent of the total basal area, while in South Queensland it was 16 percent. In a beech-maple forest in southern Michigan, using the same sized trees, the commonest of the ten species of trees was found to represent 51 percent of the total basal area (Cain, 1935). Each species in such a mixed tropical rain forest tends to be widely scattered. We seldom find a grove of a single species, each tree we come to seems to be different. The impression we obtain is an arrangement of great complexity.

(1966:37)

In equatorial settings like the North Queensland rain forest[21] described by MacArthur and Connell, species density and equability are frequently correlated in such a way that as species density increases, so does equability. In less equatorial settings, however, both species density and equability tend to be reduced, with the result that a few species tend to be present in large numbers while others are present in a rapidly decreasing curve of relative frequencies.

If I expand my consideration to include the differences between a grass-covered prairie and an arctic tundra instead of simply a tropical rain forest, it is immediately apparent that species density and equability also vary with differences in biomass (BIO5) and biomass accumulation ratio (BAR5) when latitude is held constant. There may be a wide variety of potential foods for hunter-gatherers occupying a habitat in which animal resources are present in high species density and high equability, but the quantity concentrated in any one place would be relatively small. In low-density and low-equability settings, fewer animal species are present, but the dominant species may occur in a number of discrete spatial aggregations so that the same basic procurement strategy can be applied in many different locations.

Further insight into the range of procurement strategies available to hunter-gatherers can be drawn from a brief exploration of the tactics of nonhuman species that result from differences in locomotor ability and placement in the vertical structure of niches within a habitat. Whether a species is a terrestrial or canopy feeder is related to its body size and to the spatial structure of primary production, which may vary with species density (Fleming 1973). Fleming's study identified a number of patterns generated by an equatorial-to-polar scaling of species density:

Several geographic trends were seen in the communities examined: (1) a southward increase in the proportion of bats; (2) a southward decrease in the proportion of carnivores; (3) a southward increase in the propor-

tion of small species; (4) a southward decrease in the proportion of terrestrial species; (5) a southward increase in the proportion of aerial species; and (6) an increased variety of food types eaten in the tropical forests.

(Fleming 1973:558)

When Fleming analyzed these trends relative to the overall increase in species density from polar to equatorial settings, he found that this increase is largely accounted for by increases in the number of species that are scansorially, arboreally, and aerially adapted. These observations point to the higher primary biomass of tropical forests and signal many of the accessibility problems that human hunters face in procuring food in these settings. Constraints on access are largely due to the vertical stratification of production in tropical forests and the role of the high canopy as the locus of greatest primary production. The human species is terrestrial in terms of locomotor skills and its body size is large compared to the most successful species occupying high-biomass tropical forests. Like many other occupants of tropical forests, human beings take advantage of the great number of fruiting trees and respond favorably to the lack of synchronized seasonality among different species in many tropical settings. (For a review of the explanatory arguments regarding these patterns see Pianka 1966; Pielou 1975; Tilman 1982:98.)

Many studies of species density and equability focus on a wide variety of secondary producers or animals. Simpson (1964) has demonstrated strong patterning in the species densities of North American mammals that appears to be related to latitude. Stehli (1968:178) has presented global data on latitudinal gradients for mosquito species and demonstrated a regular reduction in species density in both hemispheres as latitude increases. Dobzhansky (1950) illustrated a similar relationship between snake species density and latitude, and similar studies of nesting birds produced the same pattern (Schoener 1968).

The species density of organisms acting as human pathogens is similarly distributed with respect to latitude. Human beings experience the highest pathogen "stress" at roughly zero degrees latitude, while the least stress occurs in polar settings (Low 1988, 1990:334). In fact, all studies of terrestrial species confirm the generalization that species density and equability are high in the tropics and become lower as distance from tropical settings increases. The opposite pattern, however, has emerged in studies of marine birds such as penguins and puffins (Stehli 1968) and marine fauna dwelling in shallow coastal shelf areas (Thorson 1957).

Some other characteristics of high-diversity, high-equability tropical settings should be noted as part of the discussion of terrestrial animals. For instance, field studies of animals have been conducted in the same North Queensland forest in which the plant studies cited by MacArthur and Connell (1966) occurred. Table 6.02 summarizes the number of

TABLE 6.02

ANIMAL BIOMASS IN TROPICAL AND SUBTROPICAL FORESTS

		AUSTRALIA (QUEENSLAND)		MALAYA (KUALA LUMPUR)		ZAIRE (ITURI)	
EFFECTIVE TEMPERATURE (°C)		19.54		24.82		22.86	
ANNUAL RAINFALL (MM)		3750		3276		2418	
		SPECIES		SPECIES		SPECIES	
FEEDING HABITAT	ZONE/BODY SIZE	No.	Col. %	No.	Col. %	No.	Col. %
ARBOREAL	Canopy zone	8	28.6	27	26.2	10	21.7
	Middle zone	9	32.1	25	24.3	12	26.1
	Arboreal subtotal	17	60.7	52	50.5	22	47.8
GROUND	Large body size	3	10.7	21	20.4	16	34.8
	Small body size	8	28.6	30	29.1	8	17.4
	Ground subtotal	11	39.3	51	49.5	24	52.2
	Total	28		103		46	

Note: This classification of the Ituri data is based on Harako (1976:49–51). The Australian and Malayan data are drawn from Harrison (1962).

mammalian species tabulated in a sample area of unknown size in the North Queensland rain forest as well as in a tropical rain forest area near Kuala Lumpur, Malaysia. The table also includes Harako's (1976) data on animal species exploited by the Mbuti, who occupy a moderately dry tropical forest, the Ituri forest, that gradually changes into a broadleaf tropical savanna (VEGTAT = SW-2). Because the number of animals is reported relative to the Mbuti use of animals, very small terrestrial species are probably underrepresented.

Several features of the comparison in table 6.02 are informative. In Queensland, which has low levels of solar radiation but high rainfall levels, 61 percent of the mammalian species live in the forest canopy and upper strata of plant production. In contrast, only 50.5 percent of the species in the Malaysian forest are found in the upper strata and 49.5 percent are ground feeders. The Ituri forest has the lowest rainfall of the three cases in table 6.02, and tree-feeding species make up only 47.8 percent of the fauna compared with the 52.2 percent that are terrestrial feeders. Given that small ground feeders are underrepresented in the Mbuti case, ground-dwelling species are almost certainly more common than the 52 percent figure indicates.

Perhaps the best example of the increase in terrestrial species that is associated with decreasing rainfall is the Ituri forest, which is characterized by much less equably distributed plant species and higher effective temperature than the Queensland forest, but considerably lower rainfall. In comparison to descriptions of the Queensland forest, it may appear surprising that in over one-half of the Ituri forest area, 90 percent of the canopy is composed of a single tree species (Hart and Hart 1986:34).

Clearly, the structural differences of generally more complex forest settings will have a significant impact on human food procurement strategies because of the relatively easy access that human populations have to food resources in biotically different settings. This point is underscored by Eisenberg in his general comments about animal biomass in tropical and subtropical settings: "If one imagines moving along a rainfall gradient, the biomass increases progressively until the type of forest cover becomes so continuous there is very little grassland and shrub habitat. Once again, the forest will tend to support a low density of terrestrial, mammalian herbivores" (Eisenberg 1980:43).

Enough information has now been presented to warrant the development of several additional indices for making quantitative estimates of the variability in levels of demand that may be securely met in different types of habitats. The goal is to learn the attributes and range of differential success that human actors would experience as they participate in evolutionary plays in different ecological theaters.

It should be clear that the greater the biomass of a plant community such as a tropical rain forest, the more frequently human occupants must cope with two obvious problems. The first difficulty is that, given their relatively large body size, humans cannot readily gain access to the productivity of the upper canopy. Another constraint, as Eisenberg suggests, is that when primary biomass increases, the success of terrestrial animals decreases because there is simply less for them to eat on the forest floor unless the animal is a detritus feeder. Of course, Eisenberg had in mind ungulates and grazers who depend primarily on grass and other plant species in locations at which production is situated directly on the ground surface. In this specific situation, however, the human species shares a similar problem of access with ungulates, although such an overlap is not general in all habitats.

In the equations that I have constructed thus far in this chapter, all habitats have been considered equal with respect to the limitations on access that high-biomass locations impose. The components of my incomplete model constrain access in terms only of seasonal fluctuations in resources, which I propose to monitor through measures of the length and energetic intensity of the growing season. I now need to build into the model the limitations that biomass itself imposes on human access to food resources. I must also cope with the much more difficult problem of estimating the proportion of the total net aboveground productivity in a habitat whose potential food resources are available to humans.

Before I proceed, however, I must first eliminate the proportion of net aboveground productivity that increases the overall biomass of the plant community annually and is generally not available to human actors. This proportion is measured by the biomass accumulation ratio (BAR5),[22] which is determined by the metabolic rate of a particular plant community. Before I can use this value as a partial estimate of the proportion of total net aboveground productivity that is rendered inaccessible to humans, I must transform BAR5 values into a percentage scale ranging from zero to one. This is illustrated in the third component of my evolving model:

$$(6.06)$$

Components:
1. $(NAGP/1000) * 100,000,000$
2. $1.0 - [1.0 - (GROWC/12)^2] * 1.0 - [(ET - 7.0)/23]$
3. $1.0 - (BAR5/85)$

The first step in formulating the fourth component of my model is to convert biomass (BIO5) into a percentage scale encompassing all known variability in biomass ranging from zero to the highest recorded estimate, which is approximately 57,000 grams per square meter per year. I have converted biomass values into percentage values by dividing by 61,000, which ensured that there were no zero percentages given the reversed-values equation. The resulting values were squared to emphasize the curvilinear effect of high biomass and to downplay the role of biomass at lower values.

On a percentage scale, this segment of the equation identifies the extremes. The second segment of component four repeats the properties of segment one, except that it is not squared. Its function is to make the role of biomass more important than the role of biomass accumulation itself (component three) and to smooth the curve of percentage values between the two segments of the equation in favor of biomass itself, rather than the metabolic characteristics of biomass accumulation.

$$(6.07)$$

Components:
1. $(NAGP/1000) * 100,000,000$
2. $1.0 - \{10**(GROWC/12)^2 * [1.0 - (ET - 7.0)/23]\}$
3. $1.0 - (BAR/85)$
4a. $1.0 - [10**(BIO5/61,000)^2]$
4b. $1.0 - (BIO5/61,000)$

In the preceding statements I have defined four sets of empirically defensible relationships that advance my effort to estimate the quantity of resources derived from production that would be available and accessible to human feeders in any habitat. The major elements are identified as a temporal component (number 2), a spatial component (number 4), and a nonedible component (number 3). I must now quantify the impact on human consumption of one of the earth's major habitats, the great grasslands and savannas, where ungulates thrive but a majority of the production is unavailable to humans because our species does not derive any nutritional benefit from grass leaves and stems. To approximate the limitation that this habitat places on human access to plant production, I have used squared, reversed values of EXPREY that have been weighted slightly to reduce their impact relative to the drastic impact of biomass on access. I then combined this component with a "smoothing" element based on net aboveground productivity (NAGP), which is the value from which both BAR and BIO5 were partially derived, producing a reversed percentage of NAGP:

$$(6.08a)$$

Component 5: $[1.0 - (EXPREY/20,000)^2] *$
$$[1.0 - (NAGP/6300)]$$

The second segment of the equation smoothes the rough transitions that can occur when a series of independent transformations is linked together. The two segments of component 5 were combined because each time a single percentage scale is multiplied by another, the overall effect is to reduce the scale proportionally to the percentages of each. The five components required to build a model of the amount of plant production potentially accessible to human foragers per 100 square kilometers are as follows:

$$(6.08b)$$

Components:
1. $(NAGP/1000) * 100,000,000$
2. $1.0 - \{10**(GROWC/12)^2 * [1.0 - (ET - 7.0)/23]\}$
3. $1.0 - (BAR/85)$
4. $\{1.0 - [10**(BIO5/61,000)^2]\} * [1.0 - (BIO5/61,000)]$
5. $\{1.0 - [10**(EXPREY/7000)^2 *.75]\} * (1.0 - NAGP/63,000)$

Producing an estimate of the amount of production per 100 square kilometers that is potentially accessible to a human consumer is, however, somewhat more complicated than simply linking all five components sequentially. To produce meaningful results, calculations must take place in the following three separate steps:

(6.09)

EXPRIM1 = [(NAGP/1000) * 100,000,000] *
            [1.0 − (BAR5/85)] * [1.0 − (BIO5/61,000)^2] *
            [1.0 − (BIO5/61,000)]

EXPRIM2 = EXPRIM1 * [1.0 − (EXPREY/20000)^2] *
            [1.0 − (NAGP/63,000)]

EXPRIM3 = EXPRIM2 − (EXPRIM2 *
            [1.0 − (GROWC/12)^2] * 1.0 − [(ET − 7.0)/23]

The preceding three equations produce an estimate of the accessible plant production that my model's human consumer could exploit as food. Since, however, my goal is to develop a minimalist terrestrial model of hunter-gatherer resource procurement, I must also develop a comparable estimate of the animal resources, or accessible secondary biomass, that my model's hunter-gatherer could exploit.

MODELING ACCESSIBLE ANIMAL FOODS

As a first step in my efforts to model plant production, it was necessary to convert the measure of expected prey into values for the unit in terms of which human biomass will be calculated, which is 100 square kilometers. To do this we simply multiplied EXPREY values by 100:

(6.10)

EXPREYA = 100 * (EXPREY + 0.01)

Access to prey is not absolutely related to prey abundance in a reciprocal way. Rather, it is proportional, which in this context means it is relative to the number of prey organisms present in a habitat. Furthermore, the situations in which ungulates of moderate body size do best are those in which human consumers have proportionately less access. This finding is due partly to the fact that in some settings with extremely high biomass values potential prey are also extremely mobile, which often prevents humans from continuously and reliably exploiting otherwise available resources (Burch 1972).

The same conditions limiting access to the vast herds of caribou discussed by Burch also place constraints on access to the massive herds of zebra and wildebeest that move annually over huge areas of the Serengeti Plains. This is also one reason why American Indian villages were not situated on the Great Plains of North America until after the introduction of the horse in the colonial era. The places in which ungulates are most successful are the locations where they are largely migratory.

In contrast, human hunters are able to exploit ungulate prey most effectively, relative to the numbers present, in

those locations where prey is territorial. I have concluded, therefore, that access in the proportional sense of the term is essentially a reciprocal reflection of actual ungulate biomass distribution, and I have modeled this relationship in the following terms:

(6.11)

RXPREY = 1.0 − (EXPREY/20,000)

With this equation, I have now completed the first step in building a minimalist terrestrial model that will allow me to estimate the quantity of accessible plant and animal resources that would be available to hunter-gatherers in various habitats.

ADDITIONAL ASSUMPTIONS
ABOUT HUMAN ACTORS

Since my minimalist model of hunter-gatherer resource exploitation will provide a template against which to compare more complex, real-world human behavior, my human prototype must be endowed with the simplest set of strategies. For this reason I will assume that a minimalist hunter-gatherer exploits only animals and plants from the terrestrial domain. Another minimalist tactical assumption is that my hunter-gatherer is a terrestrial omnivore who exploits potential food sources as a direct function of their abundance and accessibility in any given habitat. This constraint acknowledges that, unassisted, the human species is unable to fly or otherwise readily gain access to potential food resources located on small branches high in a forest canopy. Similarly, the human species cannot eat grass and digest cellulose. These constraints mean that when I model abundance, I must take into consideration the problem of access.

I have already developed estimates of plant productivity (NAGP) and secondary biomass (EXPREY) at any location for which basic climatic data are available. I have also developed measures embodying the constraints on human access to some resources and have adjusted gross estimates of plant and animal standing crop to reflect human access problems. What I need now is a common currency for discussing human food requirements, as well as some knowledge of a few important constants affecting the relationship between the biomass of consumers and the biomass of the nutrients required to sustain these consumers. I will begin with a discussion of human nutritional requirements and the effect that these requirements have on the habitats of human consumers.

Step One: Constants and Currency

It is generally agreed that there is a meaningful relationship between the quantity of food needed to sustain an animal and its body size. Obviously, elephants require more food each day than mice. It is also known that an organism's metabolic rate conditions the quantity of food needed to sustain it. A cold-blooded animal that does not burn up energy in the process of maintaining a fairly constant body temperature requires much less food than a warm-blooded animal of equivalent body size. Crocodiles and alligators generally have higher biomass values per unit area than warm-blooded animals exploiting the same foods.

If I hold metabolic rates constant, the need for food is primarily a function of body size, with minor variations related to the quality of the foods consumed. I also need to calculate the human biomass that any given habitat could be reasonably expected to support under certain assumptions of use. In short, I need to calculate human biomass as a currency *and* as a way of translating measures of biomass into food demands that must be met by the habitat.

Although biomass may be defined simply as the number of animals multiplied by the mean body size of the tabulated animals, measures of biomass are not as straightforward as the definition might imply. One of the earliest observations of importance in this context is Kleiber's law, which is an empirical generalization describing a log-linear relationship between basic metabolic rate and body size.[23] Kleiber's law stipulates that organisms of small body size have higher basic metabolic rates per unit of body weight than large organisms. An interesting aspect of this relationship is that organisms of larger body size require more energy (food) than organisms of smaller body size, but, given some niche differences between species of different body size, one might expect there to be more individuals of smaller body size in a habitat. This means that while organisms of different body size may have equal biomass (population density multiplied by mean body weight expressed with respect to units of area), population densities of these organisms may be vastly different.

Body Size and Biomass. Human beings are quite variable in body size. For instance, the Efe pygmies of Zaire have a recorded mean body size of 39.8 kilograms or 87.7 pounds, while the mean of three samples of Eskimos is 63.63 kilograms or 140 pounds (Roberts 1953:556–57), the difference representing 60 percent of the mean for the Efe. In the United States, the mean body size of males of median height is 73.9 kilograms, and for females of median height it is 67.6 kilograms or 162.6 pounds – 148.7 pounds (Diem 1962:623), representing a weight differential of greater than 1.75 times across the human range.

A good way to illustrate the importance of this variable as a potential conditioner of population density values is to calculate the difference that body size makes in biomass values for a group of a given size, such as twenty persons. Since biomass is calculated as the number of persons multiplied by their mean body weight, in the Efe example the biomass of a group of twenty adults would be 796 kilograms, while the

biomass of a group of twenty adult American males would be 1,478 kilograms. Given that total consumer biomass conditions the amount of food required to sustain a group, it should be clear that, from an energetic perspective, a group of twenty Efe and a group of twenty American males are not at all equal.

If both of the cited groups lived in a similar amount of space—for example 65 square kilometers—they would each have a population density of 30.76 persons per 100 square kilometers. The same amount of space, however, would have to support a human biomass of 796 kilograms in the Efe example and 1,478 kilograms in the American male example. In other words, the Efe range would have to contain resources capable of supporting 12.24 kilograms of human biomass per square kilometer while the range of the American males would have to supply resources capable of supporting 22.74 kilograms of human biomass per square kilometer of resource space. Very different strategies would likely accompany differential energetic demands of this magnitude, even though population density would be the same. Clearly, body size is one property of human actors that must be controlled in my minimalist model.

Body Size and Environment. In the middle of the nineteenth century, Swedish researcher C. Bergmann argued that polytypic, warm-blooded species were distributed in a patterned way relative to latitude, with species of larger body size located where temperatures were lowest and the number of organisms of smaller body size increasing regularly as mean annual temperature increased. J. A. Allen elaborated on this observation by empirically demonstrating that the size of exposed portions of the body should decrease with decreases in mean annual temperature.

During the twentieth century, many students of anthropometry discovered that these two empirical generalizations also applied to humans, and more recent research has also confirmed these conclusions. There is, however, unexplained variability that appears to exhibit somewhat different slopes for the relationship of body size to temperature in African and European populations as opposed to Asians and American Indians. There are also some exceptional cases. (For a comparison with ancient hominid material see Stringer 1984:67–76.)

The implications of Allen's rule describing the proportions of body mass and the size of appendages have been challenged by many demonstrations of major changes in stature over relatively short periods of time (Lasker 1946; Tobias 1962), presumably in response to dietary changes occurring as a result of modern food production techniques and supply. Nevertheless, Bergmann's rule remains a "statistical law" in the nineteenth-century sense of the word.

Even if the only sources of knowledge consisted of what is known about human and other animal species, I could expect varying levels of population density among hunter-gatherers, other things being equal, in response to differences in both body size and niche characteristics resulting from trophic differences in the feeding strategies of human groups. I might also expect different relationships between range size and population density when the trophic characteristics of niche were held constant but productivity and accessibility varied. If, however, I intend to use population density as a system state indicator in my model, I must develop some analytical tools to deal with several lacunae in my knowledge base.

At this stage in the analysis I can measure population density, but I do not know how to argue about what different levels of population density imply in terms of system state. This situation is similar to being able to measure a person's body temperature but not knowing what the *normal* body temperature curve of humans might be. I need, therefore, to develop a standard or scale that will allow me to link population density values to indicators of system state. I would also like to be able to control for the effects of hunter-gatherer body size variability and to recognize differences that result from trophic feeding biases.

When I began to record the data on hunter-gatherer mean body size and stature that are summarized in table 6.03, I quickly discovered that there are far more observations in the ethnographic literature on stature than on weight. This difference probably reflects the difficulty of carrying scales into remote areas compared with the ease of transporting a tape measure. As a way of coping with missing weight data, I consulted a number of summary sources that publish data on the relationship between human body size and temperature, hoping to be able to estimate body size using its correlation with temperature. The most recent and widely cited summary of these relationships is provided by Roberts (1953), but when I examined his data I discovered that many of the cases with extreme values were hunter-gatherer groups located in Africa and the North American arctic.

In light of the common assumption that hunter-gatherers live "closer to nature" than many of the modern populations included in Roberts's studies, I wondered whether a more appropriate summary of the allometric relationship between temperature and body size might be obtained by using only the hunter-gatherer populations. It seemed reasonable that peoples using less technologically based thermal regulators might well exhibit somewhat different and more reliable correlations to habitat temperatures than nonforaging peoples.

Focusing exclusively on the small sample of hunter-gatherer cases for which body weights could be obtained (table 6.03), I tried several different analytical approaches. Using single-variable curve-fitting strategies, I found that the most meaningful fit was between body weight and the mean temperature value of the coldest month of the year. The best result was a complex polynomial equation that yielded an r^2 value of

0.61. Multiple regressions produced a much simpler fit and a somewhat more provocative equation yielding a multiple R value of 0.801 using two variables: (1) the $\log_{10}$ value of temperature range (LTRANGE) and (2) a measure of the evenness of rainfall during the year (MRAIN). The equation illustrates that as rainfall increases, so too does body weight, other things being equal:

$$Y = a + b * \text{LTRANGE} + c * \text{MRAIN}$$ **(6.12)**

Where
$a = 39.154974,$
$b = 16.276180,$ and
$c = 0.146003$

This equation allows me to project the relationship between body weight and environmental variables onto those locations for which I have hunter-gatherer cases but no information about body size. Although this estimate may be somewhat crude, it is still better than using mean human body size, which is a value that does not anticipate variability.

I now have the information I need to calculate biomass estimates for any location for which I have climatic data, and I also have population density estimates. Since biomass is the product of body weight multiplied by numbers of persons, I can now determine biomass any time I have population density estimates.

Some Important Constants Linking Consumers to Accessible Foods

Estimates of body size and biomass are important components of my evolving baseline model of terrestrial hunter-gatherer variability, but I must also develop estimates of some important constants. I have already noted that there is a meaningful relationship between the body size of different animals and the quantity of food needed to sustain them. It is also well known that metabolic rates condition the quantity of food needed to sustain an animal. If metabolic rate is held constant, then the quantity of food needed is primarily a function of body size, with minor variation related to the quality of the foods consumed. For omnivores such as humans, one can expect a relatively low-variance constant for the relationship between body size and quantity of food required to sustain the organism.

I searched the anthropological literature to find out what that constant value might be and whether it might vary with dietary quality, but I found no research dealing with this subject. This was a surprising discovery in light of all of the economic decisions that must ultimately depend upon a knowledge of the relationship between body size and food requirements (purchasing food to supply large military organizations is just one example of a relevant set of decisions).[24] Table 6.04 summarizes the only data I have been able to find, which come from a case study by Rappaport (1967:280–91),

TABLE 6.03
HUNTER-GATHERER STATURE AND WEIGHT

HUNTER-GATHERER GROUP	STATURE (CM) Male	Female	WEIGHT (KG) Male	Female	REFERENCE
PUNAN (GANG)	1498				Urquhart 1951:501
PUNAN (BUSANG)	1567	1468	52.9	37.9	Oldrey 1975:155
BATAK	1531	1432	46.5	40.6	Eder 1987:140
KUBU	1578	1462			Volz 1909:92
SHOMPEN	1597	1474	60.5	48.0	Rizvi 1990:35
	1591	1487	55.3	4.71	Agrawal 1967:84–87
AYTA (PINATUBO)	1464	1388			Reed 1904:75–77
ANDAMAN ISLANDS	1490	1371	43.5	39.5	Temple 1903:54
	1492	1393	44.5	42.3	Man 1883:73
SEMANG	1491	1408			Skeat and Blagden 1906:575
VEDDA	1533	1433			Skeat and Blagden 1906:574
	1435	1371			Bailey 1863:283
AGTA (CASIGURAN)	1520	1457	44.0	37.5	Headland 1986:544
AGTA (ISABELA)	1530	1450	41.0	34.0	Wastl 1957:805
AGTA (CAGAYAN)	1510	1425			Vanoverbergh 1925:400
		1427		34.9	Goodman et al. 1985: 1203
CHENCHU	1630				Fürer-Haimendorf 1943:17
MRABRI	1580	1444			Bernatzik 1951:165
	1529	1440	48.8		Flatz 1963, table 1
	1546	1445			Trier 1981: 292
KADAR	1580	1500			Ehrenfels 1952:6
AINU	1581	1482			Landor 1893:299
KET	1587				Shimkin 1939:149
YUKAGHIR	1560	1470			Jochelson 1926:20
SIBERIAN ESKIMO	1628		64.2		Szathmary 1984:65
YARUROS (PUME)	1599	1484			Petrullo 1939:177
GUIHIBO	1540		57.8	47.3	Hurtado and Hill 1990:329
BORORO	1680				Newman 1953:321
SIRIONO	1625	1575			Holmberg 1950:8
NAMBIKWARA	1620				Newman 1953:321
GUAYAKI (ACHE)	1610	1500	59.6	55.8	Hill et al. 1984:table 4, 132
BOTOCUDO	1585	1495			Ehrenreich 1887:16–17
HETA	1652				Kozak et al. 1979:374
TEHUELCHE	1750				Lothrop 1928:45
ALACALUF	1574	1488			Lothrop 1928:39
ONA	1754	1592			Lothrop 1928:41
YAGHAN	1581	1475			Lothrop 1928:41
AKA	1486[1]		45.1		Cavalli-Sforza 1986a:83
BAYAKA	1530	1440	46.4		Heymer 1980:178; Hiernaux et al. 1975:7
BAMBOTE	1452				Skeat and Blagden 1906:573
BAKA	1526	1441	49.5		Hiernaux et al. 1975:7; Vallois and Marquer 1976:63
EFE	1453	1363	43.1	37.9	Bailey and Peacock 1988:107
MBUTI	1440	1370	39.8		Hiernaux et al. 1975:7; Cavalli-Sforza 1986c:392; Roberts 1953: 557
HUKWE	1574	1494			Clark 1951:60
HAI//OM	1553	1497			Werner 1906:241
	1539	1491			Tobias 1962:802–3
DOROBO	1694	1587			Wayland 1931:217
SEKELE	1605	1503			Bleek 1929:106; De Castro and Almeida 1956, 1957
	1593	1488			

(continued)

TABLE 6.03 *(continued)*

HUNTER-GATHERER GROUP	STATURE (CM)		WEIGHT (KG)		REFERENCE
	Male	*Female*	*Male*	*Female*	
!KUNG	1584	1485	50.4	42.5	Howell 1979:258–59; Bleek 1929:106; Tobias 1962:802–3
AUEN	1515	1455			Kaufmann 1910:135
	1584	1493			Tobias 1962:802–3
NHARO	1570	1501			
	1593	1493			Tobias 1962:802–3
G/WI	1578	1520			Tobias 1962:802–3
KUA	1610	1523	54.43		Tobias 1962:802–3; Wyndham and Morrison 1958:221
AUNI-KHOMANI	1558	1460			Dart 1937b:184
BATWA (LAKE CHRISSIE)	1489	1347			Toerien 1958:122–23
LARIKIA	1696		55.1		Howells 1937:16
GUNWINGU			55.3	46.1	Altman 1987:34
MIRRNGADJA	1706				Macintosh 1952:213
MURNGIN	1665	1580	59.2	43.5	Howells 1937:16; Peterson 1976:269
NUMGGUGUYU	1669		55.8		Howells 1937:16
TIWI	1668		56.9		Howells 1937:16
WALMBARIA	1650	1550			Hale and Tindale 1933:71
MULLUK	1708				Stanner 1933:386
MAMU	1578		50.5		Birdsell 1967:112
WALBIRI	1698	1571	56.7	45.4	Abbie 1957:236–38
PINTUBI	1671				Campbell et al.1936:113
ALYAWARA	1661				Campbell et al.1936:113
PITJANDJARA	1687				Campbell et al.1936:113
ARANDA (SOUTHERN)			53.1		Roberts 1953:556
ARANDA (NORTHERN)	1663	1568	56.9		Roberts 1953:556; Spencer and Gillen 1899:appendix C
KARUNA	1680	1520			Cawthorn 1844:50
SOUTHWESTERN VICTORIA	1647		64.4		Birdsell 1967:113
TASMANIANS	1618	1503			Roth 1899:192
SERI		1612			McGee 1898:136
CAHUILLA	1670	1580			Gifford 1926b:232–33
CUPENO	1680	1560			Gifford 1926b:232–33
LAKE YOKUTS	1668	1550			Gifford 1926b:232–33
SERRANO	1710	1580			Gifford 1926b:232–33
LUISENO	1690	1570			Gifford 1926b:232–33
NOMLAKI	1650	1520			Gifford 1926b:232–33
YOKUTS (NORTHERN HILLS)	1640	1510			Gifford 1926b:232–33
PATWIN	1690				Gifford 1926b:232–33
EASTERN POMO	1690	1640			Gifford 1926b:232–33
SALINAN	1670				Gifford 1926b:232–33
YUKI	1570	1480			Gifford 1926b:232–33
NORTHERN POMO	1640	1540			Gifford 1926b:232–33
YANA	1690				Gifford 1926b:232–33
MIWOK (SIERRA)	1660	1550			Gifford 1926b:232–33
HUPA	1660	1520			Gifford 1926b:232–33
ATSUGEWI	1630	1540			Gifford 1926b:232–33
WIYOT	1650	1560			Gifford 1926b:232–33
MAIDU (MOUNTAIN)	1630	1530			Gifford 1926b:232–33
YUROK	1640	1530			Gifford 1926b:232–33
ACHOMAWI	1670	1530			Gifford 1926b:232–33
MODOC	1620	1550			Gifford 1926b:232–33
KLAMATH	1670	1600			Gifford 1926b:232–33
YAVAPAI	1740	1600	71.0	63.0	Corbusier 1886:278–79
WALAPAI	1684	1577			Hrdlička 1909:413

TABLE 6.03 *(continued)*

HUNTER-GATHERER GROUP	STATURE (CM)		WEIGHT (KG)		REFERENCE
	Male	Female	Male	Female	
OWENS VALLEY PAIUTE	1640	1560			Gifford 1926b:232–33
KAIBAB	1667	1521			Hrdlička 1909:408
KUYUIDODADO	1683				Boas 1899:753
UTE TIMINOGAS	1661				Boas 1899:753
NORTH PAIUTE (HONEY LAKE)	1669	1600			Gifford 1926b:232–33
WHITE KNIFE	1665				Boas 1899:753
MONO (NORTH FORK)	1650	1560			Gifford 1926b:232–33
SOUTHERN UTE	1668	1537			Hrdlička 1909:409
WASHO	1730	1580			Gifford 1926b:232–33
UINTAH UTE	1641[1]				Boas 1899:753
UNCOMPAHGRE	1628[1]				Boas 1899:753
AGAIDUKA	1665[1]				Boas 1899:753
LIPAN	1691	1568			Hrdlička 1909:412
COMANCHE	1678	1562			Goldstein 1934:299
TETON	1724	1600			Sullivan 1920:169
BANNOCK	1685				Boas 1899:753
KUTENAI	1690	1569	67.8		Chamberlain 1892:564–82
ALSEA	1652	1486			Boas 1891:433
TWANA	1651		64.4		Eells 1887:273
NOOTKA	1616				Cybulski 1990b:54
LILLOOET	1633	1532			Boas and Farrand 1899:630
STALO	1639				Cybulski 1990b:54
COWICHAN	1610	1495			Wilson 1866:278
BELLA BELLA	1637				Cybulski 1990b:54
KWAKIUTL	1633	1543			Boas and Farrand 1899:630; Cybulski 1990b:54
TSIMSHIAN	1656	1520			Boas and Farrand 1899:630; Cybulski 1990b:54
HAIDA	1625	1552			Boas and Farrand 1899:630; Cybulski 1990b:54
BELLA COOLA	1661	1573			Boas and Farrand 1899:630; Cybulski 1990b:54
GITKSAN	1659	1543			Boas and Farrand 1899:630; Cybulski 1990b:54
KUSKOWAGMUT	1660				Hrdlička 1930:251
ALEUT	1612				Newman 1960:289
NUNIVAK	1618	1531			Hrdlička 1930:251
THOMPSON	1659	1576			Boas and Farrand 1899:630
MICMAC	1747	1579			Boas 1895:574
NORTH SALTEAUX	1719				Grant 1924:302
SHUSWAP	1705	1569			Chamberlain 1892:615
PEKANGEKUM	1680				Grant 1924:302
ROUND LAKE	1709				Grant 1924:302
MISTASSINI CREE	1676	1549			Rogers 1972:92
OJIBWA WEAGAMON	1712	1574	70.3		Boas 1895:574
SEKANI	1693	1578			Jenness 1937:27
	1683	1568			Grant 1936:18
BEAVER	1683	1564			Grant 1936:13–15
CHILCOTIN	1651	1565			Boas and Farrand 1899:630
CARRIER	1679	1572			Grant 1936:18
ATTAWAPISKAT	1680	1555			Mason 1967:5
CHIPEWYAN	1647	1509			Grant 1936:13–15
KUTCHIN	1646	1521			Boas 1901:64–65; McKennan 1964:47
TAHLTAN	1704	1617			Boas 1901:61–63
NEBESNA	1699				McKennan 1964:46

(continued)

TABLE 6.03 *(continued)*

HUNTER-GATHERER GROUP	STATURE (CM)		WEIGHT (KG)		REFERENCE
	Male	*Female*	*Male*	*Female*	
DOGRIB	1654		66.6		Szathmary 1984:65
NASKAPI	1662	1546			Hallowell 1929:341
NORTON SOUND	1654	1561			Seltzer 1933:341
KOTZEBUE	1675	1607	64.3	64.3	Rodahl and Edwards 1952:243
LABRADOR ESKIMO	1583	1504			Seltzer 1933:341
NOATAK	1685	1556			Boas 1901:64–65
NUNAMIUT	1649	1549			Jamison 1978:56, 58
MACKENZIE ESKIMO	1683	1535			Seltzer 1933:341
SIVOKAMIUT	1661	1533	64.4	56.5	Rodahl and Edwards 1952:243
	1633	1514			Hrdlička 1930:251
POINT HOPE	1665				Jenness 1922:b49; Seltzer 1933:341
COPPER ESKIMO	1648	1564			Jenness 1922:b49
AIVILINGMIUT	1580[1]				Oetteking 1931:423
	1622	1583			Hrdlička 1930:230
IGLULIK	1626	65.3			Szathmary 1984
	1660	1537			Hallowell 1929:353
WEST GREENLAND	1620	1520			Hansen 1914
BAFFIN ISLAND	1602	1499	62.1		Roberts 1953:557
		1551[1]			Oetteking 1931:423
ANGMAKSALIK	1635	1521			Pooled from Hansen 1914 and Poulsen 1909:135, 144–46
TAREUMIUT (BARROW)	1665	1537	65.3		Roberts 1953:556; Seltzer 1933:341
	1615	1536	69.7	61.22	
WAINWRIGHT	1662	1558	67.1	66.2	Jamison and Zegura 1970:132, 138
POLAR ESKIMO	1574	1454	63.5		Roberts 1953:557; Steensby 1910:389

Note: 1. Instead of providing separate means of male and female stature, in this case the ethnographer reports a combined mean that includes both male and female measurements.

but it is sufficient to allow me to calculate an estimate of the relationship between human biomass and dietary intake of plant foods.

Using the data in table 6.04, I can now demonstrate the importance of developing a biomass ratio[25]: human biomass (688 kilograms) divided by a biomass ratio of 0.043748 yields the weight in kilograms of the plant resources required to sustain the quantity of measured human biomass (15,726 kilograms). This ratio now allows me to calculate the plant biomass necessary to feed a given biomass of human actors at a given level of plant dependence.

One of the intellectual benefits of building a model is that the model does not have to be accurate in every detail in order to be useful. In fact, in situations of ignorance or uncertainty, a model may be designed to be *inaccurate* so that deviations from the expected result can signal sources of ignorance and indicate in which direction the researcher might profitably invest more effort. It is important to note that the interactive properties of the relationships described by the model must be as accurate as possible, but the values that express these relationships may be off the mark in minor ways. The

reason that relationships among the cases for which the model was constructed are relatively unaffected by error in the constants is that all results are still arrayed in a regular way relative to one another.

I can therefore accept the biomass ratio derived from Rappaport's data as the human-to-plant food ratio and use it to calculate the plant biomass required to sustain that proportion of the gross human biomass that is totally supported by terrestrial plant foods. Equipped with a biomass conversion ratio and a knowledge of the quantity of plant biomass accessible to a human population at a given location, I can use the ratio to estimate the number of persons whose nutritional needs can be met at that location. The calculation is simply the amount of accessible plant food divided by the plant food required to feed a single individual of a given body size or accessible plant biomass divided by 0.043748.

I understand that one documented ethnographic case is not representative of the biomass of all human beings and that the food-to-human-biomass conversion ratios are likely to be different in New Guinea than elsewhere. In fact, variability in this ratio is one of the primary ways in which one

TABLE 6.04

CONSUMPTION OF PLANT FOODS
BY SIXTEEN PERSONS DURING A
243-DAY PERIOD AT 99 PERCENT
DEPENDENCE UPON PLANT FOODS

PLANT FOOD CLASS	WEIGHT (LB)
ROOTS	11,901.39
TREES	2,594.60
MISCELLANEOUS GARDEN	227.99
LEAVES	2,073.25
GRASS, ETC.	2,961.00
OTHER PLANTS	3,324.43
TOTAL	23,082.43 (10,469.99 kg)

Notes: Weight of plant food extrapolated to one year = 10,469.99 divided by 0.6657534 = 15,726.52 kilograms. Human biomass in adult male weight equivalents equals 688 kilograms. Biomass ratio = 0.043748 (human biomass divided by biomass of plant foods). The mean body weight of adult males was 43.0 kilograms. Data are taken from Rappaport (1967:280–91).

sociocultural system differs from another. Ironically, my admittedly imperfect model may help me to develop a better understanding of the sources of that variability.

A Model of an Exclusively Terrestrial Hunter-Gatherer Who Responds Primarily to Variability in Directly Accessible Foods

I have now developed all of the components of a minimalist model of hunter-gatherer response to the variable habitat conditions that I believe influence the number of persons who can be sustained under assumptions of constant behavioral potentials. The model itself is really very simple compared to the issues of variability that I have dealt with in estimating terrestrial plant productivity and terrestrial animal biomass. It is also simple compared to the task of developing the assumptions of the model and the constants required to make it work.

To determine the number of individuals who could be sustained by the available food base in a given area, I simply divide the accessible standing crop of either terrestrial plants or terrestrial animals by the amount of food required to sustain a single individual of a projected mean body weight. The only other essential component is the trophic conversion ratio that I discussed in preceding paragraphs. The equations for calculating expected dependence upon terrestrial plants and terrestrial animals, particularly ungulates, and for expected population densities or human biomass at different locations under the minimalist assumptions of this model are as follows:

1. *Number of persons per 100-square-kilometer unit who could be supported by ungulate resources alone:*

(6.13)

$$TERMH2 = (\{EXPREYA * [1.0 - (EXPREY/20,000)]\} * 0.026142)/(EXWGT/0.0450)$$

This equation begins with expected prey (EXPREY) values corrected to biomass units per 100 square kilometers (EXPREYA). This value is then multiplied by the reciprocal percentage value of EXPREY expressed relative to a maximum value of 20,000 grams per square meter, which is the correction for access discussed previously. This value is then multiplied by a constant of 0.026142, which was introduced after experimenting with observed values of hunting pressure among hunter-gatherer cases and accepting the mean value of the lowest-performance cases in the set, minus a full percentage point. The minimalist model is thereby standardized to a value lower than was observed among the least hunting-dependent peoples of the ethnographic present.

The resultant value is then divided by the body weight anticipated at a given location divided by the biomass conversion ratio of 0.0450, which is just slightly better than the value used for plant foods because of the generally higher-quality foods obtained from terrestrial animals. The resultant value, called TERMH2, therefore represents the model's estimate of the number of persons per 100 square kilometers who could be supported by terrestrial animal resources exclusively at the given location.

2. *Number of persons per 100-square-kilometer unit who could be supported from terrestrial plant foods alone:*

(6.14)

$$TERMG2 = (EXPRIM3 * 0.000060)/(EXWGT/0.43748)$$

The only value in the preceding equation that has not been discussed is the constant 0.000060, which is used to reduce the estimated biomass of accessible plant foods utilizable by humans, further reduced by the basic trophic conversion ratio (0.005882) used by ecologists (Odum 1959:66) to convert plant biomass into human biomass.

3. *Population density (adjusted for body size) expected at a particular location and expressed in terms of persons per 100 square kilometers:*

(6.15)

$$TERMD2 = TERMH2 + TERMG2$$

4. *Percentage dependence upon terrestrial plant foods:*

(6.16)

$$(TERMG2/TERMD2) * 100$$

5. *Percentage dependence upon terrestrial animal foods:*

(6.17)

(TERMH2/TERMD2) * 100

Thirteen of the preceding equations (6.04–6.17) taken together permit the calculation of population density values for any location for which basic weather data are available. These values reflect simple differences between the accessibility of the terrestrial plants and animals that sustain human beings who, according to the terms of the model, rely on minimal technological assistance to procure their food. The values also reflect differences among habitats in terms of the potential subsistence security offered to tactically unsophisticated humans whose procurement strategy involves the consumption of accessible food in proportion to its abundance in the habitat. The model stipulates that the habitat's abundance is limited only by the demand for food of persons practicing no storage. The model therefore provides a baseline for examining the real world of adaptive flexibility, niche differentiation, and system state diversity.

Using Models and Projections: System State Differences and Ideas about Emergent Complexity

So far in this chapter, I have identified some properties of ecosystems that make it possible to understand variability in some properties of sociocultural systems. I have also used ecological variables in my construction of a minimalist model that I will refer to hereafter as the Terrestrial Model. The model demonstrates how purely terrestrial hunters and gatherers might modify their food procurement tactics in response to the effects of environmental variability. With the model in place, I have arrived at the ultimate goal of this chapter, which is to demonstrate how the intellectual tools that I have constructed can help us address patterning in the archeological record. As the demonstration proceeds, I illustrate some of the differences that result from using a projected frame of reference and a modeled frame of reference when one studies archaeological patterning.

Patterning in archaeological data implicates the past, but if archaeologists inaccurately visualize the basic processes that operated in the past they are not likely to appreciate the implications of the patterns that they recognize. This chapter began with a discussion of relatively recent ideas about self-organization and emergence that are the subjects of macro-evolutionary theory building. Emergence studies deal with the appearance of new forms of organization and their novel properties, which cannot be anticipated from a complete knowledge of the prior organizational features of a parent system.

The appearance of new niches in the biological domain is generally addressed by researching the appearance of new species, but for human beings, as I have pointed out, a niche is a form of organization that is not linked to the physical properties that, in other species, weld species and niche together. In the human species, new niches have not been tied to biological change for at least 40,000 years. Niches may appear as a result of gradual accumulative changes, but they may also result from rapidly emergent kinds of processes that produce change. In the latter case, new niches will appear to arise out of nowhere, since the new organization that they entail may include little that would permit us to see continuity with the parent system.

Archaeologists have recognized two types of change in the archaeological record. One involves gradual, additive, or substitutive changes that seems to indicate continuity between an antecedent system and its offspring. The other type of change is swift and dramatically contrastive, and it appears to signify a lack of continuity in a temporal sequence. Conventionally, the latter pattern has been interpreted as an episode of migration or some other sort of populational replacement that interrupts the "normal" and very gradual process of descent with modification. What archaeologists often overlook is that "normal" evolutionary processes can result in dramatic restructuring of the component parts of an organization. When such a process does occur (albeit less frequently than gradual processes of change with continuity), it represents a major event in the overall history of culture change. Unfortunately, archaeologists are still very likely to interpret such events as migrations and populational replacements (Binford 1999)!

Before this chapter concludes, I will apply the referential tools that I have developed and reported on in the last several chapters to the archaeological data relating to the appearance of domesticated plants and animals in western Europe. This exercise will be interesting in and of itself, but looking at properties of the archaeological record through numerous environmental frames of reference will also allow me to introduce other problems associated with the recognition of system state differences that will help prepare the way for the subject matter presented in chapter 7.

INTENSIFICATION AND IMPORTANT SCALAR CHANGES

When I use the term *intensification,* it refers to any tactical or strategic practices that increase the production of food per unit area. Production can be increased by investing more labor in food procurement activities or by shifting exploitation to species occurring in greater concentrations in space. In terms of animal resources, one intensifying strategy would be to domesticate and breed animals whose maintenance on reduced ranges requires increasing quantities of human labor. In some environments, another strategy would be to shift from animals of larger body size, which require extensive ranges, to increased dependence upon plant species that occur in more spatially clustered distributions. In environments in which plants are not a realistic alternative to animals of larger body size, aquatic resources may be increasingly exploited when there is pressure to intensify food procurement.

Clues to intensification are found archaeologically in evidence of a reduction in the size of food procurement areas, increased labor in the form of technological aids such as traps and facilities for food procurement, and reduced mobility both in numbers of annual residential moves and in the distances traveled in the course of a seasonal round. Another measure of intensification is the increased exploitation of species that require a greater investment of labor to procure or process. For example, evidence that prehistoric foragers were leaching tannic acid from acorns may signal intensification. I have already mentioned that a shift in biome or from one trophic level to another may also signal the onset of intensification.

I am well aware that the ethnographic cases in my sample are nearly contemporary peoples, and I know that many of them experienced strong pressure to intensify. At the time of documentation, 37.2 percent were described as sedentary or semisedentary and 15.9 percent could not be described as independent groups whose subsistence depended exclusively on some combination of hunting or gathering.

I also know that even the well-known !Kung group of foragers did not live in a world composed exclusively of other hunter-gatherers but instead participated in a complex world of non-hunter-gatherers. This was a dismaying fact for those who looked to the !Kung for a realistic depiction of what life was like during the Pleistocene. Interestingly, Richard Lee presented the !Kung as an anthropological object lesson about the reliability of plant resources and their importance in the diet of all hunter-gatherers. In contrast, the Terrestrial Model projects that the !Kung would have been heavily dependent upon terrestrial animals. Lee's report of the situation at /Xai/xai pan, however, located in the very heart of !Kung territory, stresses exploitation of plant resources:

> Some 50 years before cattle had permanently been settled there, it presented a very different aspect. . . . The elephant grass that filled the basin was higher than a man's head, and hippopotamuses lived hidden in the extensive reedbeds of the pan. The pan lay in a lush valley flanked by dense stands of Grewia bushes, and the river course attracted flocks of migrating waterfowl. It is hard to believe this description when faced with the dustbowl reality that is /Xai/xai today, but the picture is true and serves to underline how rapidly a semiarid environment can degrade when cattle are introduced.
> (Lee 1979:82)

Could it be that the changes that Lee found so profoundly shocking could also have modified the world of the !Kung

sufficiently to cause them to shift their subsistence practices from the exploitation of wild animals to increased dependence upon plant resources prior to Lee's arrival? Did !Kung food procurement strategies represent a response to intensificational pressures? This would be completely consistent with events occurring at /Xai/xai since Lee's work there in the late 1960s (Brooks et al. 1984). This case should be kept in mind as I clarify and emphasize some characteristics of the frames of reference I will be using. At the same time, I suggest that the comparisons that will be made between the Terrestrial Model and my projections of ethnographic data will be very helpful to an understanding of the whole issue of intensification.

COMPARATIVE PROJECTIONS AND CLUES TO DIFFERENT KINDS OF VARIABILITY

The Terrestrial Model is a baseline frame of reference that anticipates variability that could only arise as a result of differences in effective environments. There are no components of the model that contribute to variability in different system states or to processual changes in the character of systems over time. Furthermore, no system state variability among similar habitats could be the result of overexploitation, forest clearance, or other assaults extraneous to the environment.

All environmental projections are for stable climax vegetation and relatively stable animal populations. No system state differences are modeled for the habitats themselves. Variability among hunter-gatherers in this model can arise only from variability in the fundamental input variables of solar radiation and rainfall as they are known to affect the earth's biota. The model is further restricted to purely terrestrial consumers. In almost total contrast, the ethnographic frame of reference is grounded in the variability documented among hunter-gatherers of the relatively recent era and makes no effort to standardize or control for system state variability.

The Rosetta Stone that permits me to relate these two intellectual constructions is, of course, the environment of the earth as it has been determined by climatological dynamics during the past 125 years. The environmental variables upon which the model is built and to which hunter-gatherer variability is related and correlated are the same environmental conditions to which variability among hunter-gatherer cases has been previously related.

Proposition 6.05

Differences in the ways that documented hunter-gatherers respond to the same environmental conditions that constitute the basis of the Terrestrial Model should be considered a measure of the degree to which the

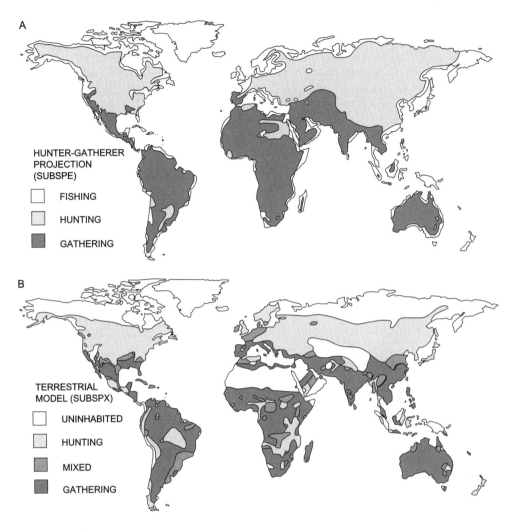

FIGURE 6.04

Global comparison of projections from ethnographically documented hunter-gatherers (A) and from the Terrestrial Model (B) for primary source of food. Markers are for SUBSPE: projection from 339 hunter-gatherer cases for subsistence bias, and SUBSPX: Terrestrial Model expected subsistence bias.

ethnographic cases diverge from the modeled conditions in the same environmental settings. This is a measure of system state variability and differentiation. In many cases, this differentiation takes the form of system state variability in response to processes of intensifiation.

***

Contrasting Patterning: Clues to Trends in Intensification

Maps A and B in figure 6.04 illustrate a global comparison between the geography of primary sources of foods projected from the data on ethnographically documented hunter-gatherers (map A) and the Terrestrial Model of hunter-gatherer subsistence (map B). The first feature requiring

comment is that the illustration of the model in map B appears much more fine-grained; patchy distributions of plants, animals, and plant-animal mixtures are visible in both sub-Saharan Africa and South America. In the projections from the ethnographically documented hunter-gatherers in map A, these same areas reflect a rather homogeneous dependency upon terrestrial plants.

In my opinion, the model has more provocative implications for these areas than the ethnographic projection, since most cases of hunter-gatherers from the tropical regions depicted are either engaged in a mutualistic partnership with agriculturists (e.g., the Mbuti [Harako 1976], Efe [Bailey 1985], and Bayaka [Heymer 1980] of Africa; the Mikea of Madagascar [Dina and Hoerner 1976]; the Yerukulas of South India [Murty 1981]; the Van Vagris of Rajasthan

TABLE 6.05

COMPARISON OF PROJECTED AND MODELED FREQUENCIES
FOR DOMINANT SUBSISTENCE SOURCES AMONG THE
WEATHER STATIONS FROM AFRICA AND SOUTH AMERICA

| | TERRESTRIAL MODEL | | | | |
	Terrestrial plants	*Terrestrial animals*	*Mixed*	*Uninhabited*	*Total*
A. Comparison of the combined data for South America and Africa for the Terrestrial Model and the projected values from the hunter-gatherer cases (counts are of weather stations).					
HUNTER-GATHERER PROJECTION					
TERRESTRIAL PLANTS	177	61	35	18	291
	(75.6)	(73.5)	(72.9)	(31.6)	(69.0)
TERRESTRIAL ANIMALS	7	4	6	16	33
	(3.0)	(4.8)	(12.5)	(28.1)	(7.8)
AQUATIC RESOURCES	50	18	7	23	98
	(21.4)	(21.7)	(14.6)	(40.4)	(23.2)
TOTAL	234	83	48	57	422
	(55.5)	(19.6)	(11.4)	(13.5)	
B. Comparison of the combined data for South America and Africa for the Terrestrial Model and the combined data from the hunter-gatherer cases from both South America and Africa.					
HUNTER-GATHERER DATA					
TERRESTRIAL PLANTS	20	5	2	0	27
	(76.9)	(71.4)	(66.6)	(00.0)	(71.1)
TERRESTRIAL ANIMALS	4	1	1	1	7
	(15.4)	(14.3)	(33.3)	(50.0)	(18.4)
AQUATIC RESOURCES	2	1	0	1	4
	(7.7)	(14.3)	(00.0)	(50.0)	(10.5)
TOTAL	26	7	3	2	38
	(68.4)	(18.4)	(7.9)	(5.3)	

Note: Percentage values are in parentheses and are column values except for the rows, which are totals. **Bold** entries show important high- and low-correspondence cells.

[Misra 1990]; the Kanjars of Uttar Pradesh [Nagar and Misra 1990]; the Kadar [Ehrenfels 1952]; the Bihor [Williams 1974]; the Paliyans [Gardner 1965]; the Chololanaickan [Bhanu 1982, 1992]; and the Mrabri of Thailand [Pookajorn 1988]) or maintain mutualistic partnerships with pastoralists (e.g., the Haddad of Chad [Nicolaisen 1968] and the Nemadi of Mauritania [Gabus 1952]) or were agriculturists at the time of documentation (e.g., the Kubu of Sumatra [Sandbukt 1988]; the Chenchu of India [Fürer-Haimendorf 1943]; and the Ayta (Pinatubo) of the Philippines [Fox 1952]) or were wage laborers acting as forest specialists (e.g., the Nayaka-Naikan of southern India [Bird 1983]).

The patterned absence of more than one group of hunter-gatherers in the same environment documents changes and pressures relating to the dominance of pastoral and agricultural subsistence in relatively recent times. In other words, a long-term trend of increasing intensification in food production characterizes these regions. Since the ethnographic projections are based on hunter-gatherer data recorded during the last two hundred years, and the Terrestrial Model is

perhaps more behaviorally germane at the very close of the Pleistocene but is displayed against recent environments, contrasts between the two maps can be viewed as providing clues to intensifying pressures on hunter-gatherer subsistence that affected the trophic level of exploited food resources during the Holocene.

Table 6.05, part A, presents data from Africa and South America illustrating the differences between the Terrestrial Model and the projected ethnographic data in terms of the consumption of animal, plant, and aquatic resources. Part B of the table summarizes the differences between the ethnographic projections of hunter-gatherer cases from Africa and South America and the expected food dependencies anticipated by the Terrestrial Model. The results confirm the patterns illustrated in figure 6.04.

Of the 234 weather stations in part A of the table that the Terrestrial Model predicts will be dominated by terrestrial plant food resources, 75.6 percent are also projected to have been dependent upon terrestrial plant sources by the equations that summarize the ethnographic data. The major difference lies in the fifty cases projected to have been dependent upon aquatic resources, which is an alternative the Terrestrial Model does not allow. This means that 21.4 percent of the cases modeled as dependent upon terrestrial plant sources in our "Pleistocene" model of hunter-gatherer behavior shifted to primary dependence upon aquatic resources. This result is consistent with the wide-scale resource shifts among intensifying hunter-gatherers that are suspected to have occurred at the close of the Pleistocene (Clarke 1976).

The big contrast, however, occurs in comparisons of locations that the Terrestrial Model predicts are predominantly dependent upon terrestrial animals.

Generalization 6.04

The hunter-gatherer equations project that 73.5 percent of these locations will be dependent upon terrestrial plants. An additional 21.7 percent are projected to be dependent upon aquatic resources. Only 4.8 percent of the cases projected by the Terrestrial Model to be dependent upon terrestrial animals are also projected by the modern hunter-gatherer data to be primarily dependent on hunting.

It is important to remember that the Terrestrial Model projects that hunter-gatherers take food from their environment in approximately the same proportions as it occurs in the habitat. In contrast, the projective equations derived from the recorded behavior of nearly contemporary hunter-gatherers demonstrate a huge bias against the exploitation of terrestrial animals and in favor of terrestrial plants and aquatic resources. The difference between the bias in the ethnographic record and the possibilities suggested by an ecological analysis of hunter-gatherer habitats has fueled many debates in the anthropological literature about the character of the past—none more germane than those of Richard Lee at the Man the Hunter Conference:

> The basis of Bushman diet is derived from sources other than meat. This emphasis makes good ecological sense to the !Kung Bushman and appears to be a common feature among hunters and gatherers in general. Since a 30 to 40 percent input of meat is such a consistent target for modern hunters in a variety of habitats, is it not reasonable to postulate a similar percentage for prehistoric hunters? . . . One gets the impression that hunting societies have been chosen by ethnologists to illustrate a theme . . . but unfortunately it has led to the assumption that a precarious hunting subsistence base was characteristic of all cultures in the Pleistocene. This view of both modern and ancient hunters ought to be reconsidered.   (Lee 1968:43)

The view that terrestrial animals were focal food targets and accounted for a substantial amount of the organized variability among hunter-gatherers has been dismissed as little more than a romantic bias, perhaps most enthusiastically by

David Clarke (1976) in his comments about the character of subsistence in Europe at the close of the Pleistocene:

> The conventional interpretation that depicts the displacement of the European meat-eating Mesolithic hunter-fishers by Neolithic cereal farmers has indeed become traditional. . . . It is a culturally induced assumption that hunted mammals were the main source of Mesolithic food supply and meat quantitatively the most important food-stuff. Modern North Europeans and North Americans come from cultures that especially esteem meat.   (Clarke 1976:449–50)

Clarke proceeds to argue that foragers in Mesolithic Europe were largely dependent upon plant resources and that cultural biases, stereotypes, and unwarranted assumptions made by archaeological investigators have conspired to distort our view of the past.[26]

Are the opinions of Richard Lee and David Clarke correct, to mention only two of the recent researchers who have made normative statements about hunter-gatherer plant-based subsistence? I have already noted that the Terrestrial Model anticipated that the !Kung—upon whom Lee based his skepticism about the importance of terrestrial mammals in the diet of ancient peoples—would be predominantly dependent upon terrestrial animals! Based on the comparisons between my two different frames of reference, it can be concluded that ethnographically documented hunter-gatherers represent a *range* of system state variability, much of which is probably referable to various mixes of exploited resources and different levels of intensification. In subsequent chapters, I concentrate on assessing more concretely some of the types of variability that hunter-gatherer systems represent.

Relational Patterning in Archaeological Observations

If one assumes that the Terrestrial Model effectively approximates the variability in trophic dependency prevalent during the Late Pleistocene, then the complicated pattern apparent throughout western Europe[27] in figure 6.05 is most provocative. Although in Clarke's opinion this vast region was "misunderstood" by researchers whose interpretative biases populated the past with "meat eaters," the patterns in figure 6.05 do not support Clarke's view.

Dependence upon terrestrial plants predominates across the zone of "Mediterranean" environments that encompasses the south coasts of Portugal and Spain, and the southern coasts of France, Italy, and most of Albania and Greece. There is, in addition, an extension of this pattern across southwestern France and into the area in the southern British Isles that is later identified as the "Wessex Culture." The area of mixed dependency upon terrestrial plants and animals is very large and includes England and Wales as well as the southeastern part of Ireland. There is a wide area of mixed dependence extending east from southwestern France and narrowing

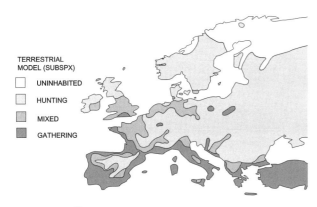

FIGURE 6.05

Projection of Terrestrial Model estimates for primary sources of foods for western Europe, using modern weather stations as the climatic baseline.

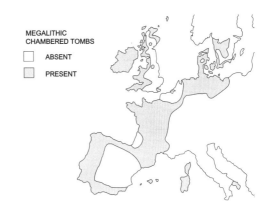

FIGURE 6.06

Distribution of Megalithic chambered tombs across western Europe. Adapted and redrawn from Piggott (1965:figure 29).

to an interior distribution across Belgium and the Netherlands. Mixed dependence extends across Lower Saxony and Schleswig-Holstein in western Germany and southwestward into the southern part of western Germany. This pattern of mixed dependence on plant and animal resources corresponds in many ways to the dispersion of "chambered tombs" that begin to appear archaeologically during the fifth millennium B.C. (figure 6.06).

The pattern of real interest, however, extends across the European continent north and east of the areas characterized by hunter-gatherer plant dependence. With some very minor exceptions, the Terrestrial Model projects that subsistence in this entire area is predominantly dependent upon terrestrial mammals. The archaeological record of this heartland region is characterized by the early appearance of domesticate-dependent societies in the southern Balkans; their presence along the Vardar, Morava, Struma, and Maritsa Rivers; and a later extension of domestication into the Danube River valley itself. The ecological and organizational dynamics underlying such a transition in subsistence have been encapsulated in the archaeological identifier "the early painted pottery cultures," and they include sites at Karanovo, Starčevo, Körös, and Criş (Tringham 1971:68–139).

A somewhat later but nonetheless interesting appearance of domesticate-dependent societies that are identified archaeologically with linear pottery or LBK materials occurs across the loess belt traversing western Moldavia, the Ukraine, Czechoslovakia, Poland, and Germany and extends into the eastern edges of the Netherlands and northern France. The Terrestrial Model anticipates that hunter-gatherer subsistence in all of these areas of temperate Europe would have been predominantly dependent upon terrestrial animals.

The broad outlines of these basic adaptive zonal patterns were identified many years ago, but when they are compared with the patterns projected from the ethnographic

data set, some major differences emerge. Along the coastal margins of western Europe,[28] for instance, there is a huge shift to dependence upon aquatic resources. Consistent with the global sample comparisons, this shift may be at the expense of dependence upon both terrestrial animals and plants.

The fit between the projected ethnographic data and the generalizations derived from data on the Mesolithic of Europe is illustrated by a comparison of the patterns in figures 6.07 and 6.08. Clearly, not only are my projections for Europe consistent with other global patterns, they are also consistent with the Mesolithic archaeological reality.[29] Nevertheless, in Europe, as maps A and B in figure 6.09 illustrate, the most dramatic reduction relative to the Terrestrial Model occurs in the regions occupied by peoples who are dependent for their subsistence on terrestrial mammals.

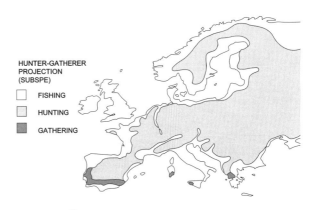

FIGURE 6.07

Projection from ethnographically documented hunter-gatherers to western Europe for primary sources of food using modern weather stations as the climatic baseline.

AQUATIC RESOURCES

☐ RIVERINE

■ ATLANTIC

■ HIGHEST
  PRODUCTIVITY

FIGURE 6.08

Distribution of estimates of aquatic resource accessibility across western Europe using modern weather stations as the climatic baseline.

A simple visual comparison of the latter two plots demonstrates that, in contrast to the projections of the Terrestrial Model presented in map A, the data from ethnographic sources (map B) project a massive reduction in the area occupied by peoples predominantly dependent upon terrestrial animals. The projections of the shape and distribution of the area in which terrestrial mammals provide more than 50 percent of the diet are even more interesting.

This region bears a striking resemblance to the area in which Paleolithic artifacts have suggested to researchers that a major alliance network provided "a safety net for dispersed populations living at low densities in such high-risk environments as those which characterized Europe after 30,000 BP" (Gamble 1982, 1983; see also Champion et al. 1984:86). For instance, both the Paleolithic dispersions of female figurines and much later distributions of the LBK culture of the Early Neolithic are very similar to the pattern in figure

6.09, map B. With these interesting patterns in mind, I now emphasize some features of the frames of reference that are being used and reiterate how these comparisons can help us understand processes of intensification.

COMPARATIVE PATTERNING: FRAME OF
REFERENCE TO FRAME OF REFERENCE

The Terrestrial Model is both a baseline model and a frame of reference that anticipates variability arising only as a result of differences in effective environment. Nothing in the model contributes to variability in system state or to processual changes in the character of systems over time. Similarly, no system state variability is modeled that might arise from overexploitation or forest clearance in otherwise similar habitats. All environmental projections are based on stable climax vegetation and relatively stable animal populations, and no system state differences are modeled for habitats themselves. According to the terms of the model, variability among hunter-gatherer groups arises exclusively from differences in the fundamental input variables of solar radiation and rainfall and their effect on the earth's biota. The model is further restricted to purely terrestrial consumers.

In almost total contrast, projections from the ethnographic frame of reference are grounded in the differences that have been documented among hunter-gatherers of the relatively recent era, and no effort has been made to control for system state variability in the sample of cases. The Rosetta Stone permitting us to relate the two frames of reference is the environment of the earth as affected by its climate during the last 20 to 125 years. The environmental variables upon which the Terrestrial Model is built are the same environmental conditions to which hunter-gatherer variability is related and correlated (see proposition 6.05).

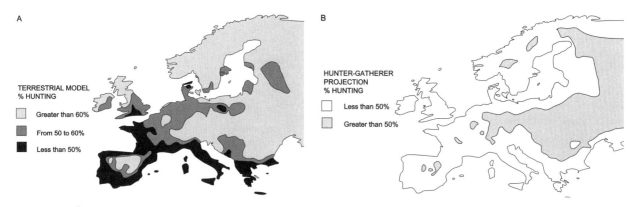

A

TERRESTRIAL MODEL
% HUNTING

☐ Greater than 60%

■ From 50 to 60%

■ Less than 50%

B

HUNTER-GATHERER
PROJECTION
% HUNTING

☐ Less than 50%

☐ Greater than 50%

FIGURE 6.09

Comparative projections of the role of hunting among hunter-gatherers projected to inhabit the environments of contemporary western Europe. Map A is the projection from the Terrestrial Model while map B is the projection from the ethnographic cases. Both use modern weather stations as the climatic baseline.

TABLE 6.06

WEATHER STATION DATA FOR CENTRAL AND WESTERN EUROPE
USING THE TERRESTRIAL MODEL AND THE PROJECTED VALUES
FROM THE HUNTER-GATHERER DATA SET

HUNTER-GATHERER PROJECTION	TERRESTRIAL MODEL				
	Terrestrial plants	*Terrestrial animals*	*Mixed*	*Uninhabited*	*Total*
TERRESTRIAL PLANTS	9 (10.7)	0 (0.0)	0 (0.0)	0 (0.0)	9 (2.2)
TERRESTRIAL ANIMALS	9 (10.7)	137 (**63.1**)	27 (36.5)	10 (33.3)	183 (45.2)
AQUATIC RESOURCES	66 (**78.6**)	80 (36.9)	47 (**63.5**)	20 (**66.7**)	213 (52.6)
TOTAL	84 (20.7)	217 (53.6)	74 (18.3)	30 (7.4)	405

Note: **Bold** entries show important high- and low-correspondence cells.

As an illustration of the utility of the "grounded" projections of system state variability, I explore briefly some features of a set of phenomena commonly referred to as "the spread of agriculture" into western Europe during the seventh and eighth centuries B.P., using an enriched sample of 405 weather stations distributed across Europe roughly west of 35 degrees east longitude and extending into the British Isles. Climatic data from this region allowed me to calculate all of the basic environmental estimates as well as the subsistence and demographic variables estimated by the Terrestrial Model. I also calculated values for many properties projected from the 339-group sample of hunter-gatherers. With these data in hand, I am now able to compare the patterns made visible by the two different frames of reference and to observe how variability among the ethnographically documented hunter-gatherers differs from the variability anticipated by the model when the only operative factors are differential productivity and accessibility of productivity in different environmental settings.

Another insight into how the two frames of reference provide clues to patterns of system state differentiation is found in a cross-tabulation in table 6.06 of how often the food sources projected from the hunter-gatherer data diverged from expectations obtained from the Terrestrial Model. If my expectations were based on the comparison in table 6.05, parts A and B, of projected and modeled data from Africa and South America, then the data in table 6.06 should certainly come as no surprise.

Generalization 6.05

In the comparison of groups from Africa and South America, approximately 75 percent of the cases dependent upon terrestrial plants are observed to be dependent upon terrestrial plants in projections of the ethnographic data set. In contrast,

in the European example only 10.7 percent of the cases that were modeled as dependent upon plants are projected to have remained plant dependent. In the European data, 78.6 percent of the model's plant-dependent cases shift to aquatic resources in the ethnographic projections.

Generalization 6.06

In Africa and South America, 73.5 percent of the cases modeled as primarily dependent upon terrestrial animals had shifted to terrestrial plants in the ethnographic projections. In contrast, in Europe, 63.1 percent of the modeled hunters remained dependent upon terrestrial mammals in the ethnographic projections, none had shifted to plants, and 36.9 percent had shifted to aquatic resources.

The most surprising contrast between the Terrestrial Model and the ethnographic projections occurs in the mixed category:

Generalization 6.07

In Africa and South America, 72.9 percent of the hunter-gatherer cases had shifted primarily to plants in the ethnographic projections, whereas in Europe no groups had shifted to plants, although 63.5 percent had shifted to aquatic resources.

As I have noted elsewhere, the ethnographic projections in general reflect cases exhibiting varying degrees of intensification relative to the Terrestrial Model.

It should be stressed that the ethnographic cases are *not* representative of forager subsistence in the Pleistocene, nor do they represent some mythical group of pristine hunter-gatherers. They are merely interesting cases whose various strategies and tactics for intensifying food production in different habitats contribute to much of the between-case variability in the sample. If I am correct, this is a valuable body of case material that is germane to unraveling the differences between system state variability and habitat adaptability.

The range of system states observable in these cases is likely to refer to different scalar states of intensification. I want to learn more about scales of intensification and differences between states in order to determine whether the variety that I can demonstrate arises from gradual, additive change or punctuated, dramatic kinds of emergent change. Considerable variability in system state may be related to changing strategies of intensification that produce different results in different habitats and contexts of regional interaction. The contrasts between Europe, in the Northern Hemisphere, and Africa and South America, in the Southern Hemisphere, underscore the important fact that initial conditions—the structure of both within- and between-habitat variability—appear to influence strongly various strategies of intensification in different settings, regardless of the factors that may be selecting for intensification itself.

LINKING THE PROBLEMS OF INTENSIFICATION AND EMERGENCE

In preceding chapters, I suggested that recent research focused on the emergence of complex systems has provided some compelling arguments for the view that emergent change can and does characterize the natural history of living systems. One of the most important characteristics of emergent change is that the outcomes of change cannot be anticipated, even if all of a system's properties are known prior to the change. In short, a break in continuity occurs between a system's composition prior to and after a change of state. Archaeologists have long recognized that two basic kinds of patterning occur in the archaeological record. Deposits often reflect long periods of continuity accompanied by gradual, substitutional, and additive changes, but abrupt discontinuities also occur, indicating that in a short period of time phenomena appear that could not be projected from a knowledge of preceding patterns. Traditionally, stable patterns have been interpreted as "normal" local developments, whereas evidence of instability is said to signal a migration or the replacement of one culture by another in a local or regional sense. I believe, however, that

Proposition 6.06
Both stable and discontinuous types of patterning may represent autochthonous phases of change within the trajectory of a single system and therefore may be a reflection of the uniquely human property of niche metamorphosis.

I have already elaborated on the point that the human species is able to occupy what might be considered an infinite variety of niches and that the essential link between niche and species in the majority of the natural world does not apply to humankind. System changes that open or create new niches are an option for any humans who might optimize or gain by moving into the new niche. This means that there need not be any continuity between the system within which an emergent change occurs, although the persons who occupy the old and new niches could be the same.

The well-documented changes that occurred on the Great Plains of North America during the historic period illustrate this point. At the time of ethnographic documentation, the Great Plains were occupied by many ethnically different groups whose clothing, housing, patterns of mobility, site structure, customs, and religious beliefs were nevertheless so similar that the term *Plains Indians* was used to describe their material culture. This relative homogeneity across a huge area was not, however, referable to a single cultural progenitor. The ethnic groups of the Plains came from practically all of the different language and ethnic groups that surrounded the Great Plains prior to the spread of the horse northward from early Spanish settlements.

Of even more interest is the fact that some of the ancestral groups were agriculturists, while others were hunter-gatherers. Groups came from regions as vastly different as boreal forests, eastern deciduous forests, and steppic and semidesertic regions adjacent to the southern plains. Yet nineteenth-century ethnographers detected very few remnants of this diverse background in the extreme homogeneity of Plains Indian culture (Wissler 1934). Perhaps even more important, if one were to look for the historical origins of classic Plains Indian cultural traits and overall characteristics, there would be little continuity between the protohistoric archaeology of the Plains regions and the archaeology of the classic Plains Indian groups.[30]

Most of the dramatic changes occurring on the Great Plains were initiated as a result of the spread, from group to group, of one domesticated species—the horse (Ewers 1955; Wissler 1914). This example can easily lead one to question whether the incorporation into the subsistence base and controlled use of several domesticated forms of plants and animals by Mesolithic hunter-gatherers of western Europe may document emergent changes in system states in some cases and yet, in others, represent simply one incremental step in a pattern of gradual intensification in the use of wild resources that produced little, if any, major system change.[31] Phenomena such as demographic migrations and radiations, which have been proposed to account for similar discontinuities in the archaeological record (Ammerman and Cavalli-Sforza 1971, 1973), require a very different kind of explanation (Binford 1999).

With regard to the linkage of emergence and intensification, however, different kinds of emergent change in European hunter-gatherer cultural systems—and the rates at which such changes occurred—should be related, at least in part, to habitat differences and to the prior or initial conditions constituting the environmental springboard for change. The characteristics of a prior or preexisting state should have much to do with whether the adoption of domesticate-based subsistence strategies solves a set of basic problems or simply increases a group's subsistence security by expanding its tactical responses to the problems it confronts. Since similar selective processes may occur in settings with very different initial conditions, one should expect trajectories of change to correspond to the way that similar processes operate in a context of different initial conditions.

A comparison of some features of the archaeological record documenting the appearance of domesticates in western Europe with projections from the Terrestrial Model and my ethnographic frame of reference may provide some insights into system state differences documented among the more contemporary hunter-gatherers. The Rosetta Stone in this comparison is the structure of variability in climatic conditions and how climatic variables affect other environmental conditions characteristic of the era for which there are climatic records.

Early historical inferences about the appearance of Neolithic societies in Europe favored migrational scenarios in which agropastoralists moved into Europe from eastern demographic centers and displaced local populations (Gimbutas 1973, 1977, 1979, 1980). More sophisticated versions of the same argument have been termed the "wave of advance model" or "demic diffusion" (Ammerman and Cavalli-Sforza 1984). In the latter argument, the spread of domesticates was not linked to system state changes or variability between resident systems but was attributed instead to the mechanical consequences of adopting domesticates. According to Cavalli-Sforza, populations tend to grow more rapidly in sedentary contexts rather than under conditions of high mobility, so domesticate-based production will take the form of a "wave of advance" as new communities are created by "excess" population.

In this kind of argument, the explanation of the spread of agriculture is very different from the explanation of its origins, which must result from conditions operative prior to the consequences of the use of domesticates. Most models of "diffusion" share with the wave of advance argument the property that new system state conditions, brought on by the introduction of domesticates, drive the spread of domesticates. Most of the time these arguments emphasize the alleged advantages conferred by domesticates on their users; therefore, the adoption of domesticates by new populations is said to be a consequence of the self-evident superiority of agriculture over the exploitation of wild foods.

More recent research explores the possibility that some "processes" operating in Europe transformed local Mesolithic societies into increasingly domesticate-dependent systems (e.g., Dennell 1983, 1992; Donahue 1992; Zvelebil 1986). Another view of the European archaeological evidence suggests that the spread of domesticated plants and animals may be a different process than the one that leads to the transformation of hunter-gatherers into agropastoralists (Cowan and Watson 1992; Dennell 1992; Zvelebil and Rowley-Conwy 1984). This view is at least predisposed to regard system state transformation as something quite distinct from accumulative gradualism and the repetitive incorporation of possible subsistence tactics and strategies, but because these distinctions have not heretofore been seriously considered, questions such as how to distinguish emergent evolutionary change from other discontinuities visible in the archaeological record have never been addressed.

Looking at the Spread of Agropastoralism with Projected Knowledge

I have taken Ammerman and Cavalli-Sforza's (1984:140–48) admittedly out-of-date suite of sites and dates documenting the appearance of domesticated forms of plants and animals across western Europe[32] and have projected onto these locations the modeled and projected properties of the hunter-gatherer data set. Using Ammerman and Cavalli-Sforza's data on longitude and latitude, I calculated values for all of the basic climatic variables summarized in chapters 4 and 5 and then projected both the modeled values from the Terrestrial Model and the properties projected from ethnographically known hunter-gatherers onto each of the European sites.

Given that, in Europe, as intensification proceeds, the number of hunter-gatherers dependent upon terrestrial mammals is greatly reduced, and *given* that intensification results in increased dependence upon aquatic resources regardless of whether initial conditions involved dependence upon terrestrial plants or animals, and last, *given* that, in the absence of aquatic resources, I expect the dependence upon hunting to increase in cooler temperate and warmer boreal zones (figures 6.04 and 6.05), I might expect that, in the absence of aquatic alternatives, intensification might be very difficult or nearly impossible in situations in which terrestrial animals are the primary food source and the area is in the higher latitudes.

I might also reasonably expect that some conditions of intensification, such as the adoption of domesticated plants and animals, would appear archaeologically as a sequence of incremental steps, the costs of which could be changing over time relative to other intensificational alternatives. The length of time between the point at which domesticated species are

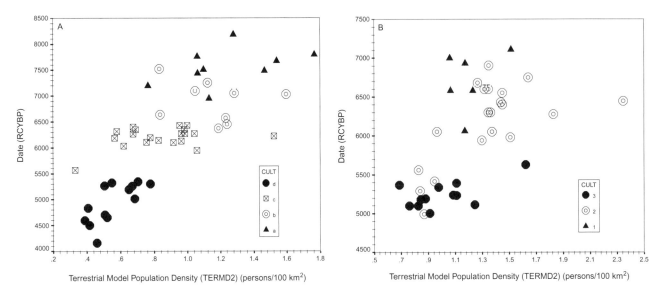

FIGURE 6.10

Comparative graphs showing the dates of the earliest appearance of cultigens in northern and southern Europe, displayed against population density estimates projected by the Terrestrial Model. Graph A shows sites along the "northern route," where the marker indicates recognized cultures (CULT): (a) early Greek; (b) Körös, Karanovo I, Starčevo, and Criş–Central European block; (c) linear pottery culture (LBK); and (d) Baltic region sites. Graph B shows sites along the "southern route": (1) eastern Mediterranean, (2) western Mediterranean and France, and (3) British Isles.

well known and accessible and the point at which they are adopted might well vary inversely with the costs of alternative intensification strategies using wild resources. If the costs of the latter are very high, I would expect rapid adoption of domesticate-based alternatives.

Conversely, if the costs of acquiring other resources are low, then I would expect considerable time to elapse between the availability of domesticated species and their adoption by any given group. I would also expect that prior conditions determining the organizational scale of social networks would affect the accessibility of either seeds or breeding pairs of a species. Knowledge of potentially useful domesticated species, and hence the speed with which lower-cost domesticate-based tactics would be adopted by hunter-gatherers, would be similarly affected in those locations in which the intensification costs of wild alternatives are relatively high.

Against the backdrop of the preceding arguments, I now examine some patterns produced by plotting archaeological properties against the frames of reference I have developed. In figure 6.10, graphs A and B, uncalibrated ^{14}C dates for the first appearance of domesticates have been plotted against population density estimates (in numbers of persons per 100 square kilometers) produced by the Terrestrial Model. In graph A of figure 6.10, sites associated with the northern route into central and northern Europe are plotted; in graph B, sites

associated with the Mediterranean route into France and from there into Great Britain appear.

A positive curvilinear relationship characterizes the central-to-northern route (graph A), illustrating that the lower the projected population density, the later the appearance of domesticates across western Europe. The curvilinear aspects of the relationship are not as evident in the data from the Mediterranean to Great Britain sites, although the positive aspects of the relationship are sustained. What makes the distribution in graph B different from the one in graph A is that the dates from Italy are not significantly different from those in Spain and France. The significant contrasts are between the dates for the continent and Great Britain and between lowland sites and those in the Alps.

These relationships between dated archaeological sites and projected population estimates suggest that initial conditions affecting population density may have contributed to the rate of intensification.[33] It would also be worthwhile to investigate the possibility that absolute numbers of persons, perhaps varying in different settings, could be a more important conditioner of intensification than the percentage increase represented. It is quite clear, however, that in figure 6.10 the patterning indicates that early intensification occurs primarily in areas in which the Terrestrial Model predicts that subsistence would be predominantly dependent upon terrestrial plants and secon-

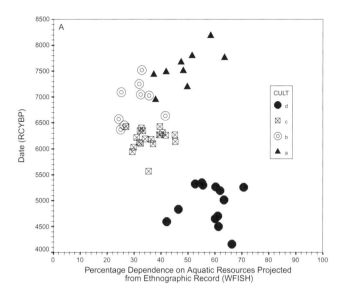
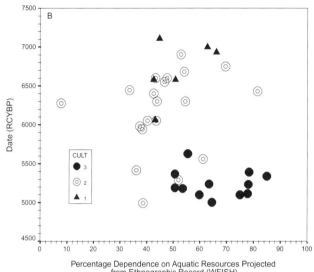

FIGURE 6.11

Comparative graphs showing the dates for the earliest appearance of cultigens in northern and southern Europe, displayed against the percentage dependence upon aquatic resources of ethnographically described hunter-gatherers projected to inhabit the environments of contemporary Europe. Graph A shows sites along the "northern route," where the marker indicates recognized cultures (CULT): (a) early Greek; (b) Körös, Karanovo I, Starčevo, and Criş–Central European block; (c) linear pottery culture (LBK); and (d) Baltic region sites. Graph B shows sites along the "southern route": (1) eastern Mediterranean, (2) western Mediterranean and France, and (3) British Isles.

darily in areas where trophically mixed strategies would have prevailed.

I have already noted that, based on comparisons between the two projections, intensification results in increased dependence upon aquatic resources in those settings in which aquatic alternatives exist. Graphs A and B in figure 6.11 illustrate projections from the ethnographic data set that plot the relationship between the percent dependence upon aquatic resources and the dates for the first use of domesticates. Both distributions are similar in shape but they differ in scale; that is, the time represented between the two horizontal arms of the open elliptical distribution is greater for the central to northern European distribution than for the Mediterranean to Great Britain distribution. In both graphs, some of the earliest groups using domesticates were also projected to include significant numbers of persons supported by aquatic resources.

This initial stage was followed by the spread of domesticates into areas in which a greatly reduced dependence upon aquatic resources is projected. There is also a correlation between the date of early documentation and a projection of less reliance upon aquatic resources. Along the central to northern European route, a considerable delay occurs between the appearance of LBK materials and dates from the northern Scandinavian and Finno-Baltic area, but this is not an original observation. In a comparative study of the appearance of domesticates in the archaeological record of Denmark and Finland, Zvelebil and Rowley-Conwy (1984:104) note that "the cases studied emphasize the long continuation of foraging adaptations, and the long delay before the appearance of a predominantly agricultural economy. This delay has been caused by the development of successful maritime adaptations, which acted as a viable alternative to farming until a specific trigger—a decline in marine resources—occurred and initiated the substitution phase of the transition."

What is impressive about the patterns in the graphs in figure 6.11 is that they were produced by projections from recent hunter-gatherer data. The fact that these patterns are at least consistent with patterning observed in the archaeological record suggests that much of the criticism directed toward the archaeological use of ethnographic data has nothing to do with the data per se but rather its inappropriate use by researchers. One of the fundamental concerns of this book is to demonstrate that prior knowledge—which in this case includes environmental, ecological, *and* ethnographic data—can be either useful or useless, depending upon what researchers try to do with it.

As far as the issue of intensification in western Europe is concerned, all of the projections have pointed to an unrelenting shift away from dependence upon terrestrial animals in those settings for which there is archaeological evidence of intensification. For example, in graphs A and B in figure 6.12, the percentages of the diet obtained from

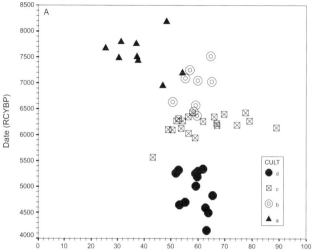

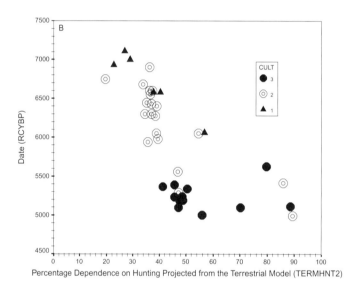

FIGURE 6.12

Comparative graphs showing the dates for the earliest appearance of domesticates in northern and southern Europe, displayed against the percentage dependence upon terrestrial animals projected from the Terrestrial Model for minimalist hunter-gatherers inhabiting the environments of contemporary Europe. Graph A shows sites along the "northern route," where the marker indicates recognized cultures (CULT): (a) early Greek; (b) Körös, Karanovo I, Starčevo, and Criş–Central European block; (c) linear pottery culture (LBK); and (d) Baltic region sites. Graph B shows sites along the "southern route": (1) eastern Mediterranean, (2) western Mediterranean and France, and (3) British Isles.

terrestrial ungulates as projected by the Terrestrial Model are shown against the dates of the first appearance of domesticates in the archaeological record for two sets of archaeological sites. Graph B, the "southern route," illustrates an inversely correlated sigmoid curve with an inflection point at a value of approximately 40 percent dependence upon terrestrial animals. The pattern in graph A, the "northern route," is analogous to that in graph B, although the inflection point deviates from its placement in the conventional sigmoid curve. (It is likely that the distribution in graph A would inscribe

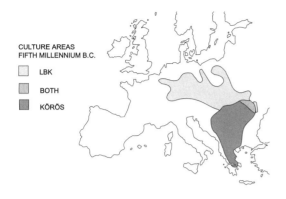

FIGURE 6.13

Early assessment of the distribution across Europe of LBK ceramics and their makers relative to earlier cultures at approximately the fifth millennium B.C.

FIGURE 6.14

More recent map of the distribution of LBK ceramics and their makers, partitioned into early and later periods.

a sigmoid curve if dated sites from Finland and northern Sweden had been included in the list of plotted locations.)

Nevertheless, the interesting feature of graph A is the horizontal scatter of LBK sites, which have been previously interpreted as classic examples of a rapid migration of agropastoralists into Europe (see figures 6.13 and 6.14 for an early assessment of LBK site distribution and a much more recent one). It is true that a very tight distribution of ^{14}C dates is evident in figure 6.12, graph A, but with only one exception all of the LBK sites were projected by the Terrestrial Model to range between 48 and 88 percent dependence upon terrestrial animals for hunter-gatherers living in the same settings. Furthermore, according to Tringham (1971:116), these LBK sites have not contained remains of fish or other aquatic resources.

These observations provide an interesting backdrop to the conventional archaeological assessment of the pre-LBK, or Mesolithic, deposits in the region. These have been characterized as nonexistent in the loess deposits in which LBK sites are found and, when present in the region, are located on sandy soils and in cave deposits. The archaeological materials recovered from the loess deposits have been identified as "typically Paleolithic" industries because they are manufactured on blades and lack a significant microlithic component.

Using their typological templates, archaeologists have decreed that since blades are by definition Paleolithic, when blade tools are found in loessic soil contexts they must have been deposited during the Paleolithic era.[34] Similarly, the Mesolithic era is defined by the presence of microlithic tools, and if no microliths are recovered from deposits then the Mesolithic is said to be absent. The lack of continuity between subsequent Neolithic materials and preceding blade-based assemblages is therefore said to be irrefutable proof of the absence of the Mesolithic.

The projections illustrated in figure 6.12 suggest that had Mesolithic populations preceded the populations responsible for the LBK materials in the region, the available subsistence base would have more than met their nutritional needs. This leads me to speculate that perhaps the blade-based assemblages assigned to the Paleolithic are, in fact, representative of the Mesolithic in this region. Tringham's (1971:117) observation that LBK lithics typify a blade industry supports the view that instead of a lack of continuity between the Mesolithic and the Neolithic, the LBK represents autochthonous system state change rather than an intrusive "culture" that spread very rapidly over the northern and central European regions characterized by loessic soil.

What other data might be brought to bear on the nature of the change in the archaeological record coincident with the appearance of LBK materials? I have already pointed out that projections from both the Terrestrial Model and the ethnographic data set suggest that hunter-gatherers in the LBK region would have been predominantly dependent upon terrestrial mammals. I have also suggested that intensification would have been very difficult in settings lacking an aquatic alternative to terrestrial animals. Plant-based intensification would have become less and less possible as latitude increased, and domestication of locally hunted wild animals would take considerable time.

On the other hand, if populations who were under pressure to intensify had access to already domesticated plants and animals that would flourish at LBK latitudes, the adoption of agropastoralist strategies could be expected to occur rapidly. In fact, the LBK may represent emergent change similar to that described for the Great Plains of North America, where a new niche opened up and peoples from many different peripheral sources converged on the region. An internally homogeneous culture area would, therefore, have been formed that had a heterogeneous origin in terms of population but a single systemic origin in the sense of the emergence of a new niche.

It is not yet certain, however, what the diagnostic criteria of episodes of emergent change would be in the archaeological record. There have been some very dramatic and rapid changes that are currently considered examples of emergence,[35] but no analysis attempting to develop criteria for accurate diagnosis has been undertaken. I am aware that doing the requisite research is required before I could convincingly evaluate the idea that LBK patterning represents an emergent phenomenon.

Searching for Clues to Process: Other Uses for Frames of Reference

In chapter 3, I noted that the only intellectual tool available to archaeologists that directly implicates past dynamics is the use of frames of reference to produce second-order or higher derivative patterning. At this juncture, I examine some additional characteristics of both the environment and the responses of ethnographically documented hunter-gatherers in an effort to learn more about the environments in which processes leading to agropastoral change occurred in the past.

Figure 6.15 consists of a property space map of the world sample of weather stations introduced in chapter 4 on which the distribution of early Neolithic data is plotted. The southern European data points occur at and below the "elbow" of the distribution, below approximately 45 degrees latitude, where productivity is low owing to water deficit or elevation or some combination of both factors. Above 45 degrees, low productivity is related to latitude and proximity to the polar regions.

The low productivity threshold in Europe is clearly demonstrated in the detailed plots of dated sites on the property space graphs in figure 6.16. The lower arm of the distribution, where productivity increases with latitude, represents the water deficit regions of the Mediterranean. A threshold is apparent between 45 and 46 degrees latitude, beyond which, except for some areas of the British Isles, there is a regular decrease in net aboveground productivity as latitude increases. All of the LBK sites occur above the threshold at which any increase in latitude corresponds to a decrease in net aboveground productivity.

The same property space distribution is displayed in graph B of figure 6.16, but now it is coded for the predominant food source projected by the Terrestrial Model. A big shift occurs from terrestrial plants to terrestrial animals at the threshold between 43 and 47 degrees latitude, which indicates that LBK sites are located in an energetically very different environment from locations containing archaeological evidence of earlier agropastoral adaptations. This is because LBK sites occur in environmental settings just above the threshold where aboveground productivity begins to diminish in a northerly direction.

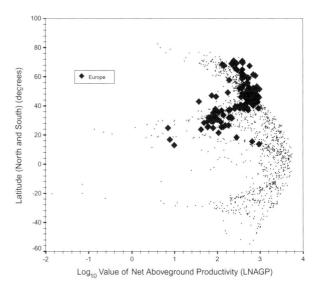

FIGURE 6.15

Property space graph of the world sample of weather stations showing the location of European sites for which ^{14}C dates document the appearance of cultigens.

What do these frames of reference say about the characteristics of the locations of LBK sites when we look at them from the perspective of ethnographically documented hunter-gatherer systems? Figure 6.17 displays the relationships between the expected size of ethnic areas (measured in 100-square-kilometer units) and the chronology (measured in uncalibrated ^{14}C dates) of the suite of archaeological locations containing the earliest evidence of the use of domesticated plants and animals in a large region that includes Greece, the Balkans, the loess deposits extending from the Paris plain to the edge of the Black Sea, and the Balto-Scandinavian region of Europe.

The points in the distribution are coded for culture group or region, and those representing early Greek agropastoralism are relatively tightly clustered at the top of the graph. The points at the bottom of the plot represent sites from Scandinavia and the Baltic states. In contrast, the LBK sites and the Karanovo I, Starčevo, Criş culture block in the north Balkan states form a continuous scatter across the entire graph with the Karanovo I, Starčevo, Criş culture block to the right and the LBK materials scattered from the middle to the left of the graph. Ethnic areas range in size from moderately small (comparable to the ethnographically documented Chimariko of California and the interior central coast, Salish-speaking Cowichan of Canada's British Columbia) to large, in the case of the projected ethnic area surrounding the site of Gyálarét. The closest ethnographic analogues to the latter area are the Coeur d'Alene of the Columbia Plateau and the Gros-Ventre of the Great Plains of North America. In North America, moderately large ethnic areas reflect sub-

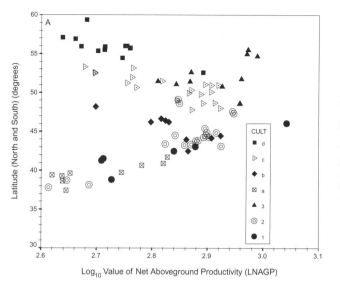
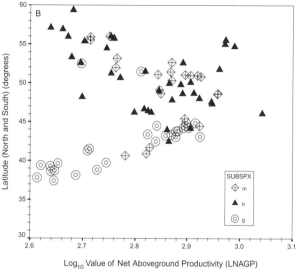

FIGURE 6.16

Comparative graphs showing the cultural identity (A) and the primary sources of food projected by the Terrestrial Model (B) for all of the dated locations in Europe yielding the earliest evidence of the systematic use of domesticates. This information is summarized in a property space defined by latitude and net aboveground productivity (NAGP). Graph A shows sites along the "northern route," where the marker indicates recognized cultures (CULT): (a) early Greek; (b) Körös, Karanovo I, Starčevo, and Criş–Central European block; (c) linear pottery culture (LBK); and (d) Baltic region sites. Graph B shows the same sites as graph A. However, the marker for Graph B is the dominant source of food as anticipated by the Terrestrial Model (SUBSPX): (g) terrestrial plants, (h) terrestrial animals, and (m) mixed sources.

stantial regional networks that developed in the context of the spread of the horse among previously agricultural or much less mobile hunter-gatherers who gave up agriculture for the new hunter-pastoralist niche that the horse made possible.

The patterning in figure 6.17 illustrates that a very wide range of variability in the anticipated size of ethnic areas characterized the hunter-gatherers who exploited the area subsequently occupied by LBK populations. This suggests that much of the cultural diversity extant among hunter-gatherers was replaced by relative homogeneity across the same range of environmental variability. It is reasonable to imagine that the appearance of a new niche, accompanied by an increase in system complexity, might well be signaled by the disappearance of some of the characteristics of the habitat that have been rendered irrelevant in the new effective environment. In short, the new niche may replace previous multiplicity and diversity with a larger but relatively more homogeneous cultural organization (compared with prior system) that is associated with a considerable shift in the effective environment.

Another feature suggested by the large ethnic areas projected in figure 6.17 is the possible role of intergroup networks as an important initial condition for the rapid adaptive transformation that may have occurred within the LBK region. In support of this assertion I note that the sizes of networks and ethnic areas seem to be related to the scales of mobility and the character of the environments in North American hunter-gatherer analogues.[36]

When I examine the projections based on the hunter-gatherer data that appear in graphs A and B in figure 6.18 and look for characteristics related to mobility that are thought to indicate the extent of social networks in the LBK and northern Balkan areas, some provocative patterns are apparent. Site dates (in uncalibrated ^{14}C determinations) are plotted against two different indicators of mobility: projections of the number of residential moves per year (in graph A) and the total distance, expressed in miles, of all residential moves made in one year (in graph B).

Once again, the LBK and northern Balkan early agro-pastoralist sites are independently distributed, varying between twelve and nineteen projected residential moves per year in graph A while in graph B (the actual distance moved residentially) there are four cases that overlap the distributions from both Greece and the Balto-Scandinavian states: Gornja-Tuzla, a Starčevo tell site in the former Yugoslavia; the two northernmost LBK sites of Eitzum and Stezelce; and Lautereck, the only LBK site that is close to the upland Alpine area. Not surprisingly, all of the sites that overlap other "culture areas" are on the periphery of the

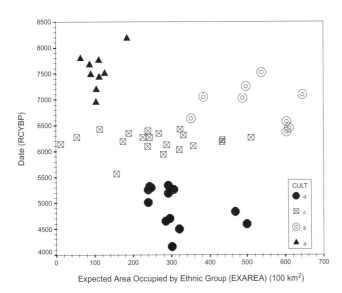

FIGURE 6.17

Dates of the earliest appearance of domesticates in northern Europe displayed relative to the area occupied by an ethnic group projected from ethnographically documented hunter-gatherers to the contemporary environments of western Europe. The marker indicates recognized cultures or cultural regions (CULT): (a) early Greek; (b) Körös, Karanovo I, Starčevo, and Criş–Central European block; (c) linear pottery culture (LBK); and (d) Baltic region sites.

LBK and Körös-Criş distributions. Considerable variability in mobility is projected for hunter-gatherers who might have lived within the distributions of the two culture areas.

Conclusion

In previous chapters, I have described in perhaps greater detail than many will find palatable the steps I have taken to assemble environmental and ethnographic frames of reference that would, I promised, eventually be applied to questions stimulated by archaeological patterning. In this chapter, I have used two of these tools, the Terrestrial Model and a set of projections based on ethnographic data, to approximate the subsistence base, degree of mobility, and ethnic diversity that might have characterized the hunter-gatherer populations preceding agricultural peoples in specific regions of Europe.

As I worked back and forth between the expectations of the model and the archaeological record, I demonstrated that what could have been an area populated by hunter-gatherer groups of considerable ethnic diversity became, in the Neolithic era, a culture area of considerable internal homogeneity. In addition, mobility values for hunter-gatherers in what would later be called the LBK and Körös-Criş culture areas are projected to be dramatically high, although archaeological evidence indicates that the LBK and Körös-Criş sites are almost, if not totally, sedentary settlements.

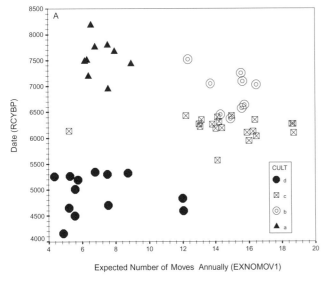
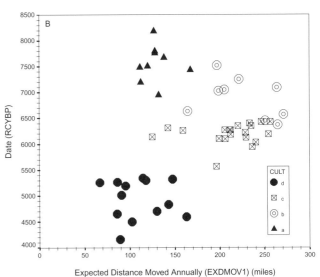

FIGURE 6.18

Comparative graphs showing the number of residential moves per year (A) and the total miles moved among residential sites on an annual basis (B) projected from ethnographically documented hunter-gatherers to the contemporary environments of western Europe. Both distributions are displayed against the dates for the first appearance of domesticates. The marker indicates recognized cultures or cultural regions (CULT): (a) early Greek; (b) Körös, Karanovo I, Starčevo, and Criş-Central European block; (c) linear pottery culture (LBK); and (d) Baltic region sites.

The absence during the Mesolithic era of any evidence of intensification in the LBK region and much of the Körös-Criş area also supports a diagnosis of rapid and dramatic systemic change. Ironically, however, the possibility of migration is not rendered any less likely by the patterns that the frames of reference have allowed us to see because there are no definitive recognition criteria that one might look for either in the archaeological record or in first- and second-order derivative patterning revealed by the frames of reference.

Unfortunately, I cannot solve in this chapter the problem posed by the LBK patterning in the archaeological record. I can, however, allow myself to be excited by the new kinds of patterning that the frames of reference have made possible and the new ways of looking at old data that implicate processes of emergence and patterns of system growth that are not simply the result of abrupt or accumulative changes. I hope that using the two projective frames of reference to study such simple features of the archaeological record as the age of sites and their "culture area" classification has suggested other trajectories of comparative research that could be investigated, provided more detailed information was available from relevant sites.

Of interest would be the archaeological evidence of a site's aquatic resource and terrestrial faunal content, variability in lithic assemblage content, the size of structures and settlements, settlement plans, and forms of mortuary practice, to name only a few categories of data. Similarly, variability in the density and character of Mesolithic sites located between early Neolithic culture areas could be profitably studied. It would also be interesting to determine if the density of Mesolithic sites varies in any regular way with differences in projected mobility based on my ethnographic frame of reference. Does the content of Mesolithic sites vary with the projections and subsequent rates of change documented among the early Neolithic sites in similar places? If so, we might begin to see the way that initial conditions influenced the direction of subsequent changes in local sequences.

"Seeing the past" is merely a figure of speech for those archaeologists who appreciate that there are no remnant dynamic processes observable in the deposits that they excavate. "Knowing the past" is, however, a realizable goal, provided that archaeologists devise and implement the kinds of analytical tools that I have been outlining in this book. In the aggregate, these intellectual tools can be thought of as constituting an *archaeoscope,*[37] a device that provides us with a range of secure knowledge about observable dynamics that can be used to examine the data from the past.

In chapter 7, I will continue to enlarge the purview of my archaeoscope by returning once again to a reexamination of the ethnographically documented hunter-gatherer data set. My goal this time will be to understand some of the patterning related to indicators of intensification and to see if I can determine what factors may pressure foragers to intensify.

Recognizing Patterns and Generalizing about What the World Is Like

The Transition from Pattern Recognition to Theory Building

In this part of the book, readers come face-to-face with the interesting problem of "what is the world of hunter-gatherers like?" Asking this question is a fundamental precondition for considering another query: "why is the world the way it appears to be?" The currency in terms of which each of these two questions is asked must be the same, but they must be answered using independently reasoned arguments.

The problem under investigation must be understood in the same terms as the answer is framed. If the problem arises in one domain and the answer is offered in another, then the linkage between the two domains may be unclear. The flaw in so many of the so-called theories of the social sciences lies in the linkage between the phenomena said to be explained and a postulated explanation that is usually based upon human agency.

Twenty-One Generalizations in Search of a Theory

I have used various metaphors in this book to illustrate the similarities between my intellectual modus operandi and the structure and presentation of theatrical productions. Now I extend the figure of speech to include the overall structure of this book, which has a lot in common with a contemporary, three-act drama. The first act of most plays is designed to orient the audience in time and space and to introduce the characters and themes that will be explored in dramatic form. In similar fashion, chapters 1–3 of this book form an introductory unit in which I review the history of hunter-gatherer studies, present my generic "human actor" and advance an argument about the role he or she plays in the events occurring in habitats and niches, and introduce the intellectual tools that I use initially in the play of ideas.

My metaphorical act 2 began in chapter 4 with a discussion of the environmental frame of reference I have used to examine some of the properties of the ecological theaters within which evolutionary plays involving human actors have occurred. In chapter 5, I explored how an environmental frame of reference can isolate the relationships between hunter-gatherer variability and environmental variables. When these relationships were robust, I demonstrated how both proportional and relational projections of hunter-gatherer variability could be applied to the entire earth and used as a baseline for comparisons with other kinds of data. Act 2 concluded with chapter 6, in which I developed the Terrestrial Model of human hunting and gathering—another basic construct to which I could compare either ethnographic or archaeological variability.

As this chapter begins, the curtain has just opened on act 3, the unit in which the dramatic action begun in the preceding acts reaches its logical conclusion. In the play of ideas in the scientific theater, this is the point at which the patterns that have been generated by projecting data against frames of reference—and the relationships that have been identified between the variables—are summarized in general statements describing *the way that the world appears to be*. The generalizations I present synthesize the patterns demonstrable

in the ethnographic and environmental data sets, so "the world," in this instance, refers to hunter-gatherers in their ecological and social contexts.

In this chapter, I describe how sets of variables relating to hunter-gatherer group size and dependency ratios behave in relation to mobility and labor organization, and how these variables may be distributed in scalar fashion when instruments for measurement are developed comparing them with some relevant standard. I begin by asking the following questions: what has been accomplished by studying ethnographic and environmental data at a global scale, by generating property space patterning, and by developing the Terrestrial Model and the projections from the hunter-gatherer data base? And what is the relationship of all of the foregoing to archaeological data? These are complex questions, and to deal with them I start by referring to figure 5.14, graphs A and B, which revealed the following patterns:

Generalization 7.01

When the variable referred to as size of the area occupied by an ethnic group was projected from the hunter-gatherer data set to the entire earth, it was correlated with environmental and geographic boundaries without apparent regard for the level of sociopolitical complexity. Small ethnic areas were usually situated in high-productivity tropical and subtropical settings, as well as in a spotty distribution across moderately dry settings. The latter cases, however, were dependent upon aquatic resources, in contrast to their neighbors, who were primarily dependent upon terrestrial plants.

Generalization 7.02

The largest ethnic areas occurred in regions in which subsistence was predominantly based on hunting, but ethnic areas of almost comparable size were found in very dry settings inhabited by highly mobile, plant-dependent peoples.

Much more information than simply the relationship between the size of an ethnic area and the many environmental variables in the data set was encoded in the equations from which generalizations 7.01 and 7.02 were derived. In order to detect some of these other relationships, I projected the data against a spatial frame of reference—in this case, geography at a global scale—and produced second-order derivative patterning. Patterns at this scale may take a variety of forms, limited only by one's imagination and ability to project complex observations against relevant, knowledge-laden frames of reference. For example, in chapter 6 I compressed the projected global data into a nominal classification of primary food sources and produced a cross-tabulation of frequencies comparing the Terrestrial Model and the ethnographic projections at the same places (table 6.05). These comparisons produced patterns that can be summarized as follows:

Generalization 7.03

Among ethnographic cases in Africa and South America that were projected by the Terrestrial Model to be primarily dependent upon terrestrial plants, 75.6 percent remained plant dependent while 21.4 percent shifted to aquatic resources. In projections from the ethnographic data set, however, only 3.0 percent shifted to terrestrial animals. In Europe, projections from the ethnographic data set revealed that only 10.7 percent remained plant dependent, 78.6 percent shifted to aquatic resources, and 10.7 percent shifted to hunting terrestrial animals.

In discussing the preceding comparisons, I claimed that differences between the projections from the Terrestrial Model and those produced by the ethnographic data set were due to system state differences resulting primarily from processes of intensification, by which I mean tactical or strategic practices that tend to increase the exploitation of resources in circumscribed or shrinking food patches. When Europe is compared with Africa and South America, there is a clear contrast in intensificational indicators, although a similar set of trends occurs in both places. The following observations are therefore justified:

Generalization 7.04

If intensification is indicated by a shift in exploitation from one type of biotic community to another, the shift will usually be to aquatic resources and rarely, if ever, to terrestrial animals. Of the biotic communities exploited by nonintensified hunter-gatherers, only terrestrial plants appear to offer much potential for intensification.

Generalization 7.04a

Furthermore, when projections were made using the ethnographic data base, for those cases projected by the Terrestrial Model to be predominantly dependent upon terrestrial animals, 4.8 percent of the African and South American groups remained animal dependent, 73.5 percent shifted to plant resources, and 21.7 percent shifted to aquatic resources. In projections from the ethnographic data set, 63.1 percent of the European cases remained animal dependent, no cases shifted to plant resources, and 36 percent had become dependent upon aquatic resources.

Generalization 7.04b

For cases in Africa and South America projected by the Terrestrial Model to exploit a mixed suite of trophically different food sources, projections from the ethnographic data indicated that 72.9 percent shifted to plant resources, only 12.5 percent shifted to terrestrial animals, and the remaining 14.6 percent shifted to aquatic resources. In Europe, on the other hand, projections from the ethnographic data indicated that no cases shifted to plant resources, whereas 36 percent shifted to exploitation of terrestrial animals and 63.5 percent were predominantly dependent on aquatic resources.

All of the details in the preceding two generalizations can be summarized in the following comprehensive statement:

Generalization 7.05

In environments in which the resource mix permits intensification, the preferred strategy of human actors experiencing subsistence stress will be increased dependence upon terrestrial plants. Human dependence upon aquatic resources occurs either as a supplement to a plant-based strategy or as the primary strategy in environments that prohibit plant-based subsistence options.

Considered as a unit, the preceding generalizations imply a set of relationships between subsistence, biotic geography, the size of ethnic groups and the areas they exploit, and intensificational processes in general. In spite of these encouraging results, however, before I can proceed with theory building itself, I must address the issue of accuracy in the hunter-gatherer data base on which my projections have been based. It would, after all, be folly to develop tactics to explain the way the world appears to be and then discover that I have been misled by appearances that are ambiguous or inaccurate. For this reason, I continue to explore the variability in subsistence, mobility, size of ethnic area, and size of ethnic units documented in the ethnographic data base, but I am also on the lookout both for errors in the data base and for additional system state indicators to use in my analysis of information in the data base.

I also want to evaluate my suggestion in chapter 6 that projections from the ethnographic data do, in fact, reflect considerable system state variability among the cases making up the hunter-gatherer data base. And, because it is my belief that processes of intensification are largely responsible for the differences in system states that have been implied by the pattern recognition work I have already conducted, I must first attempt to isolate reliable diagnostic criteria for measuring system state variability itself.

Recognizing System State Variability

A discussion of system state changes and the diagnostic criteria used to recognize them flows logically from my earlier consideration of the problem of *niche,* which was introduced in chapter 2 with the simple question: *what niche do human actors occupy in ecosystems?* My response was that— in contrast to most other species, which occupy only one or, at most, a very limited range of niches—human beings are capable of exploiting an astonishingly diverse range of articulations with the environment. In nonhuman species, changes in niche are usually accompanied by the emergence of a new species and are effected by changes in the morphological and physiological properties that equip the species to compete with both conspecifics and other species. Analogously, in order to identify what might be called the *niche state* of human cultural systems, I need to be able to recognize a change in the organizational properties of the cultural system, together with shifts in such a system's effective environment, even though the biological structure of the human participants remains the same.

With regard to the fundamental problem of recognizing system boundaries, as I have previously observed, "one way of thinking about theories is to consider them as a kind of definition of a natural system. Such a 'definition' consists of the laws and particular theoretical terms that specify how the system works. Systems that work in fundamentally different ways from the theoretical specifications of one theory require theories differing in their 'rules' of dynamics" (Binford 1983:214).

In other words, one theory may be required for treating variability among organizationally similar systems while a different theory would be required to explain variability among cases belonging to a different type of system. Additionally, a different order of theory is required for explaining how systems of one form are transformed into organizationally very different forms. "Part of our job as scientists is to identify systems characterized by fundamentally different determinant and conditioning properties" (Binford 1983:214).

Attempts to deal with this issue have stimulated an important, although controversial, literature in anthropology. For instance, Julian Steward's (1949) seminal article "Culture, Causality, and Law: A Trial Formulation of the Development of Early Civilizations" and his essay "Evolution and Process" (Steward 1953) dealt with some aspects of the issue introduced here.[1] As Steward noted, "Hunting and gathering . . . is far too broad a category. The functional relations and cultural-ecological adaptations which led to a patrilineal band, consisting of a localized lineage, were very different from those which produced a nomadic, bilateral band composed of many unrelated families" (1953:322).

If Steward was correct in surmising that patrilineal and bilateral bands represented distinct systems organizationally, it becomes important to know whether similar shifts in environmental variables would result in convergent or further divergent changes between patrilineal and bilateral bands. This would depend upon another major factor affecting the vectors of systemic change: the nature of initial system state conditions. In order to evaluate Steward's assertion that patrilineal and bilateral bands developed from very different "cultural-ecological adaptations," one would need to have reliable diagnostic indicators of a system's initial conditions and its current state.

In chapter 6, I noted that a knowledge of initial conditions is particularly important when one uses an atemporal sample of hunter-gatherer systems as the basis for making projections.[2] One attribute of science is a concern for the recognition of system boundaries, and it is important to remember that relationships among variables in dynamic and organizational terms may be different in different system states.

Because a major source of variability within the sample of hunter-gatherers is likely to be referable to system state differences, I expect attempts at correlational analysis to yield diverse results as a consequence of using cases that differ from one another in terms of their scale of complexity relative to environmental conditions. Other factors affecting the outcome of correlational analysis include using cases that have developed from different sets of prior initial conditions or that started with similar initial conditions but now vary in a scalar way with habitat differences, as I demonstrated by pointing out the variability within the Terrestrial Model. Other researches have recognized the validity of Steward's (1953:322) injunction against lumping cultural units into one broad "hunting and gathering" category and have dealt with system state differences by creating more discriminating classifications based on differences in sociopolitical organization. Two well-known typologies identify social units either as bands, tribes, chiefdoms, and states (Service 1962) or as egalitarian, ranked, stratified, and state-level systems (Fried 1967).

These and other sociocultural types are envisioned as "natural kinds" (Quine 1991:164), although the criteria of similarity usually apply only to the dimension of organizational complexity. When other criteria are applied to a broader suite of formal properties, particularly to design elements reflected in material culture, the result is a classification of entities referred to as *cultures,* and the list is endless (Anasazi, Mississippian, Natufian, Mousterian, Lungshan, Prepottery Neolithic A, Aztec, Inka, and so forth). The difference between typologies based on "natural kinds" and those grouped in terms of similar design elements resembles the distinction by Sahlins (1960) between "specific" and "general" evolution.

Specific evolution was identified with adaptation, or the process of "securing and conserving control over environment" (Harding 1960:47). When it is compared with the terminology and arguments made in this book, it could be said that specific evolution refers to the processes underlying the variability observable in the Terrestrial Model. General evolution, on the other hand, applies to the concept of culture as an open system and embraces relationships both to nature and to other cultural systems (Harding 1960:47). According to Sahlins, general evolution led the "passage from less to greater energy exploitation, lower to higher levels of integration, and less to greater all-around adaptability" (1960:22). Both specific and general evolutionary taxonomies were based on the assumption of the existence of natural kinds (Kornblith 1993; Quine 1991).

The concept of natural kinds of cultural systems is not incompatible per se with the differentiation represented by the identification of either niche differences or distinct biological organisms. I do not, however, consider that creating a scale of progressively more complex systemic organization (Carneiro 1973; Carneiro and Tobias 1963) produces the kind of information needed to recognize such sociocultural natural kinds. Although it is conceivable that systems at different levels of complexity, measured by attributes such as the presence or absence of roads, can belong to the same category of "natural kind" in terms of organization, it is equally conceivable that systems belonging to roughly similar levels of complexity could be organized quite differently. Given the uncertainty in my understanding of what criteria to use in recognizing important differences in system state, I arbitrarily choose to focus in this chapter on differences in subsistence base—in other words, where food comes from when viewed from an ecological perspective—exhibited by the hunter-gatherer groups in my ethnographic data base.

In the search for system state indicators, I will also be alert to cross-cultural differences that appear to vary with subsistence base. This focus is warranted by the demonstrable organizational repercussions that such shifts as a heavy dependence upon domesticated plants and animals have

signaled. These differences will be explored as potentially variable initial conditions that could influence the appearance of changed organizational forms with different evolutionary potential in punctuated evolutionary events, resulting in restructured organizational forms of greater complexity. In other words, I must investigate the possibility that some theories may be useful in explaining variability among some systems while other theories may be needed to address variability in systems of diverse kinds.

Since the recognition of natural kinds is an empirical issue, the ability to recognize different system states must be built into the tools that are used for pattern recognition work. I must also develop the ability to assess whether these differences refer to the relationships among a common set of variables of differing values or whether the variability exists between systems whose different variables are linked in ways affecting the differences I observe. This is what is meant by the challenge of learning: when the organizational rules of natural variability change, different theories are required to explain the resulting patterns. The issue becomes how many and what "other things" are justifiably considered "equal" when an exploratory pattern recognition study is undertaken or when an explanatory argument about variability is attempted.

My previous discussions of projection and the adequacy of the hunter-gatherer sample have not seriously addressed the probability that the sample includes many systems that are engaged in either similar or different evolutionary trajectories but occupy relatively similar habitats, when viewed strictly from the perspective of the environmental variables introduced thus far. At this point, how might system state be held constant as I examine the factors affecting the diverse sources of variability referring exclusively to differences among the ecological theaters within which evolutionary plays are produced? I pursue the answer to this question in this and subsequent chapters, but in the meantime I need to illustrate the character of the problem with an example that will underscore the important role that system state plays in the design of the samples to be used as the basis of projections, depending upon the questions I seek to address.

Exploring System State Variability among Ethnographically Documented Hunter-Gatherers

In chapter 6, the pattern recognition search was focused on the contrasting configurations of projections from both the Terrestrial Model and the hunter-gatherer data set. Because my goal in this chapter is to identify diagnostic patterning indicative of system state variability, I confine my examination to the relationships among the variables recorded for the 339 hunter-gatherer cases within the ethnographic data set.

I noted in chapter 1 that Julian Steward believed that group size had an important effect on the organizational form assumed by social units and that his distinction between lineal and composite bands was based in part upon this key criterion. Steward also believed that at least some of the differences in hunter-gatherer group size were related to such subsistence activities as the exploitation of herd mammals.

I also pointed out that other researchers believed that what was termed a group's *acculturative state* accounted for organizational diversity among hunter-gatherer groups, particularly the Shoshoni speakers of the Great Basin of North America, about whom Steward (1938:260) was the researcher of record. Other researchers cited a group's scale of mobility as a major indicator of system state, with the result that sedentary hunter-gatherers were frequently considered to be very different systemically from more mobile groups.

I thought that it might be useful to compare hunter-gatherer groups in terms of a set of coded properties relating to group size that, when applied to my data set, identified three separate "kinds" of groups: (1) the designation GROUP1 refers to the mean size of the social unit camping together during the *most dispersed* phase of the settlement-subsistence system; (2) GROUP2 refers to the mean size of the camp-sharing groups during the *most aggregated* phase of the subsistence settlement system; (3) GROUP3 designates the mean size of social aggregations occurring *annually or every several years* that assemble for other reasons than strictly subsistence-related activities.

Groups in these three categories were assigned a value for each of three coded system state indicators. The first indicator is the variable SUBSP, which identifies the primary source of food in the diet (terrestrial plants are signified by 1, terrestrial animals are coded 2, and aquatic resources have a code of 3). The variable GRPPAT refers to mobility and distinguishes between those cases for which settlement mobility is a major tactic used in the annual subsistence round (GRPPAT = 1) and groups maintaining at least semisedentary settlements that do not move as part of a group's positioning strategy throughout the year and from which subsistence activities are launched (GRPPAT = 2). Finally, the coded variable SUBPOP refers to a group's acculturative state: those that obtained their food exclusively from hunting and gathering activities at the time of ethnographic observation have been given a SUBPOP code of n. If, on the other hand, group members were working as wage laborers, or procuring forest products and exchanging them for agricultural products, or actually practicing agriculture, a SUBPOP code of x was recorded, and the cases are referred to as "suspect."

My comparison also includes data summarizing the mean value of the total population attributed to the ethnic group and summarized as "a case" (TLPOP); the size of the geo-

graphic region reported to be controlled by the ethnic group, recorded in units of 100 square kilometers (AREA); and the derivative ratio of TLPOP divided by AREA, which is a measure of population density (DENSITY). My first assessment of the variability related to system state differences is presented in table 7.01 and directs our attention to some basic demographic and spatial facts about the hunter-gatherer groups in the data set. I summarize the most striking features of this table in the following five generalizations.

--- *Generalization 7.06* ---

In all comparisons among nonsuspect cases (SUBPOP = n), there is a dramatic increase in the size of the ethnic group among sedentary peoples relative to their mobile analogues, except for those that are dependent upon terrestrial animals.

--- *Generalization 7.07* ---

In all comparisons among nonsuspect cases (SUBPOP = n), there is a dramatic decrease in the size of the area occupied by all sedentary peoples relative to that occupied by mobile peoples.

The figures in table 7.01 reveal several other interesting differences among the cases in the hunter-gatherer data set. For instance, sedentary gatherers exploit approximately one-third of the area that is required by mobile peoples who are predominantly dependent upon terrestrial plants. Correspondingly, sedentary peoples predominantly dependent upon aquatic resources are controlling only one-fourth of the area needed by mobile peoples who depend upon aquatic resources. Very different proportions result from a comparison of the numbers of persons included in an ethnic group. Groups designated as "gatherers" support 3.4 sedentary persons for every mobile person in 31 percent of the geographic area required by mobile peoples. Groups in the "fishers" category support 2.02 sedentary persons for every one supported among nonsedentary fishers in 27.0 percent of the geographic area needed by mobile peoples. The following generalization summarizes these observations:

--- *Generalization 7.08* ---

Tactically mobile and sedentary hunter-gatherer groups differ in two of the dimensions being compared in table 7.01. A larger number of people are integrated in a given sedentary ethnic unit and, even more importantly, there is a reduction in the size of the area controlled by the demographically larger sedentary groups.

Both of these conditions merge in the derived ratio of population density, one striking feature of which is the contrast

TABLE 7.01

COMPARISON OF DEMOGRAPHIC AND AREAL DATA SEGREGATING
THE HUNTER-GATHERER DATA SET BY SUBSISTENCE,
MOBILITY PATTERN, AND ACCULTURATIVE STATE

SUBPOP	GRPPAT	TERRESTRIAL PLANTS	TERRESTRIAL ANIMALS	AQUATIC RESOURCES
		Total population (TLPOP) recorded for a given ethnic group		
n	1	764.0 ± 803.6 (81)	*1,664.4 ± 2,057.4 (71)*	1,478.8 ± 1,447.4 (43)
	2	*2,613.2 ± 1,757.4 (18)*	76.0 (01)	*2,990.9 ± 3,407.3 (71)*
x	1	*1,575.5 ± 2,444.7 (30)*	124.6 ± 90.4 (05)	495.0 ± 658.6 (05)
	2	972.1 ± 973.2 (13)	—	400.0 (01)
		Total area (AREA) claimed by a given ethnic group		
n	1	179.6 ± 233.8 (81)	*1,012.0 ± 1,370.7 (71)*	541.8 ± 1,034.9 (43)
	2	55.8 ± 58.9 (18)	24.6 (01)	*146.9 ± 231.1 (71)*
x	1	*312.9 ± 524.3 (30)*	34.9 ± 24.8 (05)	24.0 ± 28.3 (05)
	2	72.1 ± 122.6 (12)	—	5.5 (01)
		Number of persons per 100 square kilometers (DENSITY)		
n	1	10.5 ± 10.7 (81)	3.4 ± 4.1 (71)	*17.9 ± 17.7 (43)*
	2	*82.7 ± 68.1 (18)*	3.09 (01)	48.8 ± 45.7 (70)
x	1	21.5 ± 22.8 (31)	3.8 ± 1.6 (05)	*28.4 ± 14.8 (05)*
	2	48.5 ± 33.2 (13)	—	*72.7 (01)*

Note: Underlined values are the highest value in the row; *italics* indicate highest value in GRPPAT comparisons among sets with identical values, e.g., 1 or 2 in a column.

in ordination between the mobile and sedentary cases when food is obtained from different trophic or biotic sources:

Generalization 7.09

Those mobile peoples dependent upon terrestrial animals have the lowest population densities, 3.4 persons per 100 square kilometers, compared with 10.5 persons for mobile plant exploiters and 17.9 persons for mobile groups exploiting aquatic resources.

Examination of the cases classified as sedentary, however, reveals marked contrasts when compared with mobile peoples:

Generalization 7.10

With only one exception, groups exploiting terrestrial plants and aquatic resources are characterized by a reversed ordination in population density, with 48.8 persons per 100 square kilometers for groups classified as fishers and 82.7 persons for terrestrial plant users.

These contrasts suggest that in those circumstances in which it becomes necessary to pursue tactics or strategies designed to increase the amount of food obtainable from a given geographic area, the greatest intensificational potential lies with terrestrial plants. Among peoples who are at least still somewhat mobile, however, aquatic resources offer the greatest return from intensificational strategies. Support for the correlation between sedentism and increased dependence upon terrestrial plants comes from the archaeological record of the Near East, where there is considerable evidence for the argument that the domestication of plants occurred in the context of dramatically reduced mobility (Bar-Yosef and Meadow 1995). I also note that the preceding observations support the comparable patterning produced by both the Terrestrial Model and the projected ethnographic data when different continents were compared.

With these generalizations in mind, I now turn to the cases classified as suspect and coded *x* in table 7.01, which represent hunter-gatherer societies living in close association with one another at the time of colonial contact. Except for cases that are predominantly dependent upon terrestrial plants, it is clear that population levels are greatly reduced compared with the cases that appear to have been relatively unexposed to other complex systems. The exceptional cases (SUBPOP = *x*) in the category of peoples dependent upon terrestrial plant resources and designated "nonsedentary" either were practicing agriculture at the time of ethnographic description (e.g., the Chenchu of India, the Pinatubo Ayta of the Phillippines, the Cahuilla of southern California) or represent groups considered suspect because of the extraordinarily high population estimates assigned to them by local researchers (e.g., some northern California cases).

Naturally, I am curious about the organizational dynamics underlying the data summarized in table 7.01. Why should sedentary ethnic groups have more people, on average, and at the same time control two-thirds less land compared with the area controlled by smaller but more mobile ethnic units? I also want to know why, when population levels are increasing within a mobile ethnic unit, the geographic area controlled by such a unit is simultaneously decreasing. Unfortunately, the summary means in table 7.01 represent gross estimates at best, and I am unable to answer these questions because I do not know how the tabulated variables are distributed with respect to other important variables. It is reasonable, however, to want to know whether the patterns in table 7.01 simply reflect biases in the frequencies of cases in different environmental areas or whether the mobile cases come from one suite of environments and the sedentary ones from another.

In order to explore these possibilities, I classified groups in table 7.02 in terms of their primary food resources and then compared mean population density values. Groups primarily dependent upon terrestrial animal resources, terrestrial plants, and aquatic resources were tabulated independently and grouped by climatic zone (CLIM) and then further partitioned into mobile versus nonmobile cases. This comparison resulted in some interesting patterns:

Generalization 7.11

Of the groups that are predominantly dependent upon terrestrial plant resources, many mobile cases are located in equatorial (11), tropical (23), and subtropical (15) regions. There are, however, only seven sedentary cases (12 percent) in all three regions combined. In warm temperate regions, mobile, plant-dependent groups still outnumber sedentary cases

TABLE 7.02

POPULATION DENSITY PARTITIONED BY CLIMATIC ZONE, MOBILITY PATTERN, AND PREDOMINANT FOOD SOURCE

CLIM	GRPPAT	TERRESTRIAL PLANTS	TERRESTRIAL ANIMALS	AQUATIC RESOURCES
		The polar region (CLIM = 1)		
1	1	—	2.9 ± 3.8 (03)	<u>4.1 ± 8.7 (10)</u>
	2	—	—	<u>9.0 ± 6.6 (06)</u>
		The boreal region (CLIM = 2)		
2	1	4.4 ± 4.4 (02)	1.9 ± 1.6 (46)	<u>6.4 ± 5.6 (12)</u>
		22.9 (01)	3.1 (01)	<u>34.8 ± 33.5 (35)</u>
		The cool temperate region (CLIM = 3)		
3	1	3.8 ± 15.2 (24)	5.3 ± 4.3 (18)	<u>21.8 ± 16.9 (10)</u>
	2	<u>100.3 ± 71.8 (13)</u>	—	79.1 ± 51.8 (25)
		The warm temperate region (CLIM = 4)		
4	1	7.6 ± 9.0 (36)	3.3 ± 0.9 (03)	<u>17.2 ± 5.4 (02)</u>
	2	37.9 ± 25.6 (10)	—	<u>64.9 (01)</u>
		The subtropical region (CLIM = 5)		
5	1	10.8 ± 15.6 (15)	3.5 ± (01)	<u>23.6 ± 2.6 (02)</u>
	2	<u>40.8 (01)</u>	—	*38.7 (01)*
		The tropical region (CLIM = 6)		
6	1	21.7 ± 21.3 (23)	8.0 ± 7.5 (03)	<u>36.6 ± 15.2 (12)</u>
	2	<u>*72.90 ± 43.8 (03)*</u>	—	48.0 ± 30.9 (03)
		The equatorial region (CLIM = 7)		
7	1	20.3 ± 12.9 (11)	—	<u>31.7 ± 10.5 (03)</u>
	2	<u>*50.8 ± 37.7 (03)*</u>	—	35.0 ± 8.7 (01)

Note: <u>Underlined</u> values are the highest value in the row; *italics* indicate highest value in GRPPAT comparisons among sets with identical values, e.g., 1 or 2 in a column.

almost 2.5 to 1.0, but 27 percent of the cases are sedentary. Boreal and polar regions are only minimally represented by plant-dependent peoples.

On the other hand, when one looks at the groups that are predominantly dependent upon either hunting or aquatic resources, a very different distribution of cases in terms of climatic zones emerges. It would appear from this exercise that even though there is not a complete segregation in which all of the mobile cases come from one environment and all of the sedentary ones come from another, there is, nevertheless, strong environmental patterning in the relationship between sedentary and mobile state frequencies. This patterning appears to be ecological in character, in that it suggests meaningfully variable initial conditions arising from ecological variability between hunter-gatherer habitats. If my inference is correct, then the factors contributing to increased intensification—indicated here by reduced mobility—appear to proceed very differently depending upon the subsistence strategies being pursued in response to intensificational pressures.

A serendipitous byproduct of exploring the possible bias in the hunter-gatherer data set has been the emergence of provocative patterning identifying unanticipated relationships between variables, such as how group mobility co-varies with the types of food resources exploited. The next generalization and its derivative proposition summarize these results:

Generalization 7.12

In the boreal region, 76.6 percent of the mobile cases exploit primarily terrestrial animals while 96.5 percent of the sedentary cases exploit primarily aquatic resources. In contrast, in tropical and equatorial regions, 69.3 percent of the mobile cases depend primarily upon terrestrial plant foods, while among the small sample of settled peoples, only 60 percent exploit plant foods and 40 percent exploit aquatic resources. There is clearly something different about aquatic resources in cold and warm environments.

Based on these observations, I now propose

Proposition 7.01

In warmer climates, there are two distinct paths leading to settled living, depending upon the type of food resource exploited: intensification based on the use of terrestrial plants and intensification based on the use of aquatic resources. In colder environments, intensification resulting from the exploitation of aquatic resources is the only pathway.

These conclusions about differences in the resource base of settled versus mobile peoples support the picture that emerged from an examination of the projected and modeled data on intensificational pathways summarized in generalization 7.04. I may, therefore, return to earlier observations and ask again if there are any systematic differences in mean total population values between mobile and sedentary hunter-gatherer systems in different environmental settings. In order to answer this question, I prepared table 7.03, in which data on the total population of an ethnic group (TLPOP) and the geographic area it occupies (AREA) are partitioned according to the primary food resource exploited by the group. The tabulation is made in terms of the abundance of water available in an environment relative to potential evapotranspiration (AVWAT), and within each environmental unit cases are tabulated independently for mobile and sedentary settlement patterns (GRPPAT).

The observation that prompted my examination of the relationship between environmental setting and a group's placement on the mobility-sedentism continuum was summarized in generalization 7.08: *A larger number of people are integrated in a given sedentary ethnic unit and, even more importantly, there is a reduction in the size of the area controlled by the demographically larger sedentary groups.* It might therefore be expected that mean ethnic group size should be smaller for the mobile hunter-gatherer cases in the data set. The data in table 7.03 illustrate, however, that there are some environments in which this expectation is not met and, furthermore, that the environmental distribution of the exceptional cases depends on the trophic level of a group's primary source of food.

In order to make this pattern more explicit, I compiled table 7.04, based on the following reasoning: if the expectation is for ethnic unit size to be smaller for groups of mobile peoples than for sedentary peoples, then—when mean mobile ethnic group size is divided by mean sedentary ethnic group size—the value of this ratio should be less than one, given the accuracy of generalization 7.08. Exceptions would, of course, exhibit values greater than one. Since I would also expect that area occupied by an ethnic unit should be smaller for sedentary peoples and larger for mobile peoples, if the mean area values for sedentary peoples are divided by the mean area values for mobile peoples, I would expect the ratio of the mean value of settled peoples divided by the mean value of mobile peoples to be less than one, and that exceptions would likewise be greater than one.

In table 7.04, expected ratios for values of total population and area have been calculated for mobile and sedentary subsets (represented by the variable GRPPAT). The matrix of cells is defined by values of the variables AVWAT—representing an ordinal scale of variability in the amount of water available to the plant community relative to the potential evapotranspiration at the same location—and SUBSP—

TABLE 7.03

TOTAL POPULATION AND AREA OCCUPIED PARTITIONED BY
CLIMATIC ZONE, MOBILITY PATTERN, AND PREDOMINANT FOOD SOURCE

AVWAT	GRPPAT	TERRESTRIAL PLANTS	TERRESTRIAL ANIMALS	AQUATIC RESOURCES
		Total population of ethnic unit (TLPOP)		
		Very dry (AVWAT = 1)		
1	1	363.9 ± 271.3 (13)	—	—
	2	*3,117.5 ± 2,666.4 (04)*	—	—
		Dry (AVWAT = 2)		
2	1	955.9 ± 1,282.3 (46)	*1,627.4 ± 2,304.0 (18)*	1,613.7 ± 1,187.7 (06)
	2	2,460.1 ± 1,631.1 (11)	—	*4,005.0 ± 1,808.9 (05)*
		Moderately dry (AVWAT = 3)		
3	1	1,161.1 ± 965.9 (17)	*1,514.1 ± 993.1 (17)*	650.4 ± 6 43.0 (11)
	2	1,602/8 ± 1,431.2 (06)	—	1,319.2 ± 1,126.2 (15)
		Transitional dry (AVWAT = 4)		
4	1	1,582.3 ± 1,457.2 (04)	*2,267.8 ± 3,264.4 (14)*	680.0 ± 287.1 (03)
	2	—	—	*1,418.8 ± 830.5 (04)*
		Transitional damp (AVWAT = 5)		
5	1	779.2 ± 725.3 (03)	—	*2,180.9 ± 2,495.9 (07)*
	2	*1,893.0 ± 2,074.7 (02)*	—	1,435.2 ± 705.5 (06)
		Damp (AVWAT = 6)		
6	1	598.2 ± 351.9 (05)	*1,975.9 ± 1,566.9 (08)*	1,466.8 ± 1,718.9 (04)
	2	1,034.5 ± 863.4 (02)	—	*2,757.0 ± 3,397.5 (16)*
		Moist (AVWAT = 7)		
7	1	915.2 ± 1,018.5 (10)	997.2 ± 1,304.4 (16)	*1,436.1 ± 1,201.9 (14)*
	2	850 (01)	—	*3,416.1 ± 3,894.6 (13)*
		Wet (AVWAT = 8)		
8	1	1,529.9 ± 3,177.9 (13)	83.0 ± 34.7 (03)	*1,983.3 ± 1,478.5 (03)*
	2	764.4 ± 713.3 (05)	76.0 (01)	*5,394.8 ± 4,822.1 (13)*
		Total area used by ethnic unit (AREA)		
		Very dry (AVWAT = 1)		
1	1	185.5 ± 213.7 (13)	—	—
	2	78.5 ± 69.9 (04)	—	—
		Dry (AVWAT = 2)		
2	1	257.4 ± 287.4 (46)	*1,118.5 ± 1,567.3 (18)*	838.9 ± 1,852.7 (06)
	2	120.4 ± 123.1 (11)	—	89.0 ± 38.0 (05)
		Moderately dry (AVWAT = 3)		
3	1	298.4 ± 594.7 (17)	*1,398.6 ± 1,642.9 (17)*	301.7 ± 651.7 (11)
	2	14.5 ± 10.3 (06)	—	*98.4 ± 165.9 (15)*

(continued)

TABLE 7.03 *(continued)*

AVWAT	GRPPAT	TERRESTRIAL PLANTS		TERRESTRIAL ANIMALS		AQUATIC RESOURCES	
		Transitional dry (AVWAT = 4)					
4	1	*117.5 ± 146.5*	*(04)*	769.4 ± 549.5	(14)	*234.0 ± 374.2*	*(03)*
	2	—		—		153.5 ± 82.0	(04)
		Transitional damp (AVWAT = 5)					
5	1	*364.4 ± 533.8*	*(03)*	—		810.5 ± 1,345.01	(07)
	2	*17.2 ± 19.5*	*(02)*	—		18.8 ± 10.9	(06)
		Damp (AVWAT = 6)					
6	1	*42.2 ± 49.2*	*(05)*	578.4 ± 399.0	(08)	*273.8 ± 312.8*	*(04)*
	2	*13.9 ± 5.7*	*(02)*	—		134.7 ± 283.1	(16)
		Moist (AVWAT = 7)					
7	1	*109.9 ± 166.3*	*(10)*	789.9 ± 1,581.9	(16)	*513.0 ± 908.6*	*(14)*
	2	*16.5*	*(01)*	—		226.4 ± 285.6	(13)
		Wet (AVWAT = 8)					
8	1	*133.9 ± 350.0*	*(13)*	26.8 ± 1.6	(03)	138.2 ± 97.6	(03)
	2	*27.8 ± 35.9*	*(05)*	24.6	(01)	206.9 ± 271.5	(13)

Note: Underlined values are the highest value in the row; *italics* indicate highest value in GRPPAT comparisons among sets with identical values, e.g., 1 or 2 in a column.

a categorical separation of cases according to the trophic level of a group's primary food resources. It is clear in table 7.04 that although the mean values for ethnic group size and area occupied vary among sedentary and mobile peoples in provocative ways, nevertheless when these relationships are examined in cases separated in terms of an ordinal scale of water availability, and by trophic bias in the source of food, there is a contrast in the ways that AREA and TLPOP distribute.

The vast majority of the comparisons between the areas occupied by sedentary and mobile peoples result in values that sustain my generalization that *area decreases markedly with*

TABLE 7.04

RATIOS INDICATING TRENDS IN THE
HUNTER-GATHERER SAMPLE FOR
TOTAL POPULATION AND AREA OCCUPIED

	TLPOP: MOBILE/SEDENTARY			AREA: SEDENTARY/MOBILE		
AVWAT	*Gathering* (1)	*Hunting* (2)	*Fishing* (3)	*Gathering* (4)	*Hunting* (5)	*Fishing* (6)
1	0.12	—	—	0.42	—	—
2	0.39	—	0.40	0.47	—	0.11
3	0.72	—	0.49	0.05	—	0.33
4	—	—	0.48	—	—	0.65
5	0.41	—	1.52	0.05	—	0.02
6	0.58	—	0.53	0.33	—	0.49
7	1.07	—	0.42	0.15	—	0.32
8	2.00	1.09	0.36	0.21	0.91	1.50

sedentism. Only one exceptional value occurs for the variable AREA, and it is found in the aquatic-dependent cell formed by the intersection of column 6 and row 8 in table 7.04. This exceptional cell compares thirteen sedentary cases, all but one from the northwest coast of North America, with only three groups of mobile peoples. Two of the latter cases are the Chono and the Alacaluf, both classic "Canoe Indians" from the west coast of Chile, and the third case is the north coastal Tasmanian group.

These three geographic regions differ dramatically in the topography of their respective coastlines. There is a vast archipelago along the Chilean coast and a moderately large archipelago along the Pacific coast of northwest North America, but the Tasmanian coast lacks a major coastal archipelago. An important difference between the coastal regions of Chile and the Pacific northwest, however, is that many major river systems drain from the interior of the latter region and support major runs of anadromous fish, while along the Chilean coast such river systems are absent, as are anadromous fish. It is also relevant that warfare and competition were common features of the life of the settled and socially more complex societies of the Pacific northwest coast, whereas no such organized competition characterizes the mobile peoples of South America and Tasmania.

An examination of the cases in this comparison suggests that the three mobile groups do not have markedly low values for size of ethnic area. The high value of the ratio results from the large ethnic areas associated with the sedentary peoples of the Pacific northwest coast relative to other sedentary peoples studied here. The question is: why are some of the coastal peoples of the Pacific northwest controlling areas that exceed the size of areas under the control of mobile peoples in roughly comparable rainfall environments?

This question can be placed in a wider context by pointing out that it is possible to identify many sedentary agricultural and industrially based ethnic groups that were much larger than the northwest coastal groups and also controlled larger geographic regions. This knowledge tells us that, at some point and under some conditions, a threshold must be reached that marks a reversal of this trend and that subsequent patterning proceeds in the opposite direction: that is, the size of an ethnic area increases with further intensification. Such a threshold appears to separate most hunter-gatherer systems from the world of larger-scale, more complex, ethnically recognizable systems. Some hunter-gatherer societies, however, have crossed this threshold without becoming non-hunter-gatherers, and the majority are found along the Pacific northwest coast of North America.

I feel that my efforts at pattern recognition have taught me something important about the relationship between the size of an ethnic group's area and its degree of intensification—and perhaps even something about system complexity, too. My conclusion (summarized in generalization 7.08) that, other things being equal, the size of the area occupied by an ethnic group decreases regularly with corresponding decreases in mobility and hence appears to be diagnostic of intensification among hunter-gatherers, is therefore strongly supported by the study of variability among the 339 hunter-gatherer cases in the study population. There are, however, notable exceptions to this regular pattern:

Generalization 7.13

In a very few cases, which differ from the patterns observable in the vast majority of hunter-gatherer groups, increases in the number of persons included in an ethnic group coincide with the acquisition and maintenance of a much larger ethnic area than is customary for mobile hunter-gatherer groups of a similar size. These exceptional groups maintain multiyear residential sites.

I must conclude, therefore, that the generalization stipulating that as the number of persons incorporated into an ethnic group increases the size of the area occupied decreases is not universally applicable. Most of the exceptions come from the northwest coast of North America and include the Nootka, Haida, Chinook, Kwakiutl, Aleut, and Thompson groups. Other cases in this category are the Gabrielino of California, the Calusa of Florida, and the Paraujano of Venezuela. The Calusa and Paraujano are, in fact, the only complex, internally stratified, large-scale hunter-gatherer systems found outside the northern Pacific rim area.

Generalization 7.14

All of the cases in which the more customary inverse relationship between group size and size of ethnic area is reversed can be categorized as socially complex and having organizational properties that justify their designation as "complex hunter-gatherers" (Price and Brown 1985; Burch and Ellanna 1994; Kelly 1995:293–331).

I believe that I can now reasonably argue that my pattern recognition studies have isolated at least one possible diagnostic criterion for a major system state boundary within the population of hunter-gatherer cases available for study. Given that most hunter-gatherer systems appear to contract in spatial scale in response to increases in the number of persons participating within the system, one could reason that:

Proposition 7.02

Most hunter-gatherer groups respond to increases in population with a kind of spatial specialization that is accompanied by an increase in the number of systems per unit area and an attendant increase in subsistence diversity and security among systems within a region.

I have noted that the process of intensification, as currently understood, could be underlying the patterns I have identified in my data set. I have also demonstrated that properties relating to intensification differ significantly, depending on what food resources ethnic groups primarily exploit. It is also important to keep in mind that I have developed very provocative equations that allow me to anticipate rather accurately, and in terms of percentages, the different food resources upon which the documented cases of hunter-gatherers in the data set primarily depend.

The data support the view that variability in subsistence practice is strongly related to the type of habitat in which a group is located, and it is therefore reasonable to expect that these differences should be explicable in any comprehensive theory dealing with intensification. If I use the equations to obtain estimates of diagnostic variables, such as the area occupied by an ethnic group, environmentally "corrected" values are obtained for the variable of interest. Other things being equal (particularly error in the data set), differences between the observed and expected values should be informative about system state differences.

Isolating these differences might, in fact, be a more provocative way of identifying cases that represent instances when the rules governing intensification change than the tabulations summarized in tables 7.02 and 7.03 that suggested system changes. Since I have used mean values for subsets within the total population of hunter-gatherer cases, there may well be cases that have not yet been identified but that belong in the set of complex societies that defy the generalizations derived from the majority of the hunter-gatherer cases.

Figure 7.01 was prepared to explore these possibilities using the observed-versus-expected-value approach. The residuals from five equations, derived from the full set of hunter-gatherer cases that best anticipated the size of ethnic areas using environmental variables, were backplotted against density only for cases with a GRPPAT value of 2 (settled or sedentary).[3] I think that the inverse relationship between density and the residuals for AREA has reference to system state variability, since expected values for area are based on relationships to the environment that are determined by differences in subsistence and mobility strategies.

The "exceptional" groups in the Poisson dispersion in figure 7.01 are, without exception, cases for which the observed value far exceeds the expected positive value for the AREA variable (size of ethnic area). Examination of the cases whose uniqueness was absorbed by the mean values used in tables 7.02 and 7.03 permits the addition of the Konaig (group 294), Tlingit (group 292), and Tsimshim (group 289) to the list of cases from the Pacific northwest coast of North America (the Aleut [group 298], Chinook [group 274], Haida [group 290], Kwakiutl [group 288], and Nootka

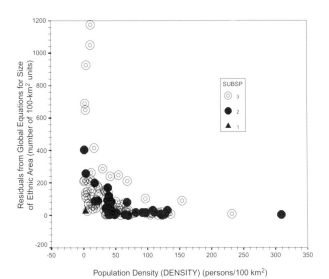

FIGURE 7.01

Demonstration of a Poisson distribution for the residuals from global equations for ethnic area sizes. Marker is dominant sources of foods (SUBSP): (1) terrestrial animals, (2) terrestrial plants, and (3) aquatic resources.

[group 273]), all of which represent a reversal of the pattern of expanding area relative to the total population included in an ethnic group (generalization 7.13).

It is also clear that there is a second set of cases in which reversal of the inverse relationship between the size of the ethnic area and increases in population is not nearly as pronounced—that is, the scale of the reversal is quantitatively less than that among the first group of cases—but this cluster nevertheless belongs in the group of exceptions to the rule. Cases in this second grouping include the Bella-Bella (group 283), Chehalis (group 272), Comox (group 282), Gitksan (group 293), Lillooet (group 276), Thompson (group 325), and Wenatchi (group 317), which are all from the Pacific northwest coast of North America. Also included are the Dorobo (group 70) of east Africa, the Tjapwurong (group 133) of south Australia (who constructed large facilities for catching eels), and the Wintu (group 160) of California. These cases, as well as the Calusa (group 46) and Paraujano (group 35), constitute a set of twenty groups that differ from all other settled hunter-gatherers in the relationship that is maintained between the size of their ethnic area and the number of persons in their ethnic group.

I believe that my examination of the cases included in the "exceptional" cell in table 7.02 provides an important clue to the recognition of system state boundaries, which were anticipated in my introduction to the problem of system state variability. As I have pointed out, "part of our job as scientists is to identify systems characterized by fundamentally different determinant and conditioning properties" (Binford 1983:214). The provocative threshold that has been isolated in patterning derived from the hunter-gatherer data set appears to correspond to differences in system state, but whether this threshold also represents the kind of system boundary that demands a change in the realm of explanatory theory remains to be seen.

I must now redirect attention to the cells in table 7.04 that failed to meet my expectations about the relationship between the total number of persons in an ethnic group and reduced mobility, which was indicated by the contrast between TLPOP values of mobile and sedentary peoples arrayed across a rainfall gradient of environments (AVWAT). For groups primarily obtaining their food from terrestrial plants and animals, the unexpected reduction in group size associated with sedentism occurs only in the wettest habitats (table 7.04, rows 7 and 8, columns 1 and 2). In drier settings, the prevailing pattern consists of larger ethnic units made up of fewer mobile peoples. Wet settings were also the loci of the exceptions to the area reduction generalization. Among plant-dependent peoples, however, increased group size in the mobile groups is producing the inversion in index value.

In the wettest environments, dependence upon terrestrial plants would not be expected to support many persons, and mobility would be expected to be high, given the scattered distribution of potential foods.[4] In these settings, the ratios indicative of reversals in overall trends are exclusively confined to both mobile and sedentary cases whose status at the time of observation was recorded as "suspect" or to groups that were alleged to have been hunter-gatherers in the past but at the time of observation had a different subsistence base and social organization. These facts, together with the very low frequency (23%) of sedentary hunter-gatherers in moist and wet settings, reinforce the view that sedentary peoples are unlikely to be found in circumstances characterized by hunter-gatherers living in an environment of other hunter-gatherers. All of the sedentary groups in this pattern were either mutualists, forest specialists, or peoples who had recently adopted horticulture.

If groups become sedentary in settings in which plant foods are the primarily available wild food, they must concentrate plant production in spatially circumscribed areas, which in its most extreme form is what is meant by horticulture or agriculture. Groups in this category are by definition no longer hunter-gatherers, and most would have been excluded from this study. The cases that *are* included were once hunter-gatherers, but in the context of modernity their subsistence base has been systemically modified, either by the adoption of agriculture or by their integration as mutualists or wage laborers into larger systems, or by their physical resettlement around mission stations.

Why should mutualists and forest product specialists have larger ethnic group sizes than mobile peoples in similar environments?

I conclude that rather than merely remaining exceptions to the generalization, these cases constitute the exceptions that prove the rule. My judgment is supported by the fact that processes leading to intensification could also occur as a result of a group's increased dependence upon aquatic resources, a pattern that, in fact, occurs in table 7.04, row 5, column 3, among peoples in transitional wet habitats who are dependent upon aquatic resources. The population levels of observed sedentary ethnic groups were smaller than those of their mobile analogues in settings with the same rainfall regimes, a finding that is a clear exception to previous generalizations. The expected pattern of larger sedentary ethnic units is found, however, in all other environmental settings in which both mobile and sedentary groups obtain their food primarily from aquatic resources.

It was not initially clear how this exceptional pattern was to be understood, since examination of the contributing cases did not reveal any obviously provocative environmental associations. The single feature that did prove to be important is the coefficient of variation, a parameter that is very high for the mobile cases and very low for the sedentary cases. In table 7.04, the cell formed by the intersection of row 5 and column 3 has a mean value of 2,180.9 persons per ethnic group for mobile cases, with the contributing cases clearly distributed in two distinct sets. Cases with more than 2,700 persons include the Baffin Island Inuit, the Karankawa of the Texas coast, and the West Greenland Inuit, while the Kaurareg, Polar Inuit, Pume, and Coast Yuki have group sizes of fewer than 750 persons.

The mean value of this cell is being inflated by the two Eskimo cases, which could better be described as macroregional populations rather than ethnic groups, and by the Karankawa, about whom not much is known. Examination of the cases from the same cell that are classified as sedentary reveals a different pattern. Only one case (the Lummi) has a TLPOP value of less than 750, while values for the remaining five cases (the Hupa, Karok, Squamish, Tolowa, and Wiyot) are over 1,000 persons. These values indicate at least a bimodal distribution in size of ethnic group, and there is a bias in favor of expected large group size in spite of the inflation of the mean by the inclusion of large regional groups of Inuit in the mobile group category.

These observations prompt me to reconsider the problems encountered when units of different sizes are considered as equals in this classification of ethnic groups.[5]

———————— *Generalization 7.15* ————————

Groups differing from one another in a number of different respects are being classified as similar units in the tabulations—derived from ethnographic data—of total population size and other properties.

For example, the name *Heta* has been given to a local group of fewer than fifty persons while the designation *Baffin Island Inuit* includes all of the people living on Baffin Island. Between these extremes are found some cases whose commonality is based on sharing a linguistic dialect or others who represent regional segments of a language group, while still other cases are discrete sociopolitical units, such as the Calusa and Paraujano.

Good science demands that generalizations and descriptions have an unambiguous referent, which in practical terms usually means a well-defined class or category of phenomena. Unfortunately, I can see no way of ensuring that all of the hunter-gatherer cases in my data base represent the same kind of unit. It may also be true that ethnicity itself is organized differently by peoples who live in organizationally different systems. If this is so, then the defining characteristics of a classification such as *ethnic unit* must be considered variables—organizationally speaking—rather than taken together to define an analytical unit or category in terms of which variability in other properties may be studied.

I believe the solution to the conflict between the exigencies of good science and the inclusion in the data base of some incomparable entities in my classification of so-called ethnic units may lie with the variable *population density*. Because population density is a ratio defined as the number of persons within the boundaries of a geographic unit of specified size, the count of persons and the area occupied is standardized and therefore comparable, regardless of the organizing principle used to identify the social unit occupying a spatial unit.

In table 7.02, I compared the population density levels of both mobile and sedentary peoples against the background of a classification of the climatic conditions of the earth. This comparison revealed that, in all climatic zones for which both sedentary and mobile peoples were available for comparison, higher population densities were found among the sedentary peoples regardless of food sources. This observation lends support to the previous correlations noted between the reduction in the total area occupied by an "ethnic group," an associated increase in the numbers of persons included in the "ethnic group," and reductions in mobility leading to sedentary settlement patterns.

Of the generalizations derived thus far from the patterns produced by analysis of the 339 cases in the hunter-gatherer data set, generalizations 7.06 and 7.07 appear the most provocative. Taken together, they claim that, other things being

equal, there is a twofold difference between tactically mobile and more stationary hunter-gatherers who live among, and are articulated primarily with, other hunter-gatherers. First, more people are included in an ethnic unit, and, even more importantly, there is a reduction in the size of the area controlled by these enlarging ethnic groups. When these observations are related to others first introduced in chapter 6, a clue emerges about how subsistence behavior changes relative to intensificational processes:

———————— *Generalization 7.16* ————————

Groups of sedentary persons who are dependent upon terrestrial animals for subsistence are very rare indeed. In fact, it could be argued that, based on the available data, it is not likely that any cases of sedentary persons who are predominantly dependent upon undomesticated terrestrial animals would occur.

———————— *Proposition 7.03* ————————

Any conditions that contribute to a reduction in area and increased ethnic group numbers will favor a shift in subsistence strategies and an accompanying reduction in dependence upon terrestrial animals.

Given what I think is secure knowledge, it is reasonable to suggest that if selective forces (such as a reduction in the area needed to sustain a group) are favoring intensification of production, there may be a progression in resource exploitation down the trophic scale in the direction of lower-level resources. In such a successional sequence, other things being equal, hunter-gatherers would shift from terrestrial animals to aquatic resources to, finally, terrestrial plants in settings in which each of these options is feasible. In settings in which some constraint renders impossible one or more options, other trajectories may be expected. In environments such as much of the arctic, in which the Terrestrial Model suggested that dependence upon terrestrial animals is not feasible, the only option for successful human occupation of such an environment is either dependence upon aquatic resources or perhaps some combination of aquatic resource exploitation augmented by hunting terrestrial animals.

If none of the preceding options is unavailable to human groups, the data from north Asia demonstrate that the only subsistence alternative is to shift to domesticated animals. In plant communities such as the boreal or other northern forests, the exploitation of terrestrial animals will support only minimal population levels and intensification is likely to occur primarily through a major shift to increased exploitation of aquatic resources. In warm temperate and equatorial settings, intensification will occur as the end product of the sequence of changes in trophic level that I originally described.

I have also identified another event sequence that can result in changes in mobility and subsistence base. In generalization 7.08, I noted that, as reductions in a group's mobility occurred, there was an associated reduction in the size of the area it occupied. At the same time, I noted an increase in the numbers of persons included within the group. This pattern persisted when the relationships between mobility and group size were examined relative to environmental variables such as temperature and rainfall (tables 7.02 and 7.03). There were, however, significant exceptions to generalization 7.08. In three of the five exceptional cells in table 7.04, the reversal of the relationship between group size and the area occupied by the group was understandable when it was learned that all of the sedentary cases were classified as "suspect" (SUB-POP = x). Such a designation indicates that the cases appeared to have been strongly conditioned by more complex, non-hunter-gatherer systems in the region.

I would argue that the suspect cases reflect the consequences of life in the colonial era, during which documentary evidence records many instances of massive decreases in population and displacement of local peoples. Colonial administrations also encouraged native peoples to settle at newly established missions and towns, where they were pressed into wage-based labor. Any or all of these factors would be expected to reduce the size of the area exploited by still-mobile peoples and to affect the size of already sedentary populations. For peoples dependent upon aquatic resources, however, the picture is a more complex.

——————— *Generalization 7.17* ———————

Under some conditions, sedentism is associated with a reduction in the area controlled by an ethnic group, whereas in other situations—which appear to be related to success in warfare or alliance building—the area controlled by an ethnic group enlarges as intensification increases.

It should be stressed that, at some point, the preceding trends must reverse themselves, since larger ethnic group sizes and control over larger areas are demonstrable in many systems with clearly identified hunter-gatherer antecedents. In answer to the question of what factors condition a reversal of the patterning seen among mobile hunter-gatherers, so far my analysis has allowed me only to suggest that warfare and sociopolitical complexity appear correlated with hunter-gatherer groups that also appear to be operating from an expansionist imperative.

It is also important to keep in mind that more research must be devoted to the cases isolated in table 7.04 that indicate there is something strange about mutualists and forest product specialists (problem 7.01). These groups have larger

ethnic units than expected and are heavily concentrated in wet environments. At this juncture, however, a better perspective on the issues of area utilized and ethnic group size can be obtained from anthropologists who have already wrestled with causality in this domain.

Relating Our Observations and Generalizations to Arguments in the Anthropological Literature

During the nearly twenty-five years between 1953 and 1975, physical anthropologist Joseph Birdsell explored the relationships between environmental variables, particularly rainfall, and a suite of demographic variables that, much later, I have referred to as AREA, TLPOP, and DENSITY (Birdsell 1953, 1957, 1958, 1968, 1975). His initial research paper (1953) demonstrated a strong relationship between "tribal area," by which he meant the size of the geographic area occupied by known groups of Australian Aborigines (referred to as "tribes" by the conventions of that era) and mean annual rainfall. Birdsell fitted an equation to the data of the form $Y = aX^b$, in which Y referred to tribal area, X to mean annual rainfall, and constants a and b were defined as 7,112.8 and −1.58451, respectively.

Birdsell was interested in whether there was a basic "self-defining limit" to the size of the extended hunter-gatherer social unit (Birdsell 1953:172) and he reasoned that, since an inverse relationship was demonstrable between mean annual rainfall and the area controlled by Australian Aboriginal ethnic units, if the numbers of persons within ethnic units approximated a constant, then ethnic area and population density would be inversely related. In other words, if ethnic areas were large, population densities would be low. Given the nature of a ratio, Birdsell suggested, population density should be positively correlated with rainfall even if there was no independent response of population to rainfall. As Kelley (1994:436) has noted, Birdsell argued against the possibility that population levels would respond independently[6]: "If for any reason the average size of the tribal population varied as a function of rainfall, the distorting influence of this factor could not be detected. Thus, for example, tribes might have consistently small-sized populations in desert areas, and larger ones in regions of high rainfall without this being apparent in the original correlation. But there is little evidence to suggest that this type of variation is important" (Birdsell 1953:178). These comments make sense only if they are linked to an assumption of a parallel relationship between ethnic area, ethnic unit size, and rainfall, thus rendering a relationship with the undocumented variable of ethnic unit size invisible and consistent with the idea that ethnic units maintain a constant, self-defining size.

All of the patterns generated by my analysis strongly contradict Birdsell's conclusions. I have demonstrated that when hunter-gatherer mobility is high, the area controlled by groups of foragers is large, whereas groups whose mobility is reduced are associated with smaller geographic regions. I have also argued that the number of persons constituting a discrete ethnic unit is small among mobile peoples and consistently larger among more sedentary groups, regardless of trophic bias in the subsistence base. These studies show that, other things being equal, population density is positively related to situations in which the variable AREA is small, a finding that directly contradicts Birdsell's expectations. These results also challenge Birdsell's argument for the existence of a self-defining unit that he later termed the "dialectical tribe." This influential construct was estimated to have a mean size of 500 persons and, at the Man the Hunter conference, it stimulated considerable discussion about demographic constants and their role as determinants of the group sizes of modern and Pleistocene hunters (Lee and DeVore 1968a:245–48).

Instead of identifying demographic constants, my data exhibit considerable variability, at least at the level of the postulated "dialectical tribe." All of this variability appears related to mobility and environment, as indicated by the variables included in the best-fit equations for AREA, which were obtained by segregating the hunter-gatherer cases in terms of subsistence base, as well as by patterning relating to mobility, as indicated by the variable GRPPAT. My study reveals that rather different environmental variables predict AREA, depending upon the character of the subsistence base. This is not what one would expect if Birdsell's relationship between area and rainfall was the only factor conditioning the size of ethnic unit areas. My pattern recognition studies also show that very different kinds of units stand behind the ethnic units included in the hunter-gatherer data base (generalization 7.13).

A comparison of my findings with Birdsell's important and visionary work[7] still leaves unconsidered two aspects of the problem that he sought to solve. First, I must deal with the issue of how density relates to environmental variables. Of equal importance is the concept of self-defining units in general, particularly the "magic number" of twenty-five, which to Birdsell and others suggested the presence of self-defining features in hunter-gatherer group formation processes.

RELATING POPULATION DENSITY TO AREA AND ENVIRONMENT

As I have already noted, the term *population density* refers to a ratio that expresses two measurements: a given number of persons *and* a spatial unit of measurement, such as one square kilometer. Ratios are extremely useful ways of summarizing observations, but when a ratio varies there is no way

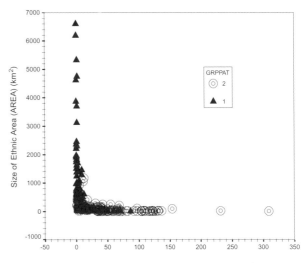

FIGURE 7.02

Demonstration of a Poisson distribution for the observed values of ethnic area sizes and population density. Marker is relative mobility of the cases (GRPPAT): (1) mobile cases and (2) relatively sedentary cases.

of knowing which term in the ratio is varying, or whether both are varying, or how they are related. This ambiguity made the possibility of self-defining demographic constants a credible idea, and it prompted Birdsell to argue that the population size of so-called tribal units varied around a mean of 500 persons. According to the logic of Birdsell's argument, such a constant was not responsive to environmental variables and was therefore "self-defining." Only the area controlled by an ethnic unit was thought to be related to environmental variables, and any correlation between density and environment arose because a constant was being divided by the environmentally responsive variable termed "tribal" or ethnic area.

In figure 7.02, the relationship between AREA and DENSITY is displayed for the cases in this study. The pattern resembles the Poisson relationship that Birdsell demonstrated between tribal area and mean annual rainfall, using cases from the interior of Australia. Undoubtedly Birdsell would have interpreted this pattern as support for his argument that the number of persons per tribal or ethnic area varied slightly around a constant value of 500 persons. Cases on the vertical axis reflect groups located in environments in which rainfall was very low and AREA was very large—circumstances in which, Birdsell argued, population density values would be very low. Cases on the horizontal axis occurred in regions where rainfall was very high and areas were very small, resulting in very high density values for tribal groups of 500 persons.

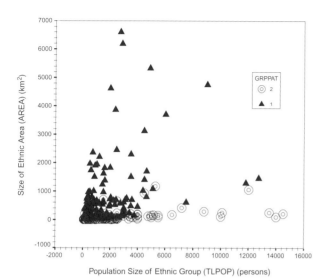

FIGURE 7.03

Demonstration of the partial independence between ethnic area and the population size of an ethnic group. Marker is relative mobility of the cases (GRPPAT): (1) mobile cases and (2) relatively sedentary cases.

In figure 7.03, however, when I display the scatter plots of the distribution of cases plotted by AREA on the *y* axis and total population (TLPOP) on the *x* axis, it is clear that there is no support for Birdsell's position. Cases with both large and small ethnic units have small areas, and those with large areas also have high population density values. In other words, both AREA and TLPOP are varying. Total population is therefore not a constant, nor is there support for the view that all variability in TLPOP is referable to different types of ethnic units within the sample.

I think it was worthwhile to compare the patterning produced by my hunter-gatherer data set with Birdsell's postulation of a self-limiting regional population unit, and I believe that I have demonstrated that his argument is not sustained.[8] The same patterning has, however, occurred in many different manifestations, and it has been summarized in generalizations 7.08–7.12. The patterns in the hunter-gatherer data set imply a process of intensification, particularly those patterns illustrating that as the area utilized by an ethnic group decreases, the number of persons within such a unit increases. This pattern is strongly reinforced by contrasts in the degree of mobility maintained by relevant hunter-gatherer cases and suggests that I may need to change the scale at which I look for patterns in the data, since mobility is not, strictly speaking, responsive to conditions at the level of the ethnic group but varies in response to circumstances affecting the local groups that together compose the ethnic unit.

Exploring System State Variability at a Smaller Scale

Before I determine whether the putative demographic constant of twenty-five persons at the local group level is imaginary or supported by the evidence in my data set, I summarize the findings about such a constant at a larger scale of social organization:

Generalization 7.18

There does not appear to be a "self-defining" constant structuring the number of persons included in hunter-gatherer regional units, dialect groups, or ethnic units. The data reveal that large-scale, collective human groups co-vary in size with environmental variables. Large-scale macro units are presumably selectively conditioned, and the extent to which they can be thought of as system state indicators is also variable.

I think, nevertheless, that the fundamental hunter-gatherer socioeconomic unit is not a language group or a dialect subgroup or an ethnic unit per se. If I want to learn something about the dynamic processes underlying hunter-gatherer social forms, I need to examine properties and units that have the potential to be more directly informative about cultural-ecological relationships. I begin by shifting scales and examining some statistics summarizing properties of hunter-gatherer systems that refer to internally variable phenomena, that is, properties that vary among the social components of the larger-scale ethnic units that I have treated as ethnographic cases. The target of this research is the size of the on-the-ground social unit, the sum total of which units constitutes an ethnic group.

I have recorded data from ethnographic sources relating to the three types of groups previously referred to in this chapter as GROUP1, GROUP2, and GROUP3. Table 7.05 summarizes the means and standard deviations of these three types of camping units that can be observed to vary within ethnic units. The cases are separated in terms of GRPPAT and SUBPOP, and means are provided for cases in terms of their primary dependence upon either terrestrial plants, terrestrial animals, or aquatic resources.

It is interesting to look at the data in table 7.05 in light of Julian Steward's (1936:344) argument that peoples who were dependent upon terrestrial animals had larger band sizes than groups dependent on other food resources. Steward believed that successful hunting was contingent upon the coordinated collaboration of numbers of hunters, and the data in table 7.05—which demonstrate that the mean group sizes of peoples dependent upon terrestrial animals are largest among mobile peoples—certainly support his assumption. Furthermore, mobile groups of terrestrial plant exploiters are in some cases approximately half the size of analogous groups

TABLE 7.05

COMPARISON OF GROUP SIZE AMONG SUBSETS OF CASES

SUBPOP	GRPPAT	TERRESTRIAL PLANTS	TERRESTRIAL ANIMALS	AQUATIC RESOURCES
		Group 1 (GRP1): Size of the most mobile residential group		
n	1	12.2 ± 4.0 (61)	$\underline{23.8 \pm 14.6}$ *(61)*	13.2 ± 4.6 (33)
	2	13.2 ± 1.5 *(05)*	—	$\underline{19.0 \pm 9.4 \ (23)}$
x	1	17.2 ± 6.0 (25)	$\underline{21.9 \pm 5.7}$ *(04)*	15.4 ± 2.1 (05)
	2	$\underline{17.5 \pm 6.2}$ *(10)*	—	16.0 (01)
		Group 2 (GRP2): Size of the most aggregated residential group		
n	1	34.5 ± 10.9 (67)	$\underline{97.6 \pm 94.3}$ *(65)*	46.7 ± 24.6 (32)
	2	87.5 ± 37.5 (14)	76.0 (01)	$\underline{126.4 \pm 131.5 \ (67)}$
x	1	40.5 ± 16.7 (28)	$\underline{57.7 \pm 13.7}$ *(03)*	39.8 ± 14.1 (05)
	2	$\underline{67.4 \pm 30.7}$ *(13)*	—	34.0 (01)
		Group 3 (GRP3): Size of periodic aggregates		
n	1	156.2 ± 92.5 (52)	$\underline{313.0 \pm 279.5 \ (58)}$	181.2 ± 89.8 (33)
	2	214.3 ± 937.7 (12)	—	$\underline{273.8 \pm 187.7 \ (18)}$
x	1	$\underline{119.3 \pm 67.8}$ *(23)*	113.3 ± 15.3 (03)	83.3 ± 22.1 (04)
	2	$\underline{166.0 \pm 65.2}$ *(08)*	—	80.0 (01)

Note: Underlined values are the highest value in the row; italics indicate highest value in GRPPAT comparisons among sets with identical values, e.g., 1 or 2 in a column.

exploiting terrestrial animals. Similar proportional differences prevail between groups in the GROUP2 and GROUP3 categories, which are only 50 percent as large as the groups of terrestrial hunters.

I noted in chapter 1 that the ethnographic records available to Steward contained relatively poor data on groups of northern boreal forest hunters. As a result, he had assumed that the large group sizes reported for these units meant that they must have been similar to the large, cooperatively organized groups of horse-mounted hunters documented on the Great Plains of North America. The provenance of Steward's assumption prompts me to investigate whether there is any systematic difference in organization between mounted hunters and peoples who exploit wild terrestrial animals using other modes of transport. Table 7.06 summarizes the data relative to this inquiry by isolating and separately tabulating the thirty cases of mounted hunters in my study (groups 23, 51, 209, 222, 227, 229, 230, 234, 240–260, and 333).

When, in fact, groups of mounted hunters are tabulated independently, the dramatic contrast in group size identified in table 7.05 disappears from summaries of the remaining hunter-gatherer cases. Nevertheless, meaningful differences distinguish hunters from peoples dependent on other food resources (for instance, nonequestrian hunters still have the largest GROUP1, GROUP2, and GROUP3 sizes). The reason why equestrian hunters have larger group sizes, however,

remains unknown. Was Steward correct in suggesting that successful hunting required cooperation at a larger organizational scale? He was thinking of the labor investment that was required to launch game drives focused on relatively large herd mammals such as bison and caribou, but perhaps hunting imposes constraints or imperatives on group size that have not yet been identified.

These questions suggest that perhaps my research might benefit from a consideration of the factors affecting hunter-gatherer group size in general before I attempt to answer more specific questions about organizational dynamics in less-inclusive situations. I will begin with the observation that in all comparisons of group size in table 7.06, peoples primarily exploiting terrestrial plants have the smallest group size, hunters of terrestrial animals have the largest group size, and peoples primarily dependent upon aquatic resources are located in between. It is also worth noting that in all on-the-ground groups—regardless of subsistence base—group size is larger for sedentary peoples than for mobile peoples.

The comparisons in table 7.06 include two very different kinds of units: ethnic groups of various sizes and smaller residential groups that together form ethnic groups. There are real differences in group size for peoples exploiting different food resources, and group size differs consistently between mobile and sedentary peoples. I must conclude that, consistent with earlier generalizations about ethnic group size and area

TABLE 7.06

COMPARISON OF GROUP SIZE BY SUBSISTENCE, MOBILITY, AND ACCULTURATIVE STATE

SUBPOP	GRPPAT	TERRESTRIAL PLANTS	TERRESTRIAL ANIMALS	AQUATIC RESOURCES
		Group 1 (GRP1): Size of the most mobile residential group		
n	1	12.0 ± 4.0 (59)	16.3 ± 5.1 (41)	15.0 ± 4.3 (32)
n—Horse	1	*16.8 ± 1.1 (02)*	*39.2 ± 15.8 (20)*	—
n	2	13.2 ± 1.5 (05)	—	*20.8 ± 5.8 (23)*
n—Horse	2	—	—	—
		Group 2 (GRP2): Size of the most aggregated residential group		
n	1	34.1 ± 10.8 (65)	46.7 ± 18.2 (43)	46.7 ± 24.6 (32)
n—Horse	1	46.5 ± 4.9 (02)	*189.4 ± 107.9 (23)*	—
n	2	*87.5 ± 37.5 (14)*	—	*127.5 ± 132.9 (65)*
n—Horse	2	—	—	108.0 (01)
		Group 3: Size of periodic aggregates		
n	1	155.9 ± 94.3 (50)	182.9 ± 71.5 (40)	178.1 ± 90.1 (30)
n—Horse	1	164.5 ± 6.4 (02)	*565.3 ± 349.9 (20)*	—
n	1	*214.3 ± 93.7 (12)*	—	*266.5 ± 185.1 (19)*
n—Horse	2	—	—	266.4 (01)

Note: Underlined values are the highest value in the row; *italics* indicate highest value in GRPPAT comparisons among sets with identical values, e.g., 1 or 2 in a column. All horse-mounted hunters were excluded from the total of "normal" cases. SUBPOP was summarized independently to signify "horse."

occupied, I was unable to discover a self-limiting group size that is characteristic of all hunter-gatherers, discussions of a magic number of twenty-five at the Man the Hunter conference notwithstanding. The presence of moderately low standard deviations for GROUP1 group sizes, however, lends support to the view that some rather regular causal relationships condition residential group size.

These observations, coupled with my earlier discussions of intensification, prompt me to argue that, other things being equal, intensification should condition group size at all scales of observation. The consequences of intensification, however, should be most regular and pronounced in those domains in which subsistence strategies are directly organized and implemented. As a way of evaluating my impressions of analogous patterning between ethnic unit areas and sizes as opposed to residential groups and their sizes, I prepared figure 7.04, which illustrates the relationship between size of ethnic group area (AREA) and the mean size of residential groups during the most aggregated phase of the annual settlement cycle (GROUP2).

The overall pattern in figure 7.04 illustrates a fuzzy Poisson relationship between the size of the area occupied by an ethnic group and the mean number of persons included in a socioeconomic group *within* the ethnic group. The scatter plot demonstrates that cases with large group sizes during

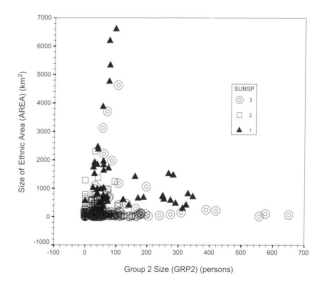

FIGURE 7.04

Demonstration of a Poisson-like relationship between GROUP2 size and the size of an ethnic area. Marker is primary source of foods (SUBSP): (1) terrestrial animals, (2) terrestrial plants, and (3) aquatic resources.

aggregated annual camps (GROUP2) are also those with the smallest ethnic areas. Cases with the smallest GROUP2 group sizes are also those that usually have the largest ethnic areas. These results support the earlier impression that at least some of the same processes not only are operating on ethnic groups but also are conditioning the size of the on-the-ground socioeconomic units that constitute ethnic groups. Both comparisons reveal that as larger numbers of people are included within groups, such groups have access to the resources of a smaller area. Since area is decreasing at the same time that numbers of people are increasing absolutely, intensificational processes must have an accelerating effect on ratios such as population density.

Even though trends in the direction of intensification are common to all hunter-gatherer cases in the data set, it is clear that the type of food resource that assumes dietary predominance strongly and differentially conditions the size of analogous groups and, therefore, the way groups are dispersed spatially. Groups that are primarily dependent upon terrestrial animals have the largest group sizes and tend to have the largest areas, whereas peoples primarily exploiting aquatic resources cluster in groups of moderate size, and peoples dependent upon terrestrial plants have the smallest group sizes.

Not only do changes in the primary food resource appear to play a role in determining group size, there also seems to be sequential patterning when hunter-gatherer cases are ordinated in terms of intensificational indicators. There are clear indications that peoples who are primarily dependent upon terrestrial animals uniformly respond to intensificational pressures by reducing their dependence upon these resources. In temperate and arctic settings, aquatic resources are exploited more heavily during periods of intensification, whereas peoples in warm-temperate and tropical settings may shift to terrestrial plants, aquatic resources, or some combination of both. Among terrestrial plant-dependent peoples, aquatic resources may assume an important role, but increased dependence upon terrestrial plants seems to be the ultimate response to intensification.

ANOTHER STEP TOWARD THE GOAL OF GOOD THEORY BUILDING

I have demonstrated so far that a suite of patterned relationships underlies the differences between hunter-gatherer systems that are mobile and those that are more sedentary. I do not know, however, whether the transition in system state from high mobility to residential stability is the kind of scalar relationship implied by the word *intensification* or whether an abrupt and rapid set of changes related to regional dynamics is set in motion by intensification (generalization 7.17). I also do not have any satisfactory measure of the area occupied by a hunter-gatherer ethnic group that can be

unambiguously related to the measure of the number of persons occupying different types of socioeconomically and reproductively integrated groups. All that I have, in fact, is a set of provocative patterns illustrating relationships between mobility, basic classes of wild food resources, and spatially defined social groups that all point to a set of causal relationships between the organization of hunter-gatherer task groups and the character of the tasks.

At the conceptual level, I have an intellectual tool—*intensification*—that defines a changing set of relationships between persons and their use of a geographic area. The challenge, at this juncture, is to develop an argument about how the world works in a dynamic sense relative to my idea of intensification. This will permit me to anticipate accurately the circumstances in which changes in the size of a geographic area, changes in the number of persons in spatially clustered groups, and changes in the target of food procurement and the labor strategies employed in food procurement would occur. If I can develop an argument about how intensification occurs, not only will I be able to identify the differences between the cases in my data set that refer to intensification, I will also be able to anticipate when intensification would and would not occur.

I am describing, of course, a theory of intensification that in principle would also account for the set of past dynamics usually referred to as *the origins of agriculture,* and perhaps other transitions in system state as well. I am, however, just beginning to explore different kinds of units and to isolate patterns that will help narrow down the character of the variability that theory building efforts will address. I can expect that a shift from pattern recognition studies to theory building will necessitate some changes in tactics, and I will illustrate what I mean by returning to the issue of the ambiguity in one of my basic units of comparison, the ethnic group.

My working definition of an ethnic unit is an association of on-the-ground hunter-gatherer groups that are economically and reproductively integrated within a wider system. In order to transform this informal definition into a meaningful component of a theory, I need to identify some specific properties of groups in terms of which I can isolate and array the cases in my data set. In chapter 4, I referred to this sorting and regrouping strategy as *dimensionalizing data,* and, in my judgment, a good place to begin this particular kind of scrutiny is with the variable I call *group size.*

At the outset, it might seem that I already have a useful measure of group size—that is, the number of persons in a group—but, as will be seen, that phrase tells us very little. I want to dimensionalize my data in informative terms by developing an instrument for measurement that will define a dimension consisting of unique units, such as inches, and provide a continuous scale of measurement that, having a referent, carries directly readable information.

Measurement of a quantity implies that a number is assigned to represent its magnitude. Usually the assignment can be made by a simple comparison. The magnitude of the quantity is compared to a "standard" quantity, the magnitude of which is arbitrarily chosen to have the measure 1.

Quantities having a scale of measurement chosen in this way arbitrarily and independently of the scales of other quantities are called "fundamental" and all other quantities are measured in units defined in relation to, or derived from fundamental quantities.

(Morris 1969:811)

Considered in these terms, what, I may ask, is the standard for measuring "group size?" Obviously it is numbers of persons, but how do I determine what a group might be? The concept of group size expresses a vague ratio in which the "group" provides the boundary conditions for counting persons. In this sense, a group is conventionally defined as "any collection or assemblage of persons or things; cluster; aggregation" (Morris 1969:582). This means that a group is defined with reference to space as a cluster or aggregation.

There are, however, other characteristics that allow us to distinguish one kind of group from another, as I illustrated in my typology of group pattern (GRPPAT) that distinguishes between mobile and sedentary residential units (table 7.05). Model building is one of the tactics available to me in my quest to identify the properties of groups that interact to produce causal responses in other variables, and at this point I will build a structure that embodies my units of interest and their germane properties in order to explore their relationships and the ways in which they respond to intensificational processes.

Building a Minimalist Model of Hunter-Gatherer Group Size as a Standard for Measurement

For heuristic purposes, the first step in building a minimalist model of hunter-gatherer group size will be to propose that

Proposition 7.04

Other things being equal, mobility costs act as the ultimate limiting factor on economically constituted hunter-gatherer group sizes.

In other words, minimizing mobility costs provides the context for understanding how other variables regularly interact. Given this limiting factor, I must identify the variables that act as fundamental conditioners of hunter-gatherer subsistence performance. This model building exercise must perforce consist of two parts. First I will explore the factors conditioning subsistence performance within hunter-gatherer

residential groups and examine how the proportional relationships between producers and dependents affect group size. Then I will demonstrate the character of the relationship between group size and mobility using modeled relationships of land use.

IDENTIFYING FUNDAMENTAL LABOR VARIABLES CONDITIONING HUNTER-GATHERER GROUP SIZE

Since a social group is minimally a unit of food procurement and consumption, the fundamental components of the group, when viewed from this perspective, consist of the persons who are active food procurers and the persons who are consumers but usually not food procurers. Empirical evidence suggests there is a rather narrow range of variability in the relationship between consumers and producers—referred to as the *dependency ratio*—which is calculated by dividing the total number of persons in the group by the number of active food producers. The resulting value represents the number of consumers, including the producers themselves, who must be fed by a single food producer.

One feature of the human life course is the extended period of maturation that juveniles experience, and any model of human economic behavior must take into consideration the consumer demands made by immature offspring on a single producer. One important source of variability in the dependency ratio is, therefore, the age structure of a population. From the populational perspective, however, which is concerned with very large aggregate units, the age structure of a population does not modify the dependency ratio as much as might be anticipated. For instance, a very young population has many children relative to the adult producer category, while the number of old persons is small. On the other hand, in populations that are classified as "old," there are fewer young children relative to the number of producers, but the number of aged dependents increases (see Wrigley 1969:23–28).

For purposes of discrimination, however, at present I am looking at hunter-gatherer groups at an entirely different scale and am concerned with actual on-the-ground group sizes, in aggregations that ethnographers would be likely to see during their field work in an ethnic territory. For instance, in the November 1968 census reported by Nancy Howell (1979:45), the dependency ratio is 1.598 persons for a !Kung population of 569 people, whereas between 1964 and 1973 the aggregate value from !Kung camps with a total population of 561 people is 1.65 persons (Lee 1979:68–70).

Table 7.07 illustrates the fact that among !Kung hunters and gatherers living in relatively small groups during 1964, the dependency ratio varied between 1.25 and 3.00 persons. In contrast, in the contemporary world of nation-states, the dependency ratio ranges between 1.10 and 1.98, based on a

TABLE 7.07

PRODUCERS AND DEPENDENTS AT SELECTED ZU/WASI !KUNG CAMPS

GROUP PLACEMENT	NUMBER OF PERSONS	NUMBER OF PRODUCERS	NUMBER OF DEPENDENTS	DEPENDENCY RATIO[1]
DOBE (N'EISHI)	11	8	3	1.37
DOBE (TOMA//GWE)	24	12	12	2.00
!KANGWA (BO)	22	14	8	1.57
BATE (!XOMA)	19	11	8	1.73
BATE (KXARU)	10	8	2	*1.25*
!KUBI (N/AHKA)	23	17	6	1.35
!GOSHE (/TISHE)	23	15	8	1.53
!GOSHE (/TI!KAY)	11	8	3	1.37
!GOSHE (BO)	19	10	9	1.90
!GOSHE KAU (DWA)	13	10	3	1.30
/XAI/XAI (//KAU)	13	5	8	2.60
/XAI/XAI (//KAIHAN!A)	9	3	6	**3.00**
/XAI/XAI (TOMA!XWA)	30	17	13	1.76
/XAI/XAI (SA//GAI)	18	8	10	2.25
/XAI/XAI (TOMAZHO)	28	17	11	1.65
TOTAL (N = 15)	273	163	110	1.68

MEAN NUMBER OF PERSONS	18.20
MEAN NUMBER OF PRODUCERS	10.86
MEAN DEPENDENCY RATIO FROM TOTALS	1.68
MEAN OF CAMP DEPENDENCY RATIOS	1.68

Notes: 1. The highest dependency ratio is indicated by **bold** type; the lowest is *italicized.*
Data were recorded by Lee (1979:68) during the high-food-density period in 1964. The term *Producers* refers to persons between the ages of fifteen and fifty-nine. The name of the group's headman, in parentheses, follows the name of the camp's location.)

definition of producers as persons older than age fifteen and younger than age sixty-five (Hawley 1959:365). The median value corrected for the definition of producers in contemporary populations is 1.57 persons. Based on Lee's (1979) data, it appears unrealistic to include hunter-gatherers older than age fifty-nine in the producer category, so I have followed Lee's convention of calculating dependency ratios based on an age span for producers of between fifteen and fifty-nine years of age.

I was able to find only eighteen cases in the ethnographic literature for which dependency ratio values were calculated, and these are listed in table 7.08. In light of such limited evidence of hunter-gatherer demography, it is difficult to extrapolate the best estimate for hunter-gatherers in general, but I believe that the contemporary global data, coupled with data available from ethnographic sources, will produce a defensible (if not ideal) mean value. Obviously, if I were omniscient, I might discover that the real dependency ratio value is different, but for purposes of model building I will use a dependency ratio of 1.75 consumers per producer.

Group Size and Dependency Ratio Interaction
The importance of the relationship between the dependency ratio and foraging activities is illustrated by data collected in

Australia by McCarthy and McArthur (1960), who reported on the work habits of two different groups of Aboriginal hunter-gatherers. The data are summarized in table 7.09. One group of thirteen people, five of whom were children (dependency ratio of 1.62), were observed foraging over a seven-day period near Hemple Bay on Groote Eyelandt. During this time, ten female foraging expeditions were observed, the average size of the foraging unit was 2.2 persons, and the average duration of each expedition was 7.0 hours. There were four adult women in the group of thirteen persons, so there were twenty-eight potential female work days during the period of observation. Of this total, women actually worked on twenty-two days, which means that each woman participated in a work group every 1.27 days.

During the same seven-day period of observation, the men in the group, who were engaged in both collecting and fishing, were observed on five fishing expeditions. The average size of the foraging unit was 2.6 men, and each expedition lasted an average of 6.26 hours. Seven collecting expeditions were observed with an average of 1.26 men per expedition and an average duration of 5.1 hours. Of the twenty-eight potential work days available to men, foraging units were actually engaged in subsistence activities on twenty-two, which means that males participated in a work

TABLE 7.08

DEPENDENCY RATIOS OF SELECTED
HUNTER-GATHERER CASES

CASE	DEPENDENCY RATIO	REFERENCE
ACHE	1.72	Hurtado 1985:39
ALYAWARA	2.03	Denham 1975:135
ASIATIC ESKIMO	1.71	Krupnik 1993:46
GROOTE EYLANDT	1.73	Rose 1960:61
GUNWINGU	1.69	Altman 1987:101–5
HADZA (1967)	1.89	Blurton-Jones et al. 1992:167
HILL PANDARAM	1.86	Morris 1982a:169
JU/WASI (1968)	1.60	Howell 1979:45
JU/WASI (1964–73)	1.65	Lee 1979:68–70
MBUTI	1.81	Ichikawa 1978:141
NORTHERN TERRITORY	1.75	Jones 1963:67
NENETS	1.69	Krupnik 1993:99
NUNAMIUT	2.09	Binford 1991a:29–89
PITJANDJARA	1.62	Yengoyan 1970:73
PUME (DORO ANA)	1.59	Gragson 1989:126–27
SIRIONO	1.70	Holmberg 1950:51
SIRIONO	1.61	Holmberg 1950:51
TIWI (1961)	1.76	Jones 1963:28

MEAN VALUE ($N = 18$)		1.75
MEDIAN VALUE		1.84
MEAN VALUE WITH NUNAMIUT AND ALYAWARA EXCLUDED		1.71

TABLE 7.09

COMPARISON OF WORK EFFORT
AND DEPENDENCY RATIO AT TWO
AUSTRALIAN HUNTER-GATHERER CAMPS

	FISH CREEK ARNHEM LAND	HEMPLE BAY GROOTE EYELANDT
NUMBER OF EXPEDITIONS	31	22
MEAN SIZE OF PARTY	3.19 persons	1.99 persons
DURATION OF EXPEDITION	3.86 hours	6.28 hours
TOTAL EXPEDITION HOURS	119.67 hours	138.27 hours
TOTAL HOURS WORKED BY ALL PRODUCERS	381.74 hours	275.15 hours
TOTAL PRODUCER-DAYS DURING RECORD	140 days	56 days
TOTAL CONSUMER-DAYS DURING RECORD	154 days	91 days
MEAN NUMBER OF HOURS WORKED PER PRODUCER DAY	2.72 hours	4.91 hours
MEAN NUMBER OF HOURS WORKED PER CONSUMER DAY	2.40 hours	3.02 hours
DAILY WORK INTERVAL FOR EACH PRODUCER	Every 1.43 days	Every 1.27 days
DEPENDENCY RATIO	1.10	1.62

group every 1.27 days. From the standpoint of labor expenditure, this value is identical to that of the women, although the duration of the male foraging expeditions was less than the duration of the female expeditions.

In contrast, table 7.09 summarizes the fourteen-day record available for a group of eleven persons (ten adults with a dependency ratio of 1.10) living in the Dry Fish Creek area of Arnhem Land, fifty miles from Oenpelli station. Observations were recorded between October 7 and 20, near the end of the long dry season, when food resources are least abundant. Twelve female collecting expeditions were observed, composed on average of 3.25 women and lasting on average for only three hours and twenty-four minutes. Of the possible fifty-six female work days, work occurred on only thirty-nine, which meant that a woman participated in a work group every 1.43 days.

On ten occasions, males were observed hunting terrestrial mammals, with an average of 3.1 persons per expedition, each of which lasted an average of five hours and ten minutes. Nine fishing expeditions were observed, lasting an average of three hours and two minutes, with an average foraging unit of 3.22 persons. Of the eighty-four potential male work days, men participated in a work group every 1.4 days, for a total of 60 work days. Once again, this value very closely approximates the work schedule of the women in the group.

The comparison of these two Australian cases in table 7.09 suggests that the dependency ratio has a significant effect on work effort. In the Fish Creek group each producer worked only 2.72 hours per day, whereas in the Hemple Bay group each producer worked 4.91 hours per day. In other words, the producers in the Fish Creek group worked only 55 percent as much as the producers in the Hemple Bay group. On the other hand, when I compare the two groups in terms of consumer days, individuals at Fish Creek worked 2.40 hours per consumer day whereas the Hemple Bay group worked 3.02 hours.

In this comparison, Fish Creek producers worked 79 percent as much as the Hemple Bay group relative to the number of consumers in the group. The difference between 55 percent and 79 percent is, other things being equal, the difference that dependency ratios of 1.10 and 1.62 make relative to the work effort required of producers. In other words, 53 percent of the observed difference in work effort expended between the two groups may be related directly to differences in the dependency ratio, while the remaining 47 percent is presumably related to differences in the availability of food resources in the two habitats. I believe that this example illustrates the importance of an additional variable that must be included in any model that might be built to demonstrate the relationship between group size and labor organization.

Division of Labor and Male and Female
Labor Schedules

The organizational character of the division of labor and the way it is reflected in daily work schedules have an important effect on the number of producers in a group and the way their labor is deployed on a daily basis. At this point in my inquiry, I want to be able to identify the factors that govern differential male and female participation in the food procurement labor force and to discover what conditions determine the size and frequency of food-getting expeditions. With regard to the former, individuals obviously vary in their capacity to perform work, but one might nevertheless expect there to be a mean number of days of effort per year that could be accepted as a standard for foragers working on foot. In fact, data on this subject are scarce, but I have been able to find some information in the ethnographic record.

Richard Lee (1969) has recorded some pertinent observations about the Dobe !Kung (Zu/wasi) Bushmen that I paraphrase because of their relevance to my present concern. Men tended to work more than women, Lee reported, but their schedules were unpredictable. A man might hunt three days in a row and then do no hunting for ten days or two weeks.

Lee's activity diary of the Dobe camp followed the eleven males of hunting age in residence at the camp over a twenty-seven-day period in July 1964. During that interval, four of the eleven men did no hunting at all, while the other seven men worked an average of three or four days per week, resulting in a total of seventy-eight man-days spent hunting. Since there were 189 potential work days for the active men and hunting occurred on only seventy-eight days, hunters were active on only 41.2 percent of the available days. In other words, during a one-year period, the average hunter would be expected to work 150.4 days. If I include the four inactive men in the calculation, I obtain a workday percentage of only 26.2 percent or an expected work budget of only 95.6 hunting days per year per man.

In his description of the Xai/Xai !Kung at /Du/da, Lee (1968) has reported that adult work routines were similar to those described for the nearby Dobe !Kung to the north. Adults preferred to work one day and stay home the next, and on a typical day one-third to one-half of the able-bodied adults were at home, either resting or doing maintenance chores. Adolescents and old people performed serious work even fewer days per week. The hunting patterns of the men at /Du/da were also different from those observed in the north. Lee has recorded that, on occasion, parties of hunters stayed out several nights tracking down and butchering an antelope, although the more usual pattern of adult male work consisted of a day of hunting followed by a day spent in camp.

All of the able-bodied men at /Du/da hunted on a regular basis, although there were differences among them in skill, luck, and the numbers of antelope they killed. Draper (personal communication April 1974) has noted that the women of /Du/da spent more hours per week gathering than did the women of Dobe or Mahopa. Their gathering trips lasted six to eight hours per day, reflecting the fact that they walked farther in a day and that they searched for a greater variety and volume of bush foods.

Holmberg reported that, half a world away, the Siriono hunters of Bolivia maintained a very different schedule: "The most persistent hunter was out for 16 of the 31 days in August, 12 of the 30 days in September, and 19 of the 31 days in October. The majority of the hunters averaged from 11–12 days a month" (1950:31). According to these observations, the most active Siriono hunter was engaged in food production for forty-seven of the ninety-two days on which observations were made, or 51.0 percent of the total period. If this proportion of days worked to days not worked was maintained on a yearly basis, this Siriono hunter would have been engaged in food production for 186.1 days of the year. The other men in Holmberg's study would have hunted approximately 35.8 percent of the days in the period of observation or an estimated 130.7 days of the year. The mean estimate of the total number of days during which observation occurred would approximate 138 days per year. Holmberg noted, however, that "to be sure the conditions at Tibaera were not in all respects aboriginal. Informants told me, however, and my observations under aboriginal conditions seem to bear them out, that a man goes hunting on the average of every other day throughout the year. On the odd days he rests, repairs arrows, eats" (1950:32).

Clearly the Siriono are more persistent hunters than the !Kung. An estimate of their level of activity would be between 138 and 186 days per year under aboriginal conditions, although I doubt that the average of every other day reported by Holmberg's informant applied to all of the men in the labor pool. As the best estimate, therefore, I will accept a value halfway between the two reported values, or 162 days per year.

Another on-the-ground group for which data on food production exist are the Nunamiut caribou hunters of north central Alaska. I have restricted my consideration of the Nunamiut data to a twenty-six-day period during which the Eskimo engaged in intense hunting at the peak of the fall 1971 caribou migration (Binford 1978). Because of several coincidences, the number of hunters in the village was low, the caribou migration was smaller than normal in terms of animal density, and the animals were more dispersed than usual. For these reasons, the data from this period should be a fair approximation of the level of a hunter's performance when operating at maximum capacity. My records show that there were nineteen active hunters during the caribou migration and, therefore, 494 potential hunter-days in the record. Of those 494 days, the men hunted 237 days or 47.9 percent of the time. If this level of investment were to be maintained throughout the year, the men would have hunted 174.8 days per year.

Using the records of the three preceding cases, I have determined that an energetic !Kung hunter would invest 150.4 days each year in terrestrial animal procurement, an average Siriono would work 162 days per year at the same activity, and a Nunamiut Eskimo working at peak performance would be expected to hunt about 174.8 days per year. Although these estimates are not conclusive and are based on limited data, I would argue that the maximum effort that might be expected of a hunter would result in a hunting schedule of approximately 180 days per year or, on average, every other day. This estimate appears reasonable since foraging groups also need time to move camp and to cope with illness and the varying capabilities of individuals who differ in age and state of health.

Since a hunter's weekly schedule does not proceed with the regularity of an office worker's, a day of strenuous hunting is likely to be followed by a day spent recuperating and repairing gear. Although I have suggested that the maximum number of days of active hunting that males in a hunter-gatherer society might be expected to maintain is 180, a more realistic estimate of the level of performance that could be sustained over long periods of time might be closer to between 165 and 175 days per year. For purposes of model building, therefore, I have decided that 170 days per year is a reasonable estimate of the time an average hunter will invest in the procurement of terrestrial animal resources.

A Minimalist Model of Hunter-Gatherer Group Size

If I assume, for purposes of model building, the existence of a "normal" division of labor between males and females—that is, both males and females are food producers but are involved in different, complementary subsistence tasks—I may argue that a local group capable of sustained subsistence procurement tasks would be composed of approximately 20.47 persons. This estimate depends for its accuracy upon the correctness of the constants I have already discussed, coupled with an assumption that the food produced each day is consumed daily. Such an assumption entails that a group would have to be large enough to engage in an average of two foraging expeditions per day, one male and one female. This means that there would be at least five producers available for work each day, since male groups consist, on average, of two men while female work groups are slightly larger.

Given that producers work an average of 170 days each year, or 46.5 percent of the time, over the long run the group would have to include 11.7 producers, given a dependency ratio of 1.75, for a total group size of 20.47 persons.[9] If a group were smaller, it would have to either collapse the division of labor or boost its effectiveness level so that a single foraging expedition produced food for more than one day, thereby reducing expedition frequency. Other options would be to maintain a supply of stored food that was procured under different labor conditions or to organize labor in different ways during the course of the year.

My estimate of group size represents a mean calculated over a full year, since for short periods of time only 10 producers instead of 11.7 would be necessary. If there were only ten producers in a group (five of whom could work each day), at a dependency ratio of 1.75, a minimal group size of 17.5 persons could be maintained. If group size falls below this level and at least a partial collapse of the male-female division of labor occurs, group sizes of 10.23 persons (for a long-term group) or 8.75 persons, based on group members working 50 percent of the time, could be maintained.[10] A group size of 8.75 persons approximates a modal value when the group is at a truly minimal level and maintains a somewhat increased work load by dispensing with the male-female division of labor. It is likely, however, that these conditions would occur only during a relatively short period of the annual settlement round and that during the majority of the year minimal group size values of between 17.5 and 20.47 persons would be more common.

The Terrestrial Model is designed to explore the relationships between the variables that condition group size under certain assumed initial conditions. The model is static in that minimal labor and producer relationships are considered constants when calculating the interaction among the variables in the model. I have therefore defined a standardized measurement of group size that has direct meaning for hunter-gatherer labor organization and the relationships between food procurement and consumption.

I refer to this measure as a COHAB because it represents the minimal size of a local group that camps and forages together and is capable of sustained subsistence procurement tasks. One COHAB represents 20.47 persons, and I can determine the number of COHABs that any particular hunter-gatherer group represents by dividing the number of persons in that group by 20.47. For instance, if a group includes 57 persons, its group size would be 2.784 COHABs (57 divided by 20.47).

By modeling the relationships among a suite of variables that demonstrably condition hunter-gatherer group size under certain assumed initial conditions, I have now created a *dimension* in terms of which I can array and compare data. And because the COHAB standard is not defined with respect to any spatial or geographic properties, it is unambiguous as measured. The model is minimalist because it assumes that some very important conditions favor minimal group size among mobile hunter-gatherers—the primary limiting factor being mobility itself.

MOBILITY AS A FACTOR LIMITING GROUP SIZE

The linkage between mobility and group size is relatively straightforward and is summarized in the following generalization:

———————— *Generalization 7.19* ————————

At a given level of food availability in the habitat, the larger the group size, the greater the demand on the available food supply per unit of occupied area. Therefore, other things being equal, in the absence of intensification, the larger the group size, the greater the number of moves a group must make during a year in order to meet subsistence needs.

This statement makes sense, however, only if there is some basic limitation affecting the size of the area that a group is able to exploit on a daily basis. By convention, this important variable has been referred to as a *foraging radius*.

Modeling the Minimal Subsistence Area

From the short-term perspective of a single day, it is reasonable to ask if there are certain limits on the size of the area that human beings can readily cover in the course of their food procurement activities. I assume that those human attributes affecting levels of physical performance, such as stature, metabolic rate, musculature, and so forth, would be primary conditioners of the distance a human being could comfortably cover in a single day, other things (e.g., health, age) being equal.

Geographic and seasonal differences in the number of daylight hours might also be expected to affect the number of hours a forager could devote to acquiring food resources, as would regional temperatures and the foraging distance. These factors would affect foraging schedules and ranges in any given setting but would not have a direct effect on the physiologically based optimal foraging distance for human beings, other things being equal. I also expect optimal foraging distance to form a normal distribution for which the standard deviation of the mean would be relatively low.

I turned to ethnographic sources in an attempt to assign an empirical value to optimal foraging distance but was surprised to discover that most ethnographers have failed to provide data on the number of hours worked or the distances covered by the peoples they observed. The body of relevant data (which includes my own field observations) turns out to have been collected by only a small number of persons: Robert Altman, Patricia Draper, Richard Gould, Russell Greaves, Kristen Hawkes, Kim Hill, Betty Meehan, and John Yellen. Data from these researchers are presented in tables 7.10–7.12, which also include summarizing statements from a number of sources and information supplied to me by Woodie Denham, Rhys Jones, Mervin Meggitt, and James O'Connell. Although these data are clearly limited, they will allow me to make a reasonable estimate of hunter-gatherer foraging ranges for inclusion in the model.

It should be noted that some of the foraging expeditions quantified and presented in tables 7.10–7.12 occurred under special circumstances that require elaboration. For instance,

TABLE 7.10

EMPIRICAL OBSERVATIONS OF FORAGING DISTANCES
FOR FEMALE-ONLY FORAGING PARTIES

NUMBER IN PARTY	ROUND-TRIP DISTANCE (KM)	DURATION OF EXPEDITION (HR)	RATE OF TRAVEL (KM/HR)
1. Ten berry-picking foraging expeditions by Nunamiut Eskimo women during late summer 1972 and 1973 (Binford, unpublished data)			
3	13.5	6.7	2.01
5	14.3	5.9	2.41
3 WOMEN AND 2 GIRLS	14.6	7.3	1.99
1 WOMAN AND 2 GIRLS	9.3	2.9	3.21
2	9.5	3.1	3.05
3	15.9	4.7	3.38
4	13.0	6.1	2.12
2 WOMEN AND 2 GIRLS	10.8	5.5	1.94
2	11.9	5.6	2.12
4 WOMEN AND 3 GIRLS	12.4	5.7	2.17
TOTAL	125.3	53.5	21.54
NUMBER	10.0	10.0	10.0
MEAN	12.5	5.35	2.16
STANDARD DEVIATION	2.2	1.42	0.92
MEAN FORAGING RADIUS = 5.36 ± 0.98 KILOMETERS			
MEAN NUMBER OF ADULTS PER EXPEDITION = 3.2			
2. Three foraging expeditions by Alyawara-speaking Australian women to collect seed and bush potatoes at MacDonald Downs, Northern Territories, 1974 (Binford, unpublished data)			
4	11.3	3.6	3.06
2	12.9	6.3	2.03
3 WOMEN AND AN UNKNOWN NUMBER OF CHILDREN	8.0	4.0	2.01
TOTAL	20.0	13.97	7.10
NUMBER	3.0	3.0	3.0
MEAN	6.66	4.65	2.37
STANDARD DEVIATION	1.22	1.43	0.59
MEAN FORAGING RADIUS = 3.33 ± 0.61 KILOMETERS			
MEAN NUMBER OF ADULTS PER EXPEDITION EQUALS 3.0			
3. Miscellaneous female foraging data			
3 PITJANDJARA-SPEAKING AUSTRALIAN WOMEN AND 5 CHILDREN (GOULD 1969A:3–15)	16.89	6.6	2.56
ANBARRA WOMEN COLLECTING SHELLFISH (NUMBER NOT SPECIFIED) (64 DAY-TRIPS) (MEEHAN 1982:126–29)	6.1875	—	—
PUME (VENEZUELA) WOMEN (HILTON AND GREAVES 1995: TABLE 1)	6.767	—	—

the data on Nunamiut male foraging parties were collected during the summer, when daylight is continuous in the high arctic. The settlement was subsisting primarily on stored foods and hunting expeditions were rare (during the summer months, a single hunter might make only one foraging trip). These circumstances account for the high values recorded for round-trip distance and foraging radius, as well as the mean number of participants in a trip, and must not be mistaken for a normal, day-to-day foraging strategy. In this case, the record of 408 trips by males with an average of 1.44 participants per trip, which was compiled over an eighteen-month period, is a more accurate indicator of the size of male hunting trips.

TABLE 7.11

EMPIRICAL OBSERVATIONS OF FORAGING DISTANCES FOR MALE-ONLY FORAGING PARTIES

NUMBER IN PARTY	ROUND-TRIP DISTANCE (KM)	DURATION OF EXPEDITION (HR)	RATE OF TRAVEL (KM/HR)
1. Eight sheep- and caribou-hunting expeditions by Nunamiut Eskimo men during mid-summer 1972[1]			
2	27.4	5.6	4.89
3	25.1	9.6	2.61
2	27.7	13.6	2.03
4	23.7	10.6	2.23
2	29.7	18.7	1.58
1	15.0	5.1	2.94
2	23.5	10.5	2.24
1	24.9	11.5	2.17
TOTAL	197.0	95.1	20.69
NUMBER	8.0	8.0	8.0
MEAN	24.62	1.8	2.59
STANDARD DEVIATION	7.93	4.11	0.40
MEAN FORAGING RADIUS = 12.31 ± 3.96 KILOMETERS			
MEAN NUMBER OF PRODUCERS PER EXPEDITION = 2.13			
2. Sixteen hunting expeditions by Dobe !Kung males with same-day return, May 24–June 9, 1968 (Yellen 1972)			
1 MALE AND 1 BOY	3.7		
1 MALE AND 1 BOY	15.9		
2	11.1		
1	11.4		
2	18.5		
4	6.8		
2 MALES AND 1 BOY	9.2		
2	19.6		
5	15.6		
3	16.7		
2	20.4		
3	18.8		
2	14.0		
1	6.4		
3	4.2		
3	15.9		
TOTAL	208.2		
NUMBER	16.0		
MEAN	12.2		
STANDARD DEVIATION	5.57		
MEAN FORAGING RADIUS = 6.1 ± 2.78 KILOMETERS			
MEAN NUMBER OF PRODUCERS PER EXPEDITION = 3.0			
3. Miscellaneous male foraging data			
1.44 (MEAN NUMBER FOR NUNAMIUT) (408 TRIPS) (BINFORD 1991a:102–7)	—	—	—
ACHE (PARAGUAY) (NUMBER NOT SPECIFIED) (HILL AND HAWKES 1983:159, 176)	—	6.91	4
PUME (VENEZUELA) (NUMBER NOT SPECIFIED) (HILTON AND GREAVES 1995:TABLE 1)	12.0	—	—

Note: 1. All participants were on foot. The sample is biased in favor of multiperson trips (Binford unpublished data).

TABLE 7.12

SIZE OF FORAGING AREA FOR SEVEN HUNTER-GATHERER GROUPS
AND TIME NEEDED FOR COVERAGE

GROUP	FORAGING DATA	REFERENCE
HADZA OF TANZANIA	Walking time = 4.15 kilometers per hour Foraging area of a single camp = 20 km^2 Foraging radius = 2.52 kilometers Annual foraging range = 75 km^2 Annual foraging radius = 4.89 kilometers.	O'Connell et al. 1992:329–30
AKA OF THE CENTRAL AFRICAN REPUBLIC	Adult daily work schedule = 6 hours Foraging radius of a single camp = 4.279 kilometers Foraging area of three "bands" = 280, 210, and 265 km^2, respectively Mean foraging area = 250 km^2 Mean foraging radius = 8.92 kilometers	Bahuchet 1990:30 Bahuchet 1979: 1009
BAMBOTE OF ZAIRE (NET HUNTERS)	Work interval is every other day with an average workday of 10.2 hours Foraging area of a single camp = 80 km^2 Foraging radius = 5.05 kilometers	Terashima 1980:245
EFE OF ZAIRE (BOW HUNTERS)	Observed spear hunts involve 10.7 men and last 9 hours 49 monkey hunts average 3.31 hours each with an additional 3.6 hours devoted to arrow-making 45 ambush hunting episodes averaged 1.87 hours each 71 group hunts averaged 5.49 hours each Average daily distance of hunting trips = 4.61 kilometers	Bailey 1985:173 Bailey 1985:175 Bailey 1985:178 Bailey 1985:181 Bailey 1985:184
MBUTI OF ZAIRE (NET HUNTERS)	Band foraging area = 133 km^2 Foraging radius = 6.50 kilometers Average number of hours per day spent hunting = 7.33 Average number of hours per day spent hunting = 7.47 Band foraging area = 107 km^2 Foraging radius = 5.84 kilometers Foraging area = 88.8 km^2 Foraging radius = 5.32 kilometers	Ichikawa 1983:56 Ichikawa 1983:58 Tanno 1976:112 Hart 1978:327
HILL PANDARAM	Mean local community group size = 55.6 persons Foraging area = 79.66 km^2 Foraging radius = 5.04 kilometers	Morris 1982:169
PEKANGEKUM	Dependency ratio = 2.04 persons	Dunning 1959:68

Note: Data are categorized differently for different groups. Data do not discriminate by gender of foraging parties.

It is much more likely that the !Kung data reflect a normal, day-to-day hunting pattern, since they were taken from records of male foraging parties whose mobility was directed expressly toward meeting subsistence goals. The large size of !Kung male hunting parties (3.0 males) is not, however, directly comparable to the Nunamiut data, in which values refer strictly to the size of male foraging parties. Data for the !Kung represent the number of males from the same camp who went hunting on a given day, although these hunters were not necessarily all hunting together.

In contrast, the data on female foraging parties is remarkably similar in all cases. The female work groups in table 7.10 had a smaller foraging radius and lower standard deviations than either of the male cases in table 7.11. The size of the female work group—on average three adults per work party—also differed significantly from the size of the average two-person male hunting party. Consistent with the foregoing data is the contrast between men and women in the rate of travel; the rate documented for men is 2.59 kilometers per hour while for women two rates were recorded,

TABLE 7.13

SUMMARY OF DATA ON HUNTER-GATHERER FORAGING TRIPS

GROUP	NUMBER IN PARTY	ROUND-TRIP DISTANCE (KM)	DURATION OF EXPEDITION (HR)	RATE OF TRAVEL (KM/HR)	FORAGING RADIUS (KM)
			1. Data on women		
NUNAMIUT	2.9 (1.19)	15.9 (2.19)	5.35 (1.42)	2.16 (0.92)	6.26 (1.09)
ALYAWARA	3.01 (1.00)	10.72 (1.96)	4.65 (1.43)	2.36 (0.60)	5.36 (0.98)
PITJANDJARA	3.0	16.89	6.6	2.53	8.37
ANBARRA		6.19			
PUME		6.77			
MEAN	2.97	14.50	5.53	2.35	6.66
			2. Data on men		
NUNAMIUT	2.1 (0.99)	26.4 (7.93)	11.8 (4.11)	2.26 (0.40)	13.2 (3.96)
!KUNG	2.1 (1.43)	13.4 (5.57)			6.6 (2.78)
PUME		12.3			
MEAN	2.1	17.37	11.8	2.26	9.9
MALES AND FEMALES COMBINED	5.07	15.94		2.31	8.28

Note: Individual values are means with standard deviations in parentheses.

2.16 and 2.37 kilometers per hour. Time lost by women in collecting is not directly comparable to time lost by men searching for prey and waiting in lookout locations.

Table 7.13 records the mean foraging radius for male and female work parties in very different environmental settings. Because the terms of the Group Size Model being constructed require that I produce a single value from the combined record of male and female foraging activities, I used the mean of the female (6.66 kilometers) and male (9.9 kilometers) foraging radiuses. The combined mean value of 8.28 kilometers applies to the radius of a circle encompassing 215.38 square kilometers or 2.15 100-square-kilometer units. Since this figure is itself an approximation, I have chosen to accept as the standard a circle forming the boundary of 2.25 100-square-kilometer units.

I made this adjustment because the data from the Kalahari applied to a group that at the time of documentation was rapidly becoming more sedentary, and I have tried to account for this ongoing change in system state in my approximated, rather than measured, mean value for foraging area. For purposes of model building, therefore, the standard foraging radius was arbitrarily set at 8.469 kilometers, which corresponds to a foraging area of 225.33 square kilometers. I have termed this arbitrary unit of hunter-gatherer foraging space a FORAD, one FORAD being equal to a circle with a radius of 8.459 kilometers and a total area of 225.33 square kilometers.

My estimate of foraging area is greater than the estimates offered by Henry (1964:11–12), Holmberg (1950:40), and Williams (1974:147), but in the cases documented by these three researchers either processes of intensification were suspected to be occurring or an inference was required to obtain an estimate of foraging radius. The same logical structure underlies the standards that I am proposing in the Group Size Model, for—I repeat—the values I have chosen to work with are not empirical generalizations applying to all hunter-gatherers. They represent, instead, a summary of available information that I believe is germane to mobile hunter-gatherers, and they are used as instruments for measurement in an effort to reduce ambiguity.

In this chapter so far, I have developed two analytical tools. One is the COHAB, which represents 20.47 persons and serves as the standard in terms of which I will measure the size of a foraging group. I will also use the FORAD, which corresponds to a 225-square-kilometer circular area that serves as a standard for the unit of geographic space within which a COHAB operates. Equipped with these instruments for measurement, I can now give meaning and significance to population density values.

For instance, if a given ethnic group had a population density value of 13.45 persons per 100 square kilometers, and since one FORAD is larger than the standard unit for expressing density in this study (100 square kilometers), then the number of persons within a FORAD would be determined by multiplying the population density by 2.25, or, in this example, 30.26 persons, representing 1.478 COHABs. Since population density refers to an ethnic group, I can also visualize the structure of the population in space. If the population was distributed in FORAD-sized units, there would be a single settlement of 30.26 persons evenly spaced every 16.94 kilometers (10.53 miles) across the entire ethnic territory. In addition, I would know that the group was rather sedentary since a population density value that exceeds 9.098 persons (20.47 divided by 2.25) per 100 square kilometers would be circumscribed by groups living in FORAD-sized units on all sides.

Exploring Variability in the Modeled Units and Their Contributing Variables

If I consider the problem of mobility from the perspective of the number of moves that occur as well as the pattern of movement, several factors become important. First of all, the more abundant the food supply—other things being equal—the lower the mobility level required to support a given number of people. As a demonstration, let us consider a situation in which all of the basic constants that I have previously discussed are, in fact, constant: the foraging area consists of 225.33 square kilometers (or 86.83 square miles), the dependency ratio is 1.75 persons, an average producer works 170 days per year, and a normal foraging expedition is composed of 2.5035 persons.

Given these values and a knowledge of (1) the area needed to feed a single person, (2) the number of persons, and (3) the average area covered by a single foraging expedition (8.33 square kilometers), I can calculate the following variables:

1. The total area that must be searched (group size multiplied by area needed per person).
2. The number of moves per year (total area divided by the foraging area constant of 215.383 square kilometers).
3. The duration of stay at any one camp (365 days divided by the number of moves).
4. The number of producers in the group (total group size divided by the dependency ratio of 1.75).
5. The number of producers available to work each day (the number of producers multiplied by 0.465).
6. The number of expeditions per day (the number of producers available per day divided by the average expedition size of 2.5 persons).
7. The frequency of foraging area coverage, which is another way of saying the number of times during a stay that an area will be searched (8.33 square kilometers covered by a single expedition or 27.05 expeditions that cover 225.33 square kilometers).

The relationships between mobility and the variables just enumerated have been calculated for groups of 20 and 50 people and are presented in table 7.14. The food abundance variable is indicated by the number of square kilometers needed to support a single person (column 2).

The information in table 7.14 clearly demonstrates that as food abundance decreases, mobility increases, regardless

of group size. For instance, a group of twenty persons in a food-abundant setting (19.9 square kilometers per person) would have to move only 1.77 times per year, while a similar group in a food-scarce setting (79.9 square kilometers per person) would need to move 7.1 times during a year to meet their nutritional requirements. This finding is a graphic illustration of the generalization that search time increases as food resources become less abundant. As an example, at an abundance level of 19.9 square kilometers per person, a group of twenty persons could meet their nutritional requirements in a single FORAD for a period of 206 expedition days. In contrast, at a food abundance level of 79.9 square kilometers per person, food resources would be depleted after only 51 expedition days.

Other things being equal, the data in table 7.14 also indicate that, the larger the group size, the more annual mobility increases. This relationship can be seen by comparing the number of moves for a group of fifty persons at a given level of abundance with a group of twenty persons. For instance, in settings in which 79.9 square kilometers are required to support a single person for a year, a group of twenty persons would have to move only 7.10 times whereas a group of fifty persons would move 17.7 times.

The relationship between group size and mobility is explored further in table 7.15, in which food abundance is held constant at 15.4 square kilometers per person per year and the size of the group is allowed to vary. This scenario demonstrates that increases in group size do not result in increased coverage of a foraging area. Rather, groups in all size categories cover a foraging area approximately 20.8 times during their occupation of any one FORAD. The scale of annual coverage of the territory is simply increased and the time spent at any one resource location is reduced.

The preceding exercise has illustrated several relationships between variables and constants in the Group Size Model, which I will now summarize in two generalizations and two related propositions:

Generalization 7.20

The energy required to move from one foraging area to another is minimized by living in small groups, regardless of the level of food abundance.

Proposition 7.05

Therefore, other things being equal, I anticipate that there is a minimum group size and an optimal small group size that should be characteristic of mobile hunters and gatherers regardless of other variable conditions.

TABLE 7.14

DEMONSTRATION OF THE RELATIONSHIP BETWEEN MOBILITY AND FOOD ABUNDANCE FOR 20- AND 50-PERSON GROUPS OF FORAGERS

GROUP SIZE	AREA PER PERSON (KM²) (1)	TOTAL AREA NEEDED (KM²) (2)	NO. MOVES PER YEAR (3)	DURATION OF STAY (DAYS) (4)	TOTAL PRODUCERS IN GROUP (5)	NO. AVAILABLE PER DAY (6)	NO. TRIPS PER DAY (7)	FREQUENCY OF FORAGING AREA COVERAGE (8)
20	19.9	398	1.77	206	11.4	5.3	2	15.2
	39.9	798	3.55	103	11.4	5.3	2	7.6
	59.9	1,198	5.32	69	11.4	5.3	2	5.1
	79.9	1,598	7.10	51	11.4	5.3	2	3.8
50	19.9	995	4.4	83	28.6	13.3	5.3	16.9
	39.9	1,995	8.8	41	28.6	13.3	5.3	8.3
	59.9	2,995	13.3	27	28.6	13.3	5.3	5.5
	79.9	3,995	17.7	21	28.6	13.3	5.3	4.3

TABLE 7.15

DEMONSTRATION OF THE RELATIONSHIP BETWEEN FORAGER MOBILITY AND GROUP SIZE
WHEN ABUNDANCE OF FOOD IS HELD CONSTANT

GROUP SIZE	AREA PER PERSON (KM²) (1)	TOTAL AREA NEEDED (KM²) (2)	NO. MOVES PER YEAR (3)	DURATION OF STAY (DAYS) (4)	TOTAL PRODUCERS IN GROUP (5)	NO. AVAILABLE PER DAY (6)	NO. TRIPS PER DAY (7)	FREQUENCY OF FORAGING AREA COVERAGE (8)
10	15.4	154	0.7	521	5.7	2.7	1.1	21.2
20	15.4	308	1.4	261	11.4	5.3	2.1	20.3
30	15.4	462	2.1	174	17.1	7.9	3.2	20.6
40	15.4	616	2.7	135	22.9	10.6	4.2	20.9
50	15.4	770	3.4	107	28.6	13.3	5.3	21.0
60	15.4	924	4.1	89	34.3	15.9	6.4	21.0
70	15.4	1,078	4.8	76	40.0	18.6	7.4	20.8
80	15.4	1,232	5.5	66	45.7	21.2	8.5	20.7
90	15.4	1,386	6.2	59	51.4	23.9	9.5	20.7
100	15.4	1,540	6.8	54	57.1	26.6	10.6	21.2

Generalization 7.21

As the abundance of food in a habitat decreases, of necessity a group's mobility increases. Other things being equal, it is certain that greater net benefit is associated with small group sizes in food-poor settings.

Proposition 7.06

Therefore, I expect the smallest groups and the most consistent relationships between mobility and group size to occur among peoples living in low-productivity habitats.

This modeling exercise has allowed me to define two instruments for measurement, the COHAB and the FORAD, by means of which I can now relate such abstract measures as population density to more easily understood properties of mobile hunter-gatherers. I can also explore the relational consequences of shifts in the values of the variables and dimensions that I have discussed and explored thus far. I am now in a position to apply the intellectual tools that have been developed to the empirical data on group size to see if my expectations about the world of dynamics, which I have presented in the form of generalizations, will be confirmed.

Conclusion

In this chapter I have demonstrated provocative patterns in the relationships between several categories of information in the ethnographic data set. I have illustrated that the size of the geographic area occupied by ethnic groups, as well as the number of persons included in such groups, is linked in provocative ways to properties of the habitats that are exploited for food. I have also suggested that the human unit implied by use of the term *ethnic group* is ambiguous and that any generalizations I might develop that would incorporate such a term are equally ambiguous.

I have also demonstrated what I mean by the term *system state* and its linkage to thresholds where "the rules change." I have argued that building theories to explain transitions in system state could require different types of arguments than building theories to explain variability among cases in which a reversal in the relationships between variables does not occur. I have tried to show that being able to identify exceptions to the regularities summarized by generalizations is a good way to recognize such transitional situations, but I did not systematically follow up on this argument. I did demon-

strate, however, that equestrian hunters differ markedly in group size parameters from all other hunters and that they had uniformly larger group sizes than foragers who were dependent upon terrestrial animals. In light of the generalizations summarized in this chapter, I would also expect mounted hunters to be highly mobile, and (as will be seen in chapters 10 and 11) my expectation is confirmed.

One might then ask why equestrian hunters did not reduce their group sizes and thereby lower their mobility costs. The answer is that domesticated horses allowed hunters to reduce their mobility costs drastically—which in turn prompts me to ask what is the advantage, given such reduced costs, of maintaining large group sizes. The answer to this question is important, but of even greater significance is the point that the data on equestrian hunters highlight: mode of transport is yet another variable that must be controlled, both in comparative experiments and in theory building. In both instances, one must either hold mode of transport constant or permit it to vary as a way of exploring the interactions between such variables as the costs of transport and the scale of territorial coverage relative to the body size of prey, the shifts in food resources, and human energy budgets relative to labor requirements.

I noted that not only should a theory anticipate accurately when something will occur, it must also anticipate when it will not. For example, many of the ancestors of the Plains Indians had responded to intensificational pressures by becoming horticulturists, but when a new subsistence technology (represented by the horse) became available, they reversed direction and once again became hunter-gatherers (or hunter-pastoralists, as some would say). At the same time that these groups changed from a higher to a lower state of intensification, their trajectory was toward a more complex form of social integration that featured secret societies and other kinds of sodalities.[11] By developing a good theory, it should be possible to anticipate when exceptional forms of organization should occur rather than categorically dismissing groups as bogus or somehow not "real" hunter-gatherers.

I do not mean to suggest that I cannot use a limited number of hunter-gatherer cases as the basis for a model that will act as a standard to clarify both what is being measured and how cases may differ from the standard. In chapter 8, I intend to use the generalizations and exceptions developed in this chapter, as well as the Group Size Model, in the analysis of the hunter-gatherer data set. My goal is to explain the patterns already identified and the relationships that I expect to see when operationalizing the knowledge developed in this chapter. I will also develop some further refinements to apply to the investigation of what the world appears to be like with respect to an increased focus on intensification.

A Flat Earth or a "Thick Rotundity"?

Investigating What The World Is Like before Attempting to Explain It

Theory building is not for sissies! It is a rigorous, time-consuming process, and there is no guarantee that a comprehensive, defensible theory will result from the effort that has been invested in its development. Thankfully, intellectual tactics do exist that can make the process less daunting, as a review of the sequence of steps I have taken in this study thus far will illustrate.[1]

I argued in chapter 2 that successful use of the human capacity to plan for the future is made possible by a knowledge of stabilities in the world of experience. In attempting to build theories about the patterned interactions among various recurring dynamic properties in the world of experience, I am using my own reasoning capacity to structure the stabilities I have observed in a particular set of dynamics. I must also take care to look at the world unambiguously, so that I can see how independently varying features of experience actually interact as part of event sequences in the external world. Theory building is as heavily dependent upon the use of prior knowledge as is the construction of frames of reference and projections.

Because, however, a theory is a *causal* argument about patterning in nature,[2] theories operate at a higher explanatory level than simple projections in the hierarchy of a scientist's intellectual tools. A good example of the confusion that still exists on this point, even in rarified scientific circles, occurs in the following account of Per Bak's encounter with eminent paleontologist Stephen J. Gould at a meeting of the Harvard Society of Fellows:

> I happened to be sitting next to the president of the society, and on the other side of the president was a smiling gentleman. I introduced myself. "Stephen Jay Gould," the gentleman responded. What a coincidence—the very person I wanted to meet was my neighbor at the table. That should not be wasted. "Wouldn't it be nice if there were a theory of punctuated equilibria?" I started. "Punctuated equilibria is a theory!" Gould

responded. Where do you go from there? Not much communication took place, and I had to run to catch my plane. (1996:162–63)

I would have to agree with Per Bak that the relatively sudden appearance and disappearance of now-extinct species in the fossil record constitute an evolutionary pattern that demands an explanation and that, as such, is not a theory at all.

In chapter 7, I presented and commented on many provocative, patterned relationships among the variables in the hunter-gatherer data set. These ranged from the observation that small ethnic areas were usually situated in high-productivity tropical and subtropical localities (generalization 7.01) to the association of higher mobility levels with decreases in the abundance of a habitat's food supply (generalization 7.21). Throughout the chapter, I suggested which variables might be interacting to shape the patterns I had isolated, I narrowed my focus to patterning in the size of economically important residential groups, and I addressed the issue of measurement and model building.

In this chapter, I am searching for ideas. I once again explore patterns in the hunter-gatherer data, but this time I am interested in how the different patterns relate to my ideas about how the world works and why it might work that way. In chapter 7, I built a bold model. Now I evaluate how well that model permits me to anticipate classes of data that I intentionally did not use in the construction of the model. I also discover whether or not the model enables me to see new patterning.

In the process of model building, I tried to identify the factors that could be contributing to variability in group size. Based upon prior knowledge of the exigencies of hunter-gatherer life, I chose to look more closely at dependency ratios and the organization and scheduling of the division of labor among food producers. Despite the lacunae in the ethnographic literature on the subject of dependency ratio values

243

(summarized in table 7.08), I was able to calculate a defensible, if less than ideal, mean value for this important variable. I also explored the effect of dependency ratios on the organization and intensity of male and female food-related labor (table 7.09).

At this juncture, I want to determine how these factors are affected by the different trophic levels targeted by hunter-gatherers and to identify the degree of mobility that results from their various subsistence strategies. I will, in fact, extend my evaluation of mobility, begun in chapter 7, by focusing on the effect that differences in degree and mode of mobility have on group sizes. Along the way, I hope to refine and develop my understanding of the processes contributing to adaptive differentiation among peoples making use of different habitats as well as variability arising from intensification.

My more specific goal includes an examination of the available information on group size relative to the models and dimensions that I developed in chapter 7. Does the real world correspond in any way to my hunter-gatherer Group Size Model? If it becomes clear that the model is an imperfect recreation of real-world dynamics, then I must search for sources that will enlighten me about why the variables represented by the model's constants diverge from my projections and what the factors responsible for the variation may be. I also want to identify any additional sources of data that are relevant to the already identified patterns and model I have built.

Variability in GROUP1 Size: The Model versus the Documented Cases

One problem with pursuing an interest in hunter-gatherer group size and the organization of an annual settlement cycle is that ethnographic observers have often failed to note whether they were discussing a "task group" or a "residential group." Their reports are also notoriously deficient in information about a group's total settlement system. Since, however, I am aware of the limitations of my data and am committed to its judicious use, I have compiled table 8.01, which summarizes data on group size values and provides bibliographic citations for the ethnographic groups for which data are available. In most cases, the estimates are based on information supplied by an individual ethnographer, but these assessments frequently do not occur in the same descriptive context. Often it is not possible to point to one statement in which group size is discretely specified. In many instances, group size values are approximated in several different statements that are dispersed throughout an ethnographer's monograph.

The data on the hunter-gatherer cases presented in table 8.01 constitute an impressive array of group size estimates. The obvious question is how they compare to the values

modeled in chapter 7 for COHAB, my standardized unit in terms of which data on group size were dimensionalized. The assumptions underlying the COHAB variable are most likely to be met by hunter-gatherer cases that are predominantly dependent upon terrestrial plants (SUBSP = 2), classified as mobile (GRPPAT = 1), only moderately disrupted by colonial expansion (SUBPOP = n), and not included in the "mounted hunters of the Americas" category (HUNTFIL2 = 1). GROUP1 size was available for fifty-nine of the cases in table 8.01 that met all of the assumptions about COHAB units. All are designated as foragers (sensu Binford 1980) with respect to the variable MOBP2, which classifies cases according to the way that labor is organized and positioned to exploit resources.

Figure 8.01 illustrates that there is a bimodal distribution of GROUP1 sizes among the cases that are predominantly dependent upon terrestrial plants, are mobile, and are not heavily affected by non-hunter-gatherer systems. The smaller of the two distributions has a mean of 9.95 ± 1.58 persons while the mean of the larger distribution is 17.49 ± 3.39 persons. It should be recalled that, for smaller groups, the model anticipated a GROUP1 size of 10.23 persons in groups with a partially collapsed division of labor. For larger groups with a normal division of labor, I modeled a GROUP1 size of 20.47 persons. The short-term version of the basic model anticipated a value of 8.75 persons for groups with a collapsed division of labor and a minimal group size of 17.5 persons when the division of labor was normal. In this instance, the empirical case material corresponds quite well to the modeled values, and I think it is a good demonstration of the model's likely utility.

It should also be noted that the smaller of the model's two variants of minimal group size, which I anticipated would be characterized by a collapsed division of labor, is more prevalent among plant-dependent peoples by a factor of 2.28 to 1.0. This proportion is not restricted to the Great Basin of North America, even though Steward (1955:101–21) initially identified the family level of organization in this region, at least partly because of the frequency of groups of this type.[3]

Among the groups in the global hunter-gatherer sample that are dependent upon terrestrial plant resources, social units with a collapsed division of labor are more prevalent by a ratio of 1.71 to 1.0, even when the Great Basin cases are excluded. This frequency bias should not be surprising since I argued in proposition 7.06 that the greatest net gain from smaller group sizes would accrue to peoples in habitats with relatively low primary productivity, since greater mobility would be expected in such settings, other things being equal.

On the left side of the graph in figure 8.02, which represents low-productivity settings, GROUP1 size values for most of the cases are in the range of the collapsed division of labor variant (mean size = 9.95 ± 1.58 persons). There is

TABLE 8.01

HUNTER-GATHERER GROUP SIZE DURING THE MOST DISPERSED
AND MOST AGGREGATED PHASES OF THE ANNUAL CYCLE
AND AT PERIODIC REGIONAL AGGREGATIONS

CASES	GROUP1 MOST DISPERSED	GROUP2 MOST AGGREGATED	GROUP3 PERIODIC REGIONAL AGGREGATIONS	REFERENCE(S)
Tropical-subtropical Asia				
PUNAN		30	62	Harrison 1949:135, 139; Urquart 1951:515,
		26		505; Brosius 1986:174
	22	30		Sellato 1994:143–44
BATEK (PALAWAN)	19	58		Eder 1978:56, 1987:105
KUBU	12			Hagen 1908:25–28; Persoon 1989:511
SHOMPEN	19.3	31		Rizvi 1990:8
ANDAMAN ISLANDS (ONGE)	10	23	70	Bose 1964:305
ANDAMAN ISLANDS (JARWA)	8.6	25.8	65	Temple 1903:62, 77, 84
AYTA (PINATUBO)	11	35	200	Fox, 1952:188; Reed 1904:19
BIG ANDAMAN ISLAND	11	43	80	Radcliffe-Brown 1948:28
SEMANG	17	34	71	Schebesta 1962a:17, 220; Rambo 1985:4, 33; Brandt 1961:131–33
VEDDAH	14	29	72	Bailey 1863:296, 308; Seligmann and Seligmann 1911:43–44
HILL PANDARAM	10	34	141	Morris 1982a:36–37, 174
AGTA (CASIGURAN)	17	30	82	Headland pers. comm. 1993
AGTA (ISABELA)	12	21	70	Rai 1982:63, 66, 119
AGTA (CAGAYAN)	18.9	43.3		Vanoverbergh 1925:195, 196–98, 432
CHENCHU	19.3	48		Fürer-Haimendorf 1943:366
MRABRI	19.5	40		Pookajorn 1985:187, 207; Velder 1963:186–87
PALIYANS	14	25	107	Gardner 1965:101, 1988:93, 94
BIRHOR	26.8	46	160	Sen and Sen 1955:172; Williams 1974:79
KADAR	17.5	31.7	187	Ehrenfels 1952:66–67
CHOLANAICKAN	10.2	20.5		Bhanu 1992:table 1.1
NAYAKA	13.8	69		Bird 1983:58
AINU				
HOKKAIDO	15.1	30.3	122.6	Watanabe 1964:8–9
KURIL ISLAND	15.1	30.3	122.6	Landor 1893:89, 125
	22.0	68		
OROGENS	20	60	265	Qiu 1983 (estimates only)
KET	24	33	182	Lee 1967:24; Shimkin 1939:150
GILYAK	23	90		Shternberg 1933:385
YUKAGHIR	12.3	55	180	Kreynovich 1979:191–92, 196
NGANASAN	14	29	116	Popov 1966:12, 103
SIBERIAN ESKIMO	15	35	90	Krupnik 1983:94–95
Tropical-subtropical South America				
SHIRIANA		50		Métraux 1948:863
AKURIYO	18.5	28	66	Kloos 1977:116
YARURO-PUME	15.1	57	70	Greaves pers. comm. 1993; Gragson 1989:289–90
GUAHIBO	20	60	179	Wilbert 1957:90
NUKAK	18.8	47	94	Politis 1992:3, pers. comm. 1992
BORORO		118		Baldus 1937:115–23; Lévi-Strauss 1936:269
GUATO	16.6	37		Métraux 1946a:410
SIRIONO	16	70		Holmberg 1950:51
YUQUI	18.0	43		Stearman 1989a:26, 31
NAMBIKWARA	17.5	47	75	Lévi-Strauss 1970:288; Oberg 1953:86
CALUSA	35	62	700	Hann 1991:42, 159, 168
GUAYAKI (ACHE)	17.5	50		Clastres 1972:163; Oberg 1953:18, 38

(continued)

TABLE 8.01 *(continued)*

CASES	MOST DISPERSED	MOST AGGREGATED	PERIODIC REGIONAL AGGREGATIONS	REFERENCE(S)
BOTOCUDO		50	84	Métraux 1946:534
HETA	20	30		Kozak et al. 1979:360
AWEIKOMO	27		110	Henry 1964:11, 50, 159
TEHUELCHE	25	75	225	Cooper 1946c:150; Goni 1988:145
ALACALUF	13.4			Bird pers. comm. 1970
ONA	20	45	290	Chapman 1982:58; Cooper 1946b:117; Gusinde 1931:205
YAHGAN	13	24	250	Gusinde 1937:384, 387

Tropical-subtropical Africa

CASES	MOST DISPERSED	MOST AGGREGATED	PERIODIC REGIONAL AGGREGATIONS	REFERENCE(S)
AKA	18	36	111	Bahuchet 1988:131; Hudson 1990:58, 63, 71
BAYAKA	19.7	30	73	Heymer 1980:178, 193–96
BAMBOTE	19.7	60	95	Terashima 1980:234, 235, 262
BAKA	17.5	32.6	104	Cavalli-Sforza 1986c:32–33
	16	31.75	90	Vallois and Marquer 1976:113
EFE	17.8	33	100	Bailey and Peacock 1988:99–100; Fisher and Strickland 1989:476
MBUTI				
MAWAMBO	30.7	60	87	Tanno 1976:107, 108, 130
EPULA	30.2	104	252	Turnbull 1965:97, 98
MIKEA		40		Kelly and Poyer 1993:1
HUKWE		23	70	Clark 1951:65
HAI//OM		60	166	Fourie 1927:51
HADZA	16.5	42		Blurton-Jones et al. 1992:164; Hawkes et al. 1989:344; Woodburn 1968:104
DOROBO	17	46	75	Huntingford 1951:8; 1954:128
SEKELE	12	31	65	Bleek 1929:109; De Castro and Alemeida 1956:9
!KUNG (NYAE NYAE)	10.4	24.3	130	Marshall 1960:328
!KUNG (DOBE)	11	23	45	Lee 1972a:330
NHARO	6	20	70	Guenther 1986:186; Schapera 1930:78
G/WI	5.6	36	85	Silberbauer 1972:296, 1981a:195–98
KUA	8	21	42	Kent and Vierich 1989
!KO	13	54	111	Eibl-Eibelsfeldt 1972:32–33
/AUNI (KHOMANI)	9	21	77	Steyn 1984:118; Dart 1937b:160–65
//XEGWI			100	Potgieter 1955:8
/XAM	8	24		Bleek 1924:viii, ix

Australia: subtropical desert through temperate settings

CASES	MOST DISPERSED	MOST AGGREGATED	PERIODIC REGIONAL AGGREGATIONS	REFERENCE(S)
KAURAREG	17.5	50	116	Moore 1979:39
GUNWINGGU	18.5	44	128	Altman 1987:15–27; Berndt and Berndt 1970:3–14
MIRRNGADJA	16	34	77	Peterson 1973:185; 1970:11; pers. comm. 1992; Peterson and Long 1986:40
ANBARRA	10	35	250	Meehan 1982:31–41
GIDJINGALI	16	34	80	Peterson 1972:26; Peterson and Long 1986:40
MURNGIN	18	36	290	Thomson 1949:16; Warner 1958:127–28
JEIDJI	17	32	125	Kaberry 1935:428
WIKMUNKAN	8	45	150	Wills 1980:85 (LRB estimates from photos)
KAKADU	9	32	200	Leichardt 1847:507; McCarthy and MacArthur 1960:90–96
NUNGGUBUYU	17	30	225	Biernoff 1979:12; MacArthur 1960:95; Thompson 1949:4
YINTJINGGA	15			Thomson 1934:241

TABLE 8.01 *(continued)*

CASES	MOST DISPERSED	MOST AGGREGATED	PERIODIC REGIONAL AGGREGATIONS	REFERENCE(S)
YIR-YORONT	14	30		Peterson and Long 1986:88–89, 95–99; Sharp 1934a:425
TIWI	18	32		Hart and Piling 1960:35, 36, 65, 66
KUKU (YALANJI)	14.3		250	Anderson and Robins 1988: 187, 191–92
GROOTE EYELANDT	10	32		Peterson and Long 1986:78–79
WALMBARIA		35	60	Hale and Tindale 1933:77–78
MULLUK	18	30	150	Stanner 1933:393 (estimate)
WORORA	18	35	150	Blundell 1980:106–7; Love 1936:93
LARDIL		45		Memmott 1983a:367
KAIADILT	15.4	29	85	Tindale 1962a:269
MAMU	20	45	285	Harris 1978:128
KARIERA	11	31		Radcliffe-Brown 1912:146
WARUNGGU	19	25	250	Brayshaw 1990:31; Lumholtz 1889:194
DJARU	16	50		Nind 1831:22
WALBIRI	9	42	200	Meggitt 1962:47, 50, 56
NGATJAN	16	32	250	Harris 1978:128
MARDUDJARA	8	25	130	Peterson and Long 1986:116–17; Tonkinson 1978:53
ILDAWONGGA	11.5			Peterson and Long 1986:112–15, 124
PINTUBI	8.5	21	300	Long 1971:264–65; Meggitt 1962:55; Peterson and Long 1986:104–11
UNDANBI			150	Colliver and Woolston 1975:93
JINIBARRA	20	60	400	Morwood 1987:339; Winterbotham 1980:41
ALYAWARA	16	30	230	Binford field notes 1974; Denham 1975:120; O'Connell 1987:85
NGATATJARA	11	25	150	Gould 1977:21–22
BADJALANG	14	90	250	W. Gardner 1978:239–46
PITJANDJARA	10	23	256	Brokensha 1975:19, 33; Layton 1983:26; Peterson and Long 1986:127; Tindale 1972:224, 244
DIERI	7	22	350	Gason 1879:257, 264; Sturt 1849a, 1:254, 261, 296, 316, 407, 414; 2:70,74
JANKUNDJARA	9.5	28	225	Tindale pers. comm. 1965
NORTHERN ARENDA	9.6	30	310	Spencer and Gillen 1927:15, 506
NAKAKO	10.6			Peterson and Long 1986:129–34
MINENG	9	50	300	Nind 1831:28
TJAPWURONG	25	175	350	Williams 1985:75
BUNURONG	7.3	44	275	Gaughwin and Sullivan 1984:92, 94
KURNAI	10	50	270	Fison and Howitt 1880:209; Howitt 1904:773–77
TASMANIANS (EASTERN)	7.5	35	52	Hiatt 1967:201; Jones 1971:278, 279
TASMANIANS (WESTERN)	7.5	33	75	Hiatt 1967:201; Jones 1971:278, 279

North America: California and Northern Mexico

CASES	MOST DISPERSED	MOST AGGREGATED	PERIODIC REGIONAL AGGREGATIONS	REFERENCE(S)
SERI	17	45	188	Bowen 1976:24–30; Griffen 1959:vii
CAHUILLA	20	75	180	Bean 1972:76; Kroeber 1925:692, 706–7; Strong 1929:43–56
CUPENO		97	195	Strong 1929:187–19
KILIWA		62	130	Meigs 1939:18–20
DIEGUENO		39	120	Kroeber 1925:712, 719; Luomala 1978:597
LAKE YOKUTS		91	150	Cook 1955:40
SERRANO		68		Kroeber 1925:617–18
LUISENO	1	110	300	Oxendine 1983:50–57
WUKCHUMI		40	350	Cook 1955:40
TUBATULABAL	14	21	110	Voegelin 1938:39–43

(continued)

CASES	MOST DISPERSED	MOST AGGREGATED	PERIODIC REGIONAL AGGREGATIONS	REFERENCE(S)
NOMLAKI	13	65	130	Goldschmidt 1948:445
NORTH FOOTHILL YOKUTS	16	40	130	Cook 1955:35
PATWIN		53	189	P. J. Johnson 1978:352
MONACHE	13	32	70	Gifford 1932b:42–47
CLEAR LAKE POMO		150	450	Cook 1956:116–17
WINTU	20	50	150	DuBois 1935:28, 29
CHUMASH		557		Cook and Heizer 1965:71
NISENAN	11	45	165	Wilson and Towne 1978:388
SOUTHERN POMO		150		Cook 1956:118
SINKYONE		23		Cook 1956:103–5
MIWOK (COAST)		26		Collier and Thalman 1991:72, 177–78
MATTOLE		45		Cook 1956:102
MIWOK (LAKE)		90	192	Cook 1955:122
YUKI (PROPER)		25	150	Cook 1956:107
WAPPO		95	154	Cook 1956:124
NORTHERN POMO		127		Cook 1956:114
MIWOK (MOUNTAIN)	19	45	250	Cook 1955:36
TOLOWA	18	96		Cook 1956:101; Drucker 1940:226–27
SHASTA		48		Cook and Heizer 1965:70
HUPA		113		Cook 1956:100
KAROK		30		Cook 1956:98
WIYOT		33		Cook 1956:97
MAIDU (MOUNTAIN)		40		Cook and Heizer 1965:71
YUROK		45		Cook 1956:101; Schalk 1978:125
ACHUMAWI		23	275	Kroeber 1962:36–37
MODOC	15	92	157	Ray 1963:204
KLAMATH	18	31	97	Spier 1930:5–8, 23

North America: desert and desert scrub

CASES	MOST DISPERSED	MOST AGGREGATED	PERIODIC REGIONAL AGGREGATIONS	REFERENCE(S)
GUAICURA	11.7	45	128	Aschmann 1967:122
DEATH VALLEY SHOSHONI	7.5	22.5	45	Steward 1938:85–91
KARANKAWA			225	Stiles 1906:80–87
PANAMINT VALLEY SHOSHONI	7.5	22.5		Steward 1938:84
YAVAPAI		107		Gifford 1932a:180–89
KOSO MOUNTAIN SHOSHONI	13.5	55		Steward 1938:80–84
WALAPAI	7	28	60	Hayden 1936:142, 165–68, 70; Kroeber 1935:45
KAWAIISU	15	31	45	Voegelin 1938:48
SALINE VALLEY SHOSHONI	9	30	65	Steward 1938:77, 78, 80
OWENS VALLEY PAIUTE	13	64	300	Liljeblad and Fowler 1986:414–15; Steward 1938:110
KAWICH MOUNTAIN SHOSHONI	9.5	19.5	42	Steward 1938:110
KAIBAB SOUTHERN PAIUTE				
1860S	10.1	21.2	70	Kelly 1964:11–22
KAIBAB	9.6	27	116	Euler and Fowler 1966:35; Stoffle and Evans 1978:183
LAS VEGAS		26	200	Euler and Fowler 1966:35, 101
MONO LAKE PAIUTE	9.6	25		Davis 1965:36
DEEP SPRINGS PAIUTE		23		Steward 1938:58–59
SALMON-EATER SHOSHONI	11.2	34	119	Gould pers. comm. 1992
PYRAMID LAKE PAIUTE		50	320	Fowler and Liljeblad 1986:443, 457
TIMANOGAS UTE	17.5	50	160	Janetski 1983:53–54, 75
CATTAIL PAIUTE	18	46	130	Fowler 1992:35–37, 154
FISH LAKE VALLEY PAIUTE	10.5	27	101	Steward 1938:61
HUKUNDUKA SHOSHONI		24	138	Steward 1938:177
GOSIUTE SHOSHONI	10	33	150	Steward 1938:132

TABLE 8.01 (*continued*)

CASES	MOST DISPERSED	MOST AGGREGATED	PERIODIC REGIONAL AGGREGATIONS	REFERENCE(S)
SPRING VALLEY SHOSHONI	11	24	130	Steward 1938:124–27
WHITE KNIFE SHOSHONI	12	23	180	Lowie 1924:284; Steward 1938:161
RAILROAD VALLEY SHOSHONI	11	32	70	Steward 1938:117
REESE RIVER SHOSHONI	10	30	132	Steward 1938:101, 108
MONO-NORTH FORK PAIUTE		29		Cook 1955:37
GROUSE CREEK SHOSHONI	16	38	78	Steward 1938:174
WIMONANTCI UTE		37	102	Callaway et al. 1986:352; Smith 1974:123
BEAR CREEK PAIUTE	16	40		Lowie 1924:284
ANTELOPE VALLEY SHOSHONI	12.5	20	110	Steward 1938:130
WASHO	9	29		Price 1962:40
SURPRISE VALLEY PAIUTE	13	28	100	Kelly 1932:78, 105
WIND RIVER SHOSHONI	16	50	200	Shimkin 1947:255; Steward 1974:373
WADADUKA (RUBY VALLEY SHOSHONI)	21	48	65	Steward 1938:145–46
BOHOGUE NORTHERN SHOSHONI	12	60		Steward 1938:209
UINTAH UTE	16	43	169	Steward 1974:147
WADADOKADO PAIUTE	11			Whiting 1950:19
AGAIDUKA SHOSHONI	18.3		300	Steward 1938:186–89
LITTLE SMOKEY SHOSHONI	16		96	Steward 1938:113
UNCOMPAHGRE UTE	17	45	150	Steward 1974:147

Mounted hunters from steppic regions of North America

CASES	MOST DISPERSED	MOST AGGREGATED	PERIODIC REGIONAL AGGREGATIONS	REFERENCE(S)
LIPAN APACHE	25	75	166	Basehart pers. comm. 1972; Swanton 1952:323
COMANCHE	60	269	650	Wallace and Hoebel 1952:23
CHIRICAHUA APACHE	34	95	200	Basehart 1972:5; Morice 1906b:496; Opler 1937:177–82
KIOWA APACHE	35	313	620	Bamforth 1988:106–9
KIOWA		291		Bamforth 1988:106–9
CHEYENNE	45	275	687	Moore 1987:180–86, 194
ARAPAHOE	36	325	750	Flannery 1953:54; Gussow et al. 1974:23
CROW	66	330	1,500	Bamforth 1988:106–9; Denig 1961:165
TETON LAKOTA	38	283	500	Culbertson 1952:135
KUTENAI		122		Chamberlain 1892:551
BANNOCK	43	170	650	Steward 1938:201–6
GROS-VENTRE	34	188	445	Bamforth 1988:106–9; Swanton 1952:278
PLAINS OJIBWA	40	250	500	Skinner 1914:477
PEIGAN	45	254	762	Ewers 1955:303
BLACKFOOT	70	346	1,100	Bushnell 1922:26; Ewers 1955:303
ASSINIBOINE	55	159	850	Bushnell 1922:32–33; Culbertson 1952:107; Lowrie and Clarke 1832
PLAINS CREE	40	75	285	Bamforth 1988:106–109; Bushnell 1922:20, 21
BLOOD	42	250	800	Bamforth 1988:106–109
SARSI	43	140	300	Bamforth 1988:106–109; Jenness 1938:10–11

North Pacific coastal areas of North America and Asia

CASES	MOST DISPERSED	MOST AGGREGATED	PERIODIC REGIONAL AGGREGATIONS	REFERENCE(S)
TAKELMA	18	50		Gray 1987:37–40
TUTUTNI		60		Gray 1987:56
SQUAMISH		106		Suttles 1990:453, 473
PUYALLUP	28	145		Smith 1940a:7–14
TWANA		80		Elmendorf 1960:32–55

(*continued*)

TABLE 8.01 *(continued)*

CASES	MOST DISPERSED	MOST AGGREGATED	PERIODIC REGIONAL AGGREGATIONS	REFERENCE(S)
CHEHALIS		110		Taylor 1974a:187
NOOTKA (1881)		195		Drucker 1951:222–49; Koppert 1930b:53
CHINOOK		52		Ray 1938:38–41
COOS		58		Boyd 1990:136; Zenk 1990:572
LILLOOETZ		85		Teit 1906:199
LUMMI		140		Stern 1934:7
QUINAULT		36		Schalk 1978:165
STALO		37		Duff 1952:45
COWICHAN		48		Suttles 1990: 462; Wilson 1866:286
TILLAMOOK		65		Seaburg and Miller 1990:561
COMOX		240		Kennedy and Bouchard 1990:450–51
BELLA-BELLA		181		Hilton 1990:313
QUILEUTE	29	112	225	Pettitt 1950:3–5
CLALLAM		166		Boyd 1990:136; Suttles 1990:456
MAKAH		164		Swan 1870:2
HAISLA		650		Schalk 1978:165
SOUTHERN KWAKIUTL		420		Schalk 1978:165
TSIMSHIM		389		Schalk 1978:126, 165
HAIDA		577		Schalk 1978:126, 165
BELLA-COOLA		58		Schalk 1978:165
SOUTHERN TLINGIT		197		Schalk 1978:127, 165
GITKSAN		179		Adams 1973:8
KONAIG		162		Knecht and Jordan 1985:21
EYAK		57	130	Birket-Smith and de Laguna 1938:19
KUSKOWAGMUT	19	108		Michael 1967:306
CHUGASH				
1843		40		Michael 1967:306
1890		67		de Laguna 1956:256
ALEUT		55		Lantis 1970:178; Mitchell and Donald 1988:319–21
NUNIVAK		54.6	133	Lantis 1946:163–64

Subarctic and continental midlatitude forests of North America and Asia

CASES	MOST DISPERSED	MOST AGGREGATED	PERIODIC REGIONAL AGGREGATIONS	REFERENCE(S)
TENINO			212	Murdock 1980:130
WENATCHI		275	500	Teit 1928:93–108
WISHRAM	25	205	700	Spier and Sapir 1930:166–67
COEUR D'ALENE	21	60	350	Teit 1930:39, 331
SINKAIETK	20	83	230	Cline et al. 1938:87
OKANAGON	23	50	245	Teit 1930:207–11
SANPOIL		50		Teit 1930:211
NEZ PERCE		134	438	Spinden 1908:174–75, 196, 240
THOMPSON	18	113	265	Teit 1900:241–48
KALISPEL	22	75	350	Teit 1930:331
KITCHIBUAN	15	65	200	Jenness 1935:13
KATIKITEGON		76		Kinietz 1947:247
MICMAC	15	25	190	Speck 1922:143–44
FLATHEAD	24	73	300	Teit 1930:331; Turney-High 1937:98
RAINY RIVER OJIBWA	21	57	210	Hickerson 1967:54–55
NORTH SALTEAUX	15	45	185	Bishop 1978:222–26
SHUSWAP		108	266	Teit 1905:457–66
PEKANGEKUM OJIBWA	22	55	160	Dunning 1959:57, 58, 84; Rogers 1969:31
ROUND LAKE OJIBWA	7	50	150	Rogers 1963:67, 76, 88; 1969:25, 31
ALKATCHO	20	85	235	Goldman 1940:334
NIPIGON OJIBWA	18	36	126	Hickerson 1962:30–33
MISTASSINI CREE	15	37	215	Rogers 1962a: 23, 1969:30
NORTH ALBANY OJIBWA		50	225	Rogers 1969:43
WASWANIPPI CREE	12	58	235	Rogers 1969:31; Morantz 1983:89, 106

TABLE 8.01 (*continued*)

CASES	MOST DISPERSED	MOST AGGREGATED	PERIODIC REGIONAL AGGREGATIONS	REFERENCE(S)
WEAGAMON OJIBWA	10	50	140	Rogers and Black 1976:19
MONTAGNAIS	22	95	245	Tanner 1944:592–609
SEKANI	18	40	164	Dennison 1981:434–35; Jenness 1937:14
BEAVER	20	58	110	Ives 1985:166–67
SLAVE	13	39	220	Helm 1961:50–52, 169; Ives 1985:166–67; Janes 1983:50–51
KASKA	16	58	139	Honigmann 1949:33–37
TAHLTAN		71	165	MacLachlan 1981:460–61
CARRIER	18	54	170	Jenness 1943:485–86
MOUNTAIN	15	60		Gillespie 1981:334–35
HAN			214	Crow and Obley 1981:511
HARE	13	26	120	Helm 1961: 169; Savishinsky 1974:47, 54
ATTAWAPISKAT CREE	17	55	172	Honigmann 1956:58; 1981:228–29
KOYUKON	14	38	105	Clark 1974:96
CHIPPEWYAN (1800)	23	75	295	Smith 1981:275, 1978:81, 1976:19
KUTCHIN	32	78	210	Slobodin 1969:58–59, 64
INGALIK				
KUSK	8	29		Michael 1967:307; Sullivan 1942:10
YUKON		77		Michael 1967:307
SATUDENE-BEAR LAKE	12	29		MacKenzie 1966:49–56
NABESNA	17	39		McKennan 1959:18
RUPERT HOUSE CREE	12	55	225	Morantz 1983:106
DOGRIB	22	60	162	Helm 1968:120
TANAINA (1843)		68		Michael 1967:306
TUTCHONE	17	60		Legros 1982:68–69
HOLIKACHUK		66	300	Snow 1981:615
NASKAPI	23	39	117	Henriksen 1973:58–59, 68

Arctic

NORTON SOUND INUIT	27.5	48		Ray 1992:295
KOBUK INUIT	18	30		Burch 1975:257–58
KOTZEBUE SOUND INUIT	24.5	49	350	Burch 1975:269–72, 1984:305
LABRADOR INUIT	11	35	158	Taylor 1974:15–19, 64
GREAT WHALE INUIT	20	40	65	Willmot 1960:48, 53
CARIBOU INUIT	19.5	40	75	Birket-Smith 1929:67–69
NOATAK INUIT	17.5	30	105	Binford 1971 field notes; Burch 1975:255
NUNAMUIT INUIT				
1898–1909	8.9	31.1	75	Amsden 1977:224
1934–1950	18.5	25.1		Amsden 1977:224
1951–1959	7.8	40.5	71	Amsden 1977:224; Binford 1991:80
MACKENZIE INUIT	12	45	135	McGhee 1988:11; Tyrrell 1897:167
SIVOKAMIUT INUIT	19	121		Moore 1923:340
POINT HOPE INUIT	13	179		Burch 1975:260–69
COPPER INUIT	18	105	264	Jenness 1922:30, 55, 57; Rasmussen 1932:70, 78–85
UTKUHIKHALINGMIUT	18	35		Briggs 1970:15, 372–74
AIVILINGMIUT INUIT	13	26	64	Rae 1850:40, 48, 49
INGULIK INUIT	12	60	120	Mathiassen 1928:32
WEST GREENLAND	16.2	31.5		Perry 1898:131, 171–72, 267–68, 336, 386, 431; York 1875:179
BAFFIN ISLAND INUIT	12	70	144	Boas 1888:426; Hantzsch 1977:39, 99; Low 1906:57–58
NETSILIK INUIT	22	85	150	M'Clintock 1860:8, 230, 232, 235, 239, 240
ANGMAKASLIK	14	31	137	Mirsky 1937:53; Peterson 1984:623
TAREUMIUT INUIT	14	309		Simpson 1875:237; Spencer 1959:15
POLAR INUIT	11.5	35	150	Ekblaw 1948:3, Steensby 1910:266, 296, 324

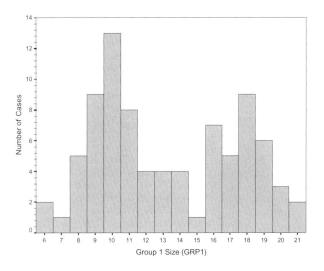

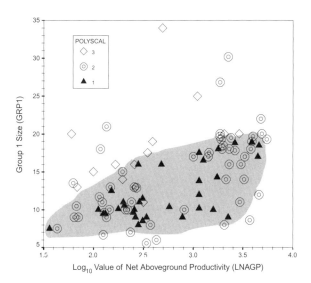

FIGURE 8.01

Bar graph illustrating the differences in GROUP1 size of mobile groups dependent upon terrestrial plants.

FIGURE 8.02

Scatter plot with GROUP1 size and the $\log_{10}$ value of net aboveground productivity defining the property space. The marker is coded ordinally for political development (POLY-SCAL): (1) groups with strict local autonomy, in which senior males provide informal, advisory leadership; (2) groups with strict local autonomy but with performance-based leadership; and (3) groups with strict local autonomy but with a council of advisors that is convened by a recognized leader who has specific corporate duties. Shading defines the zone for cases in which POLYSCAL = 1.

also a trend—which is steeper among more politically complex peoples—toward larger group size in more productive habitats. This pattern is inversely related to mobility-adapted peoples and, thus far, seems to support the mobility-minimizing assumption of the Group Size Model.

Another way to demonstrate the relationship between net aboveground productivity and GROUP1 size is to compare the plant-dependent cases illustrated in figure 8.02 with other subsistence-based subsets in a cross-tabulation such as the one in table 8.02. Arraying the data in this format suggests that groups living in food-poor environments would derive the greatest benefit from the reduced mobility that smaller group size facilitates. Another way to summarize the patterns in figure 8.02 and table 8.02 is to say that

Generalization 8.01

Among terrestrial plant–dependent peoples, smaller GROUP1 sizes predominate in settings in which net aboveground productivity is low. The reverse is true for settings with substantial net aboveground productivity.

Generalization 8.02

Politically complex cases have larger GROUP1 sizes regardless of environment. In this instance, however, political complexity may be autocorrelated with sedentism, since increased ethnic group sizes and decreased ethnic group areas were both documented (generalization 7.08).

Proposition 8.01

GROUP1 size may also increase regularly with intensification and therefore be autocorrelated with other responses to intensification, such as sedentism and political complexity.

The inverse relationship between the abundance of food in a habitat and group mobility, summarized in generalization 7.20 and proposition 7.06, is supported by the patterns in figure 8.02 and table 8.02. These illustrate that greater benefits would accrue to terrestrial plant–dependent peoples in marginal habitats who maintained minimal group sizes and reduced their mobility costs.

Because table 8.02 also includes data on groups that were primarily dependent upon terrestrial animals and aquatic resources, the two graphs in figure 8.03 present a more focused comparison of group size among peoples practicing these different subsistence strategies. In frequency histograms referring to the GROUP1 sizes of mobile peoples, those groups dependent upon aquatic resources are plotted in graph A while groups dependent upon terrestrial animals are

TABLE 8.02

COMPARISON OF GROUP1 SIZE BY CLASSES
OF NET ABOVEGROUND PRODUCTIVITY

	LOG_{10} NET ABOVEGROUND PRODUCTIVITY		
GROUP1 SIZE	<2.75	>2.75	TOTAL
A. Cases dependent upon terrestrial plants			
>15 PERSONS	10 (06)	**33 (03)**	43
<15 PERSONS	**43 (05)**	15 (00)	58
TOTAL	53	48	101
B. Cases dependent upon terrestrial animals			
>15 PERSONS	**38 (17)**	**08 (03)**	46
<15 PERSONS	19 (01)	01 (00)	20
TOTAL	57	09	66
C. Cases dependent upon aquatic resources			
>15 PERSONS	**26 (12)**	**13 (01)**	39
<15 PERSONS	10 (00)	12 (00)	22
TOTAL	57	09	66

Note: Values in parentheses indicate the number of cases that are politically complex and whose POLYSC value is greater than 3. **Boldface** denotes the most common frequency in each paired comparison.

plotted in graph B. Given the effect that inclusion of horse-assisted hunters of the North American plains had on summary values in previous comparisons (tables 7.05 and 7.06), the frequency histogram of groups predominantly dependent upon terrestrial animals in figure 8.03, graph B, does not include mounted plains hunters.

In figure 8.03, graph A, the bimodal pattern in figure 8.01 that was associated with plant-dependent peoples does not occur. There is, instead, a strongly skewed, unimodal distribution with a mean of 15.10 persons and a mode of 18 persons. The larger GROUP1 size that is less frequently associated with plant-dependent peoples is most common, and there are

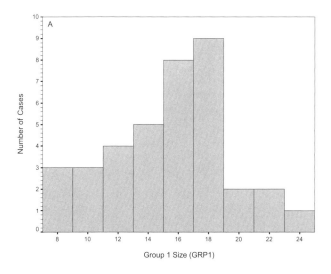

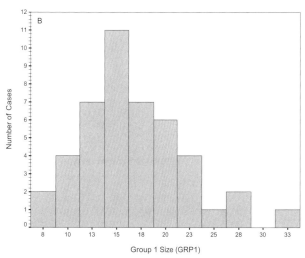

FIGURE 8.03

Comparative bar graphs illustrating the frequency of cases with different GROUP1 sizes displayed relative to subsistence dominance: aquatic resources (A) and terrestrial animal resources (B).

only a few cases in the range of the smaller GROUP1 unit that typifies plant-dependent groups. A similar unimodal distribution occurs in graph B of figure 8.03; most of the cases fall in the distribution that includes GROUP1 sizes of fewer than thirty persons. Thirty-nine cases in this subset have sufficient data to record a value in each of the categories being tabulated; 90 percent of the groups are classified as foragers and 10 percent as collectors.

There is a statistical difference between the mean GROUP1 value of 16.87 recorded for all groups in this category and the means calculated separately for groups of collectors (mean = 17.45 persons, $n = 35$) and foragers (11.75 persons, $n = 4$). The mean GROUP1 value for groups depending primarily upon terrestrial animal resources falls in the trough separating the two components of the bimodal distribution of plant dependent peoples. This is a strong indication that significant organizational differences exist between terrestrial hunters and plant-dependent peoples.

I believe that the observable difference in GROUP1 sizes between figures 8.03 and 8.01 is not likely to be due to differences in initial conditions affecting foragers and collectors. It is more likely that the assumptions underlying the model regarding sexual division of labor and the number of parties searching daily for food may not be characteristic of groups exploiting terrestrial animal resources.

Generalization 8.03

All of the groups depending primarily upon the exploitation of terrestrial plants for which relevant information is available (fifty-nine cases) were classified as foragers. A strategy of residential mobility positioned consumers in proximity to the sources of food in their habitat. In marked contrast, thirty-five of the thirty-nine groups primarily exploiting terrestrial animal resources were classified as collectors, which means that food resources were available at sufficient distances from residential sites to require acquisition and transport to residentially based consumers.

The tactical differences in residential mobility demonstrable between foragers and collectors, particularly the collector strategy of transporting consumable products to residential sites, also result in a very different organization of male and female labor. I discuss these differences in subsequent sections of this chapter.

The data in table 8.02 also illustrate another contrast between groups that are dependent upon aquatic resources and those primarily exploiting terrestrial plant resources:

Generalization 8.04

I have emphasized that groups primarily exploiting terrestrial plant resources are associated with small GROUP1 units

that are situated in habitats with low primary productivity. On the other hand, groups primarily exploiting aquatic resources have higher frequencies of large GROUP1 sizes, regardless of the productivity of the habitat. Among the latter there are roughly equal numbers of small and large GROUP1 cases. With regard to the degree of political complexity, the pattern is identical to, but more robust than, that noted among plant-dependent peoples, and politically complex cases are exclusively characterized by the larger GROUP1 variant.

Examination of the groups primarily dependent upon terrestrial animals, however, reveals a third pattern:

Generalization 8.05

Among groups of hunters, regardless of the net above-ground productivity of their habitat, large GROUP1 sizes are indicated. When small GROUP1 sizes do occur, they are located almost exclusively in low-primary-productivity settings, which is similar to the pattern observed among plant-dependent peoples. The difference lies in the greater frequency of large GROUP1 cases, regardless of environment, and the correspondingly reduced number of small GROUP1 cases located in settings with high primary productivity.

This pattern could be accounted for by the fact that few opportunities for hunting occur in high-biomass settings such as tropical rain forests. On the other hand, the prevalence of large GROUP1 sizes among hunters in settings with low primary productivity does not support my argument that smaller group sizes should decrease mobility costs. Since small GROUP1 size is not common among hunters in low-productivity settings, mobility costs do not appear to be the primary conditioner here.

Since a preponderance of the evidence indicates that hunters are more mobile than foragers who exploit terrestrial plant resources, why are their GROUP1 sizes larger? When I examine the overall patterning in the subsistence subset, I note that, except for hunters, there appears to be a consistent pattern of large GROUP1 sizes associated with high-productivity habitats. Small GROUP1 sizes are, however, regularly found in nearly equal numbers in high- and low-productivity settings among groups that are primarily dependent upon aquatic resources and occur in 6 percent of the cases in which terrestrial plant exploitation predominates. These patterns demand that I search for the conditions that appear to be responsible for displacing mobility as the sole driving force behind the variability in GROUP1 size in groups of non-plant-dependent peoples.

Identifying Other Conditioners of Group Size Variability

It is clear that the Group Size Model works fairly well when it is applied to groups that are primarily dependent upon terrestrial plant resources, but it does not anticipate the variability among either groups of hunters or peoples dependent upon aquatic resources. At this point, I want to find out what additional factors contribute to variability in group size and why they have a different effect on groups that primarily exploit terrestrial plant resources.

I might begin by focusing on mobility itself. I have argued elsewhere (Binford 1980) that mobility is one of the fundamental adaptive tactics available to and characteristic of hunter-gatherers. The introduction of the idea of tactics directs my inquiry away from a strictly linear or scalar view of mobility and implies instead what has been termed hunter-gatherer "mapping on" or positioning strategies relative to the spatial structure of the resources in a habitat. The form that these cooperative strategies assume is determined by the demand for food relative to the distribution and abundance of potential foods in a habitat. From this perspective, on the one hand, mobility is more likely to be differentiated in scale and tempo as a consequence of the interaction between variability in the structure and abundance of differently ranked food targets, and, on the other, the various ways that labor can be organized and tactics for positioning food producers can be optimized to exploit wild resources, given variable demand for food. This means that

---

Proposition 8.02

Mobility in its quantitative characteristics—for example, how far people move in a year or how far they move between residential locations—is a byproduct of strategic articulations between the structure of the habitat and the demand for resources, when both are adjusted by variability in labor organization and positioning tactics within the habitat.

This is a different view of the world than the one underlying my earlier suggestion that hunter-gatherers adjusted their group size to minimize the physical costs of mobility. If proposition 8.02 has merit, it shifts attention away from expectations about correlations between group size and distance moved to a consideration of how demands for food may vary independently of the simple relationship between the number of consumers in a group and their average daily food requirements, which were fundamental components of the Group Size Model. Another important factor is the range of ways that labor can be organized to meet demand curves that may vary independently of the simple daily food needs of the workers involved in procuring and processing foods. All of these factors may vary interactively with the changing spatial distributions and abundance of potential foods within a habitat. And last, the technological aids available for moving across the landscape and transporting procured resources certainly constitute a variable that must be acknowledged as I try to understand the relationship between group size and mobility.

THE DEMAND CURVE

In the Group Size Model, the demand curve for food was a simple linear relationship between the number of consumers in a group and the amount of food each consumer needs per day. Other things being equal, the larger the number of consumers, the greater the demand for food. The only source of variability in consumer food demand resulted from differences in the age, body size, and reproductive status of the persons in a group.

One of the factors that would significantly modify the relationships specified in the model would be the procurement and storage of foods for consumption over periods of time greatly exceeding the simple assumption of same-day procurement and consumption that was built into the model. This modification would only occur, however, if food for storage was being procured during the most dispersed phase of the settlement cycle.[4] Such a tactic results in the number of persons in the group being equal to the number of consumer-days for which food is obtained by the labor of the group. Once the storage of food becomes the tactic of choice, the number of consumer-days for which food is procured each day is no longer necessarily equal to the number of persons in the group actively engaged in food production.

It often happens that a group organizes to obtain large quantities of food that is destined for consumption by a group of a *different* size over a long period of time. In other words, a producer unit may well be large in order to meet the nutritional needs of the labor unit required to obtain and process a large amount of food, which would then be consumed by a smaller group over a very long period of time. The one-to-one relationship between both the size of the producer and consumer units and the daily production and consumption of food may therefore be disrupted by the practice of storage.

These changes in fundamental relationships ensure that one could observe large GROUP1 labor units engaged in procuring and processing foods that are destined for consumption over extended periods of time by groups of differing sizes. The large group size may be a response to the sheer bulk of the materials being processed per unit of time and not to the consumer demands of the labor group itself over the same period of time.

I have referred to storage as a basic strategy for gaining time utility from resources (Binford 1978:91, 1990). Expressed in this way, storage can be considered an entropy reduction strategy of a given consumer or group of consumers. In habitats with resources that occur periodically in huge abundance, if a group uses only what its members can consume during the period of availability, from a consumer viewpoint much potential food is going to be wasted. Processing and storage would make possible the exploitation of large quantities of food over a relatively short period and thereby extend the time over which those resources could be consumed. In summary,

Generalization 8.06

Storage breaks the one-to-one link between group size and the size of the consumer unit. Given a storage strategy, GROUP1 size could well reflect the labor demands of bulk procurement and processing rather than simply an attempt to minimize the consumer demand upon localized resources.

It follows, therefore, that

Proposition 8.03

In situations in which storage occurs, GROUP1 size— or the size of the social unit during the most dispersed phase of the annual cycle—could represent one of two tactics: (1) an organizational response to the season of least food abundance, during which small GROUP1 size would most likely reflect minimal mobility and minimal food demand per unit area; or (2) an organizational response to the number and spatial distribution of patches of concentrated resources and to temporal variability in the availability at such patches. In the latter situation, there may be few direct mobility correlates to GROUP1 size.

Assessing the Effects of Storage on GROUP1 Size
Being able to recognize the implications of storage—which breaks the linkage between the number of persons in a group and the demand for resources—requires that one know where to look for such effects. In the recent anthropological literature, several authors have made vigorous arguments that storage plays a causal role in the appearance of complex societies (Testart 1982a). I have already shown that GROUP1 size tends to be larger among politically complex hunter-gatherers (table 8.02 and generalization 8.02) and that these groups are usually sedentary and practice storage. Correlations such as these tend to occur because, like storage, they reflect some aspects of intensification. The search for causes, therefore, must be concerned with the factors that precipitate intensification in its many manifestations.

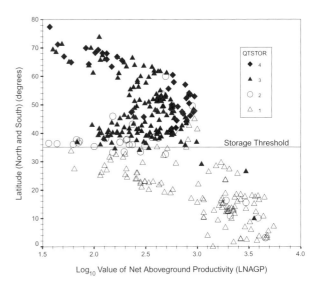

FIGURE 8.04

Property space map defined by latitude and net aboveground productivity relative to the quantity of stored food (all hunter-gatherer cases included). Cases are coded for the quantity of food stored (QTSTOR): (1) no regular storage or minor, very-short-term storage of two or three days; (2) moderate investment in storage, in both quantity and period of potential use; (3) major investment in storage and in the duration of anticipated use; and (4) massive investment in storage from the standpoint of both species stored and duration of use.

Woodburn's arguments (1980) are not as single-minded as those of Testart, but they also assign considerable causal importance to contrasts—very similar to ones pointed out much earlier by Meillassoux (1973)[5]—between immediate-return and delayed-return systems. This distinction expands the concept of storage to include other tactics for maximizing the time utility of human labor, such as the construction of traps and other types of *facilities* (in Wagner's [1960] terms [Binford 1968]) and reliance on delayed social obligations. Most of these tactics are common among sedentary peoples with high population densities and represent the effects of intensificational processes. Since storage often functions as a very important intensificational strategy, it ought to be clear that storage itself cannot therefore *cause* intensification.

I have argued elsewhere (Binford 1990:140–50) that storage and many features of "delayed return societies" may represent cost-benefit responses to environmental variations that are strongly tied to the length of the growing season. I explore this linkage in figure 8.04, which dramatically documents the relationship between storage and latitude—the latter acting as a measure of the length of the growing season. In this figure, I am using the property space map introduced in figure 4.13 and used productively in chapter 5 (figure 5.14).

At latitudes of less than 35 degrees, 108 (87.8 percent) of the 123 hunter-gatherer cases in the sample generally do not store food. Only fifteen cases below this boundary are reported to use storage, of which nine are classified as having *minor insurance* storage and seven store surpluses produced by domesticated plants. The remaining two cases in this category, and all six cases classified as exhibiting *moderate investments* in storage, either are complex hunter-gatherers or practice some agriculture and would therefore be considered intensified. Thus,

Proposition 8.04

Consistent with earlier arguments, the practice of storage in low-latitude (less than 35 degrees) settings may be regarded as an intensificational indicator.

Of somewhat greater interest at this juncture are those cases located between 35 and 90 degrees latitude (the boundary of the polar areas). Within this area 214 cases occur, and 191 (89.25 percent) of these make moderate to major investments in stored foods. An additional seven cases are classified as practicing minor, short-term insurance storage, and only six cases are classified as practicing no storage. I believe that the scale of comparison clearly demonstrates that the practice of storage is related to latitude.

The six cases whose subsistence tactics do not include storage are the Kurnai and Jaralde of South Australia, both the Eastern and Western Tasmanians, and the Chono and Yahgan of southwestern Chile and Argentina. All six exceptions occupy a relatively rare environmental zone that has comparatively little variation in annual temperature, with MTEMP values ranging between 81 and 86 and TEMP values of between 62 and 73°C. These cases are all located in the plant community dominated by northofagus vegetation found at the southern tip of South America and on the Island of Tasmania, and this habitat includes many other common features as well. Environments with the highest temperateness values (figure 4.05) are usually clustered in zones close to the earth's mean biotemperature (ET = 14.84), although there are exceptions.

In figure 8.05, the property space defined by the relationship between temperateness (TEMP) and latitude is displayed, along with markers coded to indicate the quantity of stored food (QTSTOR). The same threshold between storage and nonstorage that was observed in figure 8.04 is very clear at 35 degrees latitude. I have also indicated the threshold between temperate and nontemperate settings at the TEMP value of 50°C. There is also a provocative threshold at a TEMP value of 66°C, where a cluster of cases practicing considerable food storage occurs. This pattern then gives

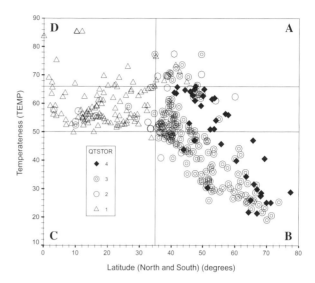

FIGURE 8.05

Property space map defined by temperateness and latitude relative to the quantity of stored food (all hunter-gatherer cases included). Cases are coded for the quantity of food stored (QTSTOR): (1) no regular storage or minor, very-short-term storage of two or three days; (2) moderate investment in storage, in both quantity and period of potential use; (3) major investment in storage and in the duration of anticipated use; and (4) massive investment in storage from the standpoint of both species stored and duration of use.

way to cases with higher TEMP values but no storage and a scattering of cases with minimal to moderate storage.

The obvious question is why such an abrupt drop-off in dependence on storage occurs at a temperateness value of 66°C. High temperateness, as measured by the variable TEMP, seems to elicit very different tactical subsistence responses. One might even surmise that at similar latitudes high temperateness would tend to reduce the probability that heavy storage would occur. If this conjecture is true, it could account for the six cases from South America and Tasmania that rarely if ever resorted to storage.[6] This simple view seems very unlikely given the strong clustering of heavy dependence upon storage found between TEMP values of 60 and 66°C in figure 8.05.

An examination of the geographic distribution of the global sample of weather stations reveals that the environmental settings in which hunter-gatherer groups practice little or no storage occur in the following regions: along the southeast coast of Australia from Sydney to Melbourne, throughout most of Tasmania, across the southern portion of New Zealand's South Island, on the Chatham Islands (approximately 400 miles off the eastern coast of New Zealand), and around the southern tip of South America along

TABLE 8.03

COMPARISON OF "EXCEPTIONAL" HUNTER-GATHERER CASES
IN TERMS OF SELECTED ENVIRONMENTAL VARIABLES,
POPULATION DENSITY, AND DEPENDENCE UPON STORED FOODS

GROUPS	LATITUDE	ET	BAR5	TEMP	GROWC	DENSITY	QTSTOR
A. Growing season = three months							
ONA	53.00	9.76	19.41	61.02	3.00	7.27	2
(ALEUT)	55.00	10.28	19.86	54.60	3.00	54.42	3
YAHGAN	60.00	9.60	21.90	62.43	3.00	28.42	2
B. Growing season = six to seven months							
BELLA-BELLA	52.87	12.08	36.80	61.45	6.00	20.51	4
ALACALUF	49.55	11.13	37.57	70.27	6.00	14.98	2
HAIDA	53.54	11.71	38.67	61.93	6.00	97.09	4
KWAKIUTL	50.42	11.74	40.25	64.99	6.00	68.70	4
(BALTASOUND—UNITED KINGDOM)	60.77	11.18	41.80	65.95	6.00	—	—
COMOX	50.00	12.15	60.82	62.68	6.00	55.00	4
CHONO	45.00	12.12	36.70	67.57	7.00	13.67	1
C. Growing seasons = nine months							
TASMANIANS—EAST	42.62	12.74	14.46	71.12	9.00	8.17	1
CHATHAM ISLANDS	44.00	12.00	18.00	65.00	8.00	(51.66)	1
(BORDEAUX—FRANCE)	44.83	13.85	19.04	61.84	9.00	—	—
(KAINGAROA—NEW ZEALAND)	38.40	12.77	33.98	67.05	9.00	—	—
(HOKIYIKA—NEW ZEALAND)	42.72	12.52	34.24	72.53	9.00	—	—
TASMANIANS—WEST	41.38	12.53	34.96	73.42	9.00	13.35	1
TUTUTNI	42.61	13.01	50.11	69.73	9.00	67.07	3
YUROK	41.40	12.55	51.18	72.59	9.00	131.00	3
TOLOWA	41.87	13.35	57.72	65.67	9.00	122.00	4
D. Growing season = twelve months							
JARALDE	35.06	14.95	8.08	68.11	12.00	40.00	1
TJAPWURONG	35.86	14.12	10.11	65.02	12.00	35.00	(?)
SALINAN	35.47	14.29	15.33	69.52	12.00	37.40	2
BUNURONG	49.46	20.42	19.53	77.83	12.00	25.04	1
COAST MIWOK	38.24	13.82	26.98	69.89	12.00	53.57	2
SOUTHERN POMO	39.34	13.71	64.99	70.68	12.00	108.40	3

Notes: **Boldface** indicates cases from the Subantarctic Zone. Cases in *italics* indicate hunter-gatherers whose regions share many environmental characteristics with cases in **boldface**. Parentheses indicate weather stations that share many environmental characteristics with cases in **boldface**.

both the Chilean and Argentine coasts, south of approximately 47.5 degrees south latitude. All of these regions occur within the convergence zone formed by the Antarctic and subtropical oceanic temperature and salinity regimes. This area is noted for unpredictable weather patterns, oceanic storms, strong winds, and an associated chill factor,[7] all of which drive the convergent pattern of ocean dynamics between surface and deep water.

No analogous conditions exist in the Northern Hemisphere because continental landmasses interfere with their formation. Nevertheless, convergent zones in the oceans north of the equator roughly coincide with the two great clockwise currents of the northern Pacific and the Atlantic: the Japan Current and the Gulf Stream, respectively. The former strikes the west coast of North America between southern British Columbia and northern California. The Gulf Stream similarly affects the coastal areas of western Europe, although with somewhat less force since the convergence zone between arctic and subtropical waters is less distinct along the European coast. Even so, the Canaries Current modifies the climate along the Portuguese coast and the Norwegian Coastal Current has an impact on conditions in the Bay of Biscay, the Irish Sea, and the Hebrides Islands west of Scotland (Stowe 1979:184).

The north central Pacific coast of North America experiences similar temperateness at comparable latitudes, but storms in this region are characterized by milder temperatures than those affecting coastal regions in the Southern Hemisphere. Locations of interest include the west coast of Portugal and the northern coast of Spain, extending roughly to the French city of Biarritz and northward. Another patch of high temperateness occurs in the southern Irish sea and along the coast of Wales as far south as Cardiff. The Hebrides Islands are also characterized by high temperateness values (greater than 66°C). These occur in the same property space as shown in the second quadrant of figure 8.05, in which cases from the Southern Hemisphere that were minimally dependent upon storage as a subsistence tactic were observed. In North America, an area of comparable temperateness extends northward along the California coast from just north of San Luis Obispo to the central coast of Oregon. Thereafter, temperateness drops steadily as latitude increases, until the TEMP values equal 50°C at approximately 54 degrees north latitude.

Keeping in mind my synopsis of the factors conditioning climatic features of both coastal and insular locations, as well as analogous locations elsewhere, I look again at the hunter-gatherer cases that were identified as exceptional from the distribution in figure 8.05. Table 8.03 presents these exceptional cases in sets grouped according to the number of months in the growing season. When arranged in this fashion, the exceptional cases scale with the length of the growing season; all cases in localities with a growing season of more than six months have been observed to practice no storage. In contrast, cases in areas with a growing season of less than or equal to six months practice some storage.

When I compare the exceptional cases to other hunter-gatherer groups occupying localities that are very similar in temperateness and latitude to regions in which exceptional cases are found, it is clear that—although the scale of dependence on storage is different—a relationship between storage and the length of the growing season is nonetheless noticeable. The mean values for the storage index (QTSTOR) are 2.3 for a twelve-month growing season, 3.3 for a nine-month growing season, and 4.0 when the growing season equals six months. The single comparative case in group A (three-month growing season) has a QTSTOR value of 3.0. These results clearly indicate that, even though the scale at which storage is practiced by highly and moderately intensified hunter-gatherer groups is different, the underlying relationship between storage and length of the growing season is maintained.[8] The character of this relationship, however, is more apparent when the intensified cases are eliminated.

Figure 8.06 uses the same property space as figure 8.04, but all of the sedentary cases have been eliminated. As a result, the cluster of cases in figure 8.04 that are heavily dependent on storage disappears, and the remaining mobile cases are distributed along the ordinal scale of storage depen-

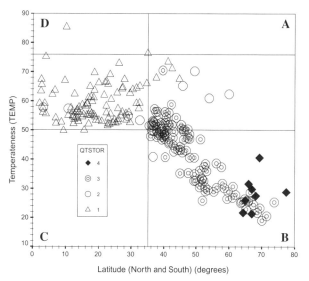

FIGURE 8.06

Property space map defined by temperateness and latitude relative to the quantity of stored food (only mobile hunter-gatherer cases included). Cases are coded for the quantity of food stored (QTSTOR): (1) no regular storage or minor, very-short-term storage of two or three days; (2) moderate investment in storage, in both quantity and period of potential use; (3) major investment in storage and in the duration of anticipated use; and (4) massive investment in storage from the standpoint of both species stored and duration of use.

dence. This distribution indicates that temperateness (TEMP) does moderate the normal effects of latitude on the length of the growing season. Settings with high temperateness tend to have very moderate winter temperatures, and they can therefore be regarded as a measure of minimal extremes in temperature. Storage becomes important at approximately 35 to 36 degrees latitude for the majority of cases. This threshold appears to be delayed until between 40 and 43 degrees latitude when temperateness (TEMP) values are high.

The effects of temperateness are further illustrated in figure 8.07, graphs A and B, in which the role of temperateness in expanding the growing season relative to effective temperature values is strongly indicated. Two very different environmental contexts were chosen to illustrate the importance of temperateness. In graph A, which includes all of the mobile cases that have twelve-month growing seasons, it is clear that those cases located in areas in which effective temperatures correspond to cool climatic regimes also have high values for temperateness. In fact, 64 percent of the cases whose ET values are greater than 16 have TEMP values greater than 60°C. Graph B illustrates the same effect, but this plot includes only cases with a three-month growing season. Here the majority of the cases are clustered between ET val-

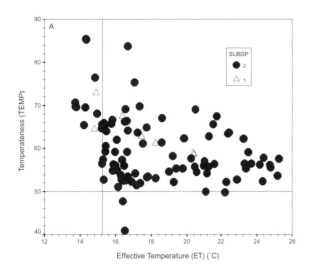
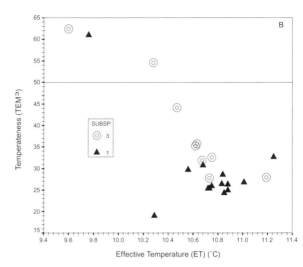

FIGURE 8.07

Comparative graphs of mobile hunter-gatherer cases displayed in property space defined by temperateness and effective temperature: graph A includes only cases with a twelve-month growing season; graph B includes only cases with a three-month growing season. Both graphs are coded for primary source of food (SUBSP): (1) terrestrial animals, (2) terrestrial plants, and (3) aquatic resources.

ues of 11.0 and 10.5, but two extraordinary cases have ET values of 9.0 or less and TEMP values of more than 60°C.

Generalization 8.07

Other things being equal, higher-latitude settings in which meteorological and climatic conditions have a moderating effect on temperature extremes also have longer growing seasons. Temperateness values greater than 60°C are a good indicator of such effects.

It is also true that

Generalization 8.08

Other things being equal, there will be a curvilinear relationship between the quantity of food stored and the length of the growing season for mobile hunter-gatherer groups that experience little or no intensificational pressure. The first appearance of storage will be noted at approximately 35 degrees latitude, hereafter referred to as the *storage threshold* and corresponding to an ET value of 15.25. Greater reliance on stored foods should be associated with decreases in the length of the growing season.

In the following settings, two major factors may precipitate a decrease in a group's investment in storage relative to the latitude of its home range:

Generalization 8.09

The habitats of some localities at 35 degrees latitude or higher are characterized by temperateness values that exceed 60°C. These locations are usually affected by oceanic conditions associated with a convergence zone between subtropical and polar ocean temperature and salinity regimes.[9] Less commonly, resources can be exploited throughout the winter at some higher-latitude locations, such as places in the high arctic where breathing hole sealing is a productive tactic. In both of these kinds of settings, there may be a considerable reduction in a group's dependence upon stored foods.

My discussion thus far of the factors that may promote storage but do not result from the concentration of social units into increasingly smaller geographic patches—and therefore are not accompanied by intensification—prompts the following postulation:

Proposition 8.05

Other things being equal, GROUP1 size should vary somewhat independently of mobility costs among hunter-gatherer groups practicing storage. Considerable variance in GROUP1 sizes might be expected as dependence upon storage increases, but larger GROUP1 sizes might be expected to occur in systems that process for storage materials with greater bulk per unit of processing time.

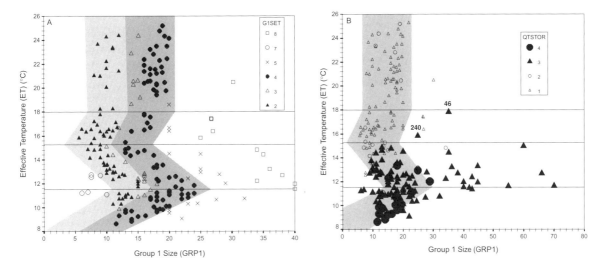

FIGURE 8.08

Comparative plots of GROUP1 size displayed relative to effective temperature: graph A focuses on the pattern defined by the small- to moderate-body-size cases relative to a series of environmental thresholds, while graph B displays the total distribution. Graph A is coded for an ordination and classification of GROUP1 sizes: (2) small, (3) medium, (4) large, (5) oversized, (7) exceptional cases, and (8) very large. Graph B is coded for the quantity of food stored (QTSTOR): (1) no regular storage or minor, very-short-term storage of two or three days; (2) moderate investment in storage, in both quantity and period of potential use; (3) major investment in storage and in the duration of anticipated use; and (4) massive investment in storage from the standpoint of both species stored and duration of use.

It might therefore be expected that GROUP1 size would track increased dependence upon storage. I would also expect increases in dependence to be disproportionately higher in settings with a short access window for obtaining storable foods or when the time between food procurement and spoilage is short. This would be particularly true for groups exploiting aquatic resources, for whom the size of GROUP1 labor units would vary inversely with the time between procurement and the onset of spoilage. Figure 8.08, graphs A and B, provides provocative insights into the modifying effects on GROUP1 size of storage and scalar differences in primary productivity, such as the length of the growing season, as indicated by effective temperature.

In graph A, the patterns of variability in GROUP1 size relative to the earth's effective temperature range are illustrated. The overall sawtoothed shape has a range of variability of approximately twelve persons and remains fairly constant across the earth's range of temperatures. Variability in the pattern is introduced in the mode of the absolute values of the maximum and minimum group sizes. High values (G1SET = 3 and 4) are concentrated just above the ET indicator of 18 degrees, which marks the shift in the length of the growing season from twelve to fewer months, and at a threshold of 11.53 degrees ET. Such a value is common within the boreal forest or—at lower altitudes—along the margin between boreal forests and grassland steppes. This pattern indi-

cates that GROUP1 size is clearly distributed differentially relative to environmental variables, but it is unclear what is the linking mechanism in a causal sense.

Graph B illustrates the linkage between GROUP1 size and storage. Between the storage threshold at an ET value of 15.25 and the threshold within the boreal forest at ET 11.53, there are many cases whose GROUP1 size is much larger than the "normal" range of variability of plus or minus six persons from the mode. Almost all of these groups are reported to be heavily dependent upon storage.

It is tempting to attribute the increase in GROUP1 size in this temperature interval as primarily related to the processing and storage of fish for winter consumption. More importantly, the cases with the largest GROUP1 sizes also primarily exploited anadromous fish, which are only available in the Northern Hemisphere. It is interesting to note that of the ten cases from the Southern Hemisphere from settings with cooler temperatures than those at the storage threshold, none falls outside of the range of variability of groups in figure 8.08, graph A, that are situated in climates with warmer temperatures than at the storage threshold. These facts support the view that GROUP1 size gets larger when high bulk processing for storage becomes necessary and when—without substantial processing—there is a very small temporal window between food procurement and the onset of spoilage.

The threshold at ET 11.53, which marks a reduction in GROUP1 size as effective temperature drops lower and lower, can be seen as defining the point at which freezing becomes a viable storage alternative. At these temperatures, creatures of larger body size requiring much less labor-intensive preparation for storage become the most-sought-after food resources.

An exception to this general rule would be the cases in the G1SET = 7 category (figure 8.08, graph A), which do not follow the larger pattern. This class of exceptional cases includes both the Eastern and Western Tasmanian groups, for which data have come exclusively from early contact situations. Consequently, not only is the group type far from clear but, since children were rarely counted by colonial observers, group size is seriously underrepresented as well. Nonetheless, these are cases with high temperateness values, which means that storage should not drive up group size (generalizations 8.07 and 8.09). Other groups in this cluster of exceptional cases come from the Canadian boreal forest and include the Round Lake Ojibwa, the Weagamon Lake Ojibwa, and the Mistassini Cree, who were trappers at the time of documentation and therefore share characteristics with other groups in the atomistic category (Rogers and Black 1976). One common feature of these three cases is that their groups were most widely dispersed during the winter, which is not characteristic of the other cases in similar environments.

In the two graphs in figure 8.09, segments of figure 8.08 are examined in more detail. The plot in graph A includes cases

from latitudes above 35 degrees (ET approximately 15.00 degrees) that are fully mobile (GRPPAT = 1) and "normal" hunter-gatherers (SUBPOP = *n*). Groups of mounted hunters (HUNTFIL2 = 1) from the New World plains areas are excluded. By looking initially only at cases of this type, it will be possible to evaluate the degree to which intensification and sedentism influence patterning in GROUP1 size and growing season indicators. Figure 8.09, graph A, reveals that

Generalization 8.10

Between ET values of 15.25 and 11.53 there is a significant increase in GROUP1 size from a median value of approximately 10.0 persons at ET 15.00 to a median value of 19.5 persons at ET 11.53. A distinct threshold occurs at 11.53 below which, as ET values decrease, there is a corresponding reduction in GROUP1 size.

The reversal in GROUP1 size was a totally unexpected result, given my arguments about storage, according to which the greatest environmentally conditioned dependence upon storage was expected to coincide with the lowest ET values![10]

The variables in figure 8.09, graph B, are identical to those in graph A, but the plot now represents patterning among only those cases that were considered to be intensified based on their status as nonmobile groups that were essentially sedentary in their overall settlement pattern. GROUP1 values would therefore refer to social units within the

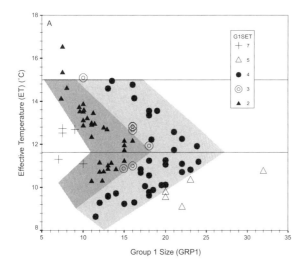
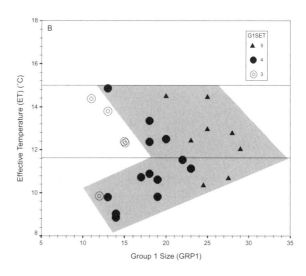

FIGURE 8.09

Comparative plots of GROUP1 size displayed relative to effective temperature; cases are restricted to those occurring in settings with ET values of less than 16 degrees. Both graphs apply to hunter-gatherers unmodified by adjacent complex societies and to nonmounted hunters. Graph A displays only mobile cases while graph B displays only cases that are not mobile. Both graphs are coded for an ordination and classification of GROUP1 sizes: (2) small, (3) medium, (4) large, (5) oversized, (7) exceptional cases, and (8) very large.

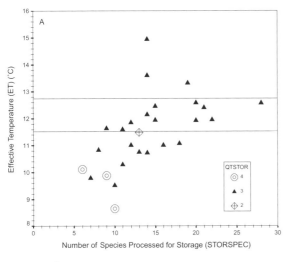
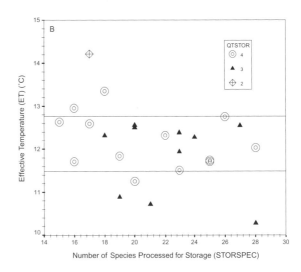

FIGURE 8.10

Comparative plots of the number of species processed for storage displayed relative to effective temperature: graph A includes only mobile hunter-gatherer groups and graph B includes only sedentary hunter-gatherer cases. Both graphs are coded for the quantity of food stored (QTSTOR):(2) moderate investment in storage, in both quantity and period of potential use; (3) major investment in storage and in the duration of anticipated use; and (4) massive investment in storage from the standpoint of both species stored and duration of use.

otherwise sedentary settlement that seasonally moved their temporary residences. The same threshold in group size observed in graph A also occurs here at the ET values of 15.25 and 11.53, although—in this instance—the distribution of GROUP1 values at the thresholds is higher. It can therefore be said of the pattern in graph B of figure 8.09 that

Generalization 8.11

Among groups in localities with ET values of less than 15.25 degrees, mobile residential work groups originating in sedentary settlements are larger, on average, than the maximally dispersed components of residentially mobile peoples at similar locations.

I have already taken exception to the proposition that storage is a causal factor in the evolution of complex societies; at this juncture, I think it is more accurate to say that storage might be expected to increase as pressure to intensify increases. Furthermore, if I am correct about the interaction between GROUP1 size and processing food resources for storage, increases in GROUP1 size among intensified peoples could be seen as reflecting increased dependence on storage.

One of the few studies attempting to relate dependence upon stored foods to political complexity was undertaken by Eileen Panowski (1985). She found that there is a correlation among hunter-gatherers between measures of political complexity (visualized as a scale of social stratification) and the number of species processed for storage. Another interest-

ing observation is that the number of aquatic foods utilized is positively correlated with both the size of labor groups and Panowski's ranking of political development (1985:21–31, 42–56). In figure 8.10, graphs A and B, the relationships between effective temperature and Panowski's tabulations of the numbers of different species prepared for storage (STOR-SPEC) are demonstrated. Markers indicate the dependence upon storage (QTSTOR) coded in this study.

In figure 8.10, mobile cases are arrayed in graph A and sedentary cases appear in graph B. In the graph of mobile cases, there is a threshold similar to the one observed in the plot of ET and GROUP1 size in figure 8.09, which anticipates major changes between mobile and sedentary hunter-gatherer cases. In graph A in figure 8.09, when GROUP1 size was plotted on the x axis, the threshold occurred at a value of 11.53, which is between the mean ET value of the boreal forest (11.33) and that of the lake forests of east central Canada (11.88).

In figure 8.10, the GROUP1 size threshold occurs within the coniferous evergreen northern forests, while the threshold for the number of species processed for storage occurs within the coastal redwood forests of California or within the transitional deciduous–northern coniferous forest zones. This positioning corresponds to the boundary between the boreal and cool temperate climate categories in the classification of plant communities summarized by the variable CLIM and presented in chapter 4.

Clearly, major changes in many aspects of hunter-gatherer adaptations occur at the 11.53 threshold. The graph in

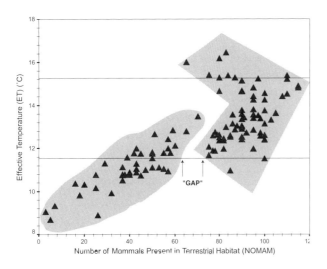

FIGURE 8.11

A property space plot of the number of mammalian species present in the terrestrial habitat displayed relative to the effective temperature for only North American cases in settings of lower than 17 degrees latitude.

figure 8.11 illustrates that, within this zone, the relationship between the expected number of terrestrial mammal species[11] and ET values has important organizational consequences for the ethnic units residing there. This figure identifies the presence of a major biological boundary with a zone of overlap corresponding to the two thresholds previously identified—the hunter-gatherer GROUP1 size data (figure 8.09, graph A) and the number of species processed for storage (figure 8.10, graphs A and B)—when both are arrayed against ET. The threshold patterning in both GROUP1 size and numbers of species processed for storage strongly suggests either the operation of a new variable or a major point of diminishing returns for the labor strategies that worked successfully in environments with ET values between approximately 15 and 12 degrees.

Unfortunately, a knowledge of only the patterns documented in figures 8.09 and 8.10 provides no clear indication of what factors may be conditioning the reversal in GROUP1 size and number of species stored. The demonstration in figure 8.11 suggests that hunter-gatherers are responding, at least partially, to a set of environmental conditions that also affect the number of terrestrial mammal species present in the habitat. This is indicated by the gap in the number of species that appears at the threshold at approximately ET 11.53 degrees. The threshold itself could mark a major change in biotic communities, with the result that the niches for animals on either side of the gap would be very different indeed.

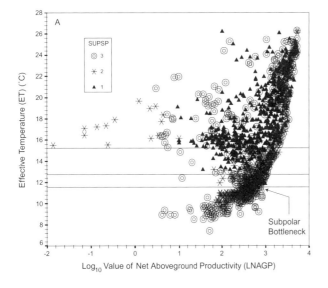

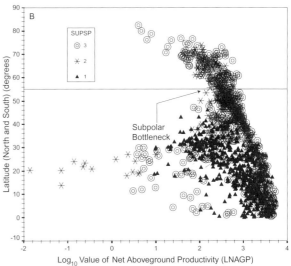

FIGURE 8.12

Comparative property space maps defined by temperature indicators and the log_{10} value of net aboveground productivity using the world sample of 1,429 weather stations. Graph A displays the pattern when effective temperature (ET) is used, while graph B displays the pattern when latitude is used as an indicator of solar energy. Coding for both graphs is the primary source of food (SUBSP): (1) terrestrial animals, (2) terrestrial plants, and (3) aquatic resources.

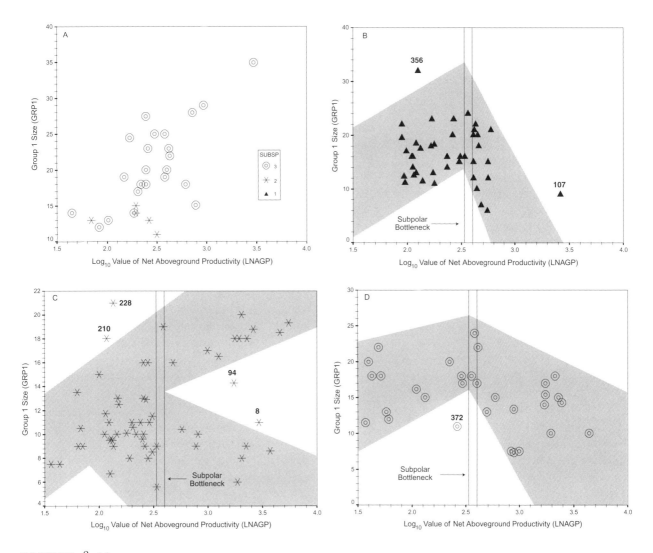

FIGURE 8.13

Four graphs displaying the log₁₀ value of net aboveground productivity relative to GROUP1 size. In all comparisons, mounted hunters and groups heavily affected by colonial presence have been eliminated from the data plotted. Differential responses to the subpolar bottleneck are demonstrated. Graph A is coded for the primary sources of food (SUBSP): (1) terrestrial animals, (2) terrestrial plants, and (3) aquatic resources. Graphs B, C, and D are each differentiated by the primary source of food: terrestrial animals (A), terrestrial plants (B), and aquatic resources (C).

Fortunately, the global sample of the earth's environments will help me examine climatic conditions at the crucial ET threshold of 11.53 degrees. In figure 8.12, graph A, I look first at the basic relationship between temperature and the availability of water to support terrestrial plant life (the log₁₀ value of net aboveground productivity). The variables on the y axis of both graphs A and B are temperature indicators, and therefore the spread of values in net aboveground productivity at any given temperature indicator represents the controlling effects of moisture on annual plant productivity.

The greatest diversity in plant productivity occurs at approximately 20 degrees latitude or 15.5 degrees ET, which

corresponds closely to the storage threshold. As one moves in the direction of higher latitude and lower ET values, the diversity is significantly reduced until a bottleneck in net aboveground productivity is reached at approximately 55 degrees latitude or 11.45 to 11.60 degrees ET. At the bottleneck, which implies only various forms of northern forest, all of the earth's environmental settings with an ET of approximately 11.53 degrees have log₁₀ net aboveground productivity values of between 2.31 and 2.89. These are moderately high productivity values, but they represent relatively high biomass values (5,000 to 10,000 grams per square meter) at these latitudes.

On the lower-ET side of the bottleneck, the productivity curve drops off sharply to the left, indicating that an accelerating reduction in net aboveground productivity occurs as ET decreases. This pattern also represents a pronounced, curvilinear decrease in biomass compared with the values occurring at the bottleneck.

I believe that the patterning in figure 8.12 shows that the provocative thresholds in GROUP1 size visible in figures 8.10, graphs A and B, and 8.11 reflect important environmental dynamics and are therefore *not* attributable to the operation of new causal variables. Indeed, the thresholds refer to patterns previously associated with groups dependent upon terrestrial plant resources that maintain larger group sizes in higher primary productivity habitats (generalization 8.01).

The four graphs in figure 8.13 illustrate several additional features of the relationship between GROUP1 size and the $\log_{10}$ value of net aboveground productivity. The less ambiguous view of the relationship appears in graph A, where only groups whose basic settlement pattern is nonmobile have been plotted. Most of the cases that are dependent primarily upon plants occur on the lower end of the distribution, while the majority of the cases are primarily dependent upon aquatic resources. The overall pattern in graph A of figure 8.13 is positive. In the other graphs a positive pattern is found to the left of the subpolar bottleneck, suggesting that, other things being equal, as the $\log_{10}$ value of net aboveground productivity increases, GROUP1 size also increases.

The only difference among graphs B, C, and D is the primary source of food, but all three graphs differ substantially from graph A. Graphs B, C, and D exhibit major changes of direction consistent with the range of LNAGP values that identified the bottleneck in the number of mammalian species in figure 8.12, graph A. In graph B (dependence upon terrestrial animals) and graph D (dependence upon aquatic resources), GROUP1 size falls off precipitously as productivity increases beyond a threshold at $\log_{10}$ values of between 2.525 and 2.600 for primary productivity. Is it a coincidence that this approximates the median value of the bottleneck identified in figure 8.12, which—incidentally—coincides with the threshold clearly demonstrated in figure 8.09 at an effective temperature of 11.53?

Values of primary productivity *within* the bottleneck are found across the full range of ET values that are warmer than those of the bottleneck itself (figure 8.12, graph B). This means that a threshold defined in terms of productivity could be ambiguous in any areas warmer than the bottleneck. Another implication is that the patterns in graphs B, C, and D in figure 8.13 could represent either autocorrelations or ambiguous information arising from sample bias in the environments represented in the controlled sample of cases displayed in the graphs.

In order to clarify which of these possibilities might be involved, the three comparative graphs in figure 8.14 were prepared, using the same property space defined by effective temperature on the *y* axis and the $\log_{10}$ value of net aboveground productivity on the *x* axis. All plots feature the same marker, which is the GROUP1 size ordinal variable G1SET that was developed for figure 8.08. The only difference between the three graphs is that, for groups whose GRPPAT = 1, SUBPOP = *n*, and HUNTFIL = 1, they plot a subset of the cases based on the class of food resources upon which each ethnic group in the controlled sample primarily depends.

The results of this exercise certainly help to clarify the significance of the patterning at or near the ET threshold of 11.53. For instance, in figure 8.14, graph A, among hunter-gatherer groups that are primarily dependent upon terrestrial animals, there is a much higher percentage of larger GROUP1 size cases in settings with ET values that are lower than the 11.53 threshold. Only one case, the Warunggu from Australia, is located in a setting with high net aboveground productivity, which indicates that the case was probably misclassified. The information about this group's diet came from Brayshaw (1990:55) and summarizes the reports of explorers who observed the food procurement choices made by these aboriginal groups.

Brayshaw also provides information on native diets relative to the variability in rainfall in the region. I chose to use values from settings with greater than 1,500 millimeters of rainfall. Comparison of graph A (hunters) with graph B (gatherers) shows that the Warunggu (graph A, 107) are more consistent with other plant-dependent peoples. Brayshaw estimated that plant dependence would account for 50 percent or more of the diet of groups in the more moderate-rainfall settings, an estimate that is likely to complement the group size observations more accurately.

The pattern formed in figure 8.14, graph B, by the groups primarily dependent upon terrestrial plants clarifies patterns seen earlier in figure 8.13, graph C. Most importantly, there are few cases with plant-dominated diets in settings with ET values of less than 12.75 degrees. I suspect that the few cases that occur below this limit come from unusual settings in which the length of the growing season is not reliably indicated by temperature values at the beginning and end of the growing season. The fact that the majority of groups that are dependent upon plant resources are found in settings with ET values of greater than 12.75 degrees simply reflects the uneven distribution of plant resources throughout the earth's environments.

Most readers were, I suspect, already aware of global variability in the availability of edible plant species, but when the focus is on variables such as GROUP1 size, the distribution of this bias is clearer. When we compare graphs B and C in figure 8.14, for example, it is apparent that larger GROUP1 sizes are more common among plant-dependent peoples in

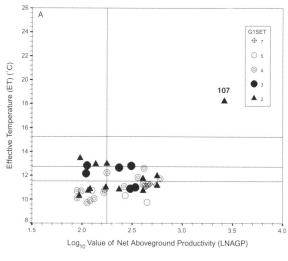

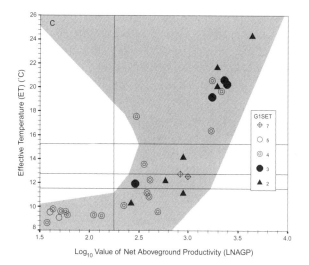

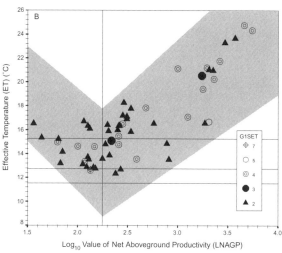

FIGURE 8.14

Three graphs comparing patterns among mobile cases differing in the trophic level of their primary food resources and displayed in the same property space, defined by effective temperature and the $\log_{10}$ value of net aboveground productivity. Coding for all three graphs is an ordination and classification of GROUP1 sizes: (2) small, (3) medium, (4) large, (5) oversized, and (7) exceptional cases.

high-productivity settings, while smaller GROUP1 sizes occur only among aquatically dependent groups living in relatively high-plant-productivity settings.

Pattern recognition studies have taught us a great deal about the interaction between habitat, subsistence practice, and the size of the groups practicing those subsistence strategies for at least some part of the year. One could say that

─────── *Generalization 8.12* ───────

Several thresholds at which major changes in the behavior of hunter-gatherers regularly occur have been identified. These include the following:

1. The *growing season threshold,* which was actually modeled by Bailey (1960) as part of his development of the effective temperature variable. The transition from environmental settings with the potential for a twelve-month growing season to settings with shorter growing seasons occurs at an ET value of 18 degrees. The importance of this pivotal point was demonstrated in figure 8.08.

2. The *storage threshold,* which occurs at approximately 35 degrees latitude (figure 8.04 and proposition 8.04) or at 15.25 degrees ET (generalization 8.11).

3. The *terrestrial plant threshold,* which occurs at an ET value of 12.75 degrees (generalization 8.12 and figure 8.14). In warmer settings than this threshold, plant-dominated subsistence strategies can be expected. In cooler settings, plant-dominated subsistence strategies are not expected, except in rare instances in which temperateness extends the growing season in spite of lowered temperatures during the growing season (generalizations 8.08–8.10 and proposition 8.05).

4. The *subpolar bottleneck,* which occurs at an ET value of 11.53 degrees and corresponds to a global constriction in the range of variability in net aboveground productivity. Locations with this ET setting exhibit a very narrow range of net aboveground productivity values ($\log_{10}$ value = 2.31 to 2.89), representing forest biomes with substantial biomass but very little species diversity (figures 8.08, 8.09, and 8.12, and generalization 8.12).

Not only have pattern changes at four major transition points become apparent, but we have also inquired into what exactly happens at these thresholds and, in some cases, what may be conditioning the shifts:

─────────── *Proposition 8.06* ───────────

Beginning at the storage threshold and continuing until the subpolar bottleneck (figures 8.08 and 8.09, and generalization 8.11), increases in GROUP1 size among mobile hunter-gatherers seem to represent a response to at least two conditioning variables. The first is an increased dependence upon stored foods in response to the shorter growing season that occurs between these two thresholds (generalizations 8.08 and 8.06). As dependence upon stored foods for longer periods of the year increases, one can expect larger and larger quantities of food to be procured during the relatively short segments of the growing season. The food is then processed for storage and later consumption during the nongrowing seasonal segment of the annual cycle. The size of the localized labor force should increase as a simple function of the increase in procurement potential per access location in the habitat. The size of the task-specific labor force should also vary inversely with the number of different resources exploited simultaneously in the habitat, for either storage or consumption.

The second factor contributing to the regular increase in group size occurring between the storage threshold and the subpolar bottleneck is the presence of the terrestrial plant threshold at an ET value of 12.75. The latter threshold occurs at one-third of the ET range below the subpolar bottleneck, which is where the empirical shift to a diet that is primarily dependent upon terrestrial animals occurs. It has been regularly demonstrated that GROUP1 size tends to be larger among hunters of terrestrial animals (generalization 8.06). Among the cases arrayed between the storage threshold and the subpolar bottleneck, it might be expected that terrestrial animals would contribute more to the total diet as the terrestrial plant threshold is approached and then replace plants as the primary component of the diet once the terrestrial plant threshold is reached, other things being equal.

─────────────────────────

I think it should be clear that

─────────── *Generalization 8.13* ───────────

Increases in GROUP1 size among mobile hunter-gatherers between the storage threshold and the subpolar bottleneck are to be referred to increased dependence upon storage and increased exploitation of terrestrial animals in direct response to environmental variables, other things being equal.

A Review of the Demand Curve as a Variable Distinct from the Consumer Demand Represented by Food-Procuring and -Processing Task Groups

The patterns I have been illustrating indicate a set of strongly linked relationships involving the trophic level of the food resources that foragers exploit, which (at least partially) implicates GROUP1 size, reliance on storage, and intensification. One clue to the character of this linkage can be found in Panowski's research into the species counts of stored foods demonstrated earlier in figure 8.10. The same set of thresholds in GROUP1 size marks changes in the number of species stored relative to ET. Both of these patterns appear to be related to primary productivity and the complex relationships between primary production and the proportion between temperature and moisture that sustains biomass in the plant community. Panowski herself observes:

> It seems to me that the number of stored foods is an indicator of the number and extent of conflicts encountered in scheduling major food procurement activities, conflicts that involve not only the time element, but also the division of labor required, and the storage options available.   (1985:41)

She provides several examples from the ethnographic literature:

> The busiest time of the year for the Southern Pomo was from August to November when two primary resources, salmon and acorns, were harvested. The most utilized oak groves were those on the slopes and valleys near the river. To avoid quarrels, the people recognized ownership of certain trees or groups of trees.... Since salmon and nuts were procured in the same general area, men, women, and children helped with both procedures. The intensive work of drying salmon could be done in two-to-three-week periods, with acorn and buckeye gathering taking place between the peaks of the fish runs and also afterwards. If it was felt necessary to do both at the same time, women could cut fish and dry them while men and children collected nuts. All helped carry the winter stores back to the village where most of the group congregated for the colder months.   (1985:41)

In the example that Panowski describes, the Pomo were dispersed in residentially based work groups that were organized as coordinated, multitask labor units. Men and women performed different tasks related to the procurement and processing of the same species, except in those instances in which simultaneous exploitation and processing of several different species were required.[12] This difference may assume considerable importance in my continued investigation of the sources of variability in GROUP1 size.

I have already discussed the fact that the demand curve is drastically modified once a group is engaged in food production for storage, trade, or wages. Groups engaged in food production are no longer constituted to meet their daily consumption requirements. They are, instead, organized in terms of the labor needed to procure and process the amount of food necessary to meet the nutrient requirements of groups whose size and duration of consumption may vary quite independently of their own.

Recognition of this set of conditions, which were not embodied in the Group Size Model, led me to investigate the phenomenon of storage and is responsible for my expectation that dependence on storage tactics should increase as the length of the growing season decreases. This relationship leads to the expectation, summarized in proposition 8.05, that GROUP1 size should increase as the bulk processing of foods for storage increases. It was assumed that, other things being equal, GROUP1 size should also increase as the length of the growing season decreases.

The discovery of an unanticipated and significant reversal in the relationship between GROUP1 size and the number of species processed for storage prompted me to reexamine the assumptions underlying the model. (It should be remembered that the model described the behavior of a classic forager [Binford 1980], who practiced no storage and consumed food at roughly the rate at which it was introduced to the camp on a daily basis. Foraging parties would procure food in terms of a normal daily return strategy, which would ensure that, as returns diminished, consumers would be moved to another patch in the habitat.) Thus far, my research strongly suggests that deviations from the characteristic sexual division of labor and the work schedules of each gender-defined work party—such as simultaneous multitasking at single locations rather than gender-based differentiation at different locations—may account for differences between observed GROUP1 sizes and the values built into the Group Size Model.

MOBILITY AND LABOR ORGANIZATION:
IMPLICATIONS OF FORAGER-COLLECTOR
DIFFERENCES AND GROUP1 SIZE VARIABILITY

In my discussion in chapter 7 of the development of a minimalist Group Size Model, I argued that a fundamental linkage existed between group size and mobility. Data presented in tables 7.06 and 7.14 have led me to conclude that

Generalization 8.14

Other things being equal, increases in group size may result in increased mobility since, when food resources are available at a constant level, the number of residential moves per year increases as group size increases.

It is possible to evaluate this generalization by referring to ethnographic estimates of residential mobility for the hunter-gatherer groups in the global sample of cases. The basic data on the number of moves per year and the distances moved by the groups in the sample, as well as the sources from which these data are taken, are presented in table 8.04. Now that these data have been compiled and made accessible, I can begin to address the implication in generalization 8.14 that GROUP1 size should increase with mobility, other things being equal.

The data displayed in the scatter plots in figure 8.15 consist of the hunter-gatherer cases for which I have both GROUP1 size and an estimate of the total number of kilometers traversed by a group during an average annual round of residential movement. These groups are also mobile (GRPPAT = 1), are not heavily affected by more complex cultural systems (SUBPOP = n), and do not use horses for hunting (HUNTFIL2 = 1). A threshold seems indicated at approximately 400 kilometers, below which groups making residential moves show a high variance trend toward reduced GROUP1 size with increased distance moved. Above the 400-kilometer threshold, GROUP1 size increases as the distance moved increases, a finding that contradicts the assumptions underlying the Group Size Model but supports generalization 8.14.

The seven relatively tightly clustered collector cases to the left of the threshold, which move 100 kilometers or less each year, are also the groups that are most intensified. The five scattered cases that move between 100 and 350 kilometers annually very likely represent nonintensified cases. The seventeen collector cases that represent 61 percent of the total number of groups cluster above the point at which distance moved exceeds 350 kilometers.

I have argued (Binford 1980) that groups adopt collector (also referred to as logistical) strategies in two sets of circumstances. Logistical strategies represent the reorganization of labor to cope with the incongruent distribution of critical resources, such as when consumers are located near one critical resource but far from another equally critical resource like water or food, firewood, or shelter (Binford 1980, 1983:344). The widely scattered collector cases in figure 8.15 whose annual moves are equal to or greater than 200 kilometers are likely to have a problem with congruence. I have suggested that these conditions tend to occur at places in which the number of critical resources is greatest, such as in the polar region and northern temperate zones.

Collector strategies might also be adopted in situations in which some restrictions are placed on consumer or residential mobility (Binford 1983:353). In such settings, various kinds of resources have very different spatial scales of dispersion and clustering. Collector strategies could be favored if groups were limited in their mobility (Binford 1983:353) by the presence of competing groups, or if there were only a few

TABLE 8.04

DATA ON HUNTER-GATHERER MOBILITY, INCLUDING NUMBER OF MOVES AND DISTANCE MOVED PER YEAR

CASE	NUMBER OF MOVES PER YEAR	DISTANCE MOVED PER YEAR (MILES)	REFERENCE(S)
Tropical-subtropical Asia			
PUNAN	45	240	Harrison 1949:135, 139; Urquart 1951:505, 515
BATEK (PALAWAN)	6	50	Eder 1984:843
KUBU	7	140	Persoon 1989:512; Volz 1909:96–101
ANDMAN ISLANDS (ONGE)	8	40	Cooper 1991
ANDAMAN ISLANDS (JARWA)	9	59	Temple 1903:69–90
AYTA (PINATUBO)	0.1[1]	0	Reed 1904:39–43
BIG ANDAMAN ISLAND	12	76	Radcliffe-Brown 1948:28
SEMANG	36	147	Schebesta 1962a:143–44
VEDDAH	3	36	Seligmann and Seligmann 1911:43–44
HILL PANDARAM	45	150	Morris 1982a:136, 174–80
AGTA (CASIGURAN)	27	135	Headland pers. comm. 1992
AGTA (ISABELA)	10	170	Rai 1982:105, 107
AGTA (CAGAYAN)	29	120	Vanoverbergh 1925:195, 196–98, 432
CHENCHU	4	14	Fürer-Haimendorf 1943:366
MRABRI	12	95	Bernatzik 1951:140; Pookajorn 1988, figures 75–77
PALIYANS	5	55	Gardner 1965:27–28, 33
BIRHOR	8	90	Williams 1974:76–77
KADAR	1.5	19	Ehrenfels 1952:8
CHOLANAICKAN	4	75	Bhanu 1982:225; 1992:31
NAYAKA	0.1	0.1	Bird 1983:57–59; Bird-David 1987:153–56
AINU (HOKKAIDO)	1.5	8	Watanabe 1964:8–9
OROGENS	15	350	Qiu 1983 (LRB estimate)
KET	13	420	Lee 1967:23–44
GILYAKA	0.1	0.1	Shternberg 1933:67
YUKAGHIR	17	410	Kreynovich 1979:194–209
NGANASAN	12	375	Chard 1963:106–8
SIBERIAN ESKIMO	3	90	Krupnik 1983:96
Tropical-subtropical South America			
SHIRIANA	33	171	LRB estimate
AKURIYO	49	285	Kloos 1977:119; pers. comm. 1982
YARURO-PUME	7	33	Gragson 1989:285–88
GUAHIBO	40	175	Kirchhoff 1945:449
MACU NUKAK	55	225	Politis pers. comm. 1992
NAMBIKWARA	13	70	Lévi-Strauss 1948b:266, 288; Aspelin 1976:9–16
BORORO	0.1	0.1	Lévi-Strauss 1936:269, 1970:140; Baldus 1937:123–24
SIRIONO	17	110	Holmberg 1950:51
YUQUI	53	312	Stearman 1989a (estimate)
NAMBIKWARA	13	70	Lévi-Strauss 1948:266, 288
CALUSA	0.1	0.1	Widmer 1983:15–18
GUAYAKI	58	290	Clastres 1972:163; Oberg 1953:18, 38
BOTOCUDO	7	135	LRB estimate
AWEIKOMO	30	170	Henry 1964:159
TEHUELCHE	17	360	LRB estimate
ONA	24	320	Chapman 1982:19
YAHGAN	7	90	Gusinde 1937:366, 511

CASE	NUMBER OF MOVES PER YEAR	DISTANCE MOVED PER YEAR (MILES)	REFERENCE(S)
Tropical-subtropical Africa			
AKA	6	75	Hudson 1990:57–80
BAYAKA	10	37	Heymer 1980:189
BAMBOTE	7	60	Terashima 1980:241, 261
BAKA	16	85	Vallois and Marquer 1976:112–19
EFE	12	65	Bailey 1985:48–58; Peacock 1985:47–48
MBUTI	13	64	Harako 1976:44, 114–17
MAWAMBO	11	65	Tanno 1976:123
TETRI AREA	18	145	Ichikawa 1978:173–75
HUKWE	8	125	LRB estimate
HADZA	7	80	Lee and Devore 1968a:194
DOROBO	0.1	0.1	Huntingford 1929:340, 1955:623–34
!KUNG (NYAE NYAE)	11	300	Hitchcock and Ebert 1989:55
!KUNG (DOBE)	5.5	75	Lee 1972a:330, 1979:168, 182–204
NHARO	2	31	Hitchcock and Ebert 1989:55
G/WI	11.5	270	Silberbauer 1972:295–97; 1981:193, 196, 246; 1981b:460
//GANA	11	250	Tanaka 1976:100, 113, 1980:79–81
KUA	9	215	Hitchcock and Ebert 1989:55
!KO	12	310	Hitchcock and Ebert 1989:55
/AUNI (KHOMANI)	13	352	Informant from Molopo River
Australia: subtropical desert through temperate settings			
KUARAREG	4	32	Moore 1979:238
LARIKIA	7	60	Parkhouse 1895:639–41
GUNWINGGU	14	140	Altman 1987:22–27
MIRRNGADJA	6	14	Peterson 1973:185, 1970:11
ANBARRA	3	17	Meehan 1982:26–41
GIDJINGALI	0.1		Hiatt 1965:31–32
MURNGIN	15	180	Tindale pers. comm. 1967
JEIDJI	14	218	LRB estimate
WIKMUNKAN	14	238	Thomson 1939:211–20
KAKADU	12	150	Chaloupka 1981:163–71
NUNGGUBUYU	10	85	Biernoff 1979:156
YINTJINGGA	6	25	Thomson 1934:241
YIR (YORONT)	13	145	LRB estimate
TIWI	10	75	Hart and Pilling 1960:35, 36, 66
KUKU (YALANJI)	6	18	Anderson and Robins 1988:184–87
GROOTE EYELANDT	8	60	Tindale, pers. comm. 1967
WALMBARIA	4	30	Hale and Tindale 1933:64, 77
MULLUK	7	40	LRB estimate
WORORA	13	150	Blundell 1975:127–29.
LARDIL	4	35	Memmott 1983a:121–26
KAIADILT	7	35	LRB estimate
MAMU	12	70	Harris 1982:378–82
KARIERA	8	130	Radcliffe-Brown 1912:144–47
WALBIRI	14	380	Meggitt pers. comm. 1973
MARDUDJARA	15	416	LRB estimate
ILDAWONGGA	15	380	LRB estimate
PINTUBI	15	325	Myers 1986:77–89
JINIBARRA	8	32	Winterbotham 1980:41
KARUWALI	13	275	Duncan-Kemp 1964:129
ALYAWARA	14	325	Binford field notes 1974
NGATATJARA	14	373	Gould 1968:104–12

(continued)

TABLE 8.04 *(continued)*

CASE	NUMBER OF MOVES PER YEAR	DISTANCE MOVED PER YEAR (MILES)	REFERENCE(S)
BADJALANG	8	90	Belshaw 1978:74–78
PITJANDJARA	15	289	Tindale 1972:233–38
JANKUNDJARA	12	298	Tindale pers. comm. 1966–67
NORTHERN ARENDA	14	285	Binford field notes 1993; Spencer and Gillen 1927
NAKAKO	17	360	Tindale pers. comm. 1966.
KARUNA	8	100	Draper pers. comm. 1993
BUNURONG	10	90	Gaughwin and Sullivan 1984:90
TASMANIANS (EASTERN)	12	165	Jones 1972:4
TASMANIANS (WESTERN)	7	65	Jones 1972:4
North America: California and Northern Mexico			
SERI	7	95	McGee 1898:152
CAHUILLA	4	40	LRB estimate
CUPENO	0.1	0.1	LRB estimate
KILIWA	7	90	LRB estimate
DIEGUENO	7	80	LRB estimate
LAKE YOKUTS	1	4	Gayton 1948a:7–14; Kroeber 1925:484
SERRANO	7	90	LRB estimate
LUISENO	2	18	Sparkman 1908:212
WUKCHUMI	5	50	LRB estimate
TUBATULABAL	9	110	Voegelin 1938:2–4
NOMLAKI	3	33	Goldschmidt 1948:445
NORTH FOOTHILL YOKUTS	6	70	Gayton 1948a:56–64, 70–76
PATWIN	2	14	Kroeber 1932:259–62
GABRIELINO	0.1	0.1	LRB estimate
MONACHE	9	85	Gayton 1948a:254–63; Gifford 1932b
EASTERN POMO	3	36	Barrett 1908:182–204
WINTU	6	139	DuBois 1935:28–29
CHUMASH	0.1	0.1	LRB estimate
CHIMARIKO	2	34	Dixon 1910:295–302
NISENAN SOUTHERN MAIDU	1	5	Kroeber 1929:407–8
SOUTHERN POMO	0.1	0.1	Barrett 1908:210–26
SINKYONE	4	60	Nomland 1935:149–78
WAPPO	2	8	Driver 1936:179–220
NORTHERN POMO	0.1	0.1	Barrett 1908:124–35; Loeb 1926:172
YANA	4	85	Waterman 1918:37–60
MIWOK	4	32	Barrett and Gifford 1933:198–206
TAKELMA	6	70	Gray 1987:37–40
COAST YUKI	8	100	Gifford 1939:294, 329–30
TOLOWA	5	60	Drucker 1940:226–35
SHASTA	3	55	Dixon 1907:421–22
HUPA	0.1	0.1	Goddard 1904:12–16, 21–29
TUTUTNI	5	75	Gray 1987:48–51
KAROK	0.1	0.1	Schenck and Gifford 1952:387–92
WIYOT	1	12	Schalk 1978:125
MAIDU (MOUNTAIN)	4	28	Dixon 1905:201, 225
YUROK	2	24	Schalk 1978:125
ACHUMAWI	3	64	Kniffen 1926:303
MODOC	9	45	Ray 1963:180–211
KLAMATH	6	84	Spier 1930:11
North America: desert and desert scrub			
GUAICURA	8	135	Baegert 1863:361–65; 1865:391
DEATH VALLEY SHOSHONI	13	225	Steward 1938:91–93
PANAMINT VALLEY SHOSHONI	11	220	Steward 1938:84–85

CASE	NUMBER OF MOVES PER YEAR	DISTANCE MOVED PER YEAR (MILES)	REFERENCE(S)
YAVAPAI	9	18	Corbusier 1886:283; Gifford 1932:206–13
KOSO MOUNTAIN SHOSHONI	14	220	Steward 1936:81–83
WALAPAI	4	105	Knifen 1935:38–45
KAWAIISU	9	150	LRB estimate
SALINE VALLEY SHOSHONI	14	180	Steward 1936:76–80
ANTARIANUNT SOUTHERN PAIUTE	10	200	LRB estimate
OWENS VALLEY PAIUTE	2	17	Steward 1933:238–39, 263–66
KAWICH MOUNTAIN SHOSHONI	12	270	Thomas 1983:29–30
KAIBAB SOUTHERN PAIUTE	8	200	Kelly 1964:12, 14
MONO LAKE PAIUTE	11	215	Davis 1965:29–31
DEEP SPRINGS PAIUTE	8	195	Steward 1938:58–60
SALMON-EATER SHOSHONI	12	210	Gould and Plew 1996:64–66; Steward 1938:165–72
PYRAMID LAKE PAIUTE	3	33	LRB estimate
CATTAIL PAIUTE	5	90	Fowler 1992:25–42
FISH LAKE VALLEY PAIUTE	9	150	Steward 1938:64–68
HONEY LAKE PAIUTE	9	165	Riddell 196o:21–44
HUKUNDUKA SHOSHONI	12	250	Steward 1938:178–79
GOSIUTE SHOSHONI	13	228	Steward 1938:132–39
RAILROAD VALLEY SHOSHONI	5	90	Steward 1938:118–21
REESE RIVER SHOSHONI	8	130	Steward 1938:100–5
GROUSE CREEK SHOSHONI	14	315	Steward 1938:173–77
WASHO	7	198	Downs 1966:12–37
KIDUTOKADO	9	210	Kelly 1932:78, 105–6
RUBY VALLEY SHOSHONI	7	120	Steward 1938:figure 11, 147–49
WADADOKADO PAIUTE	11	250	Whiting 1950:17–19
AGAIDUKA SHOSHONI	13	270	Steward 1938:187–92
LITTLE SMOKEY SHOSHONI	11	260	Steward 1938:114–15, figure 8

Mounted hunters from steppic regions of North America

CASE	NUMBER OF MOVES PER YEAR	DISTANCE MOVED PER YEAR (MILES)	REFERENCE(S)
LIPAN APACHE	18	480	Basehart pers. comm. 1972
CHEYENNE	18	390	Gussow 1954; Moore 1987:163–75
CROW	31	570	Denig 1961:159; Kelly 1995:table 4.1
KUTENAI	13	285	Turney-High 1941:53–55
GROS-VENTRE	24	420	Flannery 1953:23–24
PEIGAN	28	840	Ewers 1955:125–27
	21	560	Kehoe 1993:89
BLACKFOOT	30	540	Ewers 1955:123–29
SARSI	18	440	Jenness 1938:12

North Pacific coastal areas of North America and Asia

CASE	NUMBER OF MOVES PER YEAR	DISTANCE MOVED PER YEAR (MILES)	REFERENCE(S)
SQUAMISH	2	34	Drucker 1990:464; Kelly 1995:table 4.1
ALSEA	3	22	Drucker 1939
PUYALLUP	2	50	Smith 1940a:7–32, 1940b:138–42
TWANA	4	65	Elmendorf 1960:253–65; Kelley 1995: table 4.1
NOOTKA	3	25	Schalk 1978:126
CHINOOK	2	28	Ray 1937:366, 1938:38–42, 55
COOS	0.1	0.1	Zenk 1990:572–74
LILLOOET	8	90	Hayden 1997:18–22
LUMMI	2	20	Stern 1934:43–53
QUINAULT	2	12	Olson 1936:93–94
STALO	4	40	Schalk 1978:126
COWICHAN	6	60	Wilson 1866:286
TILLAMOOK	2	16	Taylor 1974a:33–41

(continued)

TABLE 8.04 *(continued)*

CASE	NUMBER OF MOVES PER YEAR	DISTANCE MOVED PER YEAR (MILES)	REFERENCE(S)
QUILEUTE	0.1	0.1	Pettitt 1950:5–7
CLALLAM	4	45	Schalk 1978:126
MAKAH	2	15	Schalk 1978:125, 165
HAISLA	0.1	0.1	Olson 1940:170
SOUTHERN KWAKIUTL	3.5	31	Schalk 1978:165
TSHIMSHIAN	3.5	85	Halpin and Sequin 1990:269–71; Schalk 1978:126, 165
SOUTHERN TLINGIT	3	30	Schalk 1978:127, 165
CHILKAT TLINGIT	2	55	Mitchell and Donald 1988:310
GITKSAN	4	45	Halpin and Seguin 1990:269–71
KONAIG	0.1	0.1	LRB estimate
EYAK	2	25	de Laguna 1990:190–91
KUSKOWAGAMIUT	.01	0.1	Oswalt pers. comm. 1966
CHUGASH	2	15	Birket-Smith 1953:123–28
ALEUT	0.1		Lantis 1970:174–82
NUNIVAK	0.1	0.1	Lantis 1946:163

Subarctic and continental midlatitude forests of North America and Asia

CASE	NUMBER OF MOVES PER YEAR	DISTANCE MOVED PER YEAR (MILES)	REFERENCE(S)
TENINO	6	70	Murdock 1980:131
WENATCHI	2	19	Teit 1928:104, 114–15
WISHRAM	0.1	0.1	Spier and Sapir 1930:164–67, 202–5
COEUR D'ALENE	11	300	Teit 1930:95–97, 150–52
SINKAIETK	7	90	Cline et al. 1938:11
OKANAGAN	3	40	Grabert 1974:8
SANPOIL	5	75	Kelly 1995:table 4.1; Ray 1932:15–24, 27–28
KITCHIBUAN	14	225	Jenness 1935:13–14
KATIKITEGON	14	280	Kinietz 1947:43–55
MICMAC	12	252	Speck and Dester 1951:251–55; Wallis and Wallis 1955:64–66, 172
RAINY RIVER OJIBWA	13	350	Hickerson 1967:48–52; Landes 1937b:88–95
NORTH SALTEAUX	15	375	LRB estimate
SHUSWAP	4	60	Dawson 1891:7–10
ALKATCHO	5.5	90	Goldman 1940:351–52
NIPIGON	14	350	Cameron 1890:256
MISTASSINI CREE	16	450	Rogers 1972:107–11
NORTH ALBANY OJIBWA	14	275	Dunning 1959; LRB estimate
MONTAGNAIS	19	318	Lane 1952:13
SEKANI	15	400	Jenness 1937:32–37, 58
BEAVER	20	400	Goddard 1916:212; Ridington 1982:472
SLAVE	13	445	Helm 1961:16–27
KASKA	9	280	Honigmann 1954:12, 31–68
CARRIER	12	275	Jenness 1943:531–39
HARE	16	450	Savishinsky 1974:86–138
ATTAWAPISKAT CREE	8	215	Honigmann 1956:32
KOYUKON	14	350	McFadyer1981:593, 588–89
CHIPPEWYAN	18	496	Fidler 1934
KUTCHIN	16	450	Slobodin 1969:58–64, 78–83
INGALIK	4	64	Michael 1967:307
SATUDENE	14	375	Hooper 1853
NABESNA	14	320	McKennan 1959
RUPERT HOUSE CREE	16	340	Morantz 1983:33–37
DOGRIB	13	450	Helm 1972:63–72
TANAINA (1843)	2	36	Michael 1967:306
TUTCHONE	19	450	Legros 1982:67–69
HOLIKACHUK	0.1	0.1	Snow 1981:615–16
NASKAPI	16	420	Henriksen 1973:2, 4

TABLE 8.04 *(continued)*

CASE	NUMBER OF MOVES PER YEAR	DISTANCE MOVED PER YEAR (MILES)	REFERENCE(S)
		Arctic	
NORTON SOUND INUIT	0.1	0.1	LRB estimate
KOBUK INUIT	9	225	Giddings 1956:5–55
KOTZEBUE SOUND INUIT	0.1		LRB estimate
LABRADOR INUIT	4	135	Taylor 1974:51–58
GREAT WHALE INUIT	3	85	Saladin d'Anglure 1984:497–99
CARIBOU INUIT	16	440	LRB estimate
NOATAK INUIT	12	360	Binford 1972 field notes
NUNAMIUT INUIT	11	501	Amsden 1977:159, 163
MACKENZIE INUIT	6	145	McGhee 1988:7–24
SIVOKAMIUT INUIT	1	16	Moore 1923:349
POINT HOPE INUIT	2	75	Burch 1975:260–69; Rainey 1947:240, 244–67
COPPER INUIT	14	444	Jenness 1932:32, 55, 56
UTKUHIKHALINGMIUT	15	380	Briggs 1970:30, 32–40
AIVILINGMIUT INUIT	14	400	Mathiassen 1928:15–17, 24
INGULIK INUIT	12	385	Mathiassen 1928:29–36
WEST GREENLAND	3	70	Grønnow et al. 1983:13–37
BAFFIN ISLAND INUIT	4	175	Boas 1888:422–24; Hantzsch 1977:39, 99
NETSILIK INUIT	11	307	Balikci 1970:23–90
ANGMAKASLIK	2	13	Holm 1914:97, Thalbitzer 1914: 618–26
TAREUMIUT INUIT	3	60	Simpson 1875:237; Spencer 1959:139–46
POLAR INUIT	11	350	Steensby 1910:279, 289–305

Note: 1. A value of 0.1 indicates no residential mobility (a convention to differentiate missing data from zero moves).

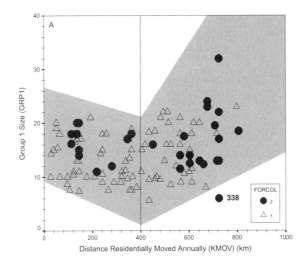
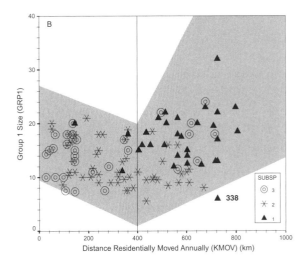

FIGURE 8.15

A two-graph comparison of subsistence and tactical differences among mobile cases only. Each graph is displayed in identical property space defined by GROUP1 size and the number of kilometers associated with residential moves on an annual basis. Graph A is coded for the forager-collector distinction (FORCOL): (1) forager and (2) collector. Graph B is coded for the primary source of food (SUBSP): (1) terrestrial animals, (2) terrestrial plants, and (3) aquatic resources.

sources of water in a region, or if a group lived on a small island. In settings in which resources are scattered over a wide area, their exploitation is likely to be organized logistically.

The residential mobility patterns of collectors have been referred to as point-to-point movement (Binford 1982, 1983:362). This designation reflects the fact that residential sites are not positioned in the landscape to facilitate the search for food on an encounter basis, as with foragers. Instead, they are placed at known locations that provide a set of critical resources. The acquisition of other critical resources (primarily migratory animals in the colder settings) is assigned to work groups that logistically target their acquisition. This organizational strategy prompts the following expectations:

Proposition 8.07

Point-to-point movement should result in higher mean distances traveled per move; it is, in reality, most often accomplished by means of transportation aids such as domesticated animals (dogs in North America and reindeer as well as horses in Asia).

Proposition 8.08

The logistical mobility of sedentary collectors is expected to be organized in terms of a central place, usually a central settlement that is maintained and used over a multiyear period. This strategy does not preclude some residential mobility within the basic foraging radius of the central place, although the distances are expected to be relatively short and the moves considerably fewer than is the case with moves between different FORAD units.

In order to develop further my argument linking group size and mobility pattern, I must first present some interesting data from the hunter-gatherer world sample that will provide a baseline for the discussion. Table 8.05 compares data on the primary food resources of forager and collector cases that are arrayed according to the ordinal scale of climatic regime represented by the variable CLIM. The table confirms my earlier postulations about the distribution of foragers and collectors:

Generalization 8.15

Collector strategies predominate among the groups that are dependent upon animal resources in polar and boreal forest climates, while in cool temperate and all warmer settings, peoples who depend on terrestrial animal resources are organized in terms of forager strategies.

Generalization 8.16

Plant-dependent peoples in all environments rely on forager strategies, although plant-dependent collectors occur in both cool temperate and warm temperate climates. In even warmer settings, some classic, tethered foragers whose mobility is constrained are known to have settled around limited, localized water sources.

Generalization 8.17

In all environments cooler than the subtropics, collector strategies are employed by those groups that rely primarily upon aquatic resources. In the tropics, forager strategies are common, although some clusters of foragers exploiting aquatic resources are found in cooler settings. For example, some central arctic peoples—such as the Copper, Netsilik, and Iglulik Inuit—practice breathing hole sealing during the winter months by building winter snow houses on the frozen surface of the ocean.[13]

The patterning in the three preceding generalizations provides a background against which to continue my discussion of the relationship between GROUP1 size and mobility. At this point, however, I want to link mobility more directly to the Group Size Model I built in chapter 7 and its constituent unit, the FORAD, which is a measure of the size of a group's foraging area. I can compare the average distance of a single residential move to the minimal distance a group could move without overlap while establishing a new foraging area (16.938 kilometers or 10.53 miles). An estimate of the minimal distance one could move within the modeled FORAD unit is 53.21 kilometers (33.07 miles), and the distance one would travel while moving around the circumference of the modeled area is 60.148 kilometers, assuming movement from the center of the FORAD and return.

In addition to a foraging radius (FORAD), one of the constants that applies to collector systems is the *logistical radius* (COLRAD), which represents the area between the 8.469-kilometer foraging radius and the approximately 17.7-kilometer radius within which overnight trips most often occur. As I have noted, a common residential move among those collectors who are primarily dependent upon terrestrial animals is a point-to-point move, which would commonly exceed the 35.4-kilometer diameter of the logistical circle.

In order to evaluate how realistic the model of hunter-gatherer positioning on the landscape might be for both foragers and collectors, I have prepared table 8.06, which summarizes mean values for GROUP1 size, the number of annual residential moves (NOMOV), and the average distance of each residential move (KSPMOV). These values are provided for

TABLE 8.05

CROSS-TABULATIONS OF FORAGERS AND COLLECTORS
ACCORDING TO CLIMATE (CLIM) AND PRIMARY FOOD RESOURCES

| | TERRESTRIAL RESOURCES | | | | | | | | |
| | Animals | | | Plants | | | Aquatic resources | | |
	FORCOL 1	FORCOL 2	TOTAL	FORCOL 1	FORCOL 2	TOTAL	FORCOL 1	FORCOL 2	TOTAL
	Polar climate (CLIM = 1)								
COUNT	1.00	2.00	3.00	0.00	0.00	0.00	5.00	11.00	16.00
EXPECTED	1.20	1.80	3.00	0.00	0.00	0.00	5.30	10.70	16.00
ROW PERCENTAGE	33.30	**66.70**		0.00	0.00		31.30	**68.80**	
COLUMN PERCENTAGE	3.10	4.3		0.00	0.00		12.50	13.80	
	Boreal climate (CLIM = 2)								
COUNT	13.00	34.00	47.00	2.00	1.00	3.00	4.00	42.00	46.00
EXPECTED	19.30	27.70	47.00	2.50	0.50	3.00	15.30	30.70	46.00
ROW PERCENTAGE	27.70	**72.30**		**66.70**	33.30		8.70	**91.30**	
COLUMN PERCENTAGE	40.60	73.90		1.70	4.80		10.00	52.50	
	Cool temperate climate (CLIM = 3)								
COUNT	12.00	8.00	20.00	27.00	10.00	37.00	11.00	22.00	33.00
EXPECTED	8.20	11.80	25.60	31.50	27.00	26.40	11.00	22.00	33.00
ROW PERCENTAGE	60.00	40.00		73.00	27.00		33.30	66.70	
COLUMN PERCENTAGE	37.50	17.40		22.70	47.60		27.50	27.50	
	Warm temperate climate (CLIM = 4)								
COUNT	2.00	2.00	4.00	37.00	8.00	45.00	0.00	3.00	3.00
EXPECTED	1.60	2.40	5.10	38.30	6.80	45.00	1.00	2.00	3.00
ROW PERCENTAGE	**50.00**	**50.00**		**82.20**	17.80		0.00	100.00	
COLUMN PERCENTAGE	6.30	4.30		31.10	38.10		0.00	3.80	
	Subtropical climate (CLIM = 5)								
COUNT	1.00	0.00	1.00	15.00	0.00	15.00	2.00	1.00	3.00
EXPECTED	0.40	0.60	1.00	12.80	2.30	15.00	1.00	2.00	3.00
ROW PERCENTAGE	**100.00**	0.00		**100.00**	0.00		66.70	33.30	
COLUMN PERCENTAGE	3.10	0.00		12.60	0.00		5.00	1.30	
	Tropical climate (CLIM = 6)								
COUNT	3.00	0.00	3.00	25.00	1.00	26.00	15.00	0.00	15.00
EXPECTED	1.20	1.80	3.00	22.10	3.90	26.00	5.00	10.00	15.00
ROW PERCENTAGE	**100.00**	0.00		**96.20**	3.80		**100.00**	0.00	
COLUMN PERCENTAGE	9.40	0.00		21.00	4.80		37.50	0.00	
	Equatorial climate (CLIM = 7)								
COUNT	0.00	0.00	0.00	13.00	1.00	14.00	3.00	1.00	4.00
EXPECTED	0.00	0.00	0.00	11.90	2.10	14.00	1.30	2.70	4.00
ROW PERCENTAGE	0.00	0.00		**92.90**	7.10		**75.00**	25.00	
COLUMN PERCENTAGE	0.00	0.00		10.90	4.80		7.50	1.30	
TOTAL[1]	32.00	46.00	78.00	119.00	21.00	140.00	40.00	60.00	120.00
PERCENT	41.00	59.00	(23.10)	85.00	15.00	(41.40)	33.30	66.70	(35.50)

Notes: The variable CLIM is discussed in chapter 4. For the variable FORCOL, a value of 1 designates forager status and a value of 2 designates collector status. **Boldface** denotes the dominant frequency.
1. Total is for sum of column count only.

TABLE 8.06

MEAN VALUES FOR HUNTER-GATHERER GROUP1 SIZE,
NUMBER OF RESIDENTIAL MOVES ANNUALLY,
AND AVERAGE NUMBER OF KILOMETERS PER MOVE,
GROUPED BY SUBSISTENCE BASE

	TACTICALLY MOBILE		TACTICALLY STATIONARY	
Terrestrial animal exploiters				
1. FORAGERS				
GROUP1 SIZE	16.29 ± 4.90	(23)		(0)
NUMBER OF MOVES	18.53 ± 13.81	(18)		(0)
KM PER MOVE	32.16 ± 10.82	(19)		(0)
2. COLLECTORS				
GROUP1 SIZE	17.32 ± 5.55	(23)		(0)
NUMBER OF MOVES	14.34 ± 4.99	(19)	14.00	(1)
KM PER MOVE	42.72 ± 11.92	(20)	32.18	(1)
Terrestrial plant exploiters				
1. FORAGERS				
GROUP1 SIZE	13.48 ± 4.61	(81)	15.09 ± 4.74	(7)
NUMBER OF MOVES	12.64 ± 9.90	(86)	6.59 ± 12.15	(10)
KM PER MOVE	25.49 ± 13.70	(79)	8.69 ± 13.17	(10)
2. COLLECTORS				
GROUP1 SIZE		(0)	16.90 ± 6.19	(08)
NUMBER OF MOVES		(0)	3.22 ± 3.61	(15)
KM PER MOVE		(0)	10.71 ± 4.84	(15)
Aquatic resource exploiters				
1. FORAGERS				
GROUP1 SIZE	14.40 ± 4.03	(24)	20.33 ± 3.78	(03)
NUMBER OF MOVES	8.31 ± 3.17	(26)	2.62 ± 1.63	(05)
KM PER MOVE	20.55 ± 15.14	(28)	17.32 ± 10.47	(05)
2. COLLECTORS				
GROUP1 SIZE	16.28 ± 4.07	(13)	20.67 ± 6.03	(21)
NUMBER OF MOVES	6.77 ± 3.81	(13)	2.53 ± 2.91	(54)
KM PER MOVE	36.59 ± 13.70	(15)	17.08 ± 14.88	(52)

Notes: Reference values: The diameter of a FORAD unit, which is the smallest residential move that can be made without producing overlapping areas of exploitation, is 16.938 kilometers. Among stationary groups who live in FORAD units, 60.148 kilometers is the maximum distance that can be covered residentially within a single year without repeating the coverage of an area within the FORAD, assuming that residential movement is linear. Among collectors, the size of the basic unit of space is larger since it includes the "logistical area" (Binford 1983:358–66). The range of increase is from a diameter of 16.938 to one of 35.4 kilometers.

mobile cases as well as for those that are tactically localized, whose residential mobility is not a fundamental part of the subsistence strategy.[14] Cases classified as foragers and collectors (and excluding mounted hunters) are summarized independently under three major headings separating cases according to the trophic level of exploited food resources (SUBSP).

Perhaps the first item of interest in table 8.06 is that the mean distance of each residential move among foraging peoples dependent upon terrestrial animals is 1.9 times greater than the value in my model for nonoverlapping site catchment movement based on the FORAD. In fact, all values for groups classified as hunters cluster around the 35.4-kilometer value modeled for collectors. And although foragers have a smaller mean distance per move (32.18 kilometers),

it is nevertheless much larger than the minimum value of 16.94 kilometers modeled for foragers. On the other hand, within the mobile hunter category, collectors have a mean value of 42.7 kilometers per move. It appears, therefore, that the model significantly underestimates the distance moved for groups dependent upon terrestrial animals. These results lead me to suggest that

Generalization 8.18

Groups primarily exploiting terrestrial animal resources, regardless of labor strategy, are uniformly more mobile and have considerably more spatial separation between residential catchment areas (FORADs or COLRADs) than was modeled for peoples *not* primarily dependent upon terrestrial animals. Hunters, in particular, make point-to-point residential moves (Binford 1983:362).

As I scan table 8.06 for other mobile collectors, I note that they occur only among groups that primarily exploit aquatic resources. Cases in this category have a mean distance per move of 36.59 kilometers. This value is not significantly different from the 35.4 kilometers modeled for collectors using a nonoverlapping or "complete leapfrog" pattern of residential mobility when the COLRAD is the size of the catchment area.

Shifting from the contrasts between forager and collector strategies among mobile peoples to a focus upon the differences between tactically stationary and mobile cases, I note additional patterning:

Generalization 8.19

GROUP1 sizes of tactically stationary groups, regardless of subsistence base, are larger than those recorded for mobile cases, a finding that supports the view that small GROUP1 sizes are most compatible with higher mobility. The number of moves and the distances moved are dramatically lower for stationary cases (which is not surprising), but the mean values for total distance moved (NOMOV * KM/MOVE) are all either very close to or below the modeled value of 53.21 kilometers for a FORAD unit. Nevertheless, among stationary groups of plant-dependent peoples, the mean total distance moved is significantly less for collectors than for foragers.

This observation is not unreasonable if, as I expected, the greater part of the effective mobility of a group of collectors takes the form of nonresidential task groups. If I accept this supposition, then the data on tactically stationary peoples who exploit aquatic resources assume a different significance. There are no probabilistic differences between any of the values recorded for foragers, as opposed to collectors, among the stationary groups dependent upon aquatic resources. I think this may indicate that among stationary, aquatically dependent peoples, the distinction between foragers and collectors is irrelevant.

Only seven cases were classified as sedentary foragers in the sample of aquatically dependent peoples. One was a resettled Australian group—the Gidjindgali—that participated in a very nonaboriginal settlement system at the time of description (Hiatt 1965:10–13). For an analogous group—the Pekangekum Ojibwa—data on mobility were scant, but it is likely that they were misclassified as stationary. Four groups—the Chimariko, Sinkyone, Coast Miwok, and Mattole—are from California, and all were probably misclassified as foragers, although there is insufficient information on mobility or labor organization to be certain. The final group, the Walmbaria from Princess Charlotte Bay, Queensland, Australia, turned out upon reexamination (Hale and Tindale 1933) not to be stationary, and their GRPPAT classification was incorrect.[15]

Reflecting on the question of whether groups dependent upon aquatic resources were ever stationary foragers leads me to conclude that hunter-gatherers were rarely if ever organized in such a way.[16] Most people who rely upon aquatic resources for food usually obtain the equally critical raw materials for clothing, housing, and technology primarily from terrestrial locations. The lack of congruence between the locations where food is available and the sites where other resources essential for life could be found strongly favors a collector strategy for the procurement of nonfood resources (Binford 1983:344). In contrast, groups that depend upon terrestrial resources (e.g., big game hunters) frequently obtain raw materials for food, clothing, and shelter from the same species as those from which food comes, or from related species.

It is also interesting to note that in table 8.05 there is no probabilistic difference between the mean GROUP1 sizes of mobile foragers who depend primarily upon either terrestrial plants or aquatic resources. There are, however, very real differences between the number of annual residential moves and the distance traveled per move.

This pattern can be viewed in more than one way. The lack of difference in means could indicate that the difference between terrestrial plant and aquatic resource procurement is irrelevant as a conditioner of GROUP1 size. It is also possible that a group's primary subsistence activity during the most dispersed phase of the annual cycle is biased in favor of terrestrial resource exploitation. In the latter case, the similarity in the means would lend strong support to the conclusion that the structure of the resource distribution heavily conditions group size.

If, on the other hand, the former alternative is correct and the trophic level of resources per se is perhaps irrelevant, then the structure of resource distribution in terms of abundance and clustering would have the greater effect upon GROUP1 size and therefore be the most important variable. In that case, correlations between the types of resource targets would actually be autocorrelations arising from different "normative" patch structures. Support for the argument of referral based on patch structure rather than on resource category comes from the previously demonstrated relationship between GROUP1 size and the $\log_{10}$ value of net aboveground productivity.[17]

THE ORGANIZATION OF LABOR: EXPLORING THE RELATIONSHIPS BETWEEN FOOD TYPE AND SYSTEM STATE AS CONDITIONERS OF GROUP SIZE

In the Group Size Model, the character of the sexual division of labor and the work schedules maintained by each gender-based labor unit were major parameters in the determination of group size. In considering subsistence tactics that primarily target aquatic resources or terrestrial animals, groups are encountered for whom storage is common and mobility is organized differently from season to season. Fewer of the assumptions directing the construction of the Group Size Model are met among peoples who depend upon aquatic and terrestrial animals, particularly the assumption about the sexual division of labor.

Female-Biased Labor Units: Polygyny and Group Size

In hunter-gatherer cases practicing polygyny—for example, the Tiwi of Australia (Hart and Pilling 1960:66)—the proportion of male to female producers in the group deviates from the fifty-fifty balance assumed by the Group Size Model.

Generalization 8.20

When the number of female food producers within polygynous families increases, GROUP1 size does not grow as rapidly with the addition of each new wife as it does in groups in which males procure the preponderance of the food. The difference is that with males, group size increases as a function of the male dependency ratio within families.

In other words, because adult males tend also to be heads of families,[18] additional numbers of adult males in a group both enlarge the work force and increase the dependency ratio, both of which affect group size.[19] There is an exception to this pattern, however:

Generalization 8.21

Within polygynous groups, the dependency ratio does not necessarily increase greatly in families made up of multiple wives, despite the fact that family size may increase dramatically.

Generalization 8.20 applies to those polygynous groups in which each new wife is also a new food producer, whose contribution to the family's resource base actually decreases the dependency ratio. In such a situation, the total number of children in the group may increase, but this will not greatly change the dependency ratio because the same proportion between children and female food producers is being maintained.

The impact of polygyny on hunter-gatherer GROUP1 size may also be affected by another variable: the age at first marriage of both males and females. I have summarized these data in table 8.07 and provided bibliographic references for each ethnographic case. There is one methodological caveat that I must discuss prior to examining the table itself, and that relates to the way my measurements of the sexual division of labor were calculated. For instance, when the division of labor is measured by the variable used in this study, which I have termed MDIVLAB, it is based on estimates of the male and female contributions to the diet in terms of the plant or animal species normally exploited by each gender.

For example, an ethnographic observer will note that "males hunt rabbits and females gather grains," but no estimate is available that measures the quantitative contribution of individual male hunters and individual female gatherers who are organized in on-the-ground groups actually engaged in obtaining food. It might therefore be suspected that polygyny would bias the estimate of MDIVLAB toward the high side when females outnumber males in the adult labor force within food-procuring groups composed of polygynous households.

A dramatic set of analogous patterns occurs in the three identical property space plots in figure 8.16. Graphs A, B, and C feature mobile hunter-gatherer groups and differ only in the kind of food resources that constitute the primary component of the diet. All three graphs exhibit multiple, converging linear and inverse relationships between the percentage of polygynous males and the percentage of the diet produced exclusively by male labor. It is clear that, among groups that are dependent upon either aquatic resources or terrestrial plants, the highest levels of polygyny occur when women obtain more than 50 percent of the total food resources. The groups that depend most heavily upon terrestrial animals have a pattern that is most like that of peoples dependent upon aquatic resources, except that in all but one case—the Warunggu of Australia—the absolute levels of polygyny are all less than 30 percent. The Warunggu also stood out in the plot of GROUP1 size in graph A of figure 8.14, and I mentioned that I thought they must have been misclassified—a judgment that their placement in figure 8.16 supports. Therefore

---
Generalization 8.22

Other things being equal, the frequency of polygyny declines among mobile peoples as the contribution of males to the diet goes up. Another way of saying this is that polygyny is most common among groups in which female labor makes the greater contribution to the diet. In the case of groups that are primarily dependent upon terrestrial plants and aquatic resources, the highest levels of polygyny coincide with situations in which more than 50 percent of the total diet is obtained by females.

TABLE 8.07

PERCENTAGE OF POLYGYNY AND AGE AT MARRIAGE
IN HUNTER-GATHERER GROUPS PRACTICING POLYGYNOUS MARRIAGE

CASE	PERCENTAGE OF POLYGYNY	AGE AT MARRIAGE		REFERENCE(S)
		Male	*Female*	
Tropical-subtropical Asia				
PUNAN	4			Kedit 1982:261–64
BATEK (PALAWAN)	5	19.9	15.1	Cadelina 1982:72–74; Warren 1964:28, 76
SHOMPEN	7	18.0	15.0	Rizvi 1990:20, 41
ANDAMAN ISLANDS (ONGE)	0			Temple 1903:65
AYTA (PINATUBO)	8	14.0	12.0	Reed 1904:57, 60
ANDAMAN ISLANDS	0	20	18	Man 1883:81; Whiting 1964:529
SEMANG	3	19.0	14.5	Evans 1937:250; Whiting 1964:529; Schebesta 1962a:220, 239
VEDDAH	<5		14.0	Spittel 1945:8, 65
HILL PANDARAM	9	15	9.0	Morris 1982a:150, 250
AGTA (CASIGURAN)	<5	21.7	18.4	Headland 1986:146, 366–67
AGTA (ISABELA)	2			Rai 1982:67
AGTA (CAGAYAN)	0	15.0	13.0	Vanoverbergh 1925:425–26; Goodman et al.
		19.0	17.0	1985:171
CHENCHU	3	16.0	14.0	Fürer-Heimendorf 1943:134, 142
MRABRI	0	15.5	13.0	Bernatzik 1951:145–46
PALIYANS	4	25.0	11.0	Gardner 1965:18, 100; Gardner 1972:421
BIRHOR	2			Williams 1974:73
KADAR	6	27.0	16.0	Ehrenfels 1952:66–68, 139–40
NAYAKA			14	Bird-David 1987:157
AINU (HOKKAIDO)	6	18.0	16.0	Hitchcock 1891:465
		19.5	16.0	Batchelor 1927:196
OROGENS	5	16.0	13.0	Qiu 1983:37
KET	0		14.5	Lee 1967:52; Shimkin 1939:155
GILYAK	5.3	16.0	5.0	Shternberg 1933:165, 167
YUKAGHIR	3	22.0	16.0	Jochelson 1924:79–85, 110–11
SIBERIAN ESKIMO	3	23.0	15.0	Bogoras 1904:30; Moore 1923:367
Tropical-subtropical South America				
AKURIYO		12.0	9.0	Kloos 1977:117
YARURO-PUME	23	15.0	13.0	Gragson 1989:123; Petrullo 1939:232
GUAHIBO	3	17.0	13.0	Metzger 1968:83, 85; Wilbert 1957:89
NUKAK	16	17.5	12.0	Politis pers. comm. 1993
BORORO	5		11.0	Cook 1908:387; Lévi-Strauss 1936:276
GUATO	25	16.0	14.0	Métraux 1946a:417
SIRIONO	28	15.0	12.5	Holmberg 1950:51, 82–83, 216
YUQUI	4			Stearman 1989a:94
NAMBIKWARA	17	14.5	13.0	Lévi-Strauss 1948a:366; 1970:269; Oberg 1953:103–04
CALUSA	12			Goggin and Sturtevant 1964:189
GUAYAKI (ACHE)	6	19.0	10.0	Clastres 1968:19–23; Métraux and Baldus 1946:442
BOTOCUDO	8		13.0	Métraux 1946b:537
HETA	30			Kozak et al. 1979:360
AWEIKOMO	32	19.0	9.0	Henry 1964:45
TEHUELCHE	<4	20.0	15.0	Cooper 1946c:149
CHONO	2			Cooper 1946d:52
ALACALUF	4			Bird 1946:77
ONA	8	19.0	17.0	Chapman 1982:58; Cooper 1946b:115
	28	20.0	17.0	Gusinde 1931:444, 479

(continued)

CASE	PECENTAGE OF POLYGYNY	AGE AT MARRIAGE		REFERENCE(S)
		Male	*Female*	
YAHGAN	3	18.0	15.5	Cooper 1946a:92

Tropical-subtropical Africa

AKA	5			Bahuchet 1979:1001
BAYAKA	0			Heymer 1980:200; Lalouel 1950:179
BAMBOTE	4			Terashima 1980:233
BAKA PYGMIES	16	18.0	16.0	Cavalli-Sforza 1986a:37
EFE	36	18.0	15.0	Bailey 1988:59 Schebesta 1962a:244
MBUTI	11	17.0	14.5	Harako 1976:46–47; Putnam 1948:336
HAI//OM		20.0	15.0	Fourie 1928:92
HADZA	3	20.0	16.0	Bleek 1931:427; O'Connell pers. comm. 1982
DOROBO	0.5	23.0	15.0	Blackburn 1971:266
!KUNG				
NYAE NYAE (1950S)	10	19.5	13.5	Marshall 1959:336, 350
DOBE AREA (1960S)	5	25.0	17.0	Howell 1979:243–44; Lee 1972a:358
SOUTHERN "AUEN"	3	17.0	14.5	Kaufmann 1910:156; Schapera 1930:104
NHARO	<4	19.0	17.0	Bleek 1928:33–34; Schapera 1930:104
G/WI	12	15.0	8.0	Silberbauer 1981:149, 155
//GANA	25			Cashdan 1980:119
KUA	12			Vierich 1981:146
!KO	2			Eibl-Eibelsfeldt 1948:29–34
/AUNI (KHOMANI)	3	18.0	14.0	Dart 1937b

Australia: subtropical desert through temperate settings

KAURAREG		23.0	21.0	Moore 1979:146
LARIKIA			13.0	Basedow 1907:14
GUNWINGGU	45	33.0	14.0	Berndt and Berndt 1970:95; Peterson and Long 1986:137
MIRRNGADJA	45			Long 1970:303
ANBARRA	42	25.0	13.5	Peterson and Long 1986:137
GIDJINGALI	38	25.0	13.0	Hiatt 1965:36, 77
	36.2			Long 1970:302
MURNGIN	43	29.0	11.0	Long 1970:303; Peterson and Long 1986:154
JEIDJI		26.0	14.5	Kaberry 1939:420
WIKMUNKAN	18			Peterson and Long 1986:137
KAKADU	40			Spencer 1966:49
YINTJINGGA		22.0	9.0	Thomson 1933:509
YIR-YORONT	43	30.0	13.0	Peterson and Long 1986:95–99; Sharp 1940:490; Sharp 1934a:427
TIWI	53.8	35.0	9.0	Goodale 1962:455; Hart 1970:296; Hart and Piling 1960:16, 36, 66; Peterson and Long 1986:137
YUKU (YALANJI)			13.0	Roth 1909:5
GROOTE EYLANDT	48	33.0	9.0	Rose 1960:12, 69, 248
WALMBARIA			13.0	Roth 1909:4
MULLUK	40	28.0	13.0	Stanner 1933:391
WORORA	35	31.0	11.0	Love 1917:21, 1936:36
LUNGGA	12.6	23.0	13.0	Kaberry 1939:113–15
LARDIL	33			Memmott 1983b:53–54
KAIADILT	52	30.0	14.0	Tindale 1962b:319–21
MAMU			10.0	Roth 1909:12
KARIERA	36		13.0	Clement 1903:13; Radcliffe-Brown 1912:158
WARUNGGU	45	29.0	9.5	Lumholtz 1889:179, 201
DJARU	7.4	19.0	11.0	Kaberry 1939:114
WALBIRI	38	24.0	11.0	Meggitt 1962:77–79

TABLE 8.07 *(continued)*

CASE	PECENTAGE OF POLYGYNY	AGE AT MARRIAGE		REFERENCE(S)
		Male	*Female*	
NGATJAN		30.0	16.0	Harris 1978:128
MARDUDJARA	30	24.0	13.5	Tonkinson 1978:67
ILDAWONGGA	41			Peterson and Long 1986:112–15
PINTUBI	31	25.0	12.0	Hayden pers. comm. 1990, 1992; Long 1970:296–97
JINIBARRA		23.0	14.0	Winterbotham 1980:34
ALYAWARA	30	27.0	13.0	Denham 1975:137–38
NGATATJARA	13	23.0	15.0	Gould 1969a:184
PITJANDJARA	25	27.0	16.0	Long 1970:299; Tindale 1972:259, 260; Yengoyan 1970:89
BADJALANG		20.0	12.5	de Bertrodano 1978:283
DIERI		25.0	13.0	Howitt 1891:79–87
SOUTHERN ARENDA		24.0	8.0	Schulze 1891:236
JANKUNDJARA	27	26.0	12.0	Tindale 1965 pers. comm.; White 1915:726–28
NORTHERN ARENDA	26		14.0	Long 1970:293; Spencer and Gillen 1927:70–71, 472
UALARIA		28.0	13.5	Parker 1905:56
OOLDEA (1941)	21		15.0	Long 1970:298; Berndt and Berndt 1944 14(3):232
KARUNA		25.0	12.0	Cawthorn 1844:76
MINENG		30.0	11.5	Nind 1831:38–39
BUNURONG	18			Cannon 1983:606–7
EAST TASMANIA	29			Plomley 1983:166

North America: California and Northern Mexico

CASE	PECENTAGE OF POLYGYNY	*Male*	*Female*	REFERENCE(S)
SERI	20			McGee 1898:279
	0	17.0		Kroeber 1931:8; Gilg 1965:51
CAHUILLA		17.5	12.5	Strong 1929:74
CUPENO		17.0	13.0	Strong 1929:239
KILIWA	3	18.0	14.0	Meigs 1939:47–50
DIGUENO		17.0	14.0	Luomala 1978:602
LAKE YOKUTS		13.0	11.0	Wallace 1978b:455
SERRANO	2		14.5	Benedict 1924:371–74
LUISENO	5		14.0	Sparkman 1908:214, 225
WUKCHUMI	<4.0	12.5	11.0	Gayton 1948b:105
TUBATULABAL	0	20.0	16.0	Voegelin 1938:43–44
NORTH FOOTHILL YOKUTS		15.0	13.5	Spier 1978:479
MONACHE	7	16.0	14.0	Gayton 1948b:235
EASTERN POMO		22.0	20.0	Loeb 1926:277–79
CLEAR LAKE POMO	9.0			Gifford 1926a:299
WINTU	<5			DuBois 1935:55
NISENAN SOUTHERN MAIDU		14.5	14.5	Faye 1923:36
SINKYONE	<7			Nomland 1935:159
MATTOLE	<3	21.0	18.0	Nomland 1938:100
YUKI (PROPER)	<3	18.0	15.0	Foster 1944:184, 185
WAPPO	0	16.5	13.5	Driver 1936:208
NORTHERN POMO		32.0	20.0	Loeb 1926:280
MIWOK	<7			Gifford 1916:162
COAST YUKI	<3			Miller 1978:250
SHASTA			15.0	Dixon 1907:462
HUPA	<4	17.0	15.5	Wallace 1978:173
MAIDU		17.5	15.5	Dixon 1905:370
YUROK	4	18.0	14.5	Heizer and Mills 1952:145
MODOC	5	18.0	15.0	Ray 1963:83, 90

(continued)

TABLE 8.07 *(continued)*

CASE	PECENTAGE OF POLYGYNY	AGE AT MARRIAGE Male	Female	REFERENCE(S)
KLAMATH	20		14.5	Spier 1930:45, 52–54

North America: desert and desert scrub

CASE	PECENTAGE OF POLYGYNY	AGE AT MARRIAGE Male	Female	REFERENCE(S)
GUAICURA	18		12.0	Baegert 1863:367–68
DEATH VALLEY SHOSHONI	13	20.0	18.0	Smith 1978:439; Steward 1938:87–88, 91
KARANKAWA	<2			Schaedel 1949:124
PANAMINT VALLEY SHOSHONI	5			Steward 1938:85
YAVAPAI	4.5	17.0	14.5	Corbusier 1886:330; Gifford 1932a:191, 195
WALAPAI	4.5	21.0	18.5	Kroeber 1935:141, 143
KAWAIISU	3			Zigmond 1986:404
ANTARIANUNT SOUTHERN PAIUTE	3.5	15.0	12.0	Kelly 1964:100; Kelly and Fowler 1986:377–80
OWENS VALLEY PAIUTE	4	15.0	12.0	Lowie 1909:210
			13.0	Steward 1933:295
KAIBAB SOUTHERN PAIUTE	3	19.0	15.5	Kelly 1964:99–100; Kelly and Fowler 1986:377
NORTHERN PAIUTE	18			Whiting 1964:531
MONO LAKE PAIUTE	<10			Davis 1965:17
DEEP SPRINGS PAIUTE	11	18.0	15.0	Fowler and Liljeblad 1986:449; Steward 1938:58–59
KIDUTOKADO	14.5	20.0	13.5	Kelly 1932:163, 164
		18.0	15.0	Brink 1969:70–72
TIMANOGAS UTE	10			Callaway et al. 1986:352
CATTAIL PAIUTE	17	18.0	16.0	Fowler 1992:152, 155
FISH LAKE VALLEY PAIUTE	5			Steward 1938:62–64
WHITE KNIFE SHOSHONI	<10			Harris 1940:49
RAILROAD VALLEY SHOSHONI	20			Steward 1938:118
GROUSE CREEK SHOSHONI	15			Steward 1938:174–75
WASHO	6.6	14.5	13.0	d'Azevedo 1963:109; Price 1962:8–9
WIND RIVER SHOSHONI			17.5	Lowie 1924:227
UINTAH UTE			15.5	Stewart 1941:296
WADADOKADO PAIUTE	12	19.0	16.5	Whiting 1950:100
AGAIDUKA SHOSHONI			14.0	Steward 1938:195
LITTLE SMOKEY SHOSHONI	10			Steward 1938:113–14

Mounted hunters from steppic regions of North America

CASE	PECENTAGE OF POLYGYNY	AGE AT MARRIAGE Male	Female	REFERENCE(S)
COMANCHE	25	27.0	16.0	Wallace and Hoebel 1952:126, 133, 142
CHIRICAHUA APACHE	17.5	21.0	18.5	Opler 1937:201, 204
KIOWA (1800s)	57	16.0	14.0	Miskin 1940:55; Newcomb 1961:201
CHEYENNE	26			Moore 1987:178, 179, 320
ARAPAHO	22	27.0	15.0	Eggan 1937:61–62; Hilger 1952:193, 197, 198
CROW	48	27.0	16.0	Denig 1953:34
KUTENAI		20.0	16.0	Turney-High 1941:119, 130
GROS-VENTRE		20.0	10.5	Flannery 1953:171
PEIGAN	20			DeJong 1912:192–97
BLACKFOOT	21			Wissler 1911:11
1787	23	23.0	1700	Lewis 1973:40
1875		35.0	13.0	Lewis 1973:40
ASSINIBOINE	25	23.0	14.0	Denig 1930:504, 511
PLAINS CREE		25.0	17.5	Mandelbaum 1940:246
SARSI		16.5	14.0	Jenness 1938:21–24

North Pacific coastal areas of North America and Asia

CASE	PECENTAGE OF POLYGYNY	AGE AT MARRIAGE Male	Female	REFERENCE(S)
PUYALLUP	10	20.0	14.0	Smith 1940b:38–39, 166
TWANA	6			Eells 1887:612–15
NOOTKA	9	20.0	16.0	Drucker 1951:281, 284, 287, 297
CHINOOK	8	19.0	15.0	Ray 1938:63–67, 73
LILLOOET		26.0	17.0	Teit 1906:264–65

TABLE 8.07 (*continued*)

CASE	PECENTAGE OF POLYGYNY	AGE AT MARRIAGE		REFERENCE(S)
		Male	*Female*	
LUMMI		19.0	15.0	Stern 1934:23–26
STALO		17.0	14.0	Duff 1952:52, 92
COWICHAN		17.0	15.0	Hill-Tout 1904:319
COMOX		17.0	14.0	Kennedy and Bouchard 1990:448
QUILEUTE		22.0	17.0	Pettitt 1950:16
CLALLAM	8			Eells 1884:35–36
MAKAH	6		15.0	Swan 1870:12, 13
BELLA-COOLA	9	14.5	16.0	McIlwraith 1948:371–72, 379
KONAIG			14.0	Holmberg 1985:53
EYAK			13.0	Birket-Smith and de Laguna 1938:133
KUSKOWAGAMIUT		18.0	14.04–5.0	Oswalt 1966:107; Nelson 1899:292
ALEUT	20	18.0	13.0	Lantis 1984:179; Mickey 1955:15
NUNIVAK	19	20.0	12.0	Lantis 1960:204–14, 233

Subarctic and continental midlatitude forests of North America and Asia

CASE	PECENTAGE OF POLYGYNY	Male	Female	REFERENCE(S)
TENINO	12	20.0	16.5	Murdock 1980:130, 141
WISHRAM	10		14.5	Spier and Sapir 1930:22, 171, 218
COEUR D'ALENE			14.5	Teit 1930:170
SINKAIETK		14.5	14.5	Cline et al. 1938:113
SANPOIL		18.0	15.0	Ray 1932:137
NEZ PERCE	40	14.0	12.0	Spinden 1908:250
THOMPSON	25	24.0	20.0	Teit 1900:321, 326
KITCHIBUAN		19.0	16.0	Jenness 1935:98
KATIKITEGON	12	15.0	12.5	Kinietz 1947:31–33, 128, 137
MICMAC	13	25.0	16.0	Speck 1922:144; Wallis and Wallis 1955:233, 237, 240
FLATHEAD	20	21.0	17.0	Teit 1930:382; Turney-High 1937:86, 94
RAINY RIVER (EMO)	17	27.0	22.0	Hickerson 1967:56; Landes 1937:69–71
NORTH SAULTEAUX	15	21.0	13.0	Hallowell 1938:240, 1955:300; Skinner 1911:151
1871–88	8			
SHUSWAP	23	23	17.5	Teit 1900:324
PEKANGEKUM	13			Dunning 1959:138
ROUND LAKE OJIBWA		21.7	16.7	Rogers 1962a:B54
NIPIGON	13	15.0	6.5	Cameron 1890:265; Grant 1960:320
MISTASSINI CREE (1828)	16.3	21.0	18.0	Lips 1947:419–54; Rogers 1962a
WASWANIPI CREE	16			Morantz 1983:87, 89
WEGAMON OJIBWA	17			Rogers and Black 1976:19
MONTAGNAIS	7			Lane 1952:29
SEKANI	10			Jenness 1937:52
BEAVER (1880)	24	14.0	11.0	Goddard 1916:221; Ives 1985:156
SLAVE	9	25.0	17.5	Helm 1961:48, 53, 72
KASKA	>6	18.0	16.0	Honigmann 1954:131
TAHLTAN	<5	19.0	15.0	Emmons 1911:98; MacLachlan 1981:464
CHILCOTIN	3	17.0	16.0	Lane 1981:405
CARRIER		21.0	17.5	Jenness 1937:524–25
HAN	3	19.0	14.0	Crow and Obley 1981:509
HARE	<5	16.0	13.0	Savishinsky and Hara 1981:319; Whiting 1964:530
ATTAWAPISKAT CREE	<5	19.0	16.5	Honigmann 1956:61, 62
KOYUKON		19.5	14.5	Clark 1975:174–75
CHIPPEWYAN	11	26.0	12.0	Smith 1981:277–79
KUTCHIN	4	16.0	15.0	Osgood 1936:142; Slobodin 1981:524
INGALIK	3	24.0	15.0	Osgood 1958:160; Snow 1981:609, 610
SATUDENE-BEAR LAKE		24.0	10.0	Rushforth 1977:119–21
NABESNA		28.0	14.0	McKennan 1959:118

(*continued*)

TABLE 8.07 *(continued)*

CASE	PECENTAGE OF POLYGYNY	AGE AT MARRIAGE		REFERENCE(S)
		Male	*Female*	
RUPERT HOUSE CREE	18	21.0	14.0	Morantz 1983:87; Skinner 1911:151
DOGRIB (1807)	4	18.0	12.0	Helm 1972:74; Keith 1960:114
TANAINA	8	30.0	16.5	Osgood 1937:161, 164; Townsend 1963:214; 1981:633
TUTCHONE		25.0	16.0	McClellan 1981:500
HOLIKACHUK		24.0	14.5	Snow 1981:615
NASKAPI		22.0	15.0	Tanner 1944:685

Arctic

CASE	PECENTAGE OF POLYGYNY	AGE AT MARRIAGE		REFERENCE(S)
		Male	*Female*	
NORTON SOUND INUIT	4		13.0	Ray 1992:286
KOBUK INUIT	2	24.0	15.0	Giddings 1956:26, pers. comm. 1963
KOTZEBUE SOUND INUIT	9			Burch 1975:269–72
LABRADOR INUIT	36	24.0	13.0	Taylor 1974:68–69
GREAT WHALE INUIT	25			Saladin d'Anglure 1984:493
CARIBOU INUIT (1922)	22	19.0	14.5	Arima 1984:455; Rasmussen 1930:11–13, 22–23, 37–38
NOATAK INUIT	10	25.0	16.0	Binford field notes 1969 (July)
NUNAMIUT INUIT	12	28.0	15.0	Binford and Chasko 1976:73–77
MACKENZIE DELTA INUIT	5			Smith 1984:353
SIVOKAMIUT INUIT	12	23.0	15.0	Moore 1923:367
COPPER INUIT	5.6	25.0	13.0	Damas 1972:42, 1984:401; Rasmussen 1932:78–85
POINT HOPE INUIT	2			Burch 1975:260–69
UTKUHIKHALINGMIUT	3.1	19.0	14.0	Rasmussen 1931:85–90
AIVILINGMIUT INUIT	3	18.0	12.5	Mathiassen 1928:15–17; Van de Velde et al. 1992:3
INGLULIK INUIT	13			Mathiassen 1928:29–36
WEST GREENLAND	5			Rink 1875:23
BAFFIN ISLAND INUIT	3			Boas 1964:18, 69, 115
NETSILIK INUIT	6.3	20.0	14.0	Balikci 1970:102, 156; Rasmussen 1931:85–90
TAREUMIUT INUIT (1852)	<12 7.4	17.0	14.5 15.5	Burch 1975:102; Simpson 1875:254; Spencer 1959:250
POLAR INUIT	0.5	25.0	14.0	Gilberg 1984:587; Steensby 1910:325, 369

I am not yet sure what to make of the presence in figure 8.16 of suites of linear relationships with different intercept values. I will have to keep these relationships in mind as I do further pattern recognition studies, but, based on the preceding observations, it is reasonable to investigate the likelihood that polygyny is strongly tied to the organization of a group's labor base and may represent a way of organizing female labor under some circumstances.

More insight into the nature of those circumstances may come from an examination of the cases that are not mobile but are, instead, largely sedentary and so present a very different pattern. The vast majority of these cases—regardless of the contribution made by males to the diet—are polygynous only 10 percent of the time or less. Among those groups that are primarily dependent upon either terrestrial plants or aquatic resources, within each subset of cases there is a minor decrease in polygyny with increases in the male con-

tribution to the diet. There are a few exceptional cases, but these also reflect the inverse relationship between polygyny and the percentage of the diet contributed by males. These include the Aleut, the Eskimo peoples of Nunivak and Saint Lawrence Islands, and the Thompson and Shuswap.

The effects of polygyny should also be visible in the data on hunter-gatherer family size, a variable that was calculated by dividing the population of an ethnographically observed unit by the total number of married males. It is presented here in table 8.08, along with data on mean household size (MHS) and the bibliographic sources of the data.

Figure 8.17 explores the relationship between polygyny and group size as it may be conditioned by family size. There appears to be a clear break, indicated by a reference line across the graph, between family size and GROUP1 size at a FAMSZ value of five. The majority of cases to the right of the five-person line have small GROUP1 sizes (G1SET = 2)

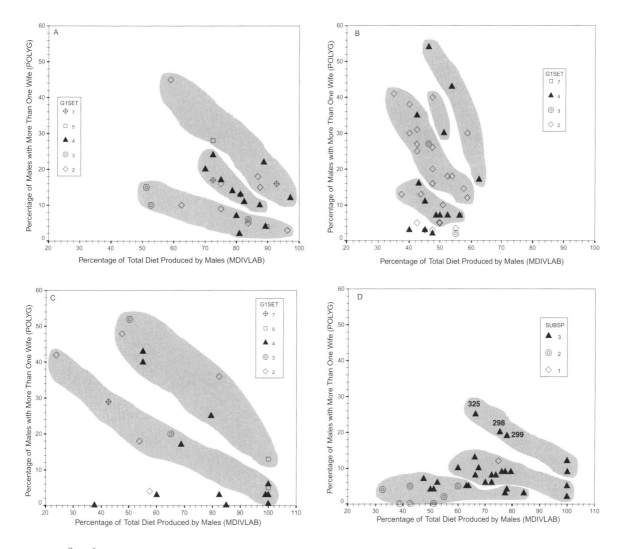

FIGURE 8.16

A four-graph comparison: graphs A, B, and C illustrate the primary source of food for mobile cases exclusively: terrestrial animals (A), terrestrial plants (B), and aquatic resources (C). Graph D displays the same information for nonmobile groups exclusively. All graphs feature the same property space, defined by the percentage of married males with more than one wife and the percentage of the total diet procured by males. Graphs A, B, and C are coded for an ordination and classification of GROUP1 sizes: (2) small, (3) medium, (4) large, (5) oversized, and (7) exceptional cases. Graph D is coded for the primary source of food (SUBSP): (1) terrestrial animals, (2) terrestrial plants, and (3) aquatic resources.

but large family sizes. It is quite likely that those with a G1SET value of 2 are GROUP1 units consisting almost exclusively of a single polygynous family. Cases to the left of the five-person line having large GROUP1 sizes would consist of multiple-family units with less bias in favor of females in the family labor force.

Two very different relationships between polygyny and family size are suggested by the shaded areas of the graph. The area on the left defines the zone in which polygyny is associated with small families. In these groups, as family size increases, polygyny tends to decrease. The shaded oval to the right identifies groups in which family size is large and

polygyny increases as group size increases, although GROUP1 units tend to be small. In the latter cases, the GROUP1 unit is largely isomorphic with one polygynous family and is biased in favor of female labor. These groups are expected to be heavily dependent upon terrestrial plants or relatively low-risk aquatic resources, such as shellfish. Two cases in this sample (the two dark triangles with small family size and POLYG = 30 or greater) are treated as suspect cases and were not used as part of the definition of the shaded areas.

The first type of polygynous family is exemplified by the Walbiri (group 109), for whom data on family size came from a census of households at Hooker Creek in 1953 (Meggitt

TABLE 8.08

MEAN HOUSEHOLD SIZE (PERSONS RESIDING IN A SINGLE STRUCTURE)
AND FAMILY SIZE FOR A SAMPLE OF ETHNOGRAPHICALLY
DOCUMENTED HUNTER-GATHERER CASES

CASES	PERSONS PER HOUSEHOLD	PERSONS PER FAMILY	HOUSEHOLD TYPE	REFERENCE(S)
		Tropical-subtropical Asia		
PUNAN				
SETTLED	6.59	3.47	(Fn)	Kedit 1982:261–71
MOBILE	2.91		(Fn)	Harrison 1949:139
SETTLED	5.76	3.75	(Fn)	Avadhani 1975:131
	5.91			Harrison 1949:139
BATEK (PALAWAN)	5.06	3.89	Fn	Eder 1987:105
BATEK (NEGROS)		4.00		Cadelina 1982:68
SHOMPEN	3.05	3.62	(N)	Rizvi 1990:16–18
ANDAMAN ISLANDS				
ONGE		3.15	(M)	Heine-Geldern and Hoehn-Gerlachstein 1958:25
ONGE		3.06	(M)	Sen 1962:72
ONGE: DRY SEASON	2.08			Cooper 1991:17, figures 3 and 4
ONGE: WET SEASON	(26.00)			Cooper 1991:17, figures 3 and 4
JARWA				
DRY SEASON	4.10			Temple 1903:62
OPEN CAMP	3.57			Temple 1903:61
DRY SEASON	3.50		M	Temple 1903:61
WET SEASON	(32.00)		M	Temple 1903:61
ANDAMAN ISLANDS	4.10	3.77	M	Radcliffe-Brown 1948:28–35
SEMANG				
DRY SEASON	3.01	3.20		Schebesta 1954:10, 17, 220
	2.81		N	Skeat and Blagden 1906:176
WET SEASON	(19.00)		N	Skeat and Blagden 1906:176
	(28.00)	3.33		Schebesta 1954:11, 222
SEMANG				
SEMAQ BERI (1980S)		3.81		Kuchikura 1988:277
VEDDAH	4.23	3.85	Fm	Bailey 1863:292; Seligmann and Seligman 1911:63; Spittel 1945:8
HILL PANDARAM	4.64	3.33	(N)	Morris 1982a:97–98, 174
AGTA (CASIGURAN)	4.33	3.57	(M)	Headland 1986:141, pers. comm. 1992
AGTA (ISABELA)	4.11			Rai 1982:228
AGTA (CAGAYAN)	5.96	4.81		Vanoverbergh 1925:196
CHENCHU	3.98	3.98	N	Fürer-Hamendorf 1943:366
MRABRI	6.05	4.00	(Fn)	Nimmanahaeminda and Hartland-Swam 1962:173; Pookajorn 1988:187; Velder 1963:186–88
PALIYANS 1962	3.31	4.08	(N)	Gardner 1972:420
BIRHOR (RANCHI)	2.60	4.88	(G)	Sen and Sen 1955:170, 174–75
BIRHOR	2.91	4.49	(G)	Williams 1974:79
KADAR				
1946–47 BASE CAMP	(9.10)	4.43	(Fn)	Ehrenfels 1952:65–67
DRY SEASON	2.89			Ehrenfels 1952:50
CHOLANAICKAN	3.59	3.59		Bhanu 1992:33
NAYAKA	3.60			Bird-David 1987:153
AINU				
HOKKAIDO 1822	4.55		Fn	Watanabe 1972:449
HOKKAIDO 1854	4.73		Fn	Watanabe 1972:449
HOKKAIDO 1873	4.52		Fn	Watanabe 1972:449
SAKHALIN 1822	–7.20–			Watanabe 1972:449
SAKHALIN 1854	–7.16–			Watanabe 1972:449

TABLE 8.08 *(continued)*

CASES	PERSONS PER HOUSEHOLD	PERSONS PER FAMILY	HOUSEHOLD TYPE	REFERENCE(S)
OROGENS	–6.31–			Qiu 1983 (photo estimate)
KET (1800S)	5.00		M	Shimkin 1939:155
GILYAK				
SUMMER	5.28	4.15		Shternberg 1933:288, 387
WINTER	(10.40)	4.15		Shternberg 1933:288, 387
YUKAGHIR				
SUMMER	–7.85–	4.08	Gn	Kreynovich 1979:191–92
WINTER	(24.00)			Kreynovich 1979:196
NGANASAN (1930S)	(9.40)			Chard 1963:112
SIBERIAN ESKIMO	(10.00)	4.72		Hayden et al. 1996:154

Tropical-subtropical South America

CASES	PERSONS PER HOUSEHOLD	PERSONS PER FAMILY	HOUSEHOLD TYPE	REFERENCE(S)
SHIRIANA	5.50			Métraux 1948:863
YARURO-PUME				
BASE CAMP, WET SEASON	(7.4)	3.92		Gragson 1989:127, 288–89
BASE CAMP, DRY SEASON	4.25			Gragson 1989:288–89
MOBILE, DRY SEASON	2.71			Gragson 1989:288–89
GUAHIBO: HIWI BASE CAMP	(10.28)		Fn	Hurtado and Hill 1986:18
GUAHIBO	6.94	5.84	Fn	Metzger 1968:268–71
NUKAK				
DRY SEASON	5.20	4.00		Politis 1992:3
COMMUNAL	(20.60)	3.97		Politis 1992:3
BORORO	(16.66)	4.9		Baldus 1937:115, 123–24; Lévi-
	9.8			Strauss 1936:269
GUATO	4.00			Schmidt 1942:47
SIRIONO	(16.88)	3.97	Er	Holmberg 1950:51, 82–83
YUQUI (SETTLED)	4.62	4.43		Stearman 1989:113–15
NAMBIKWARA				
DRY SEASON	5.15	3.60	N	Lévi-Strauss 1970:268–69, 288
WET SEASON	(15.00)			Lévi-Strauss 1970:288
	(15.80)			Oberg 1953:88
GUAYAKI (ACHE)	4.16	3.50	(N)	Jones 1983:176
BOTOCUDO	6.25			Métraux 1946b:534–36
WET SEASON	(19.00)			Ehrenreich 1887:22
HETA	4.75		(N)	Kozak et al. 1979:369
AWEIKOMO	(27.00)	6.80	P	Henry 1964:10–11, 159
TEHUELCHE	–9.80–	5.00	Fn	Boschin and Macuzzi 1979:33;
				Cooper 1946c:150
ALACALUF	–7.25–	4.8		Bird 1988:16–19
ONA	–8.20–		N	Chapman 1982:19; Gusinde 1931:205
YAHGAN	–7.0–	3.50	N	Gusinde 1937:32

Tropical-subtropical Africa

CASES	PERSONS PER HOUSEHOLD	PERSONS PER FAMILY	HOUSEHOLD TYPE	REFERENCE(S)
AKA	2.98		N	Hudson 1990:88
BAYAKA	2.82	3.88		Heymer 1980:193–97
BAMBOTE	3.16	4.87		Terashima 1980:233, 235
BAKA	3.40		(N)	Cavalli-Sforza 1986c:33
	3.47	4.39		Vallois and Marquer 1976:113, 123
EFE	3.26		(N)	Fisher 1987:104, 111
MBUTI				
NET HUNTERS	4.48		N	Harako 1976:46–47
MAWAMBO	4.63	4.28		Tanno 1976:108
HUKWE: DRY SEASON	2.86			Clark 1951:58, 65

(continued)

CASES	PERSONS PER HOUSEHOLD	PERSONS PER FAMILY	HOUSEHOLD TYPE	REFERENCE(S)
HADZA	3.63	4.50	N	O'Connell pers. comm. 1977; O'Connell et al. 1991:63, table 1
DOROBO	5.07	5.14		Huntingford 1955:631–34, 1942:183
SEKELE: DRY SEASON	2.50			Bleek 1929:109–12
!KUNG				
GENERAL	2.51	3.37	Fn	Howell 1979:43, 45
MOBILE, RAINY SEASON, CAMPS 1, 3, 5, 6, 9	4.46	5.58	Fn	Yellen 1977:237–53
MOBILE, DRY SEASON, CAMPS 2, 4, 7, 10–16	3.38	4.57	Fn	Yellen 1977:237–53
DOBE, DRY SEASON	2.53			Brooks et al. 1984:300–5; Gould and Yellen 1987:86, 93
DOBE, DRY SEASON	2.60			Lee 1979:254
NHARO	3.46			Guenther 1986:186
G/WI				
WET SEASON HUNTING CAMP	4.552.92		Gn	Hitchcock pers. comm. 1990
//GANA-G/WI	4.60		Gn	Weissner and Hitchcock pers. comm. 1991
KUA				
GENERAL	4.54			Hitchcock pers. comm. 1990
MOBILE, RAINY SEASON	4.28			
MOBILE, DRY SEASON	6.65			
!KO	3.99			Hitchcock pers. comm. 1990
BASE CAMP	3.53			Eibl-Eibesfeldt 1972:32–34

Australia: subtropical desert through temperate settings

CASES	PERSONS PER HOUSEHOLD	PERSONS PER FAMILY	HOUSEHOLD TYPE	REFERENCE(S)
GUNWINGGU	3.94	6.42		Altman 1987:100
WET SEASON	4.50			Altman 1987:100
APRIL-MAY	3.83			Altman 1987:106
MIRRNGADJA				
GENERAL	5.54	6.10		Peterson 1976:268, pers. comm. 1992; Peterson and Long 1986:135; Peterson pers. comm. 1994
RAINY SEASON	6.66			
DRY SEASON	5.00			
GIDJINGALI	5.94	6.90	(R)	Hiatt 1965:33–37
YIR-YORONT	3.69	4.20		Peterson and Long 1986:87–89
TIWI		7.40	Fp	Hart 1970:299; Hart and Pilling 1960:66; Peterson and Long 1986:135
KUKU-YALANJI	7.00			Anderson and Robins 1988:191–92
GROOTE EYELANDT	4.65	6.00		Peterson and Long 1986:80–83, 135
WALMBARIA	3.71	6.20		Hale and Tindale 1933:77
LARDIL	3.47	6.33		Memmott 1983:123
KAIADILT		6.68		Tindale 1962b:319–21
WALBIRI	3.86	4.51	R	Meggitt 1962:81
MARDUDJARA	4.12	5.20		Peterson and Long 1986:116–17
ILDAWONGGA		6.94		Peterson and Long 1986:112–15, 124
PINTUBI	4.33	5.80	(R)	Myers 1986:45; Peterson and Long 1986:104–11
PAPUNYA, SETTLED	4.42	6.68	(R)	Gargett and Hayden 1991:13–22; Hayden pers. comm. 1992
ALYAWARA	4.93	6.75	(R)	O'Connell 1987:77
	5.20			Denham 1975:142
NGATATJARA	3.55	6.18	(N)	Gould 1971:168, 1977:43
LARGE, SETTLED GROUPS				
WANAMPI WELL	4.46	6.29		Gould 1977:85

TABLE 8.08 *(continued)*

CASES	PERSONS PER HOUSEHOLD	PERSONS PER FAMILY	HOUSEHOLD TYPE	REFERENCE(S)
WARBURTON	4.50	9.00		Gould 1977:43
LEVERTON	4.62			Gould 1977:43
SUMMER ENCAMPMENTS				
MULYANGIRI	2.76	8.28		Gould 1977:43
PARTJAR (12/27/66)	3.50	4.66		Gould 1977:43
WINTER ENCAMPMENTS				
TIKA-TIKA (7/22/66)	3.33	5.00		Gould 1977:43
PARTJAR (7/22/66)	3.33	5.00		Gould 1977:43
PULYKARA (4/23/70)	3.00	5.00		Gould 1977:43
PITJANDJARA	5.75	6.96	(R)	Tindale 1972:243
JANKUNDJARA		6.26		Tindale pers. comm. 1966
NORTHERN ARENDA		6.40		Spencer and Gillen 1927:70–71
NAKAKO		8.0		Peterson and Long 1986:129–34
MINENG	3.50	6.66		Nind 1831:22
TJAPWURONG	5.00	5.61		Williams 1985:74–75
BNUNURONG	5.00			Gaughwin and Sullivan 1984:94
TASMANIANS				
EAST COAST	6.86			Plomley 1983:166
WEST COAST	8.50			Jones 1972:6

North America: California and Northern Mexico

CASES	PERSONS PER HOUSEHOLD	PERSONS PER FAMILY	HOUSEHOLD TYPE	REFERENCE(S)
SERI CA. 1938	–6.48–	5.53	Fm	Griffin 1959:vii, 50, 188
CAHUILLA	(9.30)			Strong 1929:45
CUPENO 1865	–6.45–		N	Strong 1929:189–214
KILIWA	–7.20–		N	Meigs 1939:1
WUKCHUMI	3.81		N	Gayton 1948a:57
TUBATULABAL	–7.00–	3.81	M	Voegelin 1938:43–44
NOMLAKI	3.88			Goldschmidt pers. comm. 1966
NORTH FOOTHILL YOKUTS	–6.43–			Cook 1955:54
PATWIN (1850S)	3.47		M	Barrett 1908:290–92
EASTERN POMO	(11.70)	4.33	Fn	Barrett 1908:186, 191
CLEAR LAKE POMO	(13.06)	4.75		Gifford 1926a:292–97
WINTU	6.00			Cook and Heizer 1965:71
1850S	4.00		M	Barrett 1908:289
CHUMASH	(9.50)		(E)	Cook and Heizer 1965:51
NISEMAN	3.61			Cook and Heizer 1965:71
SOUTHERN POMO	3.81			Barrett 1908:205, 214
SOUTHWEST DIALECT	2.91		Fm	Barrett 1908:235–36, 244
SINKYONE	4.40		Fn	Goddard 1923:97–101
COAST MIWOK	6.25			Collier and Thalman 1991:331–33
YUKI (PROPER)	5.62			Cook 1956:107
WAPPO				
HILL	3.75		Fm	Barrett 1908:268
VALLEY	(8.36)	4.50		Driver 1936:201
VALLEY (ESTIMATE OF TRADITIONAL HOUSEHOLDS)	(12.00)			Cook and Heizer 1965:71
NORTHERN POMO	3.76		Fp	Barrett 1908:131–32
MIWOK				
MOUNTAIN (ESTIMATE)	6.00			Cook and Heizer 1965:71
1850S	4.16			Barrett 1908:316
TEKELMA	8.34			Gray 1987:37–38
TOLOWA	–8.00–			Cook 1956:101
SHASTA	–8.00–			Cook and Heizer 1965:70

(continued)

TABLE 8.08 *(continued)*

CASES	PERSONS PER HOUSEHOLD	PERSONS PER FAMILY	HOUSEHOLD TYPE	REFERENCE(S)
HUPA	6.40		Fp	Kroeber 1925:131, 138
KAROK	–7.50–			Cook and Heizer 1965:70
WIYOT	(9.20)		Fp	Loud 1918:266, 339
MAIDU (MOUNTAIN)	6.00			Cook and Heizer 1965:71
YUROK	–7.46–		Fp	Kroeber 1925:16
MODOC (1934)	5.50		Fn	Ray 1963:159
TRADITIONAL	(13.08)			Ray 1963:149
KLAMATH (1890)	(9.90)		Fn	Spier 1930:54

North America: desert and desert scrub

CASES	PERSONS PER HOUSEHOLD	PERSONS PER FAMILY	HOUSEHOLD TYPE	REFERENCE(S)
DEATH VALLEY SHOSHONI	3.94		N	Steward 1938:87–88, 94[1]
KARANKAWA	–7.50–	3.70		Bolton 1916:199; Schaedel 1949:124
PANAMINT VALLEY SHOSHONI	4.01			Steward 1938:84, 87–88
YAVAPAI	3.30			Corbusier 1886:283; Gifford 1932a:180–81
WALAPAI	5.61	3.53		Hayden 1936:70, 165–68
KAWAIISU	4.27			Steward 1938:79
OWENS VALLEY PAIUTE	4.90	305		Steward 1933:290, 1977:127
SOUTHERN PAIUTE				
KAIBAB (1860S)	5.66			Kelly 1964:13
	7.60		N	Euler 1972:100
RESERVATION (1973)	5.40			Knack 1975:115
MONO LAKE PAIUTE	3.82			Davis 1965:36 (LRB estimate)
DEEP SPRINGS PAIUTE	4.60		N	Steward 1938:58
PYRAMID LAKE PAIUTE	4.40			Fowler 1966:61–62
SOUTHERN UTE	5.00			Smith 1974:123
CATTAIL EATER PAIUTE	4.40			Fowler 1992:36–38
FISH LAKE VALLEY PAIUTE	4.38	3.67		Steward 1938:62–64
HUKUNDUKA SHOSHONI	4.33			Steward 1938:178
SPRING VALLEY SHOSHONI	4.53			Steward 1938:124
WHITE KNIFE SHOSHONI (1827)	4.12	5.00		Ewers 1955:26
BATTLE MOUNTAIN	5.70		N	Steward 1938:163
RAILROAD VALLEY SHOSHONI	4.19		N	Steward 1938:118
NORTH FORK MONO PAIUTE	4.27	4.93	(N)	Cook 1955:37; Gayton 1948:145
POST-1850	5.15		(N)	Gifford 1932b:57–61
GROUSE CREEK SHOSHONI	4.17	4.38		Steward 1938:174–75
ANTELOPE VALLEY SHOSHONI	4.27	4.37		Steward 1938:126, 129
WASHO 1895	4.00		(N)	Price 1962:8–10
UINTAH UTE	7.77	3.06		Smith 1974:123; Steward 1974b:117
WADADOKADO PAIUTE	4.19	5.28	N	Whiting 1950:19–20
AGAIDUKA-LEMHI	9.00			Murphy and Murphy 1960:325
LITTLE SMOKEY SHOSHONI	6.85		N	Steward 1938:114
UNCOMPAHGRE UTE	5.96			Steward 1974b:140, 147

Mounted hunters from steppic regions of North and South America

CASES	PERSONS PER HOUSEHOLD	PERSONS PER FAMILY	HOUSEHOLD TYPE	REFERENCE(S)
COMANCHE	6.28			Wallace and Hoebel 1952:27
KIOWA APACHE	7.81		Er	Ewers 1955:25
CHEYENNE				
1806	7.93			Bushnell 1922:24
1880	5.60	7.72	Sp	Moore 1991:179, 298, 320
ARAPAHO (1860)	7.36			Gussow et al. 1974:23
CROW (1833)	(8.80)		R	Ewers 1955:25
TETON				
1849	7.50			Bushnell 1922:50
1850	(10.00)			Culbertson 1952:135

TABLE 8.08 *(continued)*

CASES	PERSONS PER HOUSEHOLD	PERSONS PER FAMILY	HOUSEHOLD TYPE	REFERENCE(S)
BANNOCK 1834	6.00			Murphy and Murphy 1960:325
GROS-VENTRE				
1850	8.24			Culbertson 1952:137
1860	7.92		R	Ewers 1955:25
PEIGAN	8.04			Ewers 1955:21
BLACKFOOT				
1921	4.91		Er	Robbins 1971:42
1860	8.00		Er	Ewers 1955:21
	8.00			Ewers 1971:94
ASSINIBOINE				
1800	7.95		R	Lowrie and Clarke 1832: 716
1854	4.50		R	Denig 1930:431
PLAINS CREE (SPRING)	4.28			Bushnell 1922:20
BLOOD (1860)	8.00			Ewers 1955:21
SARSI (1800S)	7.55		R	Jenness 1938:2

North Pacific coastal areas of North America and Asia				
ALSEA	(12.00)			Drucker 1939:85
PUYALLUP	(30.00)	5.0		Smith 1940a:6–7
TWANA		3.61		Eells 1884:37
CHEHALIS 1824	(26.00)			Schalk 1978:187; Taylor 1974b:431
NOOTKA	(40.00)	4.44	Fn	Drucker 1951:71, 280–81
CHINOOK	(20.00)			Ray 1938:124–27
WINTER	(15.80)			Silverstein 1990:538
SUMMER	7.00			Silverstein 1990:538
LILLOOET	(9.50)			Teit 1906:199
LUMMI	(16.00)			Stern 1934:7
QUINAULT	(18.44)	4.61	Fn	Olson 1936:22, 96
STALO		4.75		Duff 1952:130
QUILEUTE	(24.00)			Pettitt 1950:5
CLALLAM	(14.97)			Eells 1884:35
MAKAH	(14.56)	3.13	Fn	Gunther 1962:544; Swan 1870:5–6
1942	4.23			Gunther 1962:544
KWAKIUTL (COMMUNAL)	(26.40)		Fn	Kane 1859:appendix
TSIMSHIM (COMMUNAL)	(9.63)		Ep	Kane 1859:appendix
HAIDA (COMMUNAL)	(15.50)		En	Kane 1859:appendix
TLINGIT (COMMUNAL)	(19.00)		Fn	Kane 1859:appendix
GITKSAN	(8.53)			Kane 1859:appendix
1920	(16.00)			Adams 1973:28
KONAIG	(17.00)			Knecht and Jordan 1985:21
EYAK (1884)	(16.40)	5.2		Birket-Smith and de Laguna 1938:19–20, 123
KUSKOWAGMUT				
1890	(13.65)			Porter 1893:Table 6
1843	(19.90)			Michael 1967:306
	(18.00)			Oswalt and Van Stone 1967:4
CHUGASH (1843)	(11.79)			Michael 1967:306
ALEUT				
1790	(17.55)		Ep	Lantis 1970:173
UNALASKA	–7.32–			Lantis 1970:173
AKUN	–5.71–			Lantis 1970:173
BORKA	–7.33–			Lantis 1970:173
UNALGA	–7.67–			Lantis 1970:173
AVATANAK	–9.80–			Lantis 1970:173

(continued)

TABLE 8.08 *(continued)*

CASES	PERSONS PER HOUSEHOLD	PERSONS PER FAMILY	HOUSEHOLD TYPE	REFERENCE(S)
AKUTAN	–6.50–			Lantis 1970:173
ALASKA MAIN	–8.45–			Lantis 1970:173
UNGA	–8.92–			Lantis 1970:173
NUNIVAK	(10.70)			
SUMMER	(11.30)			Lantis 1946:164
TRADITIONAL	(10.10)			Lantis 1946:164
1940S SPRING CAMP	–7.20–			Lantis 1946:164
1940S LARGE VILLAGE	5.13	4.17		Lantis 1946:164, 317

Subarctic and continental midlatitude forests of North America and Asia

CASES	PERSONS PER HOUSEHOLD	PERSONS PER FAMILY	HOUSEHOLD TYPE	REFERENCE(S)
WISHRAM	(10.50)			Spier and Sapir 1930:164–67, 221
COEUR D'ALENE	–7.16–	3.58		Teit 1930:331
SINKAIETK	(20.90)	3.66		Cline et al. 1938:87
SANPOIL	(11.10)			Ray 1932:16
THOMPSON	(22.50)			Hayden et al. 1996:154, table 1
KALISPEL	–7.24–	3.62		Teit 1930:331
CHIPPEWA				
1784	–7.00–		Fn	Tyrrell 1908:276
KATIKITEGON 1939	5.43		Fn	Kinietz 1947:246–47
KITCHEBUAN 1763	–7.00–	3.5		Quimby 1962:219
MICMAC	–7.20–	5.45		Speck 1922:143; Wallis and Wallis 1953:104
FLATHEAD (1805)	(12.12)		R	Ewers 1955:25
RAINY RIVER OJIBWA	–8.20–	4.20		Hickerson 1967:57
NORTH SAULTEAUX (1965)	–6.82–		Fn	Bishop 1969:52 (mean)
"WELFARE HOUSE"	–6.82–		Fn	Bishop 1969:52
"NATIVE HOUSE"	4.40		Fn	Bishop 1969:52
PEKANGEKUM OJIBWA	–8.20–		Gp	Dunning 1959:63–64
ROUND LAKE OJIBWA	5.10	N		Rogers 1963:75–77
1952	4.63	5.59	En	Rogers 1962a:B8, 67
ALCATCHO	(18.00)			Jenness 1943:486 (Smith field notes on file, National Museum of Canada)
MISTASSINI CREE				
1823		4.55	Fn	Morantz 1982:89
1828	5.30			Lips 1947a:397–98, 453–54
1910	6.03	3.11	Fn	Rogers 1962:23
1953–54 (AUTUMN)	3.25		Fn	Speck 1923:454 Rogers 1973:3–4
WASWANIPI (CREE) 1823		5.65	Fn	Morantz 1983:89
MONTAGNAIS (WINTER 1633)	(15.00)	6.6		Lane 1952:12–13
BEAVER 1807		3.874.12	N	Keith 1960:68; Nicks 1980:34–43
SLAVE				
1951–54	6.22		R	Helm 1961:48
WILLOW LAKE 1974	5.00			Janes 1983:102
1789	4.50		R	MacKenzie 1966:56
	5.83		R	MacKenzie 1966:57
KASKA (1945)		3.43	Ee	Honigmann 1949:37
CARRIER (1870)	(13.00)		Fo	Jenness 1943:486–87
MOUNTAIN	–5.87–	4.72		Gillespie 1981
HAN	–9.00–	4.50		Adney 1900:500
HARE				
1967	5.06			Savishinsky 1974:60, 230
1789 SUMMER CAMP	4.99			MacKenzie 1966:58–59
	4.50			MacKenzie 1966:59
ATTAWAPISKAT CREE	6.00		Np	Honigmann 1956:35
1947		4.18	Np	Honigmann 1949:20
KOYUKON	(15.27)			

TABLE 8.08 *(continued)*

CASES	PERSONS PER HOUSEHOLD	PERSONS PER FAMILY	HOUSEHOLD TYPE	REFERENCE(S)
1843	(14.45)			Michael 1967:306
TENTS	(4.0)			Sullivan 1942:10
WINTER	(11.20)			Sullivan 1942:10
	(11.56)			Clark 1974:124
CHIPPEWYAN				
1800S	–9.00–			Smith 1981:276
1838		4.52	N	Brumbach and Jarvenpa 1989:54
1881		3.71	N	Brumbach and Jarvenpa 1989:64
1920–46	5.23	4.34	N	Brumbach and Jarvenpa 1989:250–58
1930S FALL CAMP	4.25			Irimoto 1981:73
1930S EARLY WINTER	4.17			Irimoto 1981:73
1930S LATE WINTER	3.79			Irimoto 1981:73
1972–73 BASE CAMP	6.81			Muller-Wille 1974:7
1975 UPER AL NU-1	5.57			Irimoto 1981:59
1975 LOWER AL NU-1	4.75	6.57		Irimoto 1981:60
1975 BE NUE-2	5.00			Irimoto 1981:61
1975 NU-2	4.66			Irimoto 1981:61
KUTCHIN	–7.80–			McKennan 1965b:20, 43
INGALIK				
1890	–6.08–		N	Porter 1893:164
1843 PROPER	(11.00)		N	Michael 1967:306
1843 YUKON	(17.90)		N	Michael 1967:306
1843 CROW VILLAGE	(18.00)		N	Oswalt and VanStone 1967:4
NABESNA				
1929	–8.00–	4.00	M	McKennan 1965a:106; Pitts 1972:118
1938 SCOTTY CREEK		4.50	M	Pitts 1972:229
1938 NABESNA		4.38	M	Pitts 1972:229–31
1938 TETLIN		5.78	M	Pitts 1972:232–34
1938 TANACROSS		3.66	M	Pitts 1972:235–38
1938 HEALY LAKE		3.93	M	Pitts 1972:239–40
RUPERT HOUSE CREE (1823)	–5.13–		Fn	Morantz 1983:89
DOGRIB (1789 SUMMER CAMP)	–5.76–		N	MacKenzie 1966:49–56
TANAINA (1843)	(17.92)		Fp	Michael 1967:306
TUTCHONE		3.33		O'Leary 1985:88
HOLIKACHUK	(15.00)			Michael 1967:307
1890		4.07		Snow 1981:615
NASKAPI				
1937–38	–8.30–	4.81		Tanner 1944:593, 627–28
1966–68	5.10		Fn	Henriksen 1973:58

Arctic

CASES	PERSONS PER HOUSEHOLD	PERSONS PER FAMILY	HOUSEHOLD TYPE	REFERENCE(S)
KOBUK INUIT	7.25			
1890	6.00	4.50		Burch 1975:257–58
1910–40 SHUNGNAK	4.73		(Gn)	Foote 1966:43
1950–65 SHUNGNAK	5.42		(Gn)	Foote 1966:43
1950–65 KOBUK	5.80		(Gn)	Foote 1966:43
1959–65 AMBLER	6.30		(Gn)	Foote 1966:43
KOTZEBUE SOUND INUIT (1900)	9.80	4.90		Burch 1975:269–72
LABRADOR INUIT				
WINTER	(22.80)		Fn	Taylor 1974:71
SPRING	7.36		Fn	Taylor 1974:71
EARLY SUMMER	7.14		Fn	Taylor 1974:71
LATE SUMMER	7.50		Fn	Taylor 1974:71

(continued)

TABLE 8.08 (*continued*)

CASES	PERSONS PER HOUSEHOLD	PERSONS PER FAMILY	HOUSEHOLD TYPE	REFERENCE(S)
1882		5.70		Turner 1894:176
1964 SUGLUK	7.49		Fn	Graburn 1969:148, 169
GREAT WHALE INUIT				
1958	5.76			Willmot 1960:53
1970	5.82	4.72		Barger 1981:675
CARIBOU INUIT				
1893 SUMMER TENTS	7.10		Gp	Hayden et al. 1996:154, table 1;
WINTER IGLOO	4.30			Tyrrell 1897:167
MAY 1922 GENERAL		3.54	Gp	Rasmussen 1930:11–13
AAERNERMUIT		3.60	Gp	Birket-Smith 1929:67–68
HAUNE TORMIUT		4.50	Gp	Birket-Smith 1929:67–68
PADLIMIUT COAST		4.86	Gp	Birket-Smith 1929:67–68
HARVA TORMIUT		4.47	Gp	Birket-Smith 1929:67–68
1947 SUMMER TENTS		2.71		Harper 1964:10
1960 BAKER LAKE	4.19		(Gm)	Vallee 1967:17
1960 SUMMER TENTS	4.35		(Gm)	Vallee 1967:60–63
NOATAK INUIT 1885	7.5	3.00		Burch 1975:255
NUNAMIUT INUIT				
1880	7.50			Binford 1971 (field notes)
1947–48		4.69		Binford 1991a:90
1947–48 SUMMER	3.81		Gn	Binford 1991a:89
1947–48 WINTER	5.75		Gn	Binford 1991a:89
MACKENZIE INUIT-LAND	(20.00)			Hayden et al. 1996:154, table 1
IGLOO	5			
SIVOKAMIUT INUIT	6.75			Hughes 1960:14–48
POINT HOPE INUIT (1909)	8.15	3.39	(Fn)	Burch 1975:260–69
COPPER INUIT				
WINTER IGLOO	5.00			Hayden et al. 1996: 154, table 1
WINTER CAMP	6.06			Jenness 1932:30
SUMMER TENTS	3.60			Jenness 1932:66, 71
SUMMER	3.48	3.42		Rasmussen 1932:78–85
UTKUHIKHALINGMIUT		3.33		Amundsen 1908:281
1963		4.37		Briggs 1970:15
AUGUST 1963 TENTS	3.66		(G)	Briggs 1970:30, 170–71
	5.50		(G)	Briggs 1970:24, 370–71
WINTER 1963 SNOW	8.33		(Fm)	Briggs 1970:372
AIVILINGMIUT				
JULY 1846	6.50			Rae 1850:40
AUGUST 1846 TENTS	5.50			Rae 1850:49
AUGUST 1921		3.03		Mathiassen 1928:15–16
1921 SOUTHAMPTON ISLAND		3.03		Mathiassen 1928:16
1959 SOUTHAMPTON ISLAND	7.07			VanStone 1960:82
CORAL HARBOUR		6.00		VanStone 1960:82
SNAFU	(12.66)			VanStone 1960:82
INGULIK INUIT				
JULY 1822	7.05		Fn	Lyon 1924:230
1921	7.50	3.05		Mathiassen 1928:17, 19, 32
1960S WINTER	8.14			Damas, letter 7/6/92
WEST GREENLAND				
1870 WINTER	9.73	5.10		Rink 1877:166, 182, 191
1896 SUMMER	8.75	4.57		Perry 1898:131, 171–72
1897 WINTER	6.25			Perry 1898:336, 386
TENTS	7.5		(Fn)	Birket-Smith 1928:78
BAFFIN ISLAND INUIT				
1615 SUMMER TENTS	7.00			Christy 1894:208
		4.11	Gr	Low 1906:57–58

TABLE 8.08 *(continued)*

CASES	PERSONS PER HOUSEHOLD	PERSONS PER FAMILY	HOUSEHOLD TYPE	REFERENCE(S)
		3.41	Gr	Boas 1964:18 (1888)
1909	4.38	3.96		Hantzsch 1977:39, 99
NETSILIK INUIT				
1830 SNOW HOUSES	5.50		(Fn)	Savelle 1987:229
AUGUST 1831 TENTS	5.75		(Fn)	Ross 1835:589; Savelle 1987a:429–31
AUGUST 1846 TENTS	5.50			Rae 1850:49
AUGUST 1858 TENTS	3.57		(Fn)	M'Clintock 1860:141–43
WINTER 1859	3.18		(Fn)	M'Clintock 1860:235
1898		3.74		Boas 1907:377–78
WINTER 1956		3.93	(Fn)	Van der Steenhoven 1959:2
ANGMAKASLIK				
1890s	(22.00)		En	Birket-Smith 1928:79
	(25.80)			Hayden et al. 1996: 154, table 1
SUMMER	9.50			Mirsky 1937:53
TAREUMIUT INUIT				
1850s NUVUK	5.72			Simpson 1875:237
1880s POINT BELCHER	6.20			Ray 1885:41
POLAR INUIT		3.74	N	Ekblaw 1928:41
1890s	5.80	4.83	N	Steensby 1910:324

Miscellaneous data on household and family size

CASES	PERSONS PER HOUSEHOLD	PERSONS PER FAMILY	HOUSEHOLD TYPE	REFERENCE(S)
ALLABAD (IRAN)		6.70		Kramer 1982:72–73
HASANABAD (IRAN)		4.59		Watson 1979:47
KEBKEBIYA		3.74		Tobert 1985:280–82
FULANI	0.84			David 1971:125
HERERO	2.50	4.30		Harpending and Pennington 1990:419
NAVAJO (1910)		4.90		Kelly 1986:45
DASSANETCH	4.22			Gifford 1977:94
JIVARO	(9.00)		Er	Harner 1973:78
YORA	6.16			Hill and Kaplan 1989:323
CONTEMPORARY USA		3.60		Glick 1959:596

Notes: Parentheses around values in column 2 (number of persons per household) indicate the presence of a communal structure; dashes in column 2 indicate a joint household made up of two nuclear families. The symbols used in column 4 are taken from Murdock (1967:155) and refer to the following properties of family units:

E   A large extended family, that is, a cooperating aggregation of smaller family units occupying a single dwelling or a number of adjacent dwellings and normally including the families of procreation of at least two siblings or cousins in each of at least two adjacent generations.

F   A small extended family, normally including the family of procreation of only one individual in the senior generation but at least two individuals in the following generation. This type of family usually dissolves upon the death of the head of the family.

G   A minimally extended or *stem* family, consisting of only two related families of procreation (excluding polygamous unions), particularly of adjacent generations.

M   An independent monogamous nuclear family.

N   An independent nuclear family with occasional or limited polygyny.

O   An independent polyandrous family.

P   An independent polygynous family in which polygyny is general and not reported to be preferentially sororal. In family units of this type, co-wives are not reported to occupy separate quarters.

Q   The same as type P, except the co-wives typically occupy separate quarters.

R   Independent polygynous families, in which polygyny is common and preferentially sororal. In families of this type, co-wives are not reported to occupy separate quarters.

S   The same as type R, except that co-wives typically occupy separate quarters.

Lowercase letters following capital letters refer to the same phenomena as the capital letters and they operate as modifiers of the extended family cases. Symbols with no parentheses reflect Murdock's (1967:155) original classification of family types; symbols in parentheses were classified by the senior author using Murdock's terms.

1. The values for "households" are proportionally reduced for the cases documented by Steward, since he apparently counted the size of an economic unit as a household rather than the literal occupants of a house. Throughout the early literature there are clear indications of "house clusters," which were apparently what Steward considered the "household."

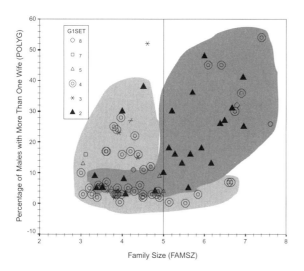

FIGURE 8.17

GROUP1 size classes in a property space defined by the percentage of males participating in polygynous marriages relative to family size. The marker indicates an ordination and classification of GROUP1 sizes: (2) small, (3) medium, (4) large, (5) oversized, (7) exceptional cases, and (8) very large.

1962:81). The estimates of Walbiri polygynous households, however, were generalized from data collected by Long (1970) from a number of sources that may or may not have been reliable. Data on the second type of polygynous family, the Kaiadilt (group 103), are based on reconstructed family histories (Tindale 1962b) that document the polygynous households of adults belonging to the generation of the interviewees. Since children were rarely mentioned in these family histories, estimates of family size are likely to be misleading.

Experimentation with the cases exhibiting an increase in both family size and polygyny revealed that they did not appear to vary much in the slope of the line but differed primarily in the value of the intercept. In other words, the intercept represents the average size of the family that existed at the point at which polygynous marriages begin to appear in a hypothetical group of monogamous families. Looking at the relationships in this way, I found that the best estimate of the slope of the lines that may vary with the means of family size when polygyny has a value of zero—but did not vary in slope—was a value of $b = 0.79085$. The straight-line equation of the relationship between family size (FAMSZ) and the percentage of males in polygynous marriages is, therefore,

(8.01)

FAMSZ = a + 0.79085(POLYG)

In the sample of hunter-gatherers for which equation 8.01 was developed, values of the intercept a may range between 3.00 and 6.00, with multimodal peaks at 3.00, 3.83,

4.36, and 5.30. These differences in family size are likely to reflect the differential age structure of a population varying with the group's rate of natural increase, as well as small-group effects of reproductive performance.[20] All these observations justify the following generalization:

Generalization 8.23

In general, family size increases as the percentage of married males with multiple wives increases.

In table 8.09, I explore the effect of polygyny on GROUP1 size when the number of married males in a group is held constant. Only the percentage of males practicing polygyny and the age and reproductive state of the group, as indicated by differences in the value of a, vary in this tabulation. When both the number of married males in a group and the reproductive state of the group are held constant, polygyny alone can account for differences in GROUP1 size of between 9.77 and 19.85 persons. If the reproductive state of the system is allowed to vary, the difference in GROUP1 size can range between 9.77 and 23.75 persons. If a is allowed to go even higher, GROUP1 sizes may be even larger.

With reference again to figure 8.17, the shaded area to the left of the graph displays a set of relationships that differ significantly from those summarized in generalization 8.23. In this sector of the plot, high percentages of polygynous marriages occur in groups with relatively small family sizes, and large family sizes are associated with lower percentages of polygynous marriage in all but one case—the Alyawara (group 117).[21]

The data in table 8.09 and figure 8.17 raise a number of questions. For instance, why should a reversal of relationship occur between polygyny and family size, coinciding more or less with the larger (normal division of labor) as opposed to the smaller (collapsed division of labor) group size variants

TABLE 8.09

EFFECT OF POLYGYNY ON GROUP1 SIZE

NUMBER OF MALES IN GROUP	PERCENTAGE OF POLYGYNY	EXPECTED GROUP1 SIZES	
		$A = 3.83$	$A = 5.36$
2.55	00.00%	9.77	13.67
2.55	10.00%	11.78	15.68
2.55	20.00%	13.80	17.70
2.55	30.00%	15.82	19.71
2.55	40.00%	17.83	21.73
2.55	50.00%	19.85	23.75

Note: Expected GROUP1 size is calculated as follows: 2.55 * (a + [0.79085 * POLYG]).

of the Group Size Model? Responding to these issues sequentially, I note that

---
Generalization 8.24

When polygyny occurs frequently among groups in warm climates that primarily exploit terrestrial plants or aquatic resources, these are also usually the settings in which a species-focused division of labor ensures a much-reduced role for males in food provisioning on a daily basis.

If polygyny is a way of recruiting productive females to participate in a relatively stable, family-based labor unit, then, of necessity, family size should be positively correlated with the frequency of polygyny. Such a pattern was, in fact, demonstrated in the distribution on the right side of the graph in figure 8.17. It might also be expected that, since polygyny provides an organized, female-biased labor force, there would be differences in the age at marriage of males and females, in the role of betrothal in marriage arrangements, and perhaps in preferences for mates when viewed from a kinship perspective.

These suppositions are based on the recognition that the incorporation of females into organized labor units through marriage sets up the very real possibility that males will be organized into cooperative labor units differently, since polygyny's mirror image—polyandry, or the organization of males into co-spousal labor units through marriage—is neither common nor very important among known hunter-gatherer peoples.[22] It is well documented that, in groups practicing polyandry, kin biases in marriage partners (at least among cooperating males) appear to result in several different kinds of linkages as the basis for the formation of male labor parties. These relationships can be nepotistic (father-son or brother-brother) or affinal (brother-in-law pairing [Binford 1990]) linkages, or they may be based on bonds formed during events, such as male initiation ceremonies.

In figure 8.18, I explore the relationships between the percentage of males in polygynous marriages and differences in the mean age at first marriage of males and females. In this figure, the cases are coded in terms of the GROUP1 size sets first identified in figure 8.08. Most of the cases fall into the small (subset 2) and large (subset 4) GROUP1 size variants relative to environmental setting. The similarity is apparent between this patterning and the inverse relationship of subset 4 to family size in figure 8.17, in which subset 2 varied in a strongly positive way with family size. In figure 8.18, however, subset 4 is primarily characterized by a strongly negative relationship between the percentage of polygynous marriages in a group and differences in the ages of males and females at first marriage. As the latter increases, the percentage of polygyny in the group decreases, although just the reverse pattern applies to the cluster of cases in which levels of polygyny are near to or greater than 30 percent.

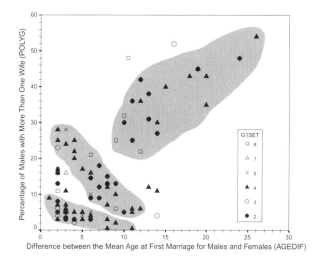

FIGURE 8.18

A property space map defined by the percentage of males participating in polygynous marriages relative to differences between the mean age at first marriage of males and females. The marker indicates an ordination and classification of GROUP1 sizes: (2) small, (3) medium, (4) large, (5) oversized, (7) exceptional cases, and (8) very large.

I have already noted that, when a marked reduction in mobility occurs, there is a corresponding increase in GROUP1 size (generalization 8.13). What meaning should be assigned to this patterning? Perhaps the first point to be emphasized is that the age differences plotted in figure 8.18 represent an average for each gender and do not refer to the actual age difference between two spouses at the first marriage of either males or females. It is not uncommon, for example, for the first wife of a relatively young Australian aboriginal male to be a widow who is considerably older than her new husband. The older widow, however, may have been very young at the time of her first marriage. The AGEDIF variable does not include information of this kind.

I think the pattern in figure 8.18 is provocative and suggests the presence of a threshold at a polygyny level of approximately 25 percent that marks a dramatic shift to a positive relationship between mean age differences and polygyny. To clarify this possibility, I have prepared the two graphs in figure 8.19, contrasting the distribution of the mean age at first marriage for males (graph A) and females (graph B). Both of these variables are plotted relative to the percentage of males whose marriages are polygynous. In both graphs, the marker codes a group's primary source of food.

The overall patterns in the graphs are very different. Among males, the higher the percentage of polygyny in a group, the greater the age at first marriage. As the percentage of polygyny decreases, however, the greater the variation is in the age of males at the time of their first marriage. One

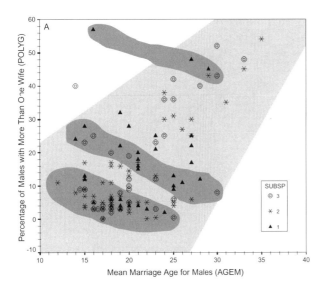
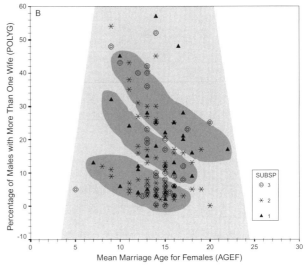

FIGURE 8.19

A paired-graph comparison between the mean age at marriage of males (A) and females (B). Both variables are expressed relative to the percentage of males participating in polygynous marriages. The marker indicates the primary source of food (SUBSP): (1) terrestrial animals, (2) terrestrial plants, and (3) aquatic resources. Light shading shows the gross overall trend.

could also argue that there is a tendency for the age at first marriage to increase as polygyny decreases within what appear to be recognizable subsets based on subsistence, such as the groups depending primarily upon hunting and aquatic resources in the central shaded area of graph A.

In contrast, the overall pattern among females is for age at first marriage to increase as polygyny decreases. In groups with high levels of polygyny, females tend to be younger at the time of their first marriage. It is therefore not surprising that in figure 8.18 the variable AGEDIF embodies the properties demonstrated in both graphs in figure 8.19.

Generalization 8.25

Other things being equal, higher levels of polygyny are associated with an earlier age at marriage for females, whereas males tend to be older at the time of their first marriage. Other things clearly are *not* equal, however, since the positive relationship among males occurs unambiguously only among cases in which polygyny is greater than 20 percent and the age at first marriage is at twenty-five years or older.

In an attempt to isolate what some of the other factors affecting these relationships might be, I did a case-by-case comparison and discovered that males were the primary food producers in all of the cases with large GROUP1 sizes and an age difference between males and females of greater than 2.5 years. In these groups, either male labor accounted for more than 60 percent of the food consumed or the

groups were sedentary and had pre-existing large-GROUP1 units. In the remainder of the cases, males contributed relatively little to the diet, and much of the total dietary intake resulted from a collapse of the division of labor, from the standpoint of the exploited species.

The age differences between males and females that have been documented in this study therefore arise from at least two very different situations. GROUP1 size also has multiple conditioners, one of which is polygyny in association with both moderate and large GROUP1 units. I have already observed that similar things can be organized differently and different things can be organized similarly; the validity of this observation is easy to demonstrate using this example of patterning:

Generalization 8.26

Other factors besides polygyny favor late marriage for males and an associated increase in the age spread between males and females at first marriage. The data indicate that this pattern is characterized by a high contribution of male labor to subsistence and that this labor is highly skilled and requires considerable learning and practice time. Polygyny is generally low in this context.

My observations thus far suggest that, for some groups under certain conditions, hunter-gatherer marriage conventions function in part as labor recruitment strategies. I have also noted that polygyny is one strategy to recruit female food

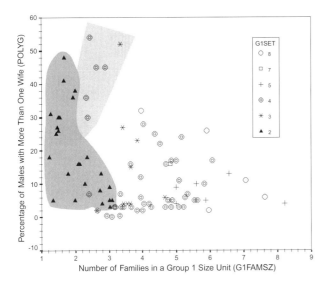

FIGURE 8.20

GROUP1 size sets shown in a property space defined by the percentage of males participating in polygynous marriages and the number of families in GROUP1 size units. The pattern demonstrates a strong relationship between polygyny and very few families per GROUP1 unit. The marker indicates an ordination and classification of GROUP1 sizes: (2) small, (3) medium, (4) large, (5) oversized, (7) exceptional cases, and (8) very large.

producers. Males, however, appear not to be recruited in a similar fashion, since—even though a large number of groups organize food procurement in terms of male-male bonding—polyandry is, in fact, quite rare among hunter-gatherers. The only region in which polyandry has been reported in any significant numbers is the Great Basin of North America (Steward 1938: 285), where it occurred with lower frequencies than sororal polygyny.

I have not yet exhausted the learning possibilities associated with the relationships between polygyny, GROUP1 size, and family size. If, for instance, polygynous families can be expected to be on average larger than nonpolygynous families, it is reasonable to conclude that in any given group made up of polygynous families there would be fewer families and, other things being equal, fewer males in each group.

Such a possibility is explored in figure 8.20, in which the shaded areas identify the cases with small GROUP1 sizes. All groups in this shaded cluster are made up of three or fewer families and at least 5 percent of the marriages are polygynous. In the zone in which polygyny ranges from low to high and the GROUP1 unit is classified as large, the number of families per unit is still three or fewer. In contrast, groups with large GROUP1 sizes (in which cases are classified as G1SET = 3, 4, 5, and 8) tend to have many more families,

although, in those instances when they do not, the level of polygyny is higher.

Generalization 8.27

When polygyny is prevalent, GROUP1 units should be made up of a small number of families. The number should decrease when the percentage of polygyny increases relative to the absolute size of the group. Other things being equal, this has the effect of increasing the size of the female labor force in a family context and, at the same time, minimizing the male presence when unmarried yet mature males live in independent camps (which occurs very frequently).

By means of several tables and figures, I have explored polygyny and the ways in which it conditions GROUP1 size. These displays of patterned data have provided a glimpse of organizational domains in which labor recruitment is biased in favor of females rather than males. I have also discussed some exceptions to my generalizations about labor organization and the practice of polygyny, and I have noted that there are ethnographic cases in which males obtain most, if not all, of the food and still practice polygyny. Other examples include the mounted hunters of the Great Plains, who are so frequently exceptions to my generalizations, and the Labrador Eskimo, who reorganized their labor force in the eighteenth century after European fur trading stations were established near their settlements. In order to explore the organizational basis of these exceptional cases, I must first focus upon male bias in the subsistence labor force.

Male Bias in Contributions to Diet and Labor
Previous researchers have recognized that groups which exploit different types of foods also organize the acquisition of resources differently in terms of the sexual division of labor. For example,

Generalization 8.28

As the proportion of a group's total dietary intake from large sea mammals increases, the proportion of the total diet that is obtained by males increases (Hiatt 1970:7).

Generalization 8.29

As a group's dependence upon terrestrial animals increases, the proportion of the total diet obtained by males increases (Murdock and Provost 1973:208).

These generalizations have prompted me to investigate how changes in the proportions of male and female labor would modify a group's dependency ratio and its important effects on group size. As an initial illustration, the best information on the male dependency ratio in situations in which males obtain most of the food consumed by an entire group comes from my data on the Nunamiut (male division of labor estimate = 97.17). These data were collected prior to the time when the Nunamiut had regular access to modern medical support and include a mean male dependency ratio of 4.044.[23] I use this value as the standard for modeling the effects of shifts in the division of labor.

If I wish to illustrate the effect on group size of a shift in tactics to predominantly male food procurement, I need values for only three variables: the male contribution to the labor force, the mean male dependency ratio at 100 percent production, and the number of producers in the group. Such a calculation also requires one constant that, in this case, represents the increase in the male dependency ratio for each increase in the percentage of the male contribution to the labor force. For the previously defined standard value of 4.044, the slope of the line is $b = 0.0458$, or an increase in the male dependency ratio of 0.0458 for each increase in the percentage of male labor. The equation for obtaining an estimate of GROUP1 size is therefore

$$\text{(8.02)}$$

$$\text{GROUP1 size} = (\text{MDIVLAB} - 50.0) * 0.0458 *$$
$$(\text{number of producers})$$

I have used this equation to obtain the GROUP1 values in table 8.10, which range from 8.92 for a group in which the male contribution to the labor force is 50.0 percent of the total group effort to a value of 20.55 for a group in which the percentage of the male division of labor reaches 99.99 percent. The number of producers has remained the same in all cases, however. Differences in group size are attributable to the number of adult female dependents relative to the number of male producers. In this example, the number of producers corre-

sponds to the numbers associated with groups of plant-dependent peoples who have a collapsed division of labor. Based on the data in table 8.10, the following conclusions can be drawn:

───────────── *Generalization 8.30* ─────────────

When the male-female division of labor is collapsed, group size decreases to roughly half of the minimal size of groups with a fifty-fifty division of labor. On the other hand, when more and more responsibility for food production is assumed by males—in groups that are primarily dependent upon aquatic resources and terrestrial mammals—minimal group size increases as a linear function of increases in the percentage of the contribution that male labor makes to the total diet.

───

Modeled GROUP1 sizes in table 8.10 are very close to the mean values in table 8.06 for a fifty-fifty division of labor in cases in which the male contribution to the division of labor is higher than 85 percent. Since the cases in table 8.06 are classified as essentially nonmobile or sedentary (only three are foragers, sensu Binford), it is very likely that they are intensified. This view is supported by the fact that twenty of the twenty-three cases with MDIVLAB values of greater than 85 percent are tabulated as collectors whose producers range outward from a central place and return with essential resources to the residential location. Even among these relatively sedentary peoples, family units do move to food procurement locations, particularly during the growing season or during fish runs. These temporary residential groups are coded as GROUP1 units, and the correspondence of the histograms in figures 8.01 and 8.03 to the 20.47 mean value of the Group Size Model is remarkable.

My experiences reading the ethnographic case material[24] have led me to conclude that although males and females

TABLE 8.10

RELATIONSHIPS BETWEEN MALE DIVISION OF LABOR AND VARIABILITY IN GROUP SIZE WHEN THE NUMBER OF PRODUCERS IS HELD CONSTANT

GROUP	MDIVLAB	MALE DEPENDENCY RATIO	NUMBER OF PRODUCERS	ESTIMATED GROUP1 SIZE	OBSERVED GROUP1 SIZE
MODEL	50.00	1.750	5.10	8.92	—
NGANASAN	74.25	2.860	5.10	12.75	14.00
SLAVE	75.00	2.895	5.10	12.91	13.00
HARE	83.75	3.295	5.10	16.80	13.00
KOYUKON	86.25	3.410	5.10	17.39	14.00
NUNAMIUT	97.17	3.910	5.10	19.96	18.50
INGULIK	99.99	4.039	5.10	20.55	20.00

Note: In column 6, the number of producers is unknown and therefore not necessarily equivalent to the estimated values in column 5.

FIGURE 8.21

Utkuhikhalingmiut fishing camp, 1963. Photo by Jean L. Briggs.

may pursue independent procurement activities in some settings, this is not the kind of rigid division of labor—in which each gender is responsible for the procurement and processing of different species or products—that is common among plant-dependent peoples.[25] Among groups that are primarily dependent upon aquatic resources, males and females frequently perform different roles while procuring and processing a single resource. In one sense, the division of labor is collapsed in comparison with the foragers who have served as my model, since males and females are both involved in the exploitation of the same species. On the other hand, in groups with a truly collapsed division of labor, males and females not only concentrate on a single species or related suite of species, they also perform identical tasks.

The last Nunamiut corporate caribou drive, held in 1944 at Chandler Lake, Alaska (Binford 1991b:33–43), is a good example of male and female task sharing.[26] In this instance—as well as in all other documented examples—equal or proportional numbers of males and females are needed to accomplish the subsistence tasks. The size of the residential group therefore reflects the contribution of both genders on a daily basis, just as it does with the larger groups of plant-dependent peoples in the original model. In figure 8.21, a communal residential site of this type is illustrated in Jean Briggs's photograph of a 1963 Utkuhikhalingmiut fishing camp (1970:88–89).

On the basis of these observations, I suggest that

Proposition 8.09

When resources must be obtained in large quantities within a comparatively short period of time, considerable processing of the products for both storage and consumption will frequently be required. In such circumstances, the division of labor will be between males, who are primarily involved in procurement, and females, who are primarily involved in processing. Under these conditions, group size will be responsive to the need for simultaneous male and female work parties (also noted among plant-dependent foragers). The labor of males and females, however, will be directed to different tasks associated with the procurement and processing of the same species instead of being channeled into separate procurement tasks for males and females. Whether the tasks are associated with procurement or processing appears to be irrelevant as a conditioner of group size. The important variable is the number of simultaneous male and female work parties that must be assembled each day in order to complete the subsistence task.

It should be clear that groups dependent upon aquatic resources have very different ways of organizing the gender-based division of labor than groups who depend primarily on plants. This fact is reflected in different frequency patterning in GROUP1 size for the two types of groups. The major determinant of both similarities to and differences from the conditions of the Group Size Model lies in the relationships between simultaneous gender-based work groups that are essential to the accomplishment of subsistence tasks conducted by the group as a whole.

Unfortunately, ever since the early cross-cultural research of Murdock and his colleagues, the division of labor has been thought of in terms of differences in the species exploited by males and females. Using this criterion meant that the character of the division of labor in a sample of social units could be distinguished by simply identifying which species were procured by males and which by females. Such a distinction never really dealt with the *organization* of labor.

Much of the ethnographic data used in this study is derived from sources that conceptualized human labor in categorical terms. For this reason, the measure that I use to estimate the percentage of the total diet obtained by males (MDIVLAB) represents an accommodation to the Murdock modus operandi. MDIVLAB is literally an estimate of the relative contribution of males and females to the total quantity of food coming from terrestrial plants, terrestrial animals, and aquatic resources that is consumed by a group. If male subsistence acquisition in a hypothetical group is concentrated on terrestrial animals, I have recorded an MDIVLAB value of 100 percent from terrestrial animals. Such a variable merely identifies the resources that males and females contribute to subsistence; it does not measure the amount of labor each gender expends in the procurement of consumables.

In figure 8.22, graph A, the relationship between GROUP1 size and the percentage of the male contribution to the acquisition of terrestrial animals is displayed for cases that are classified as "normal" hunter-gatherers (SUBPOP = n) (mounted hunters of the North American plains are excluded). The pattern in this graph is quite definite and can be described in the following terms:

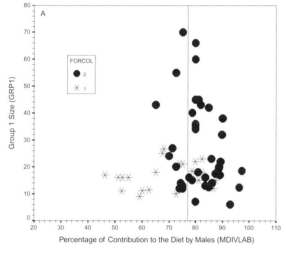

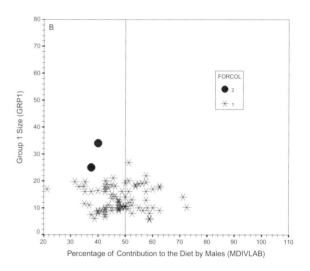

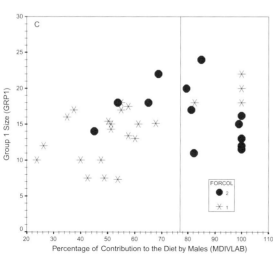

FIGURE 8.22

A three-graph comparison of forager-collector case distributions in a property space map defined by GROUP1 size and the percentage of the diet contributed by males for hunter-gatherers dependent on terrestrial animals (A), terrestrial plants (B), and aquatic resources (C). Threshold values in the male contribution to the diet are demonstrated. All graphs are coded for the forager-collector distinction (FORCOL): (1) forager and (2) collector.

―――――――― *Generalization 8.31* ――――――――

Among groups who depend upon terrestrial animals and have low values for the male division of labor variable (MDI-VLAB), the increase in group size that is expected to coincide with increases in the percentage of the male contribution to the labor pool is, in fact, visible (figure 8.22). This pattern persists until a threshold is reached at which males obtain approximately 77 percent of all food. Thereafter, further increases in MDIVLAB are accompanied by a reduction in observed values of GROUP1 size.

―――――――――――――――――――――――――――――

This distribution also documents that decreasing GROUP1 size relative to a male division of labor value of greater than 77 percent occurs in twenty-seven cases classified as collectors and only seven forager cases (a 3.86:1.00 ratio). This pattern supports the earlier observation that logistically organized hunters tend to have smaller GROUP1 sizes, a correlation that is also related to very high values for male division of labor. These relationships are accentuated by the fact that there is a 1.50:1.00 ratio of foragers to collectors among the cases that are distributed on the low side of the MDIVLAB threshold at 77 percent.

This observation is consistent with Nunamiut settlement systems data, which record that the smallest residential groups occurred during the spring and fall, coincident with caribou migrations. During these seasons, a regional food glut occurred and residential parties were often positioned relative to the locations of prior kill sites, where the animals killed in large numbers were processed and prepared for storage. Groups were small—not because hunters were trying to reduce the mobility costs incurred while obtaining food, but because the social units that were processing meat for storage were usually nuclear or slightly extended families who were working independently of other similar units to meet their subsistence needs, and they had no need for a large labor contingent.

It was not unusual, however, for Nunamiut men and their sons-in-law to cooperate in the spring and fall hunts (Binford 1991a). In these situations, more than one nuclear family was expected at kill sites, although these sites were not corporately organized. With regard to group size, such extended family units are comparable to groups at the higher end of the range of plant-dependent cases having a collapsed division of labor.

Figure 8.22, graph B, demonstrates the presence of a vague threshold at the 50 percent point on the male division of labor (MDIVLAB) axis among peoples dominantly dependent upon terrestrial plants. No meaningful relationships to the collector strategy are indicated since all the cases defining the plot's chevron pattern are foragers. A much more impressive pattern is demonstrated in graph C for groups that are primarily dependent upon aquatic resources. In the same

graph, an unambiguous threshold occurs at approximately 77 percent on the male division of labor (MDIVLAB) axis and is marked by a reference line. (I must point out that these patterns were completely unexpected. I had anticipated the simple, positive linear relationship between GROUP1 size and increases in male participation in food production that was modeled in table 8.06 and represents a view that has precedent in the anthropological literature [Hiatt 1970].)

―――――――――― *Generalization 8.32* ――――――――――

I had originally thought that increases in the male contribution to the total diet should result in increased group size. Such increases do occur as the percentage of MDIVLAB increases, but a threshold occurs in all subsistence subsets after which GROUP1 size diminishes with further increases in the male division of labor percentage. Among plant-dependent peoples, the threshold occurs at 49 to 50 percent, while for groups dependent upon either terrestrial animal or aquatic resources, the threshold is evident at an MDIVLAB level of 75 to 77 percent.

―――――――――――――――――――――――――――――

Among groups dependent upon terrestrial animal and aquatic resources, I have also noted a relationship between the number of cases that are classified as collectors and the frequencies of cases that exceed the male division of labor estimate of 75 to 77 percent:

―――――――――― *Generalization 8.33* ――――――――――

The vast majority of the groups dependent upon terrestrial plant resources (generalization 8.07) are classified as foragers, and there is no biased distribution in GROUP1 size at the 49 to 50 percent MDIVLAB threshold in the few plant-dependent cases that are classified as collectors. In contrast, groups dependent upon either terrestrial animals or aquatic resources exhibit threshold values for GROUP1 size at MDIVLAB values of between 75 and 77 percent. These cases are also strongly biased in the number of groups classified as collectors that occur on the high side of the threshold.

―――――――――――――――――――――――――――――

The presence of thresholds is not a new phenomenon in the analysis of my data. Thresholds in the distribution of hunter-gatherer groups occurred in plots of GROUP1 size and ET, as well as GROUP1 size and latitude (figures 8.08 and 8.09). These thresholds occurred in settings in which there was a major shift in the number of mammalian species, producing dramatic changes (the subpolar bottleneck) at an ET value of 11.53 (figure 8.12, graphs A and B). At this threshold in all of the earth's analogous settings, extraordinary forests occur that have the highest biomass accumulation ratios on earth but relatively low values of net aboveground productivity. At this point I ask the obvious question: does the observable threshold in GROUP1 size relative

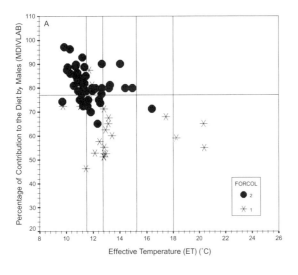

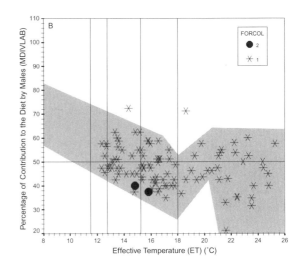

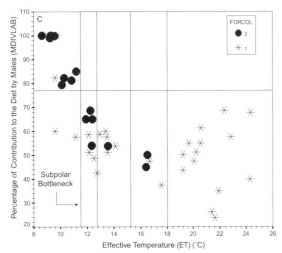

FIGURE 8.23

A three-graph comparison of forager-collector case distributions in a property space map defined by the percentage of the diet contributed by males and effective temperature. Comparisons are between the primary sources of food: terrestrial animals (A), terrestrial plants (B), and aquatic resources (C). All graphs are coded for the forager-collector distinction (FORCOL): (1) forager and (2) collector.

to the male division of labor correspond to the thresholds in GROUP1 size that were noted at the bottleneck at ET 11.53 or at other previously identified thresholds?

By counting the cases and their forager-collector percentages, it should be clear that the threshold pattern in graph A of figure 8.22 corresponds to a point that is halfway between the terrestrial plant threshold at 12.75 ET and the subpolar bottleneck at 11.53 degrees ET in figure 8.23, graph A. The minimally defined threshold for groups that are primarily dependent upon terrestrial plants is an artifact of splitting a parallelogram at the 50 percent line for male division of labor on graph B of figure 8.23. The result is that most of the cases in settings warmer than 16 degrees ET occur on the left side of the line at 50 percent MDIVLAB in figure 8.22, graph B. In contrast, most of the cases from colder settings occur to the right of the chevron. This pattern indicates that the possible threshold suggested in figure 8.22, graph B, results from a bias in the distribution of the cases on either

side of the 50 percent marker. This pattern is very different from the relationship between the threshold indicated in figure 8.22, graph C, for groups exploiting aquatic resources and its clear association with the subpolar bottleneck at an ET value of 11.53 degrees (figure 8.23, graph C).

Generalization 8.34

For mobile groups that are primarily dependent upon aquatic resources, thresholds relating to the division of labor and GROUP1 size occur at the subpolar bottleneck of 11.53 ET (generalizations 8.10 and 8.12). This threshold also anticipates major changes in the number of mammalian species present in the environment (figure 8.11). On the other hand, for hunter-gatherers who are primarily dependent upon terrestrial animals, a threshold occurs in the male division of labor at a point that is only slightly cooler than the terrestrial plant threshold at approximately ET 12.75. It would not be surprising if this pattern corresponds to increased shifts toward aquatic resources and greater female involvement in the preparation of hunted foods for storage. The absence of a marked threshold—except for the one noted at the growing season threshold in figure 8.23, graph B—is consistent with the organization of foraging among mobile peoples who are primarily dependent upon terrestrial plants and whose mobility strategy is tied to the length of the growing season. This observation amends the statement on plant-dependent peoples in generalization 8.32.

Where Are We? An Assessment

In the introduction to this chapter, I pointed out that patterning in nature prompts and defines the research problems that a scientist chooses to pursue. The bedtime prayer of many researchers is likely to be that the new day will bring ever more correspondence between his or her ideas and formulations about the world and the character of the world itself. "Please don't let me spend all of my time describing and attempting to explain a flat earth," the sleepy investigator is likely to plead, "if the world is, in fact, round!"

My initial approximations of what the world is like for small, co-resident groups of hunter-gatherers were summarized in the Group Size Model developed at the end of chapter 7. There I argued that, other things being equal,

1. A minimal group size should be favored, since among foragers mobility costs would increase as GROUP1 size increased.
2. Variability among units of minimal size will be conditioned by (a) the demand for food and (b) the organization of laborers engaged in obtaining food, with a focus on the sexual division of labor.

My model made assumptions about the most likely values for all of the preceding variables. My estimate of the demand for food was based on the assumptions that food was not stored and that the amount of food required was a simple function of the number of consumers in the group. Since the goal was to be able to model GROUP1 size—and the only way I knew to obtain group size estimates was to model the labor organization of minimal size groups—I chose the dependency ratio (the number of persons fed by a single food producer) as the means to convert the smallest organization of food producers into the minimal group size.

Two aspects of labor organization were essential to the construction of the Group Size Model: the character of the sexual division of labor in food procurement and the average work schedule of individual producers. I assumed that males and females each contributed approximately 50 percent of the total food consumed by the group. Another assumption was that the division of labor was structured so that males obtained food from one set of species, that females primarily exploited an independent range of species, and that each day males and females independently organized work parties and obtained foods. These assumptions required that I estimate the minimal mean size of such work parties as well as the number of producers needed per day. It was necessary to estimate the average individual work schedule or how many days per year the average producer worked. With this information, I could then estimate the minimum number of producers a group must have in order to meet the need for producers on a daily basis and, at the same time, maintain the work schedule (e.g., work every other day).

The preceding estimates allowed me to obtain an estimate of group size by multiplying the minimum number of producers needed in a group by the dependency ratio. The result was an estimate of 18.98 persons in the minimal group,[27] although I noted that group size would decrease to 9.49 persons if the sexual division of labor was collapsed. I found that among the hunter-gatherer groups that were primarily dependent upon terrestrial plants and were classified as foragers—therefore meeting the model's assumptions about food source, acquisition strategy, and the sexual division of labor—forty-one of the fifty-nine documented cases occurred in the smaller bimodal cluster of cases in figure 8.01 that had a mean size of 9.95 1.58 persons (compared the expected value of 9.49 persons). The remaining eighteen cases formed a larger cluster with a mean of 17.49 ± 2.36 persons (compared with an expected value of 18.98).

Without much question, the Group Size Model behaves very well for cases that meet its assumptions, but in this chapter I have been exploring variability in GROUP1 sizes among cases that violate one or more of the model's assumptions. In spite of the large number of cases of the latter kind, the actual range of variability in GROUP1 sizes is relatively slight. Of the 225 cases of hunter-gatherers in the ethnographic sample for which GROUP1 estimates were available, 87.11 percent, or 196 cases, fall between the values of five and twenty-four persons. The twenty-nine cases whose GROUP1 size exceeds twenty-four persons are almost exclusively groups of mounted hunters from the North American plains, which I have regularly referred to as "exceptional" in terms of the total sample.

I believe that the facts just presented justify the following generalization:

Generalization 8.35

During the most dispersed phase of the hunter-gatherer settlement cycle, minimal group sizes are most likely to occur.

In this chapter, I have used the Group Size Model as a screen against which I have projected a number of related variables from the ethnographic data set in order to determine whether my ideas about the "world" of hunter-gatherer subsistence organization described a sphere or a planar surface. I definitely hoped that the emerging shape would be spherical, and I have been relieved to discover that, in general, my approximation of the world has not been contradicted by any of the feedback I have received from my pattern recognition work.

I believe that the analysis has confirmed that a number of the relationships between the variables summarized in both my generalizations and my propositions strongly imply the operation of self-organizing processes underlying the variability I have been exploring. By *self-organization* I mean only that the causes of phenomena in the empirical domain are to be found in the interactions among variables and not in any individual factor or agency. As Prigogine has pointed out, "In biology, the conflict between reductionists and antireductionists has often appeared as a conflict between the assertion of an external and an internal purpose. The idea of an imminent organizing intelligence is thus often opposed by an organizational model borrowed from the technology of the time (mechanical, heat, cybernetic machines), which immediately elicits the retort: 'Who' built the machine, the automation that obeys external purpose?" (Prigogine and Stengers 1984:174).[28]

Self-organization emphasizes a view of the world that looks to processes—dynamic event sequences that may fluctuate between states of near equilibrium and near chaos—rather than to agents for causal explanations. Fluctuations may modify the normal values of equilibrium states rather than correct deviations—as in equilibrium states—so that new system state conditions are brought into being.[29] Determinant arguments apply when dealing with equilibrium states, which is why I emphasized in chapter 7 that, in the classic scientific sense of the word, theories are system specific (Binford 1983:214). In other words, theories are dependent upon certain fundamental stabilities, and when these relationships are no longer stable theories require modification, elaboration, or replacement with new theories. It is in this sense that I have used the expression "the same 'things' can be organized differently and different 'things' can be organized similarly" to describe dynamics in both the external world and the world of ideas.

Up to this point, I have approached the analysis of GROUP1 size as though this property of hunter-gatherer organization was the same "thing" and could be expected to vary across all systems in response to the same causal or conditioning circumstances. In so doing, I was hoping to be able to recognize when and if the rules changed, which would enable me to begin to specify at least some properties of systemic boundaries. Also, from the very beginning of this chapter, I have assumed that the study of on-the-ground group sizes would help me understand the patterning in

the ethnographic data and the generalizations emerging from the analysis in chapter 7.

In chapters 6 and 7, I began to discuss intensification, stressing at the same time the difference between variability related to system state dynamics and variability that was related to ecological dynamics. In the lay language of archaeology, the latter changes can be regarded as adaptive responses in the same sense as the distinction made by Sahlins and Service (1960) between "specific evolution" and "general evolution," which I discussed in chapter 7. The recognition that systems could be self-organizing while operating at the interface between cultural systems and their environmental settings and result in adjustments by cultural systems while they remain in a state of equilibrium is also very close to what those authors intended by the term *specific evolution*.

Thirteen of the generalizations presented in this chapter refer to the ecological locus of process. They deal with the following:

1. Net aboveground productivity and GROUP1 size (generalization 8.01).
2. The relationships between the basic sources of foods, the structure of the habitat, and the organization of labor as indicated by forager-collector strategies and group sizes (generalizations 8.03, 8.04, and 8.16).
3. The ecology of storage strategies (generalizations 8.08, 8.09, and 8.10).
4. Temperature—in this case warmth—as a factor affecting both the basic sources of food and the organization of labor as indicated by the forager-collector distinction (generalizations 8.15 and 8.19), and warmth and the division of labor (generalizations 8.12, 8.31, and 8.32).
5. Ways to use the patterns of interaction among environmental variables to identify system boundaries (generalization 8.10 and 8.38).

I have also been concerned with what I prefer to call *functional interactions,* but because of the ambiguity generated in anthropology by the use of the word *functional*—and the disrepute that is attached to the term at present—I now refer to this class of dynamics as "interoperating, mutually accommodating processes within cultural systems." Five of the propositions and six of the generalizations presented in this chapter have reference to these dynamic, internal, cultural processes. The generalizations deal with a number of conditions: (1) storage of food and group size (8.06); (2) group size and mobility (8.11); (3) family size and dependency ratios (8.23, 8.24); (4) the division of labor and group size (8.26); (5) marriage, polygyny, divisions of labor, and sedentism (8.33); and (6) the relationships between GROUP1 size, polygyny, the division of labor, and family size (8.27). The propositions are more complex and deal with (1) the factors affecting mobility (8.02); (2) the lack of interdependence between group size and mobility when storage is practiced (8.05); (3) the pattern, scale, and technology of mobility (8.07); and (4) strategies of resource procurement, the division of labor, and group size (8.09). Table 8.09 summarizes data relating to female producers, polygyny, and group size.

Throughout the inquiry that produced the generalizations and propositions, I consistently noted exceptions to the regularities that were enumerated. I often suspected that many deviations arose because my analytical unit—GROUP1—did not really refer to the same "thing" in the organization of ethnographically documented hunter-gatherer systems (proposition 8.03).

For example, when I asked the question "under what conditions are hunter-gatherer settlement systems maximally dispersed?" I discovered that GROUP1 units occurred under very different conditions in different systems. In the Kalahari, the G/wi were maximally dispersed during the least productive phase of the subsistence settlement cycle, the dry season (Silberbauer 1981:196). In contrast, the !Kung speakers of Dobe Pan were maximally dispersed during the rainy season, which is the habitat's most productive phase of the year (Barnard 1992:43). In the high arctic, the Nunamiut were also most dispersed residentially during the caribou migration, when their most important food resource was maximally available.

Other interesting examples include the Hadza of Tanzania, who were most dispersed during the season when honey, one of their prized foods, was most abundant (J. O'Connell, pers. comm. 1989). The availability of honey also affected the seasonal group sizes of most of the central African tropical mutualists, such as the Efe (Bailey 1985:109, 111). On the other hand, the Semang were reported to be most dispersed during the wet season, at which time flooding was likely in their normal range (Endicott and Endicott 1986:153–55; Gregg 1980).

Hunter-gatherer groups that have been referred to as "forest product specialists" are particularly interesting. These people exploit tropical forests for products that they usually do not consume but instead exchange, barter, or "turn in" as part of wage labor arrangements (see, for instance, the Nayaka or "Naikens" of South India [Bird 1983] and the Hill Pandaram from the same area [Morris 1982a]). Groups of this kind bring to mind the "tappers and trappers" argument of Murphy and Steward (1956), to which I must add another class of specialists, "traders." Here the focus is not on the products that are acquired for exchange or for wage labor but rather on the economic dependency of hunter-gatherers upon larger, non-hunter-gatherer societies whose economic concerns are organized at a much larger scale.

As I noted in chapter 1, tappers and trappers were characterized as maintaining a "family level of sociocultural integration" (Steward 1955) and as "atomistic" (Lévy 1968; Rubel and Kupferer 1968), and they have been cited as the antithesis (Speck and Eiseley 1942) of the idealized, communalis-

tic hunter-gatherer society (Leacock and Lee 1982). In almost all of the characterizations of hunter-gatherer societal organization, a contrast has been recognized between cooperative integration in economic pursuits and a more individualized, less cooperative integration, the latter designated as atomistic and the former as primitive communism.

The contrast between these characterizations illustrates the sterility of many of the anthropological approaches to variability. A much more productive approach tries to determine the factors that favor cooperation and to identify the circumstances in which it is advantageous for individuals and groups to pursue cooperative or individualistic strategies. My analysis, in fact, has been able to demonstrate that

---

Generalization 8.36

Among hunter-gatherers, societies are segmental with regard to cooperative integration.

The variability in GROUP1 size in the data set demonstrates that there is no uniformity in the size of hunter-gatherer residential units. During certain seasons or under certain conditions having to do with the scheduling of access to potential foods, small groups or minimally cooperating segments such as families or households may reside and work independently. During other phases of the subsistence settlement cycle, these segments may cooperate with other similar units in larger, integrated associations. The issue is not whether the original and persistent condition of mankind was essentially cooperative or uncooperative, but instead what factors affect the variability in and stability of a cooperative state in a cultural system. Of the several attempts to address this issue, the least profitable consideration of this subject is by Riches (1982) and the most germane and interesting one is by Eric Alden Smith (1991:287–356).[30]

The evidence strongly suggests that differences in group size are a direct indicator of the scale of cooperation during the most dispersed phase of the year. The factors that differ— such as dispersion during the least productive season of the year as opposed to dispersion during the season of greatest food abundance—are to be understood in terms of the costs and benefits between large-scale cooperation and reductions in the scale of cooperating units. I therefore do not regard differences in the conditions of dispersal as an impediment to the development of general arguments about variability in group size. I have not yet, however, developed any arguments about the scales at which cooperation per se occurs.

Returning to the issue of the locus of process, I have pointed to the interface between cultural systems and their habitats, as well as the internal articulations between cultural properties and subsystems. I have not really addressed directly the issue of intensificational processes nor the very real problem of their impact on system state differences. My focus on

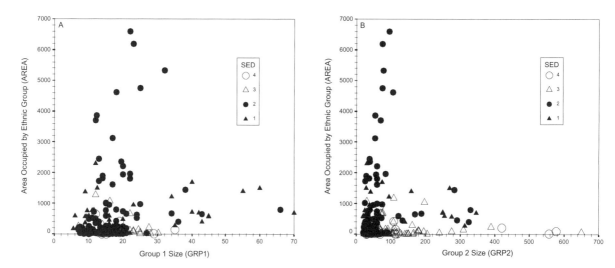

FIGURE 8.24

A paired-graph comparison featuring degrees of residential mobility in a property space map of GROUP1 (A) and GROUP2 sizes (B) expressed relative to the area occupied by an ethnic group. Both graphs are coded for degrees of residential mobility (SED): (1) fully nomadic, (2) seminomadic, (3) semisedentary, and (4) fully sedentary.

GROUP1 size was prompted by pattern recognition work in both chapters 6 and 7, in which I dealt with macro-units such as ethic groups.

In chapter 7, I demonstrated provocative patterning that seemed to justify using the concept of "intensification." The units with which I originally worked were relatively gross, however, and in the case of TLPOP the total number of individuals in an "ethnic group" was ambiguous since the term *ethnic group* is neither well defined nor consistently employed. This recognition demanded that I shift the scale of observation to a well-documented and economically important unit such as GROUP1 size.

How does the variability demonstrated in GROUP1 size relate to the patterns that have been observed for variables such as the total number of individuals in an ethnic group or the total area utilized by an ethnic group (AREA)? There are two reasons why this is an important question. The first is simply that it was patterning in the distribution of TLPOP and AREA that led me to explore the process of intensification. The second is that I recognized ambiguity in the TLPOP variable and suspected that the ethnic group was not the appropriate unit with which to explore organizational linkages between environmental variables that, in turn, had a significant impact on what hunter-gatherers were likely to eat. I also evaluated how the basic trophic sources of food might condition differential patterns of mobility, group size, and the organization of segmentally based, larger social units.

Now that I have studied hunter-gatherer groupings that I believe are more appropriate to the issues and questions that concern me, I need to make a connection between at least

some of my findings and the variables that prompted the decision to work with GROUP1 and GROUP2 units in the first place. I begin in figure 8.24 with an illustration of the relationships between the size of the area occupied by an ethnic group (AREA) and the size of GROUP1 and GROUP2 units.

For both GROUP1 and GROUP2, the overall pattern is the same: there is a minor correlation between area and group size. Huge geographic areas tend to have slightly larger GROUP1 and GROUP2 sizes, but the relationship is overshadowed by the fact that the largest documented GROUP1 and GROUP2 units occur in very small ethnic areas! These small social units exhibit the same basic pattern documented in chapter 6: that is, the smaller the size of the ethnic group area, the larger the social units that are found in that area. This pattern appears to apply across the whole range human aggregations from large ethnic units to small social segments such as GROUP1 and GROUP2 units. I feel fairly confident that

Proposition 8.10

Intensification operates throughout the range of social segmentation[31] in an ethnic group, favoring larger groups when there are constraints on geographic expansion and the area available for use becomes smaller.

Graphs A and B in figure 8.25 illustrate similar patterning in the relationships between the estimated number of persons in an ethnic group plotted against GROUP1 and

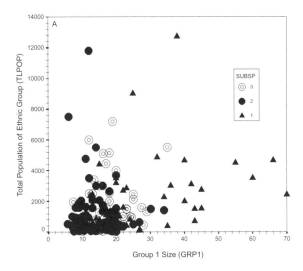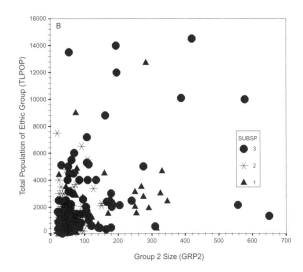

FIGURE 8.25

A paired-graph comparison featuring degrees of residential mobility in a property space map of GROUP1 (A) and GROUP2 sizes (B) expressed relative to the total population recorded for an ethnic group. The marker indicates the primary source of food (SUBSP): (1) terrestrial animals, (2) terrestrial plants, and (3) aquatic resources.

GROUP2 sizes. Here the largest GROUP1 size occurs in ethnic groups of small to moderate size, while very large ethnic groups are associated with moderate to small GROUP1 sizes. The x and y arms of the distributions in both graphs are bent closer to the diagonal, but they still form clearly distinct, inverse patterns. This suggests that perhaps there is more convergent or correlated patterning between ethnic unit sizes and GROUP2 sizes, but the considerable independence implicates different suites of causal variables.

Nevertheless, when large GROUP1 sizes occur, as was the case with area, they are associated with small to moderate ethnic group sizes. The patterning in both the largest social units considered here—"ethnic groups"—and the smallest of the segmentary[32] social units targeted for study—GROUP1—appears to behave similarly with respect to the relationships between group size and area occupied: the smaller the area utilized, the larger the group using the area. These results indicate that further investigation of intensificational processes is clearly justified.

I have noted not only an interesting relationship between group size and area utilized but also that, to the extent that mobility is a basic hunter-gatherer tactic to ensure subsistence security,

Proposition 8.11

Changed relationships should be expected between the number of people and the area utilized that would affect the effectiveness and utilization of tactical mobility as a means of ensuring subsistence security. Since population density is calculated as a ratio between ethnic

area (AREA) and the number of persons per ethnic group, increases in population density should be accompanied by decreases in the indicators of mobility.

Other ramifications of mobility are explored in graph A of figure 8.26, which displays the relationship between the $\log_{10}$ value of population density (LDEN) and the total distance of all residential moves per year, measured in kilometers. (The markers identify the primary food resources exploited by each group.) This distribution prompts me to observe that

Generalization 8.37

There is a negative linear correlation between the sum of the distance moved residentially per year and the $\log_{10}$ value of population density.

Since population density is the ratio between the total population estimated for an ethnic group (TLPOP) and the area utilized or inhabited by the ethnic group (AREA), density summarizes the interaction between these two variables, which were examined independently in previous chapters. These considerations led to a discussion of the conditions that would reward hunter-gatherers who implemented tactics to increase the net food return from smaller units of land. Graph A in figure 8.26 clearly demonstrates that as the number of persons who must be fed from a finite unit of space increases—regardless of habitat—the less frequently residential mobility is chosen as a food-getting tactic. Without doubt, residential

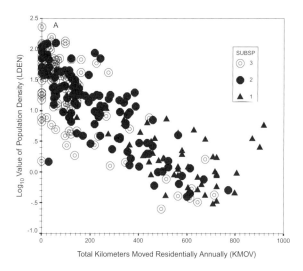
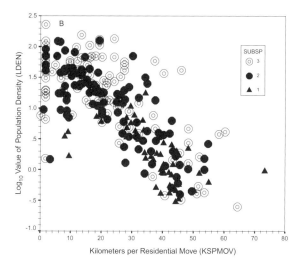

FIGURE 8.26

A paired-graph comparison between the total number of kilometers moved residentially (A) and the mean number of kilometers per residential move (B). Both variables are expressed relative to the $\log_{10}$ value of population density. Both graphs are coded for the primary source of food (SUBSP): (1) terrestrial animals, (2) terrestrial plants, and (3) aquatic resources.

mobility decreases as a function of the relationships between TLPOP and AREA.

A shift in focus to the patterning within the property space demonstrated in graph A of figure 8.20 confirms a pattern observed earlier in a different comparative context: the frequency distributions and positioning within the property space differ dramatically as the trophic level of a group's primary source of food changes. I noted in generalization 8.18 that the vast majority of hunter-gatherers whose subsistence is based primarily on terrestrial animals also rely on mobility as a major positioning strategy within their habitat. Most hunters make residential moves that total more than 300 kilometers per year. Although some plant-dependent groups move equal distances, most cases in this category actually move less than 300 kilometers annually.

Some groups exploiting aquatic resources are similar to plant-dependent peoples in that they move large distances within a year. The majority of cases, however, move less than 175 kilometers annually, and an impressive cluster of these cases have the highest population densities and the lowest mobility of all hunter-gatherer groups. These patterns support my argument that, other things being equal, processes of intensification disproportionately favor plant food resources over animal food resources, and—in many environments—aquatic resources are favored over terrestrial animal foods as well. The role of aquatic resources in continental, warm temperate, and equatorial settings appears in need of further clarification, however.

In the comparable scatter plot in figure 8.26, graph B, the indicator of mobility is the mean distance traveled per res-

idential move during a year. This is a reflection less of how mobile groups are than of how groups use mobility to position themselves on the landscape. This difference is illustrated by the wide distribution of cases across the density range, many of which travel ten or fewer kilometers per move. Cases in the lower distribution in the graph are fully sedentary, which means that settlements last longer than a single year.[33]

A parallel distribution includes groups that make, on average, very short residential moves, in many cases moving every day or two as they quite literally feed their way across the habitat.[34] This is a very different strategy from what I have referred to as "mapping on" or positioning strategies. In spite of these differences, however, there is an undeniable inverse correlation between the $\log_{10}$ value of population density and the average distance moved between residential camps. This pattern unambiguously documents an inverse scalar relationship between mobility and intensificational indicators.

I also wanted to examine larger social units relative to the male division of labor, which is one of the variables isolated in this chapter that consistently patterned with small GROUP1 units. The graphs in figure 8.27 demonstrate that there is a very complex relationship between the male division of labor and $\log_{10}$ values of population density. Two thresholds are indicated in each graph. One occurs on the x axis (male division of labor) at value for a male contribution to the diet of between 57 and 62 percent, which marks the approximate upper limit of dependence upon plants and corresponds to the terrestrial plant threshold at ET 12.75 degrees.

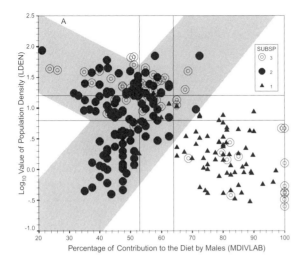
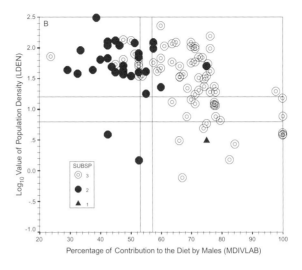

FIGURE 8.27

A paired-graph comparison between mobile hunter-gatherers (A) and sedentary hunter-gatherers (B), both expressed relative to the $\log_{10}$ value of population density. Both graphs are coded for the primary source of food (SUBSP): (1) terrestrial animals, (2) terrestrial plants, and (3) aquatic resources.

The first appearance of another threshold occurs at approximately the $\log_{10}$ value of 1.0, which is the point at which male division of labor among groups of gatherers exhibits a marked threshold. The highest values are clustered at the density threshold and diminish in a chevron pattern on either side. Most groups of terrestrial animal hunters are clustered above the MDIVLAB threshold and have a lower population density than at the threshold value around 1.0. Aquatic resource specialists are distributed across the full range of variability for the male division of labor but are noticeably absent from the quadrant of the graph in which both density and male division of labor are low. This pattern may suggest that density-dependent factors affect aquatic resource exploitation in environments in which heavy dependence upon terrestrial plants is a possibility.

Based on the information presented in figure 8.27, graph A, it appears that among mobile peoples at a density level of between approximately 10 and 32 to 35 persons (or a $\log_{10}$ value of 1 to 1.54 persons) per 100 square kilometers, who use residential mobility as a subsistence strategy, there is a vague continuation of the responses that characterized tactically more mobile peoples living at lower levels of population density. On the other hand, in figure 8.27, graph B, which only includes cases that do not use residential mobility as their primary subsistence strategy, a shift occurs in the distribution's center of gravity to cases with density values greater than 32 to 35 persons per 100 square kilometers and increased male contributions to the diet. The majority of these cases are dependent upon aquatic resources. The cases primarily dependent upon plants, like the cases with lower

population density values (graph A in figure 8.27), continue to exhibit low values for the percentage of the male contribution to the diet.

As interesting and provocative as the patterns in figure 8.27 may be, the two most important features of the graph are as follows:

1. Those cases that in my judgment use residential mobility as their primary subsistence strategy occur at uniformly lower levels of population density. In contrast, the food-getting strategies of the majority of the cases do not include residential mobility to any great extent. The threshold between the two types of strategies occurs at approximately 32 to 35 ($\log_{10}$ 1.0 to 1.54) persons per 100 square kilometers.

2. The threshold between increasing and decreasing percentages in the male contribution to the diet occurs at a $\log_{10}$ density value of 1.0 ± 0.2, which places the mean for the threshold at approximately 10 persons per 100 square kilometers. The presence and value of this threshold are even more provocative since, after I built the Group Size Model at the end of chapter 7, I noted that "a population density value that exceeds 9.098 persons (20.47 divided by 2.25) per 100 square kilometers would be circumscribed by groups living in FORAD-sized units on all sides" (page 239).

The coincidence between the threshold in MDIVLAB values and the modeled value of the level of population density (9.098 persons) at which constraints on mobility confine hunter-gatherers to FORAD-sized units *strongly suggests* that groups respond to mobility constraints by modifying the way in which their labor is organized. This coincidence suggests that I may be observing clues to the kind of systemic change—brought on by dynamic processes—that leads to the appearance of emergent conditions. In such a system state, very new properties abruptly appear that could not have been anticipated by projections from the characteristic behaviors of the parent system. I have contrasted this kind of change with gradual, accretional modifications that are the outcome of systemic growth rather than emergence.

There have already been hints that storage tactics may well respond quite differently to basic environmental gradients (figures 8.04 and 8.05) than they do to pressures to intensify. Other patterns indicate that tactical mobility plays a diminishing role in systems in which the number of persons per unit area is increasing. And, in spite of imperfect and rather mechanical techniques for estimating the character of the sexual division of labor, this variable also interacts in a patterned way with properties that vary consistently with my earlier ideas about intensification.

I feel that I have learned enough from my analysis to say with some confidence that the pattern of interest is intensification itself. If it is possible to understand the interacting factors that cause it and how the causal process stimulates new organizational properties within cultural systems—something that my investigations thus far suggest—then I will have made major progress in my search for ways to identify and explain the differences in hunter-gather system states.

Intensification was implicated in chapter 7 as a major factor underlying system state differences, and three of the generalizations and propositions enumerated in this chapter also deal with intensificational indicators. Generalizations 8.02, 8.13, and 8.19 summarize the correlations between larger GROUP1 sizes and sedentism, culturally complex cases, the logistical organization of task groups, and patterns of mobility. None of these variables is a *measure* of intensification, but most are thought to be *consequences* of intensification. Generalization 8.27 and propositions 8.01, 8.04, and 8.08 suggest other possible correlates of intensification, such as increased GROUP1 size, storage at latitudes below 35 degrees, and distances moved by small groups originating in central-place, sedentary communities.

Conclusion

As this chapter concludes, I have organized my observations into those that refer to the articulations between cultural systems and their ecological settings and those that relate to functional or interoperating, mutually accommodating processes *within* cultural systems. I have also linked my observations on GROUP1 size back to my observations at a larger scale that

were summarized in chapter 7. I continue to regard intensification as responsible for much of the organizational variability documented in hunter-gatherers groups, but two other points have been suggested by my pattern recognition studies.

The more important of the two points relates to cooperation and the factors responsible for its variability within systems. Variability in this case refers to dynamics that are both seasonal and situational (a point initially recognized by Mauss and Beuchat [1979] and discussed in chapter 1) as well as to processes affecting the way that systems vary along a scale of cooperative integration ranging from atomism to communism. Although it would be difficult to arrive at the following conclusion from a perusal of the anthropological literature, cooperation is a variable and not an expression of the essential disposition or ideological ethos of hunter-gatherers.

So far, I have only hinted at the second important point, which is my assumption in chapter 7 that small GROUP1 sizes enabled hunter-gatherers to minimize mobility costs. Two of the observations I have made in this chapter are germane to this issue:

1. The linkage of the demand for food to the size of the GROUP1 unit may be severed completely when groups resort to food storage. Once storage tactics are implemented, group size is more likely to be conditioned by the time and transport constraints that are involved in successfully procuring and processing adequate quantities of food to sustain groups over varying and sometimes considerable periods of time. In such a situation, group size is likely to be conditioned by labor demands that vary independently of the daily food needs of the group preparing food resources for storage.
2. Mobility costs may not be germane when single-species food gluts occur or during the accumulation and processing for storage of large quantities of simultaneously available foods. It might be said that mobility costs may be epiphenomenal in many contexts in which differential food accessibility or clustering occurs (proposition 8.05).

Once I begin to question the effect of mobility costs on GROUP1 sizes, I come face-to-face with the issue of system state variability and the possibility that emergent conditions are involved that change the way the world works in rather dramatic ways. Since intensification is the system state in which there is a selective advantage to tactics and strategies that increase the yield of food from spatial units of a constant or diminishing size, such a state implies an ever-decreasing role for residential mobility in the tactical sense of the word. In whatever terms intensification is conceived, however, it implies reduced mobility, at least at the GROUP2 level. If intensification is accepted as a process, then, in light of the generalizations presented in this study, one must also concede that

———————— *Generalization 8.38* ————————

Mobility is not an independent variable; it responds to changes in system state induced by intensification.

We might therefore expect that

———————— *Proposition 8.12* ————————

GROUP1 size responds to changes in the demand for food and for differently configured labor groups, particularly since at least one major intensificational strategy is to increase labor inputs in an effort to secure higher net food returns. Changes in the organization of labor would be occurring at the same time that tactical mobility was becoming an increasingly ineffective food procurement strategy.

———————————————————————————

This proposition is supported by my previous observations on the biased frequency of hunter-gatherer cases practicing collector rather than forager strategies.

The goal of this entire endeavor is to learn how—and under what conditions—changes and even reversals in the organizational properties of cultural systems occur. At this time, however, I do not yet know how processes of intensification bring into being the new status quo implied in the preceding statements! In chapter 9, however, I address this issue directly.

CHAPTER

9

The Play's the Thing in the Scientific Theater

In chapter 3, I described two very different dramatic enterprises that can be visualized as parallel dimensions in which events unfold concurrently. One domain consists of the world of dynamics that a scientist studies and attempts to explain, which in this case refers to many hunter-gatherer evolutionary plays unfolding in many different ecological theaters. In the other realm of dynamics—the scientific theater—researchers take center stage as they evaluate, elucidate, and defend their ideas about the nature of the events that they have observed in the evidentiary forum. I also noted that scientific colloquy is an essential component of the learning process, often an opportunity for the researcher to expand his or her fund of knowledge or to compare the fruits of individual research to the disciplinary canon as a whole.

In the past five chapters, I have played the role of an explorer. I have used pattern recognition techniques to peruse data about hunter-gatherer activities, environmental dynamics, and ecological relationships, and I have discovered exciting regularities in the ways that variables co-occur and interact. I hope to have illustrated that building and using models as part of the learning process is much more useful than creating a corpus of static "truths" to which the observational world is then accommodated.

I have also insisted that working with undimensionalized data simply mirrors the organization of one's own cognitive schemes. I have stressed that second-order derivative patterning offers the only hope of discovering properties that are informative about the way in which the external world is organized. Up until now, however, I have not discussed the interaction between, on the one hand, a researcher's ideas about what the world is like and why it might be that way and, on the other hand, second-order derivative patterning in general.

In chapter 3, I compared the logic of science to an equilateral triangle in which the scientist stands in the middle. One corner of the triangle is labeled "source side" and contains all of the received knowledge that can be used in argument or cited as warranting beliefs about the phenomenological world of interest to the scientist. The second corner of the triangle is labeled "subject side," and it is here that the phenomena to be studied repose. In the case of archaeology and ethnology, this includes all of the accessible properties of the archaeological and ethnographic records, the observations that offer the archaeologist the opportunity to learn about the past and the ethnologist the opportunity to learn about the near present.

The third corner of the triangle contains all of the received knowledge about techniques and strategies for productively linking source-side knowledge to subject-side observations. A major focus of this book has been the use of tactics and strategies for organizing source-side knowledge to maximize the information that can be extracted from subject-side observations. I have practiced what I preached in chapter 3, act III, scenes 1 and 2, and, as a result, in chapters 6, 7, and 8 I have been able to develop provocative, generalizable observations that implicate the dynamic world of hunter-gatherer variability.

The appropriate tactic at such a juncture, I believe, is to return to the intellectual theater and initiate a dialogue that will expose my subject-side observations, generalizations, and models to the arguments of other anthropological researchers. As always, the general goal is to learn; the specific focus in this instance is the utility of the Group Size Model viewed against the backdrop of other conceptions of variability.

I have described my work in earlier chapters as an exploratory process in which I looked for clues to relationships between and among variables as I worked back and forth between patterning in the ethnographic and ecological data sets. The direction of my research was determined to a large extent by the sequence of my observations, coupled with my prior knowledge. My incessant, ramifying exercises in pattern recognition frequently resulted in descriptive statements, or generalizations, about what the world appears to be like.

In this chapter, however, I am proceeding differently. Shortly I will examine several different schemata that purport to account for *why* the world is the way it appears to be. I am not myself engaged in theory building, however. The goal is simply to evaluate and reduce the multitude of knowledge claims and arguments that have been advanced to explain why the world, in one of its many domains, is the way it appears to be.

A little more than a decade ago, Ernest Gellner (pers. comm. 1986) astutely observed that the theoretical apple barrel is always full and that the removal of some bad apples only makes room for more apples of unknown utility. I have chosen one of many theoretical apples in the anthropological barrel to use as an intellectual frame of reference for looking at some of my own postulations as well as at some other often-cited apples, which will be examined for worms and soft spots.

I will continue to use pattern recognition techniques, but as a way of relating relevant observations about the world of hunter-gatherers to the various suppositions under scrutiny. As a result, the patterns that are generated will not necessarily appear cumulative, since they will be relative to the particular intellectual apples rather than to a general problem, such as variability in group size, that I seek to understand. It should be clear that exploring an intellectual apple barrel is very different from exploring a body of dimensionalized data. Although it is likely that some important properties about the world of hunter-gatherers will be encountered, they will have to be ignored for the moment while the focus is on a particular apple, regardless of how many other apples may be implicated by my observations. I believe that this use of intellectual capital is justified because it promises in the long run to lead to an enhanced understanding of intensificational processes.

Spotlight on the Group Size Model

My discussion in chapter 8 of the Group Size Model was confined to patterning observed in the ethnographic and environmental data sets. As such, it was unrelated to the work of other researchers who may have offered arguments about group size or debated the factors that condition group size variability. In chapter 6, however, Birdsell's research on group size at the level of the ethnic group was introduced and discussed. He argued that group size was a "self-defining unit," and he specifically addressed what he thought of as "the dialectical tribe," or the 500-person unit within which a single language dialect was spoken. Implicit in Birdsell's discussion of group size was his belief that the mean band size of twenty-five persons—the so-called "magic number" discussed at the Man the Hunter Conference (Lee and DeVore 1968a:245–48)—was also "self-defining." What Birdsell meant

by self-defining units is best understood by quoting his own words: "Some system of equilibrium forces, involving both ecological and cultural factors, tends to maintain appropriate population size for band structure for given local conditions. Since anthropologists have not defined details of the nature of the cultural forces involved and have gathered no materials which allow a detailed examination of the ecological factors, it is impossible to construct models to explore the systems occurring among various peoples" (1958:195).

Birdsell seems to be referring to the process of self-organization, which proceeds without a directing agency, similar to the dynamics responsible for the patterning in hunter-gatherer group sizes explored in chapters 7 and 8. It is unfortunate that—as Birdsell was well aware—he wanted to investigate properties that in 1958 were inadequately documented. Forty years later it is appropriate to applaud his foresight and, I hope, fulfill his expectations: "it does seem clear that band size is not primarily determined by chance factors and that systematic forces do exist. One may hope that future generations of field workers may collect enough demographic and ecological data to provide a basis for such investigation" (Birdsell 1958:195).

"JOHNSON'S CONSTANT"

Gregory Johnson is one of the researchers who has responded to Birdsell's injunction to investigate the factors contributing to patterning in group size, and he has produced an elegant and widely cited argument dealing with this issue (Johnson 1978 and, particularly, 1982). Johnson is primarily concerned with understanding the organizational variability in sociocultural systems that results from differences in the sizes of the social units so organized. In the context of these interests he has distinguished between what he terms *sequential* and *simultaneous hierarchies*. Sequential hierarchies are characteristic of societies that are considered to be egalitarian. In contrast, simultaneous hierarchies refer to "complex" societies that are internally differentiated by ever-present criteria regulating the rank or social placement of the participants in the stratified system.

Johnson organized the received knowledge side of his particular research triangle in new and provocative ways. He began with previously observed patterns that had demonstrated a positive correlation between various ways of measuring system complexity and the size—in the sense of the number of persons organized—of the systems targeted for measurement. He noted that

Generalization 9.01

There is a tendency toward positive correlations between measures of system complexity and the size of the system. This pattern holds, however, only if a very wide range of population sizes is included in the array studied. If, for example, one looks only at small-scale systems (which would include most hunter-gatherers), there does not appear to be such a correlation.

In light of these observations, Johnson reasoned that

Proposition 9.01

"This suggests that while there is an underlying process that governs the scale-complexity relationship, this process is subject to significant '*local' variation*" (Johnson 1982:391–92; emphasis added).

Johnson was particularly interested in the locus of societal decision making and in the fact that there are really no societies in which all persons must participate in order for consensus to be achieved. In reality, children rarely participate in adult decision making, and many decisions are made by sets of males independent of either females or children. Similarly, sets of females may act independently. Some decisions are made among families linked by immediate kin ties into extended families, and, if decisions must be made by a suite of extended families, the decision making is the responsibility of the elders of those extended families. Human social systems can be organized in a segmentary fashion (Middleton and Tait 1958) so that, under some conditions, nuclear families constitute a decision making suite of units. In other contexts, the same nuclear families may be "nested" within an extended family unit whose representative joins those of other extended families to form a decision making "council."

This organizational principle results in considerable flexibility in unit formation. Individual family units may be combined into sequential hierarchies, each of which maintains relatively small group sizes for decision making purposes, although these relatively small groups may represent a very large number of people. It was this patterned sequence of ever-smaller nested units—each requiring consensual decision making at each step of the nested chain—that led Johnson to focus on the organizational unit per se, rather than the number of persons in each unit, as a measure of societal scale.

Johnson warranted the idea of sequentially nested decision making by referring to observations made by nonanthropological researchers and summarizing the results of multiple investigations specifically designed to reveal the effects of group size on the performance of decision making tasks (Johnson 1982:395). These studies revealed that a limited number of persons—in this case six—could participate in consensually based decision making and, at the same time, feel satisfied with the results of that process. When more than six persons were involved, consensus was difficult to achieve, as the graph in figure 9.01 illustrates.

Johnson's investigation of this pattern led him to conclude that the impediments to consensual decision making were related to the human capacity to make judgments about "unidimensional stimuli that is limited by the amount of information (in bits) that must be processed and a span of immediate memory limited by the number of items (information chunks) that can be simultaneously retained. Both spans are fairly narrow, and average about seven" (Johnson 1982:394). More elaborate linkages have also been suggested, but the pertinent generalizations refer to human decision making capabilities in situations in which consensual decision making, or human cooperation, is expected to occur.

As I noted in chapter 2, like *all* constants, "Johnson's constant" does not explain observable events or patterns. But, as I demonstrated in the course of building my two minimalist models, a knowledge of the existence of a constant—as well as its value—is basic to understanding what the world is like and how it works. Therefore, a constant facilitates efforts to develop an explanation of observed variability in the phenomena being studied.

For the moment, let us accept Johnson's argument that human actors have a limited ability to process information and that the information load to be processed is a function of the number of paired relationships within a group of deliberating persons. It is also assumed that consensually based decisions will be more likely to occur if each person in the group shares information and opinions with all other persons in the group on a one-to-one basis. Under these conditions, the equation[1] that yields the number of paired relationships to be considered by any one person is $(n^2 - n)/2$, where n equals group size (see Johnson 1982:392 for an expanded discussion of this point).

The information summarized in figure 9.01 suggests that the optimal size of such a deliberating body is six persons. Assuming that, in a real-world situation, the six persons embodying Johnson's constant are engaged together in the execution of a series of tasks, one would simply multiply the number 6—which in my example represents two work parties available on alternate days in a group with a collapsed division of labor—by the dependency ratio of 1.75 persons used in model building. The value of 10.5 persons would represent the size of such a group, assuming that dependents were eliminated from the decision making component of the group. This is an interesting value when it is recalled that the smallest mode of the bimodal distribution of GROUP1 sizes tabulated for terrestrial plant–dependent hunter-gatherers was 9.95 ± 1.58 persons.

The Group Size Model—which was based on assumptions about mobility minimization, the character of the division of labor, and individual work schedules—yielded a value of 10.23 persons for a group with a collapsed division of labor. It is interesting that, by using the model but substituting a maximizing assumption about decision making capabili-

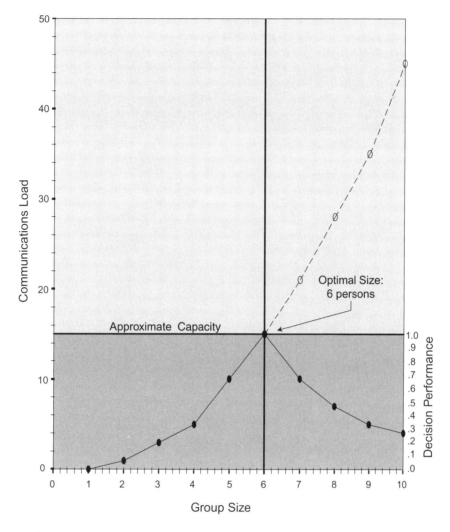

FIGURE 9.01

Scalar-communications stress and decision performance. Adapted and redrawn from Johnson (1982:395, figure 21.3).

ties in place of the assumption about mobility cost minimization, the same group size value results. Both forms of the model fit very well with the empirical data on plant-dependent peoples.

If the optimal size of a decision making group is doubled to include six adult women and six adult men—representing the labor force required in order for one-half of the producers to be available for work every other day—it must also be assumed that males make the decisions affecting male labor and females are responsible for decisions affecting female labor. The estimated size of such a group is 21 persons (12 * 1.75 or the assumed dependency ratio), while the mean group size observed in the ethnographic data set was 17.49 and the mobility-minimizing model anticipated 20.47 persons. This is another instance in which use of "Johnson's constant" results in provocative modeling and produces results that are

statistically consistent with the original estimates of my model.

EXPLORING THE DETAILS
OF JOHNSON'S ARGUMENT

In light of the excellent results produced by the Group Size Model when it includes an assumption that group size reflects efforts to maximize decision making rather than to minimize mobility costs, it becomes necessary to reexamine Johnson's argument (1982:391–92) that "population is not necessarily the best measure of scale." This statement implies that by organizing decision making activities into units made up of no more than six persons, it would be possible to integrate groups with very different total populations at similar

TABLE 9.01

PROPERTIES OF HUNTER-GATHERER SYSTEMS

GROUP NO.	NAME	SYSTATE3	MHSSET	MHSET2	FAMHOUS	G2MHS	G2MHSET2	G2MHSET3	G2BASORD	PREVALUE
1	Punan	5	2	3	1.68	4.93	1	1	3	7.98448
2	Batek	2	5	1	1.3	11.46	5	3	6	4.2059
3	Kubu	3					9			
4	Shompen	3	5	1	0.84	10.16	6	3	4	3.7508
5	Onge	4	1	2	8.5	0.88	2	4	3	6.61206
6	Jarwa	4	1	2		0.81	2	4	3	7.16103
7	Ayta (Pinatubo)	2	5	1	1.04	8.33	5	3	4	3.81822
8	Andaman	4	5	1	1.09	10.49	5	3	5	3.95306
9	Semang	3	1	2	8.77	1.19	2	4	4	8.76872
10	Vedda	4	5	1	1.1	6.86	4	2	3	5.07109
11	Hill Pandaran	3	5	1	1.39	7.35	4	2	4	5.4076
12	Agta (Casiguran)	3	5	1	1.21	6.93	4	2	3	5.13707
13	Agta (Isabela)	3	2	3		5.11	1	1	2	6.21994
14	Agta (Kagayan)	3	4	5	1.24	7.27	4	2	5	6.01463
15	Chenchu	2	5	1	1	12.06	5	3	5	4.03734
16	Mrabri	3	4	5	1.51	6.61	3	1	4	9.94507
17	Paliyans	3	5	1	0.81	7.55	5	3	3	3.64967
18	Birhor	3	5	1	0.65	15.81	6	3	5	4.00363
19	Kadar	3	2	3	2.05	3.48	1	1	4	8.31778
20	Cholanaickan	3	2	3	1	5.71	1	1	2	6.12191
21	Nayaka	3	5	1		19.17	6	3	6	4.39131
22	Ainu	5	5	1		6.59	3	1	4	8.0433
23	Orogens	1	4	5		9.51	4	2	6	7.11653
24	Ket	6	5	1		6.6	3	1	4	8.57266
25	Gilyak	6	3	4	2.51	8.65	4	2	7	9.09599
26	Yukaghir	2	3	4	1.92	7.01	4	2	6	6.78662
27	Nganasan	2	2	3		3.09	1	1	3	7.78842
28	Siberian Eskimo	6	2	3	2.12	3.5	1	1	4	8.96478
35	Paraujano	7								
36	Shiriana	4							5	
37	Akuriyo		4							
38	Pume	2	3	4	1.89	7.7	4	2	6	6.91858
39	Guahibo	2	4	5	1.19	8.65	4	2	6	7.11653
40	Nukak	4	5	1	1.3	9.04	4	2	5	6.25876
41	Bororo	2	3	4	2	12.04	4	2	8	10.94348
42	Guato	2	5	1	1.05	9.25	5	3	4	3.85193
43	Siriono	2	2	3	4.25	4.15	3	1	6	15.82685
44	Yuqui	4	5	1	1.03	9.71	5	3	5	3.95306
45	Nambikwara	2	4	5	1.6	8.16	4	2	5	6.25876
46	Calusa	7	1	2		1.72	2	4	6	14.25838
47	Guayaki (Ache)	4	5	1	1.19	14.42	6	3	6	4.23961
48	Botocudo	5	4	5		8	4	2	5	6.45671
49	Heta	4	2	3	1.19	6.32	2	1	3	7.98448
50	Aweikomo	5	2	3	3.97		1	1		
51	Tehuelche	1	3	4	1.96	7.65	4	2	7	8.10626
52	Chono	4								
53	Alacaluf	4			1.51					
54	Ona	4	2	3		5.49	2	1	5	10.92537
55	Yaghan	4	2	3		3.43	1	1	3	6.80812
60	Aka	3	5	1	0.93	12.08	6	3	4	3.83508
61	Bayaka	3	5	1	0.73	10.64	6	3	3	3.73394
62	Bambote	3	5	1	0.65	18.99	6	3	6	4.23961
63	Baka	3	5	1	0.79	9.14	5	3	4	3.7626
64	Efe	3	5	1	0	10.12	6	3	4	3.78451

PREDG2MH	G1FAMSZ	G2FAMSZ	G1MHS	POLYSCAL	POLPOS	CLASS	PEROGAT	MONEY	OCCSPE	COMMUN	COMSTFUN	OWNERS
6.35	6.09	8.31		2	3	1	2	1	1	4	1	1
4.21	4.88	14.91	3.752	2	3	1	1	1	1	2	1	4
				2	3	1	1	1	1	5	1	1
3.75	5.33	8.56	6.332	2	3	1	1	1	1	3	1	2
	3.27	7.52	0.882	2	1	1	1	1	1	1	1	1
			0.272	2	1	1	1	1	1	1	1	1
3.82	2.72	8.66	2.622	2	3	1	1	1	1	1	1	3
3.95	2.92	11.41	4.392	2	1	1	1	1	1	4	1	1
	5.21	10.43	0.592	2	3	1	1	1	1	4	1	1
5.07	3.64	7.53	3.312	2	3	1	1	1	1	5	1	1
5.41		10.24	2.161	1	3	1	1	1	1	3	1	1
5.14	4.76	8.4	3.931	1	3	1	1	1	1	1	1	1
4.48			2.921	1	3	1	1	1	1	1	1	1
6.01	3.93	9	3.171	1	3	1	1	1	1	4	1	1
4.04	4.85	12.06	4.852	2	3	1	1	1	1	5	1	1
8.42	4.88	10	3.222	2	3	1	1	1	1	3	1	1
3.65	3.43	6.13	4.232	2	3	1	1	1	1	5	1	1
4	5.97	10.24	9.212	2	3	1	1	4	1	5	1	2
6.7	3.95	7.16	1.921	1	3	1	1	1	1	5	1	1
4.37	2.84	5.71	2.84	1	3	1	1	1	1	3	1	1
4.39			3.83	1	3	1	1	4	1	5	1	2
6.41			3.28	3	1	1	2	1	2	2	1	3
7.12			3.17	2	2	2	2	1	1	1	1	1
6.97			4.8	3	2	2	3	1	1	3	1	4
9.1	5.54	21.69	2.21	3	1	2	1	1	2	2	1	2
6.79	3.01	13.48	1.57	2	2	1	1	1	1	2	1	4
6.14			1.49	2	2	1	2	1	1	2	1	3
7.39	3.18	7.42	1.5	2	1	2	2	1	2	2	1	3
				4	2	3	5	2	3	2	4	4
				2	1	1	1	1	1	1	1	1
				1	3	1	1	1	1	3	1	1
6.92	3.85	14.54	2.04	1	3	1	1	1	1	5	1	1
7.12	3.42	10.27	2.88	2	3	1	1	1	1	3	1	3
6.26	4.7	11.75	3.62	1	3	1	1	1	1	3	1	1
10.94		24.08		3	3	1	3	1	2	5	4	2
3.85	4.37	9.74	4.15	2	3	1	2	1	1	5	1	1
14.66	4.03	17.63	0.95	2	3	1	1	1	1	3	1	1
3.95	4.2	10.02	4.06	2	3	1	1	1	1	4	1	1
6.26	4.86	13.06	3.04	2	3	1	2	1	1	5	1	3
			0.97	4	3	3	5	2	3		7	4
4.24	7.63	17.14	6.42	2	1	1	1	1	1	3	1	3
6.46				3	1	1	2	1	1	4	1	1
6.35	5	7.5	2.11	2	3	1	1	1	1	4	1	1
	3.97		1	2	3	1	2	1	1	1	1	1
8.11	5	15	2.55	2	1	2	4	1	1	1	1	3
				2	1	1	1	1	1	1	1	2
	2.79		1.85	1	1	1	1	1	1	4	1	2
9.46			2.44	2	1	1	1	1	1	1	1	3
5.1			1.86	1	1	1	1	1	1	4	1	1
3.84	5.63	11.25	6.04	2	3	1	1	1	1	1	1	1
3.73	5.08	7.73	6.99	2	3	1	1	1	1	1	1	1
4.24	4.05	12.32	6.23	2	3	1	1	1	1	1	1	1
3.76	3.64	7.22	3.54	2	3	1	1	1	1	1	1	1
3.78			5.46	2	3	1	1	1	1	1	1	1

(continued)

TABLE 9.01 *(continued)*

GROUP NO.	NAME	SYSTATE3	MHSSET	MHSET2	FAMHOUS	G2MHS	G2MHSET2	G2MHSET3	G2BASORD	PREVALUE
65	Mbuti	3	5	1	1.05	23.21	6	3	8	4.98125
66	Mikea	3							4	
67	Hukwe	4							3	
68	Hai//om	2								
69	Hadza	4	5	1	0.81	11.57	5	3	5	3.93621
70	Dorobo	2	5	1	0.99	9.07	4	2	5	6.19278
71	Sekele	4	5	1		19.6	7	3	4	3.7508
72	!Kung	4	5	1	0.74	9.68	6	3	3	3.63787
73	Nharo	2	2	3		5.84	1	1	2	6.0631
74	G/wi	4	5	1		7.91	4	2	4	5.53296
75	Kua	4	2	3		4.58	1	1	2	6.18073
76	!Ko	4	5	1	0.77	14.4	6	3	6	4.13848
77	/Auni-khomani	4	2	3		4.67	1	1	2	6.21994
78	//Xegwi	4								
79	/Xam	4							3	
82	Kaurareg	2							5	
83	Larikia	4								
84	Gunwiggu	4	5	1	0.61	11.17	5	3	5	3.96992
85	Mirrngadja	4	2	3	0.91	6.14	2	1	4	8.76872
86	Anbarra	4							4	
87	Gidjingali	4	2	3	0.86	5.72	2	1	4	8.76872
88	Murngin	4							4	
89	Jeidji	4							4	
90	Wikmunkun	4							5	
91	Kakadu	4							4	
92	Nunggubuyu	4							3	
93	Yintjingga	4								
94	Yir-yoront	4	5	1	0.88	8.13	5	3	3	3.73394
95	Tiwi	4							4	
96	Kuku (Yalanji)	4								
97	Groote Eylandt	4	5	1	0.78	6.88	4	2	4	5.26904
98	Walmbaria	4	5	1		9.43	5	3	4	3.81822
99	Mulluk	6							3	
100	Worora	4							4	
101	Lungga	4								
102	Lardil	4	5	1	0.55	12.97	6	3	5	3.98678
103	Kaiadilt	4							3	
104	Karadjeri	4								
105	Mamu	4							5	
106	Kariera	4							4	
107	Warunggu	4							3	
108	Djaru	4							5	
109	Walbiri	4	5	1	0.86	10.88	5	3	5	3.93621
110	Ngatjan	4							4	
111	Mardudjara	4	2	3	0.79	6.07	2	1	3	7.00418
112	Ildawongga	4								
113	Pintubi	4	2	3	0.65	4.85	1	1	6.21994	6.22
114	Undambi	4								
115	Jinibarra	5							6	
116	Karuwali	4								
117	Alyawara	4	2	3	0.75	5.93	2	1	3	7.98448
118	Ngatatjara	4	2	3	0.72	5.58	1	1	3	7.00418
119	Badjalang	4							7	
120	Pitjandjara	4	2	3	0.83	4	1	1	3	6.61206
121	Dieri	4							2	
122	Southern Arenda	4					4	2		

PREDG2MH	G1FAMSZ	G2FAMSZ	G1MHS	POLYSCAL	POLPOS	CLASS	PEROGAT	MONEY	OCCSPE	COMMUN	COMSTFUN	OWNERS
4.98	7.06	24.3	6.74	2	3	1	1	1	1	1	1	1
				1	3	1	1	1	1	4	1	1
				2	3	1	1	3	1	3	1	1
				2	3	1	1	1	1	3	1	1
3.94	3.67	9.33	4.55	1	3	1	1	1	1	4	1	1
6.19	3.31	8.95	3.35	2	3	1	1	1	1	5	2	1
3.75			4.8	1	3	1	1	1	1	2	1	1
3.64	3.09	7.21	4.14	1	1	1	1	1	1	4	1	1
4.31				2	1	1	1	1	1	3	1	1
5.53			1.23	2	1	1	1	1	1	3	1	1
4.43			1.76	2	3	1	1	1	1	3	1	1
4.14	2.65	11.02	3.47	2	1	1	1	1	1	3	1	1
4.48			2	2	1	1	1	1	1	3	1	1
				2	3	1	1	1	1	2	1	1
				2	3	1	1	1	1	4	1	1
				2	3	1	1	1	2	1	1	2
				2	1	1	1	1	1	5	1	1
3.97	2.88	6.85	4.7	2	1	1	1	1	1	5	1	1
7.18	2.62	5.57	2.89	2	1	1	1	1	1	5	1	1
				1	1	1	1	1	1	5	1	1
7.18	2.32	4.93	2.69	1	1	1	1	1	1	5	1	1
				2	1	1	1	1	1	3	1	3
				2	1	1	1	1	1	3	1	1
				2	1	1	1	1	1	3	1	1
				1	1	1	1	1	1	3	1	2
				2	1	1	1	1	1	5	1	3
				1	1	1	1	1	1	5	1	3
3.73	3.4	7.14	3.88	1	1	1	1	1	1	3	1	1
	2.43	4.32		2	1	1	1	1	1	3	1	3
	2.04			1	1	1	1	1	1	3	1	1
5.27	1.67	5.33	2.15	2	1	1	1	1	1	3	1	1
3.82				2	1	1	1	1	1	5	1	3
				2	1	2	1	1	1	4	1	1
				1	1	1	1	1	1	5	1	1
				1	1	1	1	1	1	3	1	1
3.99		7.11		2	1	1	1	1	1	3	1	2
	3.34	6.29		2	1	1	1	1	1	3	1	2
				1	1	1	1	1	1	3	1	1
				3	1	1	1	1	1	4	1	2
				1	1	1	1	1	1	3	1	1
				2	1	1	1	1	1	3	1	1
	2.4	7.51		1	1	1	1	1	1	3	1	1
3.94	2	9.31	2.33	1	1	1	1	1	1	3	1	1
				2	1	1	1	1	1	4	1	2
5.31	1.54	4.81	1.94	1	1	1	1	1	1	3	1	1
	1.66			1	1	1	1	1	1	3	1	1
4.48	1.27	3.14	1.96	1	1	1	1	1	1	4	1	1
				3	1	1	1	1	1	5	1	1
				3	1	1	1	1	1	5	1	2
				1	1	1	1	1	1	3	1	1
6.35	2.37	4.44	3.16	1	1	1	1	1	1	3	1	1
5.31	1.78	4.05	2.46	1	1	1	1	1	1	4	1	1
				2	1	1	1	1	1	4	1	2
4.89	1.44	3.3	1.74	1	1	1	1	1	1	4	1	1
				2	1	1	1	1	1	3	1	1
				1	1	1	1	1	1	3	1	1

(continued)

GROUP NO.	NAME	SYSTATE3	MHSSET	MHSET2	FAMHOUS	G2MHS	G2MHSET2	G2MHSET3	G2BASORD	PREVALUE
123	Jankundjara	4							3	
124	Northern Arenda	4							3	
125	Ualarai	4								
126	Nakako	4								
127	Ooldea	4								
128	Barkindji	4								
129	Kaurna	4								
130	Wongaibon	4								
131	Jaralde	4								
132	Mineng	4	4	5		7.51	4	2	5	6.45671
133	Tjapwurong	6	5	1	0.89	35	7	3	10	6.178
134	Bunurong	4	5	1	0.84	8.8	4	2	5	6.06082
135	Kurnai	4							5	
136	Tasmanians (southern)	4	2	3		5.1	2	1	4	8.96478
137	Tasmanians (northwestern)	4	2	3		3.88	1	1	4	8.57266
143	Seri	5	4	5	1.17	6.94	4	2	5	6.1268
144	Cahuilla	2	3	4		8.06	4	2	7	8.10626
145	Cupeno	5	4	5		15.04	5	3	8	4.86326
146	Kiliwa	4	4	5		8.61	4	2	6	7.24849
147	Diegueno	5							4	
148	Lake Yokuts	6							7	
149	Serrano	6							6	
150	Luiseno	6							8	
151	Wukchumi	4	5	1		13.33	6	3	4	3.9025
152	Tubatulabal	5	2	3	1.84	3	1	1	2	6.21994
153	Nomlaki	6							6	
154	Yokuts (northern)	6	2	3		6.22	3	1	4	9.94507
155	Patwin	6	5	1		15.27	6	3	6	4.12162
156	Gabrieleno	7								
157	Monachi	5	2	3		6.21	2	1	4	8.3766
158	Eastern Pomo	6								
159	Pomo Clear Lake	6	3	4	2.75	11.49	4	2	9	13.05491
160	Wintu	6	5	1		12.5	5	3	5	4.07105
161	Chumash	7	4	5		58.63	6	3	13	12.61681
162	Chimariko	4							5	
163	Nisenan	6	5	1		12.47	6	3	5	3.98678
164	Salinan	6								
165	Southern Pomo	6							9	
166	Sinkyone	6	2	3		5.23	1	1	3	6.61206
167	Lassik	6								
168	Coast Miwok	5	2	3		4.16	1	1	3	7.20024
169	Mattole	6							5	
170	Lake Miwok	6							7	
171	Yuki Proper	6	2	3	1.66	4.45	1	1	3	7.00418
172	Wappo	6	4	5	1.86	11.36	4	2	8	9.425
173	Nothern Pomo	6	5	1		33.78	7	3	9	5.36893
174	Northern Yana	6								
175	Sierra Miwok	4	5	1		8.86	4	2	5	6.1268
176	Tekelma	6	2	3		6	3	1	5	11.90567
177	Coast Yuki	5								
178	Tolowa	6	4	5		12	4	2	8	9.49188
179	Shasta	6	2	3		6	3	1	5	11.51355
180	Hupa	6	5	1		17.66	5	3	8	5.13295

PREDG2MH	G1FAMSZ	G2FAMSZ	G1MHS	POLYSCAL	POLPOS	CLASS	PEROGAT	MONEY	OCCSPE	COMMUN	COMSTFUN	OWNERS
	1.46	4.31		1	1	1	1	1	1	4	1	2
	1.5	4.69		1	1	1	1	1	1	3	1	2
				2	1	1	1	1	1	3	1	1
	1.33			1	1	1	1	1	1	4	1	1
				2	1	1	1	1	1	1	1	2
				1	1	1	1	1	1	3	1	1
				1	1	1	1	1	1	5	1	2
				2	1	1	1	1	1	3	1	2
				3	1	1	1	1	1	5	1	2
6.46			1.95	1	1	1	1	1	1	3	1	2
6.18	4.46	31.19	5	3	1	1	1	1	1		1	3
6.06	1.23	7.42	1.46	1	1	1	1	1	1	4	1	3
				2	1	1	1	1	1	5	1	3
7.39			1.09	2	1	1	1	1	1		1	1
6.97			0.88	1	1	1	1	1	1		1	1
6.13	3.07	8.14	2.62	2	3	1	2	1	2	1	1	1
8.11			2.15	3	3	1	3	1	1	2	2	3
4.86				3	3	1	2	4	1	2	2	2
7.25				2	1	1	1	1	1	5	2	1
				3	1	1	2	1	1	5	1	3
				3	1	2	3	4	1	2	3	3
				3	1	2	2	3	2	5	2	2
				3	1	2	3	3	1	2	2	3
3.9				3	1	1	3	4	1	1	3	2
4.48	2.62	5.51	1.43	2	2	1	3	4	1	1	2	2
				3	1	2	2	4	2	2	5	2
8.42			2.49	3	1	2	3	3	1	2	3	3
4.12				3	1	2	4	4	2	2	6	2
				2	1	3	5	4	2	2	2	3
6.76			2.52	2	2	1	2	3	1	1	3	2
				3	1	2	4	4	2	2	4	3
13.05		31.58		3	1	2	4	4	3	2	4	4
4.07			5	3	1	2	4	4	2	2	6	3
12.62				4	1	3	5	4	3	2	2	3
				3	1	1	1	3	2	1	4	2
3.99			3.05	3	1	2	4	4	1	1	5	3
				3	1	2	4	4	3	2	3	3
				3	1	2	4	4	3	2	3	2
4.89				3	1	2	1	4	2	1	3	2
				3	1	2	2	4	3	1	3	2
5.51				3	1	1	4	4	3	1	3	2
				3	1	1	1	4	2	1	3	2
				3	1	2		4	3	2	6	2
5.31		7.4		3	1	2	4	4	2	2	5	3
9.43		21.11		3	1	2	4	4	2	2	4	2
5.37				3	1	2	4	4	2	2	6	2
				3	2	2	4	3	2	4	6	3
6.13			3.74	3	1	1	3	3	1	4	6	2
10.5			2.16	2	1	2	1	4	2	2	2	2
				2	1	1	1	3	1	1	6	2
9.49			2.25	2	1	2	1	4	3	2	3	3
10.09				2	1	2	2	3	2	5	5	3
5.13				2	2	2	1	4	3	1	5	2

(continued)

GROUP NO.	NAME	SYSTATE3	MHSSET	MHSET2	FAMHOUS	G2MHS	G2MHSET2	G2MHSET3	G2BASORD	PREVALUE
181	Coastal Tututni	6							6	
182	Karok	6	2	3		4	1	1	3	7.98448
183	Atsugewi	6								
184	Wiyot	6	2	3		3.59	1	1	4	8.57266
185	Mountain Maidu	6	4	5		6.67	3	1	4	9.94507
186	Yurok	6	2	3		6.03	3	1	5	10.92537
187	Achomawi	6							3	
188	Modoc	6	3	4		9.2	4	2	7	9.22795
189	Klamath	6	2	3		3.13	1	1	4	8.18054
190	Guaicura	4							5	
191	Chichimec	4								
192	Death Valley	4	2	3		5.71	1	1	2	6.51403
193	Karankawa	5			2.03					
194	Coahuilenos	4	5	1		14.86	6	3	5	3.91935
195	Panamint	4	2	3	0.72	5.61	1	1	2	6.51403
196	Yavapai	2	5	1		32.42	7	3	8	5.03182
197	Koso Mountain	4							6	
198	Walapai	2	2	3	1.59	4.96	1	1	3	7.55315
199	Kawaiisu	4	2	3		4.68	1	1	4	8.18054
200	Saline Valley	4							3	
201	Antarianunts	4							3	
202	Eastern Mono	4	5	1	1.34	13.06	5	3	6	4.30703
203	Kawich Mountain	4							2	
204	Kaibab	4	2	3		5.18	1	1	2	6.25916
205	Mono Lake	4	2	3		6.54	2	1	3	7.00418
206	Deep Springs	4	2	3		5	1	1	3	6.61206
207	Salmon Eater	4	5	1	1.47	7.08	4	2	4	5.401
208	Kuyuidokado	4	5	1	1.29	11.36	5	3	5	4.07105
209	Ute-timpanogas	1							5	
210	Cattail Eater	4	5	1		10.36	5	3	5	4.00363
211	Fish Lake	4	2	3	1.25	6.16	2	1	3	7.3963
212	Honey Lake	4								
213	Hukundika	4	2	3		5.54	1	1	3	6.80812
214	Gosiute	4							4	
215	Spring Valley	4	2	3		5.3	1	1	3	6.80812
216	White Knife	4	2	3	0.82	5.58	1	1	3	6.61206
217	Railroad Valley	4	5	1		7.64	4	2	4	5.26904
218	Reese River	4							3	
219	North Fork Mono	6	5	1	0.87	6.79	4	2	3	5.07109
221	Grouse Creek	4	5	1	0.95	9.11	5	3	4	3.86879
222	Southern Ute	1	5	1		7.4	4	2	4	5.59895
223	Bear Creek	4							4	
224	Antelope Valley	4	2	3	0.98	4.68	1	1	2	6.02388
225	Washo	4	5	1		7.25	4	2	3	5.07109
226	Kidutokado	5							3	
227	Wind River Shoshoni	4							5	
228	Wadadika	5							5	
229	Bohogue	1							6	
230	Uintah Ute	1	2	3	2.52	5.58	2	1	5	10.53325
231	Wadadokado	5			0.79					
232	Agaiduka	4								
233	Little Smokey	4								
234	Uncompahgre Ute	1	4	5		7.55	4	2	5	6.1268
240	Lipan Apache	1	5	1		15	5	3	7	4.49244

PREDG2MH	G1FAMSZ	G2FAMSZ	G1MHS	POLYSCAL	POLPOS	CLASS	PEROGAT	MONEY	OCCSPE	COMMUN	COMSTFUN	OWNERS
				2	1	2	4	4	2	2	3	2
6.35				3	1	2	1	4	3	2	5	2
				2	2	2	4	3	1	4	5	3
6.97				3	1	2	1	4	3	1	3	2
8.42				2	1	2	1	3	1	5	5	3
9.46				2	1	2	1	4	3	1	3	2
				2	2	2	2	3	1	4	5	3
9.23			1.5	2	1	2	1	4	2	2	2	3
6.55			1.82	2	1	2	1	3	2	2	2	3
				2	1	1	1	1	1	3	1	1
				2	3	1	1	1	1	1	1	1
4.79			1.9	1	1	1	1	3	1	1	1	1
				3	1	1	2	1	1	4	1	3
3.92			3.26	1	1	1	1	1	1	4	1	1
4.79	1.34	4.02	1.87	2	1	1	1	3	1	4	2	1
5.03				3	1	1	3	1	1	5	1	1
				2	1	1	1	3	1	4	1	1
5.89	1.98	7.88	1.25	2	1	1	3	1	1	4	2	3
6.55			1.87	3	2	1	1	3	1	1	2	1
				2	1	1	1	1	1	1	2	1
				2	1	1	1	1	1	1	1	1
4.31	3.54	17.44	2.65	3	1	1	4	3	1	2	3	1
				1	1	1	1	1	1	4	1	1
4.52			2.47	1	1	1	1	1	1	4	1	1
5.31			2.51	2	2	1	1	3	1	4	1	1
4.89				2	1	1	1	3	1	1	2	1
5.4	3.43	10.4	2.33	2	1	1	1	1	1	5	1	1
4.07		14.66		2	1	1	1	1	1	1	1	1
				3	1	1	2	1	1	1	2	1
4			4.05	2	1	1	1	1	1	1	1	1
5.72	3	7.71	2.4	2	1	1	1	1	1	1	1	1
				1	2	1	1	3	1	1	1	1
5.1				2	1	1	2	1	1	1	1	1
				1	1	1	1	1	1	1	1	1
5.1			2.43	2	1	1	1	1	1	5	1	1
4.89	2.28	4.6	2.77	1	1	1	1	1	1	5	1	1
5.27			2.63	2	1	1	1	1	1	5	1	1
				2	1	1	1	1	1	5	1	1
5.07		5.88		2	1	2	4	3	1	4	3	2
3.87	3.65	8.68	3.84	2	1	1	1	1	1	1	1	1
5.6				3	1	1	2	1	1	1	1	1
				1	1	1	1	1	1	1	1	1
4.27	2.86	4.58	2.93	1	1	1	1	1	1	5	1	1
5.07			2.25	2	1	1	1	1	1	1	1	1
				2	1	1	2	1	1	1	1	1
				3	2	1	3	1	1	2	1	1
				2	1	1	2	1	1	5	1	1
				3	1	2	2	1	1	2	1	3
9.05	5.23	14.05	2.08	3	1	1	2	1	1	1	2	1
	2.08		2.63	2	1	1	2	1	1	1	2	1
			2.03	2	1	1	1	1	1	1	1	1
			3.38	1	1	1	1	1	1	5	1	1
6.13			2.85	1	1	2	1	1	4	2	1	
4.49			5	3	1	1	1	1	1	2	1	3

(continued)

GROUP NO.	NAME	SYSTATE3	MHSSET	MHSET2	FAMHOUS	G2MHS	G2MHSET2	G2MHSET3	G2BASORD	PREVALUE
241	Comanche	1	5	1		42.83	7	3	11	7.76242
242	Chiricahua Apache	1							8	
243	Kiowa Apache	1	4	5		40.08	6	3	12	8.50406
244	Kiowa	1							12	
245	Cheyenne	1	4	5	1.04	34.68	6	3	11	7.86355
246	Arapaho	1	4	5		44.16	6	3	12	8.70633
248	Crow	1	4	5		37.5	6	3	12	8.7906
249	Teton Sioux	1	4	5		32.34	6	3	11	7.99839
250	Kutenai	1							8	
252	Bannock	1	4	5		28.33	6	3	10	6.09372
253	Gros-Ventre	1	4	5		23.27	5	3	10	6.39712
254	Bungi	1							11	
255	Peigan	1	4	5		31.59	6	3	11	7.50958
256	Blackfoot	1	4	5		43.74	6	3	12	9.06029
257	Assiniboine	1	4	5		20	5	3	9	5.90831
258	Plains Cree	1	5	1		17.52	6	3	7	4.49244
259	Blood	1	4	5		31.25	6	3	11	7.44216
260	Sarsi	1	4	5		18.54	5	3	9	5.58805
268	Squamish	6							8	
269	Alsea	6								
270	Puyallup	6	2	3	6	4.83	3	1	9	30.53131
271	Twana	6							7	
272	Chehalis	6	2	3		4.23	3	1	8	23.66923
273	Central Nootka	7	2	3	9.01	4.88	3	1	10	40.33427
274	Chinook	6	2	3		2.6	2	4	6	12.29778
275	Coos	6							6	
276	Lillooet	7	3	4		8.95	4	2	7	8.76608
277	Lummi	7	3	4		8.75	4	2	9	12.39509
278	Quinault	6			4	1.95	2	4	4	9.16083
279	Stalo	6	2	3			1	1	4	9.35689
280	Cowichan	6							4	
281	Tillamook	6	2	3		4.64	3	1	6	14.84656
282	Comox	7							11	
283	Bella-Bella	7							10	
284	Quileute	6	2	3		4.67	3	1	8	24.06135
285	Klallam	7	3	4		11.09	4	2	10	14.11062
286	Makah	7	3	4	4.65	11.26	4	2	9	13.97865
287	Haisla	7							13	
288	Kwakiutl	7	3	4		15.91	4	2	13	30.87003
289	Tsimshim	7	4	5		40.39	6	3	13	9.78508
290	Haida	7	3	4		37.23	5	3	13	12.95392
291	Bella-Coola	7							6	
292	Tlingit	7	3	4		10.37	4	2	10	16.15606
293	Gitksan	7	4	5		20.04	5	3	10	6.24542
294	Konaig	7	3	4		9.53	4	2	9	13.84669
295	Eyak	6	2	3	3.15	3.48	2	1	6	13.27808
296	Kuskowagmut	6	3	4		7.91	4	2	8	10.28366
297	Chugach	7	2	3		4.54	2	1	6	12.59187
298	Aleut	7	2	3		3.13	2	1	6	12.88596
299	Nunivak	6	2	3	2.57	5.1	2	1	6	12.80754
315	Yenino	6								
316	Umatilla	6								
317	Wenatchi	6							11	
318	Yakima	6								
319	Wishram	6	4	5		20.5	5	3	10	6.68366

PREDG2MH	G1FAMSZ	G2FAMSZ	G1MHS	POLYSCAL	POLPOS	CLASS	PEROGAT	MONEY	OCCSPE	COMMUN	COMSTFUN	OWNERS
7.76			9.55	3	1	2	3	1	1	2	1	3
				3	1	1	1	1	1	2	2	3
8.5			4.48	3	1	1	3	1	1	2	2	3
				3	1	1	3	1	1	2	2	1
7.86	5.91	36.09	5.67	4	1	2	3	1	1	2	1	3
8.71			4.89	3	1	1	2	1	1	2	1	3
8.79			7.5	3	1	2	3	1	1	3	1	3
8			4.34	4	1	2	3	1	1	3	1	3
				3	1	2	2	1	1	2	2	3
6.09			7.17	3	1	2	2	1	1	2	1	3
6.4			4.21	3	1	2	3	1	3	2	1	1
				3	1	1	3	1	1	2	1	1
7.51			5.6	3	1	2	3	1	1	2	1	1
9.06			8.85	3	1	2	3	1	1	2	1	1
5.91			6.92	3	1	1	3	1	1	2	1	1
4.49			9.35	3	1	1	2	1	1	2	1	1
7.44			5.25	3	1	2	3	1	1	2	1	1
5.59			5.7	3	1	1		1	1	2	1	1
				2	1	2	4	2	3	1	1	2
				2	1	2	4	3	2	2	2	2
30.25	5.6	29	0.93	2	1	2	4	1	3	2	5	4
		22.16		3	1	2	3	1	3	2	5	4
22.97				2	1	2	2	1	4	2	1	4
40.64		43.92		4	1	3	5	2	4	2	5	4
				3	1	2	4	4	3	1	3	4
				3	2	2	5	4	3	2	3	4
8.77				3	1	3	2	2	1	2	1	4
12.4				3	1	3	2	2	4	2	1	2
		7.81		2	1	3	4	4	3	2	2	4
7.8		7.79		2	1	2	4	2	2	2	1	4
				2	2	2	3	2	2	2	1	4
13.62				2	1	2	2	3	3	2	1	4
				3	2	3	3	3	4	2	1	4
				4	1	3	5	2	4	2	1	3
23.39			1.21	2	1	3	3	4	3	1	1	4
14.11				3	2	3	3	2	2	2	1	3
13.98		52.4		3	2	3	3	2	3	2	1	3
				3	1	3	3	2	3	2	1	3
30.87				3	1	3	4	2	4	1	1	4
9.79				4	1	3	4	2	4	2	1	4
12.95				4	1	3	4	2	4	2	1	4
				4	1	3	4	2	4	1	1	4
16.16				4	1	3	4	2	4	2	1	4
6.25				3	2	3	4	2	4	2	1	4
13.85				3	1	3	3	2	2	2	4	3
11.96		10.96		3	2	2	4	2	3	2	5	3
10.28			1.39	3	1	2	2	1	1	5	4	3
11.23				3	1	3	5	1	4	2	4	4
11.54				4	1	3	4	2	3	2	1	3
11.46		13.09		4	1	2	1	1	1	2	4	4
				2	2	2	2	1	1	2	1	3
				3	2	2	3	1	1	1	1	3
				2	2	2	3	1	1	2	2	3
				3	2	1	3	1	1	1	1	3
6.68			2.5	3	1	2	3	2	2	2	3	3

(continued)

TABLE 9.01 *(continued)*

GROUP NO.	NAME	SYSTATE3	MHSSET	MHSET2	FAMHOUS	G2MHS	G2MHSET2	G2MHSET3	G2BASORD	PREVALUE
320	Coeur d'Alene	6	4	5	2	8.38	4	2	6	7.11653
321	Sinkaietk	7	2	3	5.71	3.97	3	1	7	18.37563
322	Okanagon	6								
323	Sanpoil	5	2	3		4.5	2	1	5	11.90567
324	Nez Perce	6							9	
325	Thompson	6	2	3		5.02	3	1	8	24.25741
326	Kalispel	6	4	5	2	10.36	4	2	7	8.10626
327	Kitchibaun	5	2	3	2	3.57	1	1	6	14.84656
328	Katikitegon	4	5	1		14	5	3	7	4.5093
329	Micmac	6	2	3	1.32	3.47	1	1	3	7.00418
330	Flathead	6	2	3		6.02	3	1	7	16.41503
331	Rainy River Ojibwa	5	3	4	1.95	6.95	4	2	6	6.91858
332	North Saulteaux	5	2	3		5.36	2	1	5	10.92537
333	Shuswap	1							8	
334	Pekangekum	3	3	4		6.71	3	1	6	12.88596
335	Round Lake Ojibwa	3	5	1		9.8	5	3	5	4.07105
336	Alkatcho	7	3	4		8.1	4	2	7	8.76608
337	Ojibwa Nipigon	6							4	
338	Mistassini Cree	3	2	3	1.94	6.14	2	1	4	9.35689
339	Northern Ojibwa (Albany)	3							5	
340	Waswanipi Cree	3							6	
341	Ojibwa-weagamon	3							5	
342	Montagnais	5	2	3	2.27	6.33	3	1	8	20.72834
343	Sekani	1							4	
344	Beaver	4							6	
345	Slave	4	4	5		7.56	4	2	4	5.73091
346	Kaska	4							6	
347	Tahltan	6							7	
348	Chilcotin	7								
349	Carrier	7	2	3		4.15	2	1	6	12.6899
350	Mountain	4							6	
351	Han	6			2					
352	Hare	4	2	3		5.49	1	1	3	7.20024
353	Attawapiskat Cree	4	4	5	1.44	9.17	4	2	6	6.78662
354	Koyukon	4	2	3	3.21	2.49	2	1	4	9.55295
355	Chippewyan	4	3	4	1.99	8.33	4	2	7	8.10626
356	Kutchin	6	4	5	2	10	4	2	7	8.30421
357	Ingalik	5	2	3		4.3	3	1	7	17.19927
358	Satudene-Bear Lake	4	2	3		5.03	1	1	3	7.78842
359	Nabesna	5	2	3	1.8	4.88	2	1	4	9.74901
360	Rupert House Cree	3							6	
361	Dogrib	4	5	1		15	6	3	6	4.23961
362	Tanaina	7	2	3		3.79	3	1	6	15.43473
363	Tutchone	6							6	
364	Holikachuk	6	2	3	3.69	4.4	3	1	6	15.04262
365	Naskapi	4	2	3	1.73	4.7	2	1	4	9.74901
369	Norton Sound	6							5	
370	Kobuk Eskimo	5	2	3	1.61	4.14	1	1	3	7.98448
371	Kotzebue Sound	6	2	3	2	5	2	1	5	11.70961
372	Labrador Eskimo	5	1	2	4	1.54	2	4	4	8.96478
373	Great Whale	6	4	5		6.91	4	2	4	5.79689
374	Caribou Eskimo	4	2	3	1.65	5.63	2	1	4	9.94507
375	Noatak Eskimo	4	2	3	2.5	4	1	1	3	7.98448
377	Nunamiut Eskimo	4	2	3	1.6	3.35	1	1	3	7.02379

PREDG2MH	G1FAMSZ	G2FAMSZ	G1MHS	POLYSCAL	POLPOS	CLASS	PEROGAT	MONEY	OCCSPE	COMMUN	COMSTFUN	OWNERS
7.12	5.87	16.76	2.93	3	1	2	2	1	2	1	2	3
17.36	5.46	22.68	0.96	2	1	3	3	1	1	1	2	3
5				2	1	2	2	1	1	1	2	3
10.5				2	1	1	3	1	1	2	2	3
				3	1	2	3	1	1	2	3	3
23.6			0.8	3	2	2	3	1	1	1	2	3
8.11	6.08	20.72	3.04	3	2	1	3	1	1	1	1	3
13.62	4.29	7.14	2.14	2	1	1	2	1	1	5	1	4
4.51				3	1	1	1	1	1	2	2	4
5.31	2.75	4.59	2.08	3	1	2	4	1	1	1	1	3
15.28			1.98	3	1	2	3	1	1	2	1	3
6.92	5	13.57	2.56	2	2	1	2	1	1	5	1	1
9.46			1.79	2	3	1	2	1	1	5	1	1
				3	1	2	3	2	2	2	1	2
11.54			2.68	2	3	1	2	1	1	5	1	1
4.07			1.37	2	3	1	2	1	1	2	1	1
8.77			1.9	3	2	3	5	2	3	2	2	2
				2	3	2	2	1	1	5	1	1
7.8	4.82	11.9	2.49	2	3	1	2	1	1	2	1	3
				2	3	1	2	1	1	2	1	1
	2.12	10.27		2	3	1	2	1	1	2	1	1
				2	3	1	2	1	1	5	1	1
19.86	3.33	14.39	1.47	2	1	1	2	1	1	5	1	1
				2	1	1	1	1	1	1	1	1
	5.17	14.99		2	1	1	1	1	1	5	1	1
5.73			2.52	2	1	1	1	1	1	2	1	1
	4.66	16.91		1	2	1	1	1	1	2	1	1
				3	2	2	3	2	2	2	1	2
				2	2	3	1	2	2	2	1	2
11.33			1.38	3	2	3	5	2	2	2	1	2
	3.18	12.71		1	1	1	1	1	1	2	1	2
				2	1	2	2	2	1	2	1	2
5.51			2.74	2	1	1	1	1	1	2	1	1
6.79	4.07	13.16	2.83	2	3	1	1	1	1	2	1	1
8.01	2.95	8	0.92	2	1	1	1	2	2	2	4	2
8.11	5.09	16.59	2.56	2	1	1	1	1	1	5	1	3
8.3	8.21	20	4.1	2	1	2	2	1	1	2	1	3
16.12				3	1	1	2	1	1	1	4	4
6.14			2.17	2	1	1	1	1	1	2	1	1
8.22	3.82	8.76	2.13	3	1	1	2	1	2	2	4	2
	2.34	10.72		2	3	1	1	1	1	5	1	1
4.24			5.5	2	1	1	1	1	1	2	1	1
14.24				3	1	3	4	2	2	2	3	2
	5.11	18.02		2	2	2	1	2	1	2	2	2
13.83		16.22		3	1	2	2	1	1	2	4	2
8.22	4.78	8.11	2.77	2	1	1	1	1	1	2	1	1
				3	1	2	2	1	1	5	4	3
6.35	4	6.67	2.48	2	1	1	2	1	1	2	4	1
10.3	5	10	2.5	3	1	2	2	2	1	2	4	2
	1.93	6.14	0.48	2	1	1	2	1	1	2	4	2
5.8			3.45	2	1	2	2	1	1	2	4	1
8.42	4.52	9.28	2.75	2	1	1	1	1	1	1	1	1
6.35	5.83	10	2.33	2	1	1	1	1	1	1	1	1
5.33	3.94	5.35	2.47	2	1	1	1	1	1	1	1	1

(continued)

TABLE 9.01 *(continued)*

GROUP NO.	NAME	SYSTATE3	MHSSET	MHSET2	FAMHOUS	G2MHS	G2MHSET2	G2MHSET3	G2BASORD	PREVALUE
378	Mackenzie Eskimo	6	2	3		4.09	2	1	5	10.92537
379	Sivokamiut	6	4	5		17.93	5	3	8	5.2678
380	Point Hope Eskimo	6	4	5	2.4	21.96	5	3	10	6.24542
381	Copper Eskimo	4	5	1	1.62	18.99	5	3	8	4.99811
382	Utkuhikhalingmiut	4	2	3	2.16	4.2	1	1	4	8.96478
383	Aivilingmiut	4	2	3	1.89	4.52	1	1	3	7.20024
384	Iglulik	4	4	5	2.31	8.51	4	2	6	7.11653
385	West Greenland	4	2	3	1.71	3.82	1	1	4	8.27857
386	Baffin Island	4	4	5	1.83	10	4	2	6	7.77635
387	Netsilik Eskimo	4	5	1	1.49	15.23	5	3	7	4.661
388	Angmaksalik	4	1	2		1.29	2	4	4	8.16093
389	Tareumiut	6	5	1		54.02	7	3	12	8.43664
390	Polar Eskimo	4	2	3	1.47	6.03	2	1	4	8.96478

organizational scales. This is particularly true if there is some leeway in the demand that the optimal number of persons occur in each and every unit.

Johnson illustrated his thesis using information about seasonal variability in social groupings among the Ju/'hoans, or !Kung speakers, of the Dobe area in Botswana. He noted that during the rainy season groups were composed of segmented nuclear families (comparable to GROUP1 units), whereas in dry-season camps the basal segments of organization were extended families composed of several nuclear families. By shifting the basic decision making unit in the large camps to extended families, larger populations could be organized and, at the same time, the size of decision making units (made up of representatives of the extended families) could be maintained at six persons.

In this example, a reorganization occurs within a system of basal units involving what I would refer to as GROUP1 and GROUP2 units. Organizational dynamics of this kind are not unprecedented (see my arguments about internal organizational shifting in Binford 1972; 1983; Binford and Binford 1966) and have been reported by Gearing (1962) and Mauss and Beuchat (1979).

Another of Johnson's observations implicates between-system or "system state" variability itself. In proposition 9.01, Johnson states that if scale indicators are compared with group size population values, local variation accounts for many of the differences among small-scale systems. Support for this proposition comes from the GROUP1 data set, in which group size varies considerably between peoples exploiting different resources and living in environments with different productivity levels (generalization 8.01). GROUP1 size is also responsive to levels of political development and scales of residential mobility (generalizations 8.02 and 8.04). Much of this variability can be related to shifts in labor organization re-

flected in the division of labor and the contribution of each gender to subsistence and to differences in the level of polygyny. Presumably this is what Johnson has in mind when he speaks of "local variation."

Macroscale differences in population levels may also be important indicators of organizational and system state differences. This is particularly true if populational values are distributed multimodally or are arrayed in a punctuated pattern of change with respect to social groupings of different sizes that appear to be temporally clustered. Thus far in my analysis, however, I have not been able to see variability at this larger scale. Perhaps the fact that, up to this point, differences in population values have appeared to result from local variability—in Johnson's terms—should prompt an expansion of the purview and scale of my inquiry.

At the time that I began to read extensively in the ethnographic literature and to develop a list of attribute codes for recording relevant data, neither did I appreciate the organizational implications of the variability among hunter-gatherers nor had I developed the ideas that have been presented in this and previous chapters. I therefore did not attempt to identify "basic organizational units," in Johnson's terms, nor did I really think much about sequential hierarchies or nested segmental forms of organization. Largely for other reasons, I nevertheless made a number of observations that are germane to the issues that Johnson raises. I have already presented data on family size and mean household size (table 8.08); identified three types of on-the-ground groups, which have been labeled GROUP1, GROUP2, and GROUP3 (tables 5.01 and 8.01); and have estimated the total population of each ethnic group in the world sample (TLPOP values in table 5.01). I also coded a number of relevant variables that have not yet been formally introduced in this book, although a few of these were identified when-

PREDG2MH	G1FAMSZ	G2FAMSZ	G1MHS	POLYSCAL	POLPOS	CLASS	PEROGAT	MONEY	OCCSPE	COMMUN	COMSTFUN	OWNERS
9.46			1.09	2	1	2	1	1	1	2	4	3
5.27			2.81	2	1	2	1	1	2	2	4	1
6.25	3.83	52.8	1.6	2	1	2	2	1	1	2	4	3
5	5.26	30.7	3.25	2	1	1	1	1	1	1	1	1
7.39	4.68	9.09	2.16	2	1	1	1	1	1	2	1	1
5.51	4.26	8.52	2.26	2	1	1	1	1	1	2	1	1
7.12	6.56	19.67	2.84	2	1	1	1	1	1	5	1	1
6.66	3.35	6.52	1.97	2	1	1	1	1	1	2	1	1
7.78	3.14	18.32	1.71	2	1	1	1	1	1	1	4	1
4.66	5.88	22.73	3.94	2	1	1	1	1	1	2	1	1
			0.59	2	1	1	1	1	1	1	1	3
8.44			2.45	2	1	2	1	1	1	2	4	1
7.39	2.92	8.88	1.98	2	1	1	1	1	1	1	1	1

ever they were used as coded markers on some of the graphs.

Table 9.01 presents a suite of variables for each of the 339 ethnographic cases in the world sample. These include (1) the number of households per GROUP1 and GROUP2 unit; (2) the number of families per household, GROUP1 and GROUP2 unit, and other group unit ratios; (3) a set of coded properties referring to characteristics of leadership and the political organization of groups; (4) features of community structures and facilities; (5) whether ownership claims are asserted for particular locations of high productivity; and (6) whether there is economic role specialization beyond simple age and gender differences. Included in the community codes is a class that specifies the type of system state based on some of the criteria used in more thoughtful evolutionary classifications, such as ones by Fried (1967) and Johnson and Earle (1987). These data will be helpful in the exploration of ideas discussed in this chapter.

GROUP1 SIZE AND JOHNSON'S CONSTANT

Using the information summarized in table 9.01, it is possible to evaluate Johnson's arguments about the probability that nested basic organizational units should "fit within each other" at proportions of six to one or less. In figure 9.02, graph A, the number of families included in each GROUP1 unit (G1FAMSZ) is displayed, while in graph B the number of households in each GROUP1 unit (G1MHS) appears. The patterning in graph A demonstrates that

Generalization 9.02

All of the cases with both GROUP1 and family size data have six or fewer families in GROUP1 units except the Mbuti, Guayaki (Ache), Iglulik, and Kutchin.

A modified version of this pattern is visible in graph B, which plots data on the number of households in each GROUP1 unit. Although there are data on both GROUP1 size and mean household size for more cases than in the previous comparison of family size and GROUP1 size, the vast majority of the cases have six or fewer household-size units in each GROUP1 unit. The distribution is nevertheless very different from the pattern in graph A.

First, cases representing the mounted hunters of the Great Plains of North America are clustered in a distribution that is completely distinct from the remainder of the hunter-gatherer cases (shaded). The only group of nonmounted hunters represented in the shaded area is the Kutchin, who constitute one of the very few North American cases in which the leadership hierarchy and sodalities are analogous to those of the plains hunters (Osgood 1936:128–30). This distinctive distribution describes a region of the graph that is centered on the Johnson constant but separated from all other hunter-gatherer cases by the clustered, uniquely large size of its GROUP1 units.

The exceptional cases analogous to the mounted hunter distribution that had more than six households per GROUP1 unit include the Efe (group 64), Birhor (group 18), Bayaka (group 61), Aka (group 60), and Bambote (62). Without exception all of these groups are net-hunting mutualists of the tropics and subtropics. Two other cases, the Guayaki (Ache) (47) of Paraguay and the Shompen (4) of the Nicobar Islands, are also among the exceptional cases. Because the Shompen maintain separate structures for unmarried teenagers and other combinations of children and elders, mean household size is less than mean family size, so the family is the unit that is nested within GROUP1 units.

The Guayaki (Ache), however, are a different story. Because of disruptive events within the past few decades affecting their

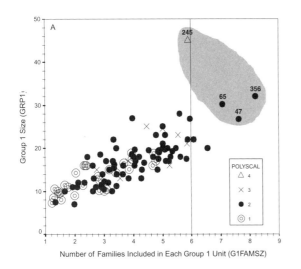
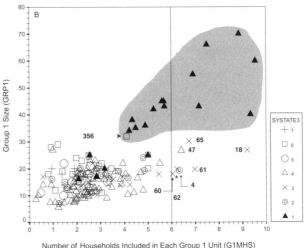

FIGURE 9.02

A paired-graph comparison between the number of families included in each GROUP1 unit (A) and the number of households included in each GROUP1 unit (B). Both are expressed relative to the size of GROUP1 units. Graph A is coded with respect to political scale (POLYSCAL): (1) local autonomy, senior male "guidance"; (2) local autonomy with performance-based leadership, leaders are acknowledged; (3) local autonomy with a formal council and a leader who assembles the council and has other group duties; and (4) neighborhoods of GROUP2 units integrated into an overarching leadership and decision making organization. Graph B is coded with respect to system states (SYSTATES): (1) mounted hunters, (2) agriculturists, (3) mutualists, (4) egalitarian without leaders, (5) egalitarian with leaders, (6) ranked wealth, and (7) ranked elites.

subsistence base and societal organization, the most dispersed phase of the Guayaki (Ache) residential cycle occurs when they are on "walkabout," moving their residential camp every day or so as they forage through the forest. Hill and Hawks (1983:175) have documented Guayaki (Ache) group size in terms of the number of male hunters, since their research interest was focused on Guayaki (Ache) hunting returns. When another colleague provided me with census information for nine Guayaki (Ache) groups (Kaplan pers. comm. 1990), it was immediately apparent that the dependency ratio was relatively low for six of these groups.

I will forgo a detailed discussion of this data, but I stress that most of these mobile groups do not appear to maintain reproductively viable units. In six of the nine cases, task groups were biased in favor of active males and there were few children (only nursing infants were regularly present) and no elderly persons.[2] Ethnographers have considered these units to be equivalent to "traditional" ethnic groups, but I strongly doubt this supposition. A more judicious reading of the data supports the view that, under normal conditions, the Guayaki (Ache) did not disperse and aggregate during different phases of a subsistence settlement cycle. (See the contrasts between the recently observed "band" sizes and earlier data [Hill and Hawkes 1983:175].) I suspect that Guayaki (Ache) GROUP1 size is large because it really represents an approximation of a traditional GROUP2 unit.[3]

Another look at the overall distribution in figure 9.02, graph B, reveals that there is a concentration of cases between 0 and 4.0 on the x axis with a modal concentration around 2.25 households. The marker symbol documents that mean household sizes in the area of the graph to the left of a value of 1.0 on the x axis represents few of the smallest household sizes. It is clear that, in most of these cases, GROUP1 size is smaller than household size. This fact alone strongly suggests that households *do not* constitute the basic organizational segments of which GROUP1 units are formed. On the other hand, the mounted hunters and the cases in the nonshaded area to the right side of a value of 6.0 on the x axis *could* represent such units. The accuracy of this suspicion can be checked by partitioning the data into classes reflecting the number of families in a household scaled relative to mean household size.

The marker symbols 3 and 4 in figure 9.03, graph A—which is the same graph illustrated in graph A of figure 9.02—now reflect an ordination of large mean household sizes in which household size exceeds the size of the GROUP1 units scattered across the full proportional array of numbers of families per GROUP1 unit. In contrast, graph B simply confirms earlier suspicions and reinforces the pattern in graph A. In the cases distributed to the right of the groups identified by a solid marker, household size and family size approximate one another. I believe that this pattern clearly indicates that

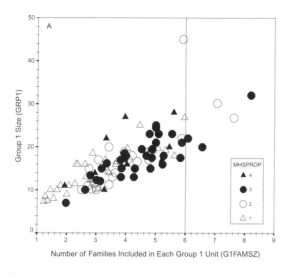 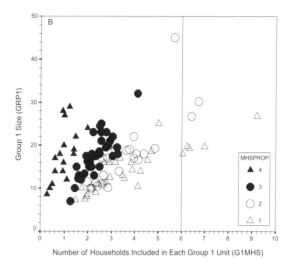

FIGURE 9.03

A paired-graph comparison between the number of families (A) and the number of households (B) in each GROUP1 unit. Both variables are expressed relative to the size of the GROUP1 unit. Both graphs are coded for the relationship between mean household size and the size of other social units (MHSPROP): (1) mean household size is less than family size; (2) mean household size is approximately equal to family size; (3) mean household size approximates GROUP1 size; and (4) mean household size exceeds GROUP1 size.

the family is the segmental form being nested to build GROUP1 units, regardless of the sheltering strategy. This conclusion strongly supports Johnson's insightful analysis of the Dobe !Kung data collected during their encampments in the rainy season. What Johnson did not know was that this is a widespread hunter-gatherer pattern.

Generalization 9.03

The household appears to be a basic organizational entity for GROUP1 units only when it is larger than GROUP1 size, or when the household is identical in size to the family. In other words, among all hunter-gatherers, the family constitutes the unit of organizational scale for GROUP1 units.

This generalization confirms Johnson's earlier observation of considerable variability in the actual size of units even when there is no variability in the *form* of the basal unit of which larger units are composed. It is also compatible with the generalizations about the variables conditioning size differences in GROUP1 units presented in chapter 8.

GROUP2 SIZE AND JOHNSON'S CONSTANT

Since GROUP2 residential locations can be thought of as the social pool out of which GROUP1 units and other task groups are formed, it is reasonable to suspect that GROUP2

units represent a segmentally organized form of GROUP1 units. This possibility is explored in the graphs in figure 9.04, which illustrate the relationship between GROUP2 size and the number of GROUP1 units that a GROUP2 unit could accommodate. Using the same cutoff criteria here as in figure 9.02, it could be argued that GROUP2 residential units consist of multiple GROUP1 units. There is, however, an overall distribution similar to the pattern in figure 9.02, graph B, in which the majority of the cases are clustered around a value just greater than two GROUP1 units per GROUP2 settlement. Although the maximum size of most GROUP2 residential units is less than six GROUP1 units, unit size is not evenly distributed across the range of the Johnson constant (see figure 9.02, graph A, for contrast). This pattern leads me to suspect that GROUP1 units are not, on average, the organizational building blocks of GROUP2 aggregations.

I had earlier entertained the idea that households were perhaps the basic organizational units of which social groups larger than GROUP1 units were composed. In order to examine the relationship between mean household size and GROUP2 size, the number of GROUP1 units included in GROUP2 units is illustrated in graph A of figure 9.04. In graph B, I plotted the number of households per GROUP2 unit on the *x* axis and the mean size of GROUP2 settlements on the *y* axis. In graph B, there is a distinct break in mean household size at a value just greater than the Johnson constant of six units, with a fairly normal distribution between one and six units that peaks at four and five units. This pattern is

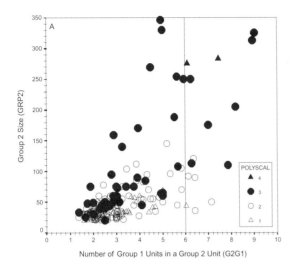
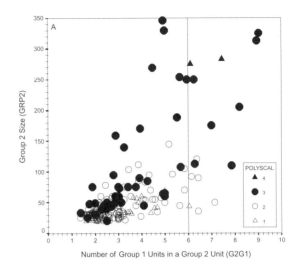

FIGURE 9.04

A paired-graph comparison of the number of GROUP1 units and the number of households included in each GROUP2 unit, both plotted against the size of GROUP2 units. Both graphs are coded with respect to political scale (POLYSCAL): (1) local autonomy, senior male "guidance"; (2) local autonomy with performance-based leadership, leaders are acknowledged; (3) local autonomy with a formal council and a leader who assembles the council and has other group duties; and (4) neighborhoods of GROUP2 units integrated into an overarching leadership and decision making organization.

repeated just prior to a value of twelve, suggesting single- and double-house basic units.

The pattern is also similar to the relationship between families and GROUP1 units that was illustrated in figure 9.02, graph A. Cases with large GROUP2 units are politically complex, and in such large GROUP2 units mean household size is large and represents more than 2.8 to 3.1 families. It therefore appears that some GROUP2 units may be composed of basic household units while others may not. At present, however, it is not known what factors are responsible for conditioning households as basal organizational units.

Given the uncertainty about the causal factors underlying the organizational patterns visible in figure 9.04, I decided to take a closer look at mean household size. I summarized the number of houses, using the variable SUBSP, for only those hunter-gatherer cases in the shaded zone of figure 9.04, graph B, in which the household appears to be the basal organizational unit of GROUP2 settlements. As table 9.02 demonstrates, statistically meaningful differences in the number of basal organizational units nested within GROUP2 units are related to the primary food resources that groups exploit. This pattern also demonstrates that type of food resource does not bias whether households do or do not function as the basal organizational unit.

Another look at the relationship between mean household size and GROUP2 size seemed justified, so I prepared the graph in figure 9.05. When I first examined this distribution, it seemed to have three major components. One group of cases is desig-

nated by sets of marker symbols numbered 5, 6, and 7 and represents a distribution in which there is substantial variability in GROUP2 size but relatively little variability in mean household size. Set 4 is the central or transitional unit, in which there is variability in both GROUP2 size and mean household size. Sets 1 through 3 are distinctive in that they exhibit little variability in GROUP2 size but impressive variability in mean household size, which is the mirror image of sets 5 through 7.

The sets themselves were defined by grouping together those hunter-gatherer cases that were best aligned in an

TABLE 9.02

ESTIMATES OF AVERAGE NUMBER OF BASAL UNITS WITHIN GROUP2 CASES, CLASSIFIED BY PRIMARY FOOD SOURCE FOR CASES IN WHICH HOUSEHOLDS ARE THE BASAL UNIT

PRIMARY FOOD SOURCE	MEAN NUMBER OF BASAL UNITS	MEAN SIZE OF BASAL UNITS	NUMBER OF CASES
TERRESTRIAL ANIMALS	4.76	9.59 ± 5.58	19
TERRESTRIAL PLANTS	5.35	5.01 ± 7.35	27
AQUATIC RESOURCES	4.45	12.66 ± 7.84	39

Note: Mounted hunters are excluded.

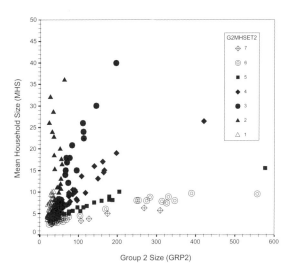

FIGURE 9.05

Justification for the definition of subsets in mean household size when studied relative to GROUP2 sizes. Cases are coded for the subsets recognized in G2MHSET2: (1) MHS is in the extended family size range and GROUP2 size is fewer than fifty persons; (2) MHS is highly variable but large, while GROUP2 sizes are regularly fifty or fewer persons; (3) MHS varies positively with GROUP2 size, but at a very seep angle due to the large size of the communal structures and the relatively small size of the GROUP2 units; (4) MHS varies linearly with GROUP2 size, with cases in the extended family range as well as the communal house range; (5) MHS is in the extended family range and group size is variable; (6) MHS is slightly larger than seven persons but GROUP2 size is much more variable; and (7) MHS is small and GROUP2 size is large and variable.

experimental series of scatter plots produced prior to figure 9.05. I had hoped to note some similarities in the sets of cases produced by this classification, but initially I failed to see anything very obvious about the cases assigned to each of the sets. My next thought was that new and relevant patterns might be revealed if I changed scale and looked at the relationship between mean household size and GROUP2 size for these sets in tabular form. Table 9.03 therefore includes values for the correlation coefficient (R^2) and the adjusted R^2, the standard error, the value of f, the number of cases used in the calculation of the regressions, the value of a (the intercept), and the value of b (the slope of the line) for each regression.

There is little doubt that all of the sets (figure 9.05), with the possible exception of number 2, exhibit substantial linear relationships between the size of the GROUP2 unit and mean household size.[4] It is also clear that household size varies with GROUP2 size, but not in a consistent and uncomplicated way. The seven sets of hunter-gatherer cases and their associated equations show that some other factor besides GROUP2 size must be strongly conditioning the interaction between GROUP2 size and mean household size. But at this point, all I know is that the dynamics underlying some as yet unidentified set of initial conditions have partitioned the hunter-gatherer cases into seven sets, and that in sets 3 through 7 the interaction between mean household size and GROUP2 size is very strong.

Another potentially informative perspective may result from looking at the seven sets of cases (G2MHSET2) in terms of the commonalities that might account for their being aggregated in one of the three clusters of sets originally identified in figure 9.04, graph B. When this is done, it becomes apparent that sets 1 through 4 each has a mix of complex and noncomplex hunter-gatherer cases. Sets 5, 6, and 7, on the other hand, seem to have relatively fewer cases that would be called socially complex, and sets 6 and 7 also include most of the mounted hunters of the Great Plains. To

TABLE 9.03

SUMMARY OF RELATIONSHIP BETWEEN MEAN HOUSEHOLD SIZE AND MEAN SIZE OF RESIDENTIAL SETTLEMENTS DURING THE MOST AGGREGATED PHASE OF THE ANNUAL SETTLEMENT CYCLE

G2MHSET IDENTITY	R^2	ADJUSTED R^2	STANDARD ERROR	SIGNIFICANCE (f)	NUMBER OF CASES	a	b
SET 1	0.28163	0.26321	1.66	0.0004	42	2.357169	0.136649
SET 2	0.03634	0.00622	8.64	0.2802	35	6.406445	0.156824
SET 3	0.93890	0.93585	2.35	0.0000	24	−1.666352	0.223166
SET 4	0.90106	0.89908	1.39	0.0000	53	3.157613	0.065982
SET 5	0.93150	0.92929	0.66	0.0000	34	3.386997	0.023763
SET 6	0.91351	0.91031	0.74	0.0000	30	2.747215	0.016218
SET 7	0.91262	0.89077	0.49	0.0030	07	2.133912	0.013513

Note: x = GROUP2 size; y = mean household size.

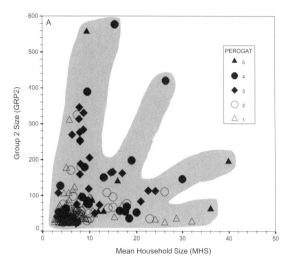
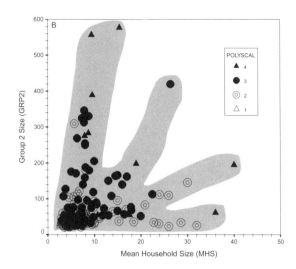

FIGURE 9.06

Displayed in the property space of GROUP2 size and mean household size is an investigation of the relationship between developed leadership (A) and "scalar differences" (B) as indicators of political complexity. Graph A is coded for the prerogatives of leadership (PEROGAT): (1) no special prerogatives; (2) no relief from subsistence and no special dress prerogatives, but messengers as regular assistants; (3) no relief from subsistence and only minor dress prerogatives, but both messengers and a talking chief or speaker for the leader; (4) some regular relief from subsistence, in-kind contributions to the leader from the "people," sometimes special labor for food production and manufactured goods contributed, messengers, a "speaker," and special roles for the leader's wife; and (5) complete relief from subsistence duties, more assistants, special roles associated with the leader, visible symbols associated with the office, perhaps a permanent "guard," perhaps special marriage rules, and very distinctive clothing. Graph B is coded for political scale (POLYSCAL): (1) local autonomy, senior male "guidance"; (2) local autonomy with performance-based leadership, leaders are acknowledged; (3) local autonomy with a formal council and a leader who assembles the council and has other group duties; and (4) neighborhoods of GROUP2 units integrated into an overarching leadership and decision making organization.

follow up on the possibility that organizational complexity contributes to the differentiation of the hunter-gatherer sample into seven sets, the two graphs in figure 9.06 were prepared. These display the same distribution as in figure 9.04, although now the cases are coded in terms of two variables that are indicative of political complexity, PEROGAT and POLYSCAL.

A general overview of both graphs in figure 9.06 indicates immediately that a very different structure of dynamics is responsible for the patterns in both scatter plots. In graph A, the ordinal variable PEROGAT (the scale is explained in the figure caption) is used to encode the prerogatives of leadership regardless of the types of leadership present in the group. Insofar as these prerogatives can be regarded as some measure of political development or investment, there appears to be little linear correlation with the size of GROUP2 residential units. On the other hand, there is an association of larger group size with a greater number of prerogatives afforded to leaders.

Another way of expressing this relationship is that prerogatives increase both with increases in GROUP2 size *and* with mean household size, but the types of prerogatives are

ordered differently. This pattern suggests that the relationship between the amount of social investment focused on persons acknowledged as leaders and the size of GROUP2 units is not a simple one. In addition, the relationship between mean household size and GROUP2 residential units is not linked in any direct or simple manner with political complexity, at least in the terms that have been used here. It appears instead that

---
Generalization 9.04

Substantial social investment in persons acknowledged as leaders can occur in systems with either very small or very large GROUP2 sizes. When leadership is present and GROUP2 size is small, mean household size is usually large. In at least some small-scale societies, politically differentiated leadership roles do not appear only in response to scalar differences.

It could be argued that there are sequential, curvilinear, inverse relationships between mean household size and the size of GROUP2 residential units among cases designated as "leadership developed." Within this group of cases, the larger

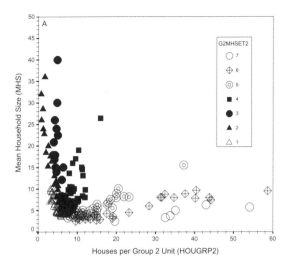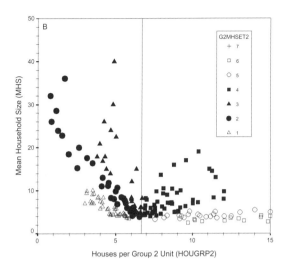

FIGURE 9.07

Investigation of mean household size as a possible "basic organizational unit," viewed as an overall distribution (A) and in finer detail (B). Cases are coded in both graphs for G2MHSET2: (1) MHS is in the extended family size range and GROUP2 size is fewer than fifty persons; (2) MHS is highly variable but large, while GROUP2 size is regularly fifty or fewer persons; (3) MHS varies positively with GROUP2 size but at a very steep angle, due to the large sizes of the communal structures and the relatively small size of the GROUP2 units; (4) MHS varies linearly with GROUP2 size, with both cases in the extended family range as well as communal house range; (5) MHS is in the extended family range and group size is variable; (6) MHS is slightly larger than seven persons but GROUP2 size is much more variable; and (7) MHS is small and GROUP2 size is large and variable.

"communal" houses are associated with smaller GROUP2 sizes. Perhaps another way of saying the same thing is that among some groups the basic organizational unit (sensu Johnson) is housed together in a single dwelling, while in other societies the members of such basic units do not occupy the same domicile. In addition to this difference, the character of leadership and associated prerogatives does not seem to be the same among cases with large GROUP2 sizes, as opposed to groups with large mean household sizes.

Graphs A and B in figure 9.07 illustrate this point by plotting mean household size against the mean number of houses per GROUP2 settlement, using markers that represent the same classificatory sets presented in table 9.03. The first notable feature of the graphs in figure 9.07 emerges from a comparison of these graphs with patterned relationships between mean household size and GROUP2 size in figure 9.05. The similarity originally noted between sets 1 through 3 (G2MHSET2) is now much more apparent, since, for all three sets (1–3), mean household size is negatively related to the number of houses in GROUP2 settlements. There also appear to be two modal peaks (1–3 and 4), suggesting two basic units with different scales of communal living. In contrast, for sets 5 through 7, mean household size is seemingly unrelated to the mean number of houses per GROUP2 settlement. This relationship is well illustrated by

the enlargement in figure 9.07, graph B, emphasizing the important distribution in the left-hand corner of graph A.

The figure 9.07 cases in which the household appears to be the basal unit have dark symbols, and some of these are identified as having the household as the GROUP2 unit. A distinct threshold occurs between 6.50 and 6.75 houses per GROUP2 settlement, marking the location where the overall distribution shifts from negative to positive. The distribution of the remaining cases is flat, except for those in which the mean household size is eight or more persons. These cases appear to represent systems in which the basal social unit involved in decision making is composed of two households (see the threshold indicated at twelve houses per GROUP2 unit). The fact that there is a clear change in the use of communal houses at the Johnson constant of six houses per GROUP2 unit strongly confirms the importance of the constant.

I pointed out earlier that in my opinion set 4 (G2MHSET2) in figure 9.05 was intermediary between a cluster that included sets 1, 2, and 3 and one including sets 5, 6, and 7. I noted that set 4 was likely to represent a mixture of two different ways of organizing basic units relative to households. In sets 2 and 3 in graph B of figure 9.07, a single household equals the GROUP2 unit in many cases, whereas three to six households make up the basic unit when cluster size is fewer than ten

TABLE 9.04

SUMMARY INFORMATION ON LINEAR REGRESSIONS CALCULATED
SEPARATELY BY G2MHSET3 SUBSET FOR THE RELATIONSHIP
BETWEEN GROUP2 SETTLEMENT SIZE AND MEAN HOUSEHOLD SIZE

G2MHSET IDENTITY	R^2	ADJUSTED R^2	STANDARD ERROR	SIGNIFICANCE (f)	NUMBER OF CASES	a	b
SET 1	0.48191	0.47646	5.66	0.0000	97	2.102697	0.196059
SET 2	0.94924	0.89908	1.39	0.0000	53	3.157613	0.065982
SET 3	0.75869	0.75504	1.19	0.0000	68	3.228277	0.016856

When eight outliers are removed and the equation for set 1 is recalculated, the following equation is obtained:

| SET 1A | 0.88767 | 0.88637 | 2.13 | 0.0000 | 90 | 0.110626 | 0.207854 |

When the equations for set 1a, set 2, and set 3 are used to obtain predicted values, and then the entire suite of values is run back against the observed values, the following equation is obtained:

| GENEQ | 0.89213 | 0.889161 | 1.68 | 0.0000 | 210 | 0.00000 | 1.00000 |

Note: x = GROUP2 size; *y* = mean household size.

persons. Among cases in set 4, eight to twelve households make up the basic organizational unit at the decision making level of societal organization. On the other hand, G2MHSET2 sets 5, 6, and 7 represent systems in which households do not constitute segmentary units defining the basic organizational units of society. I would conclude from this patterning that

Generalization 9.05

In some systems, households constitute the segmentary components that define the basic organizational units of societies integrated at the GROUP2 level, whereas in other systems they do not. Households do not appear to be the defining segments when GROUP2 units are housed in a single structure or when more than approximately six households make up the GROUP2 settlement.

When the distribution is examined from the preceding perspective—that is, relative to the number of households per GROUP2 settlement—one no longer sees the set of positive relationships that occurred when size of settlement and mean household size were compared in figure 9.05. This new perspective provides, instead, some indication of the differences in the organizational role of households themselves. The number of houses per settlement does increase, but only a very small increase in mean household size occurs with increases in the number of houses as a function of GROUP2 size. Mean household size remains below ten persons, with fewer small household examples in large communities (figure 9.07, graph A).

In light of the structure of the patterning in figures 9.06 and 9.07, it is clear that the seven sets of cases summarized

in table 9.03 are overly specific and that reality corresponds more closely to the patterning in figure 9.07. To reflect this different perception, a new variable, G2MHSET3, was developed, for which a code of 1 now includes former sets 1 through 3, a code of 2 now represents former set 4, and code 3 equals former sets 5 through 7. Regressions were calculated for the relationship between mean household size and GROUP2 size using these new categories, and the results are summarized in table 9.04.

A graphic representation in figure 9.08 of the combined values of the equations for sets 1 through 3 will facilitate a discussion of the relationships between observed and predicted values for mean household size. In the graph, the distribution of cases is relatively clustered, but there are eight obvious outliers (G2MHSET3 = 4): the Onge and Jarwa of the Andaman Islands, Semang of Malaysia, Calusa of South Florida, Chinook of Oregon, Quinault of Washington, Labrador Inuit, and East Greenland Eskimo of Angmaksalik. In all of these cases, without exception, the entire GROUP2 unit is essentially housed in a single structure, during either the rainy season or the coldest season, or when both sets of conditions occur simultaneously. This is obviously a very different sort of relationship between GROUP2 size and mean household size than commonly occurs in the majority of the hunter-gatherer cases in the sample, but it does point to an important fact:

Generalization 9.06

Shelter is not necessarily partitioned isomorphically with a society's basic organizational or segmental units. In some circumstances, all or nearly all basic organizational units may be communally housed. Investments in housing, including

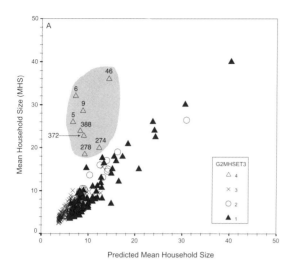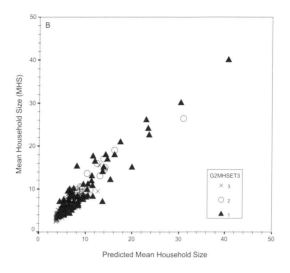

FIGURE 9.08

Two demonstrations of observed versus expected values of mean household size. Cases are coded for the size sets 1–3 defined in table 9.04; 4 designates exceptional cases.

the size of structures and expanded inclusiveness of those sheltered, may be directly responsive to the intensity of the environmental conditions that must be sheltered against.

The graphs in figure 9.08 nevertheless illustrate that all other hunter-gatherer cases in the sample exhibit a pattern of increasing household size as a function of increased GROUP2 settlement size. Although it is true that there are at least three different ways in which this interaction is expressed among hunter-gatherers—corresponding to equations for sets 1a, 2, and 3 in table 9.04—and the factors responsible for these differences have not yet been isolated, all cases exhibit increases in mean household size as their GROUP2 size increases.

Generalization 9.07

Except under the conditions enumerated in generalization 9.06, all other hunter-gatherer cases show a positive correlation between mean household size and GROUP2 size. This relationship can take two forms: one in which there is a greater increase in mean household size per unit GROUP2 increase (a tendency toward communal houses) and another in which there is much less increase in mean household size and the total number of persons housed together does not exceed eleven.

Many anthropological publications have been devoted to a discussion of the household (e.g., Bender 1967; Blanton 1994; Byrnes 1976; Sahlins 1956; Wallerstein 1984; Wilk and Rathje 1982; Wong 1984), but here I only mention the existence of

this huge and controversial literature and the provocative ideas it contains. Nevertheless, many writers have argued that household size is responsive to intensification through labor unit expansion (Netting 1993:301–19; Sahlins 1956), which is sometimes reflected in increased household size. It would certainly be reasonable to entertain the possibility that at least two economic factors could condition increased mean household size as it relates to increased GROUP2 unit settlement size.

Proposition 9.02

Mean household size may increase as GROUP2 settlement size increases if

a. Larger GROUP2 settlement size is correlated with more permanent settlements and increased labor investments in housing. Under these conditions, social units or persons (such as the elderly) whose contribution to the labor force (as well as the labor investment they receive from others) is reduced would increasingly be housed within the larger labor units to which they once contributed but upon which they now depend.

b. Larger GROUP2 settlement size is also correlated with increased intensification in production, leading to an expanded number of food sources and a greater investment of labor in the processing of both traditional and new resources, particularly if multiple work parties are required to exploit simultaneously available resources. Under these conditions there is an expected increase in the size of the basic productive unit.

TABLE 9.05
CROSS-TABULATION OF HUNTER-GATHERER CASES ACCORDING TO THE ORDINAL VARIABLES G2BAORD AND SYSTATE

SYSTATE

G2BAORD BOUNDARY ORDINAL SIZE CLASS	COMMENT	Special cases			Simultaneous cases		Sequential cases		TOTAL	COMMENTS
		MOUNTED HUNTERS (1)	AGRICUL-TURALISTS (2)	MUTUALISTS (3)	EGALITARIAN WITHOUT LEADERS (4)	EGALITARIAN WITH LEADERS (5)	RANKED WEALTH (6)	RANKED ELITES (7)		
SIZE CLASS 1	Model	0.0	1.0	2.0	9.0	1.0	0.0	0.0	13.0	Nuclear family
2.0 > 3.12 AND < 3.824		0.0	7.7	15.4	69.2	7.7	0.0	0.0	4.4	
ROW PERCENTAGE		-1.2	0.3	1.0	3.9	0.0	-2.9	-1.0		
OBSERVED – EXPECTED										
SIZE CLASS 2	Between	0.0	2.0	2.0	35.0	4.0	7.0	0.0	50.0	Nuclear family
3.0 > 3.828 AND < 5.04		0.0	4.0	4.0	70.0	8.0	14.0	0.0	16.8	
ROW PERCENTAGE		-4.7	-0.9	-1.7	15.4	0.3	-4.2	-3.9		
OBSERVED – EXPECTED										
SIZE CLASS 3	Model	2.0	2.0	9.0	32.0	5.0	11.0	0.0	61.0	Stem–polygynous family
4.0 > 5.03 AND < 6.72		3.3	3.3	14.8	52.5	8.2	18.0	1.6	20.5	
ROW PERCENTAGE		-3.7	-1.5	4.5	8.1	0.5	-3.1	-4.7		
OBSERVED – EXPECTED										
SIZE CLASS 4	Between	3.0	4.0	4.0	23.0	5.0	10.0	0.0	49.0	Stress
5.0 > 6.71 AND < 8.86		6.1	8.2	8.8	46.9	10.2	20.4	0.0	16.5	Polygynous and joint family
ROW PERCENTAGE		-1.6	1.2	0.4	3.8	1.4	-1.3	-3.8		
OBSERVED – EXPECTED										
First shift: Dominant state goes from both 6 to 6 and 8										
SIZE CLASS 5	Model	2.0	6.0	5.0	12.0	3.0	12.0	6.0	46.0	Joint–extended family
6.0 > 8.85 AND < 11.83		4.3	13.0	12.5	26.1	6.5	26.1	13.0	15.5	
ROW PERCENTAGE		-2.3	3.4	1.6	-6.1	-0.4	1.3	2.4		
OBSERVED – EXPECTED										
SIZE CLASS 6	Between	3.0	1.0	0.0	4.0	1.0	9.0	3.0	21.0	Kin clique
7.0 > 11.82 AND < 15.60		14.3	4.8	0.0	19.0	4.8	42.9	14.3	7.1	
ROW PERCENTAGE		1.0	-0.2	-1.6	-4.2	-0.6	4.1	1.4		
OBSERVED – EXPECTED										

Second shift: Secondary state goes from 6 to 3 and 8

SIZE CLASS	Type	Measure	1	2	3	4	5	6	7	Total	Annotation
SIZE CLASS 7 — 8.0 > 15.59 AND 20.00	Model	Observed	3.0	1.0	1.0	2.0	1.0	10.0	0.0	18.0	Stress / Extended kin clique
		ROW PERCENTAGE	16.6	5.5	5.5	11.1	5.5	**52.6**	0.0		
		OBSERVED − EXPECTED	1.2	−0.2	−0.4	0.6	−6.5	5.6	−1.5	6.1	
SIZE CLASS 8 — 9.0 > 20.79 AND < 27.42	Between	Observed	2.0	0.0	0.0	0.0	0.0	5.0	3.0	10.0	Stress / Descent group
		ROW PERCENTAGE	20.0	0.0	0.0	0.0	0.0	**50.0**	30.0		
		OBSERVED − EXPECTED	1.1	−0.6	−1.7	−0.7	−3.9	2.7	2.2	3.4	

Third shift: Dominant state goes from 8 to 9

SIZE CLASS	Type	Measure	1	2	3	4	5	6	7	Total	Annotation
SIZE CLASS 9 — 10.0 > 27.41 AND < 36.58	Model	Observed	2.0	0.0	0.0	0.0	0.0	3.0	5.0	10.0	Large descent group
		ROW PERCENTAGE	20.0	0.0	0.0	0.0	0.0	30.0	**50.0**		
		OBSERVED − EXPECTED	1.1	−0.6	−0.7	−0.7	−3.9	0.7	4.2	3.4	

Fourth shift: Dominant state goes from 8 to 3
Major break in character of units

SIZE CLASS	Type	Measure	1	2	3	4	5	6	7	Total	Annotation
SIZE CLASS 10 — 11.0 > 36.57 AND < 48.23	Between	Observed	6.0	0.0	0.0	0.0	0.0	1.0	1.0	8.0	"Lineage clan"
		ROW PERCENTAGE	**75.0**	0.0	0.0	0.0	0.0	12.5	12.5		
		OBSERVED − EXPECTED	5.2	−0.5	−0.6	−3.1	−0.6	−0.9	0.4	2.7	
SIZE CLASS 11 — 12.0 > 48.22 AND < 64.31	Model	Observed	5.0	0.0	0.0	0.0	0.0	1.0	0.0	6.0	Stress / "Lineage clan"
		ROW PERCENTAGE	**83.3**	0.0	0.0	0.0	0.0	16.7	0.0		
		OBSERVED − EXPECTED	4.4	−0.3	−0.4	−2.4	−0.4	−0.4	−0.5	2.0	

Fifth shift: Dominant state goes from 3 to 8
Major break in character of units

SIZE CLASS	Type	Measure	1	2	3	4	5	6	7	Total	Annotation
SIZE CLASS 12 — 13.0 > 64.3	Open	Observed	0.0	0.0	0.0	0.0	0.0	0.0	5.0	5.0	Large sodality
		ROW PERCENTAGE	0.0	0.0	0.0	0.0	0.0	0.0	**100.0**		
		OBSERVED − EXPECTED	−0.5	−0.3	−0.4	−2.0	−0.4	−1.2	4.6	1.7	
TOTALS			28	7	23	117	21	69	23	297	

Notes: Columns are as follows: (1) mounted hunters with extensive land use pattern, secret societies, and age grades; (2) agriculturalists; (3) mutualists and product specialists; (4) consensus decision makers (leadership is not politically developed); (5) consensus decision makers but with minimally supported political statuses; (6) wealth-based differentiation and minimal presence of "ownership" and economic differentiation; and (7) "class" differentiation in the society, with "noble" leadership. **Boldface** denotes highest value in row. Underscore denotes second highest value in row.

I will return to these and other provocative possibilities once I have examined the data relative to Johnson's ideas and arguments. For the moment, it is necessary to stick with an examination of Johnson's "apple," which postulates a fundamental constant of six as an approximation of the upper limit on the number of persons who can participate in consensus-based decision making and a size threshold at which point scalar stress conditions organizational change. Exploration of the idea of basal organizational units might benefit from the enumeration of a few assumptions about such units, followed by an examination of the composition of GROUP2 social units based on the parameters that Johnson has proposed.

MODELING BASAL UNIT VALUES

Working back and forth between the data set and the patterns visible when Johnson's constant is applied to a search for regularities in group size, I still do not know what the building blocks of social organization—which, following Johnson's lead, I am referring to as basal units—might look like in the real world of hunter-gatherer dynamics. In order to approximate this reality, I have decided to use my knowledge of group size means and medians to produce an array of units that are consistent with what is already known. For instance, it has been established that the mean of the largest GROUP1 unit is 17.49 persons and that the smallest GROUP1 unit consists of 9.95 persons. Dividing 9.95 by 17.49 results in a proportional estimator of 0.5668. It should be noted that this value is not very different from the value of 0.5024, which accommodates the empirical material used in constructing figure 9.08. By using this proportional estimator as a constant, the following array of values can be produced, representing the mean numbers of basal units that Johnson's arguments anticipate: 1.812, 3.196, 5.64, 9.95, 17.49, 30.85, 54.44, 96.05, and 169.46. These numbers represent actual group sizes of 10.87, 19.176, 33.84, 59.70, 104.94, 185.1, 326.64, 576.3, and 1,016.76, provided that all group sizes were segmented into six units of equal size.

It should be clear that I have begun to build a model of the sizes of decision making segments, or basal units, but in order to isolate these values more clearly it is necessary to construct intervals of equal proportional value between the higher and lower paired values that define the size range between the values in the array of modeled basal units. This is done in three steps, by (1) dividing the differences between the paired values by four, (2) assigning one-fourth to the positive side of the lowest of the pair being considered, and (3) subtracting one-fourth from the larger of the two values defining the high and low boundaries of a new ordinal unit situated between the two modeled basal units. (The ordinal classification that results from this process is presented in table 9.05.) With this new model of basal units, it is now possible to examine how various properties that might be indicative

of related scalar changes in organization correspond to or diverge from junctures in the modeled array of basal unit approximations.

I have said that it is difficult to imagine that households actually represent basal units in very many situations, but now there is a way to evaluate this judgment. Graph A in figure 9.09 replicates the distribution illustrated in figure 9.04, graph B, but in this case the symbols identifying hunter-gatherer cases refer to classifications in the ordinal scale of modeled basal units presented in table 9.05.

The demonstration in figure 9.09, graph A, is simple: a given GROUP2 "basal demographic unit" is distributed across varying ranges of "houses per basal units," which means that houses are sheltering different numbers of basal demographic units. For instance, an examination (G2BASE) of basal unit "eighteen per GROUP2 unit" reveals that, in some instances, basal units occur in houses that shelter more than one such unit, although in some cases almost six houses are required to shelter one basal unit. This range of variability suggests that other factors must be conditioning house size and the number of occupants sheltered per house.

This point is reinforced by graph B in figure 9.09, which plots mean household size (MHS) on the y axis and the number of houses per GROUP2 unit (HOUGRP2) on the x axis. Case markers refer to classes defined by the ordinal sets for GROUP2 (G2MHSET2). In graph B, cases in size class 6 illustrate that the range of mean household sizes required to accommodate a single basal unit is extensive, ranging from thirty-five to approximately two persons per house. This pattern illustrates that

Generalization 9.08

Variations in the size of the basal unit are not necessarily responsible for differences in mean household size among hunter-gatherers.

Since my interest at the moment is in identifying basic organizational units and how they may relate to the size of systems and to system states, I will defer until later a consideration of the interesting issues of how such units are housed and what factors account for variability in the size of the units sheltered together (household size). There is, however, an obvious question that follows from generalizations 9.03 and 9.05, which will now be stated in the form of a problem:

Problem 9.01

What factors are conditioning the differential size of hunter-gatherer households?

The juxtaposition of hunter-gatherer variability and Johnson's postulations of scalar stress has focused attention on the

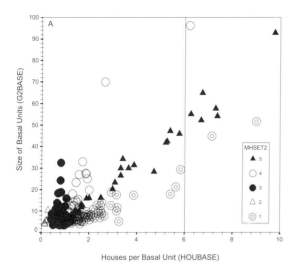
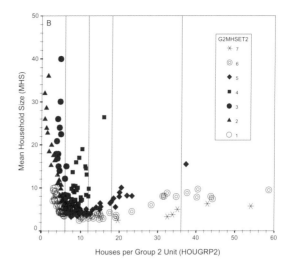

FIGURE 9.09

Modeled GROUP2 "basal unit sizes" (A) and mean household sizes (B) compared with houses per modeled basal unit. These graphs illustrate that differences in "basal unit" size do not account for differences in mean household size. Graph A is coded for the classification of the relationship between mean household size and the houses per GROUP2 unit (MHSET2): (1) MHS is fewer than five persons and HOUGRP2 is greater than 0.60; (2) MHS is between twenty and thirty-eight persons and HOUGRP2 is fewer than 0.30; (3) MHS is over the full range and HOUGRP2 is fewer than 0.60; (4) MHS is greater than eight persons and HOUGRP2 is greater than 0.60; and (5) MHS is greater than five and fewer than eleven persons and HOUGRP2 is greater than 0.60. Graph B is coded for G2MHSET2: (1) MHS is in the extended family size range and GROUP2 size is fewer than fifty persons; (2) MHS is highly variable but large while GROUP2 sizes are regularly fifty or fewer persons; (3) MHS varies positively with GROUP2 size, but at a very steep angle due to the large sizes of the communal structures and the relatively small size of the GROUP2 units; (4) MHS varies linearly with GROUP2 size, with both cases in the extended family range as well as communal house range; (5) MHS is in the extended family range and group size is variable; (6) MHS is slightly larger than seven persons but GROUP2 size is much more variable; and (7) MHS is small and GROUP size is large and variable.

question of whether system state differences might be related to punctuated stress arising from scalar phenomena. Although Johnson's suggestion that scalar thresholds should be associated with changes in system state did not figure in the original dimensionalization of the hunter-gatherer data, I have been prompted by my exploration of Johnson's work to come up with one or more ways of dimensionalizing the available data in a new format that incorporates concerns about both system state and scalar stress.

A new variable, SYSTATE, is introduced in the cross-tabulation in table 9.05 and represents a combination of data embodied in four other variables: CLASS, PEROGAT, HUNTFIL2, and POLPOS. (In some instances it was necessary to refer to the ethnographic literature to resolve ambiguity in the classifications or to supply missing data on key variables.) SYSTATE refers to formal properties of organization, which include leadership, internal differentiation of leadership status, associated roles relative to participation in decision making, and the exercise of power within the society. Cases that are clearly in different "states" relative to the overall world of hunter-gatherers are also identified; these include the mounted hunters of the North American plains

and other regions (column 1)—such as the Teton Sioux, the Comanche, and the Blackfoot peoples—who have emerged as exceptions in several previous comparisons.

Hunter-gatherer groups who were agriculturists at the time of ethnographic documentation are also listed separately in table 9.05 (column 2). These include the Chenchu of India, the Cahuilla of southern California, and the Bororo of South America. Groups that maintain mutualistic relationships with nearby agriculturists or exchange forest products for goods or money with representatives of more complex systems or at regional markets are also identified and tabulated separately (column 3). Since many of these groups are the subjects of extensive discussion in the hunter-gatherer literature, it must be determined if and in what ways they differ from hunter-gatherer groups that are not as involved with non-hunter-gatherers.

Comparison of the columns in table 9.05 provides a number of interesting insights into the relationships between scalar ordination and system state organizational differences. Focusing initially on the group of exceptional cases, the *most* exceptional with regard to the scalar distribution of the size of basal social units are the mounted hunters.

EXTENSIFICATION: WHAT MAKES THE MOUNTED HUNTERS OF THE NORTH AMERICAN PLAINS EXCEPTIONAL?

As a group, the mounted hunters have the highest row percentages (size classes 10 and 11), not only of the cases in the exceptional category but in all of table 9.05.[5] These cases are also represented in size classes greater than size class 5, and there is no question that many of the mounted hunter groups have large GROUP2 sizes. Values for the mounted hunter cases also occur between the distributions of ranked societies (columns 6 and 7). This is not too surprising, since wealth is also a prerequisite for prominence among the mounted hunters, and they could quite easily have been classified with the groups in column 8 had not another property—their use of domesticated animals in hunting—been given taxonomic priority.

EXTENSIFICATION IMPLIES DIFFERENT PROCESSES THAN INTENSIFICATION

Beginning with generalizations 7.06 and 7.07 and continuing in chapter 8 with generalizations 8.02, 8.04, and 8.19, I have referred repeatedly to conditions that strongly implicate very regular patterning that co-varies with intensification. In generalization 7.08 and proposition 7.02, intensification was defined as a process that results in a reduction in the area available for exploitation at the same time that an increase in population occurs. Processes of intensification therefore require an increase in the net amount of food that must be extracted from a given geographic area.

A good example of the impact of intensifying pressures on population density can be seen in a comparison of the data in table 9.05 for mounted hunter groups and ranked societies (columns 1 and 7). The mounted hunters have GROUP2 sizes that are roughly equivalent to those of ranked societies, but the mean values of population density in all categories of the table are 3.69 persons per 100 square kilometers for mounted hunters, 29.60 for agriculturists, 23.97 for mutualists, 13.15 for egalitarian groups, 14.8 for egalitarian groups with institutionalized leadership, 46.74 for ranked societies with no elite leadership, and 51.08 for ranked societies with elite leadership.

Even though the GROUP2 sizes of mounted hunters and groups with elite-based leadership are roughly equivalent, there is a stark contrast in population density between 3.69 persons per 100 square kilometers for mounted hunter groups and 51.08 persons for groups with elite leadership. As these values indicate, there is no necessary relationship between intensification and increases in the size of social units or, in Johnson's terms, social scale. In the world sample, groups at opposite ends of the population density scale have roughly equal GROUP2 sizes. Increases in social scale may, in fact, be

associated with dramatic increases in population density or intensification, or they may occur as a result of system changes in the direction of extensification, which the mounted hunter cases illustrate quite well. This means that, in order to explain the former, the factors involved in processes of extensification must be explained as well.

Almost all of the discussion of system change and the evolution of cultural systems in the anthropological literature has focused on and attempted to generalize about processes of intensification, even though researchers have been aware of the many tactics, tools, and strategies available to hunter-gatherers to facilitate the role played by mobility in their societies. Sleds and toboggans have enhanced the ability of hunter-gatherers to move gear and products as part of an extensive land use strategy. So have all kinds of boats and water craft, which not only make transport of persons and gear feasible but also provide the opportunity to extend mobile hunting and gathering strategies to new aquatic habitats. Boats made possible the radiation of the ancestors of modern Eskimo peoples, whose high-latitude voyages along the Arctic sea and adjacent archipelago extended from Point Barrow, Alaska, to Greenland.

The domestication of animals to serve as transport aids was an important development in the history of hunter-gatherers. Dogs and domesticated reindeer were used to move sleds and toboggans and also served as pack animals. Sled dogs were much more important in the New World than across the Russian arctic region, where reindeer were the only draft animals. Unfortunately, the domestication of the reindeer is undocumented, but in 892 A.D. (Krupnik 1993:161), Tungusic-speaking peoples are postulated to have migrated from the Amur River region and encountered reindeer for the first time. It is argued that the prior experience of these groups with domesticated horses "stimulated" them to domesticate the analogous reindeer species.[6] In this context, the domestication of ungulates produced a draft animal that enhanced human efforts to hunt wild reindeer (Krupnik 1993:162–66) and at the same time served as a means of transportation.

The use of dogs in the New World to pull sleds is not documented until the beginning of the Thule era at approximately 800 to 1,000 A.D., although large dogs, traditionally thought to assist in hunting and as pack animals, are documented during the earliest human radiation eastward across the arctic region.[7] If the traditional view of reindeer domestication is correct, it does not represent a response to intensificational pressures, but instead facilitated extensification and the ability to exploit larger ranges than was possible when humans could travel only by foot. Boats and the use of domesticated dogs as pack and draft animals also served as extensificational devices.

Throughout this study I have repeatedly stated that mounted hunters, particularly those from North America, are exceptions to many of the patterns in the hunter-gatherer data set that have been summarized as generalizations. The primary ways in which they behave differently from the majority of the groups in the sample include (1) the large size of their GROUP1 and GROUP2 units, (2) the huge geographic areas they utilized relative to their large group sizes, and (3) the simultaneous presence of indicators of social complexity *and* very low population densities.

I have pointed out that the mounted plains hunters represent an outstanding example of new niche creation—the dramatic emergence of what was clearly a region of great cultural integrity molded from a historically documented, diverse set of original participants. The new niche was unquestionably stimulated by the availability of domesticated horses, which increased the scale of range use and provided a transport advantage to peoples who were formerly semi-sedentary horticulturists. It is paradoxical, however, that as the plains became occupied at an unprecedented scale by groups of mounted hunters, the population density of these groups was *lower* than the densities characterizing the ancestral horticultural groups that originally adopted the horse and began to exploit bison as their primary source of food.

The process standing behind the appearance of the vital plains culture area (sensu Lowie 1954) was extensification,[8] which was also responsible for analogous changes in hunter-gatherer life ways in the steppic regions of Argentina after the reintroduction of the horse. Unfortunately, rather than searching for the important variables operative in diversity-producing situations, it has been customary in anthropology to dismiss these organizational changes, as well as those of the American plains, as "historically" caused, rather than the result of basic systemic processes. For example, Fried speaks of events in Patagonia in the following terms: "perhaps the largest bands [were] those of the Patagonian Tehuelche, running 400 and 500. These last can easily be discounted, however, as occurring in response to European influence, which included, among other tangibles, the Tehuelche acquisition of domesticated horses" (1967:68). This kind of response by a self-proclaimed evolutionist—who considers some organizational variants as pristine consequences of adaptive processes and other social forms as historically conditioned and of no interest to process-oriented researchers—is baffling.

Generalization 9.09

The process of extensification responds to very different conditioning variables than intensification. Changes in social scale, such as the larger group size of the Plains Indians, are nevertheless produced quite independently of any changes in population that might be measured by population density. This pattern supports Johnson's view that scale is distinct from populational variables. The recognition that extensificational processes are to some extent conditioned independently of

intensificational process allows the study of scalar effects in a controlled manner relative to populational variables.

Processes of extensification have played important roles in other times and places in the world, almost certainly in the regions in which the horse and camel were domesticated. One could speculate about other historical contexts, but in this study the plains mounted hunters provide an almost perfect experimental opportunity to use a comparative approach to investigate the features of social change that appear particularly responsive to scalar change, independent of contexts (such as systems with elite and sequential hierarchies) in which intensificational processes are at work.

OBSERVATIONS ON HORTICULTURISTS IN THE DATA BASE

I continue the comparison between Johnson's "apple" and my own observations by noting that in table 9.05 agriculturists are most often found in ordinal class 5 and occur less frequently in class 6, both of which categories have moderately large GROUP2 and basal unit sizes. A concentration of cases occurs within the "stress" category, which contradicts my expectation that this class would be avoided if scalar stress was the only factor at issue. Such a situation could occur if (1) variables other than scalar stress are conditioning GROUP2 sizes among agriculturists or (2) some ways of organizing basal units are more available to agriculturists than to peoples relying on other strategies of food procurement. In this regard, it is interesting that the only other systems showing an analogous pattern are those in which wealth-based ranking is an important component of leadership (column 6).

As a way of examining this situation more closely, I review all of the cases in the agriculturist category that have basal unit sizes within the range in which most of the noncomplex hunter-gatherers are clustered, all of which are recognizable as exceptional in various ways. For instance, a single case, the Nharo of the Kalahari, occurs in ordinal size class 1. At the time of observation, group members were working as laborers on Ghanzi farms in Botswana (Guenther 1986:120–33), so this case would have fit equally well in the wage laborer category along with other product specialists (column 3).

The two cases in ordinal size class 2 are the Walapai and the Nganasan, but I think in retrospect that the latter group is misclassified since they are reindeer herders in northernmost Siberia who use their domestic reindeer primarily for transport and as draft animals.[9] The Nganasan should be included in the mounted hunter class and almost certainly represent an instance of extensification. The inclusion of the Walapai is provocative since this group lived in small groups (Kniffen 1935:45) in a region of low rainfall along the

Colorado river in Arizona, adjacent to the Grand Canyon, where they were tethered to the few springs and soaks in the area. Agriculture was practiced around these water sources—ownership of which was hereditary—and often involved the investment of low levels of labor in irrigation (Kniffen 1935:44). No cultivated products were stored, and crops were consumed at harvest. Hunted and gathered resources constituted a major component of the diet, and families spent considerable time moving through the landscape in search of food.

The Walapai maintained very low population densities, usually between 3.86 (Kroeber 1953:136) and 4.89 (Kniffen 1935:44–45) persons per 100 square kilometers.[10] In this case, the adoption of domesticated plants may represent a diversificational strategy—an example of Flannery's "broad-spectrum revolution" (1986:8)—or an expansion of niche breadth in response to seasonal instability in natural productivity (Johnson 1997:87–90) rather than population growth and subsequent demographic packing (Binford 1983:203). Of course, this particular strategy is likely to be adopted only when initial conditions include such an option, as in the presence of agriculturists in a region when adoption becomes necessary or, alternatively, when a daughter community of agriculturists takes up residence in an unoccupied or very sparsely occupied region.

One of the groups in ordinal size class 3 is the Ayta from the Pinatubo region of the island of Luzon in the Philippines. The Ayta were reported to be hunter-gatherers at the turn of the century, but they were practicing agriculture at the time of the most detailed ethnographic description. In marked contrast to the Walapai, Ayta population density was 91.9 persons per 100 square kilometers, and they practiced no irrigation. For these reasons, this case must be regarded as an example of intensification. The second case in ordinal class 3 is a poorly documented group from South America, the Guato, who traditionally exploited aquatic resources in an swampy, inland area. This case would have fit equally well in a "remnant group" category since, at the time of ethnographic observation, their numbers were greatly reduced and they were practicing horticulture.

Last, the four cases in ordinal size class 4 are the Chenchu of India (population density 125.29 persons per 100 square kilometers), the Nambikwara of South America (7.78), the Dorobo of Africa (40.8), and the Kaurareg (35.0), who lived on the island of Mabuiag off the coast of the Prince of Wales Island in the southern Torres Straits between Australia and Papua New Guinea. All of these cases are considered hunter-gatherers who have adopted the cultivation of domestic plants in very recent times. Some controversy has surrounded the degree to which the Nambikwara were dependent upon cultivation (Aspelin 1976, 1979; Lévi-Strauss 1948), but the other cases were clearly intensified, judging from their population densities—although there are no obvious indica-

tors of an organizational response to scalar stress. This examination suggests that

––––––   —   *Generalization 9.10*   ––––––

There may be two systemic contexts in which hunter-gatherers use cultivars. One is a context of diversification or an expansion of niche breadth in the face of productive instability in the habitat, whereas the other seems to be a consequence of intensification based on population packing as a density-dependent response.

For cases in the latter context, where scalar stress is anticipated, cultivars may be playing very different roles for participants within the system, and members of any one basal unit may not consistently invest in the whole range of available subsistence strategies. Intensification may well have an "atomizing" effect on the components of a system undergoing major subsistence change, since, as Netting (1993) has compellingly reported, it is the small household or family-based unit that actually intensifies and expands productivity from cultivars.[11] In other words, all households may not invest in similar strategies during transitional episodes of responsive change.[12]

Although a review of these cases has produced provocative results, there is still no direct evidence identifying the practice of horticulture as a specific response to increases in group size and accompanying scalar stress, in Johnson's terms. In most of the cases in the ethnographic sample, intensification among horticulturists is indicated by increases in population density, but unambiguous evidence of scalar stress has not yet been observed. Instead, most of the variability might be due to what Johnson would term local effects among small-scale societies.

MUTUALISTS AND PRODUCT SPECIALISTS

Groups of mutualists (the Efe and Aka) and product specialists (the Hill Pandaram and Birhor) are listed in column 3 of table 9.05 and have a proportional distribution of frequencies similar to that of the cases in column 4. There are, however, small differences between the two categories: estimated basal units are larger and proportionally more cases occur in size classes 3 and 5. I have also noted that many of the cases tabulated in column 3, particularly the product specialists, have been identified as atomistic[13]—with an emphasis on individualism—while at the same time conventional leadership roles were undeveloped. The Epulu Mbuti, one of the exceptions noted in figure 9.02, are mutualists and have the largest basal unit (G2BASORD = 6). The next largest basal units occur in five product specialist cases, all size class 5, that include the allegedly atomistic Nayaka of southern India, who were essentially wage laborers (Bird 1983). The logical question to ask at this juncture can be expressed in the form of a problem:

——————— *Problem 9.02* ———————

Why should atomistic societies have larger GROUP2 sizes than the majority of egalitarian hunter-gatherers, while the majority of mutualists have GROUP2 sizes that are consistent with the egalitarian hunter-gatherer groups tabulated in column 4—except, of course, for the Epulu Mbuti?

————————————————————————

One answer that comes immediately to mind is that ethnographically documented mutualists are rather tightly knit social units who are strongly dependent upon cooperative action and all that it implies organizationally. Net hunting as a subsistence strategy is a particularly striking example of an effort that depends for its success on large-scale cooperation and labor integration.

The differences between mutualists and product specialists could be due partly to the very different role that cooperation plays in the labor organization of the two sets of cases. This contrast is striking in light of Murphy and Steward's comments on the effect of wage labor or an exchange economy on foraging peoples: "When the people of an unstratified native society barter wild products found in extensive distribution and obtained through individual effort, the structure of the native culture will be destroyed, and the final culmination will be a culture type characterized by individual families" (1956:353).

One might imagine that, under the conditions described by Murphy and Steward, GROUP2 size might not matter, at least insofar as decision making and cooperation are concerned. In fact, atomists argued that, when mutual helpfulness occurred in an atomistic social setting, one individual helped another with his or her endeavor to the same degree that they had received help. There was no permanently constituted group that engaged in common pursuits whose byproducts were regarded as common property (Honigmann 1968:220–21). Another possibility, however, is that

——————— *Proposition 9.03* ———————

Among forest product specialists, GROUP2 units might be considered equivalent to the GROUP3 units maintained by mobile hunter-gatherers, which served primarily to maintain social relationships between persons at a much larger scale (the connubium, for instance) than the normal social unit of cooperation around which everyday subsistence tactics and strategies were organized. In circumstances in which the execution of such strategies is reduced to the level of a single fam-

ily, the next largest aggregation would be the functional equivalent of GROUP3 units among many mobile hunter-gatherers.

————————————————————————

Regardless of the taxonomic status of GROUP2 units among forest product specialists, the differences between product specialist and mutualist groups are likely to refer to dissimilarities in the organization and division of labor and the scales of cooperation. In general, these same factors affect variability in hunter-gatherer group size. Therefore, given the present level of knowledge, these cases do not represent system states distinctly different from those observed among other "generic" hunter-gatherer cases. (In this and all future instances, "generic" refers only to the fact that hunter-gatherers with this designation use mobility as their primary means of ensuring subsistence security).

It should be kept in mind that the Group Size Model and the groups in the world sample of hunter-gatherer cases do not differ greatly in scale except for, as previously noted, the mounted hunters and perhaps systems with ranked elites who monopolize leadership roles. Using the Group Size Model as a standard revealed that most of the variability in group size within the ethnographic sample appeared related to the organization of labor and provided a more comprehensive understanding of the effects of changes in the division of labor, polygyny, and the relationships between fundamental social units. Similar issues appear to be involved in the contrasts between mutualists and product specialists, although the Group Size Model is unable to anticipate the states of these systems relative to their neighbors. The model and its modifiers—the division of labor and polygyny—assumed a fundamental equivalence between labor organization and what people ate. With mutualists, however, this assumption was regularly violated when groups in this category were organized to procure animal resources even though their primary source of food consisted of terrestrial plants, and domesticated plants at that.

In chapter 8, I demonstrated that storage breaks the link between group size and the demand for food at a given time (generalization 8.06), and it may be equally true that a formalized exchange of foods breaks the link between food getting, labor organization, and what people actually eat. This recognition permits the identification of systems in which the relationships among variables are different and prompts me to think about cooperation itself. The subsistence success of net-hunting mutualists is based on cooperation at the point of food production, as they coordinate the use of a number of nets, each owned by a different social unit, in the pursuit of specific prey. In contrast, forest product specialists either independently accumulate the forest products upon which their subsistence depends or receive only minimal cooperation from others.

These distinctions prompt me to regard the research of earlier anthropologists in a somewhat different light, particularly the work of the atomists. These researchers accounted for the absence of cooperative labor efforts by postulating the existence of hidden properties of the hunter-gatherer personality, which were knowable through the same observable behaviors that led to the recognition of atomism in the first place.[14] Unfortunately for those who habitually resort to characterizing life in small-scale societies, there is considerable diversity in which aspects of life hunter-gatherers organize cooperatively. A good example would be the polar differences in the level of cooperation in resource procurement between most mutualists and forest product specialists. I hope that more attention to issues of this kind will resolve some of the pointless, normative discussions of sharing—and degrees thereof—among hunter-gatherers, as well as arguments about the social postures of hunter-gatherer groups throughout an annual cycle.

The issue of how cooperation is organized and what kinds of units and lower-order organizations are nested in cooperative and other forms of organization also has not been productively explored. For instance, one assumption of this study has been that hunter-gatherers have a three-tiered structure of group aggregation and dispersal. For that reason, as I researched the ethnographic literature I tried to find estimates of three different group sizes for each hunter-gatherer case. Speculation about the organizational equivalence of the relatively large GROUP2 settlements of some forest product specialists led to the suggestion that there might not be genuine functional equivalents of GROUP2 units among these groups. This would be particularly true if the atomists were correct in their view that the basic or fundamental unit of labor cooperation in such societies was the family and that larger social units did not exist. This possibility leads to another research problem:

Problem 9.03

Is it possible that one of the sources of organizational variability among hunter-gatherers is the character of the group aggregation and dispersion hierarchy itself?

Earlier in this chapter, as part of the discussion of the Guayaki (Ache) of Paraguay, I wondered about the possibility that this group had no GROUP1 pattern of dispersal and that all basal subsistence units were GROUP2 units. I have now suggested that, for forest product specialists, what appear to be GROUP2 units may well be the organizational equivalent of the GROUP3 units of mobile hunter-gatherers. Once this idea occurred to me, a check of the cases that report no values for GROUP3 units revealed that twenty-eight of the thirty-two cases from the Pacific northwest coast of North America have no aggregations comparable to GROUP3 units

as specified by my classification. (Australian Aborigines provide a good example of GROUP3 units every three to seven years, when members of local groups from a large region aggregate for special events such as male initiations.)

Northwest Coast groups were not the only cases lacking GROUP3 units. Seven of the eight Eskimo cases from coastal arctic regions that maintained permanent winter villages also reported no GROUP3 units. Only the Mackenzie Delta Eskimo had a GROUP3-size unit, and it occurred only occasionally, whenever whale hunting was not sufficiently productive to provide stored food for winter consumption (McGhee 1988:4–5). Under these conditions, permanent winter villages were abandoned and temporary snow houses were built on the sea ice, where people from several settlements cooperated to kill seals at their breathing holes. The reported group size at these settlements was, of course, much larger than at the separate settlements from which people had moved.

The aggregation pattern of the Eskimo cases is certainly different from the pattern of the Australian Aborigines who served as a model for the definition of GROUP3 units (breathing hole sealing settlements represent an alternative kind of GROUP2 settlement). Nevertheless, I have learned that all hunter-gatherers do not necessarily have GROUP3 units, and I have identified some cases that either do not have GROUP1 units, such as the Guayaki (Ache), or have what appear to be GROUP2 units that, functionally speaking, are GROUP3 units, such as the Nayaka. I think, therefore, that

Proposition 9.04

One source of variability among hunter-gatherers is the character of the group unit hierarchy. All hunter-gatherer groups do not have the same types of units, and the units they have may serve different functions.

Proposition 9.05

An additional source of variability in hunter-gatherer GROUP2 sizes is the number of alternative subsistence strategies that could be implemented at the time of the greatest annual aggregation of basic subsistence-oriented social units. The Mackenzie Eskimo provide an example of alternative winter strategies that result in different GROUP2 sizes. Similarly, the Southern Tutchone peoples had the option to return regularly to good salmon fishing locations and put up stores for winter or to depend more upon moose hunted during the winter for food. Each subsistence option resulted in different GROUP2 sizes at different seasons (O'Leary pers. comm. 1990; see also O'Leary 1985).

Risk Pooling or Nested Hierarchies of Decision Makers?

I have already pointed out that hunter-gatherer groups in the central arctic have anomalously high GROUP2 sizes (Balikci 1964:17, 36; Damas 1963:116). A look at the values recorded for egalitarian hunter-gatherers with limited leadership (table 9.05, column 7) reveals that the group with the largest basal unit is another central arctic case, the Copper Eskimo. Winter seal hunters of the central Canadian arctic, such as the Mackenzie Eskimo, inspired Mauss and Beuchat (1979) to point out the strong, seasonal, within-system, organizational contrasts in religious observance, family composition, and economics. My analysis has led me to wonder whether the groups from the central arctic that fascinated Mauss and Beuchat and are reported to aggregate in large communities on winter sea ice (Riches 1982:29–31) actually represent a distinct form of organization.

A pertinent field study by Erik Alden Smith (1991:329) determined that, relative to other hunting strategies, breathing hole sealing is characterized by uncertainty. This conclusion helps explain why the preferred subsistence strategy of the Mackenzie Delta Eskimo was the accumulation of stored resources acquired through whale hunting. Based on the strong evidence showing that labor organization is a major conditioner of group size, I would expect that a shift in the way cooperative effort is organized would be associated with a change from whale hunting and associated storage to seal hunting for direct consumption.[15] In fact, recent research has proposed just such an organizational restructuring in the breathing hole sealing context as a basis for large group size: "The hypothesis here is that winter aggregations reduce variation in seal consumption rather than seal harvest, through cooperative distribution rather than cooperative production. . . . I have also pointed to household food storage as an alternative means of variance reduction, but am now less convinced that it is equal or superior to sharing in a situation where poor hunting luck could and sometimes did result in starvation" (Smith 1991:330).

Smith's argument is informed by the excellent research of Bruce Winterhalder (1990). He also explored the issue of comparability between the demand for and the production of resources. He has contrasted the strategy of diversification among productive venues by a single labor-consumer unit to reduce risk with that of diversification among small labor units working in different places as a way of reducing risk for a larger, risk-pooling consumer unit within which sharing is organized. Smith suggests simply that the latter two strategies can be nested, or practiced simultaneously, to use Johnson's term.

Labor units may exploit different venues to reduce the risk experienced by a consumer unit within which shared averaging of returns occurs. At the same time, these consumer units

may be sharing among a larger set of similarly organized units. The classic central arctic hunter-gatherers may be engaged in a similar arrangement with regular seal-sharing partners, which would contribute to large group sizes, in spite of the fact that available information shows that risk does not vary independently of the net return rate in breathing hole sealing field studies (Smith 1991:327). Under the latter conditions, there is no way that maintaining a very large, cooperative hunting party could reduce risk per se.

Winterhalder's work also demonstrates the presence of an economy of scale among small hunting parties whose highest return rate is reached when an average hunting party consists of 3.0 to 3.5 hunters. On the other hand, nested risk pools—which the snow house settlements of the central arctic breathing hole sealers may represent—would be a different story. Smith determined that optimally organized hunting parties engaged in breathing hole sealing would consist of approximately 3.5 hunters. The basal unit of production in large camps—the unit from which daily hunting parties were drawn—would be organized into a risk pool with other basal social units among which there would be formalized sharing conventions. Winterhalder concluded from his study of risk that "80% of the potential risk reduction from pooling and division can be gained by only 6 cooperating foragers. For modestly negative values of R, even smaller numbers of individuals (e.g., 3–5 foragers) can achieve dramatic reductions in the variation of their pooled catch" (1990:79).

The importance of Winterhalder's "magic number" of six should not escape the notice of those who have followed my discussion of Johnson's constant. Equally provocative is the realization that Johnson's empirical example illustrating his constant, and the idea of scalar stress itself, were based on Lee's work with the !Kung speakers of Dobe! This is the same group of people who have been proclaimed by many anthropologists to be the quintessential example of an egalitarian society based on food-sharing principles. Among the !Kung, sharing occurs both in large camps, in which extended families make up the basal unit, and in small rainy season camps in which nuclear families define the basal unit. Given Winterhalder's magic number, the patterning cited by Johnson to support his argument that scalar stress determines group size among the !Kung could just as easily be related to risk pooling and could therefore account for the sharing pools with which the !Kung peoples of Dobe are identified. In that case, I would expect sharing to be organized differently in dry and rainy season camps. This expectation, in fact, appears to be the case.

Too Many Models and Constants!

In spite of the fact that the Group Size Model developed in chapter 7 did not include scalar stress as a variable, my use of the Johnson constant produces a nearly perfect fit between group size and the values anticipated by the model. Now another constant with a value of six has been introduced, which appears to be a factor in the totally different domain of risk reduction. At this juncture I find myself working with three arguments, all of which seem to accommodate at least some of the data on group size. My predicament reminds me that in science it is not uncommon to have two or more "theories" that accommodate the same facts equally well. In such a situation, a researcher usually stops everything and attempts to determine which is the best causal construction, while at the same time he or she may also be attempting to discover under what different initial conditions each explanation may be correct and germane.

The best strategy would be to make some new observations that would help resolve three crucial issues: (1) the effect of group size on the division of labor as discussed in chapter 8; (2) the optimal size of task groups in the context of a division of labor; and (3) the extent to which different tasks affect optimal group size measured in terms of return rates. I also want to clarify the circumstances in which organizational mediation of risk is achieved by the integration of nested risk pooling units and to determine whether group size is modified by decision making procedures in circumstances in which scalar stress is being minimized. These concerns are stated more explicitly in problem 9.04:

Problem 9.04

I have identified three different approaches to building an explanation of variability in hunter-gatherer group size: (1) the Group Size Model developed in chapter 7, (2) the argument based on Johnson's decision making constant of six persons and his postulations about scalar stress, and (3) the arguments of evolutionary biologists who cite optimal task group sizes that are conditioned primarily by return rates and risk reduction strategies. The latter regularly result in Winterhalder's constant of a group of six persons, which, like Johnson's sequential hierarchies, can be nested or segmentary. I want to determine which of these arguments has the maximum explanatory utility and what are the boundaries of such utility.

As tempting as it is, however, to follow up these issues, I feel that this is not the time to abandon the strategy that has brought me this far in my study—that is, to continue to expand my knowledge about what may be germane to know about the world before I attempt to explain patterning already observed.

More Interesting Problems Raised by the Frequency Distributions of "Basal Units"

The hunter-gatherer cases in column 4 of table 9.05 were articulated with or living in a regional environment with other hunter-gatherers whose subsistence strategies were autochthonous. These groups (e.g., the Polar Eskimo, Nunamiut, G/wi, Hadza, Ona, and Nukak), which have been classified as egalitarian on the basis of their decision making procedures, are also the groups with the smallest basal unit values. Most groups meet the criteria of size class 2, but some, to a lesser extent, belong to size class 3 of the basal unit scale (G2BAORD). The same range of variability is observable in the comparison of columns 4 and 5, although the latter suggest a slight shift in the mean unit size with proportionally more cases in size classes 4 and 5.

The cases in column 5 are hunter-gatherers, but their groups feature instituted leadership or headmen whose primary role is to cope with visitors and to organize messengers who monitor dispersed units and inform them of conditions in the society at large. Events involving the entire settlement may be organized by these leaders and social events may be held at the headman's house, but, these activities notwithstanding, leaders are not exempt from subsistence production.

The sequential contrasts in the size of GROUP2 units, with increased size relating to increased investments in leadership status, support the view that a greater emphasis on leadership and role differentiation may be a response to increases in social scale. The frequency shifts from egalitarian to ranked cases following size class 5 also support the view that scalar increases could play a role in the development of leadership and decision making institutions. It is quite provocative that this shift occurs at a level subsequent to the identification by Johnson's model of a size threshold associated with scalar stress (size class 4).

It may be important to point out that only 16.5 percent of the cases classified as egalitarian have basal unit sizes greater than those of size class 4. On the other hand, 59.42 percent of the ranked cases (column 6) have basic unit sizes larger than the stressful size class 4 and 100 percent of the groups with ranked elite (column 7) are larger than those in the stressful zone. This suggests that whatever factors are positively conditioning ranking, the primary basis for differentiation appears to occur before stressful scalar levels are reached and therefore seems unlikely to be an organizational response to scalar stress per se. Another possibility is that these cases could be ranked societies in which declining population levels have resulted in smaller GROUP2 sizes, although it is unclear why decreases in population should affect GROUP2 size rather than the number of such groups.

—————— *Problem 9.05* ——————

Why do more than 25 percent of the hunter-gatherer cases in which wealth and ranking (sensu Fried 1967) play important roles in both leadership and decision making have small GROUP2 units, when these are the units that would facilitate consensual decision making among participating families? It seems unlikely that scalar stress would be responsible for organizational differentiation in these cases as opposed to other egalitarian societies included in table 9.05, column 4. Other conditioning variables must be at work here.

The problem of identifying what these variables may be is exacerbated by the fact that wealth and associated social ranking are characteristic of the mounted plains hunters who demonstrably exemplify groups that have responded to extensificational processes and are also organized at a social scale that is far larger than the majority of hunter-gatherer cases. There is considerably less ambiguity, however, about the expected locus of scalar stress in the ranked societies with elite leadership and simultaneous hierarchies tabulated in column 7 of table 9.05: 100 percent of the basal unit size classes of these cases are larger than the set in size class 4 of table 9.05, and no cases occur in the size classes typical of egalitarian hunter-gatherer groups.

The range of variability is also proportionally extended so that five stratified cases define the upper limit of GROUP2 sizes for all of the hunter-gatherer cases studied here. In fact, these cases dominate the frequencies from size classes 5 through 9 and size class 12 as well. Size classes 10 and 11 include only one case of stratified hunter-gatherers and are dominated by column 3—the mounted hunters—with which I began my comparisons. As I have already noted, mounted hunter groups could also be classified on the basis of wealth differentiation, and therefore some cases, particularly the large ones, could also be included in column 6.

—————— *Generalization 9.11* ——————

Stratification usually occurs in sociopolitical systems that exceed the scale at which most hunter-gatherer societies are organized. A related term, *complexity,* has been defined as the degree of internal differentiation, both structural and functional, within a system. It appears that for internal differentiation to occur, at least a minimal level of group size and social connectivity must be present. This minimal scalar threshold seems to be present in regularly integrated labor-based, social cooperatives of greater than 53.16 persons, or 8.86 persons per basal unit (see table 9.05, size class 4).

Another feature of the overall distribution of elite-based systems in table 9.05, column 7, is that it is uneven and less

graduated than most of the distributions in columns 1 through 6. One could also argue that there is a multimodal distribution to the frequency patterning of the cases in table 9.05, with one suite of cases in size classes 5 and 6, then a gap, followed by another cluster in size classes 8 and 9, followed by another gap, and finally five cases in size class 12 representing the larger-scale GROUP2 units in the 339-case sample. Earlier indications foreshadowing this pattern occurred in chapter 7 (generalization 7.14, proposition 7.02, and the discussion of figure 7.01), where it was noted that the most politically developed cases scaled at very different levels of population relative to size of ethnic territory. It is possible that these dissimilarities in overall scale are played out in the discontinuous distribution of GROUP2 sizes for systems with elite-based leadership. If so, then generalization 9.09 will at least have to be amended and perhaps even considerably modified to account for the impact of scalar conditioning on variability in GROUP2 size.

Some of the features of the relationship between social scale and complexity—as measured by internal social differentiation (generalizations 9.01, 9.04, 9.09, and 9.11)—have already been summarized, but these relationships are easier to visualize using the distributions in table 9.05. For example, those sets of cases that were designed to control for differences in the degree of status and role differentiation, as well as the presence of class differentiation and the concentration of differential access to goods and services in the hands of a few elite families, are scaled with respect to GROUP2 basal unit sizes (the mean size of the largest annual aggregated settlement). This overall pattern should not be surprising, since various researchers have generalized about scale as a diagnostic correlate of complexity in human societies (Johnson 1982; Johnson and Earle 1987; Kosse 1990, 1994; and many others). Nevertheless, the fact that many researchers have "sensed" patterned regularity in the size of social units—and have argued that it implies organizational changes that are causally linked to scalar levels in group size itself—is not the same thing as arriving inductively at similar conclusions based on the analysis of a global sample of hunter-gatherer cases.

Looking back over this particular discussion, I can see that it is necessary to relate the issues enunciated in problem 9.04 to the observations in generalization 9.09. I will begin by noting that wealth, as a precondition for leadership or a characteristic of leaders, did not exhibit any regular correlation with societal scale as indicated by GROUP2 size. On the other hand, stratification or differential access to goods and services by virtue of inherited social position was distributed exclusively among cases for which GROUP2 size exceeded fifty-three persons. Large GROUP2 sizes were not, however, exclusively a feature of systems with elite-based leadership. GROUP2 sizes among the Great Plains mounted hunters overlapped the upper size range of "generic" hunter-gatherers and spanned almost the entire range of values for systems with elite-based leadership, even though these groups are the epitome of societies that were simultaneously large and "egalitarian." I must therefore conclude that

---

Proposition 9.06

While the factors invoked by the use of the term *scale* may be necessary initial conditions, they are not sufficient to account for the appearance of social stratification (which would include caste systems and slavery as well as elite monopolies of leadership and the control of resource-based internal differentiation).

I am now face-to-face with one of the issues that has plagued anthropology since its inception: how do we classify or characterize the observable variability in cultural systems? Often when cultural variability has been considered at a larger comparative scale, many anthropologists have been content to characterize hunter-gatherers in normative terms and then place them on the lowest rung of a taxonomic ladder that ascends to ever-increasing levels of social complexity. In chapter 1, I criticized the intellectual habit of characterizing, and it is no more productive an alternative in this chapter.[16]

It is clear that the integrative institutions of the Great Plains mounted hunters constituted what anthropologists have called "secret societies," which admitted members based on the criterion of age. A search of the hunter-gatherer data set for other similarly organized groups reveals that the Pomo of west central California have similar institutions, even though these groups were primarily dependent for subsistence upon aquatic resources and the exploitation of native plants, particularly acorns. Searching again for institutional analogues, I find that some of the agricultural Pueblo peoples of the American Southwest also had secret societies,[17] although others did not. A quick survey of the data base suggests that secret societies and weak leadership might be associated in large-scale social entities regardless of the character of the food base. The feature that seems to be shared by these otherwise dissimilar societies is social scale, in Johnson's sense of the term.

Clearly, population density levels are very different in all three examples, and different conditioning factors are also involved. The genesis of the life style of the mounted hunters was due in some part to extensificational processes, whereas the factors affecting the Pomo and Pueblo groups were intensificational in character. These dissimilarities tend to support Johnson's view that, at least in some contexts, there are important conditioning differences and therefore potential independence between social scale and populational variables. These factors may appear as autocorrelations, but their quantitative relationship to one another may range from complete independence (in a Plains-Pomo comparison), through par-

tial correlation (in a comparison of the Pomo to at least some Pueblo groups), to a stable, high-level autocorrelation.

Johnson's research has forced me to recognize a very important parameter, but it does not help me deal with other differences between egalitarian or "generic" and more complex systems, particularly those with, on the one hand, internal divisions such as moieties, secret societies, and incipient age-grades and, on the other, hereditary elite leadership and associated control over production. Before issues of this magnitude can be addressed, however, it is necessary to prepare intellectually by focusing on the contrast between scale and populational parameters.

The "Population Pressure" Controversy and the General Issue of Density-Dependent Changes in Organization

Johnson (1982:390) denies any necessary relationship between scalar change in group size and population growth, and he cites Hassan (1975:38) approvingly for distinguishing between population density and group size. Johnson warrants this position by claiming that "there is much less variability in group size than in environmental conditions" (Johnson 1982:390), but the logic underlying this claim is at best opaque. The argumentative sequence begins with a denial of a systematic relationship between group size and population growth, then moves to a discussion of population density (which, I would like to emphasize, is not a direct measure of population growth), and ultimately focuses on variability in environmental conditions! The only way this semantic slipperiness can appear to make sense is if the real argument is about what Johnson (1982:391) calls "subsistence stress," or demand pressure on resources, which is a very controversial subject.

Regardless of terminology, arguments about subsistence stress are arguments about evolutionary processes, which inhabit an entirely different explanatory domain from the views about evolution expounded by early anthropologists. According to their world view, technology caused sociocultural change, and therefore the history of inventions and differential exposure to the knowledge of inventions explained cultural variability. In contrast, Johnson's research explores relationships within sociocultural systems, and in his view "scale" and "scalar stress" refer to size in an organizational sense but not necessarily to overall demographic growth. Johnson's research also operates as a not altogether negative response to the anthropological literature of the 1960s. That corpus sought to reverse the arguments of traditional anthropology by claiming that technological change represents a response to systemic processes that have been triggered by increases in the numbers of persons occupying a habitat and decreases in the capacity of the habitat to sustain them.

Arguments demanding that demographic factors be considered in discussions of traditional problems such as the origins of agriculture (Binford 1968)—or more appropriately the causes of intensificational processes—were common in the literature of the 1960s. I argued that the options available to growing communities were either to channel excess population into separate, geographically dispersed, daughter communities or to intensify production. In regions in which some populations were growing faster than others, I argued that the intensificational responses of expanding systems reduced the foraging ranges of slower-growing hunter-gatherer groups.

At roughly the same time, Ester Boserup (1965) claimed that her research contradicted classic Malthusian arguments (see Banks and Glass 1953 for references to Malthus's work) postulating that population growth resulted in diminished food supplies, which inhibited further growth. Boserup argued instead that increases in population stimulated technological changes, which boosted agricultural production and stimulated economic growth. I was never convinced by Boserup's scenario, which denied that competition and increasing implementation of short-term strategies would occur in a spatially bounded system with increasing population and demand on limited and delimited resources. Boserup's utopian vision, which assumed that long-term sets of future-oriented strategies would be implemented to deal with immediate, pressing problems, seemed to me to be based on a misplaced motivational idealism that made no attempt to account for dynamics in a very material world.[18]

Initially Boserup's arguments enjoyed a brief period of popularity during which they were applied to various archaeological sequences (Smith 1976; Smith and Young 1972) and elaborated upon (Flannery 1969, 1972). Acceptance, however, was short-lived, and numerous negative responses followed (Bender 1975; Bronson 1975; Brumfiel 1976; Cowgill 1975; Hassan 1978, 1981:161–75; Hayden 1972, 1975; and many others). Rejection of the demographic arguments took one of several forms: either a dismissal of the "population as cause" position based on an opposing paradigm or an internal criticism directed against specific assumptions associated with demographic arguments. I will briefly summarize these two approaches.

Neo-Marxists were particularly uncomfortable with demographic arguments, but because their discourse has been well summarized elsewhere in the anthropological literature (Johnson and Earle 1987:6–15), I focus here on a narrower suite of arguments that were presented specifically to challenge postulations about population pressure as a causal engine. I deal first with Barbara Bender (1978, 1981, 1985), who professed that the locus of cause of societal change could be found in the "relations of production." This placement of cause ensured that "demographic pressure will be perceived when the social structure comes under threat rather

than in terms of population survival—it may therefore have nothing to do with an increase in numbers" (Bender 1978:208–9).

Given this perspective on prehistory, Bender (1978:211) searched for "potential internal pressure that might make increasing demands on production." She found her causal motor in the "alliance theory" of Lévi-Strauss and the economic arguments of Sahlins, which were briefly reviewed in chapter 1. For Bender, the link between alliance and economics was exchange, which she pronounced the engine of internal pressure responsible for social change. Increased sedentism would further speed up the internal societal motor, and at this point in her upward theoretical spiral Bender speculated about the contexts in which technological change would be stimulated by alliance exchange: "In areas where resources are bountiful, as along the Northwest Coast, it may lead to increased investment in durable facilities, weirs, dams etc. (further enhancing the leader's status since he organizes the construction and controls access). In other areas, where potential domesticates are available, it may lead to an increased commitment of food production" (Bender 1978:214).

Bender has made a vitalistic argument in which the behaviors and activities of individuals are ascribed to an inherent, irrepressible property of human life, in this case the social relations of production. Her argument is reminiscent of the ideas outlined by Gregory Bateson (1958) in his fascinating ethnographic study *Naven*, in which he claimed to have identified a vital process, which he called *schismogenesis*, that underlies social change. Schismogenesis was defined as "a process of differentiation in the norms of individual behavior resulting from cumulative interaction between individuals," enlightened by the study of "the reactions of individuals to the reactions of other individuals" (Bateson 1958:175). In the ensuing years, similar arguments have attributed major intensificational changes in the organization of cultural systems (including the origins of agriculture) to various schismogenetic linkages between trade, prestige seeking, and increases in productive surplus.

Another kind of argument usually begins with a recitation of the universal properties of human beings and then moves to a schismogenetic formulation: "We argue that the transition from egalitarian to rank societies was a process that occurred on a regional scale under special historical and techno-environmental circumstances. The engine for change was self-interested competition among political actors vying for prestige or social esteem" (Clark and Blake 1996:259).

The similarities between this statement and the "reactions of individuals to the reactions of other individuals" are striking and suggest a vitalistic process of internal feedback. The problem with such arguments is that there is no cause, only consequence, if cause is admitted as vital to the process. This is a variant of what I have called the "Garden of Eden" argument, which is given full expression by Brian Hayden

(1986, 1992; Gargett and Hayden 1991) among others. Human psychology is considered a constant, and therefore all groups contain individuals who are prestige seekers. Groups find themselves in environments that will "sustain escalating exploitation by an aggrandizer. . . . The environment must be productive enough to support a rapidly growing labor force, the followers attached to an aggrandizer. In other words, aggrandizers fare best in 'intensifiable habitats'" (Clark and Blake 1996:261). One would have to conclude that the aggrandizing personality is a societal constant that requires only a fertile environment to produce the transition from egalitarian to ranked society. To say that I am underwhelmed by the preceding arguments is an understatement.

A second suite of objections to the demographic arguments of the mid-1960s was not so much a set of alternative propositions as critiques of the use these arguments made of the related concepts of carrying capacity and population pressure. The linkage between these concepts was reputed to take the form of a ratio between carrying capacity and the demand made on a habitat by a given level of population. The greater the demand relative to the habitat's supply of food resources, the greater the pressure that a population was thought to exert. A corollary of this axiom was that population growth itself regulated the size of the population and, ultimately, the demand for sustaining products.

I have long referred to this formulation of the relationship between carrying capacity and population pressure as "the petri dish view of niches." Given the link between the size of a population attempting to meet its needs and an inflexible "carrying capacity," the hidden assumption is that group fission and expansion of range—the mechanisms that sustained hunter-gatherers and resulted in the peopling of the earth—are somehow no longer feasible. Population levels are assumed to increase within a bounded space, and therefore changes in population density are considered to be surrogate indicators of population pressure. The human response to this putative pressure is to invent new adaptive strategies and techniques that, when implemented, change a region's carrying capacity.

In a very insightful paper, Dewar (1984) has pointed out that this formulation visualized carrying capacity very differently from the meaning given the term by demographers in studies using Lotka's curve (Odum 1959:232). For demographers, the symbol k refers to all density-dependent properties operating to modify the rates at which populations grow. The difficulties inherent in isolating the density-dependent from the density-independent conditioners of population growth have been pointed out numerous times (Dewar 1984:602–5). Intellectual obstacles do not, however, prevent researchers from wondering what the density-dependent consequences are that would suppress rates of population growth and whether such suppression would have any effect

on the problems arising from threats to a region's food supply in the form of increasing population levels.

It should be apparent that if there are too many people relative to the food supply, the problem will not be solved by reducing the rate of population growth, because populations would still continue to grow, unless a catastrophic situation occurred. And, under such extreme conditions, it is hard to imagine that much effort would be invested in developing new strategies and tactics designed to solve future problems, because people would be trying to cope with critical, short-term situations.[19] At bottom, scenarios about carrying capacity, on the one hand, and attempts to determine which density-dependent conditions might depress growth rates, on the other, reflect two very different approaches to process.

These interesting features of the demographic literature aside, the central issue facing anthropologists working from a demographic perspective has to do with "population pressure" and two other related event sequences: diminishing returns and populations that hover on the edge of a food crisis. When I initially began to investigate problems of subsistence and demographic change (Binford 1968), I assumed that population growth in the ancient past had occurred at relatively slow rates. I tried to imagine the conditions that might concentrate temporally the consequences of slow growth and produce rapid changes in population relative to the productive character of finite habitats. I proposed emigrations from more rapidly growing populations into the subsistence space of more stable populations as one possible situation in which gross interference with the subsistence base of resident peoples might occur. Such a scenario might also create the necessity for adaptive change on the part of the migrant population.

What I had in mind was largely unstated: that is, increasing interference with, and therefore increasing costs to, traditional tactics of food procurement should force exploration of and perhaps shifts to alternative or new tactics. If diminishing returns were the only currency for evaluating tactics, then it seemed likely that people would pay the costs and increase their labor investment through traditional means and thereby increase net returns. Such a response seemed to be standing behind Flannery's (1969:77–79) broad-spectrum revolution, which represented a simple expansion of the scope of existing procurement techniques through increased labor. The same techniques would remain in use, but a tactical shift would favor an expansion of diet breadth.

The shift to cultivation represents both a change in subsistence techniques and an altered tactical strategy. In order to evaluate the rationality of tactics and strategies—the reasons why some work and others do not—more factors than simply the relationship between abundance in the habitat and the demand for food generated by population levels must be considered. The techniques and tactics of food procurement themselves have mediating efficiencies and optimal settings for implementation that drastically modify the relationship between simple, gross demand for food and the abundance of potential foods. These efficiencies vary with the scale of the environment over which they can be implemented and the structure of the distribution of potential foods in that environment.

A set of tactics may work quite well under one set of demographic conditions, but when they are employed in conjunction with a different regional demographic structure, the same techniques may be counterproductive. For instance, some groups of hunter-gatherers—such as the Tubatulabal, whose range was east of the current city of Bakersfield, California—set fires on a regular basis as part of their rabbit drives (Smith 1978:444). The fires would eventually burn out before they threatened neighboring settlements or negatively affected the subsistence practices of adjacent groups.

It does not require much imagination, however, to anticipate the reaction to a fire set today by a Tubatulabal who wanted to hunt rabbits in the valleys of the Kern River. This is what is meant by saying that some tactics and strategies are density-dependent in terms of their utility and efficiency. It may well be that many basic tactical and strategic changes, such as the adoption of techniques of plant cultivation, could have more to do with thresholds conditioning the utility of earlier tactics and strategies than the actual long-term, nutritional state of a population or its absolute level of demand on resources.

In preceding chapters, I have argued that intensification is a process of extracting greater nutritional benefit from parcels of land of decreasing size. This process can be thought of as a response to increased numbers of failures in the time-tested strategy of hunter-gatherer adaptation, which is mobility. In this regard I have written elsewhere:

> the driving forces of change lie in the interaction between the environment and the adaptive system being considered. Given such a view, the systems of adaptation may enjoy relatively stable periods of varying duration, representing times when it is able to cope successfully with the perturbations of the environment. Selection for change occurs when the system is unable to continue previously successful tactics in the face of changed conditions in the environment. The source of such change may be the accumulated effects of the system's history, but such effects are buildups of changed ecological relationships rather than the continuous operation of either some inner vital principles or of unrelenting external pressures.   (Binford 1983:203)

The challenge to archaeologists is therefore to be able to isolate density-dependent processes that render traditional subsistence strategies and techniques ineffective and obsolete. In such a context, innovations would become mandatory considerably before starvation and social chaos ensued, which is the condition most often implied by the proponents of population pressure as a mechanism for change.

Reflections

I had two goals in mind when I began this chapter. I wanted to illustrate that it is sometimes useful to contrast apparently conflicting ideas with one another and then to use ideas developed in the context of one argument as a frame of reference for looking at the ethnographic data base in ways that had not previously been considered. A related goal was to accumulate intellectual ammunition for my engagement in the next chapter with the issue of intensification. I hoped that my goals would interact synergistically, prompting me to think new thoughts and to imagine new ways of organizing the observations at my disposal.

The first thing I learned was that Johnson's constant of six entities matched the frequency distribution of the number of basic family units making up GROUP1 units (generalization 9.02). This congruence makes a great deal of sense and supports Johnson and Earle's claim that "the family or hearth group is the primary subsistence group. It is capable of great self-sufficiency, but moves in and out of extended family camps or hamlets opportunistically as problems or opportunities arise" (1987:19). The independence of the basal family as defined in my study[20] provided the basis for many generalizations attesting to the flexibility of hunter-gatherer groupings. With regard to GROUP1 units, my findings provide substance for pronouncements by many anthropologists, and they support Johnson's constant as fundamental to segmentally organized social units.

When patterning in the distribution of GROUP2 units was examined, however, the identity of basal units and the importance of a constant of six became less clear. My expectations were similar to those enunciated by Johnson (1982:396–97) and Johnson and Earle (1987): that hunter-gatherer social segmentation corresponded to what is termed the "extended family," a much-discussed but elusive entity. According to Murdock (1949:23), the extended family consisted of "two or more nuclear families united by consanguineal kinship bonds such as those between parents and child or between two siblings." Although segmental organizations of nuclear families certainly existed among the cases in the global sample of hunter-gatherer cases, such forms were not documented at the time of data production for the basic hunter-gatherer file. That such forms were probably germane is supported by the observation that neither GROUP1 units nor basal family units were the basal units of GROUP2 settlements (see the discussion following figure 9.04).

I therefore investigated the possibility that households might provide a surrogate clue to the character of the basal unit segments making up GROUP2 units. Generalizations 9.05 and 9.07 point out that household size responds to environmental variables affecting the primary function of houses, which is to provide shelter, as well as to the size and composition of the segmental units in need of shelter. The as yet undefined interaction between these two very different suites of conditioning variables makes the role that households play in the formation of basal organizational units ambiguous.

Quite unexpectedly, I found that, except for cases in which households equaled GROUP2 or basic organizational units, household size increased in a regular way with increases in GROUP2 size. I also discovered that this patterned increase was not identical in all hunter-gatherer cases but that it instead took three different forms. Although I did not pursue these provocative observations, the possible linkage between household size and environmental and social correlates, particularly GROUP2 unit size, suggests that archaeologists should investigate these relationships further. The study of household variability relative to variability in house size is an obvious place to begin, and it should be followed up by a search for patterning linking these two variables to household composition and GROUP2 size.

My strategy in this chapter has paid off in several other ways besides what I learned about basal organizational units. The decision to assume that basal units were defined by Johnson's constant of six led me to the realization that very different conditioning factors were involved in processes of extensification and intensification. The mounted hunters of the Great Plains—who have consistently emerged as different from other hunter-gatherer groups in many comparisons and tabulations of variables—again demonstrated their divergence from the norm with large-scale social units and very low population densities. These groups also had more of the attributes associated with complexity, a process that appears to be responsive to social scale rather than to population levels and the density-dependent variables usually cited in discussions of social complexity.

In this regard, I pointed out in chapter 5 that, contrary to conventional wisdom, pastoralists—rather than hunter-gatherers—occupied the world's most marginal environments. This fact illustrates that the growth and development of social systems on which extensificational pressures have operated is a neglected domain of anthropological research. In how many textbooks is it possible to find pastoralists[21] and other systems that respond to processes of extensification listed as examples of the linear model of cultural evolution?

One of the most interesting results of my pattern recognition work was the identification of systems practicing alternative subsistence strategies during the most aggregated phase of their annual cycle. As an example, I pointed to the experience of the Mackenzie Delta Eskimo, who one winter were forced to relocate to larger than usual, temporary settlements on the Arctic sea ice, where they hunted seals at breathing holes—a tactic that required the establishment of new working relationships emphasizing cooperative labor. This singular event, which was recorded by an observer, prompted me to take another look at the circumstances associated with the anomalously large GROUP2 sizes of the

central arctic Eskimo, and I discovered that for these groups breathing hole sealing was the customary winter subsistence strategy.

Evolutionary biologists have tried to explain the popularity of this alternative, beginning with the argument that because risk pooling could be segmentally organized by the central arctic Eskimo, the large size of their winter sealing villages could not be understood exclusively in terms of pooling the risk associated with food acquisition. It appeared more likely that a two-stage, nested set of risk-pooling organizations was at work: the smaller unit was a labor-sharing pool for reducing the risk in food procurement, while the larger, more inclusive, more reticulate risk pool was designed to reduce the risk of food shortages among consumers.[22] The presence of the latter, larger risk pool, it was argued, conditioned the larger GROUP2 winter settlements.

These observations and arguments were fascinating in themselves, but I discovered that the upper limit on the number of units participating in the larger risk pool designed to cope with food shortages corresponded to the Johnson constant of six. The ubiquitous presence of the constant six finally clarified several observations that had originally seemed inconsistent.

First of all, Johnson used the !Kung as an example of what he termed sequential hierarchies. He noted that the nuclear family was the basic social unit in rainy season GROUP1 camps, whereas the extended family formed the basic unit at dry season GROUP2 camps. In Johnson's data, the mean size of the nuclear family was 3.43 persons and mean extended family size was 11.43 persons. The latter unit consisted of 3.33 basal units (11.43 divided by 3.43), a figure that does not have much in common with a constant of six. Johnson also reported that !Kung dry season camps were made up of extended family basal units and had a mean size of forty persons. Dividing the size of the dry season camps by the mean value of their basal units (40.0 divided by 11.43) produces a value of 3.49 as the number of basal units, which—again—is not in the same ballpark as the Johnson constant.

On the other hand, 3.33 and 3.49 are not very different from the value of 3.55 that Smith (1991:327–30) found was the optimal size of the labor unit designed to reduce the risks resulting from differential hunting success by averaging returns, or sharing, among the participating hunters. The social units of the Dobe !Kung have been reported as modular in structure, associated with a sequential hierarchy of shifting sizes of basal units, as Johnson argued.

The difference in the !Kung case appears to be that the nested hierarchy is organized in terms of labor cooperatives and risk pools that function at the level of both food procurement and food consumption. For example, food sharing in rainy season camps was based on the pooling of procurement risk among all cooperating males in the camp. In dry season camps, however, a pattern of meat sharing and averaging of returns among cooperating hunters was followed by a pattern of distribution in which individual hunters shared their portions with others, based on egocentric criteria.

The only well-documented case of two-stage sharing among the !Kung was recorded by DeVore and published by Yellen (1977b:285–90). In this record, sharing among hunters takes the form of a pooled average of returns, while each hunter's sharing with consumers is biased toward sharing with members of the preceding or parental generation. Any campwide distributions of food result from subsequent sharing by members of the senior generation. Each extended family is represented in the daily hunting cooperatives of short duration by males of the younger generation.

It is this linkage between labor and the size of the risk pool units in each of the different ways of organizing risk that accounts for the strong fit of the Group Size Model with the empirical material. The provocative fit of GROUP1 data to the Johnson constant of six is due to the fact that nuclear families made up the basal units and that group sizes were a function of labor cooperatives with alternating daily work schedules, which required six units in order to meet the target of three different male or female workers each day.

This understanding of the sequential hierarchies prevalent among many small-scale hunter-gatherer groups is also consistent with Johnson's astute observation (generalization 9.01 and proposition 9.01) that the correlation between a system's complexity and the size of its population is only really apparent if a very wide range of variability in population is considered. Johnson also pointed out that, when relatively minor differences in population were involved, there was significant "local" variation, and I agree with this assessment. All of the variability in GROUP1 sizes is conditioned by labor organization, work schedules, and the sexual division of labor.

There is a much greater range in the size of GROUP2 units, and they are also less well understood. When GROUP2 size exceeds a threshold of between forty and fifty-three persons (generalization 9.11), scalar-based changes may appear. This threshold, however, has been determined by assuming that the smallest of the elite-based systems in my sample of ethnographic cases have been subjected to scalar stresses subsequent to documented population growth or reductions in the size of their ranges. Since my method recognizes

only those systems that have been successful in coping with stress or other intensificational pressures, there are still many questions about the systems that fail and become extinct, such as: What would failing systems look like? Are organizational responses to scalar change or intensificational processes reversible?

If the answer to the latter question is "no," then it raises the possibility of abnormally small-scale systems that have overblown organizational features and presents another challenging aspect of system state variability to investigate. As part of the discussion of intensification in the next chapter, I will need to control for more variables and design the analysis with issues such as these in mind.

A preoccupation with system state issues in the last section of this chapter stimulated my discussion of population pressure—which was contrasted with Johnson's concept of scalar change—and some of the difficulties associated with identifying the sector within a system where density-dependent variables operate. It has been widely assumed that these factors operate at the consumer level and that reductions in the accessible food base exacerbate the stereotypical hunter-gatherer condition in which, as Sahlins (1968:85) said, "starvation stalks the stalker." I discussed Boserup's (1965) argument that food scarcity was the stimulus for technological changes that, in turn, increased agricultural production and prompted further demographic growth. I also commented on the controversial literature arguing that populational variables were causal conditioners of change and suggested that density dependence is a state that has direct impact on hunter-gatherer tactics and strategies of food procurement, perhaps partially independently of reductions in return rates that result from their implementation.

My contribution to this important discussion briefly introduced ideas that take a wider view and attempted to argue that the costs of tactical implementation are conditioned by more variables than simply the standing crop of available resources at any given time. For instance, although competition with neighbors can be costly and result in an increase in the standing crop of resources, competition may also drive down the return rate and result in a shift to alternative foods. In the next chapter, discussion of the complicated interaction of density-dependent variables continues as the issue of intensification is addressed directly.

Putting Ideas, Second-Order Derivative Patterning, and Generalizations Together

Explorations in Theory Building

In this final section, the focus is on analysis and integration, with the goal of learning more about what appear to be the germane characteristics of the world of hunter-gatherers. At the same time, I hope to integrate the picture of that world with arguments about why it is the way it appears to be. My conclusions may or may not represent a formal theory, because what I have learned by using frames of reference—coupled with how the world I have observed is organized—may change my view of what the "subject-side" world is like. The focus of theory building can be said to shift as our learning strategies lead to the development of more secure, subject-side knowledge.

One challenge remains unchanged, however, and that is to explain the cultural variability that has been documented ethnographically among hunter-gatherer peoples. In the final chapter of this book, we come face-to-face with the realization that cultural variability may have arisen in response to dynamics operating in two or more semi-independent causal domains. I have demonstrated, for instance, how the domain of habitat variability impinges upon hunter-gatherer life ways. Environments are not static but fluctuate at some scale all of the time. The question becomes: how do changes in the environmental domain differentially affect cultural systems that vary in terms of social scale, adaptive organization, and packing state? I believe that I have made some progress toward understanding and beginning to explain the causal processes that operate upon these domains.

I have not been able to deal substantively with the issues of reversibility and irreversibility, but I hope that the exercises in environmental reconstruction make it clear that this subject is critically important, since the real world is not static but changes at an ecosystemic level at different rates and tempos. The importance of dynamics of this kind must be appreciated prior to developing a theory that will predict both when something will happen and when it will not.

I have stressed, however, the importance of initial conditions in structuring trajectories of change, since, to a large extent, they affect the way that similar density-dependent processes or ecologically induced changes in habitat play out for different hunter-gatherer groups. A greater understanding of these dynamics should put us in a position to address systematically the issue of irreversibility and the mechanisms underlying emergent patterns of punctuated change represented by new niche formation.

CHAPTER
10

A Disembodied Observer Looks at
Hunter-Gatherer Responses to Packing

The flow of ideas in this chapter has much in common with the rush-hour traffic patterns seen from a helicopter that hovers over and monitors the vehicles streaming through the confluence of two or more multilane highways. These big interchanges are often given names like "the spaghetti bowl" or "the mix-master" because some roads turn and twist and disappear while others wrap around themselves and emerge from the jumble oriented in a different direction from the one they were following when they entered the interchange.

In the first half of this book, it was fairly easy to distinguish between the events taking place in the scientific theater and those on the hunter-gatherer stage, but in the last three chapters it has seemed increasingly artificial to separate the two arenas. Tactics and strategies initiated in the scientific domain have become increasingly important to an understanding of events that once occurred in the hunter-gatherer theater. A marked shift in tempo between the two domains should be apparent to the reader: discussions of themes in the scientific theater flow smoothly and quickly, but the pace slows in the sections in which dynamics in the hunter-gatherer theater are monitored through pattern recognition studies.

The justification for the "spaghetti bowl" metaphor comes from the feedback between the slow and sometimes laborious episodes of pattern recognition work and subsequent events in the scientific theater. Ideas often change, commitments to particular ways of looking at the world are frequently modified, and, in the full light of knowledge growth, what had appeared to be helpful "natural units" are revealed as expedient, rather than essential, analytical tools.

This chapter is about the synergy between a scientist's use of prior knowledge and the patterns that are exposed through structured, source-side observations that directly implicate the characteristics of dynamics taking place in the hunter-gatherer theater. To illustrate the synergetic method, I shift

back and forth between two roles: at one moment I participate as an actor in the scientific play, while at another I become a disembodied observer who floats above the stage and comments on the action. In the former role, I provide a commentary on the developing plot of the scientific play. As a disembodied observer, on the other hand, from the vantage point of my metaphorical helicopter, I describe the complicated traffic patterns moving through the analytical spaghetti bowl and point out the feedback loops that characterize the synergistic learning experience.

The term *intensification* has been used many times in previous chapters. I think of it as the process that impels hunter-gatherers to increase the amount of food they extract from smaller and smaller segments of the landscape. The linkage between intensification and increases in population has already been identified, and I have presented arguments outlining the factors that govern group size among mobile hunter-gatherers. I and others have suggested that small group size is advantageous for mobile peoples and that, as population increases, new groups will be formed, resulting in increasingly packed ranges and circumscription of the economic space used by any given group.

In this chapter, the effect of reduced range size on hunter-gatherer habitats will be explored, as will the responses of hunter-gatherers to the inevitable impact of range reduction on their subsistence strategies. Another feature of this chapter is an expansion of the scope in terms of which intensification is investigated. Obviously, intensification applies both to horticultural practices and to the seminal issue of the origins of agriculture. It was, after all, hunter-gatherers who became prehistory's horticulturists, pastoralists, and agriculturists. I increasingly explore clues derived from a study of hunter-gatherer variability to determine how, in the past, intensification might have promoted the exploration of new ways to satisfy human nutritional requirements using plant and animal resources.

Habitat Variability, Potential Niche Diversity, and the Spatial Structure of Resource Accessibility

Disembodied Observer: The title of this section makes sense only to readers who know that in the scientific theater many behind-the-scenes discussions and late-night brainstorming sessions have preceded the opening curtain. One argument claims that, thus far, environmental information has been used in a relatively static way, usually as a stable frame of reference against which variability in hunter-gatherer plays has been projected. A more realistic view holds that environments are not static and that there are likely to be dynamic links between habitats—defined exclusively in terms of nonhuman ecology and biology— and the scales at which human beings fit into these habitats.

At this point in the scientific play, this idea is explored by drawing upon prior knowledge available from nonanthropological research to develop a number of provocative generalizations. Then the audience is exposed to the impact that new information can have on previous research, as a number of propositions are developed that stipulate the possible consequences for hunter-gatherers of changes in their effective environments. These ideas appear consistent with what I already know, but they nevertheless extend beyond my current analytical abilities.

If niche diversity is considered not as a formal property of a habitat but as a variable condition of hyperspace (see chapter 2)—that is, variable with respect to the spatial clumping and availability of diverse food resources—it might be possible to isolate some consequences of intensification that I have not previously considered. As a bonus, other clues pointing to the factors responsible for various forms of adaptation might also be recognized, as well as differences in system state levels of complexity.

I have already demonstrated that variance in hunter-gatherer subsistence practices is strongly related to the habitats within which such groups live (see generalizations 7.01 through 7.05, 7.11, 7.12, 8.04, 8.08, 8.09, 8.12, 8.17, 8.18, and 8.33 as well as propositions 7.01 and 8.02). I have not yet considered the changes in hunter-gatherer habitats that result from their own different density-dependent states. It would be worthwhile to consider the character of changes in the habitat that inevitably arise from reductions in the subsistence range or the area from which hunter-gatherers obtain their food. This is because changes in the effective environments of peoples living in the same ecological space are indeed habitat changes, even if they result from shifts in the size of the subsistence range and changes in the way labor is organized.

Investments in technology usually have a similar effect as they enlarge and render more productive a particular set of windows giving access to resources. This kind of change may occur without affecting the environment, lowering the nutritional returns, or degrading the ecosystem and reducing its complexity. On the other hand, there are no free meals, and intensification can lead to a reduction of the energetic level of segments of the ecosystem.

CHANGES IN EFFECTIVE HABITAT ARISING FROM REDUCTIONS IN SUBSISTENCE RANGE

It is a well-known fact that the number of plant species in a given area varies exponentially with the size of the area within which the species count is made (Cailleux 1953; Williams 1964). This relationship is well illustrated in table 10.01, which presents Cailleux's data from various regions in France. The exponential relationship between the number of species and the area ensures that changes in range size will restructure the effective environment of a group of foragers, even if there is no change in group size. As an example, by using the equation in table 10.01, the number of species that would be available for exploitation by groups of foragers living at different density levels in France—whose range size is between approximately 140 and more than 4,000 square kilometers—can be determined.

These relationships are explicated further by the data in table 10.02, which illustrate that range reduction can dramatically modify the effective environments of human groups as measured by the number of species available for potential exploitation. It should be noted, however, that the number of species tells only part of the story. In most settings, abundant species account for approximately 20 percent of the total species present in an area (Williams 1964:60). Plentiful species also yield higher nutritional returns—other things, such as handling time, being equal— than relatively rare species because of the greater search time and mobility costs associated with acquiring fewer available resources.

TABLE 10.01

NUMBER OF SPECIES OF FLOWERING PLANTS COMPARED WITH SIZE OF AREA SURVEYED

	AREA IN KM^2	SPECIES COUNT
ALL OF FRANCE	550,000	4,400
PARIS REGION	30,000	2,871
PAS DE CALAIS	6,605	1,400
HAXEBROUCH	708	980
LE FAZEL, OISE	7	516

Note: These data fit an exponential curve according to $y = 2.71828^{**}[a + b^* \log N(x)]$, where $a = 5.7393514$ and $b = 0.19559006$, $y =$ number of species, and $x =$ area in square kilometers.

TABLE 10.02

EXPECTED NUMBER OF SPECIES OF FLOWERING PLANTS OCCURRING IN RANGES OF DIFFERENT SIZE AND OCCUPIED BY HUNTER-GATHERER GROUPS OF TWENTY PERSONS

POPULATION DENSITY	AREA OF RANGE (KM^2)	EXPECTED NUMBER OF SPECIES	NUMBER OF ABUNDANT SPECIES
200.00	10	490	98
66.66	30	607	121
40.00	50	671	134
28.57	70	716	143
14.28	140	821	164
8.00	250	920	184
5.71	350	983	196
4.44	450	1,033	206
2.00	2,000	1,209	215
1.00	1,000	1,386	277
0.50	4,000	1,588	318

TABLE 10.03

RESIDUAL SPECIES IN AREAS OF COMPARABLE SIZE LOCATED IN DIFFERENT ENVIRONMENTAL ZONES, USING FRENCH FLOWERING PLANTS AS A BASELINE FOR MEASUREMENT

SAMPLE AREA	NUMBER OF EXPECTED SPECIES	NUMBER OF OBSERVED SPECIES	PERCENTAGE DIFFERENCE BETWEEN OBSERVED AND EXPECTED	NUMBER
BAFFIN ISLAND	4,207	129	−96.93	−4,143
NEW MEXICAN DESERT	1,127	62	−94.50	−1,065
MANITOBA, CANADA	4,307	1,029	−76.11	−3,278
DENMARK	2,838	1,084	−61.81	−1,754
TASMANIA	2,773	1,096	−60.48	−1,677
KANGAROO ISLAND, AUSTRALIA	1,615	653	−59.57	−962
CALIFORNIA	3,949	3,727	−5.63	−222
JAPAN	3,907	4,000	7.00	93
CONNECTICUT	1,998	2,228	10.32	250
MANILA AREA	769	1,007	23.64	238
TRINIDAD	1,628	2,500	34.88	872
SOUTH AFRICA—CAPE	1,127	1,750	35.60	623
MALAY PENINSULA	2,935	5,100	42.45	2,165
JAVA	385	2,400	83.5	2,015

Notes: All values were calculated using the formula in table 10.01. Data on area and number of observed species were taken from Williams (1964:312–17). Area (x) was then used to solve for expected species, using the same equation.

Changes in range size often result in different consequences for foragers, depending upon their environment. Table 10.03 illustrates the significant differences in the number of species per unit area associated with a variety of climatic and geographic regimes, using flowering species from France as a baseline for measurement. The locations for which species counts were available are arranged ordinally in table 10.03 in terms of the difference—expressed as a percentage—between observed and expected values. The term *expected values*, of course, refers to expected abundance of species in France. It is clear that very warm locations with high rainfall have observed values that exceed expected levels by as much as 83 percent, whereas observed values are lower than expected by 97 and 94 percent, respectively, for Baffin Island (in the arctic) and the desert of New Mexico, both places with very low productivity. In the case of Baffin Island, diminished solar radiation accounts for reduced productivity and species richness; low rainfall is responsible for the same result in the New Mexican desert.[1]

The species density of habitats prior to intensification is a crucial component of the complex set of circumstances encompassed by the term *initial conditions,* and clearly differences in species density levels can be expected to produce different outcomes in response to reductions in the size of hunter-gatherer ranges. The fact that aquatic resources play such a predominant role in the subsistence of foragers in arctic zones, and that most of these cases are also packed, supports the view that a shift to aquatic resources is the most viable hunting and gathering response to intensificational pressure in high-latitude settings.[2]

THE RELATIONSHIP BETWEEN ANIMAL BODY SIZE AND RANGE SIZE: FURTHER CHANGES REFERABLE TO INTENSIFICATION

The investigation of the relationship between animal body size and home range has a long history in ecological research (Damuth and MacFadden 1990), one result of which has been the discovery of an overall logarithmic relationship between these two variables (Damuth 1982; Eisenberg 1990; Gittleman and Harvey 1982; Harestad and Bunnell 1979; McNab 1963; Peters 1983; Schoener 1968, 1981; Swihart et al. 1988). When animal species are segregated into trophic subclasses, the empirical relationships are much tighter and differ according to feeding strategy.

Animals that are direct consumers of primary plant production, such as ungulates, have a smaller home range per unit of body size and more animals are supported per unit area, resulting in a relatively high population density. On the other hand, carnivores that feed primarily on other animals have much larger home ranges than herbivores of similar body size and correspondingly lower population densities (Harestad and Bunnell 1979:390; Peters 1983:167; Schoener 1968:135).

In a given area, therefore, approximately 86 percent of the total animal biomass will consist of feeders on primary production and the remaining 14 percent will be carnivores. This relationship demonstrates that, at the scale of trophic differentiation, there is a correlation between range size and habitat abundance: the less abundant the habitat, the larger the size of the range.

Even these two trophic classes can be broken down into more niche-specific terms. For instance, McNab (1963) found that herbivorous animals that consume primarily the photosynthetic organs of plants (e.g., bovids) have higher population densities than herbivores subsisting on the reproductive organs of plants and related plant products, such as seeds and nectar. It was also apparent that for the latter class of herbivores population densities are lower relative to body size than among blade and leaf feeders. Similarly, primate species that are fruit and insect feeders have larger home ranges than leaf-eating species (Harvey and Read 1992:156).

Unlike the relationships between range size, body size, and species abundance in trophically distinct forms, such as herbivores and carnivores, among species that feed on primary production the feeding specialties are more numerous and body sizes and ranges are smaller. This means that, in some areas with low plant productivity, the number of animal species is greater—other things being equal—and average body size is smaller. For example, of the forty-eight contiguous United States, New Mexico has the highest number of different mammalian species (Simpson 1964), even though plant productivity is not particularly high. New Mexico does, however, have considerable between-habitat diversity that is related to altitudinal differences, but this factor is not enough to account for the high level of animal species richness. In this case, species diversity appears to be associated with the presence of many creatures of very small body size that have small home ranges and correspondingly reduced niche distributions.

More recent ecological research has tended to study the relationship between body size and species density rather than range size itself (Currie and Fritz 1993; Demuth 1981, 1987; Maurer and Brown 1988; Peters and Raelson 1984), and the results indicate that more than 80 percent of the variation in the $\log_{10}$ value of animal population densities is accounted for by body size.

--- *Generalization 10.01* ---

As hunter-gatherer range size is reduced, exploitation of animals of large body size also decreases. It follows that, the greater the reduction in subsistence area, other things being equal, the more dependent upon animals of smaller and smaller body size hunter-gatherers must become.

Body size is not the only issue, however. Species density or richness also exhibits great geographic variability. Recent research has shown that once the strong relationship to body size is controlled and animals are separated into different metabolic groups (invertebrates, ectotherms, birds, and mammals), the single variable that best accounts for most of the residual variability is potential evapotranspiration (PET). Currie and Fritz (1993) have demonstrated the strength of this variable's patterning using global positioning techniques applied to sample locations.

The preceding discussion of the geographic patterning in and relationships between animal density and richness can be summarized in the following terms:

Generalization 10.02

As subsistence area and species richness are reduced as a power function of area, hunter-gatherers normally rely more heavily on fewer animal species of smaller and smaller body size, other things being equal.

The patterns summarized in generalizations 10.01 and 10.02 correspond to niche differences relative to the abundance of targeted foods in a habitat. The frequencies of species of large body size decrease as net aboveground productivity declines, but they increase as the turnover rate in the plant community increases. If most of a habitat's biotic production is in the form of plant biomass, less food is available to those plant feeders that consume new growth, particularly photosynthetic and reproductive organs and related products. The smaller an animal's body size, the shorter its life span, which means that its period of reproductive maturity is very short. Most short-lived species produce mature offspring annually, and their populations change in very short growth intervals.[3] This results in long-term stability in the food supply for species that exploit such animal populations.[4]

The preceding discussion of habitat differences exemplified by variability in the species abundance of plants and animals was intended to demonstrate that, as far as the exploitation of prey species is concerned, a reduction in the size of subsistence ranges will have inevitable consequences:

Generalization 10.03

Given a reduction in the size of a group's effective subsistence range, the number of plant species available for exploitation decreases as a power function of the scale of the reduction in area.

These relationships are further complicated by the fact that habitats differ dramatically in the number of species per unit area. The range of difference in plant species was illustrated in table 10.02 (see also Currie and Paquin 1987), and it applies to animals of all kinds (Currie and Fritz 1993). The

species richness or density of trees (the numbers of species per standard unit area) appears to be strongly related, as a curvilinear function of actual evapotranspiration (AE), to the usable energy available to a plant community. This energy is partitioned among species within the community, and the total available amount acts as a limit on species richness itself (Currie and Paquin 1987:327). Regardless of the dynamics that are postulated to account for these patterns, however, the point is that the number of plant species varies in response to the same environmental variable (AE) as net aboveground productivity. In highly productive environments, there are a greater number of species per unit area than in low-productivity settings.

The pattern of reduction in species numbers in response to conditions suggested in generalization 10.02 is not expected to vary linearly but rather as a power function relative to the availability of solar radiation, since the metabolic rates of plants vary considerably with latitude or PET. As the metabolic levels of the plant community are reduced in conjunction with reduced levels of solar radiation, the number of species appears to decrease as a power function of metabolic levels, semi-independently of productivity. In other words,

Generalization 10.04

The scalar consequences of range reduction for hunter-gatherers will vary among habitats as a function of the species richness and structure of equability within the plant community where the range reduction occurs.

These patterns in the distribution of species richness and (in animal species) the relationship between body size and density ensure that range reduction results in a decrease in the number of species and the number of potential food sources. In the case of animals, range reduction results in fewer opportunities for exploiting animals of large body size, other things being equal. Another important feature is that species richness is strongly conditioned by the global patterning in energy distribution.

Generalization 10.05

Other things being equal, when climate changes from colder to warmer conditions, as it did at the close of the Pleistocene, it is reasonable to expect increases in diet breadth and the appearance of a *broad-spectrum revolution* as a simple function of environmental change. Subsistence change by hunter-gatherers in this instance represents a response to environmental change and is not a "strategic change" per se.

Against the background of the preceding cursory description of the relationship between range size and species richness, as well as changes in the accessibility of terrestrial animals, I now turn to a consideration of hunter-gatherer responses to intensification and packing. My focus remains, however, on subsistence practices and correlative relationships.

SOME CONSEQUENCES OF INTENSIFICATION AND ADDITIONAL LINKS TO HABITAT, TECHNOLOGY, AND EMERGENT COMPLEXITY

I have already pointed out that no successful hunter-gatherers in my ethnographic data base were, at the same time, primarily dependent upon terrestrial animals and either sedentary (generalization 7.10) or characterized by population densities exceeding the packing threshold (generalization 7.09). I have also contended that the only significant, long-term intensificational response of hunters to packed conditions is to reduce their dependence upon larger terrestrial animals and to shift to terrestrial animals of smaller body size (generalization 10.02). For hunter-gatherer groups in cool to cold environments, the only option is to shift to aquatic resources, which, along with an increased dependence upon plants, is also an option for groups in warm-temperate to equatorial settings.

In settings in which foragers are expected to be primarily dependent upon terrestrial plant resources (see figures 5.11 and 6.07), intensification may condition expansion of diet breadth through increased use of terrestrial plants and at the same time also result in experimentation with aquatic resources. An expansion of both diet breadth and niche breadth is therefore possible when pressures to intensify occur.

Proposition 10.01

Increased use of aquatic resources by groups dependent upon terrestrial plants would reduce risk as a function of the increased probability that accessing schedules are not likely to be synchronous (Binford 1991c:33–40, 232). Under these conditions, greater stability in meeting consumer demands for food could be anticipated. Greater niche breadth would also reduce the rate at which intensification of plant use, including cultivars, would proceed relative to (1) scalar changes in social organization and (2) other, as yet unidentified, factors favoring ranking or other nonegalitarian social features.

Applying these expectations to the issue of the transformation of hunter-gatherers into horticulturists, it is reasonable to suggest that, other things being equal,

Proposition 10.02

The earliest use of domesticated plants and animals should occur in already packed regions that lack sub-

stantial aquatic alternatives, in spite of growing intensificational pressures in nearby areas in which foragers already exploit aquatic resources.

By expanding the investigation still further, we learn that a cross-tabulation of the hunter-gatherer cases reveals that twenty-five of the twenty-six cases classified as stratified or characterized by elite and privileged leaders (SYSTATE3 = 7) are primarily dependent upon aquatic resources. The single exception is a group of mounted hunters who are also heavily dependent upon aquatic resources. It is justified to generalize that there is a strong association in my data set between nonegalitarian social characteristics and the use of aquatic resources. If it can be assumed that this is a general condition and not a regional bias in the modern hunter-gatherer data, then I would venture an additional expectation that, other things being equal,

Proposition 10.03

During the earliest stages of intensification in which domesticated plants were being adopted, evidence of nonegalitarian social features should not appear in those groups for whom the exploitation of alternative aquatic resources is not feasible.

In this instance, perhaps the most important feature of the conditional statement "other things being equal" is that the domesticated plants and animals that were used experimentally *were not native to aquatic biomes*. A good example is wet rice cultivation in Asia. The exploitation and eventual domestication of this cultivar may have been part of a process of intensification that was focused upon a freshwater aquatic biome. It is not surprising that population growth in China was accompanied by expansion of the number and size of sites in "new low-lying areas . . . [with] access to regularly flooded land where clearing and planting would have produced appropriate conditions for rice" (Higham 1995:154).

An interesting aspect of wet rice cultivation is that it may well demonstrate an important point about aquatic resource exploitation in general. The patches or access windows for the procurement of aquatic resources are largely determined by the nature of the habitat, as modified, of course, by the available technology for accessing food from the biome. This means that expansion of the geographic scale of an aquatic adaptation is limited by the characteristics of the access windows to the biome, as well as differences within the habitat— from location to location within the biome—in the frequency and clustering of access windows. Relative to the terrestrial habitat, accessible resources are distributed in an extremely concentrated or clustered fashion, which almost certainly conditions the way human beings organize their exploitation of resources.

FIGURE 10.01

A fish drive on the Nata River, Botswana. Photo by Robert Hitchcock.

Add to these features of the environment the fact that a technological filter stands between many resources and the human ability to access or exploit the aquatic milieu. In such circumstances, the extraction of resources is frequently dependent upon not only the prior investment of substantial labor in technology but also the fact that there are only a limited number of places or contexts in which such investments of labor will result in needed food yields. Most people would agree that, in a marine context, shellfish in general and species isolated in tidal pools or made accessible from a terrestrial vantage point by tidal variation are the only resources that could be exploited without tools of some kind.

Aquatic birds that nest terrestrially, as well as some sea mammals who mate and give birth terrestrially, would be accessible from a terrestrial base; their capture would require some simple technological aids.[5] In riparian and lacustrine contexts, factors such as the restricted width of some streams would make fish drives and wading-based strategies (figure 10.01), such as the hand capture of fish, occasionally feasible. Riparian analogies to tidal phenomena (particularly the rise and fall of flood conditions) that would make it possible to take naturally trapped fish and turtles in flood ponds are another example.

When the exploitation of aquatic resources is intensified much beyond the situations described in the preceding paragraph, it is likely to be technology-driven. Increased labor investments might be expected in both the production of technology (figure 10.02) and the procurement and processing

time associated with implementing technology, but these tactics, as well as the gross returns from their implementation, are poorly understood. I nevertheless venture to say that, other things being equal, given an increase in the exploitation of aquatic resources resulting primarily from range reductions due to population increase and associated increases in the number of groups in the region,

Proposition 10.04

The greater the prior investment of labor in implements and facilities used to extract resources from a particular venue, the more access to the venue will be restricted to particular persons and the more the products derived from the venue will be restricted to the persons contributing their labor to construct the facilities. Moreover, the fewer the locations for productive access to the aquatic biome, the greater the limitation on the persons who have acknowledged rights to use the venue.

If the preceding supposition is correct, it is also reasonable to suppose that

Proposition 10.05

In settings characterized by demographic packing, the expansion of diet breadth and niche breadth through the use of aquatic resources necessarily results in organized and institutionalized stewardship or ownership

FIGURE 10.02

Hupa fish weir, California. Photo by Goddard (1906), courtesy of the Phoebe Apperson Hearst Museum of Anthropology and the Regents of the University of California.

of the critical and often rare locations used for accessing aquatic resources.

Let me emphasize that I do not wish to suggest that the *only* context in which ownership occurs is the exploitation of aquatic resources.

────────── *Proposition 10.06* ──────────

The expansion of aquatic diet breadth is more likely to involve increasing technological innovation and labor investment in technology, and the latter factor could well contribute to ownership as much as do the unique locations for accessing aquatic resources.

────────────────────────────────────

If we accept the probability that proposition 8.04 is accurate, another consequence of high population density, other things being equal, is likely to be that

────────── *Proposition 10.07* ──────────

As intensification increases, the dependence upon storage should also increase.

────────────────────────────────────

This expectation derives from a biogeographical expectation that

────────── *Proposition 10.08* ──────────

As the size of a group's range decreases, variance in the seasons of availability of accessible resources should also decrease.

────────────────────────────────────

And, if the assumptions in propositions 10.06, 10.07, and 10.08, as well as 8.05 and 8.07, are correct, it is also reasonable to assume that

────────── *Proposition 10.09* ──────────

With a given technology, there will be increased exploitation of resources that are accessible in bulk and there will be an accompanying development of techniques for gaining time utility from such resources through storage strategies.

────────────────────────────────────

The preceding propositions apply to a series of linked situations in which, as the area containing exploitable resources is reduced, it is likely that variance in the variables conditioning semi-independent, seasonal production schedules of accessible foods would also be reduced. Reductions in the size of the range from which foods can be extracted can be visualized as cone-shaped; as the "power" of the focus (e.g., degrees of packing) changes, fewer things are visible, but they appear much more important and dominate our field of view. As the area of the cone is reduced, there is a corresponding reduction in the range of values of variables conditioning both differences in productivity schedules and the diverse pool of species from which foods must be drawn. As the area of the cone is reduced still further, it contains fewer and fewer resources that must, therefore, be exploited in greater and greater quantities.

Looking at dynamics from this perspective brings us back to some of the topics I have already discussed. For instance, in chapters 7 and 8, I have shown how important labor organization is to an understanding of group size (generalizations 7.14, 8.30, and 8.31; propositions 8.09 and 10.05). In situations in which demographic packing is not a problem, I have argued that the larger the group size, the greater the mobility costs required to provide sufficient food (generalizations 7.19 and 7.21; proposition 8.02). On the other hand, among politically complex hunter-gatherer groups, GROUP1 and GROUP2 sizes are larger (generalization 8.02; proposition 8.01). These groups are also usually sedentary, so mobility is not a realistic tactical option for expanding diet and niche breadth (generalizations 8.02 and 8.11; propositions 8.01, 8.05, 8.10, and 8.12). The larger group sizes, particularly GROUP1, seem to represent an increase in the size of productive labor units. At the same time, an increase in GROUP2 size seems to be an aggregating response associated with greater microhabitat specification within the productive ranges of relatively independent, fundamental units of production.

Among most of the groups of the Pacific northwest coast that distinguished between elite and non-elite persons and featured social ranking, the house was identified as the fundamental unit of production. In these societies, the social hierarchy consisted of nested, integrated units, with GROUP2 communities made up of multiple, independent, food-producing units or houses, situated at the peak of the size range. The houses were, in turn, composed of multiple, cooperating families, who "owned" various access windows to resources that were the venues where different types of aquatic resources were exploited. The transactional hierarchy was, however, only a two-stage segmentary system. Heads of houses organized intergroup exchanges of goods, most of which took place within the community or among the units that wintered together in a single GROUP2 settlement.

Among these groups, the transfer of goods always represented a debt incurred by the recipient that had to be settled at a future date. This transactional scheme has been referred to as "social storage" (O'Shea 1981) because, at a future date, the host or gift-giver could expect a return, and even an increase, on his investment from those who were indebted to him.[6] This approach to donor-debtor transactions emphasizes the fact that they are unidirectional transfers in any specific transactional episode.

In some cases, this type of scheme was extended to exchanges between independent communities and was sim-

ilar to the internal differentiation within the community regarding the scale of marriage networks. Some heads of houses tended to seek mates outside the community or winter village, although most people married endogamously within the winter village community. Internal differentiation between the social and geographic scales of economic transactions, parallel differentiation in kin networks among persons of low and high rank, and socioeconomic stratification itself (indicated by a system state value of SYSTATE3 = 7) are the characteristics usually considered as indicative of "complex hunter-gatherers."[7]

I hope to show that hunter-gatherer sociopolitical complexity assumes quite different forms when viewed from an organizational perspective. For instance, in contrast to the transactional exchanges[8] that I have briefly described, there are many hunter-gatherer cases in which the transfers were bidirectional. That is, in a given exchange episode, craft goods and food tended to move in opposite directions. Arrangements of this sort were particularly characteristic of hunter-gatherer systems in California, in which various types of craft items, particularly shell beads, were exchanged for food. The transfers were simultaneous and no debts or obligations to exchange items again in the future were incurred.

In this context, possessing durable goods meant that at a later time they could be exchanged for food, if necessary, while the consumption of food provided an incentive to produce more goods as "money in the bank" (Dalton 1967) with which to buy food in case of future shortfalls. In hunter-gatherer organizations, such a risk-buffering, transactional strategy has the effect of breaking the linkage between the short-term demand curve for food products and the normal consumer demand set by the number of cooperating producers and their dependents.

In this sense, the relationship between "social storage" and the size of producer units is similar to strategies that I discussed in chapter 8 (see generalization 8.06 and proposition 8.03) regulating the use of physical storage and breaking the linkage between producers and immediate consumer demand. Under these conditions, when access to sufficient food-yielding patches is cut off as a consequence of reductions in group mobility, security results from increased labor inputs. The "ownership" of food-yielding venues goes hand in hand with packing and intensification.

Ownership in this context represents an increasing monopoly over resources, or more realistically an accelerating exclusion of one's kin from access[9] to food-producing venues, although these family members were usually welcome under less packed conditions. This process of exclusion results in an increasing segmentation of kinpersons into smaller and smaller units that have more and more restricted functions. At the same time, integrative mechanisms such as moieties and secret societies may begin to function at larger social scales. Although these mechanisms may be quite independently conceived in their linkages between kin distance and economic cooperation, they nevertheless serve inclusive social functions that in less complex systems were embedded directly within the kinship system itself. This uncoupling of scale and function is one manifestation of complexity.

Although I have made some progress toward the goal of viewing complexity as the consequence of variations in the scales of intensification, I have not yet developed a convincing account of the kinds and different levels of complexity that are demonstrable among hunter-gatherer peoples. To address complexity properly, however, it is also necessary to address variability.

With regard to the idea of reducing the habitat space from which a forager obtains basic foods, groups primarily dependent upon aquatic resources may well be fundamentally different from hunter-gatherers who pursue a truly terrestrial adaptation. For instance, the way a forager searches the ecological space of exploited aquatic species is not at all analogous to the way a forager searches terrestrial space. Clearly, the role of mobility is likely to be very different for each forager, and the packing argument—which is derived from the minimal group size argument—may therefore not be equally relevant to each subsistence mode.

Additionally, the arguments about species richness and the relationship to body size presented in this chapter are difficult to translate into statements about the access space of aquatic resources. Strictly speaking, the coverage of space in an aquatic context is exclusively dependent upon technology, whereas the most common technique used by terrestrially dependent foragers for covering the landscape is walking. This distinction simply points out that the idea of "range" is very different, energetically speaking, for groups dependent upon aquatic resources than for foragers primarily exploiting terrestrial resources (Osborn 1977, 1980).[10]

Disembodied Observer: A focus on the impact of range reduction on the effective environments of hunter-gatherers resulted in three important generalizations that are useful in anticipating responses to intensification (generalizations 10.01, 10.02, and 10.03). A study of the patterning leading to the first three generalizations directed attention to the issue of habitat differences, particularly in terms of "richness" (generalization 10.04). Speculation about the consequences of differences in habitat was more fruitful when climatic change over time was considered (generalization 10.05).

Generalization 10.05 made it possible to explore ideas that went beyond the specifics of the generalizations dealing with the synergy between habitat scale itself and the scale at which a habitat is utilized by a group of hunter-gatherers. Two problems surfaced several times during this consideration, the most recurrent being the clear difference between hunter-gatherers who specialize to some extent on aquatic resources (propositions 10.01, 10.03, 10.05, and 10.06) and

those whose terrestrial adaptation is governed by a toggle switch that directs their focus back and forth between animals and plants.

The other concern that began to surface was a clear expansion of interest beyond hunter-gatherers to processes of intensification that could ultimately lead to a non–hunting and gathering adaptation. Speculations were introduced that focused on the contexts in which domesticated plants and animals might appear in response to pressures to intensify (propositions 10.02 and 10.03). Subsequent explorations focused on the synergy between such practices as storage and intensification (proposition 10.07), storage and technology (proposition 10.09), habitat and technology (proposition 10.06), and intensification and diet breadth (proposition 10.08).

These discussions led to a reexamination of diet breadth and niche breadth, and the links between labor, "social storage," and other transactional exchanges of food products. These considerations prompted the focus to shift again to hunter-gatherer adaptations based on aquatic resources and associated issues of complexity. It became apparent that at least some of the earlier difficulties of dealing with complexity may have resulted from the lack of specific techniques for measuring intensifiation, particularly packing, as well as some measurement that would make it possible to cope more directly with habitat diversity and richness. This train of thought makes it imperative to turn now to the development of two crucial instruments for measurement.

Two New Instruments for Measurement: Spatial Packing and Niche Effectiveness

In chapter 7, I suggested that models could serve important functions in a discussion of system state variability, and as an illustration I developed the Group Size Model and demonstrated how it could be used. In chapter 8, I applied the model to the question of variability in ethnographically documented GROUP1 sizes. The model served a useful analytical function and made it possible to expand my understanding of variables, particularly foraging area and the cohabitational unit, that had first been introduced in the Group Size Model. I hope in this chapter to be able to demonstrate that these two variables can be used to standardize an instrument for measuring intensification.

Building a compelling argument about the causes of intensification begins with an operational definition: in the simplest of terms, intensification is the process that results in an increase in net food returns from a given area. If, therefore, it is possible to measure such increases, then it can be said that intensification has occurred. These simple tools will make it possible to proceed with the search for clues to how and under what conditions intensification occurs and,

I hope, to develop an understanding of the character of the organizational changes that intensification stimulates.

MEASURING NICHE EFFECTIVENESS

The expression *measuring niche effectiveness* is an indirect way of saying that I am measuring the deviation of a particular ethnographic group from the baseline system state standardized in the Terrestrial Model. In this instance, the effectiveness of the niche occupied by any given system will be measured in a currency consisting of the number of persons per 100 square kilometers. In other words, the population density of an ethnographically documented hunter-gatherer group will be scaled according to the following standard: the number of persons reported by the Terrestrial Model to be present in 100 square kilometers and situated in the identical environment of the group to be measured.

In practical terms, the population density of an ethnographic case is simply divided by the variable TERMD, which is the population density estimated by the Terrestrial Model at the center of the territory occupied by the group in question. The result is a measure in basic units generated by the Terrestrial Model of how many such units, plus or minus the observed case, are positioned relative to the standard. This variable is called NICHEFF; it refers to how the ethnographic case in question differs, in its ability to convert food into people, from a group in an identical habitat as anticipated by the Terrestrial Model.

(10.01)

Ratio of niche effectiveness:
NICHEFF = Population density/TERMD2

(10.02)

Ratio of niche effectiveness in exploitation of terrestrial plant resources: NICHEFFG = DENG/TERMG2

(10.03)

Ratio of niche effectiveness in exploiting terrestrial animal resources: NICHEFFH = DENH/TERMH2

(10.04)

DENG = DENSITY * (GATHERIN/100)

DENH = DENSITY * (HUNTING/100)

DENA = DENSITY * (FISHING/100)

where DENG is the number of persons per 100 square kilometers who could be supported exclusively by plant foods, given the known proportions of dependence upon terrestrial

plants and the population density of an ethnographic case. DENH and DENA are determined the same way, given the known proportions of dependence upon terrestrial animals and aquatic resources, respectively. All of the measures outlined in the preceding six equations are expressions of modeled demographic expectations for any given location for which basic weather data are available.

This approach to carrying capacity provides a measure of the role played by cultural tactics and strategies in exploiting environments at different levels of effectiveness, as indicated by the number of persons supported per unit area. It includes a correction for the fact that environments differ in their capacity to produce foods that are readily accessible to human foragers. Although NICHEFF measures niche effectiveness, it is not a direct measurement of population pressure. The latter condition refers to a state that is *expected* to occur prior to major changes in technology or organization, but to my knowledge there are no convincing, independent identifiers of population pressure that are not tautologies.

Most arguments alluding to "population pressure" have focused on population growth,[11] which—as the basic Lotka curve anticipates—is assumed to be density-limited and expected to decelerate, or at least not to increase appreciably. Growth rates are enormously difficult to measure,[12] and even if it was possible to approximate them there is little agreement on the relationships between the number of persons (density) and the conditions of growth that would bring about population pressure.

The same problem also applies to measurements of niche effectiveness, but I can use the scale of deviations from a known standard—the NICHEFF component of the Terrestrial Model—to study the system state variability that I suspect indicates the presence of intensification. The model holds habitat variability relatively constant, but this instrument will not single-handedly solve the problem of tracking evolutionary system state phases. It should, however, be very helpful when used in conjunction with another instrument for measurement that I now discuss.

MEASURING SPATIAL PACKING

Unlike NICHEFF, which relates niche differences to the differential support human consumers receive in a productively finite environmental setting, packing relates human groups to the geographic space they use, regardless of niche. This variable is designed to evaluate the probability that mobility is a major tactical component of the food-getting strategies in the niche that a given group occupies. Since hunter-gatherers are often characterized as mobile and "nomadic"—whereas intensified populations are usually described as sedentary and "settled"—some factors must be responsible for the obsolescence of mobility as an effective strategy for ensuring an adequate food supply. Casting things in these terms removes the argument from the arena in which starvation and food shortages are said to foster invention and new tactics.

I strongly suspect that the really important density-dependent factors conditioning subsistence change are those that negatively affect the tactics and strategies of food procurement. I am, therefore, skeptical about arguments that postulate some sort of failure that results in starvation or other events that dramatically modify the mortality and fertility rates of the population. As I have previously suggested, it is more likely that the latter scenarios would have the effect of prolonging the use of precatastrophic strategies and reducing the pressure to intensify, therefore rendering density-dependent change less likely.

Clearly, there is a great need for an independent dimension that measures the relationship between the number of persons participating in a social unit and the units of space they occupy. As part of the development of the Group Size Model in chapter 7, I devised such a baseline sociospatial unit, the FORAD (225.33 square kilometers), which was utilized in the model by a minimalist extractive social unit called the COHAB (20.47 persons). I was able to show that, given a regional value for population density—for example 13.75 persons per 100 square kilometers—I could deduce the spatial structure of the FORAD units within the region. This was achieved by dividing the COHAB value of 20.47 persons by the number of 100-square-kilometer units in a FORAD (2.2533), which yields a value of 9.098 persons living in a 100-square-kilometer unit.

When population density is calculated relative to the 100-square-kilometer unit convention I use in this study, the result can be divided by 9.098 persons to obtain a re-scaled value of population density that is expressed relative to FORAD-COHAB standards. This value is called PACKINX and represents the number of standard COHAB units per FORAD in the region. Values greater than 1.0 would indicate circumscription of the FORAD and hence regional packing within the ethnic area.

By re-scaling population density values in this way, it is possible to measure directly the intensity of packing within a region relative to a known standard. At the same time, one can provide a measure of the differences in the packing levels of groups within a region, quite independently of considerations of the carrying capacity or effective productivity of different habitats. A $\log_{10}$ value of 0.0 for the PACKINX variable approximates the boundary of circumscribed FORAD units in a region. Values greater than 0.0 are, therefore, a direct indication of packing pressure among the circumscribed units within the ethnic territory. A $\log_{10}$ value of less than 0.0 records minimal or low levels of circumscription and therefore identifies groups for whom residential mobility is a realistic tactical means of exploiting regional food resources, regardless of their abundance.

INTENSIFICATION AND OTHER DIMENSIONS OF HUNTER-GATHERER VARIABILITY

Disembodied Observer: The requisite instruments for measurement have now been developed, and it is time to embark on a long and perhaps tedious trip through the pattern recognition "spaghetti bowl." It was suggested earlier in this chapter that the point of entry into the spaghetti bowl is not a very good indicator of where the exit will be. I now enter with new tools for measuring several aspects of intensification, and I apply them first to group size, building on previous knowledge and expanding my interests in other directions.

My current knowledge, however, in no way allows me to anticipate where my interest will be focused when I exit. Pattern recognition is a learning strategy, and, although I may follow the group-size route at first, I have already indicated that the origin of system complexity and diversity is one desired destination. Previous research prompts me to want to determine whether the vague concept of environmental richness plays a role as a conditioner of complexity itself and whether it has any modifying effect on rates of intensification and the diversity of responses to pressures to intensify. The goals are clear, but it is less than certain what will be foremost in my mind when I exit from the spaghetti bowl.

My search for relevant patterning must be approached with several things in mind. The first is that the Terrestrial Model refers only to terrestrial adaptations; no exploitation of aquatic resources was permitted in the specifications of the model. This means that when groups that are dependent upon aquatic resources are examined, the intensification indicator NICHEFF applies only to the terrestrial habitat. Any expansion into the aquatic domain may push the potential effectiveness to levels considerably above that modeled for the terrestrial habitat.

The second point to remember is that the Group Size Model is identified as minimalist because it is based largely on information taken from foragers of the Kalahari and areas in central Australia. Therefore it might be expected that the model is most accurate as a standard when examining foragers. When the focus is on other cases, deviations from the modeled conditions should be examined carefully for indications that the forager organization assumed by the model is not applicable. The utility of these measures for investigating questions of regional packing and niche effectiveness rests with the fact that the former is anchored by the Group Size Model whereas the latter is bound to the Terrestrial Model.

Another way of thinking about these measures is that they are differentially scaled expressions of population density and are useful precisely because they express population density in different terms. Using NICHEFF and PACKINX should reveal minor differences in patterning in response to different questions. For instance, does the threshold of the packing index actually anticipate major changes in group size? Is there an analogous threshold on the NICHEFF scale? Is there patterned regularity among the cases designated as exceptional relative to the patterns observed in NICHEFF property space? I also examine any properties that may result from processes of intensification that are revealed in the course of using the packing and niche effectiveness scales as the basis for defining new property space matrices.

Pattern Recognition Using Instruments for Measurement

RESPONSES TO INTENSIFICATION BY PEOPLES DEPENDENT UPON TERRESTRIAL PLANT RESOURCES

The effect of packing on the process of intensification is perhaps not as easy to appreciate as one might have assumed. Packing affects the ability of foragers to cover space readily in search of food and to accomplish this task reliably on a daily basis. The Terrestrial Model assumes that group size consists of the minimum number of laborers needed to search for and obtain food and to return to a residential location in a single day. The area needed for subsistence is modeled in terms of the modal distance walked by foragers carrying out these tasks. If the population density of a region is such that the area available annually to a modeled group is only a single foraging area with a radius of 8.469 kilometers, then the region is packed.

It is possible to imagine a very productive environment in which the modeled group is able to obtain all the food it needs from a single foraging area, in which case the group would not necessarily be intensified. The group would only be intensified if it were under pressure to increase the food yield from its single foraging area, a situation that is easy to imagine in a much less abundant environment than the one envisioned in the previous example. What is unknown is the scale of land use required for a given set of food procurement tactics to be cost-effective.

It could be that the use of some tactics, regardless of the richness of the habitat, would result in intensification pressure if the foragers were constrained to a single foraging area. Obviously, one topic to be researched is what factors trigger pressures to intensify. With these issues in mind, it is time to turn to an examination of GROUP1 size among the hunter-gatherer groups that are primarily dependent upon terrestrial plant resources.

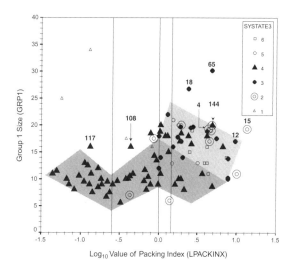

FIGURE 10.03

Demonstration of the packing threshold for GROUP1 size among terrestrial plant-dependent groups. Marker is a classification of systems state (SYSTATE3): (1) mounted hunters, (2) horticulturally augmented cases, (3) mutualists and forest product specialists, (4) generic hunter-gatherers, (5) generic hunter-gatherers with instituted leadership, and (6) wealth-differentiated hunter-gatherers.

In figure 10.03, the overall pattern is somewhat surprising, given the basis for the modeled values. Hunter-gatherer cases from the least packed settings have GROUP1 values of between roughly nine and fourteen persons, but as packing increases GROUP1 size drops to between five and ten persons at an LPACKINX value of –0.60. This is equivalent to a population density of 2.27 persons per 100 square kilometers. At this point, the distribution reverses, and with further increases in the packing index GROUP1 size increases up to a point at the $\log_{10}$ value of 0.0. This is the value at which foraging area circumscription is modeled, associated with a population density of 9.098 persons per 100 square kilometers.[13]

After this point in the graph, two separate trends are visible. One is a continuation of the pattern in which GROUP1 size increases to a maximum of approximately twenty-two persons. The other trend reverses the earlier pattern, and another threshold occurs at approximately a $\log_{10}$(PACKINX) value of 0.16, which translates into a population density value of 13.19 persons per 100 square kilometers. On the positive side of this threshold, GROUP1 size decreases in a regular manner.

Generalization 10.06

Among peoples who are dependent upon terrestrial plant resources, GROUP1 sizes greater than approximately fifteen persons are found only just prior to and immediately after circumscription.[14]

Larger GROUP1 size has been shown to co-occur with maximum values for the male contribution to the labor force, a variable that increases as temperature decreases across the temperate zone (figure 8.23, graph B). It has also been shown to achieve maximum size among sedentary peoples (figure 8.13, graph A).

Proposition 10.10

The pattern displayed in figure 10.03 documents the fact that as packing increases and the option of moving into a new foraging area decreases, there is an increase in male efforts to maintain the previous levels of net returns from terrestrial animals and an expansion of male exploitation of aquatic resources. Males also share more of the labor costs with females, as both sexes pursue food resources that may have previously either been obtained primarily by females or not been exploited at all. Strategies of this kind indicate that the broad-spectrum revolution may be in operation.

According to the terms of the Group Size Model, after the packing threshold is passed, the division of labor is restructured. One possible implication of this restructuring is that species traditionally obtained by males constitute less and less of the diet.

Eleven hunter-gatherer cases in three locations of the graph in figure 10.03 do not conform to the overall pattern. The first two exceptional cases, the Djaru (group 108) and the Alyawara (group 117) are aligned on the left side of the graph, above the cases with low GROUP1 size values around −0.5 on the x axis. Both of these Australian cases have high levels of polygynous marriage, so inflated family sizes are not too surprising. The cases differ from others in the array because GROUP1 values were recorded after both groups had been resettled—the Djaru at a mission and the Alyawara at several cattle stations. Population density values were calculated, however, using the size of their traditional areas and not the area surrounding their resettled communities. If data on the latter areas could have been included, the density values would have been inflated and the cases would shift to the right side of the graph, into the sector of the packing threshold and larger GROUP1 sizes associated with intensification.[15]

The second set of cases with exceptionally high GROUP1 values consists of two net-hunting groups of mutualists, the Birhor (group 18) from India and the Mbuti (group 65) from Africa. In both of these groups, the organization of labor is structured to facilitate hunting, even though the diet is biased

in favor of plant foods. Although the placement of these groups in the graph is consistent with generalization 8.25, which states that GROUP1 size is higher among hunting peoples, another characteristic of these groups is affecting their position in the array of cases.

Population densities were calculated only for each ethnic group itself and do not reflect their status as partners in a mutualist suite that includes agriculturists living within the subsistence ranges of the hunter-gatherers. If persons living in the agricultural groups among which the hunter-gatherers move and exchange goods were included, density levels would be considerably higher, and these cases would be found in the area of the graph in which high levels of packing are documented, which would reinforce the overall pattern in figure 10.03.

Last, several cases on the right side of the graph are all circumscribed, have GROUP1 sizes of between fifteen and twenty persons, and appear to have inflated PACKINX values. These four groups include (1) the Chenchu (group 15) of India, who practiced horticulture at the time of ethnographic observation; (2) the Agta (Casiguran) (group 12), a mutualist group that exchanged labor and forest products with their neighbors in return for agricultural products, making them analogous to the Mbuti and Birhor as far as population density is concerned; (3) the Cahuilla (group 144) of California, who were horticultural at the time of initial ethnographic documentation; and (4) the Shompen (group 4) of Great Nicobar Island, who were also horticultural, depending heavily upon pandanus at the time of recording.

These exceptional cases can be separated into three different categories based on their contexts:

1. Two groups lived as noncircumscribed peoples during the traditional era for which the density estimate applies. These groups were resettled in the context of European expansion, and their GROUP1 size was observed in the resettled or packed context. These cases are ambiguous because they were polygynous, a characteristic that has been demonstrated to inflate family size and therefore GROUP1 size (see generalizations 8.17, 8.19, and 8.20).
2. Two groups were circumscribed net-hunting specialists whose diet was based primarily on plant products. The organization of GROUP1 units, however, was in terms of hunting, which conditions large GROUP1 sizes. Although these groups were mutualists, their density values did not include the agricultural peoples living within their ranges, who were treated by their ethnographers as independent systems.
3. Four groups were circumscribed horticultural peoples at the time that their group size and population density levels were recorded. These values fall near the upper range of the array in figure 10.03 and beyond those of more typical hunter-gatherers.

The very obvious relationship between GROUP1 size and the packing index in figure 10.03 is important, and the modeled threshold for the circumscription of a single foraging area is clearly evident in the GROUP1 size patterning. At the anticipated value of 1.0, the direction of the relationships between the packing index and GROUP1 size both reverses on itself and accelerates, indicating that the principles of labor organization among hunter-gatherers appear to change dramatically at this threshold. At least in this initial illustration, which is restricted to groups that are primarily dependent upon terrestrial plants, packing appears to structure all of the previous relationships defined in chapter 8 as the fundamental conditioners of GROUP1 size. Shifts in labor organization, the division of labor, and relative dependence upon other food resources pattern nicely with the packing index, which, it should be recalled, ignores differences in food richness among habitats.

A relevant question to ask at this juncture is: what would patterning in niche effectiveness look like when the values are standardized across habitat differences in potential food abundance? Should a dramatic threshold be visible or is a high-variance scatter correlated with habitat differences to be expected?

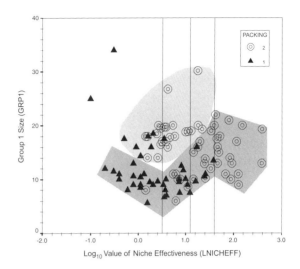

FIGURE 10.04

Niche effectiveness and threshold-related patterning in GROUP1 size among terrestrial plant-dependent groups. Cases are coded for packing (PACKING): (1) nonpacked and (2) packed.

Proposition 10.11

If intensification is being triggered by differences in the natural richness of habitats, coupled with differences in the ease with which niche effectiveness could be expanded, the pressure to intensify could be expected to be less in rich habitats and considerably greater in food-poor settings with lower values for packing.

Generalization 10.07

Increases in spatial packing and niche effectiveness beyond a $\log_{10}$ threshold value of 0.0 for the packing index (PACKINX) and 1.6 for the niche effectiveness index result in decreases in GROUP1 size and increased frequencies of GROUP1 units of fewer than fifteen persons. The observed modal range suggests units composed of joint or extended families.

In order to explore the difference between packing and niche effectiveness as indicators of intensification, niche effectiveness was plotted for the same group of cases presented in figure 10.03. In the results displayed in the graph in figure 10.04, the cases that are packed and have a population density of greater than 9.098 persons per 100 square kilometers are indicated by small, solid traiangles. The pattern in figure 10.04 differs in some details from that in figure 10.03, but it also retains some familiar features. These include the lower concave distribution that rises to a threshold of slightly greater than 1.6 $\log_{10}$ value of NICHEFF, which is forty times the population density anticipated by the Terrestrial Model. At this point, the modal range of GROUP1 sizes is between thirteen and twenty-two persons, and the upper part of this range is clearly within the size range conventionally accepted for band size. As in figure 10.03, increases in the indicators of intensification should fall to the right of the threshold that records proportional decreases in GROUP1 size.

Continued focus on only the lower arc of cases in figure 10.04 reveals that the transition between packed and unpacked cases, as indicated by the markers, occurs at a $\log_{10}$ value of 1.0934 or about 12.4 times the value in the Terrestrial Model. It is also clear that niche effectiveness interacts with packing only between 12.4 and 40 times the Terrestrial Model population density values. This is the zone of overlap between the two indicators of intensification.

In contrast to the packing index distribution in figure 10.03, there is a separate, upper convex arc of thirty-two cases in figure 10.04 that rises very gradually from the low values on the left of the graph to the threshold at approximately a $\log_{10}$ value of 1.60 (emphasized by shading). All of these cases have relatively large GROUP1 sizes but are not intensified with respect to accessible foods, as are other large GROUP1 cases clustered at the threshold value of $\log_{10}$ 1.60 or beyond. Twenty-five cases (83 percent) are packed but have relatively low values for niche effectiveness, particularly relative to the rather clear threshold distribution. The presence of cases

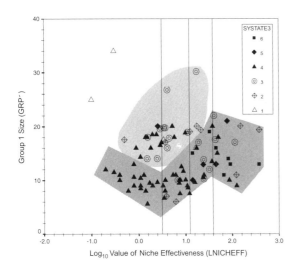

FIGURE 10.05

Relationships between niche effectiveness and GROUP1 size illustrating system state differences at a demonstrable threshold among terrestrial plant-dependent groups. Marker is a classification of systems state (SYSTATE3): (1) mounted hunters, (2) horticulturally augmented cases, (3) mutualists and forest product specialists, (4) generic hunter-gatherers, (5) generic hunter-gatherers with instituted leadership, and (6) wealth-differentiated hunter-gatherers.

with low values for niche effectiveness, but with sufficient density to be considered packed, may indicate the presence of high habitat productivity that is depressing the effects of packing (see proposition 10.04).

To clarify this ambiguity, the same property space graph in figure 10.04 was used in figure 10.05, but the marker variable has been changed to indicate the system state of the cases. This change makes it apparent that 62 percent of the twenty-nine cases clustered in the upper arc were organizationally articulated to populations that were not hunter-gatherers or were mutualists or forest product specialists (SYSTATE3 = 3) or, at the time of observation. Groups in the former category include the Batek of the Philippines (Cadelina 1982) and the Chenchu of India (Fürer-Haimendorf 1943). Thirteen of the cases in this group unquestionably shared territory with other non–hunting and gathering populations, and—like the exceptional cases in my examination of the packing index in figure 10.03—they prove the rule. In both graphs, when the exceptional cases are viewed from an ecological perspective, the population densities calculated only for hunter-gatherers are energetically inappropriate.

For example, the Efe population density value of 16.33 persons per 100 square kilometers is calculated only for Efe living in a territory defined by Efe settlements, but these communities are all associated with villages of Lese horti-

culturists. The demographic information supplied by Bailey (1985:36) states that for every Efe person there are 1.17 Lese persons in the same territory, which means that the ecological population density of the Efe is 35.46 persons per 100 square kilometers. An increase of this magnitude would shift the Efe toward the cluster of cases surrounding the packing threshold in figures 10.03 and 10.04.[16] If all thirteen cases could be corrected to reflect the ecological density in their ranges, they would move to the right of the graph and much, if not all, of the upper distribution of exceptional cases would disappear. This same effect would also shift the two uppermost, shaded cases (which were identified in figure 10.05 as having exceptionally large GROUP1 units) into the threshold zone.

It is worth reiterating that the organizational complexity of the system within which mutualist cases are integrated would be more complex and larger in scale than that recorded for its subsystemic components.[17] It must be recognized that some cases may be components of a complex, caste-based system,[18] whereas others should be considered as differentiated hunter-gatherer specialists who are mutualistically articulated with non-hunter-gatherer peoples in the same region. A third alternative is that members of some groups may be true economic specialists (wage laborers) in a much larger, internally differentiated system, such as a complex state or colonial system.

Generalization 10.08

Systemic complexity can be organized at very different scales when viewed from the perspective of the cultural or political autonomy of the basal units integrated into a more complex system. In some situations, societies with similar cultural characteristics may be politically and economically autonomous. A more complex, emergent system could, however, integrate these culturally similar units into a larger, more complex political or economic system. Conversely, a region that is strongly differentiated ethnically and culturally could also be integrated by an emergent, complex system in such a way as to permit the initial cultural differentiations to persist, thereby creating the impression that culturally independent systems were incorporated into a larger system of economic interdependencies.[19]

Consistent with the preceding generalizations in this chapter, the importance of the information in figure 10.05 cannot be overestimated. Regardless of the *type* of complex system—that is to say, the degree of cultural similarity within a complex system—the threshold at which a major response in GROUP1 size appears is the same for systems composed of culturally homogeneous or heterogeneous communities.

The patterned distributions in figures 10.03, 10.04, and 10.05 are consistent with the following statement:

Proposition 10.12

Organizational change in group size appears to be a density-dependent response, at least among peoples that are dependent upon terrestrial plant resources. A major threshold in density dependence is centered at a $\log_{10}$ value of 1.60 for niche effectiveness, suggesting that there is a point at which the "laws" of variability governing GROUP1 size change for hunter-gatherer groups so positioned. A sudden increase in systemic complexity is suspected to occur at this threshold and should continue subsequent to it. The systemic scale at which an increase in complexity will occur, however, is not controlled by the threshold conditions. Complexity could occur at the regional level or at the local group level at the same threshold.

The conclusions summarized in proposition 10.12 lead to the suggestion that

Problem 10.01

The factors that are responsible for complexity at a regional scale of internal differentiation (e.g., mutualism and patron-client relationships) need to be identified, as do those governing the occurrence of internal changes in local group structure that lead to stratification or ranking within otherwise small, culturally homogeneous groups.

I amplify this problem in the form of another proposition:

Proposition 10.13

Mutualism must be considered a form of organization that occurs in response to intensification pressure, but it is only one of several possible responses. There must be specific conditions that would favor mutualism, along with other forms of ethnic incorporation such as caste systems. More traditional forms of internal differentiation and functional specialization would arise within an ethnically similar population under other conditions. It is important to search for clues to what these conditions might be.

So far in this chapter, I have synthesized the results of several pattern recognition episodes. I have recast them as a set of generalizations and propositions that prompts me to identify some challenging problems not usually acknowledged in most discussions of complex systems. The most striking feature of the work thus far is the recognition of another kind of variability that has not previously been considered but must

be dealt with. Complex systems may differ in terms of the cultural homogeneity of the fundamental basal sociocultural units making up the internally differentiated system (proposition 10.08). In short, complexity within systems that are integrated at very different scales can occur in response to the same level of intensificational pressure. This means that the scale at which organizational responses to such pressures are apparent may be conditioned by variables that have not yet been considered.

Problem 10.02

Is it possible that mutualism is not usually a realistic response to regional, systemic diversity? Does it occur in all environments? Is it a predictable phenomenon in any region with cultural and between-habitat diversity in the ecosystem? The assumption has been made in several studies that mutualism is a reasonable organizational response whenever the two preceding conditions are met (Gregg 1988; Spielmann 1991).

I will return to this point when I have completed the pattern recognition studies that explore variability in group size relative to indicators of intensification, packing, and niche effectiveness.

To some extent, the discovery that mutualism is probably a density-dependent phenomenon has distracted attention from a question that originally prompted this exploration of data from my hunter-gatherer world sample. I began my research with a very different problem, one more directly related to niche effectiveness and packing. In proposition 10.11, I addressed the issue of environmental richness and responses to packing out of a concern with whether or not environmental richness diminishes or delays organizational responses to packing. I also want to know whether, other things being equal, environmental richness—by supporting inflated rates of population growth—accelerates the time required for packing to occur.

One promising source of information consists of the exceptional cases in figure 10.05 that were ignored during the discussion of patterning related to mutualism. Eleven cases were distributed in an upper arc with the mutualist cases, and these were characterized by larger GROUP1 sizes and low niche effectiveness scores. Six of these—the !Ko, Yir-Yoront, Djaru, Alyawara, Akuriyo, and Heta—either were remnant groups (Akuriyo and Heta), had been resettled at missions (Yir-Yoront and Djaru) or on cattle stations (Alyawara), or had lived in some other nonvoluntary context at the time of demographic study (see Heinz and Lee 1979 for a participant's description of the events behind an artificial aggregation of !Ko foragers; see Eibl-Eibelsfeldt 1972:33–37 for, more strictly speaking, a demographic summary of the same group). These were all artificially aggregated groups that no longer used mobility as a primary subsistence strategy—or at least not in the same way as when they had lived independently.

Of the remaining five cases, the Hadza have undergone rapid population growth in recent years, but only the least settled groups of Hadza have been the subjects of ethnographic description. The Gunwinggu of Australia have also experienced considerable population growth, which has been accommodated by territorial expansion into the "countries" of other aboriginal peoples who became extinct during the colonial era. The data on Gunwinggu group size have, however, come from relatively recent, mission-focused settlements. This is also true of the Wororo of northwestern Australia and the Tiwi of northern Australia. The Murngin of north central Australia were studied during a period of intense local warfare.

In none of these cases does richness of the environment seem to account for either the exceptionally high group size values or the lower values of niche effectiveness. In all cases, the exceptional values at the time of observation appear to be referable to the impact of western colonization as well as the lack of direct fit between the regional population as counted by demographers and local group sizes.

Generalization 10.09

There is no indication of a reduction in the definition of thresholds—a condition that would be expected if richness mitigated the effects of packing—at which marked changes in group size are recognizable among plant-dependent peoples. It remains to be seen whether primary dependence upon other food resources, when studied relative to the packing index, might be associated with less definite thresholds and possibly implicate richness as a mitigating phenomenon.

RESPONSES TO INTENSIFICATION BY PEOPLES DEPENDENT UPON TERRESTRIAL ANIMAL RESOURCES: A COMPARISON WITH PEOPLES PRIMARILY EXPLOITING TERRESTRIAL PLANTS

I have already demonstrated that both labor organization and the division of labor vary significantly with the niche occupied by hunter-gatherers (generalizations 8.26, 8.28, 8.29, 8.31, and 8.32). I can therefore expect that, for groups dependent upon terrestrial animals or aquatic resources, the threshold effects relative to both packing and niche effectiveness measures could well be different, not only from one another but also from those for plant-dependent peoples. In order to achieve a better perspective on these possibilities, I prepared the graphs in figure 10.06.

My expectations for differences in threshold effects are supported by the pattern in figure 10.06, graph A, which deals with hunter-gatherers who are primarily dependent upon terrestrial animals. A striking 94.525 percent of the cases fall on the low side of the $\log_{10}$ packing threshold of 0.0 posited by the Group Size Model, which was shown to be germane to group size variability among peoples who are primarily dependent upon plants (figure 10.04). In other words, heavy exploitation of terrestrial animals is simply not done under packed conditions. In fact, there appears to be a threshold at a $\log_{10}$ value of –0.803 for the packing index (LPACKINX), which corresponds to 1.59 persons per 100 square kilometers. Beyond this point, group size increases dramatically among groups of mounted hunters but reverses and then decreases for nonmounted hunters as the $\log_{10}$ value of zero is approached.

There are four exceptional cases of hunting peoples in the zone of the graph corresponding to packed conditions. These include the Warunggu of the Herbert River area in the Queensland region of Australia, which is the only Australian group classified as primarily dependent upon terrestrials animals.[20] Two groups from California, the Achumawi and the North Fork Paiute, are both classified as primarily dependent upon terrestrial animals, although there is little direct observational data to justify this classification. That they were packed, however, seems likely.

The fourth exception is the White Knife group of the North American Great Basin. According to the primary source (Harris 1940), this group was primarily dependent upon plant foods, and their classification as hunters of terrestrial animals represents a coding error in my data set.[21] The presence of these four cases is not sufficient to modify the overall pattern that has been generalized, that is, that peoples primarily dependent upon terrestrial mammals are not found under packed conditions.

Two other exceptional cases located above the basic distribution in graph A—the Siriono (group 43) and the Alcatcho Carrier (group 336)—appear to be related to the earlier packing threshold noted among plant-dependent peoples. This is not surprising since the Siriono were practicing agriculture at the time of initial observation, and their subsistence classification should have reflected their status as agriculturists. They were, instead, classified in terms of "reconstructed" subsistence, which was an error. The Alcatcho, on the other hand, were economically linked to the Bella-Coola, and their diet is reported to have consisted of an equal mixture of terrestrial animals and aquatic species (Goldman 1940:351). It is quite likely that the ethnographer's report is correct in terms of the resources they procured, but Goldman reports that meat figured prominently in their exchanges with the coastal peoples. It is therefore more likely that aquatic resources were the primary source of food for the Alcatcho.

In spite of cases that appear to be exceptions to the basic pattern, I would say that

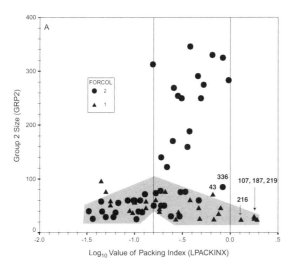
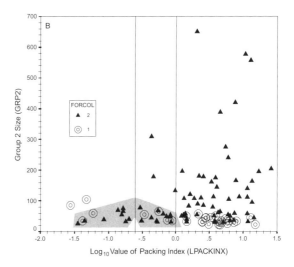

FIGURE 10.06

Paired property space plots comparing groups dependent upon terrestrial animal resources (A) and aquatic resources (B). Both graphs are coded for the forager-collector distinction (FORCOL): (1) forager and (2) collector.

Generalization 10.10

The hunter-gatherer groups dependent upon terrestrial animals that are displayed against the packing index provide a strong confirmation of earlier generalizations (7.10, 7.12, 7.16, 8.18, 10.01, and 10.02) and propositions (7.01 and 7.03), which state that intensification results in a reduced dependence upon terrestrial animals. The distribution in figure 10.06, graph A, further documents that GROUP2 size exhibits a threshold with respect to the packing index at a value equal to 1.57 persons per 100 square kilometers. Given what is known about the sexual division of labor and group size (generalizations 8.31 and 8.32; propositions 8.10, 8.11, and 8.12), the observed threshold—equal to 1.59 persons per 100 square kilometers—corresponds to the point in the division of labor at which more female labor begins to be employed. This threshold is also associated with decreased dependence upon big game and greater use of smaller animals or aquatic resources in northern temperate and more polar settings. In warmer climates, groups dependent upon terrestrial animals that are undergoing intensification will exhibit increased dependence upon terrestrial plant foods or aquatic resources, and the proportion of female labor devoted to food procurement will also increase.

The difference in the packing thresholds between groups dependent upon terrestrial animals and those dependent upon plants (a $\log_{10}$ value of −0.803 as opposed to 0.0) directly reflects the differences in the spatial requirements of individual mobile animals and individual stationary plants. Different patterns of aggregation and dispersion of the

species themselves are also implicated. These ultimately reflect the trophic differences between primary and secondary productivity and the overall structure of energetic relationships between plants and animals. The spatial stability and degree of clumping in the structure of species distributions are the factors that directly condition differences in the geographic scale of hunter-gatherer ranges and the patterns of mobility that characterize peoples who exploit trophically distinct species as basic resources.

Two packing thresholds, each with a different impact, have now been identified. The new threshold applies to hunter-gatherers who are primarily dependent upon terrestrial animal resources, and it is identified at a population density of 1.59 persons per 100 square kilometers. Once this density level is reached, two different responses are indicated. First, GROUP2 size will decrease as packing increases, which would be expected if, as I have suggested, there is an increased dependence upon animals of smaller body size and mobility costs are being minimized. The second response is that new energy sources, such as animals for riding or transport, make possible extensificational strategies and accompanying reductions in density.

Once these effects occur, the second threshold associated with groups dependent upon terrestrial plant resources kicks in at a population density of 9.098 persons per 100 square kilometers, and, it should be noted, dependence upon terrestrial animal resources disappears. Clearly, one threshold does not replace the other; rather, different constraints on group size and subsistence strategy operate on groups whose diets are made up of resources from different trophic levels. These observations reinforce the conclusion that environmental richness does not appear to be germane as a mediating variable when demographic packing occurs.

RESPONSES TO INTENSIFICATION BY PEOPLES DEPENDENT UPON AQUATIC RESOURCES: A COMPARISON WITH PEOPLES PRIMARILY EXPLOITING TERRESTRIAL ANIMALS AND PLANTS

The distribution of GROUP2 values for peoples dependent upon aquatic resources is markedly different from the $\log_{10}$ values for packing of groups primarily dependent upon terrestrial resources (figure 10.06, graph B). The most obvious contrast is the fact that the majority of the aquatically dependent cases fall to the right or on the high side of the 0.0 $\log_{10}$ threshold value of the packing index identified for plant-dependent peoples (figure 10.03).

If a threshold value is recognizable within the distribution of aquatically dependent cases, it is coincident with the shift from smaller ($\log_{10}$ value of –0.6 for packing) to larger GROUP1 sizes for groups dependent upon terrestrial plants as one approaches the packing threshold of 0.0 (figure 10.03). On the other hand, the direction of this –0.6 threshold is reversed relative to that for plant-dependent peoples, exhibiting a shift similar to the $\log_{10}$ packing value of –0.8 for peoples dependent upon terrestrial animals (figure 10.06, graph A).

Because these comparisons are difficult to keep in mind, the three graphs in figure 10.07 were prepared, one for each subsistence specialty (SUBSP1, SUBSP2, SUBSP3). Each graph has been standardized to the same scale and uses the same markers. Vertical reference lines have been placed on each graph at the low and high thresholds for groups dependent upon terrestrial plant resources. A horizontal reference line indicates the group size at which scalar stress may have conditioned some aspects of the relationship between group

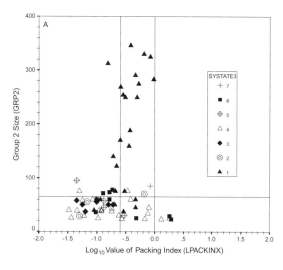

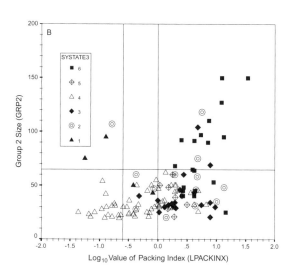

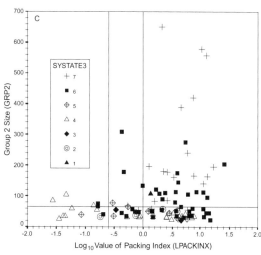

FIGURE 10.07

A three-graph comparison of groups dependent upon terrestrial animals (A), terrestrial plants (B), and aquatic resources (C); GROUP2 sizes are displayed relative to the packing index. Marker is a classification of systems state (SYSTATE3): (1) mounted hunters, (2) horticulturally augmented cases, (3) mutualists and forest product specialists, (4) generic hunter-gatherers, (5) generic hunter-gatherers with instituted leadership, (6) wealth-differentiated hunter-gatherers, and (7) internally ranked hunter-gatherers.

size and social complexity. These variables are considered independently of density-dependent conditions as measured by the packing index (generalization 9.11 and proposition 9.06), although the latter may be autocorrelated in many instances.

By looking discretely at hunter-gatherer groups that primarily exploit either plants or animals or aquatic resources—but using the same pair of lenses in each instance—important differences can be seen in the relationship between the indicators of complexity, and thresholds can be recognized as they emerge. In figure 10.07, graph A, for example, groups dependent upon terrestrial animals are primarily positioned to the left of the major threshold at $\log_{10}$ 0.0, which indicates that demographic packing has not yet occurred. I have already discussed the four exceptions to this pattern in connection with figure 10.05, graph A, even though it has been established that no groups primarily exploiting terrestrial animals are able to survive under packed conditions.

In figure 10.07, graph B, groups of foragers who are primarily dependent upon terrestrial plants have a very different distribution. I noted previously that many cases are found to the right of the $\log_{10}$ packing threshold value of 0.0 and that mutualists and supplemental agriculturists tend to fall below the horizontal reference line for a GROUP2 size of sixty-five or more persons. This pattern indicates that, in spite of the fact that mutualists and product specialists are organized into larger regional systems,

———————— *Generalization 10.11* ————————

There are no increases in social scale within the ethnic components of larger, more complex regional systems. The consequences of scalar increases are therefore not manifested in the social organization of the ethnic components of larger, regionally integrated systems.

———————————————————————————

On the other hand, plant-dependent cases in which ranking and wealth figure importantly in social differentiation fall almost exclusively above the reference line indicating GROUP2 sizes of more than sixty-five persons. As Gregory Johnson (1982) initially suggested, these cases are likely to be experiencing organizational changes in response to scalar stress.

In figure 10.07, graph C, foraging groups dependent upon aquatic resources exhibit an even higher percentage of cases to the right of the packing threshold. Also, in a much higher proportion of the cases below the scalar stress line, wealth and ranking are features of the social organization. I noted in generalizations 9.04 and 9.09, and in problem 9.05, that this type of social differentiation does not appear to be related to a scalar phenomenon and seems, instead, to indicate a more labor-based linkage to the resource structure within the habitat. The other striking difference in graph C is the number of cases whose GROUP2 size dramatically exceeds the size range of most other hunter-gatherers. This suggests that at least two

major sources are conditioning complexity among groups dependent upon aquatic resources.

By substituting niche effectiveness (NICHEFF) for the variable LPACKINX featured in figure 10.07, a useful comparison across trophic levels is apparent in the three graphs in figure 10.08. One of the most interesting features of a comparison of the graphs in figures 10.07 and 10.08 is the difference in the distribution of groups dependent upon terrestrial animals. In figure 10.08, graph A, the dispersion of the cases adopting an extensificational strategy (the mounted hunters) ascends from the left side of the graph and terminates at or near the middle of the transitional segment leading to the $\log_{10}$ value of 1.6. This makes a great deal of sense since

———————— *Proposition 10.14* ————————

Hunting terrestrial animals as a major subsistence strategy will decrease in response to increased packing pressure after a population density value of approximately 1.57 persons per 100 square kilometers is exceeded. Hunting will continue to decrease as density increases until the level of 9.098 persons per 100 square kilometers is reached, by which time the primary source of food should have shifted to either terrestrial plants or aquatic resources, depending upon the environmental setting. In cases in which, for whatever reason, such shifts are not feasible, a demand for food that exceeds the effective carrying capacity will ensure that populations are reduced owing to nutritional and disease-related stress.

———————————————————————————

In the context of the exploitation of terrestrial animals, these costs probably ensure the onset of a classic Malthusian scenario (see chapter 9 for a discussion of the population pressure controversy) in which competitive restrictions on mobility could condition still larger group sizes and result in extreme packing. Dependence upon a limited food resource, such as bison, could well initiate a negative feedback system with attendant decreases in the number of bison as a result of increased demand per unit area.

The near extinction of the bison on the Great Plains of North America is probably not exclusively a consequence of the predation by buffalo hunters employed by the railroads. The success of extensificational processes as measured by population increases—in conjunction with competitive exclusion in many areas of the plains that reduced the effective mobility of many Native American groups—resulted in increased demand on diminishing areas of the bison's former range. These thoughts also suggest that the initial domestication of the horse on the Pontic steppe would make a fascinating subject within which to investigate further clues provided by comparative ethnography.

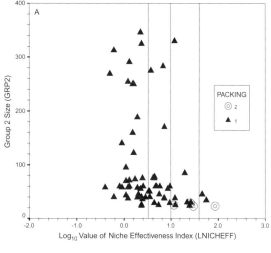

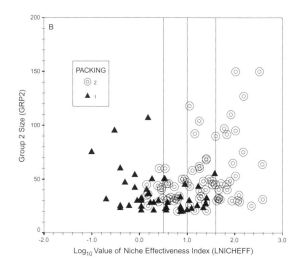

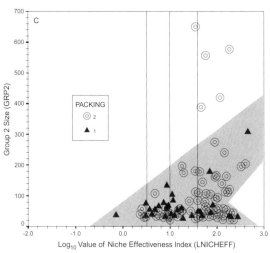

FIGURE 10.08

A three-graph comparison of groups dependent upon terrestrial animals (A), terrestrial plants (B), and aquatic resources (C); GROUP2 sizes are displayed relative to the niche effectiveness index. Cases are coded for packing (PACKING): (1) non-packed and (2) packed.

Another interesting feature of figure 10.08, graph A, is that there are only three groups dependent upon animal resources to the right of the $\log_{10}$ threshold of 1.6, which is analogous to the structure of the packing graph in figure 10.07 (graph A). All evidence (see generalization 10.08) supports the view summarized by proposition 10.14. The pattern in figure 10.08, graph B, for plant-dependent groups is familiar since it appeared in figures 10.04 and 10.05. The distribution of cases in figure 10.08, graph C—all of which are groups dependent upon aquatic resources—represents a new pattern with respect to the niche effectiveness index. There is a distinct chevron-shaped threshold at the niche effectiveness value of $\log_{10}$ 1.6, which prompts the speculation that

Proposition 10.15

Although packing appears to be a very important conditioner of the *shift* by foragers to aquatic resources, it is not nearly as important a conditioner of *variability* among aquatically dependent groups as it is among groups that are primarily dependent upon terrestrial resources. This pattern may, however, result at least partially from an autocorrelation with increasing use of aquatic resources by intensified peoples.

Increased exploitation of aquatic resources shifts land use to a more linear distribution of settlements along shorelines. Following such a range shift, increases in packing result not so much from increased population as from its spatial restructuring. Unfortunately, there is insufficient information currently available to explore the potential ambiguity of this suggestion.

Nevertheless, proposition 10.15 is strongly supported by the additional observation that only seven cases occur to the left of the low group-size threshold for niche effectiveness noted among plant-dependent groups. This is another way of saying that there are very few groups that are dependent upon aquatic resources which would not also be classified as intensified, based on the packing threshold.

────────── *Proposition 10.16* ──────────

Exploitation of aquatic resources, other things being equal, appears to be a density-dependent response to terrestrial packing. It may result from the costs associated with maintaining high mobility in low-food-yielding terrestrial habitats. In such situations, experimentation with aquatic resources could reduce mobility costs. Nevertheless, packing is a general characteristic of documented hunter-gatherers who are dependent upon aquatic resources.

It must be kept in mind that the marked transition at the $\log_{10}$ value of 1.6 for LNICHEFF in figure 10.08, graph C, has properties that are similar to those of terrestrial packing thresholds. For example, increasing group sizes are located to the left of the threshold and both accelerating and decreasing group sizes fall to the right. It should be remembered that the threshold associated with the LNICHEFF axis occurs at a value that is approximately forty times the population density modeled by the Terrestrial Model.

The majority of groups dependent upon aquatic resources with niche effectiveness values of less than 12.4 are found in tropical monsoon forests; the second most common habitat is the boreal forest. The majority of cases with niche effectiveness values of between 12.4 and 40.0 are from boreal forests and midlatitude coastal forests (the redwood and Douglas fir forests of the Pacific northwest coast of North America). It is perhaps not surprising that of the fifty-seven groups dependent upon aquatic resources that had niche effectiveness values greater than 40.0, 84 percent (forty-eight cases) are from midlatitude coastal forest, boreal forest, and tundra biomes.

During the discussions of high-biomass forests in chapters 4 and 5, it was noted that these forests do not offer abundant resources to hunter-gatherers. With regard to the tundra biome, it was suggested that when hunter-gatherers radiated into uninhabited arctic coastal regions, they were already pursuing an aquatic adaptation. These comparisons suggest that

────────── *Generalization 10.12* ──────────

The majority of the global sample of hunter-gatherer groups that are dependent upon aquatic resources are situated in forest plant communities. In general, these habitats offer relatively little accessible food for hunter-gatherers, and this is particularly true of forests in cool and cold environments, where species diversity is much lower than in subtropical and tropical forests with comparable biomass. Forests in warmer climates offer more food opportunities to hunter-gatherers because of their greater species diversity and, in many instances, longer growing seasons.

The arctic coastal tundra is one of the earth's least productive habitats in terms of providing food for human beings, so it is not surprising that many of the hunter-gatherers who are dependent upon aquatic resources are found there. Although no ethnographically documented hunter-gatherers have inhabited true deserts, archaeological deposits in the deserts along the coasts of Peru and Chile, and in Mauritania and the Spanish Sahara, contain sites produced by peoples who were heavy exploiters of aquatic resources in the past. These distributions, and the patterns associated with cases having high niche effectiveness values, strongly support the assertion in generalization 10.12 that the exploitation of aquatic resources is primarily a density-dependent response.

────────── *Proposition 10.17* ──────────

Relative niche effectiveness appears to be the major factor determining how intensification affects system state variability among groups dependent upon aquatic resources. In principle, this variability reflects the diversity of aquatic species and the heavy investment in technological aids employed in intensive food extraction from aquatic biomes.[22]

Other things being equal, this means that

────────── *Proposition 10.18* ──────────

The abundance and distributional structure of aquatic resources and the periodicity in access to them, together with the technology used to access them, will be the major factors determining the broad outlines of variability in social organization among groups dependent upon aquatic resources (see, e.g., Cohen 1981; Schalk 1981).

The preceding comparisons have demonstrated that

────────── *Generalization 10.13* ──────────

Packing appears to be an important conditioner of system state variability regardless of the character of the subsistence base. The character of the variability produced in response to packing, however, differs from one group to another, depending upon the specialized resources that become the dietary focus.

I have argued in generalization 10.11 and proposition 10.14 that increased packing produces intensificational pressures that force a reduction in the dependence upon terrestrial animals. I have also suggested in generalization 10.12 and proposition 10.16 that conditions approaching packing, as defined by a population density of 9.098 persons per 100 square kilometers, may well initiate intensification by increasing a group's dependence upon aquatic resources in settings where this is a realistic alternative.

─────────────── *Generalization 10.14* ───────────────

Among groups dependent upon terrestrial plants, packing drives the buildup of intensificational pressures. The only available responses are to increase the net returns per unit area from plant resources and to expand niche breadth by increasingly exploiting aquatic resources, wherever possible.

───

Aside from providing an increased understanding of the linkages between subsistence, the organization and division of labor, and the impact of both of these factors on group structure, the patterning characteristic of groups dependent upon aquatic resources has led me to suggest links to technology. It is an appropriate juncture for me to turn now to the issue of intensification and its impact upon technological variability and change:

─────────────── *Problem 10.03* ───────────────

Is the role of technology in facilitating intensification the same for groups subsisting upon fundamentally different types of resources?

───

Disembodied Observer: Although I appear to have emerged from the spaghetti bowl and to be getting ready to head purposefully toward a consideration of the relationship between intensification and technology, it is also possible that I am a bit lost. At this point, questions such as "Where was I going when I entered the bowl?" "Where am I now?" and "Did I take a wrong turn?" might well be on my mind. I entered with the intent of exploring the variable termed environmental richness, particularly the role it might play in conditioning different responses to intensificational pressure. I also intended to pursue what is meant by social or cultural "complexity," a term that is often discussed by anthropologists but is still quite ambiguous.

Almost immediately, I learned that the packing index did, in fact, isolate a major threshold of system change in the group size of hunter-gatherers who were primarily dependent upon terrestrial plant resources (generalization 10.06). This clarified earlier observations relating sociopolitical complexity and group size (generalizations 8.01 and 8.02; proposition 8.01). Since I had earlier demonstrated some strong relationships between group size and the division of labor (generalizations 8.32 and 8.33), as well as group size and changes in the labor costs of subsistence (proposition 8.12), I was prompted to speculate further about the division of labor and the organization of labor in general (proposition 10.10). When I turned to the use of my second instrument for measurement—niche effectiveness values—I encountered the issue of habitat "richness" and its role, if any, in modifying responses to intensification (proposition 10.11). Although I had some expectations about patterning if richness was an important conditioner, no clear or unambiguous indicators were revealed.

An investigation of exceptional hunter-gatherer cases led quite unexpectedly to the issue of complexity as I focused on groups that were classified as mutualists. It became clear that complexity can be "built" in different ways. It most commonly occurs within systems undergoing restructuring, but the mutualist cases document an integrational pathway along which relatively independent systems are integrated into higher-order systems while maintaining their ethnic and cultural "independence" (generalization 10.08 and problem 10.01). The evidence at hand was consistent with the view that mutualism itself was a density-dependent response (proposition 10.13), which prompted me to ask what factors produce that type of response instead of, for instance, internal system restructuring (problem 10.01 and proposition 10.13). An investigation of the distribution of mutualist cases relative to habitat variability revealed such pronounced environmental bias in the distribution of cases that it seemed reasonable to question whether similar responses might be expected in all types of environments (problem 10.02). Finally, an application of instruments for measuring habitat richness to groups dependent upon terrestrial plants did not clarify the issue at all. On the contrary, there was no indication that this variable played any role whatsoever in conditioning the occurrence of major intensificational responses (generalization 10.09).

Pattern recognition studies were expanded to include, first, hunters who were primarily dependent upon terrestrial animals, followed by groups dependent upon aquatic resources. Among the groups exploiting animal resources, I found that no cases in my sampling of the past survived the packing threshold that has been identified as affecting groups dependent upon terrestrial plants. This was very strong confirmation of earlier observations and arguments in this chapter asserting that intensification selects against terrestrial animals as food resources (generalizations 10.01, 10.02, and 10.10). An additional threshold was unexpectedly identified at a low value of 1.59 persons per 100 square kilometers as the point at which reductions in group size occurred. This threshold implicates dependence upon terrestrial animals since I demonstrated earlier that group size was particularly sensitive to the relative dependence upon terrestrial animals (generalizations 8.18, 8.29, 8.31, and 8.32).

Although groups dependent upon either terrestrial animals or plants were usually found on the low side of the packing threshold, foragers primarily dependent upon aquatic resources were more common on the high side of the packing threshold. This bias among groups primarily exploiting aquatic resources led to the suggestion that the shift to aquatic resources was a density-dependent response (proposition 10.16).

In light of these conclusions, it should come as no surprise that my pattern recognition work with sets of cases grouped in terms of subsistence base concluded by demonstrating a bias in the habitats in which aquatic resources play major roles (generalization 10.12). I initiated a discussion of the factors responsible for system state variability among groups dependent upon aquatic resources (proposition10.18) and summarized what I had learned about packing as the force driving intensificational processes (generalizations 10.13 and 10.14). I concluded with a question about the role of technology, which was prompted during my consideration of differences between aquatic and essentially terrestrial adaptations.

Intensification and Technology: More Responses to Packing

Disembodied Observer: The question about technology introduced at the end of the preceding section, coupled with the overarching goal of this book—to put in place a usable body of prior knowledge and analytical tactics appropriate for use by archaeologists—are the concerns behind the rather abrupt shift to pattern recognition studies using data on hunter-gatherer technology. Ever since the inception of their discipline, anthropologists have speculated about the role technology plays in bringing about culture change, and archaeologists have often identified culture change by invoking technological criteria.

Although I am known to use a somewhat different lexicon, like my archaeological colleagues I find the issues embodied by the cultural historical paradigm bedeviling. How does technology respond to intensification pressures? Are clues to system state changes and variability to be found in technological variability? Certainly a much larger sample of cases than are included here is desirable and necessary to reach a comprehensive understanding of technological change and the forces producing it.

Another aspect of such an inquiry that must be kept in mind relative to archaeological interests is that, in this study, I tabulated only tools used directly in the procurement of food. In order to develop a comprehensive data base of hunter-gatherer technology, a significant investment of time, effort, and expense would be required to tabulate tools used to make tools and tools used to fabricate tended and untended food procurement facilities.

In 1973, Oswalt introduced his first effort to summarize systematically hunter-gatherer technological richness in terms of the number of basic tools and the number of components from which such tools were constructed (see also Oswalt 1976). In this important early study, the operative principle was simple: through time, the complexity of a tool assemblage increased. The challenge to the researcher was to measure this trend and to recognize major junctures at which advance occurred.

Oswalt's interpretation of the technologies that he reviewed is not important here, but his research—which made available a number of ethnographic cases that were studied and described in the same terms—offered other researchers the opportunity to undertake comparative studies. This opportunity was seized initially by Robin Torrence (1983), who demonstrated a compelling relationship between latitude and the measured complexity of ethnographically documented tools used to obtain foods. Simply put, in Torrence's study complexity increased as latitude increased.

This correlation is demonstrated in figure 10.09, graphs A and B, using thirty-one cases[23] instead of the twenty that were available to Torrence in 1983. Interestingly, the relationship between latitude and number of weapons is even more robust than in Torrence's earlier work (1983:figs. 3.1 and 3.2). The cases in figure 10.09, graph A, are identified in terms of the ordinal variable "leader," for which a code of 1 indicates that leadership status is based on the relevance of a person's knowledge and the quality of his or her advice and is often embedded in the roles played by older persons.[24] A code of 2 indicates that leaders are quite visible and are recognized by everyone. Usually the latter kind of leadership status is derived from performance, and recognized leaders have "followers." I have thought of category 2 as "show me" leadership because—unlike "consulting" leaders who are sought out for advice but never really have a following—followers of "show me" leaders shift their allegiance in response to a leader's "performance in role."[25]

Both graphs in figure 10.09 clearly indicate that there is a positive curvilinear relationship between the number of weapons and latitude.[26] There is also a threshold at approximately 40 degrees latitude above which "show me" leadership prevails in the higher latitudes and below which "consulting" leadership is characteristic. These differences are likely to reflect important initial conditions for changes in subsequent social forms initiated by intensification.

A similar distribution in figure 10.09, graph B, demonstrates the relationship between latitude and the number of weapons for ethnographic cases coded to reflect the primary source of food. Groups characterized by relatively few weapons dominate the graph below 40 degrees latitude and are primarily dependent upon terrestrial plants, in whose acquisition weapons would not be very useful. Above 40 degrees, there is a pronounced shift in the orientation of the graph, as rapid increases in the number of tools occur with increases in latitude. The groups featured in this pattern are

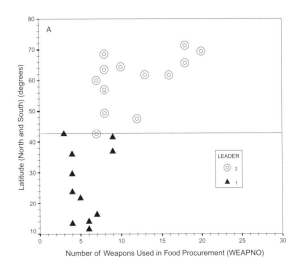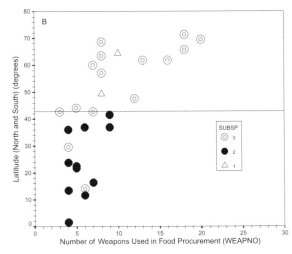

FIGURE 10.09

A two-graph comparison of the relationship between latitude and the number of weapons used in food procurement. Graph A is coded for leadership (LEADER): (1) an elaboration of achieved social status judged in terms of knowledge and "good advice" criteria, leadership may be said to be embedded in the roles of elder persons; (2) leaders are quite visible, everyone recognizes them, and the role is performance-based; there are "followers" of given leaders. Graph B is coded for the primary source of food (SUBSP): (1) terrestrial animals, (2) terrestrial plants, and (3) aquatic resources.

all primarily dependent upon terrestrial animals or aquatic resources, which is not surprising since the procurement of these two types of resources usually involves weapons and dependence upon them is documented to increase with latitude (generalizations 7.05, 7.11, and 7.12). The higher latitudes are also where "performance in role" is crucial to subsistence security. Knowledge and its tactical use in planning for the capture of both terrestrial and aquatic animals,[27] coupled with skill in using the technology, are the two essential qualities that a leader must possess.

The evidence for increasing numbers of weapons[28] used in direct procurement subsistence activities in higher latitudes has been convincingly demonstrated in figure 10.09. To pursue further my interest in the tool-task relationship, figure 10.10 was prepared to show the patterned distribution between latitude and the number of tended facilities used in obtaining food. *Tended facilities* have been defined by Oswalt (1976:106–7) as tools that control the movement of a species to man's advantage but require a human presence to either initiate the use of or take advantage of the controlled animal movements. Tended facilities include game blinds, hunting disguises, items thrown to direct or control animal movement (such as the boomerangs used by Australian Aborigines to restrict the flight of birds), fish weirs, fish nets, fish hooks, and similar devices.

In figure 10.10, a positive relationship is visible between latitude and the number of tended facilities (FACNO) up to a threshold at approximately 42.6 degrees, after which the pat-

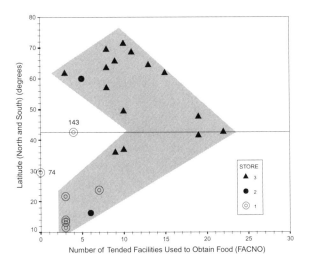

FIGURE 10.10

The threshold in the number of tended facilities used in obtaining food relative to latitude. Cases are coded for dependence upon storage (STORE): (1) storage beyond a day or two is not present; (2) special event storage only (food is processed and accumulated prior to a special event at which guests are supplemented with food gifts); and (3) food is stored for use during seasonal and other low-productivity phases of the year.

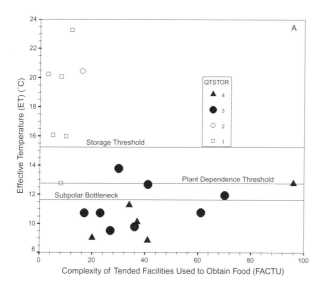
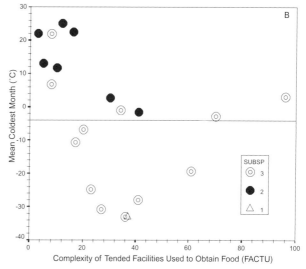

FIGURE 10.11

A two-graph comparison of two measures of temperature and the relationship between these measures and the complexity of tended facilities (A) used to obtain food. A threshold is suggested relative to a mean of –4.0°C for the coldest month (B). Graph A is coded for the quantity of food stored (QTSTOR): (1) no regular storage or minor, very-short-term storage of two or three days; (2) moderate investment in storage in both quantity and period of potential use; (3) major investment in storage and in the duration of anticipated use; and (4) massive investment in storage from the standpoint of both species stored and duration of use. Graph B is coded for the primary source of food (SUBSP): (1) terrestrial animals, (2) terrestrial plants, and (3) aquatic resources.

tern reverses and the number of tended facilities decreases. Relating this pattern to the distribution in figure 10.09, it is clear that, although the number of tended facilities goes down at latitudes of approximately 42.6 degrees, the number of weapons increases dramatically. It should be emphasized that the 42.6-degree threshold corresponds to the terrestrial plant threshold—noted earlier in proposition 8.06—at 12.75 degrees ET, at which point accessible plant resources become less available. As subsistence shifts to the pursuit of large game and sea mammals—supplemented by fish—weapons and mobility become more important.

Other interesting observations emerge that refer to generalization 8.10, which notes that a threshold in GROUP1 size occurs at an ET value of 11.53, and to figure 3.10, which records a threshold in the number of species stored at an ET value of 12.75 degrees. The latter threshold corresponds to the latitudinal threshold in figure 10.10 marking the transitional zone of reversal in the relationship between weapons and tended facilities.

GROUP1 size also goes up as the number of weapons and dependence upon storage increase until a threshold occurs at ET 12.75 (generalization 8.12), after which GROUP1 size and the use of tended facilities both decrease. Other relationships between ET and complexity in the design of tools and facilities (FACTU) are explored in figure 10.11, graphs A and B, which illustrate that a transitional zone in ET values corresponds to a habitat in which the temperature during the coldest month of the year is –4°C (figure 10.11, graph B). This is also roughly coincidental with the terrestrial plant threshold at ET 12.75 degrees.[29]

Presumably, a reduction in the use of tended facilities is linked to the size of the labor force in environments in which the plants are no longer expected to provide most of the food. Another possibility is that the reduction in the number of mammalian species that occurs in arctic regions may also decrease the number of contexts in which different types of species might occur.

Generalization 10.15

The observed relationship between tools and latitude is referable to the character of the targeted food resources, to the organization and deployment of labor, and to an investment of labor in the facilities that are best suited to the capture of different targeted food resources.

These facilities are autocorrelated with latitude, given the niches occupied by human groups, but this autocorrelation does not, as Torrence suggested, directly reveal causal linkages. Support for this point is found in the patterned coincidences between contrasts in leadership (figure 10.09, graph A) and primary sources of food (figure 10.09, graph B) when each of these variables is plotted against increased complexity in the design and number of weapons. Tended facilities (figure 10.10) are parallel to this pattern, diverging at the point at which a reduction occurs in the size of the basic units engaged in food procurement. This point coincides with important shifts in the primary sources of food.

Figures 10.10 and 10.11 demonstrate that the number of tended facilities and the complexity of their design vary with group size and cold temperatures in a different way relative to weapons. The numbers accelerate dramatically at approximately 39 degrees latitude, then a threshold occurs at a mean of close to –4°C for the coldest month of the year, at which point the pattern reverses. Thereafter, as latitude increases, the number of tended facilities and the complexity of their design decrease.

I originally thought that this pattern could reflect two different determinant conditions: an increased dependence upon aquatic resources as one moves in a polar direction and an increase in sociopolitically complex groups that are dependent upon aquatic resources at approximately 45 degrees latitude, followed by diminishing complexity above 60 degrees. This pattern prompts me to ask whether complexity somehow drives down the use of tended facilities. This possibility echoes the claims made by other researchers, the work of one of whom I will now discuss.

Using only five of Oswalt's original ethnographic cases and eliminating the high-latitude arctic cases,[30] Michael Shott (1986) compared Oswalt's measures to the number of annual residential moves and the total distance moved residentially by the five groups. He argued that "mobility frequency (number of annual residential moves) may limit the number of tools and, correspondingly, the number of tool classes that can be carried between residences" (Shott 1986:23).[31] Shott illustrated a rough, inverse, curvilinear relationship between the number of residential moves and his data on the number of "weapons and instruments," to use Oswalt's terms. The pattern in figure 10.12 is analogous to that reported by Shott, but it tabulates only the number of weapons (using the variable WEAPNO), rather than tool classes, and the number of residential moves made annually (NOMOV). The ethnographic cases have been coded according to their primary source of food.

The most obvious pattern in the graph relates food source to mobility. Groups primarily dependent upon terrestrial animal resources are most mobile, plant-dependent cases are less mobile, and although groups primarily dependent upon aquatic resources overlap with plant-dependent peoples, on the whole they are even less mobile. A general increase in the number of weapons corresponds to a decrease in residential mobility for groups dependent upon either plants or terrestrial animals. It is clear, however, that the most emphatic pattern shows that, among exploiters of aquatic resources, the number of weapons increases as mobility decreases. Com-

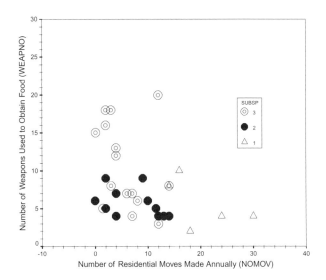

FIGURE 10.12

The relationship between the number of weapons used to obtain food and the number of residential moves made annually. Cases are coded for dominant sources of foods (SUBSP): (1) terrestrial animals, (2) terrestrial plants, and (3) aquatic resources.

parable reductions in the mobility of plant-dependent peoples result in a much smaller increase in the number of weapons. In general, groups dependent upon terrestrial animal resources are more mobile and have fewer weapons.

Shott interpreted the patterned relationship between hunter-gatherer mobility and the number of weapons as directly related to transport limitations or the high portability costs incurred when many moves were being made (Shott 1986:23, 45). He argued that these constraints ensured that the equation of tool type to task was less likely in sedentary contexts in which tool diversity was subject to fewer utilitarian constraints. According to Shott, in such a context tool differentiation could be referable to an increasing number of "social reasons" (Shott 1986:45). Given the patterns in figure 10.09, one wonders why groups dependent upon terrestrial plants should feel more bound by utilitarian constraints or endow their tools with fewer social meanings than peoples who depend primarily upon aquatic resources. Contrary to Shott's argument, I think the answer to such a dilemma lies elsewhere:

Generalization 10.16

Variability in the number of tool-assisted tasks that are central to food procurement and—when the character and distribution of potential food resources in the habitat differ—the specificity of the role of tools in such events condition the number and the complexity of design of fundamentally different kinds of tools.

The pursuit of aquatic resources is directed toward many food targets that must be both constrained in their movement and extracted from the aquatic milieu. It is the latter demand on the forager which ensures that differentiated tool design will vary more discretely with the character of the access window and the size and behavior of the creatures being extracted from the aquatic milieu. In contrast, the extraction of edible plant components from their location requires relatively simple tools—digging sticks or poles for knocking down fruit—compared with the variety of implements used to extract fish and sea mammals from aquatic biomes.

─────────── *Generalization 10.17* ───────────

Differences in the character of capture and extraction events are the major stimuli for the design differences in tools used to obtain resources directly.

With regard to the equation of task and tool, accurately anticipating changes and shifts in tool frequency and design is complicated further by differences in food procurement tactics. In fact, one could argue that many of the differences between the biased use of weapons and tended or untended facilities are tactical and correlated with the size of the labor group (generalizations 8.31 and 8.32) and variability in group organization (generalizations 8.03, 8.12, 8.13, 8.14, and 8.27).

I have already suggested that tactical changes are likely to occur when system state conditions change, and I have also focused on changes that are driven by pressures per square kilometer to intensify. When these pressures operate on diverse systems that exploit profoundly different food resources, foragers would be expected to vary significantly in the way they design and use tools, depending upon the organization of the system coming under intensificational pressure. This point underscores a central theme in this book: that one should expect marked variability that relates in regular ways to the character of the initial conditions prevailing at the time that change-inducing pressures arise. The identification of relevant initial conditions is fundamental to understanding variability itself and to the successful investigation of patterned variability in the temporal trajectories of systems with different initial conditions.

I have already suggested that packing is an important initial condition underlying the shift by hunter-gatherers to heavy exploitation of aquatic resources (generalization 10.07). I also argued earlier that niche effectiveness directly measures the extent to which a given group of hunter-gatherers exceeds the extractive effectiveness anticipated by the Terrestrial Model. It was implied that increases in effectiveness would be driven primarily by technology and associated tactical changes in the organization of food procurement activities. The graphs in figure 10.13 demonstrate the relationship between the niche effectiveness index (NICHEFF) and

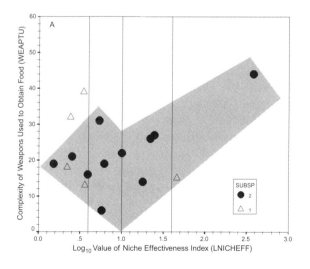 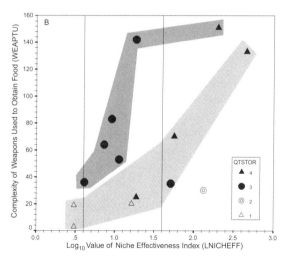

FIGURE 10.13

A comparison between the technological responses to niche effectiveness of groups primarily dependent upon terrestrial (A) and aquatic (B) resources. Graph A is coded for the primary source of food (SUBSP): (1) terrestrial animals and (2) terrestrial plants. Graph B is coded for the quantity of food stored (QTSTOR): (1) no regular storage or minor, very-short-term storage of two or three days; (2) moderate investment in storage in both quantity and period of potential use; (3) major investment in storage and in the duration of anticipated use; and (4) massive investment in storage from the standpoint of both species stored and duration of use.

the total number of techno-units[32] (WEAPTU) incorporated into the design of weapons used by a given group. Cases are represented by the ordinal variable SUBSP in graph A and by the variable QTSTOR in graph B.

This figure confirms the pattern in figure 10.09, which illustrated that weapons play minor roles among hunter-gatherer groups that are primarily dependent upon terrestrial plants, but that their importance accelerates as hunting contributes more significantly to the diet. One could argue that in the zone in figure 10.13, graph A, in which packing and therefore increased niche effectiveness would be expected to increase (indicating that intensification is occurring), the complexity of weapons decreases and then increases again once the threshold zone has been traversed. The latter increase could reflect the higher cost of obtaining essential animal protein and, consequently, greater weapons specialization, as well as increased competition or warfare. The number of cases tabulated for technology is, unfortunately, too small to make these observations compelling.

What is obvious is the contrast between the two graphs in figure 10.13, both of which feature the same scale. In graph B—which records only groups that are primarily dependent upon aquatic resources—as the niche effectiveness threshold range (0.6–1.6) is approached, there is a pronounced increase in the complexity of weapons measured in terms of the numbers of techno-units. The acceleration proceeds as a curvilinear function and, as in earlier graphs, a shadow effect occurs with acceleration, beginning at a threshold of approximately 0.6 on the $\log_{10}$ scale of niche effectiveness. As the graph indicates, all of the cases clustered in the darker shaded area are groups from latitudes at or above 60 degrees. Most of these groups were located in areas projected by the Terrestrial Model to have been uninhabited or to have had very low population densities. It is quite likely that intensificational pressures were felt earlier (in niche effectiveness terms) in these settings because of the extremely low level of accessible terrestrial food sources. In environments that are more hospitable to hunter-gatherers, the major threshold for intensification is delayed until approximately 1.6 on the niche effectiveness scale.[33]

The only hunter-gatherer group that falls outside the basic pattern in figure 10.13, graph B, is the Yahgan, located at the southern tip of South America. Although it is my impression that the available population density estimates are maximum values, the Terrestrial Model projects a very low value for this case. At the time that the variable *temperateness* was modeled (see generalization 8.07), this case was noted as an exception relative to the quantity of food stored.[34] In spite of these technical problems, there seems little doubt that

Generalization 10.18

Increasing complexity in the design of weapons responds positively to intensificational pressures when aquatic resources

are the primary source of food. Since dependence upon terrestrial animals diminishes as pressures to intensify increase, there is a corresponding decrease in both the use and the complexity of weapons used for subsistence purposes as the exploitation of terrestrial animal resources decreases.

The split between the left and right reference lines distinguishes between the intensified cases (right line) and those cases that are intensified relative to their terrestrial settings (left line), which are projected by the Terrestrial Model to be uninhabited. The role technology plays in maintaining groups in such low-productivity settings is clear, and it should be noted that the vast majority of the weapons produced in these settings are used to exploit sea mammals. This graph is considered strong support for the earlier proposition that

Generalization 10.19

Increasing niche effectiveness among groups that are primarily dependent upon aquatic resources is made possible by the increased complexity and diversity of their food-procuring technology.

Since system state has been documented in numerous instances (generalizations 10.01, 10.03, 10.04, and 10.08; proposition 10.17) to vary significantly with the packing index, which is also related in a very general way to the niche effectiveness index, it can be expected that

Proposition 10.19

As packing increases, groups that are dependent upon aquatic resources should resort to more complex subsistence technology. Increasing complexity in the design of weapons should also be associated with hunter-gatherer groups that are not primarily dependent upon aquatic resources as a function of their more specialized exploitation of a reduced number of high-yield species (see generalizations 10.15 and 10.16).

To help evaluate this proposition, figure 10.14 plots the number of techno-units (sensu Oswalt) relative to the packing index. All groups display a reduction in design complexity as the packing threshold is approached. This finding is almost certainly related to an earlier demonstration of a patterned reduction in hunting (compare to figure 10.08, graph A) as groups dependent upon terrestrial resources approached the packing threshold. Once systems become packed, there is an increase in weapon complexity among groups who depend primarily upon aquatic resources, as well as those that are dependent upon terrestrial plant resources.

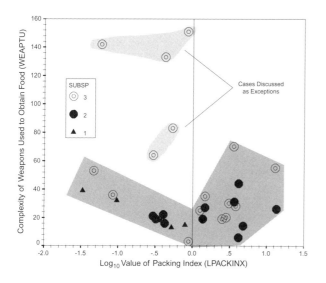

FIGURE 10.14

An overview of the relationship between the complexity of weapons design used in obtaining food and the $\log_{10}$ value of the packing index. Cases are coded for the primary source of food (SUBSP): (1) terrestrial animals, (2) terrestrial plants, and (3) aquatic resources.

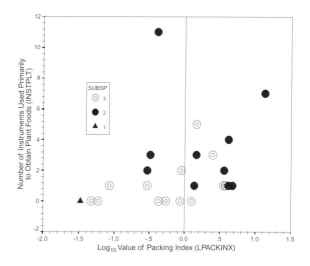

FIGURE 10.15

The number of instruments used primarily to obtain plant foods displayed relative to the $\log_{10}$ value of the packing index. Cases are coded for the primary source of food (SUBSP): (1) terrestrial animals, (2) terrestrial plants, and (3) aquatic resources.

Further examination of these cases reveals that this trend also associates packing with an increase in the exploitation of aquatic resources. The groups that are dependent upon aquatic resources, have low PACKINX values, and are located in the upper shaded area of the graph are all sea mammal hunters of the high Arctic. The Terrestrial Model projects that such a habitat would be uninhabited, and it is only the development of a complex technology for exploiting marine resources that made successful penetration of this habitat possible.

The two cases above 60 degrees latitude in the lower shaded area of figure 10.14—the Ingalik and the Tanaina of Alaska—are adjacent geographically, occupying the lower riparian zone just inland from coastal groups. Both of these groups hunted and fished, but only very rough estimates of aboriginal populations can be found in the ethnographic record (Snow 1981; Townsend 1981).[35] Nevertheless, given what is known about the archaeological record in northern latitudes, I propose that

Proposition 10.20

The development of weapons technology can open up new niches and facilitate radiations into previously unoccupied geographic regions.

As a further demonstration of the relationship between tools and the contexts of tool use, in figure 10.15 I have plotted hunter-gatherer cases coded for their primary source of subsistence in a matrix with the $\log_{10}$ value of the packing index (LPACKINX) on the *x* axis and the number of instruments used primarily in obtaining plant foods on the *y* axis. Oswalt (1976:64) defined these instruments as "hand-manipulated [tools] that customarily are used to impinge on masses incapable of significant motion and are relatively harmless to people."

Two features of the graph are provocative. First, once the packing threshold is passed, there is in increase in the number of "instruments," which should correspond to increased intensification and the exploitation of a greater number of plant species. The second important feature of the graph is that relatively few of the groups dependent upon aquatic resources exhibit such a threshold-related increase. Those that do are cases in warm temperate and subtropical habitats in which aquatic dependence expands simultaneously with dependence upon plants. Clearly, increasing numbers of instruments appear to relate directly to intensification.

Weapons and instruments are not the only kinds of tools that may be critical to obtaining food resources. Oswalt also made a distinction between two types of facilities (Wagner 1960). In addition to tended facilities, which I have already discussed, he referred to untended facilities, a category that includes items such as snares and mechanically activated traps (either deadfall or pitfall), which do not require manipulation to be activated.

In figure 10.16, the relationship between the number of untended facilities and the $\log_{10}$ value of the packing index

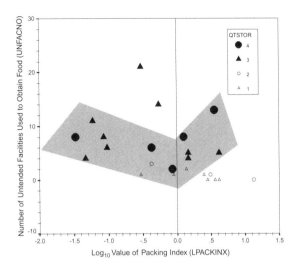

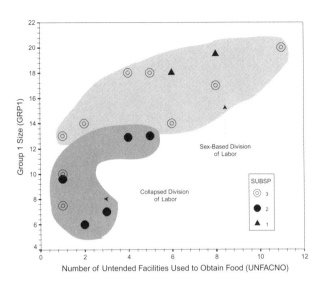

FIGURE 10.16

The relationships between packing, storage, and increased numbers of untended facilities. Cases are coded for the quantity of food stored (QTSTOR): (1) no regular storage or minor, very-short-term storage of two or three days; (2) moderate investment in storage in both quantity and period of potential use; (3) major investment in storage and in the duration of anticipated use; and (4) massive investment in storage from the standpoint of both species stored and duration of use.

is illustrated for hunter-gatherer cases coded in terms of the variable QTSTOR (the quantity of food that is stored). The chevron pattern in the graph is reminiscent of the way group size and the packing threshold interacted in figure 10.14. Here the number of untended facilities goes down as the packing threshold is approached, but once that threshold is crossed the number of facilities increases again. Although the sample size in figure 10.16 is small, it appears that this distinctive pattern does not apply to groups that do not store food. The increased investment in untended facilities therefore seems to be a response to packing primarily when stored foods make an important contribution to the diet.[36]

Untended traps can be regarded as mechanical hunters; by placing them in many different locations, hunter-gatherers increase both their potential animal encounter rate and their net return. This strategy should pay off in situations in which either there is insufficient labor or the labor demands increase the demand curve for foods, which raises the bar on net returns and possibly increases mobility costs as well.

An exploration of the relationship between GROUP1 size and the number of different untended facilities coded for the primary resources exploited by hunter-gatherers is presented in figure 10.17. The pattern in this graph suggests that

FIGURE 10.17

The relationship between GROUP1 size and the number of untended facilities used to obtain food, with implications for the division of labor. Cases are coded for the primary source of food (SUBSP): (1) terrestrial animals, (2) terrestrial plants, and (3) aquatic resources.

Generalization 10.20

There are apparently two contexts in which untended facilities play a significant role in food procurement. The first occurs when the division of labor is collapsed (see generalization 8.30) and labor is therefore in very short supply (see the lower left segment of figure 10.17). In the second context, GROUP1 size and gender-based differentiation in subsistence roles both increase with packing. The number of untended facilities increases positively and linearly as GROUP1 size increases above the level of a collapsed division of labor.

It is relevant to note that the vast majority of groups in the latter context are primarily dependent upon either terrestrial animals, aquatic resources, or both (see marker code for cases in the higher-GROUP1-size range in figure 10.17). I have demonstrated earlier that the amount of labor contributed by males increases dramatically as dependence upon terrestrial and aquatic resources increases (generalizations 8.28, 8.29, and 8.30). During my own field experience in the arctic, I learned that under these conditions females do, in fact, invest substantial labor in the use of untended trapping facilities, particularly during summer months. This kind of activity—along with other, more direct labor contributions (proposition 8.09)—accounts for a reversal in the relationship between estimates of the percentage of the total food obtained by males (MDIVLAB) and GROUP1 size (gener-

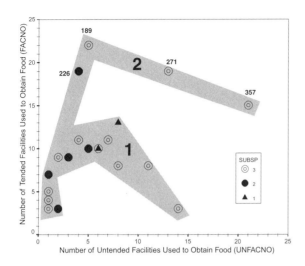

FIGURE 10.18

The relationship between the number of tended and untended facilities used in obtaining food. Cases are coded for the primary source of food (SUBSP): (1) terrestrial animals, (2) terrestrial plants, and (3) aquatic resources.

alization 8.12). This reversal occurs at the same point in the graph as the threshold for tended facilities (see the discussion of figure 8.23).

The absence of a reversal in the pattern in figure 10.17 and the regular linear relationship with male contribution to the total labor effort demonstrate that untended facilities track shifts in group size and the proportion of the total division of labor represented by male effort. This is true regardless of directional changes in that effort at the threshold of a mean temperature of approximately –4°C for the coldest month of the year (see figure 10.11, graph B), which roughly corresponds to the terrestrial plant threshold (generalization 8.12).

A good illustration of this pattern occurs in figure 10.18, in which the number of tended facilities behaves similarly to group size and the male contribution to the labor force relative to the terrestrial plant threshold that has now been identified with an approximate value of –4°C as the mean of the coldest month. This coincidence is important to changes in both the number and complexity of tended facilities (figures 10.10 and 10.11). Figure 10.18 shows that the number of tended facilities increases as the number of untended facilities increases up to a point between 5.0 and 7.75 untended facilities. Thereafter, tended facilities decrease as untended facilities increase. This pattern occurs at two different orders of magnitude for tended facilities, labeled 1 and 2 in figure 10.18.[37]

Generalization 10.21

Situations in which untended facilities of many kinds contribute significantly to subsistence are situations in which there

is not much opportunity to expand the numbers of tended facilities.

I have already pointed out that the design complexity of tended facilities expands dramatically from warm environmental settings up to locations in which the mean temperature of the coldest month of the year is –4°C or warmer, which corresponds to the plant threshold at 12.75°C (ET) (figure 10.11, graph B). Thereafter, in environments with short growing seasons and cold winters, obtaining high net returns in relatively short periods of time is crucial to the success of storage strategies. The subsistence base in such settings consists of terrestrial animals and, under increasingly packed conditions, greater dependence upon aquatic resources. In such settings, tended facilities are used less and less.

A former student of mine, Trent Holliday (1998), undertook a comparative study of trapping and found that the use of untended traps was low when both residential mobility and ungulate biomass were high. It tended to be high, however, in habitats in which animal biomass was relatively low and animals were dispersed. He also noted that the primary context of reduced mobility was associated with the increased utilization of aquatic resources. This was also the setting in which the use of untended traps among recent hunter-gatherers was highest. Holliday's findings amplify and support the relationships between tended and untended facilities demonstrated in figure 10.18, and they form the basis of the expectation that

---

Proposition 10.21

Tended facilities are increasingly successful in settings in which artiodactyl biomass is moderate to high and animals are at least periodically aggregated. The same distributional principles apply to smaller species. The use of tended facilities will also increase in settings in which packing occurs and residential mobility is reduced, depending primarily on the feasibility of the use of aquatic resources.

The preceding pattern recognition studies have provided some ideas about the circumstances in which the use of tended and untended facilities is likely to be selected for. As the final step in my examination of variability in subsistence technology using Oswalt's conventions, it is time for a direct examination of the facilities that are tended or activated by hunter-gatherers. I have already pointed out that these facilities include many types of fish weirs, the use of seine netting, and most netting equipment used in a terrestrial context, including many but not all of the types of game drive facilities. On the other hand, the forms most frequently recorded are various kinds of fish hooks and gorges, items used in game drives such as torches and beating sticks, and basket traps used in conjunction with weirs. The use of some of these kinds of facilities also implies communal hunting (sensu Hayden 1981:371), although the vast majority of forms do not.

The preceding comparisons of tended and untended facilities, coupled with cross-cultural ethnographic studies, are not the only sources that provide useful intellectual capital in my examination of tended facilities. A discussion of one of the relatively few instances in contemporary archaeology in which problem-oriented research is actually derived from pattern recognition studies conducted on the archaeological record is germane at this juncture. This research touches directly upon the subject of tended facilities and is pertinent to the broader issue of intensification as well. In his 1982 doctoral thesis, Frank Bayham pointed out that, in the long sequence at Arizona's Ventana Cave, evidence for the use of plant materials diminishes through time and the exploitation of artiodactyls of large to moderate body size increases. Simultaneously, there is an unrelenting trend in the region toward increased sedentism and dependence upon horticulture, culminating in irrigation horticulture.

Bayham has stated his expectation that, over time, a reduction in body size and an overall decrease in the contribution to the diet from animal sources would be expected. Bayham continued to research this proposition, and later Speth and Scott (1985) undertook a comprehensive investigation of the patterns isolated by Bayham. Speth and Scott found that in many, mostly New World settings involving horticultural and settled peoples, a counterintuitive increase in artiodactyls relative to animals of small body size was demonstrable (for relevant discussions see Kent 1989; Speth and Scott 1989; Szuter and Bayham 1989). Speth and Scott (1989:75–76) linked this pattern to an increase in communal hunting. Against this background of provocative results from almost two decades of research, it seems reasonable to ask why at least some hunter-gatherers have responded to intensification by using tended facilities.

This question is explored in figure 10.19, which shows the patterned interaction between the complexity of tended facilities and the $\log_{10}$ value of the packing index for ethnographic cases that are categorized in terms of their degree of class differentiation. Unlike most of the other graphs in which tools or techno-units are plotted against the packing index, in figure 10.19 the number of techno-units does not decrease as the packing threshold is approached and then increase as packing continues to increase. Instead, three relatively independent distributions of cases occur.

In the two distributions designated 1 and 2, there is an overall decrease in the number of tended techno-units across the packing index threshold. The two lines then converge at a value of ten times the packing threshold, or ten times the population occurring at the time a packed condition is first reached, where tended units drop to zero. In contrast, cases

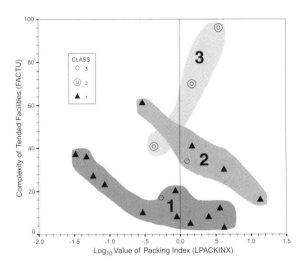

FIGURE 10.19

The relationship between the complexity of tended facilities and the packing index. Cases are coded for class distinctions (CLASS): (1) absence of any significant class distinctions, (2) wealth distinctions only, (3) dual stratification into a hereditary aristocracy and a lower class of ordinary people.

that have only wealth distinctions (distribution 3) behave completely differently: the number of techno-units increases sharply as the packing threshold is crossed. What is to be made of such an anomalous pattern?

Examination of the cases in terms of Oswalt's tool typology reveals that the majority of the tended facilities are used as part of a "wait and hope" procurement strategy. Good examples of this kind of technology include hook and line fishing, human-activated snares, and traps that involve the use of a lure. Tools of a very different character are associated with game drives: torches and beating sticks might be used, or musical instruments (such as drums) might be played, or fire itself could be used to control the movement of game. Some groups construct features such as lines of rocks or fences of vegetation to influence the behavior of their prey.

Between twenty and thirty-two of the tended facilities listed in Oswalt's typology result in the capture of only individual animals or a small number of animals or fish at one time. Only six of these forms (Oswalt 1976:110–11) are used by groups in their communal hunting activities. As intensification increases, I can therefore expect that decreasing numbers of less complex tended facilities may well co-vary with a shift to communal hunting tactics or the abandonment of some techniques that are not "rate-maximizing" (Beckerman 1994:179) with regard to labor investments, such as a shift from tended facilities to untended facilities (figure 10.18). An increase in the use of tended facilities in contexts associated with wealth differentiation could reflect the rejection of a rate-maximizing strategy by persons without wealth in favor of a strategy of maximizing net returns under stress. Nevertheless, I do not know what stands behind the contrary distribution 3 in figure 10.19.

In other contexts, an increase in the use of tended facilities maintained by communal labor may not necessarily occur in the early stages of intensification. The hunter-gatherer data in figure 10.19 indicate a general reduction in tended facilities, culminating in a low-end convergence on the Chenchu of India, an agricultural group with a population density of 123.3 persons per 100 square kilometers (thirteen times the number of persons associated with the packing threshold). Among the Chenchu, the use of fish poison is reported to be prevalent, and communal use of tended facilities accounts for over half of the recorded techno-units. These observations support the conclusion that heavily intensified groups use relatively few tended facilities but that, when present, they are biased in favor of communal use of such facilities.

Additionally, the overall return from these communally organized activities may be expected to exceed the returns from tended facilities that are individually organized. Since the available information is insufficient to account for the pattern in figure 10.19, these accommodations to the data are only offered as provocative examples. Conclusive evidence would require additional research using the original sources, which amounts to undertaking an entirely new investigation.

There is, however, another speculation that could stimulate research. If I had included a number of horticultural societies in my study, such as those cases referenced by Speth and Scott (1989) and discussed in the book edited by Kent (1989), would an increase in tended facilities have appeared on the high side of the graph in figure 10.19, associated with packing index values of a little more than 10.0? Of course this question cannot be answered, but it is possible to examine the small sample of available cases for which the state of the system relative to packing is known and to plot them against the niche effectiveness index.

When I do this in figure 10.20, a provocative pattern emerges. Packed cases are associated with a remarkable increase in tended facilities as the niche effectiveness threshold—identified through the comparative study of group sizes—approaches a $\log_{10}$ value of 1.6. Immediately thereafter, the number of tended facilities drops off considerably. Unpacked cases that have a niche effectiveness value of approximately 0.6—which marks the lower edge of the intensification-driven transition zone noted for group sizes (see proposition 10.10)—tend to rely more on tended facilities than do packed cases at the same relatively low niche effectiveness level. These relationships buffer the argument in generalization 10.10 about the role of different food sources as conditioners of responses to packing and other intensificational pressures.

When, however, the cases included in figure 10.20 were examined relative to their primary food resources, no com-

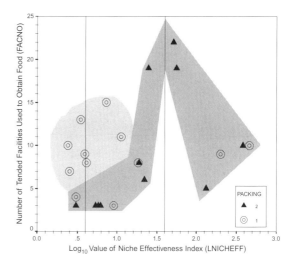

FIGURE 10.20

The relationship between the number of tended facilities and the niche effectiveness index. Cases are coded for packing (PACKING): (1) nonpacked and (2) packed.

pelling patterning emerged. This finding suggests that the character of the habitat is more likely the conditioning variable—a conclusion that is supported by the patterning in figure 10.21. In this figure, ethnographic cases are classified in terms of an ordinal ranking of their dependence upon stored food. This information is plotted in a matrix defined by the number of tended facilities and niche effectiveness.

Although the number of hunter-gatherer cases in figure 10.21 is small, the pattern is robust. The groups that are dependent upon storage define a chevron pattern of increasing numbers of tended facilities up to just beyond the already identified threshold of a $\log_{10}$ value of 1.6 on the niche effectiveness index. Thereafter, the familiar pattern of a decreased use of tended facilities on the high side of the threshold is visible. It is also clear that, as the niche effectiveness value increases, the use of tended facilities *decreases* among those hunter-gatherer groups that did not depend on storage.

Generalization 10.22

Substantial dependence upon storage—expressed relative to the productivity of accessible food in the habitat, or niche effectiveness—appears to be a necessary initial condition for the accelerating use of tended facilities in response to intensificational pressures.

I suspect that

Proposition 10.22

The declining number of tended facilities following a recognizable threshold of intensification indicates a

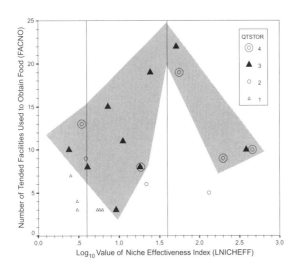

FIGURE 10.21

The relationship between the number of tended facilities and the niche effectiveness index. Cases are coded for the quantity of food stored (QTSTOR): (1) no regular storage or minor, very-short-term storage of two or three days; (2) moderate investment in storage in both quantity and period of potential use; (3) major investment in storage and in the duration of anticipated use; and (4) massive investment in storage from the standpoint of both species stored and duration of use.

change in both the organization and size of the labor units using the facilities.[38]

At this juncture, by changing the focus from specific patterned relationships between types of technological aids and their richness and complexity of design to the implications of the overall shifts in technology in response to packing, I am able to look at technological change in somewhat non-traditional ways. When early anthropologists attempted to account for technological change, they imagined discoveries that, it was thought, changed the course of history. These innovations appeared abruptly and were truly novel phenomena. More recently, technological change has been visualized as a set of responses to problem-solving challenges. The search for patterns in this chapter has demonstrated that similar kinds of tool technology, including weapons and both tended and untended facilities, are developed and used by hunter-gatherer groups that live in vastly different system state conditions.

Proposition 10.23

Density-dependent system state changes prompt modifications in the ways that various kinds of tools are combined with one another, in the ways that tools are used relative to changing tasks, and in the choices of

tools that are emphasized numerically relative to their labor requirements for activation. In short, technological change in a system consists most often of tactical change—a redistribution of technological variety among systems—rather than a series of discoveries or the recognition of new technological principles per se.

Disembodied Observer: A review of the preceding section of this chapter reveals that the first sets of observations and generalizations concluded simply that variability in tools is a consequence of the variability in tasks and the labor strategies associated with successful task performance (generalizations 10.15 and 10.16). This conclusion is not surprising if one thinks of tool use in subsistence activities as primarily a means to successful task performance. The importance of technology in ensuring effective task performance is well illustrated by the relationship between niche effectiveness, technological complexity, and aquatic resource dependence (generalizations and propositions 10.19, 10.20, and 10.21).

The use of untended facilities, such as deadfall traps and snares, increases in situations in which the division of labor has collapsed and packing is not a factor. The most common context of increased use of tended facilities occurs when groups are experiencing demographic packing. Traps are most often used by groups at the packing threshold when GROUP1 size is increasing (generalization 10.20 and proposition 10.22), although traps usually vary inversely with tended facilities in packed situations. Tended facilities are generally used in conjunction with game drives and facilities such as large fish traps and seine nets, but heavy dependence upon storage appears to be a necessary precondition to an increase in tended facilities when intensification pressures are mounting. Groups with a heavy dependence upon storage are all also primarily dependent upon aquatic resources (proposition 10.22 and generalization 10.22).

Perhaps the most provocative patterning in the discussion of technology demonstrates that tool types and frequencies, as well as design complexity, vary in response to density-dependent system states. Demographic packing quite directly affects tool variability, as does the source for food, particularly when the focus is on species that can be accessed in large bulk units. Tools change in tandem with changes in subsistence strategies and the food resources exploited more intensively (proposition 10.23).

The pattern recognition work in this section supports the assertion that expanding one's dependence upon aquatic resources is contingent upon technological development in association with demographic packing. These factors appear to have less of an effect upon hunter-gatherers who are primarily dependent upon plants. As far as terrestrial hunters are concerned, packing reduces dependence upon animal resources and results in a corresponding decrease in weapon utilization. These observations certainly have implications for the archaeological record.

Conclusion

Exploration of the relationships between the variables developed from my ethnographic and ecological data sets has been a significant learning experience. It has taught me a great deal about the connections between hunter-gatherers and their habitats and how these vary under different density-dependent system state conditions. I have advanced an argument about the fundamental tactical role mobility plays in hunter-gatherer subsistence and how demographic packing provokes intensificational pressures that increasingly render mobility obsolete as a tactical subsistence strategy. I have touched upon the processes that play an active part in the evolution of small-scale systems into increasingly complex organizations, citing mutualism as one kind of complex system that is usually overlooked by anthropologists in their discussions of the development of complex societies.

Even so, organizational complexity and the factors that condition various complex sociopolitical forms are topics that have not been adequately addressed. Also left unfinished is the discussion of habitat richness, which appears to play an insignificant role as a modifier of responses to packing, judging from the specificity of the packing threshold values. On the other hand, the range of values for niche effectiveness is considerable—although why there is ambiguity in the location of thresholds for this measure is unclear. This problem is further complicated by the fact that most of the cases clustering at the high end of the niche effectiveness scale are demographically packed and dependent upon aquatic resources, prompting me to wonder what factors are forcing a threshold in niche effectiveness among already packed groups. It is possible that habitat richness, coupled with other habitat variables, may condition the rate of demographic change, but it is likely that *packing*—which is the outcome of differential growth—is the factor forcing major adaptive changes. At this point, however, there are no convincing explanations for many of these problems.

Finally, I have not used the habitat-related variability that is documented among hunter-gatherers as a tool to study the chronology of culture change. In fact, I have not directly addressed the question of how the analytical techniques and knowledge presented so far in this book can serve archaeological goals. I hope, however, to weave together many of these important loose strands in the next analytical chapter of this book.

CHAPTER

11

The Evolution of System States

Complexity, Stability, Symmetry, and System Change

The Once and Future Processual Archaeology

It was with a certain sense of déja vu that, in chapter 1 of this book, I found myself exhorting the discipline of archaeology to direct its attention to the study and explanation of variability among cultural systems. It will soon be forty years since I observed that our task was to "*explicate* and *explain* the total range of physical and cultural similarities and differences characteristic of the entire spatial-temporal span of man's existence" (Binford 1962:218). I went on to say, so long ago, that by explanation I meant "the *demonstration* of a constant articulation of variables within a system and the measurement of the concomitant variability among the variables within the system."

In light of my youthful, exuberant embrace of the broad sweep of the processual explanatory imperative, is my narrow focus in the previous chapter on group size—and a somewhat more expansive concern for system state variability—not somewhat perplexing? Surely a concern with more variables than group size or regional differences in integration is implicit in the phrase "differences among cultural systems." What about kinship conventions, technology, shamanism, forms of ritual expression, and ideology—to mention only a few components of societal organization? Why have I devoted so much effort to so few characteristics of cultural systems? Clues to the answers to these questions can be found in the longer-term view of science.

Since I am concerned with exploring and understanding how the world works with the goal of explaining why it is that way, an increase in my knowledge of such processes cannot help but increase my ability to explore other aspects of systemic variability in the future. When, in the early seventeenth century, William Harvey (1578–1657) began to lecture on the dynamics of the circulation of blood in the human body and demonstrated that the heart functions as a pump, he introduced a new vector for understanding human vari-

ability in the domains of disease and nutrition. Today, the exploration of variability in the human body continues, much of it dependent upon a prior knowledge of the physiology of the circulatory system. Contemporary research focused on the cause and treatment of high blood pressure, the reduction of atherosclerotic deposits in the arterial system, and the links between obesity and circulatory problems is built on the kind of growth of knowledge exemplified by Harvey's early endeavors.

Of course, there are properties of the human condition that a knowledge of the circulatory system is not likely to address in any causal sense. But only research focused on *process* will lead to sufficient knowledge to enable one to say with confidence that variability in x and y is independent and unaffected by variability in a and b, when each is a characteristic of cultural systems. Most intellectual variability among archaeological and anthropological researchers can be explained by differences of opinion about the causal priority that should be assigned to various characteristics of cultural systems.

For instance, do innovations in ideology drive culture change? If ideology is preeminent in the causal domain, as many researchers prior to Harvey would have argued (even about the function of the heart), can we not imitate Harvey's inquiry—what makes the heart central and what does it do?—but ask instead what makes ideology central and what does it do? Unfortunately, few persons could answer these questions today by citing convincing empirical research.

Processual archaeology anticipates that, in the future, our understanding of the dynamics of cultural processes will grow and that we may be able to make compelling, empirically based arguments about the origin and function of ideology. In the meantime, processual archaeology acknowledges that it is impossible to study everything at once. We must build up a relevant knowledge base through cumulative, accretional research.

It should be kept in mind that Harvey's understanding of the circulatory system was significantly incomplete since, prior to the invention of the microscope, the capillary had never been observed, and of course it is in the capillary that the fundamental exchange of oxygen for carbon dioxide and other waste products takes place. Just as a knowledge of the structure and function of capillaries was developed many years after Harvey's work, contemporary processual research in archaeology ensures productive research in the future. Since we can never achieve a complete understanding at a single point in time, the growth of knowledge that science makes possible assumes fundamental links between today's research and the paths it paves for work tomorrow.

The passage of time changes what is "once" and what is in the future. Archaeology "once" embraced the idea of progress, and this concept has become a constant source of controversy and debate in today's evolutionary literature (Gould 1996:135–230). Researchers frequently clash over what is meant by *complexity,* and arguments abound about the meaning of the directional patterning observable in the formal properties of entities that undergo evolutionary processes when these are arrayed against a temporal frame of reference.

One of the most provocative, thoughtful discussions of this issue occurs in the concluding chapter of a book by J. T. Bonner (1988) entitled *The Evolution of Complexity: A Conclusion with Three Insights.* Bonner distinguishes between two different kinds of systemic change. The first refers to the differences that occur *within* units as a result of internal structural differentiation and functional specialization. The other kind of organizational complexity results from an integrating process that merges already differentiated entities into a new level of systemic organization. Although Bonner's research is focused on complexity in noncultural systems, I argue in this chapter that these two pathways to complexity also occur in cultural systems.

Bonner is interested not only in the structural differences between various trajectories of increasing complexity but also in the correlates of complexity. He offers a convincing argument that although "size, internal differentiation, and species diversity could each be independently acted upon by selection," these variables nevertheless tend to behave in tandem, since "if one is altered it may automatically affect the others" (1988:226). From this perspective, complexity might even be described as the emergence of new and more synergistically linked components of a system.

In chapter 10, I pointed out that complexity that appears to arise within a unit such as a cultural system is perhaps different from complexity arising from the integration of previously independently organized units. In this chapter, I begin with an examination of complexity that arises from the additive, integrative pathway, or—to put it another way—

complexity arrived at by means of the integration of previously independent systems. After addressing this subject, I examine the process of emergence, which can also be described as the transformation that results in sociocultural complexity within a system that did not previously appear to be complex. Emergence, however, presupposes a temporal sequence, and at the moment I am concerned with essentially atemporal phenomena.

Even when we are, strictly speaking, thinking about trajectories and temporal sequences, we can certainly learn things that are strongly suspected to imply emergent change, although these processual implications remain regrettably atemporal. In light of this reality, but informed by the patterning that has been generated so far, I then examine other important characteristics of culturally variable systems. Domains of variability so far unaddressed analytically will be examined to see how they vary with the properties that have already been demonstrated to strongly suggest systemic processes. Some of these characteristics are chosen because they occupy a place in the archaeological literature reserved for "reliable indicators of complexity." My question at this juncture is simply "are they?" Along the way, I discuss additional facts that may appear to point to processes, although these do not represent a departure from the world of atemporal phenomena.

Recent Archaeological Research on Complexity: Issues of Stability and Instability

An exploration of some recent research, coupled with available hunter-gatherer data that is germane to the issue of multiple trajectories to complexity, may suggest greater parallels between the biological and cultural worlds than have been previously suspected. Four recent studies of cultural variability, all of which addressed aspects of the "complexification" process, have yielded important findings that together cast light on some of the patterns I have identified in this book. Considering these studies in chronological order, the first one has already been cited in chapter 8 and deals with hunter-gatherer societies of the Northern Pacific Coast of North America (Panowski 1985), about whom the author observes:

Generalization 11.01

There is a strong relationship between the number of species prepared for storage and the degree of ranking and complexity in the jurisdictional hierarchies of the social system.

Although this pattern is somewhat ambiguous, it still points to a linkage between the diversity of the food base and the complexity of the society.

402 PART IV — IDEAS, DERIVATIVE PATTERNING, AND GENERALIZATIONS

Proposition 11.01

Given a correlation between the number of species prepared for storage and the complexity of the society, as indicated by the centralized roles of leaders in the jurisdictional hierarchy, this suggests that, other things being equal, there is a relationship between a diverse diet that requires substantial labor input prior to consumption and the power vested in social hierarchies.

In the case of hunter-gatherers of the Northwest Coast, most of the species came from the aquatic biome, and therefore dietary diversity was not the result of differences in trophic level but rather of species diversity within the single biotic domain from which the primary food resources came.

The next provocative research link was made by Carol Raish (1988, 1992), who took as her problem the demonstrable differences in the onset and duration of an archaeological phenomenon that has been termed the *village farming period,* which occurs in sequences around the world. This period is identified by the appearance of domesticated species in association with more or less permanent settlements of small-scale horticulturists. It lasted until the appearance of major public buildings and other facilities that are usually cited as evidence of a complex social organization featuring social ranking or stratification and major institutional supports for a multilevel, jurisdictional hierarchy.

Raish found dramatic differences in the duration of the village farming system state in ten Old World sequences ranging from 6,200 years in central Europe to 1,900 years in southern Mesopotamia. Five of the six New World sequences she examined were shorter than any of the Old World sequences, the longest being 1,750 years and the shortest 800 years. Only the sequence from Peru, with a duration of 3,650 years, fit comfortably within the range of variability from the Old World. Why, asked Raish, was there such a contrast between the New and Old Worlds, except for the Peruvian sequence?

Raish argued that the only important difference was that Old World systems were based on domesticated plants, with the addition of domesticated animals, whereas subsistence in New World systems with village farming periods of short duration was based only on domesticated plants. High-quality animal protein had to be obtained from hunting. For Raish, the exception that proved the rule was Peru, which had both domesticated animals and a village farming period of longer duration than any other New World sequence. One thing seems clear from Raish's (1992) research:

Generalization 11.02

The addition of domesticated animals of moderate to large body size to the diet of groups that were intensified to the point of utilizing domesticated plants *does* seem to stabilize the system and reduce the rates of change as measured by major system state indicators.

More recently in this sequence of research, the Ph.D. thesis of Richard Wojcik (1992) reviews the ethnohistoric records of hunter-gatherers from California northward to the arctic regions of North America. Wojcik identifies a number of interesting relationships and patterns linking the scale and character of labor organization as it relates to the procurement of food resources with the character of the habitat and selected ecological variables. He also argues that subsistence-focused labor organization was strongly linked to socially organized transactional structures. Wojcik demonstrates that forms of leadership and the social scales at which transactions related to the exchange of goods were differentially organized in different systems and appear to be strongly conditioned by basic ecological variables.

Four years later, Ph.D. research by Amber Johnson (1997) was based on the premise that

---

Proposition 11.02

"Other things being equal, systems with greater niche breadth, or subsistence diversity, are more stable than those which are more specialized" (Johnson 1997:iv).

The fundamental warranting argument for the accuracy of this proposition was presented in chapter 6. It maintains that the cycles of abundance, accessibility, and utility of potential food resources obtained from different trophic levels (e.g., terrestrial plants as opposed to terrestrial animals) and biomes (e.g., terrestrial versus aquatic) are likely to be at least semi-independent. In many instances, the patterns are totally independent, as in the example of arctic groups, for whom the accessibility of marine mammals in winter is not positively correlated with the lack of edible terrestrial plants. Synergistic interactions also enhance stability, as Raish (1992: 45–51) pointed out in her discussion of the relationships in the annual diet of agriculturists between the production of domestic plants, the use of traction and fertilizer, and the secondary products derived from animals.

Given my discussion thus far, there may be some ambiguity about the kind of diversity implied by the term *niche breadth.* The more familiar term *diet breadth* usually refers to the species richness of the diet or the number of different species that are regularly included in the diet. Niche breadth or diversity, on the other hand, does not refer to the inventory of exploited species but instead to the scale, complexity, and energetic connectivity among the components of the ecosystem tapped for food and energy resources.

For instance, if a group of hunter-gatherers exclusively exploits only annually occurring terrestrial plants, then all of these species are likely to be linked to the temperature and rainfall levels that are characteristic of the growing season. The productive cycles of the exploited plants would be generally synchronized and food would only be available during the growing season, broadly defined. On the other hand, if the same group of hunter-gatherers exploited both annual and perennial plants, some of the latter kind, such as oak trees, would dependably provide food at the close of or after the growing season.

In order to actually measure niche breadth, it would be necessary to know the species being exploited, the length of their period of availability, and how frequently these periods occur. One would have to know something about the connectivity or linkages between all of the different species included in the diet. Niche breadth would not be increased if a group exploited fifteen species instead of ten if all fifteen species were directly tied to the temperature and rainfall regimes characteristic of a single place. Changes in either or both regimes would result in comparable increases or decreases in the diet breadth but would not affect niche breadth[1] and would not contribute to system stability unless storage was being practiced.

On the other hand, if a group exploited the preceding hypothetical ten species and *also* exploited twenty-two species from a marine biome, the chances of synchrony in the schedule of accessibility would be greatly reduced. Even more importantly, it is unlikely that the dynamic response of a terrestrial biome to basic variables such as temperature and rainfall would correspond to that of an adjacent marine biome, particularly in colder climates. As Johnson has pointed out, the principle of risk reduction is the same for subsistence as for investors in the stock market—diversify the income base: "If one resource fails or is seasonally unavailable, there are others to fall back on" (1997:80).

The analogy to investing in the stock market is perhaps less appropriate than it might seem, however, because—where subsistence is concerned—there is a demand curve for food that must be met on a daily or weekly basis. Regularity in making investments is not the only way to build a portfolio, but if for some reason it is, then additional stock purchases are usually made at quarterly or annual intervals, while meeting subsistence needs is regulated by a demand curve with critically shorter intervals.

During the period in which Raish (1992) carried out her thesis research, she and her committee understood the important connection between subsistence stability and the exploitation of species with different or semi-independent limiting factors (Binford 1964b, 1991c). An equally important factor in her research was the recognition of how synergistic links had been developed in the past between different sources of food, such as the energy transfer inherent in the use of animal manure to enhance soil fertility and the use of animals for traction and transport.

One of the features of early animal domestication that was not appreciated, however, was the relationship between the reproductive cycles of mammals and plants in the same habitat. Most mammals give birth prior to or at the very beginning of the growing season, which means that as plant foods become increasingly abundant, the demand for food from spring-born young is increasingly met. For hunter-gatherers, on the other hand, spring is a season (particularly in latitudes other than tropical and subtropical zones) when food from terrestrial sources is least available. Controlling reproduction means controlling access to secondary production, and once groups take this step, the proliferation of synergistic links and the development of alternative exploitative strategies illustrated by the "secondary products revolution"—and others summarized by Raish (1992:60–72)—can be expected to follow.

In neither of the preceding two studies, however, did the exploitation of aquatic resources play much of a role in argument. In contrast, the role of aquatic resources is very important in my analysis, both by contributing to subsistence diversity among hunter-gatherer groups and also by providing clues to explanatory variables and important initial conditions.

One of the indicators of niche breadth that A. Johnson found to be informative was the calculation of standard deviation using estimates (in percentages) of the relative contribution to the diet coming from different trophic and biotic sources, including both wild resources and domesticated plants and animals. For my study, it was possible to calculate the standard deviation[2] of the quantity of terrestrial plants, animals, and aquatic resources estimated for each hunter-gatherer case. Unfortunately, at the time of coding I did not distinguish between domesticated and wild animals and plants and included both categories in one estimate. I am able, nevertheless, to identify the cases that include both categories of resources.

In figure 11.01, hunter-gatherer groups that are primarily dependent upon terrestrial plant resources (SUBSP = 2) are plotted in a matrix measuring subsistence diversity on the *y* axis and the $\log_{10}$ value of population density on the *x* axis. Two distinct threshold patterns are visible in the upper portion of this plot. There is also a lower circular pattern, identified as C and composed almost exclusively of cases situated in regions containing both hunter-gatherers and non-hunter-gatherers. All of the mutualists and many of the forest product specialists in my data set live in such regions and have low values for subsistence diversity, which indicates that their niche breadth is limited.

Two other interesting patterns in figure 11.01 can be seen in the shaded areas marked A and B. These have parallel patterns but different intercepts on the *y* axis. Cases in the smaller cluster with the larger *y* intercept value of approximately 68.0 are all from relatively dry but temperate envi-

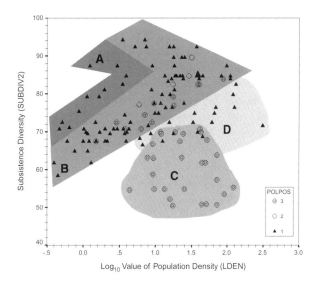

FIGURE 11.01

Exploring the relationship between population density and subsistence diversity. Cases are coded for political encroachment (POLPOS): (1) group is autonomous and exists in a matrix of similarly scaled hunter-gatherer systems; (2) group is autonomous but is articulated to a socially or politically more complex group of hunter-gatherers; and (3) group exists in a culturally heterogeneous region and is articulated to a non-hunter-gatherer society, either mutualistically or in a patron-client relationship.

ronments in the southern Kalahari, the American Great Basin, and southern Australia. There appears to be a threshold at a value of $y = 85$, below which the cases increase in a linear manner as population density increases. Above this threshold, cases with lower values for density and higher values for subsistence diversity (SUBDIV2) are also increasing. In the distribution marked B, the pattern is similar but the y intercept is lower and population density values are much higher at a threshold on the y axis at SUBDIV2 = 85. As in the A distribution, subsistence diversity increases linearly and at regular intervals as density increases, until the relationship reverses at a subsistence diversity value of 85.0. Both of these patterned distributions are telling a similar story:

Generalization 11.03

Other things being equal, when density-dependent spatial packing increases among hunter-gatherers who primarily exploit terrestrial plant resources, subsistence diversity increases at regular intervals up to a threshold value of 85.0, after which packing decreases in value for groups whose subsistence diversity indicator continues to increase.

Given the assumption that the domestication of plants and animals was a response to intensification, these measured rela-

tionships support Flannery's (1969:77–79) suggestion that just prior to early experiments with domestication, a "broad-spectrum revolution" occurred. As originally presented by Flannery, the broad-spectrum revolution primarily entailed an increase in diet breadth as more and more species were exploited. The data from hunter-gatherers summarized in figure 11.01 suggest, however, that, along with increased population density, there is a regular increase in niche breadth. The latter would have the additional effect of stabilizing the system as food resources were restricted to smaller spatial units. In both instances, it is reasonable to expect that

Proposition 11.03

Increases in both niche and diet breadth may well be accompanied by increased labor costs per unit of additional net return obtained from smaller units of space.

An examination of the dispersion of cases in figure 11.01 to the right of the modeled[3] packing threshold at a log_{10} value for x of 1.0 reveals that the regular patterning notable on the left of the threshold disappears dramatically. In its place is a scattering of cases in a shaded area of the graph that appears to be pulled down and to the right. I have already noted that the adjacent circular distribution with low values for subsistence diversity, designated as area C, contains cases that share a geographic region with ethnic units that are organizationally very different, such as agricultural peoples or trading representatives of larger industrial systems. There is little doubt that once systems become packed, as anticipated by the Group Size Model, many hunter-gatherer groups have lower subsistence diversity values.

Figure 11.02 was prepared in order to clarify the relationship between subsistence diversity and the mutualist cases in area C. In this graph, mutualist cases are, once again, primarily situated in a circular distribution similar to area C in figure 11.01. Cases with increased social complexity—particularly ones featuring special prerogatives associated with leadership—have greater subsistence diversity and are clustered around the threshold at a value of 85.0 on the y axis. A scatter of cases, however, tails off to the left, and all of these have lower subsistence diversity values (between 70.0 and 80.0) and higher population densities. This scatter appears to link the distribution of cases with values of between 64.0 and 75.0 on the y axis (shown in figure 11.02 as the "zone of horticultural dietary supplement").

There are some interesting contrasts among these cases in terms of their responses to packing. At identical values of the log_{10} value of population density (−0.50 through 1.0), no cases are identified as "complex," although complex cases predominate when subsistence diversity values exceed the upper

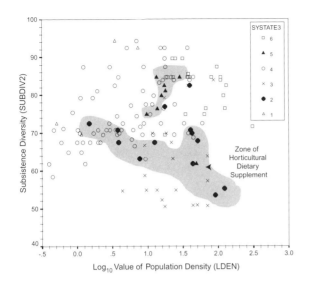

FIGURE 11.02

Partitioning the property space of population density and subsistence diversity by means of system state indicators. Cases are coded for system state differences (SYSTATE3): (1) mounted hunters, (2) horticulturally augmented cases, (3) mutualists and forest product specialists, (4) generic hunter-gatherers, (5) generic hunter-gatherers with instituted leadership, and (6) wealth-differentiated hunter-gatherers.

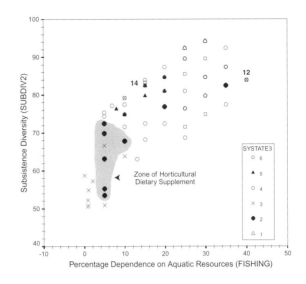

FIGURE 11.03

Subsistence diversity as conditioned by aquatic resource dependence. There is more to learn from system state indicators. Cases are coded for system state differences (SYSTATE3): (1) mounted hunters, (2) horticulturally augmented cases, (3) mutualists and forest product specialists, (4) generic hunter-gatherers, (5) generic hunter-gatherers with instituted leadership, (6) wealth differentiated hunter-gatherers, and (7) internally ranked hunter-gatherers.

limit of the "zone of horticultural dietary supplement." This pattern suggests that

---
Proposition 11.04

Packing is not the only factor contributing to social complexity—as measured by ranking and special privileges for leaders—among hunter-gatherers primarily dependent upon terrestrial plant resources (compare this statement to generalization 9.13).

In figure 11.03, subsistence diversity (SUBDIV2) is plotted against aquatic resources using the same marker variable (SYSTATE3) that was included in figure 11.02. In this graph, all but two cases of mutualists (the Casiguran Agta [group 12] and the coastal Agta from Kagayan province [group 14]) derive less than 10 percent of their diet from aquatic resources. Both of these exceptional cases share territories with peoples engaged in very different subsistence strategies and regularly interact with them, but it is certainly questionable whether they are mutualists or represent an economic caste or class. In any case, the organizational status of these two groups at the regional level is unclear,[4] although it does appear that

---
Proposition 11.05

Among hunter-gatherers who are primarily dependent upon terrestrial plant resources, mutualists and product specialists appear to represent a response to packing. This response is more likely to occur in environmental settings in which an aquatic alternative for expanding diet and niche breadth is not feasible. This usually means interior continental settings or areas associated with the upper reaches of river drainages.

Among the cases in figure 11.03 in which aquatic resources contribute more than 15 percent of the total diet, the majority have leaders who enjoy special prerogatives denied to the rank and file, or they are societies with institutionalized, internal social ranking. Exceptions to the association of aquatic dependence and nonegalitarian social characteristics include cases such as the Guahibo, who have recently adopted agriculture and exploit primarily riparian fish in the interior of the continent. This description also applies to the Guato and the Yaruro-Pume, who are remnant groups that have recently adopted horticulture but lack any evidence of nonegalitarian social features. Although the patterning in the exceptional cases in figure 11.03 is complicated by the use of riparian resources, these groups are not "complex" and are consistent with other horticulturists in their lack of ranking. In fact

―――――――――― *Generalization 11.04* ――――――――――

Social ranking and leadership prerogatives such as assistants and relief from production are not present in the hunter-gatherer cases that practice horticulture and are primarily dependent upon terrestrial plants. This is not to say that they are not "complex"; they are just different, organizationally speaking. Most of these groups are organized into sodalities such as moieties—or into a nested hierarchy of sodalities— and may have secret societies as well. All of these units are socially reticulate ways of integrating large associations of persons, many of whose members may live in different, but nevertheless large, residential groups.

―――――――――――――――――――――――――――――――――――――

Good examples of this kind of group would be the Bororo, Cahuilla, Cupeño, Guahibo, and Serrano, who also serve as a reminder that we have encountered a similar form of "complexity" among the mounted hunters of the North American Great Plains. Packing was not demonstrable among the mounted hunters, but large group sizes were characteristic (see generalizations 9.08 and 9.10 as well as proposition 9.04). I suggest, therefore that

―――――――――――― *Proposition 11.06* ――――――――――――

Organizational features such as secret societies and reticulate sodalities represent a scalar response to the large size of residentially associated social groups that may cooperate in a segmentary fashion. Such large units regularly occur and frequently represent relatively sedentary settlements.

―――――――――――――――――――――――――――――――――――――

An interesting feature of the hunter-gatherer cases within the "zone of horticultural supplement" in figures 11.02 and 11.03 is that, unlike the mounted hunters, they have high population densities. In fact, densities in these groups exceed the modeled packing threshold as much or more than they do in most hunter-gatherer groups that are significantly dependent upon aquatic resources, yet there is little evidence of this pattern if the focus is simply on leadership privileges, economic differentiation, or social ranking. I must conclude that

―――――――――――― *Proposition 11.07* ――――――――――――

Although packing may condition larger GROUP1 and GROUP2 sizes (figures 10.05 and 10.06, graph B), it does not directly condition the presence of social ranking and leaders with considerable power and special prerogatives (problem 9.05 and proposition 10.06). On the other hand, scalar responses to larger group sizes

do appear to condition the presence of sodalities and secret societies that may be integrating multilocal social groups and fostering nested hierarchies of decision making as well as status and role differentiation, particularly in terms of age.

―――――――――――――――――――――――――――――――――――――

In situations in which ranking and strong leadership prerogatives are favored, scalar stress (see chapter 9) may also favor the formation of sodalities that serve larger-scale social functions of integration. Therefore

―――――――――――― *Proposition 11.08* ――――――――――――

Systems with and without ranking may be integrated by sodalities, depending upon the presence of scalar trends toward larger group sizes and associated cooperative endeavors.

―――――――――――――――――――――――――――――――――――――

Applying New Knowledge about Stability and Instability to Questions of Specialization and Diversification

I have made some headway in isolating several of the contexts in which different forms of complexity are situated. Mutualism, for example, is apparently a density-dependent response that is rather clearly based upon specialization. But as I have demonstrated, stability also appears to result from diversification. Resolving this apparent paradox would seem to be the next order of business. A quick review of previous generalizations and propositions demonstrates that we have learned about some interesting characteristics of variability that appear to arise along different paths to complexity. At the same time, this variability appears to occur as a response to intensificational pressures.

It is also true that many of the archetypal features of complex societies, such as a leadership hierarchy that enjoys "elite" privileges, are not characteristic of the mutualist hunter-gatherers or those who have recently adopted horticulture. Neither do they occur among groups that are dependent upon terrestrial plant resources, clearly packed, and already coping with scalar stress. Additionally, social ranking and other nonegalitarian features of leadership hierarchies have thus far not been unambiguously implicated as density-dependent or scalar phenomena. Intensification seems to be involved, however, in spite of the absence of a clear packing threshold in cases in which wealth differentials and ranking appear. One suspects that there are other unidentified initial conditions and variables that favor ranking when pressures to intensify are present.

As I suggested in the introductory paragraphs of this chapter, such a wide range of problems cannot all be addressed

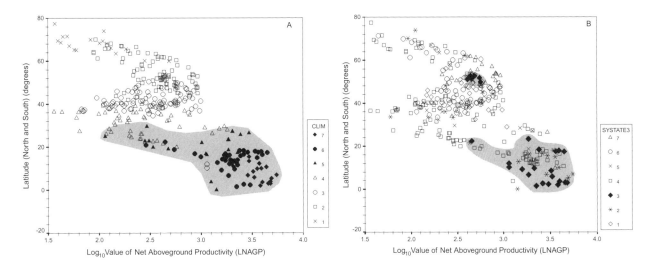

FIGURE 11.04

Paired property space plots illustrating the environmental "geography" of mutualists and tropical settings. Graph A is coded for temperature ordination (CLIM). The shaded markers are: (7) equatorial climate, (6) tropical climate, and (5) subtropical climate. The scale of climate categories ends with a code of (1) corresponding to polar conditions. Graph B is coded for system state differences (SYSTATE3): (1) mounted hunters, (2) horticulturally augmented cases, (3) mutualists and forest product specialists, (4) generic hunter-gatherers, (5) generic hunter-gatherers with instituted leadership, (6) wealth-differentiated hunter-gatherers, and (7) internally ranked hunter-gatherers.

simultaneously. At this point, therefore, I again take up the issue of mutualism, which clearly occupies a unique position in the property space charts of figures 11.01, 11.02, and 11.03. These particular specialists appear to represent an organizational variant that is usually ignored when the subject of complex societies is discussed.

Perhaps the most obvious indication of the pathway to complexity defined by accretive integration of differentiated units lies with hunter-gatherers who are mutualists or forest product specialists, both of whom exhibit interesting patterning summarized in generalization 10.04 and proposition 10.05. The first question to be answered is simply: is there any habitat bias affecting the occurrence of these subsistence specialties?

The property space maps in figure 11.04, graphs A and B, address this issue. In graph A, climate is classified in terms of temperature and features a zone of subtropical, tropical and equatorial temperatures that is emphasized by shading. The map in graph B features a shaded area in which mutualist societies are concentrated in two localizations. The smaller of the two, situated at a latitude of approximately 50 degrees, includes hunter-gatherers who originally were primarily dependent upon terrestrial animals and aquatic resources but were transformed by forces of colonial expansion into product specialists—in this instance, fur trappers. It seems to me that

Proposition 11.09

Product specialists might occur in any environment in which representatives from an expansive, eclectic, product-using system intrude into a region of largely small-scale societies.

The interesting distribution of cases in figure 11.04, therefore, is the lower one, which includes product specialists and mutualist groups that are articulated with relatively small-scale horticultural societies. In fact,

Generalization 11.05

With the exception of the northern-latitude fur-trapping specialists, all of the mutualistic societies involving alleged hunter-gatherers occur in equatorial to subtropical habitats.

Given such a biased distribution, two questions come to mind:

Problem 11.01

(1) Why have so many hunting specialists and groups using forager tactics survived in subtropical and equatorial zones and not in localities in which agriculturists and horticulturists have been most successful? (2)

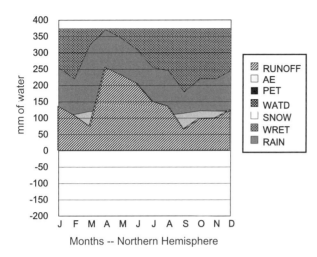

FIGURE 11.05

Water balance graph for a typical tropical rain forest.

Why have so few cases of nonmutualistic hunter-gatherers survived in the same range of environments in which midlatitude horticulturists have predominated?

In chapter 6, I discussed at some length the issue of within-habitat diversity and the relationships between species density, system stability, and feeding specialists. The patterning in figure 11.04 makes me wonder whether the survival of "conservative" cultural forms in certain habitats is fostered by the advantages that cultural diversity offers in some habitats. It is possible that this phenomenon may just reflect analogies or even homologies between cultural systems and some properties of the ecosystems themselves. As I noted in chapter 6 (paraphrasing Ernst Mayr):

Generalization 11.06

Environmental "steadiness" or lack of high-amplitude variability in basic climatic variables fostered ecological stability.

A comment of relevance to the second question raised in problem 11.01—why have so few cases of independent hunter-gatherers who are not articulated in symbiotic ways with other ethnic groups survived in the same regions?—also occurred in chapter 6:

Generalization 11.07

Omnivores and trophic generalists tend to reduce systemwide stability, whereas an increase in the number of specialists seems to enhance it.

In tropical rain forests, the two basic ingredients needed to maximize biotic activity, water and solar radiation, are present in maximum amounts. The seasonally flat pattern on the water balance graph in figure 11.05, for example, is diagnostic of settings with the kind of maximum stability referred to in generalization 11.06. These relatively stable, high-biomass tropical rain forests are characterized by the presence of many feeding specialists. In chapter 6, I also noted that, in the biological domain, niche is generally synonymous with species, but that among human actors organized into cultural systems, species offers no clues to niche. Therefore, when speaking of numerous species that occupy different niches but nevertheless

TABLE 11.01

CROSS-TABULATION OF HUNTER-GATHERER SYSTEM STATES
AND GLOBAL WARMTH VARIABLE (CLIM)

			SYSTEM STATES				
CLIM	REMNANT GROUPS	HORTICUL- TURIST	MUTUALIST	COMPLEX	INDEPEN- DENT	TOTAL	PERCENT
SUBTROPICAL	0.00	2.00	1.00	16.00	20.00		
ROW PERCENTAGE	0.00	10.00	5.00	5.00	**80.00**		24.69
COLUMN PERCENTAGE	0.00	13.13	6.25	50.00	35.55		
TROPICAL	1.00	5.00	11.00	0.00	26.00	43.00	
ROW PERCENTAGE	2.32	11.62	**25.58**	0.00	60.46		53.09
COLUMN PERCENTAGE	66.66	53.33	25.00	50.00	6.66		
EQUATORIAL	2.00	8.00	4.00	1.00	3.00	18.00	
ROW PERCENTAGE	**11.11**	**44.44**	22.22	5.55	16.66		22.00
COLUMN PERCENTAGE	66.66	53.33	25.00	50.00	6.66		
TOTAL	3.00	15.00	16.00	2.00	45.00	81.00	
PERCENT	3.70	18.51	22.22	2.47	55.00	100.00	

Note: **Boldface** indicates the highest row percentage in each column.

A
Onge
GroupNo = 5

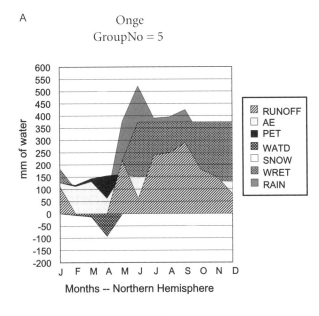

B
Jarwa
GroupNo = 6

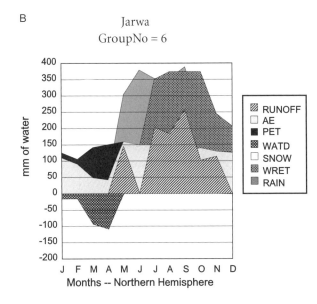

C
North Andaman Island
GroupNo = 8

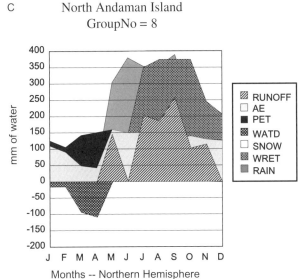

FIGURE 11.06

Comparative water balance graphs for three ethnic groups from the Andaman Islands.

behave as feeding specialists, it is important to remember that, among human beings, niches must be considered quite independently of species. The relevant question then becomes: are there more food procurement specialists among hunter-gatherers in the tropics than elsewhere?

To answer this question, table 11.01 was prepared by summarizing data on the frequencies of different types of system state indicators for hunter-gatherers living in subtropical, tropical, and equatorial habitats. These have been classified according to the amount of solar radiation they receive, calculated in terms of temperature using the global warmth variable CLIM. One of the most obvious points embedded in table 11.01 is that groups classified as "horticulturist" and "remnant groups" are most common in the

earth's warmest settings. Here economically independent groups of hunter-gatherers, as well as those in symbiotic relationships with agriculturists, each represent approximately 22 percent of the sample.

Of the independent hunter-gatherers, three of the four cases are from the Andaman Islands and include the Onge (plant biomass of 57,386.48 grams per square meter and population density of 40.10 persons per 100 square kilometers), the Jarwa (plant biomass of 29,082.34 grams per square meter and population density of 44.65 persons per 100 square kilometers), and the Aka-Bo of North Andaman Island (plant biomass of 20,875.0 grams per square meter and population density of 33.38 persons per 100 square kilometers). Members of the remaining group, the Shiriana of

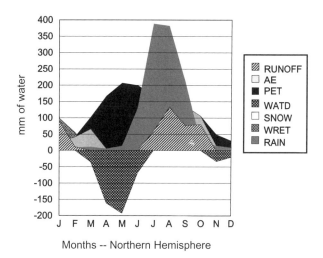

FIGURE 11.07

Water balance graph for a typical tropical monsoon forest.

deficit (indicated by the coded distribution below the zero line), and there is also a corresponding zone in which potential evapotranspiration (PET) does not correspond to actual evapotranspiration (AE). The habitats of all groups experience a minimal but nevertheless noticeable seasonality, conditioned by rainfall, which roughly corresponds to a small decrease in warmth. Although these habitats are extremely productive and are technically classified as tropical forest settings, they are not—except for that of the Onge—localities in which the greatest ecological stability would be expected to occur. In tropical rain forests, biologically speaking, feeding specialists would be expected in the zone of reduced equability in rainfall but would not be expected to extend into the much less stable tropical monsoon forest region in which pronounced seasonality in rainfall occurs.

South America (plant biomass of 36,721.40 grams per square meter and population density of 15.60 persons per 100 square kilometers) have become horticulturists in relatively recent years, leaving the Andaman Island groups as the only economically independent hunter-gatherers documented in the equatorial zone.

The water balance graphs in figure 11.06 illustrate that the habitats of each of the economically independent hunter-gatherer cases from the Andaman Islands have some water

A comparison of the graphs in figures 11.07 and 11.08 illustrates that the scale of the water deficit experienced by the hunter-gatherers in the Andaman Islands is much greater than the deficit experienced in their habitats by most warm climate mutualists, such as the Aka and Bayaka. The Jarwa and North Island Andamanese are situated at the drier end of the range of variability in tropical rain forest habitats, while the Onge of Little Andaman Island enjoy a better-watered setting. The small size of these islands, however, makes it impossible to accommodate human feeding specialists exploiting separate ranges. It should also be noted that on North Andaman Island, conditions differ for interior and coastal peoples (Radcliffe-Brown 1948:26), but the character of the relationships between these groups is unknown.

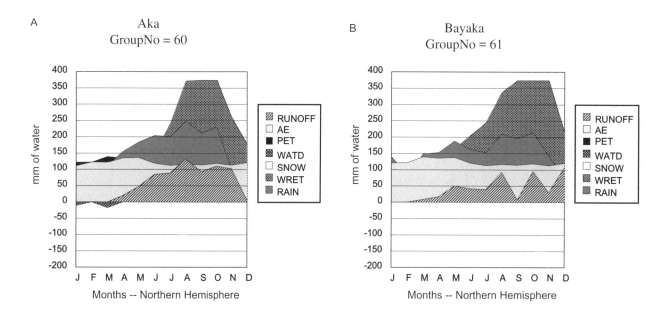

FIGURE 11.08

Comparative water balance graphs for two mutualist groups from tropical Africa.

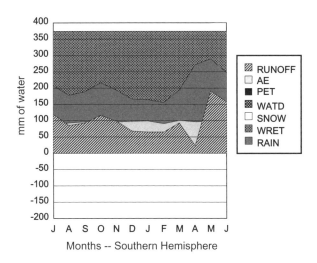

FIGURE 11.09

Water balance graph for the Nukak of tropical South America.

In contrast, the Aka and Bayaka groups, who live in the world's warmest settings in the Central African Republic and the Cameroons, experience only minor water-regulated seasonality, which begins to approximate the conditions illustrated in figure 11.07 for tropical monsoon forests. In these seasonally drier variants of the tropical rain forest, greater amounts of sunlight reach the ground through the canopy, at least during the drier months. The result is more under-story plant growth and therefore more terrestrial fauna than in the kind of classic tropical rain forest depicted in figure 11.05, in which the flat top and bottom lines are a distinc-tive feature. In such settings, hunter-gatherers tend to be more dependent upon terrestrial plant resources. The water balance graph in figure 11.09 illustrating the Nukak range in Colombia provides an example.

It is interesting that the African cases are both localized along the boundary between seasonally variable and ener-getically stable habitats. The Aka region experiences a min-imal and relatively insignificant water deficit between January and the beginning of April, but in both the Aka and Bayaka habi-tats there is a marked reduction in excess water or runoff dur-ing this period. Although the abundance of available water during the entire year provides the necessary conditions for a maximally high-biomass, tropical rain forest to flourish in these regions, the marked reduction in runoff ensures that standing biomass will be reduced. The Aka habitat is estimated to have 25,461.31 grams of plant biomass per square meter, enabling the Aka to be less dependent upon agriculturists than all of the other African mutualist groups, whereas the Bayaka habitat is slightly more productive at 28,448.64 grams of plant biomass per square meter. Both habitats have sufficiently low biomass for the Terrestrial Model to indicate that primary dietary dependence should be upon terrestrial plant resources.

A very different hydrological regime drives conditions in the region of Malaysia occupied by the Semang. Although the essential properties required for plant production—water and solar radiation—are more or less constant, there is regular runoff all year round that supports continuously flowing streams. The lack of seasonality in these two environmental variables creates an abundance of water not available to the Aka and Bayaka. Not surprisingly, the region is estimated to have almost twice the biomass of the Aka habitat (50,350.34 grams per square meter). The wide range in conditions that can characterize the habitats of groups that are involved in mutualism and other types of complex interregional artic-ulations is documented in figure 11.10, graphs A–D.

Of the four groups whose water balance graphs are included in figure 11.10, the Semang have the lowest plant biomass levels. The Kubu, Punan,[5] and Shompen have plant biomass estimates of 56,157.12, 56,660.51, and 59,274.80 grams per square meter, respectively. All four groups live in "true" tropical rain forests and have population densities that coincide with or exceed the packing threshold (the pop-ulation density of the Kubu is 9.20 persons per 100 square kilometers and the others exceed this amount). If the pop-ulation densities of the agricultural peoples with whom these groups share their ranges were available and had been included, then—from a regional perspective—all four groups would be considered extremely packed. As an example of the processes of intensification these groups are experiencing, even without these figures, the Shompen have a density of 39.54 persons per 100 square kilometers, which is more than four and one-third times the packing threshold value.

Dietary criteria can be used to differentiate "true" rain for-est dwellers from groups such as the Aka and Bayaka, who live in somewhat drier tropical forests. These include the greater importance of riparian resources, particularly fish, among the Kubu (Persoon 1989: Sandbukt 1988:133), Punan (Nicolaisen 1976:209–10), Semang (Gregg 1980:128), and Shompen (Rizvi 1990:31). Plant foods are biased in favor of sago palm or pandanus and various fruits. Yams and other bulb or root plants are well represented in the diet, and pigs and monkeys are major sources of meat, depending upon the local setting. The Kubu, Punan, Semang, and Shompen may all invest to varying degrees in "on again, off again" horti-cultural activity. Although all of these groups have trade relationships with local horticulturists, none has the relatively stable, institutionalized, mutualist relationships that char-acterize groups in the central African area.

There is a considerable contrast in organizational scale between the hunter-gatherers and the horticultural groups with whom they interact symbiotically within a culturally complex, regional setting. This also applies to other groups that are commonly lumped together in categories with names like "commercial hunter-gatherers" (Headland 1986:545) or "professional primitives" (Fox 1969). A more detailed

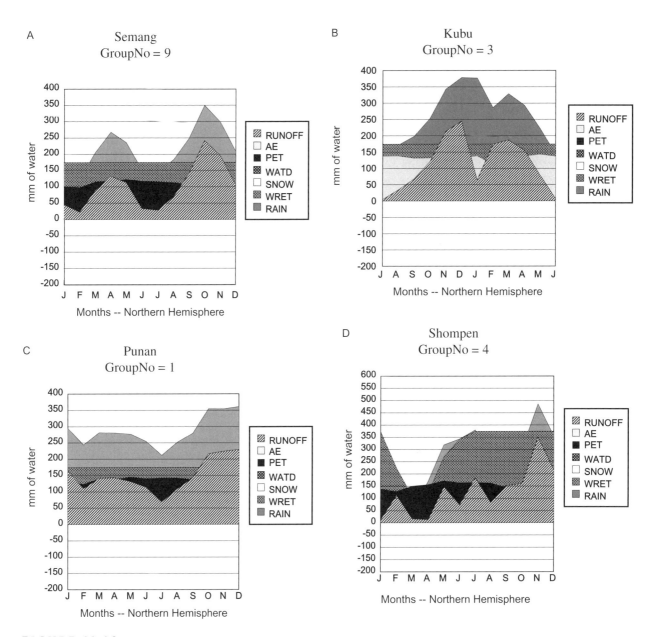

FIGURE 11.10

Comparative water balance graphs for four mutualist groups from Southeast Asia.

examination of the latter cases reveals that the character of the intergroup articulations may be quite variable. The patterns of connectance between those groups filling a specialist hunter-gatherer niche relative to adjacent groups—who may occupy very different economic niches within the same environment and territory—may also vary considerably.

Another complication occurs between groups that differ in terms of within-habitat and between-habitat social articulations. In the preceding examples, I was talking about niche differentiation within a broadly defined habitat. Some hunter-gatherer groups may articulate across large regions with social units that have noncomplementary consumer roles.

Alternatively, they may maintain relationships with representatives of larger-scale systems that have different ways of organizing the procurement, processing, and eventual sale of goods to consumers. Good examples of "wage-gatherer" groups, such as the Nayaka or Naikens, have been reported in southern India (Bird 1983), and it seems to me that

Proposition 11.10

Economic relationships integrated by high levels of connectance should be expected to vary temporally in response to density-dependent pressures at the regional level. Scalar differences between articulated units would produce different local problems and opportunities, depending upon the character and diversity of the regional cultural-economic environments within which pressures build up. In those regions in which economic diversity is high among adjacent social units, the rates of change in any one socioethnic component within such a complex regional system should vary over time with the scales of absolute change in niche density.

Taking a clue from the ecological literature regarding niche diversification and system stability, I would expect that

Proposition 11.11

Greater stability and therefore slower rates of change should be coupled with greater niche specialization. This implies that more socially independent economic specializations, or at least semispecializations. should be found among independent sociocultural systems that are embedded within more stable ecosystems, e.g., those with the least fluctuation in temperature and rainfall inputs.

If proposition 11.11 is correct, a complex organization integrating a number of cultural-economic systems might function within the broader ecosystem as a "megageneralist," with the following consequences for the larger ecosystem:

Proposition 11.12

As mutualist and product specializations in resource procurement are organized into socioeconomic articulations of larger and larger scale, "megageneralist" units will act to decrease the stability in the broader ecosystem to the extent that they cut down forests, overexploit biomass for construction and fuel, and overexploit targeted species.

On the other hand, in ecological settings in which marked seasonality in production is conditioned by high month-to-month variability in rainfall or temperature, the response to demographic packing should be to increase niche breadth. This means that, in such settings, ethnic units should behave increasingly like generalists vis-à-vis the ecosystem, which ensures that

Proposition 11.13

As annual and interannual variability in basic climatic variables increases, the presence of more trophic gen-

eralists—and all that they imply in terms of reduced ecosystem stability—would be expected. Ecological stability would be diminished regardless of the scale at which the cultural-economic system was organized. Regional mutualism would affect ecosystems in the same way as a "megageneralist" might, if the organizational unit was either a species or several independent ethnic groups.

In other words, I am arguing that cultural systems may be organized like ecosystems and at the same time participate in ecosystems! Assuming the accuracy of the preceding propositions, I would say that

Proposition 11.14

The more that cultural systems are integrated like ecosystems, the greater their stability—*but* the greater their potential for degrading the parent ecosystem. Therefore, the organizational scale of the overall system, and that of the participants in such a larger integration, represents a trade-off between what is stabilized and the pattern of entropic flow within the larger system. The closer the scale of a participating subsystem comes to the scale of the larger ecosystem, the greater the risk of ecosystemic instability and therefore potential crisis in the subsystem.

As an aid to visualizing the relevance of the preceding propositions to the cases classified as hunter-gatherers but probably integrated into larger regional systems as internally differentiated specialists, I have prepared table 11.02. This table lists the groups that are thought to be embedded within larger cultural systems and provides other germane information.

Given recent claims in the anthropological literature that hunter-gatherers could not exist in tropical rain forests[6] except as mutualists or in other roles embedded in larger cultural systems, perhaps the first item of interest is the realization that the vast majority of the cases that are cited as germane to this controversy are not found primarily in true tropical rain forests! They are, in fact, included in a temperature category that is referred to as "tropical" to distinguish it from the warmest, or *equatorial*, habitats.[7] All of the mutualist and forest specialist cases in this category are listed in part I of table 11.02.

When this list is compared with the independent hunter-gatherer cases from subtropical and warmer climates, the most striking observation is the vast difference in the role played by aquatic resources in equatorial climates. Among mutualists, only 27 percent of the cases are reported to depend on aquatic resources for more than 15 percent of their diet,

TABLE 11.02

COMPARATIVE INFORMATION ON HUNTER-GATHERER CASES IN TROPICAL AND EQUATORIAL SETTINGS:
CLUES TO COMPLEXITY AND NICHE BREADTH

GROUP	PLANT BIOMASS	TERRESTRIAL MODEL DENSITY	POPULATION DENSITY	PACKIX	NICHEFF	GROWING SEASON		SYSTEM STATE PROPERTIES	PERCENT AQUATIC DEPENDENCE
						GROWC	WILT		
I. Cases considered to be mutualistic or product specialists									
MIKEA	1,065.74	3.13	4.36	0.48	1.39	12	10	Embedded, occasional horticulture	0.0
HILL PANDARAM	3,916.20	10.33	70.37	7.74	6.81	12	5	Embedded, horticulture rare	0.2
MRABRI	9,571.19	8.05	23.16	2.54	2.87	12	3	Mutualist, relations vague	0.5
BIHOR	13,839.00	5.37	22.00	2.42	4.09	12	3	Embedded, production for market	0.0
BAMBOTE	16,752.04	7.24	25.00	2.75	3.45	12	3	Mutual dependency	1.0
AGTA (ISABELA)	23,670.98	4.14	42.00	4.62	10.14	12	1	Embedded, complex symbiosis	45.0
AKA	25,461.31	5.78	9.06	0.99	1.56	12	0	Mutual, some independence	0.4
AGTA (CAGAYAN)	29,951.88	3.35	37.94	4.17	11.32	12	0	Embedded, complex symbiosis	15.0
BAYAKA	28,448.64	4.71	17.47	1.92	3.70	12	0	Mutual dependency	0.7
EFE	30,072.33	3.55	15.96	1.75	4.49	12	0	Mutual dependency	0.8
BAKA	30,880.64	3.34	13.63	1.83	4.08	12	0	Mutual dependency	1.0
MBUTI	33,168.24	2.46	44.00	4.84	17.88	12	0	Mutual dependency and aggregation	1.0
AGTA (CASIGURAN)	47,941.20	0.76	87.00	9.57	114.47	12	0	Embedded, complex symbiosis	40.0
MAKU	51,576.72	0.60	4.60	0.51	7.66	12	0	Mutual semidependency	18.0
SEMANG	50,350.34	0.89	17.57	1.93	19.74	12	0	Embedded, situational symbiosis	10.0
KUBU	56,157.12	0.28	9.20	1.01	32.85	12	0	Embedded, incorporation-decline	5.0
PUNAN	56,550.51	0.28	11.50	1.26	41.07	12	0	Embedded, situational symbiosis	5.0
SHOMPEN	59,274.80	0.10	39.54	4.35	395.40	12	0	Embedded, situational symbiosis	35.0
II. Independent hunter-gatherers from subtropical and warmer settings									
KARIERA	657.35	1.56	9.50	1.04	6.08	12	10	Independent	35.0
JEIDJI	2,131.21	5.45	17.00	1.87	3.11	12	8	Independent	25.0
WALMBARIA	9,113.49	6.97	58.00	6.38	8.32	12	7	Independent	70.0
MURNGIN	9,420.35	7.72	11.76	1.29	1.52	12	6	Independent, endemic warfare	10.0
LARDIL	9,481.53	7.07	30.0	3.30	4.24	12	7	Independent	60.0
WORORO	9,543.11	7.93	11.00	1.21	1.38	12	7	Independent	10.0
GROOTE EYELANDT	10,129.69	7.53	22.90	2.52	3.04	12	5	Independent	60.0
KAKADU	11,138.53	7.93	8.30	0.96	1.04	12	6	Independent	25.0
GUNWINGGU	11,366.31	7.30	17.84	1.96	2.44	12	6	Independent, expanding	25.0
MULLUK	13,576.86	6.45	45.00	4.95	5.66	12	5	Independent, trading system	60.0

TIWI	16,400.11	6.62	37.50	4.13	5.66	12	5	Independent	35.0
WIKMUNKAN	16,648.36	5.98	19.31	2.12	3.22	12	5	Independent	20.0
YINTJINGGA	18,003.14	5.83	31.00	3.41	5.32	12	4	Independent	75.0
NORTH ISLAND	20,875.11	6.13	33.38	3.67	5.44	12	3	Independent, use of drugs	5.0
KUKUALANJI	21,477.13	5.37	50.00	5.50	9.31	12	3	Independent	55.0
JARWA	29,082.34	3.96	44.65	4.91	11.35	12	2	Independent, expanding warfare	30.0
NUKAK	46,251.29	0.93	9.34	1.03	10.04	12	0	Independent	13.0
WARUNGGU	47,746.43	1.38	16.28	1.79	11.79	12	0	Independent, unknown	34.0
MAMU	47,864.82	1.17	45.00	4.95	38.46	12	0	Independent, alkaloid processing	25.0
ONGE	57,386.48	0.21	40.10	4.41	190.95	12	0	Independent	30.0

III. Former hunter-gatherers who have recently adopted horticulture

NAMBIKWARA	4,806.06	14.85	7.78	0.86	0.52	12	4	Independent, hunter-gatherer horticulture	5.0
GUATO	13,715.39	9.84	6.74	0.74	0.69	12	0	Independent, remnant group	70.0
CHENCHU	15,645.89	5.61	123.30	13.57	21.97	12	3	Independent, heavy horticulture	5.0
KAURAREG	17,620.21	6.36	35.00	3.85	5.50	12	4	Independent, horticulture	65.0
SIRIONO	18,304.27	5.27	6.00	0.66	1.14	12	0	Independent, remnant, horticulture	5.0
YARURO-PUME	18,920.42	7.86	19.95	2.20	2.54	12	4	Independent, horticulture	53.0
BORORO	26,175.82	4.52	51.36	5.65	11.36	12	1	Independent, heavy horticulture	10.0
BATEK	30,378.80	3.37	43.00	4.73	12.75	12	3	Independent, horticulture	5.0
SHIRIANA	36,721.40	1.73	15.00	1.71	9.01	12	0	Independent, warfare, horticulture	0.0
GUAHIBO	42,207.45	0.96	17.47	1.90	18.19	12	0	Independent, primarily horticulture	5.0
AYTA (PINATUBO)	57,366.23	0.76	91.89	10.11	120.90	12	4	Independent, heavy horticulture	5.0

Note: Underlined figures represent instances in which population density exceeds the packing threshold, except for values in the aquatic dependence column, in which case underlined percentages represent 15 percent or more of the total diet.

while an impressive 80 percent of the independent hunter-gatherers in such warm settings are heavily dependent upon aquatic resources. These percentages are especially meaningful considering that the hunter-gatherer cases situated in tropical and equatorial settings are overwhelmingly intensified. Forty of the forty-nine cases in this category (81.6 percent) have population densities in excess of the packing threshold. Given that such an overwhelming proportion of these cases are intensified, it is interesting that aquatic resources contribute only a small percentage to the total diet of groups acting as mutualists and forest product specialists, as well as those that have recently begun to supplement their diets with horticultural products. In only 27 percent of the former and 36 percent of the latter cases do aquatic supplements contribute significantly to the diet. These data indicate that

Proposition 11.15

Other things being equal, mutualist and forest product specializations appear to be intensificational responses in environmental settings in which aquatic resources are not viable subsistence alternatives for otherwise moderately mobile peoples.

The content of the "other things being equal" stipulation now becomes critical for understanding the environmental contexts in which mutualist and forest product specializations might be expected to occur. If I reason exclusively from what I know about these issues, the answer to problem 11.01 seems clear. There are many mutualists and economic specialists in tropical and subtropical regions that are characterized by the highest environmental "steadiness" in temperature and rainfall, which are the two fundamental ingredients supporting the plant community. Biological productivity is greatest where there is the most thermal energy and water and, most importantly, where there is the least variance—both annually and interannually—in these vital necessities. Specialists must be able to rely completely upon the species or niches that they exploit and exchange for other vital necessities. Mutualistic arrangements among product specialists are driven by the same imperative: partners must be able to depend upon one another for some portion of the nutrients essential for life.

Proposition 11.16

Unstable ecosystems that regularly exhibit high-amplitude variability in fundamental climatic variables such as rainfall and solar radiation will not support mutualistic or other symbiotic relationships between culturally distinct units. It seems likely that the probability of mutualistic articulation between culturally differentiated units is reduced as a nonlinear function of the

interannual variance in rainfall and temperature. Conversely, as variance in rainfall and solar radiation increases, the optimal buffering strategy would be to expand one's niche breadth—rather than to contract it—through specialization and by increased dependence upon another group that occupies a different niche in the same unstable setting.

If this response to problem 11.01 is correct, then recent arguments stating that mutualism is an equally rational strategy for intersystemic articulation in any environmental setting (Baugh 1991; Gregg 1988; Speth 1991; Spielmann 1991) or at any geographic scale are likely to be incorrect.[8] Central to warranting these arguments has been the belief that mutualism can be defined as simple exchanges of goods and that such exchanges across habitat boundaries are evidence of mutualism (Spielmann 1991a:5, 1991b:37). In the language of this book, the terms used by recent researchers refer to between-habitat exchanges, but this is not what is meant by mutualism. As I have pointed out, documented cases of mutualism among hunter-gatherers occur among specialists within the same habitat and constitute articulations between niches within a habitat rather than interactions between social units living in different habitats.[9] Between-habitat articulations are best viewed as trade relationships and not as the kind of organizationally stable instances of symbiosis exemplified by the mutualist groups of central Africa, who nevertheless are cited as prototypical of mutualistic relationships everywhere!

Regardless of these academic problems, the patterning observable among hunter-gatherer mutualists may mean, at least in part, that differences in both internal organization and inter–ethnic unit complexity could well be a simple extension of similar variability in the organization of ecosystems themselves. As such, they would not represent a different kind of evolution unique to cultural systems. If we admit this possibility, some types of variability in complexity arising in response to intensification may be referable to habitat differences as initial conditions rather than to emergent phenomena at the level of cultural systems themselves.

These observations are provocative, but I have not yet finished with the issue of niche breadth. My initial exploration of groups that were exclusively dependent upon terrestrial plants produced interesting results that supported the identification of mutualist groups as representatives of a different kind of complexity. Researching them meant, however, that I have ignored many interesting hunter-gatherer cases that were not primarily dependent upon terrestrial plants, particularly those that were primarily dependent upon aquatic resources. Many of these groups are also considered to be complex hunter-gatherers and are of great interest to archaeologists. It has even been suggested that becoming "complex"

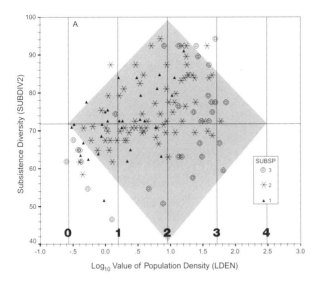 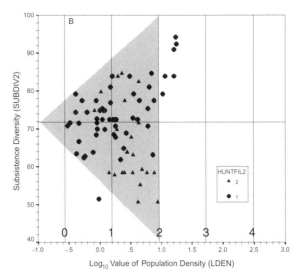

FIGURE 11.11

Comparative property space maps defined by subsistence diversity and log$_{10}$ values of population density; comparison is between generic hunter-gatherers only (A) and those primarily dependent upon terrestrial animals (B). Graph A cases are coded for the primary source of food (SUBSP): (1) terrestrial animals, (2) terrestrial plants, and (3) aquatic resources. Graph B is coded for HUNTFIL2, which distinguishes between (1) generic hunter-gatherers and (2) mounted hunters.

was a necessary precondition to the experimental use of the plants and animals that were ultimately domesticated (Price and Gebauer 1995:8). Is it accurate, however, to imagine that organizational complexity is a prerequisite to intensifying the production of foods through cultivation and herding? Perhaps such a linear idea of process is shortsighted because, when different habitats and initial conditions are examined, other alternatives come to mind when the focus is on differential responses to causal factors such as packing.

One Route to Complexity: Emergence through Internal Differentiation

It is commonly thought that complexity represents a trend away from egalitarian society and toward social differentiation in such sociopolitical terms as ranking or stratification. My research indicates, however, that the integration of mutualistic hunter-gatherer groups into larger, symbiotically linked systems has little impact within such a system in terms of either scale-related changes or changes that represent new forms of structural differentiation or functional specialization. These prevalent ideas stem from assumptions about the transformations that are imagined to occur within systems.

I have outlined how I might expect subsistence diversity to contribute to system stability, and I have had some success in combining subsistence diversity and the packing index in a property space frame of reference to study the sys-

tem state differences among mutualists. In previous discussions of system state (table 9.05), I created a nominal variable (SYSTATE3) that identified various properties of hunter-gatherer cases that I thought might indicate different system states. At this juncture, it seems reasonable to use the seven different system state groupings as data subsets to be explored for additional relationships, using property space maps that are defined by subsistence diversity (SUBDIV2) and the log$_{10}$ value of population density (LDEN).[10]

NORMAL OR GENERIC HUNTER-GATHERERS:
FINDING REGULARITY THROUGH THE
RECOGNITION OF SYMMETRY

The most appropriate set of cases to examine first are the hunter-gatherers who, at the time of ethnographic documentation, were thought to be using mobility as their primary strategy for maintaining subsistence security (simply for convenience, I have referred to groups in this category as "generic"). Further, only those mobile groups were included that exhibited none of the characteristics normally used to identify sociocultural complexity. These cases are displayed in the graphs in figure 11.11, which feature the same variables to define property space that were used in figures 11.01 and 11.02 to examine patterning in groups dependent upon terrestrial plants. It should be recalled that this approach to graphing led to interesting conclusions about the mutualist cases. In order to emphasize the patterns in the graphs, lines were placed on the *x* axis at the $\log_{10}$ values of three previously recognized density thresholds:

1. Line 0 occurs at the $\log_{10}$ value of –0.57, which identifies the lower threshold for the presence of hunter-gatherers, based on estimates taken from the Terrestrial Model.[11]
2. Line 1 occurs at the $\log_{10}$ value of 1.57, which is the threshold in group size values among terrestrial hunters.
3. Line 2 occurs at the $\log_{10}$ value of 9.098, which is the threshold anticipated by the Group Size Model for packed conditions among foragers dependent upon terrestrial plants.

The thresholds corresponding to lines 3 and 4 will be clarified subsequently.

Interpreting the patterning in figure 11.11, graph A, is a challenging intellectual exercise. Groups dependent upon aquatic resources are located around the lower and right-hand edges of the distribution, while hunter-gatherers who primarily exploit terrestrial plants and animal are arrayed in the center and upper part of the graph. Although this is an interesting distribution, an even more unexpected pattern is evident among the groups primarily exploiting aquatic resources. It should be recalled that high values for the subsistence diversity variable point to wide niche breadth, whereas niche specialization is indicated by lower values of SUBDIV2. The pattern in figure 11.11, graph A, suggests that

Generalization 11.08

The only indication of niche specialization under nonpacked conditions among mobile groups with no wealth differentials or special prerogatives accorded to leaders occurs in groups that are primarily dependent upon aquatic resources.

This specialization is dramatic at low population density levels and reaches a maximum at the reference line indicative of the threshold among terrestrial hunters first seen in figure 10.06, graph A. It seems clear that the factor responsible for the weak threshold in this graph was the contrast between nonmounted hunters who dominated the data prior to the threshold (figure 11.11, graph B) and the mounted hunters with their large group sizes who defined the distribution between the 1.57 and 9.098 thresholds. This bias in the frequency distribution of extensified cases conditioned the threshold in group size seen earlier. What I did not appreciate earlier is that this threshold identifies a bias in niche specialization as well.

I have already pointed out that, among groups that are primarily dependent upon terrestrial animals, specialists occur more often among extensified cases prior to the packing threshold (line 2 in figure 11.11, graph A). In the plot of terrestrial hunters in figure 11.11, graph B, the extensified cases that use horses are identified by a distinctive marker, and it is clear that only with extensification is there much niche spe-

cialization. In graph A, the same threshold value of 1.57 persons occurs, but it is the reverse of the pattern of specialization found among groups primarily exploiting aquatic resources. At the point of reversal (line 1) and thereafter, an undeviating pattern of decreasing specialization occurs as population density continues to increase. The co-occurrence of two patterned reversals at the same population density threshold for two different sets of cases is provocative and supports the belief that this density value is an important threshold for system characteristics among groups dependent upon both aquatic and terrestrial resources.

On the other hand, there is a lack of symmetry in the dispersal of groups of extreme specialists who are dependent upon either terrestrial animals and aquatic resources (inclusive of the mounted hunters). Among terrestrial hunters, specialists are most common above the 1.57-person threshold, whereas specialists exploiting aquatic resources occur below the 1.57-person threshold. These contrasts ensure a very different symmetry for the two distributions. It is clear in figure 11.11, graph B, that terrestrial hunters define a nearly perfect triangular distribution, and both specialization and expanded niche breadth increase as the packing threshold is approached. Among the generic cases, specialization increases among exploiters of aquatic resources only up to the 1.57-person threshold and thereafter diminishes. What should we make of this contrast?

In searching for an answer to this question, it seems reasonable to examine the content of the property space distribution described by the so-called generic cases. In figure 11.12, the distribution of cases is split into two subsets. Graph A displays hunter-gatherer cases that live in environments anticipated by the Terrestrial Model to be incapable of supporting a minimalist terrestrial human adaptation. In graph B, groups living in environments capable of sustaining a minimalist human adaptation are presented. When the diamond-shaped distribution that occurs in graph B is superimposed over the distributions in both graphs A and B, it is clear that the overall distribution of groups who live in environments that would support a viable terrestrial adaptation according to modeled conditions fits within the diamond pattern. Almost without exception, the distribution of cases that in figure 11.11, graph A, looked like a ragged parallelogram represents groups that live in environments modeled to be uninhabited (figure 11.12, graph A).

Another look at figure 11.11, graph A, reveals that these are the same cases that are primarily, if not exclusively, dependent upon aquatic resources and in which specialization and population density both increase until the LDEN threshold at #1 is reached. (These are hunter-gatherers from the high arctic for whom a specialized niche was the only alternative.) It is also noteworthy that only seven out of thirty-two of these cases were documented to have population densities that exceeded the packing threshold. The exceptions

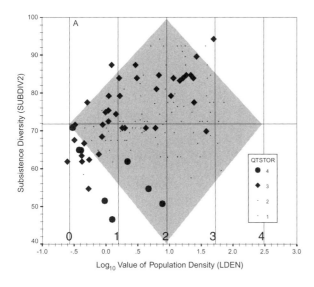
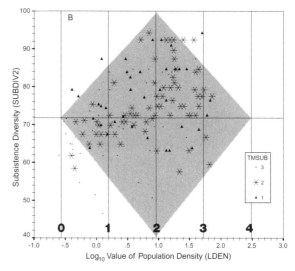

FIGURE 11.12

Comparative property space maps defined by subsistence diversity and log_{10} values of population density; comparison is between cases in settings projected to be uninhabited (A) and those living in more supportive environments (B). Graph A cases are coded for the quantity of food stored (QTSTOR): (1) no regular storage or minor, very-short-term storage of two or three days; (2) moderate investment in storage, in both quantity and period of potential use; (3) major investment in storage and in the duration of anticipated use; and (4) massive investment in storage from the standpoint of both species stored and duration of use. Graph B is coded for Terrestrial Model subsistence (TMSUB): (1) terrestrial animals, (2) terrestrial plants, and (3) uninhabited.

include the Onge of Little Andaman Island, who are primarily dependent upon aquatic resources, and the Yaghan of Tierra del Fuego, who also primarily exploited aquatic resources. The remaining exceptions are from the driest parts of Southern California and the Great Basin of North America.[12] Of equal interest is the fact that five of the seven exceptional cases enjoyed substantial niche breadth and only two fell minimally below the median line for subsistence diversity. These patterns suggest that

Generalization 11.09

If so-called generic hunter-gatherers successfully radiate into environments that are modeled to be uninhabited by the Terrestrial Model, the majority succeed through specializations with relatively narrow niche breadth. Extremely specialized cases occur in environments in which there are few if any resource alternatives, such as the high arctic or extremely dry locations.

Not only is narrow niche breadth a feature of extremely low-productivity settings, it is also true that

Generalization 11.10

Very low achieved population densities, implying very low rates of population increase, are also characteristic of generic

hunter-gatherers who inhabit the lowest-productivity settings, such as those projected by the Terrestrial Model to be uninhabited.

If the argument presented in proposition 11.16 is correct, then there should be no instances of balanced mutualism—that is, mutualistic connections between ethnic groups at roughly similar levels of complexity who differ only in terms of scalar characteristics. My research indicates that no such instances have been documented in "uninhabited" TM zones. Similarly, if the arguments presented in proposition 11.13 are correct, I would expect to see trophic generalists or groups with wide niche breadth in the most warm and productive settings. If this expectation is not confirmed, then the adaptations should be very unstable and subject to extreme cyclicity in terms of demographic growth and decline.

There have been repeated claims that these dynamics occur in the northern boreal forests, in the high arctic, and in low-productivity, dry habitats where, as I have noted, hunter-gatherer groups have extremely to only moderately narrow niche breadth, which implies instability. These groups have been reported to experience famine regularly (Balikci 1968:81–82; Henriksen 1973:67; Leacock 1969:13–15; Meggitt 1962:24; Rogers 1962b:16–32; Watanabe 1969), which indicates that my arguments about stability and instability anticipate the facts quite well.

By focusing on hunter-gatherer cases in more user-friendly habitats—such as in settings that are projected to support terrestrial adaptations (figure 11.12, graph B)—we see a biased distribution with few intensely specialized cases. This pattern is accommodated comfortably within the diamond distribution noted earlier, and a feature becomes visible that was not as clear in the original distribution in figure 11.11, graph A:

Generalization 11.11

Prior to the onset of the packing threshold, a general increase in subsistence diversity occurs concurrently with growing population density, which implies increased niche breadth. After the packing threshold is reached, however, there is a general reduction in niche breadth and a regular increase in moderate levels of specialization.

This chevron pattern is consistent with earlier suggestions in propositions 11.02 and 11.13 that subsistence diversity fosters stability. It must be kept in mind that no mutualist groups—which are demonstrably common in tropical and equatorial settings—appear in the array of cases displayed in figure 11.12, graph B. The vast majority of the displayed cases are from midlatitude temperate regions or from the world's subtropics, where expanding one's niche breadth is generally feasible and tends to stabilize a system that is increasingly constrained in its mobility options. At the packing threshold, however, a different set of conditions develops, and mobility is essentially no longer a feasible strategy for ensuring adequate net food returns.

I have already suggested that attempts to increase the net returns from a smaller home range present the hunter-gatherer with a dilemma. I have shown how, with decreases in range size, an inevitable reduction occurs in dependence upon terrestrial animals (generalization 10.01). The number of accessible terrestrial plant and animal species is also reduced as a power function of reductions in the size of a group's range (generalizations 10.02 and 10.03). These consequences of density-dependent range reduction should be regarded as marking the transition between expending labor on mobility and expending labor on intensificational tactics.

Generalization 11.12

The consequences of reducing range size in response to density-dependent pressures are usually accompanied by accelerated labor costs per unit increase in the net returns (propositions 10.09 and 11.03). It is suggested that these increased labor costs break down into four major types: (1) labor invested up front in increasing, through technological means, the probabilities of prey capture as well as the bulk returns per capture event (proposition 10.09); (2) labor invested in designing or enhancing the habitat to yield higher returns from key species; (3) labor invested in rendering the resources edible, such as removal of toxins; (4) labor invested in extending the time utility for resources obtained—e.g., preparation for storage and investments in storage facilities (propositions 10.07 and 10.09).

The choices hunter-gatherers make about how to invest labor to increase net returns from a more limited geographic area and array of productive food resources ensure that, once the packing threshold is reached, reduced subsistence diversity will result when only wild species are being exploited. This specialization might be expected to increase further if pressures are mounting for still higher net returns in response to further increases in population density.

Generalization 11.13

Other things be equal, it is expected that if, following packing, the only choices are to procure either wild terrestrial plants, animals, or aquatic resources, then subsistence diversity among generic hunter-gatherers should be reduced as a log function of increases in population density. *Relative* diet breadth may increase, however, given the likelihood that accessible but lower-return species would increasingly be exploited.

One remaining task is to examine those hunter-gatherer cases that display some minor indications of increasing social complexity and to inquire whether they provide clues to the emergence of complex forms. There are a few cases of somewhat mobile, egalitarian hunter-gatherers that maintain institutionally acknowledged leaders who are responsible for organizing and coordinating community activities not necessarily dealing directly with subsistence. These leaders may be in charge of providing hospitality to visitors and organizing social events to which other communities are invited or to which the local GROUP2 unit has been invited by faraway groups.

Although the role of leader carries with it corporate expectations, there are few prerogatives associated with the status. Persons in leadership positions are not relieved of their subsistence responsibilities and there are no unique sartorial or ornamental prerogatives. Special messengers may be available, however, to assist the leader with both gathering and distributing information, since one of a leader's primary tasks is to keep track of the well-being of GROUP1 units that may be dispersed in a variety of locations.

A look at the graph in figure 11.13, which plots the groups in the hunter-gatherer data base that meet these criteria, indicates that leaders of this type are characteristic of societies that cannot be considered to have a narrow niche breadth. All cases occur in the upper half of the distribution and represent a homologous, symmetrical version of the pattern in figure 11.11, graph A, in which the packing thresh-

55

6

66666666666ont

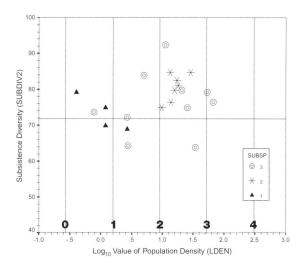

FIGURE 11.13

Distribution of generic hunter-gatherer cases with some institutional leadership roles displayed in the property space defined by subsistence diversity and the $\log_{10}$ value of population density. Cases are coded for dominant sources of foods (SUBSP): (1) terrestrial animals, (2) terrestrial plants, and (3) aquatic resources.

old (line 2) marks a point of reversal in subsistence diversity. It seems clear that, among noncomplex hunter-gatherer groups with community leaders, the response to packing is no different than in cases without community leaders. This kind of leadership can occur either below or above the packing threshold, which means that it does not arise as a response to density-dependent conditions.

An examination of other variables reveals an inverse relationship between GROUP2 size and population density among these cases. Large GROUP2 sizes are found among the nonpacked groups with the lowest population density, whereas small GROUP2 sizes are characteristic of packed cases with the highest population density. All groups in the latter category are, without exception, dependent upon either aquatic resources or a nearly equal mix of aquatic and terrestrial animal resources, so it would seem that reductions in subsistence diversity in this instance are referable to increases in the exploitation of aquatic resources.

A reduction in GROUP2 size is associated with the postpacking response and, coupled with increased specialization in aquatic resources, is possibly related to the changes in GROUP2 size that were noted earlier in figure 10.06, graph B. Among these cases, once the packing threshold was reached, some groups had smaller GROUP2 sizes whereas other GROUP2 units increased in size. To help sort out the ambiguity in postpacking GROUP2 patterning, I have prepared figure 11.14, which, in graph A, displays a scatter of generic hunter-gatherer groups that are primarily dependent upon terrestrial plant resources. The y axis is defined by

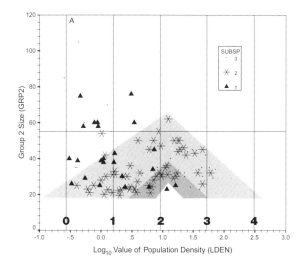 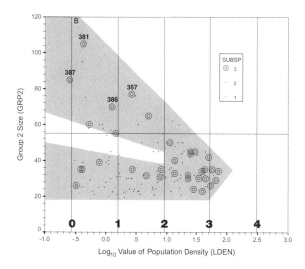

FIGURE 11.14

Comparative property space maps defined by GROUP2 size and the $\log_{10}$ value of population density. Contrasts are illustrated in the response to packing by groups dependent upon terrestrial (A) and aquatic resources (B). Both graphs are coded for the primary source of food (SUBSP): (1) terrestrial animals, (2) terrestrial plants, and (3) aquatic resources.

GROUP2 size and population density remains on the *x* axis. In contrast, graph B in figure 11.14 displays the generic cases that are primarily dependent upon aquatic resources.

The distribution in graph A of generic hunter-gatherer groups obtaining most of their food from terrestrial plants documents that

Generalization 11.14

Increases in GROUP2 size correspond to increases in population density until just beyond the packing threshold, at which point GROUP2 size decreases at the same time that population density continues to increase. The largest GROUP2 sizes occur around the packing threshold, and there are no generic cases in which group size increases once the packing threshold is reached. Given the observations summarized in generalization 11.11, this means that GROUP2 size increases as subsistence diversity increases, although above the packing threshold, as subsistence diversity decreases, there is a correlated decrease in GROUP2 size.

This pattern appears to suggest that

Scenario 11.01

As a system whose components are primarily dependent upon terrestrial plant resources approaches packing, more than two work groups may be organized each day. The former pattern of minimizing group size to reduce mobility costs becomes irrelevant, and as packing is approached increased daily labor is required to increase the subsistence diversity within a smaller home range. Once population exceeds the packing threshold, group size is reduced further as a function of decreases in subsistence diversity and attendant splintering of groups into new residential units. The latter units are situated adjacent to the resources (either bulk-return species or a suite of species) upon which each group focuses. Splintering is accompanied by the concentration of labor upon those resources that respond best to increased input of labor with increased net returns.

This scenario seems quite plausible, but I began this investigation with the observation that, among generic hunter-gatherers, leaders whose service was community-oriented rather than subsistence-oriented were associated with large GROUP2 sizes prior to packing and that, after packing, group size decreased. Looking back at the data on leadership, I realized that all the groups with leaders and population densities below the packing threshold were equally split between terrestrial animal hunters—known to have large GROUP2 sizes—and groups in boreal forest and arctic settings that were dependent upon aquatic resources and also documented to have large GROUP2 sizes. In contrast, those groups above the

packing threshold were primarily dependent upon either plant or aquatic resources.

In order to see how groups that are "generic," dependent upon aquatic resources, and subject to packing respond to increases in population density, graph B of figure 11.14 was generated. In this plot, there is at best a very minor response in group size to increases in population density, and there is essentially no response to the packing threshold. Another interesting feature of the graph is the scatter of cases occurring above the scalar threshold for group size. It comes as no surprise that the Copper Eskimo and the Netsilik, Iglulik, and Baffin Island Eskimo cases are among the overly large GROUP2 cases. In chapter 9, I described these groups of breathing hole sealers whose large winter settlements are really GROUP3 units within which a network of sharing partners acts as a risk-buffering mechanism by crosscutting the relatively small units into which cooperative labor is organized.

Some of the consequences of this type of settlement structure include the fact that—although it is not mandatory—most marriages tend to be endogamous within the GROUP3 unit. On the other hand, settlements may be segmented into units that in other circumstances would probably be separated into GROUP2 clusters or barrios within the larger settlement. Overall, as the packing threshold is approached, the size of these units decreases. All of the cases that are known to represent GROUP3 units are in the high shaded area of graph B. The cases in both shaded arms form a linear distribution in which the size of GROUP2 units decreases as the $\log_{10}$ value of population density increases and there is no response whatsoever to the packing threshold. Twelve of the packed cases are from Australia and five of the non-Australian cases are the Ainu, Chimariko, Onge, Seri, and Yahgan.[13]

Generalization 11.15

Among generic hunter-gatherers who are dependent upon aquatic resources, an unrelenting linear reduction in group size accompanies increases in the $\log_{10}$ value of population density. This pattern applies particularly to GROUP2 sizes, but when GROUP3 units replace GROUP2 units the former may be similarly affected. At the packing threshold, however, there is no group size response.

Coupled with what is already known about the use of aquatic resources, these conditions prompt some suggestions about process:

Scenario 11.02

If generic hunter-gatherers become dependent upon aquatic resources before their populations reach the packing threshold, there is probably little opportunity for them to expand subsistence diversity by developing new terrestrial opportunities for hunting and gathering once populations increase (generalization11.09). These factors ensure that increased specialization directed toward aquatic resources also requires that heroic labor investments will be attempted (generalization 11.12) in order to expand niche breadth in the face of population growth.

As specialization increases in response to density-dependent pressures, new settlements will increasingly be located in settings that, under unpacked conditions, were considered to be only marginally productive. Group size is likely to be smaller at these locations, and therefore mean GROUP2 size should regularly decrease as places with more and more marginal access windows are occupied. The same steps toward specialization that, once the packing threshold is crossed, favor reduced group size among groups dependent upon terrestrial plants (scenario 11.01) also condition reduced GROUP2 sizes among many groups dependent upon aquatic resources. The only difference lies in the inability of many of the latter groups to increase their niche breadth in response to packing pressures.

SYMMETRY AND REGULARITY: SOME CLUES
FOR USE IN FURTHER STUDIES

I have pursued the subject of symmetry as a clue to regularity among generic hunter-gatherer groups by examining patterns that appeared to demonstrate symmetrical relationships between subsistence diversity and population density, as well as population density and GROUP2 size. As I suggested in generalization 11.14, among groups primarily dependent upon terrestrial plant resources there is a parallel increase in both niche diversity and GROUP2 size as both variables approach the packing threshold. Similarly, both variables decrease once the threshold is passed. A comparable symmetry is observable in the pattern of subsistence diversity relative to a threshold of 71.75 on the niche diversity index once the packing threshold is approached. This is particularly striking since dependence upon terrestrial animals does not survive the packing threshold.

This balanced pattern is disrupted by scatters of cases that are all dependent upon aquatic resources, particularly ones situated in habitats that were projected by the Terrestrial Model to have been uninhabitable. These habitats turn out to be settings in which niche breadth cannot be expanded, provided the three simple domains of resource procurement (terrestrial plants, animals, and aquatic resources) are used as measures for niche expansion. Obviously if this were true, then increased niche breadth as a response to increased population density, followed by a reversal in the direction of greater niche specialization, could not occur, and the only pos-

sibility would be an unrelenting pattern of increased specialization.

An attempt to understand the apparent symmetry drove my effort to make sense of the exceptions to this pattern—the cases that did not behave by the same rules of symmetry (see proposition 10.15)—but there are even further implications. Earlier in my pattern recognition work, I observed that most of the groups dependent upon aquatic resources were also packed and only a few cases had density levels below the packing threshold. I proposed that, other things being equal, heavy use of aquatic resources was itself a density-dependent response (proposition 10.16). Although at present there is little additional support for this assertion, I will keep it in mind as I continue to explore these patterns in an attempt to account for complexity and its emergence.

It is also true that the symmetry between population density and niche specialization would not appear to be so striking if I were not using a frame of reference of great regularity to view the distributions of cases. In order to discuss the issue of regularity I must go back to graph A in figure 11.11, which was the first array of generic hunter-gatherer cases. Among the most interesting features of the graph is the presence of a third vertical reference line, which identifies the truncated right side of the distribution—although I did not simply place the line there to emphasize the truncation.

I had noticed that the distance, measured in population density, between thresholds 1 and 2 was very similar to the distance between the uninhabited line—the threshold at line 0[14]—and the threshold at line 1. When the value estimated from the hunter-gatherer data (0.27107) was used instead of the arbitrary value of 0.30, which set a lower limit on hunter-gatherer presence in the Terrestrial Model, the result was a value of 5.7919 for the number of times the value of the threshold at line 1 can be divided by the threshold at line 0. This is so close to the comparable value of 5.7949 obtained when the threshold at line 2 is divided by threshold at line 1 that a regular set of relationships was easy to imagine.

Two cases and three points, however, are not compelling evidence of a pattern, so, as an experiment, I decided to multiply the packing threshold of 9.098 by 5.79, which yields a value of 52.677—or a $\log_{10}$ value of 1.7216. It is the latter value that is plotted on figure 11.11, graph A, as the threshold at line 3, and it seems to define nicely the average point at which the distribution of generic hunter-gatherers, as measured by population density, ends. On the basis of this computation, it appears more reasonable to suspect a regular pattern to the distribution of thresholds.

Generalization 11.16

A regular pattern occurs in population density thresholds such that each higher threshold is 5.79 times the value of the next lower threshold. In the case of generic hunter-gatherers, the upper limit of population density is 5.79 times the packing threshold of 9.098 persons, or a density of 52.677 persons per 100 square kilometers.

As a simple experiment, a multiplier of 5.79 was used to calculate an additional threshold with a value of 304.99 persons per 100 square kilometers, which represents the population density level beyond which hunter-gatherer subsistence efforts should disappear. Realizing that there were minor differences in the multiplier for the intervals originally recognized, I developed the following exponential equation describing the relationship between the ordinal value of the threshold and the density in persons per 100 hundred square kilometers:[15]

$$(11.01)$$

$$y = \exp(a + bx)$$

where   the exponential constant $\exp = 2.71828$,
the intercept $a = -1.3053703$,
the slope of the line $b = 1.7564672$,
x = the threshold ordinal value (e.g., 1, 2, 3, . . . , N), and
y = density in persons per 100 square kilometers.

I have used this equation to obtain the best estimates of the threshold values[16] that are plotted on the graphs in this chapter because it allows me to anticipate thresholds for which there are no empirical referents at the present time. Will these projected thresholds correspond to features of hunter-gatherer distributions that have not yet been recognized? It is impossible to say at this juncture, but I can now proceed with analysis armed with two new robust patterns to help in the exploration of cases that exhibit properties commonly referred to as evidence of "complexity" and invoked to define "complex" hunter-gatherers.

COMPLEX HUNTER-GATHERERS: SOCIAL DIFFERENTIATION IN TERMS OF WEALTH AMONG CASES WITH SOCIAL RANKING AND INHERITED STATUS

Compared with the kind of leadership customary in generic hunter-gatherer groups (see figure 11.12), leaders of groups characterized by wealth differentials may enjoy some relief from subsistence tasks and be able to delegate some duties to messengers and perhaps to an assistant "talking chief." In other words, clearly designated staff persons are associated with leadership status and, in some instances, special roles are also ascribed to the leader's wife. These enhanced prerogatives of leadership are usually linked with perquisites of wealth or economic well-being as a basis for social differentiation within the group.

In the graph in figure 11.15, wealth-conscious hunter-gatherer cases are arrayed relative to the familiar dimen-

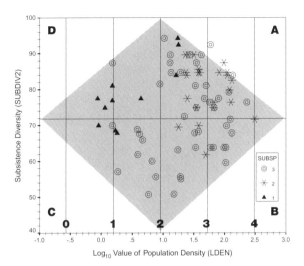

FIGURE 11.15

Wealth-differentiated cases arrayed relative to the property space defined by subsistence diversity and the $\log_{10}$ value of population density. Contrasts are illustrated in the response to packing. Cases are coded for the primary source of food (SUBSP): (1) terrestrial animals, (2) terrestrial plants, and (3) aquatic resources.

sions of subsistence diversity and the $\log_{10}$ value of population density. The distribution of cases defines an almost perfectly symmetrical, diamond-shaped pattern whose long, vertical axis is centered on the packing threshold (line 2) and horizontal axis coincides with a mean subsistence diversity value of 71.75. The eye is immediately drawn to the fourth reference line on the x axis, which is placed at the value of the fourth interval calculated by equation (11.01) and passes through the hunter-gatherer case with the highest population density. Does this placement correspond to "the last hunter-gatherer"—the value beyond which there are only "other" types of societies, such as horticulturists, agriculturists, pastoralists, and state-level societies of increasing size? The answer would appear to be "yes."

Just as the third threshold marks the point beyond which there are no longer generic hunter-gatherers and the packing threshold identifies the point at which mobility can no longer be used to ensure subsistence security, the first threshold indicates the end of groups primarily dependent upon terrestrial animals. (Of course, the initial threshold of zero defines the point of minimal population density for occupation by hunter-gatherers [see figure 11.16].) If there are no hunter-gatherer cases beyond the threshold at line 4, then "complex" hunter-gatherers must be situated to the left of this threshold. These are the groups defined by internal social ranking, inherited leadership among elite segments of the society, and many properties that some researchers cite as the initial conditions upon which a transition to the "next" step are based:

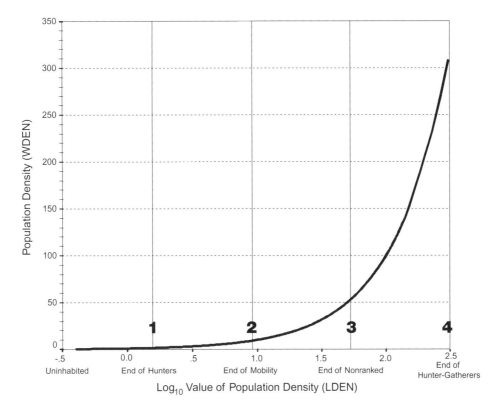

FIGURE 11.16

Demonstration of the curvilinear pattern expressed between population density as anticipated for the world sample of weather stations and the $\log_{10}$ value of population density among hunter-gatherer cases. The four density thresholds that mark major systemic changes in hunter-gatherer organization are identified.

the development of cultivation, the domestication of plants and animals, and the inevitable march to civilization!

The following statement is an illustrative example of this kind of domino effect:

> One reason I view the socioeconomic competition model of domestication as so attractive is that it is capable of providing a plausible and powerful single explanation for non-food as well as food domesticates. . . . the model posits that these items were all used in prestige contexts, as demonstrations of wealth or as motivators in their own right—special items that some people would exert themselves to a greater extent than normal to obtain. They therefore fit in with the other aspects of "prestige technology" that became prevalent only among complex hunter-gatherers, in contrast to the overwhelmingly practical technologies of generalized hunter-gatherers. (Hayden 1995:294)

Claims of this kind can be evaluated by focusing on the content of the distributions in figures 11.15 and 11.17. These graphs feature relationships between important variables characteristic of the kind of complex hunter-gatherers that, in Hayden's mind, preceded the "Neolithic revolution." The social organization of these groups, which share their region

of residence with noncomplex hunter-gatherers, is characterized by ranking; elite status is inherited; and common people enjoy few of the responsibilities and privileges of their elite leaders. In many of these groups, the lowest social class is reserved for "slaves," but "disenfranchised" might be a better description of these persons. All of the most socially complex ethnic groups from the Northwest Coast of North America usually come to mind when the phrase "complex hunter-gatherers" is used.[17]

The contrast in figure 11.17 between ranked and non-ranked cases (all of the hunter-gatherer groups *not* included in figure 11.17) corresponds roughly to Johnson's (1982: 396, 407–10) distinction between simultaneous and sequential hierarchies, if the word *hierarchy* is truly applicable in this instance. Figure 11.17 displays these cases, which have a value of 7 for SYSTATE3 or of 3 for SYSTATE4, in a property space defined by the $\log_{10}$ value of population density on the *x* axis and subsistence diversity (SUBDIV2) on the *y* axis. The case codes refer to the ownership of resource locations.

The remarkable feature of this distribution is that almost all of the cases are arrayed between the packing threshold (line

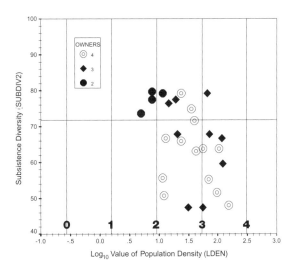

FIGURE 11.17

Property space map defined by subsistence diversity and log₁₀ values of population density displaying only internally ranked hunter-gatherer cases. Cases are coded for ownership of resource locations (OWNER): (1) no ownership reported, use rights recognized by others; (2) the local group claims exclusive use rights over resource location, residential sites, while households may claim special trees and similar features of the landscape; (3) local group claims for hunting areas, dominant animals, fishing sites, and animal drive locations, such claims administered by a group leader, but smaller segments may claim exclusive access to resource locations; and (4) elite ownership of land and resources.

2) and the fourth threshold, which marks the end of all hunter-gatherer distributions. The ranked cases, which are of particular interest here, all occur within the range of variability of nonranked hunter-gatherers, and the only factor that marks them as different is that they are specialized. As I have already pointed out, niche diversity decreases as population density increases beyond the packing threshold and approaches the level of groups residing in habitats that were projected by the Terrestrial Model to be uninhabited. An examination of the cases reveals that all except two have Terrestrial Model densities ranging from just above 0.30 to just below 0.9 persons per 100 square kilometers. The most specialized cases are those with the lowest Terrestrial Model densities, representing forest settings that are barely able to support a local population without the exploitation of aquatic resources.

The Terrestrial Model anticipates that all but the four cases with the highest diversity measures would initially be dependent upon terrestrial animals. In contrast, the vast majority of the cases have low subsistence diversity values and are specialized in their subsistence practices in a rather dramatic way. The tendency for increased specialization to fol-

low increased population density occurs in this group of cases, but it begins at a slightly lower level of subsistence diversity prior to packing. Increased exploitation of aquatic resources would have tended to increase subsistence diversity prior to packing, but, since hunting is no longer an option once the packing threshold is reached, further increases in dependence upon aquatic resources would reduce the subsistence diversity measure to lower, more specialized values. This expectation is consistent with Terrestrial Model projections that, under conditions of low population density, these groups would be primarily terrestrial animal specialists. It is also consistent with the relationship demonstrated by Panowski (1985)—and summarized previously in generalization 11.01—between the complexity of the jurisdictional hierarchies in Northwest Coast societies and the number of mostly aquatic species regularly prepared for storage.

The other dramatic feature of the distribution is that all but one of the cases to the right of the packing threshold have monopolistic strategies for restricting access to resource locations. The majority of these cases exhibit the highest level of all the groups in the hunter-gatherer data set of resource "ownership" through inheritance and elite control of access to productive locations. It is tempting to ask why elite control of resource locations in this instance is heavily biased in favor of aquatically dependent peoples, but this question will have to be put on hold until I complete my discussion of wealth differentials and the possibility that they may be a precondition to elite monopolies.

Looking for a moment at the distributions in figures 11.15 and 11.17, it is clear that, as I indicated in propositions 9.04 and 11.04, the presence of wealth differentials does not appear to be a density-dependent phenomenon. The groups in figure 11.15 are distributed across the full range of variability in density known for hunter-gatherers. A similar lack of association between population density and wealth differentials characterized the mounted hunters of the Great Plains of North America (generalization 9.07). In these extensified groups, wealth signified important social distinctions even though population density values were below the packing threshold.

Generalization 11.17

Wealth-based social differentiation is not exclusively a density-dependent phenomenon. It can appear in hunter-gatherer groups at any level of packing or population density between 0.03 and a maximum of 300 persons per 100 square kilometers.

A pattern of symmetry in the distribution of cases—which was suggested in figure 11.11, graph A, was more apparent in figure 11.12, and was strongly confirmed in figure 11.13, graph A—can be summarized as follows:

Generalization 11.18

There is a sharp reduction in the range of variability in subsistence diversity among wealth-differentiated hunter-gatherers who survive as hunter-gatherers despite increased levels of population pressure that exceed the packing threshold. Both generalist and specialist cases converge at a subsistence diversity value of 71.75 with maximum population density. *Beyond this point, no hunter-gatherers of this type remain in the nearly contemporary world.*

This type of symmetry is surprising, and—as one confronts the last hunter-gatherer survivors but has no idea about what kind of society might have replaced them—it evokes a kind of closure or finality. Nonetheless, the pattern seems to have added the "other half" to the symmetrical distribution of hunter-gatherers who are primarily dependent upon terrestrial animal resources. The pattern provided here is an overall distribution of wealth-differentiated cases that forms a nearly perfect diamond shape with a vertical axis centered on the packing threshold.

Figure 11.15 contains even more interesting patterning, however. Among those groups in which differences in wealth contribute to status differentiation, there is a huge bias in the types of resources that are exploited. Among the cases in figure 11.15 that are not packed and may be considered specialized (i.e., having a subsistence diversity value of less than 71.75 and located in segment C of the graph), nine are dependent upon aquatic resources and three exploit terrestrial animals but are also heavily dependent upon aquatic resources. *All of the groups that are packed and specialized are also dependent upon aquatic resources.*

In contrast, among groups that primarily exploit terrestrial plants, all cases with wealth differentiation have both a diversified diet and population density levels that are considerably beyond the packing threshold (segment A). These groups also have large GROUP2 units, secret societies, and some age grading. Leaders are primarily responsible for arranging intergroup events, providing hospitality to visiting dignitaries, and coordinating activities among families in the residential group. Leaders in this setting are more like "headmen" who have increased corporate responsibilities and expanded roles in a social environment in which wealth and its display are important.

In groups that are primarily dependent upon aquatic resources, leaders can assume two different kinds of roles. Achieved leadership status is a function of exceptional performance in subsistence activities and is associated with technological and tactical sophistication. Such men usually act as hosts at social events occurring in the men's house or they organize "inviting in" feasts. Wealth in this context is usually a correlate of success. The other kind of leadership is inherited, and persons in this position act as the head of a sib or

lineage, a "house," or some other social unit associated with the exploitation of "owned" locations for obtaining resources. In this situation, wealth is once again correlated with productivity, but it is now maintained by limitations that are placed on access to resource locations. It appears that

---
Proposition 11.17

Wealth differentials can result either from (1) differences in the skill and consistency of individual performance among those involved in food production or (2) efforts that increasingly monopolize access to locations with productive resources by restricting access to them based on kinship conventions. In context (1), non-density-dependent wealth differentiation can occur at any time. Context (2) is density-dependent and occurs only under packed conditions.

The dynamics described in proposition 11.17 represent a good example of the rule of thumb that the same things can be organized differently and that different things can be organized similarly. That this proposition is realistic is supported by the data displayed in figure 11.18, in which the marker distinguishes between hunter-gather cases in terms of the form their ownership of resource locations assumes.

First, it should be pointed out that overall there is a greater interest in ownership among groups in which wealth is important than among generic hunter-gatherer cases. In fact, only 7 of the 102 cases that are not packed have ownership codes of 3 or 4. Without exception, these cases either were documented after they had experienced considerable decline in their population levels during the colonial period or represent resettled, remnant populations that were not living in their original homelands. In any case, I suspect that both types of groups differed significantly from their aboriginal ancestors. Of the total of 156 generic hunter-gatherer cases, only 18 had ownership codes of 3 or 4, whereas among groups with wealth differentiation 48 of the 79 groups had developed institutions of ownership.

Perhaps of greater interest is the concentration of cases with a code of 4 (elite ownership of resource locations) in the distribution of specialized cases represented in the lower right graph segment. All of these packed groups are dependent upon aquatic resources and have a subsistence diversity factor of less than 71.75. In addition to a huge bias in favor of elite ownership of resource locations, the second germane observation relative to the cases illustrated in figure 11.15 is that those with high subsistence diversity values and the highest population densities are most often groups that are dependent upon terrestrial plant resources. Most of these groups have a classification code of 2 on the scale of ownership of resource locations. The high subsistence diversity values of groups in the code 3 category are conditioned by considerable sec-

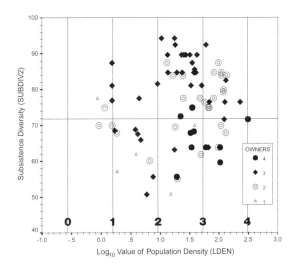

FIGURE 11.18

Property space map defined by subsistence diversity and $\log_{10}$ values of population density displaying only wealth-differentiated hunter-gatherer cases. Cases are coded for ownership of resource locations (OWNERS): (1) no ownership reported; use rights recognized by others; (2) the local group claims exclusive use rights over resource location and residential sites; households may claim special trees and similar features of the landscape; (3) local group claims for hunting areas, dominant animals, fishing sites, and animal drive locations; such claims administered by a group leader, but smaller segments may claim exclusive access to resource locations; and (4) elite ownership of land and resources.

ondary use of aquatic resources. These patterns support the view that the structure of aquatic resource access windows and their probable links to technology greatly affect monopolistic access strategies, so it is reasonable to conclude that

Generalization 11.19

When hunter-gatherers respond to packing by concentrating their subsistence efforts on aquatic resources, increasingly monopolistic control over resource locations is expected. On the other hand, when the response to packing is increased dependence upon terrestrial plants, the ownership of resource locations—when it occurs—is vested in units that are much smaller than GROUP2 units.

With regard to the conditions associated with wealth differentiation summarized in proposition 11.17, I suggest that

Proposition 11.18

When wealth differentiation occurs within nonpacked systems, it results primarily from differential participation by individuals in subsistence pursuits owing to age or

health status and secondarily from differences in performance, given normal, labor-based sharing among producers. In this situation, wealth differentials arise because productive individuals attract followers and, when groups are mobile, there are limits on how large they can become.[18]

Under these conditions, wealth is primarily a matter of comparison between GROUP2 units, and therefore much of the character of nonegalitarian societies is manifest between such units. On the other hand, in systems in which monopolies are maintained by ranking persons in terms of their kinship distance from, for instance, an original settler at a place or the first ancestor to learn how to build larger salmon traps at a given location, one would expect wealth differentiation not only between GROUP2 units but also within them.

Given the provocative results of group size comparisons among generic hunter-gatherer cases in figure 11.14, graphs A and B, a reexamination of the data on GROUP2 size for ranked and wealth-differentiated cases is presented in figure 11.19, graphs A and B, in the hope of determining why there is such a strong bias toward ownership of resource locations by elite leaders in hunter-gatherer groups that are aquatic specialists. From a comparison of graph A in both figures, it is clear that the distribution of generic cases in figure 11.14 is elaborated in figure 11.19, and as density increases GROUP2 size gets smaller once the packing threshold is crossed.

In another array of cases, the pattern is reversed and increasing GROUP2 size is correlated with increases in population density. Twelve cases or 63 percent belong to the latter grouping, which exceeds the scalar threshold, while decreasing group size occurs in only seven or 37 percent of the cases. Of the twelve cases, ownership is developed to the level of codes 3 to 4 in only four (33.3 percent) of the cases, whereas among the smaller GROUP2 units, only two (28.6 percent) of the cases have ownership codes of less than 3 to 4. This pattern suggests that at the GROUP2 level, ownership is most evident when units are small.

It should be recalled that, among generic cases, dependence upon aquatic resources was associated with a regular pattern of minor reduction in GROUP2 size with no response to the packing threshold. In contrast, large GROUP2 size was observed in hunter-gatherer cases that I knew had been misclassified and should have been designated as "special case" GROUP3 units. I have already noted that there are important substantive differences between these two types of aggregations. GROUP2 units create integrative networks for food sharing and subsistence risk reduction, whereas GROUP3 units aggregate periodically and coordinate networks that articulate marriage and educational responsibilities. Within both

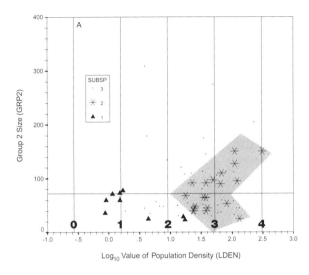 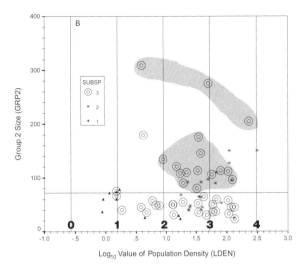

FIGURE 11.19

Subsistence-based comparative property space plots featuring only wealth-differentiated hunter-gatherer cases. Property space is defined by GROUP2 size relative to the $\log_{10}$ value of population density. Comparison is between groups primarily dependent upon terrestrial (A) and aquatic (B) resources. Cases are coded for the primary source of food (SUBSP): (1) terrestrial animals, (2) terrestrial plants, and (3) aquatic resources.

sets of cases with an aquatic specialization, however, there was a decrease in group size associated with increased population density.

The pattern in figure 11.19, graph B, resembles the distribution of egalitarian cases and features a minor reduction in group size with increased population density. Smaller group size appears to be independent of dynamics that are activated at the packing threshold. There are two clusters of cases with larger group sizes that also experience a reduction in size as population density increases. Of the three cases in the upper part of the distribution, the Tareumiut whale hunters of Point Barrow, Alaska, are distinctive because of their single-settlement ethnic group, and one could say they represent another instance in which the members of a GROUP3 unit now reside together permanently.

Two other interesting cases—the Wenatchi and the Wishram—are from the Columbia River drainage, which becomes a focal point for regional aggregations during the annual salmon runs upriver to spawning sites. The human aggregations that are distributed along the river to capture and process salmon are not really GROUP3 units, but neither are they normal GROUP2 units. They resemble the Tareumiut in that they are essentially one-village ethnic units, but the big difference is that the Wanatchi and Wishram welcome all who choose to come to their ethnic territory during the salmon runs. In contrast, the Tareumiut maintain their ethnic identity by excluding not only visitors but also residents who leave the village from participating in the integrated activities of the local community. Relatives and trading part-

ners from other communities are welcome to visit, but they are guests of individual residents and are not integrated into the structure of activities within the settlement.

The larger cluster in graph B of figure 11.19 is composed of eleven groups with GROUP2 units of moderate size. These include (1) the Eskimo village of Point Hope, which is similar to the Tareumiut; (2) the Eskimo of St. Lawrence Island, who are also similar to the Tareumiut but have a number of different settlements; (3) the contemporary Kuskowagmut, whose communities are artificially aggregated around established churches; (4) the Hupa and Tolowa of northern California; and (5) five Salish-speaking groups—the Quileute of Oregon and the Chehalis, Puyallup, Squamish, and Thompson. A single Australian case, the Tjapwurong of southwestern Victoria, adds a keystone to the list.[19]

None of these cases responds to crossing the packing threshold with anything other than an unrelenting reduction in group size as population density increases. There appear, however, to be four different scales of village size, which I have tried—with little success—to relate to most of the more than 100 coded ethnographic variables. There are autocorrelations, to be sure, but the obvious patterned relationships are between subsistence diversity and population density. Given this experience, I am reminded of the pattern recognition work in chapter 8 that examined relationships in the male-female division of labor (MDIVLAB) and polygyny as a strategy for increasing the female labor force. It occurs to me that these two variables may well make important contributions to an understanding of wealth-differentiated peoples, as outlined in the following scenario:

<hr>

Scenario 11.03

Another feature to be considered when thinking about the relationship between division of labor and polygyny is the coordination of male and female labor during the bulk processing of food for storage (proposition 8.09). In such a situation, temperature determines the time that is available for processing many meaty foods. The higher the temperature, the more imperative it becomes to process food resources at the same time that they are being procured. When groups establish simultaneous labor parties, the males are usually involved in procurement and the females in processing.

<hr>

If males can obtain huge quantities of fish using dams, weirs, or nets, the translation of large bulk returns into usable food is a function of the time that elapses between procurement and the onset of spoilage. Other things being equal, the duration of this temporal window is a function of the size and skill of the female labor force.

Another consideration is that most groups that are dependent upon fish and shellfish do not obtain the basic raw materials for making clothing from their major food resource. The use of nets and storage baskets, as well as baskets for transporting processed foods to their final storage places, increases the importance of adequate supplies of fiber. Obtaining materials for the manufacture of clothing, nets, and baskets—and the manufacturing process itself—is usually the responsibility of the female labor force when aquatic resources are the primary sources of food.

The limitations on the accumulation of large quantities of meaty foods, as well as their stabilization through processing and storage for consumption in the future, can be seen as a triangle, with outside temperatures and humidity, the size and performance of the male labor force, and the size and performance of the female labor force as its three angles. Under conditions of easy accessibility to meat-yielding species, the colder the outside temperature is at the time of meat procurement, the less the female labor force will influence the scale of the delivery of meat into storage. Limitations on availability will rest with the performance of the male labor force and fluctuations in resource accessibility.

On the other hand, the warmer and more humid the local conditions become, the more the pattern will reverse and the performance of the female labor force will increasingly become the limiting factor in the delivery of meaty foods into storage. This will be true regardless of the quantities in which one or more species are accessible for exploitation by males. If the rate of procurement far exceeds the rate at which items can be processed and rendered into storage, then the males must either slow their procurement rate or

become increasingly involved in processing. In either case, limitations on the quantity of food delivered to storage rest with the female labor force, and this is increasingly true if the access window for procuring resources in large numbers is relatively short.

One suspects that in warmer and warmer settings, regardless of the quantities in which terrestrial animal and aquatic resources are available, they will not be selected for long-term storage. If pressures to intensify force hunter-gatherers to adopt a storage strategy, other species—particularly terrestrial plants—will become the stored resources because animal resources (either terrestrial or aquatic), even though more abundant, are very likely to spoil.

<hr>

Generalization 11.20

The problems associated with attempting to store aquatic resources and meat in warm and humid settings probably favor productive specialists who fish daily for small yields and then distribute or sell their products to a particular set of customers. In more packed settings, markets are at least partially a response to the necessity for a structure to facilitate the prompt distribution and consumption of fragile food resources.

<hr>

I have calculated an equation from data obtained by Lynch and Poole (1979:220) that could well be germane to the problem of identifying the environmentally limited zones of highest storage potential for meaty resources. I refer to it as the *codfish equation* because it defines the relationship between temperature and the number of days that a codfish would remain edible prior to spoilage, if the only sources of pathogens were the fish itself and those it has accumulated while in the aquatic medium. If the fish has been cleaned and processed in any way, the time would be shortened by the risk of contamination from handlers, insects, and rodents, which are the common sources of salmonella that—together with *Clostridium botulinum,* the source of botulism poisoning—should account for most episodes of microbial contamination.

(11.02)

$$Y = \exp(a + bx)$$

where
$$\exp = 2.71829,$$
$$Y = \text{number days between catch and spoilage},$$
$$x = \text{ambient temperature},$$
$$a = 2.7725887,$$
$$\text{and } b = -0.13862944.$$

The graphs in figure 11.20 demonstrate the results of solving equation (11.02) using the mean temperature at the beginning and end of the growing season (ET). I chose this variable because food resources selected for storage are usually obtained near or at the end of the growing season. On the y axis, the variable CODAY represents the number of days that are likely to elapse between the procurement of fresh cod-

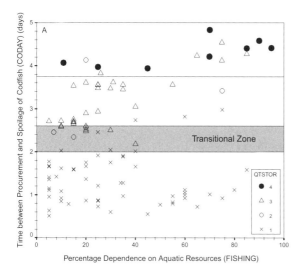

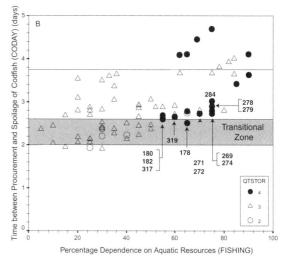

FIGURE 11.20

Comparative property space plots for generic, wealth-differentiated, and internally ranked hunter-gatherer groups. Property space is defined by the number of days between procurement of fish and the onset of spoilage and the percentage of the diet obtained from aquatic resources. Cases are coded for the quantity of food stored (QTSTOR): (1) no regular storage or minor, very-short-term storage of two or three days; (2) moderate investment in storage in both quantity and period of potential use; (3) major investment in storage and in the duration of anticipated use; and (4) massive investment in storage from the standpoint of both species stored and the duration of use.

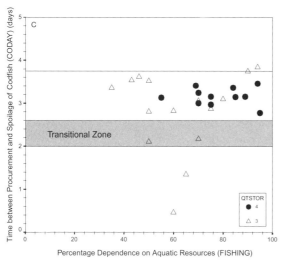

fish and the onset of spoilage, given ET values at the end of the growing season. On the *x* axis, a group's dependence upon aquatic resources, calculated in percentages, is arrayed.[20] The marker represents hunter-gatherer cases in terms of the quantity of food stored, but it refers to all foods and not just fish or other aquatic resources that we might be interested in learning about, given the preceding context.[21]

I have added reference lines to the *y* axis of all three graphs in figure 11.20 to indicate critical thresholds in the CODAY variable. For instance, the line at the 2.0-day point marks the transition between no storage and the appearance of minor storage of foods. The line at 2.6 days is the upper boundary of a temporal period beginning at 2.0 days in which—in the majority of hunter-gatherer groups—less than 30 percent of the diet comes from aquatic resources. The 2.6-day boundary also appears to mark the transition to regular dependence upon stored foods, although above this line aquatic resources usually constitute less than 45 percent

of the diet. The line at 3.75 days indicates a transition to heavy dependence upon storage and, in many cases, very heavy dependence upon aquatic resources.

When I compare the distribution of generic hunter-gatherers in figure 11.20, graph A, to the plot of wealth-differentiated hunter-gatherer cases in graph B, it is clear that almost all of the groups in the latter graph occur in environments at or above the 2.0-day line on the CODAY axis. There are many cases above the 2.6-day line, beyond which aquatic resources make up most of the diet, and these are also the cases with the maximum dependence upon stored foods. The groups clustered just above the 2.6-day boundary include the Hupa, Karok, and Tolowa of California and more northern groups of Salish speakers from along the coasts of Oregon and Washington, as well as interior peoples from the Frazier and Columbia River drainages. These groups include the Alsea, Chehalis, Chinook, Quileute, Quinault, Stalo, Twana, Wenatchi, and Wishram. This rather tight cluster of cases is distinctly out of place when compared with the generic hunter-gatherer groups for whom heavy dependence upon storage only occurs in settings with greater than 3.75 days between procurement and storage.

These patterns reinforce my earlier supposition that dependence upon aquatic resources is associated with density-dependent conditions but, more importantly, that the interval between procurement of resources and spoilage is very much less when groups rely increasingly on aquatic resources that are processed for storage. The groups in figure 11.20, graph B, are, of course, the hunter-gatherer cases with wealth differentials and polygamous privileges for the elite. For some heads of elite houses, these prerogatives are linked to the custom of "debt slaves" and "half-marriages," thereby providing these leaders with more labor—particularly female labor—to devote to resource extraction and preservation (for a good description see Gould 1978c:129–33).

Proposition 11.19

When, for any given group, packed conditions reduce the number of access locations at which critical resources can be obtained—which occurs frequently with high-yielding aquatic species—and this condition is linked to exclusionary tactics for reducing the scale of kin-based access to productive locations, the means for expanding the "legitimate" labor force at these locations is also dramatically reduced. Increasingly restricted ownership results in a labor crunch, particularly when access is being restricted to locations that provide crucial bulk resources for storage.

I am suggesting that

Proposition 11.20

The linkages between labor and ownership monopolies over resource-yielding venues form the basis for still further differentiation in social ranking through generational dilution that reduces the number of elites and increases the number of marginalized, disenfranchised persons (sometimes referred to as "slaves") in a society.

The ranked cases in graph C of figure 11.20 are located in higher latitudes, where colder temperatures mean that more time can elapse between procurement and the onset of spoilage. In these settings, processing can be extended over three to four days, so the demand for labor is less intense than when resources are processed at lower latitudes where food spoils more quickly. In regions with groups of ranked hunter-gatherers, the primary fish that is prepared for winter storage is the chum salmon, which tends to run in late fall. The heaviest investment of labor is, however, required by the

eulachon, which becomes available in February and March, when it is exploited for its oil, which is used as a condiment for lean dried fish.[22]

These two types of hunter-gatherers differ in other significant ways, such as warfare, which is much more prevalent among ranked hunter-gatherer groups than among groups with wealth-based distinctions. The size of winter villages is much larger among ranked groups and the level of complexity related to scale effects is much greater. Diet breadth is also much greater. The differences between these types of cases are directly related to conditions other than small group size and may have more to do with increased segmentation and decreased mean sizes. Among those groups who have crossed the packing threshold and now have differences in wealth but not ranking, strong ownership claims are asserted. Because of smaller group sizes, however, there are often difficulties mobilizing the labor corps needed for resource processing.

In my opinion, the comparative study of these cases may provide further clues to the causes of internal differentiation and ranking. It is, however, safe to say that cases with developed ranking are more complex in response to complications arising from scalar changes, regional competition, and the increased instability that results from greater exploitation of aquatic resources.

Conclusion

Perhaps the most important conclusion from this exploration of the conditions associated with the emergence of complexity is that complexity appears to take two different forms. One is associated with scalar changes in group size as, for example, among hunter-gatherers who are primarily dependent upon terrestrial plants and have the highest values for population density. In these groups, increased complexity is represented by secret societies and social differentiation based on an individual's progress through a series of age-graded sodalities.

These societal structures are also embedded in a social fabric that features the ownership or unchallenged association of persons with specific, highly productive locations for resource exploitation. Intensification is apparent in the increased labor inputs required at the time of harvest and preparation for storage, as well as during the food processing required for immediate consumption. This pathway to intensification is associated with decreased dependence upon terrestrial animals of large body size and a shift of male labor into roles previously assumed by female laborers, particularly the collection and processing of plant materials.

At the same time that group size increases, there is an institutionalization of regular regional interactions among the growing communities. Round-robin hosting and mutual participation in mortuary rites and educational events are major expressions of the development of regional, institutionalized interaction, as are moieties, which perform complementary functions that crosscut at least some of the residential units. This is well illustrated by many of the California hunter-gatherer groups, although there are differences between groups from the southern and northern regions. In northern California, in addition to more intensified exploitation of plant resources, greater niche breadth is possible because of abundant aquatic resources.

When I think about all of the different factors that contribute to variability among hunter-gatherer groups, I am impressed with how much the character of the subsistence base has contributed to my explorations. This megavariable is of paramount importance to a consideration of the appearance of more complex social forms. I have already suggested that complex forms arise from processes of internal intensification that are primarily related to density-dependent shifts and the synergistic interaction of limitations and changed potentials. Some of these were suggested in the preceding discussion of the causal contexts of the appearance of wealth differentiation and institutionalized ranking.

The resources exploited at the time that density-dependent pressures to intensify are first detected are fundamental, not only to the character of subsequent responses but also, apparently, to how the responses further condition the character of the society that emerges. Internally ranked and ultimately stratified societies do not just appear at the end of a linear trajectory toward complexity. These characteristics are not diagnostic of large hunter-gatherer groups, at least not initially. The contrast between, on the one hand, large soci-

eties that lacked internal ranking and council-based decision making and, on the other, internally ranked and socially stratified societies that were more dependent upon aquatic resources was noted among horticultural societies in the Virginia–North Carolina region over forty years ago (Binford 1964, 1991b:65–127).

The similarities between the horticulturists of the eastern seaboard of North America—with their secret societies, age grades, and multicommunity networking—and the social institutions of plant-dependent hunter-gatherers of California—and even the Pueblo people of the American Southwest (Johnson 1997)—strongly suggest that these organizationally diverse societies had been subjected to similar kinds of density-dependent changes and that the result was even greater diversity. This point is emphasized by the regionally complex systems within which many of the equatorial mutualists participate and that are not really perceived as complex within their specialized social units.

Julian Steward (1955:11–29) was correct in his expectation that causal processes could result in different organizational trajectories. The attempt to identify adaptive variation exclusively with diversity and multilinear patterning—and general evolutionary change with a generalized sequence of indicators of sociocultural complexity (Sahlins and Service 1960:ix)—fails in any scientific sense to explain either variability or emergence. This criticism applies as much to the anthropological literature of the 1960s as to more recent examples of linear arguments (Hayden 1995:294), even though the latter are expressed in more humanistic terms. In recent arguments, humanism only drapes soft cognitive cloaks around vitalistic nonexplanations.

CHAPTER
12

The Last Act Crowns the Play

How Hunter-Gatherers Become
Non-Hunter-Gatherers

The pattern recognition studies in this book have taught me many things about hunter-gatherer variability—too many, in fact, for me to be able to summarize them all in this chapter. My goal is less to condense than to expand the scale of generalization so that what has been learned begins to resonate more clearly and to implicate the way in which archaeologists approach the archaeological record. I shift at this juncture to a consideration of the spatial and temporal patterning of different system state conditions, beginning with the recognition of density-dependent thresholds that mark major interruptions in the character of the variability of hunter-gatherer groups.[1]

I have referred to such an investigation and its results as a search for regularities in process. The findings are dramatically summarized in equation (11.01), which organizes the placement of significant thresholds at which major changes occur in the character, complexity, and tactical behavior of hunter-gatherers. The first threshold demarcates the minimum population density that is required before hunter-gatherers can viably occupy a habitat. The second threshold indicates the point at which changes of direction occur among relatively specialized hunter-gatherers who exploit settings with relatively narrow niche breadth, either as aquatic resource or terrestrial animal specialists. Among the former, there is a change in direction toward expanded niche breadth. Among the latter, however, either a similar response occurs *or* there is a shift toward extensification rather than intensification. The basic pattern at this point, however, is unrelentingly in favor of expanded niche breadth, but with certain geographic correlates:

Generalization 12.01

Under conditions of low population density, narrow niche breadth (trophic or biotic specialization) is restricted to regions in which occupation is possible only if aquatic resources are exploited. No viable terrestrial adaptation exists in regions of this kind, examples of which include the high arctic and relatively unique places like the north coast of Chile and the south coast of Peru, where there is no indication that rainfall has occurred in recent geologic time.

On the other hand,

Generalization 12.02

In regions that can support local human populations who exploit exclusively terrestrial resources and in which population density has not yet reduced mobility options to movement within a small foraging area (i.e., areas that have not yet reached the packing threshold), the gross tendency is to increase subsistence diversity as a linear function of the $\log_{10}$ value of population density.

Many changes tend to cluster around the next threshold at a population density of 9.098 persons per 100 square kilometers. This is the point at which the maximum diversity in niche breadth occurs among known hunter-gatherers. It is also where a reversal occurs in many trends that were characteristic of hunter-gatherers in lower-density regimes who used mobility as their primary means to adjust the demands for food to the sequencing and differential spatial clumping of needed resources. At this packing threshold, mobility as the basic adaptive strategy underlying hunter-gatherer subsistence security disappears and many patterns emerge as populations continue to increase in density. Niche diversity is reduced at the high end of the variability spectrum at the same time that specialization also tends to disappear among generic hunter-gatherers. Beyond this point, there are no cases of hunter-gatherers who are primarily dependent upon terrestrial animals.

434

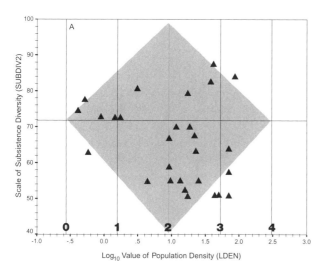
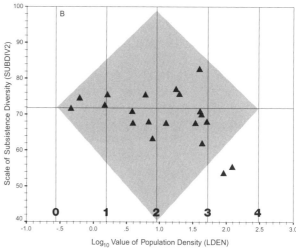

FIGURE 12.01

A two-graph property space comparison of the distribution of mutualists and forest product specialists (A) and groups practicing some horticulture (B).

I strongly suspect that the packing threshold identifies what has been called a point of "self-organized criticality" (Bak 1996). This term refers to the transition from a state of relative stability in the patterns of variability among generic hunter-gatherers, which were based on a limited number of tactical accommodations to habitat variability, to a state of greater nonequilibrium that develops as a result of increasing population density that the adaptive tactics used by hunter-gatherers do nothing to arrest.

The thresholds I have just described mark major changes in the character of organized variability among hunter-gatherers, and they describe a curvilinear law, marking points of criticality in the trajectory of evolution among hunter-gatherer systems. Since the cases in my data set were, with very few exceptions, restricted to hunter-gatherers, there is no way to monitor directly the emergence of *non*-hunter-gatherer systems without expanding the sample enormously. I did, however, include cases that, during my analysis, I discovered were non-hunter-gatherer systems in that they appeared to be new forms that had emerged in response to processes of self-organized criticality centered on the packing threshold. These mutualist cases and the few groups who had expanded their niche breadth by adopting horticultural strategies are arrayed in graphs A and B in figure 12.01.

It is known that the majority of the mutualist cases in graph A are packed. The exceptions are all fur trappers from the boreal forests of North America. Almost half of the cases using domesticated animals or plants are not packed, but the majority of these are herders of domesticated reindeer in Siberia. These groups must be considered extensified, since the reindeer were primarily used for transport in aboriginal times (Krupnik 1993:162). Only two of the groups in graph

B subsisting on domesticated plants are not packed and both of these are resettled, remnant North American groups, the Walapai and Yavapai, who had been encouraged by the U.S. government to adopt horticulture on their reservations.

The important characteristic of the patterning in graphs A and B is that, given the conditions specified in proposition 11.05,

---
Generalization 12.03

As packing increases among those groups in which horticulture has been included in the subsistence strategy, there is an increased specialization upon terrestrial plants. The same dynamics affect mutualists and product specialists, with the result that as population density increases beyond the packing threshold—regardless of the products exploited for exchange with patrons, hosts, or employers—dietary specialization upon terrestrial plants increases.[2]

These tendencies toward niche breadth specialization have the effect of breaking up the second pattern—the symmetry in the distribution of cases in the two-dimensional property space—that seemed apparent when the hunter-gatherer cases were examined relative to the dimensions of population density and subsistence diversity (see the nearly perfect, diamond-shaped distribution in figure 11.15). Apparently some subsistence specialists have emerged very quickly from the packing threshold—a pattern that is illustrated by the ranked cases in figure 11.17—a finding that tends to deprive the pattern of wealth-differentiated cases in figure 11.15 of its symmetry along the lower part of the diamond shape.

The other interesting feature of figure 12.01, graph B, is that, among horticulturists, scalar group size thresholds appear to elicit organizational responses similar to those of specialists such as mounted hunters and other hunter-gatherers with relatively high subsistence diversity but no domesticates. Groups in this category include the Pomo of northern and central California and ranked groups from the Pacific Northwest Coast who maintained secret societies and large winter villages. Hints about these conditions occurred previously in generalization 11.04 and proposition 11.06, and I think that it is safe to conclude that

Generalization 12.04

The diamond pattern anticipated in figure 11.11, graph B, and realized in figure 11.13 is not necessarily expected to occur beyond the packing threshold. It has been clearly demonstrated that niche breadth reduction is one response to the obsolescence of mobility as the major means of adjusting consumer demand to the differential spatial distribution of edible products in the habitat during a seasonal cycle, which occurs at the packing threshold.

I expect that a new diamond-shaped pattern may well be forming, centered on the packing threshold and with a subsistence diversity value of approximately 71.75, which represents the new kinds of systems that emerge from the point of criticality when mobility becomes impossible. In addition, the obsolescence of hunting at this point also ensures that more packed cases will necessarily have subsistence diversity values indicative of increased specialization. It must be realized, however, that, as coded in my data set, mutualists, forest product specialists, and horticulturists present something of a problem. If I were to consider horticulture and domesticated animals as new food resources, it would be necessary to calculate the SUBDIV2 value for five rather than the three alternative classes that applied to all the other cases in the hunter-gatherer file.[3] This would have the effect of raising the mean for the subsistence diversity index from approximately 71.75 (a real value of 72.3425) to approximately 84.56, which would lead me to expect the diamond-shaped pattern to translate upward as the new suite of systems appeared.

Assuming a recalculation with five classes of subsistence, the upward translation would probably take many of the horticultural, mutualist, and forest product specialists out of the specialist range illustrated in figure 12.01. On the imaginary new graph, only hunter-gatherer cases with ranked social classes would remain as unambiguously specialized cases.[4]

Proposition 12.01

Reasonable responses to packing and the obsolescence of subsistence-oriented mobility would include

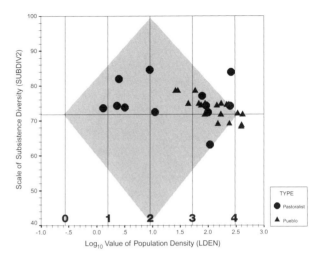

FIGURE 12.02

A property space plot identical to that of figure 12.01 but displaying non-hunter-gatherer cases represented by Pueblo groups from the American Southwest and pastoralist groups from several locations.

shifts to horticulture and pastoral pursuits. Such shifts should not define new property space diamonds, or even new forms of patterning. Instead, the new emergent forms should share the same property space as the modified hunter-gatherers themselves. A pure hunter-gatherer response to packing is in no way a necessary, linear antecedent to horticulture or to increased reproductive management of animals, but—like the latter—is a direct response to packing in different settings. It is also suspected that some habitat-related biases would favor differential responses to packing by emergent non-hunter-gatherers.

Confirmation of the expectations in proposition 12.01 is provided by figure 12.02. In this graph, data from Pueblo peoples dependent upon domesticated plants, as well as a number of pastoralist systems, are plotted on a property space graph defined by hunter-gatherer cases. The full implications of the provocative pattern are not immediately clear. For instance, many recent discussions that refer to the "origins of agriculture" or the "origins of pastoral systems" have tended to imagine specific, linear, formal properties of hunter-gatherers as necessary preconditions for the emergence of non-hunter-gatherer life ways.

These discussions begin with the fundamental premise that early cultivation and other activities leading to the domestication of plants and animals were uniquely new and that therefore a unique explanation—a history—is both demanded and expected. If, however, what I have learned about hunter-gatherers is correct and the packing threshold defines the denouement of the fundamental strategies of hunting and gathering—particularly as residential mobility becomes obsolete as a positioning strategy for obtaining food—then as all hunter-gatherers crossed the packing threshold they were equally "on the edge of chaos," or, more appropriately, in a state of criticality at that threshold.

As I have already suggested, almost half of the known hunter-gatherer adaptations are, in fact, *postpacking adaptations,* and this is especially true of all of the cases referred to as "complex hunter-gatherers" and "mutualists." There is a zone of minor overlap between the packing threshold and the third density-related threshold in which both generic and complex hunter-gatherers are found—with some complex hunter-gatherers maintaining their way of life until the fourth threshold—but those cases overlap in terms of population density and subsistence diversity with the Pueblo peoples of the southwestern United States (figure 12.02).

I have argued that the heavy bias in favor of aquatic resource dependence among already-packed hunter-gatherer groups relates to the particular spatial characteristics of the access locations from which foods may be extracted from aquatic biomes. Reduced mobility has a very different impact on groups that are dependent upon aquatic resources by forcing them to a more specialized adaptation in settings in which aquatic productivity is high. I expect that specialization in this context results in increased instability, but it is considerably less than would be experienced by specialists exploiting terrestrial animals, who would be unable to continue hunting once they had crossed the packing threshold. The domestication of terrestrial plants and animals is primarily a terrestrial response, although there are some exceptions, such as wet rice farming, which is linked to an aquatic biome. Nevertheless, the vast majority of the hunter-gatherer groups that are discussed in the context of the origins of agriculture turn out to be groups focused on the intensification of terrestrial species. I also expect that most cases of "primary" domestication will represent packing responses by terrestrially adapted peoples.

EMERGENCE IN THE CONTEXT OF OTHER
CONTEMPORARY VIEWS OF CHANGE

Many years ago, I invested considerable time and energy in learning about the archaeological sites for which claims about the first exploitation of domesticated species were made (Binford 1968). After that early immersion in data and supporting arguments, I kept up with the subject less attentively. Recently, I thought that it would be interesting to see how thirty years of work by other dedicated researchers had changed what is known about the past and the important issues surrounding agriculture's origins.

I scoured the library, combed through bibliographies, ordered books, made copies of journal articles, and began to build a wall of research materials around my desk. I read about many new sites, better field methods, potentially fruitful collaborations between pollen specialists, climatologists, authorities on phytoliths and macroplant materials, and taphonomists. I was impressed by the vast number of new archaeological observations that had accumulated since my initial research in the late 1960s.

I discovered that chronologies have been refined and more extensive information about site structure and settlement systems has been made available. But, as the initial thrill of all the new observations began to fade, I felt a growing detachment and intellectual disappointment taking its place. I had so eagerly anticipated a new understanding, a new enlightenment about the causes of change in organized life ways that are documented prior to, during, and after the shifts to cultivation agriculture and pastoralism.

Disappointment accompanied my gradual realization that the new observations and the more highly defined patterning had not produced much change in the ideas of causal process that were being debated and accommodated to these new data. Environmental change, population pressure, and little scenarios about rational human responses to various situational stimuli—such as rich resources or dwindling food supplies—seemed old hat and indicated that not much intellectual change had occurred during the past three decades. It depressed me that archaeologists seemed no closer to having an explanatory theory of intensification than they had been in the 1960s.

After examining the contemporary research, I realized that one idea—population pressure—is discussed by everyone, even by me in this book. It should be clear, however, that in my view—which I will label "the processual position"—population pressure (as it is usually conceived) probably does not contribute very much to an understanding of the appearance of horticulture and other adaptive changes. This is not to say that demographic variability is not important or that density-dependent demographic conditions are not central to the issue. It is not necessary here to revisit my argument about the packing threshold because I have already dealt with this particular preoccupation of contemporary researchers, and I can therefore move on to several other contemporary postulations that can be critiqued by relevant knowledge already presented in this book. I have singled out for comment four statements about alleged causes or preconditions of the origins of agriculture that are prominently featured in the contemporary archaeological literature:

1. Sedentism as a cause or necessary precondition (Price and Gebauer 1995:6,8; Smith 1995:211; Watson 1995:37).
2. Environmental richness as a necessary precondition to the adoption of horticulture (Hayden 1995:282–83; Price

and Gebauer 1995:7,8; Smith 1987:37).

3. The importance of assumptions about the prior hunter-gatherer subsistence base as both a "cause" and an initial condition (Bar-Yosef and Meadow 1995:50).

4. Environmental change as a fundamental causal agent or at least a subsistence destabilizer (Bar-Yosef and Meadow 1995:68).

What does my research into variability among hunter-gatherers—the systemic context out of which horticultural and pastoral systems arose—contribute to the discussion of these four explanatory postulations?

Reduced Mobility and Sedentism: Cause or Effect?

Many persons writing about hunter-gatherers have tended to think of mobility as the "soft underbelly" of the foraging way of life. Such a viewpoint frequently assumes that mobility is eventually abandoned because hunter-gatherers finally appreciate the obviously superior way of life that sedentism facilitates.[5] It is argued that sedentism is the stimulus for intensification as well as the basis for increasing rates of population growth that further accelerate the intensification process (Harris 1990:19–28, 1996:557). Implicit in most of the recent arguments citing Harris's work is an assumption that sedentism is a "better" or more economical approach to living.

This vitalistic, progressive view must give way to the warranted understanding of the causes of reduced mobility and, ultimately, sedentism demonstrated in chapter 11. I have clearly shown that hunter-gatherers living at population densities below the packing threshold vary in their group sizes, subsistence bases, patterns of mobility, and labor organization, and they may live in a wide variety of habitats. None of these groups, however, whose populations are below the packing threshold are sedentary. Even among those groups that have exceeded this threshold, few are fully sedentary unless they are aquatic specialists.

After packing occurs and mobility is severely constrained, affected groups position their labor units adjacent to resources, and their sites are usually organized in terms of residential units. Prior to reaching the packing threshold, there are only two contexts in which hunter-gatherers are engaged in very little intraseasonal residential mobility. The first is exemplified by Eskimo peoples who are primarily engaged in aquatic resource exploitation with a particular emphasis upon sea mammals. The second applies to those plant-dependent people who live in low-productivity settings and are dispersed into social units of minimum size (e.g., the dry season settlements of the G/wi). Otherwise, mobility appears to be the mechanism for ensuring accessible foods year-round among hunter-gatherers whose populations are below the packing threshold, regardless of variability in habitat richness or climatic instability.

Constraints on mobility result from intensificational pressures that arise from the presence of increasing numbers of social units within a region. As each new group establishes its own independent subsistence base, there is an automatic reduction in the mobility options that are now available within the region. As mobility becomes less and less feasible, other ways of ensuring subsistence security are required. Sedentism is the end product of intensificational pressures that render residential mobility obsolete as the primary annual or short-term food procurement strategy. It frequently occurs in the context of tactics that localize labor at a particular venue, once packing has occurred. At least with regard to cultivation and horticulture, total sedentism would not be expected until a nearly exclusive investment of labor has been made in a single venue for the production of non-mobile food resources. This means, basically, specialized subsistence from cultivated plants that are localized in a single accessible area. I therefore argue that

---

Proposition 12.02

Sedentism is a response to intensificational pressures, as are such strategies as an increased investment of labor in rendering plants edible, an expansion of the temporal usefulness of food resources by means of storage techniques, the cultivation of plants themselves, and the selection of a limited number of domesticated plants for cultivation. At some scale, all of these strategies result from the same determinant processes; one is not the cause of the other.

Environmental Richness as a Precondition to Horticulture and Pastoralism

I have demonstrated that dramatic changes occur in systems relative to the packing threshold constant of 9.098 persons per 100 square kilometers. There is an analogous point of change in the niche effectiveness index at the $\log_{10}$ value of 1.62 for the ratio between observed population density and the density anticipated by the Terrestrial Model. Changes registered more or less simultaneously relative to the number of times that observed density was divided by the density value stipulated by the Terrestrial Model. Of course, Terrestrial Model densities varied with the accessibility of food in the habitat, so the more people that are anticipated by the model the richer the environment when observed from the perspective of a technologically unaided human actor. Conversely, fewer people were supported in poor habitats.

Major cultural changes in group size, mobility, and technology did not scale with the quality of the habitat but were instead arrayed relative to a sequence of thresholds related to packing at 9.098 persons per 100 square kilometers. The contrast between initial conditions and achieved differences in population density was a more important indicator of major cultural changes than the actual quality of the habitat, which probably only affects the rates at which packing and critical levels of niche effectiveness may occur. Systemic changes and adaptive responses are associated, however, with critical threshold values and not the rates of change per se. This means that

Proposition 12.03

Insofar as the quality of the habitat for human use is related positively to rates of population growth, it might be expected, other things being equal, that indicators of intensification would appear earlier in "optimal" habitats and later in other, less user-friendly settings. The cause of these changes is not population pressure in the traditional sense of the word but packing, which constrains mobility—the primary food-getting strategy among nonintensified hunter-gatherers.

As usual, the use of the phrase *other things being equal* in proposition 12.03 is very important. It is easy to imagine a number of different conditions that could ensure that the demographic state of one group of people relative to the packing threshold might be very different from that of others, even if all groups had identical rates of population growth. For instance:

Proposition 12.04

Since packing is an achieved state that reflects the number of persons in an area rather than the rate of growth at any given time, differences in the length of time that discrete populations resided in a region could produce different levels of packing at any given time, in spite of identical rates of growth. Similarly, identical levels of packing could be found among populations with very different rates of growth, depending upon the length of time that each population had resided in the same region. In this way, founder's effects would constitute one set of processes covered by the *other things being equal* phrase.

It should be clear that, since packing is an achieved state, comparisons between indicators of rates of population growth need not directly reflect the level of intensification of any system.[6] A population whose rate of reproductive growth was nearly zero could be under heavy, density-dependent, intensificational pressure, as could a local population whose range was being infringed upon by an intrusive population (Binford 1968), even if its own rate of growth was very low. It is also important to realize that the timing of the onset of packing pressures is relative to the events and conditions occurring in the regions and land masses adjacent to where a particular group resides.

Generalization 12.05

It has been argued in this book that group size is homeostatically conditioned and that, given population growth, the expected result is increasing numbers of hunter-gatherer groups. In regions with uninhabited land and in which occupation is within the techno-informational scope of the parent population, excess population can be expected to radiate into uninhabited areas. The process of fission would considerably slow the rate at which populations increase and create packed conditions within the subsistence range of the parent population. On the other hand, any condition that would circumscribe the geographic expansion of a growing population, such as the finite size of an island or peninsula—or extreme clustering and concentration of basic resources—would favor constriction of a group's range and reorganization of its annual subsistence cycle. All of these conditions would speed up the packing process and place constraints on new group formation, other things being equal.[7]

The process of intensification is strongly related to habitat variability insofar as it conditions not only differential rates of population growth but also the spatial properties of habitats, as I have already suggested. Given the strong links to habitat variability, it is reasonable to expect that

Proposition 12.05

The temporal sequencing of packing-related events across geographic space should pattern strongly with habitat variability. Other things being equal, packing-related events—as well as other density-dependent phenomena—should appear later in settings that are less conducive to high rates of population growth and more quickly in geotopographic settings such as islands, where there are physical constraints on population expansion.

DIVERSIFICATION THROUGH INTENSIFICATION

Intensification is a dynamic process in which different levels of packing pressure result in different responses in different habitats. Depending upon the initial conditions, in some regions intensification results in increased exploitation of terrestrial plants, while in others an increase in the use of aquatic resources is an analogous response. In fact, adaptational variability is expected to relate rather directly to habitat variability. On the other hand, I have isolated several thresholds corresponding to increases in population density that identify points of major adaptational change among groups who live in very different habitats but experience similar levels of intensificational pressure. These thresholds indicate where many organizational and behavioral parallels are expected to occur among historically independent developmental sequences. These are the flashpoints of change, providing what Steward (1955:11–29) called the parallels between otherwise unrelated sequences, such as the historically independent appearance of domesticated plants in very different places.

One of my first demonstrations of the utility of frames of reference for archaeological research concerned the geographically graded, temporal sequences that provide evidence of the initial appearance of domesticates in Europe (in chapter 6, see "Looking at the Spread of Agropastoralism with Projected Knowledge"). The fit in these sequences between chronology and environmental variables was impressive, and I identified what may be an example of "niche metamorphosis," by which I meant the appearance of something very different or a new niche. At the time that chapter 6 was written, I did not know about the density-dependent thresholds demonstrated in figures 10.03, 10.04, 10.05, 10.06, and 11.01. I had suspected that the appearance of new niches could be rapid, but I did not know about the threshold-related responses to packing and growth in group size that are now so well documented.

I think it can now be reasonably imagined that these geographically graded, temporal sequences do not represent an expansion across Europe of peoples bringing their distinctive languages (Renfrew 1987, 1996) and the "good news" of domesticated plants and animals (Cavalli-Sforza 1996). I think the pattern identified archaeologically is much more likely to represent a graded distribution of differential rates of indigenous population growth in which the disparity is at least partly the result of differences in the length of time that initial human populations were present in central and western Europe. Variability in these two conditions alone could result in a geographically patterned, temporal sequence corresponding to habitat variability and reflecting differences in the timing at which local groups crossed packing and other scalar thresholds!

Proposition 12.06

Geographic patterning in the temporal appearance of tactics and behaviors reasonably viewed as responses to intensification should vary in regular ways with habitat variability. Other things being equal, earlier dates should be associated with "better" habitats and later dates with less optimal habitats.[8] The timing of responses to intensification should also vary with the time that has elapsed since initial human occupation, other things being equal, or with major climatic events that would have depressed the rates of population growth or even resulted in population declines.

Proposition 12.06 instantly directs our focus to the question of what are the "best" habitats for humans. Although I do not address this issue in detail in this book, I have previously made suggestions along these lines (Binford 1983:208–13) and, earlier in this book, I made the following comments:

Proposition 12.07

Other things being equal, "optimum security would be possible in environmental settings with minimal temporal variability in the availability and abundance of potential foods" (proposition 6.01).

Proposition 12.08

Other things being equal, "potential subsistence security will decrease as a direct result of seasonality in primary production stemming from either annual periodicity or long-term variability in rainfall or from reduced concentrations of solar radiation at terrestrial locations" (generalization 6.03, proposition 6.02).

It must be acknowledged, however, that for a habitat to be optimal for human reproductive success more than food resources are required. Other factors that affect differential fecundity and mortality are fundamentally important to a consideration of reproductively optimal habitats. Interesting discussions of these issues are available (Groube 1996; Low 1988, 1990), but, to my knowledge, no convincing modeling of the idea of optimal habitats has been attempted (see, however, Binford 1999).

From my perspective, pathogen diversity is likely to be similar to other patterns of species diversity in general because the reproductive success of pathogens, like that of other species, is regulated by moisture and temperature. For this reason I would expect that

Proposition 12.09

Other things being equal, the greatest disease burden for human beings would be in those settings in which very high and regularly present moisture occurs and where temperatures are unvaryingly high. These conditions would occur in habitats in which actual evapotranspiration was roughly equal to potential evapotranspiration and the latter was very high. The lowest pathogenic disease load would be expected where temperatures were regularly low and where rainfall was low relative to potential evapotranspiration.

If the views summarized in propositions 12.07 and 12.08 are used as approximate guides to modeling the optimal

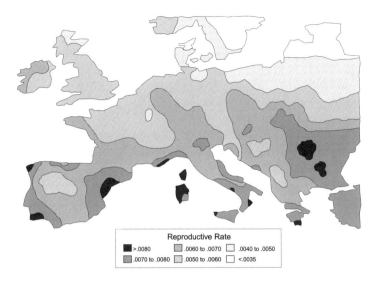

FIGURE 12.03

Isopleth map of western Europe showing modeled reproductive rates. This map is based on weather data from 472 contemporary weather stations distributed across the region.

habitats for humans and are then linked to proposition 12.09, it should be clear that the places that offer optimal security in food resources are likely to overlap only partially with those locations in which there is optimal relief from disease. In fact, it is quite likely that

---

Proposition 12.10

In very dry and very cold settings, the rates of human population growth are primarily food limited. On the other hand, in warm and moist settings, the reinforcing interaction between disease and food limitations ensures that in very-high-biomass, hot, and wet forests rates of population growth are likely to be relatively low.[9]

If the expectations in proposition 12.10 are sustained, the zones of optimal population growth should occur in cool subtropical and warm temperate zones, which would be water stressed at the warm end of that range of environments and, at the cool end, somewhat more water rich. It is certainly possible to imagine a structured distribution that yields different rates of population growth as a function of habitat variability, but it must be kept in mind that such variability, when examined in greater detail, will also vary with initial founding conditions.

Figure 12.03 illustrates the results of using an early-stage model of reproductive rates projected across western Europe, based on data from a total of 472 modern weather stations. It should be said at the outset that the model's projections are constrained by three factors: (1) the necessity of using an incomplete model of reproductive rates, (2) my ignorance of the baseline population levels at the time that biotic conditions initially stabilized, and (3) inadequate information about how the newly stabilized biotic conditions would have affected rates of population growth. The point here, however, is not the accuracy of the modeled values but the issue of initial conditions and the differential buildup of density-dependent causal conditions. It should be clear that there would have been geographic differences in the effect of density-dependent pressures across Europe and that, over time, there should have been corresponding differences in the trajectories of organizational change as well.

Other things being equal, the earliest density-dependent changes should have occurred between Valencia and Barcelona on the southern coast of Spain, as well as in an area (which played a central role in the spread of agriculture into western Europe) centered on the Romanian Plain with extensions into the Hungarian Plain and eastward toward the western shore of the Black Sea. The model projects analogously high rates in Turkey, southern Greece, southern Italy and Sicily, and along the northern coast of the Mediterranean between Genoa and Nice (Liguria). North of the Mediterranean zone, reproductive rates are projected to have declined relatively gradually with increases in latitude. The gradual geographic distribution of archaeological phenomena associated with these early rates of population growth would traditionally have been interpreted as diffusion, and in turn diffusion would have been cited as the explanation for the distribution.

I argue that the rates of change of various cultural phenomena are likely to be contingent upon the interaction of underlying conditioning variables and that so-called diffusion therefore represents patterns that require explanation rather than sets of phenomena that operate independently of underlying processual dynamics. Graded spatial patterns are most likely to represent the consequences of differential temporal sequencing in the forcing effects of causal processes. In the context of this demonstration, the idea of "environmental richness" should take on a different significance. Environments are neither rich nor poor; instead, the interactions between variables affecting the characteristics of habitat space are responsible for different rates of change in the spatial components of adaptive niches.

I have taken some pains to explore the subject of habitat richness as a precondition for the development of cultivation, subsequent horticulture, and pastoralism. To think of "richness" as a property of the environment is simplistic in the extreme since whether or not an environment is considered rich depends very much on one's niche. After all, a rich habitat for a termite would present a primate with poor pickings indeed. If those who appeal to richness are given the benefit of the doubt on this point, however, the problem of localities that are pathogen limited rather than food limited must still be dealt with. Under these conditions, richness would have none of the effects imagined by those who claim it acts as a catalyst in the development of "prestige economies."

The analytical imperative is to isolate the relationships that must exist at critical thresholds between different temporal and spatial distributions, for it is these relationships that force culture change. I would expect societies that are distributed across major geographic regions to cross the packing threshold—and other critical demographic boundaries—at different times. It is also reasonable to expect that human systems in different habitats will become packed at different rates, some quickly and others much more slowly. Those archaeologists who plot the geographic distribution of material traits that I would identify as responses to packing, and then demonstrate a temporal gradient in these traits, and *then* "explain" the pattern as a reflection of either diffusion or migration never address the issue of process and the factors that are responsible for the distribution of such responses to intensification as horticultural or pastoral life ways.

One might ask why populations should unrelentingly radiate into already occupied subsistence ranges, bringing with them a set of techniques that require less space and can feed more people. It is much more likely that horticultural techniques would spread rather rapidly across a region in which strong pressures to intensify are at work. If, on the other hand, groups were not under heavy intensificational pressure, the rates of change in subsistence tactics would be quite slow. This is not to say that there are no situations in which populations might expand quite rapidly into new territory. I have already cited the example of the radiation of the mounted hunters

of the North American Great Plains, for whom an extensificational strategy was made possible by transport technology. But it is possible to envision the appearance of new niches that could result in a relatively rapid dispersion of people into areas that were minimally used or unoccupied by hunter-gatherers.

Hunter-Gatherer Subsistence Base: Initial Conditions

I have repeatedly stressed how much initial conditions contribute to the different trajectories of change that hunter-gatherer systems undergo. I have also taken pains to emphasize that differential rates of population growth are not the only ways in which hunter-gatherer systems differ initially. It should be clear by now that another fundamental difference that directs the course of change for hunter-gatherers is the composition of their subsistence base, particularly the primary resource that is exploited when packing pressure begins to increase. Sadly, many researchers have ignored the issue of dietary initial conditions beyond pointing out that, prior to the appearance of agriculture, human subsistence was based on hunting and gathering. Similarly, in the not too distant past, it was assumed that Pleistocene hunter-gatherers were primarily hunters of large terrestrial animals. One of the longest-lived arguments maintains that environmental changes at the end of the Pleistocene reduced the population levels of animals of large body size (Miller 1992:52) and that hunter-gatherers thereafter pursued a more eclectic, "broad-spectrum" diet.

On the other hand, in regions in which "pristine" agricultural adaptations developed, several researchers have dealt more explicitly with the initial conditions immediately antecedent to the development of agriculture. For instance, Cowan and Watson (1992:209) have observed that "archaic economies dependent upon wild plant foods developed during the early Holocene in each of these areas, and in each area the archaic adaptation was dominated by a few staple species." Similarly, Bar-Yosef and Meadow (1995:50) note that "Most hunter-gatherer diets in middle latitudes and up to 1,500 m above sea level are based on vegetal resources." Clarke (1976) also assumes that the hunter-gatherer societies that became dependent upon cultigens were, initially, predominantly dependent upon plant resources—an expectation that underlies Rindos's (1984) gradualistic scenario of the domestication of plants.

I believe that the pattern recognition studies undertaken in this book can provide a relevant comment on these views. First, packing—or the patterned reduction in subsistence range arising from a regional increase in population—is a universal conditioner of change in both subsistence strategies and the labor base operationalizing them. Changes in these domains are reflected in a group's size and pattern of mobility. I have also shown that technology, gender roles, and the resources targeted for exploitation respond as linked sets to the packing level of a hunter-gatherer system.

The thresholds for the initiation of subsistence shifts occur at different values on the packing or niche effectiveness scales, depending upon the initial conditions associated with the primary source of exploited food resources. Groups that are dependent upon terrestrial animal resources appear to respond to packing pressures at a population density level of 1.57 persons per 100 square kilometers.[10] When population levels of 9.098 persons per 100 square kilometers are reached, the shift away from primary dependence upon animal resources has already occurred and dependence upon either terrestrial plants or aquatic resources has increased correspondingly. This kind of processual understanding renders the frequently cited !Kung "preference" for "reliable" terrestrial plants (Lee 1968:42) not only wrong[11] but also totally irrelevant to the achievement of any realistic understanding of hunter-gatherer variability.

The data from my global sample of hunter-gatherer groups not only correct past inaccuracies but also—when they are used analytically to develop patterns between variables—demonstrate regularities, such as the fact that the packing threshold coincides with changes in both group size and technology, regardless of habitat variability. There are, at the same time, major correlates between hunter-gatherer habitats, exploited food resources, and the technology used to obtain resources (generalizations 10.10 and 10.13, proposition 10.13). The greatest contrast in group size and mobility patterns occurs between groups that are dependent upon terrestrial animal resources and those who exploit terrestrial plants. Linked to these differences is an extreme bias against terrestrial animals as the primary food resource under packed conditions. It can be argued that

Proposition 12.11

Other things being equal, packing results in greater and more drastic changes in group size and mobility patterns among peoples who were initially heavily dependent upon terrestrial animals (generalization 10.10, proposition 10.14). It might be expected that such changes would also be more rapid,[12] and this expectation is justified by the patterning in figure 10.04. This graph demonstrates that, after a threshold of 1.57 persons per 100 square kilometers is reached, GROUP2 size decreases and no cases survive as dependent upon terrestrial animals once the packing threshold of 9.098 persons per 100 kilometers square is reached.

Proposition 12.12

If the shift in food resources is from terrestrial animals to terrestrial plants, certain consequences occur that

seem to ensure greater rates of change per unit of time. First, group size can be expected to decrease and, even if there is no overall change in the regional population level, there will be an increase in the number of economically independent groups in the region. Second, as the shift to increased dependence upon plants occurs, range size will also contract. Insofar as there is a restructuring of the population relative to the patch structure of accessible terrestrial plants—and given the preceding conditions—a retraction of population can be expected from segments of the former range with less accessible plant foods and their concentration at and around the locations where reliable plant foods can be obtained.

The preceding conditions should have the effect of accelerating the consequences of packing, regardless of the role, if any, of population growth per se within the region.

Proposition 12.13

In the case of groups that were originally dependent upon terrestrial animals, the adaptive responses to increased packing that favor a shift from animals to plants accelerate the packing state as a consequence of restructuring to increase plant dependence itself. This "doubling" of effects ensures that the major organizational changes among such systems will occur at a more rapid rate.

On the other hand,

Proposition 12.14

If packing increases in a region occupied by groups dependent upon terrestrial plants and there are no alternative aquatic resources, the only available response is to increase the dependence upon plants. Normally this tactic involves (1) expanding the diet breadth to include species that increase the net return but are obtained less efficiently, or (2) increasing the labor inputs for processing and incurring the costs associated with building and maintaining facilities, including the costs connected with the storage and logistical transport of resources. These tactics will enable groups to gain time and space utility from high-return resource patches. In either case, the labor costs increase with intensification.

Regardless of which choice groups make and their attendant costs, the likelihood of their producing distinctive archaeological patterning is substantial. Groups that were originally dependent upon animal resources go through a two-step process, beginning with rapid change rates that are a consequence of spatial restructuring, which does not necessarily accompany intensification among groups that were originally plant dependent. Changes in subsistence produce dramatically different settlement patterns, as do the newly organized changes in division of labor and group size. I also would expect major changes in technology.

For groups originally dependent upon terrestrial plants, there is only an unrelenting pattern of increasing intensification pressure favoring the extraction of greater net returns from smaller areas that reliably produce plant foods. Technological change may be minimal and settlement patterns should indicate reduced mobility, but the overall pattern of land use may appear to be relatively unchanged.

Using traditional interpretative conventions, archaeologists are likely to infer that the archaeological record produced by a group of hunter-gatherers that is primarily dependent upon terrestrial plants but undergoing an intensification-driven shift to the use of cultivars reflects culture change with continuity. For groups originally dependent upon terrestrial animals, the process begins at much lower population levels but quickly accelerates with intensification. Accompanying the acceleration will be drastic changes in the archaeological record, initially reflecting the major restructuring responses of the shift to plant dependence and, subsequently, to cultivars. If cultivars are accessible from neighboring regions, the change might well be so drastic as to suggest a discontinuity or break with tradition and be interpreted in conventional terms as the replacement of one group by, perhaps, an expanding population.

If, as I have suggested, the group of interest is one in which hunter-gatherers were originally dependent upon aquatic resources, it is very likely that such a subsistence focus is density dependent and therefore represents an earlier response to packed conditions. Particularly in cooler habitats, the initial shift from terrestrial animals in response to intensificational pressures would have resulted in increased dependence upon aquatic resources. As pressures to intensify continue to build and scalar responses become activated, experimentation with cultigens seems to represent a simple technique for expanding niche diversity. Subsequent developments could even be more complicated.

Finally, in some settings with considerable niche breadth, aquatic resources have already been incorporated into the diet as part of the normal increase in niche breadth associated with increased population density prior to reaching the packing threshold (generalization 11.11). Under such conditions, it is unclear exactly what changes might be expected at the packing threshold. I have argued, for instance, that dependence upon aquatic resources is fundamentally a response to packing (propositions 10.14, 10.15, and 10.16), but aquatic resources could also be tapped as part of the stabilizing

increase in niche breadth that some groups experience prior to packing. Based on my ethnographically documented hunter-gatherer sample, this tactic would be expected in settings with unearned water, or where rivers carry water through regions with little rainfall, or where there are substantial internal drainages leading to lakes in otherwise dry settings.

It has also been argued that

Generalization 12.06

Forests tend to offer less accessible food resources than many other types of plant formations, so in well-watered forest settings (generalization 10.12), rivers and streams offer an obvious opportunity to expand niche breadth as population increases prior to packing. Such a strategy would stabilize the system and produce an archaeological record that had continuity in both settlement locations and the basic materials and tactics of adaptation.

Under these sets of conditions, the archaeological consequences of a group's response to the packing threshold are ambiguous, since most of the hunter-gatherers dependent upon aquatic resources in my sample were already packed when they were observed by ethnographers. This led to my argument that dependence upon aquatic resources was a response to packing (propositions 10.15 and 10.16). My assumption still seems justified, since primary dependence is a move toward niche specialization, and, as I have argued, expanding the diet breadth in an aquatic biome is a technology-dependent strategy (generalization 10.18). These cases, however, do not tell us much about settings in which terrestrial food alternatives are complementary to aquatic alternatives rather than, strictly speaking, a substitution of one for the other. For example, figure 12.04 (data from Binford 1964) illustrates that the availability of fish increases in the spring, which is also the period of lowest food accessibility in the terrestrial biome (proposition 6.03).

I have now encountered a situation in which there appears to be a strong bias in the data from ethnographically documented hunter-gatherers. Groups living in packed conditions with a wide niche breadth to which aquatic resources make an important contribution—particularly in forested settings that have a substantial river drainage—are rare in the sample. This seems an excellent opportunity to reason deductively from the patterns I have isolated and the theory I have been building:

Scenario 12.01

In settings with warm to hot temperatures, if packing reduces easy access to foods that are accessible during the least productive phases of the annual cycle of terrestrial resources, the

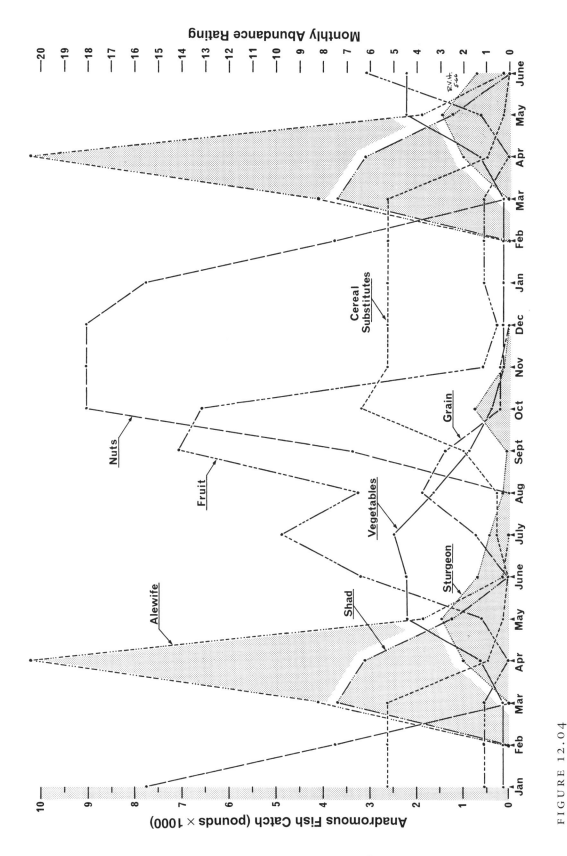

FIGURE 12.04

Yearly cycle of abundance for three species of anadromous fish (as well as plants) in the southern Chesapeake Bay region.

exploitation of aquatic resources—if they are available—will be increased to provide food during that phase of the annual cycle (figure 12.04). If packing has proceeded to the point that there is reduced dependence upon terrestrial animals during the nongrowing season in temperate settings, then the tactical response would be to initiate or increase dependence upon storage. If temperatures are warm during the period in which bulk aquatic resources are accessible or during the storage-dependent months, then there will be a shift to the storage of dried plant seeds to reduce the risk of disease from consuming in warm seasons aquatic products that were processed during cold periods but may now be hazardous to consume (scenario 11.03, equation (11.02), and figure 11.20).

Further increases in population density will force groups to depend increasingly upon terrestrial plants, particularly dried seeds. In this context, a door will open for the inadvertent domestication of plants, as Smith (1995) has argued in the "floodplain weed theory" of domestication. Insofar as domesticated weeds derive from the same habitat as the one exploited by groups that have reached the packing threshold, this step must be seen as an intensificational response. It is, however, one that will not necessarily lead to a truly new niche, since it represents an expansion or restructuring of niche breadth (proposition 11.03) and would have a stabilizing effect rather than bring about change (propositions 11.02 and 11.11). Concentrating subsistence upon floodplain "weeds" would be the functional equivalent of increasing one's labor investment in the removal of toxins from available, but initially inedible, acorns. Such a tactic may increase subsistence security, but it does not necessarily shift a system into a new niche.

Given the patterns that have already been demonstrated, in situations in which aquatic resources represent a narrow niche breadth specialization (generalization 11.08)—which occurs along the coasts in subtropical and temperate zones or in large river systems in northern temperate regions that lack many terrestrial alternatives—one would expect the appearance of settlement hierarchies (proposition 10.04) with "village-hamlet" distributions (Binford 1991b:83) and some social differentiation in terms of wealth (proposition 10.05). Ranking may even occur in such circumstances if post-packing pressures to intensify have been significant (proposition 11.20). Relatively permanent occupancy, substantial houses, and—in large settlements where scalar effects have resulted in integrative institutions—community buildings and prominent constructions might also be expected to occur. All of these conditions, which are often associated with "complex hunter-gatherers," could precede the appearance of cultivation or the exploitation of domesticated animals.

Other things being equal, the "level" of complexity should be a linear function of the $\log_{10}$ values of population density that exceed the packing threshold. The primary qualifier resulting in variability would be increases in storage dependence relative to the length of the growing season (proposition 11.19). The shorter the growing season, other things being equal, the greater the quantity of resources processed for storage must be. As bulk requirements increase, the number of access locations yielding such returns should decrease and the size of the labor force needed to process the resources should increase. These patterns force social differentiation and monopolistic control of access locations.

I cannot emphasize strongly enough the fundamental importance of studying the differences that initial conditions precipitate when a general process is operative across a diversified sample of adaptive responses. A review of the literature discussing the origins of cultivation and the domestication of plants and animals reveals that, in spite of endless arguments against linear evolutionary models, most researchers are in fact arguing that their particular sequence or area of expertise provides the correct model or "theory" of the origins of cultivation and domestication. Intellectually, they are offering an event sequence as a model of process even though an event sequence is simply a pattern in need of explanation. Postulations about dynamics do not equal process.

The term *process* refers to the underlying causal factors that condition dynamics, whereas theories consist of relational statements about the necessary patterns of interaction and synergy among variables that would produce event sequences. It is a common misconception to believe that a single, clear, descriptive event sequence provides a prototype for all examples, but this assumption is simply wrong. Archaeologists should expect a wide range of variability in the paths to cultivation and domestication. Only through comparative study and theory building about underlying processes such as intensification can we even begin to explain the event sequences in the archaeological record and to anticipate when events will and will not happen.

It is not uncommon for archaeologists to argue that an observed change in the archaeological record could be a response to environmental change or population pressure. When these alternatives are appealed to, the term *stress model* is frequently used to label the argument (Hayden 1995:289). I have tried to develop an argument that exposes the explanatory poverty of the population pressure argument by focusing on the process of intensification, in which increases in population density are only one component. Arguments that focus exclusively on population pressure stress food shortages and overexploitation of the food supply, but it should be clear that the packing argument points to limitations on mobility that create population densities that force hunter-gatherers to intensify. Overexploitation of the food supply is conspicuously absent in my argument.

Given the necessary links between the habitat and the fundamental energetic infrastructure of a cultural system, it is hard to imagine that packing or any other aspect of system state conditions would remain unaffected by climatic change. The synergy between changes in climate and human adaptive responses ensures that demographic and climatic dimensions will not act alone, nor will they present themselves as simple alternative causes. It is imperative to understand in more detail the character of the interactive process between habitat change and adaptive response, when the system state is expected to represent a set of varying initial conditions.

Problem 12.01

Anticipating the scale as well as the character of responses to differing degrees of climatic change, given varying initial system state conditions prior to the climatic event, is a theory building challenge.

What Happens When Climates Change?

Although the two most frequently cited "causes" of significant culture change in prehistory are population growth and environmental change, and although objections to the primacy of each of these dimensions of dynamics in causal arguments have been regularly voiced, it has rarely been suggested that progress in developing theories about culture change would result from considering both of these dimensions together. While it is true that changes in weather patterns of some type and at some scale are always occurring, to assume that there is a connection between all instances of climatic and cultural change is short-sighted. On the other hand, it is reasonable to expect that major climatic changes will elicit adaptive responses or, at the very least, destabilize well-established adaptive systems—but how does this work and what actually happens in nature?

Until recently, exploration of the cultural responses that might be expected to occur during periods of climatic change has been a frustrating experience for me. Recently, however, it became possible to apply the results of research by Reid Bryson (1989a, 1989b, 1992, 1997) to archaeological patterning. Bryson and his colleagues at the Center for Climatic Research at the University of Wisconsin (Bryson and Goodman 1980, 1986; Bryson and Bryson 1995, 1997) have developed a method of reconstructing past climates in a high-resolution, site-specific manner. Using the Bryson method,[13] monthly mean estimates of temperature and rainfall are produced for a specific archaeological site or for any location about which longitude, latitude, and elevation are known.[14] These summary monthly mean estimates are generated in two-hundred-year intervals continuously from the present backwards in time to 14,000 B.P., and in five-hundred-year intervals thereafter to 40,000 years ago.

I was very excited when I learned about the Brysons' research, because all of the equations that were developed for the environmental variables presented in chapters 4 and 5, as well as those that project information from the hunter-gatherer variables, depend upon values for mean monthly rainfall, temperature, and elevation. With the Brysons' procedure, I can provide estimates of the habitat variables developed in this book—such as net aboveground productivity, length of the growing season, amount of snow accumulation, and plant biomass—by two-hundred- and five-hundred-year intervals projected 40,000 years into the past. Similarly, it is possible to project summary information about hunter-gatherers not only onto space—using information from present climates (as I did in chapter 6 for Europe and for the earth in chapters 5 and 6)—but also onto climatic sequences at particular places. Doing this provides a picture of how hunter-gatherers *as we know them* would respond to specific climatic changes.

I have chosen to illustrate this capability using data from two locations: (1) Jerusalem, which represents the upland region adjacent to the Dead Sea basin that has been studied by Bar-Yosef and Meadow (1995), and (2) the Zagros region, represented by the site of Zeribar, where available pollen samples have provided clues to past environments in the vicinity of the archaeological sites of Jarmo, Karim, Palegawra, Shahir, and Zarzi. The two graphs in figure 12.05 illustrate the relationships between three different variables at these two locations: (1) potential evapotranspiration (PET), or the total amount of water in millimeters that could be evaporated or transpired if unlimited water was available at the location; (2) mean annual rainfall (CRR), or the total amount of rainfall in millimeters that falls annually; and (3) the amount of rainfall that occurs as runoff in either rivers, lakes, or other bodies of water (RUNOFF) and is lost to the botanical habitat.

On both graphs, three vertical shaded columns represent major glacial episodes at the close of the Pleistocene. The column farthest to the left marks the interstadial episode between stages 3 and 2 of the oxygen isotope glacial sequence. The wide column that occurs between 24,000 and 15,000 years ago identifies the most recent glacial period, which reached its maximum at approximately 18,000 years ago. The third column identifies the Younger Dryas episode, which in the Near East occurred between approximately 11,350 and 10,000 years ago.[15] In the Levant, two other climatic episodes are important in local sequences, and these are identified by short, more lightly shaded columns on either side of the Younger Dryas. In graph A (Jerusalem), these columns are labeled "increasing rain–A," to indicate a climatic regime particular to the Mediterranean Levant, according to Bar-Yosef and Meadow (1995:44).

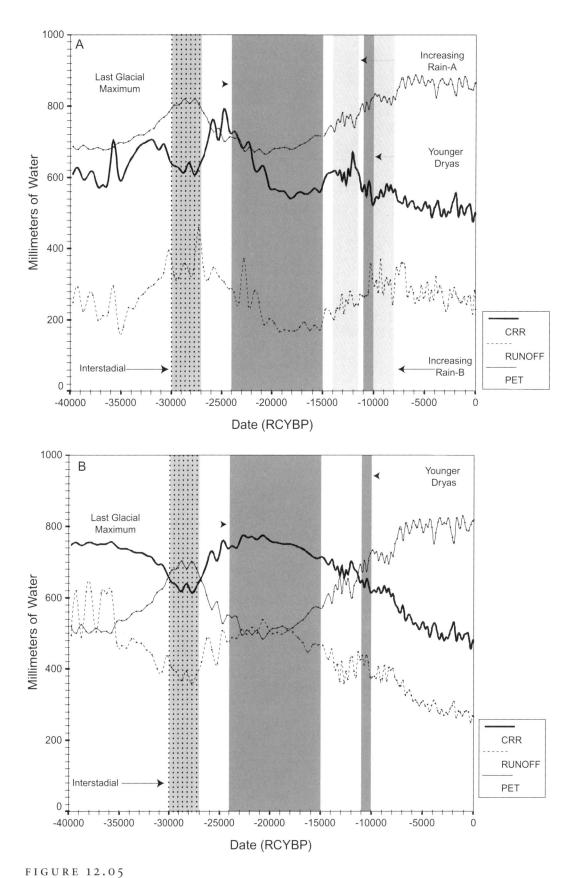

FIGURE 12.05

Paired property space graphs comparing the values of three reconstructed environmental variables at Jerusalem, Israel (A), and Zeribar, Iran (B).

Some of the complexity in the interaction between rainfall and temperature is clearly demonstrated by a comparison of the two graphs in figure 12.05. For instance, there are interesting contrasts between the graphs for the interstadial that occurred between 30,000 and 27,000 years ago. There was a pronounced rise in temperature (PET) at Jerusalem and a corresponding decrease in rainfall (CRR), even though there was an increase in runoff (RUNOFF). This situation appears contradictory but results from a shift to winter rainfall at Jerusalem during the peak of the interstadial. The graph indicates that runoff was greatest at Jerusalem during and immediately following the interstadial, whereas the pattern is reversed at Zeribar, where most runoff occurred during glacial events.

Figure 12.06 provides a further appreciation of how basic variability in weather translates into differences over time in the character of the plant communities at Jerusalem and Zeribar. Perhaps the first notable feature is that the two periods of increased rainfall that are said to have occurred only in the Mediterranean zone of the Levant are shown to have anticipated periods of increased rainfall and runoff at

Jerusalem (figure 12.05, graph A) but did not translate into increased plant productivity at this location! This situation is the result of a simultaneous increase in temperature that actually offset the effects of increased rainfall and resulted in greater evaporation and transpiration per unit of available water and therefore less productivity within the plant community. The difference in millimeters between the PET line and the CRR line on graph A is some measure of reduced productivity.

The importance of these differences is shown by a comparison with figure 12.05, graph B (Zeribar), in which rainfall actually exceeded PET values between 14,000 and 11,400 B.P. and again between 10,000 and 8,000 B.P., after which PET reversed and exceeded CRR by about 95 millimeters of water. These differences in conditions are responsible for the dramatic drop in net aboveground productivity at Jerusalem illustrated in figure 12.06, even though productivity at Zeribar increased throughout the Younger Dryas, except for a dip between 10,000 and 8,000 B.P., when potential evapotranspiration exceeded rainfall.

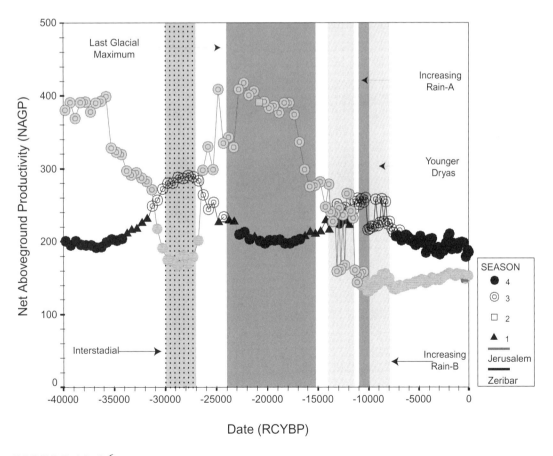

FIGURE 12.06

A property space graph comparing projected net aboveground productivity at Jerusalem, Israel, and Zeribar, Iran, arrayed over 40,000 years. Marker is for season of greatest rainfall: (1) spring, (2) summer, (3) fall, and (4) winter.

The most striking difference in the comparison in figure 12.06 of climatic regimes at Jerusalem and Zeribar concerns the overall climatic pattern, which is almost totally reversed. This means that when productivity in the plant community was high at Jerusalem it was low at Zeribar. Plant productivity at Zeribar was highest during the interstadial and immediately after the last glacial event, but then it dropped regularly between 8,000 and 3,000 years ago. At Jerusalem, plant productivity was highest during glacial events and dropped dramatically during the interstadial. It also dropped dramatically at the end of the "increasing rain–A" period that terminated about 11,400 years ago and signaled the beginning of the Younger Dryas, during which productivity at Jerusalem dropped to its all-time low. At Zeribar, however, productivity was higher during the Younger Dryas than during any other postglacial period.

According to the environmental reconstruction I have presented here, there is little doubt that conditions at Zeribar were very different from those at Jerusalem. In spite of the differences in both sequences, however, gross chronological markers—such as the interglacial, the last glacial maximum, the periods marked "increased rain," and the Younger Dryas—do identify recognizable climatic episodes. In fact, the fit between the episodes that were identified by independent researchers working in the Jerusalem area (Bar-Yosef and Meadow 1995:44) and those produced by reconstructing climatic patterns are quite remarkable, and this congruence encourages a serious consideration of the reconstructed sequences.

Nevertheless, my concern is not with reconstructed environments per se but with the issue of how a knowledge of hunter-gatherers—projected by means of environmentally based equations to the changing climates indicated in the reconstructed sequences—may enlighten us about the archaeological remains recovered from the Near East and any other area. There is also the possibility that, by using the techniques described in this book, new things will be learned by observing how the world that we know responds to condensed climatic changes that neither we nor the hunter-gatherers in my data set have ever experienced. It should be kept in mind that

Generalization 12.07

The equations in this book are completely reversible, so that, for instance, the environmental conditions that are related to small group size will yield small size projections whenever the appropriate environmental conditions are encountered, regardless of sequence. The second feature of the hunter-gatherer equations is that most include all of the cases in my data set—the mobile peoples as well as the intensified groups—and therefore the environmental correlates of intensification are also built into the equations developed early in the book.

I certainly expect that many changes are likely to be irreversible in the world of evolutionary processes. Under certain selective conditions, the coping strategies of hunter-gatherer groups are likely to have failed, causing them to disappear or change in ways that would have made it impossible to return to the niche they had occupied prior to the onset of destabilizing processes. When archaeologists have seen directional change in cultural deposits, if it has not appeared to reverse direction, we have assumed that change itself was irreversible.

Now the hunter-gatherer projections can tell us when, other things being equal, conditions *should have* reversed. We can then refer to the archaeological record, which can tell us when and if they did not. Using our prior knowledge as a frame of reference opens up many new research opportunities, and we should be able to discern when—and in response to what magnitude of climatic change—"stress" would be an appropriate way to define the selective context of a system.

What should the archaeological record at Jerusalem and Zeribar look like when we project our knowledge of nearly contemporary hunter-gatherers onto the environmental changes reconstructed for these locations? In figure 12.07, graph A displays the projected population density anticipated by the Terrestrial Model at Jerusalem. Graph B refers to the same location, but the projection is based on the scale of egocentric social networks and correlated levels of mobility of the mobile hunter-gatherer cases in my global sample. The variable NETP1 is calculated from projected values for the total ethnic population and for the area used by the total ethnic population,[16] yielding an inverse value for the percentage of the total ethnic population utilizing an area of 100 square kilometers.

High values of NETP1 indicate large ethnic areas and lower values indicate small ethnic areas. High values can be interpreted as an indication of the presence of extensive egocentric social networks that in ethnographic contexts are associated with moderate to high mobility. Low values, on the other hand, suggest trends toward a cellular distribution of ethnic groups. These values are correlated with packing in such a way that an NETP1 value of 91.42 is the mean of all packed hunter-gatherer cases. The mean value of all *nonpacked* hunter-gatherer cases is 99.126 ± 1.74. For all practical purposes, as values decrease from 99.0, intensification pressures are mounting. By the time the values are reduced to 91.42, there is a greater than 75 percent chance that the packing threshold has been reached. If networks exist beyond this point, they tend to be socially negotiated networks maintained among "representatives" of social or ethnic groups or specialists of various types.[17]

Perhaps the first observation of interest in figure 12.07 is that in graph A the Terrestrial Model anticipates that prior to approximately 10,000 B.P., when cultivation is suspected to have begun, the primary food resources consisted of a

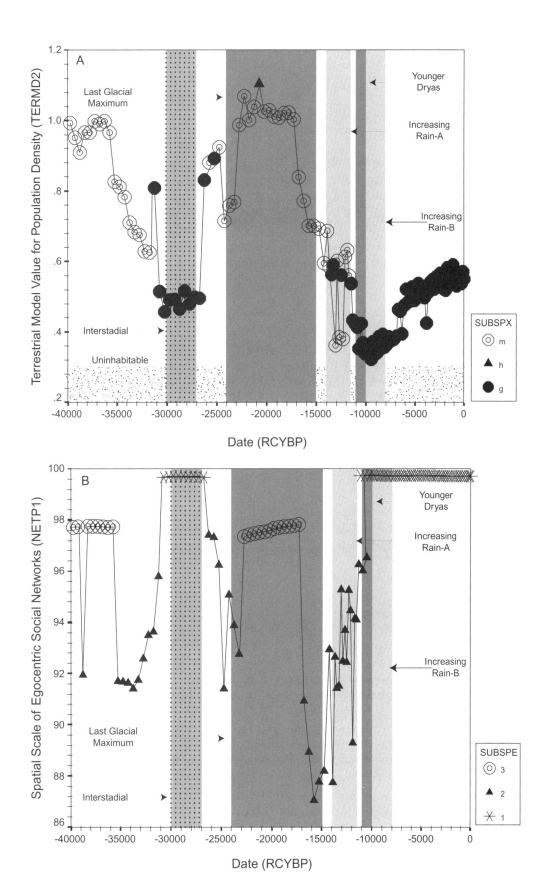

FIGURE 12.07

Modeled and projected characteristics of hunter-gatherer systems over the past 40,000 years at Jerusalem, based on reconstructed climatic variables. Graph A features population density and graph B records scale of social networks. Graph A marker identifies the dominant sources of food anticipated by the Terrestrial Model: (g) plants, (h) animals, and (m) mixed sources. Graph B marker is for dominant sources of food as projected from 339 hunter-gatherer cases: (1) plants, (2) animals, and (3) aquatic sources.

roughly equivalent mix of both terrestrial plant and animal resources. During the earlier interglacial, hunter-gatherers are projected to have been primarily dependent upon terrestrial plants. An unstable period in which shifts between plants and animals occurred is anticipated from the earliest "increasing rain–A" period through the Younger Dryas, after which dependence upon terrestrial plants is anticipated. I have already argued in propositions 12.11, 12.12, 12.13, and 12.14 that such a change could be rapid and dramatic, and it is interesting that at least some of the anticipated events appear to have actually happened, at least during the period from about 14,000 B.P. until the present.

The shift to plant cultivation represents an extreme form of dependence upon terrestrial plants (proposition 12.14). In this instance, however, the players were not the minimalist hunter-gatherers stipulated by the Terrestrial Model but were instead groups that had abandoned mobility as their primary food-getting strategy and substituted an increased investment of labor in food production and infrastructure. The Terrestrial Model also assumes technologically unaided, "minimally performing" humans and, given technological aids, we might expect a greater dependence upon terrestrial animals than the model allows. In graph B of figure 12.07, the points are coded with subsistence expectations projected from nearly contemporary hunter-gatherers. As anticipated, during the six thousand years prior to the transition to plant cultivation, groups that were primarily dependent upon terrestrial animal resources are projected to have occupied the area around Jerusalem.[18]

This projection is at odds with the assumptions and interpretations that have guided researchers in the region (Bar-Yosef and Meadow 1995:50), particularly the view that the hunter-gatherers who were transformed into intensified cultivators of plants were originally primarily dependent upon terrestrial plants. It is possible that the peoples who first practiced cultivation were previously hunters who responded to intensificational pressures by shifting to a greater dependence upon plants and then simply extended their exploitation of plants to cultivation. Propositions 12.11 through 12.14, generalization 12.02, and proposition 12.01 deal with the rapidity of change when hunters become intensified and could be germane to areas of the Levant, particularly areas north of Jerusalem, at the critical period between 10,000 and 11,400 years ago.[19]

An understanding of initial conditions and adaptive differences among hunter-gatherer systems is crucial to any considerations of system change, but when we shift our attention to the change events themselves, as documented archaeologically, many frames of reference become available to use in our research. These include the frame of reference provided by reconstructed climatic conditions, the one provided by modern environments as they vary with climatic conditions, and the frame of reference provided by our

knowledge of the adaptive variability of contemporary hunter-gatherers and the ways in which their behavior differs according to environmental conditions.

The Terrestrial Model anticipates dramatic adaptive responses among hunter-gatherers during the last glacial period. At that time, a population of approximately one person per 100 square kilometers is projected for technologically unaided hunter-gatherers and, beginning at about 16,000 years ago, the expected population drops precipitously to an absolute low[20] just at the end of the Younger Dryas episode. At that time—if the Terrestrial Model can be accepted as an indicator of a "user-friendly" environment—hunter-gatherers would have had great difficulty making a living along the upland western border of the Jordan River valley. This is strong support for the contention that the "stress" model is germane in this region, despite strong criticism (Hayden 1995:286–88).

In the archaeological sequence on the eastern side of the Jordan valley, the Natufian sequence appears between 11,000 and 12,000 years ago,[21] corresponding to an upturn in population at the end of the oldest "increasing rain–A" period just prior to the Younger Dryas (during the Younger Dryas itself, there are no dated archaeological remains). At the low point of the plot of population density in figure 12.07, graph A, corresponding to the beginning of the most recent "increasing rain–A" period, the prepottery Neolithic A appears. During the latter half of this era, prepottery Neolithic B predominates. The patterns in figure 12.07 make the case that environmental changes must have strongly affected the hunter-gatherers living in the region during the time that archaeological remains from the Natufian to prepottery Neolithic B were deposited.

Since it is already known that rainfall increased during the "increasing rain–B" period, it is reasonable to ask why hunter-gatherer population density in the region is projected to be so low. The answer is that at the beginning of the Younger Dryas a shift is predicted from summer to winter rainfall (figure 12.06) with more runoff and therefore less water available to drive production in the plant community. This projected shift corresponds exactly with the reported history of the Dead Sea: "the Dead Sea began ca. 15,000 years ago, during a period with a low runoff/evaporation ratio, which indicated a dry climate. Shortly after this, pluvial conditions caused the lake to rise, reaching its maximum between 12,000 and 10,000 B.P. and continuing to ca 6,500 B.P., when desiccation ensued" (Goldberg 1994:90).

Near the end of the Younger Dryas, there should have been many new springs and seeps that would have made water much more available along Jordan's western border with the Dead Sea basin. Maximum runoff is indicated toward the end of the Younger Dryas and during the first half of the "increasing rain–B" period, which coincides exactly with the appearance of prepottery Neolithic A. As Waterbolk

(1994:358) notes, "traditionally, the Jordan Valley . . . is associated with PPNA."

In data projected from the mobile hunter-gatherers in figure 12.07, graph B, an overall reduction in the scale of networks that is positively autocorrelated with reduced mobility is projected by NETP1 and is consistent with a general pattern of anticipated intensification. There are, however, several other features of this graph that demand attention. For instance, during two major glacial periods (from 40,000 to 36,000 B.P. and from 24,000 to 17,000 B.P.), subsistence is projected to be dominated by aquatic resources.[22] Nevertheless, populations are projected to be highly mobile and to maintain only slightly less extensive networks than during the interstadial and the interglacial. As I have said many times, the use of aquatic resources is a response to intensification (proposition 10.16). The projection for aquatic resources should therefore be read as a consequence of the interaction between cool climates and the preliminary responses to intensification that are anticipated among groups dependent upon terrestrial animal resources (proposition 10.14).

It should be noted that archaeological remains associated with glacial periods are generally rare in the Levant region. If we consider only dated sites, then the controversial "Early Ahmarian" and the "Levantine Aurignacian" assemblages occurred during interstadial or interglacial periods with only two possible exceptions, Boker A and Ein Agev, both of which are at the very end of glacial events. This pattern is not conclusive, but it suggests that large populations were never coincident with the glacial events occurring to the north.

Consistent with low population levels, a similar lack of sites also occurs in the Jordan basin, where the best-dated site suggesting occupancy during a glacial period is Ohalo II (Bar-Yosef and Meadow 1995:54; Waterbolk 1994:355), a lakeside settlement near the Sea of Galilee. It is quite possible that, instead of the region having been occupied during glacial events by highly stressed local populations of hunter-gatherers who were dependent on terrestrial animal resources, it experienced a marked decline in population. In such a scenario, only small pockets of hunter-gatherers survived in relatively unique refugia such as the Ohalo II site, where waterfowl and other aquatic species are represented in the deposits.

During both glacial eras, the mean effective temperature (ET) values during these cool periods are estimated to have been between 12.9 and 13.10°C during the maximum. These ET values are approximately the contemporary temperature equivalents of the area in North America from the Washington-Oregon border down to central Oregon, or along the east coast near Philadelphia.[23] Nonpacked ethnographic cases located in analogous settings and temperatures would be the Honey Lake Paiute of northern California and the Gosiute of northern Utah. In Europe, a comparable temperature zone extends across France from the French-Italian border at the Mediterranean coast to the mouth of the Loire on the Atlantic coast.

The values estimated for Jerusalem do not correspond to "glacial conditions," but the temperatures were approximately 5°C lower than current mean annual temperatures in the region. This is sufficient to have replicated, in parts of the Levant, the major shifts in subsistence documented among contemporary hunter-gatherers at an ET value of approximately 12.75, which is the terrestrial plant threshold. Many other dramatic changes in technology and group size are also clustered just prior to and around this threshold (propositions 10.02 to 10.09 and 10.20 to 10.23, and also generalizations 10.15 to 10.22). The important question at this juncture is whether similar changes occurred in the Levant during Pleistocene glacial events or whether the region became largely devoid of population.

Proposition 12.15

At 18,000 years ago, the world certainly had fewer people than the global population of 7,032,402 hunter-gatherers that was projected in chapter 5 to have occurred at approximately 11,000 to 12,000 B.P. We must imagine a patchily inhabited world in which large, uninhabited areas separated localizations of very mobile, adaptively successful populations that exploited extensive areas in order to maintain their subsistence security.

In figure 12.07, graph B, packed conditions are projected as possible for the first time at approximately 16,900 B.P. Based on NETP1 values, this projection is best understood as indicating that populations were likely to have been higher than at the earlier low, which occurred at 17,250 years B.P. It should be kept in mind that projections from modern hunter-gatherer data are not processual but represent, quite literally, the peopling of habitat space with conditions experienced by more nearly contemporary peoples. These conditions are projected instantaneously and not processually. This means that when packing *actually* occurred is not necessarily the same as when it *could* have occurred, based on projections from environmental conditions correlated with population density data from nearly contemporary hunter-gatherers. The projection of packed conditions between 13,150 and 16,750 B.P. does, nevertheless, suggest that conditions may have been conducive to population growth over those 3,500 years, following what were most certainly low population levels during the last glacial maximum.[24]

Archaeological sequences in the Near East first provide evidence of packed conditions in the coastal zone north of Jerusalem at the end of the first "increasing rain–A" period at approximately 11,700 years B.P. and continuing into the early years of the Younger Dryas. These sequences are called the "early Natufian" at Ain Mallaha and Hayonim (Byrd 1994:218) and are characterized by well-defined houses, storage pits, and a rich and diverse archaeological assemblage. These deposits correspond to a high spike in packing indicators and a reduction in egocentric networks (figure 12.07, graph B, NETP1 = approximately 89). Events thereafter are dramatic: NETP1 estimates rise precipitously, indicating higher mobility and an increased probability of egocentric networks during the late Natufian: "Radiometric dates, stratified sites, and additional archaeological traits indicate that a subdivision into early and late Natufian is of crucial importance. Early Natufian base camps are characterized by semi-subterranean dwellings. Late Natufian sites have yielded flimsier remains" (Bar-Yosef and Meadow 1995:55–56).

The environmental changes between the early and late Natufian that are suggested by the environmental reconstructions lead me to expect that recently packed hunter-gatherers would try to increase their mobility and explore previously avoided areas to see if conditions were better than those where they were localized. Their world had changed and the conditions of stability upon which their strategic planning depended were no longer reliable. If the reliability of persons in positions of leadership was questioned, the result would be group fission (Binford 1991a), but if conditions were causing subsistence stress, mobility would still appear to be a reasonable alternative to coping with decreasing returns where one was tethered.[25] The archaeological record of the late Natufian appears to represent the generic hunter-gatherer response to stress: the dispersal of populations in search of better conditions, particularly those who, at the onset of the environmental changes, had been primarily, or at least heavily, dependent upon terrestrial animals (generalization 10.10, proposition 10.14), which, after all, were experiencing severe stress themselves.

Events in the Levant are of crucial importance between the early Natufian and the appearance of prepottery Neolithic A immediately following the Younger Dryas. Projections based on the mobile hunter-gatherer cases in my global sample unequivocally anticipate a return to maximum mobility and extensive egocentric networks. The archaeological record instead documents a period of settlement instability—which suggests that institutionalized networks were no longer operational—followed by intensification and the appearance of a new niche in the region.

In order to arrive at a different perspective on the preceding projected events and archaeological sequences, projections of the variable NETP2 were calculated, using a completely different set of hunter-gatherer cases that were sedentary or semi-sedentary at the time of ethnographic observation. When the equations derived from these cases were projected onto the environmental sequence from Jerusalem, a simple dichotomous classification of high and low values resulted. Values of zero indicated hyperpacked conditions during the inter-

stadial and the period following the end of the Younger Dryas. Values fluctuating into the range projected for mobile peoples in graph B of figure 12.07 were very close to 99.12 and only slightly higher than values for the cases during the glacial events. Both sets of higher values were indicative of mobile hunter-gatherers. These results are remarkable since, with two very different subsets of hunter-gatherer cases, I obtained reinforcing results regarding the important role of the Younger Dryas as the switching point between mobile and hyperintensified hunter-gatherers. That these projected conditions represent stress indicators is supported by the archaeological record.

It seems clear that in the Jerusalem area the climatic effect of the Younger Dryas would have destabilized hunter-gatherer adaptations, particularly for those groups that were close to or beyond the packing threshold. Such an event sequence is consistent with an open systems viewpoint, which maintains that equilibrium systems never evolve to the point of emergence or a "state of criticality," because this state is precipitated by variables that vary independently of the homeostatic organization of a system. Although demography operates independently of the homeostatically organized relationships between group size and mobility among generic hunter-gatherers, adaptations adjust to climatic variability across geographic space. The ranges of variability that adaptations are able to accommodate, however, are likely to be a function of the scale of the subsistence area available to hunter-gatherers and the range of climatic variability that a "dynamic steady state" can tolerate. My observation in chapter 2 is relevant in this context:

Generalization 12.08

The tactics and strategies guiding human adaptive behaviors are based on projections from past experience. In turn, the success of planned strategies and tactics is a function of stability in the variables that are assumed to be similar to past experiences.

It is reasonable to presume that

Proposition 12.16

When climatic changes exceed the range of variability projected by hunter-gatherers to be stable and predictable, based on their prior experience, their adaptive strategies and tactics tend to fail and the system is cast into a critical state. Extreme diversity of behavior is anticipated and controversy occurs within societies about why tactics are failing, who is responsible, and, more importantly, what is the best course to follow in the face of such extreme uncertainty. The crisis tends to destroy the stable patterns of organized behavior that were characteristic of the earlier "noncritical" state.

One can imagine that there would be a high level of entropy during these chaotic episodes and that many more decisions would be made at the level of smaller group segments, which would result in considerable diversity in the responses to the disaster. Are there any clues about the steps that might be taken to produce a positive adaptive readjustment following a systemically critical state? Logic tells us that the answer lies in the discovery of a new but nevertheless similar habitat that allows hunter-gatherers to translate their prior knowledge to a different set of habitat conditions.

For instance, in the context of discussing the abnormally large GROUP2 sizes of contemporary arctic peoples in chapter 9, I mentioned that the occurrence of the last Thule cultural materials in North America is coincident with the onset of cooler conditions in the Arctic Sea. As a result, once open sea "leads" in which whales were able to breathe during the winter were closed following the formation of deeper sea ice. Thule culture had been based on whale hunting and the storage of whale meat and blubber on land for winter use, and substantial Thule winter houses had dotted the high arctic coastal areas. Climatic change ensured that continued

attempts to hunt whales and store their meat would bring the Thule way of life to a precipitous end, so these hunters very quickly reorganized their subsistence efforts and established themselves in snow houses that were situated on the sea ice during the winter. From this vantage point they could exploit the region's seal population from facilities at seal breathing holes. Climatic change had ensured that the old, reliable, subsistence techniques would fail, but the new adaptation was presumably based on prior knowledge that remained germane regardless of climatic changes that (fortunately for the Thule) did not affect seals as radically as they did whales.

I think it is reasonable to view the appearance of the prepottery Neolithic A as a similar translation of germane prior knowledge to the context of a new habitat. I also suspect that this process was not undertaken by the same social units that had occupied the earlier Natufian settlements characterized by substantial houses and storage pits. The integrity of those settlements almost certainly dissolved in the context of habitat uncertainty during the Younger Dryas, and it is also quite likely that the prepottery Neolithic A was not the only successful response to the Younger Dryas. It is likely that

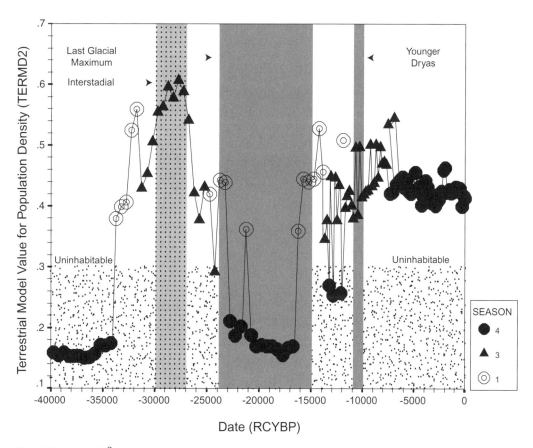

FIGURE 12.08

Modeled population density of hunter-gatherer systems and environmental conditions at Zeribar, Iran, over the past 40,000 years, based on reconstructed climatic variables. Marker is for season of greatest rainfall: (1) spring, (3) fall, and (4) winter.

uncertainty resulted in many instances of subsistence insecurity, lower reproductive rates, and, in some situations,
higher disease and nutritional stress, depending upon the character of earlier responses to dramatic climatic changes.

It is unlikely that the apparently packed, regional demographic patterns that characterized the early Natufian lasted
very long in the Younger Dryas. Instead, mobility may well
have become a viable alternative for some of the survivors,
particularly in the late Natufian. I think the indications that,
at the end of the Younger Dryas, plants were cultivated
around the increased number of soaks and springs along the
east side of the Jordan valley represent a translation of knowledge from prior experience to new, very different habitat conditions. A new niche had appeared in the region that changed
not only plants but also the way foragers in many regions
responded to intensificational pressures. This new opportunity
resulted in a restructuring of the population in the region and
a relatively quick filling of the niche space (propositions
10.12, 12.12, and 12.14).

In the search for further insights into the role that climatic
change plays in human adaptations, I now shift my focus to
the area surrounding Zeribar Lake in western Iran. This
venue is approximately 1,180 kilometers northeast of Jerusalem,
at an elevation of 1,300 meters. Given that Jerusalem is considerably south of Zeribar and has an elevation of only 760
meters, it can be assumed that the habitats surrounding
Zeribar Lake and Jerusalem were very different. In figure
12.06, graphs A and B, I demonstrated that the patterns of productivity at these two sites were radically different from one
another, and this pattern of dissimilarity continues. When figure
12.08 is compared with graph A in figure 12.07, the population densities projected for these two sites by the Terrestrial
Model show the same reversal of pattern that was noted in net
aboveground productivity in figure 12.06.

The Zeribar estimates in figure 11.08 indicate that overall population density is almost half that of Jerusalem. This
point is underscored by the projection that, during the glacial
phases between 40,000 and 34,000 B.P., and again between
24,000 and 16,500 B.P., the region was uninhabited. A further
contrast is observed in the estimates of increasing population density in Zeribar between 15,000 and 6,000 B.P., while
the opposite pattern is indicated for Jerusalem. In addition
to these differences, it is important to note that no snow accumulation was projected for Jerusalem.

In figure 12.09, however, it is clear that in Zeribar snow
accumulation could be measured in millimeters, except during the last 4,000 years, when no snow accumulation occurred.
In both Zeribar and Jerusalem, it would seem, the Younger
Dryas was a period of considerable climatic instability, but
only in Zeribar were there alternating periods of high and low
snow accumulation. In Zeribar, however, there do not appear
to have been any human populations present to experience
the instability.

The archaeological sequence in this region is very spotty
at high altitudes. Hole (1996:263–64) notes that Zarzian
materials, as those of the local Epipaleolithic are called, are
present just prior to 15,000 B.P. at altitudes above 1,000
meters. Thereafter, a gap occurs and no archaeological materials are found at high altitudes until approximately 8,000 B.P.
At lower altitudes, however, a local variant of the prepottery
Neolithic sequence occurs, termed the Mlefatian, during
which a change from round to rectangular houses took place
prior to the first ceramics (Kozlowski 1994:255–58). At lower
altitudes, clearly intensified hunter-gatherer occupations
appear to begin during the close of the Younger Dryas (Hole
1996:264). They seem to have been restricted to a relatively
narrow band of elevation between 300 and 850 meters,
which is considerably below Zeribar. One of the big differences between this area and Jerusalem is the timing of the
major changes in archaeological continuity and the demographic scale of the projected populations.

In the Jerusalem area, most of the action begins prior to
the Younger Dryas with the early Natufian, but there is nothing comparable to this in the Zeribar region, at either higher
or lower elevations. The appearance of the prepottery
Neolithic A in the vicinity of Jerusalem immediately after the
Younger Dryas corresponds roughly to the aceramic Mlefatian in Zeribar's lower altitudes, but there is no equivalent of
the prepottery Neolithic B in this region. The higher altitudes
around Zeribar seem to be uninhabited during this period
as well, and it is only later, between 6,000 and 8,000 B.P., that
settlements with remains of domesticated species occurred
at high altitudes.

Local events in Jerusalem have been successfully anticipated by using equations that simultaneously project the
likelihood of high mobility and large, egocentric social
networks (NETP1) based on nonpacked hunter-gatherer
cases. Using reconstructed climatic data, I have organized
similar projections for Zeribar in the graphs in figure 12.10,
and these differ significantly from the patterns for Jerusalem
in figure 12.07, graph B. In the latter area, there were indications of population growth and steps in the direction of
packing during the sequence, whereas in figure 12.10, graph
A, NETP1 values for the entire sequence are considerably
higher than the mean value for mobile hunter-gatherers
(99.1256). This suggests that population density was far lower
than 0.3 person per 100 square kilometers, an estimate
that was anticipated by Terrestrial Model densities (figure
12.08).

Projected values in this range are consistent with a largely
uninhabited region and are supported by archaeological
evidence. Beginning at around 7,000 B.P., NETP1 values
drop to the middle and lower part of the 98.0 range, which
is roughly coincident with a shift in the region to winter rainfall (figure 12.10, graph B) and an eight-month growing
season. Although this is the juncture at which we might

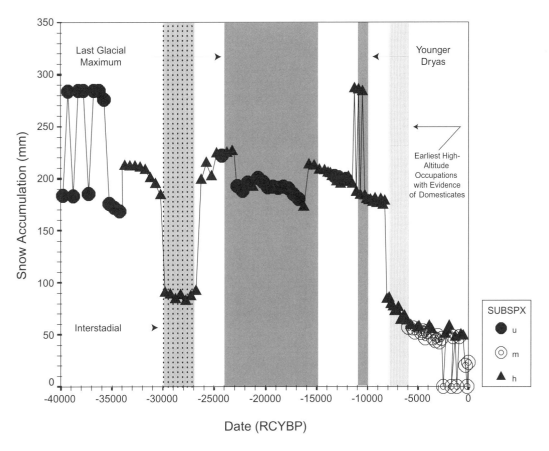

FIGURE 12.09

Modeled snow accumulation at Zeribar, Iran, over the past 40,000 years, based on reconstructed climatic variables. Marker identifies the dominant sources of food anticipated by the Terrestrial Model: (h) animals, (m) mixed sources, and (u) uninhabited.

expect mobile hunter-gatherers to radiate into this region, the archaeological sequence at lower altitudes indicates that only already intensified peoples represented by the aceramic Neolithic were poised for radiation. The appearance of sites in the higher altitudes does reflect a radiation, but one by groups whose previously established adaptation at lower altitudes now worked at higher elevations.

Processes of climatic change had made the region more "user-friendly" for this established niche and it had expanded geographically (figure 12.08), so whereas the Zeribar region tells us nothing relevant to a shift from hunting and gathering to a new niche, it does reveal something important about radiations.

Proposition 12.17

The successful radiation of a particular adaptive niche depends upon the presence of a critical set of values for a suite of fundamental environmental variables that tend to define the basic conditions for, and the outer limits to, successful functioning of the niche. Deviations

from these critical values ensure that the niche cannot be directly transferred to a new area. Environmental change can, however, trigger niche radiation once the limiting variables reach nonlimiting values.

Since my examination of Jerusalem and Zeribar was so instructive, I could not resist the temptation to introduce another site to see what might have happened at a location for which the projected initial conditions predicted that the primary food resources would have come from terrestrial plants. I chose to examine the site of Khartoum in the Sudan, since it is close enough to the equator to be well beyond the zone in which hunter-gatherers were primarily dependent upon terrestrial animals. In figure 12.11, graphs A and B illustrate several features of the history of Khartoum, beginning with the fact that, during the Pleistocene, viable human populations that were dependent upon locally earned resources could not have existed in the region. The first successful occupation is projected to have occurred after 11,400

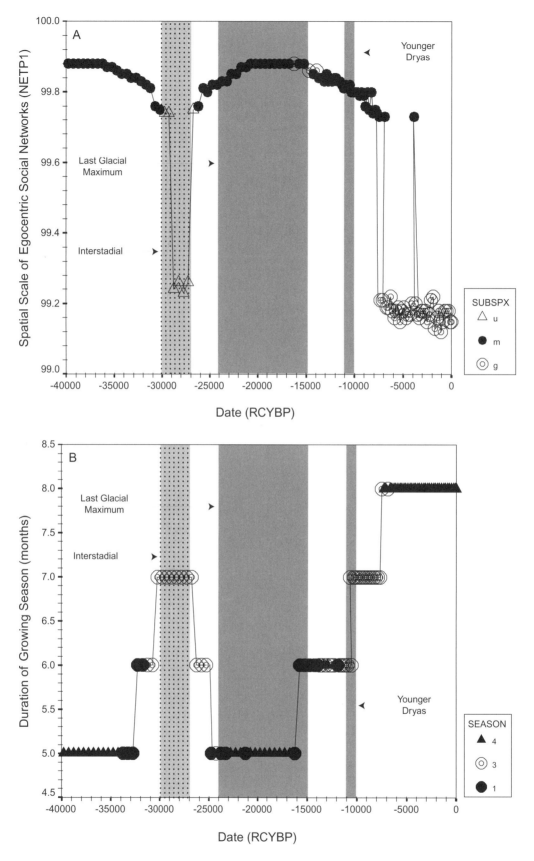

FIGURE 12.10

Modeled characteristics of hunter-gatherer systems and environmental conditions at Zeribar, Iran, over the past 40,000 years, based on reconstructed climatic variables. Graph A features scale of social networks and graph B records duration of growing season. Graph A marker identifies the dominant sources of food anticipated by the Terrestrial Model: (g) plants, (m) mixed sources, and (u) uninhabited. Graph B marker is for season of greatest rainfall: (1) spring, (3) fall, and (4) winter.

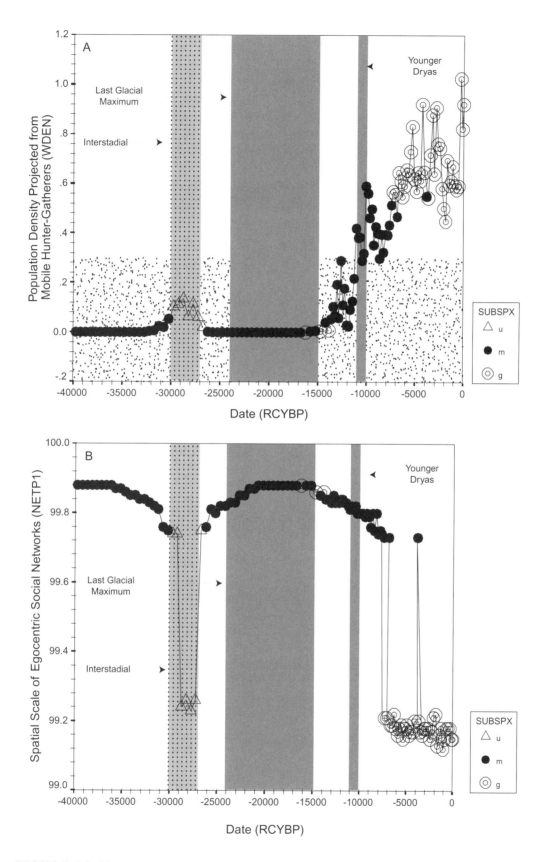

FIGURE 12.11

Projected characteristics of hunter-gatherer systems at Khartoum, Sudan, over the past 40,000 years, based on reconstructed climatic variables. Graph A features population density and graph B records scale of social networks. Marker identifies the dominant sources of food anticipated by the Terrestrial Model: (g) plants, (m) mixed sources, and (u) uninhabited.

years B.P., when hunter-gatherers might have been expected, although at very low population densities and at low levels of niche effectiveness.

Archaeological deposits in the Khartoum area have yielded no evidence of human presence between 80,000 B.P. and the appearance of the "Khartoum Complex" at approximately 9,300 B.P. (F. Wendorf, pers. comm. 1998), at which point it occurs over a wide area and "in a fully developed state" (Clark 1984:115). In other words, there is a nearly perfect fit between the archaeological record and the environmental reconstructions, integrated by means of my hunter-gatherer projections. The appearance of the archaeological remains in Khartoum apparently documents a niche radiation similar to the one at Zeribar, but with differences that are due to the character of the niche and the prior state of the systems that occupied the niche.

Scenario 12.03

Archaeologists have tended to think of migrations as ethnic phenomena, although radiations such as the horse-facilitated expansion of peoples into the Great Plains are actually niche-filling phenomena. In that example, ethnically and linguistically diverse groups moved to take up a new niche and occupy a relatively empty niche space. The result was the emergence of a new organizational collectivity that displayed a great deal of internal homogeneity in material culture and behavior.

New niches attract peoples with diverse prior identities if they open up new opportunities for increased subsistence security. A statement that expresses the idea of niche-filling is "nature abhors a vacuum." In this case, cultural systems abhor empty niche space, since it represents relief from packing pressures and an opportunity for greater independence from social restrictions on access to resource locations, which inevitably accompany reductions in between-unit competition.

As graph B in figure 12.11 illustrates, the projected subsistence dependence at Khartoum was based exclusively on terrestrial plants. This pattern is not reflected in the archaeological record, which contains evidence of a diverse food base that is rich in aquatic resources:

> They lived from taking from the river large quantities of fish . . . as well as hippopotamus, crocodile, reed rats, python and turtle. In the gallery forest they hunted buffalo; from the swampy backwaters they took Nile lechwe and, from the grass plains and open forest, kob, Equus, elephant, rhinoceros, and various medium- to small-sized antelope, among which the oribi is certainly identified. . . . the diet was rounded off with large quantities of . . . snails, the shells of which were ubiquitous on the site. . . . Grain was also collected and upper grindstones . . . were comparatively numerous.
> (Clark 1984:115)

People in Khartoum were also using ceramics when they made their first appearance in the region, which is considerably earlier than the appearance of pottery in the Levant. During the fifth millennium B.P., the first domesticated animals show up in archaeological deposits. The term for this and other changes is "the Shaheinab Complex," which occurs in the Khartoum area at the same time that groups in the predynastic phase in Egyptian prehistory were cultivating the first domestic plants. Given current information, the use of domesticated plants in the Khartoum area occurred between 4,500 and 4,000 B.P., and, only slightly more recently, domesticated animals became the primary source of meat.

The events at Khartoum, as at Zeribar, do not represent instances of initial domestication, but they are compelling nonetheless. In the first place, the environmental reconstructions projected that, initially, groups in the region should have been primarily dependent upon terrestrial plants. Generalization 8.03 states that, in settings below a latitude of approximately 35 degrees, plant-dependent groups are primarily foragers. According to generalization 7.05, when these groups are subjected to intensificational pressures, they respond by exploiting aquatic resources, if possible, and by increasing their dependence upon plants (proposition 7.01). Generalizations 7.04 and 10.04 state that, other things being equal, intensification ensures reduced dependence upon terrestrial wild animals. Groups that are dependent upon terrestrial plant resources and move toward aquatic resources in response to pressures to intensify (proposition 10.16) also tend to adopt collector strategies that move consumer goods from resource patches to consumers (generalization 8.17). In terms of scale-related phenomena, the response to packing is less immediate when aquatic resources are targeted (proposition 10.06).

Essentially all of the preceding generalizations are consistent with the archeological sequence at Khartoum. The missing bit of crucial knowledge is that, at the time of the radiation of the "Khartoum complex" into the area, the site and its environs were situated in a large floodplain of the Nile River that had a much higher water level than later on in the sequence (Clark 1984:114). The adaptation at Khartoum was primarily dependent upon unearned water during an especially bountiful period in the local hydrology. Not surprisingly, as conditions changed and water became less plentiful, the character of the land use around Khartoum also changed, prompting still other responsive changes in the cultural system.

This observation brings us back to the question I began with when I introduced the reconstructed climatic sequences at Jerusalem, Zeribar, and Khartoum: do environmental changes *cause* culture change? I could have begun to answer this question prior to my historical examination of these three locations, since I have stressed that

——————— *Scenario 12.04* ———————

Many features of cultural variability are correlated quite directly with environmental variables. In fact, it is reasonable to refer to much of the variability observable among known hunter-gatherers as adaptive variability, in other words, differences that reflect the adjustments of human groups to various properties of the habitats in which they find themselves. It should not be surprising that the same types of adaptive variability that can be demonstrated across an atemporal geographic landscape are also characteristic of a temporally changing habitat structure at a single place.

———————————————————————

Climatic change can potentially restructure cultural variability, but the lessons learned about initial conditions still apply. This means that the same climatic shift can produce different responses depending upon the various system states that are acted upon. Of particular importance is the degree to which the system is approaching, or is in, a state of self-organized criticality (Bak 1996:167–70).

The comparison of three different locations has allowed me to examine the effects of climatic stasis and change in greater depth. It has reinforced the observation that climate is strongly correlated with features of geography and varies with such geographic variables as latitude, elevation, and particular features of position relative to dynamics at the centers of climatic "action." The positions of high- and low-center weather systems, as well as of phenomena such as the jet stream, all affect habitat variability in fundamental ways.

I have also repeatedly demonstrated the strong determinant influence of habitat variability on the adaptive strategies undertaken by different cultural systems. The fit between projections drawn from contemporary hunter-gatherers and major changes in the archaeological record demonstrates that, other things being equal, adaptive variability follows habitat variability. Insofar as climatic changes restructure the character and form of habitats, it is to be expected that adaptive responses track such changes.

I have demonstrated[26] that some niches are much broader than others, have greater niche breadth, and can function across a greater range of habitat variability. This kind of system state variability has direct reference to ecostrategies. I have also shown that other types of system state variability can occur, particularly self-organizing variability. This I have explored by focusing on intensification, although it may also represent a response to the size of social units.

Other differences in cultural systems appear to be density-dependent in origin and represent a response to self-organized critical conditions in which mobility no longer ensures subsistence security. I have identified in equation (11.01) the points or thresholds in population density at which critical states are expected to occur, given an adaptation based on mobility. The importance of recognizing the preceding types of variability, including habitat-related adaptive variability, in conjunction with initial conditions should be apparent.

——————— *Scenario 12.05* ———————

When one is attempting to explain dramatic types of culture changes, it is crucial to understand the initial conditions of the system—including the character of the adaptation—relative to the habitat, the qualitative and quantitative composition of the effective environment, the technology available for exploiting the effective environment, and the character of the labor organization engaged in exploiting the habitat. This knowledge is needed prior to a consideration of the impact on the system of self-organizing processes or thresholds of criticality. All of the preceding properties and states may be differentially affected by habitat changes that are themselves driven by climatic change. It is the synergistic interactions between prior conditions, unfolding thresholds, and changes in habitat that condition organizational restructuring and result in a proliferation of new forms of complexity in cultural systems.

———————————————————————

Conclusion

In this chapter, I have attempted to build a theory about the self-organizing process of intensification among hunter-gatherers. A theory of packing makes it possible to anticipate many of the kinds of responses that occur during important episodes of change and self-organized criticality. What cannot be anticipated accurately is the range of systemic variability that may be generated during the period of criticality when the laws of self-organization themselves also change. In spite of this limitation, adaptive variability among hunter-gatherers can still be expected to follow habitat variability. This expectation was modeled by the projected information in my global sample of nearly contemporary hunter-gatherers, facilitated by the equations describing the interaction among habitat variables that best anticipated the variability among modern hunter-gatherers. Some of the properties projected in this manner were population density, number of residential moves, mean household size, size of single-family houses, and different types of group sizes. Demonstrating some relationships among them has been relatively easy.

I hope that my pattern recognition work has also demonstrated that our knowledge of the dynamics of adaptation itself is limited. Projections from the hunter-gatherer cases anticipate some of the responses of human groups to varying environmental conditions in rather provocative ways. In fact, these projections anticipate a tremendous increase in mobility and a huge increase in the scale of landscape use by a single group (figure 10.22, graph B), corresponding to the archaeological evidence up to and including the early Natufian period (propositions 8.02, 8.04, 10.08, 10.10, 10.20, 10.21, 11.07, and 11.20 and generalizations 8.37, 8.38, 9.09, 10.07, 10.22, 11.04, 11.12, 11.14, 11.20). Unfortunately, our knowledge of prior conditions and the laws governing the self-organizing properties that lead to a critical system state during the Younger Dryas do not permit us to anticipate accurately the prepottery Neolithic A.

Similarly, gradualist ideas about incremental change and descent with modification do not help us. There is no archaeological continuity between the Early Natufian of Ain Mallaha and the beginning of cultivation in the Jordan valley. On the other hand, the apparent break in continuity signaled by the Late Natufian appears to be a response to the same rules guiding hunter-gatherer adaptive changes—in this case the imperative to expand the spatial scale of land use. The response to the Younger Dryas suggests that the system changes indicated by the early Natufian[27] at or just beyond the packing threshold were not yet irreversible. Conditions during the Younger Dryas modified the scale of near-criticality extant at the time, which produced diverse responses, some of which were anticipated by our prior knowledge of the habitat variability of modern hunter-gatherers.

To those who at this juncture are prompted to ask whether environmental change can be said to cause the cultural response referred to as the prepottery Neolithic A, my response is no, but environmental change forced an already packed system into a critical state. There were probably many different adaptive responses, some of which failed and some of which survived and established a new niche by exploring and discovering new habitat characteristics in old subsistence ranges. To do this, however, Natufian groups had to imagine events not yet experienced and use their prior knowledge about the growth requirements and food potential of plants in habitat contexts that were different from those in which the plants had been originally exploited.[28]

This is not to say that I agree with Stephen Jay Gould, who argues that the methods of science are inadequate to deal with the realities of history (Gould 1989:277–79). My views are more aligned with those of Per Bak (1996:79), who refers to Gould's approach as "story telling." I have applied the same criticism to archeologists who insist on "interpreting sites" and "reconstructing history" through the use of unfounded interpretative conventions or, less often, by appeals to "contingency," as Gould might say.

The relevant question is: can archaeologists use what we have learned about the causes of hunter-gatherer variability to help us see that the prepottery Neolithic A is not a unique phenomenon, but rather one case among many? Actually, I doubt that there are many sequences in which identical events occurred, but there were *many* situations like the Early Natufian in which, in response to pressures to intensify, groups experimented with greater dependence upon

plant foods and storage. I think it is quite likely that the first cultivation, or at least the first manipulation of plants, occurred as a result of intensificational pressures at this time.

In spite of dramatic uncertainty during the Younger Dryas, which made successful planning very difficult and resulted in increased mobility and probably a decrease in regional population, cultural transmission of the adaptive strategies pursued during the early Natufian period probably occurred. I think, in fact, that much of the searching during the period of increased mobility during the late Natufian was for places where the successful adaptive techniques of the early Natufian could be implemented "with modifications." The springs and seeps that became available at the end of the Younger Dryas provided half of the solution in the form of reliable water sources for previously utilized productive plants. All that was needed was to transport the seeds.

Given the limited distribution of springs and seeps, it did not take long for the processes of intensification to force further changes that ensured higher yields from a smaller productive area. During the early Natufian, the cultural transmission of knowledge about intensified use of plant resources led to successful implementation in a new setting in which subsistence security was no longer provided by mobility. I think that there were many other instances in which the same basic process occurred, although I am also convinced that all specific historical paths to cultivation and domestication are unique. As I have argued throughout this book, all historical variety arose, nevertheless, from an antecedent set of density-dependent responses to packing.

If the arguments I have presented accurately reflect dynamics in the past, they are not only consistent with the trajectory of change reflected in archaeological sequences from Jerusalem. They also anticipate archaeological sequences in locations where gradual incremental change occurred in response to packing-related processes of intensification, provided the initial conditions included primary dependence upon terrestrial plants and very little in the way of alternative aquatic resources (generalizations 9.10, 10.01, 10.02, 10.15, 10.21, and 12.02 and propositions 10.02, 10.03, 10.07, 10.09, 11.03, 11.04, and 12.14).

Archaeological sequences in the Tehuacan Valley (Pearsall 1995:166–75) appear to meet these criteria, and it is interesting that, during the early archaic period, Flannery (1986a:11) estimates that population density levels in the Tehuacan and Oaxacan regions were between 3.45 and 11.11 persons per 100 square kilometers. The upper one-third of this range would include peoples living at or above the packing threshold. This is exactly where my arguments would expect attempts to squeeze greater plant productivity from less land to have been critical to an adaptation that could no longer rely on mobility for subsistence security.

My arguments would anticipate similar sequences, proceeding at different rates, in interior continental areas where groups were already primarily dependent upon terrestrial plants and had no realistic aquatic alternative. My arguments also anticipate still other paths to cultivation and domestication, or at least to the use of domesticated species (scenario 12.01), when increased dependence upon aquatic resources was the initial response to packing pressures.

I argued earlier that substantial houses, some social differentiation in terms of wealth, and even some movement toward inherited "ownership" of important access windows for obtaining aquatic resources could already be in place. A settlement hierarchy consisting of a few large settlements may have developed, followed by increasing numbers of small hamlets, like the one reported for the Valdivia sequence in Ecuador (Pearsall 1995:183–89) that included both coastal and riparian settlements. Many possible combinations and permutations are expected to characterize societies with considerable niche breadth or greater energetic complexity, and I would expect a wide range of organized niche diversity among these cases.

It should be recalled that hunter-gatherer groups with high subsistence diversity and sociocultural complexity did not tend to be status-based, internally ranked hierarchies. Instead, they used age-graded secret societies and other social forms to partition society into units that provided institutionalized services, such as supplying wives, organizing funeral rites, or arranging periodic ritual events. The idea that complexity always results in the division of leadership into elite or privileged persons and the disenfranchised is a vestige of linear evolutionary trajectories.

Despite the length of these remarks, I have in no way exhausted the potential of the packing argument, nor have I begun to discuss the variety of adaptive responses that could be anticipated, given a knowledge of the subsistence base prior to intensification and of the available alternatives in different habitats. I also have not addressed the domestication of animals because I do not know enough about the ecology of this process to anticipate the types of responses and the limitations that context might place on possible responses. As a result, my colleague Amber Johnson has initiated a project to study pastoralists and agropastoralists using the same methods that I applied to my hunter-gatherer research.[29]

I started research by trying to build up an accurate body of knowledge about what the world is like. Beyond this consideration, the possible variety in unknown processual relationships goes up appreciably if we permit the rates of intensification to vary based on different reproductive rates. Some alternatives may be strongly favored over others simply because of the likelihood that, as Rindos argued (1984), they require long temporal intervals to achieve appreciable returns. We do not know what effects different scales of

intensificational pressure, conditioned by differential reproductive rates, might favor. Do "quick-fix," short-term strategies with immediate returns tend to reduce the probability that long-term strategies with low initial returns would be undertaken by a system? This is a research question that we can address in the future.

Still other unresolved issues relating to ecological and cultural processes must be researched, and the criteria for recognizing a new niche—as opposed to an elaborated niche—are still to be determined. I mentioned this issue in chapter 6 in connection with my discussion of patterning in European archaeological sequences. There I suggested that new niches could make possible a totally different way of organizing an adaptation within an otherwise unchanging environment, producing dramatic breaks in the continuity of the archaeological record through time.

Let us imagine that the dynamics underlying the Zeribar sequence could have occurred in a different environmental setting, one in which a resident population of hunter-gatherers was present at the time of the climatic amelioration that permitted the radiation of a niche and accompanying population into the Zeribar area at approximately 7,000 B.P. What would have happened: "diffusion" of cultivation techniques to the hunter-gatherers and their transformation into horticulturists, or a replacement of the hunter-gatherer population by horticulturists from lower altitudes?

Arguments about this scenario are legion in anthropology, but it must be realized that neither diffusion nor migration explains the events described. Partisans for each position simply line up advocates for and against their preferred event sequences without realizing that an archaeologist's job is to explain the event sequences. The debate remains unresolved because few researchers have addressed the problem of what a "diffusion event" as opposed to a "migration event" would look like in archaeological deposits.[30] Even if it can be taken for granted that archaeologists can identify when events related to "diffusion" or "migration" have occurred, advocates of these sets of processes still must face the problem of explaining why they happened.

I have already made a few observations and suggestions that represent only elementary probes in this direction (generalization 12.05 and propositions 12.03, 12.04, 12.05, and 12.06). These statements deal primarily with environmental and temporal gradients in the distribution of cultural "traits," since patterns such as these—particularly the distribution of temporal sequences across geographic space—are usually offered as evidence for both migration and diffusion. I do not expect this issue to be resolved, however, until some accommodation is reached in the debate between science and humanism in archaeology and anthropology (Wilson 1998).

The three cases that I have used to illustrate climatic reconstructions are pertinent to this discussion. As Bar-Yosef and Meadow (1995:60) have correctly pointed out in the Jerusalem example, the critical climatic event is the Younger Dryas. A typical historian might be content with the statement that the Younger Dryas "caused" the shift to cultivation, since one event causes another event for most historians. But if we look at the data from Zeribar, the Younger Dryas can in no way be said to have caused any human response at that elevation. The appearance of peoples using domesticated species was greatly delayed at that location and, when it occurred, was facilitated by changes in the climate that can only be interpreted as making the area more user-friendly to the niche that had appeared initially at lower elevations. The situation at Khartoum is analogous since at present there is no evidence of a human presence in the area during the Younger Dryas.

The appearance of the Khartoum complex seems to have resulted from a radiation, but it was a radiation of hunter-gatherers. Once these groups were established in the region, a sequence of events occurred that was probably driven by intensification. It appears to have been a gradual, additive process in which domesticated animals were introduced first, after which domesticated plants were integrated into the system. Judging from the reconstructed climatic information, this sequence took place as the habitat deteriorated. A comparative study of these specific temporal sequences would establish that the cultivation of plants appears to have preceded the domestication of animals in the Jerusalem area, whereas at Khartoum the use of domesticated animals preceded the introduction of domesticated plants.

Should I therefore argue that a secondary adoption of domesticates is a different process than the initial context of domestication, particularly if the slow, transitional process documented in the Tehuacan Valley of Mexico represents a record of a precritical, self-organizing process of intensification? If, as I suspect, it is, would the adoption of previously domesticated species as part of a critical state leading to a new self-organizing set of relationships with new variables be only a "secondary event" in the context of a fundamental and primary change? In such a situation, the availability of domesticated species through borrowing would be a condition external to the system state during criticality, just as would be any other "independent" event or condition, such as climatic change. It may push or pull the system during criticality, but it is not what put the system in a position of change in the first place. The relationship between the precipitating variables is fundamental to an explanation of why change occurs, but the system state that results from an episode of criticality cannot be anticipated from the rules and conditions of prior self-organization.

What about the possibility that cattle were domesticated at Nabta Playa between 9,200 and 8,500 B.P.? Such events would have been contemporary with the prepottery Neolithic A and B materials in the Jerusalem area, but no evidence of contemporaneous domesticated plants occurred in the Nabta archaeological deposits. The Nabta example would be a rival "primary context" of domestication, but with a different sequence—animals first and plants much later. In the current arguments about domesticated resources in the Zagros area of Iran, the domestication of sheep and goats is believed to have occurred considerably later than the use of domesticated plants (Hole 1996:273).

The point I am trying to make is really very simple: tremendous variability can be generated during periods of self-organized criticality, and much of this variability can be anticipated if the fundamental organizational components of the prior period of relative stasis can be identified. In short, by knowing the rules of self-organization, we can anticipate many variants, although the emergent forms of *new* self-organization cannot be anticipated. Once hunter-gatherers reached the packing threshold, not only did some groups emerge from episodes of criticality organized in very different ways and with new niches and basic forms of organization, but their niche structure was also reshaped.

Based on the evidence provided by ethnographic and historical records, a truly vast array of system state variability emerged once hunter-gatherers crossed the packing threshold. We call some of the groups who experienced these adaptive transitions pastoralists, some agropastoralists, some horticulturists (slash-and-burn and otherwise), and some, perhaps, even agriculturists. And then there are all of the groups in the latter category who utilized at least some domesticated animals in ways different from pastoralists.

What are the self-organizing principles that moved so many different postforaging adaptations toward new critical states? Just because a thorough knowledge of ethnographically documented hunter-gatherers does not equip us to anticipate what these principles might be does not mean that the variability among these systems cannot be explained. As I have demonstrated in this book, we can study the variability and proceed with learning strategies that will allow us to isolate the self-organizing principles affecting peoples who do not use mobility to map onto naturally occurring distributions of accessible foods as hunter-gatherers do. This research teaches us about new principles of adaptation and intensification, since it is unlikely that such processes would cease with the obsolescence of mobile hunter-gatherer strategies.

We can expect that self-organizing processes will become more complex as the number of variables involved and the range of forms of complex systems proliferate. And, if we succeed in recognizing new thresholds arising from different forms of self-organizing systems, we may begin to develop an appreciation for the laws that govern different forms of criticality. Although these goals are certainly beyond the reach of anthropological science at present, they are not beyond the capabilities of science when the tools for learning I have presented here are used analytically.

Epilogue

There's no business like show business.
—Irving Berlin

It is said that at the conclusion of dramatic presentations in ancient Rome a person was designated to intone the words "Acta es fabula" (the play is over). Such an announcement is appropriate at this juncture since the final acts of both the hunter-gatherer play in the ecological theater and the drama of science have concluded. Like theater performances in the real world, my effort here will eventually be reviewed, but the sternest critic of a work is often the playwright him- or herself—and this certainly also applies to the authors of monographs.

After the euphoria of having completed the last chapter of this book faded, I began to assess just what it is that I am offering to the world for its contemplation. My first impression is that even though I have presented a detailed analysis of many aspects of my hunter-gatherer data, a number of important points have not been synthesized. For instance, I have demonstrated that major organizational changes have occurred when groups in any given region have reached and exceeded the packing threshold, but I have not discussed some of the broader implications of these changes for other cultural practices of generic hunter-gatherers.

I have argued that self-organized, nonpacked hunter-gatherers maintain minimal group sizes primarily by structuring their labor investments with respect to their dependence upon various food resources at different trophic levels. What also seems clear is that nonpacked hunter-gatherers are organized in terms of networks and not the more cellular kinds of social units that might be imagined when the word *band* is used to characterize their basic social attachments (see chapter 1, pages 12–17). In my view, individuals and families are *not* members of a band, even though regular cooperation, association, and shared responsibilities to the land may result in

a core group of persons who tend to move together. The important point is that the composition of on-the-ground groups and the regularity of the association of particular families or persons in these groups is quite variable.[1]

Other things being equal, decisions about the persons with whom to cooperate and where to position oneself in order to maximize subsistence security are made by the family, which is the organizational entity making up larger, on-the-ground groups. A larger—usually GROUP2-size—unit tends to occupy a subsistence range or area over which the group moves, even though the composition of the group may change as this movement occurs. A seasonally related segmentation of the group into smaller units may also occur, after which these units may reassemble into a GROUP2 unit. In such a situation, however, the newly formed group is rarely identical to the GROUP2 unit that predated the dispersal into smaller units.

Basically, generic hunter-gatherers are integrated into their social world through egocentric, reticulate patterns of extended, kin-based relationships. Persons who associate together in on-the-ground groups consider one another to be "trustworthy" because of their long-term experiences with one another in kin-based associations. In other words, persons are reasonably certain that the behavior of their groupmates will fulfill their expectations in matters relating to social responsibility and reliability. In groups articulated in this way, individuals may participate in what I earlier termed risk-pooling units, some of which may be relationships of long standing while others may represent ad hoc units that are formed on a daily basis and dissolve when the cooperative task has been completed.

The organization of a group of mobile hunter-gatherers must be viewed as a continuously shifting combination of "sequentially scaled," risk-pooling, cooperative associations. Any given individual may participate in a variety of risk-pooling relationships, including those that form and dissolve daily and others that are a function of longer-term cooperative ventures between families or individuals. The latter may last for the duration of the group or even, in some cases, beyond the life of within-group, face-to-face association. Risk-pooling associations of this type are not necessarily directly structured by kinship. They may be conditioned by compatibility in age and physical ability, commonalities having to do with family maturation, or individual states such as pregnancy (Binford 1991a).

It is my impression that female labor groups and risk-pooling units have stronger links to ego-centered kin networks than do male risk pools and labor units, except when polygyny is prevalent (greater than 20 percent of the marriages). In such circumstances, female work groups are usually composed of co-wives who are structurally integrated as a long-term risk-pooling unit.[2] As far as subsistence labor is concerned, the lack of extensive female networks in small, multifamily camps among highly polygynous peoples is expected to condition the character of the camp layout of houses or domestic spaces.[3] Variability in the organizational structure of the group is conditioned by the character of the risk-pooling associations extant at any given time. This determines the ratio of families to the number of domestic spaces, work areas, and consumption areas and results in very different patterns of camp layout.

The character of the risk pool hierarchy operating at any given time in turn conditions how necessary raw materials will be obtained, accumulated, and distributed within and among camps. To understand the variables that govern the latter sequence of subsistence-related events, we must know whether camps, families, or individuals are the units that are being provisioned. It is important to remember that generic hunter-gatherers are segmentary societies, even though the segments are most commonly individuals and families rather than larger-scale units. (Generalization 9.04 notes that GROUP1 units do not correspond to the segments out of which GROUP2 units are formed.)

If I shift scales for a moment and consider the role that egocentric kin networks play at the regional level, another set of interesting features becomes apparent. My ethnographic field work with mobile hunters and gatherers has convinced me that one of the most important forms of culturally organized behavior, other than subsistence activities, is the maintenance of social networks that are designed to facilitate family mobility and reproduction. I have also noted that most of the behavior that anthropologists have described as associated with ritual or religious observance is more accurately identified as an aspect of the educational subsystem. In turn, my conclusions have influenced my view of the traditional ways in which anthropologists have described kinship and its variants.

I have focused upon what a child receives by virtue of societal conventions for providing him or her with a full compliment of kin. Although it is true that many anthropologists have described hunter-gatherers as living primarily in kinship-based societies, most will acknowledge the existence of only a very limited set of kinship forms, which have been designated lineal, ambilateral, and bilateral. My reading of many hunter-gatherer ethnographies, including ones that report on most of the Australian Aboriginal groups, leads me to conclude that this three-part cognitive scheme misses a fundamental premise of kinship reckoning.

The traditional classification represents an expectation that kinship distance is a unidimensional phenomenon, whereas in my view kinship reckoning is fundamentally at least a bidimensional phenomenon[4] that differs significantly from bilateral systems. The latter appear to organize analogous kin of the paternal and maternal lines as if they were homologous or at least undifferentiated with regard to certain scales of kinship distance. Bidimensional systems, on the other hand, organize relationships in such a way that different features of an individual's social persona are conveyed to recipients from the "female" and "male" dimensions quite independently. For example, in some Australian groups the relationship of a person to geographic space and the social responsibilities for educating male persons are conveyed through paternal kinship conventions. The properties of individuals that by convention identify potential mates result from the conjunction of the property space defined by both female and male kinship dimensions. (Relationships of this kind are worked out in terms of the "section" systems of Australian Aborigines.)

Finally, the aspects of an individual's persona that define the appropriate etiquette governing how he or she may meet and relate to potentially marriageable persons are organized through maternal kinship conventions. Female kinship may also allocate to adult women their educational responsibilities for particular female offspring. In general, then, males are responsible for transmitting to their offspring critical aspects of identity and information that deal with the social reproduction of the society, while females transmit critical aspects of identify and information having to do with the biological reproduction of society. The conjunction between these two dimensions largely defines the appropriate social domain in which their offspring can look for mates, so that both social and biological reproduction is ensured.

The preceding example represents only one form of kinship structure. Many other forms that organize an individual's privileges and responsibilities to other persons and places in the landscape are well documented, but the important point is that an individual's inheritance is differentiated between paternal and material kinship dimensions, and both male and female offspring receive different cultural conventions, information, and social relationships from both dimensions.

If I am correct in my assessment of the way in which the Australian Aboriginal cognitive world is constituted, then the dissonance produced by anthropological classifications that feature patrilineal clans with matrimoieties but posit that the society is based on unilineal kinship conventions could well be resolved. My view of Australian kinship would place Aboriginal hunter-gatherers in the same general world as most other hunter-gatherer groups that are classified as bilateral and have a dual dimensional system, but at some levels of kin distance paternal and maternal kin may be merged while at other levels they may not. These two variants are different, however; each would be a morph of nonlinear or multidimensional kin reckoning systems.

Most of the hunter-gatherer cases that are reported to be linear have turned out, on close reading, to be either bilateral or bidimensional. In fact, all but four of the generic hunter-gatherer groups have either bilateral or bidimensional kinship systems, and a large number of these could be called affinal inclusive systems[5] in which affinal relatives are terminologically merged with lineal or bidimensional relatives. I must point out that my world sample of hunter-gatherer groups includes cases with varying degrees of bias in which numerically greater or more socially important features were transmitted through the male or female lines, resulting in what I have called an imbalanced dimensional structure. In terms of population density, however, the overwhelming number of these groups were located either right at or beyond the packing threshold.

The details are not as important here as the realization that kinship does much more than calculate kin distance for purposes of identifying potential mates. Among generic hunter-gatherers, kinship conventions link adults to children in terms of socially recognized educational responsibilities. To be effective, the education of juvenile hunter-gatherers requires that the appropriate adults make a major investment of time and energy in providing a child with instructive experiences in a wide range of environmental and geographic settings. This usually means repeated visits to relevant places during which the child assumes the role of an apprentice and is guided by a very knowledgeable person in each local area. This wide dispersal of necessary educational experience is made possible by a kin-based network of persons that is regularly maintained over a vast expanse of space. These extensive networks in turn facilitate mobility, not for a "band" but for the more fundamental units of the family or the individual.

A network-based system sometimes extends over very large areas through overlapping paths in an individual's egocentric kinship system. The correspondence between the scale of kinship networks and the scale of the social pool represented at periodic aggregations such as male initiation ceremonies in the Australian central desert is, however, unclear ethnographically. When observed from the per-

spective of individual groups in a region, these networks are clearly the conduits through which gifts and other items are circulated over very large areas, and the circulated items help maintain social ties over long periods during which no face-to-face contact occurs.

When observed from the perspective of the circulation of goods, the organizational basis of kinship networks varies. Among groups that are dependent upon terrestrial animal and aquatic resources, there is a bias toward personally initiated trading partners. These adjunct networks frequently link nonkin or affinal kin rather than consanguine kin. Among groups that are primarily dependent upon terrestrial plants, various gifts are circulated through kin-based networks. In either instance, it is my impression that the activities that archaeologists would presume relate to the trade and exchange of material items actually result from the everyday investments that persons make in maintaining their network of kin-based relationships. The volume of items flowing through a network is usually relatively low but the scale of dispersion can be very great. The items that circulate are biased in favor of "value-added" goods in which labor has been invested to modify the basic materials, such as skins that have been processed or lithic raw material that has been worked into nearly finished tools.

I feel I need to comment on the degree to which generic hunter-gatherers represent a form of society that is often referred to as egalitarian and sometimes as communalistic.[6] When I first wrote the early chapters of this book, I originally referred to generic hunter-gatherers as "egalitarian," but I stopped using this designation since I thought that it was confusing and, in the long run, misleading. It is true that sharing is very common among hunter-gatherer groups that have not approached the packing threshold, as is the practice—when necessary—of using tools and supplies that belong to other persons. It is equally common, however, for individuals to be treated differently in some circumstances and appealed to in terms of perceived differences in their skills, intelligence, athletic abilities, age, sex, and even family credentials.

There is truth in the claim that, below the packing threshold, hunter-gatherers are organized so that all participating individuals have maximum access to the vital resources that are accessible in their subsistence ranges. Participation in an economically integrated group means that all individuals endeavor to minimize the risk and maximize the returns from cooperative labor that is directed toward obtaining the vital resources needed to sustain the group as a whole. It is also true that nonpacked hunter-gatherers do not live in societies in which equal "rights" are assured by the society. Rather, in their social world, trust and respect are built upon the lifelong associations and interactions of individual members. Persons who are not considered trustworthy or "respectable" by the community may be denied not only equal access to resources but even their very right to exist, which is hardly compatible with the idea of an egalitarian society in which all individuals have rights to the corporately shared largesse.

Glimpses of Processes beyond the Packing Threshold

If we consider the preceding characteristics as usually applicable to hunter-gatherer groups below the packing threshold, it is now possible to think in different terms about hunter-gatherer groups as a general class. I have already demonstrated that major, dramatic changes appear coincidentally with and subsequent to a group's reaching the packing threshold. In equation (11.01), I summarized a partitioning of hunter-gatherers into subsets defined by a series of demonstrable, quantitative relationships having to do with thresholds in population density such that cases occurring before and after the threshold exhibit very different organizational properties.

An even more interesting observation demonstrated that prehistoric, horticultural Pueblo groups in the southwestern United States, as well as a number of pastoral societies, overlap with hunter-gatherer societies whose population density occurs between the packing threshold and the point at which the range of variability among hunter-gatherer cases terminates. This fact suggests that the hunter-gatherer groups that survived the packing threshold probably represent only a very limited component of the total range of new organizational variability that arose at or above the packing threshold. My understanding of intensification certainly suggests that the cultivation of domesticated plants and the exploitation of domesticated animals were likely to have been a response to intensification contributing to the collapse of non-packed hunter-gatherer organization, once population levels approached and exceeded the packing threshold.

I have argued earlier that the packing threshold represents the point at which residential group mobility is no longer a viable strategy for ensuring subsistence security from naturally distributed food resources. I have also demonstrated that mobility is linked to a narrow, self-organized range of variability in group size. Some part of the range of variability occurs when group size increases beyond certain parameters and individuals respond by detaching themselves from the parent group and forming new groups. In settings in which groups are dependent upon terrestrial resources, parent and daughter groups compete for resource space until the region is packed and mobility can no longer ensure subsistence security. For groups primarily dependent upon terrestrial animal resources, the pressure to intensify begins earlier than that for plant-dependent peoples, but once population density levels restrict mobility, primary dependence upon animal resources is no longer a viable option.[7]

I have also argued that the vast majority of ethnographically documented hunter-gatherers who are primarily dependant upon aquatic resources live below 60 degrees latitude and have population densities in excess of the packing threshold. It is quite likely that groups dependent upon aquatic resources arrived at their adaptive destinations by one of two routes: (1) they had been hunters of terrestrial animals who shifted their subsistence base when pressure to intensity made dependence on hunting no longer feasible; or (2) they were once exploiters of terrestrial plants who expanded their subsistence base to include aquatic resources in response to pressures to intensify.

Once population levels in warmer environments expand further and storage becomes necessary, these groups must increase their dependence upon terrestrial plants because of the risks associated with storing aquatic products. In cool-temperate, boreal, or polar zones, reduced temperatures tend to increase the probability that aquatic species can be safely stored, which makes continued specialization possible. Aquatic resource dependence may expand prior to the packing threshold and continue as population density increases, if no plant alternative is feasible. This means that groups that are dependent upon aquatic resources in settings in which terrestrial animals are expected to be heavily represented in the diet will have population levels that range from less than to greater than the packing threshold.

This pattern provides a clue to some of the processes that may be operating during the critical state occurring at the packing threshold and that may include increased specialization focused on aquatic resources and gradual expansion of aquatic diet breadth. This alternative is not possible for plant-dependent peoples under packed conditions in warm settings, however. The latter groups must specialize, to be sure, but the option of expanding the diet breadth is limited unless there is an aquatic alternative. A focus on aquatic resources would, in fact, be reversed if increasing population pressure were to force greater dependence upon storage.

A very different picture has emerged for the thirty-two groups of aquatically dependent peoples that had not yet reached the packing threshold. Twenty-one were located above 60 degrees latitude, nine occurred between 60 and 45 degrees latitude, and only two occurred below 45 degrees. The great majority of these groups were heavily dependent upon sea mammals, and their specialized strategy made it possible for them to radiate into environments that had not been occupied prior to their arrival. Unfortunately, my ethnographic sample does not allow me to evaluate the degree to which the Arctic groups can provide clues to the organization of the exclusively aquatic adaptations of archaeologically documented groups that were once located near the equator along the coasts of northern Chile, Peru, and southern Ecuador.

I was able to demonstrate that the terrestrially adapted hunter-gatherer groups in my world sample increased in size once packing occurred, but no such pattern is demonstrated among aquatically dependent peoples who continued to segment under such conditions. In these settings, daughter units were required to settle adjacent to reliable clusters of resources or near access windows where resources were obtainable, usually within the subsistence range of the parent group.[8] The linkage of groups to particular resource patches in already packed territories ensures that some of the more recently separated groups would, at least periodically, experience subsistence shortfalls, while the larger parental settlements located at the best access windows might not be so disadvantaged. In some situations, this kind of spatial infilling, characterized by increased numbers of essentially nonmobile units, seems to have resulted in ethnogenesis within a region and the partitioning of groups into a greater number of competitive ethnic units. Alternatively, a group may have become integrated, or at least maintained, within an ethnically identified unit that was itself expanding in size. This trajectory is often associated with warfare.

Other interesting consequences of arriving at the packing threshold were that (1) those hunter-gatherers who were primarily dependent upon terrestrial animals were no longer able to maintain their way of life, and (2) below the packing threshold, all cases of hunter-gatherers who were dependent upon plant resources lacked any type of wealth or social ranking in their societies. Some of the groups dependent upon aquatic resources, on the other hand, exhibited wealth distinctions prior to reaching the packing threshold. These groups were the only hunter-gatherers with internally ranked social distinctions and some type of "big man" leadership structure, as well as secret societies and an increased ritual emphasis upon individual maturational events. All groups of plant-dependent hunter-gatherers that maintained their adaptation after crossing the packing threshold began to display differences in wealth. These groups began to depend upon aquatic resources to a considerable extent, although their societies were organized very differently from the big man systems maintained by groups of aquatic resource specialists. Many of these groups developed secret societies and some distinctions based on age, but a focus on prominent leaders and an emphasis on internal ranking was not evident. These are also the packed cases with the greatest subsistence diversity and are therefore expected to be the most stable.

Regardless of some of the differences pointed out in the preceding paragraphs, regional packing radically changes the scale of kinship articulations as an overall function of reductions in mobility. Among aquatically dependent peoples, bidimensional systems tend to become imbalanced once packing occurs, as it does in groups of plant-dependent peoples who maintain their adaptation after crossing the packing threshold. Bidimensional kinship systems occur in groups dependent upon terrestrial animals about as often as do bilateral systems, but there is a cluster of imbalanced, bi-

dimensional systems at the threshold prior to packing. Between this point on the population density scale and the packing threshold, bilateral conventions with affinal inclusive terminology tended to occur, but beyond the packing threshold no groups primarily dependent upon terrestrial animals remained.

No one should be shocked to learn that, as mobility is reduced, kin conventions extending food procurement rights to distant kinsmen tend to disappear. Neither should it come as any surprise that marriages between persons who share rights of residence to common territories become more common and that conventions restricting access to resources become more prevalent.[9] Under normal circumstances, this means that the kin distance between prospective spouses becomes shorter and shorter and various forms of cross-cousin marriage become more common. As population density increases, the geographic scale of the educational systems that are organized through kinship connections are also reduced, and the rules enforced by members of secret societies that govern inclusion in and exclusion from education become more stringent.

At this point, in the few aquatically dependent groups that remain hunter-gatherers,[10] control over resources becomes critical. When the effects of packing become severe, regional networks become greatly constricted or even disappear, and only with the later appearance of ranked and politically centralized authorities do kinship-based networks reappear. Under these new conditions, however, egocentric networks are replaced by sociocentric alliances based on elite kinship ties. This pattern occurs only among hunter-gatherer groups that are dependent upon aquatic resources, although different conditions might prompt other emergent, non-hunter-gatherer responses to packing.

There has been considerable speculation about the role that trade has played in societal transformation, particularly the role of emerging elites in stimulating trade. I have previously discussed how trade and the circulation of items among nonpacked hunter-gatherers can be organized in one of two ways: (1) the circulation of gifts through highly conventionalized kinship links, and (2) exchanges within trading partnerships, which usually represent pairings of individuals or families, frequently in terms other than those of conventional kinship.

As the packing threshold is approached, a reduction in the scale and incidence of network-based exchanges usually occurs. In some settings, this is accompanied by roughly contemporary increases in short-distance, family-initiated trading expeditions. These trips are usually associated with the appearance of some form of money or with an increased investment of labor in the production of craft items or primitive valuables (Dalton 1967:278; Polanyi 1968), with the result that a family with subsistence shortfalls will try to exchange their craft items for food.

This kind of behavior is well documented in data from California and adjacent regions (Goldschmidt 1951:417; Voegelin 1938:57),[11] which record that subsistence-stressed families initiated transactions after they had invested their labor in craft items in the hope of exchanging their products for food with families not experiencing shortfalls. These exchanges were balanced and no "social storage," delayed reciprocity, or debt was incurred. This kind of system ensured that settlements with a broader subsistence base, located adjacent to highly productive patches, would accumulate craft "wealth" and that families so situated would almost automatically become the patrons in patron-client relationships as a simple function of the reliable productivity of their subsistence ranges.

It should therefore not be surprising that, in fact, longer-term patron-client relationships of exchange actually represent the next most common new form of exchange and circulation relationship appearing at and immediately following packing. The big man phenomenon may be the inevitable result of a continuation of the spatial segmentation that characterizes nonpacked hunter-gatherer organization beyond the point at which maintenance of small group size actually facilitates subsistence security through mobility. The more change there is from a settlement system to a settlement hierarchy composed of residential clusters of different size, the more the system resembles a big man organization.

Generic hunter-gatherers do not give up an egalitarian way of life. They may be surprised to discover that their adherence to a pattern of small-unit cooperation literally moves them into an emerging regional structure in which nonegalitarian relationships in subsistence security among basic, on-the-ground social units is an inevitable result of habitat patchiness. Territoriality becomes organizationally important in this context, and limits on territorial trespass and actual defense of territory are likely to increase as the quantity and volume of craft items increase. The value of many items is based on the scarcity of the materials and the quality and quantity of "value-added" labor underlying their procurement and production.

The preceding dynamics are likely to occur most frequently in systems that are substantially dependent upon aquatic resources or in situations in which the mix of exploited resources is nearly equally divided between the aquatic and terrestrial biomes. I have observed that most of the hunter-gatherer groups that depend heavily upon terrestrial plants, even those whose diets reflect a substantial contribution from aquatic resources, do not seem to continue the "old," generic pattern of segmentation into small settlements. We see instead the increasing growth of settlements that are situated at locations where greater subsistence diversity is possible and where there tends to be less interannual variability in food availability. In short, there is a change in residential density in the direction of "megapacking" at high-productivity locations. The contemporaneous appearance of secret societies and sodalities of various kinds suggests that scalar stress is conditioning the formation of broad, integrative institutions under the preceding conditions.

I am well aware that the preceding suppositions reflect only a limited understanding of the dynamic contexts in which new organizational variability arose following the state of criticality experienced by hunter-gatherer groups as they crossed the packing threshold at different places and at different times in the past. On the far side of this organizational Rubicon, most of world's prehistoric populations of hunter-gatherers were integrated into forms of organization based on completely different subsistence strategies and are, therefore, not represented in this study. Even so, it is very tempting to ask what the new systems looked like and whether there are any clues about subsequent organizational trajectories to be discovered in an examination of the initial conditions of ancestral hunter-gatherer systems.

In the last section of chapter 12, I briefly explored three archaeological sequences and found the exercise to be exciting and provocative. We may anticipate that, once hunter-gatherer populations in a region crossed the packing threshold, a vast amount of variability appeared rather suddenly, associated with a high rate of systemic extinction. We should also expect a fair rate of extinction among the new, non–hunter-gatherer organizational variants, and the archaeological record of this era should reflect not a single, punctuated episode but, in some places, a succession of quick, punctuated phases that precede a new period of substantial stability.

The empirical support for the major thresholds demonstrated in this book should provide a substantial basis for the serious consideration of patterns in the tempo and mode of cultural evolution. Why do some archaeological sequences change rapidly while others seem to present us with a chronological sequence representing slow, gradual change? Still other sequences exhibit an orderly succession of related but nevertheless substantial changes, but we can also point to archaeological patterns of dramatic, punctuated changes followed by long periods of stasis. If we were to undertake a comparative study of ethnographically documented horticulturists and pastoralists using the packing theory developed in this book, would we see another point of criticality among non–hunting and gathering peoples at the fourth threshold specified by equation (11.01)? Or do the rules change and does a new, self-organizing form of homeostatic mechanism appear that alters the scale of demographically based thresholds of stress on the high side of the packing threshold? I do not know—but at least now there is a basis for asking such potentially productive questions.

Have I Established a General Research Procedure?

In the prologue to this book I noted that one of my major goals has been "*the development of a method for productively using ethnographic data in the service of archaeological goals.*" I hope that the logic I have followed is clear, but just in case readers are left with any lingering bewilderment, let me review several underlying principles. The first is that if one wants to use arguments based on ethnographic data to "interpret" archeological observations, it is much better to proceed with arguments from homology rather than from analogy. If it is possible to explain the variability among hunter-gatherers, or any other class of ethnographically documented cultural systems, then we should be able to deduce hypotheses—dealing with the conditional relationships between specified variables—that state when particular phenomena should or should not appear in the archeological record.

I have focused upon subsistence base and group size in this book, but along the way I have shown that other properties also appear or disappear in tandem with changes in some of the basic variables. It must be recognized, however, that the correlations I have identified appear to be general ones but that the particular mechanisms that condition their linkages to the variables that received the most attention in this book remain poorly researched. I have nonetheless initiated a process of theory building, and what I have learned now moves us to the point of being able to argue from homology about some issues.

In order to arrive at this point, considerable higher-level pattern recognition work has been fundamental. It is critical that readers understand that *second-order derivative patterning* implicates the past and the processes that operated in the past. The patterned relationships between subject-side data and organized prior knowledge cannot be seen unless prior knowledge is organized into a frame of reference for use in research. I would go so far as to suggest that, in the absence of research rooted in the rigorous use of frames of reference, successful theory building cannot be accomplished. One must keep in mind that theories attempt to explain why the world is the way it appears to be. Accuracy in the description of the world is essential to successful theory building; otherwise one is simply engaged in producing cognitively accommodating stories about a world that may not exist.

The second principle is that a person who is engaged in the act of theory building cannot appeal to authority or to a prior theory directed at the same subject matter for his or her intellectual inspiration. The learning opportunity in such a situation rests with being able to do pattern recognition research. This means comprehensively projecting what is known about a focal subject matter against a frame of reference made up of variables that are known or suspected to be relevant and about which there is some secure knowledge about the factors that condition variability in each. If one obtains robust patterns—as I did in this book between environmental variables and the ethnographically warranted variables related to hunter-gatherer systems—then it is possible to project one's knowledge about the ethnographic conditions onto environmental variability in the real world.

Doing this puts us in the position of being able to evaluate the degree to which relationships observed in the present are germane or irrelevant to dynamics in the past. If relationships between linked variables accurately anticipate patterning in the archaeological record, then we have identified a learning opportunity. This procedure allows us to transform some properties of hunter-gatherers into frames of reference in terms of which the archaeological record can be studied comparatively and unambiguously with respect to current knowledge.

It is important to realize that much of what I currently envision as useful to archaeologists was not demonstrated directly in this book. In the act of exploring my initial ideas, I learned a great deal that offers the prospect of greater learning but also requires substantial future work. For instance, when the initial equations that define the relationships between ethnographic and environmental variables were first developed, I either used my total ethnographic sample of 339 cases or divided them into subsets that seemed to make sense or that I thought might turn out to reflect important ways of partitioning the obvious variability. I actually knew very little about the organizational differences that corresponded to important system state differences in the cases.

Between then and now I have learned a great deal about system state differences in many of the places on earth about which researchers are curious. I will certainly be able to develop a series of equations that will project current knowledge about the sequential relationships among systems in different states onto targeted locations to see if my inferences about sequences, based on roughly synchronic data, are sustained by chronological data when the conditioning variables are controlled geographically and in terms of climatic reconstructions.

During the course of my research I became aware of many new features of the environments and habitats in which hunter-gatherers have lived that strongly influenced the success or failure of some of their strategies. For instance, the conditions modeled by the "codfish equation" (11.02) are not yet definitive, and substantial research is needed to understand the response of pathogens to variability in both temperature and moisture. I would also like to learn how these factors contribute to health risks in different kinds of stored products. I am particularly looking forward to discovering the many other areas of research that readers of this book will be inspired to pursue.

I fear, though, that some readers may accept some of the points I have made and still ask how archaeologists will be able to use the procedures and the knowledge developed up to this point. In response, let me point out that it is possible for archaeologists to study comparatively archaeological sites, assemblages, and even artifacts relative to the same habitat variables that I used in my study of ethnographic cases. To be sure, the scale of patterns of variability will be different when one is studying archaeological sites rather than ethnic groups, but this very difference, other things being equal, could well provide clues to the kind of interassemblage variability that is referable to within- as distinct from between-system variety. I also think more light could be shed on the question of "parts and wholes"—that is, the degree to which the contents of archaeological sites are conditioned by the varying roles played by items of material culture *within* a cultural system at different times and places, as opposed to fundamental changes in the organization of similar features and artifacts in *different* systems. We should also begin to see different scales of space and habitat characteristic of these two systemic scales of variability.

Archaeologists can begin to use the synthesized information now available about hunter-gatherers as an additional frame of reference. We will never learn what causes variability in the archaeological record by simply providing a behavioral "interpretation" of our sites or, if we are fortunate to have chronological data, by "reconstructing culture histories." We must strive to learn what factors have conditioned cultural variability in the recent as well as in the distant past. This goal requires that we embrace research strategies that permit us, for purposes of learning, to use our prior knowledge analytically rather than simply apply it to the archaeological record in an accommodative, piecemeal fashion. Such a procedure results in the creation of a past that is only as comprehensive as the current state of our knowledge or—perhaps more frighteningly—that reflects only what we choose to believe about humankind and culture.

Notes

PROLOGUE

1.   When I use the word *dimension,* I am invoking the definition that is used in physics and mathematics, which refers to one of the least number of independent coordinates required to specify a point in space uniquely. By extension, the term *property space* refers to any space that is dimensionally defined.

CHAPTER 1

1.   I do not mean to suggest that Fortes is the primary advocate of this position, for many others have also adopted this view of kinship. I simply cite Fortes because he is a convenient example.

2.   This issue has been addressed by Ives (1985) with provocative results.

3.   During Steward's era, the major challenge to this assumption was the argument presented initially by Frank Speck (1915) stating that among the Northern Algonkian hunter-gatherers of eastern Canada nuclear families were "landowning units."

4.   It is interesting that Steward's citations in support of linking large Athapaskan group size to the availability of migratory animals come exclusively from Morice (1906a, 1906b, 1907, 1909, 1910). Although these articles are quite informative, Morice discusses Athapaskans in terms of an ethnic group—or what June Helm (1968) would later call "regional bands"—and group size is referred to as large (220 persons for the Slave and 287 persons for the Dog Rib) (Steward 1936:342). Steward appears to conclude that groups of this size actually cooperated in large, communally organized caribou drives, but I know of no ethnographic documentation supporting such a conclusion. The single possible exception might be the Chippewayan, if one accepts Heffley (1981:137–38), although J. G. E. Smith (1978:77) reported that the size of the "contact-traditional" hunting group varied between eleven and forty-one persons. Small Copper Eskimo units engaged in caribou drives are also reported by Jenness (1932:58). Riches (1982:21–55) is a more recent proponent of the view that very large groups were characteristic of societies undertaking caribou drives. He assumes that the term *band* as used by Gubser (1965:167) referred to hunting groups assembled at cari-

bou drive locations. Gubser's use of the term was similar to that of Morice, whose reports misled Steward about the size of cooperating units engaged in communal hunting. It is interesting that Riches has simply assumed, as did Steward, that cooperating groups were very large and then has proceeded to explain why they should be large. There are, in fact, good reasons to believe that communal hunting groups were not generally as large as Riches imagined.

5.   Fred Eggan has discussed in general terms the spatial correlates of the family level of sociocultural integration: "Each family may camp one-quarter of a mile away from the others. The people do not actually come into close house-to-house contact, but they are within shouting distance of one another in the same valley" (Damas 1969:199).

6.   For an excellent review of the history of ideas with regard to kinship and the arguments between Julian Steward and Omer Stewart, particularly on the subject of landownership and the character of the groups being discussed under the "band" rubric, see Shapiro (1986:620–29).

7.   In spite of forceful arguments to the contrary, this view has its defenders in the contemporary literature (Bishop 1970), and the issue remains unresolved in any scientific sense of the word.

8.   This treatment of the !Kung provides a preview of the current debate questioning whether this group should be viewed as a model for hunter-gatherers of the past (Wilmsen 1983).

9.   Like Service, Lee attributed organizational divergence from a "pristine" band state to the destructive effects of contact with state-level societies. Interestingly, Wilmsen's criticism of Lee's work invokes the same argument (Wilmsen 1989).

10.   Sahlins has many critics. For example, Sahlins's incorporation of Chayanov's work and his defense of the "substantivist" economic position have been criticized from the perspective of neoclassical economics (Donham 1981). Evolutionary biologists have addressed his argument of "limited needs" by presenting evidence that hunters do not stop hunting when they "have enough" but instead hunt longer hours when hunting returns are high (Hawkes et al. 1985). Although this is an important point, Sahlins was addressing the issue of the accumulation of wealth rather than the question of increasing one's fitness, a concern that does not directly relate to the wealth issue.

11.   For a complete misunderstanding of the goals of science as a structured learning process, see the distorted description of "processual" archaeology and the claims for the value of a particularistic historical view of causation presented by McGuire (1992:146–78).

12.   I do not mean to imply that all of the ideas or research leading to the position summarized here were exclusively the work of these authors. Many other researchers have made basic contributions to the development of the views reviewed here. I have chosen this body of work because it is the most comprehensive treatment of the issue of sharing that I know of.

13.   The term *risk* has been used in a number of ways in the anthropological literature. In many cases it is used to denote either insecurity or low productivity in a habitat, or periodic failure in subsistence strategies when compared with the overall security of a system. This usage is common in the work of Richard Gould (1980:85–87, 1981:436) and John Yellen (1986), among others, but it has little analytical value and represents, at best, a vague characterization of a system state.

14.   In my opinion, most of what is discussed as *theory* in contemporary archaeology and anthropology is not theory in any scientific sense of the term. At best, the term *theory* is used to refer to a series of abstract characterizations of experience that are often indistinguishable from essentialist propositions about what the world is like. These characterizations are usually consistent with some broader moral or political philosophy to which the theorists subscribe. Theory in this context consists of the conceptual terms used by the theorist to accommodate the world of experience to his or her prior beliefs.

15.   The typological approach to hunter-gatherer variability remains alive and well: Woodburn (1988) is perhaps the most visible writer currently adhering to this essentialist approach.

16.   Historicism—and its preoccupation with event sequences—underlies many currently debated issues in the anthropological literature (Headland and Reid 1989; Schrire 1984b; Solway and Lee 1990; Wilmsen 1989).

CHAPTER 2

1.   This problem is directly implied by the discussions of atomism that have arisen in the comparative study of hunter-gatherers.

2.   Postprocessualists justify their claims for a superior archaeology by adopting the methodology of critical divination. They call for a reconstruction of the rationality of a past cultural system because their vision dictates that knowledge of the thoughts of past actors must precede an interpretation of the archaeological record. Reasons, however, are always relative to the socioculturally constituted matrix within which persons live and act and—given commonalities in belief, values, and moral and ethical positions—can be derived from any experiences in terms of which one evaluates the actions and reasons of others. The rules for creating the past in postprocessualist terms, therefore, must be arbitrary in order to accommodate the fact that reasons are difficult to access even *after* archaeological investigation.

3.   Leach's assertion that prediction of human behavior is impossible places him in the relativist category, but is this judgment made with respect to the variety and novelty observable in human action, and does Leach believe that it is uniquely referable to human abilities? If so, then quite unintentionally Leach has placed the human species in the same research context as nonhuman animals, since all researchers consider the unique properties of the subjects of their research.

4.   Ironically, in the sense of physical dynamics the products of scientific learning strategies are neither static nor dynamic. Rather they are emergent and have many of the same properties that the critics of science have claimed require a different way of learning!

5.   For Leach and other humanistic anthropologists, the problem is not one of emergence, since their ideological perspective is associated with an anti-evolutionary stance and a denial of emergence as a natural process. Unanticipated change is explained by the unpredictability of human actors and their alleged ability to change the nature of their own social organizations. According to this viewpoint, human actors are endowed with the capacity to choose their futures and then to make them happen without the impingement of natural processes.

6.   From the perspective of biological evolution, models of kin selection and inclusive fitness may be more appropriate to arguments about group stabilities than to risk reduction, since successful risk reduction strategies appear to be based upon a reasonable certainty about the future behavior of other actors in the risk pool.

7.   The research value of a maximizing assumption is well illustrated by Hurtado and Hill (1990:337–39), who noted a low level of work effort and a far from optimal nutritional state among the Hiwi (Guihibo) of Venezuela. These observations led them to look for other variables and states that could have produced a trade-off situation in which maximizing one currency resulted in a reduction in security because of other niche-related interactions.

8.   There is considerable controversy over the meaning and correct usage of the term *optimality* (Richerson and Boyd 1987). In the context of this discussion, it can be used in two ways: to refer either to the best or most desirable outcome or to a state that is better than the current state. When I use the currency of "maximizing vital security," I have in mind the stabilization of a currently unstable situation or a restructuring of niche to increase overall stability. Either of these meanings simply represents an improvement in some condition. I do not mean to imply that a sentient organism can seek an optimal state in some absolute sense, since the knowledge necessary to imagine such a state and the stabilities prerequisite to realize that state will never co-occur. This is simply another way of stating the principle of scientific indeterminism (Popper 1988:29–86).

9.   Anthropology involves a built-in conflict for practitioners. In order to do anthropological research with living peoples, it is necessary to concentrate on learning the meanings assigned to actions, as well as the values, beliefs, and customs that are shared by the peoples with whom one interacts. In short, one must become an authority on the reasons prompting the behaviors that one observes. The ability to fit in socially and to convey to others the rationality of one's own very different and sometimes shocking ways of doing things is critically dependent upon an appreciation of the "other" and their mores. Anthropologists must never assume, however, that accurately recorded emic statements about the meaning of life and the reasons for different kinds of behavior constitute an explanation of cultural variability itself. Archaeologists are perhaps uniquely positioned to undertake explanatory ventures

since it is not necessary to work out a mutually satisfying modus vivendi in order to study human material remains. Our task is the explanation of documented variability that was created in dynamic contexts to which the human capacity for generating reasons was only one of many contributing factors.

CHAPTER 3

1.   Pattern recognition has been described as a skill at which human beings excel (see Watanabe 1985:20). This apparently innate facility has been enhanced by the development of numerous tactics and strategies directed toward increasing the reliability of human recognition skills (Grenander 1981; Patrick 1972). It would not be an exaggeration to say that the development of enhanced pattern recognition skills has been crucial to the development of science as a strategy for learning.

2.   I and another researcher (Binford 1991a; Helm 1993) reported using diaries to produce data about the past that the authors of the diaries would have been unaware of or would have had no interest in.

3.   One of the features of inductively reasoned arguments is the degree of *inductive ambiguity* of the observations used in the argument. Since induction can be the basis for propositions of either great utility or sheer nonsense, scientific strategies for evaluating the utility of ideas make a major contribution to intellectual success.

4.   One of the best examples of the transition from "cognitive attachment" to explanation occurs in an article by Timothy Earle (1991) in which he argues that individual choice can be assumed to be responsible for human behavior and that "behavioralism" therefore explains archaeological patterning. The author provides an example of how the "processes of choice" might be examined archaeologically by observing a number of changes in the archaeological record of the Mantaro River in Peru subsequent to the Inka conquest. Earle then says that "the lesson appears to be quite obvious. In terms of status-defining material culture, objects with local and regional reference were largely replaced by objects that refer explicitly to the state styles. Following conquest, the Wanka elites identified themselves explicitly with the state rather than with their regional networks important prior to conquest. Eliteness derived, if you will, not from a class of elites connected horizontally by networks of alliance but from a group identified vertically by their ties to the state" (Earle 1991:95).

It appears obvious to me that at the most superficial, explanatory level, "processes of choice" underlie *most* if not all of the changes in the formal properties of items of material culture found in the archaeological record. This is because human agency and motivation are correlated with these formal properties, whether one is making the items oneself or importing them from some other source. In this example, Earle stipulates that "behavioralism" (the physical manifestation of processes of choice) is the explanatory fulcrum of archaeological theory building. He then cites the change in Wanka material culture and imputes a set of attitudes and behaviors to the Wanka (they identify themselves with the larger political system) that is said to "explain" the archaeological patterning. This is a textbook example of stipulative thinking, which simply translates all phenomena into a different set of terms with zero explanatory value—unless, of course, one believes that the intellectual content of sentences spoken in English is "explained" by a translation of the English into French.

5.   The postmodernist criticism that "interpretation" is a logical extension of the researcher's original observational bias is correct when it applies to first-order patterning. Focus on first-order observations guarantees that the original justifications for making the observations will also justify the interpretations. Unfortunately, these same critics offer alternative interpretations that make them appropriate targets of their own criticism. Apparently they do not understand that when analysis proceeds to second- and third-order derivative patterning, a strict inductive pattern of inference is established, the components of which must be independently justified.

6.   The so-called "culture war" in anthropology (Geertz 1995) derives from opinions about the correct way to articulate source- and subject-side knowledge. This debate also questions what is a "proper" subject-side focus of study and what is germane source-side knowledge. My position with respect to these issues should be clear from my attempt to develop rational and productive tactics for using source-side knowledge in a scientific search for greater knowledge and causal understanding of archaeological and ethnographic variability, with a special pragmatic focus on hunter-gatherers.

7.   I realize that all prior processes are not necessarily germane to the ancient events about which the archaeologist wishes to learn. Many kinds of events—and the processes that cause the modification of an archaeological deposit—leave residual patterning that does not directly implicate the organization of past cultural systems.

8.   First-order patterning may be recognized without the use of a frame of reference per se. For example, when two variables are plotted in two-dimensional space by means of a range of values of variable X on the X axis and a range of values of variable Y on the Y axis, the swarm of points in the area defined by the X and Y axes can represent a property space map of the relationships between the two variables. In situations in which there is a good understanding of the basis for the patterning on such a property space map, by adding one or more variables one can use the property space as a frame of reference for exploring the possibility of differential or regular patterning. I might, for instance, code with a third variable all of the points where variable X and variable Y (whose interactive relationships are generally understood) intersect in order to see if the third variable exhibits any general patterning with regard to the property space defined by the better-understood referential variables.

Property space maps can be thought of as something like geographic maps. In a distribution of points that defines the outline and features of the continent of South America, for instance, coding all points for another variable such as elevation would make it possible to transform the "flat" space of the original distribution into a property space map of elevation. Depending upon the conventions I have chosen to observe, I could now depict the South American continent not only in terms of north-south, east-west extension but also in terms of topography.

9.   As Wylie has pointed out (1985:100–105), it must be demonstrated that the subject-side phenomena (the observations or data being analyzed) and the source-side knowledge that is used to construct arguments or offer interpretations are linked in a germane or relevant real-world fashion.

10.   I hope to illustrate how projection may be used in an argument from analogy in order to permit the evaluation of analogical implications. By so doing one is able to answer a

question such as: do data from the location of interest support the expectations projected from ethnographic data? An answer of either "yes" or "no" is directly informative about the projection's limits of relevance and might also provide clues to causal conditions not considered in the original projection.

11.   Students taking a course on statistics are invariably introduced to the subject of probability by a coin-flipping demonstration. The reason that there is an equal probability distribution for the frequency of heads and tails is because the choice of heads and tails as properties to observe have nothing to do with the physics of coin-flipping, which is related to the coin's center of gravity. If the coin is tampered with in such a way that one or the other face of the coin is differentially weighted, then the coin's surface becomes relevant to the outcome. Statistics do not inform us about the external world in any direct sense; they only give us feedback about how germane the properties we have chosen to observe may be to the way the world might work. In this sense, it is not possible to prove that a random distribution really exists anywhere in nature—only that one exists with respect to the irrelevant terms with which we have chosen to describe experience!

12.   Failure to consider all these options is what has made Richard Gould's proposals (1980:138–68) for "arguments from anomaly" misleading and certain to result in false interpretations.

13.   For an interesting discussion of ethnographic analogy see the article by Rensink (1995) entitled "On Magdalenian Mobility and Land Use in North-west Europe." The author is clearly frustrated with inferential identifications by other researchers of site types that are based on my argument (resulting from ethnographic comparisons) for the presence of differences in settlement pattern and site composition that are related to logistical and foraging forms of subsistence organization. The author's support for "a return to the data" reflects the posture of other critics of analogy, such as Richard Gould (1971, 1974, 1977, 1978a, 1978b, 1980, 1985) and Gould and Watson (1982). I suggest that they all refer to my comments on this debate (Binford 1985, 1989; Binford and Stone 1985). Although I am sympathetic to these reactions, I remain unimpressed, since almost all of them derive from an empiricist paradigm. I would argue, instead, that it is imperative to learn how to use prior (source-side) knowledge more profitably to address the (subject-side) object of our research, which is the archaeological record.

14.   See, for example, the discussion by Carr (1985:384–452).

15.   I have tried to illustrate how ambiguity should be regarded as a tip-off to learning opportunities (Binford 1987), but, more often than not, ambiguity is cited as the reason that generalizations and cross-cultural comparisons are invalid.

16.   For instance, it is common to read in the archaeological literature that one's "theoretical orientation" biases what one considers to be causes. "Binford . . . attributes cross-culturally consistent relationships to environmental factors or causes, whereas I attribute cross-culturally consistent relationships to social-cultural factors" (Kent 1994:6). Unfortunately, Kent appears to misunderstand my research. I have frequently demonstrated the correlation between cultural data and environmental data. This is an empirical observation, and my "theoretical orientation" does not modify the reality of the demonstrated correlations. In fact, many of the variables that Kent focused upon in her research at Kutse were the very same variables that I have studied in many different contexts!

"Interpretations" of archaeological data are, at best, opinions about what is germane, what is relevant, and what may be linked to a researcher's knowledge and beliefs. Insofar as interpretations become the sole intellectual goal, then one's personal biases and knowledge constraints most certainly condition the kinds of interpretations offered.

17.   This tactic may appear to be similar to Gould's (1985:642) "argument from analogy," but in explanatory terms it is altogether different. Gould stipulates the significance of archaeological phenomena that he terms "anomalies" and claims that they deviate from a materialist expectation. In fact, such deviations are potential sources of new knowledge since the "causes" of the deviations were not considered in the original argument. There is, however, absolutely no basis for the assumption that a lack of inclusiveness in the original argument must refer to mental or ideological phenomena, as Gould claims.

18.   The presence of different system states directly implies that there are organizational differences: similar things can be organized differently and different things can be organized similarly. For instance, it has been said (Bender 1985:21) that the hunter-gatherers of the Northwest Coast of North America were as "complex" as, or exhibited organizational forms more like, horticultural peoples. This assertion was then used to justify their exclusion from the category of "true" hunter-gatherers. Northwest Coast groups have also been used to support the claim that subsistence base is not a meaningful conditioner of societal form because these groups more closely resemble horticultural peoples in organizational properties. One of the unresolved issues in anthropology concerns the issue of system state comparisons and the question of what types of processes produce organizational similarities and differences.

In the 1960s, the formulations of Sahlins and Service (1960:12–44) distinguished between "general" and "specific" evolution. The latter referred to "phylogenetic classification" and the former referred to "shifts in the character of process itself." These shifts resulted in "forms . . . classed in stages or levels of development without reference to phylogeny" (Sahlins 1960:13). Subsequent attempts to classify patterns of general evolution have been strongly challenged and rejected, particularly by neo-Marxists, who embrace ideological and historically particularistic approaches. Traditional "normative" archaeologists frequently support historical approaches, while so-called "selectionists"—represented by Dunnell (1992), Leonard and Jones (1987), and O'Brien and Holland (1990, 1995)—seek to eliminate inference from archaeological method and arrive at theoretical certainty directly from a classification of empirical materials!

19.   With one significant exception, archaeologists have invested little effort in the investigation of different tempos and modes of change in their data from different geographic settings. The doctoral thesis of Carol Raish (1992), however, takes a global view of important differences in the rate and mode of organizational change.

CHAPTER 4

1.   The data on the 1,429 weather stations included in my study were originally published by Wernstedt (1972), who reported values for the following variables: name of the weather station, location by country, station elevation, longitude, and latitude. Mean monthly values for temperature and mean

monthly rainfall levels are also reported, as well as summary values for total annual rainfall and mean annual temperature.

2.   An ET value was also calculated for the sample of weather stations used here as a frame of reference against which to compare hunter-gatherer systems, as well as for all other locations that are used comparatively throughout the book. All other described variables were also calculated for all hunter-gatherer cases and any other comparative materials included in the study.

3.   The most important measure of solar radiation used in biological calculations is potential evapotranspiration. Strictly speaking, this is a measurement of solar radiation expressed in terms of the amount of water that *could* be either evaporated or transpired, given the solar energy available at any given location. This measure, which is referred to as PET, will be discussed subsequently.

4.   A value of forty-five is added so that there will be no negative values in any calculations.

5.   The moisture index was developed by Thornthwaite and Mather to facilitate evaluation of the suitability of environments for agricultural production (Mather 1962:120). The index is calculated as follows: MI = 100 * (CRR/PET − 1). This value is distributed between −100 and an open scale of positive values. The following classification of habitats was proposed by the original researchers: (a) perhumid: values from 100 and greater; (b4) humid-4: values from 80 through 99.99; (b3) humid-3: values from 60 through 79.99; (b2) humid-2: values from 40 through 59.99; (b1) humid-1: values from 20 through 39.99; (c2) moist subhumid: values from 0 through 19.99; (c1) dry subhumid: values from −33.30 through −0.01; (d) semi-arid: values from −66.7 through −33.31; (e) arid: values from −100 through −66.71. It should be noted that the transition point between water-starved habitats such as desert, savanna, grassland, and some dry, scrub forests (versus "true" forests) occurs at a value of zero in this scheme.

6.   This index was developed by Holdridge (1959) for use in classifying plant communities from climatic data. It is calculated using the following equation: HIRX = PET/CRR. At this point in the discussion, PET has not been defined. It represents, however, potential evapotranspiration: the total amount of water in millimeters that could be both evaporated or transpired at a particular location, given the amount of available solar energy measured by temperature. Holdridge developed the following nine-step classification of habitats: 1, superhumid: values from zero to 0.255; 2, perhumid: values from 0.256 through 0.555; 3, humid: values from 0.556 through 1.00; 4, subhumid: values from 1.01 through 2.00; 5, semiarid: values from 2.01 through 4.00; 6, arid: values from 4.01 through 8.00; 7, periarid: values from 8.01 through 16.00; 8, superarid: values from 16.01 through 32.00; 9, desiccated: values above 32.00. It should be noted that the cutoff or transition value between forests and forms of desert, savanna, grassland, and tropical raingreen dry forests is 1.0 on this scale. All true forests have values greater than 1.0.

7.   This statement refers to the tables dealing with soil moisture retention, in which the properties of soils are related to agricultural crops and not to natural plant communities (Thornthwaite and Mather 1957:244).

8.   Most of this very difficult work was done in several time-consuming steps by Russell Gould. First, all of Thornthwaite and Mather's (1957) tables of meteorological data were scanned into the computer. Then, long iterations were run on that data relative to values read from the tables. Equations were then obtained for the relationships between the results and the variables that had been used to create the tables in the first place. Excellent results were obtained, and the equations made it possible to write a computer program that produced measures of potential evapotranspiration (PET) and actual evapotranspiration (AE), both of which are essential in calculations of water balance.

9.   In order to produce these values, the following data had to be included in the meteorological file: 1, NAME: the weather station or source of the data; 2, LATITUDE: the latitude of the weather station in degrees and tenths of degrees; 3, LAT: S = south latitude, N = north latitude; 4, LONGITUDE: the longitude of the weather station in degrees and tenths of degrees; 5, LONG: E = east longitude, W = west longitude; 6, ELEV: the elevation of the weather station in feet; 7, RJAN: mean rainfall for January in millimeters; 8–18, similar rainfall values for the months February through December; 19, TJAN: mean temperature for the month of January in degrees Celsius; 20–30, similar temperature values for the months February through December.

In addition to these basic data, the following variables were entered to facilitate subsequent calculations: 31, MCM: temperature of the coldest month of the year in degrees Celsius; 32, MWM: temperature of the warmest month of the year in degrees Celsius; 33, RHIGH: rainfall for the wettest month of the year in millimeters; 34, RLOW: rainfall for the driest month of the year in millimeters; 35, RRCORR: number of months (positive or negative from the warmest month of the year) of the wettest month of the year (positive values range from 1 to 6 while negative values range from 1 to 5).

In reality, the meteorological data used in this study were obtained largely by geographic extrapolation from the data of several weather stations because only in rare instances was a weather station located exactly in the center of the range of a known group of hunter-gatherers. When extrapolation was required, a minimum of three stations were chosen that were roughly equidistant from the point to be estimated. If equidistant stations were not available, data from other stations were weighted as a function of their distance from the longitude and latitude of the point of interest.

10.   The equations and procedures for calculating all of the necessary variables (based solely on meteorological data) for an analysis of the water balance at any given location are currently stored on the computer in my laboratory at Southern Methodist University in Dallas. In the near future I hope to be able to make these files available to interested researchers.

11.   One feature of the water balance approach is the consideration given to the properties of soils. In order to use this method, the researcher needs to know the character of the soils at the various locations for which calculations will be performed. In turn, the different types of soils are weighted so that varying amounts of water retained within the soil are estimated differentially, depending upon the mix of soil properties. The following values for water storage (WSTORAGE) have been used for the basic soil types: S = 62.72; A1 = 59.96; A2 = 108.75; A3 = 196.84; A4 = 103.86; A5 = 196.84; A = (59.96 + 108.75 + 196.84 + 103.86)/4; U = 174.52; U2 = 174.52; U4 = 174.52; O = 383.93; V = 161.20; M = 195.92; M5 = 195.92; D = 69.95; T = 66.72; H = 143.03.

12.   I had originally planned to use existing systems of vegetation classification based on climatic data. On investigation, however, I discovered that while the Strahler and Strahler classification (1984:chapter 10 and appendix I) was based on Thornthwaite and Mather (1957), it was ambiguous in a number of ways and did not take advantage of the latter authors' strengths. For example, water storage was considered to be a potential of all soil types, which was totally unrealistic. My large data set described here was used to generate a climatic classification more consistent with Thornthwaite and Mather's water balance approach.

13.   This relationship is documented in the values of PET divided by annual precipitation, which range between 0.25 and zero. This interval defines the world's rain forest zone in Holdridge's scheme of plant community classification. Similarly, in Thornthwaite's moisture index, values in excess of 80.00 define the "b4 humid-plus" zone containing the highest-biomass plant communities on earth.

14.   This was achieved by fitting a curve for the relationship between the maximum biomass and the net aboveground productivity recorded at several locations. The value of net aboveground productivity would be the same as the value of net aboveground productivity resulting from an actual evapotranspiration (AE) value that was equal to potential evapotranspiration (PET).

15.   Eyre's classification has been widely used and serves as the basis of a number of texts in physical geography (e.g., Strahler and Strahler 1984). The accompanying maps were scanned into a computer, enlarged to a uniform scale, and then printed. These standardized maps were then used to measure the area of the earth covered by the different vegetative formations distinguished by Eyre's classification.

16.   It is true that hunter-gatherers in some predominantly dry environments are reported to have set fire to the landscape as a routine response to a cycle of annual desiccation. The regions in which this practice has occurred are also subject to fires of natural origin, and, not surprisingly, the climax plant community consists of species that are rejuvenated rather than destroyed by fire. Fire in this setting, regardless of agency, is one of the natural conditions that helps to maintain a climax plant formation.

16.   On Strahler and Strahler's maps (1984:424–25), latitude was indicated by straight lines, so that it was relatively easy to project them fairly accurately across areas of the map representing land surfaces. A bigger problem was accurately projecting the curved lines representing longitude, for which I used a Keuffel and Esser flexcurve drafting edge (#57-2817-18).

17.   Porcupine grass refers to various species of spinifex that are restricted to Australia, which means that, unlike Mediterranean types of vegetation, this formation is provincial.

18.   Amber Johnson worked for several days measuring the areas on Eyre's maps occupied by different vegetative zones. On the basis of her work, I then selected the areally proportional sample of the earth's weather stations presented in table 4.08, as well as the information on plant communities that the table summarizes. This information on the earth's area will be referred to extensively in chapter 5.

19.   Eyre's maps acknowledge that his projections were adaptations of the work of a well-known person named "Goode" at the University of Chicago, but I have been unable to find an accurate bibliographic citation to Goode's work.

20.   Eisenberg, who is one of the foremost researchers of animal biomass, kindly shared with me his vast knowledge of the ecological literature as well as his understanding of the problem that I was researching.

21.   SPSS for Windows version 5.0 was programmed to perform this analysis, using a stepwise method with a 0.05 F probability for entry and a 0.10 F probability for removal.

22.   These results are expected when the sample size is reduced for cases in which the basic relationships between the dependent and independent variables are strong. There is no necessary implication of increased accuracy, however.

23.   As a check against the production of impossible values, which my experience has demonstrated could be a consequence of using such an equation, I developed the following procedure:

   1. I would reject any value requiring that more plant food be available to feed the projected animal biomass than was projected as present, given certain corrections for the difference between accessible and available plant food, as well as the trophic exchange ratio. I used the following equation, which produced the ratio (APLRTO):

   $$(\{[100 * (EXPREY + 0.001)] * 2.15\}/0.043748)/NAGPP$$

   where 2.15 is simply an estimate of the niche-related fauna in addition to ungulates that might be present, and 0.043748 is a conversion ratio that tells how much plant biomass is required to support the amount of animal biomass into which it is divided. The variable NAGPP is simply the value of NAGP scaled up to equal the amount present in an area measuring 100 square kilometers. This scaling requires that EXPREY be multiplied by 100 since it is calculated in the equation in units of square kilometers.

   2. Any cases in which the preceding equation produced a value greater than 0.39—or greater than 39 percent of available plant productivity—were considered unrealistic and were identified in the output by an expected value of –99.0.

24.   This equation was calculated using 98 of the 103 cases listed in the animal biomass file. The five omitted cases were consistent outliers regardless of how I calculated the equations. They include the Gir in India, Sengwa Park in Zimbabwe, Queen Elizabeth Park in Uganda, and Hlu-Hluhluwe in South Africa.

25.   The inclusion of WSTORAGE in this equation is interesting since the criticism by Oesterheld et al. (1992) of Fritz and Duncan's work (1993) appears to be justified. This may well be a situation in which Fritz and Duncan are correct, but for the wrong reasons. Another possibility is that Fritz and Duncan's use of different data at different scales was not the serious blunder that Oesterheld et al. (1992) alleged.

26.   Coe et al. (1976) report that the park's total biomass, including elephants, is 3,909 kilograms per square kilometer. Barnes and Douglas-Hamilton (1982:415), however, report that of 5,422 kilograms of animal biomass per square kilometer, only 912 kilograms were from species other than elephants. Since most of my data on Africa came from Coe et al., I reasoned that approximately the same percentage of total biomass represented by elephants was eliminated from the BIOSMALL estimates, and I chose a BIOSMALL value of 664 kilograms per square

kilometer as the base estimate for the time period covered by the data of Coe et al.

It is clear in retrospect that this was not a good strategy. Barnes and Douglas-Hamilton have reported a 9 percent per year increase in the Park's elephant population since 1972, which is attributed by the authors to "human pressure." It should be noted that, prior to 1946, over thirty settlements were established in the area that now constitutes the park, although currently there are no resident settlements. Since 1946, the abundance and distribution of animal populations has been changing dramatically.

CHAPTER 5

1. Despite my efforts to inject clarity into the confused discussion in the archaeological literature about the nature and importance of middle-range research, many misconceptions about this term remain (Binford 1981:21–30, 1987:449–55, 503–8, 1989:12–23). In general, however, all research on source-side subjects that is applied to subject-side problems to facilitate secure inferences about the character of the past is embraced by the term *middle-range research.*

2. See Lee and DeVore (1968b) for a statement about the importance of hunter-gatherer data.

3. Since there is no such thing as a $\log_{10}$ value of zero, by convention a value of 0.01 has been entered in all cells that would otherwise have been coded zero. In order to have the total value of the three subsistence-related variables equal 100 percent, a fractional correction of 0.99 is entered in one of the three columns instead of a whole number.

4. Use of the terms *hunting, gathering,* and *fishing* is not an accurate indication of what these variables represent. The three terms refer to what a person does to get food, whereas the variables refer to *where in the natural world one gets food.* I have kept Murdock's terms because they are recognizable and because the phrase *terrestrial plants* or *terrestrial animals* is cumbersome in tables.

5. Considerable debate has been initiated by the post-processual faction in archaeology, much of it focused on this issue. Clearly it is possible to choose one of many different problems as the starting point for analysis. I realize that not everyone is interested in demographic and subsistence variables. In fact, postprocessualists labeled my concerns as illegitimate based on their ontological beliefs about the locus of cause. It was argued that science was an invalid strategy for learning because postprocessual interests reside in domains that require unique epistemological underpinnings. Instead of engaging in counterproductive debate, a more reasonable course is to admit that, just as research focus may vary from researcher to researcher, solutions to different problems may also be different.

6. Hunter-gatherer penetration of the challenging environment of the polar tundra resulted from dynamic processes occurring just prior to and contemporary with the appearance of the earliest use of domesticated plants and animals, which was itself a response to causal processes in other hunter-gatherer systems. Successful occupation of the arctic tundra was a remarkable feat of adaptive ingenuity and should not be "marginalized" by ill-informed interpreters of the recent distribution of peoples and cultures.

7. See Vierich (1982) for information relevant to an answer to this question.

8. An examination of the ethnographic record casts doubt on the assertion that "with agriculture . . . humans could harness labour by using food as a currency and a medium of exchange" (Hole 1992:378). True money was a currency used regularly by many of the hunter-gatherers of California, and food was the major commodity purchased with that money (Wojcik 1992).

9. See Shott (1992) for a review of such arguments.

10. This concern has extended to the question of what is the proper "status" of the peoples of the Northwest Coast of North America and the Ainu of Japan. Since all of these groups share characteristics with horticultural peoples, it has been argued that they should be excluded from the class of hunter-gatherers.

11. For a philosophical exploration of the issue of natural units and their importance in science see Kornblith (1993).

12. Technically, the grasslands of California are components of an oak savanna that is typically conditioned by predominantly winter rainfall. These should not be equated with grasslands that do not have predominantly winter rainfall. This is a distinction that, unfortunately, Eyre fails to make.

13. Each time one adjusts the basis of a projection—as in map A in figure 5.12, for which I used only nonsedentary hunter-gatherer cases—it is also necessary to reconfigure the projection in order to maintain proportionality relative to the vegetative communities. This adjustment was not made in these examples since I was simply trying to illustrate the utility of using a frame of reference and making projections from the known to the unknown. In this case, these projections correspond to what the world would look like if it were peopled by hunter-gatherers.

14. The analogy here is with subspecies as opposed to species, which are separated by reproductively isolating mechanisms.

CHAPTER 6

1. Marshall Sahlins and Elman Service (1960) dealt with a similar question but did not address the issue of process. Sahlins and Service distinguished between *specific* and *general evolution* and argued that *adaptation* was the mechanism underlying specific evolution. In contrast, general evolution was identified with the emergence of complex political systems. Reaction to this distinction was not generally supportive; the prevailing view was that the problem of variability could best be understood as arising from the same processes that produce differential complexity, either between or among cases drawn from similar or different "culture areas."

2. Although some archaeologists have recently expressed sympathy with or a poorly reasoned enthusiasm for recent research on the evolutionary processes resulting in complexification (e.g., Tainter and Tainter 1996), no publication in the archaeological literature has yet dealt with this issue incisively.

3. White was an inspiring but frustrating teacher. He argued vigorously on behalf of the holistic belief that cultural variability could not be explained by reductionist reasoning. At the same time, he worked with a general currency—energy—as the basis of all system dynamics, regardless of the level of organizational complexity and ordered "uniqueness," as he would say. However, the position outlined by Sahlins (1976:13), which claimed that, because culture was an emergent phenomenon, cultural variability had to be explained in cultural terms,

seemed equally unwarranted. And similar ideas, vented contemporaneously by Dunnell (1971:133) and Leach (1973), made unproductive ontological claims about the locus of cause based on the taxonomic implications of a holistic viewpoint, although they were expressed in terms of human characteristics or human nature, rather than culture.

4. See MacArthur (1968, 1972); MacArthur et al. (1966); and MacArthur and Wilson (1967).

5. The work of Boyd and Richerson (1985) dealing with the heritability of culture is an exception to this generalization and represents a major step forward in the development of evolutionary theory that is germane to the concerns of anthropologists.

6. The arguments presented in the articles listed have recently been characterized as an appeal to the uniqueness hypothesis of human behavior (Jones et al. 1995:13). This claim is rather silly since there are at least two contexts within which a claim of uniqueness might be warranted: (1) The differences between mice and men have consequences for the way equal selective pressures will operate on two such populations, which is another way of saying that *initial conditions* are important considerations in any attempted explanation. (2) There are important differences between domains of phenomena, as Mayr argued forcefully with regard to biological versus physical domains, which were said to require different methods and even different types of epistemology! I assume that the selectionist criticism is of the latter position, which has been called "Whiggish" by Wicken (1990) and other insightful thinkers. I support Wicken's criticism and therefore support point (1) and reject point (2). Mayr, however, is one of the selectionists' revered "ancestors," and one can only wonder what Jones et al. could be talking about.

7. Risk in this context does not refer to danger or insecurity, but rather to variability in the success rates of individuals who are attempting to procure resources. Success or failure does not result from differences in the skills of the producers or variability in the abundance of resources present. Risk can be characterized as the differential "luck" of hunters on a given day.

8. In chapter 7, the Terrestrial Model will make it possible to traverse the interesting zone of uncertainty between what I allegedly know about the range of variability in the types of plays in which human actors could have participated when they were rigidly constrained by specified conditions and my knowledge of the plays that have actually been produced.

9. The word *adaptation* has been misunderstood and misrepresented in the anthropological literature. My use of the term does not refer to some optimal state of a system (Rindos 1989:35), nor is it an "uncomfortable synonym" for natural selection (Dunnell 1980:49). I believe instead that adaptation refers to the state of a cultural system at the time it is observed or becomes the focus of research. When I refer to variability among cultural systems or in the niches occupied by cultural systems, I would, therefore, mean variability in the cultural *adaptations* under discussion. An adaptation has reference to the *ecological state* of a cultural system and *not* to its stability or pattern of change, nor to any absolute criteria of optimality, as implied by Rindos (1989:22).

10. Anthropology's unscientific character is nowhere better illustrated than by the outbursts of name-calling evoked by the results of human ecology research. In contrast to the scientific method, which attempts to evaluate the utility and accuracy of a set of arguments, name-calling attempts to dismiss those arguments with which the name-caller disagrees by claiming that they are flawed, not in their logic or content but because they deal with arguments of cause and effect in terms of domains that are considered inappropriate to a discussion of human behavior.

11. See note 9.

12. There are certainly exceptions, such as Rostlund's (1952) comprehensive study, which should be of interest to archaeologists and ethnologists alike. Not all studies of this kind, however, provide the information needed to work with habitat variables.

13. This term is adopted from Birdsell (1953:184).

14. For an excellent illustration of the relationship between understory growth and animal body size see DuBost (1979).

15. The global pattern of plant community destruction due to fire is a fascinating study in itself. Storms are major conditioners of successional dynamics, particularly in areas subject to cyclones. High-biomass tropical forests also experience this type of perturbation. See Webb (1958) for a description of the effect on the Queensland rain forests referred to in this chapter.

16. Not surprisingly, archaeologists have been concerned with some of the issues raised by the generalist-specialist debate (Cleland 1976). More recent literature has expanded considerably on this subject (Bettinger 1980; Dunnell 1980; Meltzer and Smith 1986), but the discussion of specialists and generalists in the anthropological literature is unconnected intellectually to the discussion by ecologists of within-habitat diversity and structural complexity. The ecological arguments specify a set of initial conditions and define the phenotypes of the species within the habitat of interest. Like MacArthur's broken stick model, these arguments often include irreversible conditions and subsequent outcomes that change the structure of the ecosystem as a result of selective pressures favoring or leading to the extinction of specialists or generalists. When archaeologists infer that their data indicate relatively narrow niche breadth ("focal strategies" is Cleland's term), which means that few species are exploited instead of many, they search the ecological literature for information about specialization and "jack-of-all-trades" strategies. This application of ecological principles is inappropriate since the issue is not whether a habitat is dominated by either feeding specialists or generalists, but rather what factors are conditioning differences in diet breadth in an omnivorous species occupying different habitats. Another relevant question is what factors contribute to shifts in diet breadth when gross environmental conditions are considered similar. Archaeologists want to know why changes occur in diet breadth over time or in the trophic strata from which foods are obtained or from greater dependence upon hunting to increased use of plant species (Bettinger and Baumhoff 1982; Hayden 1990; Meltzer and Smith 1986). The ecological literature addresses instead the issue of niche dynamics and variability within species and not the problem of within-habitat diversity, which is the context for a discussion of generalists and specialists when the issue is human niches.

17. The Nunamiut have often been identified as feeding specialists since most of their food comes from one species, the caribou. Considering the number of species present in their habitat, however, and the differential accessibility of species (lemming versus caribou, for instance), it is clear that they are

almost perfect generalists. In fact, the Nunamiut feeding strategy is consistent with Pielou's previously cited generalization. Perhaps the most ill-advised use of the terms *specialist* and *generalist* is found in discussions of the alleged "specialist" behavior of Paleoindian societies in the New World, which is contrasted with the "generalist" strategies of hunter-gatherer groups in subsequent Archaic time periods. I think that these assessments are probably wrong and that the contrasts that archaeologists have noted refer to differences in habitat and *not* differences in the strategic behaviors of hunter-gatherers. In all likelihood, groups during both time periods were generalists.

18.   Honey is a major source of food in many tropical settings, where it is collected—usually by males—from the nests of bees. In many ethnographic reports honey is classified as an animal product, but it is really a plant product that is accumulated by bees. The energetics of production and the level of the bee population are a function of net aboveground productivity in the plant community.

19.   By dividing NAGP by 1,000, the equation transforms measures of NAGP from grams to kilograms. Anticipating the later use of human population density values that are expressed in units consisting of the number of persons per 100 square kilometers, I converted the measure of net aboveground productivity to a comparable unit by multiplying by 100,000,000 square meters (the number of square meters in 100 square kilometers).

20.   This is the environment of three of the hunter-gatherer groups included in this study: the Djaru, Mamu, and Ngatjan of the Queensland rain forest.

21.   Two of the hunter-gatherer groups included in this study inhabited the North Queensland rain forests or forest margins. The Mamu were forest-dwellers (VEGTAT = FE-1) whereas the Ngatjan lived in the slightly drier broadleaf evergreen forests nearby (VEGTAT = FBE-4).

22.   BAR2 is simply total estimated biomass (BIO5) divided by net aboveground productivity. Values of this indicator range from zero to sixty.

23.   Human beings fall nearly perfectly on the fitted line describing this relationship (Aiello 1992a:41).

24.   I had hoped that the recent interest in food procurement and consumption that figures prominently in the literature on optimal foraging theory might be a source of the information I needed for my model. Researchers monitoring food consumption had to weigh all consumables in order to calculate calories and kilocalories, which are the currency used in these studies. Unfortunately, primary observations of the weights of food items are usually unreported, and, in the rare instances when they are reported, they refer to labor efficiency values and not to the contribution a food item makes to the overall diet.

25.   This value is very close to the value of 0.0466 used by Odum (1971:83) when he calculated the ecological pyramids of a boy, beef, and alfalfa plants.

26.   This view has been presented yet again in the anthropological literature by Kornfeld (1996).

27.   The maps of Europe in this chapter are based upon a sample of 405 weather stations covering Europe west of 35 degrees east longitude.

28.   It should be kept in mind that the projections for aquatic dependence are not modified by information about rivers or lakes and are not related to the differential productivity of the marine environment. They are, instead, related to number of kilometers from the coast, as well as other environmental variables that are correlated with the locations of aquatically dependent peoples during the historic period.

29.   The equations used to project world weather station data and the expanded sample of stations used to project information to Europe do not include the information on rivers, lakes, and streams that was introduced in the section of this chapter entitled "Aquatic Biomes and Human Habitats." In my judgment, a prohibitive amount of time would have been required to measure the global distribution (on maps providing sufficient detail, which were rarely available) of values for DRAIN, HEADWAT, DRANK, DPOSIT, and other similar variables. Instead, I provided values for those variables only in those regions in which the hunter-gatherer groups in my sample were located. Equations in subsequent chapters will project both ethnographic data and more detailed information on rivers; other researchers working in specific local areas will be able to apply these equations to their own data with increased accuracy.

30.   Of course, the presence of many items of European manufacture would mark the historic period, although these items would not explain either the origin and the character of the Plains Indian culture area or its fascinating internal cohesiveness at the level of similarities in material culture.

31.   The suggestion that there were very different trajectories of intensification in the past—some gradual and others transformational—is at least partially acknowledged in discussions of the European Neolithic "problem" (Zvelebil 1986; Zvelebil and Dolukhanov 1991).

32.   The dates from these sites do not all refer to the same phenomena. Some refer to the first appearance of forms of domesticated plants and animals, while others have reference to the earliest dependence on agropastoral strategies. In the latter case the date tentatively has reference to major system changes, and in the former the presence of major transformational changes is either unclear or undemonstrated. In addition, new dates have been obtained on some of these sites, and a wealth of new information has been made available since the data used here were published. I initially planned to update the information on the spread of agropastoralism but realized that this is a highly specialized literature, published in many languages. I therefore decided that specialists in the field are much more qualified than I am to take on this project.

33.   This pattern has been recognized by many different researchers (e.g., Keeley 1988, 1995; Schalk 1981).

34.   "Long blade" materials have been identified in Great Britain and are believed to date to the terminal Pleistocene or early Holocene. These industries are thought to have been prevalent in regions in which herd mammals survived longest in Europe, and they were common in Britain as late as the early Pre-Boreal period (Barton 1989).

35.   The rapid and dramatic appearance of Middle Mississippian materials in the central Mississippi valley is usually considered to be such a phenomenon. The alleged lack of continuity with earlier materials was cited as evidence for migrations.

36.   If the changes that the adoption of the horse stimulated among the peoples who became the Plains Indians of North America were to be viewed simply in archaeological terms—rather than historical terms—would the result not be similar to the LBK? Would archaeologists see few sites on the Plains proper from the period immediately prior to the appearance

of European goods and horse-related changes followed by a florescence of very similar materials distributed across a huge area? The phenomenon was not caused by a migration or a "wave of advance," nor does it reflect a pattern of local, gradual change. It represents instead an infilling of a huge area by populations from many different sources moving into sparsely occupied areas, all of which was made possible by the creation of a new niche.

37.   According to *Webster's Encyclopedic Unabridged Dictionary of the English Language,* the suffix *-scope* is "a learned borrowing from Greek used, with the meaning 'instrument for viewing,' in the formation of compound words."

CHAPTER 7

1.   See also Steward (1955).

2.   Almost all of the authors of so-called "cross-cultural" studies in anthropology have failed to include a consideration of system state variability in their correlational approaches to pattern recognition. This is particularly true of the studies pioneered by Murdock (1949) and summarized by Levinson and Malone (1980).

3.   In the five equations used to generate the patterning represented in figure 7.01, I used only hunter-gatherer cases with a value of *n* for the SUBPOP variable, because I had discovered that cases classified as "suspect" were usually outliers in any patterned relationship. It also became clear that cases classified as "mobile" hunter-gatherers exhibited very different relationships to environmental variables than those in the "settled" GRPPAT category. It is also important to note that very different relationships prevailed between AREA and environmental variables depending on the predominant source of food. Among mobile peoples, the multiple *R* values for groups primarily dependent upon terrestrial plant, terrestrial animal, and aquatic resources were 0.8785, 0.9221, and 0.9504, respectively. For groups in the settled category, the values were 0.9769 and 0.9224 for those primarily dependent upon terrestrial plant and aquatic resources (there are no sedentary groups primarily dependent upon terrestrial animals).

4.   The spatial distribution of potential foods was discussed in chapter 5.

5.   This issue has been dealt with by Naroll (1964).

6.   I have reviewed Kelly's arguments in detail and find that his scholarship with respect to these issues is accurate.

7.   I was privileged to team-teach both undergraduate and graduate courses with Joseph Birdsell at UCLA during the 1960s. Birdsell was one of anthropology's master teachers; not only did he teach his students about hunter-gatherers, he taught his junior colleagues how to teach. His early work linking environmental and cultural variables was and remains an inspiration to me.

8.   Birdsell was well aware that exceptions to his argument could be found among peoples who were not excluded because of unearned water (personal communication 1965). Additionally, he noted that interior groups, such as the Kamilaroi, Wongaibon, Wiradjuri, and Barkendji—all located in New South Wales—were "bilateral" in their kinship conventions and thus appeared as exceptions to his arguments about "patrilineal" bands. Based on more recent research, one could now argue that all Australian Aboriginal groups were bilateral in their kinship conventions.

9.   The value of 11.7 producers is the minimal labor pool required for a one-year period, since each producer works only 46.5 percent of the time and extra producers are needed as stand-in workers during the course of an entire year. Mobile hunter-gatherers meet these labor requirements by the regular movement of families and even young individuals among groups during the annual round.

10.   Most of the values for "family camps" provided by Julian Steward (1938:58, 63, 69, 80, 94, 114, 214) refer to numbers of adults; children are only rarely mentioned. For the twenty-four camps documented in the preceding citation, 140 persons are tabulated. When this total is divided by twenty-four, it yields a value of 5.83 as the mean number of adults per camp. Multiplying this value by 1.75 results in an estimate of 10.20 for mean camp size. This is very close to my modeled value for residential groups with a collapsed division of labor. This variable is documented by Steward for much of the year in the Great Basin and was the unit that he referred to as the "family." Obviously, the members of such a unit are likely to be related but are unlikely to represent a single reproductive unit or "family."

11.   There is a big difference between seeking an explanation for variability and seeking a model for the past. For instance, about the "band" size of the Tehuelche of Patagonia, Fried (1967:68) opines: "these . . . can easily be discounted, however, as occurring in response to European influence, which included, among other tangibles, the Tehuelche acquisition of domesticated horses." Fried dismisses the data on the Tehuelche because "European influence" makes them irrelevant to a model of the past. In my view, the Tehuelche contribute important data relevant to my interest in the cost-of-transport variable and illustrate how the availability of horses changed the cost and ease of transport.

CHAPTER 8

1.   The title of this chapter was suggested by "Strike flat the thick rotundity o' the world" (*King Lear,* act 3, scene 2, line 7).

2.   In theory building, one of the more common errors is the belief that it is possible to observe causes. Although the act of looking enables human beings to see events, entities, material structures, and all sorts of other phenomena, to build theories one must reason and make an argument about the character of the necessary relationships among specified variables. It cannot be stated too often or with too much emphasis that it is not possible to see a cause. A cause is a relational statement developed through argument.

3.   Steward himself never attempted to relate the dichotomy between units with a collapsed division of labor and those with regular gender role differentiation to the species these differently organized groups either exploited or targeted. He was fascinated by his observation that "in the few forms of collective activity the same group of [Shoshonean] families did not cooperate with one another or accept the same leader on successive occasions" (Steward 1955:109). Using Steward's criteria, many different groups of hunter-gatherers, particularly plant-dependent groups, would have to be considered representatives of the "family level of sociocultural integration."

4.   At the time that I researched GROUP1 sizes in the ethnographic literature, I did not appreciate how valuable it would be to know what the dispersed group was doing during this phase of the settlement cycle. This oversight demonstrates

how, in the process of analyzing data, scientists learn a great deal about what it is germane to know.

5.   Meillassoux's propositions (1973) about the relationship between reproduction and production later appeared in Woodburn's work (1980) as the justification for the inclusion of Australian Aborigines in Woodburn's category of "delayed return societies," based exclusively on the character of their kin relationships. The astute reader is aware that most authors who assign explanatory power to such variables as storage, who create dichotomous categories such as immediate and delayed return societies, and who cite similarities between the relations of production and the structure of kinship organization tend to subscribe to a Marxist world view.

6.   Three of these cases were identified earlier in the discussion of table 7.04. I concluded that they were not necessarily exceptional, even though they inhabited environments analogous to the Northwest Pacific Coast of North America, where a concentration of complex hunter-gatherers has been documented. It now appears that there may well be some significant environmental differences between the Northwest Coast and similar environments in the Southern Hemisphere.

7.   In 1982, Douglas G. Sutton published a fascinating paper in *Current Anthropology* in which he called attention to the same locations that I have cited in the context of the minimal interest displayed by indigenous hunter-gatherers in the tactical use of stored foods and the temperateness of the climatic regime relative to its latitude.

8.   Another, and perhaps equally important, observation is that all of the analogous cases with biomass accumulation ratios in excess of 35.0 also have the highest contrast in storage dependence relative to the exceptional cases. When I examine the population density values from these cases, the highest values also tend to track the biomass accumulation ratios. Storage dependence and population density seem to be equally inflated in high-primary-biomass settings. Intensification, therefore, seems greatest where high primary biomass limits both animal and human feeding success and there is a productive aquatic alternative.

9.   I have briefly summarized these locations in the discussion preceding citation of table 8.03. The reduced investment in stored foods in these settings is probably referable to two conditions: the increased length of the growing season and the response of marine organisms and birds to a longer growing season. A reduction in extreme winter temperatures also increases the accessibility of foods during periods of the year when there would otherwise be less abundance owing to the effects of latitude.

10.   This same pattern was clearly evident in one of my earlier studies (Binford 1980, 1983:figure 23.4). At the time I did not comment on the pattern because I was uncertain about the conditions to which it might refer.

11.   In this study, I include only information on North American species. My source was Simpson's (1964) series of isopleth maps depicting the species density of terrestrial mammals.

12.   Some of the features of Pomo labor organization described by Panowski are also components of Marshall Sahlins's (1956) argument about family size on Moala, Fiji. He notes that if simultaneous labor is needed at different locations, then the size of the overall task group must be larger, other things being equal.

13.   An excellent discussion of the foraging strategies of these interesting peoples is found in Savelle (1987b).

14.   Tactical localization means that although families do move in the course of resource acquisition, their primary residence is not abandoned or moved as part of this strategy.

15.   These erroneous classifications have not been changed in the basic data set used in this analysis. To make such changes would require that I go back and redo all of the previous analyses, which defeats the dual purpose of analysis conducted to recognize patterning and expose coding errors. Coding misjudgments will be dealt with after the analysis has been completed.

16.   The anthropological literature on this subject is somewhat confused. For instance, in an excellent behavioral study of mobility among the Batak, Eder uses the individual person as his unit of study (Eder 1984:838, table 1), although in other places the household becomes his unit. As a result, it is unclear whether household moves or individual moves are being counted. Nevertheless, he concludes that some mobility distinctions are not valid because humans can change their units of observation (Eder 1984:846), with the effect that there are in reality different units. Eder seems to believe that it is possible to look at the world in terms of a wide range of units but that other researchers are unaware of such multiple units. Eder's ontological view of the scientific use of units borders on the absurd. Similarly, the view that a sedentary settlement system should include only nonmobile people is an equally irrational use of units. It is much more profitable in terms of the growth of knowledge to generalize about identifiable units than to attempt to capture the "essence" of the personal state of motion.

17.   Arguments of referral generate considerable controversy in archaeology. More often than not they represent the opinions of persons who interpret the archaeological record according to their personal biases—which, as a class, have recently been raised to the level of theory by postmodernist writers (Preucel and Hodder 1996). In spite of the relativist view of alternatives that forms the centerpiece of these authors' paradigm, alternative arguments of referral *can* be evaluated and the utility of their claims determined.

18.   Of course, this generalization is not always true since it is possible that a group will include adult unmarried males as well as persons involved in polyandrous marriages. Both of these situations occur less frequently than the presence in the work force of males who are heads of families.

19.   In this study, family size is measured by dividing the total population of a group by the number of married males within that population. Although this figure does not coincide exactly with the male dependency ratio, in many situations it could be very close indeed.

20.   For an excellent discussion of the complexities inherent in measuring the reproductive performance of different populations, see Howell (1979), particularly chapters 11 and 15.

21.   At the time of documentation, the Alyawara were essentially sedentary, and the larger GROUP1 size that was recorded probably relates to my observations in generalization 8.01. Because of their inflated GROUP1 size, therefore, the Alyawara occur as an exception in size subset 4.

22.   In those instances in which polyandry occurs, it is almost always fraternal polyandry, which means that two brothers share the same wife. Most often, the senior brother marries a woman

to whom the younger brother then has sexual access. This kind of arrangement does not appear to represent a labor recruitment strategy.

23. Although this value is for a male dependency ratio of 97.17, I am using it in place of a 100 percent level of male production since the data come from a rapidly growing population.

24. A good example of residential mobility occurs in Briggs (1970:88), who has described a late summer fishing camp "at the Rapids," occupied by the Utkuhikhalingmiut.

25. Gender roles are frequently distinguished in terms of "catch and process" activities, which are well summarized by Balikci (1970:34–37) in his description of Netsilik Eskimo activities at a stone fishing weir. It should be pointed out that camps in which gender role distinctions in the treatment of a single species are documented are also usually arranged with very tight tent spacing. (See, for instance, the photograph by Jean Briggs entitled "Late Summer at the Rapids" [1970:an unnumbered photographic plate between pages 108 and 109].) A similar, though poorly documented, pattern seems to have occurred among the Copper Eskimo (Condon 1996: 73–77; Damas 1972:25).

26. I was unable to locate this site during my field work in Alaska in the 1970s, but I gave Alaskan archaeologists the information provided to me by Nunamiut informants. In 1989, I was notified by Grant Spearman that the site had been found, and I was able to obtain a modest research grant, which enabled Spearman to take the last three living participants in the 1944 events to the site for interviews. They provided excellent supplementary documentation of the caribou hunt from which Spearman was able to make a map of the area, including the locations of the residential camp, the butchering and processing location, and the placement of caribou fences. During the hunting and processing of the caribou, the twenty-two occupants of the site ate communally. Each day a different female family head was responsible for the preparation of the food for the entire camp. A striking feature of the camp at Chandler Lake was the very close spacing of the tents, which differed completely from the wide spacing characteristic of residential sites in other seasons (Binford 1991a).

27. This and the following values represent an average of the two versions of the model: one which is the same over an entire year and the second, which allows group size to vary over a year relative to differences in work schedules between an even and a fractional number.

28. The view that Prigogine describes is alive and well in anthropology. The popular answer to the question of "who built the machine" is, of course, that individual human beings cause culture and culture change. A restatement of this view appears in the article by O'Meara (1997).

29. It is important to recognize that many other features of contemporary archaeology and anthropology provide classic examples of the use of bad or inappropriate models from physics, as Prigogine states: "The foremost example of this is the paradigm of optimization. It is obvious that the management of human society as well as the action of selective pressures tends to optimize some aspects of behaviors or modes of connection. To consider optimization as the key to understanding how populations and individuals survive is to risk confusing causes with effects" (Prigogine and Stengers 1984:207).

30. Smith's remarks do not devote much consideration to synergistic interactions among such features as work schedules, the division of labor, and other organizationally important variables of which labor recruitment strategies constitute one example. It also seems that there is a hidden assumption of stability built into the argument since, as net returns or other measures of optimality diminish, mobile hunter-gatherers most commonly move rather than break up the cooperative unit in terms of such considerations as the "joiners" or "members" rules.

31. This pattern suggests that units such as the family, the household, and groups periodically aggregated within a region should all be investigated in order to understand how these segmentally agglomerated units respond to intensification.

32. In the case of GROUP1 segments, smaller units would most commonly be households or families.

33. Sedentism is frequently discussed in the anthropological literature, but almost exclusively in ontological terms. Eder (1984) insists that there can be no segmental mobility by components of a community who maintain a community settlement throughout a single year or season cycle. Rafferty (1985) recognizes that sedentism is not an ontological issue but rather one of convention and analytical utility. I might agree with Rafferty were she not adamantly opposed to the use of the term *semisedentary*. I find this a useful term when it is used to refer to a settlement system, rather than to a particular settlement within a system. Rafferty's hard and fast distinction (1985:116) is perhaps more germane to specific "sites," but sites do not a settlement system make in any unambiguous, taxonomic sense of the word.

34. These cases frequently move in what I (Binford 1982, 1983:362) have called a "half radius continuous pattern," which is also characteristic of "routed foragers" (Kloos 1977). The phrase "residentially constricted mobility" has also been used for analogous patterning (Graham and Roberts 1986). For a more recent review see Kelly (1992).

CHAPTER 9

1. This is the variable on the *y* axis of figure 9.01.

2. These Guayaki (Ache) foraging groups are, in fact, made up of residents of a permanent horticultural settlement who appear to be newly established families exploiting wild resources, thereby reducing the demand on food supplies at or near the settlement. Hill and Hawkes (1983) report that larger "bands" were typical during the pre-mission period, but it is unclear how these units—which were classified by size into three categories—relate to patterns of dispersal and aggregation. In fact, the Guayaki (Ache) may be one of the very few hunter-gatherer groups who did not have a seasonal cycle of aggregation and dispersal. Their anomalous status is due to repeated attacks during relatively recent decades and their subsequent aggregation in large groups for their own protection. It seems more likely that bands were equivalent to GROUP2 units and did not disperse into small groups during the seasonal cycle.

3. In chapter 1, the first set of generalizations and descriptions of organizational variability was based on the research of Mauss and Beuchat, who pointed out the dramatic difference in group size and behavior observable in North American hunter-gatherers. They related within-system variability to seasonal changes in climate and associated resource availability; over the years, the unquestioned assumption has developed that organizational shifting is a fundamental characteristic of hunter-gatherers. Such an assumption clearly stood behind

the decision to tabulate group size during the most dispersed as well as the most aggregated phases of the subsistence settlement cycle. One should at least entertain the possibility that—in some environments—an annual pulsation in organization should not occur if the relationship to seasonal habitat variability noted by Mauss and Beuchat is reduced or nonexistent. There may, in fact, be systems that do not have GROUP1 units!

4.   This result is not surprising since similarity in linear distribution was the criterion for classification in the first place.

5.   Although these totals are the result of the relative sample size at this scale, the comparison is nevertheless still relevant.

6.   One of the cases in my sample of 339 ethnographic groups, the Orogens, is an ethnic group of mounted hunters that has a long history in the forested region of the Amur drainage along the Chinese-Russian border (Qiu 1983). Groups such as the Orogens served as the basis for the supposition that migrating peoples would take their knowledge of the utility of domesticated animals as transportation aids to a new locality and apply it to an analogous species. For basic regional arguments see Laufer (1917).

7.   In north Asia and Siberia, dogs were used to herd reindeer, particularly in eastern regions (Bogoras 1930:plate 1).

8.   The use of this terms is appropriate and analogous to Netting's distinction (1968:135, 205) between intensive and extensive land use patterns. It is certainly germane to the difference in land use being discussed on a very different scale and with respect to very different production techniques. Amber Johnson has pointed out the relevance of Netting's distinctions to this analysis.

9.   The classification of the Nganasan was not accidental. They were considered distinct from the plains hunters since they did not ride their domesticated animals while hunting. The process of extensification focuses on transport capability and not the particular context in which that capability is utilized.

10.   This is only slightly better than the mean for the mounted peoples of the Great Plains.

11.   Netting's discussion of the literature and the reality of intensification in the ethnographic world is required reading for those who would address the issue of units, stress, and pressure on resources as well as the theoretical literature of demography and social change (particularly see Netting 1993:261–324).

12.   What I have in mind was well documented among the people of Dobe Pan by Richard Lee (1979:412–14). He noted that all families did not have domesticated animals and that the tactical differences between caring for livestock and maintaining a traditional expectation of food-sharing by some former hunter-gatherer families worked against the easy transition to animal husbandry.

13.   See the discussion of atomism in chapter 1.

14.   One can see this as a foreshadowing of the methods of structuralism and later varieties of postmodernist thought.

15.   The archaeological record suggests that this shift occurred in the central arctic between 1200 and 1300 A.D. Sites created by earlier whale-hunting peoples are followed by sites attributable to the neo-Eskimo peoples, who were observed by ethnographers to depend primarily upon the exploitation of ringed seal during the winter. The timing of these changes in subsistence strategy corresponds to environmental changes that reduced the arctic habitat of migratory sea mammals of all kinds, but particularly whales (Savelle 1987b).

16.   At best, characterizing is based on a single distinguishing criterion in terms of which other systems are postulated to be "characteristically different," and the criterion is usually considered to be causal with respect to the differences characterized! Two good examples include the distinction between immediate and delayed return systems (Woodburn 1980) and more recent derivatives, such as the distinction between the "root metaphor" in terms of which participants in a culture view themselves, others, and the environment in general. The distinction in such a metaphor between the "giving environment" and the "reciprocating environment" is then argued to explain the alleged differences in economic behaviors such as sharing and the exchange of goods. This "culturalist" point of view is the ultimate in the "functionalist" fallacy (*function* is used here in the social anthropological sense of the word). In such a view, stability is always accommodated and change is never contemplated.

17.   For a discussion of the role of secret societies in Pueblo life, see Johnson (1997, particularly pages 68–71).

18.   Fekri Hassan (1981:162 footnote) has pointed out that this position is not inconsistent with Malthus's humanistic views.

19.   Aside from fundamental differences between the two views of carrying capacity, another aspect of the demographers' "*k*-based" view of carrying capacity has struck a chord with the romantic idealists in our midst. The state of being "in balance" with nature is frequently attributed to ancient or small-scale populations, particularly hunter-gatherers (McDonald 1977; Redford 1991). This alleged state is often associated with ideological viewpoints based on "respect for nature," which are contrasted with behaviors and ideologies that are said to degrade nature as part of a negative feedback spiral. The latter are often viewed as properties distinctive to the modern world (see Alvard 1993 for an excellent discussion of this issue).

20.   The total population divided by the number of married males. This approach builds in the effects of polygyny and different marriage strategies on size differences.

21.   Pastoral systems present a wonderful comparative opportunity. Some are almost certainly the byproducts of extensificational processes, after which intensificational pressures begin to operate. Others may result solely from internal specialization and contribute to complexity in an otherwise intensificationally driven regional system. The diversity in pastoral systems is staggering and ranges from the Hottentots of southern Africa, to the Kazak and Kalmulk Mongols, to the "Tatar State" (Krader 1968:82–103). There are also many other specialty castes and groups of mutualists at varying levels of autochthonous complexity.

22.   I observed this kind of nested hierarchy of risk pooling among the Nunamiut, for whom the smaller segment consisted of food producers or hunters. The larger unit of longer duration was composed of families who pooled when the stored foods of a participating family had been destroyed by bears or, if stored underground, by water seepage.

CHAPTER 10

1.   In chapter 6, see the section entitled "A More Dynamic View of Between-Habitat Variability" for a more general dis-

cussion of between-habitat variability, particularly its relationship to species density.

2.   An extensificational response would be the development of transport technology that would make previously uninhabited regions accessible. For example, the domestication of reindeer in the Old World and the use of dog traction in North America permitted exploitation of previously uninhabited zones.

3.   For instance, the turnover rate of rabbit populations can be quite high, yielding reliable food over the long term.

4.   It is reasonable to ask whether the very late adoption of horticulture in southern New Mexico and northwest Texas is related to the stability of the habitats exploited by prehistoric hunter-gatherers in these regions.

5.   I do not wish to imply that accessing such resources would be easy, or even very frequently done. My only point here is that they may occasionally be obtained without technological aids.

6.   For a number of interesting discussions of this kind of organization, see Halstead and O'Shea (1989). The chapter in that book by Rowley-Conwy and Zvelebil 1989) contains a good discussion of issues germane to hunter-gatherers.

7.   Hayden (1990) argues that this kind of system is the context for the domestication of plants and animals. I find the suggestion that the Pacific northwest coast—which maintained hunter-gatherer populations until very recently—was a context for the development of domesticates to be overwhelmingly uncompelling.

8.   I am indebted to Richard Wojcik (1992), whose research was very helpful as I formed much of my discussion of transactional strategies and scales.

9.   Exclusion is largely achieved by manipulating the conventions of kin inclusiveness. It can also result from an increasing elaboration in the differentiation of functions that operate at different scales of inclusiveness.

10.   This idea has met heavy resistance (Perlman 1980; Renouf 1984; Yesner 1980), as has the idea that ecology is relevant to understanding the differences between groups dependent upon aquatic resources and foragers who are more terrestrially oriented (Pálsson 1988). More recently, Kelly (1995: 293–331) has productively discussed the problem of complex, aquatically dependent peoples.

11.   For an introduction to the many problems associated with trying to measure prehistoric population growth using archaeological remains, see Sutton and Molloy (1989). The term *density dependence* literally means density and refers to how populations are distributed with respect to essential nutrients. Another aspect of the problem is that, although the growth rate in a particular area may be going down, the number of persons per unit area can be increasing.

12.   See Sutton and Molloy (1989) for a fine example of this analytical can of worms. These authors generate skepticism about the demographic arguments that they criticize, but they are unable to make any progress toward the goal of measuring population pressure.

13.   Actually, the population density value for packing is 9.098 or a $\log_{10}$ value of −0.9589, which is slightly less than the 0.0 value.

14.   This operational definition of circumscription makes it possible to use the available data base to evaluate some of Carneiro's (1970) provocative arguments about state forma-

tion. It is also likely to be germane to systems at very different levels of complexity.

15.   It should be remembered that the number of families in each GROUP1 unit was determined by dividing the total group size by the number of married males. Polygyny commonly results in large basal units and therefore large GROUP1 units. Nevertheless, the packing levels associated with resettlement are probably more responsible for the large sizes since this appears to be a general condition.

16.   The relationship is even more important to a group like the Casiguran Agta of the Philippines. Headland (1986:96) reports that 609 Agta live among 35,000 non-Agta. Although I am convinced that this estimate is incorrect, it is still relevant to the point I am making about ecological density.

17.   It has recently become a popular pastime to postulate the presence of mutualistic relationships among archaeologically documented hunter-gatherers, as well as between Neolithic societies and hunter-gatherers (see particularly Gregg 1988). The justification for these kinds of interpretative searches is based on well-recorded instances of mutualists in the ethnographic record, the most notable being the Mbuti and similar groups from equatorial Africa. The argument postulates that, since mutualism is known to exist, it should be an alternative in any setting in which culturally distinct groups practice different strategies for obtaining food. This argument fails to consider the causes of mutualism and assumes, or even argues, that there is a self-evident advantage to organizing subsistence in this way. Based on my data, I would point out that there is a strong concentration of mutualist cases in high-biomass, equatorial, and tropical forest settings. These habitats tend to be stable and very diverse in terms of species density, while the distribution of plant species would justify a high equability index. Given current knowledge, the stability of these regimes appears to be at least partially, if not exclusively, a function of connectivity.

18.   See, for instance, the Van Vagris (Misra 1990) and the Kanjars (Nagar and Misra 1990). The only reason that these cases were not included in this study is because I had no information about them at the time that I compiled my basic list of cases.

19.   This issue has been explored by Headland (1986:402–40, 545).

20.   This characterization of the Warunggu is based on the report by Brayshaw (1990:table 5:4, columns 6 and 7). The data consisted of species counts rather than body size or contribution to the diet by weight or calories. The author also noted that the primary observer in the region was a zoologist (Lumholtz 1889) whose observations were biased in favor of animals, most of which were very small. It seems likely that animals are overrepresented relative to their actual contribution by weight to the diet, but I have more confidence in the density values and the characterization of this system as packed. These attributes are supported by the type of leadership, the presence of institutions of conflict resolution, and the practice of cannibalism.

21.   This error almost certainly results from the fact that the ordination of the subsistence specialty category was changed during the course of this study. Originally, plants had a code of 1, animals a code of 2, and aquatic resources a code of 3. When an attempt was made to convert this nominal scale to an ordinal scale relative to social variables, the numbering of plants and animals was reversed and a mechanical error was introduced. Most errors were detected early, but this case was

overlooked and was only recently changed in the data file. Earlier analysis, however, did not include this change.

22.   By intensive exploitation of aquatic resources I mean regular exploitation of resources that are unobtainable in tidal pools or on rocks intermittently exposed by tidal fluctuations, or from wading depths. These resources must be quite literally *extracted* from the aquatic biome in settings in which foragers are unable to have direct access to the biome.

23.   Over the years, my former students have studied the technology of another eleven hunter-gatherer cases. Susan G. Miller (1984) added seven new cases and Alan Osborn (1999) has added four more, for a total of thirty-one cases in my data set. The values for the variables developed by Oswalt differ slightly in some cases from his original values because I have examined more ethnographic sources for the cases he studied and have found some errors in his original tabulations.

24.   This observation is by no means unique to me; differences in leadership have long been recognized by anthropologists (see, e.g., Lowie 1920:359–61).

25.   See Binford (1991a) for a historical description of the social dynamics that this type of leadership evokes.

26.   A gross awareness of this type of relationship is not new. In an essay entitled "Some Problems of Methodology in the Social Sciences" (reprinted in Boas 1940:267), Boas long ago generalized that "we have simple industries and complex organization, or diverse industries and simple organization." In his lectures, Boas usually made this point by citing the complex technology and simple social organization of Eskimos in contrast to the complex social organization and simple technology of Australian Aborigines (L. A. White, pers. comm. 1956).

27.   See the descriptions of leadership in Henriksen (1973) as well as in Binford (1991a).

28.   Weapons are defined as tools designed to kill, wound, or maim animals that are capable of significant motion (Oswalt 1976:76–103).

29.   When this threshold was first encountered in chapter 8 (figure 8.10), I did not realize it was very close to the point at which the temperature of the mean coldest month shifted from positive to negative. As graph B in figure 10.11 illustrates, this is certainly the case. The coincidence of so many threshold patterns here marks a major transition point in the character of hunter-gatherer adaptational systems.

30.   All cases located at higher than 57 degrees latitude were eliminated, but this strategy does not explain why the Tiwi and Ingura of northern Australia were not included. The Tasmanians, the Naron of west central Botswana, and the Owens Valley Paiute were also eliminated, but an unspecified "Paiute" case (almost certainly the Surprise Valley Paiute, since Kelly [1932] is cited) was included—although the values are very different from those provided by Oswalt!

31.   This argument totally ignores the fact that mobile peoples routinely cache items. For instance, the Nunamiut did not carry a kayak with them when they moved. Instead, they cached it near the lake where it was last used, along with other gear and tools used at the lake. Perhaps the only items that might be relevant to Shott's argument would be personal gear.

32.   See Oswalt (1976:38) for a definition of this term, which refers to the total number of design features that are characteristic of the total number of weapons produced by a given group.

33.   When the Terrestrial Model was constructed, the weighting factors used to anticipate population density were based on gross estimates of primary and secondary biomass, turnover rates, and productivity values. Although these estimates were functional, now that it is possible to isolate the lack of registration indicated in figure 10.13, I can make adjustments to the Terrestrial Model to bring these two lines on the graph into better registration. This also applies to various properties in selected cases that were either miscoded or misclassified. This has not yet been done because the tools developed in the early part of the book are still being used as learning devices—and, of course, one of the things I have learned is the limit of their utility.

34.   I probably should include temperateness as a modifier in the Terrestrial Model.

35.   It is not really clear why these two cases occupy this placement on the property space map in figure 10.14.

36.   The dynamics underlying this pattern can be viewed in several ways. Traps may be used to provide food when foragers are busy processing other species that provide the majority of stored foods. This tactic reduces the demand on the species being processed so that it will be available to meet food demands at some future time. Although this is likely to be true in some situations, the cases that appear as exceptions in figure 10.16—the Ingalik and Tanaina—were both engaged in fur trading, and traps were primarily used in the latter context. I would also expect that, as mobility decreased, the use of untended traps should have increased, even if the number of different types did not.

37.   In my opinion, the differences in magnitude reflect the fact that ethnographers differed in the amount of attention they paid to tools and their uses. In all of the cases occurring in the area marked 2, there was a heavy research investment in technology, particularly the technology of food procurement. The other cases included in figure 10.18 did not benefit from the same attention to technology.

38.   In spite of the very limited sample of cases coded for technological variables, very provocative patterns have emerged in the figures in chapter 10. Clearly, the number of coded cases must be expanded to include the useful categories originally developed by Oswalt (1973, 1976). There are doubtless many new relationships between technology, ecological variables, and other aspects of the organization of cultural systems remaining to be discovered.

CHAPTER 11

1.   The importance of these distinctions—as well as the relationship of both terms to the frequently misunderstood concepts of *generalist* and *specialist* currently in vogue in the archeological literature—is discussed in chapter 6 and in notes 16 and 17 of that chapter.

2.   The standard deviation is lower for cases with relatively equal contributions from all three kinds of resources and higher for cases that are primarily dependent upon only one source of food, such as terrestrial plants. The process of calculating an increase in niche breadth using a measurement that *decreases* as values increase is difficult to think about. For this reason, standard deviations were calculated using the percentage values of terrestrial plant, animal, and aquatic resources. These values were then subtracted from 100, yielding an inverted value, so that an increase in niche breadth corresponds to an increase in the value of 100 minus the standard deviation.

3.   I am referring here to the Group Size Model developed in chapter 7, which demonstrates that a population density value that exceeds 9.098 persons per 100 square kilometers would be "packed." At such a level, persons would be unable to move freely since they would be surrounded on all sides by groups of equal size (see the discussion following table 7.13).

4.   It is nearly impossible to scale this variable, but the time spent in host villages and the distance moved away from these villages appear to provide a clue (Bahuchet 1988:131). Nevertheless, it has been observed that the strength of the symbiosis varies regionally in Africa, particularly in western regions such as Cameroon (Vallois and Marquer 1976). Exchange has been more common in the east, whereas true mutualism has predominated in the west (Lalouel 1950:209).

5.   For discussions of Punan economic activities, see Endicott and Endicott (1986), Hoffman (1984), Rambo (1985), and Sellato (1994), who reflect slightly different interests in their discussions of the Semang.

6.   See Headland (1987), Headland and Bailey (1991), and Headland and Reid (1989).

7.   *Equatorial* is the term chosen to designate the warmest habitats on earth. Ironically, the mutualist cases that are, in fact, situated very near the equator do not live in the warmest of these forests, but are found in cooler settings that are referred to as *tropical* in this study.

8.   Susan Gregg (1988) was one of the first to cite the hunter-gatherer cases in figure 8.17 as ethnographic justifications for proposing mutualist articulations between hunter-gatherers and agriculturists in temperate zone settings. This idea was not new, but the serious consideration it received certainly was. Since Gregg's book was published, there has been a major expansion of publications that not only appeal to these ideas (Spielmann 1991) but also expand the intellectual scope of the argument to "world systems theory" and other contemporary nontheories (e.g., Baugh 1982, 1984; Kohl 1987; Schortman and Urban 1987).

9.   I do not wish to suggest that articulations between systems exploiting different habitats are not possible. My point is that the conditions favoring articulations of this kind are likely to be very different from the ones that occur among species in moderate- to high-biomass subtropical to tropical ecosystems. In such settings, there are analogous mutualist interactions between small-scale societies composed of ethnically different people. Features of interregional trade and exchange are likely to be organized very differently, to be conducted among different types of units, and to represent a response to very different conditioning variables.

10.   It should be remembered that the packing index is simply a re-scaled expression of population density. Since population density is the variable most people are familiar with, I will use population in this exercise.

11.   The actual value used here is 0.27107, which was obtained by adjusting the Terrestrial Model estimate in light of actual values recorded for hunter-gatherers. The rather overprecise value used is a derivative of the method of estimating the probable error in actual density values at such low numbers among hunter-gatherers.

12.   The great altitudinal differences in the territories of these people are not adequately represented. Most of the weather stations are in the lowlands, and hence the environmental data are biased in favor of these more arid locations.

13.   A comparative study of these interesting cases is in order, but unfortunately the importance of this set of ethnographic cases was not recognized until this book was almost finished.

14.   When the density value of the packing threshold (9.098) is divided by the value of the threshold at line 1 (1.57), the result is a value of 5.7949. This is 5.7949 times the line 1 value. When 1.57 is divided by the arbitrary value of 0.30 estimated for the lower limit of hunter-gatherer occupation in an area, the result is a value of 5.2333. This is a very close fit since the 0.30 value was an arbitrary estimate and—after the hunter-gatherer data were examined—a value of 0.27107 was identified as the best estimate based on the data (see endnote 11).

15.   The initial threshold between uninhabited land and land occupied by hunter-gatherers is given the ordinal value of zero and each threshold thereafter is numbered sequentially. For instance, the last threshold, which defines the density boundary for hunter-gatherers, is threshold 4.

16.   The values obtained are listed for the following numbered thresholds: $0 = 0.27107$, $1 = 1.57000$, $2 = 9.09935$, $3 = 52.66922$, $4 = 305.05695$, $5 = 1,766.87142$, $6 = 10,233.61225$.

17.   See particularly Arnold (1996), Hayden (1997), Price and Brown (1985), and Price and Feinman (1995).

18.   In chapter 8, I discussed the limits on group size in relation to the Group Size Model, but for another point of view see Eric Alden Smith's (1991) discussion of cooperative foraging, particularly pages 287–410.

19.   The Tjapwurong built stone-lined ditches and used complicated constructions to flush eels out of swamps and into artificial drains, where capture was relatively easy. The large group sizes reported for these locations almost certainly do not represent GROUP2 units but are more likely GROUP3 units (Lourandos 1980:255) that, over the years, produced the remarkable archeological remains at Mount William and Toolondo swamp.

20.   This equation can be solved for each monthly temperature, resulting in a curve of storage potential for all four seasons that can then be compared with the period of procurement for given resources, such as the timing of salmon runs at different places.

21.   One of the consequences of my extensive analysis is my recognition of the inadequacy of the information coded for the hunter-gatherer cases in my data base. Having learned what I needed to know to resolve ambiguities, most of the time the initial codes and dimensionalized data were rendered obsolete.

22.   Fish that are lean and have little fat dry better and are less subject to spoilage. They become more palatable and nutritious, however, if oil is served when they are consumed.

CHAPTER 12

1.   The title of this chapter is a quote from Francis Quarles, "Respice Finem" (Epigram).

2.   It must be kept in mind that my analysis admits only three possibilities for increasing niche breadth. Horticulture itself may be considered another possibility, as is the domestication of animals. Economic diversification is both a measure of complexity and a conditioner of stability and instability (propositions 11.10, 11.11, 11.12, 11.13, and 11.14). The inclusion of more alternative niche breadth strategies changes the range of variability of the standard deviation, which in turn changes the distribution of the limits of scatter for subsistence

diversity as measured here. Clearly, a better way of measuring subsistence diversity must be devised. The coefficient of variability might be a better measure except for the fact that it does not really measure niche diversity. A solution to the problem of dealing with cases beyond the basics of hunter-gatherer variability is currently being researched by Johnson (2000).

3.   The means from each class would be reduced from approximately 33.33 to 20.00, assuming an array of cases in which all possible combinations were given equal probability of being present.

4.   The problem of measurement, which really only affects the emergent possibilities, is one of diversity as opposed to equability, and it has been dealt with in ecological studies. In this book, the variable SUBDIV2 has worked very well, although I am sure that greater refinement will result from future work.

5.   Brian Hayden is one of the few contemporary researchers who still believes that sedentism is the preferred state in which to live (Hayden 1995: 279). As support for his view of progress, he cites the preferences of sedentary peoples—but do any of us really know any life ways that are not defended as the best by the majority of the participants?

6.   This point has been lost on both advocates and critics of arguments about population pressure and its role in cultural process. The work of Sutton and Molloy (1989) provides an excellent example of missing the point of selection.

7.   This point has been argued quite convincingly at a larger scale by Sherratt (1996:130–31).

8.   I have not used the word *marginal* since its original reference to relativity has been lost in our literature. See, for instance, the discussion by Garrard et al. (1996), in which *marginal* is equated with low productivity in general and the productivity of arid lands in particular. I originally used the term, as did Flannery a bit later, to refer to areas around centers of rapid population growth that were capable of supporting peoples with a different subsistence strategy than was characteristic of the rapidly growing "center."

9.   See chapter 6 for a discussion of food access in such settings (propositions 6.02, 6.03, and 6.04).

10.   The value is far below the 10.00 persons per 100 square kilometers frequently cited as a mean for hunter-gatherers in general (Bender 1975:6; Flannery 1983:35).

11.   Frequency tabulations of modern hunter-gatherer cases are often cited as proof of the importance to hunter-gatherers, in general and in the past, of primary dependence upon terrestrial plant resources. My data show that of the 339 cases included in this study, 52.5 percent (178) are intensified and have population densities exceeding the packing threshold. Among the nonpacked cases, 72 (44.7 percent) are primarily dependent upon terrestrial animals, 58 (36.0 percent) are primarily dependent upon terrestrial plants, and only 31 (19.3 percent) are primarily dependent upon aquatic resources. The latter cases are concentrated in areas that are projected to be uninhabited by the Terrestrial Model. Any uncritical tabulation of contemporary hunter-gatherers will be biased in favor of intensified cases. In fact, depending upon which article is cited, the !Kung either are very close to being packed or were already packed at the time of Richard Lee's (1968, 1972a, 1972b) early studies! Many authors have been taken in completely by such distortions (Clarke 1976; Kornfeld 1996).

12.   Recent research in the American Southwest supports this claim. Hunter-gatherers who are believed to have been pri-

marily dependent upon terrestrial animals changed more, per unit of time, after the adoption or onset of regular use of domesticated plants than did hunter-gatherers who were originally primarily dependent upon plant resources (Johnson 1997:76–90).

13.   In December 1997, the Brysons came to Southern Methodist University and conducted an archaeoclimatological workshop, during which they taught interested faculty and students how to use their methods of climatic reconstruction. Amber Johnson then worked one-on-one with the Brysons at the University of Wisconsin in order to clarify some technical ambiguities in their procedures. The Brysons have made two additional trips to Dallas to work out ways to link their reconstructive procedures and my work on calculating derivative values for a variety of ecologically relevant variables. This collaboration on the development of predictive models is expected to continue.

14.   The procedure is straightforward for locations monitored by contemporary weather stations, but for sites and other locations of archaeological interest for which only pollen data are available, extrapolations from contemporary weather summaries become necessary.

15.   All dates used in this section have reference to uncalibrated ^{14}C dates for every event.

16.   To get this result, I divided the expected total ethnic population projected from only mobile hunter-gatherer cases by the total area occupied by the ethnic group measured in 100-square-kilometer units and divided the result by the total expected ethnic population multiplied by 100. The product of this calculation was then subtracted from 100: NETP1 = 100 − [100 * (EXTLPOP1/EXAREA1)/EXTLOPOP1]. The result is the inverse of the percentage of the total population accommodated in a 100-square-kilometer unit. The inverse percentage was used so that large values would indicate extensive areas and large, egocentric, social networks.

17.   This generalization is consistent with observations made by Kelly (1995:313) and adopted by Bar-Yosef and Meadow (1995:53).

18.   It is likely that a more fine-grained classification with perhaps a mixed category would yield results similar to those of the Terrestrial Model for some periods. The projections from modern hunter-gatherers include, however, the use of weapons such as the bow and arrow and other implements that are likely to have driven the dependence upon high-quality food in the direction of terrestrial animals.

19.   Generalizations 11.12 and 11.14 may also be relevant to the Natufian situation, as might scenario 11.01.

20.   The criterion for identifying an area as unoccupied is 0.3 person per 100 square kilometers. Values of only 0.32 person are indicated from the period immediately following the Younger Dryas.

21.   This information is summarized from Waterbolk (1994:369). It should be noted that the early Natufian tends to be concentrated in the coastal zone to the north of Jerusalem. Interestingly, prepottery Neolithic A deposits are absent from the coastal zone and prepottery Neolithic B represents the initial Neolithic in this zone. Late Natufian deposits are dated to the Younger Dryas and are found in the coastal regions, but their general character is a matter of some speculation. Bar-Yosef considers the late Natufian to have been associated with mobility and a land-extensive settlement pattern, particularly

in coastal areas south of Jerusalem (Bar-Yosef and Meadow 1995:59–61).

22.   This feature of the projected hunter-gatherer data is fascinating. The equations on which these projections are based were developed at the time I was beginning the research reported in this book, but prior to beginning the actual writing. The analysis and pattern recognition work reported in the book after chapter 4, and some of the material at the beginning of chapter 5, were all done as part of the writing of the book. The equations, therefore, were completed prior to the development of the Terrestrial Model and long before I had imagined that a Group Size Model would be useful. It now appears that the equation for mobile hunter-gatherer population density had picked up the threshold at 1.59 persons for groups dependent upon terrestrial animals. This threshold became more germane as climates became colder, because the colder the climate, the less possible it became to increase one's dependence upon terrestrial plants. In the archaeological sequences from the Near East, we are seeing a dramatic drop in projected densities to just slightly more than two persons per 100 square kilometers. This is only possible if an aquatic alternative is present in such settings.

23.   At the time of European contact in eastern North America, this zone corresponded to the northernmost extension of the use of domesticated plants. At the colder end of this zone, hunter-gatherers were largely dependent upon aquatic resources.

24.   To calculate the rate of population growth when one knows the size of the beginning population (P_1), the size of the ending population (P_2), and the length of time between the two (Y), the equation is: Rate per annum = $\log_{10}P_2 - (\log_{10}P_1/\log_{10}Y)$.

25.   When groups are faced with short-term, extreme changes in their habitat, mobility is often the response, as persons search for better circumstances. For instance, during the crash of the caribou population at the beginning of the twentieth century, the Nunamiut Eskimo actually split up into search parties made up of adult and younger males who went on long trips to look for caribou. Some of these trips lasted over eighteen months, and in some cases the information obtained resulted in the fission and movement of groups over long distances into new areas.

26.   The niche breadth of linear pottery cultures, as opposed to the variability anticipated for mobile hunter-gatherers in the same settings, is discussed following figure 6.17.

27.   New evidence of decreased mobility in early Natufian sites has become available (Lieberman 1993). The author's data on Natufian era gazelle are fascinating and understandable, given the data on technology reported in chapter 10. Because the author has no framework to evaluate these data, however, his ideas about intensification and hunting are in the realm of science fiction.

28.   I strongly urge readers to refer at this point to chapter 2. One of the characteristics of the actors in the hunter-gatherer play I am discussing is the capacity to learn, to plan in terms of future outcomes—in short to plan for events not yet in evidence. Cultural life itself is only possible because of the human ability to reason using symbols. Imagining events not yet experienced is also the capability that makes scientific learning possible. This capability is not always homeostatically regulated by means of ideology. It may be expected to be manifested when cultural systems are in critical states. The only prerequisite for the adaptive shift to seeps and soaks, for instance, was

to be able to project what was already known about the biotic requirements of plants and to imagine the contribution that human labor could make to meeting these needs. Of course, this insight was followed by an enormous investment of energy to learn about how to make the new adaptation work.

29.   Alex Applegate and Amber Johnson of Southern Methodist University researched this issue with the assistance of Jessica Patti during the summer of 1998 (Johnson 2000).

30.   In the environment of postmodernist nihilism, many persons interpret the reluctance of some archaeologists to postulate diffusion or migration as "paradigm bias." See, for instance, Blumler (1996:36–37), who labels many rational attempts to dispel our own ignorance as paradigm bias, despite the fact that Blumler shares this ignorance with the rest of us.

EPILOGUE

1.   For an excellent description see Galindo (1997:30–40).

2.   This generalization may not apply to large camps, particularly if they include both men's and women's camps, which is common in Australia. Under such conditions, female ego-centered kin may participate in risk-pooling units with or without co-wives, as long as sharing includes the family of procreation.

3.   In another pattern among generic hunter-gatherers, which I have not followed up as thoroughly, wide interhousehold spacing in camps is related to high levels of polygyny. There are a few exceptions to this generalization, but these groups have all either been resettled or for many years been strongly pressured by missionaries to give up the practice of polygyny. Only one polygynous group is known that maintains tight camp spacing (Altman 1987:29), but the level of polygyny and the nature of the risk-pooling associations have not been well documented. The reader should be cautioned that groups with or without polygynous arrangements may actually be organized as labor-based risk pools of differing scales in particular types of camps that may have extraordinarily tight spacing when compared with normal residential camps. Such arrangements have been documented among the Nunamiut during cooperative caribou drives (unpublished site plan 1944: Caribou Drive at Chandler Lake) and among the southern Netsilik during episodes of cooperative netting of fish for storage (Briggs 1970:108–9:photo 3). Northern Netsilik and Copper Eskimo groups also camp in tight clusters when doing breathing hole sealing, which is associated with a nested hierarchy of risk-pooling networks.

4.   Bidimensionality is appropriate from the perspective of birth as the event that endows an individual with a full compliment of kin. In all cases, however, this event has been preceded by some form of marriage event incorporating or merging affinal kin with bidimensional kin. In some instances, a third dimension has even been added that relates to how the affines of an individual's parents have been conceptualized.

5.   See Heinrich (1963:88).

6.   In my opinion, neither of these terms is appropriately applied to generic hunter-gatherers, particularly if the only source of information is ethnography. The term *egalitarian* makes sense only relative to stratified systems with centralized, authoritarian, power-based decision making. A more appropriate term for generic hunter-gatherers is *nonstratified* or *nonranked*.

7.   These observations strongly affect arguments such as those by Bettinger and Baumhoff (1982) postulating a "Numic spread."

8.   Other possibilities include moving considerable distances to find uninhabited areas, or a new niche might open up within the subsistence range of the parent unit. This could lead to a huge increase in carrying capacity as well as some interesting possibilities for increased systemic and regional complexity. In general, these alternatives may represent possibilities standing behind many new kinds of systems that would not appear in my global sample of hunter-gatherers.

9.   These processes are well documented in the ethnographies of Australian hunter-gatherers. For instance, at the time of the first European contact, the northern part of the region near the coast of New South Wales contained many ethnic groups. (A good example would be the Jinibara [Winterbotham 1980], who were in the process of coping quite directly with packing.) A variety of groups in southeast Queensland (Morwood 1987) were similarly affected. Important information on groups experiencing packing along Australia's north coast was published by Galindo (1997), who reports that the population density within the clan estate where she conducted research was 23.31 persons per 100 square kilometers, which is well beyond the packing threshold. The marriage preferences and conventions for access to other clan territories had essentially collapsed, so that a person's mate did not make territory accessible to affines who were not already considered to have access rights.

10.   Owens and Hayden (1997) have provided an excellent review of the rituals and events at the center of maturational episodes among "transegalitarian" hunter-gatherers (these groups are usually classified as internally ranked in my study). Following their review, the authors attempt to argue that the late Upper Paleolithic painted caves of western Europe are to be understood as locations for maturational rituals—which seems likely—but they assume that the Paleolithic societies were internally ranked or transegalitarian! It is interesting that in my sample of hunter-gatherers, maturational rituals are either the most important annual social ritual or the second most important social ritual in 57 percent of the nonpacked hunter-gatherer cases that are primarily dependent upon terrestrial plants, in 35 percent of the groups dependent upon terrestrial animals, and in only 10 percent of the groups dependent upon aquatic resources. Among hunter-gatherer groups that have reached the packing threshold and do not exhibit evidence of either wealth differentials or ranking, the percentages increase considerably to 66 percent, 50 percent, and 80 percent, respectively. Among aquatically dependent cases, population densities above the packing threshold correspond to large differences in the character of social rituals. In groups whose population density level is *below* the packing threshold, wealth differentiation and ranking do not occur when the primary subsistence focus is terrestrial plants or aquatic resources. Wealth differentiation may be present among groups of terrestrial hunters, 42 percent of whom engage in maturational rituals. These data mean that in my global sample of hunter-gatherers maturational rituals are very common among groups that are packed but are found less often among packed, nonranked groups. On the other hand, remarkably few maturational rituals occur among groups of nonpacked, aquatically dependent peoples, whereas the highest frequencies occur in ranked cases. So, to return to Owens and Hayden's postulation, when making projections about behavior in the Pleistocene it is imperative to know whether or not the groups were packed. If the answer is affirmative, then they could not be primarily dependent upon terrestrial animal resources, and if they were dependent upon terrestrial plants, they would not be internally ranked. The remaining possibility—that the groups were dependent upon aquatic resources and packed—can only be made with confidence if there is some confirmatory evidence. Hayden himself has argued that there was minimal use of aquatic resources by "classic" Upper Paleolithic hunter-gatherers (Hayden et al. 1987), so I think it is much more likely that the Upper Paleolithic groups were not packed and that they were not primarily dependent upon aquatic resources. They could have been nonpacked and dependent upon terrestrial animals, with or without wealth differentials, but plant-dependent Upper Paleolithic peoples in western Europe would not have been likely. Data on modern hunter-gatherers, therefore, offer no support for Hayden's arguments about Upper Paleolithic artists.

11.   I do not mean to imply that the only context in which money was used and labor-added craft items were exchanged was a single-family expedition. These kinds of exchanges could occur at trade fairs, which were sometimes organized in a region as part of settlement-sponsored social events.

References

Abbie, A. A.
1957 Metrical Characters of a Central Australian Tribe. *Oceania* 27:220–243.

Adams, J. W.
1973 *The Gitksan Potlatch: Population Flux, Resource Ownership and Reciprocity.* Holt, Rinehart and Winston of Canada, Toronto.

Adney, T.
1900 Moose Hunting with the Tro-Kutchin. *Harpers Magazine* 100:495–507.

Agrawal, H. N.
1967 Physical Characteristics of the Shompen of Great Nicobar. *Bulletin of the Anthropological Survey of India* 16(1–2):83–97.

Aiello, L. C.
1992a Body Size and Energy Requirements. In *The Cambridge Encyclopedia of Human Evolution,* edited by S. Jones, R. Martin, and D. Pilbeam, pp. 41–44. Cambridge University Press, Cambridge.
1992b Human Body Size and Energy. In *The Cambridge Encyclopedia of Human Evolution,* edited by S. Jones, R. Martin, and D. Pilbeam, pp. 44–45. Cambridge University Press, Cambridge.

Allen, P. M.
1982 The Genesis of Structure in Social Systems: The Paradigm of Self-Organization. In *Theory and Explanation in Archaeology: The Southampton Conference,* edited by C. Renfrew, M. Rowlands, and B. A. Segraves, pp. 347–374. Academic Press, New York.

Altman, J. C.
1987 *Hunter-Gatherers Today: An Aboriginal Economy in North Australia.* Australian Institute of Aboriginal Studies, Canberra.

Alvard, M. S.
1993 Testing the "Ecologically Noble Savage" hypothesis: Interspecific prey choice by Piro hunters of Amazonian Peru. *Human Ecology* 21(3):355–387.

Ammerman, A. J., and L. L. Cavalli-Sforza
1971 Measuring the Rate of Spread of Early Farming in Europe. *Man* 6:674–688.
1973 A Population Model for the Diffusion of Early Farming in Europe. In *The Explanation of Culture Change,* edited by C. Renfrew, pp. 345–357. Duckworth, London.
1984 *The Neolithic Transition and the Population Genetics of Populations in Europe.* Princeton University Press, Princeton, N.J.

Amsden, C. W.
1977 A Quantitative Analysis of Nunamiut Eskimo Settlement Dynamics: 1898 to 1969. Ph.D. dissertation, Department of Anthropology, University of New Mexico, Albuquerque. University Microfilms, Ann Arbor, Mich.

Amundsen, R. E. G.
1908 *Roald Amundsen's "The Northwest Passage." Being the Record of a Voyage of Exploration of the Ship "Gjöa," 1903–1907.* 2 vols. E. P. Dutton, New York.

Anderson, C., and R. Robins
1988 Dismissed Due to Lack of Evidence? Kuku-Yalanji Sites and the Archaeological Record. In *Archaeology with Ethnography: An Australian Perspective,* edited by B. Meenan and R. Jones, pp. 182–205. Australian National University, Canberra.

Andrewartha, H. G., and L. C. Birch
1954 *The Distribution and Abundance of Animals.* University of Chicago Press, Chicago.

Arima, E. Y.
1984 Caribou Eskimo. In *Arctic,* edited by D. Damas, pp. 447–462. Handbook of North American Indians, Vol. 5. Smithsonian Institution, Washington, D.C.

Arnold, J. E. (editor)
1996 *Emergent Complexity: The Evolution of Intermediate Societies.* Archaeological Series No. 9. International Monographs in Prehistory No. 127. International Monographs in Prehistory, Ann Arbor, Mich.

Aschmann, H.
1967 *The Central Desert of Baja California: Demography and Ecology.* Manessier, Riverside, Calif.

Ashby, W. R.
1964 The Set Theory of Mechanism and Homeostasis. *General Systems* 9:83–97.

Aspelin, P. L.
1976 Nambicuara Economic Dualism: Lévi-Strauss in the Garden Once Again, Bijdragen tot de taal-land-en. *Volkenkunde* 132:1–31.
1979 Food Distribution and Social Bonding among the Mamaindé of Mato Grosso, Brazil. *Journal of Anthropological Research* 35:309–327.

Atkinson, R. J. C.
1964   Peasant Farmers in Europe. In *Man before History,* edited by C. Gabel, pp. 115–119. Prentice Hall, Englewood Cliffs, N.J.

Auerbach, M. J.
1984   Stability, Probability, and the Topology of Food Webs. In *Ecological Communities: Conceptual Issues and the Evidence,* edited by D. R. Strong, Jr., D. Simberloff, L. G. Abele, and A. B. Thistle, pp. 413–436. Princeton University Press, Princeton, N.J.

Axelrod, R.
1981   The Emergence of Cooperation among Egoists. *American Political Science Review* 75:306–318.

Axelrod, R., and W. D. Hamilton
1981   The Evolution of Cooperation. *Science* 211:1390–1396.

Baegert, J.
1863   An Account of the Aboriginal Inhabitants of the California Peninsula. In *Smithsonian Institution Annual Report, 1863,* pp. 352–369. Smithsonian Institution, Washington, D.C.

1865   An Account of the Aboriginal Inhabitants of the California Peninsula. In *Smithsonian Institution Annual Report, 1864,* pp. 378–399. Smithsonian Institution, Washington, D.C.

Bahuchet, S.
1979   Utilisation de l'espace forestier par les Pygmées Aka, Chasseurs-sueilleurs d'Afrique Centrale. *Information sur les sciences sociales* 18(6):999–1019.

1988   Food Supply Uncertainty among the Aka Pygmies (Lobaye, Central African Republic). In *Coping with Uncertainty in the Food Supply,* edited by I. de Garine and G. A. Harrison, pp. 118–149. Clarendon Press, Oxford.

1990   Food Sharing among the Pygmies of Central Africa. *African Study Monographs* (Kyoto) 11(1):27–53.

Bailey, H. P.
1960   A Method of Determining the Warmth and Temperateness of Climate. *Geografiska Annaler* 42(1):1–16.

Bailey, J.
1863   An Account of the Wild Tribes of the Veddahs of Ceylon: Their Habits, Customs and Superstitions. *Transactions of the Ethnological Society of London* 2:278–320.

Bailey, R. C.
1985   The Socioecology of the Efe Pygmy Men in the Ituri Forest, Zaire. Ph.D. dissertation, Department of Social Relations, Harvard University, Cambridge. University Microfilms, Ann Arbor, Mich.

1988   The Significance of Hypergyny for Understanding Subsistence Behavior among Contemporary Hunters and Gatherers. In *Diet and Subsistence: Current Archaeological Perspectives,* edited by B. V. Kennedy and G. M. LeMoine, pp. 57–65. University of Calgary Press, Calgary.

Bailey, R. C., and N. R. Peacock
1988   Efe Pygmies of Northeast Zaire: Subsistence Strategies in the Ituri Forest. In *Coping with Uncertainty in the Food Supply,* edited by I. de Garine and G. A. Harrison, pp. 88–117. Clarendon Press, Oxford.

Bak, P.
1996   *How Nature Works: The Science of Self-Organized Criticality.* Copernicus, New York.

Baldus, H.
1937   The Social Position of the Woman among the Eastern Bororo (transl. I. Lillios). *Ensaios de Etnologia Brasileira Brasiliana* 101:112–162.

Balikci, A.
1964   *Development of Basic Socioeconomic Units in Two Eskimo Communities.* National Museums of Canada Bulletin No. 202. Anthropological Series No. 69. National Museums of Canada, Ottawa.

1968   The Netsilik Eskimos: Adaptive Processes. In *Man the Hunter,* edited by R. B. Lee and I. DeVore, pp. 78–82. Aldine, Chicago.

1970   *The Netsilik Eskimo.* Natural History Press, Garden City, N.Y.

Bamforth, D. B.
1988   *Ecology and Human Organization on the Great Plains.* Plenum Press, New York.

Banks, J. A., and D. Glass
1953   A List of Books, Pamphlets, and Articles on the Population Question . . . Britain . . . 1793–1800. In *Introduction to Malthus,* edited by D. Glass, pp. 81–112. John Wiley and Sons, New York.

Barger, W. K.
1981   Great Whale River, Quebec. In *SubArctic,* edited by J. Helm, pp. 673–682. Handbook of North American Indians, Vol. 6. Smithsonian Institution, Washington, D.C.

Barnard, A.
1992   *Hunters and Herders of Southern Africa: A Comparative Ethnography of the Khoisan Peoples.* Cambridge University Press, Cambridge.

Barnes, R. F. W., and I. Douglas-Hamilton
1982   The Numbers and Distribution Patterns of Large Mammals in the Ruaha-Rungwa Area of Southern Tanzania. *Journal of Applied Ecology* 19(3):411–425.

Barrett, S. A.
1908   *The Ethno-Geography of the Pomo and Neighboring Indians.* University of California Publications in American Archaeology and Ethnology, Vol. 6. University of California Press, Berkeley.

Barrett, S. A., and E. W. Gifford
1933   *Miwok Material Culture: Indian Life of the Yosemite Region.* Bulletin of the Milwaukee Public Museum, Vol. 2, No. 4. Yosemite Natural History Association, Yosemite National Park, Calif.

Barth, F.
1966   Models of Social Organization. Occasional Papers of the Royal Anthropological Society No. 23. Royal Anthropological Institute, London.

1967   On the Study of Social Change. *American Anthropologist* 69:661–669.

Barton, R. N. E.
1989   Long Blade Technology in Southern Britain. In *The Mesolithic in Europe,* edited by C. Bonsall, pp. 264–271. John Donald, Edinburgh.

Bar-Yosef, O., and R. H. Meadow
1995   The Origins of Agriculture in the Near East. In *Last Hunters–First Farmers,* edited by T. D. Price and A. B. Gebauer, pp. 39–94. School of American Research Press, Santa Fe, N.M.

Basedow, H.
1907   Anthropological Notes on the Western Coastal Tribes of the Northern Territory of South Australia. *Trans-*

actions and Proceedings and Report of the Royal Society of South Australia 31:1–62.

Basehart, H. W.
1972   Band Organization and Leadership among the Mescalero Apache. Ms. on file, Department of Anthropology, Southern Methodist University, Dallas.

Batchelor, J.
1927   *Ainu Life and Lore: Echos of a Departing Race.* Kyobunkwan, Tokyo.

Bateson, G.
1958   *Naven: A Survey of the Problems Suggested by a Composite Picture of the Culture of a New Guinea Tribe Drawn from Three Points of View,* 2nd ed. Stanford University Press, Stanford, Calif.

Baugh, T. G.
1982   *Edwards I(34BK2): Southern Plains Adaptations in the Protohistoric Period.* Studies in Oklahoma's Past No. 8. Oklahoma Archaeological Survey, Norman.
1984   Southern Plains Societies and Eastern Frontier Pueblo Exchange during the Protohistoric Period. *Papers of the Archaeological Society of New Mexico* 9:154–167.
1991   Ecology and Exchange: The Dynamics of Plains-Pueblo Interaction. In *Farmers, Hunters, and Colonists,* edited by K. A. Spielmann, pp. 107–127. University of Arizona Press, Tucson.

Baumhoff, M. A.
1963   *Ecological Determinants of Aboriginal California Populations.* University of California Publications in American Archaeology and Ethnology, Vol. 49, No. 2, pp. 155–236. University of California Press, Berkeley.

Bean, L. J.
1972   *Mukat's People: The Cahuilla Indians of Southern California.* University of California Press, Berkeley.

Beatty, J.
1987   Natural Selection and the Null Hypothesis. In *The Latest on the Best: Essays on Evolution and Optimality,* edited by J. Dupré, pp. 53–75. MIT Press, Cambridge, Mass.

Beckerman, S.
1994   Hunting and Fishing in Amazonia: Hold the Answers, What Are the Questions? In *Amazonian Indians from Prehistory to the Present,* edited by A. Roosevelt, pp. 177–200. University of Arizona Press, Tucson.

Begon, M., J. L. Harper, and C. R. Townsend
1990   *Ecology: Individuals, Populations and Communities,* 2nd ed. Blackwell, Boston.

Belshaw, J.
1978   Population Distribution and the Pattern of Seasonal Movement in Northern New South Wales. In *Records of Times Past: Ethnohistorical Essays on the Culture and Ecology of the New England Tribes,* edited by I. McBryde, pp. 65–81. Australian Institute of Aboriginal Studies, Canberra.

Bender, B.
1975   *Farming in Prehistory: From Hunter-Gatherer to Food Producer.* St. Martin's Press, New York.
1978   Gatherer-Hunter to Farmer: A Social Perspective. *World Archaeology* 10:204–222.
1981   Gatherer-Hunter Intensification. In *Economic Archaeology,* edited by A. Sheridan and G. Bailey, pp.149–157. BAR International Series No. 96. British Archaeological Reports, Oxford.
1985   Prehistoric Developments in the American Midcontinent and in Brittany, Northwest France. In *Prehis-*

toric Hunter-Gatherers: The Emergence of Cultural Complexity, edited by T. D. Price and J. A. Brown, pp. 21–57. Academic Press, Orlando, Fla.

Bender, D. R.
1967   A Refinement of the Concept of Household: Families, Co-Residence, and Domestic Function. *American Anthropologist* 69:493–504.

Benedict, R. F.
1924   A Brief Sketch of Serrano Culture. *American Anthropologist* 26:366–392.

Bergerud, A. T.
1963   Aerial Winter Census of Caribou. *Journal of Wildlife Management* 27(3):438–449.
1974   The Role of the Environment in the Aggregation, Movement and Disturbance Behavior of Caribou. In *The Behavior of Ungulates and Its Relation to Management,* edited by V. Geist and F. Walther, pp. 552–581. IUCN Publications New Series No. 24, Vol. 2. International Union for Conservation of Nature and Natural Resources, Morges, Switzerland.

Bergerud, A. T., and F. Manuel
1969   Aerial Census of Moose in Central Newfoundland. *Journal of Wildlife Management* 33(4):910–916.

Bernatzik, H. A.
1951   *The Spirits of the Yellow Leaves.* In collaboration with E. Bernatzik. Robert Hale, London.

Berndt, R. M., and C. H. Berndt
1944   A Preliminary Report of Field Work in the Ooldea Region, Western South Australia: Women's Life. *Oceania* 14:220–249.
1970   *Man, Land and Myth in North Australia: The Gunwinggu People.* Michigan State University Press, East Lansing.

Bertalanffy, L. von
1950   The Theory of Open Systems in Physics and Biology. *Science* 3:23–29.
1968   *General System Theory: Foundations, Development, Applications.* George Braziller, New York.

Bettinger, R. L.
1980   Explanatory/predictive models of hunter-gatherer adaptation. In *Advances in Archaeological Method and Theory,* Vol. 3, edited by M. B. Schiffer, pp. 189–255. Academic Press, New York.
1991   *Hunter-Gatherers: Archaeological and Evolutionary Theory.* Plenum Press, New York.

Bettinger, R. L., and M. A. Baumhoff
1982   The Numic Spread: Great Basin Cultures in Competition. *American Antiquity* 47(3):485–503.

Bhanu, B. A.
1982   The Nomadic Cholanaickans of Kerala: An Analysis of Their Movements. In *Nomads in India,* edited by P. K. Misra and K. C. Malhotra, pp. 215–226. Anthropological Survey of India, Calcutta.
1992   Boundaries, Obligations, and Reciprocity: Levels of Territoriality among the Cholanaickan of South India. In *Mobility and Territoriality: Social and Spatial Boundaries among Foragers, Fishers, Pastoralists, and Peripatetics,* edited by M. J. Casimir and A. Rao, pp. 29–54. Berg, New York.

Biernoff, D.
1979   Traditional and Contemporary Structures and Settlement in Eastern Arnhem Land with Particular Reference to the Nunggubuyu. In *A Black Reality— Aboriginal Camps and Housing in Remote Australia,*

edited by M. Heppell, pp. 153–179. Australian Institute of Aboriginal Studies, Canberra.

Binford, L. R.
1962 Archaeology as Anthropology. *American Antiquity* 28(2):217–225.

1964 Cultural Diversity among Aboriginal Cultures of Coastal Virginia and North Carolina. Ph.D. dissertation, Department of Anthropology, University of Michigan, Ann Arbor. University Microfilms, Ann Arbor, Mich.

1968 Post-Pleistocene Adaptations. In *New Perspectives in Archeology,* edited by S. R. Binford and L. R. Binford, pp. 313–341. Aldine, Chicago.

1971 Field notes (Book 3) on file, Department of Anthropology, Southern Methodist University, Dallas, Texas.

1972 *An Archaeological Perspective.* Seminar Press, New York.

1974 Field notes (Alyawara, July) on file, Department of Anthropology, Southern Methodist University, Dallas, Texas.

1978 *Nunamiut Ethnoarchaeology.* Academic Press, New York.

1980 Willow Smoke and Dog's Tails: Hunter-Gatherer Settlement Systems and Archaeological Site Formation. *American Antiquity* 45(1):1–17.

1981 *Bones: Ancient Men and Modern Myths.* Academic Press, New York.

1982 Objectivity–Explanation–Archaeology, 1981. In *Theory and Explanation in Archaeology,* edited by C. Renfrew, M. J. Rowlands, and B. A. Segraves, pp. 125–138. Academic Press, New York.

1983 *In Pursuit of the Past: Decoding the Archaeological Record.* Thames and Hudson, New York.

1985 Brand-X versus the Recommended Product. *American Antiquity* 40(3):157–182.

1987 Researching Ambiguity: Frames of Reference and Site Structure. In *Method and Theory for Activity Area Research: An Ethnoarchaeological Approach,* edited by S. Kent, pp. 449–512. Columbia University Press, New York.

1989 *Debating Archaeology.* Academic Press, New York.

1990 Mobility, Housing, and Environment: A Comparative Study. *Journal of Anthropological Research* 46:119–152.

1991a When the Going Gets Tough, the Tough Get Going: Nunamiut Local Groups, Camping Patterns, and Economic Organization. In *Ethnoarchaeological Approaches to Mobile Campsites: Hunter-Gatherer and Pastoralist Case Studies,* edited by W. A. Boismier and C. S. Gamble, pp. 25–137. Ethnoarchaeology Series No. 1. International Monographs in Prehistory, Ann Arbor, Mich.

1991b *Cultural Diversity among Aboriginal Cultures of Coastal Virginia and North Carolina.* Garland, New York.

1991c A Corporate Caribou Hunt: Documenting the Archaeology of Past Lifeways. *Expedition* 33(1):33–43.

1992 Subsistence, a Key to the Past. In *The Cambridge Encyclopedia of Human Evolution,* edited by S. Jones, R. Martin, and D. Pilbeam, pp. 365–368. Cambridge University Press, Cambridge.

1999 Time as a Clue to Cause? *Proceedings of the British Academy* 101:1–35.

Binford, L. R., and S. R. Binford
1966 A Preliminary Analysis of Functional Variability in the Mousterian of Levallois Facies. *American Anthropologist* 68:238–295.

Binford, L. R., and W. J. Chasko
1976 Nunamiut Demographic History. In *Demographic Anthropology: Quantitative Approaches,* edited by E. B. Zubrow, pp. 63–143. University of New Mexico Press, Albuquerque.

Binford, L. R., and J. A. Sabloff
1982 Paradigms, Systematics, and Archaeology. *Journal of Anthropological Research* 38:137–153.

Binford, L. R., and N. M. Stone
1985 "Righteous Rocks" and Richard Gould: Some Observations on Misguided "Debate." *American Antiquity* 50(1):151–153.

Bird, J. B.
1946 The Alacaluf. In *The Marginal Tribes,* edited by J. H. Steward, pp. 55–80. Handbook of South American Indians, Vol. 1. Bureau of American Ethnology Bulletin No. 143. Smithsonian Institution, Washington, D.C.

1988 *Travels and Archaeology in South Chile,* edited by J. Hyslop. University of Iowa Press, Iowa City.

Bird, N.
1983 Wage-Gathering: Socio-Economic Changes and the Case of the Food-Gatherer Naikens of South India. In *Rural South Asia: Linkages, Change and Development,* edited by P. Robb, pp. 57–88. Curzon Press, London.

Bird-David, N.
1987 Single Persons and Social Cohesion in a Hunter-Gatherer Society. In *Dimensions of Social Life: Essays in Honor of David G. Mandelbaum,* edited by P. Hockings, pp. 151–166. Mouton de Gruyter, Berlin.

Birdsell, J. B.
1953 Some Environmental and Cultural Factors Influencing the Structuring of Australian Aboriginal Populations. *American Naturalist* 87:171–207.

1957 Some Population Problems Involving Pleistocene Man. *Cold Spring Harbor Symposia on Quantitative Biology* 22:47–69.

1958 On Population Structure in Generalized Hunting and Collecting Populations. *Evolution* 12:189–205.

1967 Preliminary Data on the Trihybrid Origin of the Australian Aborigines. *Archaeology and Physical Anthropology in Oceania* 2:100–155.

1968 Some Predictions for the Pleistocene Based on Equilibria Systems among Recent Hunters and Gatherers. In *Man the Hunter,* edited by R. B. Lee and I. DeVore, pp. 229–240. Aldine, Chicago.

1972 *Human Evolution: An Introduction to the New Physical Anthropology.* Rand McNally, Chicago.

1975 A Preliminary Report on New Research on Man-Land Relations in Aboriginal Australia. In *Population Studies in Archaeology and Physical Anthropology,* edited by A. C. Swedlund, pp. 34–37. Society for American Archaeology Memoir No. 30. *American Antiquity* 40(2, pt. 2).

Birket-Smith, K.
1928 The Greenlanders of the Present Day. *Greenland* 2:1–207.

1929 *The Caribou Eskimos: Material and Social Life and Their Cultural Position.* Report of the Fifth Thule Expedition, 1921–24, Vol. 5. Nordisk Forlag, Copenhagen.

1953 *The Chugach Eskimo.* Nationalmuseets Skrifter, Etnografisk Raekke 6. Copenhagen.

Birket-Smith, K., and F. de Laguna
1938   *The Eyak Indians of the Copper River Delta, Alaska.* Levin and Munksgaard, Copenhagen.

Bishop, C. A.
1969   The Northern Chippewa: An Ethnohistorical Study. Ph.D. dissertation, Department of Anthropology, State University of New York, Buffalo. University Microfilms, Ann Arbor, Mich.
1970   The Emergence of Hunting Territories among the Northern Ojibwa. *Ethnology* 9(1):1–15.
1978   Cultural and Biological Adaptations to Deprivation: The Northern Ojibwa Case. In *Extinction and Survival in Human Populations,* edited by C. D. Laughlin, Jr., and I. A. Brady, pp. 208–230. Columbia University Press, New York.

Blackburn, R. H.
1971   Honey in Okiek Personality, Culture and Society. Ph.D. dissertation, Department of Anthropology, Michigan State University, East Lansing. University Microfilms, Ann Arbor, Mich.

Blanton, R. E.
1994   *Houses and Households.* Plenum Press, New York.

Bleek, D. F.
1924   *The Mantis and His Friends.* Maskew Miller, Cape Town.
1928   *The Naron: A Bushman Tribe of the Central Kalahari.* Cambridge University Press, Cambridge.
1929   Bushmen of Central Angola. *Bantu Studies* 3:105–125.
1931   Traces of Former Bushmen Occupation in Tanganyika Territory. *South African Journal of Science* 28:423–429.

Blumler, M. A.
1996   Ecology, Evolutionary Theory and Agricultural Origins. In *The Origins and Spread of Agriculture and Pastoralism in Eurasia,* edited by D. R. Harris, pp. 25–50. Smithsonian Institution Press, Washington, D.C.

Blundell, V. J.
1975   Aboriginal Adaptation in Northwest Australia. Ph.D. dissertation, Department of Anthropology, University of Wisconsin, Madison. University Microfilms, Ann Arbor, Mich.
1980   Hunter-Gatherer Territoriality: Ideology and Behavior in Northwest Australia. *Ethnohistory* 27(2):103–117.

Blurton-Jones, N. G., L. C. Smith, J. F. O'Connell, K. Hawkes, and C. L. Kamuzora
1992   Demography of the Hadza, an Increasing and High-Density Population of Savanna Foragers. *American Journal of Physical Anthropology* 89:159–181.

Boas, F.
1888   The Central Eskimo. In *Sixth Annual Report of the Bureau of Ethnology to the Smithsonian Institution,* pp. 409–670. U.S. Government Printing Office, Washington, D.C.
1890   The Shushwap. In *Report of the 60th Meeting of the British Association for the Advancement of Science,* Part IV, pp. 632–647. Leeds.
1891   Physical Characteristics of the Tribes of the North Pacific Coast. *Annual Report of the British Association for the Advancement of Science* 61:424–449.
1895   The Indians of British Columbia: Physical Characteristics of the Tribes of the North Pacific Coast, the Tinnch Tribe of Nicola Valley, the Ts'ets'ā'ut, the Nisk'a', Linguistics of Nisk'a' and Ts'ets'ā'ut and Vocabulary of the Tinnch Tribes of Canada. In *Report of the 65th Meeting of the British Association for the Advancement of Science,* pp. 523–592. Leeds.
1899   Anthropometry of the Shoshonean Tribes. *American Anthropologist* 1:751–758.
1901   A. J. Stone's Measurements of the Natives of Northwestern Territories. *Bulletin of the American Museum of Natural History* 14:53–68.
1907   The Eskimo of Baffin Land and Hudson Bay. *Bulletin of the American Museum of Natural History* 15.
1940   *Race, Language, and Culture.* Free Press, New York.
1964   *The Central Eskimo.* University of Nebraska Press, Lincoln.

Boas, F., and L. Farrand
1899   Physical Characteristics of the Tribes of British Columbia. *Report of the 68th Meeting of the British Association for the Advancement of Science* 68:628–645.

Bogoras, W.
1904   *The Chukchee.* The Jesup North Pacific Expedition, Vol. 7. Memoirs of the American Museum of Natural History, Vol. 11. E. J. Brill, Leiden, the Netherlands.
1930   New Data on the Types and Distribution of Reindeer Breeding in Northern Eurasia. *Proceedings of the 23rd International Congress of Americanists,* pp. 403–410. New York.

Bolton, H. E. (editor)
1916   *Spanish Exploration in the Southwest, 1542–1706.* Charles Scribner's Sons, New York.

Bonner, J. T.
198   *The Evolution of Complexity.* Princeton University Press, Princeton, N.J.

Bonnichsen, R.
1973   Millie's Camp: An Experiment in Archaeology. *World Archaeology* 4:277–291.

Boschín, M. T., and L. R. Macuzzi
1979   Ensayo metodologico para la reconstruccion ethnohistorica: su aplicacion a la coprension del modelo Tehuelche Meridional. *Colegio de Graduados en Antropología, Serie Monografica* (Buenos Aires) 4:3–37.

Bose, S.
1964   Economy of the Onge of Little Andaman. *Man in India* 44(4):298–310.

Boserup, E.
1965   *The Conditions of Agricultural Growth: The Economics of Agrarian Change under Population Pressure.* Aldine, Chicago.

Boulding, K.
1956   General Systems Theory—The Skeleton of Science. *Management Science* 2:197–208.

Bourquin, O., J. Vincent, and P. M. Hitchins
1971   The Vertebrates of the Hluhluwe Game Reserve–Corridor–Umfolozi Game Reserve Complex. *Lammergeyer* 14:5–58.

Bowen, T.
1976   *Seri Prehistory: The Archaeology of the Central Coast of Sonora, Mexico.* Anthropological Papers of the University of Arizona No. 27. University of Arizona Press, Tucson.

Bower, B.
1989   A World That Never Existed. *Science News* 135:264–266.

Boyd, R. T.
1990   Demographic History, 1774–1874. In *Northwest Coast,* edited by W. Suttles, pp. 135–148. Handbook of North

American Indians, Vol. 7. Smithsonian Institution, Washington, D.C.

Boyd, R. T., and P. J. Richerson
1985   *Culture and the Evolutionary Process.* University of Chicago Press, Chicago.

Brandt, J. H.
1961   The Negrito of Peninsular Thailand. *Journal of the Siam Society* 49(2):123–160.

Brayshaw, H.
1990   *Well Beaten Paths.* Studies in North Queensland History No. 10. Department of History, James Cook University of North Queensland, Cairns.

Briggs, J.
1970   *Never in Anger: Portrait of an Eskimo Family.* Harvard University Press, Cambridge, Mass.

Brink, P. J.
1969   The Pyramid Lake Paiute of Nevada. Ph.D. dissertation, Department of Anthropology, Boston University, Boston. University Microfilms, Ann Arbor, Mich.

Brokensha, P.
1975   *The Pitjantjatjara and Their Crafts.* Aboriginal Arts Board, North Sydney.

Bronson, B.
1975   The Earliest Farming: Demography as Cause and Consequence. In *Population, Ecology and Social Evolution,* edited by S. Polgar, pp. 53–78. Mouton, the Hague.

Brooks, A. S., D. E. Gelburd, and J. E. Yellen
1984   Food Production and Culture Change among the !Kung San: Implications for Prehistoric Research. In *From Hunters to Farmers: The Causes and Consequences of Food Production in Africa,* edited by J. D. Clark and S. A. Brandt, pp. 293–310. University of California Press, Berkeley.

Brosius, J. P.
1986   River, Forest and Mountain: the Penan Gang Landscape. *Sarawak Museum Journal* 36(57):173–184.
1988   A Separate Reality: Comments on Hoffman's *The Punan: Hunters and Gatherers of Borneo. Borneo Research Bulletin* 20:81–106.

Brumbach, H. J., and R. Jarvnpa
1989   *Ethnoarchaeological and Cultural Frontiers.* Peter Lang, New York.

Brumfiel, E.
1976   Regional Growth on the Eastern Valley of Mexico: A Test of the Population Pressure Hypothesis. In *The Early Mesoamerican Village,* edited by K. V. Flannery, pp. 243–249. Academic Press, New York.

Bryson, R. A.
1989a   Late Quaternary Volcanic Modulation of Milankovitch Climate Forcing. *Theoretical and Applied Climatology* 39:115–125.
1989b   Modeling the NW India Monsoon for the Last 40,000 Years. *Climate Dynamics* 3:169–177.
1992   A Macrophysical Model of the Holocene Intertropical Convergence and Jetstream Positions and Rainfall for the Saharan Region. *Meteorology and Atmospheric Physics* 47:247–258.
1997   The Paradigm of Climatology: An Essay. *Bulletin of the American Meteorological Society* 78(3):449–455.

Bryson, R. A., and R. Bryson
1995   *An Archaeoclimatology Workbook: High-Resolution, Site-Specific Climate Modeling for Field Scientists.*

Center for Climatic Research, Madison, Wisc.
1997   High-Resolution Simulations of Regional Holocene Climate: North Africa and the Near East. In *Proceedings: Third Millennium B.C. Climate Change and Old World Collapse,* edited by H. N. Dalfes, G. Kukla, and H. Weiss, pp. 566–593. NATO ASI Series I, Vol. 49. Springer-Verlag, Berlin.

Bryson, R. A., and B. M. Goodman
1980   Volcanic Activity and Climatic Changes. *Science* 207:1040–1044.
1986   Milankovitch and Global Ice Volume Simulation. *Theoretical and Applied Climatology* 37:22–28.

Burch, E. S., Jr.
1972   The Caribou/Wild Reindeer as a Human Resource. *American Antiquity* 37(3):339–368.
1975   *Eskimo Kinsmen: Changing Family Relationships in Northwest Alaska.* West, St. Paul, Minn.

Burch, E. S., Jr., and L. J. Ellanna (editors)
1994   *Key Issues in Hunter-Gatherer Research.* Berg, Oxford.

Bushnell, D. I., Jr.
1922   *Villages of the Algonquian, Siouian and Caddoan Tribes West of the Mississippi.* Bureau of American Ethnology Bulletin No. 77. Smithsonian Institution, Washington, D.C.

Byrnes, R. F.
1976   *The Zadruga.* University of Notre Dame Press, South Bend, Ind.

Cadelina, R. V.
1982   Batak Interhousehold Food Sharing: A Systematic Analysis of Food Management of Marginal Agriculturalists in the Philippines. Ph.D. dissertation, Department of Anthropology, University of Hawaii, Honolulu. University Microfilms, Ann Arbor, Mich.

Cailleux, A.
1953   *Biogeographie Mondiale.* Presses Universitaires, Paris.

Cain, S.
1935   Studies of Virgin Hardwood Forest. III. Warren's Woods, a Beech-Maple Climax Forest in Berrien County, Michigan. *Ecology* 15:500–513.

Callaway, D. G., J. C. Janetski, and O. C. Stewart
1986   Ute. In *Great Basin,* edited by W. L. d'Azevedo, pp. 336–367. Handbook of North American Indians, Vol. 11. Smithsonian Institution, Washington, D.C.

Cameron, D.
1890   A sketch of the customs, manners, and way of living of the natives in the barren country about Nipigon. In "Les Bourgeois de la Compagnie du Nord-Ouest." *A Côté et Cie* 2:239–265.

Campbell, T. D., J. H. Gray, and C. J. Hackett
1936   Physical Anthropology of the Aborigines of Central Australia. *Oceania* 7:106–139, 246–261.

Cannon, M. (editor)
1983   *Historical Records of Victoria, Foundation Series,* Vol. 2B: *Aborigines and Protectors 1838–1839.* Victorian Government Printing Office, Melbourne.

Carneiro, R. L.
1970   A Theory of the Origin of the State. *Science* 169:733–738.
1973   The Four Faces of Evolution. In *The Handbook of Social and Cultural Anthropology,* edited by J. J. Honigmann, pp. 89–110. Rand McNally, Chicago.

Carneiro, R. L., and S. F. Tobias
1963   The Application of Scale Analysis to the Study of Cultural Evolution. *Transactions of the New York Academy of Sciences* (ser. 2) 26:196–207.

Carr, C.
1985   Alternative Models, Alternative Techniques: Variable Approaches to Intrasite Spatial Analysis. In *For Concordance in Archaeological Analysis: Bridging Data Structure, Quantitative Technique and Theory,* edited by C. Carr, pp. 302–459. Waveland Press, Prospect Heights, Ill.

Case, T. J., M. E. Gilpin, and J. M. Diamond
1979   Overexploitation, Interference Competition, and Excess Density Compensation in Insular Faunas. *American Naturalist* 113:843–854.

Cashdan, E.
1980   Egalitarianism among Hunters and Gatherers. *American Anthropologist* 82:116–120.

Caughley, W. A., and J. Goddard
1975   Abundance and Distribution of Elephants in the Luangwa Valley, Zambia. *East African Wildlife Journal* 13:39–48.

Cavalli-Sforza, L. L.
1986a   Demographic Data. In *African Pygmies,* edited by L. L. Cavalli-Sforza, pp. 23–45. Academic Press, Orlando, Fla.
1986b   Introduction. In *African Pygmies,* edited by L. L. Cavalli-Sforza, pp. 1–22. Academic Press, Orlando, Fla.
1996   The Spread of Agriculture and Nomadic Pastoralism: Insights from Genetics, Linguistics and Archaeology. In *The Origins and Spread of Agriculture and Pastoralism in Eurasia,* edited by D. R. Harris, pp. 51–69. Smithsonian Institution Press, Washington, D.C.

Cavalli-Sforza, L. L. (editor)
1986c   *African Pygmies.* Academic Press, Orlando, Fla.

Cawthorne, W. A.
1844   Rough Notes on the Manners and Customs of the Natives. Reprinted in *Proceedings of the Royal Geographical Society of South Australia* 27:47–77.

Chaloupka, G.
1981   The Traditional Movement of a Band of Aboriginals in Kakadu. In *Kakadu National Park Education Resources,* edited by T. Stokes, pp. 162–171. Australian National Parks and Wildlife Service, Canberra.

Chamberlain, A. F.
1892   Report on the Kootenay Indians of South-Eastern British Columbia. *Reports of the British Association for the Advancement of Science* 62:549–615.

Champion, T., C. Gamble, S. Shennan, and A. Whittle
1984   *Prehistoric Europe.* Academic Press, London.

Chang, K. C.
1962   A Typology of Settlement and Community Patterns in Some Circumpolar Societies. *Arctic Anthropology* 1:28–41.

Chapman, A.
1982   *Drama and Power in a Hunting Society: The Selk'nam of Tierra del Fuego.* Cambridge University Press, Cambridge.

Chard, C. S.
1963   The Nganasan—Wild Reindeer Hunters of the Taimyr Peninsula. *Arctic Anthropology* 1:105–121.

Christy, M. (editor)
1894   *The Voyages of Captain Luke Fox of Hull and Captain Thomas James of Bristol in Search of a Northwest Passage, in 1631–1632.* Hakluyt Society, London.

Clark, A. McF.
1974   *Koyukuk River Culture.* National Museum of Man Mercury Series, Canadian Ethnology Service Paper No. 18. National Museums of Canada, Ottawa.

1975   Upper Koyukon River Koyukon Athapaskan Social Culture: An Overview. In *Proceedings: Northern Athapaskan Conference, 1971,* Vol. 1, edited by A. McF. Clark, pp. 147–180. National Museum of Man Mercury Series, Canadian Ethnology Service Paper No. 27. National Museums of Canada, Ottawa.

Clark, J. D.
1951   Bushman Hunters of the Barotse Forests. *Northern Rhodesia Journal* 1(3):56–65.
1984   Prehistoric Cultural Continuity and Economic Change in the Central Sudan in the Early Holocene. In *From Hunters to Farmers,* edited by J. D. Clark and S. A. Brandt, pp. 113–126. University of California Press, Berkeley.

Clark, J. E., and M. Blake
1996   The Power of Prestige: Competitive Generosity and the Emergence of Rank Societies in Lowland Mesoamerica. In *Contemporary Archaeology in Theory,* edited by R. W. Preucel and I. Hodder, pp. 258–281. Blackwell, Oxford.

Clarke, D.
1976   Mesolithic Europe: The Economic Basis. In *Problems in Economic and Social Archaeology,* edited by G. G. Sieveking, I. H. Longworth, and K. E. Wilson, pp. 449–481. Duckworth, London.

Clastres, P.
1968   Ethnographie des Indiens Guayaki. *Journal de la Société des Américanistes* 57:8–61.
1972   The Guayaki. In *Hunters and Gatherers Today: A Socioeconomic Study of Eleven Such Cultures in the Twentieth Century,* edited by M. Bicchieri, pp. 138–174. Holt, Rinehart and Winston, New York.

Cleland, C. E.
1976   The Focal-Diffuse Model: An Evolutionary Perspective in the Prehistoric Cultural Adaptations of the Eastern United States. *Mid-Continental Journal of Archaeology* 1:59–76.

Clement, E.
1903   Ethnographical Notes of the Western-Australian Aborigines. *Internationales Archiv für Ethnographie* 16(I/II):1–29.

Cline, W., R. S. Commons, M. Mandelbaum, R. H. Post, and L. V. W. Walters
1938   The Sinkaietk or Southern Okanagon of Washington. In *Contributions from the Laboratory of Anthropology,* No. 2, edited by L. Spier, pp. 11–129. General Series in Anthropology No. 6. George Banta, Menasha, Wisconsin.

Clutton-Brock, T. H., F. E. Guinness, and S. D. Albon
1982   *Red Deer: Behavior and Ecology of Two Sexes.* University of Chicago Press, Chicago.

Codere, H.
1990   Kwakiutl: Traditional Culture. In *Northwest Coast,* edited by W. Suttles, pp. 359–377. Handbook of North American Indians, Vol. 7. Smithsonian Institution, Washington, D.C.

Coe, M. J., D. H. Cumming, and J. Phillipson
1976   Biomass and Production of Large African Herbivores in Relation to Rainfall and Primary Production. *Oecologia* 22:341–354.

Cohen, M. N.
1977   *The Food Crisis in Prehistory: Overpopulation and the Origins of Agriculture.* Yale University Press, New Haven, Conn.

1981   Pacific Coast Foragers: Affluent or Overcrowded? In *Affluent Foragers,* edited by S. Koyama and D. H. Thomas, pp. 275–295. Senri Ethnological Studies No. 9. National Museum of Ethnology, Osaka.

Collier, M. E. T., and S. B. Thalman (editors)
1991   *Interviews with Tom Smith and Maria Copa: Isabel Kelly's Ethnographic Notes on the Coast Miwok Indians of Marin and Southern Sonoma Counties, California.* Miwok Archaeological Preserve of Marin, Occasional Papers No. 6. MAPOM, San Rafael, Calif.

Collins, W. B.
1958   *The Perpetual Forest.* Staples Press, London.

Colliver, F. S., and F. P. Woolston
1975   The Aborigines of Stradbroke Island. *Proceedings of the Royal Society of Queensland* 86(16):91–104.

Condon, R. G.
1996   *The Northern Copper Inuit.* University of Toronto Press, Toronto.

Connell, J., and E. Orias
1964   The Ecological Regulation of Species Diversity. *American Naturalist* 98:399–414.

Connell, J., J. G. Tracey, and L. J. Webb
1964   Studies of Species Diversity of Rainforests in Queensland, Australia. Unpublished report cited in MacArthur and Connell (1966:37).

Cook, S. F.
1955   *The Aboriginal Population of the San Joaquin Valley, California.* Anthropological Records, Vol. 16, No. 2. University of California Press, Berkeley.
1956   *The Aboriginal Population of the North Coast of California.* Anthropological Records, Vol. 16, No. 3. University of California Press, Berkeley.

Cook, S. F., and R. F. Heizer
1965   *The Quantitative Approach to the Relation between Population and Settlement Size.* Contributions of the University of the California Archaeological Research Facility No. 64. University of California Press, Berkeley.

Cook, W. A.
1908   The Bororó Indians of Matto Grosso, Brazil. *Smithsonian Miscellaneous Collections* 50:48–62.

Cooper, J. M.
1939   Is the Algonquin Family Hunting Ground System Pre-Columbian? *American Anthropologist* 41:66–90.
1946a   The Yahgan. In *The Marginal Tribes,* edited by J. H. Steward, pp. 81–106. Handbook of South American Indians, Vol. 1. Bureau of American Ethnology Bulletin No. 143. Smithsonian Institution, Washington, D.C.
1946b   The Ona. In *The Marginal Tribes,* edited by J. H. Steward, pp. 107–125. Handbook of South American Indians, Vol. 1. Bureau of American Ethnology Bulletin No. 143. Smithsonian Institution, Washington, D.C.
1946c   The Patagonian and Pampean Hunters. In *The Marginal Tribes,* edited by J. H. Steward, pp. 127–168. Handbook of South American Indians, Vol. 1. Bureau of American Ethnology Bulletin No. 143. Smithsonian Institution, Washington, D.C.
1946d   The Chono. In *The Marginal Tribes,* edited by J. H. Steward, pp. 47–55. Handbook of South American Indians, Vol. 1. Bureau of American Ethnology No. 143. Smithsonian Institution, Washington, D.C.

Cooper, Z.
1991   Abandoned Onge Encampments and Their Relevance in Understanding the Archaeological Record in the Andaman Islands. Prepared for the Symposium on Living Traditions: South Asian Ethnoarchaeology, Cambridge, U.K., September 23–25. Manuscript on file, Department of Anthropology, Southern Methodist University, Dallas, Texas.

Corbusier, Wm. F.
1886   The Apache-Yumas and Apache-Mojaves. *American Antiquarian* 8:276–284, 325–339.

Cowan, C. S., and P. J. Watson
1992   *The Origins of Agriculture.* Smithsonian Institution Press, Washington, D.C.

Cowgill, G. L.
1975   Population Pressure as a Non-Explanation. In *Population Studies in Archaeology and Physical Anthropology,* edited by A. C. Swedlund, pp. 127–131. Society for American Archaeology Memoir No. 30. Issued as *American Antiquity* 40(2, pt. 2).

Crow, J. R., and P. R. Obley
1981   Han. In *Subarctic,* edited by J. Helm, pp. 506–513. Handbook of North American Indians, Vol. 6. Smithsonian Institution, Washington, D.C.

Crowder, L. B.
1980   Ecological Convergence of Community Structure: A Neutral Model Analysis. *Ecology* 61:194–198.

Culbertson, T. A.
1952   *Journal of an Expedition to the Mauvaises Terres and the Upper Missouri in 1850,* edited by J. F. McDermott. Bureau of American Ethnology Bulletin No. 147. Smithsonian Institution, Washington, D.C.

Currie, D. J., and J. T. Fritz
1993   Global Patterns of Animal Abundance and Species Energy Use. *Oikos* 57:56–68.

Currie, D. J., and V. Paquin
1987   Large-Scale Biogeographical Patterns of Species Richness of Trees. *Nature* 329:326–327.

Curtis, J. T.
1959   *The Vegetation of Wisconsin: An Ordination of Plant Communities.* University of Wisconsin Press, Madison.

Cybulski, J. S.
1990a   History of Research in Physical Anthropology. In *Northwest Coast,* edited by W. Suttles, pp. 116–118. Handbook of North American Indians, Vol. 7. Smithsonian Institution, Washington, D.C.
1990b   Human Biology. In *Northwest Coast,* edited by W. Suttles, pp. 52–59. Handbook of North American Indians, Vol. 7. Smithsonian Institution, Washington, D. C.

Dalton, G.
1967   Primitive Money. In *Tribal and Peasant Economies: Readings in Economic Anthropology,* edited by G. Dalton, pp. 254–281. Natural History Press, Garden City, N.Y.

Damas, D.
1963   *Iglugligmiut Kinship and Local Groupings: A Structural Approach.* Anthropological Series No. 64, Natural Museum of Canada Bulletin 196. Natural Museum of Canada, Ottawa.
1972   The Copper Eskimo. In *Hunters and Gatherers Today: A Socioeconomic Study of Eleven Such Cultures in the Twentieth Century,* edited by M. G. Bicchieri, pp. 3–50. Holt, Rinehart and Winston, New York.

1984   Copper Eskimo. In *Arctic,* edited by D. Damas, pp. 397–414. Handbook of North American Indians, Vol. 5. Smithsonian Institution Press, Washington, D.C.

Damas, D. (editor)
1969   *Contributions to Anthropology: Band Societies.* National Museums of Canada Bulletin No. 228. Anthropological Series No. 84. National Museums of Canada, Ottawa.

Damuth, J.
1981   Population Density and Body Size in Mammals. *Nature* 290:699–700.
1982   Analysis of the Preservation of Community Structure in Assemblages of Fossil Mammals. *Paleobiology* 8:434–446.
1987   Interspecific Allometry of Population Density in Mammals and Other Animals: The Independence of Body Mass and Population Energy Use. *Biological Journal of the Linnean Society* 31:193–246.

Damuth, J., and B. J. MacFadden (editors)
1990   *Body Size in Mammalian Paleobiology: Estimation and Biological Implications.* Cambridge University Press, Cambridge.

Dansereau, P.
1957   *Biogeography: An Ecological Perspective.* Ronald Press, New York.

Dart, R. A.
1937a   The Hut Distribution Genealogy and Homogeneity of the /'Auni-/Khomani bushmen. *Bantu Studies* 6:159–174.
1937b   The physical characters of the /?Auni=Khomani Bushmen. *Bantu Studies* 11:176–246.

Dasmann, R. F., and A. S. Mossman
1962   Abundance and Population Structure of Wild Ungulates in Some Areas of Southern Rhodesia. *Journal of Wildlife Management* 26:262–268.

David, N.
1971   The Fulani Compound and the Archaeologist. *World Archaeology* 3:111–131.

Davis, E. L.
1965   *An Ethnography of the Kuzedika Paiute of Mono Lake, Mono County, California.* University of Utah Anthropological Papers No. 75. University of Utah Press, Salt Lake City.

Dawson, G. M.
1891   Notes on the Shuswap People of British Columbia. *Proceedings and Transactions of the Royal Society of Canada* 9(2):3–44.

D'Azevedo, W. L. (editor)
1963   *The Washo Indians of California and Nevada.* University of Utah Anthropological Papers No. 67. University of Utah Press, Salt Lake City.

De Bertrodano, R. E.
1978   Description of an Aboriginal Tribe. In *Records of Times Past,* edited by I. McBryde, pp. 281–286. Australian Institute of Aboriginal Studies, Canberra.

De Castro, M. E., and A. Alemeida
1956   Canones de mulheres indigenas de Angola. *Progresso Cien* 23:6–16.
1957   Subsidio para a estudo anthropological dos Mucussos e mangares (Angolo). *Ultram* 6:1–14.

Deevey, E., Jr.
1960   The Human Population, *Scientific American* 203(3):195–204.

DeJong, J.
1912   Social Organization of the Southern Peigans. *Internationales Archiv für Ethnographie* 20:191–197.

De Laguna, F.
1956   *Chugash Prehistory: The Archaeology of Prince William Sound, Alaska.* University of Washington Press, Seattle.
1990   Eyak. In *Northwest Coast,* edited by W. Suttles, pp. 189–196. Handbook of North American Indians, Vol. 7. Smithsonian Institution, Washington, D.C.

Denham, W. W.
1975   Population Properties of Physical Groups among the Alyawara Tribe of Central Australia. *Archaeology and Physical Anthropology in Oceania* 10:115–159.

Denig, E. T.
1930   Indian Tribes of the Upper Missouri. In *Forty-Sixth Annual Report of the Bureau of American Ethnology, 1928–1929,* edited by J. N. B. Hewitt, pp. 375–628. Smithsonian Institution, Washington, D.C.
1953   *Of the Crow Nation.* Smithsonian Anthropological Papers No. 33. Bureau of American Ethnology Bulletin No. 151. Smithsonian Institution, Washington, D.C.
1961   *Five Indian Tribes of the Upper Missouri: Sioux, Arickaras, Assiniboines, Crees, Crows,* edited by J. C. Ewers. University of Oklahoma Press, Norman.

Dennell, R. W.
1983   *European Economic Prehistory.* Academic Press, London.
1992   The Origins of Crop Agriculture in Europe. In *The Origins of Agriculture: An International Perspective,* edited by C. W. Cowan and P. J. Watson, pp. 71–100. Smithsonian Institution Press, Washington.

Dennison, G.
1981   Sekani. In *Subarctic,* edited by J. Helm, pp. 433–441. Handbook of North American Indians, Vol. 6. Smithsonian Institution, Washington, D.C.

Dewar, R. E.
1984   Environmental Productivity, Population Regulation, and Carrying Capacity. *American Anthropologist* 86:601–614.

Diem, K. (editor)
1962   *Documenta Geigy Scientific Tables.* Geigy Pharmaceuticals. Ardsley, New York.

Dina, J., and J. M. Hoerner
1976   Etude sur les populations Mikea du sud-ouest de Madagascar. *Omaly sy Anid Hier et Aujourd'hui* 34:269–286.

Dixon, R. B.
1905   The Northern Maidu. *Bulletin of the American Museum of Natural History* 17, Pt. 3.
1907   *The Shasta.* Anthropological Papers, Vol. 17, Pt. 5. American Museum of Natural History, New York.
1910   *The Chimikaro Indians and Language.* University of California Publications in American Archaeology and Ethnology, Vol. 5, No. 5. University of California Press, Berkeley.

Dobzhansky, T.
1950   Evolution in the Tropics. *American Scientist* 38:209–221.

Donahue, R. E.
1992   Desperately Seeking Ceres: A Critical Examination of Current Models for the Transition to Agriculture in

Mediterranean Europe. In *Transitions to Agriculture in Prehistory,* edited by A. B. Gebauer and J. D. Price. Monographs in World Archaeology No. 4. Prehistory Press, Madison, Wisc.

Donham, D. L.
1981   Beyond the Domestic Mode of Production. *Man* 16:515–541.

Douglas, M.
1972   Symbolic Orders in the Use of Domestic Space. In *Man, Settlement and Urbanism,* edited by P. J. Ucko, R. Tringham, and G. W. Dimbleby, pp. 512–514. Duckworth, London.

Downs, J. F.
1966   *The Two Worlds of the Washo: An Indian tribe of California and Nevada.* Holt, Rinehart and Winston, New York.

Draper, P.
1975   !Kung Women: Contrasts in Sexual Egalitarianism in the Foraging and Sedentary Contexts. In *Toward an Anthropology of Women,* edited by R. Reiter, pp. 77–109. Monthly Review Press, New York.

Driver, H. E.
1936   *Wappo Ethnography.* University of California Publications in American Archaeology and Ethnology, Vol. 36, No. 3. University of California Press, Berkeley.

Drucker, P.
1939   *Contributions to Alsea Ethnography.* University of California Publications in American Archaeology and Ethnology, Vol. 35, No. 7, pp. 81–101. University of California Press, Berkeley
1940   *The Tolowa and Their Southwest Oregon Kin.* University of California Publications in American Archaeology and Ethnology, Vol. 36, No. 4. University of California Press, Berkeley.
1951   *The Northern and Central Nootkan Tribes.* Bureau of American Ethnology Bulletin No. 144. Smithsonian Institution, Washington, D.C.
1965   *Cultures of the North Pacific Coast.* Chandler, San Francisco.
1990   Central Coast Salish. In *Northwest Coast,* edited by W. Suttles, pp. 453–475. Handbook of North American Indians, Vol. 7. Smithsonian Institution, Washington, D.C.

DuBois, C. A.
1935   *Wintu Ethnography.* University of California Publications in American Archaeology and Ethnology, Vol. 36, No. 1. University of California Press, Berkeley.

DuBost, G.
1979   The Size of African Forest Artiodactyls as Determined by the Vegetation Structure. *African Journal of Ecology* 17:1–17.

Duff, W.
1952   *The Upper Stalo Indians.* Anthropology in British Columbia Memoir No. 1, pp. 1–136. British Columbia Provincial Museum, Victoria.
1981   Testsaut. In *Subarctic,* edited by J. Helm, pp. 454–457. Handbook of North American Indians, Vol. 6. Smithsonian Institution, Washington, D. C.

Duncan-Kemp, A. M.
1964   *Where Strange Paths Go Down.* W. R. Smith and Paterson, Brisbane.

Dunnell, R. C.
1971   *Systematics in Prehistory.* Free Press, New York.
1980   Evolutionary Theory and Archaeology. In *Advances in Archaeological Method and Theory,* Vol. 3, edited by M. B. Schiffer, pp. 35–99. Academic Press, New York.
1989   Aspects of the Application of Evolutionary Theory in Archaeology. In *Archaeological Thought in America,* edited by C. C. Lamberg-Karlovsky, pp. 35–49. Cambridge University Press, New York.
1992   Archaeology and Evolutionary Science. In *Quandaries and Quests: Visions of Archaeology's Future,* edited by L. Wandsnider, pp. 209–224. Center for Archaeological Investigations Occasional Paper No. 20. Southern Illinois University Press, Carbondale.
1995   What Is It That Actually Evolves? In *Evolutionary Archaeology,* edited by P. A. Teltser, pp. 33–50. University of Arizona Press, Tucson.

Dunning, R. W.
1959   *Social and Economic Change among the Northern Ojibwa.* University of Toronto Press, Toronto.

Dupré, J. (editor)
1987   *The Latest on the Best: Essays on Evolution and Optimality.* Bradford Books/MIT Press, Cambridge, Mass.

Earle, T. K.
1991   Toward a Behavioral Archaeology. In *Processual and Postprocessual Archaeologies: Multiple Ways of Knowing the Past,* edited by R. W. Preucel, pp. 83–95. Center For Archaeological Investigations Occasional Paper No. 10. Southern Illinois University Press, Carbondale.

East, R.
1984   Rainfall, Soil Nutrient Status, and Biomass of Large African Savanna Mammals. *African Journal of Ecology* 22:245–270.

Eder, J. F.
1978   The Caloric Returns to Food Collecting: Disruption and Change among the Batak of the Philippine Tropical Forest. *Human Ecology* 6(1):55–69.
1984   The Impact of Subsistence Change on Mobility and Settlement Pattern in a Tropical Forest Foraging Economy: Some Implications for Archeology. *American Anthropologist* 86:837–853.
1987   *On the Road to Tribal Extinction: Depopulation, Deculturation, and Adaptive Well-Being among the Batak of the Philippines.* University of California Press, Berkeley.

Eells, M.
1884   Census of the Challam and Twana Indians of Washington. *American Antiquarian and Oriental Journal* 6:35–38.
1887   Decrease of Population among the Indians of Puget Sound. *American Antiquarian and Oriental Journal* 9:271–276.

Eggan, F.
1937   The Cheyenne and Arapaho Kinship System. In *Social Anthropology of North American Tribes: Essays in Social Organization, Law and Religion,* edited by F. Eggan, pp. 35–98. University of Chicago Press, Chicago.
1968   Comments. In *Man the Hunter,* edited by R. B. Lee and I. DeVore, p. 85. Aldine, Chicago.

Ehrenfels, U. R.
1952   *The Kadar of Cochin.* University of Madras Press, Madras.

Ehrenreich, P.
1887   Ueber die Botocudos der Brasilianischen Provinzen Espiritu Santo und Minas Geraes. *Zeitschrift für Ethnologie* 19:1–46.

Eibl-Eibelsfeldt, I.
1972   *Die !Ko-Buschmann-Gesellschaft.* R. Piper, Munich.

Eisenberg, J. F.
1980   The Density and Biomass of Tropical Animals. In *Conservation Biology: An Evolutionary-Ecological Perspective,* edited by M. E. Soulé and B. A. Wilcox, pp. 35–55. Sinauer Associates, Sunderland, Mass.
1990   The Behavior/Ecological Significance of Body Size in the Mammalia. In *Body Size in Mammalian Paleobiology: Estimation and Biological Implications,* edited by J. Damuth and B. J. MacFadden, pp. 25–37. Cambridge University Press, Cambridge.

Eisenberg, J. F., and G. M. McKay
1974   Comparison of Ungulate Adaptations in the New World and Old World Tropical Forests with Special Reference to Ceylon and the Rainforests of Central America. In *The Behavior of Ungulates and Its Relation to Management,* edited by V. Geist and F. Walther, pp. 585–602. IUCN Publications New Series, Vol. 2, No. 24. International Union for Conservation of Nature and Natural Resources, Morges, Switzerland.

Eisenberg, J. F., and J. Seidensticker
1976   Ungulates in Southern Asia: A Consideration of Biomass Estimates for Selected Habitats. *Biological Conservation* 10:293–308.

Eisenberg, J. F., and J. Thorington
1973   A Preliminary Analysis of a Neotropical Mammal Fauna. *Biotropica* 5:150–161.

Eisenberg, J. F., M. A. O'Connell, and P. V. August
1979   Density, Productivity, and Distribution of Mammals in Two Venezuelan Habitats. In *Vertebrate Ecology in the Northern Neotropics,* edited by J. F. Eisenberg, pp. 187–207. Smithsonian Institution Press, Washington, D.C.

Ekblaw, W. E.
1927   The Material Response of the Polar Eskimo to Their Far Arctic Environment. *Annals of the Association of American Geographers* 17(4):148–198.
1928   The Material Response of the Polar Eskimo to Their Far Arctic Environment (Continued). *Annals of the Association of American Geographers* 18(1):1–44.
1948   Significance of Movement among the Polar Eskimo. *Bulletin of the Massachusetts Archaeological Society* 10:1–4.

Eldredge, N., and S. J. Gould
1972   Punctuated Equilibria: An Alternative to Phyletic Gradualism. In *Models in Paleobiology,* edited by T. J. M. Schoph, pp. 82–115. Freeman, Cooper, San Francisco.

Eldredge, N., and I. Tattersall
1982   *The Myths of Human Evolution.* Columbia University Press, New York.

Elmendorf, W. W.
1960   *The Structure of Twana Culture.* Research Studies Monographic Supplement No. 2. Washington State University, Pullman.

Emmons, G. T.
1911   *The Tahltan Indians.* University of Pennsylvania Museum Anthropological Publications 4(1). University of Pennsylvania Museum, Philadelphia.

Endicott, K., and K. L Endicott
1986   The Question of Hunter-Gatherer Territoriality: The Case of the Batek of Malaysia. In *The Past and Future of !Kung Ethnography,* edited by M. Biesele, R. Lee, and R. Gordon. Helmut Buske Verlag, Hamburg.

Euler, R. C.
1972   *The Paiute People.* Indian Tribal Series, Phoenix.

Euler, R. C., and C. Fowler
1966   *Southern Paiute Ethnohistory.* Glen Canyon Series No. 28. University of Utah Anthropological Papers No. 78. University of Utah Press, Salt Lake City.

Evans, C. D., W. A. Troyer, and C. J. Lensink
1966   Aerial Census of Moose by Quadrat Sampling Units. *Journal of Wildlife Management* 38:767–776.

Evans, I. H. N.
1937   *The Negritos of Malaya.* Cambridge University Press, Cambridge.

Ewers, J. C.
1955   *The Horse in Blackfoot Indian Culture.* Bureau of American Ethnology Bulletin No. 159. Smithsonian Institution, Washington, D.C.
1971   *The Blackfeet: Raiders on The Northwestern Plains.* University of Oklahoma Press, Norman.

Eyre, S. R.
1968   *Vegetation and Soils: A World Picture,* 2nd ed. Aldine, Chicago.

Faye, P. L.
1923   Notes on the Southern Maidu. In *Phoebe Apperson Hearst Memorial Volume,* edited by A. L. Kroeber, pp. 35–53. University of California Publications in American Archaeology and Ethnology, Vol. 20. University of California Press, Berkeley.

Fidler, P.
1934   Journal of a Journey with the Chepawyans, or Northern Indians, to the Slave Lake, and to the East and West of the Slave River in 1791 & 2. In *Publications,* Vol. 21, pp. 495–555. Champlain Society, Toronto.

Field, C. R., and R. M. Laws
1970   The Distribution of Large Herbivores in the Queen Elizabeth National Park, Uganda. *Journal of Applied Ecology* 7(2):273–294.

Fisher, J. W.
1987   *Shadows in the Forest: Ethnoarchaeology among the Efe Pygmies.* Ph.D. dissertation, Department of Anthropology, University of California, Berkeley. University Microfilms, Ann Arbor, Mich.

Fisher, J. W., and H. C. Strickland
1989   Ethnoarchaeology among the Efe Pygmies, Zaire: Spatial Organization of Campsites. *American Journal of Physical Anthropology* 78:473–484.

Fison, L., and A. W. Howitt
1880   *Kamilaroi and Kurnai.* George Robertson, Melbourne.

Fittkau, E. J., and H. Klinge
1973   On Biomass and Trophic Structure of the Central Amazonian Rain Forest System. *Biotropica* 5:2–14.

Flannery, K. V.
1969   Origins and Ecological Effects of Early Domestication in Iran and the Near East. In *The Domestication and Exploitation of Plants and Animals,* edited by P. J. Ucko and G. W. Dimbleby, pp. 73–100. Aldine, Chicago.
1972   The Origins of the Village as a Settlement Type in Mesoamerica and the Near East: A Comparative

Study. In *Man, Settlement and Urbanism*, edited by P. J. Ucko, R. Tringham, and G. W. Dimbleby, pp. 23–53. Duckworth, London.

1983   Settlement, Subsistence, and Social Organization of the Proto-Otomangueans. In *The Cloud People: Divergent Evolution of the Zapotec and Mixtec Civilizations,* edited by K. V. Flannery and J. Marcus, pp. 32–36. Academic Press, New York.

1986a   The Research Problem. In *Guilá Naquitz: Archaic Foraging and Early Agriculture in Oaxaca, Mexico,* edited by K. V. Flannery, pp. 3–18. Academic Press, Orlando, Fla.

1986b   A Visit to the Master. In *Guilá Naquitz: Archaic Foraging and Early Agriculture in Oaxaca, Mexico,* edited by K. V. Flannery, pp. 511–519. Academic Press, Orlando, Fla.

Flannery, R.
1953   *The Gros Ventres of Montana*, Pt. I: *Social Life.* Catholic University of America Anthropological Series No. 15. Catholic University of America Press, Washington, D.C.

Flatz, G.
1963   The Mrabri: Anthropometric, Genetic, and Medical Examinations. *Journal of the Siam Society* 51(2): 161–170.

Fleming, T. H.
1973   Numbers of Mammal Species in North and Central American Forest Communities. *Ecology* 54:555–563.

Floyd, T. J., L. D. Mech, and M. E. Nelson
1979   An Improved Method of Censussing Deer in Deciduous-Coniferous Forests. *Journal of Wildlife Management* 43:258–261.

Foley, R.
1988   Hominids, Humans and Hunter-Gatherers: An Evolutionary Perspective. In *History, Evolution and Social Change,* edited by T. Ingold, D. Riches, and J. Woodburn, pp. 207–221. Hunters and Gatherers, Vol. 1. Berg, Oxford.

Foote, D. C.
1966   *Human Biographical Studies in Northwestern Arctic Alaska:The Upper Kobuk River Project, 1965.* Final Report to the Association on American Indian Affairs, New York.

Fortes, M.
1969   *Kinship and the Social Order.* Aldine, Chicago.

Foster, G. M.
1944   *A Summary of Yuki Culture.* Anthropological Records, Vol. 5, No. 3, pp. 155–244. University of California Press, Berkeley.

Fourie, L.
1927   Preliminary Notes on Certain Customs of the Hei-//om Bushmen. *Veröffentlichungen der Wissenschaftlichen Vereinigung in Südwestafrika* 1:19–63.

1928   The Bushmen of South West Africa. In *The Native Tribes of South West Africa,* edited by C. H. Hahn, H. Vedder, and L. Fourie, pp. 79–106. Frank Cass, London.

Fowler, C. S.
1992   *In the Shadow of Fox Peak: An Ethnography of the Cattail-Eater Northern Paiute People of Stillwater Marsh.* Cultural Resource Series No. 5, U.S. Department of Interior, Fish and Wildlife Service, Region 1. U.S. Government Printing Office, Washington, D.C.

Fowler, C. S., and S. Liljeblad
1986   Northern Paiute. In *Great Basin,* edited by W. L. d'Azevedo, pp. 435–465. Handbook of North American Indians, Vol.11. Smithsonian Institution, Washington, D.C.

Fowler, D.
1966   Great Basin Social Organization. In *The Current Status of Anthropological Research in the Great Basin: 1964,* edited by W. L. d'Azevedo, pp. 57–73. Publications in the Social Sciences 1. Desert Research Institute, University of Nevada, Reno.

Fox, J. J.
1979   Foreword. In *Seasonal Variations of the Eskimo: A Study in Social Morphology,* by M. Mauss and H. Beuchat, translated by J. J. Fox, pp. 1–18. Routledge and Kegan Paul, London.

Fox, R. B.
1952   The Pinatubo Negritos: Their Useful Plants and Material Culture. *Philippine Journal of Science* 81(3–4):173–394.

1969   "Professional Primitives": Hunters and Gatherers of Nuclear South Asia. *Man in India* 49(2):139–160.

Fried, M. H.
1967   *The Evolution of Political Society.* Random House, New York.

Fritz, H., and P. Duncan
1993   Large Herbivores in Rangelands. *Nature* 364:292–293.

Fürer-Haimendorf, C. von
1943   *The Chenchus.* The Aboriginal Tribes of Hyderabad, Vol. 1. Macmillan, London.

Gabus, J.
1952   Contribution à l'étude des Namadi, chasseurs archaïques du Djout. *Bulletin der Schweizerischen Gesellschaft für Anthropologie und Ethnologie* 28:29–83.

Galindo, J. L.
1997   Scales of Human Organization and Rock Art Distributions: An Ethnoarchaeological Study among the Kunwinjku People of Arnhem Land, Australia. M.A. thesis, Department of Anthropology, University of Nebraska, Lincoln.

Gamble, C. S.
1982   Interaction and Alliance in Paleolithic Society. *Man* 17:92–107.

1983   Culture and Society in the Upper Paleolithic of Europe. In *Hunter-Gatherer Economy in Prehistoric Europe,* edited by G. N. Bailey, pp. 201–211. Cambridge University Press, Cambridge.

Gardner, P. M.
1965   Ecology and Social Structure in Refugee Populations: The Paliyans of South India. Ph.D. dissertation, Department of Anthropology, University of Pennsylvania, Philadelphia. University Microfilms, Ann Arbor, Mich.

1966   Symmetric Respect and Memorate Knowledge: The Structure and Ecology of Individualistic Culture. *Southwestern Journal of Anthropology* 22:389–415.

1969   Paliyan Social Structure. In *Contributions to Anthropology: Band Societies,* edited by D. Damas, pp. 153–167. National Museums of Canada Bulletin No. 228. Anthropological Series No. 84. National Museums of Canada, Ottawa.

1972   The Paliyans. In *Hunters and Gatherers Today: A Socioeconomic Study of Eleven Such Cultures in the*

Twentieth Century, edited by M. Bicchieri, pp. 404–450. Holt, Rinehart and Winston, New York.

1978   India's Changing Tribes: Identity and Interaction in Crises. In *Cohesion and Conflict in Modern India,* edited by G. R. Gupta, pp. 289–318. Main Currents in Indian Sociology, Vol. 3. Carolina Academic Press, Durham, N.C.

1982   Ascribed Austerity: A Tribal Path to Purity. *Man* 17:462–469.

1983   Cyclical Adaptations on Variable Cultural Frontiers. *Nomadic Peoples* 12:14–19.

1985   Bicultural Oscillation as a Long-Term Adaptation to Cultural Frontiers: Cases and Questions. *Human Ecology* 13(4):411–432.

1988   Pressures for Tamil Propriety in Paliyan Social Organization. In *History, Evolution and Social Change,* edited by T. Ingold, D. Riches, and J. Woodburn, pp. 91–106. Hunters and Gatherers, Vol. 1. Berg, Oxford.

Gardner, W.
1978   Productions and Resources of the Northern and Western Districts of New South Wales (1842–54). In *Records of Past Times: Ethnohistorical Essays on the Culture and Ecology of the New England Tribes,* edited by I. McBryde, pp. 239–246. Australian Institute of Aboriginal Studies, Canberra.

Gargett, R., and B. Hayden
1991   Site Structure, Kinship and Sharing in Aboriginal Australia: Implications for Archaeology. In *The Interpretation of Archaeological Spatial Patterning,* edited by E. Kroll and D. Price, pp. 11–32. Plenum Press, New York.

Garrard, A., S. Colledge, and L. Martin
1996   The Emergence of Crop Cultivation and Caprine Herding in the "Marginal Zone" of the Southern Levant. In *The Origins and Spread of Agriculture and Pastoralism in Eurasia,* edited by D. R. Harris, pp. 204–226. Smithsonian Institution Press, Washington, D.C.

Gason, S.
1879   The Dieyerie Tribe. In *The Native Tribes of South Australia,* edited by J. D. Woods, pp. 257–286. E. S. Wigg and Son, Adelaide.

Gaughwin, D., and H. Sullivan
1984   Aboriginal Boundaries and Movements in Western Port, Victoria. *Aboriginal History* 8:80–98.

Gayton, A. H.
1948a   *Yokuts and Western Mono Ethnography. I. Tulare Lake, Southern Valley, and Central Foothill Yokuts.* Anthropological Records, Vol. 10, No. 1. University of California Press, Berkeley.

1948b   *Yokuts and Western Mono Ethnography. II. Northern Foothill Yokuts and Western Mono.* Anthropological Records, Vol. 10, No. 2. University of California Press, Berkeley.

Gearing, F.
1962   *Priests and Warriors: Social Structure for Cherokee Politics in the 18th Century.* American Anthropological Association Memoir No. 93. *American Anthropologist* 64(5, pt. 2).

Geerling, C., and J. Bokdam
1973   Fauna of the Comoé National Park, Ivory Coast. *Biological Conservation* 5(4):251–257.

Geertz, C.
1995   Culture War. *New York Review of Books* 42(19):4–6.

Gellner, E.
1973   Primitive Communism. *Man* 8:536–540.

Gibson, T.
1988   Meat Sharing as a Political Ritual: Forms of Transaction versus Modes of Subsistence. In *Property, Power and Ideology,* edited by T. Ingold, D. Riches, and J. Woodburn, pp. 165–179. Hunters and Gatherers, Vol. 2. Berg, Oxford.

Giddings, J. L.
1956   Forest Eskimos: An Ethnographic Sketch of Kobuk River People in the 1880's. *University Museum Bulletin* (Philadelphia) 20(2):1–55.

Gifford, D. P.
1977   Observations of Modern Human Settlements as an Aid to Archaeological Interpretation. Ph.D. dissertation, Department of Anthropology, University of California, Berkeley. University Microfilms, Ann Arbor, Mich.

Gifford, E. W.
1916   *Miwok Moieties.* University of California Publications in American Archaeology and Ethnology, Vol. 12. University of California Press, Berkeley.

1926a   *Clear Lake Pomo Society.* University of California Publications in American Archaeology and Ethnology, Vol. 18, No. 2, pp 287–390. University of California Press, Berkeley.

1926b   *California Anthropometry.* University of California Publications in American Archaeology and Ethnology, Vol. 22. University of California Press, Berkeley.

1932a   *The Southeastern Yavapai.* University of California Publications in American Archaeology and Ethnology, Vol. 29. University of California Press, Berkeley.

1932b   *The Northfork Mono.* University of California Publications in American Archaeology and Ethnology, Vol. 31, No. 2. University of California Press, Berkeley.

1939   The Coast Yuki. *Anthropos* 34:292–375.

Gilberg, R.
1984   Polar Eskimo. In *Arctic,* edited by D. Damas, pp. 577–594. Handbook of North American Indians, Vol. 5. Smithsonian Institution, Washington, D.C.

Gilg, A.
1965   The Seri Indians in 1692, translated and edited by C. C. DiPeso and D. S. Matson. *Arizona and the West* 7(1):33–56.

Gillespie, B. C.
1981   Mountain Indians. In *Subarctic,* edited by J. Helm, pp. 326–337. Handbook of North American Indians, Vol. 6. Smithsonian Institution, Washington, D.C.

Gimbutas, M.
1973   The Beginning of the Bronze Age in Europe and the Indo-Europeans 3500–2500 B.C. *Journal of Indo-European Studies* 1:163–214.

1977   The First Wave of Eurasian Steppe Pastoralists into Copper Age Europe. *Journal of Indo-European Studies* 5:277–338.

1979   The Three Waves of the Kurgan People into Old Europe. *Archives Suisses d'Anthropologie Générale* 43:113–117.

1980   The Kurgan Wave Migration (c. 3400–3200 B.C.) into Europe and the Following Transformation of Culture. *Journal of Near Eastern Studies* 8:273–315.

Gittleman, J. L., and P. H. Harvey
1982 Carnivore Home-Range Size, Metabolic Needs and Ecology. *Behavioral Ecology and Sociobiology* 10:57–63.
Gleick, J.
1987 *Chaos: Making a New Science.* Penguin, New York.
Glick, P. C.
1959 Family Statistics. In *The Study of Population: An Inventory and Appraisal,* edited by P. M. Hauser and O. D. Duncan, pp. 576–603. University of Chicago Press, Chicago.
Goddard, P. E.
1904 *Hupa Texts.* University of California Publications in American Archaeology and Ethnology, Vol. 1, No. 2. University of California Press, Berkeley.
1916 *The Beaver Indians.* Anthropological Papers, Vol. 10, Pt. 4. American Museum of Natural History, New York.
Goggin, J. M., and W. C. Sturtevant
1964 The Calusa: A Stratified, Nonagricultural Society (with Notes on Sibling Marriage). In *Explorations in Cultural Anthropology: Essays in Honor of George Peter Murdock,* edited by W. H. Goodenough, pp. 179–219. McGraw-Hill, New York.
Goldberg, P.
1994 Interpreting Late Quaternary Continental Sequences In Israel. In *Late Quaternary Chronology and Paleoclimates of the Eastern Mediterranean,* edited by O. Bar-Yosef and R. S. Kra, pp. 89–102. RadioCarbon, Vol. 45. Department of Geosciences, University of Arizona, Tucson.
Goldman, I.
1940 The Alkatcho Carrier of British Columbia. In *Acculturation in Seven American Indian Tribes,* edited by R. Linton, pp. 333–386. D. Appleton–Century, New York.
1941 The Alkatcho Carrier: Historical Background of Crest Prerogatives. *American Anthropologist* (n.s.) 43(3): 396–418.
Goldschmidt, W.
1948 Social Organization in Native California and the Origin of Clans. *American Anthropologist* 50:444–456.
1951 *Nomlaki Ethnography.* University of California Publications in American Archaeology and Ethnology, Vol. 42, No. 4. University of California Press, Berkeley.
Goldstein, M. S.
1934 Anthropometry of the Comanches. *American Journal of Physical Anthropology* 19:289–319.
Goni, R. A.
1988 Arqueologia de momentos tardios en el Parque Nacional Perito Moreno (Santa Cruz, Argentina). In *Precirculados de las Ponencias Cientificas presentada a los Simposios del IX Congreso nacional de Arquelogia Argentina,* pp. 140–151. Universidad de Buenos Aires, Buenos Aires.
Goodale, J. C.
1962 Marriage Contacts among the Tiwi. *Ethnology* 1:452–466.
Goodman, M. J., A. Estioko-Griffin, P. B. Griffin, and J. S. Grove
1985 The Compatibility of Hunting and Mothering among Agta Hunter Gatherers of the Philippines. *Sex Roles* 12(11–12):1199–1209.
Gould, R. A.
1968 Living Archaeology: The Ngatatjara of Western Australia. *Southwestern Journal of Anthropology* 24: 101–122.
1969 *Yiwara: Foragers of the Australian Desert.* Charles Scribner's Sons, New York.
1971 The Archaeologist as Ethnographer: A Case Study from the Western Desert of Australia. *World Archaeology* 3:143–177.
1974 Some Current Problems in Ethnoarchaeology. In *Ethnoarchaeology,* edited by C. B. Donnan and C. W. Clewlow, pp. 29–48. Archaeological Survey Monograph No. 4. Institute of Archaeology, University of California, Los Angeles.
1977 *Puntutjarpa Rockshelter and the Australian Desert Culture.* Anthropological Papers, Vol. 54. American Museum of Natural History, New York.
1978a From Tasmania to Tucson. In *New Directions in Ethnoarchaeology,* edited by R. A. Gould, pp. 1–10. University of New Mexico Press, Albuquerque.
1978b Beyond Analogy in Ethnoarchaeology. In *Explorations in Ethnoarchaeology,* edited by R. A. Gould, pp. 249–293. University of New Mexico Press, Albuquerque.
1978c Tolowa. In *California,* edited by R. F. Heizer, pp. 128–136. Handbook of North American Indians, Vol. 8, pp. 128–136. Smithsonian Institution, Washington, D.C.
1980 *Living Archaeology.* Cambridge University Press, Cambridge.
1981 Comparative Ecology of Food-Sharing in Australia and Northwest California. In *Omnivorous Primates: Gathering and Hunting in Human Evolution,* edited by R. S. O. Harding and G. Teleki, pp. 422–454. Columbia University Press, New York.
1985 The Empiricist Strikes Back: Reply to Binford. *American Antiquity* 50(4):638–644.
Gould, R. A., and P. J. Watson
1982 A Dialogue on the Meaning and Use of Analogy in Ethnoarchaeological Reasoning. *Journal of Anthropological Archaeology* 1:355–381.
Gould, R. A., and J. E. Yellen
1987 Man the Hunted: Determinants of Household Spacing in Desert and Tropical Foraging Societies. *Journal of Anthropological Archaeology* 6:77–103.
Gould, R. T., and M. G. Plew
1996 Late Archaic Fishing along the Middle Snake River, Southwestern Idaho. In *Prehistoric Hunter-Gatherer Fishing Strategies,* edited by M. G. Plew, pp. 64–83. Department of Anthropology, Boise State University, Boise, Idaho.
Gould, S. J.
1989 *Wonderful Life: The Burgess Shale and the Nature of History.* W. W. Norton, New York.
1996 *Full House: The Spread of Excellence from Plato to Darwin.* Harmony, New York.
Grabert, G. F.
1974 Okanagan Archaeology: 1966–67. *Syesis* 7(2):1–83.
Graburn, N. H. H.
1969 *Eskimos without Igloos: Social and Economic Development in Sugluk.* Little, Brown, Boston.
Gragson, T.
1989 Allocation of Time to Subsistence and Settlement in a Ciri Khonome Pume Village of the Llanos of Apure, Venezuela. Ph.D. dissertation, Department of Anthropology, Pennsylvania State University, College Station. University Microfilms, Ann Arbor, Mich.

Graham, M., and A. Roberts
1986   Residentially-Constricted Mobility: A Preliminary Investigation of Variability in Settlement Organization. *Haliksa'i* (Albuquerque) 5:105–116.

Grant, J. C. B.
1924   Anthropometry of the Lake Winnipeg Indians. *American Journal of Physical Anthropology* 7:299–315.
1936   *Anthropometry of the Beaver, Sekani, and Carrier Indians.* National Museums of Canada Bulletin No. 81. Anthropological Series No. 18. Canada Department of Mines, Ottawa.

Grant, P.
1960   The Saulteux Indians. In *Les Bourgeois de la Compagnie du Nord-Ouest,* edited by L. R. Masson, pp. 307–366. Antiquarian Press, New York.

Gray, D. J.
1987   *The Takelma and Their Athapascan Neighbors.* Anthropological Papers No. 37. University of Oregon, Eugene.

Greaves, R. D.
1996   Ethnoarchaeological Investigation of Technological Organization, Subsistence Mobility and Resource Targeting among Pume Foragers of Venezuela. Ph.D. dissertation, Department of Anthropology, University of New Mexico, Albuquerque. University Microfilms, Ann Arbor, Mich.

Green, A. A.
1979   Density Estimate of the Larger Mammals of Arli National Park, Upper Volta. *Mammalia* 43(1):59–70.

Gregg, S. A.
1980   A Material Perspective of Tropical Rainforest Hunter-Gatherers: The Semang of Malaysia. In *The Archaeological Correlates of Hunter-Gatherer Societies: Studies from the Ethnographic Record,* edited by F. E. Smiley, C. M. Singpoli, H. E. Jackson, W. H. Wills, and S. A. Gregg, pp. 117–135. Michigan Discussions in Anthropology, Vol. 5, Nos. 1–2. Department of Anthroplogy, University of Michigan, Ann Arbor.
1988   *Foragers and Farmers: Population Interaction and Agricultural Expansion in Prehistoric Europe.* University of Chicago Press, Chicago.

Griffen, B.
1959   *Notes on Seri Indian Culture, Sonora, Mexico.* Latin American Monograph Series No. 10. University of Florida Press, Gainesville.

Griffin, P. B.
1981   Northern Luzon Agta Subsistence and Settlement. *Filipinas* 2:26–42.

Grønnow, B., M. Melgaard, and J. B. Nielsen
1983   *Aasivissuit—The Great Summer Camp: Archaeological, Ethnographical and Zoo-Archaeological Studies of a Caribou-Hunting Site in West Greenland.* Meddelelser om Grønland, Man and Society, Vol. 5. Commission for Scientific Research in Greenland, Odense.

Groube, L.
1996   The Impact of Diseases upon the Emergence of Agriculture. In *The Origins and Spread of Agriculture and Pastoralism in Eurasia,* edited by D. R. Harris, pp. 101–129. Smithsonian Institution Press, Washington, D.C.

Gubser, N. J.
1965   *The Nunamiut Eskimos: Hunters of Caribou.* Yale University Press, New Haven, Conn.

Guenther, M.
1986   *The Nharo Bushmen of Botswana: Tradition and Change.* Helmut Buske Verlag, Hamburg.

Guggisberg, C. A. W.
1970   *Man and Wildlife.* Arco, New York.

Gunther, E.
1962   Makah Marriage Patterns and Population Stability. In *Akten des 34th Internationalen Amerikanisten Kongress,* pp. 538–545. Verlag Ferdinand Berger, Vienna.

Gusinde, M.
1931   *The Selk'nam: On the Life and Thought of a Hunting People on the Great Land of Tierra del Fuego,* translated by F. Schütze. Die Feuerland-Indianer, Vol. 1. Human Relations Area Files, New Haven, Conn.
1937   *The Yahgan: The Life and Thought of the Water Nomads of Cape Horn,* translated by F. Schütze. Die Feuerland-Indianer, Vol. 2. Human Relations Area Files, New Haven, Conn.

Gussow, Z.
1954   Cheyenne and Arapaho: Aboriginal Occupations. In *American Indian Ethnohistory: Plains Indians,* edited by D. Horr, pp. 27–96. Garland, New York.

Gussow, Z., L. R. Hafen, and A. A. Ekirch
1974   *Cheyenne and Arapaho: Commission Findings, Indian Claims Commission.* American Indian Ethnohistory: Plains Indians Series. Garland, New York.

Hagen, B.
1908   *Die Orang Kubu auf Sumatra.* Veröffentlichungen aus dem Städtischen Völker-Museum No. 2. Joseph Baer, Frankfurt.

Hale, H. M., and N. B. Tindale
1933   Aborigines of the Princess Charlotte Bay, North Queensland. *Records of the South Australia Museum* 5:63–107.

Hallett, J. G.
1982   Habitat Selection and the Community Matrix of a Desert Small-Mammal Fauna. *Ecology* 63:1400–1410.

Hallowell, A. I.
1929   The Physical Characteristics of the Indians of Labrador. *Journal de la Société des Américanistes de Paris* (n.s.) 21:337–371.
1938   The Incidence, Character, and Decline of Polygyny among the Lake Winnipeg Cree and Saulteaux. *American Anthropologist* 40:235–256.
1955   *Culture and Experience.* University of Pennsylvania Press, Philadelphia.

Halpin, M. M., and M. Seguin
1990   Tsimshian Peoples: Southern Tsimshian, Coast Tsimshian, Nishga, and Gitksan. In *Northwest Coast,* edited by W. Suttles, pp. 267–284. Handbook of North American Indians, Vol. 7. Smithsonian Institution, Washington, D.C.

Halstead, P., and J. O'Shea (editors)
1989   *Bad Year Economics.* Cambridge University Press, Cambridge.

Hamilton, W. D.
1963   The Evolution of Altruistic Behavior. *American Naturalist* 97:354–356.

Hann, J. H. (editor and translator)
1991   *Missions to the Calusa.* Florida Museum of Natural History and University of Florida Press, Gainesville.

Hansen, S.
1886   Bidrag til Østgronlaendernes Anthropologi. *Meddelelser om Grønland* 10:1–41.

1914   Contributions to the Anthropology of the East Green-landers. *Meddelelser om Grønland* 39(2).

Hantzsch, B.
1977   *My Life among the Eskimos: Baffin Island Journeys in the Years 1909–1911.* Institute for Northern Studies Mawdsley Memoir Series No. 3. University of Saskatchewan, Saskatoon.

Harako, R.
1976   *The Mbuti as Hunters: A Study of Ecological Anthropology of the Mbuti Pygmies (I).* Kyoto University African Studies No. 10. Kyoto University, Kyoto.

Harding, T. G.
1960   Adaptation and Stability. In *Evolution and Culture,* edited by M. D. Sahlins and E. R. Service, pp. 45–68. University of Michigan Press, Ann Arbor.

Hardy, C. E., and J. W. Franks
1963   Forest Fires in Alaska. Manuscript on file, U.S. Forest Service, Fairbanks, Alaska.

Harestad, A. S., and F. L. Bunnell
1979   Home Range and Body Weight—A Reevaluation. *Ecology* 60:389–402.

Harner, M. J.
1970   Population Pressure and the Social Evolution of Agriculturalists. *Southwestern Journal of Anthropology* 26:67–86.
1973   *The Jívaro: People of the Sacred Waterfalls.* Doubleday, Garden City, N.Y.

Harpending, H., and R. Pennington
1990   Herero Households. *Human Ecology* 18(4):417–439.

Harper, F.
1964   *Caribou Eskimos of the Upper Kazan River, Keewatin.* University of Kansas Museum of Natural History Miscellaneous Publication No. 36. Allen Press, Lawrence, Kans.

Harper, J. A., J. H. Harn, W. W. Bentley, and C. F. Yocom
1967   *The Status and Ecology of the Roosevelt Elk in California.* Wildlife Monographs No. 16. Wildlife Society, Washington, D. C.

Harris, D. R.
1978   Adaptation to a Tropical Rain-Forest Environment: Aboriginal Subsistence in Northeastern Queensland. In *Human Behavior and Adaptation,* edited by N. Blurton-Jones and V. Reynolds, pp. 113–133. Taylor and Francis, London.
1982   Aboriginal Subsistence in a Tropical Rain Forest Environment: Food Procurement, Cannibalism, and Population Regulation in Northeastern Australia. In *Food and Evolution: Toward a Theory of Human Food Habits,* edited by M. Harris and E. B. Ross, pp. 357–385. Temple University Press, Philadelphia.
1990   *Settling Down and Breaking Ground: Rethinking the Neolithic Revolution.* Stichting Nederlands Museum voor Antropologie en Praehistorie. Twaalfde Kroon Voordracht, Amsterdam.
1996   The Origins and Spread of Agriculture and Pastoralism in Eurasia: An Overview. In *The Origins and Spread of Agriculture and Pastoralism in Eurasia,* edited by D. R. Harris, pp. 552–573. Smithsonian Institution Press, Washington, D.C.

Harris, J.
1940   The White Knife Shoshoni of Nevada. In *Acculturation in Seven American Indian Tribes,* edited by R. Linton, pp. 39–166. D. Appleton–Century, New York.

Harrison, J. L.
1962   The Distribution of Feeding Habits among Animals in a Tropical Rainforest. *Journal of Animal Ecology* 31:53–63.

Harrison, T.
1949   Notes on Some Nomadic Punans. *Sarawak Museum Journal* 5(1):130–146.

Hart, C. W. M.
1970   Some Factors Affecting Residence among the Tiwi. *Oceania* 40:296–303.

Hart, C. W. M., and A. R. Pilling
1960   *The Tiwi of North Australia.* Holt, Rinehart and Winston, New York.

Hart, J. A.
1978   From Subsistence to Market: A Case Study of the Mbuti Net Hunters. *Human Ecology* 6(3):325–353.

Hart, T. B., and J. A. Hart
1986   The Ecological Basis of Hunter-Gatherer Subsistence in African Rain Forests: The Mbuti of Eastern Zaire. *Human Ecology* 14(1):29–55.

Harvey, P. H., and A. F. Read
1992   Home Range and Territory. In *The Cambridge Encyclopedia of Human Evolution,* edited by S. Jones, R. Martin, and D. Pilbeam, pp. 155–156. Cambridge University Press, Cambridge.

Hassan, F. A.
1975   Determinants of the Size, Density, and Growth Rates of Hunting-Gathering Populations. In *Human Ecology and Evolution,* edited by S. Polgar, pp. 27–53. Mouton, the Hague.
1978   Demographic Archaeology. In *Advances in Archaeological Theory and Method,* Vol. 1, edited by M. B. Schiffer, pp. 49–103. Academic Press, New York.
1981   *Demographic Archaeology.* Academic Press, New York.

Hauge, T. M., and L. B. Keith
1981   Dynamics of Moose Populations in Northeastern Alberta. *Journal of Wildlife Management* 45:573–597.

Hawkes, C., J. F. O'Connell, and N. B. Jones
1989   Hardworking Hadza Grandmothers. In *Comparative Socioecology: The Behavioral Ecology of Humans and Other Mammals,* edited by V. Standen and R. A. Foley, pp. 341–366. Blackwell, London.

Hawkes, K., and J. F. O'Connell
1981   Affluent Hunters? Some Comments in Light of the Alyawara Case. *American Anthropologist* 83:622–626.

Hawkes, K., K. Hill, and J. F. O'Connell
1982   Why Hunters Gather: Optimal Foraging and the Ache of Eastern Paraguay. *American Ethnologist* 9:379–398.

Hawkes, K., J. F. O'Connell, K. Hill, and E. L. Charnov
1985   How Much Is Enough? Hunters and Limited Needs. *Ethnology and Sociobiology* 6:3–15.

Hawley, A.
1959   Population Composition. In *The Study of Population: An Inventory and Appraisal,* edited by P. S. Hauser and O. D. Duncan, pp. 361–382. University of Chicago Press, Chicago.

Hayden, B.
1972   Population Control among Hunter/Gatherers. *World Archaeology* 4:205–221.
1975   The Carrying Capacity Dilemma. In *Population Studies in Archaeology and Physical Anthropology,* edited by A. C. Swedlund, pp. 11–21. Society for American Archaeology. Memoir No. 30. Issued as *American Antiquity* 40(2, pt. 2).

1981   Subsistence and Ecological Adaptations of Modern Hunter/Gatherers. In *Omnivorous Primates: Gathering and Hunting in Human Evolution,* edited by R. S. O. Harding and G. Teleki, pp. 344–421. Columbia University Press, New York.

1986   Resources, Rivalry, and Reproduction: The Influence of Basic Resource Characteristics on Reproductive Behavior. In *Culture and Reproduction,* edited by P. Handwerker, pp. 176–196. Westview Press, Boulder, Colo.

1990   Nimrods, Piscators, Pluckers, and Planters: The Emergence of Food Production. *Journal of Anthropological Archaeology* 9:31–69.

1992   Models of Domestication. In *Transitions to Agriculture in Prehistory,* edited by A. B. Gebauer and T. C. Price, pp. 11–19. Prehistory Press, Madison, Wisc.

1995   A New Overview of Domestication. In *Last Hunters–First Farmers,* edited by T. D. Price and A. B. Gebauer, pp. 273–299. School of American Research Press, Santa Fe, N.M.

1997   *The Pithouses of Keatley Creek.* Harcourt Brace College Publishers, Orlando, Fla.

Hayden, B., B. Chisholm, and H. P. Schwarcz
1987   Fishing and Foraging: Marine Resources in the Upper Paleolithic of France. In *The Pleistocene Old World: Regional Perspectives,* edited by O. Soffer, pp. 279–292. Plenum Press, New York.

Hayden, B., G. A. Reinhardt, R. MacDonald, D. Holmberg, and D. Crellin
1996   Space per Capita and the Optimal Size of Housepits. In *People Who Lived in Big Houses: Archaeological Perspectives on Large Domestic Structures,* edited by G. Coupland and E. B. Banning, pp. 151–164. Monographs in World Archaeology No. 27. Prehistory Press, Madison, Wisc.

Hayden, C. (compiler)
1936   *Walapai Papers: Historical Reports, Documents, and Extracts from Publications Relating to the Walapai Indians of Arizona.* Seventy-Fourth Congress, Second Session, Senate Document No. 273. U.S. Government Printing Office, Washington, D.C.

Headland, T. N.
1986   Why Foragers Do Not Become Farmers: A Historical Study of a Changing Ecosystem and Its Effect on a Negrito Hunter-Gatherer Group in the Philippines. Ph.D. dissertation, Department of Anthropology, University of Hawaii, Honolulu. University Microfilms, Ann Arbor, Mich.

1987   The Wild Yam Question: How Well Could Independent Hunter-Gatherers Live in a Tropical Rain Forest Ecosystem? *Human Ecology* 15(4):463–491.

Headland, T. N., and R. C. Bailey
1991   Introduction: Have Hunter-Gatherers Ever Lived in Tropical Rain Forests Independently of Agriculture? *Human Ecology* 19(1):115–122.

Headland, T. N., and L. A. Reid
1989   Hunter-Gatherers and Their Neighbors from Prehistory to the Present. *Current Anthropology* 30:43–66.

Heffley, S.
1981   The Relationship between Northern Athapaskan Settlement Patterns and Resource Distribution: An Application of Horn's Model. In *Hunter-Gatherer Foraging Strategies: Ethnographic and Archeological Analyses,* edited by B. Winterhalder and E. A. Smith, pp. 126–147. University of Chicago Press, Chicago.

Heine-Geldern, R., and A. Hoehnwart-Gerlachstein (editors)
1958   *Bulletin of the International Committee on Urgent Anthropological and Ethnological Research,* No. 1. International Union of Anthropological and Ethnological Sciences and UNESCO, Vienna.

Heinrich, A. C.
1963   Eskimo Type Kinship and Eskimo Kinship: An Evaluation and a Provisional Model for Presenting Data Pertaining to Inupiaq Kinship Systems. Ph.D. dissertation, Department of Anthropology, University of Washington. University Microfilms, Ann Arbor, Mich.

Heinz, H. J., and M. Lee
1979   *Namkwa: Life among the Bushman.* Houghton Mifflin, Boston.

Heizer, R. F., and J. E. Mills
1952   *The Four Ages of Tsurai: A Documentary History of the Indian Village on Trinidad Bay.* University of California Press, Berkeley.

Helm, J.
1961   *The Lynx Point People: The Dynamics of a Northern Athapaskan Band.* National Museums of Canada Bulletin No. 176. Anthropological Series No. 53. Department of Northern Affairs and National Resources, Ottawa.

1968   The Nature of Dogrib Socioterritorial Groups. In *Man the Hunter,* edited by R. B. Lee and I. DeVore, pp. 118–125. Aldine, Chicago.

1969   Remarks on the Methodology of Band Composition Analysis. In *Contributions to Anthropology: Band Societies,* edited by D. Damas, pp. 212–217. National Museums of Canada Bulletin No. 228. Anthropological Series No. 84. National Museums of Canada, Ottawa.

1972   The Dogrib Indians. In *Hunters and Gatherers Today,* edited by M. G. Bicchieri, pp. 51–89. Holt, Rinehart and Winston, New York.

1993   "Always with Them Either a Feast or a Famine": Living Off the Land with Chipewyan Indians, 1791–1792. *Arctic Anthropology* 30:46–60.

Hemming, J. E.
1971   *The Distribution and Movement Patterns of Caribou in Alaska.* Wildlife Technical Bulletin No. 1. Alaska Department of Fish and Game, Juneau.

Henriksen, G.
1973   *Hunters in the Barrens: The Naskapi on the Edge of the White Man's World.* Newfoundland Social and Economic Studies No. 12. Memorial University of Newfoundland and University of Toronto Press, St. Johns.

Henry, J.
1964   *Jungle People: A Kaingang Tribe of the Highlands of Brazil.* Vintage Books, New York.

Hexter, J. H.
1971   Chapter 1: The Cases of the Muddy Pants, the Dead Mr. Sweet, and the Convergence of Particles, or Explanation Why and Prediction in History. In *The History Primer,* by J. H. Hexter, pp. 21–42. Basic Books, New York.

Heymer, A.
1980   The Bayaka Pygmies of Central Africa in the Light of Human Ethnological Research Work. *Mankind Quarterly* 20(3–4):173–204.

Hiatt, B.
1967   The Food Quest and the Economy of the Tasmanian Aborigines. *Oceania* 38(2):99–133, 38(3):190–219.
1970   Woman the Gatherer. In *Woman's Role in Aboriginal Society,* edited by F. Gale. Australian Aboriginal Studies No. 36. University of Adelaide, Adelaide.

Hiatt, L. R.
1962   Local Organization among the Australian Aborigines. *Oceania* 32:267–286.
1965   *Kinship and Conflict: A Study of an Aboriginal Community in Northern Arnhem Land.* Australian National University, Canberra.

Hickerson, H.
1962   *The Southwestern Chippewa: An Ethnohistorical Study.* Memoirs of the American Anthropological Association No. 92. American Anthropological Association, Menasha, Wisc.
1967   *Land Tenure of the Rainy Lake Chippewa at the Beginning of the 19th Century.* Smithsonian Contributions to Anthropology, Vol. 2, No. 4. Smithsonian Institution, Washington, D.C.

Hiernaux, J., P. Rudan, and A. Brambati
1975   Climate and the Weight/Height Relationship in Sub-Sahara Africa. *Annals of Human Biology* 2:3–12.

Higham, C.
1995   The Transition to Rice Cultivation in Southeast Asia. In *Last Hunters–First Farmers,* edited by T. D. Price and A. B. Gebauer, pp. 127–156. School of American Research Press, Santa Fe, N.M.

Hilger, M. I.
1952   *Arapaho Child Life and Its Cultural Background.* Bureau of American Ethnology Bulletin No. 148. Smithsonian Institution, Washington, D.C.

Hill, K.
1982   Hunting and Human Evolution. *Journal of Human Evolution* 11:521–544.

Hill, K., and K. Hawkes
1983   Neotropical Hunting among the Ache of Eastern Paraguay. In *Adaptations of Native Amazonians,* edited by R. Hames and W. Vickers, pp. 139–188. Academic Press, New York.

Hill, K., and H. Kaplan
1989   Population and Dry-Season Subsistence Strategies of the Recently Contacted Yora of Peru. *National Geographic Research* 5:317–334.

Hill, K., C. Hawkes, A. M. Hurtado, and H. Kaplan
1984   Seasonal Variance in the Diet of Ache Hunter-Gatherers of Eastern Paraguay. *Human Ecology* 12(2): 101–135.

Hill-Tout, C.
1904   Ethnological Report on the Stseélis and Skaúlits Tribes of the Halōkmēlem Division of the Salish of British Columbia. *Journal of the Royal Anthropological Institute of Great Britain and Ireland* 34:311–376.

Hilton, C. E., and R. D. Greaves
1995   Mobility Patterns in Modern Human Foragers. Presented at the 64th Annual Meeting of the American Anthropological Association of Physical Anthropologists, Oakland, Calif. Abstract published in *American Journal of Physical Anthropology,* Supplement 20:111.

Hilton, S.
1990   Haihais, Bella Bella and Oowekeeno. In *Northwest Coast,* edited by W. Suttles, pp. 312–322. Handbook of North American Indians, Vol. 7. Smithsonian Institution, Washington, D.C.

Hitchcock, R. K., and J. I. Ebert
1989   Modeling Kalahari Hunter-Gatherer Subsistence and Settlement Systems: Implications for Development Policy and Land Use Planning. *Anthropos* 84:47–62.

Hodder, I.
1982a   Theoretical Archaeology: A Reactionary View. In *Symbolic and Structural Archaeology,* edited by I. Hodder, pp. 1–16. Cambridge University Press, Cambridge.
1986   *Reading the Past: Current Approaches to Interpretation in Archaeology.* Cambridge University Press, Cambridge.

Hoffman, C. L.
1984   Punan Foragers in the Trading Networks of Southeast Asia. In *Past and Present in Hunter-Gatherer Studies,* edited by C. Schrire, pp. 123–149. Academic Press, Orlando, Fla.

Hoffmeyer, I.
1980   Rhino Count. *African Wild Life* 34(5):37–38.

Holdridge, L. R.
1947   Determination of World Plant Formations from Simple Climatic Data. *Science* 105:367–368.
1959   Simple Method for Determining Potential Evapotranspiration from Temperature Data. *Science* 130: 572.

Hole, F.
1992   Origins of Agriculture. In *The Cambridge Encyclopedia of Human Evolution,* edited by S. Jones, R. Martin, and D. Pilbeam, pp. 373–379. Cambridge University Press, Cambridge.
1996   The Context of Caprine Domestication in the Zagros Region. In *The Origins and Spread of Agriculture and Pastoralism in Eurasia,* edited by D. R. Harris, pp. 263–281. Smithsonian Institution Press, Washington, D.C.

Holliday, T. W.
1998   The Ecological Context of Trapping among Recent Hunter-Gatherers: Implications for Subsistence in Terminal Pleistocene Europe. *Current Anthropology* 39(5):711–719.

Holm, G.
1914   Ethnological Sketch of the Angmagsalik Eskimo. *Meddelelser om Grønland* 39:1–147.

Holmberg, A. R.
1950   *Nomads of the Long Bow: The Siriono of Eastern Bolivia.* Smithsonian Institution Institute of Social Anthropology Publication No. 10. U.S. Government Printing Office, Washington, D.C.

Holmberg, H. J.
1985   *Holmberg's Ethnographic Sketches,* edited by M. W. Falk, translated by F. Jaensch. University of Alaska Press, Fairbanks.

Honigmann, J. J.
1949   *Culture and Ethos of Kaska Society.* Yale University Publications in Anthropology No. 40. Yale University Press, New Haven, Conn.
1954   *The Kaska Indians: An Ethnographic Reconstruction.* Yale University Publications in Anthropology No. 51. Yale University Press, New Haven, Conn.
1956   The Attawapiskat Swampy Cree: An Ethnographic Reconstruction. *Anthropological Papers of the University of Alaska* 5:23–82.

1968 Perspectives on the Atomistic-Type Society: Interpersonal Relations in Atomistic Communities. *Human Organization* 27:220–235.

1981 West Main Cree. In *Subarctic,* edited by J. Helm, pp. 217–230. Handbook of North American Indians, Vol. 6. Smithsonian Institution, Washington, D.C.

Hoogerwerf, A.

1970 *Udjung Kulon: Land of the Last Javan Rhinoceros.* E. J. Briss, Leiden.

Hooper, W. H.

1853 *Ten Months among the Tents of the Tuski: With Incidents of an Arctic Boat Expedition in Search of Sir John Franklin, as Far as the Mackenzie River, and Cape Bathurst.* John Murray, London.

Howell, N.

1979 *Demography of the Dobe !Kung.* Academic Press, New York.

Howells, W. W.

1937 *Anthropometry of the Natives of Arnhem Land and the Australian Race Problem.* Papers of the Peabody Museum of American Archaeology and Ethnology, Vol. 16, No. 1. Peabody Museum, Cambridge, Mass.

Howitt, A. W.

1891 The Dieri and Other Kindred Tribes of Central Australia. *Journal of the Royal Anthropological Institute of Great Britain and Ireland* 20:30–104.

Hrdlička, A.

1909 On the Stature of the Indians of the Southwest and of Northern Mexico. In *Putnam Anniversary Volume: Anthropological Essays Presented to Fredric Ward Putnam in Honor of His Seventieth Birthday, April 16, 1909,* edited by S. Williams, pp. 405–426. AMS Press, New York.

1930 Older Anthropometric Data on the Western Eskimo: Stature and Other Measurements. In *46th Annual Report of the Bureau of American Ethnology, 1928–1929,* pp. 228–253. Smithsonian Institution, Washington, D.C.

Hudson, J. L.

1990 Advancing Methods in Zooarchaeology: An Ethnoarchaeological Study among the Aka. Ph.D. dissertation, Department of Anthropology, University of California, Santa Barbara. University Microfilms, Ann Arbor, Mich.

Hughes, C. C.

1960 *The Eskimo Village in the Modern World.* Cornell University Press, Ithaca, New York.

Hull, D.

1974 *Philosophy of Biological Science.* Prentice Hall, Englewood Cliffs, N.J.

Huntingford, G. W. B.

1929 Modern Hunters: Some Accounts of the Kamelilo-Kapchepkendi Dorobo (Okiek) of Kenya Colony. *Journal of the Royal Anthropological Institute of Great Britain and Ireland* 59:333–378.

1942 The Social Organization of the Dorobo. *African Studies* (1):183–200.

1951 The Social Institutions of the Dorobo. *Anthropos* 46:1–48.

1954 The Political Organization of the Dorobo. *Anthropos* 46:123–148.

1955 The Economic Life of the Dorobo. *Anthropos* 50:602–634.

Hurtado, A. M.

1985 Women's Subsistence Strategies among Ache Hunter-Gatherers of Eastern Paraguay. Ph.D. dissertation, Department of Anthropology, University of Utah, Salt Lake City.

Hurtado, A. M., and K. R. Hill

1986 The Cuiva: Hunter-Gatherers of Western Venezuela. *Anthroquest* 36:1,14–22.

1990 Seasonality in a Foraging Society: Variation in Diet, Work Effort, Fertility and Sexual Division of Labor among the Hiwi of Venezuela. *Journal of Anthropological Research* 46:293–346.

Hurtado, A. M., K. Hawkes, K. Hill, and H. Kaplan

1985 Female Subsistence Strategies among Ache Hunter-Gatherers of Eastern Paraguay. *Human Ecology* 13(1):1–28.

Hutchinson, G. E.

1953 The Concept of Pattern in Ecology. *American Academy of Natural Science Proceedings* 105:1–12.

1958 Concluding Remarks. *Cold Spring Harbor Symposia on Quantitative Biology* 22:415–427.

1959 Homage to *Santa Rosalia,* or Why Are There So Many Kinds of Animals? *American Naturalist* 93:145–159.

1965 *The Ecological Theater and the Evolutionary Play.* Yale University Press, New Haven, Conn.

1967 *A Treatise on Limnology,* Vol. 2: *Introduction to Lake Biology and the Limnoplankton.* John Wiley and Sons, New York.

Ichikawa, M.

1978 *The Residential Groups of the Mbuti Pygmies,* Vol. 1: *Africa.* Senri Ethnological Studies No. 1. National Museum of Ethnology, Osaka.

1983 An Examination of the Hunting-Dependent Life of the Mbuti Pygmies: Eastern Zaire. *African Study Monographs* (Kyoto) 4(1):55–76.

Ingold, T.

1981 The Hunter and His Spear: Notes on the Cultural Mediation of Social and Ecological Systems. In *Economic Archaeology: Towards an Integration of Ecological and Social Approaches,* edited by A. Sheridan and G. Bailey, pp. 119–130. BAR International Series No. 96. British Archaeological Reports, Oxford.

1986 *Evolution and Social Life.* Cambridge University Press, Cambridge.

Irimoto, T.

1981 *Chipewyan Ecology: Group Structure and Caribou Hunting System.* Senri Ethnological Studies No. 8. National Museum of Ethnology, Osaka.

Isaac, G. Ll.

1978a The Food-Sharing Behavior of Protohuman Hominids. *Scientific American* 238(4):90–106.

1978b Food Sharing and Human Evolution: Archaeological Evidence from the Plio-Pleistocene of East Africa. *Journal of Anthropological Research* 34:311–325.

Itô, T.

1967 Ecological Studies on the Japanese Deer, *Cervus nippon centralis* Kishida, on Kinkazan Island. I. The Distribution and Population Structure. *Bulletin of the Marine Biological Station of Asamushi* 13(1):57–62.

Ives, J. W.

1985 Northern Athapaskan Social and Economic Variability. Ph.D. dissertation, University of Michigan, Ann Arbor. University Microfilms, Ann Arbor, Mich.

Jamison, P. L.
  1978   Anthropometric Variation. In *Eskimos of Northwest-ern Alaska: A Biological Perspective,* edited by P. L. Jamison, S. L. Zegura, and F. A. Milan, pp. 40–78. Dowden, Hutchison and Ross, Stroudsburg, Penn.

Jamison, P. L., and S. L. Zegura
  1970   An Anthropometric Study of the Eskimos of Wainwright, Alaska. *Arctic Anthropology* 7:125–143.

Janes, R. R.
  1983   *Archaeological Ethnography among Mackenzie Basin Déné, Canada.* Arctic Institute of North America Technical Paper No. 28. University of Calgary, Calgary.

Janetski, J. C.
  1983   The Western Ute of Utah Valley: An Ethnohistoric Model of Lakeside Adaptation. Ph.D. dissertation, Department of Anthropology, University of Utah, Salt Lake City. University Microfilms, Ann Arbor, Mich.

Jenness, D.
  1922   The Life of the Copper Eskimo. *Report of the Canadian Arctic Expedition 1913–1918.* Voliza, Ottawa.
  1932   *The Indians of Canada.* National Museums of Canada Bulletin No. 65. Canada Department of Mines and Resources, Ottawa.
  1935   *The Ojibwa Indians of Parry Island: Their Social and Religious Life.* National Museums of Canada Bulletin No. 78. Canada Department of Mines and Resources, Ottawa.
  1937   *The Sekani Indians of British Columbia.* National Museums of Canada Bulletin No. 84. Canada Department of Mines and Resources, Ottawa.
  1938   *The Sarcee Indians of Alberta.* Canada Department of Mines and Natural Resources Bulletin No. 90. National Museum of Canada, Ottawa.
  1943   The Carrier Indians of the Bulkley River: Their Social and Religious Life. In *Smithsonian Institution Anthropological Papers,* No. 19-26, pp. 469–586. Bureau of American Ethnology Bulletin No. 133. U.S. Government Printing Office, Washington, D.C.

Jochelson, W.
  1924   *The Yukaghir and Yukaghirized Tungus.* Memoirs of the American Museum of Natural History, Vol. 13, Pt. 2. G. E. Stechert, New York.
  1926   *The Yukaghir and Yukaghirized Tungus.* Memoirs of the American Museum of Natural History, Vol. 13, Pt. 1. G. E. Stechert, New York.

Johnson, A. L.
  1997   Explaining Variability in the Pace and Pattern of Cultural Evolution in the North American Southwest: An Exercise in Theory Building. Ph.D. dissertation, Department of Anthropology, Southern Methodist University, Dallas. University Microfilms, Ann Arbor, Mich.
  2000   Distinguishing Organizational States of Pastoral Adaptations. Paper delivered at the 65th Annual Meeting of the Society for American Archaeology, April, Philadelphia.

Johnson, A. W., and T. Earle
  1987   *The Evolution of Human Societies: From Foraging Group to Agrarian State.* Stanford University Press, Stanford, Calif.

Johnson, G. A.
  1978   Information Sources and the Development of Decision-Making Organizations. In *Social Archaeology: Beyond Subsistence and Dating,* edited by C. L. Redman, pp. 87–112. Academic Press, New York.
  1982   Organizational Structure and Scalar Stress. In *Theory and Explanation in Archaeology,* edited by C. Renfrew, M. J. Rowlands, and B. A. Segraves, pp. 389–421. Academic Press, New York.

Johnson, P. J.
  1978   Patwin. In *California,* edited by R. Heizer, pp. 350–360. Handbook of North American Indians, Vol. 8. Smithsonian Institution, Washington, D.C.

Jones, F. L.
  1963   *A Demographic Study of the Aboriginal Population of the Northern Territory, with Special Reference to Bathurst Island Misson.* Occasional Papers in Aboriginal Studies No. 1. Social Anthropology Series No. 1. Australian Institute of Aboriginal Studies, Canberra.

Jones, G. T., R. D. Leonard, and A. L. Abbott
  1995   The Structure of Selectionist Explanations in Archaeology. In *Evolutionary Archaeology: Methodological Issues,* edited by P. A. Teltser, pp. 13–32. University of Arizona Press, Tucson.

Jones, K. T.
  1983   Forager Archaeology: The Ache of Eastern Paraguay. In *Carnivores, Human Scavengers, and Predators: A Question of Bone Technology,* edited by G. M. LeMoine and A. S. MacEachern, pp. 171–191. University of Calgary, Calgary.

Jones, R.
  1971   The Demography of Hunters and Farmers in Tasmania. In *Aboriginal Man and Environment in Australia,* edited by D. J. Mulvaney and J. Golson, pp. 271–287. Australian National University Press, Canberra.
  1972   A Hunting Landscape. Prepared for the Australian Association of Social Anthropologists Annual Conference, Symposium on Space and Territory, Monash University. Manuscript on file, Department of Anthropology, Southern Methodist University, Dallas, Texas.

Joubert, E., and P.K.N. Mostert
  1975   Distribution Patterns and Status of Some Mammals in South West Africa. *Madoqua* 9:5–44

Kaberry, P. M.
  1935   The Forest River and Lyne River Tribes of North-West Australia: A Report on Field Work. *Oceania* 5:408–435.
  1939   *Aboriginal Woman: Sacred and Profane.* George Routledge and Sons, London.

Kane, P.
  1859   *Wanderings of an Artist among the Indians of North America.* Longman, Brown, Green, Longmans and Roberts, London.

Kaplan, H.
  1983   The Evolution of Food Sharing among Adult Conspecifics: Research with Ache Hunter-Gatherers of Eastern Paraguay. Ph.D. dissertation, Department of Anthropology, University of Utah, Salt Lake City. University Microfilms, Ann Arbor, Mich.

Kaplan, H., and K. Hill
  1985   Food Sharing among Ache Foragers: Tests of Explanatory Hypotheses. *Current Anthropology* 26:223–246.

Kaplan, H., K. Hill, K. Hawkes, and A. M. Hurtado
  1984   Food Sharing among Ache Hunter-Gatherers of Eastern Paraguay. *Current Anthropology* 25:113–115.

Kaplan, H., K. Hill, and A. M. Hurtado
  1990   Risk, Foraging, and Food Sharing among the Ache. In *Risk and Uncertainty in Tribal and Peasant Societies,*

edited by E. Cashdan, pp. 107–141. Westview Press, Boulder, Colo.

Kaufmann, H.
1910   The Auen, a Contribution to the Study of the Bushmen. *Mitteilungen aus den Deutschen Schutzgebieten* 23:135–160.

Kedit, P. M.
1982   An Ecological Survey of the Penan. *Sarawak Museum Journal* 30(51):226–279.

Keeley, L. H.
1988   Hunter-Gatherer Economic Complexity and "Population Pressure": A Cross-Cultural Analysis. *Journal of Anthropological Archaeology* 7(4):373–411.
1995   Proto-Agricultural Practice among Hunter-Gatherers: A Cross-Cultural Survey. In *Last Hunters–First Farmers,* edited by T. D. Price and A. B. Gebauer, pp. 243–272. School of American Research Press, Sante Fe, N.M.

Kehoe, A. B.
1993   How the Ancient Peigans Lived. *Research in Economic Anthropology* 14:87–105.

Keith, G.
1960   Letters to Mr. Roderic McKenzie, 1807–1817. In *Les Bourgeois de la Compagnie du Nord Ouest,* Vol. 2, edited by L. R. Masson, pp. 65–132. Antiquarian Press, New York.

Kelley, K. M.
1994   On the Magic Number 500: An Expostulation. *Current Anthropology* 34(4):435–439.

Kelly, I. T.
1932   *Ethnography of the Surprise Valley Paiute.* University of California Publications in American Archaeology and Ethnology, Vol. 31, Pt. 3. University of California Press, Berkeley.
1934   Southern Paiute Bands. *American Anthropologist* 36(4):548–560.
1964   *Southern Paiute Ethnography.* Glen Canyon Series No. 21. University of Utah Anthropological Papers No. 69. University of Utah Press, Salt Lake City.

Kelly, I. T., and C. S. Fowler
1986   Southern Paiute. In *Great Basin,* edited by W. L. d'Azevedo, pp. 368–397. Handbook of North American Indians, Vol. 11. Smithsonian Institution Press, Washington, D.C.

Kelly, K. B.
1986   *Navajo Land Use: An Ethnoarchaeological Study.* Academic Press, New York.

Kelly, R. L.
1992   Mobility/Sedentism: Concepts, Archaeological Measures, and Effects. *Annual Review of Anthropology* 21:43–66.
1995   *The Foraging Spectrum: Diversity in Hunter-Gatherer Lifeways.* Smithsonian Institution Press, Washington, D.C.

Kelly, R. L., and L. A. Poyer
1993   Ethnoarchaeology among the Mikea of Southwestern Madagascar: Report of Activities, July-August, 1993. Manuscript on file, Department of Anthropology, Southern Methodist University, Dallas, Texas.

Kennedy, D. I. D., and R. T. Bouchard
1990   Northcoast Salish. In *Northwest Coast,* edited by W. Suttles, pp. 441–452. Handbook of North American Indians, Vol. 7. Smithsonian Institution Press, Washington, D.C.

Kent, S.
1991   The Relationship between Mobility Strategies and Site Structure. In *The Interpretation of Archaeological Spatial Patterning,* edited by E. M. Kroll and T. D. Price, pp. 33–59. Plenum Press, New York.
1992   The Current Forager Controversy: Real versus Ideal Views of Hunter-Gatherers. *Man* (n.s.) 27:40–65.

Kent, S. (editor)
1989   *Farmers as Hunters: The Implications of Sedentism.* Cambridge University Press, Cambridge.

Kent, S., and H. Vierich
1989   The Myth of Ecological Determinism: Anticipated Mobility and Site Organization of Space. In *Farmers as Hunters: The Implications of Sedentism,* edited by S. Kent, pp. 96–130. Cambridge University Press, Cambridge.

Kinietz, W. V.
1947   *Chippewa Village: The Story of Kitikitegon.* Cranbrook Institute of Science Bulletin No. 25. Cranbrook Institute of Science, Bloomfield Hills, Mich.

Kirchhoff, P.
1945   Food Gathering Tribes of the Venezuelan Llanos. In *Handbook of South American Indians,* Vol. 4: *The Circum-Caribbean Tribes,* edited by J. H. Steward, pp. 445–468. Bureau of American Ethnology Bulletin No. 143. Smithsonian Institution, Washington, D.C.

Kitts, D. B.
1977   *The Structure of Geology.* Southern Methodist University Press, Dallas, Texas.

Kloos, P.
1977   The Akuriyo Way of Death. In *Carib-Speaking Indians: Culture, Society, and Language,* edited by E. B. Basso, pp. 114–122. University of Arizona Press, Tucson.

Knack, M. C.
1975   Contemporary Southern Paiute Household Structure and Bilateral Kinship Clusters. Ph.D. dissertation, Department of Anthropology, University of Michigan, Ann Arbor. University Microfilms, Ann Arbor.

Knecht, R. A., and R. H. Jordan
1985   Nunakakhnak, an Historic Period Koniag Village in Karluk, Kodiak Island, Alaska. *Arctic Anthropology* 22:17–35.

Kniffen, F. B.
1926   *Achomawi Geography.* University of California Publications in American Archaeology and Ethnology, Vol. 23, No. 5, pp. 297–332. University of California Press, Berkeley.
1935   Geography. In *Walapai Ethnography,* edited by A. L. Kroeber, pp. 27–47. American Anthropological Association Memoir No. 42. American Anthropological Association, Menasha, Wisc.
1940   *Pomo Geography.* University of California Publications in American Archaeology and Ethnology, Vol. 36, No. 6. University of California Press, Berkeley.

Knight, R. R.
1970   *The Sun River Elk Herd.* Wildlife Monographs No. 23. Wildlife Society, Washington, D.C.

Kohl, P.L.
1987   The Use and Abuse of World Systems Theory: The Case of the Pristine West Asian State. In *Advances in Archaeological Method and Theory,* Vol. 11, edited by M. B. Schiffer, pp. 1–35. Academic Press, New York.

Komarek, E. V.
1964 The Natural History of Lightning. In *Proceedings of the Third Annual Tall Timbers Fire Ecology Conference,* pp. 139–183. Tall Timbers Research Station, Tallahassee, Fla.

Koppert, V. A.
1930 The Nootka Family. *Primitive Man* 3(3/4):49–55.

Kornblith, H.
1993 *Inductive Inference and Its Natural Ground: An Essay in Naturalistic Epistemology.* MIT Press, Cambridge, Mass.

Kornfeld, M.
1996 The Big-Game Focus: Reinterpreting the Archaeological Record of Cantabrian Upper Paleolithic Economy. *Current Anthropology* 37(4):629-657.

Kosse, K.
1990 Group Size and Societal Complexity: Thresholds in Long Term Memory. *Journal of Anthropological Archaeology* 9:275–303.
1994 The Evolution of Large, Complex Groups: An Hypothesis. *Journal of Anthropological Archaeology* 13:35–50.

Kozak, V., D. Baxter, L. Williamson, and R. L. Carneiro
1979 *The Heta Indians: Fish in a Dry Pond.* Anthropological Papers, Vol. 55, Pt. 6. American Museum of Natural History, New York.

Kozlowski, S. K.
1994 Radiocarbon Dates from Aceramic Iraq. In *Late Quaternary Chronology and Paleoclimates of the Eastern Mediterranean,* edited by O. Bar-Yosef and R. S. Kra, pp. 255–264. RadioCarbon, Vol. 45. Department of Geosciences, University of Arizona, Tucson.

Krader, L.
1968 *Formation of the State.* Foundations of Modern Anthropology. Prentice Hall, Englewood Cliffs, N.J.

Kramer, C.
1982 *Village Ethnoarchaeology: Rural Iran in Archaeological Perspective.* Academic Press, New York.

Krebs, C. J.
1972 *Ecology: The Experimental Analysis of Distribution and Abundance.* Harper and Row, New York.

Kreynovich, E. A.
1979 The Tundra Yukagirs at the Turn of the Century. *Arctic Anthropology* 16:187–216.

Krishnan, M.
1984 *The Handbook of India's Wildlife.* Nagraj, Madras.

Kroeber, A. L.
1925 *Handbook of the Indians of California.* Bureau of American Ethnology Bulletin No. 78. Smithsonian Institution, Washington, D.C.
1929 *The Valley Nisenan.* University of California Publications in American Archaeology and Ethnology, Vol. 24, No. 4. University of California Press, Berkeley.
1931 *The Seri.* Southwest Museum Papers No. 6. Southwest Museum, Los Angeles.
1932 *The Patwin and Their Neighbors.* University of California Publications in American Archaeology and Ethnology, Vol. 29, No. 4. University of California Press, Berkeley.
1953 *Cultural and Natural Areas of Native North America.* University of California Press, Berkeley.
1962 The Nature of Land-Holding Groups in Aboriginal California. *Reports of the University of California Archaeological Survey* 56(2):19–58.

Kroeber, A. L. (editor)
1935 *Walapai Ethnography.* Memoirs of the American Anthropological Association No. 42. Contributions from the Laboratory of Anthropology No. 1. American Anthropological Association, Menasha, Wisc.

Kroll, E., and D. Price (editors)
1991 *The Interpretation of Archaeological Spatial Patterning.* Plenum Press, New York.

Krupnik, I. I.
1983 Early Settlements and the Demographic History of Asian Eskimos of Southeastern Chukotka (Including St. Lawrence Island). In *Cultures of the Bering Sea Region: Papers from an International Symposium,* edited by H. N. Michael and J. W. Van Stone, pp. 84–111. International Research and Exchange Board, New York.
1993 *Arctic Adaptations: Native Whalers and Reindeer Herders of Northern Eurasia.* University Press of New England, Hanover, N.H.

Kuchikura, Y.
1988 Efficiency and Focus of Blowpipe Hunting among Semaq Beri Hunter-Gatherers of Peninsula Malaysia. *Human Ecology* 16(2):271–305.

Kufeld, R. C., J. H. Olterman, and D. C. Bowden
1980 A Helicopter Quadrat Census for Mule Deer on Uncompahgre Plateau, Colorado. *Journal of Wildlife Management* 43:632–639.

Lalouel, J.
1950 Les Babinga Ethnographique des Négrilles Baka et Bayaka. *Bulletins et mémoires de la Société d'Anthropologie de Paris* 1(10):75–211.

Lamprey, H. F.
1964 Estimation of the Large Mammal Densities, Biomass and Energy Exchange in the Tarangire Game Reserve and the Masai Steppe in Tanganyika. *East African Wildlife Journal* 2:1–46.

Landor, A. H. S.
1893 *Alone with the Hairy Ainu, or 3800 Miles on a Pack Saddle in Yezo and a Cruise to the Kurile Islands.* John Murray, London.

Lane, K. S.
1952 *The Montagnais Indians 1600–1640.* Kroeber Anthropological Society Papers No. 7. Kroeber Anthropological Society, Berkeley, Calif.

Lane, R. B.
1981 Chilcotin. In *Subarctic,* edited by J. Helm, pp. 402–412. Handbook of North American Indians, Vol. 6. Smithsonian Institution, Washington, D.C.

Lantis, M.
1946 The Social Culture of the Nunivak Eskimo. *Transactions of the American Philosophical Society* (Philadelphia) 35(3):29–328.
1960 *Eskimo Childhood and Interpersonal Relationships: Nunivak Biographies and Genealogies.* Monographs of the American Ethnological Society No. 33. University of Washington Press, Seattle.
1970 The Aleut Social System, 1750 to 1810, from Early Historical Sources. In *Ethnohistory in Southwestern Alaska and the Southern Yukon: Method and Content,* edited by M. Lantis, pp. 139–302. University Press of Kentucky, Lexington.
1984 Aleut. In *Arctic,* edited by D. Damas, pp. 161–184. Handbook of North American Indians, Vol. 5. Smithsonian Institution, Washington, D.C.

Lasker, G. W.
1946 Migration and Physical Differentiation: A Comparison of Immigrant with American-Born Chinese. *American Journal of Physical Anthropology* 4:273–300.

Laszlo, E.
1987 *Evolution: The Grand Synthesis.* New Science Library, Boston.

Laufer, B.
1917 The Reindeer and Its Domestication. *Memoirs of the American Anthropological Association* 4(2):91–147.

Layton, R.
1983 Ambilineal Descent and Traditional Pitjantjatjara Rights to Land. In *Aborigines, Land and Land Rights,* edited by N. Peterson and M. Langton, pp. 15–32. Australian Institute of Aboriginal Studies, Canberra.

Leach, E.
1973 Concluding Address. In *The Explanation of Culture Change: Models in Prehistory,* edited by C. Renfrew, pp. 761–771. Duckworth, Gloucester Crescent.

Leacock, E.
1954 *The Montagnais "Hunting Territory" and the Fur Trade.* American Anthropological Association Memoir No. 78. American Anthropological Association, Washington, D.C.
1969 The Naskapi Band. In *Contributions to Anthropology: Band Societies,* edited by D. Damas, pp. 1–17. National Museums of Canada Bulletin No. 228. Anthropological Series No. 84. National Museums of Canada, Ottawa.

Leacock, E., and R. B. Lee (editors)
1982 *Politics and History in Band Societies.* Cambridge University Press, Cambridge.

Leakey, R., and R. Lewin
1977 *Origins.* E. P. Dutton, New York.

Lee, P. T.
1967 The Ket: A Contribution to the Ethnography of a Central Siberian Tribe. Ph.D. dissertation, Department of Anthropology, Stanford University. University Microfilms, Ann Arbor, Mich.

Lee, R. B.
1968 What Hunters Do for a Living, or How to Make Out on Scarce Resources. In *Man the Hunter,* edited by R. B. Lee and I. DeVore, pp. 30–48. Aldine, Chicago.
1969a !Kung Bushman Subsistence: An Input-Output Analysis. In *Contributions to Anthropology: Ecological Essays,* edited by D. Damas, pp. 73–94. National Museums of Canada Bulletin No. 230. Anthropological Series No. 86. National Museums of Canada, Ottawa.
1969b Eating Christmas in the Kalahari. *Natural History* (Dec):14–22, 60–63.
1972a The !Kung Bushmen of Botswana. In *Hunters and Gatherers Today: A Socioeconomic Study of Eleven Such Cultures in the Twentieth Century,* edited by M. G. Bicchieri, pp. 327–368. Holt, Rinehart and Winston, New York.
1972b Work Effort, Group Structure, and Land Use in Contemporary Hunter-Gatherers. In *Man, Settlement and Urbanism,* edited by P. J. Ucko, R. Tringham, and G. W. Dimbleby, pp. 177–185. Duckworth, London.
1979 *The !Kung San: Men, Women, and Work in a Foraging Society.* Cambridge University Press, Cambridge.
1988 Reflections on Primitive Communism. In *History, Evolution and Social Change,* edited by T. Ingold, D. Riches, and J. Woodburn, pp. 252–268. Hunters and Gatherers, Vol. 1. Berg, Oxford.
1990 Primitive Communism and the Origin of Social Inequality. In *The Evolution of Political Systems: Sociopolitics in Small-Scale Sedentary Societies,* edited by S. Upham, pp. 225–246. Cambridge University Press, Cambridge.
1992 Art, Science or Politics? The Crisis in Hunter-Gatherer Studies. *American Anthropologist* 94:31–54.

Lee, R. B., and I. DeVore (editors)
1968a *Man the Hunter.* Aldine, Chicago.

Lee, R. B., and I. DeVore
1968b Problems in the Study of Hunters and Gatherers. In *Man the Hunter,* edited by R. B. Lee and I. DeVore, pp. 3–12. Aldine, Chicago.

Legros, D.
1982 Réflexions sur l'Origine des Inégalités Sociales à Partir du Cas des Athapaskan Tutchone. *Culture* 2(3): 65–84.

Leichhardt, L.
1847 *Journal of an Overland Expedition in Australia from Moreton Bay to Port Essington, a Distance of Upwards of 3000 Miles, during the Years 1844–1845.* T. & W. Boone, London.

Leonard, R. D., and G. T. Jones
1987 Elements of an Inclusive Evolutionary Model for Archaeology. *Journal of Anthropological Archaeology* 6:199–219.

Leopold, A. S., T. Riney, R. McCain, and Ll. Tevis, Jr.
1951 *The Jawbone Deer Herd.* Game Bulletin No. 4. State of California, Department of Natural Resources, Division of Fish and Game, Sacramento.

Lévi-Strauss, C.
1936 Contribution à l'Etude de l'Organisation Sociale des Indiens Bororo. *Journal de la Société des Américanistes de Paris* (n.s.) 28:269–304.
1948a The Nambicuara. In *The Tropical Forest Tribes,* edited by J. H. Steward, pp. 361–370. Handbook of South American Indians, Vol. 3. Bureau of American Ethnology Bulletin No. 143. Smithsonian Institution, Washington, D.C.
1948b La Vie Familiale et Sociale des Indiens Nambikwara. *Journal de la Société des Américanistes de Paris* (n.s.) 37:1–132.
1970 *Tristes Tropiques: An Anthropological Study of Primitive Societies in Brazil.* Atheneum, New York.

Levinson, D., and M. J. Malone
1980 *Toward Explaining Human Culture: A Critical Review of the Findings of Worldwide Cross-Cultural Research.* HRAF Press, New Haven, Conn.

Lévy, J. E.
1968 Some Anaxagorian Thoughts on Atomism, Dualism, and the Effect on the Mind of the Monad. *Human Organization* 27:230–235.

Lewin, R.
1988 New Views Emerge on Hunters and Gatherers. *Science* 240:1146–1147.
1992 *Life at the Edge of Chaos.* Macmillan, New York.

Lewis, O.
1973 *The Effects of White Contact upon Blackfoot Culture with Special Reference to the Role of the Fur Trade.* Monographs of the American Ethnological Society, Vol. 6. University of Washington Press, Seattle.

Lieberman, D. E.
1993   The Rise and Fall of Seasonal Mobility among Hunter-Gatherers: The Case of the Southern Levant. *Current Anthropology* 34:599–631.

Liljeblad, S., and C. Fowler
1986   Owens Valley Paiute. In *Great Basin,* edited by W. L. d'Azevedo, pp. 412–434. Handbook of North American Indians, Vol. 11. Smithsonian Institution, Washington, D.C.

Lips, J. E.
1947   Naskapi Law. *Transactions of the American Philosophical Society* (Philadelphia) 37(4):381–491.

Lock, J. M.
1977   Preliminary Results from Fire and Elephant Exclusion Plots in Kabaliga National Park, Uganda. *East African Wildlife Journal* 15:229–232.

Loeb, E. M.
1926   *Pomo Folkways.* University of California Publications in American Archaeology and Ethnology, Vol. 19, Pt. 2. University of California Press, Berkeley.

Long, J. P. M.
1970   Polygyny, Acculturation and Contact: Aspects of Aboriginal Marriage in Central Australia. In *Australian Aboriginal Anthropology: Modern Studies in the Social Anthropology of the Australian Aborigines,* edited by R. M. Berndt, pp. 292–304. University of Western Australia Press, Perth.
1971   Arid Region Aborigines: The Pintubi. In *Aboriginal Man and Environment in Australia,* edited by D. J. Mulvaney and J. Golson, pp. 262–270. Australian National University Press, Canberra.

Longhurst, Wm. M., A. S. Leopold, and R. F. Dasmann
1952   *A Survey of California Deer Herds: Their Ranges and Management Problems.* Game Bulletin No. 6. State of California, Department of Fish and Game, Bureau of Game Conservation, Sacramento.

Lothrop, S. K.
1928   *The Indians of Tierra del Fuego.* Museum of the American Indian Heye Foundation, New York.

Loucks, O. L.
1970   Evolution of Diversity, Efficiency, and Community Stability. *American Zoologist* 10:17–25.

Loud, L. L.
1918   *Ethnogeography and Archaeology of the Wiyot.* University of California Publications in American Archaeology and Ethnology, Vol. 14, Pt. 3. University of California Press, Berkeley.

Lourandos, H.
1980   Change or Stability? Hydraulics, Hunter-Gatherers and Population in Temperate Australia. *World Archaeology* 2:245–264.

Love, J. R. B.
1917   Notes on the Wororra Tribe of North-Western Australia. *Transactions of the Royal Society of South Australia* 41:21–38.
1936   *Stone-Age Bushmen of To-day: Life and Adventure among a Tribe of Savages in North-Western Australia.* Blackie and Son, London.

Loveless, C. M.
1959   *The Everglades Deer Herd: Life History and Management.* Technical Bulletin No. 6. Florida Game and Fresh Water Fish Commission, Gainesville.

Low, A. P.
1906   *The Cruise of the Neptune: Report of the Dominion Government Expedition to the Hudson Bay and the Arctic Islands on Board the D.G.S.* Neptune, *1903–1904.* Government Printing Bureau, Ottawa.

Low, B. S.
1988   Pathogen Stress and Polygyny in Humans. In *Human Reproductive Behavior: A Darwinian Perspective,* edited by P. Turke and M. B. Mulder, pp. 115–127. Cambridge University Press, Cambridge.
1990   Marriage Systems and Pathogen Stress in Human Societies. *American Zoologist* 30:325–339.

Lowie, R. H.
1909   *The Northern Shoshone.* Anthropological Papers, Vol. 2, Pt. 2. American Museum of Natural History, New York.
1920   *Primitive Society.* Liveright, New York.
1924   *Notes on Shoshonean Ethnography.* Anthropological Papers, Vol. 20, Pt. 3. American Museum of Natural History, New York.
1954   *Indians of the Plains.* McGraw-Hill, New York.

Lowrie, W., and M. St. C. Clarke (editors)
1832   Indian Affairs—Lewis and Clarke's Expedition Communicated to Congress, Feb. 19, 1806—9th Congress 1st Session. In *American State Papers: Documents, Legislative and Executive, of the Congress of the United States . . . Commencing March 3, 1789, and ending March 3, 1815,* Vol. IV, pp. 705–743. Gales and Seaton, Washington, D.C.

Lumholtz, C.
1889   *Among Cannibals: Four Years' Travels in Australia and of the Camp Life with the Aborigines of Queensland.* John Murray, London.

Luomala, K.
1978   Tipai and Ipai. In *California,* edited by R. Heizer, pp. 592–609. Handbook of North American Indians, Vol. 8. Smithsonian Institution, Washington, D.C.

Lynch, J. M, and N. J. Poole (editors)
1979   *Microbial Ecology: A Conceptual Approach.* John Wiley and Sons, New York.

Lyon, G. F.
1924   *The Private Journal of G. F. Lyon of H.M.S.* Hecla *during the Recent Voyage of Discovery under Captain Parry, 1821–1823.* Imprint Society, Barre, Vermont.

MacArthur, R. H.
1965   Patterns of Species Diversity. *Biological Review* 40:510–533.
1968   The Theory of Niche. In *Population Biology and Evolution,* edited by R. C. Lewontin, pp. 159–176. Syracuse University Press, Syracuse, N.Y.
1972   *Geographical Ecology: Patterns in the Distribution of Species.* Harper and Row, New York.

MacArthur, R. H., and J. Connell
1966   *The Biology of Populations.* John Wiley and Sons, New York.

MacArthur, R. H., and E. O. Wilson.
1967   *The Theory of Island Biogeography.* Princeton University Press, Princeton, N.J.

MacArthur, R. H., H. Recher, and M. Cody
1966   On the Relations between Habitat Selection and Species Diversity. *American Naturalist* 100:319–332.

MacIntosh, N. W. G.
1952   Stature in Some Aboriginal Tribes in South-West Arnhem Land. *Oceania* 22:208–215.

MacKenzie, A.
1966   *Exploring the Northwest Territory: Sir Alexander Mackenzie's Journal of a Voyage by Bark Canoe from Lake Athabaska to the Pacific Ocean in the Summer of 1789,* edited by T. H. McDonald. University of Oklahoma Press, Norman.

Mackie, R.
1970   Range Ecology and Relations of Mule Deer, Elk and Cattle in the Missouri River Breaks, Montana. *Wildlife Monographs* 20.

MacLachlan, B. B.
1981   Tahltan. In *Subarctic,* edited by J. Helm, pp. 458–468. Handbook of North American Indians, Vol. 6. Smithsonian Institution, Washington, D.C.

Man, E. H.
1883   On the Aboriginal Inhabitants of the Andaman Islands. *Journal of the Anthropological Institute of Great Britain and Ireland* 12(1):69–116.

Mandelbaum, D. G.
1940   *The Plains Cree.* Anthropological Papers, Vol. 37, Pt. 2. American Museum of Natural History, New York.

Margalef, R.
1968   *Perspectives in Ecological Theory.* University of Chicago Press, Chicago.

Marshall, L.
1959   Marriage among !Kung Bushmen. *Africa* 29:335–365.
1960   !Kung Bushman Bands. *Africa* 30:325–355.
1976   *The !Kung of Nyae Nyae.* Harvard University Press, Cambridge, Mass.

Martin, M. K.
1969   South American Foragers: A Case Study in Cultural Devolution. *American Anthropologist* 71:243–260.

Maslow, A. H., and J. J. Honigmann
1970   Synergy: Some Notes of Ruth Benedict. *American Anthropologist* 72:320–333.

Mason, L.
1967   *The Swampu Cree: A Study in Acculturation.* Anthropology Papers of the National Museum of Canada No. 13. Department of the Secretary of State, Ottawa.

Mather, J. R.
1962a   Introduction. In *Average Climatic Water Balance Data of the Continents,* Part I: *Africa,* pp. 115–123. Publications in Climatology, Vol. 15, No. 2. C. W. Thornthwaite Associates Laboratory of Climatology, Centerton, N.J.
1962b   *Average Climatic Water Balance Data of the Continents,* Part I: *Africa.* Publications in Climatology, Vol. 15, No. 2. C. W. Thornthwaite Associates Laboratory of Climatology, Centerton, N.J.
1963a   *Average Climatic Water Balance Data of the Continents,* Part II: *Asia (Excluding U.S.S.R.).* Publications in Climatology, Vol. 16, No. 1. C. W. Thornthwaite Associates Laboratory of Climatology, Centerton, N.J.
1963b   *Average Climatic Water Balance Data of the Continents,* Part III: *U.S.S.R.* Publications in Climatology, Vol. 16, No. 2. C. W. Thornthwaite Associates Laboratory of Climatology, Centerton, N.J.
1963c   *Average Climatic Water Balance Data of the Continents,* Part IV: *Australia, New Zealand, and Oceania.* Publi-

cations in Climatology, Vol. 16, No. 3. C. W. Thornthwaite Associates Laboratory of Climatology, Centerton, N.J.
1964   *Average Climatic Water Balance Data of the Continents,* Part I: *North America (Excluding United States).* Publications in Climatology, Vol. 17, No. 2. C. W. Thornthwaite Associates Laboratory of Climatology, Centerton, N.J.
1965a   *Average Climatic Water Balance Data of the Continents,* Part VII: *The United States of America.* Publications in Climatology, Vol. 18, No. 1. Laboratory of Climatology, Elmer, N.J.
1965b   *Average Climatic Water Balance Data of the Continents,* Part I: *South America.* Publications in Climatology, Vol. 18, No. 2. C. W. Thornthwaite Associates Laboratory of Climatology, Centerton, N.J.

Mathiassen, T.
1928   *Material Culture of the Iglulik Eskimos.* Report of the Fifth Thule Expedition, 1921–24, Vol. 6, No. 1. Nordisk Forlag, Copenhagen.

Maurer, B. A., and J. H. Brown
1988   Distribution of Energy Use and Biomass among Species of North American Terrestrial Birds. *Ecology* 69:1923–1932.

Mauss, M., and H. Beuchat
1979   *Seasonal Variations of the Eskimo: A Study in Social Morphology.* Routledge and Kegan Paul, London.

May, R. M.
1972   Will a Large Complex System Be Stable? *Nature* 238:413–414.
1973   *Stability and Complexity in Model Ecosystems.* Princeton University Press, Princeton, N.J.

Mayr, E.
1982   *The Growth of Biological Thought.* Harvard University Press, Cambridge, Mass.

McArthur, M.
1960   Food Consumption and Dietary Levels of Groups of Aborigines Living on Naturally Occurring Foods. In *Arnhem Land: Anthropology and Nutrition,* edited by C. Mountford, pp. 90–144. Records of the American-Australian Scientific Expedition, Vol. 2. University of Melbourne Press, Melbourne.

McCarthy, F. D., and M. McArthur
1960   The Food Quest and the Time Factor in Aboriginal Economic Life. In *Arnhem Land: Anthropology and Nutrition,* edited by C. Mountford, pp. 145–194. Records of the American-Australian Scientific Expedition, Vol. 2. University of Melbourne Press, Melbourne.

McClellan, C.
1981   Tutchone. In *Subarctic,* edited by J. Helm, pp. 493–505. Handbook of North American Indians, Vol. 6. Smithsonian Institution, Washington, D.C.

McCullough, D. R.
1979   *The George Reserve Deer Herd: Population Ecology of a K-Selected Species.* University of Michigan Press, Ann Arbor.

McDonald, D.
1977   Food Taboos: A Primitive Environmental Protection Agency. *Anthropos* 72:734–748.

McFayden-Clark, A.
1981   Koyukon. In *Subarctic,* edited by J. Helm, pp. 582–601. Handbook of North American Indians, Vol. 6. Smithsonian Institution, Washington, D. C.

McGee, M. J.
1898   The Seri Indians. In *Seventeenth Annual Report of the Bureau of American Ethnology to the Secretary of the Smithsonian Institution, 1895–1896,* pp. 9–341. Smithsonian Institution, Washington, D.C.

McGhee, R.
1988   *Baluga Hunters: An Archaeological Reconstruction of the History and Culture of the Mackenzie Delta Kittegaryumiut.* Canadian Museum of Civilization, Hull, Quebec.

McGuire, R. H.
1992   *A Marxist Archaeology.* Academic Press, San Diego.

McHugh, T.
1958   Social Behavior of American Bison. *Zoologica* 43:1–40.

McIlwraith, T. F.
1948   *The Bella Coola Indians* (2 vols.). University of Toronto Press, Toronto.

McKay, G. M., and J. F. Eisenberg
1974   Movement Patterns and Habitat Utilization of Ungulates in Ceylon. In *The Behavior of Ungulates and Its Relation to Management,* edited by V. Geist and F. Walther, pp. 708–721. IUCN Publications New Series, Vol. 2, No. 24. International Union for Conservation of Nature and Natural Resources, Morges, Switzerland.

McKennan, R. A.
1959   *The Upper Tanana Indians.* Yale University Publications in Anthropology No. 55. Department of Anthropology, Yale University, New Haven, Conn.
1964   The Physical Anthropology of Two Alaskan Athapaskan Groups. *American Journal of Physical Anthropology* 22:43–52.
1965   *The Chandalar Kutchin.* Arctic Institute of North America Technical Paper No. 17. Arctic Institute of North America, Montreal.

McLaren, I. A. (editor)
1971   *Natural Regulation of Animal Populations.* Atherton Press, New York.

M'Clintock, R. N.
1860   *A Narrative of the Discovery of the Fate of Sir John Franklin and His Companions.* Ticknor and Fields, Boston.

McNab, B. K.
1963   Bioenergetics and the Determination of Home Range Size. *American Naturalist* 97:133–140.

McNaughton, S. J., M. Oesterheld, D. A. Frank, and K. J. Williams
1989   Ecosystem-Level Patterns of Primary Productivity and Herbivory in Terrestrial Habitats. *Nature* 341:142–144.

Mech, L. D.
1966   *The Wolves of Isle Royale.* Fauna of the National Parks of the United States, Fauna Series No. 7. U.S. Government Printing Office, Washington, D.C.

Medway, L., and D. R. Wells
1971   Diversity and Density of Birds and Mammals in Kuala Lompat, Pahang. *Malay Nature Journal* 24:238–247.

Meehan, B.
1982   *Shell Bed to Shell Midden.* Australian Institute of Aboriginal Studies, Canberra.

Meggitt, M. J.
1962   *A Study of the Walbiri Aborigines of Central Australia.* University of Chicago Press, Chicago.
1964   Aboriginal Food-Gatherers of Tropical Australia. In *Proceedings and Papers of the International Union for Conservation of Nature Ninth Technical Meeting: Pre-Industrial Man in the Tropical Environment,* pp. 30–37. IUCN Publications No. 4, Pt. 1. Nairobi, Kenya.
1965   Marriage among the Walbiri of Central Australia: A Statistical Examination. In *Aboriginal Man in Australia,* edited by R. M Berndt and C. H. Berndt, pp. 146–166. Angus and Robertson, Sydney.

Meigs, P.
1939   *The Kiliwa Indians of Lower California.* University of California Press, Berkeley.

Meillassoux, C.
1972   From Reproduction to Production: A Marxist Approach to Economic Anthropology. *Economy and Society* 1:99–105.
1973   On the Mode of Production of the Hunting Band. In *French Perspectives in African Studies,* edited by P. Alexandre, pp. 187–203. Oxford University Press, Oxford.

Meltzer, D. J., and B. D. Smith
1986   Paleoindian and Early Archaic Subsistence Strategies in Eastern North America. In *Foraging, Collecting, Harvesting: Archaic Period Subsistence and Settlement in the Eastern Woodlands,* edited by S. W. Neusius, pp. 3–31. Center for Archaeological Investigations Occasional Paper No. 6. Southern Illinois University Press, Carbondale.

Memmott, P.
1983a   Lardil Artifacts and Shelters. In *Aborigines, Land and Land Rights,* edited by N. Peterson and M. Langton, pp. 107–142. Australian Institute of Aboriginal Studies, Canberra.
1983b   Social Structure and Use of Space amongst the Lardil. In *Aborigines, Land and Land Rights,* edited by N. Peterson and M. Langton, pp. 33–65. Australian Institute of Aboriginal Studies, Canberra.

Mentis, M. T.
1970   Estimates of Natural Biomasses of Large Herbivores in the Umfolozi Game Reserve Area. *Mammalia* 34(3):363–393.
1980   Towards a Scientific Management of Terrestrial Ecosystems. *South African Journal of Science* 76:536–540.

Métraux, A
1946a   The Guato. In *The Marginal Tribes,* edited by J. H. Steward, pp. 409–418. Handbook of South American Indians, Vol. 1. Bureau of American Ethnology Bulletin No. 143. Smithsonian Institution, Washington, D.C.
1946b   The Botocudo. In *The Marginal Tribes,* edited by J. H. Steward, pp. 531–540. Handbook of South American Indians, Vol. 1. Bureau of American Ethnology Bulletin No. 143. Smithsonian Institution, Washington, D.C.
1948   The Shirianá, Waica, and Guaharibo. In *The Tropical Forest Tribes,* edited by J. H. Steward, pp. 861–864. Handbook of South American Indians, Vol. 3. Bureau of American Ethnology Bulletin No. 143, Smithsonian Institution, Washington, D.C.

Métraux, A., and H. Baldus
1946   The Guayaki. In *The Marginal Tribes,* edited by J. H. Steward, pp. 435–444. Handbook of South American Indians, Vol. 1. Bureau of American Ethnology Bulletin No. 143. Smithsonian Institution, Washington, D.C.

Metzger, D. J.
1968   Social Organization of the Guahibo Indians. Ph.D. dissertation, Department of Anthropology, University of Pittsburgh. University Microfilms, Ann Arbor, Mich.

Michael, H. N. (editor)
1967   *Lieutenant Zagoskin's Travels in Russian America, 1842–1844: The First Ethnographic and Geographic Investigations in the Yukon and Kuskokwim Valleys of Alaska.* University of Toronto Press, Toronto.

Mickey, B. H.
1955   The Family among the Western Eskimo. *Anthropological Papers of the University of Alaska* 4:13–22.

Middleton, J., and D. Tait (editors)
1958   *Tribes without Rulers: Studies in African Segmentary Systems.* Routledge and Kegan Paul, London.

Miller, N. F.
1992   The Origins of Plant Cultivation in the Near East. In *The Origins of Agriculture: An International Perspective,* edited by C. W. Cowan and P. J. Watson, pp. 39–58. Smithsonian Institution Press, Washington, D.C.

Miller, S. G.
1984   Building Theory: Hunter-Gatherer Subsistant Technology and Conditioned Interaction. Manuscript on file, Department of Anthropology, Southern Methodist University, Dallas.

Miller, V. P.
1978   Yuki, Huchnom, and Coast Yuki. In *California,* edited by R. Heizer, pp. 249–255. Handbook of North American Indians, Vol. 8. Smithsonian Institution, Washington, D.C.

Milligan, K., S. S. Ajayi, and J. B. Hall
1982   Density and Biomass of the Large Herbivore Community in Kainji Lake National Park, Nigeria. *African Journal of Ecology* 20:1–12.

Mirsky, J.
1937   The Eskimo of Greenland. In *Cooperation and Competition among Primitive Peoples,* edited by M. Mead, pp. 51–85. McGraw-Hill, New York.

Mishkin, B.
1940   *Rank and Warfare among the Plains Indians.* Monographs of the American Ethnological Society 3. J. J. Augustine, New York.

Misra, P. K., and B.A. Bhanu
1980   Boundary Maintenance among Cholanaickan: The Cave-Men of Kerala. *Man in India* 60(1–2): 51–59.

Misra, V. N.
1990   The Van Vagris—"Lost" Hunters of the Thar Desert, Rajastan. *Man and Environment* 15:89–108.

Mitchell, D., and L. Donald
1988   Archaeology and the Study of Northwest Coast Economics. *Research in Economic Anthropology,* Supplement 3:293–351.

Mithen, S. J.
1990   *Thoughtful Foragers: A Study in Prehistoric Decision-Making.* Cambridge University Press, Cambridge.

Monk, C. D.
1967   Tree Species Diversity in the Eastern Deciduous Forest with Particular Reference to North Central Florida. *American Naturalist* 101:173–187.

Moore, D. R.
1979   *Islanders and Aborigines at Cape York.* Australian Institute of Aboriginal Studies, Canberra.

Moore, J. H.
1987   *The Cheyenne Nation: A Social and Demographic History.* University of Nebraska Press, Lincoln.
1991   The Developmental Cycle of Cheyenne Polygyny. *American Indian Quarterly* 15:312–328.

Moore, R. D.
1923   Social Life of the Eskimo of St. Lawrence Island. *American Anthropologist* 25:339–375.

Morantz, T.
1983   *An Ethnohistoric Study of Eastern James Bay Cree Social Organization.* National Museum of Man Mercury Series, Canadian Ethnology Service Paper No. 88. National Museums of Canada, Ottawa.

Morgan, L. H.
1881   *Houses and House-Life of the American Aborigines.* Contributions to North American Ethnology, Vol. 4. U.S. Geographical and Geological Survey of the Rocky Mountain Region, Department of the Interior, Washington, D.C.

Morice, A. G.
1906a   The Great Déné Race: Introduction. *Anthropos* 1:229–277.
1906b   The Great Déné Race: The Southern Dénés. *Anthropos* 1:483–508.
1907   The Great Déné Race: Economic Conditions. *Anthropos* 2: 181–200.
1909   The Great Déné Race: Habitations. *Anthropos* 4:582–606.
1910   The Great Déné Race. *Anthropos* 5:113–142, 419–443, 643–653.

Morris, B.
1982a   *Forest Traders: A Socio-Economic Study of the Hill Pandaram.* London School of Economics Monographs on Social Anthropology No. 55. Athlone Press, London.
1982b   The Family, Group Structuring, and Trade among South Indian Hunter-Gatherers. In *Politics and History in Band Societies,* edited by E. Leacock and R. B. Lee, pp. 171–188. Cambridge University Press, Cambridge.

Morris, W. (editor)
1969   *The American Heritage Dictionary.* Houghton Mifflin, Boston.

Morwood, M. J.
1987   The Archaeology of Social Complexity in South-East Queensland. *Proceedings of the Prehistoric Society* 53:337–350.

Movius, H.
1965   Upper Périgordian and Aurignacian Hearths at Abri Pataud, Les Eyzies (Dordogne). In *Miscelánea en Homage al Abate Henri Breuil (1877–1961),* Vol. 2, pp. 181–189. Instituto de Prehistoria y Arqueología, Barcelona.
1966   The Hearths of the Upper Perigordian and Aurignacian Horizons at the Abri Pataud, Les Eyzies (Dordogne), and Their Possible Significance. *American Anthropologist* 2(2):296–325.

Muller-Wille, L.
1974   Caribou Never Die! Modern Caribou Hunting Economy of the Déné (Chipewyan) of the Fond du Lac, Saskatchewan and N.W.T. *Musk Ox* 14(1):7–19.

Munch, P. A., and C. E. Marske
1981   Atomism and Social Integration. *Journal of Anthropological Research* 37:158–171.

Murdock, G. P.
1949   *Social Structure*. Macmillan, New York.
1967   *Ethnographic Atlas*. University of Pittsburgh Press, Pittsburgh.
1980   The Tenino Indians. *Ethnography* 19:129–149.

Murdock, G. P, and C. Provost
1973   Factors in the Division of Labor by Sex: A Cross-Cultural Analysis. *Ethnology* 12(2):203–225.

Murphy, R. F., and Y. Murphy
1960   *Shoshone-Bannock Subsistence and Society*. Anthropological Records, Vol. 16, No. 7. University of California Press, Berkeley.

Murphy, R. F., and J. H. Steward
1956   Tappers and Trappers: Parallel Process in Acculturation. *Economic Development and Cultural Change* 4:335–355.

Murty, M. L. K.
1981   Symbiosis and Traditional Behavior in the Subsistence Economies of the Kanchapuri Yerukulas of South India: A Predictive Model. *Puratattva* 10: 50–61.

Myers, F.
1986   *Pintupi Country, Pintupi Self: Sentiment, Place and Politics among Western Desert Aborigines*. Smithsonian Institution Press and Australian Institute of Aboriginal Studies, Washington, D.C.

Nagar, M., and V. N. Misra
1990   The Kanjars—A Hunting-Gathering Community of the Ganga Valley, Uttar Pradesh. *Man and Environment* 15(2):71–88.

Naroll, R.
1961   Two Solutions to Galton's problem. *Philosophy of Science* 28:15–39.
1964   On Ethnic Unit Classification. *Current Anthropology* 5(4)283–312.

Naylor, J. N., G. J. Caughley, and O. Liberg
1973   Luangwa Valley Conservation and Development Project, Zambia. *Game Management and Habitat Manipulation*.

Nelson, E. W.
1899   The Eskimo about Bering Strait. In *18th Annual Report of the Bureau of American Ethnology for the Years 1896–1897*, pp. 3–518. U.S. Government Printing Office, Washington, D.C.

Netting, R. McC.
1968   *Hill Farmers of Nigeria: Cultural Ecology of the Kofyar of the Jos Plateau*. University of Washington Press, Seattle.
1993   *Smallholders, Householders: Farm Families and the Ecology of Intensive, Sustainable Agriculture*. Stanford University Press, Stanford, Calif.

Newcomb, W. W.
1961   *The Indians of Texas*. University of Texas Press, Austin.

Newman, M. T.
1953   The Application of Ecological Rules to the Racial Anthropology of the Aboriginal New World. *American Anthropologist* 55:311–327.
1960   Adaptations in the Physique of American Aborigines to Nutritional Factors. *Human Biology* 32:288–313.

Newsome, A. E.
1965a   The Abundance of Red Kangaroos, *Megaleia rufa* (Desmarest), in Central Australia. *Australian Journal of Zoology* 13:269–287.

1965b   The Distribution of Red Kangaroos, *Megaleia rufa* (Desmarest), about Sources of Persistent Food and Water in Central Australia. *Australian Journal of Zoology* 13:289–299.

Nicholson, A. J.
1933   The Balance of Animal Populations. *Journal of Animal Ecology* 2:131–178.
1954a   Compensatory Reactions of Populations to Stress, and Their Evolutionary Significance. *Australian Journal of Zoology* 2:1–8.
1954b   An Outline of the Dynamics of Animal Populations. *Australian Journal of Zoology* 2:9–65.
1957   The Self-Adjustment of Populations to Change. *Cold Spring Harbor Symposia on Quantitative Biology* 22:153–172.
1958   Dynamics of Insect Populations. *Annual Review of Entomology* 3:107–136.

Nicks, G. C.
1980   Demographic Anthropology of Native Populations in Western Canada, 1800–1975. Ph.D. dissertation, Department of Anthropology, University of Alberta.

Nicolaisen, J.
1968   The Haddad—A Hunting People in Tchad. *Folk* 10:91–109.
1976   The Penan of Sarawak. *Folk* 18:205–236.

Nimmanahaeminda, K., and J. Hartland-Swann
1962   Expedition to the "Khon Pa" (or Phi Tong Luang?). *Journal of the Siam Society* 50(2):165–186.

Nind, S.
1831   Description of the Natives of King George's Sound (Swan River Colony) and Adjoining Country. *Journal of the Royal Geographical Society of London* 1:21–51.

Nomland, G. A.
1935   *Sinkyone Notes*. University of California Publications in American Archaeology and Ethnology, Vol. 36. University of California Press, Berkeley.
1938   *Bear River Ethnography*. Anthropological Records, Vol. 2, No. 2, pp. 91–125. University of California Press, Berkeley.

Oberg, K.
1953   *Indian Tribes of Northern Mato, Brazil*. Smithsonian Institute of Social Anthropology Publication No. 15. Smithsonian Institution, Washington, D.C.

O'Brien, M. J., and T. D. Holland
1990   Variation, Selection, and the Archaeological Record. In *Advances in Archaeological Method and Theory*, Vol. 2, edited by M. B. Schiffer, pp. 31–79. University of Arizona Press, Tucson.
1995   The Nature and Premise of a Selection-Based Archaeology. In *Evolutionary Archaeology: Methodological Issues*, edited by P. A. Teltser, pp. 175–200. University of Arizona Press, Tucson.

O'Connell, J. F.
1987   Alyawara Site Structure and Its Archaeological Implications. *American Antiquity* 52(1):74–108.
1995   Ethnoarchaeology Needs a General Theory of Behavior. *Journal of Archaeological Research* 3(3): 205–255.

O'Connell, J. F., K. Hawkes, and N. G. Blurton-Jones
1991   Distribution of Refuse-Producing Activities at Hadza Residential Base Camps: Implications for Analyses of Archaeological Site Structure. In *The Interpretation of*

Archaeological Spatial Patterning, edited by E. M. Kroll and T. D. Price, pp. 61–76. Plenum Press, New York.

1992   Patterns in the Distribution, Site Structure and Assemblage Composition of Hadza Kill-Butchering Sites. *Journal of Archaeological Science* 19:319–345.

Odum, E. P.
1959   *Fundamentals of Ecology.* W. B. Saunders, Philadelphia.
1971   *Fundamentals of Ecology,* 3rd ed. W. B. Saunders, Philadelphia.

Oesterheld, M., O. E. Sala, and S. J. McNaughton
1992   Effect of Animal Husbandry on Herbivore-Carrying Capacity at a Regional Scale. *Nature* 256:234–236.

Oetteking, B.
1931   A Contribution to the Physical Anthropology of Baffin Island, Based on Somatometrical Data and Skeletal Material Collected by the Putnam Baffin Island Expedition of 1927. *American Journal of Physical Anthropology* 15(3):421–468.

O'Leary, B.
1985   Salmon and Storage: Southern Tutchone Use of an "Abundant" Resource. Ph.D. dissertation, Department of Anthropology, University of New Mexico, Albuquerque. University Microfilms, Ann Arbor, Mich.

Oldrey, T. B. N.
1975   A Study of the Punan Busang IV. Medical Report. *Malay Nature Journal* 28(3–4):152–159.

Olson, R. L.
1936   *The Quinault Indians.* University of Washington Publications in Anthropology, Vol. 6, No. 1. University of Washington Press, Seattle.
1940   *The Social Organization of the Haisla of British Columbia.* Anthropological Records, Vol. 2, No. 5. University of California Press, Berkeley.

O'Meara, T.
1997   Causation and the Struggle for a Science of Culture. *Current Anthropology* 38(3):399–418.

Opler, M.
1937   An Outline of Chiricahua Apache Social Organization. In *Social Anthropology of North American Tribes: Essays in Social Organization, Law and Religion,* edited by F. Eggan, pp. 173–242. University of Chicago Press, Chicago.

Osborn, A. J.
1977   Strand Loopers, Mermaids, and Other Fairy Tales: Ecological Determinants of Marine Resource Utilization—The Peruvian Case. In *For Theory Building in Archaeology: Essays on Faunal Remains, Aquatic Resources, Spatial Analysis, and Systemic Modeling,* edited by L. R. Binford, pp. 157–205. Academic Press, New York.
1981   Aboriginal Coastal Population Density: Toward the Resolution of a Paradox. Presented at the 45th Annual Society for American Archaeology Meeting, Philadelphia, May 1980. Revised August 1981. Manuscript on file, Department of Anthropology, Southern Methodist University, Dallas, Texas.
1999   From Global Models to Regional Patterns: Possible Determinants of Folsom Hunting Weapon Design, Diversity and Complexity. In *Exploring Variation in Folsom Lithic Technology,* edited by D. Amick, pp. 188–213. International Monographs in Prehistory, Ann Arbor, Mich.

Osgood, C.
1936   *Contributions to the Ethnography of the Kutchin.* Yale University Publications in Anthropology No. 14. Yale University Press, New Haven, Conn.
1937   *The Ethnography of the Tanaina.* Yale University Publications in Anthropology No. 16. Yale University Press, New Haven, Conn.
1958   *Ingalik Social Culture.* Yale University Publications in Anthropology No. 53. Yale University Press, New Haven, Conn.

O'Shea, J.
1981   Coping with Scarcity: Exchange and Social Storage. In *Economic Anthropology,* edited by A. Sheridan and G. N. Bailey, pp. 167–186. BAR International Series No. 96. British Archaeological Reports, Oxford.

Oswalt, W. H.
1966   *This Land Was Theirs.* John Wiley and Sons, New York.
1973   *Habitat and Technology: The Evolution of Hunting.* Holt, Rinehart and Winston, New York.
1976   *An Anthropological Analysis of Food Getting Technology.* Willey-Interscience, New York.

Oswalt, W. H., and J. W. VanStone
1967   *The Ethnoarchaeology of Crow Village, Alaska.* Bureau of American Ethnology Bulletin No. 199. Smithsonian Institution, Washington, D.C.

Owens, D., and B. Hayden
1997   Prehistoric Rites of Passage: A Comparative Study of Transegalitarian Hunter-Gatherers. *Journal of Anthropological Archaeology* 16(2):121–161.

Oxendine, J.
1983   The Luiseno Village during the Late Prehistoric Era. Ph.D. dissertation, Department of Anthropology, University of California, Riverside. University Microfilms, Ann Arbor, Mich.

Pálsson, G.
1988   Hunters and Gatherers of the Sea. In *History, Evolution and Social Change,* edited by T. Ingold, D. Riches, and J. Woodburn, pp. 189–204. Hunters and Gatherers, Vol. 1. Berg, Oxford.

Panowski, E. T.
1985   Analyzing Hunter-Gatherers: Population Pressure, Subsistence, Social Structure, Northwest Coast Societies, and Slavery. Ph.D. dissertation, Department of Anthropology, University of New Mexico, Albuquerque. University Microfilms, Ann Arbor, Mich.

Parker, G. R.
1972   *Total Numbers, Mortality, Recruitment, and Seasonal Distribution.* Biology of the Kaminuriak Population of Barren-Ground Caribou, Pt. 1. Report Series No. 20. Canadian Wildlife Service, Ottawa.

Parker, K. L.
1905   *The Euahlai Tribe: A Study of Aboriginal Life in Australia.* Archibald Constable, London.

Parkhouse, T. A.
1895   Native Tribes of Port Darwin and Its Neighborhood. *Australian Association for the Advancement of Science* 6:638–646.

Parkington, J., and G. Mills
1991   From Space to Place: The Architecture and Social Organisation of Southern African Mobile Communities. In *Ethnoarchaeological Approaches to Mobile*

Campsites: Hunter-Gatherer Case Studies, edited by C. S. Gamble and Wm. A. Boismier, pp. 355–370. Ethnoarchaeological Series No. 1. International Monographs in Prehistory, Ann Arbor, Mich.

Patrick, E. A.
  1972 *Fundamentals of Pattern Recognition.* Prentice Hall, Englewood Cliffs, N.J.

Pavlov, B. M., V. D. Savel'ev, G. D. Yakushkin, and V. A. Zyryanov
  1971 The Ecological Structure of the Taimyr Wild Reindeer Population. *Ecologiya* 2(1):49–57.

Peacock, N. R.
  1985 Time Allocation, Work, and Fertility among Efe Pygmy Women of Northeast Zaire. Ph.D. dissertation, Department of Social Relations, Harvard University, Cambridge, Mass. University Microfilms, Ann Arbor, Mich.

Pearsall, D. M.
  1995 Domestication and Agriculture in the New World Tropics. In *Last Hunters–First Farmers,* edited by T. D. Price and A. B. Gebauer, pp. 157–192. School of American Research Press, Santa Fe, N.M.

Perlman, S. M.
  1980 An Optimum Diet Model, Coastal Variability, and Hunter-Gatherer Behavior. In *Advances in Archaeological Method and Theory,* Vol. 3, edited by M. B. Schiffer, pp. 257–310. Academic Press, New York.

Perry, R. E.
  1898 *Northward over the "Great Ice."* Methuen, London.

Persoon, G.
  1989 The Kubu and the Outside World (South Sumatra, Indonesia): The Modification of Hunting and Gathering. *Anthropos* 84:507–519.

Peters, R. H., and J. V. Raelson
  1984 Relations between Individual Size and Mammalian Population Density. *American Naturalist* 124:498–517.

Peterson, N.
  1970 The Importance of Women in Determining the Composition of Residential Groups in Aboriginal Australia. In *Woman's Role in Aboriginal Society,* edited by F. Gale, pp. 9–16. Australian Institute of Aboriginal Studies, Canberra.
  1973 Camp Site Location amongst Australian Hunter-Gatherers: Archaeological and Ethnographic Evidence for a Key Determinant. *Archaeology and Physical Anthropology in Oceania* 8:173–193.

Peterson, N. (editor)
  1976 *Tribes and Boundaries in Australia.* Australian Institute of Aboriginal Studies, Canberra.

Peterson, N., and J. Long
  1986 *Australian Territorial Organization.* Oceania Monograph 30. University of Sydney, Sydney.

Peterson, R.
  1984 East Greenland before 1950. In *Arctic,* edited by D. Damas, pp. 622–639. Handbook of North American Indians, Vol. 5. Smithsonian Institution, Washington, D.C.

Petrullo, V.
  1939 The Yaruros of the Capanaparo River, Venezuela. In *Smithsonian Anthropological Papers,* No. 11, pp. 161–290. Bureau of American Ethnology Bulletin No. 123. Smithsonian Institution, Washington, D.C.

Pettitt, G. A.
  1950 *The Quileute of La Push: 1775–1945.* Anthropological Records, Vol. 14, No. 1, pp. 1–83. University of California Press, Berkeley.

Pianka, E. R.
  1966 Latitudinal Gradients in Species Diversity: A Review of Concepts. *American Naturalist* 100:33–46.
  1969 Habitat Specificity, Speciation, and Species Density in Australian Desert Lizards. *Ecology* 50:498–502.
  1971 Lizard Species Density in the Kalahari Desert. *Ecology* 52:1024–1029.

Pielou, E. C.
  1975 *Ecological Diversity.* John Wiley and Sons, New York.

Piggott, S.
  1965 *Ancient Europe from the Beginnings of Agriculture to Classical Antiquity.* Aldine, Chicago.

Pitts, R. S.
  1972 The Changing Settlement Patterns and Housing Types of the Upper Tanana Indians. Master's thesis, Department of Anthropology, University of Alaska, Fairbanks. University Microfilms, Ann Arbor, Mich.

Plomley, N. J. B.
  1983 *The Baudin Expedition and the Tasmanian Aborigines 1802.* Blubber Head Press, Hobart, Australia.

Polanyi, K.
  1968 The Semantics of Money-Uses. In *Primitive, Archaic and Modern Economies,* edited by G. Dalton, pp. 175–203. Doubleday, Garden City, N.Y.

Politis, G.
  1992 La Situación Actual de los Nukak. *Revista Universidad Nacional* 26:3–6.

Pookajorn, S.
  1985 Ethnoarchaeology with the Phi Tong Luang: Forest Hunters of Northern Thailand. *World Archaeology* 17:206–221.
  1988 *Archaeological Research of the Hoabinhian Culture or Technocomplex and Its Comparison with Ethnoarchaeology of the Phi Tong Luang, a Hunter-Gatherer Group of Thailand.* Archaeologica Venatoria, Tübingen.

Popov, A. A.
  1964 The Nganasans. In *The Peoples of Siberia,* edited by M. G. Levin and L. P. Patopov, pp. 571–581. University of Chicago Press, Chicago.
  1966 *The Nganasan: The Material Culture of the Tavgi Samoyeds,* translated by E. K. Ristinen. The Uralic and Altaic Series, Vol. 56. Indiana University Press, Bloomington, and Mouton, the Hague.

Popov, A. A., and B. O. Dolgikh
  1964 The Kets. In *The Peoples of Siberia,* edited by M. G. Levin and L. P. Patopov, pp. 607–619. University of Chicago Press, Chicago.

Popper, K. R.
  1988 The Open Universe: An Argument for Indeterminism. Postscript to *The Logic of Scientific Discovery,* Pt. 2, edited by W. W. Bartley, III, pp. 1–185. Routledge, London.

Porter, R. P.
  1893 *Report on Population and Resources of Alaska at the Eleventh Census: 1890.* Department of the Interior Census Office, Washington, D.C.

Potgieter, E. F.
1955 *The Disappearing Bushmen of Lake Chrissie: A Pre-liminary Survey.* J. L. Schaik, Pretoria, South Africa.

Poulsen, K.
1909 Contributions to the Anthropology and Nosology of the East-Greenlanders. *Meddelelser om Grønland* 28(4):133–150.

Preucel, R. W., and I. Hodder
1996 Communicating Present Pasts. In *Contemporary Archaeology in Theory: A Reader,* edited by R. W. Preucel and I. Hodder, pp. 3–20. Blackwell, Oxford.

Price, J. A.
1962 *Washo Economy.* Nevada State Museum Anthropological Papers No. 6. Nevada State Museum, Carson City.

Price, T. D., and J. A. Brown
1985 *Prehistoric Hunter-Gatherers: The Emergence of Cultural Complexity.* Academic Press, Orlando, Fla.

Price, T. D., and G. M. Feinman (editors)
1995 *Foundations of Social Inequality.* Plenum Press, New York.

Price, T. D., and A. B. Gebauer (editors)
1995 *Last Hunters–First Farmers.* School of American Research Press, Santa Fe, N.M.

Prigogine, I., and I. Stengers
1984 *Order Out of Chaos: Man's New Dialogue with Nature.* Bantam, New York.

Qiu, P
1983 *The Oroqens—China's Nomadic Hunters.* Foreign Languages Press, Beijing.

Quimby, G. I.
1962 A Year with a Chippewa Family, 1763–1764. *Ethnohistory* 9:217–239.

Quine, W. V. O.
1991 Natural Kinds. In *The Philosophy of Science,* edited by R. Boyd, P. Gasper, and J. D. Trout, pp. 159–170. MIT Press, Cambridge, Mass.

Radcliffe-Brown, A. R.
1912 Three Tribes of Western Australia. *Journal of the Royal Anthropological Institute of Great Britain and Ireland* 43:143–194.
1948 *The Andaman Islanders.* Free Press, Glencoe, Ill.

Rae, J.
1850 *Narrative of an Expedition to the Shores of the Arctic Sea in 1846 and 1847.* T. and W. Boone, London.

Rafferty, J. E.
1985 The Archaeological Record on Sedentariness: Recognition, Development, and Implications. In *Advances in Archaeological Method and Theory,* Vol. 8, edited by M. B. Schiffer, pp. 113–156. Academic Press, New York.

Rai, N. K.
1982 From Forest to Field: A Study of Philippine Negrito Foragers in Transition. Ph.D. dissertation, Department of Anthropology, University of Hawaii, Honolulu. University Microfilms, Ann Arbor, Mich.

Rainey, F. G.
1947 The Whale Hunters of Tigara. *Anthropological Papers of the American Museum of Natural History* 41(2):231–283.

Raish, C.
1988 Domestic Animals and Stability in Pre-State Farming Societies. Ph.D. dissertation, Department of Anthropology, University of New Mexico, Albuquerque. University Microfilms, Ann Arbor, Mich.

1992 *Domestic Animals and Stability in Pre-State Farming Societies.* BAR International Series No. 579. British Archaeological Reports, Oxford.

Rambo, A. T.
1985 *Primitive Polluters: Semang Impact on the Malaysian Tropical Rain Forest System.* Anthropological Papers of the Museum of Anthropology No. 76. University of Michigan Press, Ann Arbor.

Rapoport, A.
1953 What Is Information? *ETC* 10:247–260.
1956 The Promise and Pitfalls of Information Theory. *Behavioral Science* 1:303–309.
1966 Some Systems Approaches to Political Theory. In *Varieties of Political Theory,* edited by D. Easton, pp. 129–141. Prentice Hall, Englewood Cliffs, N.J.

Rappaport, R. A.
1967 *Pigs for the Ancestors: Ritual in the Ecology of a New Guinea People.* Yale University Press, New Haven, Conn.

Rasmussen, K.
1930 *Observations on the Intellectual Culture of the Caribou Eskimo.* Report of the Fifth Thule Expedition, 1921–24, Vol. 8(1–2). Nordisk Forlag, Copenhagen.
1931 *The Netsilik Eskimos: Social Life and Spirital Culture.* Report of the Fifth Thule Expedition, 1921–24, Vol. 8(1–2). Nordisk Forlag, Copenhagen.
1932 *Intellectual Culture of the Copper Eskimos.* Report of the Fifth Thule Expedition, 1921–24, Vol. 9. Nordisk Forlag, Copenhagen.

Ray, D. J.
1992 *The Eskimos of Bering Strait, 1650–1898.* University of Washington Press, Seattle.

Ray, P. H.
1885 Ethnographic Sketch of the Natives of Point Barrow. In *Report of the International Polar Expedition to Point Barrow, Alaska,* Pt. 3, pp. 35–87. U.S. Government Printing Office, Washington, D.C.

Ray, V. F.
1932 *The Sanpoil and Nespelem: Salishan Peoples of Northeastern Washington.* University of Washington Publications in Anthropology, Vol. 5. University of Washington Press, Seattle.
1937 The Historical Position of the Lower Chinook in the Native Culture of the Northwest. *Pacific Northwest Quarterly* 28:363–372.
1938 *Lower Chinook Ethnographic Notes.* University of Washington Publications in Anthropology, Vol. 7, No. 2. University of Washington Press, Seattle.
1963 *Primitive Pragmatists: The Modoc Indians of Northern California.* University of Washington Press, Seattle.

Redford, K.
1991 The Ecologically Noble Savage. *Orion* 9:24–29.

Reed, W.
1904 *Negritos of Zambales.* Philippine Ethnological Survey No. II. Manila, Philippines.

Renfrew, C.
1978 Trajectory Discontinuity and Morphogenesis: The Implications of Catastrophe Theory for Archaeology. *American Antiquity* 43(2):203–222.
1987 *Archaeology and Language: The Puzzle of Indo-European Origins.* Jonathan Cape, London.
1996 Language Families and the Spread of Farming. In *The Origins and Spread of Agriculture and Pastoralism in Eurasia,* edited by D. R. Harris, pp.

524   REFERENCES

70–92. Smithsonian Institution Press, Washington, D.C.

Renfrew, C., and K. L. Cooke
1979   *Transformations: Mathematical Approaches to Culture Change.* Academic Press, New York.

Renouf, M. A. P.
1984   Northern Hunter-Fishers: An Archaeological Model. *World Archaeology* 16:18–27.

Rensink, E.
1995   On Magdalenian Mobility and Land Use in North-West Europe: Some Methodological Considerations. *Archaeological Dialogues* 2(2):85–119.

Richerson, P. J., and R. Boyd
1987   Simple Models of Complex Phenomena: The Case of Cultural Evolution. In *The Latest on the Best: Essays on Evolution and Optimality,* edited by J. Dupré, pp. 27–52. MIT Press, Cambridge, Mass.

Riches, D.
1982   *Northern Nomadic Hunter-Gatherers: A Humanistic Approach.* Academic Press, New York.

Riddell, F. A.
1960   *Honey Lake Paiute Ethnography.* Nevada State Museum Anthropological Papers No. 4. Nevada State Museum, Carson City.

Ridington, R.
1981   Beaver. In *Subarctic,* edited by J. Helm, pp. 350–360. Handbook of North American Indians, Vol. 6. Smithsonian Institution, Washington, D.C.
1982   Technology, World View, and Adaptive Strategy in a Northern Hunting Society. *Canadian Review of Sociology and Anthropology* 19:469–481.

Rindos, D.
1984   *The Origins of Agriculture: An Evolutionary Perspective.* Academic Press, Orlando, Fla.
1989   Undirected Variation and the Darwinian Explanation of Cultural Change. In *Advances in Archaeological Method and Theory,* Vol. 1, edited by M. B. Schiffer, pp. 1–45. Academic Press, New York.

Rink, H.
1875   *Tales and Traditions of the Eskimo with a Sketch of Their Habits, Religion, Language and Other Peculiarities,* edited by R. Brown. William Blackwood and Sons, Edinburgh.
1877   *Danish Greenland: Its People and Its Products,* edited by R. Brown. H. S. King, London.

Rizvi, S. N. H.
1990   *The Shompen: A Vanishing Tribe of the Great Nicobar Island.* Seagull Books, Calcutta.

Robbins, L. A.
1971   Blackfeet Families and Households. Ph.D. dissertation, Department of Anthropology, University of Oregon, Eugene. University Microfilms, Ann Arbor, Mich.

Roberts, D. F.
1953   Body Weight, Race and Climate. *American Journal of Physical Anthropology* 11:533–558.

Robinette, W. L., N. V. Hancock, and D. A. Jones
1977   *The Oak Creek Mule Deer Herd in Utah.* Publication No. 77-15. Utah State Division of Wildlife Resources, Salt Lake City.

Rodahl, K., and J. Edwards
1952   The Body Surface Area of the Eskimo. *Journal of Applied Physiology* 5:242–246.

Rogers, E. S.
1962a   *The Hunting Group–Hunting Territory Complex among the Mistassini Indians.* National Museums of Canada Bulletin No. 195. Anthropology Series No. 63. National Museums of Canada, Ottawa.
1962b   *The Round Lake Ojibwa.* Occasional Paper No. 5, Art and Archaeology Division, Royal Ontario Museum. Ontario Department of Lands and Forests, Toronto.
1963   Changing Settlement Pattern of the Cree-Ojibwa of Northern Ontario. *Southwestern Journal of Anthropology* 19(1):64–88.
1969   Band Organization among the Indians of Eastern Subarctic Canada. In *Contributions to Anthropology: Band Societies,* edited by D. Damas, pp. 21–50. National Museums of Canada Bulletin No. 228. Anthropological Series No. 84. National Museums of Canada, Ottawa.
1972   The Mistassini Cree. In *Hunters and Gatherers Today: A Socioeconomic Study of Eleven Such Cultures in the Twentieth Century,* edited by M. Bicchieri, pp. 90–137. Holt, Rinehart and Winston, New York.
1973   *The Quest for Food and Furs: The Mistassini Cree, 1953–1954.* National Museum of Man Publications in Ethnology No. 5. National Museums of Canada, Ottawa.

Rogers, E. S., and M. B. Black
1976   Subsistence Strategy in the Fish and Hare Period, Northern Ontario: The Weagamon Ojibwa, 1880–1920. *Journal of Anthropological Research* 32:1–43.

Rolley, R. E., and L. B. Keith
1980   Moose Population Dynamics and Winter Habitat Use at Rochester, Alberta, 1965–1979. *Canadian Field-Naturalist* 94:9–18.

Rose, F.
1963   On the Structure of the Australian Family. In *Ethnologie: VIe Congrès International des Sciences Anthropologiques et Ethnologiques, Paris 1960,* Vol. 2, pp. 247–251. Musée de l'Homme, Paris.

Rosen, R.
1982   On a Theory of Transformations in Cultural Systems. In *Theory and Explanation in Archaeology: The Southampton Conference,* edited by C. Renfrew, M. Rowlands, and B. A. Segraves, pp. 315–346. Academic Press, New York.

Rosenberg, M.
1990   The Mother of Invention: Evolutionary Theory, Territoriality, and the Origins of Agriculture. *American Anthropologist* 92(2):399–415.

Rosenzweig, M. L.
1968   Net Primary Production of Terrestrial Communities: Prediction from Climatological Data. *American Naturalist* 102:67–74.
1995   *Species Diversity in Space and Time.* Cambridge University Press, Cambridge.

Rosenzweig, M. L., and J. Winakur
1969   Population Ecology of Desert Rodent Communities: Habitats and Environmental Complexity. *Ecology* 50:558–572.

Ross, J.
1835   *Narrative of a Second Voyage in Search of a North-West Passage, and of a Residence in the Arctic Regions during the Years 1829, 1830, 1831, 1832, 1833.* A. W. Webster, London.

Rostlund, E.
1952   *Fresh Water Fish and Fishing in Native North America.* University of California Publications in Geography, Vol. 9. University of California Press, Berkeley.

Roth, H. L.
1899   *The Aborigines of Tasmania.* Fullers Bookshop, Hobart.
1909   *Marriage Ceremonies and Infant Life.* North Queensland Ethnography Bulletin No. 10, Records of the Australian Museum. G. A. Vaughan, Sydney.

Rowley-Conwy, P., and M. Zvelebil
1989   Saving It for Later: Storage by Prehistoric Hunter-Gatherers in Europe. In *Bad Year Economics,* edited by P. Halstead and J. O'Shea, pp. 40–56. Cambridge University Press, Cambridge.

Rubel, A. J., and H. J. Kupferer
1968   Perspectives on the Atomistic-Type Society: Introduction. *Human Organization* 27:189–235.

Rue, L. L., III
1978   *The Deer of North America.* Crown, New York.

Rushforth, E. S.
1977   *Kinship and Social Organization among the Great Bear Lake Indians: A Cultural Decision-Making Model.* Ph.D. dissertation, Department of Anthropology, University of Arizona. University Microfilms, Ann Arbor, Mich.

Russo, J. P.
1964   *The Kaibab North Deer Herd—Its History, Problems and Management.* Wildlife Bulletin No. 7. State of Arizona Game and Fish Department, Phoenix.

Sahlins, M. D.
1956   Land Use and the Extended Family in Moala, Fiji. *American Anthropologist* 59:449–462.
1960   Evolution: Specific and General. In *Evolution and Culture,* edited by M. D. Sahlins and E. R. Service, pp. 12–44. University of Michigan Press, Ann Arbor.
1968   Notes on the Original Affluent Society. In *Man the Hunter,* edited by R. B. Lee and I. DeVore, pp. 85–89. Aldine, Chicago.
1972   *Stone Age Economics.* Aldine-Atherton, Chicago.
1976   *Culture and Practical Reason.* University of Chicago Press, Chicago.

Sahlins, M. D., and E. R. Service (editors)
1960   *Evolution and Culture.* University of Michigan Press, Ann Arbor.

Saladin d'Anglure, B. S.
1984   Inuit of Quebec. In *Arctic,* edited by D. Damas, pp. 476–507. Handbook of North American Indians, Vol. 5. Smithsonian Institution, Washington, D.C.

Sandbukt, Ø.
1988   Resource Constraints and Relations of Appropriation among Tropical Forest Foragers: The Case of the Sumatran Kubu. *Research in Economic Anthropology* 10:117–156.

Savelle, J. M.
1987   *Collectors and Foragers: Subsistence-Settlement System Change in the Central Canadian Arctic,* A.D. *1000–1960.* BAR International Series No. 358. British Archaeological Reports, Oxford.

Savishinsky, J. S.
1974   *The Trail of the Hare: Life and Stress in an Arctic Community.* Gordon and Breach, New York.

Savishinsky, J. S., and H. S. Hara
1981   Hare. In *Subarctic,* edited by J. Helm, pp. 314–325. Handbook of North American Indians, Vol. 6. Smithsonian Institution, Washington, D.C.

Schaedel, R. P.
1949   The Karankawa of the Texas Gulf Coast. *Southwestern Journal of Anthropology* 5:117–137.

Schalk, R. F.
1978   Foragers of the Northwest Coast of North America: The Ecology of Aboriginal Land Use Systems. Ph.D. dissertation, Department of Anthropology, University of New Mexico, Albuquerque. University Microfilms, Ann Arbor, Mich.
1981   Land Use and Organizational Complexity among Foragers of Northwestern North America. In *Affluent Foragers,* edited by S. Koyama and D. H. Thomas, pp. 53–75. Senri Ethnological Studies No. 9. National Museum of Ethnology, Osaka.

Schaller, G. B.
1967   *The Deer and the Tiger: A Study of Wildlife in India.* University of Chicago Press, Chicago.

Schapera, I.
1930   *The Khoisan Peoples of South Africa: Bushmen and Hottentots.* Routledge and Kegan Paul, London.

Schebesta, P.
1962a   *Ethnography of the Negritos 1: Economy and Sociology,* translated by F. Schütze. Human Relations Area Files, New Haven, Conn.
1962b   *Ethnography of the Negritos 2: Religion and Mythology,* translated by F. Schütze. Human Relations Area Files, New Haven, Conn.

Schenck, S. M., and Gifford, E. W.
1952   *Karok Ethnobotany.* Anthropological Records, Vol. 13, pp. 377–392. University of California Press, Berkeley.

Schmidt, M.
1942   Resultados de mi tercera expedición a los Guatos efectuada en el año de 1928. *Revista de la Sociedad Científica del Paraguay* 5(6):41–75.

Schoener, T. W.
1968   Sizes of Feeding Territories among Birds. *Ecology* 49:123–141.

Schortman, E. W., and P. A. Urban
1987   Modelling Interregional Interaction in Prehistory. In *Advances in Archaeological Method and Theory,* Vol. 2, edited by M. B. Schiffer, pp. 37–97. Academic Press, New York.

Schrire, C.
1984a   An Inquiry into the Evolutionary Status and Apparent Identity of San Hunter-Gatherers. *Human Ecology* 8(1):9–31.
1984b   Wild Surmises on Savage Thoughts. In *Past and Present in Hunter-Gatherer Studies,* edited by C. Schrire, pp. 1–26. Academic Press, Orlando, Fla.

Schulze, L.
1891   The Aborigines of the Upper and Middle Finke River: Their Habits and Customs, with Introductory Notes on the Physical and Natural-History Features of the Country. *Transactions and Proceedings and Report of the Royal Society of South Australia* 14:210–243.

Schwartz, J. E., II, and G. E. Mitchell
1945   The Roosevelt Elk on the Olympic Peninsula, Washington. *Journal of Wildlife Management* 9:295–319.

Seaburg, W. R., and J. Miller
1990   Tillamook. In *Northwest Coast,* edited by W. Suttles, pp. 560–567. Handbook of North American Indians, Vol. 7. Smithsonian Institution, Washington, D.C.

Seligmann, C. G., and B. Z. Seligmann
1911   *The Veddas.* Cambridge University Press, Cambridge.

Sellato, B.
1994   *Nomads of the Borneo Rainforest: The Economics, Politics, and Ideology of Settling Down.* University of Hawaii Press, Honolulu.

Seltzer, C. C.
1933   The Anthropometry of the Western and Copper Eskimos, Based on Data of Vilhjálmur Stefánsson. *Human Biology* 5(3):313–370.

Sen, B. K., and J. Sen
1955   Notes on the Birhors. *Man in India* 35(3):169–175.

Sen, S. P. K.
1962   *The Land and People of the Andamans: A Geographical and Socio-Economic Study with a Short Account of the Nicobar Islands.* Post-Graduate Book Mart, Calcutta.

Service, E. R.
1962   *Primitive Social Organization.* Random House, New York.
1966   *The Hunters.* Prentice Hall, Englewood Cliffs, N.J.
1971   *Primitive Social Organization: An Evolutionary Perspective,* 2nd ed. Random House, New York.

Sevelle, J. M.
1987   *Collectors and Foragers: Subsistence-Settlement System Change in the Central Canadian Arctic,* A.D. *1000–1960.* BAR International Series No. 358. British Archaeological Reports, Oxford.

Shapiro, J. R.
1986   Kinship. In *Great Basin,* edited by W. L. d'Azevedo, pp. 620–629. Handbook of North American Indians, Vol. 11. Smithsonian Institution, Washington, D.C.

Sharp, L.
1934   The Social Organization of the Yir-Yoront Tribe, Cape York Peninsula, Part I: Kinship and the Family. *Oceania* 4:404–431.

Sharp, R. L.
1940   An Australian Aboriginal Population. *Human Biology* 12:481–507.

Sherratt, A.
1996   Plate Tectonics and Imaginary Prehistories: Structure and Contingency in Agricultural Origins. In *The Origins and Spread of Agriculture and Pastoralism in Eurasia,* edited by D. R. Harris, pp. 130–141. Smithsonian Institution Press, Washington, D.C.

Shimkin, D. B.
1939   A Sketch of the Ket, or Yenisei "Ostyak." *Ethnos* 4:147–176.
1947   *Wind River Shoshone Ethnogeography.* Anthropological Records, Vol. 5, No. 4. University of California Press, Berkeley.

Shott, M. J.
1986   Technological Organization and Settlement Mobility: An Ethnographic Examination. *Journal of Anthropological Research* 42:15–51.
1992   On Recent Trends in the Anthropology of Foragers: Kalahari Revisionism and Its Archaeological Implications. *Man* 27:843–871.

Shternberg, L. I.
1933   *The Gilyak, Orochi, Negidal, Ainu: Articles and Materials,* translated by L. Bromwich and N. Ward. Human Relations Area Files, New Haven, Conn.

Sigler-Eisenberg, B., and J. F. Eisenberg
ca.   Variation in White-Tailed Deer Populations: A Note
1993   on the Southeastern Coastal Plain. Manuscript on file, Department of Anthropology, Southern Methodist University, Dallas.

Silberbauer, G. B.
1972   The G/wi Bushmen. In *Hunters and Gatherers Today: A Socioeconomic Study of Eleven Such Cultures in the Twentieth Century,* edited by M. G. Bicchieri, pp. 271–326. Holt, Rinehart and Winston, New York.
1981a   *Hunter and Habitat in the Central Kalahari Desert.* Cambridge University Press, Cambridge.
1981b   Hunter/Gatherers of the Central Kalahari. In *Omnivorous Primates: Gathering and Hunting in Human Evolution,* edited by R. S. O. Harding and G. Teleki, pp. 455–498. Columbia University Press, New York.

Silverstein, M.
1990   Chinookans of the Lower Columbia. In *Northwest Coast,* edited by W. Suttles, pp. 533–546. Handbook of North American Indians, Vol. 7. Smithsonian Institution, Washington, D.C.

Simpson, G. G.
1964   Species Density of North American Recent Mammals. *Systematic Zoology* 13:57–73.

Simpson, J.
1875   The Western Eskimo. In *Arctic Geography and Ethnology: A Selection of Papers on Arctic Geography and Ethnology,* pp. 233–275. John Murray, London.

Sinclair, A. R. E., and M. Norton-Griffiths
1979   *Serengeti: Dynamics of an Ecosystem.* The University of Chicago Press, Chicago.

Skeat, W. W., and C. O. Blagden
1906   *Pagan Races of the Malay Peninsula.* Barnes and Noble, New York.

Skinner, A.
1911   *Notes on the Eastern Cree and Northern Saulteaux.* Anthropological Papers, Vol. 9, Pt. 1. American Museum of Natural History, New York.
1914   *Political Organization, Cults, and Ceremonies of the Plains-Ojibway and Plains-Cree Indians.* Anthropological Papers, Vol. 11, Pt. 6, pp. 475–511. American Museum of Natural History, New York.

Slobodin, R.
1962   *Band Organization of the Peel River Kutchin.* National Museum of Canada Bulletin No. 179. Anthropological Series No. 55. Department of Northern Affairs and National Resources, Ottawa.
1969   Leadership and Participation in a Kutchin Trapping Party. In *Contributions to Anthropology: Band Societies,* edited by D. Damas, pp. 56–89. National Museums of Canada Bulletin No. 228. Anthropological Series No. 84. National Museums of Canada, Ottawa.
1981   Kutchin. In *Subarctic,* edited by J. Helm, pp. 514–532. Handbook of North American Indians, Vol. 6. Smithsonian Institution, Washington, D.C.

Smith, A. M.
1974   *Ethnography of the Northern Utes.* Papers in Anthropology No. 17. Museum of New Mexico Press, Sante Fe.

Smith, B. D.
1987   The Independent Domestication of Indigenous Seed-Bearing Plants in Eastern North America. In *Emergent Horticultural Economies of the Eastern Woodlands,* edited by W. Keegan, pp. 1–47. Center for Archaeological Investigations, Occasional Paper No. 7. Southern Illinois University, Carbondale.
1995   Seed Plant Domestication in Eastern North America. In *The Origins and Spread of Agriculture and Pastoralism in Eurasia,* edited by D. R. Harris, pp. 193–214. Smithsonian Institution Press, Washington, D.C.

Smith, C. R.
1978   Tubatulabal. In *California,* edited by R. Heizer, pp. 437–445. Handbook of North American Indians, Vol. 8. Smithsonian Institution, Washington, D.C.

Smith, D. G.
1984   Mackenzie Delta Eskimo. In *Arctic,* edited by D. Damas, pp. 347–358. Handbook of North American Indians, Vol. 5. Smithsonian Institution, Washington, D.C.

Smith, E. A.
1991   *Inujuamiut Foraging Strategies.* Aldine de Gruyter, New York.

Smith, E. A., and R. Boyd
1990   Risk and Reciprocity: Hunter-Gatherer Socioecology and the Problem of Collective Action. In *Risk and Uncertainty in Tribal and Peasant Economies,* edited by E. Cashdan, pp. 167–191. Westview Press, Boulder, Colo.

Smith, J. G. E.
1976   Band Organization of the Caribou Eater Chipewyan. *Arctic Anthropology* 13:12–24.
1978   Economic Uncertainty in an "Original Affluent Society": Caribou and Caribou Eater Chipewyan Adaptive Strategies. *Arctic Anthropology* 15:68–88.
1981   Chipewyan. In *Subarctic,* edited by J. Helm, pp. 271–284. Handbook of North American Indians, Vol. 6. Smithsonian Institution, Washington, D.C.

Smith, M. W.
1940a   The Puyallup of Washington. In *Acculturation in Seven American Indian Tribes,* edited by R. Linton, pp. 3–36. D. Appleton–Century, New York.
1940b   *The Puyallup-Nisqually.* Columbia University Press, New York.

Smith, P. E. L.
1976   *Food Production and Its Consequences.* Cummings, Menlo Park, Calif.

Smith, P. E. L., and C. Young
1972   The Evolution of Early Agriculture and Culture in Greater Mesopotamia: A Trial Model. In *Population Growth: Anthropological Implications,* edited by B. Spooner, pp. 1–59. MIT Press, Cambridge, Mass.

Snow, J. H.
1981   Ingalik. In *Subarctic,* edited by J. Helm, pp. 602–617. Handbook of North American Indians, Vol. 6. Smithsonian Institution, Washington, D.C.

Solway, J. S., and R. B. Lee
1990   Foragers, Genuine or Spurious? Situating the Kalahari San in History. *Current Anthropology* 31:109–146.

Sparkman, P. S.
1908   *The Culture of the Luiseno Indians.* University of California Publications in American Archaeology and Ethnology, Vol. 8. University of California Press, Berkeley.

Spaulding, A. C.
1960   The Dimensions of Archaeology. In *Essays in the Science of Culture: In Honor of Leslie A. White,* edited by G. E. Dole and R. L. Carneiro, pp. 437–456. Thomas Y. Crowell, New York.

Speck, F. G.
195   The Family Hunting Band as the Basis of Algonkian Social Organization. *American Anthropologist* 17:289–305.
1922   *Beothuk and Micmac.* Indian Notes and Monographs, Miscellaneous Series No. 22. Museum of the American Indian, Heye Foundation, New York.
1923   Mistassini Hunting Territories in the Labrador Peninsula. *American Anthropologist* 25:425–471.
1926   Land Ownership among Hunting Peoples in Primitive America and the World's Marginal Areas. *Acts of the 22nd International Congress of Americanists* (Rome) 2:232–332.

Speck, F. G., and R. W. Dexter
1951   Utilization of Animals and Plants by the Micmac Indians of New Brunswick. *Journal of the Washington Academy of Sciences* 41(8):250–259.

Speck, F. G., and L. C. Eiseley
1942   Montagnais-Naskapi Bands and Family Hunting Districts of the Central and Southeastern Labrador Districts. *Transactions of the American Philosophical Society* (Philadelphia) 85(2):215–242.

Spencer, B.
1966   *Native Tribes of the Northern Territory of Australia.* Anthropological Publications, Oosterhout, the Netherlands.

Spencer, B., and F. J. Gillen
1899   *The Native Tribes of Central Australia.* Macmillan, London.
1927   *The Aruntas: A Study of Stone Age People.* Macmillan, London.

Spencer, R. F.
1959   *The North Alaskan Eskimo: A Study in Ecology and Society.* Bureau of American Ethnology Bulletin No. 171. Smithsonian Institution, Washington, D.C.

Speth, J. D.
1990   Seasonality, Resource Stress and Food Sharing in So-Called "Egalitarian" Foraging Societies. *Journal of Anthropological Archaeology* 9:148–188.
1991   Some Unexplored Aspects of Mutualistic Plains-Pueblo Food Exchange. In *Farmers, Hunters, and Colonists,* edited by K. A. Spielmann, pp. 18–35. University of Arizona Press, Tucson.

Speth, J. D., and S. L. Scott
1989   Horticulture and Large-Mammal Hunting: The Role of Resource Depletion and the Constraints of Time and Labor. In *Farmers as Hunters,* edited by S. Kent, pp. 71–79. Cambridge University Press, Cambridge.

Spielmann, K. A.
1991a   Interaction among Nonhierarchical Societies. In *Farmers, Hunters, and Colonists,* edited by K. A. Spielmann, pp.1–17. University of Arizona Press, Tucson.
1991b   Coercion or Cooperation? Plains-Pueblo Interaction in the Protohistoric Period. In *Farmers, Hunters, and Colonists,* edited by K. A. Spielmann, pp. 36–50. University of Arizona Press, Tucson.

Spier, L.
1923   Southern Diegueño Customs. In *Phoebe Apperson Hearst Memorial Volume,* edited by A. L. Kroeber,

pp. 297–358. University of California Publications in American Archaeology and Ethnology, Vol. 20. University of California Press, Berkeley.

1930   *Klamath Ethnography.* University of California Publications in American Archaeology and Ethnography, Vol. 30. University of California Press, Berkeley.

Spier, L., and E. Sapir

1930   *Wishram Ethnography.* University of Washington Publications in Anthropology, Vol. 3, Pt. 3. University of Washington Press, Seattle.

Spier, R. F. G.

1978   Foothill Yokuts. In *California,* edited by R. Heizer, pp. 471–484. Handbook of North American Indians, Vol. 8. Smithsonian Institution, Washington, D.C.

Spillett, J. J.

1967   The Kaziranga Wild Life Sanctuary, Assam. *Journal of the Bombay Natural History Society* 63(3):494–528.

Spinage, C. A.

1982   *A Territorial Antelope: The Uganda Waterbuck.* Academic Press, London.

Spinden, H. J.

1908   *The Nez Perce Indians.* Memoirs of the American Anthropological Association, Vol. 2. American Anthropological Association, Lancaster, Penn.

Spittel, R. L.

1945   *Wild Ceylon: Describing in Particular the Lives of the Present-Day Veddahs.* General Publishers, Colombo, Ceylon.

Stanley, S. M.

1979   *Macroevolution: Pattern and Process.* W. H. Freeman, San Francisco.

Stanner, W. E. H.

1933   The Daly River Tribes: A Report of Field Work in North Australia. *Oceania* 3:377–405.

1934   Ceremonial Economics of the Mullak Mulluk and Madngella Tribes of the Daly River, North Australia: A Preliminary Report. *Oceania* 4:156–175.

1965   Aboriginal Territorial Organization: Estate, Range, Domain and Regime. *Oceania* 36:1–26.

Stearman, A. M.

1989   *Yuqui: Forest Nomads in a Changing World.* Holt, Rinehart and Winston, New York.

Steensby, H. P.

1910   *Contributions to the Ethnology and Anthropogeography of the Polar Eskimos.* Bianco Luno, Copenhagen.

Stehli, F. C.

1968   Taxonomic Diversity Gradients in Pole Location: The Recent Model. In *Evolution and Environment, Peabody Museum Centennial Symposium,* edited by E. T. Drake, pp. 163–228. Yale University Press, New Haven, Conn.

Stephens, D. W., and J. R. Krebs

1986   *Foraging Theory.* Princeton University Press, Princeton, N.J.

Stern, B. J.

1934   *The Lummi Indians of Northwestern Washington.* Columbia University Press, New York.

Steward, J. H.

1933   *Ethnography of the Owens Valley Paiute.* University of California Publications in American Archaeology and Ethnology, Vol. 33, Pt. 3. University of California Press, Berkeley.

1936   The Economic and Social Basis of Primitive Bands. In *Essays in Anthropology Presented to Alfred Louis Kroe-*

ber, edited by R. H. Lowie, pp. 331–350. University of California Press, Berkeley.

1938   *Basin-Plateau Aboriginal Sociopolitical Groups.* Bureau of American Ethnology Bulletin No. 120. Smithsonian Institution, Washington, D.C.

1949   Culture Causality and Law: A Trial Formulation of the Development of Early Civilizations. *American Anthropologist* 51:1–27.

1953   Evolution and Process. In *Anthropology Today: An Encyclopedic Inventory,* edited by A. L. Kroeber, pp. 313–326. University of Chicago Press, Chicago.

1955   *Theory of Culture Change.* University of Illinois Press, Urbana.

1969   Postscript to Bands: On Taxonomy, Processes, and Causes. In *Contributions to Anthropology: Band Societies,* edited by D. Damas, pp. 288–295. National Museums of Canada Bulletin No. 228. Anthropological Series No. 84. National Museums of Canada, Ottawa.

1970   The Foundations of Basin-Plateau Shoshonean Society. In *Languages and Cultures of Western North America: Essays in Honor of Sven S. Liljeblad,* edited by E. H. Swanson, Jr., pp. 113–151. Idaho State University, Pocatello.

1974a   Aboriginal and Historical Groups of the Ute Indians of Utah: An Analysis. In *Ute Indians I,* pp. 366–406. American Indian Ethnohistory: California and Basin Plateau Indians. Garland, New York.

1974b   Native Components of the White River Ute Indians. Supplement to Aboriginal and Historic Groups of the Ute Indians of Utah: An Analysis. In *Ute Indians I,* pp. 105–159 American Indian Ethnohistory: California and Basin Plateau Indians. Garland, New York.

Steward, J. H., and L. C. Faron

1959   *Native Peoples of South America.* McGraw-Hill, New York.

Stewart, O. C.

1941   *Culture Element Distributions. XIV. Northern Paiute.* Anthropological Records, Vol. 4, No. 3. University of California Press, Berkeley.

Steyn, H. P.

1971   Aspects of the Economic Life of Some Nomadic Nharo Bushman Groups. *Annals of the South African Museum* 56:276–322.

1984   Southern Kalahari San Subsistence Ecology: A Reconstruction. *South African Archaeological Bulletin* 39:117–124.

Stiles, H.

1906   *Joutel's Journal of La Salle's Last Voyage, 1684–1687.* J. McDonough, Albany, New York.

Stoffle, R. W., and M. J. Evans

1978   Resource Competition and Population Change: A Kaibab Paiute Ethnohistorical Case. *Ethnohistory* 23:173–197.

Stowe, K. S.

1979   *Ocean Science.* John Wiley and Sons, New York.

Strahler, A. N., and A. H. Strahler

1984   *Elements of Physical Geography,* 3rd ed. John Wiley and Sons, New York.

Stringer, C.

1984   Human Evolution and Biological Adaptation in the Pleistocene. In *Hominid Evolution and Community Ecology,* edited by R. Foley, pp. 55–83. Academic Press, London.

Strong, W. D.
1929   *Aboriginal Society in Southern California.* University of California Publications in American Archaeology and Ethnology, Vol. 26. University of California Press, Berkeley.

Sturt, C.
1849a   *Narrative of an Expedition into Australia,* Vol. 1. T. and W. Boone, London.

1849b   *Narrative of an Expedition into Australia,* Vol. 2. T. and W. Boone, London.

Sugihara, G.
1980   Minimal Community Structure: An Explanation of Species Abundance Patterns. *American Naturalist* 116:770–787.

Sullivan, L. R.
1920   *Anthropometry of the Siouan Tribes.* Anthropological Papers, Vol. 23, Pt. 3. American Museum of Natural History, New York.

Sullivan, R. J.
1942   *The Ten'a Food Quest.* Catholic University Anthropological Series No. 11. Catholic University of America Press, Washington, D.C.

Sumner, W. G., and A. G. Keller
1927   *The Science of Society,* Vol. 1. Yale University Press, New Haven, Conn.

Sumner, W. G., A. G. Keller, and M. R. Davie
1927   *The Science of Society,* Vol. 4. Yale University Press, New Haven, Conn.

Suttles, W.
1990   Central Coast Salish. In *Northwest Coast,* edited by W. Suttles, pp. 453–475. Handbook of North American Indians, Vol. 7. Smithsonian Institution, Washington, D.C.

Sutton, D. G.
1982   Towards the Recognition of Convergent Cultural Adaptation in the Subantarctic Zone. *Current Anthropology* 23(1):77–97.

Sutton, D. G., and M. A. Molloy
1989   Deconstructing Pacific Palaeodemography: A Critique of Density Dependent Causality. *Archaeology in Oceania* 24:31–36.

Swan, J. G.
1870   *The Indians of Cape Flattery at the Entrance to the Strait of Fuca, Washington Territtory.* Smithsonian Contributions to Knowledge No. 220. Smithsonian Institution, Washington, D.C.

Swank, W. G.
1958   *The Mule Deer in Arizona Chaparral.* Wildlife Bulletin No. 3. State of Arizona Game and Fish Department, Phoenix.

Swanton, J. R.
1952   *The Indian Tribes of North America.* Bureau of American Ethnology Bulletin No. 145. Smithsonian Institution, Washington, D.C.

Swihart, R. K., N. A. Slade, and B. J. Bergstrom
1988   Relating Body Size to the Rate of Home Range Use in Mammals. *Ecology* 60:393–399.

Szathmary, E. J. E.
1984   Human Biology of the Arctic. In *Arctic,* edited by D. Damas, pp. 64–71. Handbook of North American Indians, Vol. 5. Smithsonian Institution, Washington, D.C.

Szuter, C. R., and F. E. Bayham
1989   Sedentism and Prehistoric Animal Procurement among Desert Horticulturists of the North American Southwest. In *Farmers as Hunters: The Implications of Sedentism,* edited by S. Kent, pp. 80–95. Cambridge University Press, Cambridge.

Taber, R. D., and R. F. Dasmann
1957   The Dynamics of Three Natural Populations of the Deer *Odocoileus hemionus columbianus. Ecology* 38(2):233–246.

Tainter, J. A., and B. B. Tainter
1996   *Evolving Complexity and Environmental Risk in the Prehistoric Southwest.* Proceedings Volume XXIV. Santa Fe Institute Studies in the Sciences of Complexity. Addison-Wesley, Reading, Mass.

Tanaka, J.
1980   *The San, Hunter-Gatherers of the Kalahari: A Study in Ecological Anthropology.* University of Tokyo Press, Tokyo.

Tanner, D.
1965   The Big Wood River Elk Herd. *Idaho Wildlife* 18(3):3–6.

Tanner, V.
1944   *The Indians of Newfoundland Labrador.* Acta Geographica, Vol. 8, Pt. 1. Societas Geographica Fenniae, Helsinki.

Tanno, T.
1976   *The Mbuti Net-Hunters in the Ituri Forest, Eastern Zaire: Their Hunting Activities and Band Composition.* Kyoto University African Studies, Vol. 10. Kyoto University, Kyoto.

Taylor, D. L.
1969   Biotic Succession of Lodgepole Pine Forests of Fire Origin in Yellowstone National Park. Ph.D. dissertation. Department of Zoology and Physiology, University of Wyoming, Laramie.

Taylor, H. C.
1974a   Anthropological Investigation of the Tillamook Indians. In *Oregon Indians I,* edited by H. C. Taylor. Garland, New York.

1974b   Anthropological Investigation of the Medicine Creek Tribes, Relative to Tribal Identity and Aboriginal Possession of Lands. In *Coast Salish and Western Washington Indians II,* edited by H. C. Taylor, pp. 401–473. Garland, New York.

Taylor, J. G.
1974   *Labrador Eskimo Settlements of the Early Contact Period.* National Museum of Man Publications in Ethnology No. 9. National Museums of Canada, Ottawa.

Teer, J. G., J. W. Thomas, and E. A. Walker
1965   *Ecology and Management of White-Tailed Deer in the Llano Basin of Texas.* Wildlife Monographs No. 15. Wildlife Society, Washington, D.C.

Teit, J. A.
1900   The Thompson Indians of British Columbia. In *Memoirs of the American Museum of Natural History,* Vol. 1, Pt. 2, pp. 163–392. Publications of the Jessup North Pacific Expedition. American Museum of Natural History, New York.

1905   The Shushwap. In *Memoirs of the American Museum of Natural History,* Vol. 2, Pt. 7, pp. 447–594. Publications of the Jessup North Pacific Expedition. American Museum of Natural History, New York.

1906   The Lillooet Indians. In *Memoirs of the American Museum of Natural History,* Vol. 4, Pt. 5, pp. 195–300. Publications of the Jessup North Pacific Expedition. American Museum of Natural History, New York.

1928   The Middle Columbia Salish. *University of Washington Publications in Anthropology* 2(4):83–128.
1930   The Salishan Tribes of the Western Plateaus. In *Forty-Fifth Annual Report of the Bureau of American Ethnology to the Secretary of the Smithsonian Institution, 1927–1928*, pp. 23–395. Smithsonian Institution, Washington, D.C.

Teltser, P. A.
1995   The Methodological Challenge of Evolutionary Theory in Archaeology. In *Evolutionary Archaeology: Methodological Issues*, edited by P. A. Teltser, pp. 1–11. University of Arizona Press, Tucson.

Temple, R. C.
1903   *The Andaman and Nicobar Islands: Report on the Census. Census of India, 1901*, Vol. 3. Office of the Superintendent of Government Printing, Calcutta.

Terashima, H.
1980   Hunting Life of the Bambote: An Anthropological Study of Hunter-Gatherers in a Wooded Savanna. In *Africa*, Vol. 2, pp. 223–268. Senri Ethnological Studies No. 6. National Museum of Ethnology, Osaka.

Testart, A.
1982a   The Significance of Food Storage among Hunter-Gatherers: Residence Patterns, Population Densities, and Social Inequalities. *Current Anthropology* 23:523–537.
1982b   *Les Chasseurs-Cueilleurs ou l'Origine des Inégalités.* Société d'Ethnographie, Paris.

Thalbitzer, W.
1914   Ethnographical Collections from East Greenland. *Meddelelser om Grønland* 39:321–455.

Thing, H.
1981   Feeding Ecology of the West Greenland Caribou (*Rangifer tarandus grøenlandicus* Gmlin) in the Holsteinsborg-Sdr. Strømfjord area. Unpublished Ph.D. dissertation. Faculty of Natural Sciences, University of Aarhus, Denmark.

Thom, R.
1975   *Structural Stability and Morphogenesis.* W. R. Benjamin, Reading, Mass.

Thomas, D. H.
1983   *The Archaeology of Monitor Valley. 1. Epistemology.* Anthropological Papers, Vol. 58, Pt. 1. American Museum of Natural History, New York.

Thomson, D. F
1933   The Hero Cult, Initiation and Totemism on Cape York. *Journal of the Royal Anthropological Institute of Great Britain and Ireland* 63:453–537.
1934   The Dugong Hunters of Cape York. *Journal of the Royal Anthropological Institute of Great Britain and Ireland* 64:237–262.
1939   The Seasonal Factor in Human Culture. *Proceedings of the Prehistoric Society of London* 10:209–221.
1949   Arnhem Land: Explorations among an Unknown People. *Geographical Journal* 113:1–28.

Thornthwaite, C. W.
1948   An Approach toward a Rational Classification of Climate. *Geographical Review* 38(1):55–94.

Thornthwaite, C. W., and J. R. Mather
1955   *The Water Balance.* Publications in Climatology, Vol. 8, No. 1. C. W. Thornthwaite Associates Laboratory of Climatology, Centerton, N.J.
1957   Instructions and Tables for Computing Potential Evapotranspiration and Water Balance. In *Publications in Climatology*, Vol. 17, pp. 231–615. Drexel Institute of Technology, Laboratory of Climatology, Centerton, N.J.

Thorson, G
1957   Bottom Communities (Sublittoral or Shallow Shelf). In *Treatise on Marine Ecology and Paleoecology*, Vol. 1, pp. 461–534. Geological Society of America Memoir No. 67. Geological Society of America, Richmond, Va.

Tilman, D.
1982   *Resource Competition and Community Structure.* Princeton University Press, Princeton, N.J.

Tindale, N. B.
1926   Natives of the Groote Eyelandt and of the West Coast of the Gulf of Carpentaria. *Records of the South Australian Museum* 3(2):61–123.
1962a   Geographical Knowledge of the Kaiadilt People of Bentinck Island, Queensland. *Records of the South Australian Museum* 14(2):259–296.
1962b   Some Population Changes among the Kaiadilt People of Bentinck Island, Queensland. *Records of the South Australian Museum* 14(2):297–336.
1972   The Pitjandjara. In *Hunters and Gatherers Today: A Socioeconomic Study of Eleven Such Cultures in the Twentieth Century*, edited by M. G. Bicchieri, pp. 217–268. Holt, Rinehart and Winston, New York.
1977   Further Report on the Kaiadilt People of Bentinck Island, Gulf of Carpentaria, Queensland. In *Sunda and Sahul: Prehistoric Studies in Southeast Asia, Melanesia and Australia*, edited by J. Allen, J. Golson, and R. Jones, pp. 247–273. Academic Press, London.

Tobert, N.
1985   Craft Specialization: A Seasonal Camp in Kebkebiya. *World Archaeology* 17:278–288.

Tobias, P. V.
1962   On the Increasing Stature of the Bushmen. *Anthropos* 57:801–810.

Toerien, M. J.
1958   The Physical Characters of the Lake Chrissie Bushman. *South African Journal of Medical Science* 23:121–124.

Tonkinson, R.
1978   *The Mardudjara Aborigines: Living the Dream in Australia's Desert.* Holt, Rinehart and Winston, New York.

Torrence, R.
1983   Time Budgeting and Hunter-Gatherer Technology. In *Hunter-Gatherer Economy in Prehistory: A European Perspective*, edited by G. Bailey, pp. 11–22. Cambridge University Press, Cambridge.

Townsend, J. B.
1963   Ethnographic Notes on the Pedro Bay Tanaina. *Anthropologica* (n.s.) 1:209–223.
1981   Tanaina. In *Subarctic*, edited by J. Helm, pp. 623–640. Handbook of North American Indians, Vol. 6. Smithsonian Institution, Washington, D.C.

Trewartha, G. T.
1961   *The Earth's Problem Climates.* University of Wisconsin Press, Madison.

Trewartha, G. T., and L. H. Horn
1980   *An Introduction to Climate*, 5th ed. McGraw-Hill, New York.

Trier, R.
1981   The Khon Pa of Northern Thailand: An Enigma. *Current Anthropology* 22(3):291–293.

Tringham, R.
1971   *Hunters, Fishers, and Farmers of Eastern Europe, 6000–3000 B.C.* Hutchinson University Library, London.

Trivers, R. L.
1971   The Evolution of Reciprocal Altruism. *Quarterly Review of Biology* 46:35–37.

Turnbull, C. M.
1965   *Wayward Servants: The Two Worlds of the African Pygmies.* Natural History Press, Garden City, N.Y.
1968   The Importance of Flux in Two Hunting Societies. In *Man the Hunter*, edited by R. B. Lee and I. DeVore, pp. 132–137. Aldine, Chicago.

Turner, L. M.
1894   Ethnology of the Ungava District, Hudson Bay Territory. In *Eleventh Annual Report of the Bureau of American Ethnology,* edited by J. W. Powell, pp. 161–350. Smithsonian Institution, Washington, D.C.

Turney-High, H. H.
1937   *The Flathead Indians of Montana.* Memoirs of the American Anthropological Association No. 48. American Anthropological Association, Menasha, Wisc.
1941   *Ethnography of the Kutenai.* Memoirs of the American Anthropological Association No. 56. American Anthropological Association, Menasha, Wisc.

Tylor, E. B.
1871   *Primitive Culture: Researches into the Development of Mythology, Philosophy, Religion, Language, Art, and Custom.* John Murray, London.
1878   *Researches into the Early History of Mankind and the Development of Civilization.* Henry Holt, New York.

Tyrrell, J. B.
1894   An Expedition through the Barren Lands of Northern Canada. *Geographical Journal* 4:437–450.
1885   A Second Expedition through the Barren Lands of Northern Canada. *Geographical Journal* 6:438–448.
1897   Report on the Doobaunt, Kazan, and Ferguson Rivers on the North-west Coast of Hudson Bay, and on Two Overland Routes from Hudson Bay to Lake Winnipeg. *Annual Report, Geological Survey of Canada, Report F* (n.s.) 9:1–218.

Tyrrell, J. W.
1908   *Across the Sub-Arctics of Canada: A Journey of 3,200 Miles by Canoe and Snowshoe through the Hudson Bay Region.* 3rd ed. William Briggs, Toronto.

Urquhart, I.
1951   Some Notes on Jungle Punans in Kapit District. *Sarawak Museum Journal* (n.s. 3) 5:495–523.

Vallee, F. G.
1967   *Kabloona and Eskimo in the Central Kawatin.* Canadian Research Center for Anthropology and Northern Coordination and Research Center, Ottawa.

Vallois, H. V., and P. Marquer
1976   *Les Pygmées Baká du Cameroun: Anthropologie et Ethnographie avec une Annexe Démographique.* Mémoires du Muséum National d'Histoire Naturelle, Série A: Zoologie, Tome C. Editions du Muséum, Paris.

Van der Steenhoven, G.
1959   *Legal Concepts among the Netsilik Eskimos of Pelly Bay.* Northern Coordination and Research Center, Report 2. Department of Northern Affairs and National Resources, Ottawa.

Van de Velde, F., T. S. Constandse-Westermann, C. H. W. Remie, and R. R. Newell
1992   One hundred and fifteen years of demography of the Arviligjuarmiut, Central Canadian Arctic. Manuscript on file, Department of Anthropology, Southern Methodist University, Dallas, Texas.

VanLavieren, L. P., and L. P. Bosch
1977   Evaluation des densités de grands mammifères dans le Parc National de Bouba Njidah, Cameroun. *Terre Vie* 31:3–32.

Vanoverbergh, M.
1925   Negritos of Northern Luzon. *Anthropos* 20:148–199, 399–443.
1930   Negritos of Northern Luzon Again. *Anthropos* 25:527–565.

VanStone, J. W.
1960   Notes on the Economy and Population Shifts of the Eskimos of Southampton Island. *Anthropological Papers of the University of Alaska* 8(2):81–88.

Velder, C.
1963   A Description of the Mrabri Camp. *Journal of the Siam Society* 51(2):185–188.

Vierich, H. I. D.
1981   The Kua of the Southeastern Kalahari: A Study in the Socio-Ecology of Dependency. Ph.D. dissertation, Department of Anthropology, University of Toronto, Toronto.
1982   Adaptive Flexibility in a Multi-Ethnic Setting: The Basarwa of the Southern Kalahari. In *Politics and History in Band Societies,* edited by E. Leacock and R. Lee, pp. 213–222. Cambridge University Press, Cambridge.

Voegelin, E. W.
1938   *Tübatulabal Ethnography.* Anthropological Records, Vol. 2, No. 1. University of California Press, Berkeley.

Volz, W.
1909   Beiträge zur Anthropologie und Ethnographie von Indonesien. III. Zur Kenntnis der Kubus in Südsumatra. *Archiv für Anthropologie* 8:89–109.

Wadsworth, F. H.
1943   Lightning Damage in Ponderosa Pine Stands of Northern Arizona. *Journal of Forestry* 41:684–685.

Wagner, P. L.
1960   *The Human Use of the Earth.* Free Press, Glencoe, Ill.

Waldrop, M. M.
1992   *Complexity: The Emerging Science at the Edge of Order and Chaos.* Simon and Schuster, New York.

Wallace, E., and E. A. Hoebel
1952   *The Comanches, Lords of the South Plains.* University of Oklahoma Press, Norman.

Wallace, W. J.
1978a   Hupa, Chilula, and Whilkut. In *California,* edited by R. F. Heizer, pp. 164–179. Handbook of North American Indians, Vol. 8. Smithsonian Institution, Washington, D.C.
1978b   Southern Valley Yokuts. In *California,* edited by R. F. Heizer, pp. 448–470. Handbook of North American Indians, Vol. 8. Smithsonian Institution, Washington, D.C.

Wallerstein, I.
1984   Household Structures and Labor-Force Formations in the Capitalist World-Economy. In *Households and*

the World-Economy, edited by J. Smith, I. Wallerstein, and H. D. Evers, pp. 17–22. Sage, Beverly Hills, Calif.

Wallis, W. D., and R. S. Wallis
1953   *Culture Loss and Culture Change among the Micmac of the Canadian Maritime Provinces, 1912–1950.* Kroeber Anthropological Society Papers Nos. 8 and 9. Kroeber Anthropological Society, Berkeley, Calif.
1955   *The Micmac Indians of Eastern Canada.* University of Minnesota Press, Minneapolis.

Walter, H.
1973   *Vegetation of the Earth.* English Universities Press, London.

Warner, W. L.
1958   *A Black Civilization: A Social Study of an Australian Tribe.* Harper and Row, New York.

Warren, C. P.
1964   *The Batak of Palawan.* Research Series No. 3. Department of Anthropology, University of Chicago, Chicago.

Wastl, J.
1957   Beitrag zur Anthropologie der Negrito von Ost-Luzon. *Anthropos* 52:769–812.

Watanabe, H.
1964   *The Ainu: A Study of Ecology and the System of Social Solidarity between Man and Nature in Relation to Group Structure.* University of Tokyo Press, Tokyo.
1969   Famine as a Population Check: Comparative Ecology of Northern Peoples. *Journal of the Faculty of Science* (University of Tokyo) (sect. 5) 3(4):237–252.
1972   *The Ainu Ecosystem, Environment and Group Structure.* Monographs of the American Ethnological Society No. 54. University of Washington Press, Seattle.

Watanabe, S.
1985   *Pattern Recognition: Human and Mechanical.* John Wiley and Sons, New York.

Waterbolk, H. T.
1994   Radiocarbon Dating Levantine Prehistory. In *Late Quaternary Chronology and Paleoclimates of the Eastern Mediterranean,* edited by O. Bar-Yosef and R. S. Kra, pp. 351–371. RadioCarbon, Vol. 45. Department of Geosciences, University of Arizona, Tucson.

Waterman, T. T.
1918   *The Yana Indians.* University of California Publications in American Archaeology and Ethnology, Vol. 13. University of California Press, Berkeley.

Watson, P. J.
1979a   *Archaeological Ethnography in Western Iran.* Viking Fund Publications in Anthropology No. 57. University of Arizona Press, Tucson.
1979b   The Idea of Ethnoarchaeology: Notes and Comments. In *Ethnoarchaeology: Implications of Ethnography for Archaeology,* edited by C. Kramer, pp. 277–287. Columbia University Press, New York.
1986   Archaeological Interpretation, 1985. In *American Archaeology Past and Future,* edited by D. J. Meltzer, D. D. Fowler, and J. A. Sabloff, pp. 439–457. Smithsonian Institution Press, Washington, D.C.
1995   Explaining the Transition to Agriculture. In *Last Hunters–First Farmers,* edited by T. D. Price and A. B. Gebauer, pp. 21–38. School of American Research Press, Santa Fe, N.M.

Wayland, E. J.
1931   Preliminary Studies of the Tribes of Karamoja: The Labwor, the Wanderobo, the Dodotho, and Jie. *Journal of the Royal Anthropological Institute of Great Britain and Ireland* 61:187–230.

Webb, L. J.
1958   Cyclones as an Ecological Factor in Tropical Lowland Rainforest, North Queensland. *Australian Journal of Botany* 6:220–228.

Werner, H.
1906   Anthropologische, ethnologische und ethnographische Beobachtungen über die Heikum-und Kung Buschleute. *Zeitschrift für Ethnologie* 38:241–268.

Wernstedt, F. L.
1972   *World Climatic Data.* Climatic Data Press, Lemont, Penn.

Western, D.
1975   Water Availability and Its Influence on the Structure and Dynamics of a Savannah Large Mammal Community. *East African Wildlife Journal* 13:265–286.

White, L. A.
1949   Energy and the Evolution of Culture. In *The Science of Culture,* by L. A. White, pp. 363–393. Farrar, Straus and Giroux, New York.
1985   The Energy Theory of Cultural Development. In *Leslie A. White: Ethnological Essays,* edited by B. Dillingham and R. L. Carneiro, pp. 215–221. University of New Mexico Press, Albuquerque.

White, S. A.
1915   The Aborigines of the Everard Range. *Transactions of the Royal Society of South Australia* 39:725–732.

Whiting, B. B.
1950   *Paiute Sorcery.* Viking Fund Publications in Anthropology No. 15. Viking Fund, New York.

Whiting, J. W. M.
1964   Effects of Climate on Certain Cultural Practices. In *Explorations in Cultural Anthropology,* edited by W. H. Goodenough, pp. 511–544. McGraw-Hill, New York.

Whitmore, T. C.
1975   *Tropical Rainforests of the Far East.* Clarendon Press, Oxford.

Whittaker, R. H.
1956   Vegetation of the Great Smoky Mountains. *Ecological Monographs* 26(1):1–80.

Whittaker, R. H., S. A. Levin, and R. B. Root
1973   Niche, Habitat, and Ecotope. *American Naturalist* 107:321–338.

Wicken, J. S.
1990   Thermodynamics, Evolution, and Emergence: Ingredients for a New Synthesis. In *Entropy, Information, and Evolution: New Perspectives on Physical and Biological Evolution,* edited by B. H. Weber, D. J. Depew, and J. D. Smith, pp. 139–169. MIT Press, Cambridge, Mass.

Widmer, R. J.
1983   The Evolution of the Calusa, a Non-Agricultural Chiefdom on the Southwest Florida Coast. Ph.D. dissertation, Department of Anthropology, Pennsylvania State University, College Station. University Microfilms, Ann Arbor, Mich.

Wiener, N.
1954   *The Human Use of Human Beings: Cybernetics and Society,* 2nd ed. Doubleday, Garden City, N.Y.

Wiens, J. A.
1984   On Understanding a Non-Equilibrium World: Myth and Reality in Community Patterns and Processes. In *Ecological Communities: Conceptual Issues and the*

Evidence, edited by D. R Strong, Jr., D. Simberloff, L. G. Abele, and A. B. Thistle, pp. 439–457. Princeton University Press, Princeton, N.J.

Wiessner, P. W.
1977   Hxaro: A Regional System of Reciprocity for Reducing Risk among the !Kung San. Ph.D. dissertation, Department of Anthropology, University of Michigan, Ann Arbor. University Microfilms, Ann Arbor, Mich.
1982   Risk, Reciprocity and Social Influences on !Kung San Economics. In *Politics and History in Band Societies,* edited by E. Leacock and R. B. Lee, pp. 61–84. Cambridge University Press, Cambridge.

Wilbert, J.
1957   Notes on Guahibo Kinship and Social Organization. *Southwestern Journal of Anthropology* 13:88–98.

Wilk, R., and W. Rathje (editors)
1982   Archaeology and the Household. *American Behavioral Scientist* 25(6).

Williams, B. J.
1968   Some Comments on Band Organization and Data on the Birhor of Hazaribagh District, India. In *Man the Hunter,* edited by R. B. Lee and I. DeVore, pp. 126–131. Aldine, Chicago.
1974   *A Model of Band Society.* Memoirs of the Society for American Archaeology No. 29. Society for American Archaeology, Washington, D.C.

Williams, C. B.
1964   *Patterns in the Balance of Nature.* Academic Press, London.

Williams, E.
1985   Estimation of Prehistoric Populations of Archaeological Sites in Southwestern Victoria: Some Problems. *Archaeology in Oceania* 20:73–89.

Willmott, W. E.
1960   The Flexibility of Eskimo Social Organization. *Anthropologica* 2:48–59.

Wills, W. H.
1980   Ethnographic Observation and Archaeological Interpretation: The Wikmunkan of Cape York Peninsula, Australia. In *The Archaeological Correlates of Hunter-Gatherer Societies: Studies from the Ethnographic Record,* edited by F. E. Smiley, C. M. Singpoli, H. E. Jackson, W. H. Wills, and S. A. Gregg, pp. 78–99. Michigan Discussions in Anthropology, Vol. 5, Nos. 1–2. Department of Anthropology, University of Michigan, Ann Arbor.

Wilmsen, E. N.
1983   The Ecology of Illusion: Anthropological Foraging in the Kalahari. *Reviews in Anthropology* 1983(Winter):9–20.
1989   *Land Filled with Flies: A Political Economy of the Kalahari.* University of Chicago Press, Chicago.

Wilson, Capt.
1866   Report on the Indian Tribes Inhabiting the Country in the Vicinity of the 49th Parallel of North Latitude. *Transactions of the Ethnological Society of London* (n.s.) 4:275–304. London.

Wilson, D. W.
1999   *Indigenous South Americans of the Past and Present: An Ecological Perspective.* Westview Press, Boulder, Colo.

Wilson, E. O.
1975   *Sociobiology: The New Synthesis.* Belknap Press, Cambridge, Mass.
1998   *Consilience: The Unity of Knowledge.* Alfred A. Knopf, New York.

Wilson, N. L., and A. H. Towne
1978   Nisenan. In *California,* edited by R. F. Heizer, pp. 387–397. Handbook of North American Indians, Vol. 8. Smithsonian Institution Press, Washington, D.C.

Winterbotham, L. P.
1980   The Jinibara Tribe of Southeast Queensland (with Some Reference to Neighboring Tribes). Manuscript on file, Department of Anthropology, Southern Methodist University, Dallas, Texas.

Winterhalder, B. P.
1990   Open Field, Common Pot: Harvest Variability and Risk Avoidance in Agricultural and Foraging Societies. In *Risk and Uncertainty in Tribal and Peasant Economies,* edited by E. Cashdan, pp. 67–87. Westview Press, Boulder, Colo.

Wissler, C.
1911   The Social Life of the Blackfoot Indians. Anthropological Papers, Vol. 7, Pt. 1. American Museum of Natural History, New York.
1914   Material Cultures of the North American Indians. *American Anthropologist* 16:447–505.
1934   *North American Indians of the Plains.* Handbook Series No. 1. American Museum of Natural History, New York.

Wojcik, R. P.
1992   Resource Transfer Systems of Foragers of Alaska, the Northwest Coast, and California. Ph.D. dissertation, Department of Anthropology, University of New Mexico, Albuquerque. University Microfilms, Ann Arbor, Mich.

Wong, D.
1984   The Limits of Using the Household as a Unit of Analysis. In *Households and the World Economy,* edited by J. Smith, I. Wallerstein, and H. D. Evers, pp. 56–63. Sage, Beverly Hills, Calif.

Woodburn, J.
1968   Stability and Flexibility in Hadza Residential Groupings. In *Man the Hunter,* edited by R. B. Lee and I. DeVore, pp. 103–110. Aldine, Chicago.
1980   Hunters and Gatherers Today and Reconstruction of the Past. In *Soviet and Western Anthropology,* edited by E. Gellner, pp. 95–117. Columbia University Press, New York.
1988   African Hunter-Gatherer Social Organization: Is It Best Understood as a Product of Encapsulation? In *History, Evolution and Social Change,* edited by T. Ingold, D. Riches, and J. Woodburn, pp. 31–64. Hunters and Gatherers, Vol. 1. Berg, Oxford.

Woodwell, G. M., and R. H. Whittaker
1968   Primary Production in Terrestrial Ecosystems. *American Zoologist* 8:19–30.

Wrigley, E. A.
1969   *Population and History.* McGraw-Hill, New York.

Wylie, A.
1985   The Reaction against Analogy. In *Advances in Archaeological Method and Theory,* Vol. 8, edited by M. B. Schiffer, pp. 63–111. Academic Press, New York.
1989   The Interpretive Dilemma. In *Critical Traditions in Contemporary Archaeology,* edited by V. Pinsky and A. Wylie, pp. 18–27. Cambridge University Press, Cambridge.

Wyndham, C. H., and J. F. Morrison
1958   Adjustment to Cold of Bushmen in the Kalahari Desert. *Journal of Applied Physiology* 13:219–225.

Yellen, J. E.

1972   Trip V Itinerary May 24–June 9, 1968. In *Exploring Human Nature*, pp. 1–47. Educational Development Center, Cambridge, Mass.

1977a   *Archaeological Approaches to the Present: Models for Reconstructing the Past.* Academic Press, New York.

1977b   Cultural Patterning in Faunal Remains: Evidence from the !Kung Bushmen. In *Experimental Archaeology*, edited by D. Ingersoll, J. E. Yellen, and W. MacDonald, pp. 271–331. Columbia University Press, New York.

1986   Optimization and Risk in Human Foraging Strategies. *Journal of Human Evolution* 15:733–750.

Yengoyan, A. A.

1970   Demographic Factors in Pitjandjara Social Organization. In *Australian Aboriginal Anthropology: Modern Studies in the Social Anthropology of the Australian Aborigines*, edited by R. M. Berndt, pp. 70–91. University of Western Australia Press, Perth.

Yesner, D. R.

1977   Resource Diversity and Population Stability among Hunter Gatherers. *Western Canadian Journal of Anthropology* 7:18–59.

1980   Maritime Hunter-Gatherers: Ecology and Prehistory. *Current Anthropology* 21:727–750.

1982   Life in the "Garden of Eden": Causes and Consequences of the Adoption of Marine Diets by Human Societies. In *Food and Evolution: Toward a Theory of Human Food Habits*, edited by M. Harris and E. B. Ross, pp. 285–310. Temple University Press, Philadelphia.

York, E.

1875   On the Arctic Highlanders. In *Arctic Geography and Ethnology: A Selection of Papers on Arctic Geography and Ethnology*, pp. 175–189. John Murray, London.

Zeeman, E. C.

1979   A Geometrical Model of Ideologies. In *Transformations: Mathematical Approaches to Culture Change*, edited by C. Renfrew and K. L. Cooke, pp. 463–479. Academic Press, New York.

1982   Decision Making and Evolution. In *Theory and Explanation in Archaeology: The Southampton Conference*, edited by C. Renfrew, M. Rowlands, and B. A. Segraves, pp. 301–314. Academic Press, New York.

Zenk, H. B.

1990   Siuslawans and Coosans. In *Northwest Coast*, edited by W. Suttles, pp. 572–579. Handbook of North American Indians, Vol. 7. Smithsonian Institution, Washington, D.C.

Zigmond, M.

1986   Kawaiisu. In *Great Basin*, edited by W. L. d'Azevedo, pp. 398–411. Handbook of North American Indians, Vol. 11. Smithsonian Institution, Washington, D.C.

Zvelebil, M. (editor)

1986   *Hunters in Transition.* Cambridge University Press, Cambridge.

Zvelebil, M., and P. Dolukhanov

1991   Transition to Farming in Eastern and Northern Europe. *Journal of World Prehistory* 5:233–278.

Zvelebil, M., and P. Rowley-Conwy

1984   Transition to Farming in Northen Europe: A Hunter-Gatherer Perspective. *Norwegian Archaeological Review* 17(2):104–128.

Author Index

Index of Ethnographic Cases and Archaeological Sites

Subject Index

541

as response to meta-stabilities of gross environment, 172–73
as response to within ecosystems dynamics, 172–73
structure, 361
propositions regarding, 255, 385, 386
variables, 33–34, 42, 55, 116
variables, descriptive
  BAR5 (biomass accumulation ratio), 85, 94, 177, 179
  BIO5 (primary plant biomass), 85, 94, 145, 154–55, 177, 179–80, 481
    data used in calculation, 60–67, 84, 86–93
    equation for, 85
    relationship to production, 179–80
  EARTHPER (percentage of earth occupied by plant community), 135
  EXPREY (secondary animal biomass), 109–13, 137, 145, 179–80, 187, 478
    and BIOSMALL (measured biomass of ungulates of moderate body size), 110–11
    defined, 109–10
    estimates of, 109
    equation for, 109
    global distribution of, 112
    problems of measurement, 108–9
    projection of, 110–13
  HGPER (percentage of plant community occupied by hunter-gatherers), 135
  LAT and LATITUDE (latitude of case location), 109, 477
  latitude, 22, 49, 56–58, 70–74, 80–83, 85, 94–101, 109–10, 113, 155–56, 166, 168–69, 172, 175–77, 181, 197, 201–3, 256–60, 262, 264, 265, 267, 305, 314, 346, 366, 367, 385, 387–90, 392–93, 403, 407–8, 420, 432, 441–42, 447, 460–61, 468, 476, 477, 478, 483, 487
  MAXBAR (estimate of maximum biomass accumulation ratio), 85
  MAXBIO (estimate of maximum possible biomass), 85
  TURNOV (biomass turnover rate), 85
  SOIL (dominant soil type), 117, 478, 479
  SOIL2 (dominant soil type), 117, 478, 479
  VEG (secondary possibility for VEGTAT), 95
  VEGNU (discriminate function standardized VEGTAT), 117, 133, 142, 153, 156
  VEGTAT (as coded from Strahler and Strahler [1984]), 94–95, 178, 481
    defined from Eyre's classification, 94–95
within-habitat diversity, 171
  general variables

COKLM, 156, 168
CVELEV, 166
DGROSS, 168
DPOSIT, 168, 481
DRAIN, 168, 481
DRANK, 168, 481
ELEV, 109, 166, 477
HEADWAT, 168, 481
MAXRANGE, 166
SDELEV, 166
SETTING, 168
synergistic variables (water and temperature interactions)
  AE (actual evapotranspiration), 74–75, 78, 79, 80, 84, 85, 367, 410, 477, 478
    defined, 74–75
    measurement problems, 74–75
  AVWAT (ordination of water-driven ecological variability), 79, 80, 82, 83, 94, 106, 107, 216, 221
    defined, 79
  DEFPER (percentage of growing season with a water deficit), 79
    equation for, 79
  GROWC (effective growing season), 73, 79, 176, 179–80
    generalizations regarding, 259–60
    and net primary plant productivity, 176
    propositions regarding, 268
    relationship to climate, 73
  NAGP (net aboveground productivity), 79–80, 81–83, 85, 94, 96, 109, 113, 134, 135, 145, 155, 170–71, 175, 179–80, 203, 478, 481
    conversion to population units, 175, 478, 481
    equation for, 79
    propositions regarding, 239–42, 385–86
  PERWLTG (percentage of growing season with available water), 79, 154, 155, 170
    below wilting point, 79
    equation for, 79
  PERWRET (percentage of growing season with water stored in soil), 79
  PET (potential evapotranspiration), 75, 78, 79, 80, 82, 84, 85, 367, 410, 447, 449, 477, 478
    defined, 75
  POTNAGP (potential net aboveground productivity when limited only by temperature), 79–80, 81, 85
  PTOAE (ratio of potential [PET] to actual [AE] evapotranspiration), 78, 106–7
    defined, 78
  PTORUN (coefficient of potential evapotranspiration [PET] to runoff [RUNOFF]), 79
  PTOWATD (coefficient of potential evapotranspiration [PET] to water deficit [WATD]), 78–79
    defined, 78–79

RUNGRC (number of months during growing season [GROWC] in which runoff [RUNOFF] is greater than zero), 79, 154, 155
RUNOFF (water lost by local community through runoff), 75, 79, 155, 156, 447, 449
  defined, 75
SNOWAC (snow accumulation), 75
SSTAB2 (modified successional stability), 171
  equation for, 171
SUCSTAB (successional stability), 169–71, 172
  equation for, 170
  modification of, 170–71
WATD (water deficit), 75, 79
WATDGRC (number of growing season months [GROWC] with water deficits), 79
WATR (water retention in soil), 75
WILTGRC (number of growing season months [GROWC] with rainfall < 38% of potential evapotranspiration [PET]), 79
temperature and solar radiation variables, 58–70
  BT (biotemperature), 59
    compared to ET, 68
  CLIM (earth temperature zone ordinal classification), 57, 70, 80, 82, 215, 263, 276, 277, 407, 408, 409
    defined, 70
  CMAT (mean annual temperature), 58, 59, 145
  CVTEMP (coefficient of variation for mean monthly temperatures), 70
  ET (effective temperature), 58–59, 68, 80, 94, 176, 179, 180, 257, 259, 260, 261, 262, 263, 264, 265, 266, 267, 268, 305, 306, 312, 389, 395, 430, 431, 453, 477
    defined, 58
    equation for, 59
  MCM (mean temperature of coldest month), 59, 68, 477
  MTEMP (seasonal contrasts in temperature), 68–70, 257
    equation for, 68
  MWM (mean temperature of warmest month), 59, 68, 477
  SDTEMP (standard deviation of mean monthly temperature), 70, 154
  TEMP (temperateness), 59, 257, 259–60
    defined, 59
    equation for, 59
    moderating latitudinal effects, 257, 259–60
    shifts storage 10° colder (ET), 259–60
water and rainfall variables
  CRR (mean annual rainfall), 70, 71, 72, 75, 78, 79, 82, 85, 105, 106, 145, 447, 449, 477

related to wealth distinctions, 427
of resource locations, 369, 370, 427–28,
462–63

Packing, Packed. *See also* Circumscription
as universal conditioner, 442–43
cases, *propositions regarding,* 368
length of time in area and rates of population growth, 439
group size, social ranking, and forms of
leadership, 406, 420–21, 426, 439
conditions projected at 16,900 B.P. in Near
East, 453
defined, 375
general responses to, 404–51, 460
generalizations regarding, 435, 427–28,
439–40
packing threshold
generalizations regarding, 348, 375–76,
377, 380, 385–86, 403–4,
419–20, 426–27
and systems state variability, 385–86
and subsistence focus, 385–86, 41
and people dependent upon aquatic
resources, 427, 432
leader as head of unit that owns
resources, 427, 427–28
specialization, 426, 427–28
ownership, 426, 427–28
decreases basis for increasing
labor force, 432
linkage provided basis for ranking,
432
most experience reduced access to
resource locations, 432
at least two independent dimensions
condition social complexity, 383
most cases are packed, 381–82,
436–37
presence of wealth distinctions not
density dependant, 426
associated with subsistence
diversity reduction, 426
possibly a necessary precondition
to elite monopolies, 426
people primarily dependent upon
terrestrial animals, not found
under fully packed conditions,
380
threshold, GROUP2 sizes and
intensification, 381–82
GROUP2 sizes and extensification,
381–82
at packing threshold of 9.097
persons, habitat richness does
not affect threshold response,
381–82
people primarily dependent upon
terrestrial plants, all cases with
wealth differentials that are
packed also have a diversified
diet, 427
wealth differential and social ranking is clustered above 53.33
GROUP2-size threshold, 383,
427

scenario regarding, 422
propositions regarding, 369–70, 376,
383–85, 392–93, 395–96, 404–5,
406, 436, 438–39
scenario regarding, 422, 423, 444
state, 462–63
temporal sequencing of events
propositions regarding, 439–40
theory of , 461. *See also* Intensification
thresholds, 435
condition for emergence of non-
hunter-gatherers, 435, 436–37
equal points of self-organized criticality, 435, 436–37
insure parallels between historically
independent developmental
sequences, 439–40
mark major organizational changes
among hunter-gatherers, 435,
436–37, 443
describe a curvilinear law, 435
PACKINX. *See* Hunter-gatherer systems: variables used in description:
PACKINX
Paradigm, 3, 4, 355, 387, 476, 483, 484, 490
Pathogen
density, 177
stress, 177–78
Patron-client relationship, 379, 404, 435, 470
Pattern recognition, 54, 123, 182, 243–44,
316–17, 363, 374–75, 461–71
Patterning
directional, 400–401
discovery of, 316
first-, second-, and higher-order derivative,
47, 48, 51, 209–10, 316
sequential and or directional, 228
spatially graded distribution of variants,
441–42
symetrical, 417–18, 422–23
transformational, 50
PEROGAT. *See* Hunter-gatherer systems:
variables used in description:
PEROGAT
PERWLTG. *See* Habitat: within-habitat
diversity: synergistic variables:
PERWLTG
PERWRET. *See* Habitat: within-habitat
diversity: synergistic variables:
PERWRET
Phenomena
emic, 14, 23, 24–25
etic, 24–25
Polar region, 21, 56–58, 72, 80, 82, 96, 136,
137, 142, 169, 177, 202, 216, 257,
269, 276, 381, 390, 407, 468
as marginal, 136, 137, 158, 479
as recently occupied, 137, 158
Politically complex hunter-gatherers. *See also*
Hunter-gatherer society:
politically complex
generalizations regarding, 244, 252, 254, 353
and high habitat productivity, 244–52
leadership and social scale, 353–54
and primary plant productivity, 268
and number of aquatic species stored, 263

and number of species processed for storage, 263
problems regarding, 352–53, 379
propositions regarding, 252
ranking, 379
stratification, 379
and warfare, 432
POLPOS. *See* Hunter-gatherer systems:
variables used in description:
POLPOS
Polygyny, 279–80
and age difference between males and
females at marriage (AGEDIF),
299
and age structure of population, 298
division of labor and subsistence base, 280,
298–99
equation for, 298
and family size, 287–88, 298, 299
and female-based labor units, 279–80, 287,
299
generalizations regarding, 279–80 286,
298–99, 300
and group size, 279–80
and male division of labor, 286–87, 298
and relative age at marriage, 280, 299
scenario regarding, 429–30
POLYSCAL. *See* Hunter-gatherer systems:
variables used in description:
POLYSCAL
Population, 32, 33
age structure of, 229–30
controversy, 354, 355
density, 33, 239
generalizations regarding, 214, 219,
311–12, 419, 420, 422, 434
propositions regarding, 151, 311, 378–79,
383–85
dependent factors, 312–13, 354, 356,
373–74, 432
criticism of some arguments, 373–74
function at consumer level, 359
impact on tactics and strategies, 359
373–74
limitations of ratios, 222, 224–25
relationships to other variables, 224,
311, 312–13, 359
responses to, 440, 444
propositions regarding, 378–79,
383–85, 413, 427, 439–40
growth, 356, 441
as regulator of product demand, 354–55,
356
as stimulation, 355
propositions regarding, 438–39, 441
rates and regional variability, 440, 441
of earth
at 11,000–12,000 B.P., 453
at 18,000 B.P., 453
as measure of scale, 319, 332
pressure, 354, 357, 437
and carrying capacity, 356–57
as cause of development, 355
as cause of intensification, 354, 354–55,
437–38
critics of above views, 355

Designer: Princeton Editorial Associates, Inc., Scottsdale, Arizona
Compositor: Princeton Editorial Associates, Inc., Scottsdale, Arizona
Text: Minion
Display: Minion and Optima
Printer and binder: Friesens, Altona, Manitoba, Canada